YEARBOOK OF AMERICAN & CANADIAN CHURCHES 1988

Fifty-sixth issue

Annual

YEARBOOK OF AMERICAN & CANADIAN CHURCHES 1988

Constant H. Jacquet, Jr., Editor

Alice Jones, Editorial Associate

Prepared and edited in the Office of Research
and Evaluation of the National Council of the
Churches of Christ in the U.S.A., 475 Riverside Drive,
New York, NY 10115

Published and Distributed
by Abingdon Press
Nashville

Printed in the United States of America
ISBN 0-687-46643-1
ISSN 0195-9043
Library of Congress catalog card number: 16-5726

PREVIOUS ISSUES

77404

INTRODUCTION

This edition of the **Yearbook of American and Canadian Churches** is the 56th in a series that began in 1916. A listing of years of publication, titles, and editors appears on page ii, opposite. Although the title refers to "churches," it should be stressed that the **Yearbook** contains information on many different faiths, not only Christian bodies, which the term *churches* implies.

Without the cooperation of many hundreds of people in the United States and Canada a reference volume of this complexity and scope could not be produced. The editor thanks all who have made this edition possible by supplying information on their organizations, correcting directory forms, filling out statistical reports, providing articles and other materials, and passing on innovative suggestions about how to improve the **Yearbook**.

The **Yearbook** has been a binational volume since 1972 and has a Canadian Advisory Committee which meets in Toronto annually to advise the editor on the Canadian sections of the book, in the light of recent developments in organized religion in that country, and to make suggestions on deletions and additions. To these Canadian friends and advisors, the editor extends thanks.

Special recognition is due Alice Jones, editorial associate, who has worked on eighteen editions of the **Yearbook**. She has made valuable contributions to this edition by her careful and patient work.

There being no established legal definitions of churches, clergy, or religion, these concepts are always subjective. The constitutional separation of church and state has left religious organizations basically free from guidance, classification, and regulation. Religious bodies, though incorporated legally in a state in the U.S. or in a province in Canada, determine their own institutions, doctrines, and standards of conduct.

Religious life in the United States and Canada is quite complex. The dynamic nature of these two nations, the patterns of immigration, the exchange of ideas and movements across the border, religious liberty, and the high degree of affluence provide conditions supporting the development of religious organizations. This has led to the formation of a bewildering diversity of sects and cults, primarily in the U.S. We do not attempt to list these bodies in the **Yearbook**. Many other small religious bodies, numbering in the hundreds, have, of necessity, also been excluded from the listings. Other sources of information exist on many of these groups.

What we do attempt to describe and record are those major religious bodies in the United States and Canada having the great majority of churches, clergy, and membership. The editor will be grateful for knowledge of any significant omissions that fall within the categories now covered in the various directory sections in this volume.

Which religious bodies are included in each edition of the **Yearbook of American and Canadian Churches** must, for reasons stated above, be an editorial matter based upon subjective criteria to some extent, and exclusion from the **Yearbook** should not necessarily be interpreted by readers as an adverse reflection on the nature, purpose, or reputation of any religious body.

Constant H. Jacquet, Jr.
Editor

A GUIDE FOR THE USER OF CHURCH STATISTICS

This guide is placed in a prominent position in each edition of the **Yearbook** to emphasize the fact that church statistics, like those of many other groups, vary greatly in quality and reliability. Therefore, necessary qualifications concerning them must be stated clearly and without reservation.

This year in Section III, the Statistical and Historical Section, the **Yearbook of American and Canadian Churches** reports data from 220 U. S. religious bodies. Of these, 108 report current data—that is, data for the years 1987 or 1986. Current data, comprising 49.1 percent of all reports, account for 74.6 percent of recorded membership. Concerning the denominations gathering statistics, some computerize data and have an accurate bank of information on cards or tape. Perhaps the largest group of denominations still gathers statistics by conventional hand-tabulation methods. Quite a few bodies are still operating on the basis of "educated guesses" in many statistical areas.

In addition to these general observations, four major qualifications should be made:

1) Church statistics are always incomplete, and they pass through many hands, some skilled and some not so skilled, and come up through many channels in church bureaucratic structures.

2) Church statistics are not always comparable. Definitions of membership, and of other important categories, vary from denomination to denomination. Jewish statistics are estimates of the number of individuals in households where one or more Jews reside and, therefore, include non-Jews living in these households as the result of intermarriage. The total number of persons in Jewish households is estimated to be 7 percent larger than the number of Jewish persons residing in these households. It should be noted that estimates of numbers of Jews have nothing to do with membership in synagogues. Roman Catholics and some Protestant bodies count all baptized persons, including children, as members. Other Protestant bodies include as members those who make a declaration of faith and become baptized. This can happen as early as age 9.

3) Church statistical data reported in the **Yearbook** are not for a single year. Not only do the reporting years differ from denomination to denomination, but some bodies do not report regularly. Therefore the reports based on data for the year 1985 or earlier are "non-current" reports. Attempts to combine current and non-current data for purposes of interpretation or projection will lead to difficulties.

4) Many of the more important types of statistical data are simply not available for a large group of denominations. Records of church attendance are not universally kept, and there are no socioeconomic data generally available. Statistics of members' participation in church activities and programs do not exist.

Statistics form an important part of church life and are necessary for the sound development of planning and program. Therefore strong efforts should be made in each denomination to upgrade the quality of its statistics. Interdenominational cooperation leading toward standardization of categories and sharing of techniques, it is hoped, will continue to grow. New ways of adapting to church needs and programs the data gathered by the U. S. Bureau of the Census must be discovered and utilized. The use of survey methods to obtain valuable socioreligious information about American religious life should be encouraged and expanded.

CONTENTS

YEARBOOK OF
AMERICAN &
CANADIAN
CHURCHES
1988

I

A CALENDAR FOR CHURCH USE

1988–1991

This Calendar presents for a four-year period the major days of religious observance for Christians, Jews, and Muslims; and, within each of these communions many other days of observance, such as saints' days, exist, but only those regarded major are listed. Thus, for example, the Roman Catholic Church mainly the "solemnities" are listed. Dates of interest to many Protestant communions are also included.

Many days of observance, such as Christmas and Easter, do not carry the list of communions observing them since it is assumed that practically all Christian bodies do. In certain cases, a religious observance will be named differently by various communions and this is noted.

In the Orthodox dates, immovable observances are listed in accordance with the Gregorian calendar. Movable dates (those depending on the date of Easter) will differ often from Western dates, since Pascha (Easter) in the Orthodox communions does not always fall on the same day as in the Western churches. For Orthodox churches that use the old Julian calendar, observances are held thirteen days later than listed here.

Ecumenical dates, such as Week of Prayer for Christian Unity and World Communion Sunday, are also included.

For Jews and Muslims, who follow differing lunar calendars, the dates of major observances are translated into Gregorian dates. For Muslim observances, the festivals are dated according to astronomical calculations that have been published in Paris, not the United States, and this could lead to slight variations. Since the actual beginning of a new month in the Islamic calendar is determined by the appearance of the new moon, the corresponding dates given here on the Gregorian calendar may vary slightly. It is also possible for a festival to occur twice in the same Gregorian year. Only 'Id al-Fitr and the 'Id al-Adha are religious holidays that are prescribed by the texts of Islam. Other Islamic dates are nevertheless key moments in the lives of Muslim believers.

(Note: In the Calendar, "RC" stands for Roman Catholic, "O" for Orthodox, "E" for Episcopal, "L" for Lutheran, "ECU" for Ecumenical.)

	1988	1989	1990	1991
1st Sunday of Advent..............	Nov 27	Dec 3	Dec 2	Dec 1
Feast Day of St. Andrew the Apostle (RC, O, E, L)............	Nov 30	Nov 30	Nov 30	Nov 30
Immaculate Conception of the Blessed Virgin Mary (RC)......	Dec 8	Dec 8	Dec 8	Dec 8
1st Day of Hanukkah (Jewish, 8 days).................	Dec 4	Dec 23	Dec 12	Dec 2
4th Sunday of Advent (Sunday before Christmas)................	Dec 18	Dec 24	Dec 23	Dec 22
Christmas..................	Dec 25	Dec 25	Dec 25	Dec 25
New Year's Day (RC—Solemnity of Mary; O—Circumcision of Jesus Christ; E—Feast of the Holy Name; L—Name of Jesus).................	Jan 1	Jan 1	Jan 1	Jan 1
Epiphany (Armenian Christmas).................	Jan 6	Jan 6	Jan 6	Jan 6
Feast Day of St. John the Baptist (O).............................	Jan 7	Jan 7	Jan 7	Jan 7
1st Sunday After Epiphany (Feast of the Baptism of Our Lord).................	Jan 10	Jan 8	Jan 7	Jan 14
Week of Prayer for Christian Unity (ECU)........................	Jan 18 to 25	Jan 18 to 25	Jan 18 to 25	Jan 18 to 25
Week of Prayer for Christian Unity, Canada (ECU)............	Jan 24 to 31	Jan 22 to 29	Jan 21 to 28	Jan 20 to 27
Presentation of Jesus in the Temple (O—The Meeting of Our Lord and Savior Jesus Christ)......................................	Feb 2	Feb 2	Feb 2	Feb 2
Brotherhood Week (Interfaith)...........................	Feb 21 to 27	Feb 19 to 25	Feb 18 to 24	Feb 17 to 23
Last Sunday After Epiphany.................	Feb 14	Feb 5	Feb 25	Feb 10
Ash Wednesday (Western churches)...............................	Feb 17	Feb 8	Feb 28	Feb 13
Easter Lent Begins (Eastern Orthodox)............................	Feb 22	Mar 13	Feb 26	Feb 18
World Day of Prayer (ECU).................................	Mar 4	Mar 3	Mar 2	Mar 1
Purim (Jewish)........................	Mar 3	Mar 21	Mar 11	Feb 28
Joseph, Husband of Mary (RC, E, L)...............................	Mar 19	Mar 19	Mar 19	Mar 19
The Annunciation (RC, O, E, L).................................	Mar 25	Mar 25	Mar 25	Mar 25
'Id al-Fitr (Festival of the End of Ramadan, celebrated on the first day of the month of Shawwal)......................................	May 20	May 8	Apr 28	Apr 17
First Day of the Month of Ramadan...............................	Apr 18	Apr 8	Mar 29	Mar 18
Holy Week (Western Churches)................................	Mar 27 to Apr 2	Mar 19 to 25	Apr 8 to 14	Mar 24 to 30
Holy Week (Eastern Orthodox).......................................	Apr 3 to 9	Apr 23 to 29	Apr 8 to 14	Mar 31 to 6
Sunday of the Passion (Palm Sunday) (Western churches)......	Mar 27	Mar 19	Apr 8	Mar 24
Palm Sunday (Eastern Orthodox)..................................	Apr 3	Apr 23	Apr 8	Mar 31
Holy Thursday (Western churches).................................	Mar 31	Mar 23	Apr 12	Mar 28
Holy Thursday (Eastern Orthodox)................................	Apr 7	Apr 27	Apr 12	Apr 4

1

	1988	1989	1990	1991
Good Friday (Friday of the Passion of Our Lord) (Western churches)..	Apr 1	Mar 24	Apr 13	Mar
Holy (Good) Friday, Burial of Jesus Christ (Eastern Orthodox)...	Apr 8	Apr 28	Apr 13	Apr
Easter (Western churches)...	Apr 3	Mar 26	Apr 15	Mar
1st Day of Passover (Jewish, 8 days)...................................	Apr 2 to 3	Apr 20 to 21	Apr 10 to 11	Mar to
Pascha (Eastern Orthodox Easter).......................................	Apr 10	Apr 30	Apr 15	Apr
May Fellowship Day (ECU)..	May 6	May 5	May 4	May
Rural Life Sunday (ECU)...	May 8	May 14	May 13	May
Ascension Day (Western churches).......................................	May 12	May 4	May 24	May
Ascension Day (Eastern Orthodox)......................................	May 19	June 8	May 24	May
1st Day of Shavuot (Jewish, 2 days)...................................	May 22 to 23	June 9 to 10	May 30 to 31	May to
Pentecost (Whitsunday) (Western churches)...........................	May 22	May 14	June 3	May
Pentecost (Eastern Orthodox)...	May 29	May 18	June 3	May
Visitation of the Blessed Virgin Mary (RC, E, L)................	May 31	May 31	May 31	May
Holy Trinity (RC, E, L)...	May 29	May 21	June 10	May
Corpus Christi (RC)...	June 5	May 28	June 17	June
Nativity of St. John the Baptist (RC, E, L).........................	June 24	June 24	June 24	June
Sacred Heart of Jesus (RC)..	June 10	June 2	June 24	June
Saint Peter and Saint Paul, Apostles (RC, O, E, L).............	June 29	June 29	June 29	June
Feast Day of the Twelve Apostles of Christ (O)...................	June 30	June 30	June 30	June
'Id al-Adha (Festival of Sacrifice at time of annual pilgrimage to Mecca)...	July 24	July 15	July 5	July
First Day of the Month of Muharram (beginning of Muslim liturgical year)..	Aug 13	Aug 4	July 24	July
Transfiguration of the Lord (RC, O, E, L)...........................	Aug 6	Aug 6	Aug 6	Aug
Feast of the Blessed Virgin Mary (E; RC—Assumption of Blessed Mary, the Virgin; O—Falling Asleep (Dormition) of the Blessed Virgin Mary; L—Mary, Mother of Our Lord)..	Aug 15	Aug 15	Aug 15	Aug
The Birth of the Blessed Virgin (RC, O).............................	Sept 8	Sept 8	Sept 8	Sept
1st Day of Rosh Hashanah (Jewish, 2 days).........................	Sept 12 to 13	Sept 30 to Oct 1	Sept 20 to 21	Sept to
Holy Cross Day (O—The Adoration of the Holy Cross; RC—Triumph of the Cross)..	Sept 14	Sept 14	Sept 14	Sept
Yom Kippur (Jewish)...	Sept 21	Oct 9	Sept 29	Sept
1st Day of Sukkot (Jewish, 7 days).....................................	Sept 26 to 27	Oct 14 to 15	Oct 4 to 5	Sept to
World Communion Sunday (ECU).......................................	Oct 2	Oct 1	Oct 7	Oct
Mawlid al-Nabi (anniversary of Prophet Muhammad's birthday)..	Oct 24	Oct 14	Oct 3	Sept
Laity Sunday (ECU)...	Oct 9	Oct 8	Oct 14	Oct
Shemini Atzeret (Jewish)...	Oct 3	Oct 21	Oct 11	Sept
Simhat Torah (Jewish)...	Oct 4	Oct 22	Oct 12	Oct
Thanksgiving Day (Canada)..	Oct 10	Oct 9	Oct 8	Oct
Reformation Sunday (L)...	Oct 30	Oct 29	Oct 28	Oct
Reformation Day (L)..	Oct 31	Oct 31	Oct 31	Oct
All Saints (RC, E, L)..	Nov 1	Nov 1	Nov 1	Nov
World Community Day (ECU)...	Nov 4	Nov 3	Nov 2	Nov
Stewardship Day (ECU)...	Nov 13	Nov 12	Nov 11	Nov
Bible Sunday (ECU)...	Nov 20	Nov 19	Nov 18	Nov
Last Sunday After Pentecost (RC, L—Feast of Christ the King)...	Nov 20	Nov 26	Nov 25	Nov
Presentation of the Blessed Virgin Mary in the Temple (also Presentation of the Theotokos) (O)...............................	Nov 21	Nov 21	Nov 21	Nov
Thanksgiving Sunday (U.S.)...	Nov 20	Nov 19	Nov 18	Nov
Thanksgiving Day (U.S.)..	Nov 24	Nov 23	Nov 22	Nov

A TABLE OF DATES AHEAD

The following table indicates the dates of Easter and other important festival days during the next few years. It also indica
the number of Sundays after Epiphany and after Pentecost for each year of the period. Easter may come as early as March 22
as late as April 25, thus bringing a wide variation in the number of Sundays included in certain of the Christian seaso

Year	Sundays After Epiphany	Ash Wednesday	Western Easter	Pascha (Orthodox Easter)	Pentecost	Sundays After Pentecost	First Sunday of Advent
1988	6	Feb 17	Apr 3	Apr 10	May 22	26	Nov 27
1989	5	Feb 8	Mar 26	Apr 30	May 14	28	Dec 3
1990	8	Feb 28	Apr 15	Apr 15	June 3	25	Dec 2
1991	5	Feb 13	Mar 31	Apr 7	May 19	27	Dec 1

II
DIRECTORIES

1. UNITED STATES COOPERATIVE ORGANIZA-TIONS, NATIONAL

NATIONAL COUNCIL OF THE CHURCHES OF CHRIST IN THE UNITED STATES OF AMERICA

The National Council of the Churches of Christ in the United States of America is a community of Christian communions which, in response to the gospel revealed in the Scriptures, confess Jesus Christ, the incarnate Word of God, as Savior and Lord. These communions covenant with one another to manifest ever more fully the unity of the Church. Relying upon the transforming power of the Holy Spirit, the Council brings these communions into common mission, serving in all creation to the glory of God.

Semiannual Meetings of the Governing Board
Arlington, TX, May 25-26, 1988
New York City Area, Nov. 2-4, 1988
May 17-19, 1989
Nov. 15-17, 1989

Offices at 475 Riverside Dr., New York, NY 10115
except as stated below.
Tel. (212)870-2200

GENERAL OFFICERS

President, Rev. Patricia A. McClurg
President-Elect, Very Rev. Leonid Kishkovsky
Vice-Presidents, Dr. I. Carleton Faulk; JoAnne Kagiwada; Dr. Jane Cary Peck; Dr. William G. Rusch; Dr. Reuben A. Sheares, II.
Secretary, Rt. Rev. David B. Reed
Treasurer, Joyce D. Sohl
Vice-Presidents for Program, Rev. Roland Pfile (Church and Society); Elaine M. Gasser (Education and Ministry); Rev. Syngman Rhee (Overseas Ministries); Bishop Philip R. Cousin (Church World Service); Dr. Beverly J. Chain (Communication Commission); Rev. Dr. Melanie May (Faith and Order); Rev. Jeanne Audrey Powers (Regional and Local Ecumenism); Rev. E. Wayne Antworth (Stewardship); Consuelo Urquiza (Justice and Liberation); Dr. Belle Miller McMaster (International Affairs)

ELECTED STAFF
OFFICE OF THE GENERAL SECRETARY

Gen. Sec., Rev. Arie Brouwer
Assoc. Gen. Sec. for Public Policy and Legal Affairs, James A. Hamilton
Dir. of the Washington Office, James A. Hamilton, 110 Maryland Ave., NE, Washington, DC 20002. Tel. (202) 544-2350. Asst. Dir., Mary Anderson Cooper; CWS/LWR Rep. for Development Plng., Rev. Paul L. Minear
Assoc. Gen. Sec. for Media and Member Services, Rev. J. Martin Bailey
Assoc. Gen. Sec. for Unity, Economic Development and Planning, Rev. Eileen W. Lindner
Asst. Gen. Sec., Dorothy J. Marple

DIVISION OF CHURCH AND SOCIETY

Assoc. Gen. Sec. for Church and Society, Dr. Kenyon Burke
Dir., Religious and Civil Liberty, Rev. Dean M. Kelley

Dir., Racial Justice, Rev. Tyrone S. Pitts
Dir., Environmental and Human Health, _____
Dir., Domestic Hunger and Poverty, Mary Ellen Lloyd
Dir., Child Advocacy Office, Karen Collins

Related Movements Sponsored by DCS

Dir., *Interfaith Center on Corporate Responsibility,* Timothy H. Smith
Dir., *National Farm Worker Ministry,* Sr. Patricia Drydyk, O.S.F., P.O. Box 302, Delano, CA 93216. Tel. (805)725-7445

DIVISION OF EDUCATION AND MINISTRY

Assoc. Gen. Sec. for Education and Ministry, Rev. Arthur O. Van Eck
Dir. of Finance, _____
Dir., Geneva Point Center, Rev. Harry Widman, Star Rt. 62, Box 469, Center Harbor, NH 03226, Tel. (603) 253-4366

Section on Education for Christian Life and Mission

Interim Exec. Dorothy R. Savage

3

Staff Administrator, Committee Uniform Lessons, Rev. Arthur O. Van Eck

Dir., Commission on Family Ministries and Human Sexuality, _____

Dir., Special Learning Needs, Vacation, Leisure and Outdoor Education, and Children's Education, Ima Jean Kidd

Dir., Adult Ministries, Dorothy R. Savage

Section on Education for Mission

Exec. Dir., Edu. for Mission and Exec. Dir., Friendship Press, Audrey Miller; Ed., Friendship Press, Nadine Hundertmark; Audio-Visual Coordinator, Rev. David W. Pomeroy

Section on Education in the Society

Interim Exec. Margaret L. Shafer

Section on Global Education

Co-Exec. Dirs., Rev. Daniel Force, Loretta W. Force, 2115 N. Charles St., Baltimore, MD 21218. Tel. (301)727-6106

Section on Professional Church Leadership

Exec. Dir., _____

Section on Revised Standard Version of the Bible

Staff: Rev. Arthur O. Van Eck

DIVISION OF OVERSEAS MINISTRIES

Assoc. Gen. Sec. for Overseas Ministries, Rev. James A. Cogswell.

Financial Management, Dir., Howard W. Jost

Specialized Ministries

Agricultural Missions:
Dir., Rev. J. Benton Rhoades; Dir., Women in Development and Network Liaison for Latin America, Deborah Jackson; Dir., Development Economics, Sinforoso A. Atienza; Dir., Agricultural/Technical Services, Lawrence W. Lewis

Associated Mission Medical Office, Dir., John D. Frame, M.D.

Human Rights, Dir. Rev. William L. Wipfler
Intermedia
Dir., Rev. David W. Bridell; Dir. for Adult Basic Ed., Dorothy Ortner

Internat'l Congregations & Lay Ministry,
Dir., Rev. Arthur Bauer

Leadership Development, Dir., John W. Backer
Overseas Personnel, Dir., Rev. Paul W. Yount Jr.

Geographic Offices

Africa: Dir., Willis H. Logan
East Asia & the Pacific: Dir., Rev. Victor W. C. Hsu; China Program, Dir., Rev. Franklin J. Woo; Japan and Hong Kong Program, Dir., Rev. Robert W. Northup;
Caribbean and Latin America: Dir., Rev. Oscar Bolioli, Assoc. Dir., Rt. Rev. J. Antonio Ramos
Middle East: Dir. Rev. Charles Kimball
Southern Asia: Dir., Rev. Robert L. Turnipseed
Europe/U.S.S.R.: Dir., Michael G. Roshak

DIVISION OF CHURCH WORLD SERVICE

Assoc. Gen. Sec. for Church World Service, _____

Assoc. Exec. Dir./Development Prog. Dir., Ann N. Beardslee
Asst. to the CWS Dir. for Development, Nancy Nicalo
Dir., CWS Communications, Rev. Larry D. Hollon
Dir. of Creative Services, Linda Robbins, 330 W. Lexington, Elkhart, IN 46515. Tel. (219)264-3102.
Dir., Intl. Disaster Response, Rev. Gregory R. Smith
Dir., Natl. Disaster Response, Kenlynn Schroeder
Dir. of Overseas Personnel, Rev. Paul W. Yount, Jr.
Dir., Material Resources, Soon-Young Hahn
Dir., Immigration and Refugees, Dale Stuart DeHaan; Assoc. Dir. for Adm., John W. Backer
Dir., Family Life and Population Programs, Iluminada R. Rodriguez
CWS/Elkhart: Mailing Address, CWS, P.O. Box 968, Elkhart, IN 46515. Tel. (219)264-3102. Dir. of Edu. and Fund Raising Unit, Rev. John F. Schultz; Dir. of Public Appeals, Rev. Lowell H. Brown

COMMUNICATION COMMISSION

Asst. Gen. Sec. for Communication, Rev. William F. Fore
Exec. Dir. for Broadcasting and Film, _____
Dir. for Media Resources, Rev. David W. Pomeroy

COMMISSION ON FAITH AND ORDER

Asst. Gen. Sec. for Faith and Order, Bro. Jeffrey Gros

The following is a Project of the Commission on Faith and Order in Association with the Duncan Black Macdonald Center for the Study of Islam and Christian-Muslim Relations of the Hartford Seminary. Its staff are secunded to the National Council of Churches, not Elected Staff of the Council.
Office for Christian-Muslim Relations, 77 Sherman St., Hartford, CT 06105. Tel. (203) 232-4451. Dir., Dr. Byron L. Haines; Asst. Dir., Dr. R. Marston Speight.

COMMISSION ON REGIONAL AND LOCAL ECUMENISM

Asst. Gen. Sec./Exec. Dir. for Commission on Regional and Local Ecumenism, Kathleen S. Hurty
The following are programs related to the Commission. Staff members connected with these programs are not NCCC Elected Staff but are employed under professional contract.
Office on Christian Jewish Relations, 475 Riverside Dr., Rm. 870, New York, NY 10115. Tel. (212) 870-2158. Dir., Dr. Jay T. Rock
Partners in Ecumenism, 475 Riverside Dr., Rm. 870, New York, NY 10115. Tel. (212) 870-2157. Nat'l. Dir., _____

COMMISSION ON STEWARDSHIP

Asst. Gen. Sec. for Stewardship, Rev. Ronald E. Vallet

4

COMMISSION ON JUSTICE AND LIBERATION

Asst. Gen. Sec. for Justice and Liberation, Lois M. Dauway

INTERNATIONAL AFFAIRS COMMISSION

Asst. Gen. Sec. and Exec. Dir., Rev. Dwain C. Epps

ADMINISTRATION AND FINANCE

Assoc. Gen. Sec. for Administration and Finance, Ruth M. Woodcock

OFFICE OF FINANCE
AND SERVICES

Department of Financial Management

Controller, Leo Lamb
Deputy Controller, Marian Perdiz
Asst. Controller, William B. Price

Department of Business Services

Exec. Dir., Dorothy L. Weeks
Asst. Exec. Dir., Mary McAllister

Department of Publication Services

Dir of Publications, Terrence S. Taylor

Department of Data Processing

Dir., Data Processing, Thomas McCloskey
Dir., Systems and Programming, Julio Devia

OFFICE OF PERSONNEL

Asst. Gen. Sec. for Personnel, Emilio F. Carrillo, Jr.
Dir. of Compensation and Benefits, Michael W. Mazoki

OFFICE OF RESEARCH AND EVALUATION

Asst. Gen. Sec. for Research and Evaluation, Peggy L. Shriver
Staff Assoc. Information Services, Constant H. Jacquet, Jr.

OFFICE OF INFORMATION

Dir., News Services, Carol Fouke
Dir., Interpretation Resources, Sarah Vilankulu

NCC Clusters

The 265 members of the Governing Board of the Council are assigned to the following five Clusters, or groupings of NCC Program Units, as listed above in this directory. Clusters meet during each semiannual meeting of the Governing Board to review and present policies, programs, and budgets proposed by the Program Units in a form that will facilitate decision making and priority setting. The Clusters also seek to build relationships between the Governing Board and the Program Units.

Unity and Relationships: Commission on Faith and Order; Commission on Regional and Local Ecumenism; Commission on Justice and Liberation.

Church and Society: Division of Church and Society and Sponsored Related Movements.

Church Life and Witness: Division of Education and Ministry; Commission on Stewardship; Communication Commission.

Church World Service: Division of Church World Service.

International Ministries: Division of Overseas Ministries; International Affairs Commission.

Constituent Bodies of the National Council (with membership dates)

African Methodist Episcopal Church (1950)
African Methodist Episcopal Zion Church (1950)
American Baptist Churches in the U.S.A. (1950)
The Antiochian Orthodox Christian Archdiocese of North America (1966)
Armenian Church of America, Diocese of the (1957)
Christian Church (Disciples of Christ) (1950)
Christian Methodist Episcopal Church (1950)
Church of the Brethren (1950)
The Coptic Orthodox Church (1978)
The Episcopal Church (1950)
Evangelical Lutheran Church in America (1950)
Friends United Meeting (1950)
General Convention, the Swedenborgian Church (1966)
Greek Orthodox Archdiocese of North and South America (1952)
Hungarian Reformed Church in America (1957)
International Council of Community Churches (1977)
Korean Presbyterian Church in America, General Assembly of the (1986)
Moravian Church in America (1950)
National Baptist Convention of America (1950)
National Baptist Convention, U.S.A., Inc. (1950)
Orthodox Church in America (1950)
Philadelphia Yearly Meeting of the Religious Society of Friends (1950)
Polish National Catholic Church of America (1957)
Presbyterian Church (U.S.A.) (1950)
Progressive National Baptist Convention, Inc. (1966)
Reformed Church in America (1950)
Russian Orthodox Church in the U.S.A., Patriarchal Parishes of the (1966)
Serbian Orthodox Church for in U.S.A. and Canada (1957)
Syrian Orthodox Church of Antioch (1960)
Ukrainian Orthodox Church in America (1950)
United Church of Christ (1950)
The United Methodist Church (1950)

American Bible Society

More than 172 years ago, in 1816, pastors and laymen representing a variety of Christian denominations gathered in New York City to establish a truly interconfessional effort "to disseminate the Gospel of Christ throughout the habitable world." Since that time the American Bible Society (ABS) has continued to provide God's Word, without doctrinal note or comment, wherever it is needed and in the language and format the reader can most easily use and understand. The Society is, in effect, the servant of the denominations and local churches as it provides the Scriptures needed for their use at home and their worldwide outreach in mission and evangelism.

Today the ABS has the endorsement of more than 100 denominations and agencies, and its Board of Managers is composed of distinguished clergy and laity drawn from these Christian groups.

Forty-two years ago the American Bible Society played a leading role in the founding of the United Bible Societies, whose members currently are involved in Scripture translation, publication, and distribution in 180 countries and territories around the world. The ABS contributes about 45 percent of the support provided by the UBS to those national Bible Societies financially unable to meet the total Scripture needs of people in their own countries.

The work of the ABS is supported through gifts from individuals, local churches, denominations and cooperating agencies. Their generosity made possible the distribution of 289,486,970 Scriptures during 1986, out of a total of 600,128,459 Scriptures distributed by all member societies of the UBS.

Offices: National Headquarters: 1865 Broadway, New York, NY 10023. Tel. (212)581-7400

OFFICERS

Pres., James Wood
Pres. Emeritus, Edmund F. Wagner
Vice-Pres., Mrs. Norman Vincent Peale
Gen. Secs., Alice E. Ball; Rev. John D. Erickson
Treas., Daniel K. Scarberry
Exec. Officers: Rev. Boyd L. Daniels (Library); Lorraine A. Kupper (Fund Raising); Maria I. Martinez (National Distribution); Charles Nelson (Services); Earl F. Schneider (Finance)
Departmental Officers: George F. Amann (Production and Supply); Rev. J. Milton Bell (Fund Raising); Henry G. Bucher (Personnel); Mary E. Cooke (Fund Raising); Rev. Louis O. Dorn (Translations); John A. Duguid (Public Relations); Florence R. Gayer (Investments); Petra T. Greenfield (Legacies); Clifford P. Macdonald (Public Relations); Bonny L. Millar (Volunteer Activities); Rev. Barclay Newman (Translations): Vartan Sahagian (Overseas); Michael J. Valentine (Services); Richard C. Walter (Finance); Peter Wosh (Archives/Records Management)
Field Exec. Secs.: Rev. J. Edward Cunningham (National Distribution); Ursula Glander (Volunteer Activities)

PERIODICAL

Bible Society Record (m), 1865 Broadway, New York, NY 10023, Clifford P. Macdonald, Man. Ed.

American Council of Christian Churches

Founded in 1941, The American Council of Christian Churches (ACCC) is comprised of major denominations—Bible Presbyterian Church, Evangelical Methodist Church, Fellowship of Fundamental Bible Churches (formerly Bible Protestant), Fundamental Methodist Church, General Association of Regular Baptist Churches, and Independent Churches Affiliated, along with hundreds of independent churches. The total membership nears 2 million. Each denomination retains its identity and full autonomy, but cannot be associated with the World Council of Churches, National Council of Churches, or National Association of Evangelicals.

The ACCC stands as an agency for fellowship and cooperation on the part of Bible-believing churches, for the maintenance of a pure testimony to the great fundamental truths of the Word of God: the inspiration and inerrancy of Scripture; the triune God—Father, Son, and Holy Spirit; the Virgin birth; substitutionary death and resurrection of Christ, and his second coming; total depravity of man; salvation by grace through faith; and the necessity of maintaining the purity of the Church in doctrine and life.

GENERAL ORGANIZATION

Headquarters: PO. Box 816, Valley Forge, PA 19482. Tel. (215)566-8154.
Annual Convention: October

OFFICER

Exec. Sec., B. Robert Biscoe

COMMISSIONS

Chaplaincy, Education; Laymen; Literature; Missions; Radio and Audio Visual; Relief; Youth

PERIODICALS

Fundamental News Service (bi-m).

American Tract Society

The American Tract Society is a nonprofit, nonsectarian, interdenominational organization, instituted in 1825 through the merger of most of the then-existing tract societies. As one of the earliest religious publishing bodies in the United States, ATS has pioneered in the publishing of Christian books, booklets, and leaflets. The volume of distribution has risen to more than 25 million pieces of literature annually.

Office: P. O. Box 462008, Garland (Dallas), TX 75046. Tel. (214)276-9408

OFFICERS

Chpsn., Stephen E. Slocum, Jr.
Vice Chpsn., Philip E. Worth
Sec., Edgar L. Bensen
Treas., Chris Simpson

†The Associated Church Press

The Associated Church Press was organized in 1916. Its member publications include major Protestant, Anglican, and Orthodox groups in the U.S. and Canada. Some Roman Catholic publications and major ecumenical journals are also members. It is a professional religious journalistic association seeking to promote better understanding among editors, raise standards, represent the interests of the religious press. It sponsors seminars, conventions, awards programs, workshops for editors, staff people, business managers.

Pres., Linda-Marie Delloff, Man. Ed., *The ChristianCentury*, 407 South Dearborn St., Chicago, IL 60605
Exec. Dir., Donald F. Hetzler, P.O. Box 306, Geneva, IL 60134. Tel. (312)232-1055
Treas., Darrell R. Shamblin, ed., Interpreter, 810 Twelfth Ave., S., Nashville, TN 37202

†The Associated Gospel Churches

Organized in 1939, The Associated Gospel Churches is primarily a service agency for fundamental denominations, colleges, seminaries, and missions. It also provides fellowship for Bible-believing independent churches, various Christian workers, missionaries, chaplains, laymen, and students.

One of the chief functions of AGC is to endorse chaplain applicants from the various denominations it represents. It is recognized by the U.S. Department of Defense and espouses the cause of national defense.

AGC devotes considerable effort toward gaining proper recognition for fundamental colleges, seminaries, and Bible Institutes. It was one of the founders of The American Association of Christian Schools of Higher Learning.

Associated Gospel Churches believes in the sovereignty of the local church, believes in the doctrines of the historic Christian faith, and practices separation from the apostasy.

Office: 3209 Norfolk St., Hopewell, VA 23860. Tel. (804)541-2879

OFFICERS

Pres. and Chmn., Commission on Chaplains, Col H. P. Kissinger, USAR
Vice Pres., and Vice Chmn., Commission on Chaplains, Dr. George W. Baugham

Sec.-Treas., Mrs. Eva Baugham
Natl. Field Rep., Chaplain (LCDR) Patrick Doney, USNR; Chaplain (LTC) Phil Minton, USAR

Association of Regional Religious Communicators (ARRC)

ARRC is a professional association of regional, ecumenical and interfaith communicators who work with local, state and regional religious agencies to: Fulfill their needs by providing occasional syndicated TV and radio programs to members, and "ARRC Newsletter," a quarterly. ARRC also provides local representation on the Communication Commission of the National Council of Churches, before the Federal Communications Commission, and with the denominations. ARRC offers fellowship by participation at the annual convention of the North American Broadcast Section of the World Association for Christian Communication, by updating names and addresses of national and local communicators.

OFFICERS

Pres., Lydia Ann Talbot, Dir., Broadcast Communications, Church Federation of Greater Chicago, 111 E. Wacker Dr., Ste. 510, Chicago, IL 60601
Exec. Sec., J. Graley Taylor, Exec. Dir., Religious Broadcasting Commission, 500 Wall St., Ste. 415, Seattle, WA 98101. Tel. (206)441-6110

Association of Statisticians of American Religious Bodies

This Association was organized in 1934 and grew out of personal consultations held by representatives from The Yearbook of American Churches, The National (now Official) Catholic Directory, the Jewish Statistical Bureau, The Methodist (now The United Methodist), the Lutheran, and the Presbyterian churches.

ASARB has a variety of purposes: to bring together those officially and professionally responsible for gathering, compiling, and publishing denominational statistics; to provide a forum for the exchange of ideas and sharing of problems in statistical methods and procedure; and to seek such standardization as may be possible in religious statistical data.

OFFICERS

Pres., Sherri Doty, Assemblies of God, 1445 Boonville Ave., Springfield, MO 65802
First Vice-Pres., James E. Horsch, Mennonite Church, 616 Walnut Ave., Scottdale, PA 15683; Second Vice-Pres., Daniel A. Nillsen, United Methodist Church, 1200 Davis St., Evanston, IL 60201
Sec.-Treas., Norman Green, Jr., American Baptist Churches in the U.S.A., Valley Forge, PA 19481

Christian Holiness Association

The Association is a coordinating agency of those religious bodies that hold the Wesleyan-Arminian theological view. It was organized in 1867.

Central Office: CHA Center, S. Walnut St. Box 100, Wilmore, KY 40390.
120th Annual Convention, Red Lion, Jantzen Beach, Portland, OR, April 19-20, 1988.

OFFICERS

Pres., Robert F. Andrews, 2340 E. University Dr. #23, Tempe, AZ 85281
Exec. Dir., Dr. B. Edgar Johnson, Ch. of the Nazarene Int'l. Hdqrs., 6401 The Paseo, Kansas City, MO 64131

AFFILIATED ORGANIZATIONS

Bible Holiness Movement
Brethren in Christ Church

Churches of Christ in Christian Union
Evangelical Christian Church
Evangelical Church of North America
Evangelical Friends Alliance
Evangelical Methodist Church
Free Methodist Church of North America
The Church of the Nazarene
The Salvation Army
The Salvation Army in Canada
United Brethren in Christ Church
(Sandusky Conference)
The Wesleyan Church
Japan Immanuel Church

COOPERATING ORGANIZATIONS

Methodist Protestant Church
Primitive Methodist Church
The Congregational Methodist Church
The Church of God (Anderson)
The Missionary Church

A Christian Ministry in the National Parks

The Ministry is an independent ecumenical movement providing interdenominational religious services in 65 National Parks, Monuments, and Recreation Areas. For 20 years it was administered in the National Council of Churches. On January 1, 1972, it became an independent movement representing over 40 denominations, 60 local park committees, over 300 theological seminaries, and 16 separate religious organizations. The program recruits and staffs 300 positions, winter and summer, in 65 areas.
Office: 222½ E. 49th St., New York, NY 10017. Tel. (212) 758-3450

OFFICER

Dir., Dr. Warren W. Ost

PERIODICAL

Opportunities Alive (a), Warren W. Ost, Ed.

Church Women United in the U.S.A.

Church Women United in the U.S.A. is an ecumenical lay movement providing Protestant, Orthodox, and Roman Catholic and other Christian women with programs and channels of involvement in church, civic, and national affairs. CWU has some 1,800 units formally organized in communities located in all 50 states, Greater Washington, DC, and Puerto Rico.
Office: 475 Riverside Dr., Room 812, New York, NY 10115. Tel. (212)870-2347. Other Offices: 777 United Nations Plz., New York, NY 10017. Tel. (212)661-3856; Rm. 108, CWU Washington Office, 110 Maryland Ave. NE, Washington, DC 20002. Tel. (212)544-8747

OFFICERS

Pres., Dr. Sylvia Talbot, Atlanta, GA
1st Vice-Pres., Helen Jones, Parson, KS
2nd Vice-Pres., Karen Freberg, Cincinnati, OH
3rd Vice-Pres., Kathryn Gramley, Winston Salem, NC
Sec., Sybel Thomas, Chicago, IL
Treas., Lois Holmes, Hot Springs, AR
Regional Coordinators: Dorothy Headley, Northfield, MN (Central); Lillian Nunnelly, Frankfort, KY (East Central); Geraldine Glick, Broadway, VA (Mid-Atlantic); Bernice Hunt, Dedham, MA (Northeast); Marilyn Bauman, Caldwell, ID (Northwest); Oouida Dorr, Houston, TX (South Central); Josephine Walton, Tuskegee, AL (Southeast); Shirley Nilsson, Salt Lake City, UT (Southwest)

STAFF

Gen. Dir., Dr. Doris Anne Younger

Assoc. Gen. Dir./Dir. of Prog. (Citizen Action and Constituency Development), Ada Maria Isasi-Diaz
Comptroller, Anne Martin
Dir. of EcumenicalCelebration/Global Rel., Mary Cline Detrick
Staff Assoc. for the Imperative, Pam Brubaker
Ed./Art Dir., Margaret Schiffert
Dir. of Media and Interpretation, Jane Burton
Dir. of Intercontinental Grants, Patricia Roache Espy
Dir. of Financial Dev. and Computer Services, Marcia Parker
Staff, UN and Global Aff., Joyce Yu
Staff Washington Ofc., Sally Timmel

PERIODICAL
The Church Woman (4/yr.)
lead time (6/yr.)

CODEL—Coordination in Development

CODEL is a consortium of Protestant and Roman Catholic mission-sending agencies, Communions and Christian organizations working together in international development. Founded in 1969, CODEL is committed to an ecumenical approach in the development process. The 40 U.S.-based member organizations combine expertise, funds, planning, project implementation and evaluation in a spirit of Christian unity working toward self-sufficiency of the poorest peoples and communities of the world.

Presently there are about 130 projects in 45 countries in health, agriculture, community development, and informal education. Other CODEL programs include seminars on current issues, development education activities, environment and development projects and workshops. CODEL's budget for 1987/88 is $2,514.500.
Headquarters: Rm. 1842, 475 Riverside Dr., New York NY.Tel. (212)870-3000.

OFFICERS
Pres., Dr. Norman Barth
Vice-Pres., Sr. Sheila McGinnis
Sec., Lloyd Van Vactor
Treas., Rev. William Crowley, Congregation of the Holy Ghost

STAFF
Exec. Dir., Rev. Boyd Lowry
Coordinator for Africa, Sr. Margaret Rogers
Coordinator for Asia and the Pacific, Mr. Ellis Shenk
Coord. for Latin America and Caribbean, Ms. Barbara Taveras
Seminar Program/Environment and Development, Sr. Mary Ann Smith; Helen Vukasian
Ecumenical Relations/Development Education, Rev. Nathan VanderWerf
Accountant, Robert Lopulisa

PERIODICAL
CODELnews (6/yr.), Suzanne Arden, Ed.

Consultation on Church Union

Officially constituted in 1962, the Consultation on Church Union is a venture in reconciliation of nine American communions which has been authorized to explore the formation of a united church truly catholic, truly evangelical, and truly reformed. In 1986 the participating churches were African Methodist Episcopal Church, African Methodist Episcopal Zion Church, Christian Church (Disciples of Christ), Christian Methodist Episcopal Church, The Episcopal Church, International Council of Community Churches, Presbyterian Church (U.S.A.), United Church of Christ, The United Methodist Church

SECRETARIAT
Address: Research Park, 151 Wall St., Princeton, NJ 08540. Tel. (609)921-7866

Gen. Sec., Rev. Dr. Gerald F. Moede
Gen. Sec. for Strategy and Interpretation, Dr. David W. A. Taylor
Treas./Bus. Mgr., Christine V. Bilarczyk

GENERAL ORGANIZATION
The *Plenary Meeting*, which normally meets every eighteen months to two years, is composed of ten delegates and ten associate delegates from each of the participating churches. Included also are observer-consultants from over twenty other churches, other union negotiations, and conciliar bodies.

The *Executive Committee* is composed of the president, two representatives from each of the participating churches, and the secretariat.

The *Secretariat* are the full-time executive staff members at the national offices in Princeton.

Various *commissions* and *committees* are periodically set up to fulfill certain assignments (1986 commissions include Commission on Church Order, Theology Commission, Commission on Worship, Commission on Racism, Commission on Strategy and Interpretation). Special emphasis is also being given to a Women's Task Force.

OFFICERS
Pres., Rev. George H. Pike, 737 Willow St., Cranford, NJ 07016
Vice-Pres., Bishop Marshall Gilmore, 109 Holcomb Dr., Shreveport LA 71103; Rt. Rev. Donald J. Parsons, 3601 N. North St., Peoria, IL 61604
Sec., Mrs.Dorothy Bascom, 2101 Park Ave., Baltimore, MD 21217

REPRESENTATIVES FROM PARTICIPATING CHURCHES
African Methodist Episcopal Church, Bishop Vinton R. Anderson, 2767 Halleck Dr., Columbus, OH 43209
African Methodist Episcopal Zion Church, Bishop J. Clinton Hoggard, 1100 W. 42nd St., Indianapolis, IN 46206; Bishop Cecil Bishop, AME Zion Ch. 5401 Broadwater St., Temple Hill, MD 20031
Christian Church (Disciples of Christ), Rev. Dr. Paul A. Crow, Jr., P. O. Box 1986, Indianapolis, IN 46206; Rev. Dr. Albert M. Pennybacker, University Christian Church, 2720 University Dr., Ft. Worth, TX 76109
Christian Methodist Episcopal Church, Bishop Marshall Gilmore, 109 Holcomb Dr., Shreveport, LA 71103; Dr. Vivian U. Robinson, 1256 Hernlen St., Augusta, GA 30901
The Episcopal Church, Rt. Rev. Donald J. Parsons, 3601 N. North St., Peoria, IL 61604; Dr. Alice Cowan, St. Paul's School of Theology, 5123 Truman Rd., Kansas City, MO 64127
International Council of Community Churches, Rev. J. Ralph Shotwell, 900 Ridge Rd., Homewood, IL 60430; Mrs. Dorothy Bascom, 2101 Park Ave., Baltimore, MD 21217
Presbyterian Church (U.S.A.), Rev. Dr. Robert B. Smith, 501 Bouman Ct., Sarasota, FL 34235; Rev. George Pike, 737 Willow St., Cranford, NJ 07016; Rev. Anneliese K. Opitz, 2315 Merrihill Dr., SW, Rochester, MN 55901
United Church of Christ, Rev. Clyde Miller, 1370 Pennsylvania, Denver, CO 80203; Dr. Avery Post, 105 Madison Ave., New York, NY 10016
The United Methodist Church, Bishop James Lloyd Knox, 6 Office Park Circle, Ste. 301, Birmingham, AL 35223; Mrs. Margaret Sonnenday, 7490 Teasdale St., St. Louis MO 63160

PUBLICATIONS
Covenanting Toward Unity: From Consensus to Communion (1985)
The COCU Consensus: In Quest of a Church of Christ Uniting (1985)
An Order for the Celebration of Holy Baptism, with Commentary

Digest of the 16th Plenary Meeting
Congregations Uniting for Mission
Word Bread Cup (Guidelines for ecumenical worship)
In Common (occasional newsletter)
An Order of Thanksgiving for the Birth or Adoption of a Child
An Affirmation of the Baptismal Covenant
Oneness in Christ: The Quest and the Questions (1981)
Sacrament of the Lord's Supper—A New Text
God's Power and Our Weakness
The Word and Words

The Evangelical Church Alliance

The Evangelical Church Alliance was incorporated in 1928 in Missouri as The World's Faith Missionary Association and was later known as The Fundamental Ministerial Association. The title Evangelical Church Alliance was adopted in 1958.

ECA (1) licenses and ordains ministers who are qualified and provides them with credentials from a recognized ecclesiastical body; (2) provides through the Bible Extension Institute, courses of study to those who have not had seminary or Bible school training; (3) provides an organization for autonomous churches so they may have communion and association with one another; (4) provides an organization where members can find companionship through correspondence, Regional Conventions, and General Conventions; (5) cooperates with churches in finding new pastors when vacancies occur in their pulpits.

ECA is an interdenominational, nonsectarian, Evangelical organization. Total ordained and licensed clergy members—1,597.

Headquarters: Rev. Glen E. Seaborg, Exec. Dir., 1273 Cardinal Dr., P.O. Box 9, Bradley, IL 60915. Tel. (815)937-0720
International Convention: Annual, next meeting, July 26-29, 1988, Marion College, Marion, IN

OFFICERS

Pres., Dr. Charles Wesley Ewing, 321 W. Harrison St., Royal Oak, MI 48067
1st Vice-Pres., Rev. John H. Bishop, 162 Grandview Ave., S., Newport, KY 41071
Exec. Dir., Rev. Glen E. Seaborg, P.O. Box 9, Bradley, IL 60915

PERIODICAL

The Evangelical Church Alliance Evangel, (a), P.O. Box 9, Bradley, IL 60915

Evangelical Press Association

The Evangelical Press Association is an organization of editors and publishers of Christian periodicals which seeks to promote the cause of Evangelical Christianity and enhance the influence of Christian journalism.

OFFICERS

Pres., John Stapert, Church Herald, 1324 Lake Dr. S.E., Grand Rapids, MI 49506
Pres. Elect, Mavis Sanders, Scripture Press, 1825 College Ave., Wheaton, IL 60187
Sec., Becky Duvost Fish, Virtue magazine, P. O. Box 850, Sisters, OR 97759
Treas., Robert Wood, OMS Outreach, Box A, Greenwood, IN 46142
Exec. Dir., Gary Warner, P.O. Box 4550, Overland Park, KS 66204. Tel. (913)381-2017

International Christian Youth Exchange

ICYE sponsors the exchange of young people between nations as a means of international and ecumenical education in order to further commitment to and responsibility for reconciliation, justice, and peace. Exchangees 16–24 years of age spend one year in another country and participate in family, school, church, voluntary service projects and community life. Short term, ecumenical, international workcamp experiences are also available for 18-30 year olds.

The U.S. Committee works in cooperation with national committees in twenty-six other countries and the Federation of National Committees for ICYE, which has headquarters in West Berlin, Federal Republic of Germany.

Exchanges for American youth going abroad and for overseas youth coming to the U.S. are frequently sponsored by local churches and/or community groups. Participation is open to all regardless of religious affiliation. Eleven denominational agencies are sponsors of ICYE, including: American Baptist Churches in the U.S.A.; American Luthern Church; Christian Church (Disciples of Christ); Church of the Brethren; Episcopal Church; Presbyterian Church (U.S.A.); Reformed Church in America; United Church of Christ; United Methodist Church; and the Lutheran Church in America. Collaborating organizations include the National Federation of Catholic Youth Ministry and the National Catholic Education Association.

Office: 134 W. 26th St., New York, NY 10001. Tel. (212) 206-7307.

OFFICER

Exec. Dir., Edwin H. Gragert

International Society of Christian Endeavor

Christian Endeavor is an international, interracial, and interdenominational youth movement in evangelical Protestant churches. It unites its members for greater Christian growth and service under the motto "For Christ and the Church." The first society was formed by Francis E. Clark in Portland, Maine, February 2, 1881.

The movement spread rapidly and, in 1885, the United Society of Christian Endeavor was organized. In 1927 the name was changed to the International Society of Christian Endeavor, to include Canada and Mexico. The World's Union was organized in 1895; in 1981 provision was made to include the territories of the United States. The movement has thousands of societies in local churches, for all age groups. Worldwide there are societies and unions in approximately 78 nations and island groups, with over two million members.

Office: 1221 E. Broad St., P.O. Box 1110, Columbus, OH 43216. Tel. (614)258-9545.
Convention: Harlingen, TX, July 1989.

OFFICERS

Pres., Rev. Clarence A. Kopp, Jr.
Gen. Sec./Treas., Rev. David G. Jackson

PERIODICAL

The Christian Endeavor World (q) 1221 E. Broad St., P.O. Box 1110, Columbus, OH 43216, David G. Jackson, Ed.

Interreligious Foundation for Community Organization (IFCO)

IFCO is a national ecumenical agency created in 1966 by several Protestant, Roman Catholic, and Jewish organizations, to be an interreligious, interracial agency for support of community organization and education in pursuit of social justice. Through IFCO, national religious bodies collaborate in development of social-justice strategies and provide financial support and technical assistance to local, national, and international social-justice projects.

IFCO serves as a bridge between the churches and communities, and acts as a resource for ministers and congregations wishing to better understand and do more to advance the struggles of the poor and oppressed. IFCO conducts training workshops for community organizers and uses its vast national and international network of organizers, clergy, and other professionals to crystallize, publicize, and act in the interest of justice.

National Office: 402 W. 145th St., New York, NY 10031. Tel. (212)926-5757.
Exec. Dir., Rev. Lucius Walker, Jr.
Sec., Mrs. Thelma Miller

OFFICERS

Pres., Dr. Negail Riley (United Methodist Church)
Vice-Pres., Msgr. John Egan (Archdiocese of Chicago); Dr. Ernest Newborn (Christian Church [Disciples of Christ], General Reconciliation Committee)

PERIODICAL

IFCO News (occ.)

InterVarsity Christian Fellowship of the U.S.A.

InterVarsity Christian Fellowship is a nonprofit, interdenominational student movement that ministers to college and university students in the United States. InterVarsity began in the United States when students at the University of Michigan invited C. Stacey Woods, then General Secretary of the Canadian movemen, to help establish an InterVarsity chapter on their campus. InterVarsity Christian Fellowship-USA was incorporated two years later, in 1941. InterVarsity's uniqueness as a campus ministry lies in the fact that it is student-initiated and student-led. InterVarsity's purpose is to build collegiate fellowships that engage their campus with the gospel of Jesus Christ and develop disciples who live out biblical values. InterVarsity students are encouraged in evangelism, spiritual discipleship, serving the Church, human relationships, righteousness, vocational stewardship and world evangelization. Our triennial missions conference held in Urbana, IL, jointly sponsored with InterVarsity-Canada, has long been a launching point for missionary service.

National Center: 6400 Schroeder Rd., P.O.Box 7895, Madison, WI 53707. Tel. (608)274-9001

Pres. & CEO, Thomas Dunkerton
Exec. Vice Pres./CAO, C. Barney Ford
Exec. Vice Pres./Dir. of Campus Ministry, Robert A. Fryling
Sec., H. Yvonne Vinkemulder
Treas., Thomas H. Witte
Bd.Chpsn., James W. Kay

Joint Strategy and Action Committee

This is a national ecumenical agency created by several denominational home mission and program agencies. Through the JSAC system, agencies collaborate with each other about issues, develop strategy options, screen project requests, and work on joint actions. JSAC has a series of national staff coalitions which work as Task Forces, Work Groups, or Networks.

National Office: 475 Riverside Dr., Rm. 450, New York, NY 10115. Tel. (212)870-3105

OFFICERS

Pres., Rev. Elliott Zabriskie III, Reformed Church in America
Vice-Pres., Rev. William A. Norgren, Episcopal Church
Sec., Rev. William Hanson, American Lutheran Church
Treas., Rev. Louis Meyer, Church of God (Anderson, Ind.)
Coord. Chpsn., Dr. Ernestine Galloway, American Baptist Churches
Exec. Dir., Rev. Jeffrey C. Wood

MEMBER DENOMINATIONAL AGENCIES

American Baptist Churches
American Lutheran Church*
Church of God (Anderson)
Church of the Brethren
Cumberland Presbyterian Church
The Episcopal Church
Evangelical Lutheran Church in America
Presbyterian Church (U.S.A.)
Reformed Church in America
The United Church of Canada
United Methodist Church

COOPERATING DENOMINATIONAL AGENCIES

African Methodist Episcopal Church
African Methodist Episcopal Zion Church
American Friends Service Committee
American Jewish Committee
Associate Reformed Presbyterian Church
Christian Church (Disciples of Christ)
Christian Methodist Episcopal Church
Christian Reformed Church
Church Women United
Evangelical Lutheran Church in Canada
Leadership Conference of Women Religious
Mennonite Central Committee
Moravian Church in America
Presbyterian Church in Canada
Progressive National Baptist Convention
Unitarian-Universalist Church
United Church of Christ
United States Catholic Conference

PERIODICAL

Grapevine (10 times a year), James E. Solheim

The Liturgical Conference

Founded in 1940 by a group of Benedictines. The Liturgical Conference is an independent, interconfessional, international association of persons concerned about liturgical renewal and meaningful worship. The Liturgical Conference is known chiefly, for its periodicals, books, audio-visual materials, and its sponsorship of regional and local workshops on worship-related concerns in cooperation with various church groups.

Headquarters: 806 Rhode Island Ave., N.E., Washington, DC 20018. Tel. (202)529-7400

OFFICERS

Pres., Gail Ramshaw
Board Chpsn., Rev. Gerard S. Sloyan
Vice Pres., James Schellman
Sec., Winnie Crapson
Treas., Ralph Van Loon
Exec. Dir., Rachel Reeder

Liturgy (q), Rachel Reeder, Ed.
Accent on Liturgy (4/yr.) Rachel Reeder, Ed.
Homily Service (m), Rachel Reeder, Ed.

The Lord's Day Alliance of the United States

The Lord's Day Alliance of the United States has served the church and nation for 97 years. It was founded in 1888 in Washington, D.C., and is the only national organization the sole purpose of which is the preservation and cultivation of Sunday, the Lord's Day, as a day of rest and worship. The Alliance also seeks to safeguard a Day of Common Rest for all people regardless of their faith. Its Board of Managers is composed of representatives from twenty-three denominations.

It serves as an information bureau, publishes a magazine *Sunday*, furnishes speakers and a variety of materials such as pamphlets, posters, radio spot announcements, decals, books, cassettes, news releases, articles for magazines and TV programs, and a new 15-minute motion picture.

Office: Ste. 107/2930 Flowers Road, South, Atlanta, GA 30341

OFFICERS

Exec. Dir. and Ed., Dr. James P. Wesberry
Pres., Dr. Charles A. Platt
Vice-Pres., Dr. Andrew R. Bird, Jr.
Sec., Rev. Ernest A. Bergeson
Treas., Mr. E. Larry Edison

PERIODICAL

Sunday (q), Dr. James P. Wesberry, Ed.

The Mennonite Central Committee

The Mennonite Central Committee is the relief and service agency of North American Mennonite and Brethren in Christ Churches. Representatives from Mennonite and Brethren in Christ groups make up the MCC, which meets annually in January to review its program and to guide future outreach. Founded in 1920, MCC administers and participates in programs of agricultural and economic development, education, medicine, self-help, relief, peace, and disaster service. MCC has over 1000 workers serving in 50 countries in Africa, Asia, Europe, Middle East, and South, Central, and North America.

MCC has service programs in North America that focus on both urban and rural poverty areas. Additionally there are North American programs focusing on such diverse matters as handicap concerns, community conciliation, employment creation and criminal justice issues. These programs are administered by two national bodies—MCC U.S. and MCC Canada.

Contributions from North American Mennonite and Brethren in Christ churches provide the largest part of MCC's support. Other sources of financial support include the contributed earnings of volunteers, grants from private and government agencies, and contributions from Mennonite churches abroad. The total income in 1986, including material aid contributions, amounted to $25,-688,256.

In the projects it undertakes, MCC tries to strengthen local communities by working in cooperation with local churches. Many personnel are placed with other agencies, including missions. Programs are planned with sensitivity to locally felt needs.

International and U.S. headquarters: 21 S. 12th St., Akron, PA 17501. Tel. (717)859-1151
Canadian office: 134 Plaza Dr., Winnipeg, Manitoba R3T 5K9

OFFICER

Exec. Secs., John A. Lapp (International); Dan Zehr; (Canada) and J. Wilmer Heisey (U.S.)

National Association of Ecumenical Staff

This is the successor organization, to the Association of Council Secretaries, which was founded in 1940. The name change was made in 1971.

NAES is an association of professional staff in ecumenical services. It was established to provide creative relationships among them, and to encourage mutual support and personal and professional growth. This is accomplished through training programs, through exchange and discussion of common concerns at conferences, and through the publication of the journal.

Headquarters: Room 870, 475 Riverside Dr., New York, NY 10115. Tel. (212)870-2158
Annual Meeting: July 11-15, 1988, Ghost Ranch, Abiqui, NM

OFFICERS

Pres., Sylvia Farmer, Minnesota Council of Churches, 122 W. Franklin Ave., #230, Minneapolis, MN 55404. Tel. (612) 870-3600
Vice-Pres., Rev. Lawrence E. Witmer, Genesee Ecumenical Ministries, 17 South Fitzhugh St., Rochester, NY 14614. Tel (716)232-6530
1988 Program Chair, Rev. David Bloom, Church Council of Greater Seattle, 4759 15th Ave., NE, Seattle, WA 98105. Tel. (206)525-1213
Sec., Rev. Angelique Walker-Smith, Trenton Ecumenical Area Ministry, 2 Prospect St. Trenton, NJ 08618. Tel. (619)396-9166

PERIODICAL

Corletter (bi-m), Rm. 870, 475 Riverside Dr. New York, NY 10115.

The National Association of Evangelicals

The National Association of Evangelicals had its beginning on April 7-9, 1942, when 150 evangelical leaders met in St. Louis, Mo., to launch a movement to bring Christians together in united action.

Since then, NAE has provided a means of "cooperation without compromise" among Bible-believing Christians. This fellowship is based upon a statement of faith that is descriptive of the true evangelical.

The NAE represents 41 complete denominations and has within its membership individual churches from at least 28 other groups. In addition, nearly two-hundred evangelical associations, organizations and schools hold membership in the NAE. Membership numbers about 5 million.

GENERAL ORGANIZATION

Headquarters: 450 Gundersen Dr., Carol Stream, IL 60188. Tel. (312)665-0500
Office of Public Affairs: 1430 K St., N.W., Washington, DC 20005. Tel. (202)628-7911

OFFICERS

Pres., Dr. Ray H. Hughes, P. O. Box 2430, Cleveland, TN 37320
1st Vice Pres., Dr. John H. White, Geneva College, Beaver FAlls, PA 15010

2nd Vice-Pres., Dr. B. Edgar Johnson, 6401 The Paseo, Kansas city, MO 64131
Sec., Dr. Jack Estep, P. O. Box 828, Wheaton, IL 60189
Treas., Mr. Paul Steiner, 1825 Florida Dr. Ft. Wayne, IN 46805

STAFF

Exec. Dir., Dr. Billy A. Melvin
Dir. of Public Affairs, Dr. Robert P. Dugan, Jr.
Dir. of Field Services, Dr. R. Gordon Bacon
Dir. of Information, Rev. Donald R. Brown
Dir. of Business Adm., Mr. Darrell L. Fulton
Field Rep., Rev. Darrel Anderson

COMMISSIONS, AFFILIATES, SERVICE AGENCIES

Commissions: Chaplains Commission, Higher Education Commission, Evangelical Churchmen Commission, Christian Social Action Commission, Evangelism and Home Missions Association, Hispanic Commission, National Christian Education Association, Stewardship Commission, Women's Commission
Affiliates: Evangelical Child and Family Agency, American Assn. of Evangelical Students, Evangelical Foreign Missions Assn., National Religious Broadcasters
Subsidiaries: World Relief Corporation
Service Agencies: Evangelical Adoption and Family Services, Inc., Evangelical Purchasing Service.

PERIODICAL

United Evangelical Action (bi-m), P. O. Box 28, Wheaton, IL 60189, Rev. Donald R. Brown, Ed.

MEMBER DENOMINATIONS

Advent Christian
Assemblies of God
Baptist General Conference
Brethren Church (Ashland, Ohio)
Brethren in Christ Church
Christian Catholic Church (Evangelical Protestant)
Christian Church of North America
Christian and Missionary Alliance
Christian Union
Church of God (Cleveland, Tenn.)
Church of God of the Mountain Assembly
Church of the Nazarene
Church of the United Brethren in Christ
Churches of Christ in Christian Union
Conservative Congregational Christian Conference
Conservative Lutheran Association
Elim Fellowship
Evangelical Church of North America
Evangelical Congregational Church
Evangelical Free Church of America
Evangelical Friends Alliance
Evangelical Mennonite Brethren
Evangelical Mennonite Church
Evangelical Methodist Church
Evangelical Presbyterian Church
Evangelistic Missionary Fellowship
Fire-Baptized Holiness Church of God of the Americas
Free Methodist Church of North America
Full Gospel Pentecostal Assn.
International Church of the Foursquare Gospel
International Pentecostal Church of Christ
International Pentecostal Holiness Church
Mennonite Brethren Churches, USA
Midwest Congregational Christian Fellowship
Missionary Church
Open Bible Standard Churches
Pentecostal Church of God
Presbyterian Church in America
Primitive Methodist Church, USA
Reformed Presbyterian Church of North America
Wesleyan Church

National Conference of Christians and Jews

The National Conference of Christians and Jews (NCCJ) is a non-profit human relations organization engaged in a nationwide program of intergroup education so that people of different religious, racial, and ethnic backgrounds learn to live together without bigotry and discrimination and without compromising distinctive faiths or identities. Founded in 1928, the NCCJ promotes education for citizenship in a pluralistic democracy and attempts to help diverse groups discover their mutual self-interest. Primary program areas include interfaith and interracial dialogue, youth intercultural communications, training for the administration of justice, and the building of community coalitions. The NCCJ has 74 offices nationally, staffed by approximately 240 people. Nearly 300 members comprise the National Board of Trustees and members from that group form the 22-member Executive Board. Each regional office has its own local board of trustees with a total of over 3,000. The National Board of Trustees meets once annually; the Executive Board at least three times annually.

Headquarters: 71 Fifth Ave., New York, NY 10003. Tel. (212)206-0006

OFFICER

Pres., Jacqueline G. Wexler

National Conference on Ministry to the Armed Forces

The Conference is an incorporated civilian agency. Representation in the Conference with all privileges of the same is open to all endorsing or certifying agencies or groups authorized to provide chaplains for any branch of the Armed Forces.

The purpose of this organization is to provide a means of dialog to discuss concerns and objectives and, when agreed upon, to take action with the appropriate authority to support the spiritual ministry to and the moral welfare of Armed Forces personnel.

GENERAL ORGANIZATION

4141 N. Henderson Rd., Ste. 13, Arlington, VA 22203. Tel. (703)276-7905

STAFF

Coordinator, Rev. James P. Rickards
Adm. Asst., Maureen Francis

OFFICERS

Chpsn., Rev. Dr. E. D. Ellison, III; Vice Chpsn., Rev. David I. Meschke; Treas., Rev. Dr. Calvin French; Sec., Rev. Ronald D. Miller; Committee Members: Msgr. John Cunniffe, Rabbi E. David Lapp, Archpriest Nicholas T. Kiryluk, Dr. Magnus P. Lutness, Member-at-Large, Bishop Vinton R. Anderson

National Interfaith Coalition on Aging, Inc.

The National Interfaith Coalition on Aging (NICA) is composed of Protestant, Roman Catholic, Jewish, and Orthodox organizations and individuals concerned about the spiritual well-being of older people and the religious community's response to problems facing our nation's aging population. NICA was organized in 1972 in response to recommendations and concerns of the 1971 White House Conference on Aging.

Primary objectives of NICA: to promote dialogue and cooperative effort among religious organizations and individuals concerned about older people; to assist churches and synagogues to initiate and support ministries that respond to older people's needs and improve the quality of their life; to identify and promote development of programs and services for older people best implemented through the religious sector; to foster cooperation and coordinated effort between religious bodies and private and public organizations whose programs and services affect the welfare and dignity of older people; to support older people's efforts to remain active participants in religious and community life and to share with society the wealth of their experience and skill.

NICA serves as a resource and training agency for its members and others who share its concerns. Current efforts focus on development of older adult ministries by congregations and religious agencies; gerontological training for clergy and religious workers; and cooperation of public and private sectors on research, training, program development, and funding.

Office: 298 South Hull St., P.O. Box 1924, Athens, GA 30603. Tel. (404)353-1331
Assoc. Exec. Sec., Miriam S. Peifer

OFFICERS

Pres., Rev. Harry J. Ekstam
Vice Pres., Mrs. Lillian Husted; Rabbi Matthew Simon; F. Daniel Krapf
Sec., Dr. Thomas B. Robb
Treas., Lt. Col. Beatrice Combs

PERIODICAL

NICA Inform (q), P. O. Box 1924, Athens, GA 30603

National Interreligious Service Board for Conscientious Objectors

NISBCO, formed in 1940, is a nonprofit service organization sponsored by a broad coalition of national religious bodies. NISBCO responds to the needs of conscientious objectors by: providing information on how to register and document one's convictions as a conscientious objector; providing professional counseling for those who are working through convictions of conscientious objection and training religious CO counselors; alerting citizens to the latest developments in the drive to bring back the draft and the efforts to institute compulsory national service; aiding COs in the armed forces who seek noncombatant transfer or discharge; maintaining an extensive referral service to local counseling agencies in all areas of the country, and to attorneys who can aid those in need of legal counsel; acting as a national resource center for those interested in CO/peace witness of all religious bodies in the United States: encouraging citizens through articles, speaking engagements, and NISBCO publications, to decide for themselves what they believe about participation in war based upon the dictates of their own consciences.

Office: Ste. 600, 800 18th St., N.W., Washington, DC 20006. Tel. (202)293-5962

OFFICERS

Chpsn., John K. Stoner, MCC, 21 S. 12th St., Akron, PA 17501
Exec. Dir., Rev. L. William Yolton

PERIODICAL

The Reporter for Conscience' Sake (m)

National Religious Broadcasters

National Religious Broadcasters is an association of more than 1,300 organizations which produce religious programs for radio and television or operate stations carrying predominately religious programs. NRB member organizations are responsible for more than 76 percent of all religious radio and television in the United States, reaching an average weekly audience of millions by radio and television.

Dedicated to the communication of the Gospel, NRB was founded in 1944 to safeguard free and complete access to the broadcast media. By encouraging the development of Christian programs and stations, NRB helps make it possible for millions to hear the good news of Jesus Christ on the electronic media.

GENERAL ORGANIZATION

Executive Offices: CN 1926, Morristown, NJ 07960. Tel. (201)428-5400.
Exec. Dir., Ben Armstrong
Annual Meeting: 1988 National Convention, Washington, DC, Jan. 30-Feb. 3, 1988

OFFICERS

Pres., Robert A. Cook, The King's Hour
1st Vice Pres., Jerry Rose, WCFC-TV (Ch. 38)
2nd Vice Pres., Robert Ball, Salem Media Services
Sec., Edna Edwards, WFGW/WMIT, Black Mountain, NC
Treas., David Clark, CBN, Virginia Beach, VA

PERIODICALS

Religious Broadcasting (11/yr.), CN 1926, Morristown, NJ 07960, Ben Armstrong, Exec. Ed.
Directory of Religious Broadcasting (Annual)

North American Academy of Ecumenists

Organized in 1967, the stated purpose of the NAAE is: "to inform, relate, and encourage men and women professionally engaged in the study, teaching, and other practice of ecumenism."
Mailing Address: c/o Prof. Eugene Zoeller, 2001 Newburg Rd., Louisville, KY 40205

OFFICERS

Pres., Joseph Burgess
Vice-Pres., Margaret O'Gara
Sec., Walter Bildstein
Sec./Treas., Eugene Zoeller

PERIODICAL

Journal of Ecumenical Studies (q), Temple University, Philadelphia, PA 19122, Leonard Swidler, Ed. (This periodical is affiliated with the Academy.)

North American Baptist Fellowship

Organized in 1964, the North American Baptist Fellowship is a voluntary organization of Baptist Conventions in Canada, the United States, and Mexico, functioning as a regional body within the Baptist World Alliance. Its objectives are: (a) to promote fellowship and cooperation among Baptists in North America, and (b) to further the aims and objectives of the Baptist World Alliance so far as these affect the life of the Baptist churches in North America. Its membership, however, is not identical with the North American membership of the Baptist World Alliance.

Church membership of the Fellowship bodies is over 28 million.

The NABF assembles representatives of the member bodies once a year for exchange of information and views in such fields as evangelism and education, missions, stewardship promotion, laymen's activities, and theological education. It conducts occasional consultations for denominational leaders on such subjects as church extension. It encourages cooperation at the city and county level where churches of more than one member group are located.

Headquarters: 6733 Curran St., McLean VA 22101. Tel. (703)790-8980.

EXECUTIVE OFFICERS

Pres., Dr. John A. Sundquist, American Baptist Churches in the U.S.A., P. O. Box 851, Valley Forge, PA 19482
Vice-Pres., Dr. V. Simpson Turner, Ed., The Baptist Progress, 712-714 Quincy St., Brooklyn, NY 11221
Sec. and Staff Exec., Dr. Archie R. Goldie, Dir., Div. of Bapt. World Aid, 6733 Curran St., McLean VA 22101
Representing the Baptist World Alliance: Dr. Noel Vose, BWA Pres., Baptist College, Hayman Rd., Bentley, Western Australia 6102; Gerhard Claas, Gen. Sec./ Treas., Baptist World Alliance, 6733 Curran St., McLean VA 22101

MEMBER BODIES

American Baptist Churches in the U.S.A.
Canadian Baptist Federation
General Association of General Baptists
National Baptist Convention of America
National Baptist Convention of Mexico
Progressive National Baptist Convention, Inc.
Seventh Day Baptist General Conference
North American Baptist Conference
Southern Baptist Convention

Pentecostal Fellowship of North America

Organized at Des Moines, Iowa, in October, 1948 shortly after the first World Conference of Pentecostal Believers was held in Zurich, Switzerland, in May, 1947, the PFNA has the following objectives: 1) to provide a vehicle of expression and coordination of efforts in matters common to all member bodies including missionary and evangelistic effort; 2) to demonstrate to the world the essential unity of Spirit-baptized believers; 3) to provide services to its constituents to facilitate world evangelism; 4) to encourage the principles of comity for the nurture of the body of Christ, endeavoring to keep the unity of the Spirit until we all come to the unity of the faith.

The PFNA has local chapters in communities where churches of the member groups are located, and fellowship rallies are held. On the national level, representatives of the member bodies are assembled for studies and exchange of views in the fields of home missions, foreign missions, and youth.

EXECUTIVE OFFICERS

Chpsn., G. Raymond Carlson, 1445 Boonville Ave., Springfield, MO 65802
1st Vice-Chpsn., Rev. James M. McKnight, 10 Overlea Blvd., Toronto, Ontario M4H 1A5
Sec., Ray E. Smith, 2020 Bell Ave., Des Moines, IA 50315
Treas., Chester H. Heath, P. O. Box 477, Export, PA 95632

PERIODICAL

P.F.N.A. News (q), 1445 Boonville Ave., Springfield, MO 65802

MEMBER GROUPS

Anchor Bay Evangelistic Association
Apostolic Church of Canada
Assemblies of God
Christian Churches of North America
Church of God
Church of God of Apostolic Faith
Church of God, Mountain Assembly
Congregational Holiness Church
Elim Fellowship

Elim Fellowship of Evangelical Churches and Ministers of Canada
Free Gospel Church, Inc.
Garr Memorial Ch., Carolina Evangelistic Assn.
International Church of the Foursquare Gospel
International Pentecostal Church of Christ
International Pentecostal Holiness Church
Italian Pentecostal Church of Canada
Open Bible Standard Churches, Inc.
Pentecostal Assemblies of Canada
Pentecostal Assemblies of Newfoundland
Pentecostal Church of God
Pentecostal Free-Will Baptist Church
Pentecostal Holiness Church of Canada
The United Full Gospel Church and Ministers Association

Project Equality, Inc.

Project Equality is a non-profit national interfaith program for affirmative action and equal employment opportunity.

Project Equality serves as a central agency to receive and validate the equal employment commitment of suppliers of goods and services to sponsoring organizations and participating institutions, congregations, and individuals. Employers filing an accepted Annual Participation Report are included in the Project Equality *Buyer's Guide*.

Workshops, training events and consultant services in affirmative action and equal employment practices in recruitment, selection, placement, transfer, promotion, discipline and discharge are also available to sponsors and participants.

Office: Project Equality, Inc., 1020 E. 63rd St., Ste. 102, Kansas City, MO 64110. Tel. (816)361-92222

OFFICERS

Chpsn., Rev. Dr. Yvonne Delk, Exec. Dir., Office of Church & Society, United Church of Christ
Vice-Chpsn., Ms. Barbara Thompson, Gen. Sec., Comm. on Religion and Race, United Methodist Church
Sec., Ms. Consuelo Urquiza, Women's Division, United Methodist Church
Treas., Ms. Dorothy Weeks, Dir. of Business Services, National Council of Churches
Exec. Dir., Rev. Maurice E. Culver

PUBLICATIONS

Buyer's Guide; Update (m)

SPONSORS/ENDORSING ORGANIZATIONS

American Baptist Churches in the U.S.A.
American Friends Service Committee
American Jewish Committee
Christian Church (Disciples of Christ)
Church of the Brethren
Church Women United
Conference of Major Superiors of Men
Consultation on Church Union
The Episcopal Church
Evangelical Lutheran Church in America
International Council of Community Churches
National Catholic Conference for Interracial Justice
National Council of Negro Women
National Council of the Churches of Christ in the U.S.A.
National Education Association
Presbyterian Church (U.S.A.)
Reformed Church in America
Roman Catholic Dioceses and Religious Orders
Unitarian Universalist Association
United Church of Christ
United Methodist Church
Young Women's Christian Association

Religion
In American Life, Inc.

Religion In American Life (RIAL) is a unique cooperative program of some fifty major national religious groups (Catholic, Eastern Orthodox, Jewish, Protestant). It reaches the American public through advertising on TV/cable, radio, in newspapers and magazines, and in transit and outdoor media. Every year since 1949, RIAL has been one of the campaigns of The Advertising Council. This results in as much as $50 to $60 million worth of time and space in a single year, contributed by the media as a public service. The advertising is produced by a volunteer agency (Saatchi & Saatchi Compton or FCB/Leber Katz Partners), with the production/distribution and administration costs funded by business and religious groups, as well as by individuals. RIAL highlights the importance of religion in daily life as an essential extension of the worshiping community, promoting laity-clergy seminars on morality in business and religions, an awards program, and a Worship Directory service in hotels, motels, and other public places.

Office: 815 Second Ave., New York, NY 10017. Tel. (212) 697-5033

OFFICERS
Chpsn. of Bd., Rabbi Joseph B. Glaser (CCAR)
Treas., Mr. Bertram Frankenberger, Jr.
Sec., Rev. Dr. Reuben T. Swanson (ELCA)

STAFF
Pres., ——
Dir. of Communication, Lois J. Anderson
Asst. to the Pres., Linda Langergaard
Worship Directory Mgr., Mary T. Fewer

PERIODICAL
The Bulletin, 815 Second Ave., New York, NY 10017

Religion Newswriters Association

Founded in 1949, the RNA is a professional association of religion news editors and reporters on secular daily and weekly newspapers, news services, and news magazines. It sponsors four annual contests for excellence in religion news coverage in the secular press. Annual meetings during a major religious convocation.

OFFICERS
Pres., Helen Parmley, Dallas Morning News, Dallas, TX 75265
1st Vice-Pres., Bruce Buursma, Chicago Tribune, Chicago, IL 69611
2nd Vice-Pres., Ed Briggs, Richmond Times-Dispatch, Richmond, VA 23293
Sec., John Dart, Los Angeles Times, Los Angeles, CA 90053
Treas., Jeanne Pugh, St. Petersburg Times, St. Petersburg, FL 33701

PERIODICAL
News Letter, 634 Johnson Ct., Teaneck, NJ 07666, Charles M. Austin, ed.

Religious Conference Management Association, Inc.

The Religious Conference Management Association, Inc. (RCMA) is an interfaith nonprofit professional organization of men and women who have responsibility for planning and/or managing meetings, seminars, conferences, conventions, assemblies, or other gatherings for religious organizations.

Founded in 1972, RCMA is dedicated to promoting the highest professional performance by its members and associate members through the mutual exchange of ideas, techniques, and methods.

Today RCMA has more than 850 members and associate members.

The association conducts an annual conference which provides a forum for its membership to gain increased knowledge in the arts and sciences of religious meeting planning and management.

Office: One Hoosier Dome, Ste. 120, Indianapolis, IN 46225. Tel. (317)632-1888.

OFFICERS
Pres., John V. Ohlin, General Council of the Assemblies of God, 1445 Boonville Avenue, Springfield, MO 65802
Vice Pres., Melvin L. Worthington, National Association of Free Will Baptists, P.O. Box 1088, Nashville, TN 37202
Sec.-Treas., Marvin C. Wilbur, Presbyterian Church (U.S.A.) Foundation, 475 Riverside Dr., Ste. 1031, New York, NY 10115
Exec. Dir., DeWayne S. Woodring, Religious Conference Management Association, One Hoosier Dome, Suite 120, Indianapolis, IN 46225

PERIODICALS
RCMA Highlights (bi-m), One Hoosier Dome, Suite 120, Indianapolis, IN 46225
Who's Who In Religious Conference Management (Annual), One Hoosier Dome, Ste. 120, Indianapolis, IN 46225

The Religious Public Relations Council, Inc.

The Religious Public Relations Council, Inc., is an organization whose purposes are to establish, raise and maintain high standards of public relations and communication to the end that religious faith and life may be advanced; and to promote fellowship, counseling, and exchange of ideas among its members.

The Council is an interfaith non-profit professional association, founded as the Religious Publicity Council on November 27, 1929, in Washington, D.C. There were 29 charter members, representing seven denominations, the Federal Council of Churches, and four church-related agencies.

Today RPRC has over 700 members in 12 chapters, as well as over 150 members-at-large in 30 states and Canada and six nations overseas.

The Council conducts an annual convention, sponsors two awards programs: the Wilbur Awards for secular journalism and broadcasting; the other, the De Rose/Hinkhouse Memorial Awards of excellence in nine categories for its own members; and each year has a week-long continuing education program.

Office: 357 Righters Mill Rd., P.O. Box 315, Gladwyne, PA 19035. Tel. (215)642-8895

OFFICERS
Pres., Paula R. Kadel, Coordinator for Promotion and Interpretation, Lutheran Church Women, 2900 Queen Lane, Philadelphia, PA 19129
Vice Pres., Thomas S. McAnally, United Methodist Communications, 810 Twelfth Ave. S., Nashville, TN 37203
Exec. Sec., Anne M. Reimel, The Martin de Porres Fdn., P.O. Box 315, Gladwyne, PA 19035

PERIODICALS
Counselor (q), P.O. Box 315, Gladwyne, PA 19035, Debbie Laudregan, Ed.
Mediakit (bi-m), P.O. Box 315, Gladwyne, PA 19035

Standing Conference of Canonical Orthodox Bishops in the Americas

This body was established in 1960 to achieve cooperation among the various Eastern Orthodox Churches in the U.S.A. The Conference is "a voluntary association of the Bishops in the Americas established . . . to serve as an agency to centralize and coordinate the mission of the Church. It acts as a clearing house to focus the efforts of the Church on common concerns and to avoid duplication and overlapping of services and agencies. Special departments are devoted to campus work, Christian education, military and other chaplaincies, regional clergy fellowships, and ecumenical relations."

Office: 8-10 East 79th St., New York, NY 10021. Tel. (212)628-2500

OFFICERS

Chpsn., Most Rev. Archbishop Iakovos
Vice Chpsn., Most Rev. Metropolitan Philip
Sec., Archbishop Victorin
Treas., Bishop Peter (L'hullien)

MEMBER CHURCHES

Albanian Orthodox Diocese of America
American Carpatho-Russian Orthodox Greek Catholic Church
Antiochian Orthodox Christian Archdiocese of All North America
Bulgarian Eastern Orthodox Church
Greek Orthodox Archdiocese of North and South America
Orthodox Church in America
Romanian Orthodox Church in America
Serbian Orthodox Church for the U.S.A. and Canada
Ukrainian Orthodox Church of America
Ukrainian Autocephalic Orthodox Church in Exile

United Ministries in Education

United Ministries in Education (UME) is a covenant-based ministry coalition created by eight national church agencies to facilitate ministries in education. It carries forward the work of two predecessor groups, United Ministries in Higher Education and Ministries in Public Education (K-12). UME works with churches and educational institutions as they seek to express their concern about the ways in which educating forces affect quality of life. UME focuses on enabling individual development so that people can responsibly serve their communities, and on interacting with institutions and systems as they engage in the formation and transfer of values.

OFFICERS

Admn. Coord., Clyde O. Robinson, Jr., 7407 Steele Creek Rd., Charlotte, NC 28210. Tel. (704)588-2182.
Communications Coord., Betsy Alden, 1801 Las Lomas NE, Albuquerque, NM 87106. Tel. (505)842-6041
Treas., Lawrence S. Steinmetz, 11780 Borman Dr., Ste. 100, St.Louis, MO 63146. Tel. (314)991-3000

PERIODICALS

UME Connexion (3/yr.)

PARTICIPATING DENOMINATIONS

American Baptist Churches, U.S.A.
Christian Church (Disciples of Christ)
Church of the Brethren
The Episcopal Church
Moravian Church
Presbyterian Church (U.S.A.)
United Church of Christ

YMCA of the USA

The Young Men's Christian Association (YMCA) is one of the largest private voluntary organizations in the world, serving about 25 million members in 90 countries. In the United States, some 2,000 local branches, units, camps, and centers annually serve about 13 million people of all ages, religions, races, abilities, and incomes. About 45 percent of those served are female. The YMCA was begun in London, England, in 1844; the first YMCA in the U.S. was established at Boston, Mass., in 1851.

YMCAs actively promote a set of Judeo-Christian values for living. The YMCA believes that people are responsible for their own lives and actions and that they should join together in positive association with one another, serving the needs of all and preserving the key concepts of equality and justice. It operates on the principle that all people are children of God, worthy of respect.

YMCAs promote values through a diverse set of programs, including health and fitness, camping, youth sports, family events, aquatics, child care, juvenile justice, corporate health enhancement, senior citizens' activities, international education and exchange, and teen programs. Some still offer residential and hotel facilities, through that number is decreasing. The kind of programs offered at each YMCA will vary; each is controlled by volunteer board members from the community who make their own program, policy, and financial decisions, based on the needs of that community.

While each YMCA is a separate enterprise, those in the U.S.A. are tied together by five basic goals which override the differences in programs, buildings, and leaders. These goals are to promote healthy life-styles, strengthen the modern family, develop leadership qualities in youth, increase international understanding, and assist in community development.

Corporate Name: YMCA of the USA
Office: 101 N. Wacker Dr., Chicago, IL 60606. Tel. (312) 977-0031

OFFICERS

Board Chpsn., James W. Ashley
Exec. Dir., Solon B. Cousins

Young Women's Christian Association of the United States of America

The YWCA of the U.S.A. is an Association comprised of some 450 affiliates in communities and on college campuses across the United States and serving more than 2 million members and program participants. It seeks to enable women, coming together across lines of age, race, religious belief, economic and occupational status to make a significant contribution to the elimination of racism and the achievement of peace, justice, freedom and dignity for all people. Its leadership is vested in a National Board, whose functions are to unite into an effective continuing organization the autonomous member Associations for furthering the purpose of the National Association and to participate in the work of the World YWCA.

NATIONAL BOARD

Office: 726 Broadway, New York, NY 10003. Tel. (212) 614-2700

OFFICERS

Pres., Glendora McIlwain Putnam
Sec., Mary R. Brown
Exec. Dir., Gwendolyn Calvert Baker

Youth for Christ / USA

Founded in 1945, the purpose of YFC is to participate in the body of Christ in responsible evangelism of youth, presenting them with the person, work and teachings of Christ and discipling them into the church.

Locally controlled YFC programs serve in 215 cities and metropolitan areas of the U.S.

YFC's Campus Life Club program involves teens who attend approximately 1,365 high schools in the United States. YFC's highly trained staff now numbers over 1,000. In addition, approximately 8,800 part-time and volunteer staff supplement the full-time staff. Youth Guidance, a ministry for nonschool-oriented youth includes group homes, court referrals, institutional services, and neighborhood ministries. The year-round conference and camping program involves approximately 35,000 young people each year. A family oriented ministry designed to enrich individuals and church family education programs is carried on through Family Forum, a daily 5 minute radio program on over 300 stations. Independent, indigenous YFC organizations also work in 65 countries overseas.

GENERAL ORGANIZATION

Headquarters: 360 S. Main Place, Carol Stream, IL 60188.
Pres., Richard Wynn
International Organization: Singapore, Pres., Rev. Jim Groen, Gen. Dir., James Wilson.
Canadian Organization: 1180A Martin Grove Rd., Rexdale, Ontario M9W 5M9.

2. CANADIAN COOPERATIVE ORGANIZATIONS, NATIONAL

This directory of Canadian Cooperative Organizations attempts to list major organizations working interdenominationally on a national basis. The editor of the **Yearbook of American and Canadian Churches** would appreciate receiving information on any significant organizations not now included. Those directories not reviewed for this edition carry the symbol (+) in front of them

The Canadian Council of Churches

The Canadian Council of Churches was organized in 1944. Its basic purpose is to provide the churches with an agency for conference and consultation and for such common planning and common action as they desire to undertake. It encourages ecumenical understanding and action throughout Canada through local councils of churches. It also relates to the World Council of Churches and other agencies serving the worldwide ecumenical movement.

The Council has a Triennial Assembly, a General Board which meets semiannually, and an Executive Committee. Program is administered through three commissions—Faith and Order, Justice and Peace, and Ecumenical Formation.

40 St. Clair Ave. E., Toronto, Ontario M4T 1M9 Tel. (416)921-4152

OFFICERS AND STAFF

Pres., Most Rev. E. W. Scott
Vice-Pres., Rev. Dr. Robert Binhammer; Rev. Nancy Cocks
Treas., Donald McClelland
Gen. Sec., _____
Assoc. Secs., _____; Rev. Tadashi Mitsui

AFFILIATED INSTITUTION

Ecumenical Forum of Canada, 11 Madison Ave., Toronto, Ontario M5R 2S2. Co-Dirs., Mr. Michael Cooke; Dr. Lois Wilson. Tel. (416) 924-9351

MEMBERS

The Anglican Church of Canada
The Armenian Church of America—Diocese of Canada
Baptist Convention of Ontario and Quebec
Canadian Conference of Catholic Bishops*
Christian Church (Disciples of Christ)
Coptic Orthodox Church of Canada
Ethiopian Orthodox Church in Canada
Evangelical Lutheran Church in Canada
Greek Orthodox Diocese of Toronto (Canada*)
Orthodox Church in America, Diocese of Canada*
Polish National Catholic Church
Presbyterian Church in Canada
Ethiopian Orthodox Church in Canada
Reformed Church in America—Classis of Ontario
Religious Society of Friends—Canada Yearly Meeting
Salvation Army—Canada and Bermuda
The United Church of Canada
*Associate Member

Canadian Bible Society

As early as 1805 the British and Foreign Bible Society was at work in Canada. The Bible Society branch at Truro, N.S., has been functioning continually since 1810. In 1904, the various auxiliaries of the British and Foreign Bible Society in Canada joined together to form the Canadian Bible Society.

Presently, the Canadian Bible Society has 17 districts and 2,000 branches. It holds an annual meeting of its Board which consists of two or more representatives of each district plus members appointed by the General Board of the CBS. There is also a meeting of its district secretaries annually.

In 1986, the CBS distributed almost 9 million Scriptures in more than 100 languages in Canada and provided over $3.5 million for the translation, publication, and distribution of the Scriptures in some 180 other countries.

Headquarters: 10 Carnforth Road, Toronto, Ontario M4A 2S4. Tel. (416)757-4171

OFFICER

Gen. Sec., Rev. Wm. R. Russell

Canadian Council of Christians and Jews

The Canadian Council of Christians and Jews is an organization which builds bridges of understanding between Canadians. Its techniques of effecting social change are dialogue and education. The CCCJ believes that there exist in any community in Canada the reservoirs of good will, the mediating skills, and the enlightened self-interest which make accommodation to change and the creation of social justice possible.

The CCCJ was established in Toronto in 1947 by a group of prominent business, civic and religious leaders.

National Office: 49 Front St., E., Toronto, Ontario M5E 1B3. Tel. (416)364-3101.

STAFF

Pres., C.E.O., Dr. Victor C. Goldbloom

Canadian Tract Society

The Canadian Tract Society was organized in 1970 as an independent distributor of gospel leaflets to provide Canadian churches and individual Christians with quality materials proclaiming the Gospel through the printed page. It is affiliated with the American Tract Society, which encouraged its formation and assisted in its founding, and for whom it serves as an exclusive Canadian distributor. The CTS is a nonprofit international service ministry.

Address: Box 203, Port Credit P.O., Mississauga, Ontario L5G 4L7

OFFICERS

Pres., Stanley D. Mackey
Exec. Sec., Robert J. Burns

Evangelical Fellowship of Canada

The Fellowship was formed in 1964. Presently there are 23 denominations, 99 organizations, and 540 local churches.

Its purposes are threefold: "Fellowship in the gospel" (Phil. 1:5). "the defence and confirmation of the gospel" (Phil. 1:7), and "the furtherance of the gospel" (Phil. 1:12).

The Fellowship believes the Holy Scriptures, as originally given, are infallible and that salvation through the Lord Jesus Christ is by faith apart from works.

In national and regional conventions the Fellowship urges Christians to live exemplary lives and to openly challenge the evils and injustices of society. It encourages cooperation with various agencies in Canada and overseas that are sensitive to man's social and spiritual needs.

Office: 175 Riviera Dr., Markham, Ontario L3R 5J6. (416)479-5885
Mailing Address: P.O. Box 8800, Sta. B, Willowdale, Ontario M2K 2R6OFFICERS

Exec. Dir., Rev. Brian Stiller
Pres., Dr. Melvin P. Sylvester
Vice Pres., Bishop Donald Bastian; Dr. John Redekop
Treas., Robert J. Doggart
Sec., Dr. Donald Jost
Chpsn., Social Action Commission, Dr. Paul Marshall
Chpsn., Task Force on Evangelism, Rev. Alan Andrews
Committee Members at Large, Major Allan Hicks, Dr. Ian Rennie, Rev. Mervin Sanders

Inter-Church Consultative Committee on Development and Relief (ICCCDR)

The Inter-Church Consultative Committee on Development and Relief (ICCCDR) was organized in October, 1971 to assist churches to work together in the fields of relief, development, and development education, consulting together and exchanging useful information.

ICCCDR is made up of representatives from Christian Churches and Inter-Church Projects. Representatives include church titular heads; general or executive secretaries of churches, and of the Canadian Council of Churches and the Canadian Conference of Catholic Bishops; staff members or representatives from the fields of development, relief, social services and inter-church projects. By 1988, ICCCDR coordination will probably be within the Canadian Council of Churches.

CORRESPONDENTS

Rev. Donald W. Anderson, Canadian Council of Churches, 40 St. Clair Ave., E., Toronto, Ontario M4T 1M9. Tel. (416)921-4152

MEMBERS

Anglican Church of Canada
Armenian Church of America—Diocese of Canada
Baptist Convention of Ontwario and Quebec
Canadian Conference of Catholic Bishops*
Christian Church (Disciples of Christ)
Coptic Orthodox Church of Canada
Council of Christian Reformed Churches
Ethiopian Orthodox Church in Canada
Evangelical Lutheran Church inCanada
Greek Orthodox Diocese of Toronto (Canada)
Mennonite Central Committee
Orthodox Church in America
Presbyterian Church in Canada
Polish National Catholic Church
Reformed Church in America-Classis of Ontario
Religious Society of Friends, Canada Yearly Meeting
Salvation Army-Canada and Bermuda
United Church of Canada

*Associate member

Inter-Varsity Christian Fellowship of Canada

Inter-Varsity Christian Fellowship is a non-profit, interdenominational Canadian student movement centering on the witness to Jesus Christ in campus communities: universities, colleges, high schools, and through a Canada-wide Pioneer camping programme. IVCF was officially formed in 1928-29 through the enthusiastic efforts of the late Dr. Howard Guinness, whose arrival from Britain challenged students to follow the example of the Inter-Varsity Fellowship from which he came, in organising themselves in prayer and Bible Study fellowship groups. Inter-Varsity has always been a student-initiated movement, emphasizing and developing leadership on the campus to call Christians to outreach, challenging other students to a personal faith in Jesus Christ, and study of the Bible as God's revealed truth within a fellowship of believers. A strong stress has been placed on missionary activity, and the triennial conference held at Urbana, Ill. (jointly sponsored by US and Canadian IVCF) has been a means of challenging many young people to service in Christian vocation. Inter-Varsity works closely with, and is a strong believer in, the work of local and national churches.

Headquarters: 1840 Lawrence Ave., E., Scarborough, Ontario M1R 2Y4. Tel. (416)487-3431

OFFICERS

Gen. Dir., James E. Berney
Dir. of Nat'l. Ofc. Services, Reginald E. Gaskin

Lutheran Council in Canada

The Lutheran Council in Canada was organized in 1967 and is a cooperative venture of the Evangelical Lutheran Church in Canada and the Lutheran Church-Canada.

The Council's activities include communications, coordinative service and national liaison in social ministry, chaplaincy, and scout activity.

Office: 25 Old York Mills Rd., Willowdale, Ontario M2P 1B5. Tel. (416)488-9430

OFFICERS

Exec. Dir., Lawrence R. Likeness

Mennonite Central Committee Canada (MCCC)

Mennonite Central Committee Canada was organized in 1964 to continue the work which several regional Canadian inter-Mennonite agencies had been doing in relief, service, immigration, and peace. All but a few of the smaller Mennonite groups in Canada belong to MCC Canada.

MCC Canada is closely related to the international MCC organization which has its headquarters in Akron, Pennsylvania, and which administers all overseas development and relief projects. MCC Canada contributed $11,101,000 for this international ministry in 1986. Additionally, 406 Canadian volunteers were serving one to three year terms in MCCC'S program at home and abroad during that same period.

The MCC Canada office in Winnipeg administers all voluntary projects located in Canada. Domestic programs of Voluntary Service, S.A.L.T. (Serve and Learn Together), Native Concerns, Peace and Social Concerns, Food Program, Employment Concerns, Ottawa Office, Offender Ministries and immigration are all part of MCCC's Canadian ministry. Whenever it undertakes a project, MCCC attempts to relate to the church or churches in the area; it attempts in this way to support and undergird the local church.

Office: 134 Plaza Dr., Winnipeg, Manitoba R3T 5K9. Tel. (204)261-6381

OFFICER

Exec. Dir., Daniel Zehr

†People for Sunday Association of Canada

A secular organization devoted to achieving for Canada Sunday as a national common day of rest and leisure.

The Association produces its publications *Sound About Sunday* and *Update* and furnishes speakers when requested.

Office: P. O. Box 457, Islington, Ontario M9A 4X4, Tel. (416)625-8759

OFFICERS

Pres., Rev, Jake Kuipers
Exec. Dir., Les Kingdon

Student Christian Movement of Canada

The Student Christian Movement of Canada was formed in 1921 from the student arm of the YMCA. It has its roots in the Social Gospel movements of the late nineteenth and early twentieth centuries. Throughout its intellectual history, the SCM in Canada has sought to relate the Christian faith to the living realities of the social and political context of each student generation.

The present priorities are built around the need to form more and stronger critical Christian communities on Canadian campuses within which individuals may develop their social and political analyses, experience spiritual growth and fellowship, and bring Christian ecumenical witness to the university.

The Student Christian Movement of Canada is affiliated with the World Student Christian Federation.

Office: 310 Danforth Ave., Toronto, Ontario M4K 1N6

Women's Interchurch Council of Canada

An ecumenical movement through which Christians may express their unity by prayer, fellowship, study, action. The purpose is: to enable Christian women across Canada to live in love and fellowship so that all people may find fullness of life in Christ. WICC sponsors the World Day of Prayer and the Fellowship of the Least Coin in Canada. Human rights projects are supported and ecumenical study kits produced. A newsletter is issued four times a year. Membership is composed of one appointment by each participating national denomination which confesses the Lord Jesus Christ as God and Saviour and members elected through the nominating process set out in the by-laws.

Office: 77 Charles St., W., Toronto, Ontario M5S 1K5 Tel. (416)922-6177

OFFICERS

Pres., Jean Gordon
Exec. Dir., Donna Hunter

Young Men's Christian Association in Canada

The first YMCA in Canada was established in Montreal, November 25, 1851, the declared purpose being "the improvement of the spiritual and mental condition of young men." Toronto and Halifax followed in 1853. At the 125th anniversary of the Canadian movement (1976), YMCAs were found in 75 cities from St. John's, Newfoundland to Victoria, B.C., with programs for intellectual, spiritual, and physical development of all Canadians.

Originally forming a single movement with the YMCAs in the United States, the Canadian Associations formed their own National Council in 1912. However, the international outreach (assisting in the establishment of YMCA movements in Latin America, Asia, and Africa) was administered jointly with the YMCA in the U.S. through an International Committee until 1970, when an agreement recognized the Canadian YMCA's independent service abroad. Today many "partnership Programs" exist between the Canadian Associations and YMCAs in developing countries.

YMCA Canada: 2160 Yonge St., Toronto, Ontario M4S 2A9. Tel. (416)485-9447

OFFICERS

Chpsn., E. Michael Byrne
Chief Exec. Officer, Richard R. Bailey
Dir., Int'l Aff., Robert Vokey

YWCA of Canada

A voluntary organization established in Canada in 1870 to serve the needs of women and their families. Member associations in over 50 communities across the country; national membership and participation about 500,000. Dedicated to improving the status of women and influencing responsible social change. Current concerns include pornography, violence against women, economic equality of women, teen pregnancy, incest, reproductive rights, pensions for women, and health.

Office: 80 Gerrard St.E., Toronto, Ontario M5B 1G6. Tel (416)593-9886

OFFICERS

Pres., Mae Boa
Exec. Dir., Rita S. Karakas

3. RELIGIOUS BODIES IN THE UNITED STATES

Introduction

The following is a series of directories of United States religious bodies arranged alphabetically by official name. Individual denominational directories have been corrected by the religious bodies themselves. Those directories which have not been updated for this edition of the **Yearbook** by denominational officials carry the symbol (†) in front of the title of denomination.

Generally speaking, each directory listing follows the following organization: a historical or doctrinal statement: a brief statement of current statistics (data for 1987 or 1986), if any; information on general organization; officers; other organizations; and major periodicals.

More complete statistics will be found in the Statistical and Historical Section of this **Yearbook** in the table on Current and Non-Current Statistics and also in the table entitled "Some Statistics of Church Finances."

A listing of religious bodies by family groups (e.g., Baptists, Lutheran) is found at the end of this directory.

A published work by Dr. J. Gordon Melton entitled *A Directory of Religious Bodies in the United States*, New York, Garland Publishing Co., 1977 lists 1,275 "primary" religious bodies currently functioning in the United States. The title, address and principal publication is supplied. There is a typology for classification of these primary religious bodies which are then listed by family groups.

Advent Christian Church

The Advent Christian Church is a conservative, evangelical denomination, which grew out of the Millerite movement of the 1830s and 1840s. Like most evangelicals, the members stress the authority of Scripture, justification by faith in Jesus Christ alone, the importance of evangelism and world missions, and the soon visible return of Jesus Christ.

Organized in 1860, the Advent Christian Church maintains headquarters in Charlotte, North Carolina, with regional offices in Rochester, New Hampshire; Augusta, Georgia; Detroit, Michigan; Lewiston, Idaho; and Lenoir, NC. Missions are maintained in India, Nigeria, Japan, Malaysia, the Philippines, Mexico and Memphis, Tennessee. In addition the denomination is engaged in a church-planting program, hoping to establish 100 new Advent Christian congregations in the United States and Canada by the end of the decade.

While the Advent Christian Church is considered conservative and evangelical in theology, it maintains doctrinal distinctives in three areas: conditional immortality, the sleep of the dead until the return of Christ, and belief that the kingdom of God will be established on earth made new by Jesus Christ.

Churches: 352; Inclusive Membership: 19,946; Sunday or Sabbath Schools: 300; Total Enrollment: 18,874; Ordained Clergy: 568

GENERAL ORGANIZATION

General Conference: triennial
Office: P.O. Box 23152, Charlotte, NC 28212, David H. Northup, Exec. Vice-Pres. Tel. (704)545-6161
Organizations and periodicals are all at this address unless otherwise noted.

OFFICERS

Pres., Rev. Donald E. Wrigley, 219 Mt. Carmel Rd., Walterboro, SC 29488
Sec., Rev. Marshall Tidwell, 1002 Grove Ave., SW, Lenoir, NC 28645
Appalachian Vice-Pres., Rev. Orville Harvey, 305 Oliver Ave., Princeton, WV 24740
Central Vice-Pres., Rev. Dwight Carpenter, 8065 Idaho Circle, N., Minneapolis, MN 55445
Eastern Vice-Pres., Rev. Irvin Verrill, 20 Highland Cliff Rd., Windham, ME 04062
Southern Vice-Pres., Rev. Larry Withrow, 318 Crescent Dr., Clayton, NC 27520
Western Vice-Pres., Mrs. Luella Johnson, 4915 Samish Way-43, Bellingham, WA 98226
The Woman's Home & Foreign Mission Society: Pres., Mrs. Bea Moore, Route 8, Box 274, Loudon, NH 03301

PERIODICALS

The Advent Christian Witness (m), Rev. Robert Mayer, P. O. Box 23152, Charlotte, NC 28212

Advent Christian News (m), Rev. Robert Mayer, Ed.
Maranatha (q), Rev. Robert Mayer, Ed.
Insight (q), Millie Griswold, Ed.

African Methodist Episcopal Church

This church began in 1787 in Philadelphia when persons in St. George's Methodist Episcopal Church withdrew as a protest against color segregation. In 1816 the denomination was started, led by Rev. Richard Allen, who had been ordained deacon by Bishop Asbury, and who was ordained elder and elected and consecrated bishop.

GENERAL ORGANIZATION

General Conference: quadrennial (Next meeting, 1988)
General Board, Annual Meeting 3rd Monday each year, June
Council of Bishops, Annually meeting 3rd Wednesday each year, June

OFFICERS

Senior Bishop, Bishop Henry W. Murph, 8939 Sepulveda Blvd., Ste. 240, Los Angeles, CA 90045. Tel. (213)216-7561
Gen. Sec., A.M.E. Church, Dr. Richard Allen Chappelle, Sr., P.O. Box 183, St. Louis, MO 63166. Tel. (314)534 6020
Pres., Council of Bishops, Bishop Rembert E. Stokes, 400 S. Zang Blvd., Ste. 813, Dallas, TX 75208. Tel. (214)941-9323
Sec. Council of Bishops, Bishop Cornelius E. Thomas, 500 Eighth Ave., S., Ste. 201, Nashville, TN 37203. Tel. (615)242-6814
Pres. General Board, Bishop Frank M. Reid, Jr., 2101 Magnolia, Birmingham, AL 35205. Tel. (205)252-2612
Sec. General Board, Dr. Richard Allen Chappelle, Sr., P.O. Box 183, St. Louis, MO 63166
Treas., A.M.E. Church, Dr. Joseph C. McKinney, 2311 "M" St., N.W., Washington, DC 20037. Tel. (202)337-3930
Historiographer, Dr. Henderson Davis, P. O. Box 783, Indianapolis, IN 46206. Tel (317)546-9654
Pres. Judical Council, Atty, P. A. Townsend, 1010 Macvicar St., Topeka, KS 66604

DEPARTMENTS

Missions: Dr. Frederick C. Harrison, 475 Riverside Dr., Rm. 1926, New York, NY 10115. Tel. (212)870-2558
Church Extension: Dr. Hercules Miles, Sec.-Treas., 3526 Dodier, St. Louis, MO 63107. Tel. (314)534-4272
Christian Education: Dr. Edgar Mack, Sec., 500 8th Ave., S., Nashville, TN 37203. Tel. (615)242-1420
Sunday School Union: Dr. Lee Henderson, Sec-Treas., 500 Eighth Ave., S., Nashville, TN 37203. Tel. (615)256-5882

Evangelism: Yale B. Bruce, Dir., 5728 Major Blvd., Orlando, FL 82819. Tel. (305)352-6515

Publications: Dr. A. Lee Henderson, Sec.-Treas., 500 8th Ave., S., Nashville, TN 37203. Tel. (615)256-5882

Pension: Dr. Joseph L. Joiner, Sec.-Treas., 500 8th Ave., S., Nashville, TN 37203. Tel. (615)256-7725

Finance Department: Dr. Joseph C. McKinney, 2311 "M" St., NW, Washington, DC 20037. Tel. (202)337-3930

Statistical Department: Dr. Richard Allen Chappelle, Sr., P. O. Box 183, St. Louis, MO 63166. Tel. (314)534-6020

Minimum Salary: Dr. Ezra M. Johnson, 280 Hernando St., Memphis, TN 38126. Tel. (901)526-4281

Religious Literature Department: Dr. Cyrus S. Keller, Sr., Editor-in-Chief, P.O. Box 5327, St. Louis, MO 63115. Tel. (314)535-8822

Women's Missionary Society: Mrs. Delores L. K. Williams, Pres., 2311 "M" St., N.W., Washington, DC 20037. Tel. (212)337-1335

Lay Organization: Dr. Kathryn M. Brown, Connectional Pres., 171 Ashby St., Atlanta, GA 30314

PERIODICALS

A.M.E. Christian Recorder: Dr. Robert H. Reid, Ed., 500 8th Ave., S., Nashville TN 37203. Tel. (615)256-8548

A.M.E. Review: Dr. Jamye Coleman Williams, 500 Eighth Ave., S., Nashville, TN 37203. Tel. (615)320-3500

Voice of Missions: Dr. Frederick C. Harrison, Ed., 475 Riverside Dr., Rm. 1920, New York, NY 10115

Women's Missionary Magazine: Mrs. Bertha O. Fordham, 800 Risley Ave., Pleasantville, NJ, 08232

Secret Chamber: Dr. Yale B. Bruce, 5728 Major Blvd., Orlando, FL 82819. Tel. (305)352-6515

Journal of Christian Education: Dr. Edgar L. Mack, 500 Eighth Ave., S., Nashville, TN 37202. Tel. (615)242-1420

BISHOPS IN THE U.S.A.

First District: Frank C. Cummings, 5070 Parkside, Ste. 1410, Philadelphia, PA 19131. Tel. (215)877-3771

Second District: John Hurst Adams, 615 G St. S.W., Washington DC 20024. Tel. (202)554-4351

Third District: Richard Allen Hildebrand, 700 Bryden Rd., Ste. 135, Columbus, OH 43215. Tel. (614)461-6496

Fourth District: Samuel S. Morris, Jr., 4448 S. Michigan Ave., P.O. Box 53539, Chicago, IL 60653. Tel. (312)285-5500

Fifth District: Henry W. Murph, 8939 S. Sepulveda, Ste. 240, Los Angeles, CA 90045. Tel. (213)216-7561

Sixth District: Frederick Talbot, 208 Auburn Ave. N.E., Atlanta, GA 30303. Tel (404)659-2012

Seventh District: Frederick C. James, 370 Forest Dr., Ste. 402, Columbia, SC 29204

Eighth District: Donald G. Ming, 2138 St. Bernard Ave., New Orleans, LA 70119. Tel. (504)948-4251

Ninth District: Frank M. Reid, Jr., 2101 Magnolia, Birmingham, AL 35205. Tel. (205)252-2612

Tenth District: Rembert E. Stokes, 400 S. Zang Blvd., Ste. 813, Dallas, TX 75208. Tel. (214)941-9323

Eleventh District: Philip R. Cousin, P.O. Box 2140, Jacksonville, FL 32203. Tel. (904)398-3797

Twelfth District: H. Hartford Brookins, 604 Locust Ave., North, Little Rock, AR 72114. Tel. (501)375-4310

Thirteenth District: Cornelius Thomas, 500 8th Ave., So., Nashville, TN 37203. Tel. (615)242-6814

Fourteenth District: Vernon R. Byrd, 460 Waverly Pl., Orange, NJ 07050. Tel. (201)674-1177

Fifteenth District: Henry A. Belin, Jr., 1358 Laboldi, Nashville, TN 37207. Tel. (615)868-5272

Sixteenth District: James H. Mayo, 6 Morningwood Ct., Olney, MD 20232. Tel (301)774-3278

Seventeenth District: Robert L. Pruitt, 7911 13th St. NW, Washington, DC 20012

Nineteenth District: John E. Hunter, 22335 La Garonne, Southville, MI 48075. Tel. (313)559-7627

Ecumenical Officer: Vinton R. Anderson, 7748 Peachtree Lane, University City MO 63130. Tel. (314)534-4278

Retired Bishops:

D. Ward Nichols, 2295 Seventh Ave., New York, NY 10030. Tel. (516)427-0225

Ernest L. Hickman, 1320 Oakcrest Dr., S.W., Atlanta, GA 30311. Tel. (404)349-1336

Harrison J. Bryant, 4000 Bedford Rd., Baltimore, MD 21207. Tel. (301)484-7508

H. Thomas Primm, 2820 Monaco Parkway, Denver, CO 80207. Tel. (303)335-9545

Hubert N. Robinson, 357 Arden Park, Detroit, MI 48202. Tel. (313)875-4967

Bishop Harold I. Bearden, 644 Skipper Dr., Atlanta, GA 30314. Tel. (404)691-9642

African Methodist Episcopal Zion Church

The A.M.E. Zion Church is an independent body, having withdrawn from the John Street Methodist Church of New York City in 1796. The first bishop was James Varick.

Churches: 6,057; Inclusive Membership: 1,195,173; Sunday or Sabbath Schools: 6,057; Total Enrollment: 217,000; Ordained Clergy: 6,396

GENERAL ORGANIZATION

General Conference: Quadrennial

OFFICERS

Senior Bishop, Bishop William Milton Smith, 3753 Springhill Ave., Mobile, AL 36608

Sec., Board of Bishops, Bishop Charles H. Foggie, 1200 Windermere Dr., Pittsburgh, PA 15218

Asst. Sec., Bishop John H. Miller, Sr., Springdale Estates, 8605 Caswell Ct., Raleigh, NC 27612

OTHER AGENCIES

Gen. Sec.-Aud., Rev. Earle E. Johnson, P.O. Box 32843, Charlotte, NC 28232. Tel. (704)332-3851

Fin. Sec., Ms. Madie L. Simpson, P.O. Box 31005, Charlotte, NC 28230. Tel. (704)333-4847

A.M.E. Zion Publishing House: Dr. Lem Long, Jr., General Mgr., P.O. Box 30714, Charlotte, NC 28230. Tel. (704)334-9596

Dept. of Overseas Missions: Rev. Dr. Kermit J. DeGraffenreidt. Sec.-Treas, 475 Riverside Dr., Ste. 1910, New York, NY 10115. Tel. (212)870-2952

Dept. of Home Missions, Pensions, and Relief: Rev. Dr. Jewett Walker, Sec.-Treas., P.O. Box 30846, Charlotte, NC 28231. Tel. (704)333-3779

Dept. of Christian Education: Rev. G. L. Blackwell, Sec., 128 E. 58th St., Chicago, IL 60637. Tel. (312)667-0183

Dept. of Church School Literature: Ms. Mary A. Love, Ed., P. O. Box 31005, Charlotte, NC 28230. Tel. (704)332-1034

Dept. of Church Extension: Dr. Lem Long, Jr., Sec.-Treas., P. O. Box 31005, Charlotte, NC 28231. Tel. (704)334-2519

Dept. of Evangelism: Rev. J. Dallas Jenkins, Sr., Dir., 4550 Laurel Dr., Dayton, OH 45417. Tel. (513)263-2411

Dept. of Public Relations: Gregory R. Smith, Dir., 344 Hawthrone Terr., Mt. Vernon, NY 10550. Tel. (212)234-1544

Woman's Home and Overseas Missionary Society: Gen Pres., Mrs. Grace L. Holmes, 2505 Linden Ave., Knoxville, TN. Tel. (615)525-1523; Exec. Sec., Mrs. Alcenia Harps, 975 Reservoir Ave., Norfolk, VA 23504. Tel. (804)627-1727; Treas., Mrs. Gwendolyn B. Johnson, 2011 Sterns Dr., Los Angeles, CA 90034. Tel. (213)939-9417

Conventional Lay Council, Pres., Dr. C. Dupont Rippy, 1701 Patton Ave., Charlotte, NC 28216

Star of Zion (w), Rev. Morgan Tann, Ed., P.O. Box 31005, Charlotte, NC 28230

Quarterly Review (q), Dr. John H. Satterwhite, Ed., 1814 Tamarack St., N.W., Washington, DC 20012. Tel. (202) 726-7308

Missionary Seer. (m), Rev. Kermit J. DeGraffenreidt, Ed., 475 Riverside Dr., Ste. 1910, New York NY 10115. Tel. (212) 870-2952

Church School Herald (q), Ms. Mary A. Love, Ed., P. O. Box 31005, Charlotte, NC 28230

BISHOPS

First Episcopal District: Bishop William Milton Smith, 3753 Springhill Ave., Mobile, AL 36608. Tel. (205) 344-7769

Second Episcopal District: Bishop Alfred G. Dunston Jr., Presidential Commons, A 521, City Line and Presidential Blvd., Philadelphia, PA 19131. Tel. (215) 877-2659

Third Episcopal District: Bishop Charles H. Foggie, 1200 Windermere Dr., Pittsburgh, PA 15218. Tel. (412) 242-5842

Fourth Episcopal District: Bishop J. Clinton Hoggard, 1100 W. 42nd St., Rm. 344, Indianapolis, IN 46208. Tel (317) 924-1207

Fifth Episcopal District: Bishop Clinton R. Coleman, 3513 Ellamont Rd., Baltimore, MD 21215. Tel. (301) 466-2220

Sixth Episcopal District: ———, P. O. Box 41138, Ben Hill Station, Atlanta, GA 30331. Tel. (404)344-6554

Seventh Episcopal District: Bishop John H. Miller, Springdale Estates, 8605 Caswell Ave., Raliegh, NC 27612. Tel. (919)787-1346

Eighth Episcopal District: Bishop Ruben L. Speaks, 1238 Marshall St., P. O. Box 986, Salisbury, NC 28144. Tel. (704)637-1471

Ninth Episcopal District: Bishop Herman L. Anderson, 5700 Barrington Dr., Charlotte, NC 28215. Tel. (704)536-7251

Tenth Episcopal District: Bishop Cecil Bishop, 5401 Broadwater St., Temple Hill, MD 20748. Tel. (301)894-2165

Eleventh Episcopal District: Bishop Richard L. Fisher, 8015 Stanford St., St. Louis, MO 63130. Tel. (314)727-4439

Twelfth Episcopal District: Bishop Alfred E. White, 93 Ridgefield St., Hartford, CT 06112

Albanian Orthodox Archdiocese in America

The Albanian Orthodox Church in America traces its origins to the groups of Albanian immigrants which first arrived in the United States in 1886, seeking religious, cultural, and economic freedoms denied them in the homeland.

In 1908 in Boston, the Rev. Fan Stylian Noli (later Archbishop) served the first liturgy in the Albanian language in 500 years, to which Orthodox Albanians rallied, later forming their own diocese in 1919. Parishes began to spring up through New England and the Mid-Atlantic and Great Lakes states.

In 1922, clergy from the U.S. traveled to Albania to proclaim the self-governance of the Orthodox Church in the homeland at the Congress of Berat.

By the 1950s newer generations witnessed a diocesan publication of nearly 62 liturgical and hymnographic volumes of Orthodox classic works in English.

In 1971 the Albanian Archdiocese sought and gained union with the Orthodox Church in America, expressing the desire to expand the Orthodox witness to America at large, giving it an indigenous character.

The Albanian Archdiocese remains vigilant for its brothers and sisters in the homeland who are denied the lifegiving mysteries of the faith, and serves as an important

resource for human rights issues and Albanian affairs, in addition to its programs for youth, theological education, vocational interest programs, and retreats for young adults and women. A Lay Ministry program was recently formed to engage a more active witness among the laity.

OFFICERS

Metropolitan Theodosius, 529 E. Broadway Boston, MA 02127. Tel. (617)268-1275

Chancellor, Very Rev. Arthur E. Liolin, 60 Antwerp St., East Milton, MA 02186. Tel. (617)698-3366

Lay Chpsn., Thomas Sotir, 145 Highland St., Newton, MA 02102 Tel. (617)244-5670

Treas., Pauline Loukas, 58 Orchard St., Jamaica Plains, MA 02130. Tel. (617)524-6859

PERIODICAL

The Vineyard (Vreshta), (q), Rev. Stephen Siniari, 5490 Main St., Trumbull, CT 06611

Albanian Orthodox Diocese of America

This Diocese was organized in 1950 as a canonical body administering to the Albanian faithful. It is under the ecclesiastical jurisdiction of the Ecumenical Patriarchate of Constantinople (Istanbul).

GENERAL ORGANIZATION

Headquarters: Mailing Address: 270 Cabot St., Newton, MA 02160. Tel. (617)731-3500

OFFICER

Vicar General, The Rev. Ik. Ilia Katre

Allegheny Wesleyan Methodist Connection (Original Allegheny Conference)

This body was formed in 1968 by members of the Allegheny Conference (located in eastern Ohio and western Pennsylvania) of the Wesleyan Methodist Church, which merged in 1966 with the Pilgrim Holiness Church to form The Wesleyan Church.

The Allegheny Wesleyan Methodist Church is composed of persons "having the form and seeking the power of godliness, united in order to pray together, to receive the word of exhortation, and to watch over one another in love, that they may help each other to work out their salvation." There is a strong commitment to congregational government and to holiness of heart and life.

Churches: 24; Inclusive Membership: 2,474; Sunday of Sabbath Schools: 126; Total Enrollment: 6,755; Ordained Clergy: 199

GENERAL ORGANIZATION

Annual Conference: next session, June 1988

General Conference: quadrennial (next session, June 1990).

Headquarters: 1827 Allen Dr., Salem, OH 44460. Tel. (216)337-9376.

OFFICERS

Pres., Rev. John B. Durfee, 1827 Allen Dr., Salem, OH 44460

Vice-Pres., Rev. John Englant, Pittsfield, PA 16340

Sec., Rev. W. H. Cornell, Box 266, Sagamore, PA 16250

Treas., Mr. Clair Taylor, 858 E. Philadelphia Ave., Youngstown, OH 44502

PERIODICAL

The Allegheny Wesleyan Methodist (m), 1827 Allen Dr., Salem, OH 44460, Rev. John B. Durfee, Ed.

Amana Church Society

The Amana Church Society was founded by a God-fearing, God-loving, and pioneering group not associated with any other church or organization. It had its beginning as the Community of True Inspiration in the year 1714 in the province of Hesse, Germany. The members were much persecuted in Germany because of their belief in the 'power of divine inspiration,' because they would not send their children to the ten established schools, and because they were pacifistic in their beliefs and aims.

The Community of True Inspiration, which had its humble beginning under the inspired leadership of Eberhard Ludwig Gruber and Johann Friedrich Rock, was more or less dormant during the early nineteenth century until renewal came to the group when Christian Metz assumed the leadership. He, while divinely inspired, designated that their path lay to the West and the New World. This trek, begun in 1842, ended in the Ebenezer Community, which they established near Buffalo in New York state. Because of deterring and worldly influences, the Ebenezer lands were abandoned in 1854 and subsequently the Amana Colonies were founded in Iowa in 1855.

The Amana Church Society does no proselyting, does not do missionary work, and does not actively work to make converts to the faith. It believes in a peaceful, quiet, 'brotherly' way of life. Although many of the stricter church rules have been relaxed over the years, the Amana Church Society still maintains its simple, unostentatious churches and rituals; although there have been no divinely inspired leaders since the demise of Barbara Landman Heinemann in 1883, the faith is still paramount in divine revelation of the Word of God through his chosen representatives on earth, and the testimonies of the aforementioned religious leaders are still read in all the regular services. Although the Amana Church has no connection with any other church society, the permanency of this small group over the years attests to a faith in God that makes the term *Amana* truly meaningful—"as a rock" or "to remain faithful."

Churches: 4; Inclusive Membership: 890; Sunday or Sabbath Schools: 4; Total Enrollment: 83; Ordained Clergy: 14

GENERAL ORGANIZATION

Board of Trustees

OFFICERS

Pres., Charles L. Selzer, Homestead, IA 52236
Vice-Pres., Kirk Setzer, Amana, IA 52203
Sec., Martin Roemig, Amana, IA 52203
Treas., Henry Schiff, Amana, IA 52203

The American Baptist Association

The American Baptist Association (ABA) is an international fellowship of independent Baptist churches voluntarily cooperating in missionary, evangelistic, benevolent, and Christian education activities throughout the world. Its beginnings can be traced to the landmark movement of the 1850s. Led by James R. Graves and J. M. Pendleton, a significant number of Baptist churches in the South, claiming a New Testament heritage, rejected as extrascriptural the policies of the newly formed Southern Baptist Convention (SBC). Because they strongly advocated church equality, many of these churches continued doing mission and benevolent work apart from the SBC, electing to work through local associations. Meeting in Texarkana, Texas, in 1924, delegates from the various churches effectively merged two of these major associations—the Baptist Missionary Association of Texas and the General Association—forming the American Baptist Association.

Since 1924, mission efforts have been supported in Canada, Mexico, Central and South America, Australia, Africa, Europe, and Asia. An even more successful domestic mission effort has changed the ABA from a predominantly rural southern organization to one with churches in 45 states.

Through its publishing arm in Texarkana, the ABA publishes literature and books numbering into the thousands. Major seminaries include the Missionary Baptist Seminary, founded by Dr. Ben M. Bogard in Little Rock, Arkansas; Oklahoma Missionary Baptist College in Marlow, Oklahoma; and Florida Baptist Schools in Lakeland, Florida.

While no person may speak for the churches of the ABA, all accept the Bible as the inerrant Word of God. They believe Christ was the virgin-born Son of God, that God is a triune God, that the only church is the local congregation of scripturally baptized believers, and that the work of the church is to spread the gospel.

Churches: 1,705; Inclusive Membership: 250,000; Sunday or Sabbath Schools: N. R. Total Enrollment: N.R: Ordained Clergy: 1,760

GENERAL ORGANIZATION

American Baptist Association Offices: 4605 N. State Line Ave., Texarkana, TX 75503. Tel. (214) 792-2783

OFFICERS

Pres., Ken Ashlock, 333 W. Centerville Rd., Garland, TX 75041
Vice-Presidents, W. E. Norris, P.O. Box 8, Sullivan, MO 63080; J. B. Powers, 607 N. Aubrey Circle, Greenwood, MS 38930; John Owen, 104 Reynolds Rd., Bryant, AR 72022
Rec. Clks., Larry Clements, P.O. Box 234, Monticello, AR 71655; Gene Smith, 1208 W. 35th St., Pine Bluff, AR 71601
Ed.-in-Chief Publications, Dr. Bill Johnson, P.O. Box 502, Texarkana, AR 75504
Bus. Mgr., Publications, Tom Sannes, Box 1828, Texarkana, AR 75501
Dir. Meeting Arrangements, Edgar N. Sutton, P.O. Box 240, Alexander, AR 72002
Sec.-Treas., D. S. Madden, P.O. Box 1050, Texarkana, AR-TX 75504

PERIODICALS

Missionary Baptist Searchlight (s-m), Box 663, Little Rock, AR 72203
Baptist Monitor (s-m), Box 591, Henderson, TX 75652
The Missionary (m), Box 5116, Nashville, TN 37206
The Baptist Anchor (s-m), Box 1641, Lakeland, FL 33802
The Missionary Baptist News, Box 123, Minden, LA 71055
Baptist Sentinel, Box 848, Bellflower, CA 90706
The Baptist Review, Box 287, Marlow, OK 23055
Christian Education Bulletin (q), P.O. Box 901, Texarkana, AR-TX 76605
A. B. A. Missions (q), P.O. Box 1050, Texarkana, AR-TX 75504

American Baptist Churches in the U.S.A.

Originally known as the Northern Baptist Convention, this body of Baptist churches changed the name to American Baptist Convention in 1950 with a commitment to "hold the name in trust for all Christians of like faith and mind who desire to bear witness to the historical Baptist convictions in a framework of cooperative Protestantism."

In 1972 American Baptist Churches in the U.S.A. was adopted as the new name. Although national missionary organizational developments began in 1814 with the establishment of the American Baptist Foreign Mission Society and continued with the organization of the American Baptist Publication Society in 1824 and the American Baptist Home Mission Society in 1832, the general denominational body was not formed until 1907. American Baptist work at the local level dates back to the organization by Roger Williams of the First Baptist Church in Providence, R. I. in 1638.

Churches: 5,864; Inclusive Membership: 1,576,483; Sunday or Sabbath Schools: N.R.; Total Enrollment: 384,477; Ordained Clergy: 7,678

GENERAL ORGANIZATION

Convention: Biennial
Offices: P. O. Box 851, Valley Forge Pa. 19482 Tel. (215) 768-2000

OFFICERS

Pres., Harold Davis
Vice-Pres., Charles I. Hendricks
Budget Review Officer: Dorothy J. Herrin
Interim Gen. Sec., Chester J. Jump, Jr.
Assoc. Gen. Sec./Treas.: Robert J. Allen
National Secs:, William K. Cober, Ronald G. Taylor, Daniel E. Weiss, Dean R. Wright
Offic of the General Secretary: Interim Gen.Sec., Chester J. Jump, Jr.; Assoc. Gen. Sec./Treas., Robert J. Allen; Research and Planning: Deputy Gen. Sec., Richard K. Gladden; Cooperative Christianity: Interim Deputy Gen. Sec., Olive Tiller; Dir. of Acct., Donald W. Brown; Assoc. Gen. Sec. for Regional Operations, Milton E. Owens; Personnel and Special Services: Deputy Gen. Sec., George B. Williams; Assoc. Gen. Sec. for World Mission Support, Richard E. Rusbuldt

REGION/STATE/CITY ORGANIZATIONS:

Central Region, American Baptist Churches of, Fred W. Thompson, Box 4105, Topeka, KS 66604 (Kansas and Oklahoma)
Chicago Baptist Associaton, William E. Nelson, 59 E. Van Buren, Ste. 257 Chicago 60605
Cleveland Baptist Association, Richard E. Johnson, 1737 Euclid Ave., Ste. 240, Cleveland 44115
Connecticut, American Baptist Churches of, Robert H. Roberts, 100 Bloomfield Ave., Hartford 06105
District of Columbia Baptist Convention, James A. Langley, 1628 16th St., NW, 20009
Great Rivers Region, American Baptist Churches of the, J. Ralph Beaty, P.O. Box 3786, Springfield, IL 62708 (Illinois & Missouri)
Indiana, American Baptist Churches of, L. Eugene Ton, 1350 North Delaware St., Indianapolis 46202
Indianapolis Baptist Association, Larry D. Sayre, 1350 N. Delaware St., Indianapolis 46202
Los Angeles Baptist City Mission Society, Emory C. Campbell, 1212 Wilshire Blvd., Los Angeles, 90017
Maine, American Baptist Churches of, Calvin L. Moon, 107 Winthrop St., Augusta 04330
Massachusetts, American Baptist Churches of, Roscoe C. Robison, 88 Tremont St., Room 500, Boston 02108
Metropolitan New York, American Baptist Churches of Carl E. Flemister, 322 8th Ave., 2nd Fl., New York, NY 10001
Michigan, American Baptist Churches of, Robert E. Shaw, 4610 S. Hagadorn Rd., East Lansing MI 48823
Mid-American Baptist Churches, Telfer L. Epp, P. O. Box 7508, Des Moines, IA 50322, (Iowa & Minnesota)
Monroe Association, American Baptist Churches of, Carrol A. Turner, 175 Genesee St., Rochester 14611 (Rochester & vicinity)
Nebraska, American Baptist Churches of, Heinz H. Grabia, 6404 Maple St., Omaha 68104
New Hampshire, American Baptist Churches of, Robert W. Williams, P.O. Box 796, Concord 03301

New Jersey, American Baptist Churches of, George D. Younger, 161 Freeway Dr. E., East Orange, 07018
New York State, American Baptist Churches of, Sumner M. Grant, 3049 E. Genesee St., Syracuse 13224
Niagara Frontier, American Baptist Churches of the, Kathryn W. Baker, 1272 Delaware Ave., Buffalo, N.Y. 14209 (Buffalo & vicinity)
North Dakota Baptist State Convention, Richard L. Waltz, 1524 S. Summit Ave., Sioux Falls, SD 57105
Northwest, American Baptist Churches of, Robert C. Bradford, 321 First Ave. W., Seattle, 98119 (Alaska, Idaho, Montana, Utah, Washington)
Ohio Baptist Convention, Rev Robert A. Fisher, P.O. Box 376, Granville 43023
Oregon, American Baptist Churches of, Glenn E. Camper, 0245 SW Bancroft St., Portland 97201
Pacific Southwest, American Baptist Churches of the, W. Lowell Fairley, 970 Village Oaks Dr., Covina, CA 91724 (Arizona, Baja, Southern California, So. Nevada & Hawaii)
Pennsylvania & Delaware, American Baptist Churches of, R. Eugene Crow, American Baptist Churches USA, Room C-127, Valley Forge, PA 19481
Philadelphia Baptist Association, Larry K. Waltz, 1701 Arch St., Rm. 417, Philadelphia 19103
Pittsburgh Baptist Association, Carlton B. Goodwin, 1620 Allegheny Bldg., 429 Forbes Ave., Pittsburgh, PA 15219
Puerto Rico, Baptist Churches of, Pedro Hernandez, Mayaguez #21, Hato Rey, PR 00917
Rhode Island, American Baptist Churches of, Donald H. Crosby, 734 Hope St., Providence, RI 02906
Rocky Mountains, American Baptist Churches of, O. Dean Nelson, 1344 Pennsylvania St., Denver 80203 (Colorado, Wyoming & New Mexico)
South Dakota Baptist Convention, Richard L. Waltz, 1524 South Summit Ave., Sioux Falls 57105
South, American Baptist Churches of the, Walter L. Parrish II, 14440 Cherry Lane Ct., Ste. 101, Laurel, MD 20707 (Alabama, Arkansas, Florida, Georgia, Kentucky, Louisiana, Maryland, Mississippi, North Carolina, Oklahoma, South Carolina, Tennessee, Texas, Virginia)
Vermont Baptist State Convention, Paul T. Losh, 19 Orchard Terrace, Burlington 05401
West, American Baptist Churches of, Robert D. Rasmussen, P.O. Box 23204, Oakland, CA 94623 (Northern California, Northern Nevada)
West Virginia Baptist Convention, Douglas W. Hill, P.O. Box 1019, Parkersburg 26101.
Wisconsin, American Baptist Churches of, William L. Wells, 15330 W. Watertown Plank Rd., Elm Grove, 53122

Board of Educational Ministries (incorporated as the American Baptist Board of Education and Publication) including Judson Press and Judson Book Store. Office: P.O. Box 851, Valley Forge, PA 19482. Exec. Dir., Daniel E. Weiss; Treas., L. Dean Hurst; Divisional Dirs.: Christian Higher Education, Shirley M. Jones; Church Education, John L. Carroll; Publishing and Business, Arthur J. Munson, Jr.; Communication, Philip E. Jenks, Officers of the Board: Pres., Edward C. Vander Hey; Vice-Pres., Jean B. Kim; Rec. Sec., Arthur J. Munson, Jr.

American Baptist Assembly (National Training Center) Green Lake, WI 54941. Exec. Dir., Paul W. LaDue; Dir. of Programming/Scheduling, Arlo R. Reichter; Dir., of Finance, L. B. Standifer III; Officers of the Board; Pres., James A. Barnett; Vice-Pres., Royce V. Angell; Treas., William E. Jarvis; Sec., Virginia Henderson.

American Baptist Historical Society (Archives and History), 1106 S. Goodman St., Rochester, NY 14620; and P.O. Box 851, Valley Forge, PA 19482; Pres., John F. Mandt.

American Baptist Men: Exec. Dir., Richard S. McPhee,

25

P. O. Box 851, Valley Forge, PA 19482; Pres., Mark E. Erickson

American Baptist Women: Exec. Dir., Martha M. Barr, P.O. Box 851, Valley Forge, PA 19482; Pres., Marilyn J. Momose

Commission on the Ministry: Exec. Dir., Linda C. Spoolstra, P.O. Box 851, Valley Forge, PA 19482

Board of International Ministries (incorporated as American Baptist Foreign Mission Society). Office: Valley Forge, PA 19482. Pres., William L. Ebling, Jr.; Vice-Pres., Claire J. Hill; Exec. Dir., Ronald G. Taylor; Spec. Assistant, Ercel Webb; Budget Dir., Charles H. Stewart. Overseas Division: Russell E. Brown, Dir., Africa (Zaire), Ivan E. George; East Asia (Japan, Okinawa, Philippines), Raymond W. Beaver; Middle East, Alice M. Findlay; Latin America (Costa Rica, Cuba, Dominican Republic, El Salvador, Haiti, Mexico, Nicaragua), Victor M. Mercado; Caribbean (Haiti, Dominican Republic, Barbados), P. Reidar Lindland; South Asia (Bangladesh, Burma, India, Nepal) Alice M. Findlay; Southeast Asia (China, Hong Kong, Singapore, Thailand), Cecil E. Carder; Sec. for International Issues, Hunger, and Coord. for Baptist Council on World Mission, Patricia L. Magdamo; Sec. for Recruitment, Betty L. Beaman; Sec. for Personnel Development, P. Reidar Lindland;. Public Relations Division: Hugh W. Smith, Dir.; Assoc. Directors: Eleanor Menke (Church Relations); Wendy E. Ryan, (Mission Interpretation); Ronald H. Brown (Resource Development); Charlotte Gillespie (White Cross Spec. Interest Missionaries and Tours); Business and Finance Division: Dir., Treas. & Bus. Mgr., Cornelius C. Jones; Assoc. Treas. & Assoc. Dir., Austin B. Windle; Asst. to the Treas. and Dir. of Estate Planning, Cornelius C. Jones; Fund Accountant, William R. Bartlett; Dir., Estate Planning, Cornelius C. Jones; Eastern Rep. Estate Planning, Alan Williams; Western Rep., Kenneth P. Giacoletto.

Board of National Ministries (incorporated as The American Baptist Home Mission Society and Woman's American Baptist Home Mission Society). Office: Valley Forge, PA 19482. Pres., Peter F. Nicholls; Vice-Pres., J. Terry Wingate; Exec. Dir., William K. Cober; Rec. Sec., and Deputy Exec. Dir., Richard M. Jones; Mgr., Adm. Support Unit, and Treas., Harold B. Cooper; Mgr., Church & Community Development Unit, Dr. Ernestine R. Galloway; Mgr., Direct & Contract Services Unit and Natl. Dir., American Baptist Personnel Services, L. Faye Ignatius-Flemister; Mgr. Individual & Corp. Responsibility Unit, Elizabeth J. Miller; Mgr., Personal & Public Witness Unit and Evangelism Dir., Emmett V. Johnson; Mgr., Program Support Unit, Richard M. Jones.

The Ministers and Missionaries Benefit Board: Office: 475 Riverside Dr., New York, NY 10115: Pres., Howard R. Moody; Vice-Pres., Ms. Dorothy J. Herrin; Actuary: Hay/Huggins, 229 S. 18th St., Rittenhouse Sq., Philadelphia, PA 19103; Exec. Dir., Dean R. Wright; Deputy Exec. Dir. & Treas., Gordon E. Smith; Sec., Sara E. Hopkins; Assoc. Exec. Dir., Margaret Ann Cowden; Assoc. Exec. Dir., East, Richard Arnesman; Assoc. Exec. Dir., West, Terry L. Burch.

Minister Council: Exec. Dir., Harley D. Hunt; Pres., Edwina Hunter.

PERIODICALS

The American Baptist (bi-m), P.O. Box 851, Valley Forge, PA 19482. Philip Jenks, Ed.

The Baptist Leader (m), P.O. Box 851, Valley Forge, PA 19482, Linda R. Isham, Ed.

The Secret Place (q), P.O. Box 851, Valley Forge, PA 19482. Betty Lou Johnson, Guest Ed.,

American Baptist Quarterly (q), P.O. Box 851, Valley Forge, PA 19482, William R. Millar, Ed.

The American Carpatho-Russian Orthodox Greek Catholic Church

The American Carpatho-Russian Orthodox Greek Catholic Church is a self-governing diocese that is in communion with the Ecumenical Partriarchate of Constantinople. The late Patriarch Benjamin I, in an official Patriarchal Document listed as No. 1379 and dated September 19, 1938, canonized the Diocese in the name of the Orthodox Church of Christ.

GENERAL ORGANIZATION

Sobor: triennial (Next Sobor 1989, Johnstown, PA)

Headquarters: Johnstown, PA 15906. Tel. (814) 536-4207

OFFICERS

Bishop: Rt. Bishop Nicholas (Smisko)

Vicar General: Rt. Mitred Peter E. Molchany, 903 Ann St., Homestead, PA 15120

Chancellor: Very Rev. Msgr. John Yurcisin, 249 Butler Ave., Johnstown, PA 15906

Treas.: Very Rev. Msgr. Ronald A. Hazuda, 115 East Ave., Erie, PA 16503

PERIODICAL

Cerkovnyj Vistnik—Church Messenger (bi-w), 419 S. Main St., Homer City, PA 15748, Very Rev. James S. Dutko, Ed.

American Evangelical Christian Churches

Founded in 1944, the A.E.C.C. functions as a denominational body with interdoctrinal views incorporating into its ecclesiastical position both the Calvinistic and Arminian doctrines. The purpose of the organization is the propagation of the gospel through the establishment of churches, missions, and places of worship. It is not affiliated with any other religious body or organization but seeks fellowship with all who hold to the concepts set forth in the teachings of Jesus the Christ. Ministerial credentials are issued by the American Evangelical Christian Churches to men and women approved by the Credentials Committee and who subscribe to the following Articles of faith: the Bible as the written word of God; the Virgin birth; the Deity of Jesus the Christ; salvation through the atonement; the guidance of our life through prayer. Its churches operate under the name Community Churches, American Bible Churches, and Evangelical Christian Churches. Each group is an independent sovereign body. An affiliated body operates in the British Isles under the name Ministers of Evangelism by authority of the charter granted to it by the Crown. The AECC has its own Bible training school, the American Bible College. The school is interdenominational, specializing in off-campus theological studies, with numerous extension centers in various parts of the country.

National Headquarters: Chicago, IL

OFFICERS

Mod., Dr. G. W. Hyatt, Waterfront Dr., Pineland FL 33945

Sec., Dr. Ben Morgan, 64 South St., Southport, IN 46227

REGIONAL MODERATORS

Vernon Bucher, New Albany, OH

Alvin House, Bozeman, MT

Joseph Schwalb, East Northport, NY

Kenneth White, Hagerstown, MD

American Rescue Workers

Founded in 1884, this branch of the Christian Church is a national religious and social services movement which operates on a quasimilitary pattern. Membership includes officers (clergy); soldiers/adherents (laity); members of various activity groups; and volunteers who serve as advisors, associates, and committed participants in ARW service functions.

The American Rescue Workers is motivated by the love of God and a practical concern for the needs of humanity. Its purpose is to preach the gospel and undertake spiritual uplifting and provision of material aid to all persons in need, regardless of race, color, creed, sex, or age.

GENERAL ORGANIZATION

Council: annual
Headquarters: 2827 Frankford Ave., Philadelphia, PA 19134. Tel. (215) 739-6524; Washington DC Capital Area Office: 716 Ritchie Rd., Capitol Heights, MD 20743. Tel. (301)336-6200
Commander-In-Chief, General Paul Martin; Vice-Pres., Lt. Col. Claude Astin, Jr. (Chief of Staff); Natl. Sec., Col. George Gossett; Lt. Col. Robert N. Cole, National Communication/Development Dir.

PERIODICAL

The Rescue Herald (q), Box 175, Hightstown, NJ 08520, Capt. Robert Turton III, Ed.

The Anglican Orthodox Church

This body was founded on November 16, 1963, in Statesville, North Carolina, by the Most Rev. James P. Dees who is the Presiding Bishop. The church holds to 39 Articles of Religion, the 1928 Prayerbook, the King James Version of the Bible, and basic Anglican traditions and church government.

GENERAL ORGANIZATION

General Convention: Biennial (Next meeting, 1988)

OFFICER

Presiding Bishop, The Most Rev. James Parker Dees, 323 E. Walnut St., P. O. Box 128, Statesville, NC 28677. Tel. (704) 873-8365

PERIODICAL

The News (m)

The Antiochian Orthodox Christian Archdiocese of North America

The foundation of the Greek Orthodox Patriarchate of Great Antioch and all the East dates from the time of the holy apostles, the first Christian community being established there by Saints Peter and Paul. The most famous scriptural reference concerning the Church of Antioch relates that it was there that the followers of Jesus Christ were first referred to as Christians (Acts 11:26). Nicholas, one of the original seven deacons, was from Antioch and perhaps the first Christian from that ancient city (Acts 6:5). During the persecution of the church which occasioned the martyrdom of Saint Stephen the Protomartyr, members of the infant Christian community in Jerusalem fled to Antioch for refuge. Since the sixteenth century, the Antiochian patriarchate has been headquartered in Damascus, Syria. For nearly twenty centuries the gospel has been preached in and from the Antiochian Patriarchate to the glory of God and for the salvation of souls.

Since the late nineteenth century through the present, Antiochian Christians have emigrated to other parts of the world from their homelands in the Middle East. The spiritual needs of Antiochian faithful in North America were first served through the Syro-Arabian Mission of the Russian Orthodox Church. This mission was established in 1892. In 1895 the Syrian Orthodox Benevolent Society was organized by Antiochian immigrants in New York City. Dr. Ibrahim Arbeely, prominent Damascene physician, was the society's first president. Conscious of the needs of his fellow countrymen and coreligionists, Dr. Arbeely wrote to Raphael Hawaweeny, a young Damascene clergyman serving as professor of Arabic language at the Orthodox theological academy in Kazan, Russia, inviting him to come to New York to organize the first Arabic-language parish in North America. Father Raphael, a missionary at heart, went to the imperial capital of St. Petersburg to meet with His Grace Nicholas, the head of the Russian Church in North America, who happened to be visiting in Russia at that time. After being canonically received under the omophorion of Bishop Nicholas, Hawaweeny came to the United States in 1896.

Upon his arrival in New York City, Archimandrite Raphael established the first Syrian Greek Orthodox parish at 77 Washington St. in lower Manhattan, the center of the Syrian immigrant community. By 1900, approximately 3,000 Syrian immigrants had crossed the East River, establishing Brooklyn as the largest Syrian community in America at that time. Therefore, in 1902 Hawaweeny's parish purchased a larger church building in that borough. The church, placed under the heavenly patronage of Saint Nicholas the Wonderworker of Myra, was located at 301-303 Pacific St. Following renovation for Orthodox worship, the church was consecrated by Bishop Tikhon, who succeeded Nicholas as Bishop of North America on October 27, 1902. Saint Nicholas Cathedral, now located at 355 State St. in Brooklyn, is considered the "mother parish" of the Archidiocese.

At the request of Bishop Tikhon, Hawaweeny was elected his vicar bishop and head of the Syro-Arabian Mission. His consecration as Bishop of Brooklyn took place at saint Nicholas church on Pacific St. on March 12, 1904. Bishop Raphael thus became the first orthodox bishop to be consecrated in North America. He traveled throughout the continent and established new parishes for his scattered flock. He also founded *Al-Kalimat* (*The Word* magazine) in 1905 and published many liturgical books for use in his parishes. After a brief but very fruitful ministry, Bishop Raphael Hawaweeny fell asleep in Christ on February 27, 1915, at the age of 54.

With the death of Bishop Raphael and the chaos in North American church administration occasioned by the Bolshevik revolution in Russia and the First World War, the unity of Orthodoxy in the New World was ruptured. Even the small Syrian Greek Orthodox community was split into factions, each founded on differing ecclesiastical loyalties. It was not until sixty years after the death of Bishop Raphael, in June 1975, that total jurisdictional and administrative unity was restored among the children of Antioch in North America. Some of the hierarchs who have led the Syrian Greek Orthodox community in North America are Germanos Shehadi, Aftimios Ofiesh, Victor Abo-Assaley, Emmanuel Abo-Hatab, Samuel David, and Antony Bashir.

On June 24, 1975, Metropolitan Philip Saliba, of the Antiochian Archdiocese of New York, and Metropolitan Michael Shaheen of the Antiochian archdiocese of Toledo, Ohio, signed the Articles of Reunification which restored administrative unity among all Antiochian Orthodox Christians in the United States and Canada. This document was presented to the Holy Synod of the Patriarchate, which ratified the contents on August 19, 1975, recognizing Saliba as the Metropolitan Primate and Shaheen as Auxiliary Archbishop. On January 9, 1983, a second auxiliary to the Metropolitan, Bishop Antoun Khouri, was consecrated at Brooklyn's Saint Nicholas Cathedral.

The Archdiocesan Board of Trustees (consisting of 50 elected and appointed clergy and lay members) and the Metropolitan's Advisory Council (consisting of clergy and lay representatives from each parish and mission) meet regularly to assist the Primate in the administration of the Archdiocese. Each summer six regional Parish Life Conferences are convened (Canadian-American Region, New England Region, Eastern Region, Midwest Region, Southwest Region, and Western Region) which attract thousands of people of all ages from the parishes and missions.

GENERAL ORGANIZATION

General Assembly: biennial.
Headquarters: 358 Mountain Rd., Englewood, NJ 07631. Tel. (201) 871-1355

OFFICERS

Metropolitan Philip (Saliba), Primate; Archbishop Michael (Shaheen), Auxiliary; Bishop Antoun (Khouri), Auxiliary

PERIODICAL

The Word (m), V. Rev. George S. Corey

Apostolic Catholic Assyrian Church of the East, North American Dioceses

This is the ancient Christian Church, and even though the official name of the Church is the Holy Apostolic Assyrian Church of the East, there are many variations of this combination of words. It is also known as Assyrian Church, Assyrian Orthodox, Persian (Babylonian) and the misnomer "Nestorian" Church, among others.

The Church was founded in 37 A.D., the year our Lord Jesus was crucified, by Sts. Peter, Thomas, Thaddaeus and Bartholomew of the Twelve and Mari and Aggai of the Seventy, in Edessa (Urhai), state of Oshroene in the Persian Region. Prior to the Great Persecution, at the hands of Tamerlane and others that followed, the Church was said to have been the largest Christian Church in the world.

The doctrine of the Church is that of the Apostles, stressing two natures and two "Qnume" in one person, perfect God and perfect man. The Church accepts the title "Mother of Christ" for the Blessed Virgin Mary, but rejects the appelation of "Mother of God", the original Nicene Creed, the Ecumenical Councils of Nicaea and Constantinople, and the Church Fathers of those periods. The Church has maintained a line of patriarchs from the time of the Holy Apostles until the present. The Church, is governed by the patriarch, His Holiness Mar Dinkha IV, Catholicos-Patriarch of the East, the 120th successor to the See, the metropolitans and the bishops, comprising the Synod.

GENERAL ORGANIZATION

Diocesan Council of Clergy: Annual (Summer or Fall)
Diocesan Central Committee (Lay representatives of each parish): Annual
Headquarters: Apostolic Catholic Assyrian Church of the East, North American Diocese, 8908 Birch Ave., Morton Grove, IL 60053. Tel. (312) 966-0009

OFFICERS

Bishop for Eastern U.S. and Canada: His Grace, Bishop Mar Aprim Khamis, 890 Birch Ave., Morton Grove, IL 60053. Tel. (312) 966-0009
Bishop for Western U.S.: His Grace, Bishop Mar Bawai, P.O. Box 32035, San Jose, CA 95152. Tel. (408) 923-1752; Sec., Fr. Mark L. Brown, 2990 Fruitbridge Rd., Sacramento, CA 95820. Tel. (916) 428-4559

PERIODICAL

Qala Min Madinka (Voice from the East) (q), Mr. Akhitiar B. Moshi and Rev. Samuel Dinkha, Eds.

Apostolic Christian Church (Nazarene)

This body was formed in America by an immigration from various European nations, from a movement begun by Rev. S. H. Froehlich, a Swiss pastor, whose followers are still found in Switzerland and Central Europe.

OFFICERS

Apostolic Christian Church Foundation, P.O. Box 151, Tremont, IL 61568, Gen. Sec., Eugene R. Galat, P.O. Box 151, Tremont, IL 61568. Tel. (309) 925-5162

PERIODICAL

Newsletter (bi-m)

Apostolic Christian Churches in America

The Apostolic Christian Church of America consists of 17,000 members in 80 congregations in 18 states, one in Canada, and two in Japan. The church was founded in the early 1830's in Switzerland by Samuel Froehlich, a young divinity student who experienced a religious conversion based on the pattern found in the New Testament and founded a church known as Evangelical Baptist. His work resulted in the formation of 110 congregations in 35 years in various surrounding countries.

In 1847, Elder Benedict Weyeneth, an associate of Froehlich, came to America and the first church was established in upstate New York. Other churches were formed with the highest concentration today in the Midwest farm belt. In America, the church became known as Apostolic Christian.

Church doctrine is based on a literal interpretation of the Bible, the infallible Word of God. The church believes that a true faith in Christ's redemptive work at Calvary is manifested by a sincere repentance and conversion. Following baptism by immersion and the laying on of hands of the presbytery, members strive for sanctification and separation from worldliness. This is as a consequence of salvation, not a means to obtain it. Security in Christ is believed to be conditional based on faithfulness. Discipline is lovingly applied to erring members.

A high degree of brotherhood and closely knit fellowship exist throughout the denomination. The biblical ideals of likemindedness and uniform observance of scriptural standards of holiness are stressed. Holy Communion is confined to members of the church. Members do not swear oaths, but affirm. Male members are willing to serve in the military, but do not bear arms. The holy kiss is practiced and women wear headcoverings during prayer and worship.

Doctrinal authority rests with a council of elders, each of whom also serves as a local elder (bishop). Both elders and ministers are chosen from local congregations, do not attend seminary, and serve without compensation. Sermons are delivered extemporaneously as led by the Holy Spirit, using the Bible as a text.

Churches: 80; Inclusive Membership: 16,916; Sunday or Sabbath Schools: 79; Total Enrollment: 6,197; Ordained Clergy: 347

CORRESPONDENT

Elder (Bishop) Dale Eisenmann, 6913 Wilmette, Darien, IL 60559. Tel. (312)969-7021

Apostolic Faith Mission of Portland, Oregon

The Apostolic Faith Mission of Portland, Oregon, was founded in 1907. It had its beginning in the Latter Rain outpouring on Azusa street in Los Angeles, California, in 1906.

Some of the main doctrines are justification by faith; spiritual new birth, as Jesus told Nicodemus and as Martin Luther proclaimed in the Great Reformation; sanctification, a second definite work of grace, the Wesleyan teaching of holiness, which Jesus prayed for us to have in John 17; the baptism of the Holy Ghost as experienced on the Day of Pentecost, and again poured out at the beginning of the Latter Rain revival in Los Angeles.

Mrs. Florence L. Crawford, who had received the baptism of the Holy Ghost in Los Angeles, brought this Latter Rain message to Portland on Christmas Day 1906. It has spread to the world by means of literature which is still published and mailed everywhere without a subscription price. Collections are never taken in the meetings and the public is not asked for money.

Camp meetings have been held annually in Portland, Oregon, since 1907, with delegations coming from around the world.

Missionaries from the Portland headquarters have established churches in Korea, Japan, and the Philippines. In the early days, European churches were established by people of different nationalities returning with the Good News to their homelands. The message has always been that people can have their sins forgiven and go forth, as Jesus said, to "sin no more."

GENERAL ORGANIZATION

Convention: annual (July)
Headquarters: 6615 S.E. 52nd Ave., Portland, OR 97206
Tel. (503) 777-1741

OFFICER

Gen. Overseer, Rev. Loyce C. Carver; 6615 S.E. 52nd Ave., Portland, OR 97206

PERIODICAL

The Light of Hope (bi-m), 6615 S.E. 52nd Ave., Portland, OR 97206. Tel. (503) 777-1741. Rev. Loyce C. Carver, Ed.

Apostolic Faith Mission Church of God

The Apostolic Faith Mission Church of God was founded and organized July 10, 1906, by Bishop F. W. Williams in Mobile, Alabama.

Bishop Williams was saved and filled with the Holy Ghost at a revival in Los Angeles under Elder W. J. Seymour of The Divine Apostolic Faith Movement. After being called into the ministry, Bishop Williams went out to preach the gospel stopping in Mississippi, then moving on to Mobile, Alabama.

On October 9, 1915, the Apostolic Faith Mission Church of God was incorporated in Mobile, Alabama under Bishop Williams who was also the general overseer of this church.

GENERAL ORGANIZATION

General Assembly; annual in the third week in June, Birmingham, AL
Headquarters: 3344 Pearl Ave., N., Birmingham, AL 36101

OFFICERS

Board of Bishops: Presiding Bishop, Houston Ward, P. O. Box 551, Cantonment, FL 39533. Tel. (904) 587-2339; Billy Carter, J. L. Smiley, T. L. Frye, D. Brown, T. C. Tolbert, R. B. Hawthorne and N. M. Andrews.

NATIONAL DEPARTMENTS

Missionary Dept., Pres., Sr. Sarah Ward, Cantonment, FL

Youth Dept., Pres., W. J. Wills, Lincoln, AL
Sunday School Dept., Supt., Thomas Brooks, Decatur, GA
Mother Dept., Pres., Lola Robertson, Birmingham, AL

Apostolic Lutheran Church of America

Organized in 1872 as Solomon Korteniemi Lutheran Society, this Finnish body was incorporated in 1929 as the Finnish Apostolic Lutheran Church in America and changed its name to Apostolic Lutheran Church of America in 1962.

This body stresses preaching the Word of God and therefore there is an absence of liturgy and formalism in worship. A seminary education is not required of pastors. Being called by God to preach the Word is the chief requirement for clergy and laity. The church stresses personal absolution and forgiveness of sins, as practiced by Martin Luther, and the importance of bringing converts into God's kingdom.

Churches: 51; Inclusive Membership 6,353; Sunday or Sabbath Schools: 39; Total Enrollment: 2,646; Ordained Clergy: 39

GENERAL ORGANIZATION

Meets annually in June

OFFICERS

Pres., Richard E. Sakrisson, 7606 NE Vancouver Mall Dr. #14, Vancouver, WA 98662
Sec., James Johnson, Rt. 1, Box 462, Houghton, MI 49931
Treas., Rev. Richard Barney, Rt. 2, Box 210, Chassell, MI 49916

PERIODICAL

Christian Monthly (m), Apostolic Lutheran Book Concern, Rt. 1, Box 150, New York Mills, MN 56567, Mr. Alvar Helmes, Ed., Rt. 2, Box 293, Rockford, MN 55373

Apostolic Overcoming Holy Church of God, Inc.

The late Right Reverent William Thomas Phillips (1893–1973), one of the greatest religious leaders of this Christian era, was thoroughly convinced in 1912 that Holiness was a system through which God wanted him to serve. In 1916 he was led to Mobile, Alabama, where he organized the Ethiopian Overcoming Holy Church of God on March 16. Realizing that God's message was to all people, on April 1, 1941, the church was incorporated in the state of Alabama under its present title. Upon his death on November 30, 1973, Bishop Phillips had successfully served for 57 years.

The disciples of the church have retained their congregational policy, with each congregation managing its own affairs, united under districts governed by overseers and diocesan bishops, and assisted by an executive board comprised of bishops, ministers, laymen, and the National Secretary. The General Assembly convenes annually (June 1–10). Our chief objective is to enlighten people of God's holy Word and to be a blessing to every nation on earth. The main purpose of this church is to ordain elders, appoint pastors, and send out divinely called misionaries and teachers. This church enforces all ordinances enacted by Jesus Christ. We believe in water baptism according to Acts 2:38, 8:12, and 10:47. We administer the Lord's Supper and observe the washing of feet according to John 13:4-7. We believe and teach that Jesus Christ shed his blood to sanctify the people and cleanse them from all sin. Matrimonies are solemnized in accordance with Hebrews 13:4, and the burying of the dead is enacted according to Genesis 23:3-4. We believe in the resurrection of the dead and the second coming of Christ.

Churches: 175; Inclusive Membership: 12,310; Sunday or Sabbath Schools: N.R.; Total Enrollment: N.R.; Ordained Clergy: 295

OFFICERS

Senior Bishop and Exec. Head, Rt. Rev. Jasper Roby, 1120 N. 24th St., Birmingham, AL 35234
Associate Bishops: Bishop G. W. Ayers, 1717 Arlington Blvd., El Cerrito, CA 94530; Bishop L. M. Bell, 2000 Pio Nono Ave., Macon, GA 31206; Bishop E. D. Moore, 1540 E. 70th St., Cleveland, Oh 44103; Bishop Gabriel Crutcher, 526 E. Bethune St. Detroit, MI 48202; Bishop John Mathews, 12 College St., Dayton, OH 45407
Exec. Sec., Mrs. Juanita R. Arrington, 1120 N. 24th St., Birmingham, Al 35234

PERIODICAL

The People's Mouthpiece(q)

Armenian Apostolic Church of America

Widespread movement of the Armenian people over the centuries caused the development of two seats of religious jurisdiction of the Armenian Apostolic Church in the World: the See of Etchmiadzin, now in Soviet Armenia, and the See of Cilicia, in Lebanon.

In America, the Armenian Church functioned under the jurisdiction of the Etchmiadzin See from 1887 to 1933, when a division occurred within the American diocese over the condition of the church in Soviet Armenia. One group chose to remain independent until 1957, when the Holy See of Cilicia agreed to accept them under its jurisdiction.

Despite the existence of two dioceses in North America, the Armenian Church has always functioned as one church in dogma and liturgy.

Churches: 18; Inclusive Membership: 29,070; Sunday or Sabbath Schools: 13; Total Enrollment: 500; Ordained Clergy: 19

GENERAL ORGANIZATION

National Representative Assembly: annual
Headquarters: 138 E. 39 St., New York, NY 10016. Tel. (212) 689-7810

OFFICERS

Prelate, Eastern Prelacy, Archbishop Mesrob Ashjian, 138 E. 39th St., New York, NY 10016. Tel. (212) 689-7810
Prelate, Western Prelacy, Archbishop Datev Sarkissian, 4401 Russell Ave., Los Angeles, CA 90026
Chpsn., Eastern Prelacy, Nerses Chitjian
Chpsn., Western Prelacy, Vatché Mandenlian

DEPARTMENTS

AREC, Armenian Religious Educational Council, Exec. Coord., Mrs. Joanna Baghsarian
ANEC, Armenian National Educational Council, Exec. Coord., Hourig Sahagian-Papazian

PERIODICAL

Outreach (m), 138 E. 39th St., New York, NY 10016

Armenian Church of America, Diocese of the

The Armenian Apostolic Church was founded at the foot of the biblical mountain of Ararat in the ancient land of Armenia. Saints Thaddeus and Bartholomew preached Christianity in this ancient land. In 301 the historic Mother Church of Etchmiadzin was built by Saint Gregory the Illuminator, the first Catholicos of All Armenians. This cathedral still stands and serves as the center of the Armenian Church. A branch of this Church was established in North America in 1889 by the then Catholicos of All Armenians, Khrimian Hairig. Armenian immigrants built the first Armenian church in the new world in Worcester, Massachusetts, under the jurisdiction of Holy Etchmiadzin.

In 1927, as a result of the growth of the communities in California, the churches and the parishes there were formed into a separate Western Diocese under the jurisdiction of Holy Etchmiadzin, Armenia. The parishes in Canada formed their own diocese in 1984, under the jurisdiction of the Mother See of Etchmiadzin. In 1933 a few parishes seceded from the Armenian Church Diocese of America and in 1958 were formed into an illicit diocese, keeping, however, its oneness in dogma and liturgy.

The Armenian Apostolic Church, under the jurisdiction of Holy Etchmiadzin, also includes the Armenian Patriarchate of Jerusalem and the Armenian Patriarchate of Constantinople.

GENERAL ORGANIZATION

Eastern Diocese
Diocesan Assembly: Annual
Diocesan offices: 630 Second Ave., New York, NY 10016. Tel. (212) 686-0710

Western Diocese
Diocesan Assembly: Annual
Diocesan offices: 1201 N. Vine St., Hollywood, CA 90038. Tel. (213) 466-5265

OFFICERS

Eastern Diocese
Primate, His Eminence the Most Rev. Archbishop Torkom Manoogian, 630 Second Ave., New York, NY 10016
Vicar Gen., V. Rev. Fr. Khajag Barsamian, 630 Second Ave., New York, NY 10016
Chpsn., Diocesan Council, Vincent Gurahian, Macauhay Rd., RFD 2, Katonah, NY 10536
Sec., Diocesan Council: Edward Onanian, 13010 Hathaway Dr., Wheaton, MD 20906
Western Diocese
Primate, His Eminence Archbishop Vatche Hovsepian, 1201 N. Vine St., Hollywood, CA 90038, Tel. (213) 466-5265
Chpsn., Diocesan Council: The Rev. Fr. Vartan Kasparian, St. Mary Armenian Church, P.O. Box 367, Yettem, CA 93670
Sec., Diocesan Council: Armen Hampar, 6134 Pat Ave., Woodland Hills, CA 91367

PERIODICALS FOR BOTH DIOCESES

The Armenian Church, (m), 630 Second Ave., New York, NY 10016
Dept. of Religious Education Bulletin (m), 630 Second Ave., New York, NY 10016
The Mother Church (m), 1201 No. Vine St., Hollywood, CA 90038, Rev. Fr. Sipan Mekhsian, Ed

Assemblies of God

From a few hundred delegates at its founding convention in 1914 at Hot Springs, Arkansas, the Assemblies of God has become the largest church group in the modern Pentecostal movement worldwide. Throughout its existence it has emphasized the power of the Holy Spirit to change lives and the participation of all members in the work of the church.

The revival that led to the formation of the Assemblies of God and numerous other church groups early in the twentieth century began during times of intense prayer and Bible study. Believers in the United States and around the world received spiritual experiences like those described in the Book of Acts. Accompanied by baptism in the Holy Spirit and its initial physical evidence of "speaking in tongues," or a language unknown to the person, their experiences were associated with the coming of the Holy Spirit at Pentecost (Acts 2), so participants were called Pentecostals.

Along with the baptism in the Holy Spirit, the church also believes that the Bible is God's infallible Word to man, that salvation is available only through Jesus Christ, that divine healing is made possible through Christ's suffering, and that Christ will return again for those who love him. In recent years, this Pentecostal revival has spilled over into almost every denomination in a new wave of revival sometimes called the charismatic renewal.

Assemblies of God leaders credit their church's rapid and continuing growth to its acceptance of the New Testament as a model for the present-day church. Aggressive evangelism, and missionary zeal at home and abroad characterize the denomination.

Assemblies of God believers observe two ordinances—water baptism by immersion and the Lord's Supper, or Holy Communion. The church is trinitarian, holding that God exists in three persons, Father, Son, and Holy Spirit.

Churches: 10,886; Inclusive Membership: 2,135,104; Sunday or Sabbath Schools: 10,572; Total Enrollment: 1,404,974; Ordained Clergy: 26,837

GENERAL ORGANIZATION

General Council: biennial, (August)
International Headquarters: 1445 Boonville Ave., Springfield, MO 65802. Tel. (417) 862-2781

EXECUTIVE PRESBYTERY

Gen. Supt: G. Raymond Carlson; Asst. Supt.: Everett R. Stenhouse
Gen. Sec.: Joseph R. Flower
Gen. Treas.: Raymond H. Hudson
Exec. Dir., Foreign Missions: J. Philip Hogan; Great Lakes: Robert K. Schmidgall, P.O. Box 296-1155 Aurora Ave., Naperville, IL 69540; Gulf: James Harmill, 475 N. Highland, 7-B, Memphis, TN 38122; North Central: Herman H. Rohde, 1315 Portland Ave. S, Minneapolis, MN 55404; Northeast: Almon Bartholomew, P.O. Box 39, Liverpool, NY 13081; Northwest: R. L. Brandt, 1702 Colton Blvd., Billings, MT 59102; South Central: Paul Lowenberg, 6015 E. Ninth St., Wichita, KS 67208; Southeast: J. Foy Johnson, P.O. Drawer C, Lakeland, FL 33802; Southwest: Glen D. Cole, 9470 Micron Rd., Sacramento, CA 95827

INTERNATIONAL HEADQUARTERS

All departmental offices are at Assemblies of God International Headquarters, 1445 Boonville Ave., Springfield, MO 65802
General Superintendent's Office Administration: Gen. Supt., G. Raymond Carlson
Spiritual Life-Evangelism: Coord., C. W. Denton; MAPS Coord., Lamar Headley; MAPS Construction Rep. for Home Missions, Patrick J. Donadio; MAPS Construction Rep. for Foreign Missions, Glenn A. Thompson; MAPS Promotions Coord., Helen Braxton; Evangelists Field Rep., Robert M. Abbott, Conference and Convention Coord., John V. Ohlin
Personnel: Mgr., Ray F. Roepke
General Services: Administrator, Jimmy Dunn
Buildings and Properties: Administrator, Melvin Sachs
Legal Counselor: Richard R. Hammar
Research: Sec., Norma Thomas
General Secretary's Office Administration: Gen. Sec., Joseph R. Flower; Secretariat Supervisor, Linda Reece, Statistician, Sherri Doty

A/G Archives: Dir. of Archives, Wayne Warner; Archives Asst., Joyce Lee
Division of the Treasury: Gen. Treasurer, Raymond H. Hudson; Adm., Clyde L. Hawkins
Stewardship Dept.: Sec., Deferred Giving and Trusts Dept.: Sec., Mel DeVries; Deferred Giving and Trusts Regional Consultants, David Watson, Ray Loven, J. Don Ross; Troy Lyon; Promotion Coord., Freda Jackson
Finance Dept.: Administrator of Accounting Services, Kenneth Tripp
Benevolences Dept.: Sec., Stanley V. Michael; Field Representative and Church Relations Coord., Robert Bornert; Promotions Coord./Ed., Owen Wilkie
Church Loan Dept.: Sec., Glenn A. Renick, Jr.
Division of Christian Education, Natl. Dir., _____
Church School Literature Dept.: Ed., Charles W. Ford; Assoc. Ed., Gary Leggett; Adult Ed., John Maempa; Youth Ed., Nick Knoth; Elementary Ed., Cathy Ketcher; Early Childhood Ed., Sharon Ellard; Children's Church Ed., Sinda Zinn; Christian School Bible Curriculum Ed., Lorraine Mastrorio
Education Dept.: Sec., David Bundrick; Promotions Coord./Ed., Jewell Ready
Division of Church Ministries: Natl. Dir., Silas Gaither; Men's Ministries Dept.: Sec., Ken Riemenschneider; Light-for-the-Lost Sec., Billy J. Strickland; Royal Rangers Nat'l. Cdr., Johnnie Barnes; Royal Ranger Nat'l. Deputy Commander, Paul Stanek; Editor of Publications, Jim Erdmann
Music Dept.: Sec., L. B. Larsen; Music Ed./Promotions Coord., Lynette Jernigan
Sunday School Department: Sec., George Edgerly; Youth and Family Ministries Consultant, Ted Brust; Adult Ministries Consultant, William Campbell; Children's Ministries Consultant, Richard Gruber; Early Childhood Consultant/BGMC Coord., Sandra K. Askew; Growth and Admin. Consultant, Terry Lewis; Publications Ed. and Trng. Coord., Sylvia Lee; Field Services & Promotion Coord., Efraim Espinoza
Women's Ministries Dept.: Sec., Sandra Clopine; Publications Coord., Aleda Swartzendruber; Auxiliaries Coord., Linda Upton; WM Representative, Nelda Ammons; Trng. Coord., Joanne Ohlin; Off. of Fin./Field Serv. Coord., Karlene Gannon
Youth Dept.: Sec., Terrell Raburn; Evangelism/AIM Rep., College Ministry Specialist, Dennis Gaylor; High School Ministries Consultant & Bible Quiz/Teen Talent Coord., R. Barry Kolanowski; Speed-the-Light Field Rep., Brenton Osgood; Speed-the-Light Adm. Clerk, Gail Mitchell; Ed. of Youth Publications, Terry King; Asst. Ed./Promotions and Publication Coord., N. Thomas Young
Division of Communications: Natl. Dir., Leland Shultz
Advance Magazine: Ed., Gwen Jones
Audiovisual Dept.: Sec., Melvin Snyder
Office of Information: Sec., Juleen Turnage; Coord. of District/Church Relations, Terry L. Terrell; Promotions/Productions Coord., Rick Griepp
Radio and Television Dept.: Sec. and Broadcast Speaker, Dan Betzer; Sec., Don Upton; Publicity Dir., Stephen J. Vaudrey; Revivaltime Choir Dir., Cyril A. McLellan
Pentecostal Evangel Magazine: Ed., Richard G. Champion; Man. Ed., Harris Jansen; Technical and Research Ed., Ann Floyd; News Ed., Gary Speer
Division of Foreign Missions: Exec. Dir., J. Philip Hogan; Adm. Asst., Norman L. Correll
Foreign Field Dirs.: Africa, Donald R. Corbin; Eurasia, Jerry L. Parsley; Far East, Robert W. Houlihan; Latin America & West Indies, Loren Triplett; Sec. of Foreign Mission Finance, Jerry L. Burgess; Finance Office Coord., Linda Alexander; Sec. of Publications, Nick Henry; Sec. of Foreign Missionary Personnel, Ronald Iwasko; Missionary Family Specialist, Robert G. Friesen; Personnel Coord., Paul Sherman; Sec. of

31

Foreign Missions Relations in U.S., G. Edward Nelson; Spec. Service Coord., Juanita Evans; Sec. of Foreign Missions Support, Paul Brannan; Promotion Coord., Rosalie McMain; Life Publishers International: Pres., Bob D. Hoskins, International Correspondence Institute: Pres., George M. Flattery; International Media Ministries Coord., David Lee; Center for Muslim Ministries, Coord., Delmar Kingsriter

Division of Home Missions: Natl. Dir., Robert W. Pirtle; Office Supervisor, Stephen Walegir; Promotion Coord., Jeffrey Champion

Chaplaincy Dept.: Chpsn., Comm. on Chaplains, G. Raymond Carlson; Sec. Lemuel McElyea

New Church Evangelism Dept.: Sec., Robert W. Pirtle

Intercultural Ministries Dept.: Sec., James Kessler; Teen Challenge Rep., Snow Peabody; Deaf and Blind Ministries Rep., James W. Banks; Spec. Rep., American Indian, John McPherson

Division of Publication (Gospel Publishing House): Natl. Dir., William Eastlake

Production Dept.: Mgr., Merrell Cooper

Marketing and Distribution Dept.: Mgr., Thomas F. Sanders

PERIODICALS

All Assemblies of God periodicals are produced by the Gospel Publishing House, 1445 Boonville Ave., Springfield, MO 65802

Advance (m), Gwen Jones, Ed.
At Ease (bi-m), Lemuel McElyea, Ed.
Caring (8/yr.) Owen Wilkie, Ed.
Curriculum Publications (q), Charles W. Ford, Ed.
Dispatch (q), Johnnie Barnes, Ed.
High Adventure (q), Johnnie Barnes, Ed.
Missionettes Memos (q), Linda Upton, Ed.
Motif (q), L. B. Larsen, Ed.
Mountain Movers (m), Nick Henry, Ed.
Paraclete (q), David Bundrick, Ed.
Pentecostal Evangel (w), Richard G. Champion, Ed.
Sunday School Counselor (m), Sylvia Lee, Ed.
Today's Man (q), Jim Ederman, Ed.
Woman's Touch (bi-m), Sandra Clopine, Ed.
Youth Alive! (m), Terry King, Ed.

Associate Reformed Presbyterian Church (General Synod)

Associate Reformed Presbyterian Church (General Synod) stems from the 1782 merger of Associate Presbyterians. In 1822, the Synod of the Carolinas broke with the Associate Reformed Presbyterian Church (which eventually became part of the United Presbyterian Church of North America).

The story of the Synod of the Carolinas began with the Seceder Church, formed in Scotland in 1733 and representing a break from the established Church of Scotland. Seceders, in America called Associate Presbyterians, settled in South Carolina following the Revolutionary War. They were joined by a few Covenanter congregations, which, along with the Seceders, had protested Scotland's established church. The Covenanters took their name from the Solemn League and Covenant of 1643, the guiding document of Scotch Presbyterians. In 1790 some Seceders and Covenanters formed the Presbytery of the Carolinas and Georgia at Long Cane, South Carolina. Thomas Clark and John Boyse led in the formation of this presbytery, a unit within the Associate Reformed Presbyterian Church. The presbytery represented the southern segment of that church.

In 1822 the southern church became independent of the northern Associate Reformed Presbyterian Church and formed the Associate Reformed Presbyterian Church of the South. "Of the South" was dropped in 1858 when the northern group joined the United Presbyterian Church

and "General Synod" was added in 1935. The General Synod is the the denomination's highest court; it is composed of all the teaching elders and at least one ruling elder from each congregation.

Doctrinally, the church holds to the Westminster Confession of Faith. In 1959 the presbyteries approved some 15 changes in the confessions, including the arrangement of existing material into new chapters on the Holy Spirit and the gospel. Liturgically, the synod has been distinguished by its exclusive use of psalmody; in 1946 this practice became optional.

Churches: 172; Inclusive Membership: 36,543; Sunday or Sabbath Schools: 163; Total Enrollment: 16,692; Ordained Clergy: 214

GENERAL ORGANIZATION

General Synod: Annual, June.

OFFICERS

Moderator, Rev. James M. Bell, Sr., P.O. Box 397, Due West, SC 29739

Principal Clk., Rev. C. Ronald Beard, 3132 Grace Hill Rd., Columbia, SC 29204

AGENCIES AND INSTITUTIONS

Associate Reformed Presbyterian Center, One Cleveland St., Greenville, SC 29601.Tel. 803-232-8297. Office of Administrative Services, Dir., Mr. Ed. Hogan. (Headquarters for the following):

Associate Reformed Presbyterian Foundation, Inc.
Associate Reformed Presbyterian Retirement Plan
Office of Christian Education, Dir., Rev. J. B. Hendrick
Office of Church Extension, Dir., Rev. W. C. Lauderdale
Office of Synod's Treasurer, Mr. W. Herman Lesslie
Office of Secretary of World Witness, Exec. Sec., John E. Mariner. Tel. (803)233-5226

PERIODICAL

The Associate Reformed Presbyterian, Mr. Ben Johnston, Ed.

Baha'i Faith

The Baha'i Faith is an independent world religion with adherents in virtually every country. Within the continental United States, Baha'is reside in more than 7,000 localities.

Baha'is are followers of Baha'u'llah (1817-1892), whose religion upholds the basic principles of the oneness of God, the oneness of religion, and the oneness of mankind. The central aim of the Baha'i Faith is the unification of mankind.

The Baha'i administrative order consists of elected local Spiritual Assemblies, National Spiritual Assemblies and the Universal House of Justice. The Local and National Spiritual Assemblies are elected annually. The Universal House of Justice is elected every five years. There are 148 National Assemblies and over 30,000 local Local Assemblies worldwide. In the United States there are over 1,000 local Local Assemblies. The literature of the Baha'i Faith has been published in 599 languages.

GENERAL ORGANIZATION

National Spiritual Assembly, Headquarters: 536 Sheridan Rd., Wilmette, IL 60091. Tel. (312) 869-9039

OFFICERS

Chpsn., Judge James Nelson; Sec., Robert Henderson, 536 Sheridan Rd., Wilmette, IL 60091

Baptist Bible Fellowship International

Organized on May 24, 1950 in Fort Worth, Texas, the Baptist Bible Fellowship was founded by about 100 pastors and lay people who had grown disenchanted with the policies and leadership of the World Fundamental Baptist Missionary Fellowship, an outgrowth of the Baptist Bible Union formed in Kansas City in 1923 by fundamentalist leaders from the Southern Baptist, Northern Baptist, and Canadian Baptist Conventions.

The BBF elected W. E. Dowell as its first president and established offices and a three-year (now four-year with a graduate school) Baptist Bible College for training pastors, missionaries, evangelists, and other Christian workers.

The BBF statement of faith was essentially that of the Baptist Bible Union, adopted in 1923, a variation of the New Hampshire Confession of Faith. It presents an infallible Bible, belief in the substitutionary death of Christ, his physical resurrection, and his premillennial return to earth. It advocates local church autonomy and strong pastoral leadership and maintains that the fundamental basis of fellowship is a missionary outreach. The BBF vigorously stresses evangelism and the international missions office reports 668 adult missionaries working on 71 fields throughout the world in 1984.

There are BBF-related churches in every state of the U.S., with special strength in the upper South, the Great Lakes region, southern states west of the Mississippi, Kansas, and California. There are 8 related colleges and 3 graduate schools or seminaries.

A Committee of Forty-Five, elected by pastors and churches within the states, sits as a representative body, meeting in three subcommittees, each chaired by one of the principal officers: an administration committee chaired by the president; a missions committee chaired by a vice-president; an education committee chaired by a vice-president. The latter reviews the work of 8 approved schools, receiving annual reports from each.

Churches: 3,449; Inclusive Membership: 1,405,900; Sunday or Sabbath Schools: 3,400; Total Enrollment: 750,000; Ordained Clergy: 4,500

GENERAL ORGANIZATION

Annual Meeting: last week of September. In 1987 at First Baptist Church, Newcastle, DE.

Offices: Baptist Bible Fellowship Missions Building, 2157 North Prospect, Springfield, MO 65802. Mailing Address: P.O. Box 191, Springfield, MO 65801. Tel. (417) 862-5001 or (417) 831-3996.

OFFICERS

Pres., Harold Henninger, Canton Baptist Temple, 515 Whipple N.W., Canton, OH 44708

First Vice-Pres., Robert Perryman, Parkcrest Baptist Church, 816 W. Republic Rd., Springfield, MO 65807

Second Vice-Pres., Kenneth Gillming, Cherry Street Baptist Church, Springfield, MO 65803

Sec., Tyrone Adrian, Glenwood Baptist Temple, 3710 North Holmes, Kansas City, MO 64116

Treas., Donald Elmore, Springdale, AR 72765

PERIODICAL

The Baptist Bible Tribune (bi-w), P.O. Box 309 HSJ, Springfield, MO 65801, James O. Combs, Ed. Tel. (417)831-3996

Baptist General Conference

The Baptist General Conference, rooted in the pietistic movement of Sweden during the nineteenth century, traces its history to August 13, 1852. On that day a small group of believers at Rock Island, Illinois, under the leadership of Gustaf Palmquist, organized the first Swedish Baptist Church in America. Swedish Baptist churches flourished in the upper Midwest and Northeast, and by 1879, when the first annual meeting was held in Village Creek, Iowa, 65 churches had been organized,

stretching from Maine to the Dakotas and South to Kansas and Missouri.

Nearly a decade before, John Alexis Edgren, an immigrant sea captain and pastor in Chicago, had begun the first publication and a theological seminary. By 1902, the conference showed significant growth, with 324 churches and nearly 26,000 members. Succeeding years showed the membership growing from 34,000 in 1927 and 40,000 in 1945 to 135,000 in 1982.

Christian Education has played an important part. Many churches began as Sunday schools. The seminary evolved into Bethel, a four-year liberal arts college with 1,800 students and the theological seminary, with over 500 students, located in Arden Hills, Minnesota.

Missions, the planting of churches, has been a main objective both in America and overseas. Today churches have been established in the U.S., Canada, and Mexico, as well as a dozen countries overseas. In 1985 the churches of Canada founded an autonomous denomination, The Baptist General Conference of Canada.

The Baptist General Conference is a member of the Baptist World Alliance, the Baptist Joint Committee on Public Affairs, and the National Association of Evangelicals. It is characterized by the balancing of a conservative doctrine with an irenic and cooperative spirit. Its basic objective is to seek the fulfillment of the great commission and the Great Commandment.

Churches: 762; Inclusive Membership: 131,480; Sunday or Sabbath Schools: 762; Total Enrollment: 74,611; Ordained clergy: 1,700

GENERAL ORGANIZATION

General Conference: annual (June)
Headquarters: 2002 S. Arlington Heights Rd., Arlington Heights, IL 60005. Tel. (312) 228-0200

OFFICERS

Pres., Dr. Robert S. Ricker, 2002 S. Arlington Heights Rd., Arlington Heights, IL 60005

OTHER ORGANIZATIONS

Board of Overseers: Chief Exec. Officer, Dr. Robert S. Ricker

Board of Home Missions: Exec. Dir.; Dr. Clifford E. Anderson

Board of World Missions: Exec. Dir., Rev. Herbert Skoglund

Board of Church Ministries: Exec. Dir., Dr. L. Ted Johnson,

Board of Regents: Pres. of Bethel College & Seminary, Dr. George Brushaber, 3900 Bethel Dr., St. Paul, MN 55112

PERIODICAL

The Standard (m), 2002 S. Arlington Heights Rd., Arlington Heights, IL 60005, Dr. Donald Anderson, Ed.

Baptist Missionary Association of America

A group of regular Baptist churches organized in associational capacity in May, 1950, in Little Rock, Ark. as North American Baptist Association. Name changed in 1969 to Baptist Missionary Association of America. There are several state and numerous local associations of cooperating churches. In theology these churches are evangelical, missionary, fundamental, and in the main premillennial.

Churches: 1,359; Inclusive Membership: 228,125; Sunday or Sabbath Schools: 1,357; Total Enrollment: 97,564; Ordained Clergy: 2,450

GENERAL ORGANIZATION

The Association meets annually (in April). Next meeting: 12-14, 1988, Arlington, TX

PRESIDING OFFICERS

Pres., Rev. Ronald Morgan, 14517 Heartside Pl., Dallas, TX 75234

Vice-Pres.'s, Rev. Gary D. Divine, 2617 Brookcrest Dr., Garland, TX 75050; Rev. Vernon R. Lee, 4621 W. Hillsboro St., El Dorado, AR 71730

Rec. Secs.: Rev. Ralph Cottrell, P.O. Box 1203, Van, TX 75790; Rev. O. D. Christian Rt. 1, Box 267, Streetman, TX 75859 and G. H. Gordon, Rt. 7, Box 36, Lucedale, MS 39452

DEPARTMENTS

Missions: Gen. Sec., Rev. James V. Schoenrock, 721 Main St., Little Rock, AR 72201

Publications: Mgr. Scotty Karber, 712 Main St., Little Rock, AR 72201; Ed.-in-Chief, Rev. James L. Silvey, 1319 Magnolia, Texarkana, TX 75501

Christian Education: Baptist Missionary Association Theological Seminary, Seminary Heights, 1410 E. Pine St., Jacksonville, TX 75766, Dr. Philip R. Bryan, Pres., Wilbur Benningfield, Dean.

Baptist News Service: Dir., Dr. Leon Gaylor, P. O. Box 97, Jacksonville, TX 75766; Asst., James C. Blaylock, P. O. Box 97, Jacksonville, TX 75766

Radio/Television: Rev. George Reddin, Dir., P.O. Box 6, Conway, AR 72032

Armed Forces Chaplaincy: Exec. Dir., William Charles Pruitt Jr., P.O. Box 912, Jacksonville, TX 75766

National Youth Department: Bobby Tucker, P. O. Box 3376, Texarkana, TX 75504

Daniel Springs Encampment: James Speer, P.O. Box 310, Gary, TX 75643

Ministers Benefit Dept., James A. Henry, 4001 Jefferson St., Texarkana, AR 75501

OTHER ORGANIZATIONS

Baptist Missionary Association Brotherhood: Pres., Randy Boyd, Rt. 2, Box 520, Warren, AR 71671

National Women's Missionary Auxiliary: Pres., Mrs. B. J. Smith, 212 S. Foxhall Rd., Jackson, MS 39208

PERIODICALS

The Advancer (m), 712 Main St., Little Rock, AR 72201, Larry Slivey, Ed.

The Gleaner (m), 721 Main St., Little Rock; AR 72201, James V. Schoenrock, Ed.

Baptist Progress (w), P.O. Box 2085, Waxahachie, TX 85165, Danny Pope, Ed.

Baptist Trumpet (w), P.O. Box 19084, Little Rock, AR 72219, David Tidwell, Ed.

Mississippi Baptist (s-m), 4228 Hwy. 15 N., Laurel, MS 39440. Rev. D. J. Brown, Ed.

Missouri Missionary Baptist (s-m), 1170 Beverly Dr., Florissant, MO 63031, Jerome Cooper, Ed.

Louisiana Baptist Builder (m), P. O. Box 1297, Denham Springs, LA 70727. Rev. Leroy Mayfield, Ed.

Oklahoma Baptist (m), P. O. Box 727, Ada, OK 74820, Buster Hayes, Ed.

Baptist Herald (m), P.O. Box 277, Galena, KS 66739. Randy Shepherd, Ed.

Alabama Baptist Banner (m) 306 Laurie Ln., Warner Robins, GA 31093. Edward Strawmier, Ed.

The Advocate, (m) Rt. 1, Box 403, McDavid, FL 32568, Nancy Brook, Ed.

Illinois and Indiana Missionary Baptist (m), P.O. Box 5, Sandwich, IL 60548, Danny Kirk, Ed

Midwest Missionary Baptist (m), 50865 CR 652, Mattawan, MI 49071, Dennis Aho, Ed.

Beachy Amish Mennonite Churches

This group originates mostly from the Old Order Amish Mennonite Church.

Two congregations had been formed as early as 1927, but the others have all been organized since 1938.

Worship is held in meeting houses. Nearly all have Sunday schools, many have prayer meetings, and most of them either sponsor or have access to Christian day schools. They sponsor evangelical missions at home and abroad; a monthly magazine, Calvary Messenger, as an evangelical and doctrinal witness; and Calvary Bible School, nine weeks each winter, for an in-depth study of the Word of God to better equip their youth for Christian service.

Churches: 83; Inclusive Membership: 5,862; Sunday or Sabbath Schools: N.R.; Total Enrollment: N.R.; Ordained Clergy: 271

INFORMATION

Ervin N. Hershberger, R. D. 1, Meyersdale, PA 15552. Tel. (814) 662-2483

Berean Fundamental Church

Founded 1932 in Denver, Colorado, this body emphasizes conservative Protestant doctrines.

GENERAL ORGANIZATION

Headquarters: North Platte, NB 69101. Tel. (308)532-7448

Annual Conference: September

OFFICERS

Pres., Rev. Curt Lehman, 6400 South 70th St., Lincoln, NB 68516. Tel. (402)423-6512

Vice-Pres., Rev. Richard Cocker, 20th and East D, Torrington, WY 82240. Tel. (307)532-2497

Sec.-Treas., Rev. Earnest H. Skoog, P.O. Box 213, Basalt, CO 81621

Exec. Advisor, Rev. Carl M. Goltz, P.O. Box 397, North Platte, NB 69103. Tel. (308)532-6723

PERIODICAL

Berean Digest (m), Box 213, Basalt, CO 81621, Rev. Carl M. Goltz, Ed.

Bethel Ministerial Association, Inc.

Originally the Evangelistic Ministerial Alliance, founded in Evansville, Indiana, May 1934, later became Bethel Baptist Assembly, then incorporated under the laws of the State of Indiana, March 16, 1960.

GENERAL ORGANIZATION

General Conference: quarterly.

Headquarters: 4400 Lincoln Ave., Evansville, IN 47715. Tel. (812) 477-8888

OFFICERS

Chpsn., Rev. Donald E. Harath, 3575 Greenhill Rd., Decatur, IL 62521. Tel. (217)429-5990

Vice-Chpsn., Rev. James Wilson, Rt. 2 Box, 11, Richland, IN 47634. Tel. (812)359-5307

Sec., Rev. Merwyn Masters, P. O. Box 509, Mahomet, IL 61853. Tel. (217)586-5240

Treas., Rev. Don G. Matthews, 7055 S. Manker, Indianapolis, IN 46227

Chmn. Emeritus, Rev. W. B. Badger, 511 W. Cedar St., Leroy, IL 61752. Tel. (309) 962-9345

The Bible Church of Christ, Inc.

The Bible Church of Christ was founded on March 1, 1961 by Bishop Roy Bryant, Sr. Since that time, the Church has grown to include congregations in the U.S. and Jamaica. The church is trinitarian and accepts the Bible as the divinely inspired Word of God. Its doctrine includes miracles of healing and the baptism of the Holy Ghost.

Churches: 6; Inclusive Membership: 6,400; Sunday or Sabbath Schools: 6; Total Enrollment: 644; Ordained Clergy: 40

GENERAL ORGANIZATION

General Meeting: annual
Headquarters: 1358 Morris Ave., Bronx, NY 10456. Tel. (212) 588-2284

OFFICERS

Pres., Bishop Roy Bryant, Sr., 3033 Gunther Ave., Bronx, NY 10469. Tel. (212) 379-8080
Vice-Pres., Bishop Roy Bryant, Jr., 34 Tuxedo Rd., Montclair, NJ 07042. Tel. (201) 746-0063
Sec., Sissieretta Bryant
Treas, Elder Artie Burney

EXECUTIVE TRUSTEE BOARD

Chpsn., Leon T. Mims, 1358 Morris Ave.,Bronx, NY 10456. Tel. (212) 588-2284
Vice-Chpsn., Peggy Rawls, 100 W. 2nd St., Mount Vernon, NY 10550. Tel. (914) 664-4602

OTHER ORGANIZATIONS

Foreign Missions: Pres., Elder Diane Cooper
Home Missions: Pres., Evangelist Eleanor Samuel
Sunday Schools: Gen. Supt., Elder Alice Jones
Evangelism: National Pres., Evangelist Gloria Gray; Field Rep., Evangelist Elizabeth Price
Youth: Pres., Deacon Tommy Robinson
Minister of Music: Leon T. Mims
Prison Ministry Team; Pres., Evangelist Marvin Lowe
Presiding Elders: (Delaware), Elder Roland Miflin, Diamond Acre, Dagsboro, DE 19939. (North Carolina), Elder Larry Bryant, West Johnson Rd., Clinton, NC 28328. (Monticello), Elder Jesse Alston, 104 Waverly Ave., Monticello, NY 12701. (Mount Vernon), Elder Artie Burney, Sr., 100 W. 2nd St., Mount Vernon, NY 10550. (Bronx), Elder Anita Robinson, 1358 Morris Ave., Bronx, NY 10456; Annex: Elder Betty Gilliard, 1069 Morris Ave., Bronx, NY 10456
Bible School: Pres., Dr. Roy Bryant, 1358 Morris Ave., Bronx, NY 10456. Tel. (212)588-2284.
Bookstore: Mgr., Elder Elizabeth Johnson, 1358 Morris Ave., Bronx, NY 10456. Tel. (212)293-1928

PERIODICAL

The Voice (q), 1358 Morris Ave., Bronx, NY 10456. Tel. (212) 588-2284. Montrose Bushrod, Ed.

Bible Way Church of Our Lord Jesus Christ World Wide, Inc.

This body was organized in 1957 in the Pentecostal tradition for the purpose of accelerating evangelistic and foreign missionary commitment and to effect a greater degree of collective leadership than was found in the body in which they had previously participated.

The doctrine is the same as that of the Church of Our Lord Jesus Christ of the Apostolic Faith, Inc. of which some of the churches and clergy were formerly members.

The growth of this organization has been very encouraging. There are approximately 300,000 members, with 300 churches and missions located in Africa, England, Guyana, Trinidad, and Jamaica, and churches in 25 states in America.

The Bible Way Church WW is involved in humanitarian, as well as evangelical outreach, with concerns for urban housing and education and economic development.

GENERAL ORGANIZATION

Headquarters: 1100 New Jersey Ave., N.W., Washington, DC 20001

OFFICERS

Presiding Bishop, Smallwood E. Williams, 4720 16th St., N.W., Washington, DC 20011
Gen. Sec., Bishop Edward William, 5118 Clarendon Rd., Brooklyn, NY 11226

PERIODICALS

The Bible Way News Voice (q), Washington, DC

Brethren Church (Ashland, Ohio)

It was organized by progressive-minded German Baptist Brethren in 1882. They reaffirmed the teaching of the original founder of the Brethren movement, Alexander Mack, and returned to congregational government.

GENERAL ORGANIZATION

General Conference: annual (August)
Headquarters: 524 College Ave., Ashland, OH 44805. Tel. (419) 289-1708
Dir. of Pastoral Ministries: Rev. Dave Cooksey

OFFICERS

Mod., Dr. Warren K. Garner, 103 Damron Dr., North Manchester, IN 49962
Mod. Elect., Dr. Dale Stoffer, 2183 Sutter Parkway, Dublin, OH 43017
Sec., Norma Waters, RR 1, Box 421, McGaheysville, VA 22840
Treas., J. Mitchel Drushal, 133 College Ave., Ashland, OH 44805
Statistician, Dr. James Hollinger, 59147 Lower Dr., Goshen, IN 46526

BOARDS

The Brethren Publishing Company, 524 College Ave., Ashland, OH 44805. Exec. Dir. and Ed., Richard Winfield
The Missionary Board, 524 College Ave., Ashland, OH 44805. Exec. Dir., James R. Black
The Benevolent Board, 524 College Ave., Ashland, OH 44805
The Board of Christian Education, Dir., Charles Beekley, 524 College Ave., Ashland, OH 44805

Brethren in Christ Church

The Brethren in Christ Church was founded in Lancaster County, Pa. in about the year 1778 and was an outgrowth of the religious awakening which occurred in that area during the latter part of the eighteenth century. This group became known as "River Brethren" because of their original location near the Susquehanna River. The name "Brethren in Christ" was officially adopted in 1863. In theology they have accents of the Anabaptist, Armenian, and holiness movements.

Churches: 183; Inclusive Membership: 15,911; Sunday or Sabbath Schools: 167; Total Enrollment: 9,516; Ordained Clergy: 227

GENERAL ORGANIZATION

General Conference: biennial

OFFICERS

Mod., Bishop Glenn A. Ginder, P.O. Box 9587, Wichita, KS 67277

Gen. Sec., Dr. R. Donald Shafer, P.O. Box 245, Upland, CA 91785

Treas., Harold D. Chubb, P.O. Box 450, Mechanicsburg, PA 17055

OTHER ORGANIZATIONS

Board of Administration: Chpsn., Glenn A. Ginder, P.O. Box 9587, Wichita, KS 67277; Gen. Sec., Dr. R. Donald Shafer, P.O. Box 245, Upland, CA 91785; Treas., Harold D. Chubb, P.O. Box 450, Mechanicsburg, PA 17055; Personnel Sec., Merle E. Brubaker, 1865 Fruitville Pike, Lancaster, PA 17601

Board of Bishops: Chpsn., Frank Kipe, P.O. Box 349, Waynesboro, PA 17268; Sec., Harvey Sider, 2519 Stevensville Rd., Stevensville, Ontario, Canada LOS 1SO

Board of Brotherhood Concerns: Chpsn, Lenora H. Stern, 345 Gettysburg Pike, Mechanicsburg, PA 17055; Sec., Paul A. Wengert, Jr., 10 Holly Dr., New Cumberland, PA 17070; Asst. Treas., Devon Bontrager, Box 921, Waynesboro, PA 17268; U.S. Treas., Glenn Dalton, Jr., 201 S. 20th St., Harrisburg, PA 17104; Exec. Dir., Eber B. Dourte, 10 Oakwood Dr., Dillsburg, PA 17019

Board for Congregational Life: Chpsn., _____; Sec., Warren L. Hoffman, 5832 N. Harvard, Oklahoma City, OK 73122; Treas., Ronald L. Miller, Messiah College, Grantham, PA 17027; Exec. Dir., Ken Letner, 2134 Sherwal Ave., Lancaster, PA 17601

Board of Directors: Chpsn., Glenn A. Ginder, P.O. Box 9587, Wichita, KS 67277; Gen. Sec., Dr. R. Shafer, P.O. Box 245, Upland, CA 91785; Treas., Harold D. Chubb, P.O. Box 450, Mechanicsburg, PA 17055

Board for Evangelism and Church Planting: Chpsn., Doublas P. Sider, 142 Streb Cresc., Saskatoon, Sask., Canada S7M 4T8; Sec., W. Dale Allison, 996 E. High St., Elizabethtown, PA 17022; Canadian Treas., Walter J. Kelly, 32 Canora Ct., Welland, Ontario, Canada L3C 6H7; U.S. Treas., Donald J. Winters, 1727 Lincoln Hwy. E., Lancaster, PA 17602; Exec. Dir., R. Dale Shaw, 4404 Meadow Creek Cir., Sarasota, FL 34233

Board for Media Ministries: Chpsn., Dwight E. Bert, P.O. Box 216, Upland, CA 91785; Sec., J. Wilmer Heisey, R. 2, Box 1711, Mt. Joy, PA 17552; Treas., Emerson C. Frey, R.D. 1, Box 232A, Millersville, PA 17551; Exec. Dir., Roger Williams, 301-305 N. Elm St., Nappanee, IN 46550

Board for Ministry and Doctrine: Chpsn., Luke L. Keefer, Jr., 1344 Twp. Rd. #523, Ashland, OH 44805; James Ernst, 1640 Redwood Ave., Grants Pass, OR 97527; Treas, Marion J. Heisey, Box 34, Tijeras, NM 87059; Exec. Dir., Glenn A. Ginder, P.O. Box 9587, Wichita, KS 67277

Board for World Missions: Chpsn., Roger C. Sider, 1432 Clover St., Rochester, NY 14610; Sec., Harold H. Engle, 322 E. Main St., Palmyra, PA 17078; Canadian Treas., Philip D. Keefer, 5384 Sherkston Rd., Sherkston, Ontario LOS 1RO; U.S. Treas., W. Edward Rickman, 63 Opal Dr., Chambersburg, PA 17201; Exec. Dir., Donald R. Zook, P.O. Box 390, Mt. Joy, PA 17552

Commission on Christian Education Literature: Chpsn., Dale W. Engle, 1067 Foxhaven Dr., Ashland, OH 44805; Sec., Glen A. Pierce, P.O. Box 166, Nappanee, IN 46550

Commission on Education Institutions: Chpsn., John A. Brubaker, Box 68, Refton, PA 17568; Sec., Harold K. Sider, 644 Vallejo Way, Upland, CA 91786

General Conference Program Committee: Chpsn., Herb Anderson, 10535 51st St., Edmonton, Alberta; Sec./ Prog. Coord., Ann Marie Shaw, 4404 Meadow Creek Dr., Sarasota, FL 34233

Jacob Engle Foundation Board of Directors: Chpsn., Dwight E. Bert, P.O. Box 216, Upland, CA 91785; Sec., Mark S. Hess, 135 N. School Lane, Lancaster, PA 17603; Exec. Dir., Ray M. Musser, P.O. Box 1136, Upland, CA 91785

Pension Fund Trustees: Chpsn., Donald R. Zook, P.O. Box 27, Mt. Joy, PA 18552; Sec., Elbert N. Smith, 309 Woodlawn Ln., Carlisle, PA 17013; Canadian Treas., Roger J. Grant, 1234 House Rd., Ridgeway, Ontario, Canada L0S 1N0; U.S. Treas., Chester Heisey, 7271 Brydon Rd., LaVerne, CA 91750

Board for Stewardship: Dir. of Finance, Charles F. Frey, P.O. Box 284, R.R. 2, Conestoga, PA 17516; Dir. of Stewardship, Merle Brubaker, 1865 Fruitville Pk., Lancaster, PA 17601

Publishing House: Evangel Press, 301 N. Elm, Nappanee, IN 46550; Exec. Dir., Roger Williams

PERIODICAL

Evangelical Visitor (m), Nappanee, IN 46550, Glen A. Pierce, Ed.

Buddhist Churches of America

Founded in 1899, organized in 1914 as the Buddhist Mission of North America, this body was incorporated in 1942 under the present name and represents the Jodo Shinshu Sect of Buddhism affiliated with the Hongwanji-ha Hongwanji denomination in the continental United States. It is a school of Buddhism which believes in salvation by faith in the Wisdom and Compassion of Amida Buddha.

GENERAL ORGANIZATION

Conference: annual (February)

Headquarters: 1710 Octavia St., San Francisco, CA 94109. Tel. (415)776-5600

OFFICERS

Bishop Seigen H. Yamaoka

Exec. Asst. to the Bishop: Rev. Seikan Fukuma

Adm. Officer: James Nagahiro

Dir. of Development: Richard T. Schellhase

OTHER ORGANIZATIONS

Federation of Buddhist Women's Assoc

Federation of Western Buddhist Dharma School Teachers' League

Institute of Buddhist Studies, a graduate school

National Young Buddhist Association

Western Adult Buddhist League

Affiliated U.S. Organizational Jurisdiction: Honpa Hongwanji Mission of Hawaii, 1727 Pali Hwy., Honolulu, HI 96813

Affiliated Canadian Organizational Jurisdiction: Buddhist Churches of Canada, 918 Bathurst St., Toronto, Ontario, Canada M5R 3G5

Bulgarian Eastern Orthodox Church

Bulgarian immigration to the United States and Canada started around the turn of the century, and the first Bulgarian Orthodox church was built in 1907 in Madison, Illinois. In 1938, the Holy Synod of the Bulgarian E. O. Church established the diocese in New York as an Episcopate, and Bishop Andrey was sent as diocesan Bishop. In 1947, the diocese was officially incorporated in New York State and Bishop Andrey became the first elected Metropolitan.

By a decision of the Holy Synod in 1969, the Bulgarian Eastern Orthodox Church was divided into the Diocese of New York (incorporated Diocese of New York) and the

Diocese of Akron (incorporated American Bulgarian Diocese of N. & S. America and Australia, Akron, Ohio).

OFFICERS

New York Diocese, Metropolitan Joseph, 550 A, West 50th St., New York, NY 10019. Tel. (212) 581-3756
Akron Diocese, Metropolitan Joseph, 1953 Stockbridge Rd., Akron, OH 44313

Christ Catholic Church

The church is a catholic communion established in 1968 to minister to the growing number of people seeking an experiential relationship with God, and who desire to make a total commitment of their lives to him. The church is catholic in faith and tradition and its orders are recognized as valid by catholics of every tradition.

Churches: 8; Inclusive Membership: 1,320; Sunday or Sabbath Schools: 1; Total Enrollment: 9; Ordained Clergy: 13

GENERAL ORGANIZATION

Synod: annual. Next meeting, August, 1988

OFFICERS

Presiding Bishop, The Most Reverend Karl Pruter, Cathedral Church, Highlandville, MO 65669. Tel. (417) 587-3951

PERIODICAL

The Cathedral Voice, Box 98, Highlandville, MO 65669

Christadelphians

A body of people who believe the Bible to be the divinely inspired word of God, written by "Holy men who spoke as they were moved by the Holy Spirit" (II Peter 1:21); in the return of Christ to earth to establish the Kingdom of God; the resurrection from the dead; in opposition to war; spiritual rebirth requiring belief and immersion in the name of Jesus; and in a godly walk in this life.

The denomination was organized in 1844 by a medical doctor, John Thomas, who came to the United States from England in 1832, having survived a near shipwreck in a violent storm. This experience affected him profoundly, and he vowed to devote his life to a search for the Truth of God and a future hope from the Bible.

NO GENERAL ORGANIZATION

Co-Ministers, H. P. Zilmer, 834 Elma Ave., Elgin, IL 60120; Norman D. Zilmer, 1000 Mohawk Dr., Elgin, IL 60120

The Christian and Missionary Alliance

An evangelical and evangelistic church begun in 1887 when Dr. Albert B. Simpson founded two organizations, The Christian Alliance (a fellowship of Christians dedicated to the experiencing of the deeper Christian life) and the Evangelical Missionary Alliance (a missionary sending organization). The two groups were merged in 1897 and became The Christian and Missionary Alliance. The denomination stresses the sufficiency of Jesus—Savior, Sanctifier, Healer, and Coming King—and has earned a worldwide reputation for its missionary accomplishments. The Canadian districts became autonomous in 1981 and formed The Christian and Missionary Alliance in Canada.

Churches: 1,691; Inclusive Membership: 238,734; Sunday or Sabbath Schools: 1,538; Total Enrollment: 168,380; Ordained Clergy: 2,154

GENERAL ORGANIZATION

Council: annual (May or June)
Headquarters: 350 N. Highland Ave., Nyack, NY 10960. Tel. (914) 353-0750

OFFICERS

Pres., David L. Rambo
Sec., Elwood N. Nielsen
Vice Pres. for Fin./Treas., Merlin C. Feather
Vice Pres. for Church Ministries, Richard W. Bailey
Vice Pres. for Overseas Ministries, David H. Moore
Vice Pres. for Gen. Services, James A. Davey

BOARD OF MANAGERS

David L. Rambo, Chairman

DIVISIONS OF ADMINISTRATION

Division of Finance: Adminis. Staff: Vice Pres./Treas., M. C. Feather; Ass't. Vice Pres., Duane Wheeland; Trust Accountant, O. P. Nelsen; Dir. of Accounting, W. E. Stedman; Dir. of Alliance Development Fund, H. E. Maynard; Adminis. Ass't., J. C. LaBarbera
Division of Church Ministries: Adminis. Staff: Vice Pres., R. W. Bailey; Ass't. Vice Pres., D. L. Gorton; Dir. of Church Growth, F. C. King; Ass't. Dir. of Church Growth, J. Ng; Dir. of Christian Education, D. D. Dale; Dir. of Specialized Minis., E. A. Cline; Assoc. Dir. of Specialized Minis., A. E. Hall; Dir. of Missionary Deputation, R. H. Pease
Division of Overseas Ministries: Adminis. Staff: Vice Pres., D. H. Moore; Ass't. Vice Pres., Arni Shareski; Dir. for East Asia and Pacific Islands, P. N. Nanfelt; Dir. for Southeast Asia/Middle East/Europe/Australia and New Zealand, R. W. Reed; Dir. for Africa, D. L. Kennedy; Dir. for South America, D. K. Volstad; Dir. for Missionary Candidates, D. O. Young
Division of General Services: Adminis. Staff: Vice Pres., J. A. Davey; *Alliance Life*, M. R. Irvin; Dir. of Data Processing, R. N. Mapstone; Mgr. of Computer Operations, D. G. Ingram; Dir. of Stewardship, S. L. Bjornson; Dir. of Business Affairs, M. J. Reese; Dir. of Communications, J. S. Moline; Dir. of Personnel, D. M. Johnson.
Christian Publications, Inc.: Pres., J. A. Davey; Vice Pres., B. S. King; Exec. Vice Pres./Treas., H. R. Cowles; Sec., D. A. Wiggins

DISTRICTS

Central: Charles R. Holmes, Sup't., 1218 High St., Wadsworth, OH 44281, Tel. (216) 336-2911
Central Pacific: Richard C. Taylor, Sr., Sup't., 3824 Buell St., Suite A, Oakland, CA 94619, Tel. (415) 530-5410
Eastern: Rev. Leon W. Young, Sup't., 1 Sherwood Dr., Mechanicsburg, PA 17055, Tel. (717) 766-0261
Great Lakes: Dahl B. Seckinger, Sup't.
Metropolitan: Rev. Paul Hazlett, Sup't., 349 Watchung Ave., N. Plainfield, NJ 07060, Tel. (201) 668-8421
Mid-Atlantic: C. E. Mock, Sup't., Shady Grove Professional Park, 9015 Shady Grove Ct., Gaithersburg, MD 20877, Tel. (301) 258-0035
Midwest: John W. Fogal, Sup't., 260 Glen Ellyn Rd., Bloomingdale, IL 60108, Tel. (312) 893-1355
New England: Dwight G. Anderson, Sup't., Box 288, S. Easton, MA 02375, Tel. (617) 238-3820
Northeastern: Woodford C. Stemple, Jr., Sup't., 6275 Pillmore Dr., Rome, NY 13440, Tel. (315) 336-4720
Northwestern: Garfield G. Powell, Sup't., 1813 N. Lexington Ave., St. Paul, MN 55113, Tel. (612) 489-1391
Ohio Valley: Keith M. Bailey, Sup't
Pacific Northwest: Ralph M. Shellrude, Sup't., P. O. Box 640, Canby, OR 97013, Tel. (503) 226-2238
Puerto Rico: Jorge Cuevas, Sup't., P.O. Box 51394, Levittown, PR 00950. Tel. (809) 795-0101

Rocky Mountain: E. N. Nielsen, Sup't., 1215 24th W., Ste. 210, Billings, MT 59102, Tel. (406) 656-4233

South Atlantic: Edward W. Smillie, Sup't., 501 Boyce Rd., Charlotte, NC 28211, Tel. (704) 364-0388

South Pacific: R. Harold Mangham, Sup't., 614 S. Euclid St., Fullerton, CA 92632, Tel. (714) 526-5555

Southeastern: Harry J. Arnold, Sup't., P.O. Box 580708, Orlando, FL 32858, Tel. (305) 298-5460

Southern: J. W. Nabors, Sup't., P. O. Box 4484, Birmingham, AL 35206, Tel. (205) 836-4048

Southwestern: Gordon G. Copeland, Sup't., P. O. Box 120756, Arlington, TX 76012, Tel. (817) 261-9631

Western: Anthony G. Bollback, Sup't., 11909 Elm St., Suite 5, Omaha, NE 68144, Tel. (402) 330-1888

Western Pennsylvania: David K. Muir, Sup't., P. O. Box 429, Punxsutawney, PA 15767, Tel. (814) 939-6920

INTERCULTURAL MINISTRIES DISTRICTS

Cambodian: Joseph S. Kong, Dir., 1885 23rd N.E., Salem, OR 97303. Tel. (503)581-2129

Dega: c/o Rev. A. E. Hall, 350 N. Highland Ave., Nyack, NY 10960

Haitian: Rev. A. E. Hall, Acting Dir., 350 N. Highland Ave., New York 10960. Tel. (914)353-0750

Hmong: Yong Xeng Yang, Field Dir., P.O. Box 219, Brighton, CO 80601, Tel. (303) 659-1538

Jewish: Rev. Abraham Sandler, Admn. Asst., 9820 Woodfern Rd., Philadelphia, PA 19115. Tel. (215)698-9089

Native American: Craig Smith, Dir., 16001 N. 34th Ave., Phoenix, AZ 85023. Tel. (602)942-3183

Korean: Rev. John H. Pang, Dir., 3214 W. Lawrence Ave., #206, Chicago, IL 60625. Tel. (312)539-3222

Lao: Malcolm M. Sawyer, 803 Irving Ave., Wheaton, IL 60187, Tel. (312) 260-1686

Spanish: Roberto Felicie, Dir., Ogden Professional Bldg. 515 Ogden Ave., 3rd Floor, Downers Grove, IL 60515.Tel. (312)964-5593

Vietnamese: Truong Van Sang, Dir., 1436 Valencia Dr. W., Fullerton, CA 92633. Tel. (714)870-0792

PERIODICAL

Alliance Life, 350 N. Highland Ave., Nyack, NY 10960

Christian Brethren (Also known as Plymouth Brethren)

An orthodox and evangelical movement which began in the British Isles in the 1820's and is now worldwide. Congregations are usually simply called "assemblies." The name Plymouth Brethren was given by others because th group in Plymouth, England, was a large congregation. In recent years the term Christian Brethren has replaced Plymouth Brethren for the "open" branch of the movement in Canada and British Commonwealth countries, and to some extent in the U.S.

The unwillingness to establish a denominational structure makes the autonomy of local congregations an important feature of the movement. Other features are weekly observance of the Lord's Supper and adherence to the doctrinal position of conservative, evangelical Christianity.

In the 1840's the movement divided. The "exclusive" branch, led by John Darby, stressed the interdependency of congregations. Since disciplinary decisions were held to be binding on all assemblies, exclusives had sub-divided into seven or eight main groups by the end of the century. Since 1925 a trend toward reunification has reduced that number to three or four. U.S. congregations number approximately 300, with an inclusive membership estimated at 19,000.

The "open" branch of the movement, stressing evangelism and foreign missions, is now the larger of the two. Following the leadership of George Muller in rejecting the "exclusive" principle of binding discipline, this branch has escaped large-scale division. U.S. congregations number approximately 850, with an inclusive membership estimated at 79,000. There are 400 "commended" full-time ministers, not including foreign missionaries.

NO GENERAL ORGANIZATION

Correspondent: Interest, Bruce R. McNicol, Pres., 218 W. Willow, Wheaton, IL 60187. Tel. (312) 653-6573.

OTHER ORGANIZATIONS

Christian Missions in Many Lands, Box 13, Spring Lake, NJ 07762

Stewards Foundation, 218 W. Willow, Wheaton, IL 60187

International Teams, Box 203, Prospect Heights, IL 60070

PERIODICALS

Interest Magazine (m), 218 W. Willow, Wheaton, IL 60187

Missions Magazine (m), Box 13, Spring Lake, NJ 07762

Food for the Flock (bi-m), 9257 Caprice Dr., Plymouth, MI 48170

Christian Catholic Church (Evangelical-Protestant)

This church was founded by the Rev. John Alexander Dowie on February 22, 1896 at Chicago, IL. In 1901 the church opened the city of Zion, Illinois as its home and headquarters. Theologically, the church is rooted in evangelical orthodoxy. The Scriptures are accepted as the rule of faith and practice. Other doctrines call for belief in the necessity of repentance for sin and personal trust in Christ for salvation, baptism by triune immersion, and tithing as a practical method of Christian stewardship. The church teaches the Second Coming of Christ.

As a denomination, the Christian Catholic Church is a denominational member of The National Association of Evangelicals. It has work in ten other nations in addition to the United States.

Churches: 6; Inclusive Membership: 2,500; Sunday or Sabbath Schools: 6; Total Enrollment: 1,050; Ordained Clergy: 16

GENERAL ORGANIZATION

Convocation: annual (end of September) Headquarters: Dowie Memorial Dr., Zion, IL 60099. Tel. (312) 746-1411

OFFICER

Gen. Overseer, Roger W. Ottersen

PERIODICAL

Leaves of Healing (bi-m), Dowie Memorial Dr., Zion, IL 60099, Roger W. Ottersen, Ed.-in-Chief

Christian Church (Disciples of Christ)

Born on the American frontier in the early 1800s as a movement to unify Christians, this body drew its major inspiration from Thomas and Alexander Campbell in western Pennsylvania and Barton W. Stone in Kentucky. Developing separately for a quarter of a century, the "Disciples," under Alexander Campbell, and the "Christians," led by Stone, united in Lexington, Kentucky, in 1832.

The Christian Church (Disciples of Christ) is marked by informality, openness, individualism and diversity. The Disciples claim no official doctrine or dogma. Membership is granted after a simple statement of belief in Jesus Christ and baptism by immersion—although most congregations accept transfers baptized by other forms in other denominations. The Lord's Supper—generally called Communion—is open to Christians of all persuasions. The practice is weekly Communion, although no church law insists upon it.

Thoroughly ecumenical, the Disciples helped organize the National and World Councils of Churches. The church is a member of the Consultation on Church Union. The Disciples and the United Church of Christ have begun working together in an "ecumenical partnership." Theological conversations have been going on since 1967 directly with the Roman Catholic Church.

Disciples have supported vigorously world and national programs of education, agricultural assistance, urban reconciliation, care of mentally retarded, family planning, and aid to victims of war and calamity. Operating ecumenically, Disciples personnel or funds work in more than 70 countries outside North America.

Three levels of church polity (general, regional, and congregational) operate as equals, managing their own finances, property, and program, with strong but voluntary ties to one another. Local congregations own their own property and have full control of their budgets and program. A General Assembly meets every two years and has voting representation direct from each congregation.

Churches: 4,221; Inclusive Membership: 1,106,692; Sunday or Sabbath Schools: 4,221; Total Enrollment: 337,595; Ordained Clergy. 6,806

GENERAL ORGANIZATION

General Assembly, biennial
General Office: 222 S. Downey Ave., Box 1986, Indianapolis, IN 46206. Tel. (317) 353-1491

OFFICERS

Gen. Minister and Pres., John O. Humbert
Mod., Daniel L. Woods, 987 E. HeronCircle, SE, Winter Haven, FL 33884
1st Vice-Mod., Lucas Torres, 895 N. Jerico Dr., Casselberry, FL 32707
2nd Vice-Mod., Audrey Anderson, 2470 N. Hayford St., Orange, CA 92665

GENERAL OFFICERS

Gen. Minister and Pres., John O. Humbert
Deputy Gen. Minister and Pres., Claudia E. Grant
Deputy Gen. Minister and Pres., Donald B. Manworren
Assoc. Gen. Minister, John R. Foulkes
Vice-Pres. for Communication, Carolyn W. Day.

ADMINISTRATIVE UNITS

Board of Church Extension: 110 S. Downey Ave., Box 7030, Indianapolis, IN 46207. Tel. (317) 356-6333. Pres., Harold R. Watkins
Christian Board of Publication (Bethany Press): Box 179, 1316 Convention Plaza Dr., St. Louis, MO 63166. Tel. (314) 231-8500. Pres., H. B. Tomlin
Christian Church Foundation: 222 S. Downey Ave., Box 1986, Indianapolis, IN 46206 Tel. (317) 353-1491, Pres., James R. Reed
Church Finance Council, Inc.: 222 S. Downey Ave., Box 1986 Indianapolis, IN 46206. Tel. (317) 353-1491. Pres., James P. Johnson
Council on Christian Unity: 222 S. Downey Ave., Box 1986, Indianapolis, IN 46206 Tel. (317) 353-1491. Pres., Paul A. Crow, Jr.
Disciples of Christ Historical Society: 1101 19th Ave. S., Nashville, TN 37212. Tel. (615) 327-1444. Pres., James M. Seale
Division of Higher Education: 11780 Borman Dr., Ste. 100, St. Louis, MO 63146. Tel. (314) 991-3000. Pres., D. Duane Cummins
Division of Homeland Ministries: 222 S. Downey Ave., Box 1986, Indianapolis, IN 46206. Tel. (317) 353-1491. Pres., John R. Compton
Division of Overseas Ministries: 222 S. Downey Ave., Box 1986, Indianapolis, IN 46206. Tel. (317) 353-1491. Pres., William J. Nottingham
National Benevolent Association: 11780 Borman Dr., Ste. 200, St. Louis, MO 63146. Tel. (314) 993-9000. Pres. Richard R. Lance

Pension Fund: 200 Barrister Bldg., 155 E. Market St., Indianapolis, IN 46204. Tel. (317) 634-4504. Pres., Lester D. Palmer

REGIONAL UNITS OF THE CHURCH

Alabama-Northwest Florida: Christian Church (Disciples of Christ) in Alabama-Northwest Florida, 1336 Montgomery Hwy., S., Birmingham, AL 35216. Tel. (205) 823-5647. Carl R. Flock, Regional Minister
Arizona: Christian Church (Disciples of Christ) in Arizona., 4423 N. 24thSt., Phoenix, AZ 85016. Tel. (602)468-3815. Bruce L. Jones, Regional Minister
Arkansas: The Christian Church (Disciples of Christ) in Arkansas, 6100 Queensboro Dr., P.O. Box 9739, Little Rock 72219. Tel. (501)562-6053. W. Chris Hobgood, Exec. Minister
California North-Nevada: The Christian Church (Disciples of Christ) of Northern California-Nevada, 111-A Fairmount Ave., Oakland, CA 94611. Tel. (415)839-3550, Richard Lauer, Regional Minister—President.
Capital Area: Christian Church (Disciples of Christ)— Capital Area, 8901 Connecticut Ave., Chevy Chase, MD 20815. Tel. (301)654-7794. Richard L. Taylor, Regional Minister
Central Rocky Mountain Region: Christian Church (Disciples of Christ) Central Rocky Mountain Region, 1370 Pennsylvania, Ste. 400, Denver CO 80203. Tel. (303)839-0075. _____, Regional Exec. Minister
Florida: Christian Church (Disciples of Christ) in Florida, Lloyd Cox, Interim, 134 E. Colonial Dr., Orlando, FL 32801. Tel. (305) 843-4652 Jimmie L. Gentle, Regional Minister
Georgia: Christian Church (Disciples of Christ) in Georgia, Inc., 2370 Vineville Ave., Macon 31204. Tel. (912) 743-8649. David L. Alexander, Regional Minister
Idaho-South: Christian Church (Disciples of Christ) of South Idaho, 4900 No. Five Mile Rd., Boise, ID 83704. Tel. (208) 322-0538. Larry Crist, Regional Minister
Illinois-Wisconsin: Christian Church (Disciples of Christ) in Illinois and Wisconsin, 1011 N. Main St., Bloomington, IL 61701. Tel. (309) 828-6293. Nathan S. Smith, Regional Minister and President
Indiana: Christian Church (Disciples of Christ) in Indiana, 1100 W. 42nd St., Indianapolis 46208. Tel. (317) 926-6051. Howard B. Goodrich, Jr., Regional Minister
Kansas: Christian Church in Kansas (Disciples of Christ), 1010 Gage, Topeka, KS 66604. Tel. (913) 273-1381. Ralph L. Smith, Regional Minister/President
Kansas City (Greater): The ChristianChurch (Disciples of Christ) of Greater Kansas City, 7203 The Paseo, P.O. Box 17088, Kansas City, MO 64132. Tel. (816) 361-7771. David C. Downing, Regional Minister/President
Kentucky: Christian Church (Disciples of Christ) in Kentucky, 1125 Red Mile Rd., Lexington 40504. Tel. (606)233-1391. A. Guy Waldrop, General Minister
Louisiana: Christian Church (Disciples of Christ) in Louisiana, 3524 Holloway Prairie Rd., Pineville 71360. Tel. (318) 443-0304. Kenneth E. Adcock, Regional Minister
Michigan: Christian Church (Disciples of Christ) Michigan Region, 2820 Covington Ct., Lansing 48912. Tel. (517) 372-3220. Morris Finch, Jr., Regional Minister
Mid-America Region: Christian Church (Disciples of Christ) of Mid-America, Hwy. 54 S., Box 1087, Jefferson City, MO 65102. Tel. (314) 636-8149. Stephen V. Cranford, Regional Minister
Mississippi: Christian Church (Disciples of Christ), in Mississippi, 1619 N. West St., Jackson 39202. Tel. (601) 352-6774. William E. McKnight, Regional Minister
Montana: Christian Church (Disciples of Christ) in Montana, 1019 Central Ave., Great Falls 59401. Tel. (406) 452-7404. James E. Kimsey, Jr., Regional Minister

Nebraska: Christian Church (Disciples of Christ) in Nebraska, 1268 S. 20th St., Lincoln 68502. Tel. (402) 476-0359. N. Dwain Acker, Regional Minister

North Carolina: Christian Church (Disciples of Christ), in North Carolina, 509 NE Lee St., Box 1568, Wilson 27893. Tel. (919) 291-4047. Bernard C. Meece, Regional Minister

Northeastern Region: Christian Church (Disciples of Christ), Northeastern Region, Inc., 1272 Delaware Ave., Buffalo, NY 14209. Tel. (716) 886-2634. Charles F. Lamb, Regional Minister

Northwest Region: The Northwest Regional Christian Church (Disciples of Christ), 6558-35th Ave., SW, Seattle, WA 98126. Tel. (206)938-1008, Robert Clarke Brock, Regional Minister—Pres.

Ohio: The Christian Church in Ohio (Disciples of Christ) 38007 Butternut Ridge Rd., Elyria 44035. Tel. (216) 458-5112. Howard M. Ratcliff, Regional Pastor and Pres.

Oklahoma: Christian Church (Disciples of Christ) in Oklahoma, 301 N.W. 36th St., Oklahoma City 73118. Tel. (405) 528-3577. Eugene N. Frazier, Exec. Regional Minister

Oregon: Christian Church (Disciples of Christ) in Oregon, 0245 S.W. Bancroft St., Suite F, Portland 97201. Tel. (503) 226-7648, Mark K. Reid, Regional Minister

Pacific Southwest Region: Christian Church (Disciples of Christ) of the Pacific Southwest Region, 3126 Los Feliz Blvd., Los Angeles, CA 90039. Tel. (213)665-5126. Margaret Owen Clark, Regional Pastor.

Pennsylvania: Christian Church (Disciples of Christ) in Pennsylvania, 670 Rodi Rd., Pittsburgh 15235. Tel. (412) 731-7000. Dwight L. French, General Minister

South Carolina: Christian Church of South Carolina, (Disciples of Christ), 1098 E. Montague Ave., North Charleston, SC 29406. Tel (803) 554-6886. _____, Regional Minister

Southwest Region: Christian Church (Disciples of Christ) in the Southwest, 2909 Lubbock Ave., Fort Worth, TX 76109. Tel. (817) 926-4687. James C. Suggs, Regional Minister

Tennessee: Christian Church (Disciples of Christ) in Tennessee, 3700 Richland Ave., Nashville 37205. Tel. (615) 269-3409. G. Bronson Netterville, Regional Minister and Pres.

Upper Midwest Region: Christian Church (Disciples of Christ) in the Upper Midwest, 3300 University Ave., Box 1024, Des Moines, IA 50311. Tel. (515) 255-3168. William L. Miller, Jr., Regional Minister

Utah: Christian Church of Utah (Disciples of Christ), 1370 Pennsylvania, Ste. 400, Denver, CO 80203. Tel. (303) 839-0075. Lloyd Cox, Interim Regional Minister

Virginia: The Christian Church (Disciples of Christ) in Virginia, 518 Brevard St., Richmond 24501. Tel. (804) 353-9124. Jack S. Austin, Regional Minister

West Virginia: Christian Church (Disciples of Christ) in West Virginia. Rt. 5, Box 167, Parkersburg 26101. Tel. (304) 428-1681. Charles E. Crank, Jr., Regional Minister

Canada: Christian Church (Disciples of Christ) in Canada, 55 Cork St. E., Ste. 303, Guelph, Ontario N1H 2W7. Tel. (519) 823-5190. Robert W. Steffer, Exec. Regional Minister, Interim Exec. Minister

PERIODICALS

The Disciple (m), Box 179, St. Louis, MO 63166, James L. Merrell, Ed.

Vanguard (church planning), 222 S. Downey Ave., Box 1986, Indianapolis, IN 46206. John R. Compton, Ed.-in-Chief

Christian Church of North America, General Council

The root system of the General Council originates in the Italian Pentecostal Movement which had its inception in Chicago, Ill., in 1907, a part of the larger outpouring of the Holy Spirit at the turn of the century.

Luigi Francescon, who later was used of the Lord to found the thriving Congregaco Crista do Brasil in Brazil, was a principal of that early period, as were Maximilliano Tosetto, Peter Ottolini, Giacomo Lombardi, and Giuseppi Petrelli—all men with unusual zeal who spread the full gospel message to their countrymen throughout the United States, Italy, and South America.

Articles of Faith adopted at the first convention of the churches in Niagara Falls, N.Y., in 1927 brought a new sense of unity to the movement, but were not successful in surmounting suspicions about "organization." A second cohesive factor was the rather universal understanding that the churches' purpose for being was missions, a factor reflected in the movement's initial incorporation in 1948 as The Missionary Society of the Christian Church of North America.

In 1963, recognizing the emergence of the movement from a single ethnic to a multiethnic body and the obligations of growth to provide supportive ministries, as well as reaching out to the unevangelized, the movement was restructured and became known as the General Council, Christian Church of North America.

GENERAL ORGANIZATION

General Council: meets annually (September).
Headquarters: Rt. 18 & Rutledge Rd., Box 141-A, R.D. #1, Transfer, PA 16154. Tel. (412) 962-3501

OFFICERS

Executive Board: Gen. Overseer, Rev. Guy BonGiovanni, 3740 Longview Rd., W. Middlesex, PA 16159

Asst. Gen. Overseers: Exec. Vice-Pres., Rev. David Farina, 41 Sherbrooke Rd., Trenton, NJ 08638; Rev. James Demola, P.O. Box 159, Mullica Hill, NJ 08072; Rev. Andrew Farina, 3 Alhambra Pl., Greenville, PA 16125; Rev. Joseph Ronisisvalle, 1031 Hermosa Dr., Rocklege, FL 32955; Rev. Charles Guy, 26 Delafield Dr., Albany, NY 12205; Rev. Anthony Freni, 10 Elkway Ave., Norwood, MA 02062

Gen. Sec.-Treas., Rev. Richard A. Tedesco, Box 141-A R. D. #1, Transfer, PA 16154

Department Dirs.:

Publications & Promotion, Rev. Frank Bongiovanni, 561 S. Transit, Lockport, NY 14094

Faith, Order, Credentials, Unity & Standard, Rev. David Farina, 41 Sherbrooke Rd., Trenton, NJ 08638

Church Growth & Media Ministries, Rev. Charles Gay, 26 Delafield Dr., Albany, NY 12205

Youth, Sunday School & Education, Rev. Dennis Karaman, 42 Sunny Side Dr., Yonkers, NY 10705

Foreign & Home Missions, Rev. John Del Turco, Box 141-A, R. D. #1, Transfer, PA 16154

Institutions, Benevolences & Fellowships, Rev. Eugene DeMarco, 155 Scott St., New Brighton, PA 15066

Finance, Rev. Richard A. Tedesco, Box 141-A, R.D. #1, Transfer, PA 16154

Honorary Personnel:

Gen. Overseer, Rev. Frank P. Fortunato, 3167 Welsh Rd., Philadelphia, PA 19136; Carmine Saginario, P.O. Box 1048, Hermitage, PA 16148

Missions, Rev. Richard L. Corsini, 921 6th Ave., Apt. #3, New Brighton, PA 15066

PERIODICALS

Il Faro (m), 708 Jeffrey Street, Herkimer, NY 13350, Rev. Guido Scalzi, Ed.

Vista (m) R.D. #4, West Middlesex, PA 16159, Mrs. Pat Leali, Ed.

Christian Churches and Churches of Christ

The fellowship, whose churches were always strictly congregational in polity, has its origin in the American movement to "restore the New Testament church in doctrine, ordinances and life" initiated by Thomas and Alexander Campbell, Walter Scott and Barton W. Stone in the early years of the nineteenth century.

Churches: 5,556; Inclusive Membership: 1,063,469; Sunday or Sabbath Schools: N.R.: TotalEnrollment: N.R.; Ordained Clergy: 5,476

NO GENERAL ORGANIZATION

CONVENTIONS

North American Christian Convention (founded 1927), Dir., Rod Huron, 3533 Epley Rd., Cincinnati, OH 45239. NACC mailing address: Box 39456 Cincinnati, OH 45239. Tel. (513)385-2470

National Missionary Convention (founded 1947), Coord., Walter Birney, Box 11, Copeland, KS 67837. Tel. (513)668-5250

Eastern Christian Convention, 5300 Norbeck Rd., Rockville, MD 10853

PERIODICALS

Christian Standard (w), 8121 Hamilton Ave., Cincinnati, OH 45231, Sam E. Stone, Ed.

Restoration Herald (m), 5664 Cheviot Rd., Cincinnati, OH 45329. Tom Thurman, Ed.

Directory of the Ministry (a), 1525 Cherry Rd., Springfield, IL 62704. Ralph D. McLean, Ed. Tel. (217) 546-7338

Horizons (bi-w), Box 2427, Knoxville, TN 37901. Norman L. Weaver, Ed. Tel. (615)577-9740

The Christian Congregation, Inc.

The Christian Congregation is a denominational evangelistic association that originated in 1798 and was active on the frontier in areas adjacent to the Ohio River. The church was an unincorporated organization until 1887. At that time a group of ministers who desired closer cooperation formally constituted the church. The charter was revised in 1898 and again in 1970.

Governmental polity basically is congregational. Local units are semiautonomous. Doctrinal positions, strongly biblical, are essentially universalist in the sense that ethical principles, which motivate us to creative activism, transcend national boundaries and racial barriers. A central tenet, John 13:34-35, translates to such respect for sanctity of life that abortions on demand, capital punishment, and all warfare are vigorously opposed. No distinctions are made between so-called just wars and unjust ones. All are unjust. International strife of this type is obsolete as a means of resolving disputes.

Early leaders were John Chapman, John L. Puckett, and Isaac V. Smith. Bishop O. J. Read was chief administrative and ecclesiastical officer for 40 years until 1961. Rev. Dr. Ora Wilbert Eads has been general superintendent since 1961.

Ministerial affiliation for independent clergymen is provided.

Churches: 1,450; Inclusive Membership: 105,478; Sunday or Sabbath Schools: 1,316; Total Enrollment: 57,563; Ordained Clergy: 1,455

OFFICER

Gen. Supt., Rev. Ora Wilbert Eads, 804 W. Hemlock St., LaFollette, TN 37766

Christian Methodist Episcopal Church

In 1870 the General Conference of the M.E. Church, South, approved the request of its colored membership for the formation of their conferences into a separate ecclesiastical body, which became the Colored Methodist Episcopal Church.

At its General Conference in Memphis, Tenn., May 1954, it was overwhelmingly voted to change the name of the Colored Methodist Episcopal Church to the Christian Methodist Episcopal Church. This became the official name on January 3, 1956.

GENERAL ORGANIZATION

General Conference: quadrennial. (Next meeting in 1990)

OFFICERS

Exec. Sec., Dr. W. Clyde Williams, 2805 Shoreland Dr., Atlanta, GA 30331. Tel. (404)344-6738

Sec. Gen. Conf., Rev. Edgar L. Wade, P.O. Box 3403, Memphis, TN 38103

OTHER ORGANIZATIONS

Christian Education: Gen. Sec., Dr. Ronald M. Cunningham, 1474 Humber St., Memphis, TN 38106. Tel. (901)947-3144

Lay Ministry: Gen. Sec., Dr. I. Carlton Faulk, 1222 Rose St., Berkeley, CA 94702. Tel. (415)655-4106

Evangelism, Missions & Human Concerns: Gen Sec., Rev. Raymond F. Williams, P.O. Box 9067, Silver Spring, MD 20906. Tel. (301)598-2653

Finance: Sec., Mr.Joseph C. Neal, Jr., P.O. Box 75085, Los Angeles, CA 90030. Tel. (213)233-5050

Publications: Gen. Sec., Rev. Lonnie L. Napier, P.O. Box 2018, Memphis, TN 38101. Tel. (901)947-3135

Personnel Services: Gen. Sec., Dr. N. Charles Thomas, P.O. Box 74, Memphis, TN 39101. Tel. (901)947-3135

Women's Missionary Council: Pres., Dr. Thelma J. Dudley, P.O. Box 5245, Orlando, FL 35855. Tel. (305)293-8186

PERIODICALS

Christian Index, The (bi-m), P. O. Box 665, Memphis, TN 38101, Rev. L. L Reddick III, Ed.

Missionary Messenger, The (m), 1634 Garden St., Shreveport, LA 71101, Cora B. Williams, Ed.

BISHOPS

First District: Bishop William H. Graves, 564 Frank Ave., Memphis, TN 38101. Tel. (901) 947-6180

Second District: Bishop Othal H. Lakey, 6322 Elwynne Dr., Cincinnati, OH 45236. Tel. (513) 984-6825

Third District: Bishop Dotcy I. Isom, Jr., 11470 Northway Dr., St. Louis, MO 63136. Tel. (314)381-3111

Fourth District: Bishop Marshall Gilmore, 109 Holcomb Dr., Shreveport, LA 71103. Tel. (318) 222-6284

Fifth District: Bishop Richard O. Bass, 308 10th Ave. W., Birmingham, AL 35204. Tel. (205) 252-3541

Sixth District: Bishop Joseph C. Coles, Jr., 2780 Collier Dr., Atlanta, GA 30018. Tel. (404) 794-0096

Seventh District: Bishop Oree Broomfield, Sr., 6524 16th St., N.W., Washington, DC 20012. Tel. (202) 723-2660

Eighth District: Bishop C. D. Coleman, Sr., 2330 Sutter St., Dallas, TX 75216. Tel. (214) 942-5781

Ninth District: Bishop E. Lynn Brown, P.O. Box 11276, Los Angeles, CA 90011. Tel. (213)216-9278

Tenth District: Bishop Nathaniel L. Linsey, P.O. Box 170127, Atlanta, GA 30317

Retired: Bishop E. P. Murchison, 4094 Windsor Castle Way, Decatur, GA 30034; Bishop Henry C. Bunton, 853 East Dempster Ave., Memphis, TN 38106; Bishop Chester A. Kirkendoll, 10 Hurtland, Jackson, TN 38305; Bishop P. Randolph Shy, 894 Falcon Dr. S.W., Atlanta, GA 30311

Christian Nation Church U.S.A.

Organized in 1895, at Marion, Ohio, as a group of "equality evangelists," who later formed the Christian Nation Church. This church is Wesleyan and Arminian in doctrine, emphasizes the Pre-Millenial Coming of Christ, semi-congregational in government; and emphasizes evangelism. Reincorporated as Christian Nation Church U.S.A., 1961.

Churches: 5; Inclusive Membership: 200; Sunday or Sabbath Schools: 5; Total Enrollment: 170' Ordained Clergy: 23

GENERAL ORGANIZATION
Congress: annual

OFFICERS
Gen. Overseer, Rev. Harvey Monjar, Box 513, South Lebanon, OH 45036. Tel.(513)932-0360

Asst. Overseer, Rev. Ronald Justice, 11245 State Rt. 669 NE, Rosedale, OH 43777. Tel. (614)982-7827

Gen. Sec., Rev. Randy Lusk, P.O. Box 113, Fanrock, WV 24834. Tel. (304)732-7792

Christian Reformed Church in North America

The Christian Reformed Church represents the historic faith of Protestantism. Founded in the United States in 1857, it asserts its belief in the Bible as the inspired Word of God, and is creedally united in the Belgic Confession (1561), the Heidelberg Catechism (1563), and the Canons of Dort (1618-19). (Note: For total statistics for this body see also those listed under the Christian Reformed Church in North America in Directory 4, Religious Bodies in Canada, which follows.)

Churches: 650; Inclusive Membership: 219,988; Sunday or Sabbath Schools: 647; Total Enrollment: 55,594; Ordained Clergy: 1,077

GENERAL ORGANIZATION
Synod: annual (June)

OFFICERS
Stat. Clk., Rev. Leonard J. Hofman, Office Address: 2850 Kalamazoo Ave. S.E., Grand Rapids, MI 49560. Tel. (616)246-0744

Denominational Financial Coord., Harry Vander Meer, 2850 Kalamazoo Ave., SE Grand Rapids, MI 49560

OTHER ORGANIZATIONS
The Back to God Hour: Dir. of Ministries, Dr. Joel H. Nederhood; Exec. Dir., Mr. David Vander Ploeg; International Headquarters: 6555 W. College Dr., Palos Heights, IL 60463

Christian Reformed Board World Ministries: Exec. Sec. Dr. Roger S. Greenway, 2850 Kalamazoo Ave. S.E., Grand Rapids, MI 49560; Christian Reformed World Missions Cmte., Dir., Rev. William Van Tol, 2850 Kalamazoo Ave. S.E., Grand Rapids, MI 49560; Christian Reformed World Relief Committee: Exec. Dir., John De Haan, 2850 Kalamazoo Ave. S.E. Grand Rapids, MI 49560

Christian Reformed Board of Home Missions: Exec. Dir., Rev. John A. Rozeboom, 2850 Kalamazoo Ave. S.E., Grand Rapids, MI 49560

CRC Publications: Exec. Dir., Gary Mulder, 2850 Kalamazoo Ave., S.E., Grand Rapids, MI 49560

Ministers' Pension Fund, Adm., Dr. Ray Vander Weele, 2850 Kalamazoo Ave., S.E., Grand Rapids, MI 49560

PERIODICAL
The Banner (w), 2850 Kalamazoo Ave. S.E., Grand Rapids, MI 49560, Rev. Andrew Kuyvenhoven, Ed.

Christian Union

Organized in 1864 in Columbus, Ohio. It stresses the oneness of the Church with Christ as its only head. The Bible is the only rule of faith and practice and good fruits the only condition of fellowship. Each local church governs itself.

GENERAL ORGANIZATION
General Council: triennial. (Next meeting, 1989)

Home Office: 220 W. Excelsior St., Excelsior Springs, MO 64024. Tel. (816) 637-5345.

OFFICERS
Pres., Rev. Hearold McElwee, Rt. 1, Box 387, Lawson, MO 64062. Tel. (816)296-3922

Vice-Pres., Rev. Dan Williams, 2-4964-B, Delta, OH 43515 Tel. (419)822-4261

Sec., Rev. Joseph Cunningham, 1005 N. 5th St., Greenfield, OH 45123. Tel. (513)981-3476

Asst. Sec., Rev. Steve Clymer, Box 101, U696-8, Liberty Center, OH 43532. Tel. (419)533-5341

Treas., Rev. William R. Smith, 154 S. Institute, Richmond, MO 64085. Tel. (816)776-6002

PERIODICAL
Christian Union Witness (m), 106 W. Broadway, Excelsior Springs, MO 64024.

Church of Christ

Organized April 6, 1830, at Fayette, New York, by Joseph Smith and five others; in 1864 Independence, Missouri, was designated as headquarters.

GENERAL ORGANIZATION
General Conference: annual

Headquarters: Temple Lot, Independence, MO

OFFICERS
Sec. of the Council of Twelve, Apostle William A. Sheldon, 1011 Cottage, Independence, MO 64050. Tel. (816) 833-3995

Gen. Bus. Mgr., Bishop Alvin Harris, P.O. Box 472, Independence, MO 64051

General Recorder, Isaac Brockman, P.O. Box 472, Independence, MO 64051

PERIODICAL
Zion's Advocate, P.O. Box 472, Independence, MO 64051, Gary Housknecht, Ed.

Church of Christ, Scientist

The Christian Science Church was founded by New England religious leader Mary Baker Eddy in 1879 "to commemorate the word and works of our Master (Christ Jesus), which should reinstate primitive Christianity and its lost element of healing." In 1892 the church was reorganized and established as The First Church of Christ, Scientist, in Boston, also called The Mother Church, with local branch churches around the world, of which there are nearly 3,000 in 56 countries today.

The church is administered by a five-member board of directors in Boston. Local churches govern themselves democratically. Since the church has no clergy, services are conducted by laypersons elected to serve as Readers. There are also about 5,000 Christian Science practitioners who devote their full time to healing through prayer.

GENERAL ORGANIZATION
Board of Directors, Headquarters: The First Church of Christ, Scientist, 175 Huntington Ave., Boston, MA 02115

OFFICERS
Bd. of Dirs., Harvey W. Wood, Ruth Elizabeth Jenks, Hal M. Friesen, Michael B. Thorneloe, John L. Selover

Pres., Charles W. Ferris

42

Treas., Donald C. Bowersock
Clk., Mrs. Virginia S. Harris
First Reader, Timothy A. MacDonald
Second Reader, Marianne Bauer

OTHER ORGANIZATIONS

Board of Education: Teaches a class of 30 pupils once in 3 years for the purpose of providing authorized teachers of Christian Science

Board of Lectureship: Made up of 35 to 40 members, delivers free lectures worldwide

Committee on Publication: Source of public information on the denomination

Publishing Society: Publishes and/or sells the authorized literature of Christian Science

PERIODICALS

The Christian Science Monitor (d) (w), Boston, MA
The Christian Science Journal (m), Boston, MA
Christian Science Sentinel (w), Boston, MA
Christian Science Quarterly (q), Boston, MA
The Herald of Christian Science (m), in French, German, Portuguese, Spanish; (q), in Danish, Dutch, Greek, Indonesian, Italian, Japanese, Norwegian, Swedish, and Braille

Church of Daniel's Band

A body Methodistic in form and evangelistic in spirit, organized in Michigan in 1893.

GENERAL ORGANIZATION

Conference: annual

OFFICERS

Pres., Rev. Jim Hoggard, 605 N. Fifth St., Coleman, MI 48618. Tel. (517)465-6915
Vice-Pres., Rev. Jim Seaman, Adams St., Coleman, MI 48618.
Sec./Treas., Rev. Marie Berry, Roehrs St., Beaverton, MI 48612.

The Church of God

Inaugurated by Bishop A. J. Tomlinson, who served as General Overseer, 1903 to 1943, and from which many groups of the Pentecostal and Holiness Movement stemmed. Bishop Homer A. Tomlinson served as General Overseer, 1943 to 1968. Episcopal in administration, evangelical in doctrines of justification by faith, sanctification as a second work of grace, and of the baptism of the Holy Ghost, speaking with other tongues, miracles of healing.

GENERAL ORGANIZATION

National Assembly, U.S.A.: annual, Chaffee, MO
National Headquarters: U.S.A. Box 13036, 1207 Willow Brook, Apt. #2, Huntsville, AL 35802. Tel. (205) 881-9629

OFFICERS

Gen. Overseer and Bishop, Voy M. Bullen; Gen. Sec., and Treas., Marie Powell
Church of God Publishing House, Box 13036, 1207 Willow Brook Apt. #2, Huntsville, AL 35802
Bus: Mgr., _____

CHURCH AUXILIARIES

Address: Box 13036, 1207 Willow Brook, Apt. #2, Huntsville AL 35802
Assembly Band Movement: Gen. Sec., Bishop Bill Kinslaw
Women's Missionary Band: Gen. Sec., Shirley Metcalf
Theocratic Bands: Gen. Sec., Rev. Ted Carr
Victory Leader's Band, Youth: Gen. Sec., Rev. Evang. Glynn Baker

Administration for Highway and Hedge Campaign: Earnest Hoover

PERIODICALS

The Church of God (s-m), Box 13036, 1207 Willow Brook, Apt. #2, Huntsville, AL 35802
Forward With Christ (m), 144 Fifth Ave., New York, NY 10011. Christopher Economou, Ed.
The Church of God Quarterly (q), Box 13036, 1207 Willow Brook, Apt. #2, Huntsville, AL 35802; Voy M. Bullen, Ed.

Church of God (Anderson, Ind.)

The Church of God (Anderson, Ind.) began in 1881 when Daniel S. Warner and several associates in northern Indiana felt constrained to forsake all denominational hierarchies and formal creeds, trusting solely in the Holy Spirit as their overseer and the Bible as their statement of belief. Warner and those of similar persuasion saw themselves at the forefront of a movement to restore unity and holiness to the church. It was not their intention to establish yet another denomination, but to promote primary allegiance to Jesus Christ so as to transcend (and even obliterate) denominational loyalties.

Deeply influenced by Wesleyan theology and Pietism, the Church of God has emphasized conversion, holiness, and attention to the Bible. Worship services tend to be informal, accentuating expository preaching and robust singing. Although some are much larger, the typical Church of God congregation is small, with Sunday morning worship attendance averaging about 100.

Not only is the Church of God noncreedal, there is no formal membership. The contention is that "salvation makes you a member." Hence persons are assumed to be members on the basis of witness to a conversion experience and evidence that supports such witness. The basis for this is that only Christ may add members to the church. The absence of formal membership is also consistent with the church's understanding of how Christian unity is to be achieved—that is, by preferring the label *Christian* before all others.

As might be expected, the Church of God is congregational in its government. Each local congregation is autonomous and as such, may call any recognized Church of God minister to be its pastor and may retain him or her as long as is mutually pleasing. Ministers are ordained and disciplined by state or provincial assemblies made up predominantly (but not usually exclusively) of ministers. National program boards serve the church through coordination and resource materials. A growing trend is the development of state offices which perform similar functions.

The Church of God maintains a strong interest in evangelism in this country and in missions overseas. There are Church of God congregations in 73 foreign countries, most of which are resourced by one or more missionaries. There are as many Church of God adherents overseas as in North America. Heaviest concentration is in the nation of Kenya.

Churches: 2,296; Inclusive Membership: 188,662; Sunday or Sabbath Schools: 2,245; Total Enrollment: 200,180; Ordained Clergy: 3,313

GENERAL ORGANIZATION

General Assembly: annual. Chpsn., Samuel G. Hines, 9553 Fort Foote Rd., Fort Washington, MD 20744

EXECUTIVE COUNCIL

Box 2420, Anderson, IN 46018. Tel. (317) 642-0256. Exec. Sec., Paul A. Tanner
Dir. of World Service, David L. Lawson
Dir. of Church Service, Keith Huttenlocker

OTHER ORGANIZATIONS

Board of Christian Education: Acting Exec. Sec.-Treas., Kenneth G. Prunty, Box 2458, Anderson, IN 46018

Board of Church Extension and Home Missions: Pres., J. Perry Grubbs, Box 2069, Anderson, IN 46018

Foreign Missionary Board: Exec. Sec.-Treas., Doris Dale, Box 2498, Anderson, IN 46018

Women of the Church of God: Exec. Sec.-Treas., Nellie Snowden, Box 2328, Anderson, IN 46018

Board of Pensions: Exec. Sec.-Treas., Harold A. Conrad, Box 2299, Anderson, IN 46018

Mass Communications Board: Dir., Dwight L. Dye, Box 2007, Anderson, IN 46018

Warner Press, Inc.: Pres., Donald Noffsinger, Box 2499, Anderson, IN 46018

PERIODICALS

Vital Christianity (bi-w), Box 2499, Anderson, IN 46018, Arlo F. Newell, Ed.

Church of God Missions (m), Box 2337, Anderson, IN 46018, Dondeena Caldwell, Ed.

Church of God by Faith, Inc.

Founded 1919, in Jacksonville Heights, Florida, by Elder John Bright. This body believes the word of God as interpreted by Jesus Christ to be the only hope of salvation, and Jesus Christ the only mediator for man.

GENERAL ORGANIZATION

General Assembly: meets every other year.

Headquarters: 3220 Haines St., Jacksonville, FL 32206. Tel. (904)353-5111

OFFICERS

Bishop Emeritus, W. W. Matthews, P.O. Box 907, Ozark, AL 36360

Bishop James E. McKnight, Rt. 10 Box 26, Gainesville, FL 32601

Treas., Elder C. M. Fogle, 813 So. Delaney Ave., Avon Park, FL 33825

Ruling Elders: Elder John Robinson, 300 Essex Dr., Ft. Pierce, FL 33450; Elder Theodore Brown, 93 Girard Pl, Newark, NJ 07108

Exec. Sec., Elder George Matthews, 8834 Camphor Dr., Jacksonville, FL 32208

PERIODICAL

The Spiritual Guide (m), 3220 Haines St., Jacksonville, FL 32206

Church of God (Cleveland, Tenn.)

America's oldest Pentecostal Church began in 1886 as an outgrowth of the holiness revival under the name Christian Union. Reorganized in 1902 as the Holiness Church and in 1907 the church adopted the name Church of God. Its doctrine is fundamental and Pentecostal; it maintains a centralized form of government and an evangelistic and missionary program.

GENERAL ORGANIZATION

General Assembly: biennial (Next meeting, August 1988)

International Offices, Keith St. at 25th NW, Cleveland, TN 37311. Tel. (615) 472-3361

EXECUTIVES

Gen. Overseer, Raymond Crowley

Asst. Gen. Overseers, Ray H. Hughes, Cecil B. Knight, R. Lamar Vest

Gen. Sec.-Treas., John Nichols

DEPARTMENTS

World Missions: Gen. Dir., J. Herbert Walker

Youth and C. E.: Gen. Dir., W. A. Davis

Publishing House: Publisher, Floyd Carey

Public Relations: Dir., Lewis J. Willis

Television and Radio Minister: Bennie S. Triplett

Evangelism: Dir., W. C. Ratchford

Education: Dir., Don Jenkins

Ladies Ministries: Pres., Mrs. Raymond Crowley

PERIODICALS

Church of God Evangel (bi-w), O. W. Polen, Ed.

Lighted Pathway (m), Marcus V. Hand, Ed.

Leadership (q), James Humbertson, Ed.

Sow (q), Herbert J. Walker, Ed.

Flame (q), W. C. Ratchford, Ed.

The Willing Worker (m), Mrs. Raymond Crowley, Ed.

Church School Literature, James Humbertson, Ed.

The Pentecostal Minister (q), Raymond Crowley, Ed.

Church of God General Conference (Oregon, Ill.)

This church is the outgrowth of several independent local groups of similar faith. Some were in existence as early as 1800, and others date their beginnings to the arrival of British immigrants in this country around 1847. Many local churches carried the name Church of God of the Abrahamic Faith. The corporate name is Church of God General Conference, Oregon, Illinois.

State and district conferences of these groups were formed as an expression of mutual cooperation. A national organization was instituted at Philadelphia in 1888. However, because of strong convictions on the questions of congregational rights and authority, it ceased to function until 1921, when the present General Conference was formed at Waterloo, Iowa.

The Bible is accepted as the supreme standard of faith. Adventist in viewpoint, the second (premmillenial) coming of Christ is strongly emphasized. The church teaches that the kingdom of God will be literal, beginning in Jerusalem at the time of the return of Christ and extending to all nations. Emphasis is placed on the oneness of God and the Sonship of Christ, that Jesus did not preexist prior to his birth in Bethlehem, and that the Holy Spirit is the power and influence of God. It believes in the restoration of Israel, the times of restitution, the mortalityof man (asleep in death until the resurrection), the literal resurrection of the dead, the reward of the righteous on earth, and the complete destruction of the wicked in the second death. Membership is dependent on faith, repentance, and baptism (for the remission of sins) by immersion.

Delegates from each church meet annually to determine church plans and policies and to elect officers who serve as the board of directors. The General Conference operates Oregon Bible College for the training of ministers; the Oregon Bible College Development Foundation, an endowment fund for the college; a Publishing Department, which produces church literature and curriculum; an Outreach and Church Development Department, which promotes youth, Sunday school, missions, and evangelistic work.

The work of the General Conference is carried on under the direction of the board of directors, which meets as necessary throughout the year. The executive officer is a president who administers the work as a whole. Because of the congregational nature of the church's government, the General Conference exists primarily as a means of mutual cooperation and for the development of yearly projects and enterprises.

Churches: 89; Inclusive Membership: 5,652; Sunday or Sabbath Schools: 89; Total Enrollment: 3,737; Ordained Clergy: 84

GENERAL ORGANIZATION

General Conference: annual (August)

Headquarters: Oregon, IL 61061. Tel. (815) 732-7991

OFFICERS

Chpsn., Joe James, Rt. 1, Buck Dr., Piedmont, SC 29673

Vice-Chpsn., Mr. Don Oovermyer, 918 N. 87th Pl., Scottsdale, AZ 85257 (winter); P.O. Box 84, Culver, IN 46511 (summer)
Pres., David Krogh, Box 100, Oregon, IL 61061
Sec., Mrs. Brenda Wessel, RR 1 Box 100, Frederick, IL 62639
Treas., Mr. Elmo Gaspar, Box 517, Eden Valley, MN 55329

OTHER ORGANIZATIONS

(All located at Box 100, Oregon, IL 61061)
Business Adm., Wilbur Burnham
Publishing Dept., Russell Magaw
Outreach & Church Development, R. Warren Sorenson
Oregon Bible College, Dale Ramsey

PERIODICALS

The Restitution Herald (bi-m), Box 100, Oregon, IL, Russell Magaw, Ed.
Church of God Progress Journal (bi-m), Box 100, Oregon, IL 61061, Russell Magaw, Ed.

†The Church of God in Christ

The Church of God in Christ was founded in 1906 in Memphis, Tenn., and was organized by Bishop Charles Harrison Mason, a former Baptist minister who pioneered the embryonic stages of the Holiness movement beginning in 1895 in Mississippi.

The Church further developed when its founder organized four major departments between 1910–1916. These departments were (1) Womens' Department, (2) Sunday School, (3) Young Peoples Willing Workers (YPWW), (4) Home and Foreign Mission.

Doctrinally, the Church is basically trinitarian. It teaches the infallability of scripture, the need for regeneration and subsequent baptism of the Holy Ghost. It emphasizes holiness as God's standard for Christian conduct. It recognizes as ordinances Holy Communion, Water Baptism and Feet Washing. Its governmental structure is basically episcopal with the General Assembly being the Legislative body.

The Church is headquartered at Memphis, Tenn. The organization has experienced tremendous growth and expansion of its ministries under the present leadership of the Presiding Bishop, Bishop J. O. Patterson.

GENERAL ORGANIZATION

International Convocation: annual (November)
General Assembly: semi-annual (April and November)
National Headquarters: Mason Temple, 939 Mason St., Memphis, TN 38126
World Headquarters: 272 South Main St., Memphis, TN 38103. Tel. (901) 521-1163 or 527-1422
The Mother Church: Pentecostal Temple, 229 S. Danny Thomas Blvd., Memphis, TN 38126. Tel. (901) 527-9202

GENERAL OFFICES

All located at 272 S. Main St., Memphis, TN 38103. Mail: P. O. Box 320, Memphis, TN 38101
Office of the Presiding Bishop
Tel. (901) 525-2507
Presiding Bishop, Most Rev. J. O. Patterson
Adm. Asst., Elder J. O. Patterson, Jr.
Exec. Sec., Mrs. Julia Mason Atkins
Sec., Elder Alfred Z. Hall, Jr.
Adjutant, Bishop F. E. Perry
Adjutant to the Presiding Bishop, Dr. J. Delano Ellis, II
Chief of Military and Institutional Chaplains, Bishop Ithiel Clemmons
The General Board
Presiding Bishop, Most Rev. J. O. Patterson, 1774 S. Parkway, E., Memphis, TN 38114
First Assistant Presiding Bishop, Rt. Rev. L. H. Ford, 9401 M. L. King Drive, Chicago, IL 60619
Second Assistant Presiding Bishop, Rt. Rev. F. D. Washington, 1328 President St., Brooklyn, NY 11213

Bishop J. D. Husband, P.O. Box 824, Atlanta, GA 30301
Bishop C. L. Anderson, Jr., 20485 Mendota, Detroit, MI 48221
Bishop L. R. Anderson, 265 Ranch Trail West, Amherst, NY 14221
Bishop C. D. Owens, 14 Van Velsor Pl., Newark, NJ 07112
Bishop O. T. Jones, Jr., 363 N. 60th St., Philadelphia, PA 19139
Bishop Jacob Cohen, 3120 N.W. 48th Terr., Miami, FL 33142
Bishop P. A. Brooks, 30945 Wendbrook Lane, Birmingham, MI 48010
Bishop S. L. Green, 2416 Orcutt Ave., Newport News, VA 23607
Bishop J. N. Haynes, 6743 Talbot, Dallas, TX 75216
Office of the General Secretary
Tel. (901) 521-1163
General Secretary, Bishop G. R. Ross
Asst. Gen. Sec. for Registration, Bishop E. Harris Moore
Asst. Gen. Sec. for Records, Bishop Herbert J. Williams; Dr. J. Delano Ellis II, Asst. to Gen. Sec. at Headquarters; Bishop A. LaDell Thomas, Coord.
Dir. of Research and Survey, Elder Ronald A. Blumburg
Office of the Financial Secretary
Tel. (901) 744-0710
Secretary, Dr. S. Y. Burnett
Gen. Treas., Bishop Theodore Davis
Chmn. of Finance, Bishop Benjamin Crouch
Office of the Board of Trustees
Chmn., Dr. Roger L. Jones
Sec., Elder Warren Miller
Office of the Clergy Bureau
Tel. (901) 523-7045
Dir., Elder Samuel Smith
Sec., Mrs. Dorothy Motley
Office of the Superintendent of Properties
Tel. (901) 774-0710
Superintendent, Bishop W. L. Porter
Sec.,
Office of the Counsel General
Tel. (901) 527-4402
Counsel General, Bishop J. O. Patterson, Jr.
Assoc. Counsel, Attorney A. W. Willis
Board of Publications
Tel. (901) 526-3644
Chmn., Bishop Roy L. H. Winbush
Sec.-Treas., Bishop Floyde E. Perry, Jr.
Headquarters Rep., Elder David Hall
Publishing House:
Tel. (901) 521-0142
Manager, Mr. Hugheau Terry
Department of Missions
Tel. (901) 522-9221
Pres., Bishop Carlis L. Moody
Exec. Sec., Elder Jesse W. Denny
Department of Women
Tel. (901) 522-9964
Pres.-Gen. Supervisor, Dr. Mattie McGlothen
Asst. Supervisor, Mrs. Emma Crouch
Exec. Sec., Mrs. Elizabeth C. Moore
Sec. of the Women's Convention, Mrs. Freddie J. Bell
Treas., Mrs. Mary L. Belvin
Fin. Sec., Mrs. Olive Brown
Department of Evangelism
Pres., Dr. Edward L. Battles, 4310 Steeplechase rail, Arlington, TX 76016. Tel. (817) 429-7166
Department of Music
Pres., Mrs. Mattie Moss Clark, 18203 Sorrento, Detroit MI 48235
Vice Pres., Mrs. Mattie Wigley, 1726 S. Wellington, Memphis, TN 38106

Department of Youth (Youth Congress)
Pres., Bishop C. H. Brewer, 260 Roydon Rd., New Haven, CT 06511
Department of Sunday Schools
Gen. Supt., Bishop Cleveland W. Williams, 270 Division St., Derby, CT 06418
United National Auxiliaries Convention
UNAC-5; Bishop Roy L. H. Winbush, Chmn.; Bishop G. R. Ross, Sec. of Exec. Committee
Church of God in Christ Book Store
272 S. Main St., Memphis, TN 38103. Tel. (901) 525-7334
Charles Harrison Mason Foundation
272 S. Main St., Memphis, TN 38103. Tel. (901) 525-2507
Chmn., The Executive Advisory Board, Presiding Bishop, J. O. Patterson
Exec. Dir., Mrs. Julia Mason Atkins
Chmn., Bd. of Dir., Bishop P. A. Brooks
Dir. of Fine Arts Scholarships, Mrs. Sara Jordan Powell

PERIODICALS

Whole Truth, P.O. Box 2017, Memphis, TN 38101, Elder David Hall, Ed.
Sunday School Literature, Publishing House, Church of God in Christ, 272 S. Main St., Memphis, TN 38103. Bishop Roy L. H. Winbush, Ed.
Y.P.W.W. Topics, 67 Tennyson, Highland Park, MI 48203. Elder James L. Whitehead, Jr., Ed.
Sunshine Band Topics, 648 Peart St., Benton Harbor, MI 29022. Mrs. Mildred Wells, Ed.
Purity Guide, P. O. Box 1526, Gary, IN 46407, Mrs. Pearl McCullom, Ed.
International Directory, 930 Mason St., Memphis, TN 38126.
The Pentecostal Interpreter, P. O. Box 6118, Knoxville, TN 37914. Bishop H. Jenkins Bell, Ed.
The Voice of Missions, 1932 Dewey Ave., Evanston, IL 60201. Ms. Jenifer James, Ed.

BISHOPS IN THE U.S.A.

(Address: Right Rev.)
Headquarters Staff: Presiding Bishop, Most Rev. J. O. Patterson; Jurisdictional Bishop, F. D. Macklin; Supt. Nat'l Properties, W. L. Porter; Auxiliaries: Samuel L. Lowe, W. A. Patterson, E. W. Rodgers, A. E. Reed; Bishop of Chaplains, Ithiel Clemmons
All of the above are located at 272 S. Main St., Memphis, TN 38103. Tel. (901) 525-2507 or 527-2710
Alabama: *First,* Chester A. Ashworth, 2901 Snavely Ave., Birmingham,AL 35211; *Second,* W. S. Harris, 3005 Melrose Pl., N.W., Huntsville, AL 35810
Alaska: Charles D. Williams, 2212 Vanderbilt Cir., Anchorage, AK 99504
Arizona: Felton King, P. O. Box 3791, Phoenix, AZ 84030
Arkansas: *First,* L. T. Walker, 2315 Chester St., Little Rock, AR 72206; *Second,* D. L. Lindsey, 401 W. 23rd St., North Little Rock, AR 72114
California: *North-Central,* G. R. Ross, 815 Calmar Ave., Oakland, CA 94610; *Northern,* B. R. Stewart, 734 12th Ave., San Francisco, CA 94118; *Northeast,* L. B. Johnson, 3121 Patridge Ave., Oakland, CA 94605; *Evangel,* E. E. Cleveland, 31313 Braeburn Ct., Haywood, CA 96045; *Northwest,* J. O. Patterson, Interim; *Southern #1,* C. E. Blake, 1731 Wellington Rd., Los Angeles, CA 90019; *Southern #2,* George McKinney, 5848 Arboles, San Diego, CA 92120 ; *Southern Metropolitan,* Bishop B. J. Crouch, 12418 Gain St., Pacoima, CA 91331; *Southwest,* B. R. Benbow, 504 Rexford Dr., Beverly Hills, CA 90210; *Valley,* Warren S. Wilson, 1435 Modoc St., Fresno, CA 93706
Colorado: Frank Johnson, 12231 E. Arkansas Pl., Aurora, CO 80014

Connecticut: *First,* Charles H. Brewer, Jr., 180 Osborne St., New Haven, CT 06515; *Second,* H. Bordeaux, 135 Westwood Rd., New Haven, CT 06511
Delaware: Lieutenant T. Blackshear, Sr., 17 S. Booth Dr., Penn Acres, New Castle, DE 19720
District of Columbia: Samuel Kelsey, 2549 11th St., N.W., Washington, DC 20001
Florida: *Central,* Calvin D. Kensey, 9462 August Dr., Jacksonville, FL 32208; *Eastern,* Jacob Cohen, 3120 N.W. 48th Terr., Miami, FL 33142; *Southwestern,* W. E. Davis, 2008 33rd Ave., Tampa, FL 33610; *Western,* M. L. Sconiers, P.O. Box 5472, Orlando, FL 32805
Georgia: *Central* and *Southeast,* J. D. Husband, P. O. Box 824, Atlanta, GA 30301; *Northern,* J. Howard Dell, 1717 Havilon Dr., S.W., Atlanta, GA 30311; *Southern,* C. J. Hicks, 1894 Madden Ave., Macon, GA 31204
Hawaii: *First,* _____; *Second,* W. H. Reed, 1223 W. 80th St., Los Angeles, CA 90044
Idaho: Nathaniel Jones, 630 Chateau, Barstow, CA 92311
Illinois: *First,* L. H. Ford, 9401 M. L. King Dr., Chicago, IL 60619; *Fifth,* B. E. Goodwin, 286 E. 16th St., Chicago Heights, IL 60411; *Sixth,* W. Haven Bonner, 1039 Bonner Ave., Aurora, IL 60505; *Central,* T. T. Rose, 1000 Dr. Taylor Rose Sq., Springfield, IL 62703; *Northern,* Isaiah Roberts, 6214 S. Michigan Ave., Chicago, IL 60637; *Southeast,* L. E. Moore, 7840 Contour Dr., St. Louis, MO 63121; *Southern,* J. Cobb, 323-30th St., Cairo, IL 62914
Indiana: *First,* William O. Blakley, 3701 Monroe St., Gary, IN 46408; *Second,* Oscar Freeman, 1760 Taft St., Gary, IN 46404
Iowa: Hurley Bassett, 1730 4th Ave., S.E., Cedar Rapids, IA 52403
Kansas: *Central,* I. B. Brown, 1635 Hudson Blvd., Topeka, KS 66607; *East,* William H. McDonald, 1627 N. 78th St., Kansas City, KS 66112; *Southwest,* J. L. Gilkey, 2403 Shadybrook, Wichita, KS 67214
Kentucky: *First,* A. T. Moore, 662 Cecil Ave., Louisville, KY 40211; *Second,* Edward H. Ware, 1560 Willis St., Memphis, TN 38108
Louisiana: *Eastern,* W. K. Gordon, Rt. 3, Box 447, Amite City, LA 70422; *Western,* Roy L. H. Winbush, 235 Diamond Dr., Lafayette, LA 70501
Maine: R. D. Williams II, 391 Gorham Rd., Scarborough, ME 04704
Maryland: *Central,* James I. Doswell, 3401 Walbrook Ave., Baltimore, MD 21216; *Eastern Shore,* James L. Eure, 635 West Main St., Salisbury, MD 21801; *Greater,* David Spann, 5023 Gwynn Oak Ave., Baltimore, MD 21207
Massachusetts: *First,* L. C. Young, 19 Almont St., Mattanpan, MA 02126; *Second and New Hampshire,* C. W. Williams, 270 Division St., Derby, CT 06418; C. D. Williams, 2212 Vanderbilt Cir., Anchorage, AK 99504; *West,* Bryant Robinson, Sr., 1424 Plumtree Rd., Springfield, MA 01119
Michigan: *Great Lakes,* C. L. Anderson, 20485 Mendota, Detroit, MI 48221; *North Central,* Herbert J. Williams, 1600 Cedar St., Saginaw, MI 48601; *Northeast,* P. A. Brooks II, 30945 Wendbrook Lane, Birmingham, MI 48010; *Southwest, First,* W. L. Harris, 1834 Outer Dr., Detroit, MI 48234; *Second,* Earl J. Wright, 18655 Autumn Lane, Southfield, MI 48076; *Third,* Rodger L. Jones, 1118 River Forest, Flint, MI 48594; *Fourth,* N. W. Wells, 530 Sue Lane, Muskogon, MI 49442
Minnesota: _____
Mississippi: *Northern,* T. T. Scott, 1066 Barnes Ave., Clarksdale, MS 38614; *Southern First,* Theodore Roosevelt Davis, 1704 Topp Ave., Jackson, MS 39204; *Southern #2,* J. E. McDowell, 3609 20th St., Gulfport, MS 39501
Missouri: *Central, MO; Eastern #1,* R. J. Ward, 4724 Palm Ave., St. Louis, MO 63115; *Eastern #2,* W. W. Sanders, 8167 Garner Lane, Berkeley, MO 63134;

Western, E. Harris Moore, 405 E. 64th Terr., Kansas City, MO 64131

Montana: W. H. Sims, 6410 Sunriver Dr., Sacramento, CA 95828

Nebraska: *Eastern,* Monte J. Bradford, 3901 Ramelle Dr., Council Bluff, IA 51501; *Northeastern,* B. T. McDaniels, 1106 N. 31st St., Omaha, NB 68103

Nevada: E. N. Webb, 1941 Goldhill, Las Vegas, NV 89106

New Jersey: *First,* Esau Courtney, 12 Clover Hill Cir., Trenton, NJ 08538; *Third,* Chandler David Owens, 14 Van Velsor Pl., Newark, NJ 07112

New Mexico: W. C. Griffin, 3322 Montclaire, Albuquerque, NM 87110

New York: *Eastern,* Frederick Douglas Washington, 1328 President St., Brooklyn, NY 11213; *Western #1,* LeRoy R. Anderson, 265 Ranch Trail, W., Amherst, NY 14221; *Western #2,* Charles H. McCoy, 168 Brunswick Blvd., Buffalo, NY 14208

North Carolina: *Greater,* L. B. Davenport, P. O. Box 156, Plymouth, NC 28803; *Second,* J. Howard Sherman, Sr., P. O. Box 329, Charlotte, NC 28201

North Dakota: Carlis L. Moody (Mission Dept.), 272 S. Main St., Memphis, TN 38103

Ohio: *North,* Robert S. Fields, 419 Crandell Ave., Youngstown, OH 44504; *Northwest,* Robert L. Chapman, 3194 E. 18th St., Cleveland, OH 44120; *Southern,* Floyde E. Perry, Jr., 3716 Rolliston Rd., Shaker Heights, OH 44120

Oklahoma: *Northwest,* J. A. Young, P.O. Box 844, Lawton, OK 73501; *Southeast,* W. E. Jeffries, 3001 Norcrest Ave., Oklahoma City, OK 73121

Oregon: *First,* H. B. Daniels, 1234 Killingsworth, Portland, OR 97211; *Second,* J. C. Foster, 2716 N.E. 9th Ave., Portland, OR 97212

Pennsylvania: *Commonwealth,* O. T. Jones, Jr., 363 N. 60th St., Philadelphia, PA 19139; *Eastern,* DeWitt A. Burton, 1400 Wistar Dr., Wyncote, PA 19095; *Western,* Gordon E. Vaughn, 6437 Stanton Ave., Pittsburgh, PA 15206

Rhode Island: Norman Quick, 1031 E. 215th St., Brooklyn, NY 11221

South Carolina: Johnnie Johnson, 649 Liberty Hall Rd., Goose Creek, SC 29445

South Dakota: Carlis L. Moody, 2413 Lee St., Evanston, IL 60202

Tennessee: *Headquarters,* F. Douglas Macklin, 1230 Tipton, Memphis, TN 38071 ; *Second,* H. J. Bell, P.O. Box 6118, Knoxville, TN 37914; ; *Central,* W. L. Porter, 1235 East Parkway, S., Memphis, TN 38114

Texas: *Eastern,* J. E. Lee, 742 Calcutta Dr., Dallas, TX 75241; *Northeast,* J. Neauell Haynes, 6743 Talbot, Dallas, TX 75216; *Northwest,* W. H. Watson, 1301 47th St., Lubbock, TX 79412; *South Central,* Nathan H. Henderson, 15622 Rockhouse Rd., Houston, TX 77060; *Southeast #1,* Robert E. Woodard, 2614 Wichita, Houston, TX 77004; *Southeast #2,* A. LaDell Thomas, 4401 McArthur Dr., Waco, TX 76708; *Southeast,* R. E. Ranger, 6604 Sabrosa Ct., W., Fort Worth, TX 76110; *Southwest,* T. D. Iglehart, 325 Terrell Rd., San Antonio, TX 78209

Utah: Nathaniel Jones, c/o Mission Dept., 630 Chateau Rd., Barstow, CA 92311

Vermont: Frank Clemons, Sr., 1323 Carroll St., Brooklyn, NY 11216

Virginia: *First,* Ted Thomas, Sr., 4145 Sunkist Rd., Chesapeake, VA 23321; *Second,* Samuel L. Green, Jr., 2416 Orcutt Ave., Newport News, VA 23607; *Third,* Levi E. Willis, 5110 Nichal Ct., Norfolk, VA 23508

Washington: T. L. Westbrook, 1256 176th St., Spanaway, WA 98402

West Virginia: *Northern,* _____; *Southern,* William Rimson, 60 Lawrence St., Detroit, MI 48202

Wisconsin: *First,* Dennis Flakes, 3420 N. 1st St., Milwaukee, WI 53212; *Northwest,* P. J. Henderson,

1312 W. Burleigh, Milwaukee, WI 53206; *Third,* J. C. Williams, 4232 N. 24th Pl., Milwaukee, WI 53209

Wyoming: A. W. Martin, 2453 N. Fountain St., Wichita, KS 67220

Church of God in Christ, International

Organized in 1969 in Kansas City, Missouri, by fourteen bishops of the Church of God in Christ of Memphis, Tennessee. The doctrine is the same, but the separation came because of disagreement over polity and governmental authority. The Church is Wesleyan in theology (two works of grace) but stresses the experience of full baptism of the Holy Ghost with the initial evidence of speaking with other tongues as the spirit gives utterance.

GENERAL ORGANIZATION

The General Assembly: annual
College of Bishops: April and August
Headquarters: 170 Adelphi St., Brooklyn, NY 11025 Tel. (718) 625-9175

OFFICERS

Presiding Bishop: The Rt. Rev. Carl E. Williams, Sr., 170 Adelphi St., Brooklyn, NY 11205

Vice-Presiding Bishop, Rt. Rev. J. P. Lucas, 1114 Broad St., Newark, NJ 07114

Sec.-Gen. Treas., The Rt. Rev. David J. Billings, III, 315 Clinton Ave., Brooklyn, NY 11205

Nat. Supervisor-Womens' Dept., Dr. Louise Norris, 210 Elmwood Ave., Bridgeport, CT 06605

Pres. Youth Department, Evangelist Joyce Taylor, 151 N. Elliott Walk, Brooklyn, NY 11205

Nat. Super., Sunday Schools, Rev. Ronald L. Figueroa, 433 Macon St., Brooklyn, NY 11233

Pres. Music Department, Beatrice Summerville, 210 Elmwood Ave., Bridgeport, CT 06605

Chpsn., Board of Elders, Rev. Elder Henry Burton, 414 Monroe St., Passaic, NJ 07055

Chpsn., Board of Bishops, Bishop J. C. White, 360 Colorado Ave., Bridgeport, CT 06605

Nat'l. Field Sec., Bishop Thomas E. Dunlap, 584 Myrtle Ave., Brooklyn, NY 11205

Chpsn., Evangelistic Dept., Rev. Eric Figueroa, 646 Jefferson Ave., Brooklyn, NY 11221

Financial Sec., Bro. Zack Kelly, 410 Grand Ave., Brooklyn, NY 11238

Mission Dept., Pres., Bishop Thomas E. Dunlap, 584 Myrtle Ave., Brooklyn, NY 11205

Church of God in Christ (Mennonite)

A section of the Mennonite body organized in 1859, in Ohio, for the reestablishment of the order and discipline of the Church.

GENERAL ORGANIZATION

Headquarters: 420 N. Wedel St., Moundridge, KS 67107. Tel. (316) 345-2532

OFFICER

Conf. Mod., Norman Koehn, 314 Crawford Dr., Victoria, TX 77904

PERIODICAL

Messenger of Truth (bi-w), Rt. 2, Box 264, Macon, MS 39341. Gladwin Koehn, Ed.

Church of God of Prophecy

The Church of God of Prophecy (the name it has borne since 1952) historically shares some of the early years of the Holiness classical pentecostal church, The Church of

God (Cleveland). A. J. Tomlinson, a dynamic pentecostal pioneer, was the church's most prominent figure in the first half of this century. Having observed many prominent turn-of-the-century ministers, he came under the influence of holiness teaching, and, finally, classical pentecostal theology. During his leadership the Church of God became a national, then an international body, various educational, social, and ecclesiastical programs were developed.

At the death of A. J. Tomlinson in 1943, M. A. Tomlinson was duly designated as leader of the organization. His tenure as general overseer, which continues to this day, has been marked by its call for church unity and fellowship, not limited socially, racially, or nationally. The church is racially integrated on all levels and various leadership positions are occupied by women.

The official teachings include special emphasis on repentance and sanctification as well as the doctrine of Spirit-baptism, with speaking in holy unknown tongues as the initial evidence. Other prominent doctrinal commitments: an imminence-oriented eschatology involving a premillennial return of the risen Jesus, which will be preceded by a series of events; a call for the sanctity of the home which includes denial of a multiple marriage; practice of water baptism by immersion, the Lord's Supper, and washing of the saints' feet; total abstinence from intoxicating beverages and tobacco; a concern for modesty in all dimensions of life; an appreciation for various gifts of the Holy Spirit, with special attention to divine healing.

The annual general assembly held at the church's world headquarters in Cleveland, Tennessee, is a time of celebration and fellowship with church members from around the world. Various doctrinal and business concerns are addressed each year, and every resolution adopted must receive unanimous agreement from the male members in attendance. At the conclusion of the assembly, the general overseer appoints all national and international leaders, who in turn are responsible for appointing various leaders under their jurisdiction.

Churches: 2,051; Inclusive Membership: 73,952; Sunday or Sabbath Schools: 1,982; Total Enrollment: 91,585; Ordained Clergy: 7,920

GENERAL ORGANIZATION

General Assembly: Annual Conclave
Mailing Address: P.O. Box 2910, Cleveland, TN 37320. Tel. (615) 479-8511

OFFICERS

Gen. Overseer, Milton A. Tomlinson
Exec. Comm.: Gen. Overseer, Milton A. Tomlinson, Gen. Treas. Leonard Kendrick; Business Mgr., White Wing Publishing House (Printing/Publishing Div. of Church), Henry O'Neal; Field Sec. to Gen. Overseer, Harper Hunter; Asst. Ed., White Wing Messenger, Billy D. Murray

GENERAL STAFF

Field Sec. to Gen. Overseer: Harper Hunter, Jose Reyes, E. L. Jones
Department Directors:
Assembly Band Movement (Prayer and Study groups): Wm. H. Brooks
Bible Training Institute: Ray C. Wynn, Supt.; Representatives: Jose Rivera, Benjamin Lawrence
Church of Prophecy Marker Association: Perry Gillum
Communication Business Manager: Thomas Duncan
Communication Minister (English) and Music Dept. Dir.: Elwood Matthews
Communication Minister (Spanish): Jose A. Reyes, Sr.
Evangelism and Home Mission Rep.: Verlin D. Thornton
Gen. Office Mgr., Leonard Kendrick
Military Service Rep.: Bobby R. Snow

Ministerial Aid: Roy D. Mixon
Public Relations: Perry Gillum
Sunday School: Harold Hunter
Tomlinson College Pres.: Donald Newlun
Victory Leaders (Youth): William M. Wilson
World Missions: Adrian Varlack; Representatives: Bobby R. Snow, E. E. Van Deventer, Raul Torres, Arthur C. Moss
Women's Missionary Auxiliary: Elva Howard
World Language: Felix R. Garcia

PERIODICALS

Sunday School Literature (q), Jessie Cagle, Ed.
White Wing Messenger, (bi-w), Billy Murray, Asst. Ed.
Happy Harvester (m), Billy Murray, Ed.

The Church of God of the Mountain Assembly, Inc.

Founded in 1906 by J. H. Parks, S. N. Bryant, Thomas Moses, and Andrew J. Silcox.

GENERAL ORGANIZATION

Headquarters and General Offices: Florence Ave., Jellico, TN 37762. Tel. (615) 784-8260. General Assembly, annually in August

OFFICERS

Gen. Overseer, Rev. Kenneth E. Massingell, Box 157, Jellico, TN 37762
First Asst. Gen. Overseer, Rev. Jasper Walden, Box 157, Jellico, TN 37762
Second Asst. Gen. Overseer, Rev. Michael Bartee, Box 157, Jellico, TN 37762
Gen. Sec.-Treas., Rev. James L. Cox, Jr., Box 157, Jellico, TN 37762

PERIODICAL

The Gospel Herald (m), P.O. Box 157, Jellico, TN 37762, Rev. James E. Prewitt, Ed.

The Church of God (Seventh Day), Denver, Colo.

The Church of God (Seventh Day) began in southwestern Michigan in 1858, when a group of Sabbath-Keepers led by Gilbert Cranmer refused to give endorsement to the visions and writings of Mrs. Ellen G. White, a principal in the formation of the Seventh-Day Adventist Church. Another branch of Sabbath-keepers, which developed near Cedar Rapids, Iowa, in 1860, joined the Michigan church in 1863 to publish a paper called The Hope of Israel, the predecessor to the Bible Advocate, the church's present publication. As the church's membership grew and spread into Missouri and Nebraska, it organized the General Conference of the Church of God in 1884. The parenthized words (Seventh Day) were added to its name in 1923. The headquarters of the church was in Stanberry, Missouri, from 1888 until 1950, when it moved to Denver, Colorado.

The church observes the seventh day as the Sabbath; believes in the imminent, personal, and visible return of Jesus; that the dead are in an unconscious state awaiting to be resurrected, the righteous to immortality and the wicked to extinction by fire; and that the earth will be the eternal abode of the righteous. It observes two ordinances: baptism by immersion and an annual Communion service accompanied by foot washing.

Churches: 135; Inclusive Membership: 6,178; Sunday or Sabbath Schools: 135; Total Enrollment: 6,250; Ordained Clergy: 92

GENERAL ORGANIZATION

General Conference: biennial (Next meeting, 1987)
Headquarters: 330 W. 152nd Ave., P.O. Box 33677, Denver, CO 80233. Tel. (303) 452-7973

48

Chpsn., Calvin Burrell
Sec.-Treas., Jayne Kuryluk
Spring Vale Academy: Principal, Ron Grubis
Youth Agency: Dir., Jerry Moldenhauer
Bible Advocate Press: Dir., LeRoy Dais
Media Outreach Services: Dir., Jerry Moldenhauer
Women's Assoc., Pres., Mrs. Emogene Coulter
Summit School of Theology: Dir., Daniel Davila
Missions Abroad: Dir., Robert Coulter

PERIODICALS

Bible Advocate (m), Denver, CO 80233, Jerry Griffin, Ed.
Harvest Field Messenger (bi-m), Denver, CO 80233, Fred Walter, Ed.

Church of God (Which He Purchased with His Own Blood)

This body was organized in 1953 in Oklahoma City, Okla. by William Jordan Fizer after his excommunication from the Church of the Living God (C.W.F.F.) over doctrinal disagreements relating to the Lord's Supper. The first annual convention was held in Oklahoma City, November 19-21, 1954.

The Church of God (W.H.P.W.H.O.B.) believes that water is not the element to be used in the Lord's Supper but rather grape juice or wine and unleavened bread. The Lord's Supper is observed every Sunday.

This body is non-Pentecostal and does not practice speaking in tongues. Its doctrine holds that the Holy Ghost is given to those who obey the Lord. Feet washing is observed as an act of humility. Baptism must be administered in the name of the Father, Son, and Holy Ghost. The Church of God believes it is the Body of Christ, and because of scriptural doctrine and practice, that it is the church organized by Jesus Christ. The Chief Bishop organized the people into the church by calling them into the true doctrine of Christ. The members are urged to lead consecrated lives unspotted from the world. Tobacco and strong drinks are condemned. Divine healing is an article of faith, but not to the exclusion of doctors.

Churches: 7; Inclusive Membership: 800; Sunday or Sabbath Schools: N.R.; Total Enrollment: N.R.; Ordained Clergy: 10

GENERAL ORGANIZATION

Convention: Annual, ending on the second Sunday in October; Annual Sunday School and Training Union; ending on the fourth Sunday in July.
Headquarters: 1628 N.E. 50th, Oklahoma City, OK 73111. Tel. (405) 427-8264

OFFICERS

Chief Bishop, William J. Fizer, 1907 N.E. Grand Blvd., Oklahoma City, OK 73111. Tel. (405) 427-2166
Gen. Sec. and Treas., Alsie Mae Fizer
Overseers: J. W. Johnson, R.1, Box 214, Choctaw, OK 73020; F. McElwee, 509 E. 47th Pl., N., Tulsa, OK 74126; M. Roberson, Rt. 2, Box 214, Mounds, OK 74047

PERODICAL

Gospel News (m), William J. Fizer, Ed.

The Church of Illumination

Organized in 1908 for the express purpose of establishing congregations at large, offering a spiritual, esoteric, philosophic interpretation of the vital biblical teachings, thereby satisfying the inner spiritual needs of those seeking spiritual truth, yet permitting them to remain in, or return to, their former church membership.

GENERAL ORGANIZATION

The Assemblage: annual
Headquarters: "Beverly Hall," Clymer Rd., Quakertown, PA 18951

OFFICERS

Dir., Gerald E. Poesnecker, P.O. Box 220, Quakertown, PA 18951

The Church of Jesus Christ (Bickertonites)

Organized 1862 at Green Oak, Pennsylvania, by William Bickerton, who obeyed the Restored Gospel under Sidney Rigdon's following in 1845.

GENERAL ORGANIZATION

General Conference: annual (October)
Headquarters: Sixth & Lincoln Sts., Monongahela, PA 15063. Tel. (412)258-3066

OFFICERS

Pres., Dominic Thomas, 6010 Barrie, Dearborn, MI 48126
First Counselor, Nicholas Pietrangelo, 24106 Meadow Bridge Dr., Mt. Clemens, MI 48043
Second Counselor, V. James Lovalvo, 5769 Pleasant Ave., Fresno, CA 93711
Exec. Sec., Paul Palmieri, 319 Pine Dr., Aliquippa, PA 15001. Tel (412) 378-4264

PERIODICAL

The Gospel News (m), 15843 Manning, Detroit, MI 48205, Anthony Scolaro, Ed.

The Church of Jesus Christ of Latter-day Saints

Organized April 6, 1830, at Fayette, New York, by Joseph Smith. Members consider the Bible, Book of Mormon, Doctrine and Covenants, and the Pearl of Great Price to be the word of God. Their belief is summed up in thirteen Articles of Faith written by Joseph Smith. Membership is worldwide.

GENERAL ORGANIZATION

General Conference sessions, April and October, Salt Lake City, Utah
Headquarters: 50 East North Temple St., Salt Lake City, UT 84150

OFFICERS

Pres., Ezra Taft Benson
1st Presidency: Ezra Taft Benson, Gordon B. Hinckley, Thomas S. Monson
The Quorum of the Twelve: Marion G. Romney, Howard W. Hunter, Boyd K. Packer, Marvin J. Ashton, L. Tom Perry, David B. Haight, James E. Faust, Neal A. Maxwell, Russell M. Nelson, Dallin H. Oaks, M. Russell Ballard, Joseph B. Wirthlin
The First Quorum of the Seventy:
Presidents: Dean L. Larsen, Richard G. Scott, Marion D. Hanks, Wm. Grant Bangerter, Robert L. Backman, Hugh W. Pinnock, James M. Paramore
Additional Members: Franklin D. Richards, Theodore M. Burton, Paul H. Dunn, Hartman Rector, Jr., Loren C. Dunn, Robert L. Simpson, Rex D. Pinegar, J. Thomas Fyans, Adney Y. Komatsu, Gene R. Cook, Charles Didier, William R. Bradford, George P. Lee, Carlos E. Asay, John H. Groberg, Jacob de Jager, Vaughn J. Featherstone, Royden G. Derrick, Robert E. Wells, F. Enzio Busche, Yoshihiko Kikuchi, Ronald E. Poelman,

Derek A. Cuthbert, Rex C. Reeve, Sr., F. Burton Howard, Ted E. Brewerton, Jack H. Goaslind, Jr., Angel Abrea, John K. Carmack, Russell C. Taylor, Robert B. Harbertson, Devere Harris, Spencer H. Osborn, Philip T. Sonntag, John Sonnenberg, F. Arthur Kay, Keith W. Wilcox, Victor L. Brown, H. Burke Peterson, J. Richard Clarke, Hans B. Ringger, Walter Pratt Call, Helio De la Rocha Camargo, Hans Verlan Anderson, George I. Cannon, Francis M. Gibbons, Gardner H. Russell, George R. Hill III, John Roger Lasater, Douglas J. Martin, Alexander B. Morrison, L. Aldin Porter, Glen Larkin Rudd, Douglas H. Smith, Lyn Andrew Sorensen

Presiding Bishopric: Robert D. Hales, Henry B. Eyring, Glenn L. Pace

Patriarch Emeritus: Eldred G. Smith

Emeritus Members of the First Quorum of the Seventy: Sterling W. Sill, Bernard P. Brockbank, Joseph Anderson, John H. Vandenberg

Church Historian and Recorder: Dean L. Larsen

AUXILIARY ORGANIZATIONS

The Relief Society of the Church of Jesus Christ of Latter-day Saints: Gen. Pres., Barbara W. Winder

Sunday Schools: Gen. Pres., Robert L. Simpson

Young Men: Pres., Vaughn J. Featherstone

Young Women: Gen. Pres., Ardith G. Kapp

Primary Association: Gen. Pres., Dwan J. Young

Genealogical Society of The Church of Jesus Christ of Latter-day Saints: Exec. Dir.: Richard G. Scott

Board of Education: Commissioner of Education, J. Elliot Cameron

PERIODICALS

Deseret News (d), Salt Lake City, UT, Thomas S. Monson, Pres.

The Ensign of The Church of Jesus Christ of Latter-day Saints (m), Salt Lake City, UT, Jay M. Todd, Man. Ed.

New Era (m), Salt Lake City, UT, Brian K. Kelly, Man. Ed.

Friend (m), Salt Lake City, UT, Vivian Paulsen, Man. Ed.

Church of Our Lord Jesus Christ of the Apostolic Faith, Inc.

This Church as an organized body was founded by Bishop R. C. Lawson in Columbus, Ohio, and moved to New York City in 1919. It is founded upon the teachings of the Apostles and Prophets, Jesus Christ being its chief cornerstone.

GENERAL ORGANIZATION

National Convocation: annual (August)

Headquarters: 2081 Adam Clayton Powell Jr. Blvd., New York, NY 10027. Tel. (212) 866-1700

OFFICERS

Board of Apostles: Pres., Bishop William L. Bonner; Bishop J. P. Steadman; Bishop Frank S. Solomon; Bishop Henry A. Ross, Sr.; Bishop Matthew A. Norwood; Bishop Wilbur L. Jones; Bishop Arthur M. Anderson; Bishop Gentle L. Groover; Chmn., Bishop Cris Dobbins

Chpsn. Board of Presbyters, District Elder Kenneth Bligen

Exec. Gen. Sec., Bishop T. E. Woolfolk

Natl. Rec. Sec., Elder Fred Rubin, Sr

Natl. Fin. Sec., District Elder Clarence Groover

Natl. Corr. Sec., Elder Raymond J. Keith, Jr.

Natl. Treas., Bishop Thomas J. Richardson

PERIODICAL

The Contender for the Faith (semi-a)

Church of the Brethren

German pietists-anabaptists founded in 1708 under Alexander Mack, Schwarzenau, Germany, entered the colonies in 1719 and settled at Germantown, Pennsylvania. They have no other creed than the New Testament, hold to principles of nonviolence, temperance, and voluntarism, and emphasize religion in life.

Churches: 1,059; Inclusive Membership: 155,967; Sunday or Sabbath Schools: 971; Total Enrollment: 59,410; Ordained Clergy: 1,963

GENERAL ORGANIZATION

General Conference: annual

Headquarters: Church of the Brethren General Offices, 1451 Dundee Ave., Elgin, IL 60120. Tel. (312) 742-5100

New Windsor Service Center: P.O. Box 188, New Windsor, MD 21776

Washington Office: 110 Maryland Ave., NE, Box 50, Washington, DC 20002

OFFICERS

Mod., Wiliam A. Hayes

Mod.-Elect, Elaine Sollenberger

Sec., Anne Myers

GENERAL BOARD STAFF

Office of General Secretary: Gen. Sec., Donald E. Miller; Exec. of Committee on Interchurch Relations, Melanie May; Coord., Barbara Lenart

Office of Human Resources: Exec., Melanie May; Admn. Asst., Barbara Greenwald; Consultant for Ministry, Robert E. Faus; Dir. of Admn. Services, NW, Eleanor Rowe; Personnel Relations/Development, David Leatherman; Recruitment, Karen Shallenberger; Dir. of Dist. Ministries, _____

Treasurer's Office: Treas., Darryl Deardorff; Dir. Financial Operations, Judy Keyser; Dir. Bldg. and Grounds, David Ingold

General Services Commission: Assoc. Gen. Sec./Exec. of Commission, Connie S. Andes; Admn. Asst., _____; Archivist, James R. Lynch; Dir. Computer Services, David Miller; Dir. of Interpretation/Editor Source/Co-Editor Agenda, Howard E. Royer; Messenger, Ed., Kermon Thomasson; Messenger, Mgr. Ed./Dir. of New Services, Wendy C. McFadden; Dir. of Planned Giving/Direct Gifts, Donald Stern; Planned Giving Officer, SE, Ronald Wyrick; Planned Giving Officer, NE. Roy Johnson; Dir. of Stewardship Education, Connie L. Burk; Congregational Support/Direct Gifts, Dale E. Minnich; Brethren Press, Gen. Mgr., Robert Durnbaugh; Dir. Marketing, _____; Editorial Dir., David Eller.

Parish Ministries Commission: Assoc. Gen. Sec./Exec. of Commission, _____; Admn. Asst., Joan Pelletier; Education/People of Covenant/Guide for Biblical Studies, Shirley Heckman; Outdoor Ministries, Walter D. Bowman, 6987 Union Rd., Clayton, OH 45315; New Church Development, Merle Crouse, Box 296, St. Cloud, FL 32769; Youth and Young Adult Ministries/Urban Ministries, Christine Michael; Program for Women, Judith Kipp; Dir. of Ministry Training, Rick Gardner; Ministry Training Field Assoc., Larry Glick; Evangelism/Korean Ministries, Paul E. R. Mundey; Health & Welfare/Home & Hospital Ministries, Jay E. Gibble

World Ministries Commission: Assoc. Gen. Sec./Exec. of Commission, J. Robert Schrock; Admn. Asst., Barbara Ober; Africa & Middle East Rep., _____; Peace & International Affairs/Europe & Asia Rep., H. Lamar Gibble; Peace Consultant, Charles L. Boyer; Dir. of Brethren Volunteer Service, _____; Latin America/Caribbean Rep., Yvonne Dilling; Economic Justice/Rural Crisis, Shantilal P. Bhagat; Washington Rep., Leland Wilson, 110 Maryland Ave. NE, Box 50, Washington, DC 20002; Dir. SERRV, Mary Myers, Box 365, New Windsor, MD 21776; Dir. Refugee/Disaster Services, _____, P.O. Box 188, New

Windsor, MD 21776; Dir. Center Operations, D. Miller Davis, P.O. Box 188, New Windsor, MD 21776; Dir. On Earth Peace, Harold Smith, P.O. Box 188, New Windsor, MD 21776

Annual Conference: Mgr., Doris I. Lasley; Treas., Darryl Deardorff

Pension Board: Exec. and Treas., Wilfred E. Nolen; Admin. Asst., Sandra Pryde; Dir. Operations, Cheryl Ingold; Dir. Interpretation, Elizabeth Jamsa

PERIODICAL

Messenger (m), Church of the Brethren General Offices, Elgin, IL 60120. Kermon Thomasson, Ed.

Church of the Living God (Motto: Christian Workers for Fellowship)

William Christian was born a slave in Mississippi on November 10, 1856. He grew up uneducated and in 1875, united with the Missionary Baptist Church and began to preach. In 1888, he left the Baptist Church and began what was known as Christian Friendship Work. Believing himself to have been inspired by the Spirit of God, through divine revelation and close study of the Scriptures he was led to the truth that the Bible refers to the church as The Church of the Living God (I Tim. 3:15).

At Caine Creek, near Wrightsville, Arkansas, in April 1889, the Rev. William Christian became founder and organizer of The Church of the Living God, the first black church in America without Anglo-Saxon roots or not begun by white missionaries.

The church believes in the infallibility of the Scriptures, is Trinitarian, and believes there are three sacraments ordained by Christ: baptism (by immersion), the Lord's Supper (unleavened bread and water), and foot washing. The Church of the Living God, C.W.F.F., believes in holiness as a gift of God subsequent to the New Birth and manifested only by a changed life acceptable to the Lord.

GENERAL ORGANIZATION

General Assembly: every four years; Annual Assembly; Annual District Conventions.

Headquarters: 434 Forest Ave., Cincinnati, OH 45229

OFFICERS

Executive Board: Bishop W. E. Crumes, Chief Bishop, 434 Forest Ave., Cincinnati, OH 45229; Bishop I. C. Collins, Vice-Chief Bishop, 3824 - 13th Ave., Sacramento, CA 94820; Bishop C. A. Lewis, Exec. Sec., 1360 N. Boston, Tulsa, OK 73111; Gen. Sec.; Elder Milton S. Herring, 2223 S. Garden, Fresno, CA 93725; Bishop J. C. Hawkins, Gen. Treas., 3804 N. Temple Ave., Indianapolis, IN 46205; Bishop E. L. Bowie, 2037 N.E. 18th, Oklahoma City, OK 73111; Bishop L. H. Dixon, 8425 S. Damen Ave., Chicago, IL 60620; Bishop E. A. Morgan, Chaplain, 4508 N. Indiana, Oklahoma City, OK 73118; Bishop L. A. Crawford, 3711 Biglow, Dallas, TX 74216; Bishop A. L. Ponder, 5609 N. Terry, Oklahoma City, OK 73111; Bishop A. R. Powell, 8557 S. Wabash, Chicago, IL 60619; Bishop A. R. Powell, 8557 S. Wabash, Chicago, IL 60619; Bishop Jeff Ruffin, 226 S. Catamaran Ct., Pittsburg, CA 94565; Bishop R. S. Morgan, Aux. Bishop, 4508 N. Indiana, Oklahoma City, OK 73118; Elder S. E. Shannon, 6271 W. Port Ave., Milwaukee, WI 53223

NATIONAL DEPARTMENTS

Convention Planning Committee, Young Peoples Progressive Union, Christian Education Dept., Sunday School Dept., Nat'l Evangelist Board, Nat'l Nurses Guild, Nat'l Women's Work Department, Nat'l Music Department, Gen. Secretary's office.

PERIODICALS

The Gospel Truth (m)
Sunday School Quarterly (q)
Annual Convention Journal

Church of the Lutheran Brethren of America

The organization of the Church of the Lutheran Brethren occurred at the turn of the century when five independent Lutheran congregations met in Milwaukee, Wisconsin, in December 1900, to form a new synod. The constitution was patterned closely after that of the Lutheran Free Church of Norway, organized in 1877. The constituting convention elected the Rev. K. O. Lundeberg as its first president. The purpose was not divisive since the members were not splitting from any denomination. Feeling the need to join together for projects larger than one congregation could handle, they organized a new church body.

During the last decade of the nineteenth century and into the twentieth, there was a widespread spiritual awakening in the upper Midwest, characterized by a deep conviction of sin and a faith in the grace offered in Jesus Christ. Scores of people entered the kingdom of God—many of them members of the Lutheran congregations, the predominant religious faith of the region. Some were new immigrants seeking meaning for their lives and finding it through salvation in Jesus Christ.

These new converts began to live their lives with great purpose. For them church life took on new meaning. They were no longer content only with Sunday worship services, which in many rural communities were held once or twice a month. Sunday school, rarely planned with adults or new believers in mind, was considered only for children.

As scattered groups of believers studied the Scriptures, many began to ask how they should live as Christians. Guidance was sought from the Bible. Patterns began to emerge. These new converts began to see that God's will was that the believer should live a godly life patterned after the principles of Scripture. The Christian life was not only a set of teachings to confess, but a life to be lived for God in holiness. Their study further led them to questions about the church. They sought answers and found them in the Bible. Their search led them to the conclusion that the local congregation was meant to be a body of believers in which the Word of God was rightly taught and the sacraments administered in accordance with Christ's command. Membership in this body was to consist only of those who, by confession and daily life, testified to the saving power of God.

The Church of the Lutheran Brethren characterizes itself as a "fellowship of believers" organized into congregations for the purpose of worship, edification, fellowship, and ministry in harmony with the Lutheran Confessions and with the purpose of bringing the gospel to the world. It is committed to the authority of Scripture, the teaching and practise of the Lutheran understanding of the sacraments, and the imminent return of the Lord. Its worship services are nonliturgical but involve all participants. To facilitate the maximum use of spiritual gifts, education in the local congregation as well as at the schools it sponsors receives strong support.

Churches: 118; Inclusive Membership: 11,778; Sunday or Sabbath Schools: 102; Total Enrollment: 10,035; Ordained Clergy: 184

GENERAL ORGANIZATION

Convention: annual (June)
Headquarters: 1007 Westside Dr., Box 655, Fergus Falls, MN 56537. Tel. (218) 739-3336

51

Pres., Rev. Robert M. Overgard, Sr., Box 655, Fergus Falls, MN 56537

1st Vice-Pres., Rev. Bruce Vallevik, P.O. Box 929, Sidney, MT 59270

2nd Vice-Pres., Rev. Theodore Thompson, 17 Apache Dr., Mount Bethel, PA 18343

Sec., Rev. Richard Vettrus, 707 Crestview Dr., West Union, IA 52175

Treas., Exec. Dir. of Finance, Mr. Ronald Egge, Box 655, Fergus Falls, MN 56537

Pres., Lutheran Brethren Schools, Rev. Omar Gjerness, Lutheran Brethren Schools, Box 317, Fergus Falls, MN 56537

Dir. of World Missions, Rev. Jarle Olson, Box 655, Fergus Falls MN 56537

Dir. of Home Missons, Rev. Burton Bundy, Box 655, Fergus Falls, MN 56537

Editor of Publications, Rev. David Rinden, Box 655, Fergus Falls, MN 56537

Dir. of Youth Ministries, Rev. Elroy Vesta, Box 655, Fergus Falls, MN 56537

PERIODICAL

Faith and Fellowship (m), 704 Vernon Ave., W. Fergus Falls, MN 56537

Church of the Lutheran Confession

The Church of the Lutheran Confession held its constituting convention in Watertown, South Dakota, in August of 1960. The Church of the Lutheran Confession was born as a result of the people and congregations who came to their own individual convictions, based on Scripture, and were moved to withdraw from church bodies that made up what was then known as the Synodical Conference. The specific error in the Synodical Conference was the error of unionism. Following such passages as I Corinthians 1:10 and Romans 16:17-18, the Church of the Lutheran Confession holds the conviction that agreement with the doctrines of Scripture is essential and necessary before exercise of church fellowship is appropriate.

Members of the Church of the Lutheran Confession uncompromisingly believe the Holy Scriptures to be verbally inspired and therefore inerrant. It subscribes without reservation to the historic Lutheran Confessions as found in the Book of Concord of 1580, because they are a clear and correct exposition of Scripture.

The Church of the Lutheran Confession exists and holds its confessional position out of concern and appreciation for the gospel. It exists to proclaim, preserve, and spread the saving truth of the gospel of Jesus Christ, so that the redeemed of God, both here and elsewhere, may learn to know Jesus Christ as their Lord and Savior, and to follow him through this life to the life to come.

Churches: 68; Inclusive Membership: 8,852; Sunday or Sabbath Schools: 63; Total Enrollment: 1,473; Ordained Clergy: 78

GENERAL ORGANIZATION

Biennial Synodical Convention (Next meeting, 1988)

Headquarters: 460 75th Ave., NE, Minneapolis, MN 55432. Tel. (612) 784-8784

OFFICERS

Pres., Rev. Daniel Fleischer, 460 75th Ave., NE, Minneapolis, MN 55432

Vice Pres., Rev. Rollin Reim, 994 Emerald Hill Rd., Redwood City, CA 94061

Mod., Prof. Ronald Roehl, 515 Ingram Dr. W., Eau Claire, WI 54701

Sec., Rev. Paul Nolting, 620 E. 50th St., Loveland, CO 80537

Treas., Lowell Moen, 3455 Jill Ave., Eau Claire, WI 54701

Archivist-Historian, John Lau

Statistician, Harvey Callies

PERIODICALS

The Lutheran Spokesman (m), 11315 E. Broadway, Spokane, WA 99206, Rev. Paul Fleischer, Ed.

Ministry by Mail (w), 620 E. 50th St., Loveland, CO 80537. Rev. Paul Nolting, Ed.

C.L.C. Directory (a), 994 Emerald Hill Rd., Redwood City, CA 94061. Rollin Reim, Ed.

Journal of Theology (4/yr.), Immanuel Lutheran College, Eau Claire, WI 54701. Prof. John Lau, Ed.

Church of the Nazarene

The origins of the Church of the Nazarene are in the broader holiness movement which arose soon after the American Civil War. It is the result of the merging of three independent holiness groups already in existence in the United States. An eastern body, located principally in New York and New England and known as the Association of Pentecostal Churches in America, joined at Chicago in 1907 with a California body called the Church of the Nazarene; the two merging churches agreed on the name Pentecostal Church of the Nazarene. The southern group, known as the Holiness Church of Christ, united with this Pentecostal Church of the Nazarene at Pilot Point, Texas, in 1908. This is considered the birth date of the Church of the Nazarene. Principal leaders in the organization were Phineas Bresee, founder of the church in the West; William Howard Hoople and H. F. Reynolds in the East; and C. B. Jernigan in the southern group. The first Church of the Nazarene in Canada was organized in November 1902 by Dr. H. F. Reynolds, in Oxford, Nova Scotia. In 1919 the word Pentecostal was dropped from the name, leaving it as we know it today, Church of the Nazarene.

The Church of the Nazarene is distinctive in its emphasis on the doctrine of entire sanctification on the proclamation of Christian Holiness. It stresses the importance of a devout and holy life and a positive witness before the world by the power of the Holy Spirit. The church feels that caring is a way of life for its constituents.

Nazarene government is representative, a studied compromise between episcopacy and congregationalism. Quadrennially, the various districts elect delegates to a general assembly, at which 6 general superintendents are elected for a term of 4 years to supervise the work of the denomination.

The church, an international denomination, is comprised of over 248 districts, 8,417 local congregations, 10 liberal arts colleges, 2 graduate seminaries, 16 seminaries, and 24 Bible colleges. The church maintains missionaries in 83 countries around the world. The world services include medical, education, and religious ministries. Books, periodicals, and other Christian literature are published at the Nazarene Publishing House. A radio program, "Master Plan," is heard each week on more than 500 stations around the world.

The Church of the Nazarene is a member of two interchurch organizations, Christian Holiness Association and the National Association of Evangelicals.

Churches: 5,018; Inclusive Membership: 530,912; Sunday or Sabbath Schools: 4,854; Total Enrollment: 835,353; Ordained Clergy: 8,667

GENERAL ORGANIZATION

General Assembly: quadrennial (Next meeting, Indianapolis, IN, June 1989)

International Headquarters: 6401 The Paseo, Kansas City, MO 64131. Tel. (816) 333-7000

OFFICERS

Gen. Supts.: V. H. Lewis, Eugene L. Stowe, Charles Strickland, William Greathouse, John A. Knight, Raymond Hurn, and Jerald Johnson

Gen. Sec., B. Edgar Johnson
Gen. Treas., Norman O. Miller

OTHER ORGANIZATIONS

General Board: Sec., B. Edgar Johnson; Treas., Norman O. Miller

General Church Divisions and Ministry/Services: Christian Life and Sunday School Div. Dir., Phil Riley; Adult Ministries, Dir., Phil Riley; Children's Ministries, Dir., Miriam Hall; Youth Ministries, Dir., Gary Sivewright; Church Growth Div. Dir., Bill Sullivan; Church Ext. Ministries, Dir., Mike Estep; Education Services, Dir., Willis Snowbarger; Evangelism Ministries, Dir., Bill Sullivan; Pastoral Ministries, Dir., Wilbur Brannon; Communications Div., Dir. Cecil D. Paul; Media Services, Dir., Paul Skiles; Publications International, Dir., Bennett Dudney; Finance Div. Dir., D. Moody Gunter; Headquarters Services, Dir., Paul Spear; Life Income Gifts Services, Dir., Robert Hempel; Pensions & Benefits Services, Dir., Dean Wessels; Stewardship Services, Dir., D. Moody Gunter; World Mission Div. Dir., Robert H. Scott; Nazarene World Missionary Society, Dir., Nina Gunter.

PERIODICALS

Herald of Holiness (bi-m), W. E. McCumber, Ed.
World Missions (m), Robert H. Scott, Ed.
Preacher's Magazine (m) Wesley Tracy, Ed.
Bread (m), Karen DeSollar, Ed.
All published by the Nazarene Publishing House, Box 527, Kansas City, MO 64141

Churches of Christ

Churches of Christ are autonomous congregations, whose members appeal to the Bible alone to determine matters of faith and practice. There are no central offices or officers. Publications and institutions related to the churches are either under local congregational control or independent of any one congregation.

Churches of Christ shared a common fellowship in the 19th century with the Christian Churches/Churches of Christ and the Christian Church (Disciples of Christ). Fellowship was broken after the introduction of instrumental music in worship and centralization of church-wide activities through a missionary society

Members of Churches of Christ believe in the inspiration of the Scriptures, the divinity of Jesus Christ, and immersion into Christ for the remission of sins. The New Testament pattern is followed in worship and church organization.

Churches: 13,364; Inclusive 1,623,754; Sunday or Sabbath Schools: N.R.; Total Enrollment: N.R.; Ordained Clergy: N.R.

NO GENERAL ORGANIZATION

PERIODICALS

Over 100 periodicals are published by members of Churches of Christ. Below are listed representative publications.

Christian Chronicle (m), Box 1100, Oklahoma City, OK 73136, Howard W. Norton, Ed.
The Christian Echo (m), Box 37266, Los Angeles, CA 90037, R. N. Hogan, Ed.
Firm Foundation (sm), Box 17200, Pensacola, FL 32522, William Cline, Ed.
Gospel Advocate (sm), Box 150, Nashville, TN 37202, Furman Kearley, Ed.
Gospel Tidings (m), 7533 E. Easter Way, Edgewood, CO 80112, Travis Allen, Ed.
Guardian of Truth (sm), Box 9670, Bowling Green, KY 42101, Mike Willis, Ed.
Image (sm), 115 Warren Dr., Ste., D., West Monroe, LA 71291, Reuel Lemmons, Ed.

Mission Journal (m), 11223 Henge Dr., Austin, TX 78759, Bobby Lee Holley, Ed.
Old Paths Advocate (m), RR 1, Lebanon, MO 65536, Clovis T. Cook, and Edwin S. Morris, Eds.
Power for Today (q), Box 40536, Nashville, TN 37204, Steven S. and Emily Y. Lemley, Eds.
Restoration Quarterly (q), Box 8227, Abilene, TX 79699, Thomas H. Olbricht, Ed.
Twentieth Century Christian (m), Box 40526, Nashville, TN 37204, M. Norval Young, Ed.
Up Reach, Box 2001, Abilene, TX 79604, Harold Hazelip, Ed.

Churches of Christ in Christian Union

Organized in 1909 at Washington Court House, Ohio, as the Churches of Christ in Christian Union. This body believes in the new birth and the baptism of the Holy Spirit for believers. It is Wesleyan with an evangelistic and missionary emphasis.

Reformed Methodist Church merged in September, 1952, with Churches of Christ in Christian Union.

Churches: 260; Inclusive Membership: 11,400; Sunday or Sabbath Schools: 260; Total Enrollment: 19,100; Ordained Clergy: 373

GENERAL ORGANIZATION

General Council: biennial (Next meeting 1990)
District Councils: annual
General Headquarters: 1426 Lancaster Pike. (Mailing address: Box 30), Circleville, OH 43113

OFFICERS

Gen. Supt., Rev. Robert Kline, Box 30, Circleville, OH 43113
Asst. Gen. Supt., Dr. Dan Tipton, Box 30, Circleville, OH 43113
Gen. Sec., Rev. Robert Barth, P. O. Box 188, Alma, GA 31510
Gen. Treas., Bevery R. Salley, Box 30, Circleville, OH 43113
Gen. Board of Trustees: Chm., Rev. Robert Kline, Box 30, Circleville, OH 43113; Vice-Chpsn., Rev. Grover Blankenship; Sec., Rev. Robert Barth, Box 188, Alma, GA 31510
District Superintendents (all District Superintendents are also members of the Gen. Bd. of Trustees); West Central District, Rev. David Dean, P. O. Box 30, Circleville, OH 43113; South Central District, Rev. Daniel Tipton, P.O. Box 30, Circleville, OH 43113; Northeast Dist., Rev. Art Penird, Rt. 2, P.O. Box 790, Port Crane, NY 17833

PERIODICALS

Advocate (m), Don Brown, Ed.
Missionary Tidings (m), Betty Seymour, Ed.

Churches of God, General Conference

The Churches of God, General Conference, had its beginnings in Harrisburg, Penna., in 1825.

John Winebrenner, recognized founder of the Church of God movement, was an ordained minister of the German Reformed Church. His experience-centered form of Christianity, particularly the "new measures" he used to promote it, his close connection with the local Methodists, his "experience and conference meetings" in the church, and his "social prayer meetings" in parishioners' homes resulted in differences of opinion and the establishment of new congregations. Some independent congregations also began to look to Winebrenner for leadership. Extensive revivals, camp meetings, and mission endeavors led to the organization of additional congregations across central

Pennsylvania and westward through Ohio, Indiana, Illinois, and Iowa.

In 1830 the first system of cooperation between local churches was initiated as an "eldership" in eastern Pennsylvania. The organization of other elderships followed. In 1835 *The Gospel Publisher* was established as a Church of God paper; its successor since 1846 is *The Church Advocate*. A General Eldership was organized in 1845, and in 1974 the official name of the denomination was changed from General Eldership of the Churches of God in North America to its present name.

The Churches of God, General Conference, is composed of sixteen conferences in the United States. The polity of the church is presbyterial in form. The church has mission ministries in the southwest among native Americans and is extensively involved in church planting and whole life ministries in Bangladesh, Haiti, and India.

The General Conference convenes in business session triennially. An Administrative Council composed of 35 regional representatives serving on 7 commissions is responsible for the administration and ministries of the church between sessions of the General Conference.

GENERAL ORGANIZATION

General Conference: meets triennially

Legal Headquarters: United Church Center, Rm. 200, 900 So. Arlington Ave., Harrisburg, PA 17109. Tel. (717) 652-0255

Administrative Offices: General Conference Administrator, Pastor William H. Reist, 700 E. Melrose Ave., P. O. Box 926, Findlay, OH 45839. Tel. (419) 424-1961

Assoc. to the General Conference Administrator: Mrs. Linda L. Draper; Church Publications; Mr. Daniel A. Fortney, Cross-Cultural Ministries; Mr. Everett L. Falk, Finance; Dr. Royal P. Kear, Stewardship and Pensions; Rev. Marilyn Rayle Kern, Curriculum; Rev. Douglas E. Nolt, Campus Ministries; Rev. Frederick C. Quade, Evangelism and Church Development; Rev. R. Joe Roach, Education and Family Life; Pastor Dean L. Baublitz, Dir. of Youth Ministry

OFFICERS

Pres., Pastor Larry G. White, 936 W. Main, Mt. Pleasant, PA 15666. Tel. (412) 547-7110

Vice-Pres., Pastor Stephen L. Dunn, 6012 S. Bend Dr., Ft. Wayne, IN 46804

Journalizing Sec., Rev. Harry G. Cadamore, 157 Second St., West Newton, PA 15089

Treas., Mr. Everett L. Falk, 700 E. Melrose Ave., P.O. Box 926, Findlay, OH 45839. Tel. (419) 424-1961

COMMISSIONS

Church Development: Chpsn., Pastor James W. Moss, Sr., 900 S Arlington Ave., Room. 200, Harrisburg, PA 17109; Sec., Pastor Stephen L. Dunn, 6012 S. Bend Dr., Ft. Wayne, IN 46804

Church Vocations: Chpsn., Dr. A. Gail Dunn, 900 S. Arlington Ave., Rm. 200, Harrisburg, PA 17109; Sec., Pastor Duane L. Beck, 8204 Edgewood Church Rd., Frederick, MD 21701

Education: Chpsn., Pastor Ronald E. Dull, 31 E. Center St., Lititz, PA 17543; Sec., Dr. John A. Parthemore, 235 West High St., Middletown, PA 17057

Evangelism: Chpsn., Pastor Glenn E. Beatty, 1114 Circle Dr., Latrobe, PA 15650; Sec., Pastor Kenneth E. Laffin, 17 123 RDA, Bryan, OH 43506

National Ministries: Chpsn., Pastor George Reser, Jr., 405 S. College St., Mt. Carroll, IL 61053; Sec., Pastor Howard L. Ruley, 3075 Yoakam Rd., Lima, OH 45806

Stewardship: Chpsn., Dr. C. Darrell Prichard, 100 College St., Findlay, OH 45840; Sec., Pastor Kenneth W. Heffner, 2114 Jennifer Lane, Findlay, OH 45840

World Missions: Chpsn., Pastor Jim G. Martin, 2420 Scotland Rd., Chambersburg, PA 17201; Sec., Pastor Charles W. Yost, 2196 Spring Run Dr., Mechanicsburg, PA 17055

PERIODICALS

The Church Advocate (m), P. O. Box 926, Findlay, OH 45839, Mrs. Linda Draper, Ed.

The Missionary Signal (bi-m), P.O. Box 926, Findlay, OH 45839, Mrs. LaVonna Powell, Ed.

The Workman (q), P.O. Box 926, Findlay, OH 45839, Pastor Marilyn Rayle Kern, Ed.

The Gem (w), P.O. Box 926, Findlay, OH 45839, Pastor Marilyn Rayle Kern, Ed.

Community Churches, International Council of

This body is a fellowship of locally autonomous, ecumenically minded, congregationally governed, non-creedal Churches. The Council came into being in 1950 as the union of two former councils of community churches, one formed of black churches known as the Biennial Council of Community Churches, and the other of white churches known as the National Council of Community Churches.

Churches: 350; Inclusive Membership: 200,000; Sunday or Sabbath Schools: N.R.; Total Enrollment: N.R.; Ordained Clergy: 350

GENERAL ORGANIZATION

Conference: Annual

International Office: 900 Ridge Rd., LL1, Homewood, IL 60430. Tel. (312) 798-2264

OFFICERS

Pres., Robert Puckett

Vice-Pres., Paul Scott & Kermit Long

Sec., Dorothy Pace

Treas., Robert Mingus

Exec. Dir., J. Ralph Shotwell

OTHER ORGANIZATIONS

(All may be contacted through the Central Office)

Commission on Church Relations

Commission on Ecumenical Relations

Commission on Clergy Relations

Commission on Laity Relations

Commission on Faith and Order

Commission on Social Concerns

Commission on Missions

Commission on Informational Services

Women's Christian Fellowship, Pres., Eugene Aldridge

Samaritans (Men's Fellowship), Pres., Louis Joy

Young Adult Fellowship, Pres., Jacqueline Clinkscales

Youth Fellowship, Pres., Cheryl Wilson

PERIODICALS

The Christian Community (m), 900 Ridge Rd., LL1, Homewood, IL 60430. J. Ralph Shotwell, Ed.

The Pastor's Journal (q), 900 Ridge Rd., LL1 Homewood, IL 60430, Robert Puckett, Ed.

Congregational Christian Churches, National Association of

Organized 1955 in Detroit, Michigan by delegates from Congregational Christian Churches committed to continuing the Congregational way of faith and order in church life. Participation by member churches is voluntary.

GENERAL ORGANIZATION

Annual Meeting: Green Bay, WI, 1988

OFFICERS

Mod., Rev. Barbara Janikowsky; Exec. Sec., J. Fred Rennebohm; Assoc. Exec. Secs., Michael Halcomb, Rev. Harry W. Clark; Adm., Mrs. Sharon Walls, P.O. Box 1620, Oak Creek, WI 53154. Tel. (414) 764-1620

The Congregationalist, Mary Woolsey, Ed.

Congregational Holiness Church

A body which separated from the Pentecostal Holiness Church in 1921; carries on mission work in Mexico, Honduras, Costa Rica, Cuba, Brazil, Spain, Guatemala, and India.

GENERAL ORGANIZATION

General Conference, meets every two years. General Committee, meets as called. Represents ten state conferences.

General Headquarters: 3888 Fayetteville Hwy., Griffin, GA 30223. Tel. (404) 228-4833

EXECUTIVE BOARD

Gen. Supt., Bishop Cullen L. Hicks
1st Asst. Gen. Supt., Rev. Billy Anderson
2nd Asst. Gen. Supt., Rev. Terry Crews
Gen. Sec., Rev. Kenneth Law
Gen. Treas., Rev. Dennis Phillips
Supt. of World Missions, Rev. Hugh B. Skelton
Supt. of Church Ministries, Rev. Hayward Clark

PERIODICAL

The Gospel Messenger (m), 3888 Fayetteville Hwy., Griffin, GA 30223, Mrs. Donna Clark, Ed.

Conservative Baptist Association of America

Organized May 17, 1947, at Atlantic City, New Jersey. The Old and New Testaments are regarded as the divinely inspired Word of God and are therefore infallible and of supreme authority. Each local church is independent and autonomous, and free from ecclesiastical or political authority.

GENERAL ORGANIZATION

Meets annually
Headquarters: 25W560 Geneva Rd., Box 66, Wheaton, IL 60189. Tel. (312) 653-5350
Gen. Dir., Dr. Tim Blanchard, Box 66, Wheaton, IL 60189. Tel. (312) 653-5350

OTHER ORGANIZATIONS

Conservative Baptist Foreign Mission Society: Box 5, Wheaton, IL 60189, Gen. Dir., Dr. Warren W. Webster
Conservative Baptist Home Mission Society: Box 828, Wheaton, IL 60189, Gen. Dir., Dr. Jack Estep

PERIODICAL

Conservative Baptist, P.O. Box 66, Wheaton, IL 60189

Conservative Congregational Christian Conference

In the 1930s, evangelicals within the Congregational Christian Churches felt a definite need for fellowship and service. By 1945, this loose association crystalized in the Conservative Congregational Christian Fellowship, concerned to maintain a faithful, biblical witness.

In 1948 in Chicago, the Conservative Congregational Christian Conference was established to provide a continuing fellowship for evangelical churches and ministers on the national level, and after several years, entered a period of healthy growth. There are now regional fellowships throughout the United States and one in Ontario, Canada. Scores of churches participate in these groups.

In recent years, many churches have joined the Conference from backgrounds other than Congregational. These Community or Bible Churches are truly congregational in polity and thoroughly evangelical in conviction, but in many cases have never enjoyed the values of inspiration and cooperation gained in the work that Christian churches must do together. The CCCC welcomes all evangelical churches that are, in fact, congregational. The CCCC believes in the necessity of a regenerate membership, the authority of the Holy Scriptures, the Lordship of Jesus Christ, the autonomy of the local church, and the universal fellowship of all Christians.

The Conservative Congregational Christian Conference is a member of the World Evangelical Congregational Fellowship (formed in 1986 in London, England) and the National Association of Evangelicals.

Churches: 170; Inclusive Membership: 28,948; Sunday or Sabbath Schools: 161; Total Enrollment: 8,641; Ordained Clergy: 424

GENERAL ORGANIZATION

General Conference
Headquarters: 7582 Currell Blvd., Ste. #108, St. Paul MN 55125

OFFICERS

Pres., Rev. Jay Warren, Rt. 3, Box 88, Highland, IL 62249
Vice-Pres., Mr. William V. Nygren, 583 Sterling, Maplewood, MN 55119
Conf. Min., Rev. Clifford R. Christensen 57 Kipling St., St. Paul, MN 55519
Controller, Mr. Orrin H. Bailey, 4260 Eastlake Rd., Muskegon, MI 49444
Treas., Mrs. Marge Bowman, 3089 Leyland Trail, Woodbury, MN 55125
Recording Sec., Rev. Doug Jones, 2620 E. Maple Rapids Rd., Eureka, MN 48833
Editor, Rev. Robert H. Wilber, 222 E. Second St., Perry, MI 48872
Historian, Rev. Daniel E. Wray, 17 Bromley Place, Scotia, NY 12302

Conservative Lutheran Assoc.
(See World Confessional Lutheran Association)

Coptic Orthodox Church

This body is part of the ancient Coptic Orthodox Church of Egypt which is currently headed by His Holiness Pope Shenouda III. In the United States many parishes have been organized consisting of Egyptian immigrants to the United States. Copts exist outside of Egypt in Ethiopia, Europe, Asia, Australia, Canada, and the United States. In all, the world Coptic community is estimated at 8 million, the vast majority being located in Egypt, however.

Churches: 28; Inclusive Membership: 115,000; Sunday or Sabbath Schools: N.R.; Total Enrollment: N.R.; Ordained Clergy: 28

CORRESPONDENT

Archpriest Fr. Gabriel Abdelsayed, 427 West Side Ave., Jersey City, NJ 07304. Tel. (201) 333-0004; (516) 931-6242

Cumberland Presbyterian Church

The Cumberland Presbyterian Church was organized in Dickson County, Tennessee, on February 4, 1810. It was an outgrowth of the Great Revival of 1800—one of the most powerful revivals this country has ever witnessed. The founders were Finis Ewing, Samuel King, and Samuel McAdow, ministers in the Presbyterian Church who rejected the doctrine of election and reprobation as taught in the Westminster Confession of Faith. The causes that led to the formation of the church are clearly set forth in publications issued at the time, and in various tracts and books published subsequently.

The Cumberland Presbytery, constituted at the time of the organization of the Church, originally consisted of only three ministers, but in three years was sufficiently large to form three presyteries. In October 1813, these presbyteries met at the Beech Church in Sumner County, Tennessee, and constituted a synod. This synod at once formulated and published a "Brief Statement," setting forth the points wherein Cumberland Presbyterians dissented from the Westminster Confession of Faith:

1. That there are no eternal reprobates;
2. That Christ died not for a part only, but for all mankind;
3. That all those dying in infancy are saved through Christ and the sanctification of the Spirit;
4. That the Spirit of God operates on the world, or as coextensively as Christ has made atonement, in such a manner as to leave all men inexcusable.

From its birth in 1810, the Cumberland Presbyterian Church grew to a membership of 250,000 at the turn of the century. In 1906 the church voted to merge with the then Presbyterian Church. Those who dissented from the merger became the nucleus of the continuing Cumberland Presbyterian Church.

Churches: 811; Inclusive Membership: 98,037; Sunday or Sabbath Schools: 734; Total Enrollment: 46,334; Ordained Clergy: 776

GENERAL ORGANIZATION
General Assembly

OFFICERS
Mod., Wilbur S. Wood, Box 122, Palestine, AR 72372
Stated Clk., Robert Prosser, 1978 Union Ave., Memphis, TN 38104
Chpsn. of General Assembly's Executive Committee, Beverly St. John, 806 Evansdale Dr., Nashville, TN 37220

INSTITUTIONS
Cumberland Presbyterian Center, 1978 Union Ave., Memphis, TN 38104. (Headquarters for program boards, Frontier Press, and resource center.

BOARDS
Board of Christian Education: Exec. Dir., Rev. Harold Davis, 1978 Union Ave., Memphis TN 38104
Board of Missions: Exec. Dir., Rev. Joe R. Matlock, 1978 Union Ave., Memphis, TN 38104
Board of Finance: Exec. Sec., Rev. Don Alexander, 1978 Union Ave., Memphis, TN 38104

PERIODICALS
The Cumberland Presbyterian (bi-w), 1978 Union Ave., Memphis, TN 38104, Rev. Mark Brown, Interim Ed.
The Missionary Messenger (m), 1978 Union Ave., Memphis, TN 38104, Rev. Dudley Condron, Ed.
Church School Literature (q). Bd. of Christian Ed., 1978 Union Ave., Memphis, TN 38104

†Duck River (and Kindred) Associations of Baptists

A group of Baptist associations found in Tennessee, Alabama, Georgia, Kentucky, and Mississippi.

GENERAL ORGANIZATION
Meets yearly, in October

OFFICERS
Duck River Association: Mod., Elder A. B. Ray, 500 Ragan St. Tullahoma, TN 37388; Clk., Elder Marvin Davenport, Auburntown, TN
General Association: Mod., Elder Calvin Jenkins, 607 State Line Rd., Rossville, GA 30741; Clk., Elder James F. Patton, Morrison, TN 37357

Elim Fellowship

The Elim Fellowship, a Pentecostal Body, established in 1947, is an outgrowth of the Elim Ministeral Fellowship, which was formed in 1933.

It is an association of churches, ministers and missionaries seeking to serve the whole Body of Christ. It is of Pentecostal conviction and charismatic orientation providing ministerial credentials and counsel and encouraging fellowship among local churches. Elim Fellowship sponsors leadership seminars at home and abroad, and serves as a transdenominational agency sending long-term, short-term, & tent-making missionaries to work with national movements.

GENERAL ORGANIZATION
Annual Representative Assemblies; Board of Administration meets semi-annually and Council of Elders meets bimonthly.

OFFICERS
Gen. Overseer, Elmer Frink, Elim Fellowship, Lima, NY 14485. Tel. (716) 582-2790
Asst. Gen. Overseer, Bernard Evans, Box 3727A, Snowden Hill Rd., New Hartford, NY 13413. Tel (315) 737-8031
Gen. Sec., Joseph Nettleton, Elim Fellowship, Lima, NY 14485. Tel. (716) 582-2790.
Gen. Treas., Ronald Taylor, 451 Westfield Dr., Manlius, NY 13104. Tel. (315) 682-8282

The Episcopal Church

The Episcopal Church entered the colonies with the earliest settlers (Jamestown, Virginia, 1607) as the Church of England. After the American Revolution it became autonomous in 1789 as The Protestant Episcopal Church in the United States of America. (The Episcopal Church became the official alternate name in 1967.) Samuel Seabury of Connecticut was elected the first bishop and consecrated in Aberdeen by bishops of the Scottish Episcopal Church in 1784. In organizing as an independent body The Episcopal Church created a bicameral legislature, the General Convention, modeled after the new U.S. Congress. It comprises a House of Bishops and a House of Clerical and Lay Deputies and meets every three years. A 40-member Executive Council, which meets three times a year, is the interim governing body. An elected presiding bishop serves as Primate and Chief Pastor.

After severe setbacks in the years immediately following the Revolution because of its association with the British Crown and the fact that a number of its clergy and members were Loyalists, the church soon established its own identity and sense of mission. Spreading westward, it sent missionaries into the newly settled territories of the United States, establishing dioceses from coast to coast, and also undertook substantial missionary work in Africa, Latin America, and the Far East. Today the overseas dioceses are developing into independent provinces of the Anglican Communion, the worldwide fellowship of churches in communion with the Church of England the the Archbishop of Canterbury.

The beliefs and practices of The Episcopal Church, like those of other Anglican churches, are both Catholic and Reformed, with bishops in the apostolic succession and the historic creeds of Christendom regarded as essential elements of faith and order, along with the primary authority of Holy Scripture and the two chief sacraments of Baptism and Eucharist.

Churches: 7,054; Inclusive Membership: 2,504,507; Sunday or Sabbath Schools: N. R.; Total Enrollment: 557,863; Ordained Clergy: 14,111

GENERAL ORGANIZATION

General Convention: Triennial (Next meeting, July 2-11, 1988)

Headquarters: 815 Second Ave., New York, NY 10017. Tel. (212) 867-8400

OFFICERS OF THE GENERAL CONVENTION

Presiding Bishop and Primate, Most Rev. Edmond L. Browning; Sec., Ho. of Bishops, Rt. Rev. Herbert A. Donovan, Jr., Box 6120, Little Rock, AR 72216
Pres., Ho. of Deputies, V. Rev. David B. Collins, 815 Second Ave., New York, NY 10017; Vice-Pres., Ho. of Deputies, Mrs. Pamela P. Chinnis; Interim Sec., Rev. Donald A. Nickerson, Jr.
Interim Sec., of the Gen. Conv., Rev. Donald A. Nickerson, Jr.; Exec. Officer, Gen. Conv., Rev. Donald A. Nickerson, Jr.; Interim Treas., Gen. Conv., Mrs. Ellen F. Cooke

THE EXECUTIVE COUNCIL

Pres. and Chpsn., Most Rev. Edmond L. Browning
Vice-Chpsn., V. Rev. David B. Collins
Vice-Pres., _____
Treas., Mrs. Ellen F. Cooke
Interim Sec., Rev. Donald A. Nickerson, Jr.

The Domestic and Foreign Missionary Society of PECUSA:
Pres., Presiding Bishop, Most Rev. Edmond L. Browning
Vice-Pres., _____
Treas., Mrs. Ellen F. Cooke
Interim Sec., Rev. Donald A. Nickerson, Jr.
Board of Directors: Executive Council

EPISCOPAL CHURCH CENTER AND STAFF

Episcopal Church Center, 815 Second Ave., New York, NY 10017. Tel. (212)867-8400
Office of the Presiding Bishop: Presiding Bishop and Primate, Most Rev. Edmond L. Browning; Senior Exec. for Mission Operations, D. Barry Menuez; Exec. for Mission Support/Treas., Mrs. Ellen F. Cooke; Exec. for Mission Planning, _____; Deputy for Adm., Rev. Richard Chang; Deputy for Anglican Relationships, Rev. Charles Cesaretti; Suffragan Bishop for Chaplaincies to Military, Prisons, and Hospitals, Rt. Rev. Charles L. Burgreen; Asst. to Bishop Burgreen, Rev. Donald W. Beers; Suffragan Bishop for Europe and the Diaspora, Rt. Rev. A. Donald Davies; Exec. Officer, Gen. Conv., Rev. Donald A. Nickerson, Jr.
Stewardship/Development: Exec., Rev. Dr. Thomas H. Carson, Jr.; Staff Officer for Stewardship, Rev. Ronald Reed; Staff Officer for Planned Giving, Frederick H. Osborn III; Staff Officer for Congregational Development, Rev. Robert H. Bonner; Staff Officer for Stewardship Educ., Mrs. Laura E. Wright
Communication: Exec., Ms. Sonia J. Francis; News Dir., Rev. William D. Dearnaley; Deputy News Dir., Ms. Janet Vetter; Dir. Publications, Frank Tedeschi; Asst. Dir. of Publications, Br. Tobias Haller; Video & Audiovisuals Producer, Whitney Smith; Electronic Media Dir., Clement W. K. Lee; Printing Production Dir., Robert Nangle; Art Dir., Ms. Rochelle Arthur; Eds., Ms. Marcy Darin, Bruce Campbell; Electronic Media Producer, Anthony Wilson
Education for Mission and Ministry: Exec., Rev. David Perry; Adm. Asst., Mrs. Ruby Miller; Field Officer for Educ. and Training, Dr. John D. Vogelsang; Coord. for Inst. of Higher Education, _____; Youth Min. Coord., _____; Ministry Development Officer. Rev. John T. Docker; Evangelism Officer Rev. A. Wayne Schwab; Congreg. Devel., Rev. Arlin Rothauge; Prog. Resource Developer, Dr. Irene V. Jackson-Brown; Coord. for Children's Min., Rev. Dr. Barbara M. Taylor; Exec. Dir., Bd. for Theol. Educ., Rev. Preston T. Kelsey; Exec. Dir. Church Deployment Office, Mr. William A.

Thompson; Exec. Dir., Office of Pastoral Development, Rt. Rev. David E. Richards; Suffragan Bishop for Chaplaincies to Military and Prisons, Rt. Rev. Charles Burgreen; Exec. Asst. Chaplain, Rev. Donald Beers
National Mission in Church and Society: Exec., Rev. Earl A. Neil; Staff Officer for Housing and Training, Howard Quander; Staff Officer for Coalition for Human Needs Commission, Ms. Gloria Brown; Staff Officer for Social and Specialized Min., Marcia L. Newcombe; Staff Officer for Black Min., Rev. Canon Harold T. Lewis; Staff Officer for Indian Min., Ms. Owanah B. Anderson; Staff Officer for Hispanic Min., Rev. Dr. Herbert Arrunategui; Staff Officer for Asiamerica Min., Rev. Winston W. Ching; Staff Officer for National Mission Development, Rev. Richard E. Gary; Women in Mission and Ministry, Ms. Ann Smith; Assoc. Ecumenical Officer for Washington Affairs, Rev. Dr. William L. Weiler; Staff Officer for Jubilee Min., Rev. Canon Peter P. Q. Golden; Public Issues Officer, _____.
World Mission in Church and Society: Exec., Ms. Judith M. Gillespie; Adm. Asst., Br. James E. Treets, BGS; Deputy and Asia & Pacific Partnership Officer, Rev. J. Patrick Mauney; Africa Partnership Officer, Rev. Canon Burgess Carr; Latin America & Caribbean Partnership Officer, Rev. Ricardo T. Potter; Interim Mission Information and Education Officer, Mrs. Margaret S. Larom; Coordinator Overseas Personnel, Rev. Mark Harris; Assoc. Leadership Training, Ms. Sonia Kelly; Assoc. Volunteers for Mission, Mrs. Beverly Anderson; Logistics Associate, Ms. Marcella Pambrun; Overseas Development Planning Officer, Ms. Jane M. Watkins; Deputy and Development Officer, Bruce W. Woodcock; Development Officer, Ms. Kirsten M. Laursen; Development Officer, James J. Chege; Ecumenical Relations Officer, Rev. William A. Norgren; Asst. Ecumenical Staff Officer, Rev. Elizabeth Z. Turner; United Thank Offering Staff Officer, Ms. Willeen V. Smith.
Presiding Bishops Fund for World Relief: Interim Exec. Dir., Ms. Bobbie Bevill; Asst. Dir. for Migration Affairs, Mrs. Marion M. Dawson; Asst. for Admin., Mrs. Nancy Marvel; Asst. for Interpretation and Network Development, Dr. David Crean; Communications/Information Officer Refugee/Migration, Rev. Gene T. White; Sponsorship Development Officer Refugee/Migration, Ms. Sarah Dresser.
Mission Support: Exec. and Treas., Mrs. Ellen F. Cooke; Asst. Treas., Louis H. Gill, Philippe Labbe; Dir. Mission Operation Support, Robert E. Brown; Controller, Clinton F. Best; Asst. Controller, Ms. Arlissa Salamone, Internal Auditor, Dr. Christopher Cabrera; Dir., MIS., Rev. Frederick J. Howard; Data Processing Super., Ms. Barbara Price; Clerical Super., Ms. Barbara Wilson
Administration: Service Manager, Terence Adair; Assist., Richard Corney; Human Resources Officer, Ms. Barbara Quinn; Asst. Human Resources Officer, James A. Lewis.
General Convention Executive Office: Exec. Officer, Rev. Donald A. Nickerson, Jr.; Interim Sec. and Registrar, Rev. Donald A. Nickerson, Jr.; Treas., Mrs. Ellen F. Cooke; Adm., Ms. Clare Fisher; Facilities Coord., Ms. Lori M. Arnold; Ed., Rev. Charles Scott; Information Systems Mgr., Mrs. Diana Morris.

OFFICIAL AGENCIES

Church Pension Fund and Affiliates: Pres., Robert A. Robinson, 800 Second Ave., New York, NY 10017
Episcopal Church Building Fund: Exec., Rev. Sherrill Scales, Jr., 815 Second Ave., New York, NY 10017, Tel. (212) 697-6066
The Episcopal Church Foundation: Exec., Mr. Jeffrey H. Kittross, 815 Second Ave., New York, NY 10017. Tel. (212) 698-2858

Archives of The Episcopal Church: Dr. V.Nelle Bellamy, Archivist

PUBLICATIONS

The Episcopalian (m), 1201 Chestnut St., Philadelphia, PA 19107, Richard Crawford, Ed.

Forward Movement Publications: 412 Sycamore St., Cincinnati, OH 45202. Rev. Charles H. Long, Ed. Tel. (513)721-6659.

The Living Church (w), 407 E. Michigan St., Milwaukee, WI 53202, Rev. H. Boone Porter, Jr. Ed.

Historical Magazine (q), Box 2247, Austin, TX 78705, Rev. J. F. Woolverton, Ed.

The Churchman (m), 1074 23rd Ave., N., St. Petersburg, FL 33704, Edna Ruth Johnson

Anglican Theol. Review (q), 600 Haven St., Evanston, IL 60201, Rev. W. Taylor Stevenson, Seabury-Western Theological Seminary, 2122 Sheridan Rd., Evanston, IL 60201

Pan-Anglican (occ.), 1335 Asylum Ave., Hartford, CT 06105

Cathedral Age, Mt. St. Albans, Washington, DC, Nancy Montgomery, Ed.

The Episcopal Church Annual, 78 Danbury Rd., Wilton, CT 06897, E. Allen Kelly, Ed.

Episcopal Clerical Directory, Church Pension Fund, 800 Second Ave., New York, NY 10017

St. Luke's Journal of Theology, The School of Theology, University of South, Sewanee, TN 37375

ACTIVE BISHOPS IN THE U.S.A.

(Note: CO, Coadjutor; S, Suffragan; A, Assistant)
(Address: Right Reverend)

Headquarters Staff: Presiding Bishop and Primate, The Most Rev. Edmond L. Browning; Field Officer, Rt. Rev. David E. Richards, 116 Alhambra Circle, Ste. 210, Coral Gables, FL 33134; Suffragan Bishop for Chaplaincies to Military, Prisons and Hospitals, Rt. Rev. Charles L. Burgreen, 815 Second Ave., New York, NY 10017

Alabama, Furman C. Stough, Robert O. Miller (S), 521 N. 20th St., Birmingham 35203

Alaska, George C. Harris, Box 441, Fairbanks 99707

Albany, Rt. Rev. David S. Ball, 62 S. Swan St., Albany, NY 12210

Arizona, Joseph T. Heistand, P.O. Box 13647, Phoenix 85002

Arkansas, Herbert Donovan, Jr., 300 W. 17th St., P.O. Box 6120, Little Rock 72206

Atlanta, C. Judson Child, Jr., Frank Kellog Allan (CO), 2744 Peachtree Rd. N.W., Atlanta, GA 30305

Bethlehem, J. Mark Dyer, 333 Wyandotte St., Bethlehem, PA 18015

California, William E. Swing, 1055 Taylor St., San Francisco 94108

Central Florida, William H. Folwell, 324 N. Interlachen Ave., Box 790, Winter Park, 32789

Central Gulf Coast, Charles F. Duvall, P.O. Box 8547, Mobile, AL 36608

Central N.Y., O'Kelley Whitaker, 310 Montgomery St., Syracuse 13203

Central Pennsylvania, Charlie F. McNutt, 221 N. Front St., Harrisburg 17101, P.O. Box W, Harrisburg 17108

Chicago, Frank T. Griswold III, 65 E. Huron St., Chicago, IL 60611

Colorado, William C. Frey, William Harvey Wolfrum (S), P.O. Box M, Capitol Hill Sta., Denver 80218

Connecticut, Arthur E. Walmsley; Clarence N. Coleridge (S); Jeffrey William Rowthorn (S), 1335 Asylum Ave., Hartford 06105

Dallas, Donis D. Patterson; 1630 Garrett St., Dallas, TX 75206

Delaware, Calvin C. Tennis, 2020 Tatnall St., Wilmington 19802

East Carolina, B. Sidney Sanders, P.O. Box 1336, Kinston, NC 28501

Eastern Oregon, Rustin R. Kimsey, P.O. Box 620, The Dalles, OR 97058

Easton, Elliott L. Sorge, P.O. Box 1027, Easton, MD 21601

East Tennessee, William E. Sanders, Box 3807, Knoxville, TN 37917

Eau Claire, William C. Wantland, 510 S. Farwell St., Eau Claire, WI 54701

El Camino Real, C. Shannon Mallory, P.O. Box 1903, Monterey, CA 93940

Florida, Frank S. Cerveny, 325 Market St., Jacksonville 32202

Fond du Lac, William L. Stevens, P.O. Box 149, Fond du Lac, WI 54935

Fort Worth, Clarence Cullam Pope, Jr., 3572 Southwest Loop 820, Fort Worth, TX 76133

Georgia, Harry W. Shipps, 611 East Bay St., Savannah 31401

Hawaii, Donald P. Hart, Queen Emma Square, Honolulu 96813

Idaho, David B. Birney, IV, Box 936, Boise 83701

Indianapolis, Edward W. Jones, 1100 W. 42nd St., Indianapolis 46208

Iowa, Walter C. Righter, 225 37th St., Des Moines 50312

Kansas, Richard F. Grein, Bethany Place, Topeka 66612

Kentucky, David B. Reed, 421 S. 2nd St., Louisville 40202

Lexington, Don A. Wimberly, 530 Sayre Ave., Lexington, KY 40508

Long Island, Robert Campbell Witcher, Henry B. Hucles, III (S), 36 Cathedral Ave., Garden City, NY 11530

Los Angeles, _____; Oliver B. Garver, Jr. (S), 1220 W. 4th St., Los Angeles, CA 90017

Louisiana, James Barrow Brown, P.O. Box 15719, New Orleans 70175

Maine, Edward C. Chalfant, 143 State St., Portland 04101

Maryland, A. Theodore Eastman, 105 W. Monument St., Baltimore 21230

Massachusetts, David Elliott Johnson, Morris F. Arnold (S), 1 Joy St., Boston 02108

Michigan, H. Coleman McGehee, Jr., Harry Irving Mayson (S), William J. Gordon (A), 4800 Woodward Ave., Detroit 48201

Milwaukee, Roger J. White, 804 E. Juneau Ave., Milwaukee, WI 53202

Minnesota, Robert M. Anderson, 309 Clifton Ave., Minneapolis 55403

Mississippi, Duncan M. Gray, Jr., P.O. Box 1636, Jackson 39205

Missouri, William Augustus Jones, Jr., 1210 Locust St., St. Louis 63103

Montana, Charles J. Jones, 515 North Park Ave., Helena 59601

Nebraska, James Daniel Warner, 200 N. 62nd St., Omaha 68132

Nevada, Stewart C. Zabriskie, 2930 W. 7th St., Reno 89503

New Hampshire, Douglas E. Theuner, 63 Green St., Concord 03301

New Jersey, G. P. Mellick Belshaw, Vincent K. Pettit (S), 808 W. State St., Trenton 08618

New York, Paul Moore, Jr., Walter D. Dennis (S), 1047 Amsterdam Ave., New York 10025

Newark, John Shelby Spong, 24 Rector St., Newark, NJ 07102

North Carolina, Robert W. Estill; Frank Harris Vest, Jr. (S), 201 St. Alban's, P.O. Box 17025, Raleigh 27609

North Dakota, Harold A. Hopkins, Jr., 809 8th Ave. S., Fargo 58102

Northern California, John L. Thompson, III, 1322 27th St., P.O. Box 161268, Sacramento 95816

Northern Indiana, Frank C. Gray, 117 N. Lafayette Blvd., South Bend 46601

Northern Michigan, Thomas K. Ray, 131 E. Ridge St., Marquette 49855

Northwest Texas, Sam Byron Hulsey, Texas Commerce

Bank Bldg., Ste. 506, 1314 Ave. K, P.O. Box 1067, Lubbock 79408

Northwestern Pennsylvania, Donald J. Davis, 145 W. 6th St., Erie, PA 16501

Ohio, James R. Moodey, Arthur B. Williams (S), 2230 Euclid Ave., Cleveland, 44115

Oklahoma, Gerald N. McAllister P. O. Box 1098; William J. Cox (A)

Olympia, Robert H. Cochrane, 1551 Tenth Ave., East, Seattle, WA 98102

Oregon, Robert Louis Ladehoff, 11800 SW Military La., Portland 97219, P.O. Box 467, Portland, OR 97034

Pennsylvania, Allan C. Bartlett, 1700 Market St., Ste. 1600, Philadelphia 19103

Pittsburgh, Alden M. Hathaway, 325 Oliver Ave., Pittsburgh, PA 15222

Quincy, Donald J. Parsons, 3601 N. North St., Peoria, IL 61604

Rhode Island, George Hunt, 275 N. Main St., Providence 02903

Rio Grande, Richard M. Trelease, Jr., 4304 Carlisle NE, Albuquerque, NM 87107

Rochester, William G. Burrill, Jr., 935 East Ave., Rochester, NY 14607

San Diego, C. Brinkley Morton, St. Paul's Church, 2728 6th Ave., San Diego, CA 92103

San Joaquin, Victor M. Rivera, 4159 East Dakota, Fresno, CA 93726

South Carolina, C. FitzSimons Allison, 1020 King St., Drawer 2127, Charleston 29403

South Dakota, Craig B. Anderson, 200 W. 18th St., P.O. Box 517, Sioux Falls 57101

Southeast Florida, Calvin O. Schofield, Jr., 525 NE 15 St., Miami 33132

Southern Ohio, William G. Black, 412 Sycamore St., Cincinnati 45202

Southern Virginia, Claude Charles Vaché, 600 Talbot Hill Rd., Norfolk 23505

Southwest Florida, Emerson Paul Haynes, Box 20899, St. Petersburg 33742

Southwestern Virginia, A Heath Light, P.O. Box 2068, Roanoke 24009

Spokane, Leigh Allen Wallace, Jr., 245 E. 13th Ave., Spokane 99202

Springfield, Donald M. Hultstrand, 821 S. 2nd St., Springfield, IL 62704

Tennessee, George Lazenby Reynolds, Box 3807, Knoxville, TN 37917

Texas, Maurice M. Benitez, Gordon T. Charlton (S), 520 San Jacinto St., Houston 77002

Upper South Carolina, William A. Beckham; Rogers Sanders Harris, (S), P.O. Box 1789, Columbia 29202

Utah, George E. Bates, 231 E. First St. South, Salt Lake City 84111

Vermont, Daniel L. Swenson, Rock Point, Burlington 05401

Virginia, Peter J. Lee, David H. Lewis, Jr. (S), 110 W. Franklin St., Richmond 23220

Washington, John T. Walker, Ronald Haines (S), Mt. St. Alban, Washington, DC 20016

West Missouri, Arthur Vogel, 415 W. 13th St., P.O. Box 23216, Kansas City 64141

West Tennessee, Alex D. Dickson, 692 Poplar Ave., Memphis, TN 38105

West Texas, John H. McNaughton, P.O. Box 6885, San Antonio 78209

West Virginia, Robert P. Atkinson; William Franklin Carr (S), 1608 Virginia St. E., Charleston, 25311

Western Kansas, John F. Ashby, 142 S. 8th St., P.O. Box 1383, Salina 67401

Western Louisiana, Willis R. Henton, P. O. Box 4046, Alexandria, LA 71301

Western Massachusetts, Andrew F. Wissemann, 37 Chestnut St., Springfield 01103

Western Michigan, Howard S. Meeks, 2600 Vincent Ave., Kalamazoo 49001

Western New York, David C. Bowman, 1114 Delaware Ave., Buffalo 14209

Western North Carolina, William G. Weinhauer, P.O. Box 368, Black Mountain 28711

Wyoming, Bob Gordon Jones, 104 S. 4th St., Box 1007, Laramie 82070

American Churches in Europe—Jurisdiction, A. Donald Davies, The American Cathedral, 23 Avenue Georges V, 75008, Paris, France

Navajoland Area Mission, Wesley Frensdorff, P.O. Box 720, Farmington, NM 47401

The Estonian Evangelical Lutheran Church

The Estonian Evangelical Lutheran Church (EELC) was founded in 1917 in Estonia and reorganized in Sweden in 1944. The teachings of the EELC are based on the Old and New Testaments, explained through the Apostolic, Nicean and Athanasian confessions, the unaltered Confession of Augsburg and other teachings found in the Book of Concord.

Churches: 24; Inclusive Membership: 7,191; Sunday or Sabbath Schools: N.R.; Total Enrollment: N.R.; Ordained Clergy: 23

GENERAL ORGANIZATION

Executive Board headed by the Archbishop, Consisterium, Auditing Committee and District Conference.

Headquarters: Wallingatan 32, Box 45074, 10430 Stockholm 45, Sweden.

OFFICERS

Bishop in North America, Rev. Karl Raudsepp, 30 Sunrise Ave., Apt. 216, Toronto, Ontario, Canada M4A 2R3

Assts. to the Bishop: Dr. Arthur Voobus, 230 So. Euclid Ave., Oak Park, IL 60302. Tel. (312) 386-6274; Dean Rudolph Reinaru, 607 East 7th St., Lakewood, NJ 08701. Tel. (201) 364-9860

PERIODICAL

Eesti Kirik (m), Wallingatan 32, Box 45074, 10430 Stockholm 45, Sweden. Dr. E. Putsep, Ed.

Ethical Culture Movement

A national federation of Ethical Humanist Societies— religious and educational fellowships based on ethics, believing in the worth, dignity, and fine potentialities of the individual, encouraging freedom of thought, committed to the democratic ideal and method, issuing in social action.

Churches: 21; Inclusive Membership: 3,500; Sunday or Sabbath Schools: 14; Total Enrollment: 500; Ordained Clergy: 45

AMERICAN ETHICAL UNION

Assembly: annual (June)

Headquarters: 2 West 64th St., New York, NY 10023. Tel. (212) 873-6500

OFFICERS

Pres., Sophie Meyer
Vice-Pres., Harry Cohn
Treas., _____
Sec., Ron Solomon
Leader for Natl. Development, _____
Adm., Margaretha E. Jones

ORGANIZATIONS

National Leaders Council, Chpsn., Judith Espenschied
National Service Conference, Pres., Richard Risk

A.E.U. Weis Ecology Center, Dir., James Markstein
A.E.U. Race Commission, Chpsn., Robert M. Stein
International Humanist & Ethical Union, Representative, Dr. Matthew Ies Spetter, Joseph Chuman
Washington Office for Social Concern, Dir., Hebert Blinder
Rel. Ed. Dir., Patricia Hoertoerfer

The Evangelical Church

The Evangelical Church was born June 4, 1968, in Portland, Oregon, when 46 congregations and about 80 ministers, under the leadership of V. A. Ballantyne and George Millen, met in an organizing session. Within two weeks a group of about twenty churches and thirty ministers from the Evangelical United Brethren and Methodist churches in Montana and North Dakota became a part of the new church. Richard Kienitz and Robert Strutz were the superintendents.

Under the leadership of Superintendent Robert Trosen, the former Holiness Methodist Church became a part of the Evangelical Church in 1969, bringing its membership and a flourishing mission field in Bolivia. The Wesleyan Covenant Church joined in 1977, with its missionary work in Mexico, in Brownsville, Texas, and among the Navajos in New Mexico.

The Evangelical Church in Canada, where T. J. Jesske was superintendent, became an automonous organization on June 5, 1970. In 1982, after years of discussions with the Evangelical Church of North America, a founding General Convention was held at Billings, Montana, where the two churches united.

The following distinctive guide the life, program, and devotion of this church: faithful, biblical, and sensible preaching and teaching of those truths proclaimed by the scholars of the Wesleyan-Arminian viewpoint; an itinerant system which reckons with the rights of individuals and the desires of the congregations; local ownership of all local church properties and assets.

The church is affiliated with the Christian Holiness Association, the National Association of Evangelicals, World Gospel Mission, and OMS International. Through the two latter agencies and the mission in Bolivia, more than 55 of the denomination's more than 115 missionaries have been appointed. The Evangelical Church continues to grow as congregations join and new churches are planted.

Churches: 186; Inclusive Membership: 17,440; Sunday or Sabbath Schools: N.R.; Total Enrollment: 19,225; Ordained Clergy: 306

GENERAL ORGANIZATION

Denominational Council: quadrennially
Executive Council: annually

OFFICERS

Gen. Supt., Dr. George K. Millen, 3223 S.E. Deswell, Portland, OR 97267. Te. (503)659-0000
Gen. Supt. Chmn. of Denominational and Exec. Councils, Dr. George K. Millen, 7525 SE Lake Rd., Ste. #7, Milwauie OR 97267. Tel. (503)652-1029

PERIODICAL

Overview (q), George Millen, Ed.

Evangelical Congregational Church

This denomination had its beginning in the movement known as the Evangelical Association, organized by Jacob Albright in the early nineteenth century. In 1891 a division occurred in the Evangelical Association, which resulted in the organization of the United Evangelical Church in 1894.

An attempt to heal this division was made in 1922, but a portion of the United Evangelical Church was not satisfied with the plan of merger and remained apart, taking the above name in 1928. This denomination is Arminian in doctrine, evangelistic in spirit, and Methodistic in church government, with congregational ownership of local church property.

Congregations are located basically from New Jersey to Illinois. A denominational center is located in Myerstown, Penn., as well as a retirement village and a seminary, Evangelical School of Theology. Three summer youth camps and three camp meetings continue evangelistic outreach. A worldwide missions movement includes conferences in North East India, Liberia, Mexico, and Japan. The denomination is a member of National Association of Evangelicals.

Churches: 160; Inclusive Membership: 41,237; Sunday or Sabbath Schools: 159; Total Enrollment: 19,029; Ordained Clergy: 211

GENERAL ORGANIZATION

General Conference: quadrennial. (Next meeting, Sept. 1990)
Headquarters: Evangelical Congregational Church Center, 100 W. Park Ave., P. O. Box 186, Myerstown, PA 17067
Presiding Bishop, Dr. Richard A. Cattermole, Myerstown, PA 17067
Dir. of Church Ministries, Rev. Keith R. Miller, Myerstown, PA 17067
Dir. of Missions, Rev. Duane M. Ray, Myerstown, PA 17067

OFFICERS

1st Vice-Chpsn., Rev. David C. Greulich, 1717 W. Livingston St., Allentown, PA 18104
2nd Vice-Chpsn., Rev. Robert M. Daneker, Sr., 122 S. Emerson St., Allentown, PA 18104
Sec., Rev. E. J. Vondran, 130 Wyomissing Ave., Shillington, PA 19607
Asst. Sec's.: Rev. Robert Stahl, Lebanon, PA and Rev. Keigh Mong, Seneca, PA
Stat. Sec., Rev. Carl Fetterhoff, 750 N. Second St., Reading, PA 19601
Treas., Stanley Heimbach, Evangelical Congregational Church, Myerstown, PA 17067
Dir. of Missions, Rev. D. M. Ray, P.O. Box 186, Myerstown, PA 17067
Supt., E. C. Church Retirement Village, Rev. Franklin H. Schock, Myerstown, PA 17067
Pres., Evangelical School of Theology, Dr. Ray A. Seilhamer, Myerstown, PA 17067

OTHER ORGANIZATIONS

Administrative Council: Chpsn., Bishop Richard A. Cattermole; Vice-Chpsn., Rev. D. C. Greulich; Treas., Stanley Heimbach
Div. of Evangelism and Spiritual Care: Chpsn., Rev. Richard A. Cattermole, Myerstown, PA
Div. of Church Ministries: Chpsn., Rev. Keith R. Miller, Myerstown, PA
Div. of Church Services: Chpsn., R. A. Cattermole, Myerstown, PA
Div. of Missions: Chpsn., Rev. D. M. Ray, Myerstown, PA
Board of Pensions: Pres., Mr. Homer Luckenbill, Jr., Pine Grove, PA; Sec., Dr. J. D. Yoder, Myerstown, PA

PERIODICALS

The United Evangelical (m), Rev. D. H. Reed, Ed. Pub., Church Center Press, Myerstown, PA

The Evangelical Covenant Church

The Evangelical Covenant Church has its roots in historical Christianity as it emerged in the Protestant

Reformation, in the biblical instruction of the Lutheran State Church of Sweden, and in the great spiritual awakenings of the nineteenth century. These three influences have in large measure shaped its development and are to be borne in mind in seeking to understand its distinctive spirit.

The Covenant Church adheres to the affirmations of the Protestant Reformation regarding the Holy Scriptures, the Old and the New Testament, as the Word of God and the only perfect rule for faith, doctrine, and conduct. It has traditionally valued the historic confessions of the Christian church, particularly the Apostles' Creed, while at the same time it has emphasized the sovereignty of the Word over all creedal interpretations. It has especially cherished the pietistic restatement of the doctrine of justification by faith as basic to its dual task of evangelism and Christian nurture, the New Testament emphasis upon personal faith in Jesus Christ as Savior and Lord, the reality of a fellowship of believers which recognizes but transcends theological differences, and the belief in baptism and the Lord's Supper as divinely ordained sacraments of the church.

While the denomination has traditionally practiced the baptism of infants, in conformity with its principle of freedom it has given room to divergent views. The principle of personal freedom, so highly esteemed by the Covenant, is to be distinguished from the individualism that disregards the centrality of the Word of God and the mutual responsibilities and disciplines of the spiritual community.

Churches: 570; Inclusive Membership: 86,079; Sunday or Sabbath Schools: 524; Total Enrollment: 71,424; Ordained Clergy: 930

GENERAL ORGANIZATION

General Conference: annual (June 21-24, 1988)
Headquarters: 5101 N. Francisco Ave., Chicago, IL 60625. Tel. (312) 784-3000

OFFICERS

Pres., Dr. Paul E. Larsen, Chicago, IL
Vice-Pres., Rev. Glen V. Wiberg, New Brighton, MN
Sec., Rev. Timothy C. Ek, Chicago, IL
Treas., Donald E. Wahlquist, Seattle, WA

ADMINISTRATIVE BOARDS

Board of Christian Education and Discipleship. Dr. John C. Pearson; Chpsn., Sec., Rev. Mark S. Olson; Exec. Sec., Christian Education and Discipleship, Rev. Evelyn M. R. Johnson
Board of Church Growth and Evangelism: Chpsn., Dr. Darryl L. Larson; Sec., Rev. Donald G. Thomas; Exec. Sec., Dr. Robert C. Larson
Board of Covenant Women: Chpsn., Mrs. Lois M. Johnson; Sec., Mrs. Anna J. Hult; Exec. Sec., Mrs. Doris R. Johnson
Board of Human Resources:Chpsn., Rev. Everett L. Wilson; Sec., Rev.David W. Lindfors
Board of the Ministry: Chpsn., Rev. William R. Notehelfer; Sec., Dr. Jean C. Lambert; Exec. Sec. of the Ministry, Rev. Donald A. Njaa
Board of Pensions: Chpsn., Warren R. Wise; Sec. & Dir. of Pensions, Rev. Donald A. Njaa
Board of Publication: Chpsn., Harry A. Nicholls; Sec., Rev. Carl L. Taylor; Exec. Sec. of Publications, Rev. James R. Hawkinson
Board of World Mission: Chpsn., Rev. Donald E. Logue; Sec., Mrs. Naida H. Aschenbrenner; Exec. Sec., World Mission, Rev. Raymond L. Dahlberg
Board of Benevolence: Chpsn., William R. Ahlem, Jr.; Sec., Robert H. Peterson; Pres. of Covenant Benevolent Institutions, Nils G. Axelson, 5145 N. California Ave., Chicago, IL 60625
Board of Directors of North Park College and Theological Seminary: Chpsn., W. Reece Bader; Sec., Dr. Dean A.

Lundgren; Pres., Dr. David G. Horner, 3225 W. Foster Ave., Chicago, IL 60625

PERIODICALS

Covenant Companion (m), Chicago, IL, Rev. James R. Hawkinson, Ed.
Covenant Quarterly (q), Chicago, IL, Dr. Wayne C. Weld, Ed.
Covenant Home Altar (q), Chicago, IL, Rev. James R. Hawkinson, Ed.

The Evangelical Free Church of America

In October 1884, 27 representatives from Swedish churches met in Boone, Iowa, to establish the Swedish Evangelical Free Church. In the fall of that same year, two Norwegian-Danish groups began worship and fellowship (in Boston and in Tacoma) and by 1912 had established the Norwegian-Danish Evangelical Free Church Association. These two denominations, representing 275 congregations, came together at a merger conference in 1950.

The Evangelical Free Church is an association of local, autonomous churches across the United States and Canada, blended together around common principles, policies, and practices. A 12-point statement addresses the major doctrines, but also provides for differences of understanding on minor issues of faith and practice.

Overseas outreach includes 350 career and 65 short-term workers, serving on mission fields in 14 countries.

Churches: 880; Inclusive Membership: 95,722; Sunday or Sabbath Schools: N.R.; Total Enrollment: N.R.; Ordained Clergy: 1,484

GENERAL ORGANIZATION

Conference: annual
Home Office: 1515 E. 66 St., Minneapolis, MN 55423. Tel. (612) 866-3343

OFFICERS

Pres., Dr. Thomas A. McDill, 1515 E. 66th St., Minneapolis, MN 55423
Pres. Emeritus, Dr. Arnold T. Olson, 6126 Park Ave., Minneapolis, MN 55417
Mod., Dr. Gordon Addington, 670 E. Eldridge Ave , St Paul MN 55117
Vice-Mod., Mr. James A. Hagman, 1895 Hampshire La. N., Golden Valley, MN 55427
Gen. Sec., Mr. Ronald O. Sollie, 4201 13th Ave. S., Minneapolis, MN 55407
Vice-Sec., Mr. Gene Hugoson, Rt. 2, Box 218, Granada, MN 56039
Fin. Sec., Mr. Kenneth Larson, 8200 Hidden Bry Trail, Lake Elmo, MN 55042
Treas., Mr. Gordon Johnson, 4905 1st Ave. So., Minneapolis, MN 55409
Exec. Dir. of Overseas Missions, Rev. Robert Dillon, 1515 E. 66th St., Minneapolis, MN 55423
Exec. Dir. of Church Ministries, Rev. James Westgate, 1515 E. 66th St., Minneapolis, MN 55423

PERIODICAL

Evangelical Beacon (semi-m), 1515 E. 66 St., Minneapolis, MN 55423 George Keck, Ed.

Evangelical Friends Alliance

Formed in 1965 as an organization representing one corporate step of denominational unity, brought about as a result of several movements of spiritual renewal within the Society of Friends. These movements are: (1) the general evangelical renewal within Christianity, (2) the New scholarly recognition of the evangelical nature of seventeenth century Quakerism, and (3) the Association of Evangelical Friends, the predecessor to EFA.

The EFA is conservative in theology and makes use of local pastors. Sunday morning worship includes singing, Scripture reading, a period of open worship—usually—and a sermon by the pastor.

YEARLY MEETINGS

Evangelical Friends Church, Eastern Region, Ron Johnson, 1201 - 30th St. N.W., Canton, OH 44709

Rocky Mountain YM, Jack Rea, P.O. Box 9629, Colorado Springs, CO 80932

Mid-America YM, Ed Key, 2018 Maple, Wichita, KS 67213

Northwest YM, Richard H. Beebe, Box 190, Newberg, OR 97132

Evangelical Lutheran Church, in America

The Evangelical Lutheran Church in America (ELCA) was organized April 20-May 3, 1987, in Columbus, Ohio, bringing together the 2.3 million-member American Lutheran Church, the 2.9 million-member Lutheran Church in America, and the 110,000-member Association of Evangelical Lutheran Churches.

The ELCA is both the youngest and at the same time, through its predecessor church bodies, the oldest of the major U.S. Lutheran churches. Its roots stretch back to the mid-17th century when a Dutch Lutheran congregation was formed in New Amsterdam (now New York). Most of the oldest congregations, however, were the result of early German immigration, dating from the first part of the 18th century, to Eastern Pennsylvania, the Hudson and Mohawk River Valleys in New York, and the Piedmont region of the Carolinas.

The first Lutheran association of congregations, the Pennsylvania Ministerium, was organized in 1748 under Henry Melchior Muhlenberg, known as the patriarch of American Lutheranism.

In 1820, a national federation of synods, the General Synod, was formed. A split in 1867 resulted in a second major body, the General Council. Earlier, as a result of the Civil War, southern synods had broken away from the General Synod to form the United Synod in the South. These three bodies were reunited in 1918 as the United Lutheran Church in America.

In 1962, the Lutheran Church in America (LCA) was formed by a merger of the United Lutheran Church with the Augustana Lutheran Church, founded in 1860 by Swedish immigrants; the American Evangelical Lutheran Church, founded in 1872 by Danish immigrants; and the Finnish Lutheran Church or Suomi Synod, founded in 1891 by Finnish immigrants.

Two years before the LCA was formed, the American Lutheran Church (ALC) was created through a merger of an earlier American Lutheran Church, which was formed in 1930 by four synods that traced their roots primarily to German immigration; the Evangelical Lutheran Church, which dated from 1917 through a merger of churches chiefly of Norwegian ethnic heritage; and the United Evangelical Lutheran Church in America, which arose from Danish immigration. On February 1, 1963, the Lutheran Free Church merged with the ALC.

The Association of Evangelical Lutheran Churches arose in 1976 from a doctrinal split with the Lutheran Church—Missouri Synod.

The ELCA, through its predecessor church bodies, was a founding member of the Lutheran World Federation, the World Council of Churches, and the National Council of the Churches of Christ in the USA.

Churchwide office of the ELCA is in Chicago. The church is divided into 65 geographical areas, or synods.

These 65 synods, in turn, are grouped into nine regional centers for mission, joint programs, and service.

Membership: 5,307,000. Congregations: 11,174.

GENERAL ORGANIZATION

Churchwide Assembly meets biennially. Next meeting, 1989, in Chicago

Churchwide Office: 8765 West Higgins Road, Chicago, IL 60631. Tel. (312)380-2700

OFFICERS

Bishop, The Rev. Dr. Herbert W. Chilstrom
Sec., The Rev. Dr. Lowell G. Almen
Treas., George E. Aker
Vice Pres., Christine H. Grumm
Office of the Bishop: Exec. Asst. for Adm., Rev. Dr. Robert N. Bacher; Exec. Asst. for Federal Chaplaincies, Rev. Lloyd W. Lyngdal; Exec. Assts., Lita B. Johnson and Rev. Dr. Morris A. Sorenson

OFFICES

Office for Ecumenical Affairs, Exec. Dir., Rev. Dr. William G. Rusch; Stnd. Comm. Chpsn., Rev. Dr. Edward D. Schneider

Office for Finance, Treas., George Aker; Stnd. Comm. Chpsn., Richard L. McAuliffe

Office for Personnel, Exec. Dir., A. C. Stein; Stnd. Comm. Chpsn., Rev. Edward F. Weiskotten

Office for Research, Planning and Evaluation, Exec. Dir., Ruth Ann Killion; Stnd. Comm. Chpsn., Helen R. Harms

DIVISIONS

Division for Congregational Life, Exec. Dir., Rev. Eldon G. DeWeerth; Board Chpsn., Susan Hermodson; Lutheran Youth Organization, Pres., Karl Anderson

Division for Education, Exec. Dir., Rev. Dr. W. Robert Sorensen; Board Chpsn., Rev. Dennis H. Dickman

Division for Global Missions, Exec. Dir., Rev. Dr. Mark W. Thomsen; Board Chpsn., Rev. Dr. William E. Lesher

Division for Ministry, Exec. Dir., Rev. Dr. Joseph M. Wagner; Board Chpsn., E. Marlene Wilson

Division for Outreach, Exec. Dir., Rev. Dr. James A. Bergquist; Board Chpsn., Nancy Lee Atkins

Division for Social Ministry, Exec. Dir., Rev. Charles S. Miller, Board Chpsn., Pamela J. Berven

COMMISSIONS

Commission for Church in Society, Exec. Dir., Rev. Dr. Jerald L. Folk; Board Chpsn., Kathleen L. Hurty

Commission for Communication, Exec. Dir., Carol Becker Smith, Board Chpsn., Robert E. A. Lee

Commission for Financial Support, Exec. Dir., Rev. Paul A. Johns; Board Chpsn., Rev. Donald J. Hillerich; Lutheran Laity Movement, Dir., Gustave G. Smith, Jr.

Commission for Multicultural Ministries, Exec. Dir., Rev. Craig J. Lewis; Board Chpsn., Pelagie Snesrud

Commission for Women, Exec. Dir., Christine Myers Crist, Board Chpsn., Doris Pagelkopf

CHURCHWIDE UNITS

Conference of Bishops, Exec. Dir., Rev. Dr. Edwin Bersagel; Chpsn. Rev. Dr. Paul Werger

ELCA Foundation, Exec. Dir., Rev. Dr. Harvey A. Stegemoeller. ELCA Publishing House, Exec. Dir., Albert E. Anderson; Board Chpsn., Rev. Dr. H. George Anderson. Board of Pensions, Exec. Dir., John G. Kapanke; Board Chpsn., Mildred M. Berg. Women of the ELCA, Exec. Dir., Betty Lee Nyhus, Board Chpsn., Jeanne W. Rapp

SYNODICAL BISHOPS

Region 1

Alaska, Rev. Donald D. Parsons, 10830 Bragaw St., Anchorage, AK 99516, Tel. (907)345-4345

Northwestern Washington, Rev. Dr. Lowell E. Knutson, 766-B John Street, Seattle, WA 98109, Tel. (206)624-0093

Southwestern Washington, Rev. David C. Wold, 301 E. Lopez, Port Angeles, WA 98362, Tel. (206)452-2323

Eastern Washington-Idaho, Rev. Robert M. Keller, 16320 Suncrest Drive, Nine Mile Falls, WA 99026, Tel. (509)466-9336

Oregon, Rev. Paul R. Swanson, Box 248, Portland, OR 97207, Tel. (503)223-5134

Montana, Rev. Dr. Norman G. Wick, 2415 13th Ave. S., Great Falls, MT 59405, Tel. (406)453-1461

Regional Coordinator: Ronald Coen, 766-B John St., Seattle, WA 98109, Tel. (206)624-0093

Region 2

Northern California-Northern Nevada, Rev. Lyle G. Miller, 364 E. Barstow Ave., Fresno, CA 93710, Tel. (209)439-4320

Southern California (West), Rev. J. Roger Anderson, 1340 S. Bonnie Brae St., Los Angeles, CA 90006, Tel. (213)387-8183

Southern California (East)-Hawaii, Rev. Robert L. Miller, 215 N. Lemon St., Fullerton, CA 92632, Tel. (805)687-1577

Arizona-Southern Nevada, Rev. Dr. Howard E. Wennes, 20121 Ventura Blvd., Ste. 225, Woodland Hills, CA 91364, Tel. (818)888-1910

Rocky Mountain, Rev. Dr. Wayne Weissenbuehler, 2701 Alcott, Ste. 292, Denver, CO 80211, Tel. (303) 433-8417

Regional Coordinator: Patricia Robertson, 409 Del Valle Circle, El Sobrante, CA 94803, Tel. (413)222-2419

Region 3

Western North Dakota, Rev. Robert D. Lynne, 1339 Meridith Dr., Bismarck, ND 58501, Tel. (701)255-1119

Eastern North Dakota, Rev. Dr. Wesley N. Haugen, Box 207, Fargo, ND 58107, Tel. (701)232-3381

South Dakota, Rev. Norman D. Eitrheim, Augustana College, Sioux Falls, SD 57107, Tel. (605)336-4011

Northwestern Minnesota, Rev. Dr. Harold R. Lohr, 1351 Page Dr. S., Ste. 320, Fargo, ND 58103, Tel. (701)237-6444

Northwestern Minnesota, Rev. Roger L. Munson, 45th E. & Colorado St., Duluth, MN 55804, Tel. (218)525-6233

Southwestern Minnesota, Rev. Dr. Darold H. Beekmann, Box 773, Willmar, MN 56201, Tel. (612)235-5525

West Metropolitan Minnesota, Rev. David W. Olson, 105 W. University Ave., St. Paul, MN 55103, Tel. (612)224-4313

East Metropolitan Minnesota, Rev. Lowell O. Erdahl, 105 W. University Ave., St. Paul, MN 55103, Tel. (612)224-4313

Southeastern Minnesota, Rev. Glenn W. Nycklemoe, 301 First St. S.W., Austin, MN 55912, Tel. (507)433-7906

Regional Coordinator: _____

Region 4

Nebraska, Rev. Dr. Dennis A. Anderson, 124 S. 24th St., Ste. 204, Omaha, NE 68102, Tel. (402)341-4155

Missouri-Kansas, Rev. Dr. Charles H. Maahs, 9948 Metcalf Ave., Overland Park, KS 66212, Tel. (913)648-0595

Arkansas-Oklahoma, Rev. Dr. Robert H. Studtmann, 4803 S. Lewis, Tulsa, OK 74105, Tel. (918)747-8517

Northern Texas-Northern Louisiana, Rev. Mark B. Hebener, 6022 Mercedes, Dallas, TX 75206, Tel. (214)421-9825

Southwestern Texas, Rev. Arthur B. Rode, 1802 North-east Loop 410, PO Box 171270, San Antonio, TX 78217, Tel. (512)824-0068

Southeastern Texas-Southern Louisiana, Rev. Martin L. Yonts, 12130 Marbrook Dr., Dallas, TX 75230, Tel. (214)661-5544

Regional Coordinator: Bruce R. Klitzky, 2311 S. Quitman St., Denver, Co 80219, Tel. (800)525-0462

Region 5

Metropolitan Chicago, Rev. Sherman Hicks, 1700 E. 56th St., Chicago, IL 60637, Tel. (312)288-0800

Northern Illinois, Rev. Ronald K. Hasley, c/o Lutheran Social Services of Illinois, 119 N. Wyman St., Rockford, IL 61101, Tel. (815)965-6300

Central/Southern Illinois, Rev. Dr. John P. Kaitschuk, 106 Seminole, Springfield, IL 62704, Tel. (217)793-0404

Southeastern Iowa, Rev. Dr. Paul M. Werger, 3125 Cottage Grove Ave., Des Moines, IA 50311, Tel. (515)279-9795

Western Iowa, Rev. Curtis H. Miller, 1614 W. Fifth St., Storm Lake, IA 50588, Tel (712)732-4968

Northeastern Iowa, Rev. Dr. L. David Brown, 3125 Cottage Grove Ave., Des Moines, IA 50311, Tel. (515)274-3674

Northern Wisconsin-Upper Michigan, Rev. Harry S. Andersen, 12875 Rocky Point Lane, Lac Du Flambeau, WI 54538, Tel. (715)588-3771

West-Central Wisconsin, Rev. Gerhard I. Knutson, 1214 Wesley Dr., Rice Lake, WI 54868, Tel. (715)234-3373

East-Central Wisconsin, Rev. Dr. Robert H. Herder, 2800 Westhill Dr., Ste. 209, Wausau, WI 54401, Tel. (715)842-0616

Southeastern Wisconsin, Rev. Peter Rogness, 2705 Packers Ave., Madison, WI 53704, Tel. (608)244-5440

South-Central Wisconsin, Rev. Dr. Lowell H. Mays, 2705 Packers Ave., Madison, WI 53704, Tel. (608)233-1391

Southwestern Wisconsin, Rev. Stefan T. Guttormsson, 1509 King St., LaCrosse, WI 54601, Tel. (608)784-9335

Regional Coordinator: _____

Region 6

Eastern Michigan, Rev. Milton R. Reisen 19711 Greenfield Rd., Detroit, MI 48235, Tel (313)837-3522

Western Michigan, Rev. Dr. Reginald H. Holle, 801 S. Waverly Rd., Lansing, MI 48917

Indiana-Kentucky, Rev. Dr. Ralph A. Kempski, 9102 N. Meridian St., Ste. 405, Indianapolis, IN 46260, Tel. (317)846-4026

Northwestern Ohio, Rev. James A. Rave, P.O. Box 1604, Findley, OH 45839

Northeastern Ohio, Rev. Dr. Robert W. Kelley, 57 E. Main St., Columbus, OH 43215, Tel. (614)221-4366

Southern Ohio, Rev. Dr. Kenneth H. Sauer, 1233 Dublin Rd., Columbus, OH 43215, Tel. (614)486-9294

Regional Coordinator: _____

Region 7

New Jersey, Rev. Herluf M. Jensen, 1930 State Hgwy. 33, Trenton, NJ 08690, Tel. (609)586-6800

New England, Rev. Robert L. Isaksen, 360 Park Avenue S., New York, NY 10010, Tel., (212)532-6350

Metropolitan New York, Rev. Dr. William H. Lazareth, 3 W. 65th St., New York, NY 10023, Tel. (212)877-6815

Upper New York, Rev. Dr. Edward K. Perry, 3049 E. Genesse St., Syracuse, NY 13224, Tel. (315)446-2502

Northeastern Pennsylvania, Rev. Dr. Harold S. Weiss, 4865 Hamilton Blvd., Wescosville, PA 18106, Tel. (215)395-6891

Southeastern Pennsylvania, Rev. Dr. Lawrence L. Hand, 2900 Queen Lane, Philadelphia, PA 19129, Tel. (215)438-0600

Slovak Zion, Rev. Dr. John Adam, 13 Kingswood Rd., Danbury, CT 06811, Tel. (203)746-5318

Regional Coordinator: _____

Northwestern Pennsylvania, Rev. Paull E. Spring, 68 Linda Dr., Warren, PA 16365, Tel. (814)723-3651

Southwestern Pennsylvania, Rev. Donald J. McCoid, 9625 Perry Hgwy., Pittsburgh, PA 15237, Tel. (412)537-4450

Allegheny, Rev. Gerald E. Miller, 915 Hickory St., Hollidaysburg, PA 16648, Tel. (814)695-8013

Lower Susquehanna, Rev. Dr. Guy S. Edmiston Jr., 900 S. Arlington Ave., Rm. 208, Harrisburg, PA 17109, Tel. (717)652-1852

Upper Susquehanna, Rev. Dr. A. Donald Main, Box 36, Lewisburg, PA 17837, Tel. (717)524-9778

Maryland, Rev. Dr. Morris Zumbrun, 7604 York Rd., Baltimore, MD 21204, Tel. (301)825-9520

Metropolitan Washington, D.C., Rev. Dr. E. Harold Jansen, 6505 Loisdale Rd., Ste. 308, Springfield, VA 22150, Tel. (703)971-2676

West Virginia, Rev. L. Alexander Black, Atrium Mall, 503 Morgantown Avenue, Fairmont, WV 26554

Regional Coordinator: Rev. Eugene Beutel, 21 Schaeffer Lane, Freehold, NJ 07728, Tel. (201)938-5551

Region 9

Virginia, Rev. Richard F. Bansemer, Drawer 70, Salem, VA 24153, Tel. (703)389-1000

North Carolina, Rev. Dr. Michael C. D. McDaniel, 1940 Holiday Inn Dr., Salisbury, NC 28144, Tel. (704)633-4861

South Carolina, Rev. Dr. James S. Aull, P.O. Box 43, Columbia, SC 29202, Tel. (803)765-0590

Southeastern, Rev. Dr. Harold C. Skillrud, 731 Peachtree St. N.E., Atlanta, GA 30308, Tel. (404)874-8664

Florida, Rev. Lavern G. Franzen, 3838 W. Cyprus St., Tampa, FL 33607, Tel. (813)876-7660

Caribbean, Rev. Rafael Malpica-Padilla, P.O. Box 14426, Bo-Obrero Station, Santurce, PR 00916, Tel. (809)727-6015

Regional Coordinator: _____

PERIODICAL

The Lutheran (18/yr.), 8765 W. Higgins Road, Chicago, IL 60631, Editor and Exec. Dir., Rev. Dr. Edgar R. Trexler; Adv. Comm. Chpsn., William F. Chamberlin

Evangelical Lutheran Synod

The Evangelical Lutheran Synod had its beginning among the Norwegian settlers who brought with them their Lutheran heritage and established it in this country. It was organized in 1853. It was reorganized in 1917 by those who desired to adhere to these principles not only in word, but also in deed.

To carry out the above-mentioned objectives, the Synod owns and operates Bethany Lutheran College in Mankato, Minnesota. It also owns and operates Bethany Lutheran Theological Seminary for the training of pastors. The seminary is also at Mankato, MN

Churches: 120; Inclusive Membership: 19,938; Sunday or Sabbath Schools: 104; Total Enrollment: 3,483; Ordained Clergy: 128

GENERAL ORGANIZATION

Synod: annual (June)

OFFICERS

Pres., Rev. George Orvick, 447 Division St., Mankato, MN 56001

Sec., Rev. Alf Merseth, 106 13th St. S., Northwood, IA 50459

Treas., Mr. LeRoy W. Meyer, 1038 S. Lewis Ave., Lombard, IL 60148

OTHER ORGANIZATIONS

Lutheran Synod Book Co.: Office, Bethany Lutheran College, Mankato, MN 56001

PERIODICAL

Lutheran Sentinel, (m), Lake Mills, IA 50450. Rev. P. Madson, Ed., Box #3, Ulen, MN 56585

Lutheran Synod Quarterly, (q), W. W. Peterson, Ed., Bethany Lutheran College, 734 Marsh St., Mankato, MN 56001

Evangelical Mennonite Brethren Conference

(See Fellowship of Evangelical Bible Churches)

Evangelical Mennonite Church, Inc.

The Evangelical Mennonite Church traces its heritage directly to the early reformation period of the 16th century to a group known as Swiss Brethren, who believed that salvation could come only by repentance for sin and faith in Jesus Christ; that baptism was only for believers; and, that the church should be separate from controls of the state. These Swiss Brethren became known as Anabaptists. As the Anabaptist movement spread to other countries, a Dutch priest; Menno Simons, left the Catholic priesthood and became one of its leaders. Much of the Anabaptist movement became identified with the name of Menno Simons, and in the course of time the group became known as Mennonites.

Around 1700 a Mennonite minister named Jacob Ammon lead a division which came to be known as the Amish. Both the Mennonites and the Amish were much persecuted in some areas of Europe. Migrations to America took place in the early 1700's and at later times. Out of these, in the middle 1800's, emerged a minister of an Amish congregation in Indiana by the name of Henry Egly. After a deep spiritual renewal in his own life, he strongly emphasized the need of being "born again" as a prerequisite to baptism and church membership. This led to his separation from the group in 1865 and the beginning of what is now the Evangelical Mennonite Church, with congregations in Michigan, Ohio, Indiana, Illinois and Kansas.

Churches: 25; Inclusive Membership: 3,841; Sunday or Sabbath Schools: 25; Total Enrollment: 4,397; Ordained Clergy: 66

GENERAL ORGANIZATION

Conference: annual (August)

Headquarters: 1420 Kerrway Ct., Fort Wayne, IN 46805. Tel. (219) 423-3649

OFFICERS

Pres., Rev. Gary Gates, 1420 Kerrway Ct., Ft. Wayne, IN 46805

Chpsn., Rev. Doug Habegger, 1033 Lee, Morton, IL 61550

Vice-Chpsn., Rev. Charles Zimmerman, 300 Park St., Archbold, OH 43502

Sec., Gene L. Rupp, Rt. 3, Box 28D, Archbold, OH 43502

Treas., David Roth, 9006 Hollopeter Rd., Leo, IN 46765

PERIODICALS

EMC Today (m), Fort Wayne, IN 46805. Gary Gates, Ed.

Evangelical Methodist Church

Organized 1946 at Memphis, Tennessee, largely as a movement of people who opposed modern liberalism and wished for a return to the historic Wesleyan position. In 1960 merged with the Evangel Church (formerly Evangelistic Tabernacles) and with the People's Methodist Church in 1962.

GENERAL ORGANIZATION

General Conference, District Conference, and Annual Church Conference

Headquarters: 3000 West Kellogg, Wichita, KS 67213. Tel. (316) 943-3278

OFFICERS

Gen. Supt., Clyde Zehr, Wichita, KS 67213
Gen. Conf. Sec., Rev. Ronald D. Driggers, Wichita, KS 67213

Evangelical Presbyterian Church

The Evangelical Presbyterian Church (EPC), established in March 1981, is a conservative denomination of eight geographic presbyteries in the U.S. and Argentina. From its inception, with 12 churches, the EPC has grown to nearly 110 with a membership of over 30,000. In 1987 the General Assembly approved the formation of St. Andrews Presbytery, consisting of five churches in Buenos Aires, Argentina.

Planted firmly within the historic Reformed tradition, evangelical in spirit, the EPC places high priority on church planting and development along with world missions. Several missionary families serve at home and abroad. Second annual meeting of the Joint Committee on Mission between the EPC and the Presbyterian Church of Brazil (IPB) was held in the fall of 1987 in Sao Paulo, Brazil.

Based on the truth of Scripture and adhering to the Westminster Confession of Faith and the EPC *Book of Order,* the denomination is committed to certain "essentials of the faith." Freedom is allowed in areas of nonessentials, issues secondary to the gospel of Jesus Christ. The motto "In essentials, unity; In nonessentials, liberty; In all things, charity" summarizes the life of EPC, along with Ephesians 4:15, "truth in love."

The Evangelical Presbyterian Church is a member of the World Alliance of Reformed Churches, National Association of Evangelicals, World Evangelical Fellowship, and Evangelical Council for Financial Accountability. Representatives also attend the annual convocation of the National Association of Presbyterian and Reformed Churches (NAPARC)

Churches: 106; Inclusive Membership: 30,000; Sunday or Sabbath Schools: N.R.; Total Enrollment: N.R.; Ordained Clergy: 177

GENERAL ORGANIZATION

Headquarters: Office of the General Assembly, 26049 Five Mile Rd., Detroit, MI 48239. Tel. (313) 532-9555.

General Assembly: Annual (next meeting, June 20-23, Cherry Hills Community Church, Englewood, CO

OFFICERS

Moderator, Mr. Perry Mobley, Trinity Presbyterian Church, Box 3865, Florence, SC 29502

Stated Clerk, Rev. L. Edward Davis, Office of the General Assembly

GENERAL ASSEMBLY STAFF

World Outreach Exec. Dir., Rev. Ed. Randal, Office of the General Assembly

PERMANENT COMMITTEES

Committee on Administration: Chmn., Mr. Roger Vonder Bruegge, 1777 W. Adams, St. Louis, MO 63122

Committee on Church Development: Chmn., Rev. Calvin Gray, Bear Creek EPC, 3101 S. Kipling, Denver, CO 80227

Committee on World Outreach: Chmn., Mr. Richard Oestreicher, 32150 Pembroke, Livonia, MI 48152

Committee on Ministerial Vocation: Chmn., Rev. J. Thomas Shields, EPC of Anna, Box 653, Anna, IL 62906

Committee on Christian Education and Publication:

Chmn., Dr. Patricia Seraydarian, 18576 Mayfield, Livonia, MI 48152

Committee on Fraternal Relations: Chmn., Dr. David Massimi, Faith EPC, Box 143, Richmond, OH 43944

Committee on Women's Ministries: Chmn., Mrs. Colleen Rinehart, 19622 N. 130th Ave., Sun City West, AZ 85375

Permanent Judicial Commission: Chmn., Rev. Robert Ralston, Faith Presbyterian, 11373 E. Alameda Ave., Aurora, CO 80012

Committee on Theology, Chairman, Rev. Daniel Lacich, North Park EPC, 600 Ingomar Road, Wexford, PA 15090

Committee on Youth Ministries, Chairman to be determined

PRESBYTERIES

Allegheny:
Rev. Daniel Lacich, North Park EPC, 600 Ingomar Rd., Wexford, PA 10590

Central South:
Mr. Paul Lawrence, Stated Clerk, 20 Cripple Shin Bluff Dr., Rogers, AR 72756

East:
Stated Clerk to be elected

Far West:
Rev. James Brown, Jr., Stated Clerk, Santa Maria Community Church, 210 W. Fesler, Santa Maria, CA 93454

Midwest:
Rev. Larry Schmoekel, Stated Clerk, Trinity Presbyterian Church, Box 638, Columbia City, IN 46725

Southwest:
Dr. Howard Shockley, Asheville EPC, Box 9845 Asheville, NC 28815

West:

St. Andrews:
Mr. Freddie Berk, Stated Clerk, Iglesia Presbyteriana San Andres, Peru 352, 1067 Buenos Aires, Argentina

West:
Mr. Robert Bole, Stated Clerk, 1697 S. Kingston, Aurora, CO 80012

Fellowship of Evangelical Bible Churches

(**Formerly known as the Evangelical Mennonite Brethren Conference**)

Formerly known as the Defenseless Mennonite Brethren in Christ of North America, this body emanates from the Russian immigration of Mennonites into the United States, 1873–74. Established with the emphasis on true repentance, conversion, and a committed life to our Savior and Lord, the conference was founded in 1889 under the leadership of Isaac Peters and Aaron Wall. The founding churches were located in Mountain Lake, Minnesota, and in Henderson and Janzen, Nebraska. The conference has since grown to a fellowship of 36 churches with approximately 4,400 members. The churches are located in four countries—Argentina, Canada, Paraguay, and United States.

From its earliest days, foreign missions have been a most vital ingredient of the total ministry of the E.M.B. Today missions constitute about 75 percent of the total annual budget, with one missionary for every 30 members in the home churches. Since the conference does not develop and administer foreign mission fields of its own, it actively participates with existing evangelical "faith" mission societies. The conference has representation on several mission boards and has missionaries serving under approximately 32 different agencies around the world.

The Evangelical Mennonite Brethren Conference has determined to maintain doctrinal purity in holding fast to the inerrency of Scripture, the Deity of Christ, the need for spiritual regeneration of man from his sinful natural state, by faith in the death, burial, and resurrection of Jesus Christ as payment for sin. The E.M.B.s look forward to the imminent return of Jesus Christ and retain a sense of urgency to share the gospel with those who have never heard of God's redeeming love.

Churches: 14; Inclusive Membership: 2,107; Sunday or Sabbath Schools: 14; Total Enrollment: 1,418; Ordained Clergy: 46

GENERAL ORGANIZATION
Convention: annual (July)
Headquarters: 5800 S. 14th St., Omaha, NE 68107. Tel. (402)731-4780

OFFICERS
Pres., Rev. Lyle Wahl, 11 Avalon Rd., Winnipeg, Manitoba R2M 2L2
Vice-Pres., Mr. Stan Seifert, 2732 Springhill St., Clearbrook, British Columbia, Canada V2T 3V9
Rec. Sec., Rev. Melvin Epp, RR 1, Wymark, Saskatchewan, S0N 2Y0
Adm. Sec., Robert L. Frey, 5800 So. 14th, Omaha, NE 68107
Commission on Churches, Chpsn., Rev. Doug Hornok, 9001 Q Street, Omaha, NE 68127
Commission on Missions, Chpsn. Rev. Allan Wiebe, 1104 Day Dr., Omaha, NE 68005
Commission of Trustees, Chpsn., Mr. Neil C. J. DeRuiter, 298 Regal Ave., Winnipeg, Manitoba R2M 0P5
Commission on Education & Publication, Chpsn., Rev. Don Gillett, 465 Osborne St., Winnepeg, Manitoba, Canada R3L 2A4

PERIODICAL
Gospel Tidings, 5800 S. 14th St., Omaha, NE 68107. Robert L. Frey, Ed.

Fellowship of Fundamental Bible Churches

This body, until 1985, was called the Bible Protestant Church. The FFBC is a fellowship of fundamental Bible-believing local autonomous churches which believe in an inerrant and infallible Bible, is dispensational as related to the study of the Scriptures, espouses the pre-Tribulation Rapture, and is premillenial. The FFBC is evangelistic and missions-oriented. It regards itself as separatistic in areas of personal life and ecclesiastical association and believes that Baptism by immersion of believers most adequately reflects the symbolic truth of death and resurrection with Christ.

The Fellowship of Fundamental Bible Churches relates historically to the Eastern Conference of the Methodist Protestant Church, which changed its name to Bible Protestant Church at the 2nd Annual Session, held in Westville, New Jersey, September 26-30, 1940.

GENERAL ORGANIZATION
Mailing Address: P.O. Box 43, Glassboro NJ 08028

OFFICERS
Pres., Rev. Daniel Baker, RD 2 Box 378, Lake Aiel, PA 18436
Vice-Pres., Rev. Mark Franklin, RD 1 Box 415, Monroeville, NJ 08343
Sec., Rev. A. Glen Doughty, 134 Delsea Dr., Westville NJ 08093
Asst. Sec., Rev. William Williams, R.D. 5, Box 249, Moscow PA 18444
Treas., Rev. Joseph Hackett, R.D. 5, Box 6, Montague, NJ 07827

The Fire Baptized Holiness Church (Wesleyan)

This church came into being about 1890 as the result of definite preaching on the doctrine of holiness in some Methodist churches in southeastern Kansas. It became known as The Southeast Kansas Fire Baptized Holiness Association, which name in 1945 was changed to The Fire Baptized Holiness Church. It is entirely Wesleyan in doctrine, episcopal in church organization, and intensive in evangelistic zeal.

GENERAL ORGANIZATION
Headquarters: 600 College Ave., Independence, KS 67301. Tel. (316) 331-3049

OFFICERS
Gen. Supt., Gerald Broadaway
Gen. Sec., Wayne Knipmeyer, 1203 N. Penn, Independence, KS 67301
Gen. Treas., Victor White, 709 N. 13th, Independence, KS 67301

PERIODICALS
The Flaming Sword (m), 10th St. & College Ave., Independence, KS 67301
John Three Sixteen (w), 10th St. & College Ave., Independence, KS 67301

Free Christian Zion Church of Christ

Organized 1905, at Redemption, Arkansas, by a company of Negro ministers associated with various denominations, with polity in general accord with that of Methodist bodies.

GENERAL ORGANIZATION
General Assembly: annual (November)
Headquarters: 1315 Hutchinson St., Nashville, AR 71852
Chief Pastor, Willie Benson, Jr.

Free Lutheran Congregations, The Association of

The Association of Free Lutheran Congregations (AFLC), rooted in the Scandinavian revival movements, was organized in 1962 by a Lutheran Free Church remnant which rejected merger with The American Lutheran Church. The original 42 congregations were joined by other like-minded conservative Lutherans, especially from the former Evangelical Lutheran Church and the Suomi Synod. There has been a fourfold increase in the number of congregations during the AFLC's first quarter century, and concern over the current Lutheran merger has led to a new surge of growth.

Congregations subscribe to the Apostles, Nicene, and Athanasian creeds; Luther's Small Catechism; and the Unaltered Augsburg Confession. A statement of polity and practice, the Fundamental Principles and Rules for Work (1897), declaring that the local congregation is the right form of the kingdom of God on earth, subject to no authority but the Word and the Spirit of God, is also central to the life of the church body.

Distinctive emphases: (1) the infallibility and inerrancy of Holy Scriptures as the Word of God; (2) congregational polity; (3) the spiritual unity of all believers, resulting in fellowship and cooperation transcending denominational lines; (4) evangelical outreach, calling all to enter a personal relationship with Jesus Christ; (5) a wholesome Lutheran pietism that proclaims the Lordship of Jesus Christ in all areas of life and results in believers becoming the salt and light in their communities; (6) a conservative stance on current social issues.

A two-year Bible school and a theological seminary are

located on a campus in suburban Minneapolis, Minnesota. Support is channeled also to sister churches in Brazil, Mexico, and Canada.

Churches: 160; Inclusive Membership: 19,508; Sunday or Sabbath Schools: 141; Total Enrollment: 6,898; Ordained Clergy: 160

GENERAL ORGANIZATION

Conference: annual (June)
Headquarters: 3110 E. Medicine Lake Blvd., Minneapolis, MN 55441; Tel. (612) 545-5631

OFFICERS

Pres., Rev. Richard Snipstead, 3110 E. Medicine Lake Blvd, Minneapolis, MN 55441
Vice Pres., Rev. Robert L. Lee, 3430 Georgia Ave., Minneapolis, MN 55427
Sec., Rev. Ronald Knutson, 402 W. 11th St., Canton, SD 57013

PERIODICAL

The Lutheran Ambassador (bi-w), 3110 East Medicine Lake Blvd., Minneapolis, MN 55441. Rev. Raymond Huglen, Ed.

Free Methodist Church of North America

The Free Methodist Church was organized in 1860 in Western New York by ministers and laymen who had called the Methodist Episcopal Church to return to what they considered the original doctrines and life style of Methodism. The issues included human freedom (antislavery), freedom and simplicity in worship, free seats so that the poor would not be discriminated against, and freedom from secret oaths (societies) so the truth might be spoken freely at all times. They emphasized the teaching of the entire sanctification of life by means of grace through faith.

The denomination continues to be true to its founding principles. It communicates the gospel and its power to all men without discrimination through strong missionary, evangelistic, and educational programs. Six colleges, a Bible college, and numerous overseas schools train the youth of the church to serve in lay and ministerial roles.

Its members covenant to maintain simplicity in life and worship, daily devotion to Christ, and responsible stewardship of time, talent, and finance.

Churches: 1,048; Inclusive Membership: 71,682; Sunday or Sabbath Schools: 1,000; Total Enrollment: 109,844; Ordained Clergy: 1,765

GENERAL ORGANIZATION

General Conference (next meeting, 1989 in Seattle WA)
Headquarters: 901 College Ave., Winona Lake, IN 46590. Tel. (219) 267-7656
Free Methodist Publishing House: 999 College Ave., Winona Lake, IN 46590. Tel. (219) 267-7161

OFFICERS

Bishops: Robert F. Andrews, Donald N. Bastian, Gerald E. Bates, David M. Foster, Noah Nzeyimana, Clyde E. Van Valin
Gen. Conf. Sec., Melvin J. Spencer
Gen. Hdqtrs. Admin., Earl R. Schamehorn
Gen. Church Treas., Philip B. Nelson
Gen. Dir. of Christian Educ., Daniel L. Riemenschneider
Gen. Dir. of Evangelism and Church Growth, Forest C. Bush, Sr.
Gen. Dir. of FM Publishing House, Wilmer Bartel
Gen. Dir. of Higher Educ. and Ministry, Bruce L. Kline
Editor, Light and Life magazine, Robert B. Haslam
Exec. Dir., Light and Life Men Int'l, Lucien E. Behar

Gen. Dir. of Planned Giving, _____
Pres., of Women's Missionary Fellowship Int'l, Elizabeth Cryderman
Gen. Dir. of World Missions, Elmore L. Clyde

PERIODICALS

Free Methodist Pastor (q), Wayne G. McCown, Ed.
Light and Life (m), Robert B. Haslam, Ed.
Missionary Tidings (m), Marian W. Groesbeck, Ed.
Yearbook (a, October), Donald L. Payne, Ed.
901 Report/901 Review (m), Donald L Payne, Ed.

Free Will Baptists, National Association of

This evangelical group of Arminian Baptists was organized by Paul Palmer in 1727 at Chowan, North Carolina. Another movement (teaching the same doctrines of free grace, free salvation, and free will) was organized June 30, 1780, in New Durham, New Hampshire, but there was no connection with the southern organization except for a fraternal relationship.

The northern line expanded more rapidly and extended into the West and Southwest. This body merged with the Northern Baptist Convention October 5, 1911, but a remnant of churches reorganized into the Cooperative General Association of Free Will Baptists December 28, 1916, at Pattonsburg, Missouri.

Churches in the southern line were organized into various conferences from the beginning and finally united in one General Conference in 1921.

Representatives of the Cooperative General Association and the General Conference joined November 5, 1935 to form the National Association of Free Will Baptists.

Churches: 2,483; Inclusive Membership: 205,546; Sunday or Sabbath Schools: 2,483; Total Enrollment: 155,766; Ordained Clergy: 2,895

GENERAL ORGANIZATION

National Association meets annually (July)
National Offices: 1134 Murfreesboro Rd., Nashville, TN 37217. Tel. (615) 361-1010
Mailing Address: P.O. Box 1088, Nashville, TN 37202

OFFICERS

Exec. Sec., Dr. Melvin Worthington, P. O. Box 1088, Nashville, TN 37202. Tel. (615) 361-1010
Mod., Rev. Ralph Hampton, P.O. Box 50117, Nashville, TN 37205

DENOMINATIONAL AGENCIES

Executive Office, P.O. Box 1088, Nashville, TN 37202
Free Will Baptist National Offices, P.O. Box 1088, Nashville, TN 37202
Free Will Baptist Foundation: Exec. Sec., Herman Hersey
Free Will Baptist Bible College: Pres., Dr. Charles Thigpen
Foreign Missions Dept.: Dir., Rev. R. Eugene Waddell
Home Missions Dept.: Dir., Rev. Roy Thomas
Board of Retirement: Dir., Rev. Herman Hersey
Historical Commission: Chpsn., David Joslin
Commission for Theological Integrity: Chpsn., Rev. Leroy Forlines
Radio & Television Commission: Chpsn., Mr. Joseph Goodfellow, P.O. Box 50117, Nashville, TN 37205
Sunday School and Church Training Dept.: Dir., Dr. Roger Reeds
Woman's National Auxiliary Convention: Exec. Sec., Dr. Mary R. Wisehart
Master's Men Dept.:, Dir., Mr. James Vallance

PERIODICALS

Contact (m), P.O. Box 1088, Nashville, TN 37202, Jack Williams, Ed.

Free Will Baptist Gem (m), P. O. Box 991., Lebanon, MO 65536, Rev. Clarence Burton, Ed.

Bible College Bulletin (m), 3606 West End Ave., Nashville, TN 37205, Bert Tippett, Ed.

Heartbeat, Foreign Missions Office, P. O. Box 1088, Nashville, TN 37202, Don Robirds, Ed.

Mission Grams, Home Missions Office, P. O. Box 1088, Nashville, TN 37202, Pat Thomas, Ed.

Happenings (q), P.O. Box 1088, Nashville, TN 37202, Vernie Hersey, Ed.

Co-Laborer, Woman's National Auxiliary Convention (bi-m), P.O. Box 1088, Nashville, TN 37202, Lorene Miley, Ed.

Friends General Conference

Friends General Conference is an association of yearly meetings open to all Friends meetings which wish to be actively associated with its programs and services. It was organized in 1900 bringing together four associations, including the First-day School Conference (1868) and the Friends Union for Philanthropic Labor (1882). The General Conference includes Baltimore, Canadian, Illinois, Lake Erie, New England, New York, Northern, Ohio Valley, Philadelphia, South Central, and Southeastern Yearly Meetings; Southern Appalachian Yearly Meeting and Association, Piedmont Friends Fellowship (NC), Central Alaska Friends Conference, Manhattan (KS), Minneapolis (MN), Morgantown (WV), Oread (KS), and Topeka (KS) monthly meetings. From its beginning, FGC held week-long family conferences biennially at Cape May, N.J. Since 1968, the conferences, FGC Gathering of Friends, have been held annually on college campuses throughout the East and Midwest. All Friends are invited to attend.

Friends General Conference is primarily a service organization and has no authority over constituent meetings. A Central Committee, to which constituent yearly meetings name appointees approximately in proportion to membership, or its Executive Committee, is responsible for the direction of the FGC's program of year-round services. A staff of twelve administers the programs.

There are six standing program committees: Advancement & Outreach, Christian & Interfaith Relations, Long Range Conference Planning, Ministry & Nurture, Publications & Communication, and Religious Education. The Advancement & Outreach Committee actively promotes intervisitation among Friends, nurtures new worship groups, and distributes material to interpret the Religious Society of Friends and to attract seekers. The Christian & Interfaith Relations Committee fosters a dialogue with Friends United Meeting and other Quaker groups, participates in ecumenical activities, maintains an active relationship with the World Council of Churches, and is an informal participant in the Quaker Theological Discussion Group. The Long Range Conference Planning Committee is responsible for establishing the annual Gathering planing committees, and for overall Gathering policy and communication with host colleges.

The Ministry & Nurture Committee oversees the FGC Field Secretary program, and nurtures the life of the Spirit within monthly meetings, yearly meetings, and within the FGC Central Committee. It also sponsors visits by staff and Central Committee members to yearly meetings. The Publications & Communications Committee publishes and distributes a wide variety of First-day School curriculum and other Quaker materials, and publishes the FGC Quarterly, which contains inspirational and informational articles intended to strengthen monthly meeting life. It has a circulation of approximately 26,000 households. The Religious Education Committee creates curriculum for First-day School and home use, sponsors leadership training workshops, and supports religious education in junior yearly meeting programs and in monthly meetings.

The Friends Meeting House Fund, Inc., operates under its own board of directors appointed by the Central Committee, and was established to provide financial assistance to meetings wanting to build, buy, or remodel their own meeting houses. Funds are available for grant or loan. Such funds are derived from money given or invested in the Friends Meeting House Fund for that purpose.

The Friends Journal is not a publication of Friends General Conference, but is closely identified with it. The Friends Journal is managed by a board named in part by the Central Committee of Friends General Conference.

GENERAL ORGANIZATION

Gathering of Friends: annual (July)
Headquarters: 1520-B Race St., Philadelphia, PA 19102. Tel. (215) 241-7270
Gen. Sec., Meredith Walton

OFFICERS

Gen. Sec., Meredith Walton
Clk., Elizabeth H. Muench
Treas., Tyla Ann Burger-Arroyo

PERIODICAL

FGC Quarterly (q), 1520-B Race St., Philadelphia, PA 19102, Mary Moehlman, Ed.

YEARLY MEETINGS

(Note: * denotes Meetings which are also affiliated with Friends United Meeting)

Philadelphia YM, Samuel D. Caldwell, 1515 Cherry St., Philadelphia, PA 19102

Lake Erie YM, Isabel Bliss, 7700 Clark's Lake Rd., Chelsea, MI 48118

*New England YM, William Kriebel, 19 Rufus Jones Lane, No. Easton, MA 02356

*New York YM, Mary Foster Cadbury, Bulls Head Rd., Clinton Corners, NY 12514

*Baltimore YM, Winifred Walker-Jones, 17100 Quaker Lane, Sandy Spring, MD 20860

*Canadian YM, Edward Bell, 2339 Briar Hill Dr., Ottawa, ON K1H 7A7, Canada

Illinois YM, Paul Buckley, RR1, Dewey St., Matteson, IL 60443

Ohio Valley YM, Barbarie Hill, 6921 Stonington Rd., Cincinnati, OH 45230

South Central YM, Dee Rogers, 2930 Riverbend, Humble, TX 77339

*Southeastern YM, Doris Emerson, 1551 Salvatierra Dr., Coral Gables, FL 33134

Northern YM, John Martinson, 270 W. Cottage Place, St. Paul, MN 55126

Piedmont FF, Marian Beane, 7125 Cardigan Ave., Charlotte, NC 28215

Southern Appalachian YM & Assoc., Tim Lamm, Rt. 4, Box 636A, Berea, KY 40404

Central Alaska F. C., Jim Cheydleur, P.O. 81177, Fairbanks, AK 99708

Friends United Meeting

Friends United Meeting was organized in 1902 (originally Five Years Meeting of Friends, the name was changed in 1963) as a loose confederation of North American yearly meetings to facilitate a united Quaker witness in missions, peace work, and Christian education.

Today Friends United Meeting is comprised of eighteen member yearly meetings (12 North American plus Cuba, East Africa, East Africa Yearly Meeting (South) Elgon Religious Society of Friends, Nairobi and Jamaica Yearly Meetings) representing about half the Friends in the world. FUM's current work includes programs of mission and service, peace education, leadership and stewardship development, and the publication of Christian education curriculum, books of Quaker history and religious thought, and a magazine, Quaker Life.

Churches: 533; Inclusive Membership: 56,495; Sunday or Sabbath Schools: 398; Total Enrollment: 25,776; Ordained Clergy: 595

GENERAL ORGANIZATION

Friends United Meeting: triennial (next meeting, 1990)

OFFICERS

Presiding Clk., Paul Enyart, 101 Quaker Hill Dr., Richmond, IN 47374
Treas., John Norris, 101 Quaker Hill Dr., Richmond, IN 47374
Gen. Sec., Stephen Main, 101 Quaker Hill Dr., Richmond, IN 47374

DEPARTMENTS

(All located at 101 Quaker Hill Dr., Richmond, IN 47374)
World Ministries Commission, Assoc. Sec., Bill Wagoner
Meeting Ministries Commission, Assoc. Sec., Mary Glenn Hadley
Communications Commission, _____
Quaker Hill Bookstore Mgr., Ardee Talbot
Friends United Press, Barbara Mays, Ed.

PERIODICALS

Quaker Life, 101 Quaker Hill Dr., Richmond, IN 47374, J. Stanley Banker, Ed.

YEARLY MEETINGS

(Note: * denotes Meetings which are also affiliated with the Friends General Conference)
Nebraska YM, Dean Young, 417 S. Millwood, Wichita, KS 67213
*New England YM, Janet Hoffman, 343 West St., Amherst, MA 01002
*New York YM, Mary Foster Cadbury, Bulls Head Rd., Clinton Corners, NY 12514
*Baltimore YM, Winifred Walker-Jones, 17100 Quaker La., Sandy Spring, MD 20860
Iowa YM, Richard Whitehead, Box 552, Oskaloosa, IA 52577
Western YM, Lester Paulsen, P.O. Box 235, Plainfield, IN 46168
North Carolina YM Sarah Wilson, 903 New Garden Rd., Greensboro, NC 27410
Indiana YM, Horace Smith, Rt. 2, Box 291, Hagerstown, IN 47346
Wilmington YM, Robert Bevan, Sr., Box 1194, Wilmington College, Wilmington, OH 45177
Cuba YM, Ernesto Gurri Acosta, Calixto Garcia #69, Gibara, Holguin, Cuba
*Canadian YM, Donald Laitin, R. R. #5, Mono Mills, Orangeville, Ontario L9W 2Z2
Jamaica YM, Frank Davis, 11 Caledonia Ave., Kingston 5, Jamaica, W.I.
*Southeastern YM, Doris Emerson, 1551 Salvatierra Dr., Coral Gables FL 33134
Southwest YM, Lind Coop, 15915 E. Russell St., Whittier, CA 90603
East Africa YM, Peter Dembebe, P.O. Box 35, Tiriki, Kenya, East Africa
East Africa YM (South), Joseph Kisia, P.O. Box 160, Vihiga, Kenya, East Africa
Nairobi YM, Stanley Ndezwa, P.O. Box 377, Nakuru, Kenya, East Africa
Elgon Religious Society of Friends, Elisha Wakube, P.O. Box 98, Kimilili, Kenya, East Africa

Full Gospel Assemblies International

This Pentecostal body had its beginning in 1972 as an adjunct to an established school of biblical studies known as Full Gospel Bible Institute under the leadership of Dr. Charles E. Strauser.

GENERAL ORGANIZATION

Headquarters: R.D. #2, Box 520, Parkesburg, PA 19365. Tel. (215)857-2357

OFFICERS

Pres.: Dr. Charles E. Strauser
Asst.: Dr. Annamae Strauser
Executive Board: Dr. C. E. Strauser, Dr. Annamae Strauser, Rev. Simeon Strauser, Miss Carol Ann Strauser
Bd. of Directors: Rev. Harold Oswold, 340 Rand St., Rochester, NY 14611; Rev. Harry E. Constein, III, 2235 Blossom Valley Rd., Lancaster, PA 17601; Simeon Strauser, Box 38, Sadsburyville, PA 19369; Rev. Samuel Strauser, Box 450, Delaware Water Gap, PA 18327; Dr. Annamae Strauser, P.O. Box 1230, Coatesville, PA 19320

PERIODICAL

The Charisma Courier, P. O. Box 1230, Coatesville, PA 19320. C. E. Strauser, Ed. Tel. (215)857-2357

Full Gospel Fellowship of Churches and Ministers International

In the early 1960s, a conviction grew in the hearts of many ministers that there ought to be closer fellowship between the people of God who believed in the apostolic ministry. Also, a great number of independent churches were experiencing serious difficulties in receiving authority from the IRS to give governmentally accepted tax-exempt receipts for donations.

In September 1962, a group of ministers met in Dallas, Texas, to form a Fellowship to give expression to the essential unity of the Body of Christ under the leadership of the Holy Spirit—a unity that goes beyond individuals, churches, or organizations. This was not a movement to build another denomination, but rather an effort to join ministers and churches of like feeling across denominational lines.

To provide opportunities for fellowship and to support the objectives and goals of local and national ministries, regional conventions and an annual international convention are held.

Churches: 450; Inclusive Membership: 65,000; Sunday or Sabbath Schools: 450; Total Enrollment: 45,000; Ordained Clergy: 850

GENERAL ORGANIZATION

Annual Conference (next convention, July 11-14, 1988, Sheraton Hotel Downtown, Dallas, TX)
Headquarters: FGFCMI General Conference, 1545 W. Mockingbird Lane, Ste. 1012, Dallas, TX 75235. Tel. (214) 630-1941

OFFICERS

Pres., James H. Helton, 1734 S. Walnut, Muncie, IN 47302
1st Vice-Pres., Don Arnold, P. O. Box 324, Gasden, AL 35901
Treas., Dr. H. K. McKnight, 1857 Fenwick St., Augusta, GA 30904
Sec., Dr. Chester P. Jenkins, P.O. Box 309, Hamlin, PA 18427
Vice-Presidents at Large: R. Richard Edgar, 5304 Edith St., Charleston, SC 29418; Maurice Hart, P. O. Box 4316, Omaha NE 68104; Don Westbrook, 3005 Ross Rd., Durham, NC 27703
Regional Vice-Presidents: Sortheast, Don Arnold, P. O. Box 324, Gadsden, AL 35901; South Central, Turner

Scogin, 2601 Pecos, Ft. Worth, TX 76119; Southwest, Gene May, 2309 W. 227th St., Torrance CA 90501; Northeast, Dr. Ray L. Chamberlain, P.O. Box 986, Salisbury, MD 21801; North Central, Raymond Rothwell, P.O. Box 367, Eaton, OH 45320; Northwest, Ralph Trask, 3212 Hyacinth St. N.E., Salem, OR 97303

Fundamental Methodist Church, Inc.

This group traces its origin through the Methodist Protestant Church. It withdrew from The Methodist Church and organized on August 27, 1942.

Churches: 13; Inclusive Membership: 698; Sunday or Sabbath Schools: 13; Total Enrollment: 515; Ordained Clergy: 23

GENERAL ORGANIZATION

Conference: Annual (at Conference Grounds, Lawrence Country, Ash Grove, MO)
Headquarters: 1028 N. Broadway, Springfield, MO 65802
Treas., Mr. Everett Etheridge, 3844 Dover, Springfield, MO 65802. Tel. (417)865-4438
Sec., Mrs. Betty Nicholson, Rt. 2, Box 397, Ash Grove, MO 65604. Tel. (417) 672-2268
Dist. Supt., Rev. Ronnie Fieker, Rt. 2, Ash Grove, MO 65604.

PERIODICAL

Fundamental Methodist Informer (m), Rev. Leroy Pugh, Ed.

General Association of Regular Baptist Churches

Founded in May, 1932, in Chicago, Illinois, by a group of churches which had withdrawn from the Northern Baptist Convention (now the American Baptist Churches in the U.S.A.) because of doctrinal differences. Its Confession of Faith, which it requires all churches to subscribe to, is essentially the old, historic New Hampshire Confession of Faith with a premillennial ending applied to the last article.

GENERAL ORGANIZATION

Meets annually
Home Office: 1300 N. Meacham Rd., Schaumburg, IL 60173. (312) 843-1600

OFFICERS

Chpsn., Dr. David Nettleton
Vice-Chpsn., Dr. Paul Dixon
Treas., Vernon Miller
Sec., Dr. John White
National Representative, Dr. Paul Tassell, 1300 N. Meacham Rd., Schaumburg, IL 60173

PERIODICAL

Baptist Bulletin (m), 1300 N. Meacham Rd., Schaumburg, IL 60173 Vernon Miller, Ed.

General Baptists (General Association of)

Similar in doctrine to those General Baptists organized in England in the early seventeenth century, the first General Bappist churches were organized on the Midwest frontier following the Second Great Awakening. The first church was established by the group's founding father, Rev. Benoni Stinson, in 1823 at Evansville, Ind.
Stinson's major theological emphasis was general atonement—"Christ tasted death for every man." The group also allows for the possibility of apostasy. It practices open Communion and believer's baptism by immersion.

Called "liberal" Baptists because of their emphasis on the freedom of man, General Baptists organized a General Association in 1870 and invited other "liberal" Baptists (e.g., "free will" and Separate Baptists) to participate. Only a few churches did so.
Today the policy-setting body is composed of delegates from local General Baptist associations. Each local church is autonomous but belongs to an association. The group currently consists of more than 60 associations in 16 states, as well as several associations in the Philippines, Guam, Saipan, Jamaica, and India. One unique aspect of General Baptist polity is that ministers and deacons are ordained by a presbytery.
A number of boards continue a variety of missions, schools, and other support ministries. General Baptists belong to the Baptist World Alliance and the North American Baptist Fellowship.

Churches: 871; Inclusive Membership: 72,263; Sunday or Sabbath Schools: N.R.; Total Enrollment: N.R.; Ordained Clergy: 1,444

GENERAL ORGANIZATION

General Association: annual
Headquarters: 100 Stinson Dr., Poplar Bluff, MO 63901

OFFICERS

Mod., Rev. Dean Trivitt, 113A Kate Dr., Sikeston, MO 63801
Clerk, Rev. Edwin Runyon, 801 Kendall, Poplar Bluff, MO 63901
Exec. Dir., Dr. Glen O. Spence, 100 Stinson Dr., Poplar Bluff, MO 63901

OTHER ORGANIZATIONS

General Board: Sec., Rev. Edwin Runyon, 801 Kendall, Poplar Bluff, MO 63901
Foreign Mission Board: Exec. Dir., Rev. Charles Carr, 100 Stinson Dr., Poplar Bluff, MO 63901
Board of Christian Education and Publications: Exec. Dir., Rev. Vyron Yount, 100 Stinson Dr., Poplar Bluff, MO 63901
Home Mission Board Exec. Dir., Dr. Leland Duncan, 100 Stinson Dr., Poplar Bluff, MO 63901
Ministers' Aid Board: Sec., Mr. Charles Weir, 7300 Oakdale Dr., Newburgh, IN 47630
Brotherhood Board: Exec. Dir., Mr. Austin Hearon, P.O. Box 452, Clay, KY 42404
Women's Mission Board: Exec. Dir., Mrs. Brenda Kennedy, 100 Stinson Dr., Poplar Bluff, MO 63901
Stewardship Dir., Rev. Ron D. Black, 100 Stinson Dr., Poplar Bluff, MO 63901
Nursing Home Adm., Ms. Wanda Britt, Rt. #2, Box 230, Campbell, MO 63933
College Board: Pres., Dr. Jim Murray, Oakland City College, P.O. Box 235, Oakland City, IN 47660
Publishing House, General Baptist Press, 400 Stinson Dr., Poplar Bluff, MO 63901. Rev. Wayne Foust

PERIODICALS

General Baptist Messenger (m), 100 Stinson Dr., Poplar Bluff, MO 63901, Rev. Wayne Foust, Ed.
Capsule, Rev. Charles Carr, Ed.
Voice, Dr. Leland Duncan, Ed.
WMS Newsletter, Mrs. Brenda Kennedy, Ed.

General Church of the New Jerusalem

The General Church of the New Jerusalem is the result of a reorganization in 1897 of the General Church of The Advent of the Lord. It stresses the full acceptance of the doctrines contained in the theological writings of Emanuel Swedenborg.

GENERAL ORGANIZATION

General Assembly (International), meets every three or four years

Headquarters: Bryn Athyn, PA 19009. Tel. (215) 947-4660

OFFICERS

Presiding Bishop, Rt. Rev. L. B. King
Sec., Rev. Lorentz R. Soneson
Treas., Neil M. Buss

PERIODICAL

New Church Life (m), Bryn Athyn, PA 19009 Rev. Donald L. Rose, Ed.

General Conference of Mennonite Brethren Churches

A small group, which had been requesting that closer attention be paid to prayer and Bible study, withdrew in 1860 from the Mennonite Church in the Ukraine. Pietistic in organization, the group adopted a Baptistic policy. In 1874, small bodies of German-speaking Mennonites left Russia, reached Kansas in 1876, then spread to the Pacific Coast and into Canada. In 1960, the Krimmer Mennonite Brethren Conference merged with this body. Today the General Conference of Mennonite Brethren Churches conducts services in many European languages as well as in Vietnamese, Mandarin, and Hindi. It works with other denominations in missionary and development projects in 23 countries outside North America.

GENERAL ORGANIZATION

General Convention: triennial

OFFICERS

Chpsn., Herb Brandt, 1423 Vineland St., Kelowna, British Columbia V1Y 7R9
Vice-Chpsn., Edmund Janzen, 1717 S. Chestnut Ave., Fresno, CA 93727
Sec., Bill A. Wiebe, 33020 Maclure Rd., Abbotsford, British Columbia V2S 4N3

PERIODICALS

Christian Leader (bi-w), Hillsboro, KS 67063, Don Ratzlaff, Ed.
Mennonite Brethren Herald, Winnipeg, Manitoba Canada, Herb Kopp, Ed.

General Conference of the Evangelical Baptist Church, Inc.

This denomination is an Arminian, Wesleyan, premillennial group whose form of government is congregational.

It was organized in 1935, and was formerly known as the Church of the Full Gospel, Inc.

GENERAL ORGANIZATION

General Conference: annual (Third Week in October)
Headquarters: 1601 E. Rose St., Goldsboro, NC 27530. Tel. (919) 734-2482

OFFICERS

Pres., Rev. David J. Crawford, 1616 Maple St., Goldsboro, NC 27530. Tel. (919)734-2482
1st Vice-Pres., Dr. Harry E. Jones, 616 Chad Dr., Rocky Mount, NC 27801. Tel. (919)443-1239
2nd Vice-Pres., Rev. George C. Wallace, 909 W. Walnut St., Chanute, KS 66720. Tel. (316)431-0706
Sec./Treas., Mrs. Evelyn Crawford, 1616 Maple St., Goldsboro, NC 27530. Tel. (919)734-2482
Dir. of Evangelism, Rev. B. L. Proctor, Rt. 3, Box 442, Nashville, NC 27856. Tel. (919)459-2063

Dir. of Women's Work, Mrs. Elizabeth Davis, Rt. 2 Box 222, Pikesville, NC 27865
Dir. of Youth Work, Rev. Ralph Jarrell, P.O. Box 1112, Burgaw, NC 28425. Tel. (919)259-9329

General Convention of The Swedenborgian Church

Founded in North America in 1972 as the Church of the New Jerusalem, the General Convention was organized as a national body in 1817 and incorporated in the state of Illinois in 1861.

Its biblically based theology is derived from the spiritual, or mystical, experiences and exhaustive biblical studies of the Swedish scientist and philosopher Emanuel Swedenborg (1688–1772).

The church centers its worship and teachings on the historical life and the risen and glorified present reality of the Lord Jesus Christ. It looks with an ecumenical vision toward the establishment of the kingdom of God in the form of a universal Church, active in the lives of all people of good will who desire and strive for freedom, peace, and justice for all. It is a member of the NCCC and active in many local councils of churches.

With churches and groups throughout the United States and Canada, the Convention's central administrative offices and its seminary—Swedenborg School of Religion—are located in Newton, Mass. Affiliated churches are found in Africa, Asia, Australia, Europe, the United Kingdom, Japan, and South America. Many internationally prominent philosphers and writers, past and present, have acknowledged their appreciation of the teachings of Emanuel Swedenborg, which form the basis of this global church.

GENERAL ORGANIZATION

General Convention: annual (June)

OFFICERS

Pres., Rev. Randall E. Laakko, 1025 Dettling Rd., Woodland Heights, Wilmington, DE 19805
Vice-Pres., Frederick G. Perry, Jr., Jackson Ridge, Box 50, Jackson, NH 03846
Sec., Mrs. Dorothy deB. Young, 88 Turnpike St., South Easton, MA 02375
Treas., John C. Perry, RFD 2, Box 2341A, Brunswick, ME 04011
Office Dir., Miss Ethelwyn Worden, 48 Sargent St., Newton, MA 02158

PERIODICAL

The Messenger (m), 48 Sargent St., Newton, MA 02158, Rev. James Lawrence, Ed.

General Six Principle Baptists

A Baptist Group, organized in Rhode Island in 1653, drawing its name from Heb. 6:1-2.

GENERAL ORGANIZATION

Conferences in Rhode Island and Pennsylvania: annually, in September

OFFICERS

Rhode Island Conference: Pres., Rev. Edgar S. Kirk, 350 Davisville Rd., North Kingstown, RI 02852. Tel. (401)884-2750
Clk., Miss Sylvia Stoner, RR #1, Box 170, Wyoming, RI 02898
Pennsylvania Association: Pres., Elder Daniel E. Carpenetti, Nicholson, PA 18446. Tel. (717)942-6578
Clk., Mrs. Eleanor Warner, Rt. 1, Nicholson, PA 18446

Grace Brethren Churches, Fellowship of

A division occurred in the Church of the Brethren in 1882 on the question of the legislative authority of the annual meeting. It resulted in the establishment of this body under a legal charter requiring congregational government.

OFFICERS

Mod., Dr. John Davies, P.O. Box 635, Winona Lake, IN 46590
Mod. Elect, Dean Fetterhoff, 406 Truth St., Marietta, GA 30066
Conf. Coord., Charles Ashman, P.O. Box 386, Winona Lake IN 46590. Tel. (219)267-5566 or (219)267-6623
Sec., Rev. Kenneth Koontz, 855 Turnbull St., Delona FL 32725. Tel. (904)789-6512
Treas., Mr. Larry N. Chamberlain, R. 1, Box 425A, Warsaw, IN 46580
Statistician, Rev. Sherwood Durkee, Rural Rt. 8, Box 49, Warsaw, IN 46580

OTHER BOARDS

Foreign Missionary Society: Exec. Dir., Rev. Tom Julien, P.O. Box 588, Winona Lake, IN 46590; Treas., Mr. Herman J. Schumacher, R1, Lakes Estate, Lot #65, Warsaw, IN 46580
Brethren Home Missions: Exec. Dir., Dr. Robert Thompson, P.O. Box 587, Winona Lake, IN 46590
Grace Schools, 200 Seminary Dr., Winona Lake, IN 46590. Tel. (210)372-5100. Pres., Dr. John Davis
Brethren Missionary Herald Co.: Publisher & Gen. Mgr., Charles Turner, P.O. Box 544, Winona Lake, IN 46590
Women's Missionary Council: Pres., Margaret Devan, 2507 Vancouver Dr. NW, Roanoke, VA 24012
GBC Christian Education: Exec. Dir., Rev. Ed Lewis, P.O. Box 365, Winona Lake, IN 46590
Grace Brethren Men & Boys: Exec. Dir., Rev. Ed Jackson, P.O. Box 416, Winona Lake, IN 46590

PERIODICAL

Brethren Missionary Herald, P.O. Box 544, Winona Lake, IN 46590 Ed., Rev. Charles Turner

Grace Gospel Fellowship

The Grace Gospel Fellowship was organized in 1944 by a group of pastors who held to a dispensational interpretation of Scripture. Most of these men had ministries in the Midwest (Ill., Ind., Wis., Ohio, Mo.). Two prominent leaders were J. C. O'Hair of Chicago and Charles Baker of Milwaukee.

Subsequent to 1945, a Bible Institute was founded (now Grace Bible College of Grand Rapids, Mich.), and a previously organized foreign mission (now Grace Ministries International of Grand Rapids) was affiliated with the group. Churches have now been established in most sections of the country.

The body has remained a fellowship, each church being autonomous in polity. All support for its college, mission, and headquarters is on a contributary basis.

The binding force of the Fellowship has been the members' doctrinal position. They believe in the Deity and Saviorship of Jesus Christ and subscribe to the inerrant authority of Scripture. Their method of biblical interpretation is dispensational, with emphasis on the distinctive revelation to and the ministry of the apostle Paul.

Churches: 52; Inclusive Membership: 4,400; Sunday or Sabbath School: N.R.; Total Enrollment: N.R.; Ordained Clergy: 122

GENERAL ORGANIZATION

National Cabinet which recommends policies and programs to the annual convention for approval. After approval it presents them to the constituent churches for voluntary united action.

OFFICERS

Pres., Charles E. O'Connor, 1011 Aldon St., SW, Grand Rapids, MI 49509. Tel. (616) 531-0046

OTHER ORGANIZATIONS

Grace Bible College, 1011 Aldon St., S.W., Grand Rapids, MI 49509. Pres., Dr. Samval Vinton
Grace Ministries International, 2125 Martindale Ave., SW, Grand Rapids, MI 49509. Exec. Dir., Wayne Schoonover
Missionary Literature Distributors, 7514 Humbert Rd., Godfrey, IL 62305. Dir., Mrs. Betty Strelow
Prison Mission Association, P.O. Box 3397, Riverside, CA 92509. Gen. Dir., Mr. Joe Mason
Grace Publications, Inc., 2125 Martindale Ave., SW, Grand Rapids, MI 49509. Exec. Dir., Timothy Conklin
Bible Doctrines to Live By, P.O. Box 2351, Grand Rapids, MI 49501. Exec. Dir., Lee Homoki

PERIODICAL

Truth (bi-m), 1011 Aldon, S.W., Grand Rapids, MI 49509

Greek Orthodox Archdiocese of North and South America

The Greek Orthodox Archdiocese of North and South America is under the jurisdiction of the Ecumenical Patriarchate of Constantinople, in Istanbul. It was chartered in 1922 by the State of New York and has parishes in the United States, Canada, Central and South America. The first Greek Orthodox Church was founded in New Orleans, Louisiana, in 1864.

GENERAL ORGANIZATION

His Eminence Archbishop Iakovos, Primate of the Greek Orthodox Church of North and South America and Exarch of the Ecumenical Patriarchate in the Western Hemisphere
Biennial Clergy-Laity Congress—29th Congress to be held in Boston in July, 1988
Headquarters: 8-10 E. 79th St., New York, NY 10021. Tel. (212) 570-3500

ARCHDIOCESAN COUNCIL

Chpsn., Archbishop Iakovos
Officers:
Pres., Andrew A. Athens (Chicago, IL)
1st Vice-Pres., Mr. George Condakes (Boston)
2nd Vice-Pres., Mr. George Chimples (Cleveland)
Sec., Mr. Peter Kourides (New York, NY)
Asst. Sec., Mrs. Elenie Huszagh (Chicago)
Treas., Mr. Michael Jaharis, Jr. (New York City)

SYNOD OF BISHOPS

His Eminence Archbishop Iakovos, Chpsn.
His Excellency Metropolitan Silas of New Jersey, 8 East 79th St., New York, NY 10021
His Grace Bishop Iakovos of Chicago, Forty East Burton Place., Chicago, IL 60610
His Grace Bishop John of Atlanta, 2801 Buford Highway, Ste. 365, Atlanta, GA 30329
His Grace Bishop Timothy of Detroit, 19504 Renfrew, Detroit, MI 48211
His Grace Bishop Sotirios of Toronto, 40 Donlands Ave., Toronto, Ontario M4J 3N6

His Grace Bishop Anthony of San Francisco, 372 Santa Clara Ave., San Francisco, CA 94127
His Grace Bishop Maximos of Pittsburgh, 5201 Ellsworth Ave., Pittsburgh, PA 15232
His Grace Bishop Gennadios of Buenos Aires, Avenida Figueroa Alcorta 3187, Buenos Aires, Argentina
_____, 10225 East Gill Place, Denver, CO 80231
His Grace Bishop Methodios of Boston, 162 Goddard Ave., Brookline, MA 02146

ASSISTANT BISHOPS TO ARCHBISHOP IAKOVOS
(Unless otherwise indicated, located at 8-10 E. 79th St., New York, NY 10021)
His Grace Bishop Philotheos of Meloa; His Grace Bishop Kallistos of Zelon, Patriarch Athenagoras Retreat Center, Cheyenne WY 82001; His Grace Bishop Philip of Daphnousia, 27-09 Crescent St., Astoria, NY 11102; His Grace Bishop Athenagoras of Dorylaion; His Grace Bishop Isaiah of Aspendos, Chancellor; His Grace Bishop Alexios of Troas, Chorepiscopos of Astoria, 30-11 30th Dr., Astoria, NY 11102

ARCHDIOCESAN DEPARTMENTS
(Unless otherwise indicated, located at 8-10 E. 79th St., New York, NY 10021)
Rel. Ed., 50 Goddard Ave., Brookline MA 02146; Youth Ministry and Camping, 39-10 Broadway, Astoria NY 11106; Church and Society; Economic Development; Ecumenical Stewardship Registry; Ionian Village; Communications; Archives; Logos, 36-10 Broadway, Astoria, NY 11106; Church and Society Mission Center, P.O. Box 4319, St. Augustine, FL 32085

ORGANIZATIONS
(Unless otherwise indicated, located at 8-10 E. 79th St., New York, NY 10021)
Ladies Philoptochos Society
Greek Orthodox Young Adult League (GOYAL), 27-09 Crescent St., Astoria, NY 11102
Order of St. Andrew the Apostle
Archdiocesan Presbyters' Council, 707 E. Lafayette Blvd., Detroit, MI 48226
National Sisterhood of Presvyteres, 1401 Wagner Rd., Glenview, IL 60025
National Forum of Greek Orthodox Church Musicians, 1700 N. Walnut St., Bloomington, IN 47401

PERIODICAL
The Orthodox Observer (bi-w), 8-10 E. 79th St., New York, NY 10021

The Holiness Church of God, Inc.

Established at Madison, North Carolina, in 1920; incorporated in 1928 at Winston-Salem, North Carolina

GENERAL ORGANIZATION
General Assembly: annual
Headquarters: Winston-Salem, NC

OFFICERS
Pres., Bishop B. McKinney, 602 E. Elm St., Graham, NC 27253
Vice-Bishop, Melvin Charley, 140-39 172nd St., Springfield Gardens, NY 11434
Gen. Sec., Mrs. Nina B. Hash, Box 541, Galax, VA 24333
Overseer, Northern Area of N.E. Dist., Melvin Charley, 140-39 172nd St., Springfield Gardens, NY 11434
Overseer, Southern Area of N.E. Dist. Edwin D. Talor, 1523 Wilard St., High Point, NC 27260
Overseer, So. Dist., Bishop T. R. Rice, 1439 Sedgefield Dr., Winston-Salem NC 27105. Tel. (919)227-4755
Overseer, Va. & W. Va., Area of N.W. Dist., Elder Arnie Joyce, Thorpe, WV 24888
Overseer, North Carolina Area of N.W. Dist., W. H. Alston, 510 East Elm St., Graham, NC 27253. Tel. (919)227-2755

Holy Ukrainian Autocephalic Orthodox Church in Exile

Organized in a parish in New York in 1951. The laymen and clergy who organized it came from among the Ukrainians who settled in the Western Hemisphere after World War II. In 1954 two bishops, immigrants from Europe, met with clergy and laymen and formally organized the religious body.

GENERAL ORGANIZATION
Headquarters: 103 Evergreen St., W. Babylon, NY 11704
Administrator: Rt. Rev. Serhij K. Pastukhiv. Tel. (516) 669-7402

House of God, Which is the Church of the Living God, the Pillar and Ground of the Truth, Inc.

Organized 1919

GENERAL ORGANIZATION
Meets annually, in October

OFFICER
Bishop Raymond W. White, 6107 Cobbs Creek Pkwy., Philadelphia, PA 19143. Tel. (215) 748-6338

PERIODICAL
Spirit of Truth Magazine (m), 3943 Fairmont Ave., Philadelphia, PA 19104. Bishop Raymond A. White, Ed.

Hungarian Reformed Church in America

A Hungarian Reformed Church was organized in New York in 1904 in connection with the Reformed Church of Hungary. In 1922 the Church in Hungary transferred most of her congregations in the U.S. to the Reformed Church in the U.S. Some, however, preferred to continue as an autonomous, self-supporting American denomination, and these formed the Free Magyar Reformed Church in America. This group changed its name in 1958 to Hungarian Reformed Church in America.
This Church is a member of the World Alliance of Reformed Churches, Presbyterian and Congregational, the WCC and the NCCC. It is deeply involved in the Roman Catholic, Presbyterian Reformed Consultation, of which for over 10 years Dr. Andrew Harsanyi has been co-chairman.

OFFICERS
Bishop, Rt. Rev. Dr. Andrew Harsanyi, P.O. Box D, Hopatcong, NJ 07843
Chief Lay-Curator, Anthony C. Beke, Box 335, Crosswick, NJ 08515
Gen. Sec., Rt. Rev. Dezso Trombitas, 751 Crenshaw Blvd., Los Angeles, CA 90005
Gen. Sec. (Lay), Prof. Stephen Szabo, 464 Forest Ave., Paramus, NJ 07652
Dean, New York Classis, The Very Rev. Alex Forro, 13 Grove Ave., Poughkeepsie, NY 12601
Dean, Western Classis, The Very Rev. Denes Tamas, 101 University Dr., McKeesport, PA 15132
Dean, Eastern Classis, The Very Rev. Stefan M. Torok, 331 Kirkland Pl., Perth Amboy, NJ 08861.

PERIODICAL
Magyar Egyhaz (Magyar Church) (6/yr.), Stefan Torok, Perth Amboy, NJ, Ed.

73

Hutterian Brethren

Small groups of Hutterites deriving their names from an early martyr, Jacob Huter (1536). They have all things in common and share income and expenses. There are 375 colonies of Hutterites throughout the world with approximately 37,000 members, 10,000 of which are unbaptized. Ordained ministers number 600 and there are an aditional 75 unordained ministers.

CORRESPONDENT

Rev. Paul S. Gross, Rt. 1, Box 6E, Reardon WA 99029

Independent Assemblies of God, International

April 9, 1906 is the date commonly accepted by Pentecostals as the twentieth century outpouring of God's Spirit in America, which began in a humble Gospel Mission at 312 Asusa Street in Los Angeles.

This Spirit Movement spread across the U.S. and gave birth to the Independent Assemblies of God (Scandanavian). Early pioneers instrumental in guiding and shaping the fellowship of ministers and churches into a nucleus of independent churches included Pastor B. M. Johnson, founder of Lakeview Gospel Church in 1911; Rev. A. A. Holmgren, a Baptist minister who received his baptism of the Holy Spirit in the early Chicago outpourings and was publisher of *Sanningens Vittne*, a voice of the Scandanavian Independent Assemblies of God, and also served as secretary of the fellowship for many years; Gunnar Wingren, missionary pioneer in Brazil; and Arthur F. Johnson,, who served for many years as chairman of the Scandanavian Assemblies.

In 1935, the Scandanavian group dissolved its incorporation and united with the Independent Assemblies of God of the U.S. and Canada which is now known as Independent Assemblies of God, International.

GENERAL ORGANIZATION

Convention: annual
Headquarters: 8504 Commerce Ave., San Diego, CA 92121. Tel. (619)530-1727

OFFICERS

Exec. Dir., Rev. T. A. Lanes, 8504 Commerce Ave., San Diego, CA 92121
Sec., Canada: Harry Nunn, Sr., 15 White Crest Ct., St. Catherines, Ontario 62N 6Y1

PERIODICAL

The Fellowship Magazine, 8504 Commerce Ave., San Diego, CA 92121. Rev. T. A. Lanes, Ed.

Independent Fundamental Churches of America

Organized 1930 at Cicero, Illinois by representatives of the American Council of Undenominational Churches and representatives of various independent churches. The founding churches and members had separated themselves from various denominational affiliations.

The IFCA provides an advance movement among independent churches and ministers to unite in a close fellowship and cooperation, in defense of the fundamental teachings of Scripture and in the proclamation of the gospel of God's grace.

GENERAL ORGANIZATION

Headquarters: 3520 Fairlanes, Grandville, MI 49418
Mailing Address: PO. Box 810, Grandville, MI 49468

EXECUTIVE OFFICERS

National Exec. Dir., Dr. Richard Gregory, 2684 Meadow Ridge Dr., Byron Center, MI 49315
Pres., Dr. Richard Keltner, 1315 North Adams Dr., Colorado Springs, CO 80904
1st Vice-Pres., Dr. Calvin H.C. Probasco, 5640 Vega Ct., Carmichael, CA 95608
2nd Vice-Pres., Dr. Paul Reiter, PO. Box 8, Pratt, WV 25162

PERIODICAL

The Voice (m), P.O. Box 810, Grandville, MI 49468. Rev. Paul J. Dollaske, Ed.

International Church of the Foursquare Gospel

Founded by Aimee Semple McPherson in 1927, the InternationalChurch of the Foursquare Gospel proclaims the message of Jesus Christ the Savior, Healer, Baptizer with the Holy Spirit and Soon-coming King. Headquartered at Angelus Temple in Los Angeles, CA, this evangelistic missionary body of believers consists of nearly 1,300 churches in the United States and Canada.

The International Church of the Foursquare Gospel is incorporated in the State of California and governed by a Board of Directors who direct its corporate affairs. A Missionary Cabinet, consisting of the Board of Directors, District Supervisors of the various districts of Foursquare churches in the United States and other elected or appointed members, serves in an advisory capacity to the President and the Board of Directors.

Each local Foursquare church is a subordinate unit of the International Church of the Foursquare Gospel. The pastor of the church is appointed by the Board of Directors and is responsible for the spiritual and physical welfare of the church. To assist and advise the pastor, a church council is elected by the local church members.

Through a program entitled *2000 Before 2000*, the Foursquare church has envisioned 2,000 churches throughout the United States before the year 2000. Complementing this expansion, Foursquare churches seek to build strong believers through Christian education, Christian day schools, youth camping and ministry, United Foursquare Women who support and encourage Foursquare missionaries abroad, radio and television ministries, the Foursquare World ADVANCE magazine and 48 Bible Colleges worldwide.

Worldwide missions remains the focus of the Foursquare Gospel Church with nearly 15,000 churches, 14,000 national Foursquare pastors/leaders and 1 million members and adherents in 61 countries around the globe.

Churches: 1,250; Inclusive Membership: 186,213; Sunday or Sabbath Schools: 959; Total Enrollment: 42,694; Ordained Clergy: 3,482

GENERAL ORGANIZATION

International Foursquare Convention: annual
Headquarters: Angelus Temple, 1100 Glendale Blvd., Los Angeles, CA 90026. Tel. (213) 484-1100

OFFICERS

Pres., Dr. Rolf K. McPherson
Pres.-Elect, Dr. John Holland

Vice-Pres., Dr. Harold E. Helms
Actg. Gen. Supervisor, Rev. J. Eugene Kurtz
Dir. of Missions International, Dr. Leland B. Edwards
Sec., Rev. John W. Bowers
Treas., Rev. Virginia Cravans
Exec. Sec., Dr. Charles Duarte
Board of Directors: Dr. Rolf K. McPherson, Dr. Howard
P. Courtney, Dr. Leland Edwards, Dr. N. M. Van
Cleave, Rev. Lorna De McPherson, Rev. John Bowers,
Dr. Paul Risser, Dr. Harold Helms, Mr. Dan Boone,
Rev. James Ritch
District Supervisors:
Eastern, Rev. Dewey Morrow
Great Lakes, Dr. Fred Parker
Midwest, Rev. Glen Metzler
Northwest, Rev. Cliff Hanes
South Central, Dr. Sidney Westbrook
Southeast, Dr. Glenn Burris
Southern California, Dr. Paul E. Jones
Southwest, _____
Western, Dr. Fred Wymore
Missionary Cabinet: Composed of Board of Directors,
District Supervisors, Dr. Charles Duarte, Dr. Jack
Hamilton, Rev. Glenn Burris, Jr., Rev. Roger
Whitlow, Rev. Glen Bright, Rev. Phil Demetro, Dr.
Ron Mehl

SUPPORT MINISTRIES

National Department of Youth: National Youth Minister,
Rev. Gregg Johnson
National Department of Christian Education and Publica-
tions: Dir., Rev. Rick Wulfestieg
United Foursquare Women: Pres., Shirley West

MEMBER OF OTHER ORGANIZATIONS

Pentecostal Fellowship of North America
National Association of Evangelicals
World Pentecostal Fellowship

PERIODICALS

(All published at 1100 Glendale Blvd., Los Angeles. CA
90026)
Foursquare World Advance (7/yr.) Rev. Ron Williams,
Ed.
United Foursquare Women's Magazine, Shirley West

The International Pentecostal Church of Christ

At a General Conference held at London, Ohio, August
10, 1976, the International Pentecostal Assemblies and the
Pentecostal Church of Christ, after a two-year trial period,
by overwhelming majority votes from each group,
consolidated into one body, taking the name International
Pentecostal Church of Christ.

The International Pentecostal Assemblies was the
successor of the Association of Pentecostal Assemblies
and the International Pentecostal Missionary Union. The
other body involved in the merger, the Pentecostal Church
of Christ, was founded by John Stroup of Flatwoods,
Kentucky, on May 10, 1917, and was incorporated at
Portsmouth, Ohio, in 1927.

The International Pentecostal Church of Christ is an
active member of the Pentecostal Fellowship of North
America, as well as a member of the National Association
of Evangelicals.

The priorities of the International Pentecostal Church of
Christ are to be an agency of God for evangelizing the
world, to be a corporate body in which man may worship
God, and to be a channel of God's purpose to build a body
of saints being perfected in the image of his Son.

The Annual Conference is held each year during the first
full week of August on Route 42 in London, Ohio, which
houses the Conference Center offices and national
campgrounds.

Churches: 75; Inclusive Membership: 2,743; Sunday or
Sabbath Schools: 75; Total Enrollment: 4,202; Ordained Clergy: 128

GENERAL ORGANIZATION

Headquarters: 2245 St. Rt. 42 SW; Mailing Address: P. O.
Box 439, London, OH 43140. Tel. (614) 852-0348

EXECUTIVE COMMITTEE

Gen. Overseer, Tom G. Grinder, P. O. Box 439, London
OH 43140. Tel. (614) 852-0348
Asst. Gen. Overseer, Clyde M. Hughes, P.O. Box 439,
London OH 43140. Tel. (614)852-0448
Gen. Sec., Rev.Thomas Dooley, 3200 Dueber Ave. S.W.,
Canton OH 44706. Tel. (216)484-6053
Gen. Treas., Rev. Chester I. Miller, P. O. Box 439,
London, OH 43140. Tel. (614) 852-2421
Dir. of Global Missions, Dr. James B. Keiller, P. O. Box
18145, Atlanta, GA 30316. Tel. (404) 627-2681

PERIODICAL

The Bridegroom's Messenger, 121 W. Hunters Trail,
Elizabeth City, NC 27909

Israelite House of David

The Israelite House of David, commonly called House
of David, was established in 1903 in Benton Harbor,
Michigan, by Brother Benjamin, our founder and leader,
after he had preached the Life of the Body without going
to the grave, while traveling for seven years throughout a
number of mid-American states.

We are a Christian Association following Jesus'
teachings (I Tim. 1:16) and the first born among many
brethren (Rom. 8:29). We believe Brother Benjamin to
have been the voice of the seventh angel referred to in
Revelation 10:7; Malachi 3:1; Job 33:23-25. In his writings
he points out the way for the elect to receive the Life of the
Body (Hosea 13:14; Isa. 38:18; I Thess. 5:23; Matt. 7:14;
Titus 1:2; II Tim. 1:10; John 10:10, 27, 28).

Three classes are mainly referred to in the Bible—Jew,
Gentile, and Israel. The Jew and the Gentile will receive
the Soul Salvation, a free Gift (Eph. 2:8). The Elect of
Israel—a few (Matt. 5:5), numbered in the seventh and
fourteenth chapters of Revelation as 144,000 of all the
tribes of the children of Israel—will receive the Life of the
Body. In Zechariah 13:8 we read, "Two parts shall be cut
off and die, but the third part shall be left therein."
According to Isaiah 19:24, Israel will be the third.

In Brother Benjamin's writings are revealed many keys
to the Scriptures, which bring harmony to many apparent
contradictions sealed till the time of the end (Dan. 12:9; I
Cor. 10:11). We expect to gather the 12 tribes of Israel
(Jer. 31:1; Ezek. 20:34, 34:13, 14; Hosea 1:11), which will
be carried over into the millennium day of rest, 1,000 years
(Rev. 20:1, 2 and 21:2, 4; Isa. 11:6-9, 35:1, 55:13, 54:13).
Israel will be gathered from both Jew and Gentile.

GENERAL ORGANIZATION

Headquarters: P.O. Box 1067, Benton Harbor, MI 49022.
Tel. (616) 926-6695

OFFICERS

Chpsn. of Bd., Lloyd H. Dalager
Pillar & Sec., H. Thomas Dewhirst

Jehovah's Witnesses

The modern history of Jehovah's Witnesses began a
little more than 100 years ago. In the early 1870s an
inconspicuous Bible study began in Allegheny City,
Pennsylvania, now a part of Pittsburgh. Charles Taze
Russell was the prime mover of the group. In July 1879,
the first issue of Zion's Watch Tower and Herald of Christ's
Presence appeared. By 1880 scores of congregations had
spread from that one small Bible study into nearby states.
In 1881 Zion's Watch Tower Tract Society was formed,

and in 1884 was incorporated with Russell as president. The Society's name was later changed to Watch Tower Bible and Tract Society. Many witnessed from house to house, offering biblical literature.

By 1909 the work had become international, and the Society's headquarters was moved to its present location in Brooklyn, New York. Printed sermons were syndicted in newspapers, and by 1913 were in four languages in 3,000 newspapers in the United States, Canada, and Europe. Books, booklets, and tracts had been distributed by the hundreds of millions.

Russell died in 1916 and was succeeded the following year by Joseph F. Rutherford. Under his direction the magazine *Golden Age* was introduced (now called *Awake!* with a circulation of 10,610,000 in 53 languages). In 1931 the name Jehovah's Witnesses, based on Isaiah 43:10-12, was adopted.

During the 1930s and 1940s Jehovah's Witnesses fought many court cases in the interest of preserving freedom of speech, press, assembly, and worship. In the United States, appeals from lower courts resulted in the Witnesses winning 43 cases before the Supreme Court. Professor C. S. Braden stated, "In their struggle they have done much to secure those rights for every minority group in America."

When Rutherford died in 1942, he was succeeded by N. H. Knorr, who immediately instituted a concerted program of training for all Jehovah's Witnesses. The Watchtower Bible School of Gilead was established in 1943 for training missionaries. It has been primarily through the efforts of these missionaries that the word has expanded today to include 208 countries.

From that small beginning in Pennsylvania, the Witnesses have expanded to the far corners of the earth and now number more than 3 million. The present president F. W. Franz and a small group of fellow administrators serve a a governing body, overseeing the work, organized under 95 branches.

From the beginning Jehovah's Witnesses have believed in one almighty God, Jehovah, creator of heaven and earth. They believe that Christ is God's Son, the first of God's creations and subject to Jehovah. Christ's human life was paid as a ransom for obedient humans. Jehovah has assigned him a Kingdom, a government for which all Christians pray and through which Christ will rule the earth in righteousness and peace. The book of Revelation assigns 144,000 individuals "who have been bought from the earth," to rule with him. This Kingdom government will rule over the "meek who will inherit the earth" mentioned in the Sermon on the Mount. These people from all nations, along with the resurrected dead, will work to transform the earth into a global Edenic paradise. This is the "good news" Jehovah's Witnesses are commissioned to preach from house to house during these last days of the present system of things. When this has been accomplished Jesus says "the end will come" and will be followed by the righteous rule of his kingdom (Matt. 24:14).

Churches: 8,336; Inclusive Membership: 752,404; Sunday or Sabbath Schools: None; Total Enrollment: None; Ordained Clergy: None

GENERAL ORGANIZATION

Headquarters: 25 Columbia Heights, Brooklyn, NY 11201. Tel. (718) 625-3600

OFFICER

Pres. Frederick W. Franz

PERIODICALS

The Watchtower and Awake! 25 Columbia Heights, Brooklyn, NY 11201

Jewish Organizations

Jews arrived in the colonies before 1650. The first Congregation is recorded in 1654, in New York City, the Shearith Israel (Remnant of Israel).

Congregations: 3,416; Community: 5,814,000; Total Number of Rabbis: 6,500

CONGREGATIONAL AND RABBINICAL ORGANIZATIONS

Federation of Reconstructionist Congregations and Havurot: 270 W. 89th St., New York, NY 10024. Tel. (212) 496-2960; Pres., Lillian S. Kaplan; Exec. Dir., Rabbi Mordechai Liebling

*Union of American Hebrew Congregations (Reform): 838 Fifth Ave., New York, NY 10021. Tel. (212) 249-0100; Pres.,. Rabbi Alexander M. Schindler; Bd. Chpsn., Charles J. Rothschild, Jr.

*United Synagogue of America (Conservative): 155 Fifth Ave., NY 10010. Tel. (212) 533-7800; Pres., Franklin D. Kreutzer; Exec. Vice Pres., Rabbi Benjamin Z. Kreitman

*Union of Orthodox Jewish Congregations of America: 45 W. 36th St., New York, NY 10018. Tel (212)563-4000; Pres., Sidney Kwestel; Exec. Vice Pres., Rabbi Pinchas Stolper

*Central Conference of American Rabbis (Reform): 21 E. 40th St., New York, NY 10016. Tel. (212) 684-4990; Pres., Rabbi W. Jack Stern; Exec. Vice-Pres., Rabbi Joseph B. Glaser

Rabbinical Alliance of America (Orthodox): 156 Fifth Ave. Ste. 807, New York, NY 10010. Pres., Rabbi Abraham B. Hecht

*The Rabbinical Assembly (Conservative): 3080 Broadway, New York, NY 10027. Tel. (212) 678-8060; Pres., Rabbi Kassel Abelson; Exec. Vice-Pres., Rabbi Wolfe Kelman

*Rabbinical Council of America, Inc. (Orthodox): 275 Seventh Ave., New York, NY 10001. Tel. (212) 807-7888; Pres., Rabbi Milton H. Polin; Exec. Vice-Pres., Rabbi Binyamin Walfish

Reconstructionist Rabbinical Association: Church Rd. and Greenwood Ave., Wyncote, PA 19095. Tel. (215) 576-0800. Pres., Rabbi Ira Schiffer; Exec. Dir., Rabbi Lewis J. Eron

Union of Orthodox Rabbis of the United States and Canada: 235 E. Broadway, New York, NY 10002. Tel. (212) 964-6337; Dir., Rabbi Hersh M. Ginsberg

*Synagogue Council of America: 327 Lexington Ave., New York, NY 10016. Tel. (212) 686-8670; Pres., Rabbi Herbert M. Baumgard; Exec. Vice-Pres., Rabbi Henry D. Michelman

*Synagogue Council of America is the coordinating body of the organizations starred above.

EDUCATIONAL AND SOCIAL SERVICE ORGANIZATIONS

American Council for Judaism, The: 298 Fifth Ave. New York, NY 10001. Tel. (212) 947-8878; Bd. Chpsn., Clarence L. Coleman, Jr.; Pres., Alan V. Stone

American Jewish Committee: 165 E. 56th St., New York, NY 10022. Tel. (212) 751-4000; Pres., Theodore Ellenoff; Exec. Vice-Pres., David M. Gordis

American Jewish Congress: 15 E. 84th St., New York, NY 10028. Tel. (212) 879-4500; Pres., Theodore R. Mann; Exec. Dir., Henry Siegman

American Jewish Historical Society: 2 Thornton Rd., Waltham, MA 02154. Tel. (617) 891-8110; Pres., Morris Soble; Dir., Bernard Wax

American Jewish Joint Distribution Committee: 711 Third Ave., New York, NY 10017. Tel. (212) 687-6200; Pres., Heinz Eppler; Exec. Vice-Chpsn., Ralph I. Goldman

Anti-Defamation League of B'nai B'rith: 823 United Nations Plaza, New York, NY 10017, Tel. (212) 490-2525. Chpsn., Berton S. Levinson; Dir., Nathan E. Perlmutter

B'nai B'rith Hillel Foundations; Inc.: 1640 Rhode Island Ave. NW, Washington, DC 20036. Tel. (202) 857-6560; Chpsn., B'nai B'rith Hillel Cmte., Edwin Shapiro; Intl. Dir., Larry S. Moses

Conference of Presidents of Major American Jewish Organizations: 515 Park Ave., New York, NY 10022. Tel. (212) 752-1616; Chpsn., Morris B. Abram; Exec. Dir., Malcolm Hoenlein

Council for Jewish Education: 426 W. 58th St., New York, NY 10019. Tel. (212) 713-0290. Pres., Rabbi Irwin E. Witty; Exec. Dir., Philip Gorodetzer

Council of Jewish Federations: 730 Broadway, New York, NY 10003. Tel. (212) 475-5000; Pres., Shoshana S. Cardin; Exec. Vice-Pres., Carmi Schwartz

Hadassah, The Women's Zionist Organization of America: 50 W. 58th St., New York, NY 10019. Tel. (212) 355-7900; Nat'l Pres., Ruth Popkin; Exec. Dir., Zmira Goodman

HIAS, Inc. (Hebrew Immigrant Aid Society): 200 Park Ave., S., New York, NY 10003. Tel. (212) 674-6800; Pres., Robert L. Israeloff; Exec. Vice-Pres., Karl D. Zukerman

Jewish Publication Society: 1930 Chestnut St., Philadelphia, PA 19103. Tel. (215) 564-5925; Pres., Charles R. Weiner; Exec. Vice Pres., Nathan Barnett

Jewish Reconstructionist Foundation: 270 West 89th St., New York, NY 10024. Tel. (212) 496-2960. Chpsn. of Bd., Rabbi Lee Friedlander; Exec. Dir., Rabbi Mordechai Liebling

JWB (National Jewish Welfare Board): 15 E 26th St., New York, NY 10010. Tel. (212) 532-4949; Pres., Leonard Rochwarger; Exec. Vice-Pres., Arthur Rotman

Jewish War Veterans of the United States of America, Inc.: 1811 R St., Washington, DC 20009. Tel. (202) 265-6280; Natl. Comdr., Harvey S. Friedman; Natl. Exec. Dir., Steven Shaw

National Federation of Temple Brotherhoods: 838 Fifth Ave., New York, NY 10021. Tel. (212) 570-0707; Pres., Carl J. Burkona; Exec. Dir., Av Bondarin

National Federation of Temple Sisterhoods: 838 Fifth Ave., New York, NY 10021. Tel. (212) 249-0100; Pres., Delores Wilkenfeld; Exec. Dir., Eleanor R. Schwartz

National Jewish Community Relations Advisory Council: 443 Park Ave., S., 11th Fl., New York, NY 10016. Tel. (212) 684-6950; Chpsn., Michael A. Pelavin; Exec. Vice-Chpsn. Albert D. Chernin

United Jewish Appeal: 99 Park Ave., New York, NY 10016. Tel. (212) 818-9100; Pres., Stanley Horowitz; Chpsn. Board of Trustees, Alexander Gross

Women's Branch of the Union of Orthodox Jewish Congregations of America: 156 Fifth Ave., New York, NY 10010. Tel. (212) 929-8857; Pres., Gitti Needleman; Admn., Rita Siff

Women's League for Conservative Judaism: 48 E. 74th St., New York, NY 10021. Tel. (212) 628-1600; Pres. Selma Weintraub; Exec., Bernice Balter

Zionist Organization of America: 4 E. 34th St., New York, NY 10016. Tel. (212) 481-1500; Pres., Alleck A. Resnick; Natl. Exec. Dir., Paul Flacks

PERIODICALS

Orthodox

Jewish Action (q), 45 W.36th St., New York, NY 10018. Tel. (212) 563-4000; Heidi Tenzer, Ed.

Tradition (q), 275 Seventh Ave., New York, NY 10001. Tel. (212) 807-7888; Walter Wurzburger, Ed.

Conservative

United Synagogue Review (q), 155 Fifth Ave., New York, NY 10010. Tel. (212) 533-7800; Ruth M. Perry, Ed.

Conservative Judaism (q), 3080 Broadway, New York, NY 10027. Tel. (212) 678-8863; Rabbi David Silverman, Ed.

Reform

Journal of Reform Judaism, (q), 21 E. 40th St., New York 10016. Tel. (212) 684-4990; Samuel Stahl, Ed.

Reform Judaism (q), 838 5th Ave., New York, NY 10021. Tel. (212) 249-0100; Aron Hirt-Manheimer, Ed.

Reconstructionist

The Reconstructionist (m), 270 W. 89th St., New York, NY 10024. Tel. (212)496-2960. Jacob J. Staub, Ed.

___

Jewish Education (q), Council for Jewish Education, 426 W. 58th St., New York, NY 10019. Tel. (212) 245-8200; Alvin I. Schiff, Ed.

The Pedagogic Reporter (q), Jewish Education Service of North America, 730 Broadway, New York, NY 10003. Tel. (212) 529-2000; Mordecai H. Lewittes, Ed.

American Jewish History (q), American Jewish Historical Society, 2 Thornton Rd., Waltham, MA 02154. Tel. (617) 891-8110; Marc Lee Raphael, Ed.

Note: For details concerning many aspects of Jewish life and organization in the United States and throughout the world, consult *American Jewish Yearbook, 1987* prepared by the American Jewish Committee, New York, and the Jewish Publication Society of America, Philadelphia, David Singer, Ed.

Kodesh Church of Immanuel

Founded 1929 and incorporated in April 1930 by Rev. Frank Russell Killingsworth and 120 laymen, some of whom were former members of the African Methodist Episcopal Zion Church. On January 22, 1934, the Christian Tabernacle Union, a body of holy people with headquarters in Pittsburgh, merged with the Kodesh Church of Immanuel. This body is an interracial body of believers whose teachings are Wesleyan and Arminian.

GENERAL ORGANIZATION

Annual Assembly—convening once a year
General Assembly—meeting quadrennially

OFFICERS

Supervising Elders: Dr. Kenneth O. Barbour, 932 Logan Rd., Bethel Park, PA 15102. Tel. (412) 833-1351; Rev. Alphonso Benjamin, 5040 Brown St., Philadelphia, PA 19139

OTHER ORGANIZATIONS

Church Extension Board: Chmn., Mrs. Thelma P. Homes, 6537 Deary St.,Pittsburgh, PA 15206

Foreign Mission Board: Pres., Mrs. E. Lucille Lockhart, 1934 N. Charles St., Pittsburgh, PA 15214

Young People's Societies: Gen. Pres., Mrs. Catherine B. Harris, 1428 Forrester Ave., Greenhill Park, Sharon Hill, PA 19079

Harty Bible School: Dr. Kenneth O. Barbour, 932 Logan Rd., Bethel Park, PA 15102

Sunday Schools: Gen. Supt., Mrs. Bernice Williams, 47 Mt. Vernon Dr., Aliquippa, PA 15001

Korean Presbyterian Church in America, General Assembly of the

This body came into official existence in the United States in 1976 and is currently an ethnic church, using the Korean language.

Churches: 180; Inclusive Membership: 24,000; Sunday or Sabbath Schools: 150; Total Enrollment: 6,500; Ordained Clergy: 225

GENERAL ORGANIZATION

General Assembly meets annually.
Headquarters: 1251 Crenshaw Blvd., Los Angeles, CA 90019. Tel. (213)857-0361.

Mod., Rev. Hee So Park, 51 Claradon Lane, Staten Island, NY 10305

Gen. Sec., Rev. Elder Nicholas C. Chun, 1251 Crenshaw Blvd., Los Angeles, CA 90019

Chpsn., Int'l Mission Cmte., Rev. Chang Duk Choi, 1230 25th St., #2, Santa Monica, CA 90404

The Latvian Evangelical Lutheran Church in America

This body was organized into a denomination on August 22, 1975, after having existed as the Federation of Latvian Evangelical Lutheran Churches in America since 1955. This church is a regional constituent part of the Lutheran Church of Latvia in Exile, a member of the Lutheran World Federation and the World Council of Churches.

The Latvian Evangelical Lutheran Church in America works to foster religious life, traditions and customs in its congregations in harmony with the Holy Scriptures, the Apostles', Nicean and Athanasian Creeds, the unaltered Augsburg Confession, Martin Luther's Small and Large Catechisms and other documents of the Book of Concord.

The LELCA is ordered by its Synod (General Assembly), executive board, auditing committee, and district conferences. A member church in Lutheran Council in the USA since 1982.

Churches: 62; Inclusive Membership: 13,838; Sunday or Sabbath Schools: 20; Total Enrollment: 560; Ordained Clergy: 40

CORRESPONDENT

Pres., Rev. Vilis Varsbergs, 6551 W. Montrose Ave., Chicago, IL 60634. Tel. (312) 725-3820

The Liberal Catholic Church—Province of the United States of America

Founded February 13, 1916 as a reorganization of the Old Catholic Church in Great Britain, the Rt. Rev. James I. Wedgwood being the first Presiding Bishop. The first ordination of a Priest in the United States was Fr. Charles Hampton, later a Bishop. The first Regionary Bishop for the American Province was the Rt. Rev. Irving S. Cooper (1919-1935).

Churches: 34; Inclusive Membership: 2,800; Sunday or Sabbath Schools: 3; Total Enrollment: 22; Ordained Clergy: 127

GENERAL ORGANIZATION

Board of Trustees, meets July 1, annually.
Provincial Episcopal Synod and Provincial Synod: Triennial
Provincial Headquarters: 1620 San Gabriel Rd., Ojai, CA 93023. Tel. (805) 646-2960

OFFICERS

Pres. and Regionary Bishop, The Rt. Rev. Lawrence J. Smith, 9740 S. Avers, Evergreen Park IL 60642. Tel. (312) 424-8329

Vice-Pres. and Vicar Gen., Very Rev. Alfred Strauss, 10606 Parrot Ave., Apt. A, Downey, CA 90241. Tel. (213)861-7569

Sec. (Provincial), The Rt. Rev. Dr. Hein VanBeusekom, Star Route 58 Eastsound, WA 98245. Tel. (206)376-4535

Provost, The Very Rev. Wm. Holme, P.O. Box 7042, Rochester, MN 55903

Treas., Rev. David Grant, 10632 Glory Ave., Tujunga, CA 91042

Chancellor, The Rt. Rev. Dr. Gerrit Munnik, 16 Krotona, Ojai CA 93023. Tel. (805) 646-2960 (AM only)

Regionary Bishop for the American Province: The Rt. Rev. Lawrence J. Smith, 9740 S. Avers, Evergreen Park, IL 60642. Tel. (312) 424-8329.

Regionary Bishop and Ep. Vicar Gen. for the Americas: The Rt. Rev. Dr. Gerrit Munnik, 16 Krotona, Ojai, CA 93023

Auxiliary Bishops of the American Province: (Address Rt. Rev.), Dr. Ramon Mayola, 950 SW First St., Miami, FL 33130; Dr. Robert S. McGinnis, Jr., 3417 Maine Ave., Kenner, LA 70062; Joseph L. Tisch, PO. Box 1117, Melbourne, FL 23901; Dr. Hein VanBeusekom, Star Route Box 58, Eastsound, WA 98245; Raja Watson, 7541 W. Forest Preserve Ave., Chicago, IL 60634

PERIODICAL

Ubique: American Province (q), P.O. Box 1117, Melbourne, FL 32901. Rt. Rev. Joseph Tisch, Ed.

Liberty Baptist Fellowship

The Liberty Baptist Fellowship consists of independent Baptist churches and pastors organized for the purpose of planting indigenous local New Testament churches in North America. The Fellowship is in general accord with the doctrines and philosophy of the Independent Baptist movement.

GENERAL ORGANIZATION

National Meeting: Annual
International Headquarters: Candler's Mountain Rd., Lynchburg, VA 24506. Tel. (804) 237-5961, ext. 325

OFFICERS

Exec. Comm: Chmn., Jerry Falwell; A. Pierre Guillermin; Dir., Elmer L. Towns; Sec., Dennis Fields, Sr.

Nat'l Comm: Pres., George Sweet; First Vice-Pres., Steve Reynolds; Second Vice-Pres., David Brown, John Cartwright, Bob Gass, Mike Grooms, Eddie Guy, Benny Hampton, Rudy Holland, Lindsay Howan, Danny Lovett, Ray Lyons, Allen MacFarland, Daren Ritchey, David Rhodenhizer

OTHER ORGANIZATIONS

Liberty Baptist Missions: Dir., Vernon Brewer

PERIODICALS

Liberty Journal (q), Elmer Towns, Ed.
Fundamentalist Journal (q), Jerry Falwell, Ed.

The Lutheran Church— Missouri Synod

The Lutheran Church—Missouri Synod, which began in the state of Missouri in 1847, has 9,000 groups of worshipers in 33 countries. Its 2.7 million North American membership forms the second-largest Lutheran denomination.

Christian education for all ages offers an array of weekday, Sunday school and Bible-class opportunities. The 6,250-plus North American congregations operate the largest elementary and secondary school systems of any Protestant denomination in the nation and 15 colleges and seminaries in the U.S. and Canada which enroll 7,750 students.

Traditional beliefs concerning the authority and interpretation of Scripture are important. In the late 1960s, a controversy developed, but following a decade of soul-searching that resulted in the walkout of most faculty members and students from one seminary and the eventual departure of slightly more than 100,000 members, little evidence of the controversy remains.

The synod is known for mass-media outreach through "The Lutheran Hour" on radio, "This Is The Life" dramas on television, and the products of Concordia Publishing House, the third-largest Protestant publisher, whose Arch Books children's series has sold 35 million copies.

An extensive Braille volunteer network makes devotional materials for the blind; 54 of the 85 deaf congregations affiliated with U.S. denominations are LCMS; and many denominations use the Bible lessons prepared for developmentally disabled persons.

There are more blacks in the synod than in any other Lutheran church, and congregations have helped 20,000 Southeast Asians to settle in America.

The involvement of women is high, though they do not occupy clergy positions. Serving as teachers, deaconesses, and social workers, women comprise approximately 42 percent of total professional workers.

The members' responsibility for congregational leadership is a distinctive characteristic of the synod, a word that means *walking together*. Practice holds that the pastor is the equipper of the saints, but a pastor might find it difficult to locate the proper slot in a modern-day organizational chart. Power is vested in voters' assemblies, generally comprised of adults of voting age. Synod decision making is given to the delegates at national and regional conventions, where the franchise is equally divided between lay and pastoral representatives.

Churches: 5,897; Inclusive Membership: 2,630,588; Sunday or Sabbath Schools: N.R.; Total Enrollment: 657,992; Ordained Clergy: 8,044

GENERAL ORGANIZATION

General Convention: every three years, next meeting, 1989

Headquarters: The Lutheran Church—Missouri Synod, International Center, 1333 S. Kirkwood Rd., St. Louis, MO 63122

OFFICERS

Pres., Dr. Ralph A. Bohlmann
1st Vice-Pres., Dr. August T. Mennicke
2nd Vice-Pres., Dr. George Wollenburg
3rd Vice-Pres., Dr. Robert King
4th Vice-Pres., Dr. Walter A. Maier
5th Vice-Pres., Dr. Guido A. Merkens
Sec., Dr. Walter L. Rosin
Treas., Dr. Norman Sell
Adm. Officer of Bd. of Dir., Dr. John P. Schuelke
Dir. of Personnel: Mr. William J. Barge
Board of Directors: Dr. Henry L. Liepchen, Setauket, NY; Rev. Ervin R. Lemke, Menomonee Falls, WI; Rev. Victor H. Marxhausen, White Bear Lake, MN; Rev. Richard L. Thompson, Billings, MT; Mr. William E. Ludwig, Kalispell, MT; Mr. Donald J. Brosz, Laramie, WY; Mr. John L. Daniel, Emmaus, PA; Mr. George H. Mohr, Wauwatosa, WI; Dr. Florence Montz, Bismarck, ND; Dr. Harold M. Olsen, Springfield, IL; Mr. Lester W. Schultz, Green Bay, WI; Mr. Donald Snyder, Henrietta, NY

BOARDS AND COMMISSIONS

(All at The Lutheran Church—Missouri Synod International Center, 1333 S. Kirkwood Rd., St. Louis, MO 63122, unless different address is given)

Board for Communication Services: Exec. Dir., Rev. Paul Devantier
Board for Evangelism Services: Exec. Dir., Dr. Erwin J. Kolb
Board for Mission Serivces: Exec. Dir., Dr. Edward A. Westcott
Board for Parish Services: Exec. Dir., Dr. Victor Constien
Board for Higher Education Services: Exec. Dir., Dr. M. J. Stelmachowicz
Board for Youth Services: Exec. Dir., Mr. Richard W. Bimler
Board for Social Ministry Services: Exec. Dir., Dr. Eugene Linse

Board, Worker Benefit Plans: Administrator, Mr. Earl E. Haake
Lutheran Church Extension Fund-Missouri Synod: Pres., Mr. Arthur C. Haake
Ministry to the Armed Forces Standing Committee: Exec. Dir., Rev. James Shaw
Dept. of Stewardship and Financial Support: Dir., Mr. Richard L. Engdahl

AUXILIARY ORGANIZATIONS

Concordia Publishing House: 3558 S. Jefferson Ave., St. Louis, MO 63118. Pres./CEO, John Gerber
Concordia Historical Institute: Concordia Seminary, 801 De Mun Ave., St. Louis, MO 63105. Dir., Dr. August R. Suelflow
International Lutheran Laymen's League: 2185 Hampton Ave., St. Louis, MO 63110. Exec. Dir., Mr. John A. Daniels
KFUO Radio: 801 De Mun Ave., St. Louis, MO 73105. Dir. of Broadcast Ministries, Kenneth J. Lombardi
International Lutheran Women's Missionary League: 3558 S. Jefferson Ave., St. Louis, MO 63118. Pres., Mrs. John L. (Betty) Duda

PERIODICALS

The Lutheran Witness (m), Rev. David Mahsman, News and Inf. Dir. and Ed.
Reporter/Alive (w), Rev. David Mahsman, Ed.

Mennonite Church

The Mennonite Church in North America traces its beginnings back to 16th century Europe and the Protestant Reformation. Conrad Grebel, Georg Blaurock, and a small band of radical believers who felt that reformers Martin Luther and Ulrich Zwingli had not gone far enough in their break with Roman Catholic tradition and a return to New Testament discipleship Christianity, baptized one another in Zurich, Switzerland, on January 21, 1525. First nicknamed Anabaptists (Rebaptizers) by their opponents (they themselves preferred to use the term Brothers and Sisters in Christ), the Mennonites later took their name from the Dutch priest Menno Simons who joined the movement in 1536, and emerged as their leader.

The Mennonites' refusal to conform to majesterial decrees including bearing of arms and the swearing of oaths, attracted fierce animosity. Thousands were martyred for their beliefs in nearly a century of persecution. Eager to find freedom to live out their faith elsewhere, they moved to many places, including the United States and Canada where some arrived as early as 1683. Between four and five thousand Mennonites settled in southeastern Pennsylvania between 1717 and 1756 in the first major migration from Europe. Caught between the warring factions of America's struggle for independence, many moved west to Ohio, Indiana, Iowa, and especially north to upper Canada (now Ontario).

North American Mennonites began their first home mission program in Chicago, Ill., in 1893 and their first foreign mission program in India in 1899. Since the 1920s the church has established extensive emergency relief and development services in conjunction with its mission program.

Mennonites hold that the Word of God is central and that new life in Christ is available to all who believe. Adult "Believer's" baptism is practiced, symbolizing a conscious decision to follow Christ. Mennonites take seriously Christ's command to witness in word and deed. Concerned for both physical and spiritual aspects of life, they regard faith and works as two sides of the same coin. They stress that Christians need the support of a faith community for encouragement and growth. In times of crisis their "mutual aid" network makes time, money, and goods available to those in need. They view Jesus' teachings as directly applicable to their lives. Following the Prince of

Peace, Mennonites generally refuse to serve in the military or to use violent resistance.

Currently the largest body of Mennonites in North America, the denomination has approximately 91,000 members in 44 states and the District of Columbia, and 9,400 members in seven Canadian provinces (1986 statistics). The Mennonite Church is a member of the Mennonite and Brethren in Christ World Conference—a fellowship of 144 bodies in 57 countries around the world. The denomination is also a member of Mennonite Central Committee, a world-wide relief and service agency representing 17 North American churches and bodies. While the denomination does not hold membership in any major ecumenical organizations in the United States and Canada, individuals and program agencies do participate in a variety of ecumenical activities at various levels of church life.

Churches: 989; Inclusive Membership: 91,167; Sunday or Sabbath Schools: 973; Total Enrollment: 112,381; Ordained Clergy: 2,399

GENERAL ORGANIZATION

General Assembly: biennial. Next meeting, 1989
General Office: 528 E. Madison St., Lombard, IL 60148. Tel. (312) 620-7802

OFFICERS

Mod., Ralph Lebold (to Aug. 1989), George R. Brunk, II (after Aug. 1989) 528 E. Madison St., Lombard, IL 60148. Tel. (312) 620-7802

OTHER ORGANIZATIONS

General Board: Exec. Sec. James M. Lapp, 528 E. Madison St., Lombard, IL 60148. Tel. (312) 620-7802
Historical Committee: Exec. Sec., Leonard Gross, 1700 S. Main, Goshen, IN. Tel. (219) 533-3161
Council on Faith, Life, and Strategy: Chpsn., _____
Board of Congregational Ministries: Exec. Sec., Gordon D. Zook, Box 1245, Elkhart, IN 46515, Tel. (219) 294-7536
Board of Education: Exec. Sec., Albert Meyer, Box 1142, Elkhart, IN 46515. Tel. (219) 294-7531
Board of Missions: Pres., Paul M. Gingrich, Box 370, Elkhart, IN 46515. Tel. (219) 294-7523
Mutual Aid Board: Pres., James Kratz, 1110 North Main, P. O. Box 483, Goshen, IN 46526 Tel. (219) 533-9511
Mennonite Publication Board: Publisher, J. Robert Ramer, 616 Walnut Ave., Scottdale, PA 15683. Tel. (412) 887-8500

PERIODICALS

Gospel Herald (w), Scottdale, PA 15683 Daniel Hertzler, Ed.
Christian Living (m), Scottdale, PA 15683. David E. Hostetler, Ed.
Builder (m), Scottdale, PA 15683. John Rogers, Ed.
Rejoice! (q) Scottdale, PA. Marjorie Waybill Assoc. Ed.
Mennonite Historical Bulletin (q), Goshen, IN 46526. Leonard Gross, Ed.
Mennonite Yearbook (biennial), Scottdale, PA 15683. James E. Horsch, Ed.
Mennonite Quarterly Review (q), Goshen, IN 46526 John S. Oyer Ed.
With (m), Scottdale, PA 15683. John Rogers, Assoc., Ed.
Purpose (w), Scottdale, PA 15683. James E. Horsch, Ed.
On the Line (w), Scottdale PA 15683. Virginia A. Hostetler, Ed.
Sent (q), Elkhart, IN 46515. Willard E. Roth, Ed.
Sharing (q), Goshen, IN 46526. Maggie Glick, Ed.
Story Friends (w), Scottdale, PA 15683. Marjorie Waybill, Ed.
Ecos Menonitas (q), Elkhart, IN 46515. Arnoldo Casas, Ed.

United Action Newsletter (q), Lombard, IL 60148. Joy Lovett, Ed.
Voice (11/yr), Elkhart, IN 46515. Vel Shearer, Ed.
Information: James E. Horsch, Ed., Mennonite Yearbook, Scottdale, PA 15683

Mennonite Church, The General Conference

The General Conference Mennonite Church was formed in 1860, uniting Mennonites throughout the U.S. who were interested in doing missionary work together. Today 65,000 Christians in 366 congregations try to follow the way of Jesus in their daily lives.

The conference consists of people of many ethnic backgrounds—Swiss and German, Russian and Dutch, Black, Hispanic, Chinese, Vietnamese, Laotian. Some native Americans in both Canada and the U.S. also relate to the conference.

The basic belief and practice of the conference come from the life and teachings of Jesus Christ, the early church of the New Testament, and the Anabaptists of the 16th-century Reformation. Thus the conference seeks to be evangelical, guided by the Bible, led by the Holy Spirit, and supported by a praying, discerning community of believers in congregations and fellowships. Peace, or shalom, is at the very heart of members, who seek to be peacemakers in everyday life.

The goals of the conference for the next three to six years are to evangelize, teach and practice biblical principles, train and develop leaders, and work for Christian unity.

Churches: 215; Inclusive Membership: 35,170; Sunday or Sabbath Schools: N.R.; Total Enrollment: 15,705; Ordained Clergy: 365

GENERAL ORGANIZATION

General Conference: triennial. Next meeting, 1989
Central Office: 722 Main, Newton, KS 67114. Tel. (316) 283-5100

OFFICERS

Pres., Florence Driedger, 3833 Montague St., Regina, Saskatchewan S4S 3J6
Vice-Pres., James Gingerich, Box 66, Moundridge, KS 67107
Sec., Myron Schultz, Bloomfield, MT 59315
Gen. Sec., Vern Preheim, 722 Main, Newton, KS 67114

OTHER ORGANIZATIONS

(All at central office)
Commission on Home Ministries: Exec. Stanley Bohn
Commission on Overseas Mission: Exec. Sec., Erwin Rempel
Women in Mission: Coordinator, Sara Regier
Commission on Education: Exec. Sec., Norma Johnson
Division of Administration: Exec. Secs., Ted Stuckey, Ray Frey

PERIODICALS

The Mennonite (bi-w), Box 347, 722 Main St., Newton, KS 67114, Muriel Thiessen Stackley, Ed.
Builder (m), 722 Main St., Newton, KS 67114
Window to Mission (q), 722 Main St., Newton, KS 67114, Lois Deckert, Ed.
Der Bote (w) 600 Shaftesbury Blvd., Winnipeg, Manitoba, Canada R3P 0M4, Gerhard Ens, Ed.

The Metropolitan Church Association, Inc.

Organized as the result of a revival movement in

Chicago in 1894, as the Metropolitan Holiness Church, and in 1899 chartered as the Metropolitan Church Association. It has Wesleyan theology.

GENERAL ORGANIZATION

General Assembly: annual
International Headquarters: 323 Broad St., Lake Geneva, WI 53147

OFFICERS

Pres., Rev. Warren W. Bitzer
Vice-Pres. & Sec., Elbert L. Ison
Treas., Gertrude J. Puckhaber

PERIODICAL

The Burning Bush (bi-m), Lake Geneva, WI, Rev. E. L. Adams, Ed. (Publishing House, The Metropolitan Church Association, Lake Geneva, WI 53147)

Metropolitan Community Churches, Universal Fellowship of

Founded October 6, 1968 by the Rev. Troy D. Perry in Los Angeles, California with a particular but not exclusive outreach to the gay community. Since that time, the Fellowship has grown to include congregations throughout the world.

The group is trinitarian and accepts the Bible as the divinely inspired Word of God. The Fellowship has two sacraments, baptism and holy communion, as well as a number of traditionally recognized rites such as ordination.

"This Fellowship acknowledges the Holy Scriptures interpreted by the Holy Spirit in conscience and faith, as its guide in faith, discipline, and government. The government of this Fellowship is vested in its General Council (consisting of Elders and District Coordinators), Clergy and church delegates, who exert the right of control in all of its affairs, subject to the provisions of its Articles of Incorporation and By-Laws."

GENERAL ORGANIZATION

General Conference: 14th General Conference (biennial) Minneapolis, MN, July, 1989
Headquarters: 5300 Santa Monica Blvd., #304, Los Angeles, CA 90029. Tel. (213) 464-5100

OFFICERS

(All at headquarters unless otherwise noted)
Mod., Rev. Elder Troy D. Perry
Vice-Mod., Rev. Elder Freda Smith, POB 20125 Sacramento, CA 95820
Treas., Rev. Elder Donald Eastman (at headquarters)
Clk., Rev. Elder Nancy L. Wilson
Rev. Elder Jeri Ann Harvey, 5300 Santa Monica Blvd., #304, Los Angeles, CA 90029
Rev. Elder Jean A. White, 207 Streatham High Rd., London, England SW16 6EG
Dir. of Admn., Mr. Ravi Verma

DISTRICT COORDINATORS

European North Sea, Rev. Robert Arthur, 174 Edmund St., Birmingham B3 2HB, England; Eastern Canadian, Rev. Ron Bergeron, P.O. Box 2979, Sta. D., Ottawa, Ontario K1P 5W9; Southeast, Rev. Frankye White, 832 NE 17th St., Fort Lauderdale, FL 33305 ; Southwest, Rev. Judy Dahl, 33881 Manta Ct., Laguna Niguel, CA 92677; Mid-Central, Rev. Bonnie Daniel, 1605 West West 37th Terrace, #821, Topeka, KS 66609; Mid-Atlantic, Mr. R. Adam DeBaugh, P.O. Box 8835 Silver Spring, MD 20907; Australian District: Rev. Bill Hein, c/o MCC-Adelaide, 285 Flanders St., Adelaide, South Australia 5001; South Central, Mr. Clarke Friesen,

P.O. Box 262822, Houston, TX 77207; Western Canadian, Mr. Arthur Pearson, P.O. Box 5178, Vancouver, British Columbia V6B 4B2; Gulf & Lower Atlantic District: Ms. Mary Moore, POB 66101, Birmingham, AL 35210; Northwest: Rev. Edward Sherriff, c/o MCC at Boise, 805 West Idaho, #419, Boise, ID 83702; Great Lakes, Rev. LaPaula Turner, 665 Salem Ave., Dayton, OH 45406; Northeast, Rev. Willie White, POB 27, Scarborough, NY 10510

OTHER ORGANIZATIONS

Dept. of Third World Ministries: Ms. Darlene Garner, 531 North Pine St., Lancaster, PA 17603; Dept. of Ecumenical Witness and Ministry, Co-Dirs., Rev. Elder Nancy Wilson, c/o UFMCC, 5300 Santa Monica Blvd., Ste. 304, Los Angeles, CA 90029; Rev. Sandi Robinson, 655 Salem Ave., Dayton, OH 45406; Commission of Faith, Fellowship and Order, Chpsn., Rev. Jennie Boyd Bull, c/o MCC Baltimore, P.O. Box 1145, Baltimore, MD 21203; Commission of the Laity, Chpsn., Mr. Chuck Harvey, 4051 E. Burnside, Portland, OR 97214; Asst. Chpsn., Mr. Ken Frantz, 3497 Coquina Key Dr., Ft. Myers, FL 33703; Clergy Credentials and Concerns Committee (CCCC), Chpsn., _____, 5300 Santa Monica Blvd., #317, Los Angeles, CA 90029; Board of Pensions, Pres., Rev. Arthur R. Green, 3000 N.W. 125th St., N. Miami, FL 33168; Admn: Lois Lundbert, 2400-109 E. Pleasant Valley, Oxnard, CA 93033

PERIODICALS

Journey (q), 5063 Ft. Clarke, Austin, TX 78745, Rev. David Day, Ed.

The Missionary Church

The Missionary Church was formed in 1969 through a merger of the United Missionary Church (organized in 1883) and the Missionary Church Association (founded in 1898). It is evangelical and conservative with a strong emphasis on missionary work and church planting

There are three levels of church government with local, district, and general conferences. There are ten church districts in the United States. The general conference meets every two years. The denomination operates two colleges in the U. S.

Churches: 295; Inclusive Membership: 26,869; Sunday or Sabbath Schools: 282; Total Enrollment: 39,933; Ordained Clergy: 616

GENERAL ORGANIZATION

U.S. Headquarters: 3901 S. Wayne Ave., Ft. Wayne, IN 46807. Tel. (219) 456-4502
Publishing Headquarters: Bethel Publishing Co., 1819 S. Main St., Elkhart, IN 46516. Tel. (219) 293-8585

OFFICERS

Pres., Dr. John Moran
Vice-Pres., Rev. William Hossler
Sec., Rev. Paul DeMerchant
Treas., Mr. Edwin W. Crewson
Dir., Overseas Ministries, Rev. Charles Carpenter
Dir., Home Ministries, Rev. John Hedegaard
Dir., Services, Mr. Dave von Gunten
Dir., Stewardship, Rev. Ken Stucky
Dir., Educational Ministries, Rev. David Mann
Dir., Youth, Dr. Dennis D. Engbrecht
Dir., Children, Mr. Neil McFarlane
Dir., Adult, Dr. Duane Beals
Missionary Men International: Pres., Dr. Duane Beals
Women's Missionary Societies: Pres., Mrs. Willis Hunking

PERIODICAL

Emphasis on Faith and Living (m), 3901 S. Wayne Ave., Ft. Wayne, IN 46807. Rev. Michael Reynolds, Ed.

Moravian Church in America (Unitas Fratrum)

In 1735 German Moravian missionaries of the pre-Reformation faith of Jan Hus came to Georgia, in 1740 to Pennsylvania, and in 1753 to North Carolina. They established the American Moravian Church, which is broadly evangelical, ecumenical, liturgical, with an episcopacy as a spiritual office and in form of government "conferential."

GENERAL ORGANIZATION

Two Provincial Synods (Northern and Southern)

NORTHERN PROVINCE

Headquarters: 1021 Center St., P.O. Box 1245, Bethlehem, PA 18016. Tel. (215) 867-7566

Churches: 101; Inclusive Membership: 32,180; Sunday or Sabbath Schools: 98; Total Enrollment: 7,440; Ordained Clergy: 174

OFFICERS

Provincial Elders' Conference:
Pres., Dr. Gordon L. Sommers
Vice-Pres. (Eastern District) and Sec., Rev. Donald E. Fulton
Vice-Pres. (Western District), Rt. Rev. Wilbur Behrend, Sun Prairie, WI
Treas., John F. Ziegler, 1021 Center St., P.O. Box 1245, Bethlehem, PA 18016

PERIODICAL

The North American Moravian (m), 1021 Center St., P.O. Box 1245, Bethlehem, PA 18016

SOUTHERN PROVINCE

Headquarters: 459 S. Church St., Winston-Salem, NC 27108. Tel. (919) 725-5811

Churches: 56; Inclusive Membership: 21,722; Sunday or Sabbath Schools: 57; Total Enrollment: 8,850; Ordained Clergy: 83

OFFICERS

Provincial Elders' Conference:
Pres., Rev. Graham H. Rights
Vice-Pres., Dr. D. Wayne Burkette
Sec., Mrs. Becky K. Cook
Treas., Ronald R. Hendrix, 500 S. Church St., Winston-Salem, NC 27101 (Mailing Address: Drawer O. Salem Station, Winston-Salem, NC 27108)

PERIODICAL

The North American Moravian, 1021 Center St., P.O. Box 1245, Bethlehem, PA 18016, Rev. Herman I. Weinlick, Ed.

Muslims

Islam now claims approximately six million adherents in the U.S. Some of them are immigrants who represent almost every part of the world, or children of such immigrants. Others are Americans who converted to Islam or children of such converts. These are apart from those who come to America temporarily, such as Muslim diplomats, students, and those who work in international institutions such as the World Bank, the International Monetary Fund, and the United Nations.

Muslims are found in nearly every American town, and are engaged in all professions, including teaching, medicine, accounting, engineering, and business. Their number increases in large industrial and commercial cities in the East and Midwest, but there are also large numbers of Muslims in some areas on the West Coast such as Los Angeles and San Francisco.

Many Islamic organizations exist in the U.S. under such titles as Islamic Society, Islamic Center, or Muslim Mosque. The aim is to provide a group in a locality with a place of worship and of meeting for other religious, social, and educational purposes. These societies and organizations are not regarded as religious sects or divisions. Their multiplication arises from the needs of each group in a given area, long distances separating the groups, and the absence in Islam of organized hierarchy, a factor which gives liberty to ambitious personalities to start their own group. All the groups hold the same beliefs, aspire to practice the same rituals: namely, prayers, fasting, almsgiving, and pilgrimage to Makkah. The only difference that may exist between black organizations and other Muslim institutions may be that the former may mix civil rights aspirations with Islamic objectives and may, therefore, follow a rigid discipline for their members.

The main Islamic organizations are the Islamic centers which are found in all 300 large cities. Their objectives are cultural, religious, and educational; and each one has a mosque or a prayer hall.
Prominent among these is:
The Islamic Center of Washington, 2551 Massachusetts Ave. NW, Washington, DC 20008. Tel. (202) 332-8343. Dir., Dr. A. Khouj. Publication: The Bulletin (w).

REGIONAL AND NATIONAL GROUPS

Apart from the Islamic Centers, a number of regional and national groups were started with the objective of helping local groups coordinate their work, and promote closer unity among them. These include:
The Federation of Islamic Associations in the United States and Canada, 300 E. 44th St., 2nd Fl., New York, NY 10017, Tel. (212) 986-6824. Pres., Mr. Dawud Assad. Publication: The Muslim Star, 17514 Woodward Ave., Detroit, MI 48203.
The Muslim Students Association of the U.S. and Canada, P. O. Box 38, Plainfield, Indianapolis, IN 46168, Tel. (317) 839-8157. Publications: The Islamic Horizons (m); Al-Ittihad (q).
Council of Muslim Communities of Canada, P. O. Box 400, Sta. D, Toronto, Ontario M6P 3J9, Sec. Gen., Dr. Imtiaz Ali. Publication: Islam Canada, P.O. Box 771, Sta. B, Willowdale, Ontario M2K 2R1, Tel. (416) 270-9215.
The World Community of Islam in the West, 7351 South Stoney Island, Chicago, IL 60649, Leader, Mr. Wallace D. Muhammad. Publication: Bilalian News, 7801 South Cottage Groves, Chicago, IL 60619, Tel. (312) 651-7600.

National Baptist Convention of America

This is the "unincorporated" body of National Baptists which was organized in 1880 following a dispute over control of the publishing board in which another Convention was organized. Membership of the churches is largely black.

GENERAL ORGANIZATION

Convention: annual (September)

OFFICERS

Pres., E. Edward Jones, 1450 Pierre Ave., Shreveport LA 71103
Vice Pres.: 1st Vice-Pres., Dr. S. M. Lockridge, 710 Crosby St., San Diego CA 92113; 2nd Vice-Pres., Dr. Albert Chew, 2823 N. Houston St., Ft. Worth TX 76106; 3rd Vice-Pres., Dr. Wallace S. Hartsfield, 3100 E. 31st St., Kansas City MO 64128
Corr. Sec., Rev. Stephen Thurston, 740 E. 77th St., Chicago IL 60619

Gen. Rec. Sec., Dr. Clarence C. Pennywell, 2016 Russell Rd., Shreveport LA 71107

Treas., Rev. Floyd N. Williams, 5902 Bealt St., Houston TX 77091

Hist., Rev. Marvin C. Griffin, 1010 E. Tenth St., Austin, TX 78702. Tel. (512) 478-1875

Statistician, Rev. E. E. Stafford, 6614 S. Western Ave., Los Angeles CA 90047

Auditor, Rev. J. Carlton Allen, 1639 Hays St., San Antonio, TX 78202. Tel. (512)225-7907

Youth Advisor, Rev. B. W. Noble, 636 N. Fourth St., Muskogee OK 74401

Admn. Asst. to Pres., Rev. Joe R. Gant, 5823 Ledbetter, Shreveport LA 71108

Sec. of Finance, Rev. H. T. Johnson, 2807 Tanner St., Dallas TX 75215

OTHER ORGANIZATIONS

Education Board: Chpsn. Dr. T. B. Adams, 609 S.W. 9th St., Belle Glade, FL 33430; Exec. Sec., Dr. W. E. Hausey, 3538 Jackson Ave., New Orleans LA 70113

Foreign Mission Board: Chpsn., Rev. J. W. Toomer, 1905 Amelia, Orlando, FL 32805; Exec. Sec., Dr. Robert H. Wilson, P.O. Drawer 223655, Dallas, TX 75222

Home Mission Board: Chpsn., Dr. Luke Mingo, 3993 S. King Dr., Chicago, IL 60653; Exec. Sec., Dr. O. B. Williams, 3132 N. Vancouver Ave., Portland, OR 97227

Evangelical Board: Chpsn. Rev. E. Potter, 2403 Hewes St., Gulfport, MS 52303; Exec. Sec., Dr. F. H. Dunn, Sr., P.O. Box 51737, New Orleans, LA 70151

Baptist Training Union Board: Chpsn., Rev. A. Bernard, 3069 Orchard St., Indianapolis, IN 46218; Exec. Sec., Dr. J. Royster Powell, 5708 Wayne St., Houston, TX 77026

Benevolent Board: Chpsn., Rev. William Bowie, Jr., 718 E. 40th St., Houston, TX 77022; Sec./Treas., Rev. J. F. Hargrett, P.O. Box 5907, Orlando, FL 32855

Senior Women #1 Pres., Dr. Fannie C. Thompson, 516 E. Waverly St., Tucson, AZ 85705

Senior Women #2: Pres., Dr. Hattie L. E. Williams, 1166 Rapides Ave., Alexandria, LA 71301

Junior Women: Pres., Sis Frances Worthy, 705 Carver Ave., Waco, TX 76704

Brotherhood: Pres. Bro. Wayman Smith, 1449 86th Ave., Oakland, CA 94621

Ushers: Pres., Bro. Charles Walker, 3167 Boulevard Pl., Indianapolis, IN 46208

Young Men for Christ: Pres., Rev. Curtis L. Carter, 2808 Crest Ave., Austin, TX 78702

Youth: Pres., Rev. Previn Carr, 302 E. Thunderbird Trail, Phoenix, AZ 85040

National Baptist Convention, U.S.A., Inc.

The older and parent convention of black Baptists. This body is to be distinguished from the National Baptist Convention of America, usually referred to as the "unincorporated" body.

GENERAL ORGANIZATION

Convention: annual

OFFICERS

Pres., Dr. T. J. Jemison, 915 Spain St., Baton Rouge, LA 70802. Tel. (504) 383-5401

Gen. Sec., Dr. W. Franklyn Richardson, 52 South 6th Ave., Mt. Vernon, NY 10550. Tel. (914) 664-2676

Vice-Pres.-at-large, Dr. C. A. Clark, 902 N. Good St., Dallas, TX 75204

Treas., Dr. Isaac Green, 3068 Iowa St., Pittsburgh, PA 15219. Tel. (412)556-1437

Vice-Pres.: Dr. David Matthews, P.O. Box 627, Indianola, MS; Dr. A. E. Campbell, 2500 Carnes Ave.,

Memphis, TN 38114; Dr. Henry L. Lyons; Dr. E. Victor Hill; Dr. Allen Stanley

Asst. Secs., Dr. B. J. Whipper, Sr., 15 Ninth St., Charleston, SC 29403; Dr. Marshall F. Robinson, 818 Summerfield St., Mobile, AL 36617; Dr. Roger P. Derricotte, 539 Roseville Ave., Newark, NJ 07107; Dr. McKinley Dukes, 4223 S. Benton, Kansas City, MO 64130

Stat., Dr. M. L. Gabriel

Hist., Dr. Clarence Wagner

OFFICERS OF BOARDS

Foreign Mission Board: 701 S. 19th St. Philadelphia, PA 19146. Sec., Dr. William J. Harvey, III

Home Mission Board: Exec. Sec., Dr. Jerry Moore, 1612 Buchanan St. N.W., Washington, DC 20011

Sunday School Publishing Board; 330 Charlotte Ave., Nashville, TN 37201. Exec. Dir., Mrs. C. N. Adkins

B.T.U. Board: 412 4th Ave., Nashville, TN 37219. Sec., Dr. Maynard Turner

Education Board: 903 Looney St., Memphis, TN 38107. Chpsn., Dr. W. H. Brewster

Evangelism Board: Dr. Manuel Scott, 2600 S. Marsalis Ave., Dallas, TX 75216

Laymen's Movement: Pres., Mr. Walter Cade, 537 N. 82nd St., Kansas City, KS 66112

Woman's Auxiliary Convention: 584 Arden Pk., Detroit, MI 48202. Pres., Mrs. Mary O. Ross

Congress of Christian Education: 1014 East Pine St., Tulsa, OK 74106. Pres., Dr. T. Oscar Chappelle

PERIODICAL

National Baptist Voice (s-m), Dr. Roscoe Cooper, Ed. 2800 Third Ave., Richmond, VA 23222. Tel. (804)321-5115

National Primitive Baptist Convention, Inc.

Throughout the years of slavery and the Civil War, the Negro population of the South worshipped with the white population in their various churches. At the time of emancipation, their white brethren helped them to establish their own churches, granting them letters of fellowship, ordaining their deacons and ministers, and helped them in other ways.

The doctrine and polity of this body are quite similar to that of white Primitive Baptists, except that they are "opposed to all forms of church organization"; yet there are local associations and a national convention, organized in 1907.

Each church is independent and receives and controls its own membership. This body was formerly known as Colored Primitive Baptists.

GENERAL ORGANIZATION

Headquarters: P.O. Box 2355, Tallahassee, FL

CHIEF OFFICERS

National Convention: Pres., Elder F. L. Livingston, 1334 Carson St., Dallas, TX 75216. Tel. (214) 949-4650; Rec. Sec., Elder T. W. Samuels, 6433 Hidden Forest Dr., Charlotte, NC 28206, Tel. (704) 596-3153; Sec. Bd. of Dirs., Elder M. G. Miles, 1525 S. Bronough St., Tallahassee, FL 32301; Statistical Sec., Br. T. M. Batts, Jr., 4714 Walford Rd., Warrensville Heights, OH 44128

National Church School Training Union: Pres., Elder W.D. Judge, 1718 West Grand Ave., Orlando, FL 32805; Sec., Mrs. Icylene B. Horne, 2222 Metropolitan St., Dallas, TX 75215

National Ushers Congress: Pres., Deac. Sylvester McClendon, 3515 Barringer Dr., Charlotte, NC 28210; Sec., Catherine Williams, 1919 E. Shadow Lawn Ave., Tampa, FL 33610

Publishing Board: Chpsn., Elder T. W. Samuels, 6433 Hidden Forest Dr., Charlotte, NC 28206; Editorial Sec. and Chpsn. Bd. of Education, Elder J. L. Fitzgerald, 2703 Aspen Dr., Nashville, TN 37208

Women's Congress: Pres., Mrs. M. C. Batts, 4076 E. 147th St., Cleveland, OH 44128; Sec., Mrs. W. M. Miles, 1525 S. Bronough St., Tallahassee, FL 32301

National Laymen's Council: Pres., George W. Brown, 405 E. 26th St., Patterson, NJ 07514; Sec., Bro. J. L. Byrd, 4829 Fairmount Ave., Elyria, OH 44035

Young People's Congress: Pres., Levy Freeman, 3920 Gardenside Dr., NW, Huntsville, AL 35810

National Spiritualist Association of Churches

This organization is made up of believers that Spiritualism is a science, philosophy, and religion based upon the demonstrated facts of communication between this world and the next.

GENERAL ORGANIZATION

Convention: annual (October)

Pres., Joseph H. Merrill, 13 Cleveland Ave., Lily Dale, NY 14752

Vice-Pres., Evelyn Muse, 1104 Susan Dr., Edinburg, TX 78539

Sec., Elizabeth R. Edgar, P.O. Box 128, Cassadaga, FL 32706. Tel. (904) 228-2506

Treas., Rev. Alfred A. Connor, 293 Jersey St., San Francisco, CA 94114

OTHER ORGANIZATIONS

Bureau of Education: Supt., Rev. Joseph Sax, Morris Pratt Institute, 11811 Watertown Plank Rd., Milwaukee, WI 53226

Bureau of Public Relations: Rev. Anne Gehman, 9533 Jomar Dr., Fairfax, VA 22072

The Stow Memorial Foundation: Sec.-Treas., Rev. Evelyn L. Muse, 1104 Susan Drive, Edinburgh, TX 78539

Spiritualist Benevolent Society, Inc.: Cassadaga, FL 32706

PERIODICAL

The National Spiritualist Summit (m), P.O. Box 30172, Indianapolis, IN 46230. Herbert Ray Worth, Ed.

Netherlands Reformed Congregations

The Netherlands Reformed Congregations organized denominationally in 1907. In the Netherlands, the so-called Churches Under the Cross (established in 1839, after breaking away from the 1934 Secession congregations) and the so-called Ledeboerian churches (established in 1841 under the leadership of the Rev. Ledeboer, who seceded from the Reformed State Church), united in 1907 under the leadership of the then 25-year-old Rev. G. H. Kersten, to form the Netherlands Reformed Congregations. Many of the North American congregations left the Christian Reformed Church to join the Netherlands Reformed Congregations after the Kuyperian presupposed regeneration doctrine began making inroads into that denomination.

All Netherlands Reformed Congregations, officeholders, and members subscribe to three Reformed Forms of Unity: The Belgic Confession of Faith (by DeBres), the Heidelberg Catechism (by Ursinus and Olevianus), and the Canons of Dort. Both the Belgic Confession and the Canons of Dordt are read regularly at worship services, and the Heidelberg Catechism is preached weekly, except on church feast days.

GENERAL ORGANIZATION

Synod meets every two years (next meeting, 1988)

OFFICERS

Pres. of Synod: Rev. C. Vogelaar, 1152 Lakeshore Rd. W., St. Catharines, Ontario L2R 6P9

Clk. of Synod: Rev. J. R. Beeke, 55 Robin Hood, Wayne, NY 07470

OTHER ORGANIZATION

Netherlands Reformed Book and Publishing, 1020 N. Main Ave., Sioux Center, IA 51250

PERIODICALS

The Banner of Truth (m), 55 Robin Hood, Wayne NJ 07470. Rev. J. R. Beeke, Ed.

Paul (bi/m). Rev. J. R. Beeke, Ed.

Insight Into (bi-m), 108 Pratt Rd., Kalamazoo, MI 49001. Rev. H. Hofman, Ed.

New Apostolic Church of North America

This body is a variant of the Catholic Apostolic Church, which movement began in England in 1830. The New Apostolic Church distinguished itself from the parent body in 1863 by recognizing a succession of Apostles.

Churches: 473; Inclusive Membership: 34,726; Sunday or Sabbath Schools: 473; Total Enrollment: 2,062; Ordained Clergy: 795

GENERAL ORGANIZATION

Headquarters: 3753 N. Troy St., Chicago, IL 60618

OFFICERS

Pres., Rev. Michael Kraus, 267 Lincoln Rd., Waterloo, Ontario, Canada

First Vice-Pres., Rev. John W. Fendt, 36 Colony La., Manhasset, NY 11030

Second Vice-Pres., Rev. Erwin Wagner, 330 Arlene Pl., Waterloo, Ontario, Canada

Sec., Rev. William K. Schmeerbauch, 312 Ladue Woods Court, St. Louis, MO 63141

Treas. and Asst. Sec., Ellen Eckhardt, 6380 N. Indian Rd., Chicago, IL 60646

PERIODICALS

(All published at 3753 N. Troy St., Chicago, IL 60618)

Word of Life (s-m)

Youth Guide (m)

New Apostolic Review (s-m)

The Good Shepherd (m)

Our Family (m)

North American Baptist Conference

The North American Baptist Conference had its beginning through immigrants from Germany in the middle of the 19th Century. The first church was organized by the Reverend Konrad Fleischmann in Philadelphia, Pennsylvania, in 1848. Actual organization of the North American Baptist Conference took place in 1865 when delegates of the churches met in Wilmot, Ontario. Today only a few churches still use the German language, mostly in a bilingual setting.

The Conference meets in general session once every three years for fellowship, inspiration and to conduct the business of the Conference through elected delegates from the local churches. The General Council, composed of representatives of the various Associations and Conference organizations and departments, meets annually to determine the annual budget and programs for the Conference and its departments and agencies. The General Council also makes recommendations to the Triennial Conference on policies, long-range plans and election of certain personnel, boards and committees. Conference departments and agencies make their recommendations for program and finances to the General Council.

Approximately 90 missionaries serve in Cameroon and Nigeria, West Africa, in Japan, in Brazil and in the Philippines, as well as among various ethnic groups throughout the United States and Canada. They are supported through the Conference Mission and Ministry Budget and Growth Budget.

NEW DAY, a youth music and drama group, is supported by the Conference in its evangelism and training ministry among North American Baptist churches.

Nine homes for the aged are affiliated with the Conference and ten camps are operated on the association level.

Churches: 253; Inclusive Membership: 42,084; Sunday or Sabbath Schools: 253; Total Enrollment: 22,644; Ordained Clergy: 381

GENERAL ORGANIZATION

Triennial Conference: Next meeting, 1988
Headquarters: 1 S. 210 Summit Ave., Oakbrook Terrace, IL 60181. Tel. (312) 495-2000

OFFICERS

Mod., Mr. Ernie Radke
Vice-Mod., Rev. Harvey Mehlaff
Exec. Dir., Dr. John Binder
Treas., Mr. Milton Hildebrandt

OTHER ORGANIZATIONS

Missions Dept.: Dir., Mr. Ron Salzman
Church Growth Dept., Dir., Rev. David Samf
Development Dept., Dir., Mr. Walter Swanson
Financial Services: Dir., Mr. Robert Mayforth
Area Ministries: Dir., Dr. Willis Potratz

PERIODICAL

The Baptist Herald (10/yr.), Barbara J. Binder, Ed., published by the North American Baptist Conference, 1 S. 210 Summit Ave., Oakbrook Terrace, IL 60181

North American Old Roman Catholic Church

A body with the doctrine of the Old Catholic Church with right and succession of Catholic orders. Knott Missal is used for all Masses. Having assumed its present form in the early 1700s when the church in Holland underwent a truly Catholic reform, the Old Catholic Church in time spread throughout Europe. It came to Canada, Mexico, and the United States during this century.

English and Latin Masses are celebrated in traditional pre-Vatican II Liturgy. Baltimore Catechism is used in all CCD Classes; Pontificale Romanum for consecrations, ordinations, etc. The church is not under Papal jurisdiction.

Records of Succession may be found in the Vatican Library, and recorded by the Ecclesiastical Committee.

The Old Catholic Church bears witness to the fullness of the teachings of Holy Scripture; it practices the wholeness of the ancient and orthodox Catholic Faith. Its Bishops and priests, its Sacraments and services, its doctrines and practices, are universally recognized as being truly Catholic. Yet, the Church is not bound by the use of a dead language nor by a myriad of medieval customs and attitudes.

Churches: 133; Inclusive Membership: 62,611; Sunday or Sabbath Schools: 54; Total Enrollment: 8,660; Ordained Clergy: 150

OFFICERS

Archbishop Co-adjutor, Most. Rev. Theodore J. Rematt; Presiding Archbishop Emeritus. Most Rev. John E. Schweikert, 4200 N. Kedvale Ave., Chicago, IL 60641

North American Old Roman Catholic Church (Archdiocese of New York)

This body is identical with the Roman Catholic Church in faith, but differs from it in discipline and worship. The Mass is offered with the appropriate rite either in Latin or in the venacular. All other sacraments are taken from the Roman Pontifical. This jurisdiction allows for married clergy.

Churches: 5; Inclusive Membership: 750; Sunday or Sabbath Schools: 4; Total Enrollment: 81; Ordained Clergy: 12

GENERAL ORGANIZATION

Synod: biennial; next meeting, May 1989, Brooklyn NY.
Chancery Address: Box 021647, G.P.O., Brooklyn, NY 11202. Tel. (718) 855-0600

OFFICERS

Primate Metropolitan, The Most Rev. Archbishop James H. Rogers, 118-09 Farmers Blvd., St. Albans, NY 11412
Chancellor, Rev. Albert J. Berube

PERIODICAL

The Augustinian (occ), Box 021647, G.P.O., Brooklyn, NY 11202

Old German Baptist Brethren

A group which separated from the Church of the Brethren (formerly German Baptist Brethren) in 1881 as a protest against a liberalizing tendency.

GENERAL ORGANIZATION

Conference, annual

OFFICERS

Foreman, Elder Clement Skiles, Rt. 1, Box 140, Bringhurst, IN 46913. Tel. (219) 967-3367
Reading Clk., Elder Herman Shuman, Rt. 4, Box 301, Pendleton, IN 46064
Writing Clk., Elder Willard Yoder, 8 Oslo Court Brookville, OH 45309

PERIODICAL

The Vindicator, 1876 Beamsville-Union City Rd., Union City, OH 45390, M. Keith Skiles, Ed.

Old Order Amish Church

The congregations of this Old Order Amish group have no annual conference. They worship in private homes. They adhere to the older forms of worship and attire. This body has bishops, ministers, and deacons.

Churches: 696; Inclusive Membership: 62,640; Sunday or Sabbath Schools: N.R.; Total Enrollment: N.R.; Ordained Clergy: N.R.

NO GENERAL ORGANIZATION INFORMATION

Der Neue Amerikanische Calendar, c/o Raber's Book Store, 2467 C R 600, Baltic, OH 43804

Old Order (Wisler) Mennonite Church

This body arose from a separation of Mennonites dated 1870, under Jacob Wisler, in opposition to what were thought to be innovations.

At present, this group is located in the Eastern United States and Canada. There are approximately 9,850 members and 46 congregations, with 50 bishops, 110 ministers, and deacons.

Each state, or district, has its own organization or government and holds a yearly conference.

NO GENERAL ORGANIZATION INFORMATION

Arthur Van Pelt, 13550 Germantown Road, Columbiana, OH 44408. Tel. (216) 482-3691

Open Bible Standard Churches, Inc.

Open Bible Standard Churches originated from two revival movements: Bible Standard Conference, founded in Eugene, Oregon, under the leadership of Fred L. Hornshuh, in 1919, and Open Bible Evangelistic Association, founded in Des Moines, Iowa, under the leadership of John R. Richey, in 1932.

Basically similar in doctrine and government, the two groups amalgamated on July 26, 1935, taking the combined name, "Open Bible Standard Churches, Inc.," with headquarters in Des Moines, Iowa.

Two hundred ten ministers formed the original group which has enlarged to incorporate over 1,535 ministers and 670 churches in twenty-nine countries.

Historical roots of the parent groups reach back to the outpouring of the Holy Spirit in 1906 at Azusa Street Mission in Los Angeles, California, and to the great full gospel movement in the Midwest. Both groups were organized under the impetus of pentecostal revival. Simple faith, freedom from fanaticism, emphasis on evangelism and missions, and free fellowship with other groups were characteristics of the growing organizations.

From its origin, Open Bible Standard Churches has emphasized world evangelism. The first missionary left Lodi, California, for India in 1926. Since that time, the program has grown to minister in China, Japan, Philippines, Papua New Guinea, Canada, Puerto Rico, Dominican Republic, Haiti, Cuba, Jamaica, St. Vincent, Grenada, Trinidad, Mexico, Guatemala, El Salvador, Argentina, Chile, Brazil, Spain, Uruguay, Paraguay, Peru, Guinea, Liberia, Ghana, Kenya and Uganda.

The highest governing body of Open Bible Standard Churches meets biennially and is composed of all ministers and one voting delegate per 100 members, or fraction thereof, from each church. A General Board of Directors, elected by the general and divisional conferences, conducts the business of the organization. The U. S. church serves through fourteen national departments, five geographical divisions and twenty-four districts.

Official Bible College is Eugene Bible College, Eugene, Oregon.

Open Bible Standard Churches is a member of the National Association of Evangelicals and is a charter member of the Pentecostal Fellowship of North America. It is also a member of the Pentecostal World Conference. Our officers serve on the governing bodies of these organizations.

Churches: 281; Inclusive Membership: 46,000; Sunday or Sabbath Schools: 270; Total Enrollment: 25,000; Ordained Clergy: 883

GENERAL ORGANIZATION

General Conference: biennial (June)
Headquarters: 2020 Bell Ave., Des Moines, IA 50315. Tel. (515) 288-6761.

OFFICERS

Gen. Supt., Ray E. Smith, Des Moines, IA
Asst. Gen. Supt., Milton J. Stewart, Eugene, OR
Sec.-Treas., Patrick L. Bowlin, Des Moines, IA
Dir. of World Missions, Paul V. Canfield, Des Moines, IA
Dir. of Christian Education, Randall A. Bach, Des Moines, IA

PERIODICALS

Address for periodicals: 2020 Bell Ave., Des Moines, IA 50315
Message of the Open Bible (m), Betty C. Bowlin, Ed.
The Overcomer (q), Randall A. Bach, Ed.
World Vision (m), Paul V. Canfield, Ed.
Outreach Magazine (semi-a), Paul V. Canfield, Ed.

The (Original) Church of God, Inc.

This body was organized in 1886 as the first church in the U.S.A., to take the name "The Church of God." In 1917 a difference of opinion led this particular group to include the word (Original) in its name. It is a holiness body and believes in the whole Bible, rightly divided, using the New Testament as its rule and government.

GENERAL ORGANIZATION

General Convention: annual (October) at Chattanooga, TN
Headquarters: P.O. Box 3086, Chattanooga, TN 37404. Tel. (615)629-9362

OFFICERS

Gen. Overseer, Rev. W. D. Sawyer
Asst. Gen. Overseer, Rev. O. E. Lambeth
Sec.-Treas., Michael B. Mitchell
Supt. Y.P.C.U.W., Billy Perkins
Camp. Mgr., Roy Wm. Kyzer

PERIODICALS

The Messenger (m), 2214 E. 17th St., Chattanooga TN 37404, Rev. W. D. Sawyer, Ed. Tel. 615)629-9362
Youth Messenger (m), Billy Perkins, Ed.

The Orthodox Church in America

The Russian Orthodox Greek Catholic Church of America entered Alaska in 1792 before its purchase by the U.S.A. in 1867. Its canonical status of independence (autocephaly) was granted by its Mother Church, the Russian Orthodox Church, on April 10, 1970, and it is now known as The Orthodox Church in America.

GENERAL ORGANIZATION

All-American Council (Triennial, next meeting, August 1989)
Primate: The Most Blessed Theodosius, Archbishop of Washington, Metropolitan of All America and Canada
Chancellor: V. Rev. Daniel Hubiak, P. O. Box 675, Syosset, NY 11791. Tel. (516)922-0550

SYNOD

Chpsn. His Beatitude Theodosius, P.O. Box 675, Syosset NY 11791
The Rt. Rev. Kyrill, Bishop of Pittsburgh, P. O. Box R, Wexford, PA 15090
The Right Rev. Peter, Bishop of New York, 33 Hewitt Ave., Bronxville, NY 10708
The Rt. Rev. Dmitri, Bishop of Dallas, 2770 Country Club Rd., Wiley TX 75098

The Rt. Rev. Herman, Bishop of Philadelphia, St. Tikhon's Monastery, South Canaan, PA 18459

The Rt. Rev. Gregory, Bishop of Sitka, St. Michael's Cathedral, Box 697, Sitka, AK 99835

The Rt. Rev. Boris, Bishop of Chicago, 8200 S. County Line Rd., Hinsdale, IL 60521

The Rt. Rev. Nathaniel, Bishop of Detroit, 2522 Grey Tower Rd., Jackson, MI 49201

The Rt. Rev. Job, Bishop of Hartford, 6 Clark Rd., Cumberland, RI 02864

The Right Rev. Tikhon, Bishop of San Francisco, 649 North Robinson St., Los Angeles, CA 90026

The Orthodox Presbyterian Church

On June 11, 1936, certain ministers, elders, and lay members of the Presbyterian Church in the U.S.A. withdrew from that body to form a new denomination. Under the leadership of the late Rev. J. Gresham Machen, noted conservative New Testament scholar, the new church determined to continue to uphold the Westminster Confession of Faith as traditionally understood by Presbyterians, and to engage in proclamation of the gospel at home and abroad.

The church has grown modestly over the years and suffered early defections, most notably one in 1937 that resulted in the formation of the Bible Presbyterian Church under the leadership of Dr. Carl McIntire. It now has congregations in almost all the states of the continental United States.

The denomination is a member of the Reformed Ecumenical Synod and the North American Presbyterian and Reformed Council.

GENERAL ORGANIZATION

General Assembly: annual Headquarters: 7401 Old York Rd., Philadelphia, PA 19126. Tel. (215) 635-0700

OFFICERS

Mod., Mr. John O. Kinnaird, 7401 Old York Rd., Philadelphia, PA 19126

Stated Clk., Rev. John P. Galbraith, 2345 Willow Brook Dr., Huntingdon Valley, PA 19006

Pentecostal Assemblies of the World, Inc.

An interracial Pentecostal holiness of the Apostolic Faith, believing in repentance, baptism in Jesus' Name, and being filled with the Holy Ghost, with the evidence of speaking in tongues. This organization, originating in the early part of the century in the Middle West has now spread throughout the country.

GENERAL ORGANIZATION

Convention: annual (August)

Headquarters; 3939 Meadows Dr., Indianapolis, IN 46208. Tel. (317) 547-9541

OFFICERS

Presiding Bishop, James A. Johnson, 12643 Conway Downs Dr., St. Louis, MO 63141; Asst. Presiding Bishop, Paul A. Bowers, 1201 Egan Hills, Cincinnati, OH 45225; Bishops, Arthur Brazier, 500 E. 33rd St., Chicago, IL 60616; David Braziel, 10 Pineridge Dr., Rt. 2, Silver Creek, GA; David Braziel, 112 Wilson Ave., Rome, GA 30161; George Brooks, 75 Brooklynlawn Circle, Westville, CT 06515; Ramsey Butler, 4627 Clay St., Washington, DC 20019; Morris E. Golder, 7474 Holliday W. Dr., Indianapolis, IN 46260; Francis L. Smith, 783 New Castle Dr., Akron, OH 44313; Brooker T. Jones, P.O. Box 1479, Princeton, WV 24740; C. R. Lee, 533 Oak St., Mansfield, OH 44707; Robert McMurray, 1639 Wellington Rd., Los Angeles, CA 90019; Benjamin T. Moore, 8048 Hollybrook Ct., Indianapolis, IN 46250; Ross P. Paddock, 818 Dwillare Dr., Kalamazoo, MI 49001; Philip L. Scott, 7133 Blue Spruce Dr., St. Louis, MO 63110; William L. Smith, 2460 Gramercy Pk., Los Angeles, CA 90019; A. J. Street 3906 N. 32nd St., Pine Bluff, AR 70601; Samuel A. Layne, 1240 N. Euclid St., St. Louis, MO 63113; Freeman M. Thomas, 436 Fielding Dr., Penn Hills Pk., VA 15235; James E. Tyson, 6431 N. Sunset La., Indianapolis, IN 64260; Charles Watkins, 1147 Brandon Rd., Cleveland, OH 44112

Gen. Sec., Dist., Elder Richard Young, Treas. Dist., Elder James Loving, Asst. Treas., Elder Willis Ellis

PERIODICAL

Christian Outlook (m), 3939 Meadow Dr., Indianapolis, IN 46208, Jane Sims, Ed.

Pentecostal Church of God

Growing out of the pentecostal revivals at the turn of the century, the Pentecostal Church of God was organized in Chicago, Illinois, on December 30, 1919, as the Pentecostal Assemblies of the U.S.A. The name was changed to Pentecostal Church of God on February 5, 1922, in 1934 was changed again to The Pentecostal Church of God of America, Inc., and finally to Pentecostal Church of God (Incorporated) in 1979.

The International Headquarters was moved from Chicago to Ottumwa, Iowa, in 1927, then to Kansas City, Missouri, in 1933, and finally to Joplin, Missouri, in 1952.

The denomination is evangelical and pentecostal in doctrine and practice. Active membership in the National Association of Evangelicals and the Pentecostal Fellowship of North America is maintained.

Doctrinally, the church is Trinitarian and teaches the absolute inerrancy of the Scripture from Genesis to Revelation. Among its cardinal beliefs are the doctrines of salvation, which includes regeneration; divine healing, as provided for in the atonement; the baptism in the Holy Ghost, with the initial physical evidence of speaking in tongues; and the premillennial second coming of Christ.

Churches: 1,144; Inclusive Membership: 90,900; Sunday or Sabbath Schools: N.R.; Total Enrollment: 68,000; Ordained Clergy: 1,595

GENERAL ORGANIZATION

Headquarters: 4901 Pennsylvania, P.O. Box 850, Joplin MO 64802

General Convention meets biennially. (Next Convention June 1987).

OFFICERS

Gen. Supt., Dr. James D. Gee
Gen. Sec.-Treas., Dr. Ronald R. Minor

OTHER GENERAL EXECUTIVES

Dir. of World Missions, Rev. Elmer L. Redding
Dir. of Indian Missions, Dr. C. Don Burke
Gen. PYPA Pres., Rev. Vernell Ingle
Dir. of Christian Ed., Dr. Kenneth K. Foreman

ASSISTANT GENERAL SUPERINTENDENTS

Northwestern Division, Dr. Lawrence D. Haddock
Southwestern Division, Dr. Norman D. Fortenberry
North Central Division, Rev. Denzel D. Parramore
South Central Division, Dr. Jack D. Barker
Northeastern Division, Dr. H. O. "Pat" Wilson
Southeastern Division, Rev. Melvin L. West

OTHER DEPARTMENTAL OFFICERS

Gen. PLA Pres., Mrs. Diana L. Gee
Dir. of Hispanic Missions, Dr. Samuel L. Corley, Sr.

Ed., The Pentecostal Messenger, Rev. Donald K. Allen
Production Manager of MPH, Rev. Donald K. Allen
Sunday School Curriculum Ed., Mrs. Rosemarie Foreman
King's Men Fellowship Pres., Rev. Roy Little
Senior Christian Fellowship Pres., Rev. Wayne Melton
Dir. of Home Missions/Evangelism, Dr. L. Arnold
Niemeyer
Messenger Publishing House, 4901 Pennsylvania, Joplin
Mo 64802

PERIODICALS

The Pentecostal Messenger (m), Donald K. Allen, Ed.
The Helper (q), Diana L. Gee, Ed.

Pentecostal Fire-Baptized Holiness Church

Organized in 1918, consolidated with Pentecostal Free
Will Baptists in 1919. Maintains rigid discipline over
members.

GENERAL ORGANIZATION

General Convention every two years. (Next meeting,
1989)
Headquarters: Toccoa, GA 30577

OFFICERS

Gen. Treas., Kenwin (Bill) N. Johnson, P.O. Box 1528,
Laurinburg, NC 28352
Gen. Sec., W. H. Preskitt, Sr., Rt. 1 Box 169, Wetumpka,
AL 36092
Gen. Mod., Steve E. Johnson, Rt. 2 Box 204, Dry Fork,
VA 24549
Gen. Supt. Mission Bd., Jerry Powell, Rt. 1, Box 384,
Chadbourn, NC 28431

PERIODICAL

Faith and Truth (m), P.O. Box 212, Nicholson, GA 30565.
Edgar Vollrath, Rt. 5, Box 137, Commerce, GA 30529,
Ed.

The Pentecostal Free Will Baptist Church, Inc.

Organized 1855, as the Cape Fear Conference of Free
Will Baptists. Reorganized in 1959 and renamed the
Pentecostal Free Will Baptist Church, Inc. The doctrines
include regeneration, sanctification, the Pentecostal baptism of the Holy Ghost, the Second Coming of Christ, and
divine healing.

GENERAL ORGANIZATION

General Meeting: Meets Semi-Annually.
General Headquarters: P.O. Box 1568, Dunn, NC 28334.
Tel. (919) 892-4161
Heritage Bible College, P.O. Box 1628, Dunn, NC 28334.
Tel. (919) 892-4268
Crusader Youth Camp, P.O. Box 1568, Dunn, NC 28334
Mutual Benevolent Fund, P.O. Box 1568, Dunn, NC
28334
Blessings Bookstore, 1006 Cumberland St., Dunn, NC
28334. Tel. (919)892-2401

OFFICERS

Gen. Supt., Rev. Don Sauls
Asst. Gen. Supt., Dr. W. L. Ellis
Gen. Sec., Rev. J. T. Hammond
Gen. Treas., Dr. W. L. Ellis
World Witness Dir., Dr. Herbert Carter
Christian Education Dir., Rev. J. T. Hammond
Gen Services Dir., Rev. Elvin Butts
Ministerial Council Dir., Rev. Roy Savage
Ladies' Auxiliary Dir., Mrs. Shirley Hardison
Heritage Bible College: Pres., Dr. W. L. Ellis
Crusader Youth Camp Dir., Rev. J. T. Hammond

Pentecostal Holiness Church, International

This body grew out of the National Holiness Association
movement of the last century and has direct roots in
Methodism. Beginning in the South and Midwest, the
present church represents the merger of three different
holiness bodies: the Fire-Baptized Holiness Church
founded by B. H. Irwin in Iowa in 1895; the Pentecostal
Holiness Church founded by A. B. Crumpler in Goldsboro, North Carolina, in 1898; and the Tabernacle
Pentecostal Church founded by N. J. Holmes in 1898.

All three bodies joined the ranks of the pentecostal
movement as a result of the Azusa Street revival in Los
Angeles in 1906 and a 1907 pentecostal revival in Dunn,
North Carolina, conducted by G. B. Cashwell, who had
visited Azusa Street. In 1911 the Fire-Baptized and
Pentecostal Holiness bodies merged in Falcon, North
Carolina, to form the present church; the Tabernacle
Pentecostal Church was added in 1915 in Canon, Georgia.

The church stresses the new birth; the Wesleyan
experience of entire sanctification; the pentecostal baptism in the Holy Spirit, evidenced by speaking in tongues;
divine healing; and the premillennial second coming of
Christ.

GENERAL ORGANIZATION

General Conference: quadrennial (Next meeting, 1989)
Headquarters: P.O. Box 12609, Oklahoma City, OK
73157 Tel. (405) 787-7110

OFFICERS

Gen. Supt., Bishop Leon Stewart
Vice Chpsn./Asst. Gen. Supt.: Rev. B. E. Underwood
Asst. Gen. Supt., Dr. Jesse Simmons
Gen. Sec./Treas., Rev. Jack Goodson

OTHER ORGANIZATIONS

The Publishing House (Advocate Press), Franklin Springs,
GA 30639. Charles Bradshaw, Gen. Administrator
Christian Education Dept.: Gen. Dir., Rev. Doyle
Marley, P. O. Box 12609, Oklahoma City, OK 73157
General Woman's Auxiliary: Pres., Mrs. Lois Tripp, P. O.
Box 12609, Oklahoma City, OK 73157

PERIODICALS

Publications Editorial Office:
P.O. Box 12609, Oklahoma City, OK 73157
The Pentecostal Holiness Advocate (m), Mrs. Shirley
Spencer, Ed.
Helping Hand (m), Mrs. Lois Tripp, Ed.
Sunday School Literature, Rev. Charles Bradshaw, Ed.
Witness (m), Rev. Joe Iaquinta, Ed.
Worldorama (m), Rev. B. E. Underwood, Ed.

Pillar of Fire

The Pillar of Fire was founded by Alma Bridwell White
in Denver, Colorado, December 29, 1901 as the Pentecostal Union. In 1917, the name was changed to Pillar of
Fire. Alma White was born in Kentucky in 1862 and taught
school in Montana where she met her husband, Kent
White, a Methodist minister, who was a University student
in Denver.

Because of Alma White's evangelistic endeavors, she
was frowned upon by her superiors, which eventually
necessitated in her withdrawing from Methodist Church
supervision. She was ordained as Bishop and her work
spread to many states, to England, and since her decease,
Liberia, W.A.

The Pillar of Fire organization is credited with being
pioneers in Christian education, with two colleges, each
stressing Biblical studies. The church continues to thrive
throughout the United States under the present leadership
of the granddaughter, Arlene White Lawrence, with the
same goals and purposes in mind as the founder.

GENERAL ORGANIZATION

Headquarters: Zarephath, NJ 08890. Tel. (201) 356-0102
Western Headquarters: 1302 Sherman St., Denver, CO 80203

OFFICERS

Pres. and Gen. Supt., Bishop Donald J. Wolfram, 1st Vice-Pres., and Asst. Supt., Bishop Robert B. Dallenbach; Sec., Mildred E. Portune; 2nd Vice-Pres. and Treas., Lois R. Stewart; Trustees, Bishop Arlene W. Lawrence; Ellworth N. Bradford, S. Rea Crawford, June Blue

PERIODICALS

Pillar of Fire (bi-m), Zarephath, NJ 08890, Bishop Donald J. Wolfram,Ed.
Pillar of Fire Junior (w), Zarephath, NJ 08890, Bishop Donald J. Wolfram, Ed.

Plymouth Brethren (See Christian Brethren)

Polish National Catholic Church of America

After a long period of dissatisfaction with Roman Catholic administration and ideology and, in addition, through the strong desire for religious freedom, this body was organized in 1897.

GENERAL ORGANIZATION

General Synod: every four years (Next General Synod, October 1990, Toronto, Ontario)
Headquarters: 529 East Locust St., Scranton, PA 18505. Tel. (717) 346-9131

OFFICERS

Prime Bishop, Most Rev. John F. Swantek, 115 Lake, Scranton Rd., Scranton, PA 18505
Bishop of the Central Diocese, Rt. Rev. Anthony M. Rysz, 529 E. Locust St., Scranton, PA 18505
Bishop of the Eastern Diocese, Rt. Rev. Thomas J. Gnat, 635 Union St., Manchester, NH 03104
Bishop of the Buffalo-Pittsburgh Diocese, Rt. Rev. Francis G. Rowinski, 182 Sobieski St., Buffalo, NY 14212
Bishop of Western Diocese, Rt. Rev. Joseph K. Zawistowski, 2019 W. Charleston St., Chicago, IL 60647
Bishop of the Canadian Diocese, Rt. Rev. Joseph I. Nieminski, 186 Cowan Ave., Toronto, Ontario M6K 2N6
Ecumenical Officer, Very Rev. Stanley Skrzypek, 206 Main St., New York Mills, NY 13416. Tel. (315)736-9757

Presbyterian Church in America

With a strong commitment to missionary work both at home and abroad and to continuing historic Presbyterianism, this body was formally organized in December 1973 in Birmingham, Alabama. The PCA increased its size and geographic coverage in June 1982 when it received the Reformed Presbyterian Church, Evangelical Synod. RPCES had come into existence in 1965 as the result of a merger of the Reformed Presbyterian Church in North America, General Synod, and the Evangelical Presbyterian Church. Denominational antecedents existed in Colonial America. The PCA believes the Bible is the inerrant Word of God and is fully infallible and sufficient rule of faith and practice. All officers are required to subscribe, without reservation, to the Reformed faith as set forth in the Westminster Confession and Catechisms.

Churches: 913; Inclusive Membership: 188,083; Sunday or Sabbath Schools: 913; Total Enrollment: 90,710; Ordained Clergy: 1,702

GENERAL ORGANIZATION

General assembly: meets annually (Knoxville, TN, June 6-10, 1988)
Headquarters: 1852 Century Pl., Atlanta, GA 30345. Tel. (404)320-3366

OFFICERS

Mod., Gerald Sovereign, Jr., Gulf Breeze, FL
Stated Clk., Rev. Morton H. Smith, 1852 Century Pl., Ste. 202, Atlanta, GA 30345. Tel. (404) 320-3366

PERMANENT COMMITTEES

Adm., Earl W. Witmer, 1852 Century Pl., Ste. 202, Atlanta, GA 30345. Tel. (404)320-3366
Christian Education and Publications, Rev. Charles Dunahoo, 1852 Century Pl., Ste. 101, Atlanta, GA 30345. Tel. (404)320-3388
Mission to North America, Rev. Terry Gyger, 1852 Century Pl. Ste. 205, Atlanta, GA 30345
Mission to the World, John E. Kyle, 1852 Century Pl., Ste. 201, Atlanta, GA 30345

PERIODICAL

The PCA Messenger (m), 1852 Century Pl., Ste. 101, Atlanta, GA 30345, Paul R. Gilchrist, Ed.

Presbyterian Church (U.S.A.)

The Presbyterian Church (U.S.A.) was organized June 10, 1983, when the Presbyterian Church in the United States ("Southern Presbyterian Church") and the United Presbyterian Church in the United States of America merged in Atlanta, Georgia. Thus was healed the major division within American Presbyterianism, which had existed since the Civil War when the Presbyterian Church in the Confederate States of America withdrew from the Presbyterian Church in the United States of America.

The United Presbyterian Church in the United States of America had been created by the 1958 union of the Presbyterian Church in the United States of America and the United Presbyterian Church of North America. Of those two uniting bodies, the Presbyterian Church in the U.S.A. dated from the first Presbytery organized in Philadelphia about 1706. The United Presbyterian Church of North America was formed in 1858, when the Associate Reformed Presbyterian Church and the Associate Presbyterian Church united.

Strongly ecumenical in outlook, the Presbyterian Church (U.S.A.) is the result of at least ten different denominational mergers over the last two and a half centuries. A Structural Design for Mission was adopted by the General Assembly meeting in June 1986. It is anticipated that implementation of the design will begin in January 1987. Therefore, the following reflects the national denominational structure in September 1986, the deadline date for submission of material for publication in this volume.

Churches: 11,531; Inclusive Membership: 3,007,332; Sunday or Sabbath Schools: 11,531; Total Enrollment: 1,098,362; Ordained Clergy: 19,514

GENERAL ASSEMBLY

Meets annually. Next meeting: June 7-15, 1988, St. Louis, MO

OFFICERS

Mod. (1987-88), Isabel Rogers
Vice-Mod., Jaime Quionnes
Stated Clerk, James E. Andrews
Assoc. Stated Clerks, Robert T. Newbold, Jr., Margrethe B. J. Brown
Asst. Stated Clerks, Eugene D. Witherspoon, Jr., Mildred L. Wager, Catherine M. Phillippe

Note: The Presbyterian Church (U.S.A.) is in the process of moving to its new headquarters in Louisville, Kentucky. This is scheduled to take place during August, 1988 and the new address is: 100 Witherspoon St., Louisville, KY 40202.

During June and July 1988, the New York and Atlanta offices described in the 1987 Yearbook of American and Canadian Churches will be in operation and it will be possible to obtain information about personnel and functions of these offices by calling the following information number in Louisville: 1-800-UP2DATE.

After the move is completed, certain staff will still continue to function in New York, Philadelphia and Jeffersonville, Indiana and in other locations throughout the U.S. The names addresses, and telephone numbers of these persons are included in the following directory. If no address or telephone number is included, the address of that office or staff person is in Louisville as cited above. At this time, there are no headquarters or other telephone numbers available.

THE OFFICE OF THE GENERAL ASSEMBLY

100 Witherspoon St., Louisville, KY 40202. Dept. of Administration, _____. Office of History, William B. Miller, Dir., 425 Lombard St., Philadelphia, PA 19147. Tel. (215)627-1852

Presbyterian Council for Chaplains and Military Personnel (joint with the Associate Reformed Presbyterian Church, the Cumberland Presbyterian Church, and the Second Cumberland Presbyterian Church), Chprsn., Christina Randazzo; Dir., Charles E. McMillan; Assoc. Dir., E. Blant Ferguson. Tel. (202)244-4177

GENERAL ASSEMBLY COUNCIL

Exec. Dir., S. David Stoner: New York Liaison, John Lindner, 475 Riverside Dr., New York, NY 10115, Tel. (202)870-2101: Coord., Finance and Budget, Bruce Berry; Assoc. Adm., Marion Leibert

CHURCH VOCATIONS UNIT

Office of Director

Dir., Edgar W. Ward: Adm. Asst., Jewel McRae; Assoc. Dir., Enlistment, Preparation and Referral Services, Mary V. Atkinson; Assoc., Equal Employment, Lillian Anthony; Editor, *Monday Morning,* Ann Anderson, 475 Riverside Dr., New York, NY 10115: Assoc. Dir., Management and Development Human Resources, Naomi Diaz; Adm. Asst., Joyce Benedicto

Section on Enlistment, Preparation and Referral Services

Office of Enlistment and Preparation for Ministry
Assoc., Preparation of Ministry, Charles Marks; Assoc., Enlistment Services, Judy Mead-Atwell

Office of Examinations, Certification and Accreditation
Assoc., Examination Services, William Chapman

Office for Personnel Referral Services
Manager, Evelyn Hwang; Assoc. Operations, Margaret Willis; Assoc., Matching, R. Howard McCuen; Assoc., Specialized Referral and Matching, JoRene Willis; Assoc., Specialized Personnel Services, Mary Serovy

Section on the Management and Development of Human Resources

Office of Human Resource Management

Employment Manager, Sharon Chaplain; Assoc. Benefits Adm, Eva Suarez; Personnel Asst., Norman Folson

Office of Human Resources Development
Coord, Carlos Santin; Assoc., Professional Devel.; Donald Brown

EDUCATION AND CONGREGATIONAL NURTURE

Director's Office
Dir., Robert Miller; Assoc., Communication, Promotion, and Coordination, Ed Craxton; Assoc., Conferencing (Dir. Stony Point), Jim Palm, Crickettown Road, Stony Point, NY 10980, Tel. (914)786-5674; Assoc., Conferencing (Dir., Ghost Ranch), Joe Keesecker, Abiquiu, NM 87510, Tel. (505)685-4333; Asst. Adm., Linda Knight

Leadership Development
Assoc. Dir., Mary Jean McFadyen; Assoc., Church Officer/Lay Leadership Resources, Ben Lane; Assoc., Family Ministries, Lindell Sawyers; Assoc., Ministry with Men, Arthur Kamitska; Assoc., Youth, Rodger Nishioka; Assoc., Ministry with Older Adults, Tom Robb; Assoc. Dir., Resource Devel. (Hispanic), Tina Gutierrez; Assoc., Ethnic Resource Devel. (Korean), C. W. Choi; Assoc., Curriculum Devel., Preschool Resources, Martha Pillow; Assoc., Curriculum Devel., Children's Resources (Bible Discovery), Mary Duckert; Assoc. Curriculum Devel., Youth Resources (Celebrate), John Purdy; Assoc., Curriculum Devel., Youth Resources (Bible Discovery, Older Youth and selected Youth Celebrate), Barbara Withers; Assoc., Curriculum Devel., Adult Resources (Bible Discovery and others), Marvin Simmers; Assoc., Curriculum Devel., Adult Resources (Celebrate and Others), Frank Hainer; Assoc., Family Resources, Carol Ikeler; Assoc., Men's Resources, David Lewis; Assoc., Resource Center Devel., Jo Gallagher; Ed. Asst./Copy Ed., Shirley Murphy

Presbyterian Survey

Ed./Publ., Vic Jameson; Man. Ed., Catherine C. Cottingham; Assoc. Ed., Eva Stimson; Publication Services Pub./Ed., Robert McIntyre

EVANGELISM AND CHURCH DEVELOPMENT MINISTRY UNIT

Dir., Patricia M. Roach; Coord., Adm., Communication, Research and Plng., Julianne Jens-Horton; Assoc. Dir., Rural/Small Town Ministry, Judith Coats; Assoc. Dir., Mission Financial Resources, Diana Stephen; Assoc. Mission Prog. Grants, Ralph Scissions; Assoc., Small Church Devel., Thomas Dietrich; Assoc., Revitalization, Barbara Woody; Assoc., Racial Ethnic Resource, Devel. and Trng., Mildred Brown. Devel. and Trng. Assoc., Intl. Ch. Devel. and Evang. (Jt. Ofc. with Global Mission Unit), Morton Taylor

GLOBAL MISSION MINISTRY UNIT

Director, Clifton Kirkpatrick; Assoc. Dir., Unit Coord., Syngman Rhee; Assoc. Global Mission Plng., Newton Thurber; Assoc., Management and Budget, Mehdi Abhari

Ecumenical/Interfaith Office
Assoc., Ecumenical Coord., Lewis Lancaster

Health Ministries Office
Assoc. Dir., Health Ministries, Gwen Crawley

Mission to the U.S.A. Office
Assoc. Dir., Internationalization of Mission, Elizabeth McAliley; Assoc., Mission to USA Personnel, Paul

Seto; Assoc. Ecumenical Exchange, Nancy Miller

Partnership in Mission Office
Assoc. Dir., Partnership Coordination, Bruce Gannaway; Assoc., Southern Africa, Yenwith Whitney; Assoc., Northern Africa, John Pritchard; Assoc., East Asia/Pacific, Insik Kim; Assoc., Interfaith Rel., Margaret O. Thomas; Assoc., South America, Benjamin Gutierrez; Assoc., Cent. Am./Mexico/Caribbean, David Young; Assoc., Europe, Robert Lodwick; Assoc., Intl. Evangelism, Morton Taylor

People in Mission Offices
Assoc. Dir., Mission Personnel, J. Wilbur Patterson; Assoc., Volunteers in Mission (USA), Rosita Bermudez; Assoc. Volunteers in Mission (International), Mike Stuart; Assoc. Missionary-Fraternal Worker Concerns, Marcia Borgeson; Assoc., Missionary Services/Pastoral Care, Harry Phillips

RACIAL ETHNIC UNIT
Dir., James Foster Reese; Assoc. Dir., Racial Justice Ministries, Jovelino Ramos; Coord., Asian Justice Ministries, Wesley Woo; Coord., Black Justice Ministries, Otis Turner; Coord., Hispanic Justice Ministries, Jose Rodriguez; Coord., Black Congregational Enhancement, Rita Dixon

SOCIAL JUSTICE AND PEACEMAKING UNIT
Dir., Belle Miller McMaster; Assoc. Dir., Donald J. Wilson; Group Dir. - Human Devel. and Coord., Hunger Prog., Colleen Shannon; Prog. Asst. for Resourcing, Hunger Prog., Diane Hockenberry; Coordinator—World Service, William K. Duval; Assoc. for Jinishian Field Service, Haig Tilbian; Group Dir., Washington Office, Mary Jane Patterson; Deputy Group Dir., Washington, George Chauncey, 110 Maryland Ave., NE, Washington, DC 20002, Tel. (202)543-1126; Assoc. for International Issues, Walter L. Owensby; Assoc. for Peace Issues, Barbara G. Green; Assoc. for Human Services, David Zuverink; Assoc. for Social Welfare Organizations, Rodney T. Martin; Coord., Jarvie Commonweal Service, Ellsworth G. Stanton, III, 475 Riverside Dr., 4th Fl., New York, NY 10115, Tel. (212)870-2967; Assoc. Coord., Jarvie Commonweal Service, Alice W. Stutz; Social Caseworkers, Jarvie Commonweal Service, Ann Bonnell, Adele Malhorta, Hazel Schuller, Patricia Charles; Helene Walker; Group Dir., Church and Public Issues, Vernon S. Broyles, III; Assoc. for Criminal Justice, Kathy Lancaster; Assoc. for Cmty. Devel., Phillip Newell; Assoc. for Mission Responsibility Through Investments, William Somplatsky-Jarman; Assoc. for Intl. Justice, Asia and Middle East, Harry F. J. Daniel; Group Dir., Peacemaking, Richard L. Killmer; Assoc. for Peacemaking, James O. Watkins, Ollie Gannaway; Assoc. for United Nations, Church Center for the UN, Robert F. Smylie, 777 United Nations Plz., New York, NY 10017

STEWARDSHIP AND COMMUNICATION DEVELOPMENT MINISTRY UNIT
Dir., John Coffin; Assoc. Dir., Plng. Budgeting and Inf. Coord., Vivian Johnson; Assoc. Dir., Churchwide Communication, Lois Stover; Assoc., Communication, Informations Systems, Nancy Heinze; Assoc. Dir., Media Services, Betty Elam; Assoc. Media Services, Bill Gee; Asst., Media Services, Lloyd Perkins; Assoc. Media Coord. and Marketing, Bill Huie; Assoc. Dir., Mission Funding, Claude Godwin; Assoc., Church Fncl. Campaign Services Coord., Don Myer; Field Reps./Church Fncl. Campaign Services, David Johnson, Gary Hall, David McDonald, Jim Tinsley, Bill Llewelyn, Kiki Swanson, Bernie Nord; Assoc. Dir., Mission, Interpretation and Promotion, James

Magruder; Assoc., Interpretation Resources, David Eddy; Assoc., Interpretation Resources Publications, Ted Yaple; Assoc., Mission Interpretation—Speakers and Correspondence, Anne Howland; Assoc., Interpretation—Marketing Synod and Presbytery Relationships, Eileene MacFalls; Assoc., Interpretation Resources Coord., Sandra Woodcock; Assoc. Dir., Research Services, Art Bemjamin; Assoc., Research/Coordination and Survey, Keith Wulff; Asst., Research/Administration, Betty Partenheimer; Assoc. Research/Information, Wayne Thompson; Assoc. Dir., Stewardship, David McGreath

THEOLOGY AND WORSHIP MINISTRY UNIT
Director, George Telford; Assoc. Liturgical Resources, Harold Daniels; Assoc., Faith and Order, Aurelia Fule

WOMEN'S MINISTRY UNIT
Director, Mary Ann Lundy; Assoc. Dir., Jean Miller; Assoc. Presbyterian Women, Gladys Strachan; Assoc., Women Employed by the Church, Ann DuBois; Assoc., Committee of Women of Color, Patricia Gill Turner; Assoc., Mission Participation, Marilyn Clark; Associates for Regional Staff: Eastern—New York City, Irene Ng, Frances Unsell, Yolanda Hernandez, 475 Riverside Dr., Rm. 439, New York, NY 10115, Tel. (212)870-2107; East Central—Pittsburgh, Glendora Paul, Margaret Hall, 300 Sixth Ave., Ste. 1110, Pittsburgh, PA 15222; West Central—Kansas City, Judy Mead, Holly Hearon, 7850 Holmes Rd., Kansas City, MO 64131, Tel. (816)363-4226; Western—San Francisco, Lucille Rieben, Lorna Shoemaker, Joan Richardson, 330 Ellis, Rm. 414, San Francisco, CA 94102, Tel. (415)775-1454; Southeastern—Atlanta, Elizabeth Lunz

SUPPORT SERVICES
Director, Robert T. Mehrhoff; Mgr., Ofc. of News Services, Marj Carpenter; Assoc. News Services, Mary Henry; Assoc. Mgr., Purchasing and Supplies, Jacqueline McCray; Purchasing Agt., Gen. Supplies, Shari De Vonish; Assoc. Mgr., Travel and Mtg. Plng., Helen S. Malik; Mgr., Ofc. of Distribution Services, Catherine A. Stratton

CENTRAL TREASURY CORPORATION
Treasurer/President, Delmar Byler; Vice Pres./Assoc. Treas., Arthur Clark; Vice Pres., Controller, Nagy Tawfik; A.V.P./Property and Risk Management, Thomas Drake; A.V.P./Planning/Cap. Budget, Carmen Lopez; Mgr., Finance Resource Coordinator, Hope Bezold; Mgr. Central Receiving, William Partenheimer; Senior Finance Resource Coordinator, Robert Etheridge; Finance Resource Coordinators: Maria Alvarez, Hwa Ja Kim, Patricia Robbins, Jeanice Vazquez; Mgr. Accounts Payable, Thomas Abraham; Assoc. Mgr., Central Recording, William Shumate; Accountant, Finance Reporting, Gerard Van Amstel; Supervisor, G/L Accounting, Robin Allen; Supervisor, A/R Loans, Sarah Zimmerman

COMMITTEE ON SOCIAL WITNESS POLICY
Dir., Dieter T. Hessel; Assoc. Dir., Policy Devel. and Interpretation, Ruth Duba

COMMITTEE ON HIGHER EDUCATION
Dir., James W. Gunn; Assoc. Global Education and Leadership Devel., Haydn O. White; Assoc., Racial-Ethnic Schools and Colleges, George M. Conn, Jr.; Assoc., Higher Education Ministries, Clyde O. Robinson, Jr.

COMMITTEE ON THEOLOGICAL EDUCATION
Dir., Joyce Tucker; Assoc. Dir. (Volunteer), Arthur Hall; Assoc., Mission Cooperation, Roger Woods

PRESBYTERIAN CHURCH (U.S.A.) FOUNDATION

Chpsn of the Board, Herbert B. Anderson; Vice Chpsn., Paul Bell; Pres., Terry Young; Vice Pres. for Finance, Dennis J. Murphy; Vice Pres. for Development, Donn Jann *(Note: This agency has offices in Jeffersonville, Indiana. At the time of printing, the address and telephone number were not known. Those interested may call the general church number given at the front of this directory.)*

PERIODICALS

American Presbyterians: Journal of Presbyterian History (q), 425 Lombard St., Philadelphia, PA 19147. Rev. James H. Smylie, Ed.

Monday Morning (bi-m), 475 Riverside Dr., New York, NY 10115. Ms. Ann Anderson, Man. Ed.

Church & Society magazine (bi-m), 100 Witherspoon St., Louisville, KY 40202. Kathy Lancaster and Gaspar B. Langella, Eds.

Horizons (6/yr.), Presbyterian Women, Barbara Roche, Ed., 100 Witherspoon St., Louisville, KY 40202

These Days (bi-m), (jointly with the Cumberland Presbyterian Church, the Presbyterian Church in Canada, the Presbyterian Church (U.S.A.), The United Church of Canada, and the United Church of Christ), Arthur M. Field, Ed., Editorial Office, 100 Witherspoon St., Louisville, KY 40202

Presbyterian Survey, 100 Witherspoon St., Louisville, KY 40202

SYNOD EXECUTIVES

Alaska-Northwest, Rev. Elizabeth B. Knott, 720 Senaca St., Seattle, WA 98101. Tel. (206) 623-4073

Covenant, Rev. George P. Morgan, 6172 Bush Blvd., Ste. 3000, Columbus, OH 43229. Tel. (614) 436-3310

Lakes & Prairies, Rev. Robert T. Cuthill, 8012 Cedar Ave., S., Bloomington, MN 55425. Tel. (612) 854-0144

Lincoln Trails, Rev. Gordon L. Corbett, Interim, 1100 W. 42nd St., Indianapolis, IN 46208. Tel. (317) 923-3681

Living Waters, Rev. Harold J. Jackson, 441 Donelson Pike, Ste. 100, P.O. Box 290275, Nashville, TN 37229. Tel. (615)889-8280

Mid-America, Rev. John L. Williams, 6400 Glenwood, Ste. 111, Overland Park, KS 66202. Tel. (913) 384-3020

North Carolina, Dr. John D. Macleod, Jr. P.O. Box 10785, Raleigh, NC 27605. Tel. (919) 834-4379

Northeast, Rev. Eugene G. Turner, 3049 E. Genesee St., Syracuse, NY 13224. Tel. (315) 446-5990

Pacific, Rev. Kenneth C. Miller, Interim, PO.Box 1810, San Anselmo, CA 94960. Tel. (415)258-0333

Piedmont, Rev. Carroll D. Jenkins, 6600 York Rd., Ste. 205A, Baltimore, MD 21212. Tel. (301) 377-7141

Puerto Rico, Dr. Ana Ines Braulio Condominio, Medical Center Plaza, Oficina 216, Mayaguez, PR 00708. Tel. (809) 832-8375

Rocky Mountains, Rev. David T. Tomlinson, 1370 Pennsylvania Ave., Ste. 410, Denver CO 80203. Tel. (303) 830-6712

South Atlantic, Rev. John Niles Bartholomew, Interstate North Office Center, 435 Clark Rd., Ste. 404, Jacksonville, FL 32218. Tel. (904)764-5644

Southern Calif., Hawaii, Rev. Frederick J. Beebe; 1501, Wilshire Blvd., Los Angeles, CA 90017. Tel. (213) 483-3840

Southwest, Rev. Gary Skinner, 4423 N. 24th St., Ste. 800, Phoenix, AZ 85016. Tel. (602)468-3800

Sun, Rev. William J. Fogelman, 920 Stemmons Fwy., Denton, TX 76201. Tel. (817) 382-9656

Trinity, Rev. Wayne W. Allen, 3040 Market St., Camp Hill, PA 17011. Tel. (717) 737-0421

Virginias, Dr. H. Davis Yeuell, 4841 Williamson Rd., Roanoke, VA 24012. Tel. (703) 563-0393

Primitive Advent Christian Church

This body split from the Advent Christian Church. All its churches are located in West Virginia. the Primitive Advent Christian Church believes that the Bible is the only rule of faith and practice and that Christian character is the only test of fellowship and communion. The church agrees with Christian fidelity and meekness; exercises mutual watch and care; counsels, admonishes, or reproves as duty may require; and receives the same from each other as becomes the household of faith. Primitive Advent Christians do not believe in taking up arms against our fellow man in case of war.

The church believes that three ordinances are set forth by the Bible to be observed by the Christian church: (1) baptism by immersion; (2) the Lord's Supper, by partaking of unleavened bread and wine; (3) feet washing, to be observed by the saints' washing of one another's feet.

OFFICERS

Pres., Donald Young, 1640 Clay Ave., South Charleston, WV

Vice-Pres., Roger Hammons, 273 Frame Rd., Elkview, WV 25071. Tel. (304)965-6247

Sec. and Treas., Hugh W. Good, 395 Frame Rd., Elkview, WV 25071. Tel. (304) 965-1550

Primitive Baptists

A large group of Baptists, located throughout the United States, who are opposed to all centralization and to modern missionary societies. This body believes, and preaches Salvation by Grace alone.

GENERAL ORGANIZATION

Address: Cayce Publ. Co., S. Second St., Thornton, AR 71766. Tel. (501) 352-3694

OFFICER

Elder W. H. Cayce, S. Second St., Thornton, AR 71766. Tel. (501) 352-3694

PERIODICALS

Primitive Baptist (m), Thornton, AR 71766. W. H. Cayce, Ed.

For the Poor (m), Thornton, AR 71766. W. H. Cayce, Ed.

Baptist Witness, Box 17037, Cincinnati, OH 45217. L. Bradley, Jr., Ed.

Christian Baptist (m), P.O. Box 68, Atwood, TN 38220, S. T. Tolly, Ed.

Christian Pathway (m), Maryville, TN 37801, Elder Harold Hunt, Ed.

Primitive Methodist Church in the U.S.A.

Hugh Bourne and William Clowes, local preachers in the Wesleyan Church in England in the early 1800s, became interested in seeing their fellow workers converted and brought to Christ. Lorenzo Dow, a Methodist preacher from America, recounted with enthusiasm the story of the American camp meeting to Bourne and Clowes, and a whole day's meeting at Mow Cop in Staffordshire, England, on May 31, 1807, was arranged. Thousands were present and many were converted but, strange as it may seem, the church founded by that great open air preacher John Wesley refused to accept these converts and reprimanded the preachers for their evangelistic effort.

After waiting for a period of two years for a favorable action by the Wesleyan Society, Bourne and Clowes established The Society of the Primitive Methodists. The words of Bourne provide the evidence that this was not a schism, for "we did not take one from them . . . it now appeared to be the will of God that we, as a Camp Meeting Community, should form classes and take upon us the care of churches in the fear of God." The first Primitive Methodist missionaries were sent to New York in 1829, and a distinct conference in America was established on September 16, 1840.

Missionary efforts reach into Guatemala, Spain, and numerous other countries, with both Spanish and English work in the U.S.A. The denomination joins in federation with the Evangelical Congregational Church and the United Brethren in Christ Church, and is a member of the National Association of Evangelicals.

The Primitive Methodist Church believes the Bible to be the only true rule of faith and practice, the inspired Word of God, and holds its declarations final. It believes in the existence of one Triune God, the Deity of Jesus Christ, the Deity and personality of the Holy Spirit, the innocence of Adam and Eve, the Fall and corruption of the human race, the necessity of repentance, justification by faith of all who believe and regeneration witnessed by the Holy Spirit, sanctification by the Holy Spirit producing holiness of heart and life, the second coming of the Lord Jesus Christ, the resurrection of the dead and conscious future existence of all men, and future judgments and eternal rewards and punishments.

Churches: 86; Inclusive Membership: 8,625;Sunday or Sabbath Schools: 82;Total Enrollment: 5,030; Ordained Clergy: 105

GENERAL ORGANIZATION

The Conference, annual (Next Meeting, May 1988)

OFFICERS

Pres., Rev. J. William Reseigh, 500 New York Rd., Browns Mills, NJ 08015
Exec. Dir., Rev. William H. Fudge, 1045 Laurel Run Rd., Wilkes-Barre, PA 18702
Gen. Sec., Rev. K. Gene Carroll, 223 Austin Ave., Wilkes-Barre, PA 18705
Treas., Mr. Raymond C. Baldwin, 11012 Langton Arms Ct., Oakton, VA 22124

Progressive National Baptist Convention, Inc.

A body which held its organizational meeting at Cincinnati, November, 1961, and subsequent regional sessions, followed by the first annual session in Philadelphia in 1962

GENERAL ORGANIZATION

Annual Session: August.

OFFICERS

Pres., Dr. J. Alfred Smith, Sr., Allen Temple Baptist Church, 8500 A St., Oakland, CA 94621
Gen. Sec., Rev. C. J. Malloy, Jr. 601 50th St., N.E., Washington, DC 20019. Tel. (202) 396-0558

OTHER ORGANIZATIONS

Dept. of Christian Education: Sec., Rev. C. B. Lucas, 3815 W. Broadway, Louisville, KY 40211
Women's Auxiliary: Mrs. Goldie Hollie, 537 66th St., Oakland, CA 94609.
Home Mission Bd., Exec. Dir., Rev. Archie LeMone, 601 50th St., N.E., Washington, DC 20019.
Congress of Christian Education: Pres., Dr. Pauline C. Reeder, 788 E. 52nd St., Brooklyn, NY 11203
Baptist F. M. Bureau, Dr. Ronald K. Hill, 1678 Fairview Ave., Willow Grove, PA 19090

PERIODICAL

Baptist Progress (q), Tabernacle Baptist Church, 1477 Copley Rd., Akron, OH 44320. Rev. Isaiah F. Paul, Ed.

The Protestant Conference (Lutheran), Inc.

The Conference came into being in 1927 as the result of expulsions of pastors and teachers from the Wisconsin Evangelical Lutheran Synod (WELS). The underlying cause which ignited the suspensions was a rebellion against what was labeled The Wauwatosa Theology, so named after the location of the Wisconsin Synod seminary at that time and the fresh approach to Scripture study there by the faculty. This approach sought to overcome the lazy and self-serving habits of dogmatism, which overtakes any group of Christians, particularly when they have been given a true and correct exposition of Christian doctrine, and is content to postulate formula to a given situation, but this rarely with the Gospel's or the faith's true interest at heart.Chiefly responsible for this renewal was Professor John Philipp Koehler.

The Conference was formed as the result of these suspensions, which were to be followed by other suspensions, and which continue to this day. To give testimony to the issues at operation in this controversy and in particular to bear witness to the grace of the Wauwatosa Theology, the Conference has published *Faith-Life* since 1928. Our roster of congregations, currently at six, is chiefly in Wisconsin. The Conference has no official officers as such. Our purpose has not been to build yet another church body interested chiefly in its survival among the many church bodies. Chief in influence on our history have been Professor J. P. Koehler (1859-1951), his son Karl Koehler (1885-1948) who was the chief architect of *Faith-Life* with its unique Policy and Purpose, and Paul Hensel (1888-1977) who displayed the freshness of the Wauwatosa Theology in his writings and commentary.

A concise history of these things is to be found in Prof. Leigh Jordahl's Introduction to a reprinting of J. P. Koehler's "The History of the Wisconsin Synod," published by the Conference.

Churches: 7; Inclusive Membership: 979; Sunday or Sabbath Schools: 4; Total Enrollment: 118; Ordained Clergy: 7

GENERAL ORGANIZATION

Conference: meets 3 times annually

OFFICERS

Rec. Sec., Pastor Gerald Hinz, P.O. Box 86, Shiocton, WI 54170. Tel. (414)986-3918
Fin. Sec.-Treas., Michael Meler, 1023 Colan Blvd., Rice Lake, WI 54868

PERIODICAL

Faith-Life (bi-m), P.O. Box 2141, LaCrosse, WI 54601. Pastor Marcus Albrecht, Rt. 1, Mindoro, WI 54644, Ed.

Protestant Reformed Churches in America

The Protestant Reformed Churches in America were organized in 1926 as a result of doctrinal disagreement relating to such matters as world conformity, problems of higher criticism and God's grace that pervaded the Christian Reformed Church in the early 1920's.

After the passage of the formula on Three Points of Common Grace by the Synod of the Christian Reformed Church in 1924, and during the resulting storm of controversy, three clergy, and those in their congregations who agreed with them, were expelled from the Christian Reformed Church. These clergy were Herman Hoeksema of the Eastern Ave. Christian Reformed Church in Grand

93

Rapids, Mich., George Ophoff, pastor of the Hope congregation in Riverbend, Mich., and Henry Danhof in Kalamazoo.

In March 1925, the consistories of these congregations signed an Act of Agreement and adopted the temporary name of "Protesting Christian Reformed Churches." Following the Synod of the Christian Reformed Church of 1926, when the break was made final, the three consistories participating in the Act of Agreement met, and in November, 1926, organized the Protestant Reformed Churches in America.

The Protestant Reformed Churches in America hold to the doctrinal tenets of Calvinism, the Belgic Confession, the Heidelberg Catechism and the Canons of Dordrecht.

GENERAL ORGANIZATION

General Synod: meets annually (June)
Headquarters: 16515 South Park Ave., South Holland, IL 60473. Tel. (312) 333-1314

OFFICER

Stat. Clk., Rev. M. Joostens, 2016 Tekonsha, S.E., Grand Rapids, MI 49506. Tel. (616) 247-0368

Reformed Church in America

The Reformed Church in America was established in 1628 by the earliest settlers of New York. It is the oldest Protestant denomination with a continuous ministry in North America. Until 1867 it was known as the Reformed Protestant Dutch Church.

The first ordained minister, Domine Jonas Michaelius, arrived in New Amsterdam from The Netherlands in 1628. Throughout the colonial period, the Reformed Church lived under the authority of the Classis of Amsterdam. Its churches were clustered in New York and New Jersey. Under the leadership of Rev. John Livingston, it became a denomination independent of the authority of the Classis of Amsterdam in 1776. Its geographical base was broadened in the nineteenth century by the immigration of Reformed Dutch and German settlers in the midwestern United States. In the twentieth century, the Reformed Church spans the United States and Canada.

The Reformed Church accepts as its standards of faith the Heidelberg Catechism, Belgic Confession, and Canons of Dort. It has a rich heritage of world mission activity. It claims to be loyal to reformed traditions which emphasizes obedience to God in all aspects of life.

Although the Reformed Church in America has worked in close cooperation with other churches, it has never entered into merger with any other denomination. It is a member of the World Alliance of Reformed Churches, the World Council of Churches, and the National Council of the Churches of Christ in the United States of America.

Churches: 928; Inclusive Membership: 340,359; Sunday or Sabbath Schools: 900; Total Enrollment: 101,659; Ordained Clergy: 1,636

GENERAL ORGANIZATION

General Synod: annual (Next meeting, June 11-17, 1988, Bronx, NY)
Denominational Office: 475 Riverside Dr., New York, NY 10115. Tel. (212) 870-2841

OFFICERS AND STAFF OF GENERAL SYNOD

Pres., Robert L. Wise, 475 Riverside Dr., Rm. 1811, New York NY 10115
Gen. Sec., Edwin G. Mulder

OTHER ORGANIZATIONS

Board of Direction: Pres., Jerrald Redeker, 475 Riverside Dr., Rm. 1811, New York NY 10115

Board of Pensions: Pres., James A. Neevel; Sec., Edwin G. Mulder
General Program Council: Mod., Carl B. Vogelaar, 475 Riverside Dr., Rm. 1812, New York, NY 10115; Sec. for Program, Eugene P. Heideman

Office of Human Resources: Coord., Alvin J. Poppen
Office of Finance: Treas., Everett K. Hicks
Office of Promotion, Communications and Development: Dir., Wayne Antworth
Reformed Church Women: Exec Dir., Diana Paulsen
The Black Council: Exec. Dir., M. William Howard, Jr.
The Hispanic Council: Nat'l. Sec., Johnny Alicea-Baez
The American Indian Council: Sec., Roe B. Lewis
The Council for Pacific/Asian American Ministries: National Sec., Ella White

PERIODICAL

The Church Herald (bi-m), 6157 - 28th St., SE, Grand Rapids, MI, John C. Stapert, Ed.

Reformed Church in the United States

Lacking pastors, early German Reformed immigrants to the American colonies were led in worship by "readers." One reader, schoolmaster John Philip Boehm, organized the first congregations near Philadelphia in 1725. A Swiss pastor, Michael Schlatter, was sent by the Dutch Reformed Church in 1746. Strong ties with the Netherlands existed until the formation of the Synod of the Reformed High German Church in 1793.

The "Mercersburg Theology" of the 1840s was a precursor to twentieth century liberalism, and to the merger of the Reformed Church with the Evangelical Synod of North America in 1934. Conservatives vigorously opposed the union, holding that it sacrificed the Reformed heritage. (The merged Evangelical and Reformed Church became part of the United Church of Christ in 1957.)

The Eureka Classis was organized in North and South Dakota in 1910 as one of fifty-eight classes (districts) in the church. These congregations were strongly influenced by the writings of H. Kohlbruegge, P. Geyser and J. Stark, who emphasized salvation by grace through faith, not by works. Under the leadership of pastors W. Grossmann and W. J. Krieger, the Eureka Classis refused to become part of the merger of 1934, and in 1942 incorporated as the continuing Reformed Church in the United States.

The growing Eureka Classis dissolved in 1986 to form a Synod with four regional classes. An heir to the Reformation theology of Zwingli and Calvin, the Heidelberg Catechism of 1563 is used as the confessional standard of the church. The Bible is strictly held to be the inerrant, infallible Word of God.

The RCUS has close relationships with other conservative Reformed and Presbyterian bodies. It supports Westminster Theological Seminary in Philadelphia and Escondido, CA; Dordt College and Mid-America Reformed Seminary in Iowa. The RCUS is the official sponsor of the Reformed Confessing Church of Zaire.

GENERAL ORGANIZATION

Synod: annual; Classis: semi-annual

OFFICERS

Pres., Rev. Robert Stuebbe, 401 Cherry Hill Dr., Bakersfield, CA 93309
Vice-Pres., Rev. Vernon Pollema, 235 James Street, Shafter, CA 93263
Clerk, Rev. Steven Work, 5692 Seifert Ave., San Jose, CA 95118. Tel. (408)448-3239

Treas., Mr. Dennis Carlson, Rte. 2, Box 99A; Hastings, NE 68901

PERIODICAL

The Reformed Herald (m), Box 797, Eureka, SD 57437, Rev. P. Grossmann, Ed.

Reformed Episcopal Church

The Reformed Episcopal Church was founded December 2, 1873, in New York City by the Bishop George D. Cummins. Cummins was a major evangelical figure in the Protestant Episcopal church and from 1866 until 1873 was the assistant bishop of the diocese of Kentucky. However, Cummins and other evangelical Episcopalians viewed with alarm the influence of the Oxford Movement in the Protestant Episcopal Church, not only for the interest in stimulated in Roman Catholic ritual and doctrine but also for the intolerance it bred toward evangelical Protestant doctrine both within and outside the Episcopal Church. Throughout the late 1860s, evangelicals and ritualists clashed over ceremonies and vestments, exchanges of pulpits with clergy of other denominations, and the proper meaning of critical passages in the Book of Common Prayer as well as the interpretation of the sacraments and validity of the so-called Apostolic Succession. These clashes culminated in October 1873, when other bishops publicly attacked Cummins in the church newspapers for participating in an ecumenical Communion service sponsored by the Evangelical Alliance. On November 10, 1873, Cummins resigned his office and, on November 13, drafted a call to Episcopalians to organize a new Episcopal Church for the "purpose of restoring the old paths of their fathers." At the organization of the new church on December 2 (known as the First General Council), a *Declaration of Principles* was adopted and the Rev. Charles E. Cheney was elected bishop to serve with Cummins. The Second General Council, meeting in May 1874 in New York City, approved a *Constitution and Canons* and a slightly amended version of the Book of Common Prayer. In 1875, the Third General Council adopted a set of *Thirty-Five Articles* as a recast substitute to the Church of England's *Thirty-Nine Articles of Religion.*

Although Cummins died in 1876, the church had grown to seven jurisdictions in the U.S. and Canada at that time. Although substantial growth ceased after 1900, the church now comprises three synods (New York-Philadelphia, Chicago, Charleston-Atlanta-Charlotte) and a missionary jurisdiction of the West. It maintains in its doctrine the founding principles of episcopacy (as an ancient and desirable form of church polity), a Biblical liturgy, Reformed doctrine, and evangelical zeal, and in its practice it continues to recognize the validity of nonepiscopal orders of evangelical ministry. The Reformed Episcopal Church is a member of the National Association of Evangelicals; it was a long-time member of the Federal Council of Churches but withdrew, and in 1938 it rejected remerger efforts with the Protestant Episcopal Church.

Churches: 81; Inclusive Membership: 5,733; Sunday or Sabbath Schools: 76; Total Enrollment: 3,163; Ordained Clergy: 116

GENERAL ORGANIZATION

General Council: triennial (Next meeting, May, 1990)

OFFICERS

Pres. and Presid. Bishop, Rev. William H. S. Jerdan, Jr., 414 W. Second South St., Summerville, SC 29483
Vice-Pres., Bishop Franklin H. Sellers, 1629 W. 99th St., Chicago, IL 60643
Sec., Rev. Roger F. Spence, 6300 Greenwood Pkwy., #203, Sagamore Hills, OH 44067

Treas., Mr. William B. Schimpf, 67 Westaway Lane, Warrington, PA 18976

OTHER ORGANIZATIONS

Board of Foreign Missions: Pres., Rev. R. Charles Gillin, 124 Springfield Ave., Aldan PA 19018; Sec., Mrs. Lyla Wildermuth, 22 Forest Ave., Willow Grove, PA 19090; Treas., Rev. Daniel Olsen, 11 S. Andover Ave., Margate, NJ 08402
Board of National Church Extension: Pres., Rev. Robert N. McIntyre, Smithown Rd., R.R. # 1, Box 416, Pipersville, PA 18947; Sec., Rev. Dale H. Crouthamel, 14 Culberson Rd., Basking Ridge, NJ 07920; Treas., Mrs. Joan Workowski, 1162 Beverly Rd., Jenkinton, PA 19046
Trustees Sustentation Fund: Pres., Mr. E. Earl Shisler, Jr., R.D. # 2, Perkasie, PA 18944. Treas., Mr. William B. Schimpf, 67 Westaway Lane, Warrington, PA 18976
Publication Society: Pres., Rev. Allen C. Guelzo, 430 Shadeland Ave., Drexel Hill PA 19026
The Reapers: Pres., Mrs. Nancy Fleischer, R.R. #1, Box 500, Pipersville, PA 18947; Treas., Mrs. Loralee Holiman, 319 E. 50th St., New York, NY 10022

BISHOPS

William H. S. Jerdan, Summerville, SC 29483.
Sanco K. Rembert, 121 Moultrie St., Charleston, SC 29403
Leonard W. Riches, R.D. 1, Box 413, Smithown Rd., Pipersville, PA 19104
Daniel G. Cox, 9 Hilltop Pl., Baltimore, MD 21228
Royal U. Grote, Jr., 19 Heather Ct., New Providence, NJ 07974
James C. West, 91 Anson St., Charleston, SC 29401

PERIODICALS

Episcopal Recorder (bi-m), 4225 Chestnut St., Philadelphia, PA 19104. Rev. George B. Fincke, Ed.
The Reformed Episcopalian, Board of National Church Extension, 4225 Chestnut St., Philadelphia, PA 19140. Bishop Royal U. Grote, Ed.

Reformed Mennonite Church

This group was reorganized in 1812 under John Herr because they did not know of any other organization that fully carried out New Testament teachings. They believe there can be only one true church, consisting of regenerated persons who are united in love and doctrine.

OFFICER

Bishop Earl Basinger, 1036 Lincoln Heights Ave., Ephrata, PA 17522

Reformed Methodist Union Episcopal Church

The Reformed Methodist Union Episcopal church was formed after a group of ministers withdrew from the African Methodist Episcopal Church following a dispute over the election of ministerial delegates to the General Conference.

These ministers held a meeting on January 22, 1885 at Hills Chapel (now known as Mt. Hermon RMUE church), on Fishburn St. in Charleston, S.C. This four-day meeting resulted in the organization of the Reformed Methodist Union church.

In this meeting the Rev. William E. Johnson was unanimously elected president of the new church. Following the death of Rev. Johnson in 1896 an extra session of the General Conference was called to elect a new leader for the church.

It was decided in this conference that the church would conform to regular American Methodism (the Episcopacy); the first Bishop, Edward Russell Middleton, was elected, and "Episcopal" was added to the name of the church.

Bishop Middleton was consecrated on Dec. 5, 1896, by Bishop P. F. Stephens of the Reformed Episcopal Church.

GENERAL ORGANIZATION

General Conference: annual Headquarters: Charleston, SC 29407

OFFICERS

Rt. Rev. Leroy Gethers, 1136 Brody Ave., Charleston, SC 29407. Tel. (803) 766-3534
Gen. Sec., Rev. Fred H. Moore, 115 St. Margaret St., Charleston, SC 29403. Tel. (803)723-8857
Treas., Rev. Rufus German
Sec. of Education, Rev. Fred E. German
Sec. of Books Concerns, Rev. Earnest McKeever
Sec. of Pension Fund, Rev. Joseph Powell
Sec. of Church Extension, Rev. Joseph Gadsden
Sec. of Church Contingent, Sammie Mitchell
Sec. of Sunday Union, Rev. Hercules Champaigne
Sec. of Mission, Rev. Jerry M. DeBoer

Reformed Presbyterian Church of North America

Also known as the Church of the Covenanters. Origin dates back to the Reformation days of Scotland when the Covenanters signed their "Covenants" in resistance to the king and the Roman Church in the enforcement of state church practices. The Church in America has signed two "Covenants" in particular, those of 1871 and 1954.

Churches: 71; Inclusive Membership: 5,111; Sunday or Sabbath Schools: 71; Total Enrollment: 2,898;Ordained Clergy: 121

GENERAL ORGANIZATION

Synod: annual

OFFICERS

Mod., Prof. Willard McMillan, 1329 Book Ave., Beaver Falls, PA 15010. Tel. (412) 486-1041
Clk., Rev. Paul M. Martin, 1117 E. Devonshire, Phoenix, AZ 85014. Tel. (602) 277-3497
Asst. Clk., Rev. Jonathan Leach, 8344 Cadwalder Ave., Elkins Park PA 19117. Tel. (215) 635-0680
Stated Clk., Louis D. Hutmire, 7418 Penn Ave., Pittsburgh, PA 15208. Tel. (412) 731-1177

PERIODICALS

The Covenanter Witness (bi-w), 7418 Penn Ave., Pittsburgh, PA 15208. James Pennington, Ed.

Reformed Zion Union Apostolic Church

Organized in 1869, at Boydton, Va., by Elder James R. Howell of New York, a minister of the A.M.E. Zion Church; with doctrines of the Methodist Episcopal Church.

GENERAL ORGANIZATION

Annual Conferences (in August After the Third Sunday) General Conference: quadrennial (Next meeting, 1990)

OFFICER

Sec., Deacon, James C. Feggins, 416 South Hill Ave., South Hill, VA 23970. Tel. (804) 447-3374

Religious Society of Friends (Conservative)

These Friends mark their present identity from separations occurring by regions at different times from 1845 to 1904. They hold to a minimum of organization structure. Unprogrammed Meetings for Worship, which are basically silent, demonstrate the belief that all individuals may

commune directly with God and may share equally in vocal ministry.

They continue to stress the importance of the Living Christ and the experience of the Holy Spirit working with Power in the lives of individuals who obey him.

YEARLY MEETINGS

North Carolina YM, Ray Treadway, 710 E. Lake Dr., Greensboro, NC 27401
Iowa YM, John Griffith, 5745 Charlotte, Kansas City MO 64110
Ohio YM, David Nagel, 61830 Sandy Ridge Rd., Barnesville, OH 43713

Religious Society of Friends (Unaffiliated Meetings)

Though all groups of Friends acknowledge the same historical roots, 19th-century divisions in theology and experience led to some of the current organizational groupings. Many newer yearly meetings, often marked by spontaneity, variety, and experimentation and hoping for renewed Quaker unity, have chosen not to identify with past divisions by affiliating in traditional ways with the larger organizations within the Society. Some of these unaffiliated groups have begun within the past 25 years.

UNAFFILIATED YEARLY MEETINGS

Alaska Yearly Meeting, Box 687, Kotzebue, AK 99752
Amigos Central de Bolivia, Casilla 992, La Paz, Bolivia
Amigos de Santidad de Bolivia, Casilla 992, La Paz, Bolivia
Central Yearly Meeting of the Friends Church, 302 S. Black, Alexandria, IN 46001
Iglesia Evangelica Amigos, Apartado 235, Santa Rosa de Capan, Honduras
Iglesia Nacional Evangelica de Los Amigos-Bolivia, Casilla Correo 8385, La Paz, Bolivia
Iglesia Nacional Evangelica de Los Amigos-Peru, Casilla 320, Puno, Peru
Intermountain Yearly Meeting, 624 Pearl St., #302, Boulder, CO 80302
North Pacific Yearly Meeting, 503 East W St., Tumwater, WA 98501
Pacific Yearly Meeting, 258 Cherry Ave., Los Altos, CA 94022
Reunion General de Los Amigos en Mexico, J. B. Tijerinah 306 Nte., 87000 Cuidad Victoria, Tam., Mexico

Reorganized Church of Jesus Christ of Latter Day Saints

Founded April 6, 1830, by Joseph Smith, Jr., and reorganized under the leadership of the founder's son, Joseph Smith III, in 1860. The Church, with headquarters in Independence, MO, is established in 35 countries in addition to the United States and Canada. A biennial world conference is held in Independence, Missouri. The current president is Wallace B. Smith, great-grandson of the original founder.

Churches: 1,094; Inclusive Membership: 192,077; Sunday or Sabbath Schools: N.R.; Total Enrollment: N.R.; Ordained Clergy: 16,585

GENERAL ORGANIZATION

Conference: (World Conference: Biennial in April of even numbered years)
Headquarters: The Auditorium, P.O. Box 1059, Independence, MO 64051. Tel. (816) 833-1000

OFFICERS

First Presidency: Wallace B. Smith, Howard S. Sheehy, Jr., Counselor, Alan D. Tyree, Counselor

Pres. of Council of 12 Apostles: Paul W. Booth
Presiding Bishopric, Francis E. Hansen, Presiding Bishop;
Gene M. Hummel, Counselor; Ray E. McClaran,
Counselor
Presiding Patriarch: Duane E. Couey
Church Sec., W. Grant McMurray
Public Relations: Stephanie Kelley

PERIODICALS

Saints Herald (m), Independence, MO. Wallace B. Smith,
Alan D. Tyree, Howard S. Sheehy, Jr., and Roger
Yarrington, Eds.
Saints in Service (bi-m), Elbert Dempsey, Ed.
Restoration Witness (bi-m), Independence, MO, Barbara
Howard, Ed.

The Roman Catholic Church

The largest single body of Christians in the U.S., the
Roman Catholic Church, is under the spiritual leadership
of His Holiness the Pope. Its establishment in America
dates back to the priests who accompanied Columbus on
his second voyage to the New World. A settlement, later
discontinued, was made at St. Augustine, Florida. The
continuous history of this Church in the Colonies began at
St. Mary's in Maryland, in 1634.

Churches: 23,561; Inclusive Membership: 52,893,217;
Sunday or Sabbath Schools: N.R.; Total Enrollment:
7,215,948; Ordained Clergy: 53,382

(The following information has been furnished by the
editor of The Official Catholic Directory, published by P.
J. Kenedy & Sons, P.O. Box 265, Skokie, IL 60077.
Reference to this complete volume will provide more
adequate information.)

INTERNATIONAL ORGANIZATION

His Holiness the Pope, Bishop of Rome, Vicar of Jesus
Christ, Supreme Pontiff of the Catholic Church.
POPE JOHN PAUL II, Karol Wojtyla (born May 18,
1920; installed October 22, 1978)

APOSTOLIC PRO NUNCIO TO THE
UNITED STATES

Archbishop Pio Laghi, 3339 Massachusetts Ave., N.W.,
Washington, DC 20008. Tel. (202) 333-7121

U.S. ORGANIZATION

National Conference of Catholic Bishops, 1312 Massachusetts Ave., NW, Washington, DC 20005. Tel. (202)
659-6600

The National Conference of Catholic Bishops (NCCB)
is a canonical entity operating in accordance with the
Vatican II Decree, **Christus Dominus.** Its purpose is to
foster the Church's mission to mankind by providing the
Bishops of this country with an opportunity to exchange
views and insights of prudence and experience and to
exercise in a joint manner their pastoral office.

OFFICERS

Pres., Archbishop John L. May
Vice-Pres., Archbishop Daniel Pilarcyk
Sec., Bishop Eugene Marino
Treas., Archbishop Daniel Kucera

GENERAL SECRETARIAT

Gen. Sec., Msgr. Daniel F. Hoye
Assoc. Gen. Secs., Rev. Donald Heintschel, Rev. Robert
Lynch, Mr. Francis X. Doyle

COMMITTEES

Ecumenical and Interreligious Affairs (Ecumenism):
Chpsn., Archbishop J. Francis Stafford
Secretariat: Exec. Dir., Rev. John Hotchkin

Asst. Exec. Dir., _____
Liturgy:
Chpsn., Bishop Joseph Delaney
Secretariat: Dir., Rev. John Gurrieri; Assoc. Dir., Rev.
Ronald Krisman, Rev. Msgr. Alan Detscher
Priestly Formation:
Chpsn., Bishop James Keleher
Secretariat: Dir., Rev. Robert N. Sherry
Permanent Diaconate:
Chpsn., Bishop William Skylstad
Secretariat: Dir., Rev. _____
Priestly Life and Ministry:
Archbp, Thomas J. Murphy
Chpsn., Rev. Msgr. Colin A. MacDonald
Secretariat: Dir., Rev. Mr. Samuel Taub
Pro-Life Activities: Joseph Cardinal Bernardin

United States Catholic Conference, 1312 Massachusetts
Ave. NW, Washington, DC 20005, Tel. (202) 659-6600

The United States Catholic Conference (USCC) is a
civil entity of the American Catholic Bishops assisting
them in their service to the Church in this country by
uniting the people of God where voluntary, collective
action on a broad diocesan level is needed. The USCC
provides an organization structure and the resources
needed to insure coordination, cooperation, and assistance in the public, educational, and social concerns of the
Church at the national, regional, state, interdiocesan and,
as appropriate, diocesan levels.

OFFICERS

Pres., Archbishop John L. May
Vice-Pres., Archbishop Daniel Pilarcyk
Treas., Archbishop Daniel Kucera
Sec., Bishop Eugene Marino

GENERAL SECRETARIAT

Gen. Sec., Msgr. Daniel F. Hoye
Assoc. Gen. Sec., Rev. Donald Heintschel, Rev. Robert
Lynch, Mr. Francis X. Doyle
Sec. for Planning, Sr. Sharon Euart, R.S.M.
Actg. Sec. for Public Affairs, William A. Ryan
Assoc. Sec., Public Affairs, _____

STAFF OFFICES

Finance & Administration, Dir., Sister Frances A.
Mlocek, I.H.M.
Accounting, Kenneth Korotky
Human Resources, Dir., Thomas Meehan; Assoc. Dir.,
Regina Grunert
Office of Publishing Services, Dan Juday
General Counsel, Mark E. Chopko
Government Liaison, Dir., Frank Monahan

COMMITTEES AND DEPARTMENTS

Communication: Chpsn., Bishop Anthony Bosco; Sec.,
Richard Hirsch; Broadcast Productions, Rev. Joseph
Fenton, S.M.,Tel. (212)644-1896; National Catholic
News Services Richard Daw
Education: Chpsn., Bishop Francis Shulte
Social Development and World Peace: Chpsn., Bishop
Sullivan; Sec., John Carr; Domestic Social Develop-
ment, Sharon Daly; Health and Welfare Issues,
_____; Rural Energy and Food Issues, Walter
Grazer; International Justice and Peace, Fr. William
Lewers, C.S.C.; Middle East Affairs, Rev. J. Bryan
Hehir; Latin American Affairs, Thomas Quigley;
European and East Asian and Political Affairs, Robert
Hennemeyer; African Affairs and Human Rights
Issues, Rev. Rollins Lambert; Political and Military
Affairs, Dr. Gerard F. Powers

RELATED ORGANIZATIONS

Campaign for Human Development, Exec. Dir., Rev.
Alfred LoPinto
Catholic Relief Services, 1011 First Ave., New York, NY

10022. Tel. (212) 838-4700. Exec. Dir., Mr. Lawrence Pezzulo

U.S.CATHOLIC BISHOPS' ADVISORY COUNCIL
Chpsn., Mrs. Barbara Hope

CORPORATE ENTITIES AFFILIATED WITH USCC

National Council of Catholic Laity, Pres., Mr. Thomas Simmons, P. O. Box 14525, Cincinnati, OH 45214. Tel. (513) 922-2495

National Council of Catholic Women, Pres., Mrs. Toni Bishchoff ; Exec. Dir., Annette Kane, 1312 Massachusetts Ave. NW, Washington, DC 20001

ASSOCIATIONS

Canon Law Society of America, Exec. Coord., Rev. Edward Pfnausch, Catholic University, Washington, DC 20064. Tel. (202) 269-3491

Catholic Charities,-USA Exec. Dir., Rev. Thomas J. Harvey, 1319 F St., N.W., Washington, DC 20004

Conference of Major Religious Superiors of Men, Rev. Ronald Faley, T.O.R., 8808 Cameron St., Silver Spring, MD 20910. Tel. (301) 588-4030

Leadership Conference of Women Religious, Exec. Dir., Sr. Janet Roesener, C.S.J., 8808 Cameron St., Silver Spring, MD 20910. Tel. (201)588-4955

National Catholic Educational Association, Pres., Sr. Catherine McNamee, 1077 30th St., N.W., Suite 100, Washington, DC 20007. Tel. (202) 337-6232

National Office for Black Catholics, 801 Rhode Island Ave., N.E., Washington,D.C. 20018.Tel (202)635-1778

Word of God Institute, Exec. Dir., Rev. John Burke, 487 Michigan Ave., NE, Washington, DC 20017. Tel. (202) 529-0001

ARCHDIOCESES AND DIOCESES

There follows an alphabetical listing of Archdioceses and Dioceses of The Roman Catholic Church. Each Archdiocese or Diocese contains the following information in sequence: Name of incumbent Bishop; name of Auxiliary Bishop or Bishops, and the Chancellor or Vicar General of the Archdiocese or Diocese, or just the address and telephone number of the chancery office.

Cardinals are addressed as "His Eminence" and Archbishops and Bishops as "Most Reverend."

Albany, Bishop Howard J. Hubbard. Chancery Office, 465 State St., Albany, NY 12203; P.O. Box 6297 Quail Sta., Albany, NY 12206. Tel. (518) 462-5476

Alexandria-Shreveport, Bishop John C. Favolora; Chancellor, Rev. Msgr. Julius G. Walle. Office, 4400 Gardner Hwy., P.O. Box 7417, Alexandria, LA 71306. Tel. (318) 445-2401

Allentown, Bishop Thomas J. Welsh; Dir. of Inf., Rev. Stanley T. Sosnowski. Chancery Office, 202 N. 17th St., Allentown, PA 18104. Tel. (215) 437-0755

Altoona-Johnstown, Bishop Joseph V. Adamec; Chancellor, Rev. Msgr. Paul D. Panza. Chancery Office, Box 126, Logan Blvd., Hollidaysburg, PA 16648. Tel. (814) 695-5579.

Amarillo, Bishop Leroy T. Mattiesen; Chancellor, Sr. Celine Thames, O.S.F., Chancery Office, 1800 N. Spring St., P.O. Box 5644, Amarillo, TX 79117. Tel. (806) 383-2243

Archdiocese of Anchorage, Archbishop Francis T. Hurley. Chancery Office, P.O. Box 2239, Anchorage, AK 99510. Tel. (907) 338-7898. Ms. Joann White, Sec. to the Archbishop, 3925 Reka Dr., Anchorage AK 99508.

Arlington, Bishop John Richard Keating, 4600 N. Carlin Springs Rd., Arlington, VA 22203; Chancery, Ste. 704, 200 Glebe Rd., Arlington, VA 22203. Tel. (703) 841-2500

Archdiocese of Atlanta, Archbishop Eugene Antones Marino; Chancellor, Rev. E. Peter Ludden. Chancery Office, 680 West Peachtree St., N.W., Atlanta, GA 30308. Tel. (404) 888-7802

Austin, Bishop John E. McCarthy; Vicar General, Rev. Msgr. Edward C. Matocha. Chancery Office, N. Congress and 16th, P.O. Box 13327 Capital Sta. Austin, TX 78711. Tel. (512) 476-4888

Baker, Bishop Thomas J. Connolly; Chancellor, Rev. Charles T. Grant. Chancery Office, Baker and First Sts., P.O. Box 826, Baker, OR 97814. Tel. (503) 523-2373

Archdiocese of Baltimore, Archbishop William D. Borders. Auxiliary Bishops of Baltimore: Bishop William C. Newman, 5400 Roland St., Baltimore MD 21210; Bishop P. Francis Murphy, 320 Cathedral St., Baltimore MD 21201; Bishop John H. Ricard, 1501 E. Oliver St., Baltimore, MD 21210. Chancery Office, 320 Cathedral St., Baltimore, MD 21213. Tel. (301) 547-5444.

Baton Rouge, Bishop Stanley J. Ott; Chancellor, Rev. Msgr. Robert Berggreen. Chancery Office, P.O. Box 2028, Baton Rouge, LA 70821. Tel. (504) 387-0561

Beaumont, Bishop Bernard J. Ganter; Chancellor Rev. Bennie J. Patillo. Chancery Office, P.O. Box 3948, Beaumont, TX 77704, Tel. (409) 838-0451

Belleville, Bishop James J. Keleher; Vicar General, Rev. James E. Margason. Chancery Office, 222 Third, Belleville IL 62220. Tel. (618)277-8181

Biloxi, Bishop Joseph Howze; Chancellor, Rev. Michael Thornton. Chancery Office, P.O. Box 1189, Biloxi, MS 39533. Tel. (601) 374-0222

Birmingham, Bishop Joseph G. Vath; Chancellor, Rev. Paul L. Rohling. Chancery Office, P.O. Box 2086, Birmingham, AL 35201. Tel. (205) 833-0175

Bismarck, Bishop John F. Kinney, Chancery Office, 420 Raymond St., Box 1575, Bismarck, ND 58501. Tel. (701) 223-1347

Boise, Bishop Sylvester W. Treinen; Chancellor, Rev. Thomas F. Miller. Chancery Office, Box 769, 420 Idaho St., Boise, ID 83701. Tel. (208) 342-1311

Archdiocese of Boston, Bernard Cardinal Law; Auxiliary Bishops of Boston: Bishop Robert J. Banks, 2121 Commonwealth Ave., Boston, MA 02135; Bishop Daniel A. Hart, 235 N. Pearl St., Brockton MA 02401; Bishop Alfred C. Hughes, St. John Seminary, 127 Lake St., Brighton, MA 02135; Bishop John J. Mulcahy, 58 Blaney St., Swampscott MA 01907; Bishop Lawrence J. Riley, 43 Maple St., Hyde Park, Boston, MA 02136; Chancery Office, 2121 Commonwealth Ave., Brighton, MA 02135. Tel. (617) 254-0100

Bridgeport, Bishop Walter W. Curtis; Chancellor, Rev. Gregory Michael Smith. Chancery Office, 238 Jewett Ave., Bridgeport CT 06606. Tel. (203) 372-4301

Brooklyn, Bishop Francis J. Mugavero. Auxiliary Bishops of Brooklyn: Bishop Joseph M. Sullivan, 256 Clinton Ave., Brooklyn NY 11205; Bishop Rene A. Valero, 34-43 93rd St., Jackson Heights NY 11372. Chancellor, Rev. Msgr. Otto L. Garcia. Chancery Office, 75 Greene Ave., Box C, Brooklyn, NY 11202. Tel. (212) 638-5500

Brownsville, Bishop John J. Fitzpatrick, Chancery Office, P.O. Box 2279, Brownsville, TX 78522. Tel. (512) 542-2501

Buffalo, Bishop Edward D. Head. Auxiliary Bishops of Buffalo: Bishop Pius A. Benincasa, 157 Cleveland Dr., Buffalo, NY 14215; Bishop Bernard J. McLaughlin, 108 Englewood Ave., Kenmore, NY 14223; Bishop Donald M. Trautman, 5480 Main St., Williamsville, NY 14221. Chancellor, Rev. Msgr. Robert J. Cunningham. Chancery Office, 795 Main St., Buffalo, NY 14203. Tel. (716)854-0303

Burlington, Bishop John A. Marshall; Vicar for Administration, Rev. Jay C. Haskin. Chancery Office, 351 North Ave., Burlington, VT 05401. Tel. (802) 658-6110

Camden, Bishop George H. Guilfoyle; Auxiliary Bishop of Camden, Bishop James L. Schad. Chancery Office, 1845 Haddon Ave., P.O. Box 709, Camden, NJ 08101. Tel. (609) 541-2100

Charleston, Bishop Ernest L. Unterkoefler; Vicar General, Rev. Msgr. Thomas R. Duffy. Chancery Office, 119 Broad St., P.O. Box 818, Charleston, SC 29401. Tel. (803) 723-3488

Charlotte, Bishop John F. Donoghue; Chancellor, Rev. Joseph A. Kerin, Chancery Office P.O. Box 36776, Charlotte, NC 28236. Tel. (704) 377-6871

Cheyenne, Bishop Joseph H. Hart; Chancellor, Rev. Lawrence Etchingham. Chancery Office, Box 426, Cheyenne, WY 82003. Tel. (307) 638-1530

Archdiocese of Chicago, Joseph Cardinal Bernardin, 1555 North State Pkwy., Chicago, IL 60610. Auxiliary Bishops of Chicago: Bishop Alred L. Abramowicz, 4327 S. Richmond St., Chicago, IL 60632; Bishop Wilton D. Gregory, P.O. Box 733, South Holland, IL 60473; Bishop Nevin W. Hayes, O. Carm., 6949 W. Addison, Chicago, IL 60634; Bishop Timothy J. Lyne, 730 N. Wabash Ave., Chicago, IL 60611; Bishop Pacicio Rodrigues, C.M.F., 1048 N. Campbell, Chicago, IL 60622; Bishop John G. Vlazny, 724 Elder La., Deerfield IL 60015. Chancellor, Rev. Robert L. Kealy, P.O. Box 1979, Chicago, IL 60690. Chancery Office, 155 E. Superior Ave., Chicago, IL 60611. Tel. (312) 751-8200

Archdiocese of Cincinnati, Archbishop Daniel E. Pilarczyk. Auxiliary Bishop of Cincinnati: Bishop James H. Garland. Chancery Office, 100 E. 8th St., Cincinnati, OH 45202. Tel. (513) 421-3131.

Cleveland, Bishop Anthony M. Pilla. Auxiliary Bishops of Cleveland: Bishop James P. Lyke, O.F.M., 1031 Superior Ave., Cleveland, OH 44114; Bishop A. Edward Pevec, 28700 Euclid Ave., Wickliffe, OH 44055; Bishop Gilbert I. Sheldon, 40 E. Center St., Akron, OH 44308. Chancery Office, 350 Chancery Bldg., Cathedral Square, 1027 Superior Ave., Cleveland, OH 44114. Tel. (216) 696-6525

Colorado Springs, Bishop Richard C. Hanifen; Chancellor, Sr. Patricia McGreevy, O.S.B. Chancery Office, 29 West Kiowa St., Colorado Springs, CO 80903. Tel. 303-636-2345

Columbus, Bishop James A. Griffin. Chancery Office, 198 E. Broad St., Columbus, OH 43215. Tel. (614) 224-2251

Corpus Christi, Bishop Rene H. Gracida; Chancellor, Sr. Arlene A. Jekielek, I.H.M. Chancery Office, 620 Lipan St., Corpus Christi, TX 78401. Tel. (512) 882-6191

Covington, Bishop William A. Hughes; Auxiliary Bishop of Covington, Bishop J. Kendrick Williams, Seminary of St. Pius X, Erlanger, KY 41018; Chancellor, Rev. Msgr. Donald F. Hellmann. Chancery Office, 1140 Madison Ave., P.O. Box 192, Covington, KY 41012. Tel. (606) 291-4240

Crookston, Bishop Victor Balke; Chancellor, Very Rev. Michael Patnode. Chancery Office, 1200 Memorial Dr., P.O. Box 610, Crookston, MN 56716. Tel. (218) 281-4533.

Dallas, Bishop Thomas Tschoepe; Vicar General, Rev. Msgr. Robert Rehkemper. Chancery Office, 3915 Lemmon Ave., P.O. Box 19507, Dallas, TX 75219. Tel. (214) 528-2240

Davenport, Bishop Gerald Francis O'Keefe; Chancellor, Very Rev. Leo Feeney. Chancery Office, 2706 Gaines St., Davenport, IA 52804. Tel. (319) 324-1911

Archdiocese of Denver. Archbishop J. Francis Stafford; Chancellor of Denver: Rev. Edward M. Hoffman. Chancery Office, 200 Josephine St., Denver, CO 80206. Tel. (303) 388-4411

Des Moines, Bishop Maurice J. Dingman; Chancellor, Rev. Michael O'Meara. Chancery Office, 818 5th Ave., P.O. Box 1816, Des Moines, IA 50306. Tel. (515) 243-7653.

Archdiocese of Detroit, Archbishop Edmund C. Szoka. Auxiliary Bishops of Detroit: Bishop Moses B. Anderson, S.S.E., 14155 Abingdon Rd., Detroit, MI 48227; Bishop Patrick R. Cooney, 1234 Washington Blvd., Detroit, MI 48226; Bishop Thomas J. Gumbleton, 12755 Longacre, Detroit, MI 48227; Bishop Dale J. Melczek, 528 Helene Ave., Royal Oak, MI 48067; Bishop Walter J. Schoenherr, 11350 Reeck Rd., Southgate, MI 48195. Chancery Office, 1234 Washington Blvd., Detroit, MI 48226. Tel. (313) 237-5816

Dodge City, Bishop Stanley G. Schlarman; Chancellor, Rev. James E. Baker. Chancery Office, 910 Central Ave., P.O. Box 849, Dodge City, KS 67801.Tel. (316) 227-3131

Archdiocese of Dubuque, Archbishop Daniel W. Kucera; Auxiliary Bishop of Dubuque, Bishop Francis J. Dunn; Chancellor, Rev. Robert L. Ferring, P.O. Box 479, Dubuque IA 52001. Tel. (319) 556-2580.

Duluth, Bishop Robert H. Brom; Chancellor, V. Rev. Lawrence O'Shea. Chancery Office, 215 W. Fourth St., Duluth, MN 55806. Tel. (218) 727-6861

El Paso, Bishop Raymond J. Pena; Chancellor, Very Rev. David G. Fierro. Chancery Office, 499 St. Matthews, El Paso, TX 79907. Tel. (915) 593-1392

Erie, Bishop Michael J. Murphy; Chancellor, Rev. Msgr. Robert J. Smith, J.C.L. Chancery Office, 205 W. Ninth St., Erie, PA 16501. Tel. (814) 452-3610

Evansville, Bishop Francis R. Shea, 3115 Bayard Park Dr., Evansville IN 47714. Chancery Office, 4200 N. Kentucky Ave., Evansville, IN 47711. Tel. (812) 424-5536

Fairbanks, Bishop Michael Kaniecki, S.J., Chancellor, Sr. Eileen Brown. Tel. (907) 456-6753. Chancery Office, 1316 Peger Rd., Fairbanks, AK 99709. Tel. (907) 474-0753

Fall River, Bishop Daniel A. Cronin; Chancellor, Rev. Msgr. John J. Oliveira. Chancery Office, 47 Underwood St., Box 2577, Fall River, MA 02722. Tel. (617) 675-1311.

Fargo, Bishop James S. Sullivan. Chancery Office, 1310 Broadway, P.O. Box 1750, Fargo, ND 58107. Tel. (701) 235-6429

Fort Wayne-South Bend, Bishop John M. D'Arcy; Auxiliary Bishop of Fort Wayne-South Bend, Bishop Joseph R. Crowley, 1701 Miami St., South Bend IN 46613. Chancery Office, 1103 S. Calhoun St., P.O. Box 390. Fort Wayne, IN 46801. Tel. (219) 422-4611

Fort Worth, Bishop Joseph D. Delaney; Chancellor, Rev. Robert W. Wilson. Chancery Office, 800 W. Loop 820 South, Fort Worth TX 76108. Tel. (817) 560-3300

Fresno, Bishop Joseph J. Madera, M.Sp.S.; Vicar General and Chancellor, Rev. Msgr. J. Wayne Hayes. Chancery Office, P.O. Box 1668, 1550 N. Fresno St., Fresno, CA 93717. Tel. (209) 237-5125

Gallup, Bishop Jerome J. Hastrich; Chancellor, Rev. Msgr. Arthur MacDonald. Chancery Office, 711 S. Puerco Dr., P.O. Box 1338, Gallup, NM 87301. Tel. (505) 863-4406

Galveston-Houston, Bishop Joseph A. Fiorenza; Chancellor, Rev. Msgr. Daniel Scheel. Chancery Office, 1700 San Jacinto St., Houston, TX 77002. Tel. (713) 659-5461

Gary, Bishop Norbert F. Gaughan; Chancellor, Rev. Msgr. John F. Morales. Chancery Office, 9292 Broadway, Merrillville, IN 46410 Tel. (219)769-9292

Gaylord, Bishop Robert J. Rose; Chancellor, Rev. David Gemuend. Chancery Office, P.O. Box 1020, Gaylord, MI 49735. Tel. (517) 732-5147

Grand Island, Bishop Lawrence J. McNamara; P.O. Box 1531, Grand Island, NE 68802; Chancellor, Rev. Charles L. Torpey. Chancery Office, 311 W. 17th St., P.O. Box 996, Grand Island, NB 68801. Tel. (308) 382-6565

Grand Rapids, Bishop Joseph M. Breitenbeck, 660 Burton St. SE, Grand Rapids, MI 49507; Auxiliary Bishop of Grand Rapids; Bishop Joseph McKinney, 4865 Eleven Mile Rd., Rockford, MI 49341; Chancellor, Rev. John Najdowski. Chancery Office, 660 Burton St. S.E., Grand Rapids, MI 49507. Tel. (616) 243-0491.

Great Falls-Billings, Bishop Thomas J. Murphy. Chancery Office, 121 23rd St. So., P.O. Box 1399, Great Falls, MT 59403. Tel. (406) 727-6683

Green Bay, Bishop Adam J. Maida; Auxiliary Bishop of Green Bay; Bishop Robert F. Morneau, St. Norbert's Abbey, DePere WI 54115; Chancellor, Rev. Msgr. Roy M. Klister. Chancery Office, Box 66, Green Bay, WI 54305. Tel. (414) 435-4406

Greensburg, Bishop Anthony G. Bosco; Chancellor and Vicar General, Rev. Thomas L. Klinzing. Chancery Office, 723 E. Pittsburgh St., Greensburg, PA 15601. Tel. (412) 837-0901

Harrisburg, Bishop William Keeler; Chancellor, Very Rev. William M. Richardson. Chancery Office, P.O. Box 2153, 4800 Union Deposit Rd., Harrisburg, PA 17105. Tel. (717) 657-4804

Archdiocese of Hartford, Archbishop John F. Whealon. Auxiliary Bishops of Hartford: Bishop John F. Hackett, 134 Farmington Ave., Hartford, CT 06105; Bishop Peter A. Rosazza, 289 Willow St., Waterbury, CT 06710. Chancellor, Sr. Helen Margaret Feeney, C.S.J. Chancery Office, 134 Farmington Ave., Hartford, CT 06105. Tel. (203) 527-4201

Helena, Bishop Elden F. Curtiss. Chancery Office, 515 N. Ewing, P.O. Box 1729, Helena, MT 59624. Tel. (406) 442-5820

Honolulu, Bishop Joseph A. Ferrario; Vicar General, Rev. Raymond J. Nishigaya. Chancery Office, 1184 Bishop St., Honolulu, HI 96813. Tel. (808) 533-1791

Houma-Thibodaux, Bishop Warren L. Boudreaux. Chancery Office, P.O. Box 9077, Houma, LA 70361. Tel. (504) 868-7720

Archdiocese of Indianapolis, Archbishop Edward T. O'Meara; Chancellor, Rev. Msgr. Gerald A. Gettelfinger. Chancery Office, 1400 N. Meridian St., P.O. Box 1410, Indianapolis, IN 46206. Tel. (317)236-1405

Jackson, Bishop William R. Houck; Vicar General, Rev. Msgr. Noel Foley. Chancery Office, 237 E. Amite St., P.O. Box 2248, Jackson, MS 39225. Tel. (601) 969-1880

Jefferson City, Bishop Michael F. McAuliffe; Chancellor, Rev. Michael J. Wilbers. Chancery Office, 605 Clark Ave., P.O. Box 417, Jefferson City, MO 65102. Tel. (314) 635-9127

Joliet, Bishop Joseph L. Imesch. Auxiliary Bishops of Joliet: Bishop Roger L. Kaffer; Bishop Raymond J. Vonesh. Chancellor, Rev. William E. Donnelly. Chancery Office, 425 Summit St., Joliet, IL 60435. Tel. (815) 722-6606

Juneau, Bishop Michael H. Kenny. Chancery Office, 419 6th St. Juneau, AK 99801. Tel. (907) 586-2227

Kalamazoo, Bishop Paul V. Donovan, Chancery Office, P.O. Box 949, 215 N. Westnedge Ave., Kalamazoo, MI 49005. Tel. (616) 349-8714

Archdiocese of Kansas City in Kansas, Archbishop Ignatius J. Strecker, 3408 Minnesota Ave., P.O. Box 2328, Kansas City KS 66110; Auxiliary Bishop of Kansas City in Kansas, Bishop Marion F. Forst, 615 N. 7th St., Kansas City KS 66101; Chancellor, Rev. Msgr. William T. Curtin. Chancery Office, 2220 Central Ave., P.O. Box 2328, Kansas City, KS 66110. Tel. (913) 621-4131

Kansas City-St. Joseph, Bishop John J. Sullivan; Chancellor, Rev. Richard F. Carney. Chancery Office, P.O. Box 419037, Kansas City, MO 64141. Tel. (816) 756-1850

La Crosse, Bishop John J. Paul; Chancellor, Very Rev. John I. Nilles, P.O. Box 4004, LaCrosse, WI 54602. Chancery Office, 3710 East Ave., La Crosse, WI 54602. Tel. (608) 788-7700

Lafayette in Indiana, Bishop William L. Higi; Chancellor, Rev. Msgr. Arthur A. Sego.Chancery Office, P. O. Box 260, 610 Lingle Ave., Lafayette, IN 47902. Tel. (317) 742-0275

Lafayette, Bishop Gerard L. Frey. Chancellor, Sr. Joanna Valoni, S.S.N.D., Chancery Office, Diocesan Office Bldg., P.O. Drawer 3387, Lafayette, LA 70502. Tel. (318) 261-5500

Lake Charles, Bishop Jude Speyrer; Chancellor and Vicar General, Rev. Msgr. Harry Grieg. Chancery Office, 414 Iris St., P.O. Box 3223, Lake Charles, LA 70602. Tel. (318) 439-7404

Lansing, Bishop Kenneth J. Povish; Chancellor, Rev. James Murray. Chancery Office, 300 W. Ottawa, Lansing, MI 48933. Tel. (517) 372-8540

Las Cruces, Bishop Ricardo Ramirez; C.S.B.; Chancellor, Rev. Bob Getz. Chancery Office, P.O. Box 16318, Las Cruces, NM 88004. Tel. (505) 523-7577

Lincoln, Bishop Glennon P. Flavin; Vice Chancellor, Rev. Garold L. Gabel. Chancery Office, 3400 Sheridan Blvd., P.O. Box 80328, Lincoln, NE 68501. Tel. (402) 488-0921

Little Rock, Bishop Andrew J. McDonald; Chancellor, Very Rev. Royce R. Thomas. Chancery Office, 2415 N. Tyler St., P.O. Box 7239, Little Rock, AR 72217. Tel. (501) 664-0340

Archdiocese of Los Angeles, Archbishop Roger M. Mahony. Auxiliary Bishops of Los Angeles: Bishop Juan Arzube, 5223 Hastings St., Los Angeles, CA 90022; Bishop John J. Ward, 10425 W. Pico Blvd., Los Angeles, CA 90064; Chancery Office, 1531 W. Ninth St., Los Angeles, CA 90015. Tel. (213) 251-3200.

Archdiocese of Louisville, Archbishop Thomas C. Kelly, O.P.; Auxiliary Bishop of Louisville, Bishop Charles G. Maloney, P.O. Box 1073, Louisville, KY 40201; Chancellor, Rev. Bernard J. Breen, P.O. Box 1073, Louisville, KY 40201. Chancery Office, 212 E. College St., Louisville, KY 40203. Tel. (502) 585-3291

Lubbock, Bishop Michael Sheehan; Chancellor, Sr. Elena Gonzalez, R.S.M. Chancery Office. P.O. Box 98700, Lubbock, TX 79499. Tel. (806) 792-3943

Madison, Bishop Cletus F. O'Donnell; Auxiliary Bishop of Madison, Bishop George O. Wirz, 404 E. Main St., Madison, WI 53705; Chancellor, Rev. Joseph P. Higgins. Chancery Office, 15 E. Wilson St., Box 111, Madison, WI 53701. Tel. (608) 256-2677

Manchester, Bishop Odore J. Gendron. Chancery Office, 153 Ash St., Manchester, NH 03105. Tel. (603) 669-3100

Marquette, Bishop Mark F. Schmitt. Chancery Office, 444 S. Fourth St., P.O. Box 550, Marquette, MI 49855. Tel. (906) 225-1141

Memphis, Bishop Daniel Mark Buechlein, O.S.B.; Chancellor, Rev. Peter P. Buchingnani. Chancery Office, 1325 Jefferson Ave., P.O. Box 41679, Memphis, TN 38174. Tel. (901) 722-4737

Metuchen, Bishop Edward Hughes. Chancery Office, P.O. Box 191, Metuchen, NJ 08840. Tel. (201) 283-3800.

Archdiocese of Miami, Archbishop Edward A. McCarthy, 6301 Biscayne Blvd., Miami, FL 33138; Auxiliary Bishop of Miami, Bishop Agustin A. Roman.Chancery Office, 9401 Biscayne Blvd., Miami Shores, FL 33138. Tel. (305) 757-6241

Archdiocese of Milwaukee, Archbishop Rembert G. Weakland, O.S.B. Auxiliary Bishops of Milwaukee: Bishop Leo J. Brust, P.O. Box 2018, Milwaukee, WI 53201; Bishop Richard J. Sklba, 1414 W. Becher St., Milwaukee, WI 53215. Chancellor, Rev. Michael T. Newman. Chancery Office, 3501 S. Lake Dr., Milwaukee, WI 53207. Tel. (414)769-3300.

Archdiocese of Mobile, Archbishop Oscar H. Lipscomb; Chancellor, Very Rev. James W. Oberkirch. Chancery Office, 400 Government St., P.O. Box 1966, Mobile, AL 36633. Tel. (205) 433-2241

Monterey, Bishop Thaddeus Shubsda; Vicar General, Rev. Msgr. Tod D. Brown. Chancery Office, 580 Fremont Blvd., P.O. Box 2048, Monterey, CA 93940. Tel. (408) 373-4345

Nashville, Bishop James D. Niedergeses; Vicar General, Rev. J. Patrick Connor. Chancery Office, 2400 21st Ave., S., Nashville, TN 37212. Tel. (615) 383-6393

Archdiocese of Newark, Archbishop Theodore E. McCarrick; Auxiliary Bishops of Newark: Bishop David Arias, O.A.R., 502 Palisade Ave., Union City, NJ 07087; Bishop Joseph Francis, S.V.D, 139 Glenwood Ave., East Orange, NJ 07017; Bishop Robert F. Garner, 311 Prospect St., Midland Park, NJ 07432; Bishop Domonic A. Marconi, 238 E. Blanke St., Linden, NJ 07036; Bishop Jerome Pechillo, T.O.R., 691 Westside Ave., Jersey City, NJ 07304; Bishop T. McHugh; Bishop John M.Smith. Chancery Office, 31 Mulberry St., Newark, NJ 07102. Tel. (201) 596-4000

Archdiocese of New Orleans, Archbishop Philip M. Hannan. Auxiliary Bishops of New Orleans: Bishop Nicholas D'Antonio, O.F.M., 1221 Mandeville St., New Orleans, LA 70117; Bishop Harold R. Perry, S.V.D., 2916 Paris Ave., New Orleans, LA 70115. Chancery Office, 7887 Walmsley Ave., New Orleans, LA 70125. Tel. (504) 861-9521

Melkite Apostolic Exarchate of Newton, Bishop Joseph Tawil. Chancery Office, 19 Dartmouth St., West Newton, MA 02165. Tel. (617) 969-8957

New Ulm, Bishop Raymond A. Lucker. Chancery Office, 1400 Chancery Drive, New Ulm, MN 56073. Tel. (507) 359-2966

Archdiocese of New York, Archbishop John J. O'Connor, 452 Madison Ave., New York, NY 10022. Auxiliary Bishops of New York: Bishop Patrick V. Ahern, 30 Manor Rd., West New Brighton, Staten Island, NY 10310; Bishop Edward N. Egan, 1011 First Ave., New York, NY 10022; Bishop Francis Garmendia, 1900 Crotona Pkwy., Bronx, NY 10460; Bishop James P. Mahoney, 235 Msgr. O'Brien Blvd., Mahopac, NY 10541; Bishop Emerson J. Moore, 211 W. 141st St., New York, NY 10030; Bishop Joseph T. O'Keefe, 348 E. 55th St., New York, NY 10022; Bishop Austin B. Vaughan, 55 Grand St., Newburgh, NY 12550; Bishop Anthony F. Mestice, 775 Main St., Poughkeepsie, NY 12603. Vicar General, Bishop Joseph T. O'Keefe. Chancery Office, 1011 First Ave., New York, NY 10022. Tel. (212) 371-1000

Norwich, Bishop Daniel P. Reilly; Chancellor, Rev. Msgr. Thomas R. Bride. Chancery Office, 201 Broadway, P.O. Box 587, Norwich, CT 06360. Tel. (203) 887-9294

Oakland, Bishop John S. Cummins, 634 21st St., Oakland CA 94612. Chancery Office, 2900 Lakeshore Ave., Oakland, CA 94610. Tel. (415) 893-4711

Ogdensburg, Bishop Stanislaus J. Brzana. Chancery Office, Box 369, 622 Washington St., Ogdensburg, NY 13669. Tel. (315) 393-2920

Archdiocese of Oklahoma City, Archbishop Charles A. Salatka; Chancellor, Rev. John A. Steichen. Chancery Office, P.O. Box 32180, Oklahoma City, OK 73123. Tel. (405) 721-5651

Archdiocese of Omaha, Archbishop Daniel E. Sheehan; Auxiliary Bishop of Omaha, Bishop Anthony M. Milone, 7600 S. 42nd St., Omaha, NE 68147; Chancery Office, 100 N. 62nd St., Omaha, NB 68132. Tel. (402) 558-3100

Orange, Bishop Norman F. McFarland; Chancellor, Rev. Msgr. Michael P. Driscoll. Chancery Office, 2811 Villa Real Dr., Orange, CA 92667. Tel. (714) 974-7120

Orlando, Bishop Thomas J. Grady; Chancellor, Rev. Art Bendixen. Chancery Office, 421 E. Robinson, P.O. Box 1800, Orlando, FL 32802. Tel. (305) 425-3556

Owensboro, Bishop John J. McRaith, 501 W. 5th St., Owensboro, KY 42301; Chancellor, Rev. Msgr. George Hancock. Chancery Office, c/o Chancellor's Residence, 4001 Frederica St., Owensboro, KY 42301. Tel. (502) 683-1545

Palm Beach, Bishop Thomas V. Daily; Chancellor, Rev. James Murtagh. Chancery Office, 8895 N. Military Trail, Bldg. C #201, Palm Beach Gardens, FL 33418. Tel. (305) 627-8700.

Parma Eparchy, Bishop Andrew Pataki. Chancery Office, 1900 Carlton Rd., Parma, OH 44134. Tel. (216) 741-8773

Passaic (Greek Rite), Bishop Michael J. Dudick. Chancery Office, 445 Lackawanna Ave., West Paterson, NJ 07424. Tel. (201)890-7777.

Paterson, Bishop Frank J. Rodimer. Chancery Office, 777 Valley Rd., Clifton, NJ 07013. Tel. (201) 777-8818.

Pensacola-Tallahassee, Bishop J. Keith Symons, P.O. Drawer 18570, Pensacola, FL 32523; Chancellor, Rev. Msgr. Luke Hunt, P.O. Drawer 17329, Pensacola, FL 32522. Chancery Office, 11 N. "B" St., Pensacola, FL 32501. Tel. (904) 432-1515

Peoria, Bishop Edward W. O'Rourke; Vicar General, Rev. John J. Myers. Chancery Office, P.O. Box 1406, 607 NE Madison Ave., Peoria, IL 61655. Tel. (309) 671-1550

Archdiocese of Philadelphia, Archbishop Anthony J. Bevilacqua, 5700 City Ave., Philadelphia, PA 19131. Auxiliary Bishops of Philadelphia: Bishop John J. Graham, 6161 N. 5th St., Philadelphia, PA 19120; Bishop Louis A. DeSimone, 2422 S. 17th St., Philadelphia, PA 19145; Bishop Martin N. Lohmuller, 252 S. 4th St., Philadelphia, PA 19106. Chancellor, Rev. Msgr. Samuel E. Shoemaker. Chancery Office, 222 N. 17th St., Philadelphia, PA 19103. Tel. (215) 587-3550

Ukrainian Rite—Philadelphia, Archbishop Stephen Sulyk. Chancery Office, 827 N. Franklin St., Philadelphia, PA 19123. Tel. (215) 627-0143

Phoenix, Bishop Thomas J. O'Brien, 48 East Wagon Wheel Dr., Phoenix, AZ 85020; Chancellor, Rev. James E. McFadden. Chancery Office, 400 E. Monroe St., Phoenix, AZ 85004. Tel. (602) 257-0030

Pittsburgh, _____; Auxiliary Bishops of Pittsburgh: Bishop Anthony G. Bosco, 5246 Clarwin Ave. (West View), Pittsburgh, PA 15229; Bishop John B. McDowell, 1018 Centre Ave., Pittsburgh, PA 15219. Chancery Office, 111 Blvd. of Allies, Pittsburgh, PA 15222. Tel. (412) 456-3000

Metropolitan Archdiocese of Pittsburgh (Byzantine) Archbishop Stephen J. Kocisko. Chancery Office, 54 Riverview Ave., Pittsburgh, PA 15214. Tel. (412) 322-7300.

Portland, Bishop Edward C. O'Leary; Auxiliary Bishop of Portland: Bishop Amedee Proulx, 307 Congress St., Portland ME 04101; Chancellor, Rev. J. Joseph Ford. Chancery Office, 510 Ocean Ave., Portland, ME 04103. Tel. (207) 773-6471

Archdiocese of Portland in Oregon, Archbishop William J. Levada; Archbishop Cornelius M. Power; Auxiliary Bishop of Portland in Oregon, Bishop Kenneth Steiner; Bishop Paul Waldschmidt, C.S.C.,5402 N. Strong, Portland, OR 97203; Chancellor, Very Rev. Gregory Moys. Chancery Office, 2838 E. Burnside St., Portland, OR 97214. Tel. (503) 234-5334

Providence, Bishop Louis E. Gelineau; Auxiliary Bishop of Providence, Bishop Kenneth A. Angell, 493 Mt. Pleasant Ave., Providence RI 02908; Chancellor, Rev. Msgr. William I. Varsanyi. Chancery Office, 1 Cathedral Square, Providence, RI 02903. Tel. (401) 278-4500

Pueblo, Bishop Arthur N. Tafoya; Chancellor, Rev. Msgr. George L. Subotich. Chancery Office, 1001 N. Grand Ave., Pueblo, CO 81003. Tel. (303) 544-9861

Raleigh, Bishop F. Joseph Gossman; Chancellor, Rev. Jeffrey Ingham. Chancery Office, 300 Cardinal Gibbons Dr., Raleigh, NC 27606. Tel. (919) 821-9700

Rapid City, Bishop Harold J. Dimmerling; 721 West Blvd., Rapid City, SD 57701; Chancellor, Very Rev. Peter B. Wilke. Chancery Office, 606 Cathedral Dr., P.O. Box 678, Rapid City, SD 57709. Tel. (605) 343-3541

Reno-Las Vegas, Bishop Daniel F. Walsh, 843 Marsh Ave., Reno, NV 89509; Chancellor, Rev. Gilbert J. Canuel, Jr., P.O. Box 1211, Reno, NV 89504. Chancery

Office, 515 Court St., Reno, NV 89501. Tel. (702) 329-9274

Richmond, Bishop Walter F. Sullivan. Chancery Office, 811 Cathedral Pl., Suite C, Richmond, VA 23220. Tel. (804) 359-5661

Rochester, Bishop Matthew H. Clark, 296 Flower City Park, Rochester, NY 14615; Auxiliary Bishop of Rochester, Bishop Dennis W. Hickey, 415 Ames St., Rochester, NY 14611. Chancery Office, 1150 Buffalo Rd., Rochester, NY 14624. Tel. (716) 328-3210

Rockford, Bishop Arthur J. O'Neill; Vicar General, Rev. Msgr. Louis J. Franey. Chancery Office, 1245 N. Court St., Rockford, IL 61103 Tel. (815) 962-3709

Rockville Centre, Bishop John R. McGann, 29 Quealy Pl., Rockville Centre, NY 11570; Auxiliary Bishop of Rockville Centre, Bishop James J. Daly, St. Joseph's Convent, Brentwood Rd., Brentwood, NY 11717; Chancellor, Rev. Msgr. John A. Alesandro. Chancery Office, 50 N. Park Ave. Rockville Centre, NY 11570. Tel. (516) 678-5800

Sacramento, Bishop Francis A. Quinn; Auxiliary Bishop of Sacramento, Bishop Alphonse Gallegos, O.A.R., P.O. Box 1706, Sacramento, CA 95808; Chancellor, Rev. Msgr. Albert G. O'Connor. Chancery Office, 1119 K St., P.O. Box 1706, Sacramento, CA 95808. Tel. (916) 443-1996

Saginaw, Bishop Kenneth E. Untener.Chancery Office, 5800 Weiss St., Saginaw, MI 48603. Tel. (517) 799-7910

St. Augustine, Bishop John J. Snyder, 35 Treasury St., St. Augustine, FL 32084; Chancellor, Rev. Msgr. Eugene C. Kohls, P.O. Box 24000, Jacksonville, FL 32241. Tel. (904) 262-3200.

St. Cloud, Bishop Jerome Hanus, O.S.B.; Chancellor, Rev. Severin Schwieters. Chancery Office, P.O. Box 1248, St. Cloud, MN 56301. Tel. (612) 251-2340

St. Josaphat in Parma, Ukrainian Bishop Robert M. Moskal. Chancery Office 5720 State Rd., Parma, OH 44134. Tel. (216) 888-1522.

Archdiocese of St. Louis, Archbishop John L. May. Auxiliary Bishops of St. Louis: Bishop George J. Gottwald, 1264 Arch Terr., Richmond Heights, MO 63117; Bishop Charles R. Koester, 15 Plaza Sq., St. Louis MO 63103; Bishop Edward J. O'Donnell, 4445 Lindell Blvd., St. Louis, MO 63108; Bishop James Terry Steib, 4445 Lindell Blvd., St. Louis, MO 63108. Chancellor, Rev. John R. Gaydos. Chancery Office, 4445 Lindell Blvd., St. Louis, MO 63108. Tel. (314) 533-1887

St. Maron of Brooklyn, Bishop Francis M. Zayek, Chancery Office, 8120 15th Ave., Brooklyn, NY 11228. Tel. (718) 259-9200

St. Nicholas in Chicago for the Ukrainians, Bishop Innocent Lotocky, O.S.B.M. Chancery Office, 2245 W. Rice St., Chicago, IL 60622. Tel. (312) 276-5080

Archdiocese of St. Paul and Minneapolis, Archbishop John R. Roach. Auxiliary Bishop of St. Paul-Minneapolis: Bishop William H. Bullock; Bishop Robert J. Carlson; Chancellor, Bishop J. Richard Ham, M.M. Chancery Office, 226 Summit Ave., St. Paul, MN 55102. Tel. (612) 291-4400.

St. Petersburg, Bishop W. Thomas Larkin; Chancellor, Very Rev. Brendan Muldoon. Chancery Office, 6363 9th Ave. N., P.O. Box 40200. St. Petersburg, FL 33743. Tel. (813) 344-1611

Salina, Bishop George K. Fitzsimons; Chancellor, Rev. Msgr. James E. Hake, P.O. Box 980, Salina KS 67402. Chancery Office, 7th & Iron, 8th Fl., Salina, KS 67402. Tel. (913) 827-8746

Salt Lake City, Bishop William K. Weigand; Chancellor, Deacon Silvio Mayo. Chancery Office, 27 C. St., Salt Lake City, UT 84103. Tel. (801) 328-8641

San Angelo, Bishop Michael Pfeifer, O.M.I.; Chancellor, Very Rev. Larry J. Droll. Chancery Office, 116 S.

Oakes (Mailing Address Box 1829) San Angelo, TX 76901. Tel. (915) 653-2466

Archdiocese of San Antonio, Archbishop Patrick F. Flores; Auxiliary Bishop of San Antonio; Bishop Bernard F. Popp, 5015 Bayonne, San Antonio, TX 78228. Chancellor, Rev. Msgr. Patrick J. Murray, Chancery Office, 2718 W. Woodlawn Ave., PO.Box 28410, San Antonio, TX 78228. Tel. (512) 734-2620

San Bernardino, Bishop Phillip F. Straling. Chancery Office, 1450 North D St., San Bernardino, CA 92405 Tel. (714) 889-8351

San Diego, Bishop Leo T. Maher, 2031 Sunset Blvd., San Diego, CA 92103; Auxiliary Bishop of San Diego; Bishop Gilbert E. Chavez, 1535 Third Ave., San Diego, CA 92101. Chancery Office, P.O. Box 80428, San Diego, CA 92138. Tel. (619) 574-6300

Archdiocese of San Francisco, Archbishop John R. Quinn. Chancellor, Sr. Mary B. Flaherty, R.S.C.J. Chancery Office, 445 Church St., San Francisco, CA 94114. Tel. (415) 565-3600

San Jose, Bishop Pierre DuMaine. Chancery Office, 7600 St. Joseph Ave., Los Altos, CA 94022. Tel. (415) 967-8670.

Archdiocese of Santa Fe, Archbishop Robert F. Sanchez; Chancellor Rev. D. J. Starkey. Chancery Office, 202 Morningside Dr., S.E., Albuquerque, NM 87108. Tel. (505) 268-4572

Santa Rosa, Bishop Mark J. Hurley; Chancellor, Rev. Msgr. James E. Pulskamp. Chancery Office, 547 "B" St., P.O. Box 1297, Santa Rosa, CA 95402. Tel. (707) 545-7610

Savannah, Bishop Raymond W. Lessard. Chancery Office, 225 Abercorn St., P.O. Box 8789, Savannah, GA 31412. Tel. (912) 238-2320

Scranton, Bishop James C. Timlin, 300 Wyoming Ave., Scranton PA 18503; Chancellor, Rev. Gerald F. Mullally. Chancery Office, 300 Wyoming Ave., Scranton, PA 18503. Tel. (717) 346-8910

Archdiocese of Seattle, Archbishop Raymond G. Hunthausen; Chancellor, Very Rev. Michael G. Ryan. Chancery Office, 910 Marion St., Seattle, WA 98104. Tel. (206) 382-4560

Shreveport, Bishop William B. Friend. Chancellor, Sr. Margaret Daves, C.S.J., 2500 Line Ave., Shreveport, LA 71104. Tel. (318)222-2006

Sioux City, Bishop Lawrence D. Soens. Chancery Office, P.O. Box 3379, Sioux City, IA 51102. Tel. (712) 255-7933

Sioux Falls, Bishop Paul V. Dudley; Auxiliary Bishop of Sious Falls, Bishop Lambert A. Hoch; Chancellor, Rev. James M. Joyce. Chancery Office, 423 N. Duluth Ave., Box 5033, Sioux Falls, SD 57117. Tel. (605) 334-9861

Spokane, Bishop Lawrence H. Welsh, W. 1025 Cleveland Ave., Spokane, WA 99120. Chancery Office, P.O. Box 1453, Spokane, WA 99205. Tel. (509) 456-7100

Springfield-Cape Girardeau, Bishop John J. Leibrecht, P.O. Box 1957 SSS, Springfield, MO 65805; Chancellor, Rev. Thomas E. Reidy, 318 Park Central E., P.O. Box 1957 SSS, Springfield, MO 65805. Tel. (417) 866-0841

Springfield in Illinois, Bishop Daniel L. Ryan; Chancellor Rev. John Renken, P.O. Box 1667, Springfield, IL 62705. Tel. (217) 522-7781

Springfield, Bishop Joseph F. Maguire; Auxiliary Bishops of Springfield, Bishop Leo E. O'Neil, P.O. Box 798, Eden Hill, Stockbridge, MA 01262, Chancellor, Rev. Thomas L. Dupre. Chancery Office, 76 Elliot St., P.O. Box 1730, Springfield, MA 01101. Tel. (413) 732-3175

Byzantine Ukainian Rite—Stamford, Bishop Basil H. Losten. Chancery Office, 161 Glenbrook Rd., Stamford, CT 06902. Tel. (203) 324-7698

Steubenville, Bishop Albert H. Ottenweller. Chancery Office, 422 Washington St., P.O. Box 969, Steubenville, OH 43952. Tel. (614) 282-3631

Stockton, Bishop Donald W. Montrose; Chancellor, Sr. Lorraine Pagendarm, O.P. Chancery Office, 1105 N. Lincoln St., Stockton, CA 95203, P.O. Box 4237, Stockton, CA 95204. Tel. (209) 466-0636

Superior, Bishop Raphael M. Fliss; Chancellor, Rev. James R. Horath. Chancery Office, 1201 Hughitt Ave., Superior, WI 54880. Tel. (715) 392-2937

Syracuse, Bishop Joseph T. O'Keefe; Auxiliary Bishop of Syracuse; Bishop Thomas J. Costello, 240 Midland Ave., Syracuse, NY 13205. Chancery Office, P.O. Box 511, Syracuse, NY 13201. Tel. (315) 422-7203

Toledo, Bishop James R. Hoffman; Auxiliary Bishop of Toledo, Bishop Robert W. Donnelly. Chancery Office, 1933 Spielbush, Toledo, OH 43624. Tel. (419)244-6711

Trenton, Bishop John C. Reiss; Auxiliary Bishop of Trenton, Bishop Edward U. Kmiec, 215 Essex Ave., Spring Lake, NJ 07762; Chancellor, Rev. Msgr. William F. Fitzgerald. Chancery Office, P.O. Box 5309, Trenton NJ 08648. Tel. (609) 882-7125

Tucson, Bishop Manuel D. Moreno; Chancellor, Rev. John F. Allt, P.O. Box 31, Tucson AZ 85702. Chancery Office, 192 S. Stone Ave., Box 31, Tucson, AZ 85702. Tel. (602) 792-3410

Tulsa, Bishop Eusebius J. Beltran. Chancery Office, 820 S. Boulder St., P.O. Box 2009, Tulsa, OK 74101. Tel. (918) 587-3115

Van Nuys Eparchy, Bishop Thomas V. Dolinay. Chancery Office, 5335 Sepulveda Blvd., Van Nuys, CA 91411. Tel. (818) 907-1051.

Venice, Bishop John J. Nevins, P.O. Box 2006, Venice, FL 34284; Chancellor, Very Rev. Jerome A. Carosella. Chancery Office, 101 Capri Isles Blvd., Venice, FL 33595. Tel. (813)484-9543.

Victoria, Bishop Charles V. Grahmann; Chancellor, Rev. Msgr. Thomas C. McLaughlin. Chancery Office, P. O. Box 4708, Victoria, TX 77903. Tel. (512) 573-0828.

Archdiocese of Washington, Archbishop James A. Hickey. Auxiliary Bishops of Washington: Bishop Thomas W. Lyons, Rt. 7, Box 42, Waldorf, MD 20601. Chancellor, Rev. Msgr. Raymond J. Boland. Chancery Office, 5001 Eastern Ave., P. O. Box 29260, NW, Washington, DC 20017. Tel. (301) 853-3800

Wheeling-Charleston, Bishop Francis B. Schulte; Auxiliary Bishop of Wheeling-Charleston, Bishop James Michaels, S.S.C., 614 S. Oakwood Ave., Beckley, WV 25801; Chancellor, Rev. Robert C. Nash. Chancery Office, 1300 Byron St., Wheeling, WV 26003. Tel. (304) 233-0880

Wichita, Bishop Eugene J. Gerber. Chancery Office, 424 N. Broadway, Wichita, KS 67202. Tel. (316) 263-6262

Wilmington, Bishop Robert E. Mulvee; Auxiliary Bishop of Wilmington, Bishop James C. Burke, O.P., 2810 Monroe St., Wilmington, DE 19802. Chancery Office, P.O. Box 2030, 1925 Delaware Ave., Ste 1A, Wilmington, DE 19899. Tel. (302) 573-3100

Winona, Bishop John G. Vlazny; Chancellor, Rev. Donald P. Schmitz. Chancery Office, 55 W. Sanborn, P.O. Box 588, Winona, MN 55987. Tel. (507) 454-4643

Worcester, Bishop Timothy J. Harrington, 2 High Ridge Rd., Worcester MA 01602. Chancery Office, 49 Elm St., Worcester, MA 01609. Tel. (617) 791-7171

Yakima, Bishop William S. Skylstad; Chancellor, Very Rev. Perron J. Auve. Chancery Office, 5301-A Tieton Dr., Yakima, WA 98908. Tel. (509) 965-7117

Youngstown, Bishop James W. Malone, 2264 Volney Rd., Youngstown Oh 44511; Auxiliary Bishop of Youngstown: Bishop Benedict C. Franzetta, 144 West Wood St., Youngstown OH 44503; Chancellor, Rev. James Clarke. Chancery Office, 144 W. Wood St., Youngstown, OH 44503. Tel. (216) 744-8451

The Romanian Orthodox Church in America

The Romanian Orthodox Church in America is an autonomous Archdiocese chartered under the name of "Romanian Orthodox Missionary Archdiocese in America."

Diocese was founded in 1929 and approved by the Holy Synod of the Romanian Orthodox Church in Romania in 1934. A decision of the Holy Synod of the Romanian Orthodox Church of July 12, 1950, granted it ecclesiastical autonomy in America, continuing to hold only dogmatical and canonical ties with the Holy Synod and the Romanian Orthodox Patriarchate of Romania.

In 1951, a group of approximately 40 parishes with their clergy from USA and Canada separated from this church and eventually joined in 1960 the Russian Orthodox Greek Catholic Metropolia now called the Orthodox Church in America which reordained for these parishes a bishop with the title "Bishop of Detroit and Michigan."

The Holy Synod of the Romanian Orthodox Church, in its session of June 11, 1973, elevated the Bishop of Romanian Orthodox Missionary Episcopate in America to the rank of Archbishop. Consequently the Annual Congress of the Romanian Orthodox Church in America, held on July 21, 1973, at Edmonton-Boian, Alberta, decided to change the title of the Diocese from "Episcopate" to that of "Archdiocese." This decision was approved by the Holy Synod of the Romanian Orthodox Church of Romania in its session of December 12, 1974, renewing at the same time the status as an Autonomous Archdiocese with the right to elect in addition to the Archbishop an Auxiliary Bishop for the Archdiocese.

GENERAL ORGANIZATION

Headquarters: 19959 Riopelle, Detroit, MI 48203. Tel. (313) 893-7191

Annual Congress in July, and biannual Archdiocesan Council

OFFICERS

Archbishop, His Eminence The Most Rev. Archbishop Victorin (Ursache), 19959 Riopelle, Detroit, MI 48203. Tel. (313) 893-7191

Vicar, Very Rev. Archim. Dr. Vasile Vasilachi, 40-03 48th Ave., Woodside, Queens NY 11377. Tel. (718) 784-4453

Dir., Inter-Church Relations, Rev. Fr. Nicholas Apostola, 14 Hammond St., Worcester, MA 01610. Tel. (617)799-0040

Sec., Very Archim, Rev. Felix Dubneae, 19959 Riopelle St., Detroit, MI 48203. Tel. (313) 892-2402

PERIODICALS

Credinta—The Faith (m), 19959 Riopelle, Detroit, MI 48203. Very Rev. Archim, Dr. Vasile Vasilachi, Ed.

Calendarul Credinta (yearbook), 19959 Riopelle, Detroit, MI 48203. Very Rev. Archim. Dr. Vasile Vasilachi, Ed.

The Romanian Orthodox Episcopate of America

This body of Eastern Orthodox Christians of Romanian descent was organized in 1929 as an autonomous Diocese under the jurisdiction of the Romanian Patriarchate. In 1951 it severed all relations with the Orthodox Church of Romania. Now under the canonical jurisdiction of the autocephalous Orthodox Church in America, it enjoys full administrative autonomy and is headed by its own Bishop.

Churches: 34; Inclusive Membership: 60,000; Sunday or Sabbath Schools: 28; Total Enrollment: 1,612; Ordained Clergy: 67

GENERAL ORGANIZATION

Church Congress: annual (July)
Headquarters: 2522 Grey Tower Road, Jackson, MI 49201. Tel. (517) 522-4800

Ruling Bishop: His Grace Bishop Nathaniel (Popp)
The Council of the Episcopate: Sec., Rev. Fr. Laurence Lazar, 3355 Ridgewood Rd., Akron, OH 44313; Treas., Rev. Fr. Richard Grabowski, 3256 Warren Rd., Cleveland, OH 44111

OTHER ORGANIZATIONS

The American Romanian Orthodox Youth (AROY): Pres., Patrick Roach, 3739 W. 165th St., Cleveland, OH 44111; Sec., Lisa Gligor, 3531 E. Western Reserve Rd., Poland, OH 44514; Spiritual Advisor, Rev. Fr. Constantin Tofan, 28430 W. Nine Mile Rd., Southfield, MI 48075

Association of Romanian Orthodox Ladies' Auxiliaries (ARFORA): Pres. Mrs. Pauline Trutza, 1466 Waterbury Ave., Lakewood, OH 44107; SpiritualAdvisor, Rev. Fr. Romey Rosco, 625 Centralia Ave., Dearborn Hts., MI 48127

Orthodox Brotherhood U.S.A.: Chpsn., Gary Brott, 4851 Westchester Dr., Austintown, OH 44515

PERIODICALS

Solia-Herald News (m), Solia Calendar (a), 146 W. Courtland St., Jackson, MI 49201

†Russian Orthodox Church in the U.S.A., Patriarchal Parishes of the

This group of parishes is under the direct jurisdiction of the Patriarch of Moscow and All Russia, His Holiness Pimen, in the person of a Vicar Bishop, His Grace Clement, Bishop of Serpukhov.

GENERAL ORGANIZATION

Headquarters: St. Nicholas Cathedral, 15 E. 97th St., New York, NY 10029. Tel. (212) 831-6294

Vicar Bishop: The Most Rev. Clement, Bishop of Serpukhov; Adm. of The Patriarchal Parishes of the Russian Orthodox Church in Canada and Temporarily in the United States of America

PERIODICALS

One Church (bi-m), 727 Miller Ave., Youngstown, OH 44502, Rt. Rev. Feodor Kovalchuk, Ed.

Journal of the Moscow Patriachate (Eng m), subscription list, St. Nicholas Cathedral, New York, NY 10029

The Russian Orthodox Church Outside of Russia

Organized in 1920 to unite in one body of dioceses the missions and parishes of the Russian Orthodox Church outside of Russia. The Governing body was set up in Constantinople sponsored by the Ecumenical Patriarchate. In November 1950, it came to the United States. The Russian Orthodox Church Outside of Russia lays emphasis on being true to the old traditions of the Russian Church, but it does not compromise with official church leaders in Moscow, "since that would amount to being under the influence and direction of a godless State."

GENERAL ORGANIZATION

Headquarters: 75 E. 93rd St., New York, NY 10128. Tel. (212) 534-1601

Council of Bishops, Synod, His Eminence Metropolitan Vitaly

Other Members: Sec., Archbishop Laurus of Syracuse and Trinity; Dep. Sec., Hilarian, Bishop of Manhattan

Sec. of the Synod of Bishops and Director of Public and Foreign Relations Dept., Archbishop Laurus of Syracuse & Trinity, 75 E. 93rd St., New York, NY 10128

PERIODICALS

Church Life (bi-m), by Synod of Bishops, 75 E. 93rd St., New York, NY 10128

Orthodox America, Box 2132, Redding, CA 96099

Orthodox Life, Holy Trinity Monastery, Jordanville, NY 13361

Pravoslavnaya Rus (2/mo.), in Russian, Holy Trinity Monastery, Jordanville, NY 13361

Living Orthodoxy (bi-m), St. John of Kronstadt Press., Rt. #1, Box 171, Liberty, TN 37095

The Salvation Army

The Salvation Army, founded in 1865 by William Booth (1829-1912) in London, England, and introduced into America in 1880, is an international religious and charitable movement organized and operated on a paramilitary pattern, and is a branch of the Christian church. To carry out its purposes, The Salvation Army has established a widely diversified program of religious and social welfare services which are designed to meet the needs of children, youth, and adults in all age groups.

Churches: 1,092; Inclusive Membership: 432,893; Sunday or Sabbath Schools: 1,113; Total Enrollment: 108,659; Ordained Clergy: 5,195

GENERAL ORGANIZATION

National Headquarters: 799 Bloomfield Ave., Verona, NJ 07044. Tel. (201) 239-0606

OFFICERS

Natl. Commander, Commissioner Andrew S. Miller

Natl. Chief Sec., Col. Harold E. Shoults

TERRITORIAL ORGANIZATIONS

Eastern Territory, 120-130 W. 14th St., New York, NY 10011; Territorial Commander, Commissioner Stanley E. Ditmer; Chief Sec., Col. Wallace Conrath

Central Territory, 860 N. Dearborn St., Chicago, IL 60610; Territorial Commander, Commissioner Robert Rightmire; Chief Sec., Col. Robert Thomson

Western Territory, 30840 Hawthorne Blvd., Rancho Palos Verdes, CA 90274. Territorial Commander, Commissioner Willard S. Evans; Chief Sec., Col. Kenneth Hood

Southern Territory, 1424 Northeast Expressway, Atlanta, GA 30329. Territorial Commander, Commissioner James Osbone; Chief Sec., Col. Bramwell Tillsley

PERIODICALS

The War Cry (w), Young Salvationist (m), The Young Soldier (m), The Musician (m), National Publications Dept., 799 Bloomfield-Ave, Verona, NJ 07044. Lt. Col. Henry Gariepy, Ed.-in-Chief

The Schwenkfelder Church

The Schwenkfelders are the spiritual descendants of the Silesian nobleman Caspar Schwenkfeld von Ossig (1489–1561), a scholar, reformer, preacher, and prolific writer who endeavored to aid in the cause of the Protestant Reformation. A contemporary of Martin Luther, John Calvin, Ulrich Zwingli, and Phillip Melancthon, Schwenkfeld sought no following, formulated no creed, and did not attempt to organize a church based on his beliefs. He labored for liberty of religious belief—a fellowship of all believers, for one united Christian church—the ecumenical Church.

He and his cobelievers supported a movement known as the Reformation by the Middle Way. Persecuted by state churches, ultimately 180 Schwenkfelders exiled from Silesia emigrated to Pennsylvania. They landed at Philadelphia Sept. 22, 1734, affirmed their allegiance to the crown of Great Britain on the 23rd and the following day, held a service of Thanksgiving for their deliverance and safe arrival in the New World.

In 1882, the Society of Schwenkfelders, the forerunner of the present Schwenkfelder Church, was formed. The church was incorporated in 1909.

The General Conference of the Schwenkfelder Church

is a voluntary association for the Schwenkfelder Churches at Palm, Worcester, Lansdale, Norristown, and Philadelphia, Pennsylvania, with a total membership of approximately 2,900.

They practice adult baptism and dedication of children, and observe the Lord's Supper regularly with open Communion. In theology, they are Christo-centric; in polity, congregational; in missions, world-minded; in ecclesiastical organization, ecumenical.

The Schwenkfelder Church has no publishing house of its own. The ministry is recruited from graduates of colleges, universities, and accredited theological seminaries. In each community, the churches have been noted for leadership in ecumenical concerns through ministerial associations, community service and action groups, councils of Christian education, and other agencies.

Churches: 5; Inclusive Membership: 2,647; Sunday or Sabbath Schools: 5; Total Enrollment: 882; Ordained Clergy: 10

GENERAL ORGANIZATION
General Conference: semi-annual
Headquarters: Pennsburg, PA 18073

OFFICERS
Mod., Kenneth D. Slough, Jr., 197 N. Whitehall Rd., Norristown PA 19403
Sec., Miss Florence Schultz, P.O. Box 221, Palm, PA 18070
Treas., Ellis W. Kriebel, 523 Meetinghouse Rd., Harleysville, PA 19438

PERIODICAL
The Schwenkfeldian (q), Pennsburg, PA 18073. Nancy M. Byron, Ed.

Second Cumberland Presbyterian Church in U.S.

This church, originally known as the Colored Cumberland Presbyterian Church, was formed in May 1874. Prior to its founding, a convention was held on October 1868 in Henderson, Ky., at which Black ministers of the Cumberland Presbyterian Church began to speak openly about forming a new denomination.

In May 1869, at the General Assembly meeting in Murfreesboro, Tenn., Moses Weir, the spokesperson for the black delegation appealed for help in organizing a separate African church. Four reasons were cited: Blacks could learn self-reliance and independence; they could have more financial assistance; they could minister more effectively among Blacks if they existed as a separate denomination; they wanted to worship close to the altar, and not in the balconies, which symbolized restriction. Four requests were made: that the Cumberland Presbyterian Church organize Blacks into presbyteries and synods; develop schools to train Black clergy; grant loans to assist Blacks to secure hymnbooks, Bibles, and church buildings; establish a separate General Assembly. At the 1869 General Assembly, the Black churches of the Cumberland Presbyterian Church were set apart with their own ecclesiastical organization.

In 1874 the first General Assembly of the Colored Cumberland Presbyterian Church met in Nashville, Tenn. The moderator was Rev. P. Price and the stated clerk was Elder John Humphrey. At that time there were 46 ordained clergy, 20 licentiates, 30 candidates, and 3,000 communicants.

Currently, the denomination's General Assembly, the national governing body, is organized around its three program boards and agencies: Finance, Publication and Christian Education and Missons and Evangelism. Other agencies of the General Assembly are under these three program boards.

The church has four synods (Alabama, Kentucky, Tennessee, and Texas) a membership of 15,000, 15 presbyteries, 153 congregations, and 100 ordained clergy. The greatest strength of the SCPC is its Alabama synod which comprises nearly one-third of the denomination; East and Middle Tennessee areas also contain large numbers of members. The SCPC extends as far north as Cleveland, Ohio and Chicago; as far west as Marshalltown, Iowa, and Dallas, Texas; and as far south as Selma, Alabama.

GENERAL ORGANIZATION
General Assembly: annual 2nd Wed. in June

OFFICERS
Mod.: Rev. Henry Ewing, Jr., 3111 Johnson Rd., SW, Huntsville, AL 35805. Tel. (205)881-3034.
Stated Clk.: Rev. Dr. R. Stanley Wood, 226 Church St., Huntsville, AL 35801. Tel. (205)536-7481

SYNODS
Alabama, Stated Clk., Arthur Hinton, 511 10th Ave., N.W., Aliceville 35442
Kentucky, Stated Clk., Leroy Hunt, 1317 Monroe St., Paducah, Ky 42001
Tennessee, Stated Clk., Rev. Curtis C. Wood, PO. Box 202, Charleston, TN 37310
Texas, Stated Clk., Arthur King, 2435 Kristen, Dallas, TX 75216

PERIODICAL
The Cumberland Flag, 226 Church St., Huntsville, AL 35801. Rev. Robert Stanley Wood, Interim Ed.

Separate Baptists in Christ

A group of Baptists found in Indiana, Ohio, Kentucky, Tennessee, Illinois, Virginia, Florida and North Carolina, dating back to an association formed in 1758 in North Carolina and Virginia.

Today this group consists of approximately 100 churches. They believe in the infallibility of the Bible, the divine ordinances of the Lord's Supper, feetwashing, baptism, and that he who endureth to the end shall be saved.

GENERAL ORGANIZATION
General Association

OFFICERS
Mod., Rev. Jim Goff, 1020 Gagel Ave., Louisville, KY 40216
Asst. Mod., Jimmy Polston, 3127 Lesky St., Indianapolis, IN 46218
Clk., Rev. Mark Polston, 1128 Fawn Run, Somerset, KY 42501. Tel. (606)678-8753
Asst. Clk., Bro. Randy Polston, 1841 N. Hawthorne Lane, Indianapolis, IN, 46218. Tel. (317)375-9898

Serbian Orthodox Church in the U.S.A. and Canada

The Serbian Orthodox Church is an organic part of the Eastern Orthodox Church. As a local church it received its autocephaly from Constantinople in 1219 A.D. The Patriarchal seat of the church today is in Belgrade, Yugoslavia. In 1921, a Serbian Orthodox Diocese in the United States of America and Canada was organized. In 1963, it was reorganized into three dioceses, and in 1983 a fourth diocese was created for the Canadian part of the church. The Serbian Orthodox Church in the USA and Canada received its administrative autonomy in 1982. The Serbian Orthodox Church is in absolute doctrinal unity with all other local Orthodox Churches.

Churches: 68; Inclusive Membership: 67,000; Sunday or Sabbath Schools: 56; Total Enrollment: 5,010; Ordained Clergy: 82

GENERAL ORGANIZATION

Episcopal Council
Central Church Council
Chancery: St. Sava Monastery, P.O. Box 519, Liberty-
ville, IL 60048. Tel. (312) 362-2440

BISHOPS

Rt. Rev. Dr. Firmilian, Bishop of Midwestern America,
P.O. Box 519 Libertyville, IL 60048. Tel. (312) 362-2440
Rt. Rev. Dr. Sava, Bishop of Shumadija, Adm. of
Western America, 2511 W. Garvey Ave., Alhambra,
CA 91803. Tel (213) 289-9061
Rt. Rev. Christopher, Bishop of Eastern America, P.O.
Box 368, Sewickley, PA 15143. Tel. (412) 741-5686
Rt. Rev.George, Bishop of Canada, 5A Stockbridge
Ave., Toronto, Ontario M8Z 4M6. Tel. (416) 231-4409
Rt. Rev. Mitrofan, Vicar Bishop of Toplica, PO. Box 519,
Libertyville, IL 60048. Tel. (312)367-0698.

OTHER ORGANIZATIONS

Brotherhood of Serbian Orthodox Clergy in the U.S.A.
and Canada, Pres., V. Rev. Milan Savich, Schererville,
IN
Federation of Circles of Serbian Sisters
Serbian Singing Federation

PERIODICAL

The Path of Orthodoxy, P.O. Box 36 Leetsdale, PA 15056.
Tel. (412) 741-8660. Rev. Rade Merick, Eng. Ed.; V.
Rev. Uros Ocokoljich and V. Rev. Nedeljko Lunich,
Serbian Ed.

Seventh-day Adventists

The Seventh-day Adventist Church grew out of a
worldwide religious revival in the mid-19th century.
People of many religious persuasions believed Bible
prophecies indicated that the second coming or advent of
Christ was imminent.

When Christ did not come in the 1840's, a group of these
disappointed Adventists in the United States continued
their Bible studies and concluded they had misinterpreted
prophetic events and that the second coming of Christ was
still in the future. This same group of Adventists later
accepted the teaching of the seventh-day Sabbath and
became known as Seventh-day Adventists. The denomination organized formally in 1863.

The church was largely confined to North America until
1874, when its first missionary was sent to Europe. Today
25,000 congregations meet in 184 countries. Membership
exceeds 5 million and increases between six and seven
percent each year.

In addition to a vigorous mission program, the church
has the largest worldwide Protestant parochial school
system with more than 5,300 schools with nearly 680,000
students on elementary through college and university
levels.

The Adventist Development and Relief Agency
(ADRA) helps victims of war and natural disasters, and
many local congregations have Community Service
facilities to help those in need close to home.

The church also has a worldwide publishing ministry
with more than 50 printing facilities producing magazines
and other publications in nearly 190 languages and
dialects. In the United States and Canada, the church
sponsors a variety of radio and television programs,
including "Christian Lifestyle Magazine," "It Is Written,"
"Breath of Life," "Ayer, Hoy, y Mañana," "Voice of
Prophecy," and "La Voz de la Esperanza."

Churches: 4,055; Inclusive Membership: 666,199; Sunday
or Sabbath Schools: 4,180; Total Enrollment: 464,307;
Ordained Clergy: 5,481

GENERAL ORGANIZATION

General Conference: quinquennial (next meeting, 1990)
Headquarters: 6840 Eastern Ave. N.W., Washington, DC
20012. Tel. (202) 722-6000

OFFICERS

Pres., Neal C. Wilson
Sec., G. Ralph Thompson
Treas., Donald F. Gilbert

DEPARTMENTS

Church Ministries Dept.: Dir., Delmer W. Holbrook
Communication Dept.: Dir., Robert W. Nixon
Education Dept.: Dir., George H. Akers
Health and Temperance Dept.: Dir., G. Gordon Hadley
Ministerial Association: Sec., W. Floyd Bresee
Public Affairs and Religious Liberty Dept.: Dir., B. B.
Beach
Publishing Dept.: Dir., Ronald E. Appenzeller

NORTH AMERICAN ORGANIZATIONS

The North American Division of Seventh-day Adventists,
6840 Eastern Ave. N.W., Washington, DC 20012, Pres.,
Charles E. Bradford; Adm. Asst. to Pres., Gary B.
Patterson; Secretaries, Robert L. Dale, Robert L.
Woodfork; Treasurers, George H. Crumley, Frank L.
Jones. This Division includes the United States, Bermuda
and Canada and is divided into 58 Conferences which are
grouped together into 9 organized Union Conferences.
The various Conferences work under the general direction
of these Union Conferences.

Atlantic Union Conference, P.O. Box 1189, South
Lancaster, MA 01561. Pres., Philip S. Follett; Sec.,
Alvin R. Gilbourne; Treas., Dale R. Beaulieu, (Terri-
tory: Connecticut, Maine, Massachusetts, New Hamp-
shire, New York, Rhode Island, Vermont, and the
Bermuda Islands)
Canada, Seventh-day Adventist Church in Canada (See
Directory 4, **Religious Bodies in Canada**)
Columbia Union Conference, 5427 Twin Knolls Rd.,
Columbia, MD 21045. Pres., Ron M. Wisbey; Sec.,
Luther R. Palmer; Treas., D. J. Russell (Territory:
Delaware, Maryland, New Jersey, Ohio, Pennsylvania,
Virginia, West Virginia, and District of Columbia)
Lake Union Conference, P.O. Box C, Berrien Springs, MI
49103, Pres., R. H. Carter; Sec., John L. Hayward;
Treas., Herbert Pritchard (Territory: Illinois, Indiana,
Michigan, and Wisconsin)
Mid-America Union Conference, P.O. Box 6127, Lincoln,
NE 68506. Pres., Joel O. Tompkins; Sec., George W.
Timpson; Treas., Duane P. Huey (Territory: Colorado,
Iowa, Kansas, Minnesota, Missouri, Nebraska, North
Dakota, South Dakota, Wyoming, San Juan County in
New Mexico)
North Pacific Union Conference, P.O. Box 16677,
Portland, OR 97216. Pres., Bruce Johnston; Sec., H. J.
Harris; Treas., Robert L. Rawson (Territory: Alaska,
Idaho, Montana, Oregon, and Washington)
Pacific Union Conference, P. O. Box 5005, Westlake
Village, CA 91359. Pres., Thomas J. Mostert, Jr.; Sec.,
Major C. White; Treas., S. D. Bietz (Territory:
Arizona, California, Hawaii, Nevada, and Utah)
Southern Union Conference, P.O. Box 849, Decatur, GA
30031. Pres., A. C. McClure; Sec., W. D. Sumpter;
Treas., Richard P. Center (Territory: Alabama, Flori-
da, Georgia, Kentucky, Mississippi, North Carolina,
South Carolina, and Tennessee)
Southwestern Union Conference, P. O. Box 4000, Burle-
son, TX 76028. Pres., Cyril Miller; Sec., Clayton R.
Pritchett; Treas., Max A. Trevino (Territory: Arkansas,
Louisiana, New Mexico [except San Juan County],
Oklahoma, and Texas)

The Adventist Review (w), 6840 Eastern Ave. N.W., Washington, DC 20012. W. G. Johnsson, Ed.

ASI News (bi-m), 6840 Eastern Ave. N.W., Washington, DC 20012. W. C. Arnold, Ed.

Celebration! (m), 55 W. Oak Ridge Dr., Hagerstown, MD 21740. D. Ronald Watts, Ed.

Christian Record, (m), 4444 South 52nd St., Lincoln NE 68506. R. J. Kaiser, Jr., Ed.

Church Ministries Worker (q), P.O. Box 7000, Boise, ID 83707. Graham Bingham, Ed.

Collegiate Quarterly (q), P.O. Box 7000, Boise, ID 83707. Graham Bingham, Ed.

Cornerstone Connections International (q), 55 W. Oak Ridge Dr., Hagerstown MD 21740. Mrs. Lyndelle Chiomenti, Ed.

Guide (w), 55 W. Oak Ridge Dr., Hagerstown, MD 21740. Jeannette R. Johnson, Ed.

Insight, (w), 55 W. Oak Ridge Dr., Hagerstown, MD 21740. J. Christopher Blake, Ed.

Journal of Adventist Education (5/yr.), 6840 Eastern Ave. N.W., Washington, DC 20012. Victor S. Griffiths, Ed.

Liberty (bi-m), 55 W. Oak Ridge Dr., Hagerstown, MD 21740. R. R. Hegstad, Ed.

Listen (m), P. O. Box 7000, Nampa, ID 83707. Gary Swanson, Ed.

Message (8/yr), 55 W. Oak Ridge Dr., Hagerstown, MD 21740. D. W. Baker, Ed.

Ministry, The (m), 55 W. Oak Ridge Dr., Hagerstown, MD 21740. J. Robert Spangler, Ed.

Mission, Adult and Junior (q), 55 W. Oak Ridge Dr. Hagerstown, MD 21740. Noelene Johnsson, Ed.

Our Little Friend (w), P.O. Box 7000, Nampa, ID 83707. Aileen Andres Sox, Ed.

Primary Treasure (w), P.O. Box 7000, Nampa, ID 83707. Aileen Andres Sox, Ed.

Sabbath School Lesson Quarterlies, P.O. Box 7000, Nampa, ID 83707.

Shabat Shalom, 55 W. Oak Ridge Dr., Hagerstown, MD 21740. Clifford Goldstein, Ed.

Signs of the Times (m), P.O. Box 7000, Nampa, ID 83707. K. J. Holland, Ed.

Vibrant Life (bi-m), 55 W. Oak Ridge Dr., Hagerstown, MD 21740. Ralph H. Blodgett, Ed.

The Winner (9/yr), 6430 Laurel St., Washington, DC 20012. Barbara Wetherell, Ed.

Youth Ministry Accent (q), 6840 Eastern Ave., N.W., Washington, DC 20012. James Joiner, Ed.

Seventh Day Baptist General Conference, USA and Canada

Seventh Day Baptists emerged during the English Reformation, organizing their first churches in England in the mid-1600's. The oldest of them all, the Millyard Seventh Day Baptist Church of London, continues to be active over 300 years later.

The first Seventh Day Baptist in America was Stephen Mumford, who emigrated from England in 1664. He became one of several Sabbathkeepers (observers of the seventh-day Sabbath, or Saturday) who fellowshipped with the First Baptist Church of Newport, R. I. In 1671 they withdrew to form the first Seventh Day Baptist Church in America at Newport.

Other Seventh Day Baptist churches were established early in New Jersey and Pennsylvania as well as New England. It was from these three centers that the denomination grew and expanded westward.

A desire to increase their fellowship and to organize for missionary efforts led to the founding of the Seventh Day Baptist General Conference in 1801.

The organized boards and agencies of the denomination reflect Seventh Day Baptist interest in missions, publishing

and education. Women have always been encouraged to participate actively at local and denominational levels. From the earliest days religious freedom has been championed for all, and the separation of church and state advocated.

In the 20th century Seventh Day Baptists have been characterized by their ecumenical spirit, fellowshipping as in the early years with other Baptists in the Baptist World Alliance and affiliated organizations, and reaching out to other Sabbathkeeping groups. In 1965 the Seventh Day Baptist World Federation was organized with the S.D.B. General Conference in U.S.A. joining as one of many member conferences around the world.

GENERAL ORGANIZATION

General Conference: annual

Headquarters: Seventh Day Baptist Center, 3120 Kennedy Rd., P. O. Box 1678, Janesville, WI 53547. Tel. (608) 752-5055

OFFICERS

Pres., Mrs. Geraldine VanDyke, 12 Cornell, Longmont, CO 80501

Rec. Sec., Mrs. Barbara C. Green, 1328 Ruger St., Janesville, WI 53545

Exec. Sec., Rev. Dale D. Thorngate, 3120 Kennedy Rd., P. O. Box 1678, Janesville, WI 53547

Treas., Ivan H. FitzRandolph, 3120 Kennedy Rd., P. O. Box 1678, Janesville, WI 53547

OTHER ORGANIZATIONS

Seventh Day Baptist Missionary Society: Exec. Vice-Pres., Rev. Leon R. Lawton, 308 Washington Trust Bldg., Westerly, RI 02891

Seventh Day Baptist Board of Christian Education: Exec. Dir., Rev. Ernest K. Bee, Jr., P.O. Box 115, Alfred Station, NY 14803

Women's Society of the General Conference: Pres., Mrs. Dorotha Shettel, 4290 Edgewood Pl., Riverside, CA 92506

American Sabbath Tract and Communication Council: Exec. Dir., D. Scott Smith, 3120 Kennedy Rd., P. O. Box 1678, Janesville, WI 53547

Seventh Day Baptist Historical Society: Rev. Don A. Stanford, Historian; Mrs. Janet Thorngate, Librarian; 3120 Kennedy Rd., P. O. Box 1678, Janesville, WI 53547

Seventh Day Baptist Center on Ministry: Dean, Rev. J. Paul Green, 3120 Kennedy Rd., P. O. Box 1678, Janesville, WI 53547

PERIODICAL

Sabbath Recorder (m), 3120 Kennedy Rd., P. O. Box 1678, Janesville, WI 53547. D. Scott Smith, Ed.

Social Brethren

Organized 1867 among members of various bodies; confession of faith has nine articles; evangelical.

GENERAL ORGANIZATION

General Assembly: biennial

OFFICERS

Mod., of General Assembly, Rev. John Hancock, RR #3 Box 221, Harrisburg, IL 62946. Tel. (618)252-0802

Mod. (Union Association), Rev. L. L. Gullet, RR #3, Harrisburg, IL 62946. Tel. (618)662-3881

Mod. (Illinois Association), Rev. Earl E. Vaughn, R.R. 2, Flora, IL 62839

Mod. (Midwestern Association), Rev. Edward Darnell, 53 E. Newport, Pontiac, MI 48055. Tel. (313)335-9125

Southern Baptist Convention

The Southern Baptist Convention was organized on May 10, 1845, in Augusta, Georgia.

Cooperating Baptist churches are located in all 50 states, the District of Columbia, Puerto Rico, American Samoa, and the Virgin Islands. The members of the churches work together through 1,214 district associations and 37 state conventions. The Southern Baptist Convention has an Executive Committee and 20 national agencies—four boards, six seminaries, seven commissions, a foundation and two associated organizations.

The purpose of the Southern Baptist Convention is "to provide a general organization for Baptists in the United States and its territories for the promotion of Christian missions at home and abroad and any other objects such as Christian education, benevolent enterprises, and social services which it may deem proper and advisable for the furtherance of the Kingdom of God" (Constitution, Article II).

The Convention exists in order to help the churches to lead people to God through Jesus Christ.

From the beginning, there has been a burning mission desire to share the Gospel with the peoples of the world. The Cooperative Program is the basic channel of mission support. In addition, the Lottie Moon Christmas Offering for Foreign Missions and the Annie Armstrong Easter Offering for Home Missions support Southern Baptists' world mission programs.

In 1986, there were 3,756 foreign missionaries serving in 105 foreign countries and 3,637 home missionaries serving within the United States.

In 1985, the Southern Baptist Convention adopted the continuation of the major denominational emphasis of Bold Mission Thrust for 1985-90. Bold Mission Thrust is an effort to enable every person in the world to have opportunity to hear and to respond to the Gospel of Christ by the year 2000.

Churches: 37,072; Inclusive Membership: 14,613,618; Sunday or Sabbath Schools: 35,975; Total Enrollment: 7,938,479; Ordained Clergy: 63,200

GENERAL ORGANIZATION
Convention: annual

OFFICERS
Pres., Adrian P. Rogers, Bellevue Baptist Church, P. O. Box 40837, Memphis, TN 38174; Rec. Sec., Martin B. Bradley, 127 9th Ave., N., Nashville, TN 37234.
Executive Committee: Offices, 901 Commerce, Nashville TN 37203. Tel. (615) 244-2355; Pres., Harold C. Bennett; Exec. Vice-Pres., Ernest E. Mosley; Vice-Pres., Business & Finance, Tim Hedquist; Vice-Pres., Public Relations, Alvin C. Shackleford.

GENERAL BOARDS AND COMMISSIONS
Foreign Mission Board: Box 6767, Richmond, VA 23230. Tel. (804) 353-0151. Pres., R. Keith Parks
Home Mission Board: 1350 Spring St., NW, Atlanta, Ga 30367. Tel. (404) 873-4041. Pres., Larry L. Lewis
Annuity Board: P.O. Box 2190, Dallas, TX 75221. Tel. (214) 720-0511. Pres., Darold H. Morgan; Exec. Vice Pres., Pat McDaniel
Sunday School Board: 127 Ninth Ave., N., Nashville, TN 37234. Tel. (615) 251-2000. Pres., Lloyd Elder; Exec. Vice-Pres., James D. Williams.
Brotherhood Commission: 1548 Poplar Ave., Memphis, TN 38104. Tel. (901) 272-2461. Pres., James H. Smith
Southern Baptist Commission on the American Baptist Theological Seminary: Room 318, 901 Commerce St., Nashville, TN 37203. Tel. (615) 244-2362. Exec. Sec.-Treas., Arthur H. Walker, Jr.; Pres., of the Seminary, Odell McGlothian, Sr.
Christian Life Commission: 901 Commerce St., Nashville, TN 37203. Tel. (615) 244-2495. Exec. Dir.-Treas., Larry N. Baker
Education Commission; 901 Commerce St., Nashville, TN 37203. Tel. (615) 244-2362. Exec. Sec.-Treas., Arthur H. Walker, Jr.
Historical Commission: 901 Commerce St., Nashville, TN

37203. Tel. (615) 251-2662. Exec. Dir. Treas., Lynn E. May, Jr.; Asst. Exec. Dir., A. Ronald Tonks
The Radio and TV Commission: 6350 West Freeway, Ft. Worth, TX 76150. Tel. (817) 737-4011. Jimmy R. Allen, Pres.
Stewardship Commission: 901 Commerce St., Nashville, TN 37203. Tel. (615) 244-2303. Exec. Dir.-Treas., A. R. Fagan; Assoc. Exec. Dir., Harry S. Bonner

STATE CONVENTIONS
Alabama, Earl Potts, 2001 E. South Blvd., Montgomery 36198. Tel. (205) 288-2460
Alaska, Bill G. Duncan, Actg. Exec. Dir., Star Route A., Box 1791, Anchorage 99502. Tel. (907) 344-9627
Arizona, Jack Johnson, 400 East Camelback Rd., Phoenix 85013. Tel. (602) 264-9421
Arkansas, Don Moore, P.O. Box 552, Little Rock 72203. Tel. (501) 376-4791
California, William Hogue, 678 E. Shaw Ave., Fresno 93755. Tel. (Tel. (209) 229-9533
Colorado, Charles Sharp, P.O. Box 22005, Denver 80222. (Tel.) (303) 771-2480
District of Columbia, James Langley, 1628 16th St. NW, Washington 20009. Tel. (202) 265-1526
Florida, Exec. Sec., Dan C. Stringer, 1230 Hendricks Ave., Jacksonville 32207. Tel. (904) 396-2351
Georgia, James N. Griffith, 2930 Flowers Rd., S., Atlanta, GA 30341. Tel. (404) 455-0404
Hawaii, Dan H. Kong, 2042 Vancouver Dr., Honolulu 96822. Tel. (808) 946-9581
Illinois, _____, Baptist Bldg., P.O. Box 3486 Springfield, 62708. Tel. (217) 786-2626
Indiana, Lew Reynolds, Interim Exec. Dir., 900 N. High School Rd., Indianapolis 46224. Tel. (317) 241-9317
Kansas-Nebraska, R. Rex Lindsay, 5410 W. Seventh St., Topeka 66606. Tel. (913) 273-4880
Kentucky, William W. Marshall, P.O. Box 43433, Middletown 40243. Tel. (502) 245-4101
Louisiana, Mark Short, Box 311, Alexandria 71301. Tel. (318) 448-3402
Maryland, Kenneth Lyle, 1313 York Rd., Lutherville 21093. Tel. (301) 321-7900
Michigan, Robert Wilson, 15635 W. 12 Mile Rd., Southfield 48076. Tel. (313) 557-4200
Minnesota-Wisconsin, Otha Winningham, 519 16th St. SE, Rochester, MN 55901. Tel. (507) 282-3636
Mississippi, Earl Kelley, P.O. Box 530, Jackson 39205. Tel. (601) 354-3704
Missouri, Donald V. Wideman, 400 E. High, Jefferson City 65101. Tel. (314) 635-7931
Nevada, Ernest B. Myers, 895 North Center St., Reno, NV 89501. Tel. (702) 322-0895
New England, James H. Currin, Box 688, 5 Oak Ave., Northboro, MA 01532. Tel. (617) 393-6013
New Mexico, Claude Cone, P.O. Box 485, Albuquerque 87103. Tel. (505) 247-0586
New York, R. Quinn Pugh, 500 S. Salina St., Syracuse 13202. Tel. (315) 475-6173
North Carolina, Roy J. Smith, 205 Convention Dr., Cary, NC 27511, Tel. (919) 467-5100
Northern Plains, John Baker, P.O. Box 1278 Rapid City, SD 57709. Tel. (605) 343-5572
Northwest Baptist Convention, Cecil Sims, 1033 N.E. 6th Ave., Portland, OR 97232. Tel. (503) 238-4545
Ohio, Tal Bonham, 1680 E. Broad St., Columbus 43203. Tel. (614) 258-8491
Oklahoma, William G. Tanner, 1141 N. Robinson, Oklahoma City 73103. (405) 236-4341
Pennsylvania-South Jersey, J. N. Evans, Interim Exec. Dir., 4620 Fritchey St., Harrisburg 17109. Tel. (717) 652-5856
South Carolina, Ray Rust, 907 Richland St., Columbia 29201. Tel. (803) 765-0030

Tennessee, Tom Madden, P.O. Box 647, Brentwood, 37027. Tel. (615) 373-2255

Texas, William M. Pinson, Jr., 511 N. Akard, Dallas 75201. Tel. (214) 741-1991

Utah-Idaho, Darwin E. Welsh, Sec., P.O. Box 1039, Sandy, UT 84091. Tel. (801) 255-3565

Virginia, Reginald M. McDonough, Va. Baptist Bldg., P. O. Box 8568, Richmond 23226. Tel. (804) 282-9751

West Virginia, Thomas E. Kinchen, 801 Sixth Ave., St. Albans 25177. Tel. (304) 727-2974

Wyoming, John W. Thomason, Box 3074, Casper, 82602. Tel. (307) 472-4087

PERIODICALS

Accent, P.O. Box C-10, Birmingham, AL 35283 Oneta Gentry, Ed.

Alabama Baptist (w), 3310 Independence Dr., Birmingham, AL 35259. Tel. (205) 870-4720. Hudson Baggett, Ed.

Alaska Baptist Messenger, Star Rt. A, Box 1791, Anchorage, AK 99507. Bill G. Duncan, Ed. Tel. (907) 344-9627.

Ambassador Life, 1548 Poplar Ave., Memphis, TN 38104. Tel (901) 272-2461

Arkansas Baptist Newsmagazine (w), 525 W. Capitol Ave., Little Rock, AR 72203. Tel. (501) 376-4791. J. Everett Sneed, Ed.

Aware, P.O. Box C-10, Birmingham, AL 35283. Mrs. Jesse A. Tucker, Ed.

Baptist and Reflector (w), P.O. Box 347, Brentwood, TN 37027. Fletcher Allen, Ed. Tel. (615) 373-2255

Baptist Beacon (w), 400 W. Camelback Rd., Phoenix, AZ 85013. Elizabeth Young, Ed. Tel. (602) 264-9429

Baptist Courier (w), Box 2168, Greenville, SC 29602. John Roberts, Ed. Tel. (803) 232-8736

Baptist Digest (w), 5410 W. 7th, Topeka, KS 66606. John Hopkins, Ed. Tel. (913) 273-4880

Baptist Message (w), Box 311, Alexandria, LA 71301. Lynn Clayton, Ed. Tel. (318) 442-7728

Baptist Messenger (w), 1141, N. Robinson, Oklahoma City, OK 73103. Glenn A. Brown, Ed. Tel. (405) 236-4341

Baptist New Mexican (w), Box 485, Albuquerque, NM 87103. J. B. Fowler, Ed. Tel. (505) 247-0586

Baptist Program, SBC, 901 Commerce St., Nashville, TN 37203. Ernest E. Mosley, Ed. Tel. (615) 244-2355

Baptist Record (w), P.O. Box 530, Jackson, MS 39205. Don McGregor, Ed. Tel. (601) 968-3800

Baptist Standard (w), P.O. Box 226330, Dallas, TX 75266. Tel. (214) 630-4571. Presnall Wood, Ed.

Biblical Recorder (w), P.O. Box 26568, Raleigh, N. C. 27611. R. Eugene Puckett, Ed. Tel. (919) 847-2127

California Southern Baptist (w), P.O. Box 5168, Fresno, CA 93755. Herb Hollinger, Ed. Tel. (209) 229-9533

Capital Baptist, 1628 16th St. NW, Washington, DC 20009. James Langley, Ed. Tel. (202) 265-1526

Christian Index (w), 2930 Flowers Rd., S., Atlanta, GA 30341. Jack U. Harwell, Ed. Tel. (404) 455-0404

Commission, The, Box 6767, Richmond, VA 23230. Floyd North, Ed.

Contempo, P.O. Box C-10, Birmingham, AL 35283. Laurella Owens, Ed.

Discovery, P.O. Box C-10, Birmingham, AL 35283. Mrs. Jesse A. Tucker, Ed.

Florida Baptist Witness (w), 1230 Hendricks Ave., Jacksonville, FL 32207. Jack Brymer, Ed. Tel. (904) 396-2351

Hawaii Baptist, 2042 Vancouver Dr., Honolulu 96822. Dan Kong, Ed. Tel. (808) 946-9581

Illinois Baptist (w), P.O. Box 3486, Springfield, 62708. Bill Webb, Ed. Tel. (217) 786-2000

Indiana Baptist (m), P.O. Box 24038, Indianapolis, IN 46224. David Simpson, Ed. Tel. (317) 241-9317

Maryland Baptist (w), 1313 York Rd., Lutherville, MD

21093. _____, Ed. Tel. (301) 321-7900

Michigan Baptist Advocate, 15635 W. Twelve Mile Rd., Southfield MI 48076. Robert Wilson, Ed. Tel. (313) 557-4200

Minnesota-Wisconsin Southern Baptist, 519 16th St. SE, Rochester, MN 55904 Mrs. Louise Cunningham, Ed.

Missions USA, 1350 Spring St. NW, Atlanta, GA 30367. William Junker, Ed.

New York Baptist, 500 S Salina St., Syracuse, NY 13202, Quenton Lockwood, Jr., Ed. Tel. (315) 475-6173

Northern Plains News, P. O. Box 1278, Rapid City, SD 57709. June Highlan, Ed. Tel. (605) 343-5572

Northwest Baptist Witness, 1033 N. 6th Ave., Portland, OR 97232, James L. Watters, Ed. Tel. (503) 238-4545

Ohio Baptist Messenger (m), 1680 E. Broad, Columbus, OH 43203. Theo Sommerkamp Ed. Tel. (614) 258-8491

Penn.-Jersey Baptist, 900 S. Arlington Ave., Harrisburg, PA 17109. J. N. Evans, Ed. Tel. (717) 652-5856

Quarterly Review (q), 127 Ninth Ave. N., Nashville, TN 37203. Linda S. Barr, Ed. Tel. (615) 251-2000

Religious Herald (w), P.O. Box 8377, Richmond, VA 23226. Julian Pentecost, Ed. Tel. (804) 288-1973

Review and Expositor (q), 2825 Lexington Rd., Louisville, KY 40206. Tel. (502) 879-4011

Rocky Mountain Baptist, P.O. Box 22005, Denver, CO 80222. _____, Ed. Tel. (303) 771-2480

Royal Service, P.O. Box C-10, Birmingham, AL 35283. Rosanne Osborn, Ed.

Southwestern News, P.O. Box 22000, Seminary Hill, Fort Worth, TX 76122. John Seelig, Ed.

Start, P.O. Box C-10, Birmingham, AL 35283. Mrs. Helen M. Allan, Ed.

Utah-Idaho Southern Baptist Witness, P.O. Box 2545, Salt Lake City, UT 84110. Darwin E. Welsh, Ed. Tel. (801) 322-3565

Western Recorder (w), Box 43401, Middletown, KY 40243. Jack Sanford, Ed. Tel. (502) 245-4101

West Virginia Southern Baptist, 801 Sixth Ave., St. Albans, WV 25177. Jackson C. Walls, Ed. Tel. (304) 727-2974

Word and Way (w), 400 E. High, Jefferson City, MO 65101. Bob Terry, Ed. Tel. (314) 635-7931

Southern Methodist Church

Organized in 1939, this body is composed of congregations desirous of continuing in true Methodism and preserving the fundamental doctrines and beliefs of the Methodist Episcopal Church, South that declined to be a party to the merger of the Methodist Episcopal Church, The Methodist Episcopal Church, South, and the Methodist Protestant Church into The Methodist Church.

GENERAL ORGANIZATION

General Conference: quadrennial (next meeting, May 1990)

Annual Conferences: (1) The Carolinas-Virginia Conference; (2) Alabama-Florida-Georgia Conference; (3) Mid-South Conference (Mississippi, Tennessee); (4) South-Western Conference (Arkansas, Louisiana, Texas)

OFFICERS

Pres., Rev. W. Lynn Corbett, P.O. Box 132, Orangeburg, SC 29116. Tel. (803) 536-1378

Vice-Presidents:

The Carolinas-Virginia Conf., Rev. Richard G. Blank, P. O. Box 233, Turbeville, SC 29162

Alabama-Florida-Georgia Conf., Rev. George C. Howell, 2206 Gail Ave., Albany, GA 31707

Mid-South Conf., Rev. Dr. Ronald R. Carrier, P. O. Box 150002, Nashville, TN 37215

Southwestern Conf., Rev. Arthur P. Meacham, 6011 Fairfield Ave., Shreveport, LA 71106

Treas., Gen. Conference, Rev. Patrick F. Endicott, P.O. Box 132, Orangeburg, SC 29116

The Southern Methodist (m), P.O. Drawer A, Orangeburg, SC 29116

Sovereign Grace Baptists

The Sovereign Grace Baptists are a contemporary movement which began its stirrings in the mid-1950's when some pastors in traditional Baptist churches returned to a Calvinist theological perspective. But this upsurge of Calvinism among present-day Baptists is simply a return to what many Baptists used to believe.

The first "Sovereign Grace" conference was held in Ashland, KY in 1954 and since then conferences of this sort have been sponsored by various local churches on the West Coast, Southern and Northern states, and Canada.

This movement is a spontaneous phenomenon concerning reformation at the local church level. Consequently, there is no interest in establishing a Reformed Baptist "Convention" of "Denomination." Part of the oneness of doctrine of the Sovereign Grace Baptists is the conviction that each local church is to administer the keys to the kingdom. Thus any ecclesiastical structure above the local church is ruled out.

Most Sovereign Grace Baptists, formally or informally relate to the *First London* (1646), *Second London* (1689), or *Philadelphia* (1742) Confessions. Baptists who relate to these Confessions differ from other "Calvinistic" Baptists who either deny the necessity of preaching to all men (most Primitive Baptists and other hyper-Calvinists), or hold to a "Baptist succession" concept of the church (Landmark Baptists).

There is a wide variety of local church government in this movement. Many Calvinist Baptists have or desire a plurality of elders in each assembly. These elders are responsible for the spiritual oversight of the church. Deacons are primarily responsible to take care of the financial and physical needs of the flock. Other Sovereign Grace Baptists, however, prefer to function with one pastor and several deacons.

Membership procedures vary from church to church but all would require a credible profession of faith in Christ, and proper Baptism as a basis for membership.

Calvinistic Baptists financially support gospel efforts (missionaries, pastors of small churches at home and abroad, literature publication and distribution, radio programs, etc.) in various parts of the world. Some local churches have institutional training programs, advanced Bible studies, and Christian schools.

Churches: 250 Inclusive Membership: 2,000 Sunday or Sabbath Schools: 250; Total Enrollment: 3,025; Ordained Clergy: 325

GENERAL ORGANIZATION

Correspondent: Pastor Jon Zens, P. O. Box 548, St. Croix Falls, WI 54024

PERIODICALS

Searching Together, P.O. Box 548, St. Croix Falls, WI 54024.

Reformation Today (bi-m), 2817 Dashwood St., Lakewood, CA 90712. Erroll Hulse, Ed.

Syrian Orthodox Church of Antioch (Archdiocese of the United States and Canada)

An archdiocese in North America of the Syrian Orthodox Church of Antioch. The Syrian Orthodox Church, composed of several archdioceses, numerous parishes, schools and seminaries, professes the faith of the first three Ecumenical Councils of Nicaea, Constantinople, Ephesus, and numbers faithful in the Middle East, India, the Americas, Europe and Australia. The Church traces its origin to the Patriarchate established in Antioch by St. Peter the Apostle and is under the supreme ecclesiastical jurisdiction of His Holiness the Syrian Orthodox Patriarch of Antioch and All the East, now residing in Damascus, Syria.

The first Syrian Orthodox faithful came to North America during the late 1800's, and by 1907 the first Syrian Orthodox priest was ordained to tend to the community's spiritual needs. In 1949, His Eminence Archbishop Mar Athanasius Y. Samuel came to America and was soon appointed Patriarchal Vicar.

There are 18 official archdiocesan parishes in the United States located in California, Maryland, Georgia, Illinois, Massachusetts, Michigan, New Jersey, New York, Oklahoma, Pennsylvania, Rhode Island and Texas. In Canada, there are 5 official parishes three in the Province of Ontario and two in the Province of Quebec.

Churches: 22; Inclusive Membership: 30,000; Sunday or Sabbath Schools: N.R.; Total Enrollment: N.R.; Ordained Clergy: 25

ORGANIZATION

Archdiocese of the U.S. and Canada, 49 Kipp Ave., Lodi, NJ 07644. Tel. (201)778-0638

Archdiocesan Convention: Annual

OFFICERS

Primate: Archbishop MarAthanasius Y. Samuel, 49 Kipp Ave., Lodi, NJ 07644. Tel. (201)778-0638

Archdiocesan Gen. Sec., Very Rev. Chorepiscopus John Meno, 45 Fairmount Ave., Hackensack, NJ 07601. Tel. (201)646-9443

Triumph the Church and Kingdom of God in Christ (International)

This church was given through the wisdom and knowledge of God himself to the Late Apostle Elias Dempsey Smith, on October 20, 1897, at 12:00 noon in Issaquena, County, Mississippi, while he was pastor of a Methodist church.

The Triumph Church, as this body is more commonly known, was founded in 1902, its doors opened in 1904, and confirmed in Birmingham, Alabama, with 225 members in 1915. It was incorporated in Washington, DC, 1918 and currently operates in 31 states and overseas. The General Church is divided into 18 districts including the Africa District and the South American District.

Triumphant doctrine and philosophy is based on the following concepts and principles: Life, Truth and Knowledge; God in man, and being expressed through man; Manifested Wisdom; Complete and Full Understanding; Constant New Revelations. Its concepts and methods of teaching "the second coming of Christ" are based on these and all other attributes of goodness.

Triumphians put strong emphasis on the fact that God is the God of the living, and not the God of the dead.

GENERAL ORGANIZATION

Quarterly and Annual Conferences, International Religious Congress: quadrennial

National Headquarters, Birmingham, AL

International Headquarters, 213 Farrington Ave., S.E., Atlanta,GA 30315

OFFICERS

Chief Bishop, Rt. Rev. A. J. Scott

Chspn. of Bd. of Trustees, Bishop C. W. Drumond, 7114 Idlewild, Pittsburgh, PA 15208

Nat. Gen. Rec. Sec., Bishop C. H. Whittaker, 9200 Miles Ave., Cleveland, OH 44105. Tel. (216) 883-6769

True (Old Calendar) Orthodox Church of Greece (Synod of Metropolitan Cyprian), American Exarchate

The American Exarchate of the True (Old Calendar) Orthodox Church of Greece adheres to the tenets of the Eastern Orthodox Church, which considers itself the legitimate heir of the historical Apostolic Church.

When the Orthodox Church of Greece, the official state Church, adopted the New or Gregorian Calendar in 1924, many felt that this breach with tradition compromised the Church's festal calendar, which is based on the Old or Julian calendar, and its unity with world Orthodoxy. A resistance movement to the reform culminated in 1935 when three State Church Bishops returned to the Old Calendar and established Synod in Resistance, The True Orthodox Church of Greece. When the last of these Bishops died, the Russian Orthodox Church Abroad consecrated a new hierarchy for the Greek Old Calendarists and, in 1969, declared them a sister Church.

In the face of persecution by the state Church, some Old Calendarists denied the validity of the Mother Church of Greece and formed into two Synods, now under the direction of Archbishop Chrysostomos of Athens and Archbishop Andreas of Athens. A moderate faction under Metropolitan Cyprian of Oropos and Fili does not maintain communion with what it considers the ailing Mother Church of Greece, but recognizes its validity and seeks for a restoration of unity between the Old and New Calendarist factions by a return to the Julian Calendar and traditional ecclesiastical polity by the State Church. About two million Orthodox Greeks belong to the Old Calendar Church.

The first Old Calendarist communities in the U.S. were formed in the 1930s. There are about twenty thousand Old Calendarist Greeks in America, equally distributed among the Exarchates of the three Greek Synods. The Exarchate under Metropolitan Cyprian, headed by a Princeton-educated, former university professor, was established in 1986 and has attracted large numbers of the Faithful. Placing emphasis on clergy education, youth programs, and recognition of the Old Calendarist minority in American Orthodoxy, the Exarchate has encouraged the establishment of monastic communities and missions. Cordial contacts with the New Calendarist and other Orthodox communities are encouraged at the parish and administrative levels. A center for theological training and Patristic studies has been established at the Exarchate headquarters in Etna, California.

Churches: 14; Inclusive Membership: 4,532; Sunday or Sabbath Schools: None; Total Enrollment: None; Ordained Clergy: 21

GENERAL ORGANIZATION

Exarchate Headquarters: St. Gregory Palamas Monastery, P. O. Box 398, Etna, CA 96027. Tel. (916) 467-3228

OFFICERS

Synodical Exarch in America, His Grace Bishop Chrysostomos, P. O. Box 398, Etna, CA 96027
Dean of Exarchate, The Rev. James P. Thornton, P. O. Box 2833, Garden Grove, CA 92642

PERIODICALS

Orthodox Tradition (3/yr), Center for Traditionalist Orthodox Studies, Etna, CA 96027, Hieromonk Fr. Auxentios, Ed.
The Orthodox Path (bi-m), Convent of St. Elizabeth the Grand Dutchess, P. O. Box 126, Etna, CA. Mo. Elizabeth and Rev. James Thornton, Eds.

Ukrainian Orthodox Church of the U.S.A.

Formally organized in U.S.A. in 1919. Archbishop John Theodorovich arrived from Ukraine in 1924.

GENERAL ORGANIZATION

The Sobor, which elects a Council of Bishops, meets every three years. Next Sobor, 1988
Headquarters: P.O. Box 495, South Bound Brook, NJ 08880. Tel. (201) 356-0090

OFFICERS

Metropolitan: Most Rev. Mstyslav S. Skrypnyk, P.O. Box 495, South Bound Brook, NJ 08880; Archbishop Constantine Buggan, 15157 Waterman Dr., S., Holland IL 60473; Bishop Antony, 4 Von Steuben Lane, South Bound Brook, NJ 08880
Consistory: Pres., V. Rev. Michael Borysenko; Vice-Pres., V. Rev. Paul Hrynyshyn; Sec., V. Rev. Frank Estocin; Treas., Mr. Thomas Burka

PERIODICAL

Ukrainian Orthodox Word, English and Ukrainian editions, P.O. Box 495, South Bound Brook, NJ 08880

Ukrainian Orthodox Church in America (Ecumenical Patriarchate)

This body was organized in America in 1928, when the first convention was held. In 1932 Dr. Joseph Zuk was consecrated as first Bishop. His successor was the Most Rev. Bishop Bohdan, Primate, who was consecrated by the order of the Ecumenical Patriarchate of Constantinople on February 28, 1937, in New York City. He was succeeded by the Most Rev. Metropolitan Andrei Kuschak, consecrated by the blessing of Ecumenical Patriarch by Archbishop Iakovos, Metropolitan Germanos and Bishop Silas of Greek-Orthodox Church, on January 26, 1967. At the present time the position of Primate is vacant.

Churches: 27; Inclusive Membership: 5,000; Sunday or Sabbath Schools: 17; Total Enrollment: 645; Ordained Clergy: 37

GENERAL ORGANIZATION

Sobor meets every 4 years.
Headquarters: St. Andrew's Ukrainian Orthodox Diocese, 90-34 139th St., Jamaica, NY 11435. Tel. (718) 297-2407

OFFICERS

Primate: _____
Administrator: Rt. Rev. Michael Pawlyskyn
Sec.: Rt. Rev. Ivan Tkaczuk
Members of Consistory: Rt. Rev. Michael Pawlyskyn, Dr. George Hordy, Charles Prychodka, Mike Fedorak and Peter Levkovich

PERIODICAL

Ukrainian Orthodox Herald (q), Fr. Ivan Tkaczuk, Ed.

Unitarian Universalist Association

The Unitarian Universalist Association is the consolidated body of the former American Unitarian Association and the Universalist Church of America. The Unitarian movement arose in Congregationalism in the 18th century, producing the American Unitarian Association in 1825. In 1865 a national conference was organized. The philosophy of Universalism originated with the doctrine of universal salvation in the first century, and was brought to America in the 18th century. Universalists were first formally organized in 1793. In May, 1961, the Unitarian and Universalist bodies were consolidated to become the Unitarian Universalist Association. The movement is noncreedal. The UVA has observor status with the National Council of Churches.

Churches: 956; Inclusive Membership: 173,167; Sunday or Sabbath Schools: N.R.; Total Enrollment: 38,899; Ordained Clergy: 1,069

GENERAL ORGANIZATION

General Assembly: annual
Headquarters: 25 Beacon St., Boston, MA 02108. Tel. (617) 742-2100. District offices, 23 in number

OFFICERS

Pres., Rev. William Schulz
Exec. Vice-Pres., Ms. Kathleen C. Montgomery
Mod., Ms. Natalie Gulbransen
Sec., Mr. Barry Johnson-Fay
Treas., Dr. Robert Sallies
Financial Advisor, Robert T. Lavender

OTHER ORGANIZATIONS

(Address unless otherwise noted, 25 Beacon St., Boston, MA 02108)
Unitarian Universalist Ministers' Association: Pres., Rev. Jack Mendelsohn
Unitarian Universalist Women's Federation: Pres., Ms. Phyllis Rickter
Young Religious Unitarian Universalists (YRUU): Contact, Rev. Ellen Brandenburg
Unitarian Universalist Service Committee, Inc.: 78 Beacon St., Boston, MA 02108. Exec. Dir., Richard Scobie
Unitarian Universalist Historical Society, Pres., Rev. Janet Bowering
Church of the Larger Fellowship: Rev. O. Eugene Pickett

PERIODICAL

The World (6/yr), Ms. Linda C. Beyer, Man. Ed., 25 Beacon St., Boston, MA 02108

United Brethren in Christ

The Church of the United Brethren in Christ had its beginning with Philip William Otterbein and Martin Boehm, who were leaders in the revivalistic movement in Pennsylvania and Maryland during the late 1760s and which continued into the early 1800s.

On September 25, 1800, they and others associated with them, formed a society under the name of United Brethren in Christ. Subsequent conferences adopted a Confession of Faith in 1815 and a constitution in 1841. The Church of the United Brethren in Christ adheres to the original constitution as amended in 1957, 1961 and 1977.

GENERAL ORGANIZATION

General Conference, quadrennial (next meeting, 1989)
Headquarters: 302 Lake St., Huntington, IN 46750. Tel. (219) 356-2312

OFFICERS

Bishops: Chpsn., C. Ray Miller, Wilber L. Sites, Jr., Clarence A. Kopp, Jr., Jerry Datema
Adm. Asst.-Gen. Treas., Marda J. Hoffman
Dir., Dept. of Education, Dr. Eugene Habecker
Dir., Dept. of Church Services, Rev. Paul Hirschy

PERIODICAL

The United Brethren (m), Huntington, IN 46750, Steve Dennie, Ed.

United Christian Church

The United Christian Church originated during the period of the Civil War or shortly thereafter, about 1864 or 1865. There were some ministers and laymen in the United Brethren in Christ Church who were in disagreement with the position and practice of the church on issues such as infant baptism, voluntary bearing of arms and belonging to oath bound secret combinations. It was this group which formed a nucleus developing into United Christian

Church, organized at a conference held in Campbelltown, Pa., on May 9, 1877, and given its name by a conference held January 1, 1878.

The principal founders of the denomination were George Hoffman, John Stamn, and Thomas Lesher. Hoffman appears to have been predominant because before they were organized, they were called Hoffmanites.

The United Christian Church has district conferences, a general conference held yearly, a general board of trustees, a mission board, a board of directors of the United Christian Church Home, a campmeeting board, a young peoples board, and has local organized congregations.

It believes in the Holy Trinity, the inspired Holy Scriptures with the doctrines they teach, and practices the ordinances of Baptism, Holy Communion, and Foot Washing.

It welcomes all into its fold who are born again, believe in Jesus Christ our Savior and Lord, and who have received the Holy Spirit and, therefore, are a part of the Church of Jesus Christ, or His Body.

Churches: 12; Inclusive Membership: 420; Sunday or Sabbath Schools: 12; Total Enrollment: 684; Ordained Clergy: 11

GENERAL ORGANIZATION

General Conference: annual (3rd Saturday in March)

OFFICERS

Mod., Elder John Ludwig, Jr., 528 W. Walnut St., Cleona, PA 17042
Presiding Elder, Elder Henry C. Heagy, 2080 White Oak St., Lebanon, PA 17042
Conf. Sec., Elder David W. Heagy, Rt. 4, Box 100, Lebanon, PA 17042

OTHER ORGANIZATIONS

Mission Board: Pres., Elder John P. Ludwig, Jr., 528 W. Walnut St., Cleona, PA 17042; Sec., Elder Walter Knight, Jr., Rt. #1, Box 98, Palmyra, PA 17078; Treas., Elder Henry C. Heagy, Rt. 4, Box 100, Lebanon, PA 17042

United Church of Christ

The United Church of Christ was duly constituted on June 25, 1957 by the regularly chosen representatives of the Congregational Christian Churches and of the Evangelical and Reformed Church, in a Uniting General Synod held in Cleveland, Ohio.

The Preamble to the Constitution states the denomination's theological base in the following words: "The United Church of Christ acknowledges as its sole head, Jesus Christ, the Son of God and Saviour. It acknowledges as kindred in Christ all who share in this confession. It looks to the Word of God in the Scriptures, and to the presence and power of the Holy Spirit, to prosper its creative and redemptive work in the world. It claims as its own the faith of the historic Church expressed in the ancient creeds and reclaimed in the basic insights of the Protestant Reformers. It affirms the responsibility of the Church in each generation to make this faith its own in reality of worship, in honesty of thought and expression, and in purity of heart before God. In accordance with the teaching of our Lord and the practice prevailing among evangelical Christians, it recognizes two sacraments: Baptism and the Lord's Supper or Holy Communion."

The creation of the United Church of Christ brought together four unique traditions from the rich and diverse history of Christian experience:

(1) The *Congregational* Way first achieved prominence among English Protestants during the civil war of the 1640s, groundwork for the Congregational form having been laid by Calvinist Puritans and Separatists during the half-century preceding. Opposition to state control of their religious worship promoted followers of the Congregational form to emigrate to America, where an active part in colonizing New England occupied their energies throughout the 17th century. Since then, Congregationalists (self-consciously a denomination from the middle of the 19th century) have made strong contributions to the religious, civil, educational and secular dimensions of American institutions and culture.

(2) The *Christian* Churches originated as a restorationist movement in several parts of the U.S. late in the 18th century. Throughout their history the Christians emphasized Christ as the only head of the church, the New Testament as their only rule of faith, and "Christian" as their sole name. Unitive in spirit, this loosely organized denomination eventually found in the Congregational Churches a like disposition, and in 1931, the two bodies formally united as the *Congregational Christian Churches.*

(3) *The German Reformed Church* comprised an irenic aspect of the Protestant Reformation, as a second generation of Reformers drew on the insights of Zwingli, Luther and Calvin to formulate the Heidelberg Catechism of 1563. This confession of faith proved to be a unifying force, first in the German Palatinate, and then in other German lands. People of the German Reformed Church began immigrating to the New World early in the 18th century, and settlement in the middle Atlantic colonies saw the heaviest concentration locating in Pennsylvania. Independence from European supervision and the formal organization of the American denomination were completed in 1793. Succeeding years saw the church spreading across the country, and in the Mercersburg Movement, developing a strong emphasis on evangelical catholicity and Christian unity.

(4) By the opening of the 19th century in Germany, Enlightenment criticism and Pietist inwardness had worked a marked decrease in long-standing conflicts between religious groups. The change was signalized in Prussia by a royal proclamation which merged Lutheran and Reformed people of the realm into one United Evangelical Church (1817). Members of this new church way migrated to America just as earlier German migrants were moving west. The Evangelicals settled in large numbers in Missouri and Illinois, there continuing their noncontroversial emphasis on pietistic devotion and unionism; in 1840 they formed the German Evangelical Church Society in the West. Union with other Evangelical church associations further expanded the movement's membership until in 1877 it took the name of the German Evangelical Synod of North America.

On June 25, 1934, this Synod and the Reformed Church in the U.S. (formerly the German Reformed Church) united to form the Evangelical and Reformed Church. In both groups the German ethnic traits had lost their influence as the Evangelical and Reformed Church entered the mainstream of American church life. In the formation of the Evangelical and Reformed Church there is a singular blend of the Reformed tradition's passion for the unity of the church and the Evangelical tradition's commitment to the liberty of conscience inherent in the gospel. These accents were critically important for the utilization of the spirit and ethos of the ecumenical movement of that time.

Churches: 6,406; Inclusive Membership: 1,676,105; Sunday or Sabbath Schools: 6,406; Total Enrollment: 441,547; Ordained Clergy: 10,071

GENERAL ORGANIZATION

Synod: biennial

Headquarters: 105 Madison Ave., New York, NY 10016. Tel. (212) 683-5656

OFFICERS

Pres., Rev. Avery D. Post
Sec., Rev. Carol Joyce Brun
Dir. of Finance & Treas., Charles H. Lockyear
Exec. Assoc. to the Pres., Rev. David Smock
Asst. to Pres. for Planning & Correlation, Rev. Charles W. Cooper, Jr.
Affirmative Action Officer, Mr. Jesse N. Alexander, Jr.
Coord., Coordinating Center for Women, Ms. Marilyn M. Breitling
Chpsn. Exec. Council, Mr. William R. Kiesel
V-Chpsn., Ms. Ruth W. Evans
Mod., Rev. Robert Sherard
Asst. Mod., Ms. Alida Millham
Asst. Mod., Mr. David Gerth

ORGANIZATIONS

UNITED CHURCH BOARD FOR WORLD MINISTRIES: Offices, 475 Riverside Dr., New York, NY 10115. Tel. (212) 870-2637; 14 Beacon St., Boston, MA 02108; 1400 N. 7th St., Ste. E, St., Louis, MO 63106; Exec. Vice Pres., Rev. Scott S. Libbey

Planning, Correlation, and Administration Unit: Gen. Sec., Rev. Scott S. Libbey; Assoc. for Planning and Admn., Rev. Bertrice Y. Wood; Personnel Mgr., Ms. Rita E. Maslanek

Mission Program Unit: Gen.Sec., Rev. Daniel F. Romero; Assoc. Gen. Sec., Rev. Lloyd Van Vactor; Regional Sec., Africa, Ms. Andrea I. Young; Europe, Rev. Kenneth R. Ziebell; East Asia, Dr. Ching-fen Hsiao; Latin Amer./Carrib., Dr. Patricia Rumer; Middle East, Dr. Dale L. Bishop; Southern Asia Rev. Eric A. Gass; Southern Asia and Mission Assoc., Ms. Constance C. Thurber; Program Sec., Rev. Gustav H. Kuether; Overseas Pers. Sec., Rev. Elinor G. Galusha; Sec. for World Hunger Action, Rev. E. Neill Richards; Sec. for World Issues, Rev. Audrey C. Smock; Assoc. for World Issues, Rev. Kenneth R. Ziebell; Sec. for Mission Edu. and Interpretation, Ms. Sandra J. Rooney.

Support Services Unit: Treas. and Gen. Sec., Rev. Myles H. Walburn; Assoc. Treas., Mr. John F. Fairfield; Asst., Treas., Mr. Bruce C. Foresman; Mngr. of Financial Services, Ms. Dorothy E. Teffeau; Mngr. Compr. Services, Mr. Anderl Jordan; Mngr. Bus. Services, Ms. Arlene Yellen.

UNITED CHURCH BOARD FOR HOMELAND MINISTRIES: 132 W. 31 St., New York, NY 10001; Tel. (212) 239-8700.

Office of Exec. Vice-Pres., Exec. Vice-Pres., Rev. Charles Shelby Rooks; Sec. for Planning and Management, Rev. Robert P. Noble, Jr.; Sec. for Admn., Mr. Nils E. Forstner; Sec. for Res. and Eval., Ms. Marjorie H. Royle; Sec. for Information Services, Ms. Sheila Kelly; Sec. for Mission Education, _____; Clk. of the Bd. of Dirs., Ms. Amy Yoshinaga; Business Mgr., Ms. Mitzie Wang

Office of the Treasurer, Treas., Mr. Richard H. Dubie; Asst. Treas., Mr. Raymond J. Healy; Asst. Treas., Ms. Norma Robinson

Division of Education and Publication, Gen. Sec., Rev. Ansley Coe Throckmorton; Sec. for Adult Ed. and Ministries Resources, Rev. Percel O. Alston; Sec. for Higher Ed. and Higher Prog. Resources, Rev. Verlyn L. Baker; Sec. for Youth Ed. and Ministries Resources, Rev. Mark L. Burns; Sec. for Childhood Ed. and Ministries Resources, Ms. Patricia J. Goldberg; Sec. for Publication, Rev. Larry E. Klap; Sec. for Higher Ed. Relationships, Rev. Joseph T. McMillan, Jr.; Sec. for Educational Leadership Training, Ms. Lois I. Peeler; Sec. for Young Adult Ed. and Ministries Resources,

Rev. Gordon J. Svoboda; Sec. for Racial and Ethnic Educational Ministries, Rev. Barbara J. Essex; Consultant, Rev. Richard K. Chamberlain; Ed. for Curriculum Services, Rev. Jack H. Haney; Sr. Ed., Ms. Marion M. Meyer; Business Mgr., Publications Operations, Mr. Bill L. Shaw; Coord. of Church-College Relationships, Rev. James A. Smith, Jr.

Division of Evangelism and Local Church Development, Gen. Sec., Rev. Robert L. Burt; Sec. for Evangelism & Membership Growth, Rev. James W. Bidle; Sec. for Local Church Capital Development, Rev. Robert F. Haskins, Jr.; Sec. for Evangelism and Membership Growth, Rev. R. Alan Johnson; Sec. for Church Bldg., Mr. John R. Potts; Sec. for Ethnic and Minority Church Development, Rev. Henry T. Simmons; Sec. for Development, Rev. Stephen L. Sterner; Secs. for Local Church Finance Advisory Services, Ms. Beatrice H. Starrett, Rev. P. William VanderWyden; Consultant, Rev. Gary L. Miller; Telecommunication Associates, Ms. Karin Stock-Whitson, Mr. Charles Whitson.

Division of American Missionary Association, Gen. Sec., Rev. Theodore H. Erickson; Sec., Special Program and Services, Mr. Carl A. Bade; Sec., Local Churches and Community Mission, Rev. Robert T. Strommen; Sec., Human Devel. Programs and Concerns, Ms. Faith A. Johnson; Sec., Health and Welfare Program and Concerns, Mr. James A. McDaniel; Sec., Public Issues in Education, Ms. Nanette M. Roberts; Sec., Ministries to Special Groups, Rev. Alphonso A. Roman; Sec., Social and Economic Justice Programs, _____, Sec., Citizen Empowerment, Rev. Herbert D. White; Consultants, Rev. Virginia Kreyer, Mary Ellen Haines, Mr. William Stackhouse

COMMISSION FOR RACIAL JUSTICE: 105 Madison Ave., New York, NY 10016; 1106 No. Capitol St., NW, Washington, DC 20001; 4904 Professional Court, Rm. 204, Raleigh, NC 27609. Exec. Dir. (NY), Rev. Benjamin F. Chavis, Jr.; Office Mgr. (NY), Ms. Andrea Gibbs; Program Asst. (NC), Ms. Armenta Eaton; Community Organizer (NC), Ms. Margaret Ellis; Dir. Community Organization Program (NY), Ms. Lawrence Hamm; Consultant, Special Project on the Black Male (NY), Mr. Aminifu Harvey; Coord., CRJ Investigator (NY), Mr. William Jones; Dir., Washington DC Office, Ms. Toni Killings; Dir., Program Asst. (DC), Ms. Della Owens; Dir., Information and Resource Development (NY), Ms. Judy Richardson; Dir., Southern Regional Office, Rev. Leon White; Dir., Research, Mr. Charles Lee; Coord. Youth & Students, Ms. Lisa Williamson

COUNCIL FOR AMERICAN INDIAN MINISTRY: 122 W. Franklin Ave., Rm. 300, Minneapolis, MN 55405. Exec. Dir., Rev. Norman W. Jackson; Exec. Asst., Ms. Jackie Owen

COUNCIL FOR HEALTH AND HUMAN SERVICE MINISTRIES: 543 College Ave., Lancaster, PA 17603. Tel. (717)299-9945 (outside Penna., (800)844-4476). Exec. & Program Office: Exec. Dir., Rev. J. Robert Achtermann; Prog. Assoc., Ms. Susan M. Sanders; Prog. Consultant, Rev. Robert M. Glasgow; Computer Services, Ms. Leslie J. Solove; Controller, Ms. Christine Gable

OFFICE FOR CHURCH IN SOCIETY: 105 Madison Ave., New York, NY 10016; 110 Maryland Ave., N.E., Washington, DC 20002; Exec. Dir., Rev. Yvonne V. Delk, (NY); Assoc. for Church Empowerment, Rev. Charles McCollough (NY); Rev. Dale Edmunds (NY); Mr. Faith Evans (DC); Assoc. for Publications, Rev. Russell G. Claussen (NY); Dir., Washington, DC Office, Rev. James E. Lintner; Assoc. Policy Advocacy, Ms. Gretchen Cassell Eick (DC); Rev. Patrick Conover (DC), Exec. Dir., Ms.Verna Rapp Uthman (NY); Admin. Asst., Ms. Nancy Hughes (DC), Ms. Dorothy Marcus (NY)

OFFICE FOR CHURCH LIFE AND LEADERSHIP: 105 Madison Ave., New York, NY 10016; 20 Woodside

Ave., San Francisco, CA 94127; 122 W. Franklin Ave., Rm. 323, Minneapolis, MN 55404; 1400 N. Seventh St., St. Louis, MO 63106; P. O. Box 5323, Portsmouth, NH 03801; 41 Croswell Rd., Columbus, OH 43214; 666 Plainsboro Rd., Plainsboro NJ 08536; P.O. Box 29883, Atlanta, GA 30359; Exec. Dir., Rev. Reuben A. Sheares, II (NY); Exec. Assoc., Rev. Thomas R. Tupper (MO); Associates, Rev. William A. Hulteen, Jr. (OH); Rev. Kenneth K. Iha (CA); Rev. Roger D. Knight (MN); Rev. Joyce B. Myers (GA); Ms. Dorothy L. Robinson (NH); Ms. Karen Roller (NJ); Rev. Robert H. Naylor (NY)

OFFICE OF COMMUNICATION: 105 Madison Ave., New York, NY 10016. Dir., Dr. Beverly J. Chain; Deputy Dir., Rev. Eugene A. Schneider; Assoc. Dir., Mr. William C. Winslow; Public Relations Coordinator, Ms. Martha R. Gotwals; Public Relations Writer, Mr. Hans Hohznagel; Public Relations Writer, Ms. Yvette Moore, Kathi Wolfe; Ed. United Church News, Rev. W. Evan Golder; Accounts/Office Mgr., Ms. Sharon Joseph; Accounts/Office Mgr., Ms. Doris Smith; Washington DC Rep., Patricia Aufderheide. Tel. (202)262-5374

STEWARDSHIP COUNCIL: 105 Madison Ave., New York, NY 10016. (Following addresses are in New York unless otherwise stated.) Exec. Dir., Rev. George W. Otto; Adm. Assoc., Ms. Ethel M. Benish; Coordinator of Financial Planning and Development, Rev. Milton E. Gockley, Jr.; Program Assoc. Resource Information, Ms. Veronica Jefferson; Assoc. for Mission Education, Mr. Alfred H. Jones; Program Assoc., Rev. C. David Langerhans; Assoc. for Audiovisuals, Rev. Earl D. Miller; Managing Ed., Ms. Christine A. Powell; Ed., Ms. Christina Villa; Exec. Assoc., Rev. Dean O. Warburton; Assoc. for Stewardship Prog. and Adm. of UCR, Rev. Jack A. Batten, 1400 N. 7th St., St. Louis, MO 63106. **Conference-Based Staff: Illinois,** Rev. Jeffrey N. Stinehelfer, P. O. Box 7208, Westchester, IL 60153; **Connecticut,** Rev. Patricia A. Sommers, 125 Sherman St., Hartford, CT 06105; Financial Development Consultant, Rev. Paul E. Baumer, 59 E. Mount St., Columbus, OH 43215.

COMMISSION ON DEVELOPMENT: 132 W. 31st St., New York, NY 10001, Rev. Donald G. Stoner, Dir. Planned Giving, Ms. Stella Schoen, Assoc.

HISTORICAL COUNCIL: 105 Madison Ave., New York, NY 10016. Office of Archivist, Philip Schaff Library, Lancaster Theological Seminry, 555 W. James St., Lancaster, PA 17603

PENSION BOARDS: 132 W. 31st S., New York, NY 10001. Exec. Vice-Pres., Dr. John Ordway; Admn. Vice-Pres., Mrs. Joan F. Brannick; Treas., Mr. Richard H. Dubie; Sec. Treas., Sec. and Sec. Member Relations, Mr. Edmund G. Tortora; Sec., Benefits, Mr. Frank Patti; Sec., Policies and Procedures, Ms. Marie Lucia; Sec., Miniterial Asst., Rev. Donald E. Stumpf.

UNITED CHURCH FOUNDATION, Inc.: 132 W. 31st St., New York, NY 10001. Financial Vice Pres. and Treas., Richard H. Dubie.

CONFERENCES

Western Region:

California, Northern, Rev. David J. Jamieson, 20 Woodside Ave.,San Francisco, CA 94127

California, Southern, Rev. Fred P. Register, 466 E. Walnut St., Pasadena, CA 91101

Hawaii, Rev. Teruo Kawata, 2103 Nuuanu Ave., Honolulu, HI 96817

Montana/Northern Wyoming, Rev. John M. Schaeffer, 1511 Poly Dr., Billings, MT 59102

Central Pacific, Rev. Donald J. Sevetson, 0245 SW Bancroft St., Portland, OR 97201

Rocky Mountain, Rev. Clyde H. Miller, Jr., 1370 Pennsylvania St., Ste. 420, Denver, CO 80203

Southwest, Rev. Carole G. Keim, 4423 N. 24th St., Ste. 600, Phoenix, AZ 85016

Washington-North Idaho, Rev. W. James Halfaker, 720 14th Ave. E., Seattle, WA 98102

West Central Region:

Iowa, Donald A. Gall, 600 42nd St., Des Moines, IA 50312

Kansas-Oklahoma, Rev. A. Gayle Engle, 1245 Fabrique, Wichita, KS 67218

Minnesota, Rev. Murdale Leysath, 122 W. Franklin Ave., Rm. 323, Minneapolis, MN 55404

Missouri, Rev. Rueben P. Koehler, 461 E. Lockwood, Ave., St. Louis, MO 63119

Nebraska, Rev. Clarence M. Higgins, Jr.,, 2055 "E" St., Lincoln, NE 68510

North Dakota, Rev. Marwood E. Rettig, 4007 State St., Ste., Bismarck, ND 58501

South Dakota, Rev. Don Yungclas, Ste. B, 801 E. 41st St., Sioux Falls, SD 57105

Great Lakes Region:

Illinois, Rev. W. Sterling Cary, 1840 Westchester Blvd., P.O. Box 7208, Westchester, IL 60153

Illinois South, Rev. Martha Ann Baumer, Box 325 Broadway, Highland, IL 62249

Indiana-Kentucky, Rev. Ralph C. Quellhorst, 1100 W. 42nd St., Indianapolis, IN 46208

Michigan, Rev. John M. Rogers, P.O. Box 1006, East Lansing, MI 48823

Ohio, Rev. Thomas E. Dipko, 41 Croswell Rd., Columbus, OH 43214

Wisconsin, Rev. Frederick R. Trost, 2719 Marshall Ct. Madison, WI 53705

Southern Region:

Florida, Rev. Charles L. Burns Jr., 222 E. Welbourne Ave., Winter Park, FL 32789

South Central, Rev. James Tomasek, Jr., 2704 Rio Grande #8, Austin TX 78705

Southeast, Rev. Emmett O. Floyd, P.O. Box 29883, Atlanta, GA 30359

Southern, Rev. Rollin O. Russell, 2121 Edgewood Ave., P.O. Box 2410, Burlington, NC 27215

Middle Atlantic Region:

Central Atlantic, Rev. Curtis R. Clare, 620 Pershing Dr., Silver Spring, MD 20910

New York, Rev. James R. Smucker, The Church Center, Rm. 260, 3049 E. Genesee St., Syracuse, NY 13224

Penn Central, Rev. Lyle J. Weible, The United Church Center, Rm. 126, 900 South Arlington Ave., Harrisburg, PA 17109

Penn Northeast, Rev. Donald E. Overlock, 431 Delaware Ave., P.O. Box 177, Palmerton, PA 18071

Pennsylvania Southeast, Rev. Peter Doghramji, 620 Main St., Box G, Collegeville, PA 19426

Penn West, Rev. Paul L. Westcoat, Jr., 320 South Maple Ave., Greensburg, PA 15601

Puerto Rico, Rev. Jaime Rivers, Calle Allianza #617, Parada 22½, Santurce, PR 00908

New England Region:

Connecticut, Rev. Carroll E. Kann, 125 Sherman St., Hartford, CT 06105

Maine, Rev. Otto E. Sommer, 68 Main St., P.O. Box 730, Yarmouth, ME 04096

Massachusetts, Rev. Alfred E. Williams, Jr., P.O. Box 2246, Salem and Badger Rds., Farmingham, MA 01701

New Hampshire, Rev. Robert D. Fiske, Rev. Carole C. Carlson, Rev. Robert D. Witham, 85 N State St., P.O. Box 465, Concord, NH 03301

Rhode Island, Rev. H. Dahler Hayes, Interchurch Center, 734 Hope St., Providence, RI 02906

Vermont, Rev. D. Curtis Minter, 285 Maple St., Burlington, VT 05401

Nongeographic:

Calvin Synod, Rev. Zoltan Kiraly, 220 Fourth St., Passaic, NJ 07055

United Holy Church of America, Inc.

The United Holy Church of America, Inc. is an outgrowth of the great revival that began with the early outpouring of the Holy Ghost on the Day of Pentecost when 120 were filled. The church is built upon the foundation of the Apostles and Prophets, Jesus Christ himself being the chief cornerstone.

It was during this time of revival of repentence, regeneration and holiness of heart and life that swept through the South and West, that the United Holy Church was born. There was no desire on the part of the founding fathers to establish another denomination, but they were pushed out of organized churches because of this experience of holiness and testimony of the Spirit-filled life.

On the first Sunday in May 1886, in Method, NC, a meeting was held that gave birth to what is today known as the United Holy Church of America, Inc. The church was incorporated on September 25, 1918 and its work has steadily grown since that time into a great organization.

Ordinances of baptism by immersion, the Lord's Supper, and feet washing are observed. We accept the premillennial teaching of the Second Coming of Christ, Divine healing—not to the exclusion of medicine, justification by faith, sanctification as a second work of grace, and Spirit baptism.

GENERAL ORGANIZATION

Convocation: All Convocations and General Meetings held at Headquarters.

Headquarters: Route 5, Box 861, Greensboro NC

Mailing Address: 825 Fairoak Ave., Chillum, MD 20783

General Convocation, annually in May

Centennial Convocation: May 4-11, 1986

Annual Worker's Conference: August, Greensboro, NC

OFFICERS

Gen. Pres., Bishop Joseph T. Bowens, 825 Fairoak Ave., Chillum, MD 20783

1st Vice-Pres., Bishop Thomas E. Talley, P. O. Box 1035, Portsmouth, VA 23705

2nd Vice-Pres., Bishop Odell McCollum, 3206 Blue Ridge Rd., Columbus, OH 43219

Gen. Rec. Sec., Rev. A. Thomas Godfrey, P.O. Box 7940, Chicago IL 60680

Gen. Fin. Sec., Mrs. Clarice L. Chambers, P.O. Box 3327, Harrisburg, PA 17104

Gen. Asst. Fin. Sec., Mrs. Vera Perkin, 1054 E. 145th St., Cleveland, OH 44110

Gen. Asst. Rec. Sec., Mrs. Beatrice S. Faison, 224 Wenz Rd., Toledo, OH 43615

Gen. Corresponding Sec., Mrs. Carolyn Gamble, 3018 9th St., S.E., Washington, DC 20032

Gen. Treas., Mrs. Bertha Williams, 4749 Shaw Dr., Wilmington, NC 28401

Pres., Missionary Dept., Rev. Mrs. Iris C. Fischer, 28 Cooper St., Brooklyn, NY 11207

Gen. Supt., Bible Church School, Mr. C. M. Corbett, 623 Belmont Ave., Youngstown, OH 44520

Pres., Y.P.H.A. Dept., Rev. William C. Turner, Jr., 41 Sedgewood Ct., Durham, NC 27713

Gen. Education Dept., Dr. Chester Gregory, 1302 Lincoln Woods Dr., Baltimore, MD 21216

Gen. Ushers Dept., Mr. Huston Williams, 6123 Irving St., Philadelphia, PA 19139

PERIODICAL

The Holiness Union (m), Record Printing, Silver Spring MD

The United Methodist Church

The United Methodist Church was formed April 23, 1968 in Dallas, Texas, by the union of The Methodist Church and The Evangelical United Brethren Church. The two churches shared a common historical and spiritual heritage. The Methodist Church resulted in 1939 from the unification of three branches of Methodism—the Methodist Episcopal Church; the Methodist Episcopal Church, South; and the Methodist Protestant Church. The Methodist movement began in 18th-century England under the preaching of John Wesley, but the so-called Christmas Conference of 1784 in Baltimore is regarded as the date on which the organized Methodist Church was founded as an ecclesiastical organization. It was there that Francis Asbury was elected the first bishop in this country. The Evangelical United Brethren Church was formed in 1946 with the merger of the Evangelical Church and the Church of the United Brethren in Christ, both of which had their beginnings in Pennsylvania in the evangelistic movement of the 18th and early 19th centuries. Philip William Otterbein and Jacob Albright were early leaders of this movement among the German-speaking settlers of the Middle Colonies.

GENERAL ORGANIZATION

General Conference: quadrennial (next meeting will be held in Spring, 1992, Louisville, KY

OFFICERS

Sec. of Gen. Conference, Faith Richardson, 168 Mt. Vernon St., Newtonville, MA 02160

Council of Bishops: Pres., Bishop Ernest T. Dixon, Jr., PO. Box 28509, San Antonio TX 98228. Tel. (512) 432-0401; Bishop Melvin G. Talbert, 2112 Third Ave., Seattle, WA 98121. Tel. (206) 624-7674

ANNUAL CONFERENCES, BISHOPS AND CONFERENCE COUNCIL DIRECTORS (BY JURISDICTION)

North Central Jurisdiction

Central Illinois—Bishop Woodie W. White, Tel. (217) 544-4604; Donald Jones, PO Box 2050, Bloomington, IL 61701. Tel: (309) 828-5092.

Detroit—Bishop Judith Craig, Tel. (313) 961-8340; Alfred Bamsey, 155 W. Congress, Suite 200, Detroit, MI 48226. Tel: (313) 961-8340.

East Ohio—Bishop James S. Thomas, Tel. (216) 499-8471; John I. E. Buchanan, 8800 Cleveland Ave. NW, North Canton, OH 44720. Tel: (216) 499-3972.

Iowa—Bishop Reuben P. Job, Tel. (515) 283-1991; Bruce Ough, 1019 Chestnut St., Des Moines, IA 50309. Tel: (515) 283-1991.

Minnesota—Bishop Emerson S. Colaw, Tel. (612) 870-3648; Jean Dowell, 122 W. Franklin Ave., Room 400, Minneapolis, MN 55404. Tel: (612) 870-3647.

North Dakota—Bishop Edwin C. Boulton, Tel. (701) 232-2241; Gunnar Gundersen, 2410 12th St. N., Fargo, ND 58102. Tel: (701) 232-2241

North Indiana—Bishop Leroy C. Hodapp, Tel. (317) 924-1321; John L. Hopkins, PO Box 869, Marion, IN 46952. Tel: (317) 662-9444

Northern Illinois—Bishop Jesse R. DeWitt, Tel. (312) 782-1422; Carolyn H. Oehler, 77 W. Washington St., Suite 1806, Chicago, IL 60602. Tel: (312) 346-8752.

South Dakota—Bishop Edwin C. Boulton, Tel. (701)

232-2241; Robert Roth, P.O. Box 460, Mitchell, SD 57301. Tel: (605) 996-6552

South Indiana—Bishop Leroy C. Hodapp, Tel. (317) 924-1321; James Gentry, Box 5008, Bloomington, IN 47402. Tel: (812) 336-0186.

Southern Illinois—Bishop Woodie W. White, Tel. (217) 544-4604; William Frazier, 1919 Broadway, Mt. Vernon, IL 62864 Tel: (618) 242-4070.

West Michigan—Bishop Judith Craig, Tel. (313) 961-8340; John L. Francis, PO Box 6247, Grand Rapids, MI 49506. Tel: (616) 459-4503.

West Ohio—Bishop Edsel A. Ammons, Tel. (614) 228-6784; Ralph K. Shunk, 471 E. Broad St., Suite 1106, Columbus, OH 43215. Tel: (614) 228-6784.

Wisconsin—Bishop David J. Lawson, Tel. (608) 837-8526; Frank Gaylord, , PO Box 220, Sun Prairie, WI 53590. Tel: (608) 837-7328.

Northeastern Jurisdiction

Baltimore—Bishop Joseph H. Yeakel, Tel. (301) 587-9226; Susan M. Morrison, 5124 Greenwich Ave., Baltimore, MD 21229. Tel: (301) 233-7300.

Central Pennsylvania—Bishop Felton E. May, Tel. (717) 652-6705; Jay House, 900 S. Arlington Ave., Room 112, Harrisburg, PA 17109. Tel: (717) 652-0460.

Eastern Pennsylvania—Bishop F. Herbert Skeete, Tel. (215) 666-9090; Robert Daughtery, PO Box 820, Valley Forge, PA 19482. Tel: (215) 666-9090.

Maine—Bishop George W. Bashore, Tel. (617) 536-7764; Beverly Abbott, P.O. Box 277, Winthrop, ME 04364. Tel: (207) 377-2912.

New Hampshire—Bishop George W. Bashore, Tel. (617) 536-7764; Dwight Haynes, RFD # 3, Box 36, Concord, NH 03301. Tel: (603) 225-6312.

New York—Bishop C. Dale White, Tel. (914) 997-1570; Wilson Boots, 252 Bryant Ave., White Plains, NY 10605. Tel: (914) 997-1570.

North Central New York—Bishop Forrest C. Stith, Tel. (315) 446-6731; James Pollard, 317 E. Jefferson St., Syracuse, NY 13202, Tel. (315) 479-5147

Northern New Jersey—Bishop Neil L. Irons, Tel. (609) 737-3940; Barrie T. Smith, P. O. Box 546, Madison, NJ 07940. Tel: (201) 377-3800.

Peninsula—Bishop Joseph H. Yeakel, Tel. (301) 587-9226; J. Gordon Stapleton, 139 N. State St., Dover, DE 19901. Tel: (302) 674-2626.

Puerto Rico—Bishop F. Herbert Skeete, Tel. (215) 666-9090; Eduardo Martinez, P.O. Box AP, UPR Station, San Juan, PR 00931. Tel. (809) 765-3195

Southern New England—Bishop George W. Bashore, Tel. (617) 536-7764; Richard E. Wiborg, 566 Commonwealth Ave., Boston, MA 02115. Tel: (617) 266-3900

Southern New Jersey—Bishop Neil L. Irons, Tel. (609) 737-3940; John Janka, 1995 E. Marlton Pike, Cherry Hill, NJ 08003. Tel: (609) 424-1701

Troy—Bishop C. Dale White, Tel. (914) 997-1570; William A. Lasher, P. O. Box 560, Saratoga Springs, NY 12866. Tel: (518) 584-8214

West Virginia—Bishop William B. Grove, Tel. (304) 344-8330; E. Wendell Eskew, PO Box 2313, Charleston, WV 25328. Tel: (304) 344-8330

Western New York—Bishop Forrest C. Stith, Tel. (315) 446-6731; J. Fay Cleveland, 8499 Main St., Buffalo, NY 14221. Tel: (716) 633-8558

Western Pennsylvania—Bishop James M. Ault, Tel. (412) 776-2300; Paul E. Schrading, 1204 Freedom Rd., Mars, PA 16046. Tel. (412) 362-7162

Wyoming—Bishop Felton E. May, Tel. (717) 652-6705; Kenneth E. Wood, 3 Orchard Rd., Binghamton, NY 13905. Tel: (607) 772-8840

South Central Jurisdiction

Central Texas—Bishop John W. Russell, Tel. (214) 522-6741; Luther Henry, One Summit Ave., Suite 505, Ft. Worth, TX 76102. Tel: (817) 877-5222

Kansas East—Bishop Kenneth W. Hicks, Tel. (913)

272-0587; H. Sharon Howell, PO Box 4187, Topeka, KS 66604. Tel: (913) 272-9111

Kansas West—Bishop Kenneth W. Hicks, Tel. (913) 272-0587; Charles E. Winkler, 151 No. Volutsia, Wichita, KS 67214. Tel: (316) 684-0266

Little Rock—Bishop Richard B. Wilke, Tel. (501) 374-6679; Jay Lofton, 715 Center St., Suite 202, Little Rock, AR 72201. Tel: (501) 374-5027

Louisiana—Bishop Benjamin R. Oliphint, Tel. (504) 346-1646; Harvey G. Williamson, 527 North Blvd., Baton Rouge, LA 70802. Tel: (504) 346-1646.

Missouri East—Bishop W. T. Handy, Jr., Tel. (314) 367-5001; Paul Schlapbach, 4625 Lindell Blvd., Suite 424, St. Louis, MO 63108. Tel: (314) 367-7422

Missouri West—Bishop W. T. Handy, Jr., Tel. (314) 367-5001; Elroy H. Hines, 1512 Van Brunt Blvd., Kansas City, MO 64127. Tel. (816) 737-5027

Nebraska—Bishop J. Woodrow Hearn, Tel. (402) 464-5994; Robert Folkers, PO Box 4553, Lincoln, NE 68504. Tel: (402) 464-5994

New Mexico—Bishop Louis W. Schowengerdt, Tel. (505) 883-5418; Mark Dorff, 8100 Mountain Rd., N.E., Albuquerque, NM 87110. Tel. (505) 255-8786

North Arkansas—Bishop Richard B. Wilke, Tel. (501) 374-6679; Jim Meadors, 723 Center St., Little Rock, AR 72201. Tel. (501) 374-1634

North Texas—Donald E. Barnes, P.O. Box 516069, Dallas, TX 75251. Tel. (214) 490-3438

Northwest Texas—Bishop Louis W. Schowengerdt, Tel. (505) 883-5418; Rex L. Mauldin, 1415 Ave. M, Lubbock, TX 79401. Tel: (806) 762-0201

Oklahoma—Bishop John W. Hardt, Tel. (405) 525-2252; Robert Montgomery, 2420 N. Blackwelder, Oklahoma City, OK 73130. Tel: (405) 525-2252

Oklahoma Indian Missionary—Bishop John W. Hardt, Tel. (405) 525-2252; Becky Thompson, PO Box 60427, Oklahoma City, OK 73146. Tel: (405) 521-1741

Rio Grande—Bishop Ernest T. Dixon, Tel. (512) 432-0401; Arturo Mariscal, Jr., PO Box 28098, San Antonio, TX 78284. Tel: (512) 432-7875

Southwest Texas—Bishop Ernest T. Dixon, Tel. (512) 432-0401; Prenza L. Woods, PO Box 28098, San Antonio, TX 78284. Tel: (512) 432-4680

Texas—Bishop Benjamin R. Oliphint, Tel. (713) 528-6881; Joe A. Wilson, 5215 S. Main St., Houston, TX 77002. Tel: (713) 521-9383

Southeastern Jurisdiction

Alabama-West Florida—Bishop J. Lloyd Knox, Tel. (205) 879-8665; Roy T. Sublette, PO Box 700, Andalusia, AL 36420. Tel: (205) 222-3127

Florida—Bishop Earl G. Hunt, Jr., Tel. (813) 688-4427; Ray Harrison, PO Box 3767, Lakeland, FL 33802. Tel: (813) 688-5563

Holston—Bishop R. Kern Eutsler, Tel. (615) 525-1809; William J. Carter, PO Box 1178, Johnson City, TN 37601. Tel: (615) 928-2156

Kentucky—Bishop Paul A. Duffey, Tel. (502) 893-6715; Raymond W. Gibson, Jr., PO Box 5107, Lexington, KY 40555. Tel: (606) 254-7388

Louisville—Bishop Paul A. Duffey, Tel. (502) 893-6715; W. Avril Allen, 1115 S. Fourth St., Louisville, KY 40203. Tel: (502) 584-3838.

Memphis—Bishop Ernest W. Newman, Tel. (615) 327-3462; Paul Douglass, 575 Lambuth Blvd., Jackson, TN 38301. Tel: (901) 427-8589

Mississippi—Bishop Robert C. Morgan, Tel. (601) 948-4561; Warren E. Pittman, P. O. Box 1147, Jackson, MS 39205. Tel: (601) 354-0515

North Alabama—Bishop J. Lloyd Knox, Tel. (205) 879-8665; George W. Hayes, 898 Arkadelphia Rd., Birmingham, AL 35204. Tel: (205) 251-9279

North Carolina—Bishop C. P. Minnick, Jr., Tel. (919) 832-9560; F. Belton Joyner, Jr., PO Box 10955, Raleigh, NC 27605. Tel: (919) 832-9560

North Georgia—Bishop Ernest A. Fitzgerald, Tel. (404) 659-0002; Herchel Sheets, 159 Ralph McGill Blvd. NE, Atlanta, GA 30365. Tel: (404) 659-0002

North Mississippi—Bishop Robert C. Morgan, Tel. (601) 948-4561; W. S. Appelby, PO Drawer U, Grenada, MS 38901. Tel: (601) 226-5202

Red Bird Missionary—Bishop Paul A. Duffey, Tel. (502) 893-6715; David Allen, Queendale Ctr., Box 3, Beverly, KY 40913. Tel: (606) 598-5915

South Carolina—Bishop Roy C. Clark, Tel. (803) 786-9486; James S. Gadsden, 4908 Colonial Dr., Suite 101, Columbia, SC 29203. Tel: (803) 799-9627

South Georgia—Bishop Ernest A. Fitzgerald, Tel. (404) 659-0002; Alvis Waite PO Box 408, St. Simons Island, GA 31522. Tel: (912) 638-8626.

Tennessee—Bishop Ernest W. Newman, Tel. (615) 327-3462; Durward McCord, PO Box 120607, Nashville, TN 37212. Tel: (615) 329-1177

Virginia—Bishop Robert M. Blackburn, Tel. (804) 359-9451; Joseph T. Carson, Jr., PO Box 11367, Richmond, VA 23230. Tel: (804) 359-9451

Western North Carolina—Bishop L. Bevel Jones, Tel. (704) 535-2260; James W. Ferree, PO Box 18005, Charlotte, NC 28218. Tel: (704) 535-2260

Western Jurisdiction

Alaska Missionary—Bishop Calvin D. McConnell, Tel. (503) 226-7931; Dennis Holway, 3402 Wesleyan Dr., Anchorage, AK 99508. Tel: (907) 274-1571

California-Nevada—Bishop Leontine T. C. Kelly, Tel. (415) 474-3101; Donald Cunningham; PO Box 467, San Francisco, CA 94101. Tel: (415) 474-3101.

California-Pacific—Bishop Jack M. Tuell, Tel. (818) 796-6607; Hans J. Holborn, 472 E. Colorado Blvd., P.O. Box 6006, Pasadena, CA 91109. Tel. (818) 796-6607

Desert Southwest—Bishop Elias Galvin, Tel. (602) 253-0847; Michael Nickerson, 1807 N. Central Ave., Ste. 100, Phoenix, AZ 85004. Tel. (602)253-0847

Oregon-Idaho—Bishop Calvin D. McConnell, Tel. (503) 226-7931; Bill McDonald, 1505 SW 18th Ave., Portland, OR 97201. Tel: (503) 226-7931.

Pacific Northwest—Bishop Melvin G. Talbert, Tel. (206) 624-7674; Edgar C. Hersh, 2112 Third Ave., Suite 300, Seattle, WA 98121. Tel: (206) 624-7482.

Rocky Mountain—Bishop Roy I. Sano, Tel. (303) 733-3736; John Blinn, 2200 S. University Blvd., Denver, CO 80210. Tel: (303) 733-3736.

Yellowstone—Bishop Roy I. Sano, Tel. (303) 733-3736; Carolyn Straub, 335 Broadwater Ave., Billings, MT 59101. Tel: (406) 256-1385.

OTHER ORGANIZATIONS

Judicial Council: Pres., Tom Matheny; Sec., Hoover Rupert, c/o Florida Southern Univ., Lakeland, FL 33802

Council on Finance and Administration: 1200 Davis St., Evanston, IL 60201. Tel. (312) 869-3345. Pres., Bishop Joseph H. Yeakel; Vice-Pres., Bishop Robert M. Blackburn; Rec. Sec., Nancy McMullin, Gen. Sec.and Treas., Clifford Droke; Section on Episcopal Matters: Asst. Gen. Sec., Marie Kitazumi; Section on Legal Services, Gen. Counsel, Craig R. Hoskins; Section on Mgmt. Information Systems: Asst. Gen. Sec., Al Fifhause; Dir., Computer Systems, Merna Johnson; Dir. of Council Operations, Mary Simmons.

Division of Financial Services: Assoc. Gen. Sec., Gary K. Bowen; Controller, Beth Taylor; Dir. of Accounting, Daniel Schwartz; Payroll Dept., Dir., Phyllis Anderson; Service Centers: (Dayton) Asst. Gen. Treas., _____; (Nashville) Comptroller, W. C. Hawkins; (Washington) Asst. Gen. Treas., _____; (New York) Asst. Gen. Treas., Stephen F. Brimigion; Section on Investments, Gary K. Bowen

Division of Administrative Services: Assoc. Gen. Sec., John F. Norwood; Section on Records and Statistics: Asst. Gen. Sec., John L. Schreiber; Dir., Dept. of Records, Cynthia Haralson; Dir., Dept. of Statistics, Daniel A. Nielsen

Council on Ministries: 601 W. Riverview Ave., Dayton, OH 45406 Tel. (513) 227-9400. Pres., Bishop James S. Thomas; Vice-Pres., Twick Morrison, Arturo Fernandez; Sec., Loretta Young; Rec. Sec., _____; Treas., Marjorie Burns; Gen. Sec., C. David Lundquist; Assoc. Gen. Secs., Trudie Kibbe Preciphs, Royal Fishbeck, Jr., C. Leonard Miller, Mearle Griffith; Asst. Gen. Sec. for Admn., _____;

Commission on Communication/United Methodist Communications: P. O. Box 320 (810 12th Ave. S.), Nashville, TN 37202. Tel. (615) 742-5400. Pres., Bishop Louis W. Schowengerdt; Co-Vice Pres., Roy D. Barton, Ruth Daugherty; Sec., William K. Quick. Gen. Admn.: Gen. Sec., Roger L. Burgess; Assoc. Gen. Sec. Planning and Admin., Newtonia Harris Coleman; Treas., Peggy Welshans; Nat'l. Dir., Television/Telecommunications, Keith A. Muhleman; Dir. of Public Relations, William R. Richards

Division of Program and Benevolence Interpretation: Assoc. Gen. Sec., Donald E. Collier; Ed., *The Interpreter*, Darrell R. Shamblin; Ed., *El Interprete*, Edith LaFontaine; Editorial Dir., Barbara Dunlap-Berg

Division of Production and Distribution: Assoc. Gen. Sec., Peggy J. West; Dir., AV/Media Production, Wilfred V. Bane, Jr.; Dir., Media Distribution and ECUFILM, Furman York; Mgr., Technical Services and Kingswood Productions, Dixie Parman; Dir. INFOSERV, Woodley McEachern; Dir., Data Processing & Computer Based Communications, Susan Peek

Division of Public Media: 475 Riverside Dr., Ste. 1370, New York, NY 10115. Tel. (212) 663-8900. Assoc. Gen. Sec., Nelson Price. United Methodist News Service: P. O. Box 320, Nashville, TN 37202. Tel. (615) 742-5470; Dir. of News Service, Thomas S. McAnally

Board of Church and Society: 100 Maryland Ave., NE, Washington, DC. 20002. Tel. (202) 488-5600. Pres. Bishop William Boyd Grove; Vice-Pres., Lydia S. Martinez; Rec. Sec., Bradley D. Watkins; Treas., W. Astor Kirk; Gen. Sec., _____; Assoc. Gen. Secs., Donna Morton-Stout, Mary Council-Austin; Ed. of Resources and *engage/social action*, Lee Ranck; U.N. Seminars on National and International Affairs: Designers, Vincent Cobb, Jim Winkler, Andres Thomas, Carol Barton, Debra Huntington, Nan Won Kim; Business and Finance: Asst. Gen. Sec., Harold Stephens; Chpsn., Trustees, Dan E. Solomon

Dept. of Human Welfare, Dir., Beverly Jackson

Dept. of Social and Economic Justice, Dir., George Ogle

Dept. of Political and Human Rights, Dir., Guillermo Chavez

Dept. of Peace and World Order, Dir., Robert McClean, 777 United Nations Plaza, New York, NY 10017. Tel. (212) 682-3633

Dept. of Environmental Justice and Survival, Dir., Jaydee Hanson

Dept. of Ethnic Minority Local Church, Dir., Manuel Espartero

Board of Discipleship: P. O. Box 840 (1908 Grand Ave. and 1001 19th Ave. S.), Nashville, TN 37202. Tel. (615) 340-7200. Pres., Bishop George W. Bashore; Vice-Pres., Bishop Woodie W. White; Sec., William Arnold, Jr.; Treas., Isaac W. Brown; Gen Sec., Ezra Earl Jones; Assoc.Gen. Sec., Alan K. Waltz, Victor Perez-Silvestry Center for Congregational Life: Exec. Sec., L. Ray Sells Office of Human Resources and Staff Services: Exec. Sec., Jean Suiter

Office of Research: Exec. Sec., Warren J. Hartman Publishing and Interpretative Services: Exec. Sec., Neil M. Alexander

Section on the Missional Priority: Asst. Gen. Sec., David L. White

Section on Ministry of the Laity: Asst. Gen. Sec., Marilyn W. Magee

Section on Stewardship: Asst. Gen. Sec., Herbert Mather

Section on United Methodist Men: Asst. Gen. Sec., James H. Snead, Jr.

Section on Evangelism: Asst. Gen. Sec., H. Eddie Fox Section on Worship: Asst. Gen. Sec., Thomas A. Langford, III

Section on Christian Education: Asst. Gen. Sec., Duane A. Ewers

The Upper Room: World Editor, Janice T. Grana Curriculum Resources Committee: Ed., Church School Publications, Orion N. Hutchinson, Jr.; Man. Ed., Church School Publications, Howard E. Walker. Curricuphone: 1-800-351-8591; Tenn. Call collect: Tel. (615) 749-6482

Board of Global Ministries: 475 Riverside Dr., New York, NY 10115. Tel. (212) 870-3600. Pres., Bishop James M. Ault; Vice-Pres., Bishop Kenneth W. Hicks, Bishop Roy I. Sano, Carolyn W. Marshall; Gen. Sec., Randolph Nugent; Deputy Gen Secs., Rene O. Bideaux, Theressa Hoover, Peggy Billings; Assoc. Gen. Secs.: Lorene F. Wilbur, Admn.; John A. Murdock, Health & Welfare; Norma Kehrberg, United Methodist Committee on Relief; Ombudsperson, Cherryetta Williams; Gen. Treas., Stephen F. Brimigion; Assoc. and Div. Treas., Brenda Norwood, Joyce Sohl, Richard Vreeland; Gen. Comptroller, Lynette Davis Rice; Public Relations Dir., Betty Thompson; Board Planner, Robert Harman.

National Division: Pres., Bishop Kenneth W. Hicks; Deputy Gen. Sec., Rene O. Bideaux; Asst. Gen. Secs., Jane Brice Briddell, Lula Garrett, Thomas Gallen, Myong Gul Son; Treas., Brenda Norwood.

Women's Division: Pres., Carolyn Marshall; Deputy Gen. Sec., Theressa Hoover; Asst. Gen. Secs., Barbara E. Campbell, Ellen Kirby, Elizabeth Calvin, Elaine Gasser;

World Division: Pres., Bishop Roy I. Sano; Treas., Richard L. Vreeland. Deputy Gen. Sec., Peggy Billings; Asst. Gen. Secs., Charles H. Germany, Sarla Lall, Doreen Tilghman, Jiro Mizuno, Nora O. Booths

Mission Education Cultivation Dept.: Chpsn., Carolyn H. Oehler; Assoc. Gen. Sec. _____; Asst. Gen. Secs., Marian T. Martin, WilliamT. Carter

Health and Welfare Dept.: Chpsn., Bishop Edsel A. Ammons; Treas., Brenda Norwood; Assoc. Gen. Sec., John A. Murdock; Asst. Gen. Sec., Cathie Lyons; Treas., Brenda Norwood

United Methodist Committee on Relief: Chpsn., Bishop Roy C. Clark; Assoc. Gen. Secs., Norman Kehr; Treas., Richard L. Vreeland

Mission Resources Dept.: Chpsn., Sharon Brown Christopher; Treas., Stephen Brimigion

Board of Higher Education and Ministry: P.O. Box 871 (1001 Nineteenth Ave. S.), Nashville, TN 37202. Tel. (615)340-7000. Pres., Bishop F. Herbert Skeete; Vice-Pres., Bishop David J. Lawson, Jimmy Carr, Nancy M. Carruth, Rev. William O. Walker; Sec., Nina H. Reeves; Gen. Sec., _____; Assoc. Gen. Sec. for Administration, Martha Lawrence; Office of Interpretation: Assoc. Gen.Sec., David Ochoa, Dir., Terri J. Hiers; Office of Loans and Scholarships: Asst. Gen. Sec., Angella Current

Division of Chaplains and Related Ministries: Assoc. Gen. Sec., James Towshend; Dirs., Patricia Barrett, Richard Stewart

Division of Diaconal Ministry: Assoc. Gen. Sec., Rosalie Bentzinger; Dirs., Joaquin Garcia, Paul Van Buren

118

Division of Higher Education: Assoc. Gen. Sec., Julius Scott; Asst. Gen. Sec., Alan Burry; Dirs., Ken Yamada, Helen Neinast. Office of the Black College Fund: Exec. Dir., Shirley Lewis. National Methodist Foundation for Christian Higher Education: Pres., Alan Peer
Division of the Ordained Ministry: Assoc. Gen. Sec., Donald H. Treese; Dirs., Robert Kohler, Richard Yeager, Kil Sang Yoon, Kathy Nickerson
Board of Pensions: 1200 Davis St., Evanston, IL 60201. Tel. (312) 869-4550. Pres., Bishop Jack M. Tuell; Vice-Pres., Conrad M. Page, Jr.; Sec., Mona Mae Waymire; Gen. Sec., James J. Parker; Sr.Assoc.Gen.Sec., Dir. of Corp. Rel., & Spec.Asst. to Gen. Sec., Allen M. Mayes; Chief of Partic. Services, Gerald Beam; Dir. of Benefits Dept., Thomas Marston; Asst.Dir., Cheryl Haack; Chief of Operational Services, Dale Knapp; Dir. of Op. Dept., Phillip Moulden; Dir. Data Process., Bruce Slown; Data Base Coord., Mary Norman; Chief of Support Services, Kenneth Truman; Dir. Adm. Serv., Joyce E. Gilman; Dir., Communic. Dept., Deanna Armstrong; Personnel Dir., Chris Mackey; Treas., Diane Penney; Asst. Treas., G. Warren Dare; Chief Fin. Officer, F. Gale Whitson-Schmidt; Portfolio Project Adm., Chantal Nelson; Portfolio Analysis Adm., Mary Pat Kincaid; Sr. Systems Analyst, Vera Czerlinski; James Kavanagh; Internal Auditor, Wilbert Blum; Asst. Int. Auditor., Joel Deaner; Asst. Gen. Secs., Wayne L. Bondurant, Mark Conner, David L. Mohr, Vidette Bullock, Keith R. Maxwell; Auditor, Frank L. Markel; Asst. Actuary, SusanWilson; Gen. Counsel, James M. Walton-Myers
Board of Publication: Chpsn, Anita J. Burrous; Vice-Chpsn., William T. Staubach, Jr.; Sec., Cornelius L. Henderson.
The United Methodist Publishing House: P.O. Box 801, 201 Eighth Ave. So., Nashville, TN 37202. Tel. (615) 749-6000 or 1-800-672-1789. Pres. & Publisher, Robert K. Feaster; Vice Pres. and Assoc. Publisher, Thomas E. Carpenter; Treas., Vice-Pres., Fin. and Admn., Larry L. Wallace; Vice-Pres., Manufacturing, Division (Parthenon Press), Max Thomas; Vice-Pres., Retail Sales (Cokesbury) Division, Gary H. Vincent; Vice-Pres., Publishing Div., H. Claude Young, Jr.; Vice-Pres., Book Editor/Edit. Dir. Gen. Publishing, Ronald P. Patterson; Vice-Pres., Office of Planning & Research, Thomas K. Potter, Jr.; Vice-Pres., Public Relations Division, James C. Peters, Sr.; Vice-Pres., Human Resources Division, Stephen C. Tippens.
Commissions on Archives and History: P.O. Box 127, Madison, NJ 07940. Tel. (201) 822-2787. Pres., Bishop Neil L. Irons; Vice-Pres., Eunice Mathews; Rec. Sec., Thelma Boeder; Gen. Sec., Charles Yrigoyen, Jr.; Asst. Gen. Sec., Arthur Swarthout; Archivist, William C. Beal, Jr.; Dir., Women's History Project, Susan Eltsher
Commission on Christian Unity and Interreligious Concerns: 475 Riverside Dr., Rm. 1300, New York, NY 10115. Tel. (212) 749-3553. Pres., Bishop Benjamin R. Oliphint; Vice-Pres., Elise Penfield; Sec., Jorge A. Gonzales; Treas., Clifford Droke, Gen. Sec., Robert W. Huston; Assoc. Gen. Secs., Jeanne Audrey Powers, W. Dayalan Niles, Bruce W. Robbins
Commission on Religion and Race: 100 Maryland Ave., N.E., Washington, DC 20002. Tel. (202) 547-4270. Pres., Bishop Melvin G. Talbert; Vice-Pres., Bishop L. Bevel Jones; Rec. Sec., Lola Keller; Gen. Sec., Barbara R. Thompson; Assoc. Gen. Secs., Kenneth Deere, Warren Hill, Yolanda Pupo-Ortiz, Hidetoshi Tanaka, Evelyn Fitzgerald
Commission on the Status and Role of Women: 1200 Davis St., Evanston, IL 60201. Tel. (312) 869-7330. Pres., H. Sharon Howell; Vice-Pres., Ressie Bass; Rec. Sec., Albert Jones; Secretariat, Nancy G. Self, Kiyoko Fujiu, Geneva Dalton
Fellowship of United Methodists in Worship, Music, and

Other Arts: P.O. Box 6867, North Augusta, SC 29841. Tel. (803)279-4961. Exec. Sec., Jerry Henry; Pres., Robert Schilling

PERIODICALS

Arkansas United Methodist (bi-w), P.O. Box 3547, Little Rock, AR 72203. Georgia Daily, Ed.
California-Nevada United Methodist Reporter (w), 231 W. Myrtle St., Hanford, CA 93230. Ruth J. Gomes, Ed.
Central Illinois United Methodist Reporter (w), P.O. Box 515, Bloomington, IL 61702. Bettie W. Story, Ed.
Central Texas U.M. Reporter (w), One Summit Ave., Ste. 505, Ft. Worth, TX 76102. Wallace Bennett, Ed.
Circuit Rider (m), P.O. Box 801, Nashville, TN 37202. Keith Pohl, Ed.
Circuit Rider U.M. Reporter (w), 5124 Greenwich Ave., Baltimore, MD 21229. Jan Lichtenwalter, Ed.
Circuit West (w), 4249 Cedar Ave., El Monte, CA 91732. Peg Parker, Ed.
Communicator, The (w), 139 N. State St., Dover, DE 19901. Susan Keirn Kester, Ed.
Conference Connexion (m), 1919 Broadway, Mt. Vernon, IL. William Frazier,Ed.
Contact (w), 2420 N. Blackwelder, Oklahoma City, OK 73106. Boyce Bowdon, Ed.
Crossfire (bi-w), 151 N. Volutsia, Wichita, KS 67214. Kathy Kruger, Ed.
Desert Views (w), 6002 N. 43rd St., Paradise Valley, AZ 85253. Colleen Sanders-Hatfield, Ed.
Dimensions (m), P. O. Box 220, Sun Prairie, WI 53590. Kris Wilhelmi, Ed.
East Ohio Today (w), 520 Lear Rd., Avon Lake, OH 44012, Sandy Rider, Ed.
Eastern Pennsylvania United Methodist Reporter (w), P. O. Box 820, Valley Forge, PA 19482. Judy Kelfstrom, Ed.
El Interprete (q) (Spanish), P. O. Box 320, Nashville, TN 37202. Edith LaFontaine,Ed.
engage/social action (m), 100 Maryland Ave., NE, Washington, DC 20002. Lee Ranck, Ed.
Florida United Methodist Reporter (w), P.O. Box 3767, Lakeland, FL 33802. Barbara Wilcox, Ed.
Hawkeye (m), 1019 Chestnut St., Des Moines, IA 50309. Karen J. Tisinger, Ed.
Holston United Methodist Reporter (w), P.O. Box 1178, Johnson City, TN 37605. Don Sluder, Ed.
Hoosier United Methodist (m), 1100 W. 42nd St., Indianapolis, IN 46208. James Steele, Ed.
Interchange (w), P.O. Box 4187, Topeka, KS 66604. _____, Ed.
International Christian Digest, P. O. Box 801, Nashville, TN 37202. J. Richard Peck, Ed.
Interpreter, The (m), P. O. Box 320, Nashville, TN 37202. Darrell R. Shamblin, Ed.
Kentucky United Methodist Review (bi-w), P.O. Box 5107, Lexington, KY 40555. Raymond Gibson, Ed.
Link, The (m), 900 S. Arlington Ave., Rm. 112, Harrisburg, PA 17109. Gerald D. Wagner, Ed.
Louisiana United Methodist Reporter (w), P. O. Box 3057, Baton Rouge, LA 70802. Harvey G. Williamson, Ed.
Louisville U.M. Reporter, 1115 S. 4th St., Louisville, KY 40203. Tammy Harrod, Ed.
Maine United Methodist, The (bi-m), P.O. Box 277, Winthrop, ME 04364. Beverly J. Abbott, Ed.
Mature Years (q), 201 Eighth Ave. S., Nashville, TN 37202. John P. Gilbert, Ed.
Memphis Conference United Methodist Reporter (w), 575 Lambuth Blvd., Jackson, TN 38301. Cathy Farmer, Ed.
Methodist History (q), P.O. Box 127, Madison, NJ 07940. Charles Yrigoyen, Jr., Ed.
Michigan Christian Advocate (w), 316 Springbrook Ave., Adrian, MI 49221. Kay Lukins, Ed.
Minnesota United Methodist Reporter (w), 122 W. Franklin Ave., Rm. 400, Minneapolis, MN 55404. Jean Noren, Ed.

Mississippi United Methodist Advocate (bi-w), Box 1093, Jackson, MS 39205. Rayford Woodrick, Ed.

Missouri East United Methodist Reporter (w), 4625 Lindell Blvd., Suite 424, St. Louis, MO 63108. Dulcina R. McCoy, Ed.

Missouri West United Methodist Reporter (w), 1512 Van Brunt Blvd., Kansas City, MO 64127. Dale L. Pollock, Ed.

Nebraska Messenger (bi-w), P.O. Box 4553, Lincoln, NE 68504. Daniel R. Gangler, Ed.

New Mexico United Methodist Reporter (w), 209 San Pedro NE, Albuquerque, NM 87108. Julianne McAchran, Ed.

New World Outlook (m), 475 Riverside Dr., Rm. 1351, New York, NY 10115. _____, Ed.

Newscope (w), P.O. Box 801, Nashville, TN 37202. Bette E. Prestwood, Ed.

North Carolina Christian Advocate (w), P.O. Box 508, Greensboro, NC 27402. C. A. Simonton, Jr., Ed.

North Central New York United Methodist Review (bi-w), R.D. 3 Delivery 121, Elmira, NY 14903. Carla Page, Ed.

North Texas U.M. Reporter (w), 1928 Ross Ave., Dallas, TX 75201. Lillian Sills, Ed.

Northern Illinois United Methodist Review (bi-w), 77 W. Washington St., Rm. 1806, Chicago, IL 60602. Dana Jones-Yelvington, Ed.

Northwest Texas United Methodist Reporter, (w), 1415 Ave. M, Lubbock, TX 79401. Robert Giovannetti, Ed.

Northwest United Methodist (m), 2112 Third Ave., #300 Seattle, WA 98121

Pockets (m), P. O. Box 189, Nashville, TN 37202. Willie Teague, Ed.

Prairie Flame, The (w), 2410 12th St. N., Fargo, ND 58102. Cameron W. Johnson, Ed.

Quarterly Review (q), P.O. Box 871, Nashville, TN 37202. Charles E. Cole, Ed.

Reporter (w) (Spanish), P.O. Box 28098, San Antonio, TX 78284. Eradio Valverde, Jr., Ed.

response (m), 475 Riverside Dr., Room 1344, New York, NY 10115. Carol M. Herb, Ed.

Rocky Mountain United Methodist Reporter (w), 2200 S. University Blvd., Denver, CO 80210. Suzanne Calvin, Ed.

South Carolina United Methodist Advocate (w), 4908 Colonial Dr., Rm. 207, Columbia, SC 29203. Maryneal Jones, Ed.

Southern New England U.M. Reporter (w), 566 Commonwealth Ave., Boston, MA 02215. Ann Whiting, Ed.

Southwest Texas U.M. Reporter, Box 28098, San Antonio, TX 78284. Beverly Robberson, Ed.

Tennessee United Methodist Reporter (w), P.O. Box 120607, Nashville, TN 37212. Ed Britt, Jr., Ed.

Texas U.M. Reporter (w), 5215 S. Main St., Houston, TX 77002. Mary L. Krause, Ed.

United Methodist (m), 1505 SW 18th Ave., Portland, OR 97201. Barbara Sawyer, Ed.

United Methodist Christian Advocate (bi-w), 909 Ninth Ave., W., Birmingham AL 35204. Paul Ruark, Ed.

United Methodist Relay (m), 300 Ridge Rd., Fairhaven, NJ 07701. Robin E. Van Cleef, Ed.

United Methodist Reporter, The (w), P.O. Box 660275, Dallas, TX 75266. Spurgeon M. Dunnam III, Ed.

United Methodist Rural Fellowship Bulletin (q), P.O. Box 307, Louisville, TN 37777. James E. Hankins, Ed.

Update (bi-w), 252 Bryant Ave., White Plains, NY 10605. Carol Hayes, Ed.

Upper Room (bi-m), P. O. Box 189, Nashville, TN 37202. Janice T. Grana, Ed.

Virginia Advocate (bi-w), P.O. Box 11367, Richmond, VA 23230. Alvan J. Horton, Ed.

Voice, The (m), 3 Orchard Rd., Binghamton, NY 13905. Cheryl Coates, Ed.

Wesleyan Christian Advocate (w), P.O. Box 54455,

Atlanta, GA 30308. G. Ross Freeman, Ed.

West Ohio News (bi-w), 471 Broad St., Suite 1106, Columbus, OH 43215. Robert F. Storey, Ed.

West Virginia United Methodist (m), P.O. Box 2313, Charleston, WV 25328. Tom Burger, Ed.

Western New York Communicator (bi-w), 8499 Main St., Buffalo, NY 14221. Nancy Howlett, Ed.

Western Pennsylvania United Methodist Reporter (w), 1204 Freedom Rd., Mars, PA 16046. _____, Ed.

World Parish (s-m), P.O. Box 518, Lake Junaluska, NC 28745. Joseph R. Hale, Ed.

Zion's Herald (m), 566 Commonwealth Ave., Boston, MA 02215. Ann Whiting, Ed.

United Pentecostal Church International

The United Pentecostal Church International came into being through the merger of two oneness Pentecostal organizations—the Pentecostal Church, Inc., and the Pentecostal Assemblies of Jesus Christ. The first of these was known as the Pentecostal Ministerial Alliance from its inception in 1925 until 1932. The second was formed in 1931 by a merger of the Apostolic Church of Jesus Christ with the Pentecostal Assemblies of the World.

The United Pentecostal Church International contends that the Bible does not teach three separate, coequal and coeternal members of the godhead, but rather one God who manifested himself as the Father in creation, the Son in redemption, and the Holy Spirit in regeneration. It is further believed that Jesus is the name of this absolute deity and that water baptism should be administered in his name, not in the titles Father, Son, and Holy Ghost. Scriptural basis for this teaching can be found in Acts 2:38, 8:16, and 19:6. This position should not be confused with the Unitarian view, which denies the deity of Jesus Christ.

The Fundamental Doctrine of the United Pentecostal Church International, as stated in its *Articles of Faith,* is "the Bible standard of full salvation, which is repentance, baptism in water by immersion in the name of the Lord Jesus Christ for the remission of sins, and the baptism of the Holy Ghost with the initial sign of speaking with other tongues as the Spirit gives utterance."

Further doctrinal teachings concern the necessity of a life of holiness and separation, the operation of the gifts of the Spirit within the church, the second coming of the Lord, and the church's obligation to take the gospel to the whole world. The traditional slogan of the United Pentecostal Church International is The Whole Gospel to the Whole World.

Churches: 3,410; Inclusive Membership: 500,000; Sunday or Sabbath Schools: N.R.; Total Enrollment: N.R.; Ordained Clergy: 6,984

GENERAL ORGANIZATION

Conference: annual

Headquarters: 8855 Dunn Rd., Hazelwood, MO 63042. Tel. (314) 837-7300

OFFICERS

Gen. Supt., Rev. Nathaniel A. Urshan, 8855 Dunn Rd., Hazelwood, MO 63042

Asst. Gen. Supts., Rev. James Kilgore, Box 15175, Houston, TX 77020; Jesse Williams, P. O. Box 64877, Fayetteville, NC 28306

Gen. Sec.-Treas., Rev. C. M. Becton, 8855 Dunn Rd., Hazelwood, MO 63042

Dir. of For. Miss., Rev. Harry Scism, 8855 Dunn Rd., Hazelwood, MO 63042

Gen. Dir. of Home Miss., Rev. Jack E. Yonts, 8855 Dunn Rd., Hazelwood, MO 63042

Editor-in-Chief, Rev. J. L. Hall, 8855 Dunn Rd., Hazelwood, MO 63042

Gen. Sunday School Dir., Rev. E. J. McClintock, 8855 Dunn Rd., Hazelwood, MO 63042

OTHER AUXILIARIES

The Pentecostal Publishing House, Rev. J. O. Wallace, Mgr.

Youth Division (Pentecostal Conquerors), Pres., Rex Johnson, Hazelwood, MO 63042

Ladies Auxiliary: Pres., Vera Kinzie, 4840 Elm Pl., Toledo, OH 43608

Harvestime Radio Broadcast: Dir., Rev. J. Hugh Rose, 698 Kerr Ave., Cadiz, OH 43907

Stewardship Dept.: Contact Church Division, Hazelwood, MO 63042

Education Division: Supt. Rev. Arless Glass, 4502 Aztec, Pasadena, TX 77504

Public Relations Division, Contact Church Division, Hazelwood, MO 63042

Historical Society & Archives: Calvin Rigdon, 8855 Dunn Rd., Hazelwood, MO 63042

PERIODICALS

The Pentecostal Herald, Hazelwood, Rev. J. L. Hall, Ed.

The Global Witness (Foreign Mission Div.), Rev. J. S. Leaman, Ed.

The Outreach (Home Mission Div.), J. L. Fiorino, Ed.

The Ephphatha (Deaf Div.), Billie Chisholm, Ed.

Homelife (Youth Div.), Rev. Jerry Dean, Ed.

Conqueror (Youth Div.), Rev. Jerry Jones, Ed.

Reflections (Ladies Div.), Melissa Anderson, Ed.

Forward (for ministers only), Rev. J. L. Hall, Jr.

United Zion Church

A branch of the Brethren in Christ which settled in Lancaster County, Pennsylvania, and was organized under the leadership of Matthias Brinser in 1855.

GENERAL ORGANIZATION

Conference: annual

OFFICERS

Gen. Conf. Mod., Bishop J. Paul Martin, Box 212 D, RD #1, Annville, PA 17003. Tel. (717)867-4253

Asst. Mod., Rev. Amos Weidman, RD #2, Manheim, PA 17545. Tel. (717)665-6274

Gen. Conf. Sec., Eugene Kreider, RD #2, Manheim, PA 17545. Tel. (717)653-8226

Gen. Conf.Treas., Carl Good, RD #1, Denver, PA 17517

Unity of the Brethren

Czech and Moravian immigrants in Texas (beginning about 1855) established congregations which grew into an Evangelical Union in 1903, and with the accession of other Brethren in Texas, into the Evangelical Unity of the Czech-Moravian Brethren in North America. In 1959, it shortened the name to the original name used in 1457, the Unity of the Brethren (Unitas Fratrum, or Jednota Bratrska).

Churches: 26; Inclusive Membership: 3,581; Sunday or Sabbath Schools: 22; Total Enrollment: 1,055; Ordained Clergy: 21

GENERAL ORGANIZATION

Synod: Every two years.

OFFICERS

Pres., Dr. Mark L. Labaj, 4202 Ermine, Temple, TX 76501

1st Vice Pres., Rev. Daniel Marek, 403 S. Main, Caldwell, TX 77836

Sec., Elizabeth Oertli, R 3,Box 583, Brenham, TX 77833

Fin. Sec., Mr. Ed Wrinkle, Rt. 3, Box 113, Taylor, TX 76574

Treas., Roy Vajdak, 920 Malone, Houston, TX 77007

ORGANIZATIONS

Sunday School Union: Chmn., Stanley F. Mrnustik, 205

N. Shaw St., Caldwell, TX 77836; Board of Christian Education: Chpsn., Rev. James Hejl, 700 Sloan St., Taylor, TX 76574

Christian Sisters Society: Pres., Mrs. Lillian Hejl, R 1, Box 502, Granger, TX 76530

Brethren Youth Fellowship: Pres., Ricky Weise, R 3, Box 121, San Angelo, TX 76901

Young Adult Fellowship: Pres., Ray Griggs, 3200 Finfeather #204, Bryan, TX 77801

PERIODICAL

Brethren Journal (m), Milton Maly, Ed.

Vedanta Society

Followers of the Vedas, the scriptures of the Indo-Aryans, doctrines expounded by Swami Vivekananda at the Parliament of Religions, Chicago, 1893. There are altogether 13 such Centers in the U.S.A. All are under the spiritual guidance of the Ramakrishna Mission, organized by Swami Vivekananda in India.

Churches: 13 Inclusive Membership: 2,500 Sunday or Sabbath Schools: N.R. Total Enrollment: N.R. Ordained Clergy: 14

GENERAL ORGANIZATION

Correspondent: 34 W. 71st St., New York, NY 10023. Tel. (212) 877-9197

LEADER

Swami Tathagatananda

Volunteers of America

Volunteers of America, founded in 1896 by Ballington and Maud Booth, provides spiritual and material aid for those in need in more than 300 communities across the U.S. As one of the nation's largest multipurpose human-service agencies, VOA offers more than 400 programs for the elderly, families, youth, alcoholics, drug abusers, offenders, and the disabled.

GENERAL ORGANIZATION

National Headquarters: 3813 North Causeway Blvd., Metairie, LA 70002. Tel. (504) 837-2652

NATIONAL OFFICERS

Pres., Raymond C. Tremont

Vice-Pres., Jack L. Dignum, David Bordenkircher, Robert E. Nolte, John A. Hood, J. Clint Cheveallier, J. Steven Tremont

PERIODICAL

The Gazette (q), published at National Headquarters

The Wesleyan Church

The Wesleyan Church was formed on June 26, 1968, through the union of the Wesleyan Methodist Church of America (1843) and the Pilgrim Holiness Church (1897). Headquarters was established at Marion, Indiana and relocated in Indianapolis, Indiana in 1987.

The Wesleyan movement centers around the scriptural truth that the atonement in Christ provides for the regeneration of sinners and the entire sanctification of believers. A revival of these truths took place in the eighteenth century under John Wesley and continues until the present.

When a group of New England ministers led by Orange Scott began to crusade for the abolition of slavery, with which many Methodist ministers and members had become involved, the bishops and others sought to silence them. This led to a series of withdrawals from the Methodist Episcopal Church. In 1843 an organizing convention was held in Utica, New York, resulting in the organization of the Wesleyan Methodist Connection of America. Scott, Jotham Horton, LaRoy Sunderland, Luther Lee, and Lucius C. Matlack were prominent leaders in the new denomination. The crusade against slavery was carried to a successful conclusion with the Civil War.

As a result of the holiness revival which swept across many denomintions in the last half of the nineteenth century, holiness replaced social reform as the major tenet of the Connection. In 1947 the name was changed from Connection to Church and a central supervisory authority was set up.

The Pilgrim Holiness Church was one of many independent holiness churches which came into existence as a result of the holiness revival. Under the leadership of Martin Wells Knapp and Seth C. Rees, the International Holiness Union and Prayer League was inaugurated in 1897 in Cincinnati, Ohio. Its purpose was to promote worldwide holiness evangelism and the Union had a strong missionary emphasis from the beginning. Membership was open to all who subscribed to its brief constitution, and it rapidly developed into a church by 1913.

The Wesleyan Church is now spread across most of the United States and Canada and 34 other countries. The Wesleyan World Fellowship was organized in 1972 to unite Wesleyan mission bodies developing into mature churches.

The Wesleyan Church is a member of the Christian Holiness Association, the National Association of Evangelicals, and the World Methodist Council.

Churches: 1,704; Inclusive Membership: 109,196; Sunday or Sabbath Schools: 1,704; Total Enrollment: 188,620; Ordained Clergy: 2,596

GENERAL ORGANIZATION

General Conference: quadrennial (next session, 1988) International Center: P.O. Box 50434, Indianapolis, IN 46250. Tel. (317) 674-0444

OFFICERS

Gen. Supts.: Dr. J. D. Abbott, Dr. O. D. Emery, Dr. Robert W. McIntyre, Dr. Earle L. Wilson
Gen. Sec., Dr. Ronald R. Brannon
Gen. Treas., Mr. Daniel D. Busby
Gen. Ed., Dr. Wayne E. Caldwell
Gen. Publisher, Mr. Mark Batman
Gen. Sec. Extension and Evangelism, Dr. Thomas E. Phillippe
Gen. Sec. World Missions, Dr. Wayne W. Wright
Gen. Sec. Local Church Edu., Rev. David L. Keith
Gen. Sec. Youth, Rev. Keith W. Drury
Gen. Sec. Education and the Ministry, Dr. Lee M. Haines
Gen. Dir. Estate Planning, Rev. Howard B. Castle
Gen. Dir. Broadcast Ministries, Dr. Norman G. Wilson
Gen. Dir. Wesleyan Pension Fund, Mr. Leland K. Crist
Gen. Dir. Wesleyan Investment Foundation, Rev. John A. Dunn

PERIODICALS

The Wesleyan Advocate, Dr. Wayne E. Caldwell, Ed.
Wesleyan World, Rev. Stanley K. Hoover, Ed.

Wesleyan Holiness Association of Churches

This body was founded Aug. 4, 1959 near Muncie, Indiana by a group of ministers and laymen who were drawn together for the purpose of spreading and conserving sweet, radical, scriptural holiness. These men came from various church bodies. This group is Wesleyan in doctrine and standards.

GENERAL ORGANIZATION

General Conference meets every two years.
Headquarters: 108 Carter Ave., Dayton, OH 45405

OFFICERS

Gen. Supt., Rev. J. Stevan Manley, 108 Carter Ave., Dayton, OH 45405 Tel. (513) 278-3770

Asst. Gen. Supt., Rev. Leon Jackson, 7121 N. 43rd Ave., Phoenix, AZ 85021. Tel. (206) 535-0425
Gen. Sec.-Treas., Rev. Robert W. Wilson, 2315 South St., Ironton, OH 45638. Tel. (614)533-1953
Gen. Youth Pres., Rev. Roger Williard, 504 W. Tyrell, St. Louis, MI 48880. Tel. (517) 681-2591

PERIODICAL

Eleventh Hour Messenger (bi-m), Rev. J. Stevan Manley, Ed.

Wisconsin Evangelical Lutheran Synod

Organized in 1850 at Milwaukee, Wisconsin by three pastors sent to America by a German mission society. The name Wisconsin Evangelical Lutheran Synod still reflects its origins, although it has lost its local character and presently has congregations in 50 states and 3 Canadian provinces.

The Wisconsin Synod federated with the Michigan and Minnesota Synods in 1892 in order to more effectively carry on education and mission enterprises. A merger of these three Synods followed in 1917 to give the Wisconsin Evangelical Lutheran Synod its present form.

Although at its organization in 1850 the Synod turned away from conservative Lutheran theology, today it is ranked as one of the most conservative Lutheran bodies in the U.S. The Synod confesses that the Bible is the verbally inspired, infalliable Word of God and subscribes without reservation to the confessional writings of the Lutheran Church. Its interchurch relations are determined by a firm commitment to the principle that unity of doctrine and practice are the prerequisites of pulpit and altar fellowship and ecclesial cooperation. Consequently it does not hold membership in ecumenical organizations.

Churches: 1,180; Inclusive Membership: 416,493; Sunday or Sabbath Schools: 1,146; Total Enrollment: 48,461; Ordained Clergy: 1,497

GENERAL ORGANIZATION

Convention: biennial (Next meeting, 1989)
National Offices: 2929 North Mayfair Rd., Wauwatosa, WI 53222. Tel. (414) 771-9357

OFFICERS

Pres., Rev. Carl H. Mischke, 2929 N. Mayfair Rd., Wauwatosa, WI 53222
1st Vice-Pres., Rev. Richard E. Lauersdorf, 105 Aztalan Ct., Jefferson, WI 53549
2nd Vice-Pres., Rev. Robert J. Zink, S66, WI4275 Janesville Rd., Muskego, WI 53150
Sec., Prof. David Worgull, 1201 W. Tulsa, Chandler, AZ 85224

OTHER ORGANIZATIONS

Bd. of Trustees: Admn., Rev. Elton H. Huebner; Bd. for Worker Trng., Admn., Rev. Wayne Borgwardt; Bd. for Parish Admn., Donald H. Zimmerman; Gen. Bd. for Home Missions: Admn., Rev. Norman W. Berg; Gen. Bd. for World Missions: Admn., Rev. Duane K. Tomhave; Special Ministries Board: Admn., Alfons Woldt; Bd. for Evangelism: Admn., Rev. Paul E. Kelm; Public Relations: Dir., Rev. James P. Schaefer

PERIODICALS

Wisconsin Lutheran Quarterly (q), 11831 N. Seminary Dr., 65 W. Mequon, WI 53092. Prof. Wilbert R. Gawrisch, Mng. Ed.
Northwestern Lutheran (semi-m), 2929 N. Mayfair Rd., Wauwatosa, WI 53222. Rev. James P. Schaefer, Ed.
Yearbook, 1250 N. 113 St., Milwaukee WI 53226. Rev. Mentor E. Kujath, Ed.
The Lutheran Educator, 2929 N. Mayfair Rd., Wauwatosa, WI 53222. Donald H. Zimmerman, Ed.

World Confessional Lutheran Assoc.

The World Confessional Lutheran Association (WCLA) was originally named Lutheran's Alert National (LAN) when it was founded in 1965 by a small group of conservative Lutheran pastors and laymen meeting in Cedar Rapids, Iowa. Its purpose was to help preserve from erosion the basic doctrines of Christian theology, including the inerrancy of Holy Scripture. The small group of ten grew to a worldwide constituency, similarly concerned over maintaining the doctrinal integrity of the Bible and the Lutheran Confessions.

In 1969, Faith Evangelical Lutheran Seminary was established in Tacoma, Washington. Graduates from this seminary fill the needs of the World Confessional Lutheran Association congregations as well as those of several other denominational churches. In 1979 the seminary established a Korean division, which provides pastors and missionaries to Korean-speaking people throughout the world.

The media arm of the WCLA, known as "Words of Truth," provides devotional programming to individuals and congregations around the world. The original name, Lutheran's Alert National, is now assigned to the Apologetic arm of the WCLA. This agency provides timely information on what is going on in the Lutheran Church worldwide by means of a monthly magazine, regional seminars, debates, and other printed and visual media.

The outreach arm, involving missions and social service ministries, is known as Lutheran World Concerns. The work of this division is to establish links with other evangelical Christian groups and mission programs worldwide, who are willing to work with the WCLA as associate partners, agree with the Statement of Faith of the WCLA, and desire to pursue the goal of world evangelization in this generation. A new school of World Missions has now been opened to help reach this goal.

The name World Confessional Lutheran Association was adopted by the board in 1984, to reflect the growing global outreach and involvement of our movement.

Churches: 11; Inclusive Membership: 1,385; Sunday or Sabbath Schools: 11; Total Enrollment: 389; Ordained Clergy: 24

GENERAL ORGANIZATION

Board meets twice yearly (June and November).
Headquarters: 3504 N. Pearl St., P.O. Box 7186, Tacoma, WA 98407. Tel. (206) 759-1891

OFFICERS

Pres., Dr. Rueben H. Redal, 409 N. Tacoma Ave., Tacoma, WA 98403
Vice Pres., Dr. Arthur H. Braun, 341 S. Hamline Ave., St. Paul, MN 55105
Sec., Dr. Carl O. Pederson, 18284 Springdale Ct., Seattle, WA 98177
Treas., Mr. William A. Kunigk, 7902 52nd St. Ct. W., Tacoma, WA 98467
Dean, Faith Ev. Luth. Sem., Dr. John F. Falk, 7600 Juneau Ct., Port Orchard, WA 98366
Director of Ministries, Dr. Lloyd R. Nelson, 4611 N. 39th, Tacoma, WA 98407

PERIODICALS

Lutherans Alert National (m), P.O. Box 7186, Tacoma, WA 98407, Dr. Paul Vigness, Ed.
Lutheran World Concerns (q), P.O. Box 7186, Tacoma, WA 98407, Rev. Lloyd Nelson, Ed.

RELIGIOUS BODIES IN THE UNITED STATES ARRANGED BY FAMILIES

The following list of religious bodies appearing in the Directory Section of this **Yearbook** shows the "families," or related clusters into which American religious bodies can be grouped. For example, there are many communions that can be grouped under the heading "Baptist" for historical and theological reasons. It is not to be assumed, however, that all denominations under one family heading are similar in belief or practice. Often, any similarity is purely coincidental. The family clusters tend to represent historical factors more often than theological or practical ones. The family categories provided one of the major pitfalls of church statistics because of the tendency to combine the statistics by "families" for analytical and comparative purposes. Such combined totals are almost meaningless, although often used as variables for sociological analysis. **Religious bodies not grouped under family headings appear alphabetically and are not indented in the following list.**

ADVENTIST BODIES

Advent Christian Church
Church of God General Conference (Oregon, IL.)
Primitive Advent Christian Church
Seventh-day Adventists

Amana Church Society
American Evangelical Christian Churches
American Rescue Workers
Apostolic Christian Church (Nazarene)
Apostolic Christian Churches of America
The Anglican Orthodox Church
Baha'i Faith

BAPTIST BODIES

American Baptist Association
American Baptist Churches in the U.S.A.
Baptist Bible Fellowship, International
Baptist General Conference
Baptist Missionary Association of America
Bethel Ministerial Association, Inc.
Conservative Baptist Association of America
Duck River (and Kindred) Associations of Baptists
Free Will Baptists
General Association of Regular Baptist Churches
General Baptists, General Association of
General Conference of the Evangelical Baptist Church, Inc.
General Six-Principle Baptists
Liberty Baptist Fellowship
National Baptist Convention of America
National Baptist Convention, U.S.A., Inc.
National Primitive Baptist Convention, Inc.
North American Baptist General Conference
Primitive Baptists
Progressive National Baptist Convention, Inc.
Separate Baptists in Christ
Seventh Day Baptist General Conference
Southern Baptist Convention
Sovereign Grace Baptists

Berean Fundamental Church

BRETHREN (GERMAN BAPTISTS)

Brethren Church (Ashland, Ohio)
Church of the Brethren
Grace Brethren Churches, Fellowship of
Old German Baptist Brethren

BRETHREN, RIVER

Brethren in Christ Church
United Zion Church

Buddhist Churches of America,
Christadelphians
The Christian and Missionary Alliance
Christian Brethren
Christian Catholic Church

The Christian Congregation
Christian Nation Church U.S.A.
Christian Union
Church of Christ, Scientist
Church of Daniel's Band
The Church of Illumination
Church of the Living God (C.W.F.F.)
Church of the Nazarene
Churches of Christ in Christian Union

CHURCHES OF CHRIST-CHRISTIAN CHURCHES

Christian Church (Disciples of Christ)
Christian Churches and Churches of Christ
Churches of Christ

CHURCHES OF GOD

Church of God (Anderson, Ind.)
Church of God by Faith
The Church of God (Seventh Day), Denver, Colo.,
Church of God (Which He Purchased With His Own Blood)
Churches of God, General Conference

CHURCHES OF THE NEW JERUSALEM

General Church of the New Jerusalem
General Convention, The Swedenborgian Church

Community Churches, International Council of
Congregational Christian Churches, National Association of
Conservative Congregational Christian Conference

EASTERN CHURCHES

Albanian Orthodox Archdiocese in America
Albanian Orthodox Diocese of America
The American Carpatho-Russian Orthodox Greek Catholic Church
The Antiochian Orthodox Christian Archdiocese of N.A.
Apostolic Catholic Assyrian Church of the East, North American Diocese
Armenian Apostolic Church of America
Armenian Church of America, Diocese of the
Bulgarian Eastern Orthodox Church
Coptic Orthodox Church
Greek Orthodox Archdiocese of North and South America
Holy Ukrainian Autocephalic Orthodox Church in Exile
The Orthodox Church in America
Romanian Orthodox Church in America
The Romanian Orthodox Episcopate of America

Russian Orthodox Church in the U.S.A., Patriarchal Parishes of the
The Russian Orthodox Church Outside Russia
Serbian Orthodox Church in the U.S.A. and Canada
Syrian Orthodox Church of Antioch (Archdiocese of the U.S.A. and Canada)
True (Old Calendar) Orthodox Church of Greece (Synod of Metropolitan Cyprian), American Exarchate
Ukrainian Orthodox Church of the U.S.A.
Ukrainian Orthodox Church in America (Ecumenical Patriarchate)

The Episcopal Church
Ethical Culture Movement
Evangelical Church of North America
Evangelical Congregational Church
The Evangelical Covenant Church
The Evangelical Free Church of America
Fellowship of Fundamental Bible Churches
The Fire-Baptized Holiness Church (Wesleyan)
Free Christian Zion Church of Christ

FRIENDS

Evangelical Friends Alliance
Friends General Conference
Friends United Meeting
Religious Society of Friends (Conservative)
Religious Society of Friends (Unaffiliated Meetings)

Grace Gospel Fellowship
The Holiness Church of God, Inc.
House of God, Which is the Church of the Living God, the Pillar and Ground of the Truth, Inc.
Independent Fundamental Churches of America
Israelite House of David
Jehovah's Witnesses
Jews
Kodesh Church of Immanuel

LATTER DAY SAINTS

Church of Christ
The Church of Jesus Christ (Bickertonites)
The Church of Jesus Christ of Latter-day Saints
Reorganized Church of Jesus Christ of Latter Day Saints

The Liberal Catholic Church-Province of the United States of America

LUTHERANS

Apostolic Lutheran Church of America
Church of the Lutheran Brethren of America
Church of the Lutheran Confession
Estonian Evangelical Lutheran Church
Evangelical Lutheran Church in America
Evangelical Lutheran Synod
Free Lutheran Congregations, The Association of
Latvian Evangelical Lutheran Church in America
The Lutheran Church—Missouri Synod
The Protestant Conference (Lutheran)
Wisconsin Evangelical Lutheran Synod
World Confessional Lutheran Association

MENNONITE BODIES

Beachy Amish Mennonite Churches
Church of God in Christ (Mennonite)
Evangelical Mennonite Church
Fellowship of Evangelical Bible Churches

General Conference of Mennonite Brethren Churches
Hutterian Brethren
Mennonite Church
Mennonite Church, The General Conference
Old Order Amish Church
Old Order (Wisler) Mennonite Church
Reformed Mennonite Church

METHODIST BODIES

African Methodist Episcopal Church
African Methodist Episcopal Zion Church
Allegheny Wesleyan Methodist Connection (Original Allegheny Conference)
Christian Methodist Episcopal Church
Evangelical Methodist Church
Free Methodist Church of North America
Fundamental Methodist Church, Inc.
Primitive Methodist Church in the U.S.A.
Reformed Methodist Union Episcopal Church
Reformed Zion Union Apostolic Church
Southern Methodist Church
The United Methodist Church
The Wesleyan Church

The Metropolitan Church Association
Metropolitan Community Churches, Universal Fellowship of
The Missionary Church

MORAVIAN BODIES

Moravian Church in America (Unitas Fratrum)
Unity of the Brethren

Muslims
National Spiritualist Association of Churches
New Apostolic Church of North America
North American Old Roman Catholic Church (Archdiocese of New York)

OLD CATHOLIC CHURCHES

Christ Catholic Church
North American Old Roman Catholic Church

PENTECOSTAL BODIES

*Holiness-Pentecostal Denominations**
The Apostolic Faith
The Church of God
Church of God (Cleveland, Tenn.)
The Church of God in Christ
Church of God in Christ, International
The Church of God of Prophecy
The Church of God of the Mountain Assembly
Congregational Holiness Church
International Pentecostal Church of Christ
The (Original) Church of God
Pentecostal Fire-Baptized Holiness Church
Pentecostal Free-Will Baptist Church, Inc.
Pentecostal Holiness Church, International
United Holy Church of America
*Baptistic-Pentecostal Denominations**
Assemblies of God
The Bible Church of Christ, Inc.
Christian Church of North America, General Council
Elim Fellowship
Full Gospel Assemblies, International
Full Gospel Fellowship of Churches and Ministers, International
Independent Assemblies of God, International
International Church of the Foursquare Gospel

Open Bible Standard Churches
Pentecostal Church of God
*Unitarian (Oneness)-Pentecostal Denominations**
  Apostolic Faith Mission Church of God
  Apostolic Overcoming Holy Church of God
  Bible Way Church of Our Lord Jesus Christ, World
    Wide, Inc.
  Church of Our Lord Jesus Christ of the Apostolic Faith
  Pentecostal Assemblies of the World
  United Pentecostal Church, International
(*The above typology for Pentecostal Bodies was supplied
by Dr. H. Vinson Synan, Asst. Gen. Supt., International
Pentecostal Holiness Church, to whom the editor is
grateful. According to Dr. Synan, "Holiness-Pentecostal"
bodies are those that teach the three stages theory of
Christian experience [i.e., conversion, sanctification,
baptism of the Holy Spirit]. "Baptistic-Pentecostal"
denominations are those that teach a two-stage theory
[i.e., conversion and baptism of the Holy Spirit].
"Unitarian-Pentecostal" bodies deny the traditional concept of the Trinity and teach that Jesus Christ alone is
God.)

Pillar of Fire
Polish National Catholic Church of America

Presbyterian Bodies

  Associate Reformed Presbyterian Church (General
    Synod)
  Cumberland Presbyterian Church
  Evangelical Presbyterian Church
  Korean Presbyterian Church in America,
    General Assembly of the
  The Orthodox Presbyterian Church
  Presbyterian Church in America
  Presbyterian Church in (U.S.A.)
  Reformed Presbyterian Church of North America
  Second Cumberland Presbyterian Church in U.S.

Reformed Bodies

  Christian Reformed Church in North America
  Hungarian Reformed Church in America
  Netherlands Reformed Congregations
  Protestant Reformed Churches in America
  Reformed Church in America
  Reformed Church in the U.S.
  United Church of Christ

Reformed Episcopal Church
The Roman Catholic Church
The Salvation Army
The Schwenkfelder Church
Social Brethren
Triumph the Church and Kingdom of God in Christ
Unitarian Universalist Association

United Brethren Bodies

  United Brethren in Christ
  United Christian Church

Vedanta Society
Volunteers of America
Wesleyan Holiness Association of Churches

4. RELIGIOUS BODIES IN CANADA

A large number of Canadian religious bodies were organized by immigrants from Europe and elsewhere and a smaller number of them sprang up originally on Canadian soil. In the case of Canada, moreover, many denominations overlapping the U.S.-Canadian border have headquarters in the United States.

In the past year, a concerted effort has been made to develop completeness in this directory and much improvement over the previous listing has been made. The editor of the **Yearbook of American and Canadian Churches** would be grateful for information on any major Canadian religious body not now included.

What follows is, first, an alphabetical directory of religious bodies in Canada that have supplied information for this edition of the **Yearbook.** The second section is an alphabetical list, with addresses and other information, of bodies known to exist in Canada that have not yet supplied directory information. This second section is entitled "Other Religious Bodies in Canada."

Those denominations that have not checked and returned their directory for this edition carry the symbol (†) in front of the title.

A listing of Canadian religious bodies classified by family groups (e.g., Baptists) appears at the end of this directory.

Complete statistics for Canadian denominations will be found in the table "Canadian Current and Non-Current Statistics" in Section III of this **Yearbook.** Statistics appearing in the denominational directories which follow are Current only; that is, those gathered in 1987 and 1986:

The Anglican Church of Canada

Anglicanism came to Canada with the early explorers such as Martin Frobisher and Henry Hudson. Continuous services began in Newfoundland about 1700 and in Nova Scotia in 1710. The first Bishop, Charles Inglis, was appointed to Nova Scotia in 1787. The numerical strength of Anglicanism was increased by the coming of American Loyalists and by massive immigration both after the Napoleonic wars and in the later 19th and early 20th centuries.

The Anglican Church of Canada has enjoyed self-government for over a century and is an autonomous member of the worldwide Anglican Communion. The General Synod, which normally meets triennially, consists of the Archbishops, Bishops, and elected clerical and lay representatives of the 30 dioceses. Each of the Ecclesiastical Provinces—Canada, Ontario, Rupert's Land, and British Columbia—is organized under a Metropolitan and has its own Provincial Synod and Executive Council. Each diocese has its own Diocesan Synod.

Churches: 3,169; Inclusive Membership: 851,032; Sunday or Sabbath Schools: 1,913; Total Enrollment: 95,440; Ordained Clergy: 3,180

GENERAL SYNOD OFFICERS

Primate of the Anglican Church of Canada, Most Rev. M. G. Peers, 600 Jarvis St., Toronto, Ontario M4Y 2J6
Prolocutor, Dr. D. Maybee, 600 Jarvis St., Toronto, Ontario M4Y 2J6
Gen. Sec., Ven. D. J. Woeller, 600 Jarvis St., Toronto, Ontario M4Y 2J6
Treas. of Gen. Synod and all Departments, John R. Ligertwood, 600 Jarvis St., Toronto, Ontario M4Y 2J6
Exec. Dir. of Program, Rev. L. C. Raymond.

DEPARTMENTS AND DIVISIONS

Offices: Church House, 600 Jarvis St., Toronto, Ontario M4Y 2J6. Tel. (416)924-9192
Dir. and Publ., Anglican Book Centre, Rev. M. J. Lloyd Missionary Society of the Anglican Church of Canada.
Exec. Sec., Rev. J. S. Barton
Dir. of World Mission: Rev. J. S. Barton
Dir. of Planning: Rev. W. E. Lowe
Division of Pensions: Dir., J. Mason
Dir. of Administration and Finance: J. R. Ligertwood
Dir. of Communications, D. Tindal
Dir. of Resources and Ministry, Rev. D. Hodgkinson
Dir. of Social Action Ministries, Ms. J. Rowles

METROPOLITANS (ARCHBISHOPS)

(Address: The Most Reverend)

Ecclesiastical Province of:
Canada: Harold Nutter, 791 Brunswick St., Fredericton, New Brunswick E3B 1H8. Tel. (506)455-8667
Rupert's Land: _____, 10033 - 84 Ave., Edmonton, Alberta T6E 2G6. Tel. (403)439-7344
British Columbia: Douglas Hambidge, 302-814 Richards St.,Vancouver, British Columbia V6B 3A7, Tel. (604)684-6306
Ontario: John Bothwell, 67 Victoria Ave., S., Hamilton, Ontario L8N 2S8. Tel. (416)527-1117

DIOCESAN ARCHBISHOPS AND BISHOPS

(Address: The Most Reverend; The Right Reverend)
Algoma: L. Peterson, Box 1168, Sault Ste. Marie, Ontario P6A 5N7. Tel. (705)256-5061
Arctic: J. R. Sperry, 1055 Avenue Rd., Toronto, Ontario M5N 2C8. Tel. (416)481-2263
Athabasca: G. Woolsey, Box 279, Peace River, Alberta T0H 2X0. Tel. (403)624-2767
Brandon: J. F. S. Conlin, 341-13th St., Brandon, Manitoba R7A 4P8. Tel. (204)727-7550
British Columbia: R. F. Shepherd, 912 Vancouver St., Victoria, British Columbia V8V 3V7. Tel. (604)386-7781
Caledonia: J. E. Hannen, Box 278, Prince Rupert, British Columbia V8J 3P6. Tel. (604)624-6013
Calgary: J. B. Curtis, 3015 Glencoe Rd. S. W., Calgary, Alberta T2S 2L9. Tel. (403)243-3673
Cariboo: J. S. P. Snowden, 465 Victoria St., Kamloops, British Columbia. V2C 2A9. Tel. (604)374-0237
Edmonton: _____, 110033 - 84 Ave., Edmonton, Alberta T6E 2G6. Tel. (403)439-7344
Fredericton: H. L. Nutter (Archbishop), 791 Brunswick St. Fredericton, New Brunswick E3B 1H8. Tel. (506)455-8667
Huron: Derwyn Jones, 4-220 Dundas St., London, Ontario N6A 1H3, Tel. (519)434-6893
Keewatin: H. J. P. Allan, Box 118, Kenora, Ontario P9N 3X1. Tel. (807)468-7011
Kootenay: R. E. F. Berry, Box 549, Kelowna, British Columbia V1Y 7P2 Tel. (604)762-3306
Montreal: R. Hollis, 1444 Union Ave., Montreal, Quebec H3A 2B8. Tel. (514)845-6211
Moosonee: C. J. Lawrence, Box 841, Schumacher, Ontario P0N 1G0. Tel. (705)267-1129
Eastern Newfoundland and Labrador: M. Mate, 19 King's Bridge Rd., St. John's, Newfoundland A1C 3K4. Tel. (709)726-6697
Central Newfoundland: M. Genge, 34 Fraser Rd., Gander, Newfoundland A1V 1K7 Tel. (709)256-2372
Western Newfoundland, S. S. Payne, 83 West St., Corner Brook, Newfoundland A2H 6H8. Tel. (709)639-8712

New Westminster: D. W. Hambidge (Archbishop), 302-814 Richards St., Vancouver, British Columbia V6B 3A7. Tel. (604)684-6306

Niagara: J. C. Bothwell (Archbishop), 67 Victoria Ave. S., Hamilton, Ontario. L8N 2S8. Tel. (416) 527-1117

Nova Scotia: A. G. Peters, 5732 College St., Halifax, Nova Scotia B3H 1X3. Tel. (902) 420-0717

Ontario: A. A. Read, 90 Johnson St., Kingston, Ontario. K7L 1X7. Tel. (613) 544-4774

Ottawa: E. K. Lackey, 71 Bronson Ave., Ottawa, Ontario K1R 6G6. Tel. (613) 232-7124

Qu'Appelle: E. Bays, 1501 College Ave., Regina, Saskatchewan S4P 1B8. Tel. (306) 522-1608

Quebec: A. Goodings, 36 rue Desjardins, Quebec, Quebec G1R 4L5. Tel. (418) 692-3858

Rupert's Land: W. Jones, 935 Nesbitt Bay, Winnipeg, Manitoba R3T 1W6. Tel. (204) 453-6248

Saskatchewan: T. O. Morgan, Box 1088, Prince Albert, Saskatchewan S6V 5S6. Tel. (306) 763-2455

Saskatoon: R. A. Wood, Box 1965, Saskatoon, Saskatchewan S7K 3S5. Tel. (306) 244-5651

Toronto: L. S. Garnsworthy, 135 Adelaide St., E., Toronto, Ontario M5C 1L8. Tel. (416) 363-6021

Yukon: R. C. Ferris, Box 4247, Whitehorse, Yukon Y1A 3T3. Tel. (403) 667-7746

The Antiochian Orthodox Christian Archdiocese of North America

There are approximately 100,000 members of the Antiochian Orthodox community living in Canada. They are under the jurisdiction of the Patriarch of Antioch and All the East, with headquarters in Damascus, Syria. There are churches in Ottawa, Toronto, Montreal, Edmonton, Halifax, London, Windsor and new missions in Prince Edward Island and other cities.

GENERAL ORGANIZATION

Metropolitan Archbishop, Philip (Saliba), 358 Mountain Rd., Englewood, NJ 07631

In Canada: V. Rev. Anthony Gabriel, St. George's Orthodox Church, 555-575 Jean Talon St., E., Montreal, Quebec H2R 1T8. Tel. (514) 276-8533

Apostolic Christian Church (Nazarene)

This church was formed in Canada as a result of immigration from various European countries. The body began as a movement originated by the Rev. S. H. Froehlich, a Swiss pastor, whose followers are still found in Switzerland and Central Europe.

GENERAL ORGANIZATION

Headquarters: Apostolic Christian Church Foundation, P.O. Box 151, Tremont, IL 61568

OFFICER

Gen. Sec. Eugene R. Galat, P.O. Box 151, Tremont, IL 61568. Tel. (309) 925-5162

PERIODICAL

Newsletter (bi-m)

The Apostolic Church in Canada

The Apostolic Church in Canada is affiliated with the worldwide organization of the Apostolic Church with headquarters in Great Britain.

A product of the Welsh Revival (1904–1908), its Canadian beginnings originated in Nova Scotia in 1927. Today its main centers are in Nova Scotia, Ontario, and Quebec.

This church is evangelical, fundamental, and Pentecostal, with special emphasis on the ministry gifts listed in Ephesians 4:11-12.

GENERAL ORGANIZATION

The Apostolic Church Council, twice yearly.

OFFICERS

Pres., Rev. D. S. Morris, 685 Park St. South, Peterborough, Ontario K9J 3S9

Natl. Sec., Rev. J. Kristensen, 388 Gerald St., Ville La Salle, Quebec H8P 2A5

Apostolic Church of Pentecost of Canada Inc.

This body was founded in 1921 at Winnipeg, Manitoba, by Pastor Frank Small. Doctrines include belief in eternal salvation by the grace of God, baptism of the Holy Spirit with the evidence of speaking in tongues, water baptism by emersion in the name of the Lord Jesus Christ.

GENERAL ORGANIZATION

Annual Ministers Conference: Next meeting June 7-9, 1988, Regina, Saskatchewan

Headquarters: 105, 31 Manning Cres. N.E., Calgary, Alberta T2E 7M9

OFFICERS

Moderator, Rev. W. S. Schindel, 105, 31 Manning Cres. N.E., Calgary, Alberta T2E 7M9

Clerk, D. Earle Jellison, 105, 31 Manning Cres. N.E., Calgary, Alberta T2E 7M9

Missionary Council Chpsn., E. G. Bradley, Box 322, Maple Ridge, British Columbia V2X 702

PERIODICAL

End Times' Messenger (11/yr.), 105, 31 Manning Cres. N.E., Calgary, Alberta T2E 7M9. I. W. Ellis, Ed.

The Armenian Church of North America, Diocese of Canada

The Canadian branch of the ancient Church of Armenia founded in A.D. 301 by St. Gregory the Illuminator. It was established in Canada at St. Catherines, Ontario, in 1930. The diocesan organization is under the jurisdiction of the Holy See of Etchmiadzin, Armenia, U.S.S.R. The Diocese has churches in St. Catherine, Hamilton, Toronto, Scarborough, Ottawa, Vancouver, and Montreal.

GENERAL ORGANIZATION

Diocesan Offices: His Eminence Bishop Vazken Keshishian Primate, Canadian Diocese, 615 Stuart Ave., Outremont, Quebec H2V 3H2. Tel. (514) 276-9479

PERIODICALS

Nor Serount (m) in Armenian and English, 14 Woodlawn Ave., Toronto, Ontario M4V 1G7.

Pourastan (m) in Armenian, 615 Stuart Ave., Montreal, Quebec H2V 3H2

Varaka Soorp Khatch (m), 225, Van Horne Ave., #1105, Toronto, Ontario M4V 2T9

Avedaper (m) in Armenian and English, St. Mary Armenian Church, 8 Mayhurst Ave., Hamilton, Ontario L8K 3M8

Avarayr, in Armenian and English, St. Vartan Armenian Church, 1260 W. 67th Ave., Vancouver, British Columbia V6P 2T2

Armenian Evangelical Church

Founded in 1960 by immigrant Armenian evangelical families from the Middle East. This body is conservative doctrinally, with an evangelical, biblical emphasis. The polity of churches within the group differ with congregationalism being dominant, but there are Presbyterian Armenian Evangelical churches as well. Most of the local churches have joined main-line denominations. All of the Armenian Evangelical (Congregational or Presbyterian) local churches in the U.S. and Canada have joined with the Armenian Evangelical Union of North America.

GENERAL ORGANIZATION

Armenian Evangelical Union of North America. Meets every two years. Next convention, June 1988.

A.E.U.N.A. OFFICERS

Moderator, Rev. Dr. Vahan Toutigian, (1986-88), 3922 Yorba Linda, Royal Oak, MI 48072
Minister to the Union, Rev. Harry M. Missirlian, 1743 West Vartikian Ave., Fresno, CA 93711

ARMENIAN EVANGELICAL CHURCH OFFICERS

Minister, Rev. Yessayi Sarmazian, 42 Glenforest Rd., Toronto, Ontario M4N 1Z8. Tel. (416) 489-3188

PERIODICAL

Canada Armenian Press (q), 42 Glenforest Rd., Toronto, Ontario M4N 1Z8. Rev. Y. Sarmazian, Ed.

Associated Gospel Churches

The Associated Gospel Churches (A.G.C.) body traces its historical roots to the early years of the twentieth century, which were marked by the growth of liberal theology in many established denominations. Many individuals and, in many cases, whole congregations, seeking to uphold the final authority of the Scriptures in all matters of faith and conduct, withdrew from those denominations.

As a result, churches which fostered an evangelical ministry under the inspired Word of God were established. These churches defended the belief that "all Scripture is given by inspiration of God" and also declared that the Holy Spirit "gave the identical words of sacred writings of holy men of old, chosen by Him to be the channel of His revelation to man."

In 1922, four churches of similar background in Ontario banded together in fellowship for counsel and coopera- tion. Known as The Christian Workers' Church in Canada, the group consisted of the Gospel Tabernacle, Hamilton; the Winona Gospel Tabernacle; the Missionary Taberna- cle, Toronto; and West Hamilton Gospel Mission. The principal organizers were Dr. P. W. Philpott of Hamilton and H. E. Irwin, K. C., of Toronto.

In 1925 the name was changed to Associated Gospel Churches under a new Dominion Charter. Since that time the A.G.C. has grown steadily. Currently there are about 115 churches across Canada, with approximately 17,000 worshipers.

GENERAL ORGANIZATION

Annual Conference. A 13-member Cabinet acts in the interim.
Headquarters: 280 Plains Rd. W., Burlington, Ontario L7T 1G4

OFFICERS

Pres., Rev. William Sifft, RR#2, Hamilton, Ontario L8N 2Z7. Tel. (416)659-1249
Vice-Pres., Rev. A. F. Penner, 239 Maunsell Close, N.E., Calgary, Alberta. Tel. (403)277-9167
Mod., Rev. R. G. Gannett, 924 Park Ave., W., Burlington, Ontario L7T 1N7. Tel. (416)636-8266
Sec.-Treas., Rev. D. C. Ralph 976 Brucedale Ave., E., Hamilton, Ontario L8T 1M4. Tel. (416)575-9072

PERIODICALS

Advance (q), Box 3203, Sta. C, Hamilton, Ontario L8H 7K6. Rev. W. Foster, Ed.

Association of Regular Baptist Churches (Canada)

Organized in 1957 by a group of churches for the purpose of mutual cooperation in missionary activities. The Association believes the Bible to be God's word, stands for historic Baptist principles, and opposes modern ecumenism.

Headquarters: 337 Jarvis St., Toronto, Ontario, M5B 2C7. Tel. (416) 925-3261

OFFICERS

Pres., Rev. Stephen Kring, 25 Sovereen St., Delhi, Ontario N4B 1L6
Field Sec., Rev. Tom Rush, Oromocto, New Brunswick
Sec., Rev. W. P. Bauman, 337 Jarvis St., Toronto, Ontario M5B 2C7

PERIODICAL

The Gospel Witness, 130 Gerrard St. E., Toronto, Ontario M5A 3T4. Rev. N. H. Street, Ed.

Bahá'í Faith

(National Spiritual Assembly of the Bahá'ís of Canada).

Bahá'ís are followers of Bahá'u'lláh (1817-1892) whose religion teaches the essential oneness of all the great religions and promotes the oneness of mankind and racial unity.

The Bahá'í administrative order consists of nine-mem- ber elected institutions called spiritual assemblies, which function at the local and national level. The international administrative institution, the Universal House of Justice, is located in Haifa, Israel, at the Bahá'í World Centre, the spiritual headquarters of the Bahá'í community and the burial place of its founders.

In Canada, the Bahá'í Faith is administered by the National Spiritual Assembly. This body was incorporated by Act of Parliament in 1949. There are approximately 1500 Bahá'í centers in Canada, of which 350 elect local Spiritual Assemblies.

GENERAL ORGANIZATION

Bahá'í National Centre of Canada: 7200 Leslie St., Thornhill, Ontario L3T 6L8. Sec., Dr. H. B. Danesh

Baptist General Conference of Canada

Founded in Canada by missionaries from the United States. Originally a Swedish body, but no longer an ethnic body. The BGC-Canada includes people of many nation- alities and is conservative and evangelical in doctrine and practice.

Head Office: #3,9833-44 Ave., Edmonton, Alberta T6E 5E. Tel. (403) 438-9127

OFFICERS

Pres. Rev. Wayne Wicks, 52 Peacock Dr., Sherwood Park, Alberta T8A 3N6
Exec. Dir., Rev. Abe Funk, 11635-51st Ave., Edmonton, Alberta T6M OM4. Tel. (403) 435-4403

DISTRICTS

1. *The Central Canada Baptist Conference*
   Central Baptist Conference, originally a Scandinavian group, is one of three districts of the Baptist General Conference of Canada. In 1907, churches from Winni- peg—Grant Memorial, Teulon, Kenora, Port Arthur, Sprague, Erickson, and Midale—organized under the leadership of Fred Palmberg. Immigration from Sweden declined, and in 1947 only nine churches remained. In 1948

the group dropped the Swedish language, withdrew from the Baptist Union, city churches were started, and today CCBC has 37 functioning churches.

An evangelical Baptist association holding to the inerrancy of the Bible, CCBC seeks to reach Central Canada for Christ by establishing local gospel-preaching churches.

CCBC offers pastoral aid to new churches, loans for building, recommendations as to pastoral supply, counsel, and fellowship. It encourages contributions to the CCBC and BGC of Canada budgets, the purchase of CCBC Serial Notes, support of the Conference BATT program (contributions to special needs of churches), and other projects to assist needy churches and pastors.

The Annual Conference in May

Head Office: 1850 Ness Ave., Winnipeg, Manitoba R3J 3J9. Tel. (204) 837-2679

OFFICERS

Exec. Min., Roy A. Campbell, 712-376 Osborne St., S., Winnipeg, Manitoba R2L 2V3

PERIODICAL

The Christian Link (m)

2. *Baptist General Conference of Alberta*

Annual Conference in June

Head Office: #4, 9825-44 Ave., Edmonton, Alberta T6E 5E3. Tel. (403) 438-9126

OFFICERS

Exec. Sec., Virgil Olson, 1943-104A St., Edmonton, Alberta. T6J 5C1

PERIODICAL

The Alberta Alert, # 4, 9825-44th Ave., Edmonton, Alberta T6E 5E3.

†3. *British Columbia Baptist Conference*

British Columbia Baptist Conference is a district of the Baptist General Conference of Canada, with roots in Sweden, where Christians began to read the Bible in their homes. One convert, F. O. Nilsson, saw the significance of baptism subsequent to a personal commitment to Christ; he went to Hamburg, Germany, where he was baptized in the Elbe River by Rev. John Oncken. When Nilsson returned to Sweden five of his converts were baptized in the North Sea and, with him, formed the first Swedish Baptist Church. Nilsson was imprisoned by the local government for violation of state church regulations and later, when exiled from Sweden, went to the United States. As Swedish Baptists immigrated to the United States to escape persecution, they formed churches in Illinois, Iowa, Minnesota, and Wisconsin and carried on aggressive evangelism among other immigrating Swedes. In 1879 they formed the Swedish Baptist General Conference of America, later named The Baptist General Conference.

Columbia Baptist Conference, with churches in Washington, Oregon, Idaho, Montana, and Alaska, is a district of the Baptist General Conference. In 1910 Columbia Baptist Conference planted a new church in Matsqui, B.C., and by 1985 there were 20 Baptist General Conference churches in B.C. These 20 churches voted in June 1985 to become a new and separate district of the Baptist General Conference of Canada. There are strong ties of fellowship and involvement in special retreats and camping programs with the Columbia District, but the B.C. churches are a separate corporate entity, one of three districts in the Baptist General Conference of Canada, which has 70 churches, from Thunder Bay, Ontario, to Victoria, B.C.

The Swedish language is a cherished heritage of Baptist General Conference churches in the United States and Canada, but by 1935 the churches had become totally English-speaking. In recent years they have become multiethnic, ministering in Filipino, Hindi, Japanese, Chinese, and French, as well as English. A very low percentage of members have any Swedish connection.

The churches in British Columbia Baptist Conference are conservative in theology, evangelistic in activity, irenic in spirit, and pietistic in life-style. They participate with other Baptists and evangelical churches in cooperative ministries.

Annual Conference in May.

Head Office: 10330-144th St., Surrey, British Columbia V3T 4V3.

OFFICERS

Exec. Min., John H. Bergeson, 10330-144th St., Surrey, British Columbia V3T 4V3

PERIODICAL

B.C. Conference Call, 10330-144th St., Surrey, British Columbia V3T 4V3. Rev. John Bergeson, Ed.

The Bible Holiness Movement

The Bible Holiness Movement, organized in 1949 as an outgrowth of the city mission work of the late Pastor William James Elijah Wakefield, an early-day Salvation Army officer, has been headed since its inception by his son, Evangelist Wesley H. Wakefield, its bishop-general.

It derives its emphasis on the original Methodist faith of salvation and scriptural holiness from the late Bishop R. C. Horner. It adheres to the common evangelical faith in the Bible, the Deity, and the atonement of Christ, and stresses a personal experience of salvation for the repentant sinner, of being wholly sanctified for the believer, and of the fullness of the Holy Spirit for effective witness.

Membership involves a life of Christian love, evangelistic and social activism, and the disciplines of simplicity and separation. This includes total abstinence from liquor and tobacco, nonattendance at popular amusements, and no membership in secret societies. Home permanency is affirmed by forbidding divorce and remarriage while there is a living spouse. Similar to Wesley's Methodism, members are, under some circumstances, allowed to retain membership in other evangelical church fellowships.

Government and ordination within the Movement is open to both men and women and is fully interracial and international. A number of interchurch affiliations are maintained with other Wesleyan-Arminian Holiness denominations.

The Movement is activist in both evangelism and social concern. Year-round evangelistic outreach is maintained through open-air meetings, visitation, literature, and other media. Noninstitutional welfare work, including addiction counseling, is conducted among minorities. There is direct overseas famine relief, as well as civil rights action, environment protection, and antinuclearism.

Sponsored organizations include a permanent committee on religious freedom and an active promotion of Christian racial equality.

Headquartered in Vancouver, Canada, the Movement has a world outreach with branches in the United States, India, Nigeria, Philippines, Ghana, Liberia, Cameroons, Kenya, Zambia, South Korea, and Haiti. It also ministers to 89 countries in 42 languages through literature, radio, and audio-cassettes.

Churches: 11; Inclusive Membership: 632; Sunday or Sabbath Schools: N.R.; Total Enrollment: N.R.; Ordained Clergy: 10

International Headquarters: Box 223 Postal Stn. A, Vancouver, British Columbia V6C 2M3. Tel. (604)498-3895

DIRECTORS

Evangelist Wesley H. Wakefield, Bishop-General. (International Leader)

Evangelist M. J. Wakefield, Oliver, British Columbia
Evangelist Napoleon Sneed, #58, 5400 Dalhousie Rd., N.W., Calgary, Alberta
Evangelist C. C. Jamandre, Sagunto, Sison, Pangasinan, Philippines 0733
Pastor Daniel Stinnett, 1425 Mountain View W. Phoenix, AZ 85021
Pastor A. Sanon, Port-au-Prince, Haiti
Evangelist U. E. Udom, Ikona, Nigeria, West Africa
Pastor Augustus Theo Seongbae, Jr., Monrovia, Liberia
Pastor Choe Chong Dee, Cha Pa Puk, South Korea
Mr. E. Payako, Kenya, East Africa

PERIODICAL

Truth on Fire (bi-m), Box 223 Postal Stn. A., Vancouver, British Columbia V6C 2M3. Rev. Wesley H. Wakefield, Ed.

Brethren in Christ Church, Canadian Conference

The Brethren in Christ, formerly known as Tunkers in Canada, arose out of a religious awakening in Lancaster County, Pa., late in the eighteenth century. Representatives of the new denomination reached Ontario in 1788 and established the church in the southern part of the present province. Presently the conference has congregations in Ontario, Alberta, and Saskatchewan. In doctrine the body is evangelical, Arminian, holiness, and premillennial.

Churches: 34; Inclusive Membership: 3,440; Sunday or Sabbath Schools: 31; Total Enrollment: 2,941; Ordained Clergy: 48.

Headquarters: 301 N. Elm St., Nappanee, IN 46550. Tel. (219) 773-3164. Canadian Headquarters (Bishop's office): 1301 Niagara Pkwy., Ft. Erie, Ontario L2A 5M4. Tel. (416)382-3144

OFFICERS

Mod., Bishop Harvey Sider, 1301 Niagara Pkwy., Ft. Erie, Ontario L2A 5M4. Tel. (416)382-3144
Sec., Leonard J. Chester, 20 Morgandale Cres., Agincourt, Ontario M1W 1S3

PERIODICAL

Evangelical Visitor (bi-w), Nappanee, IN 46550. Glenn A. Pierce

†British Methodist Episcopal Church of Canada

The British Methodist Episcopal Church was organized in 1856 in Chatham, Ontario and incorporated in 1913. It has congregations across the Province of Ontario.

GENERAL ORGANIZATION

Annual Conference: First week in July
Headquarters: 460 Shaw St., Toronto, Ontario M6G 3L3. Tel. (416)534-3831.

OFFICERS

Gen. Supt., _____
Asst. Gen. Supt., Rev. Dr. D. D. Rupwate
Gen. Sec., Rev. Dr. W. Solomon
Treas., _____

Buddhist Churches of Canada

Founded at Vancouver, British Columbia in 1904. The first minister was the Rev. Senju Sasaki. This body is the Mahayana division of Buddhism, and its sectarian belief is the Pure Land School based on the Three Canonical Scriptures with emphasis on pure faith.

GENERAL ORGANIZATION

Registered Office: 918 Bathurst St., Toronto, Ontario M5R 3G5
Administration Headquarters: 220 Jackson Ave., Vancouver, British Columbia V6A 3B3. Tel. (604)253-7033
Office of the Bishop: Bishop Toshio Murakami, 918 Bathurst St., Toronto, Ontario M5R 3G5. Tel. (416)534-4302
B.C.C. Ministerial Association: Pres., Kyojo Ikuta; Sec., Rev. Itsuo Tesaski

OFFICERS

Pres., Mr. Roy Akune
Vice-Pres., Mr. Max Ikuta
Sec., Mr. Roy Inouye
Treas., Mr. Cy Saimoto

PERIODICAL

Canadian Buddist (m).

Canadian Baptist Federation

The Canadian Baptist Federation has four federated member bodies: (1)Baptist Convention of Ontario and Quebec, (2)Baptist Union of Western Canada, (3)the United Baptist Convention of the Atlantic Provinces, (4)Union d'Eglises Baptistes Françaises au Canada (French Baptist Union). Its main purpose is to act as a coordinating agency for the four groups.

Churches: 1,131; Inclusive Membership: 129,757; Sunday or Sabbath Schools: 901; Total Enrollment: 71,944; Ordained Clergy: 1,107

GENERAL ORGANIZATION

Office: 7185 Millcreek Dr., Mississauga, Ontario L5N 5R4 Tel. (416)826-0191

OFFICERS

Pres., Mrs. Shirley Bentall, Apt. H 202, 500 Eau Claire Ave. SW, Calgary, Alberta T2P 3R8
Vice-Presidents, Dr. Maurice Boillet, 3674 rue Ontario est, Montreal, Quebec H1W 1R9; Mr. Robert MacQuade, 54 Bessborough Ave., Moncton, New Brunswick E1E 4A2; Mrs. Lois Crofoot, 30 Edgevalley Dr., Islington, Ontario M9A 4N9
Gen. Sec.-Treas., Dr. Richard Coffin, 7185 Millcreek Dr., Mississauga, Ontario L5N 5R4
Gen. Sec., Canadian Baptist Overseas Mission Board, 7185 Millcreek Dr., Mississauga, Ontario L5N 5R4

1. *Baptist Convention of Ontario and Quebec*
The Baptist Convention of Ontario and Quebec was formally organized in 1888 as a convention of churches. McMaster University was founded in 1887.
The Convention has two educational institutions— the Baptist Leadership Education Centre at Whitby, for training lay leaders, and McMaster Divinity College in Hamilton, for training in pastoral/missionary leadership.
Overseas, the Convention works through the all-Canada missionary agency, the Canadian Baptist Overseas Mission Board. The churches also support the Sharing Way, the relief and development arm of the Canadian Baptist Federation.

Office: 217 St. George St., Toronto, Ontario M5R 2M2. Tel. (416)922-5163

Churches: 387; Inclusive Membership: 45,397; Sunday or Sabbath Schools: 319; Total Enrollment: 15,471; Ordained Clergy: 542

NOTE: *The above statistics are a subtotal for the Baptist Federation of Canada whose total statistics are reported initially.*

OFFICERS

Pres., Judge Ernest F. West, Waterloo, Ontario
1st Vice-Pres., Mr. Kenneth Barnard, , Beaconsfield, Quebec
Gen. Sec., Rev. Albert E. Coe, 217 St. George St. Toronto, Ontario M5R 2M2
Treas., Mr. Peter Kaups, Toronto, Ontario

DEPARTMENTS

Dept. of Canadian Missions: Chpsn., Rev. Murray Stovell, Stoney Creek, Ontario; Exec. Sec., Rev. Robert Wilkins, Toronto, Ontario
Dept. of Christian Education: Chpsn., Rev. Lionel Pye, Cambellford, Ontario; Actg. Exec. Sec., Rev. John Coutts, Toronto, Ontario
Dept. of Communication and Stewardship: Chpsn., Mrs. Esther Morgan, Kitchener, Ontario; Exec. Sec., Rev. Phil Karpetz, Toronto, Ontario
Dept. of Ministry: Mr. Russell Lott, Guelph, Ontario; Exec. Sec., Rev. George W. Scott, Brampton, Ontario

PERIODICAL

The Canadian Baptist, 217 St. George St., Toronto, Ontario M5R 2M2. Rev. Dr. William H. Jones, Islington, Ontario, Ed.

2. *Baptist Union of Western Canada, The*

Office: 202, 838-11th Ave. S.W., Calgary, Alberta T2R 0E5. Tel. (403) 234-9044

Churches: 162; Inclusive Membership: 21,297; Sunday or Sabbath Schools: 144; Total Enrollment: 14,137; Ordained Clergy: 228
Note: *The above statistics are a subtotal for the Baptist Federation of Canada whose total statistics are reported initially.*

OFFICERS

Pres., Mr. Lawrence Milner
Exec. Minister, Rev. Douglas N. Moffat
Assoc. Exec. Minister, Dr. C. Howard Bentall
Area Minister, Alberta, Rev. J. Dozois, 43 Strathbury Cir. SW, Calgary, Alberta T3H 1R9
Area Minister, British Columbia, Rev. William Cram, 201-7 St., New Westminster, British Columbia V3M 3K2
Area Minister, Manitoba, Saskatchewan, Rev. Ralph Orvis, 30 Eglinton Cr., Winnipeg, Manitoba R3Y 1E7; Assoc. Area Minister, Rev. Robert McLaren, 257 Laurentian Dr., Saskatoon, Saskatchewan S7H 4R8
Dir., of Stewardship and Church Growth, Rev. J. Farr, 202, 838-11 Ave. SW, Calgary, Alberta T2R 0E5
Dir. of Cong. Resources, Rev. Gerald Fisher, 14 Milford Cr., Sherwood Park, Alberta T8A 3V4
Principal, Carey Hall (Ministerial Education), Rev. Philip Collins, 5920 Iona Dr., Vancouver, British Columbia V6T 1J6; Field Edu. Dir., Rev. Philip Collins, 5920 Iona Dr., Vancouver, B.C., V6T 1J6
Principal, Baptist Leadership Training School (Lay), Rev. Ken Bellous, 4330-16 Street, SW, Calgary, Alberta T2T 4H9

3. *United Baptist Convention of the Atlantic Provinces*
The United Baptist Convention of the Atlantic Provinces is the largest Baptist Convention in Canada. Through the Canadian Baptist Federation, it is a member of the Baptist World Alliance.
Work in Canada began in the Atlantic Provinces in the 1700s when Baptists from New England began to migrate into the area. The Rev. Ebenezer Moulton organized a Baptist Church in Horton (now Wolfville, Nova Scotia) in 1763. The present church in Wolfville was formed in 1778 and is Canada's oldest continuing Baptist church. The United Baptist Convention was

formed in 1905 when Calvinistic and Free Baptist churches merged; thus the name United Baptist is often used.
The first Baptist Association in Canada met in Nova Scotia in 1800. Today there are 21 Associations (usually comprised of one or two counties) within the convention. Through the Canadian Baptist Overseas Mission Board they support more than 100 missionaries in India, Kenya, Zaire, Brazil, Bolivia, Indonesia, and Sri Lanka. They have an active program of evangelism, Christian education, and church planting. They own and operate two colleges: Atlantic Baptist College in Moncton, New Brunswick, and Acadia Divinity College in Wolfville, Nova Scotia, which provides training for those entering the ministry and overseas missions. The convention operates five senior citizens' homes and a Christian bookstore.

Office: 1655 Manawagonish Rd., Saint John, New Brunswick, E2M 3Y2

Churches: 560; Inclusive Membership: 61,972; Sunday or Sabbath Schools: 450; Total Enrollment: 41,031; Ordained Clergy: 321
Note: *The above statistics are a subtotal for the Baptist Federation of Canada whose total statistics are reported initially.*

OFFICERS

Pres., Dr. Allison Trites, Acadia Divinity College, Wolfville, Nova Scotia B0P 1X0
Exec. Min., Dr. Eugene Thompson, 1655 Manawagonish Rd., Saint John, New Brunswick E2M 3Y2
Administrator-Treas., Rev. W. E. O'Grady, 1655 Manawagonish Rd., Saint John, New Brunswick E2M 3Y2
Dir. of Evangelism, Rev. Jeff Brooks, 1655 Manawagonish Rd., Sai)nt John, New Brunswick E2M 3Y2
Dir. of Christian Training, Rev. Harold Arbo, 1655 Manawagonish Rd., Saint John, New Brunswick E2M 3Y2
Dir. of Church Extension, Rev. Harry Gardner, 1665 Manawagonish Rd., St. John, New Brunswick E2M 2Y2

PERIODICAL

The Atlantic Baptist, Box 756, Kentville, Nova Scotia B4N 3X9. Rev. Michael Lipe, Ed.

4. *Union of French Baptist Churches in Canada* (Union d'Eglises Baptistes Françaises au Canada)
Baptist churches in French Canada first came into being through the labors of two missionaries from Switzerland, Rev. Louis Roussy and Mme. Henriette Feller, who arrived in Canada in 1835. The earliest church was organized in Grande Ligne (now St-Blaise), Québec, in 1838.
By 1900, there were 7 churches in the province of Quebec, together with 13 French-language Baptist churches in the New England states, where massive immigration from Quebec had taken place. The leadership was totally French Canadian.
By 1960, the process of Americanization had caused the disappearance of the French Baptist churches. A similar, but far less drastic process of Anglicization of all French Protestants took place in Quebec through the public (Protestant) school system, which was totally English-speaking. The school language situation changed very rapidly after 1960.
During the 1960s Quebec, as a society, entered into a very rapid change in all its facets: education, politics, social values, structures, etc. This has been called The Quiet Revolution. A veritable movement of mission, evangelism and church growth has once again become possible. In 1969, desiring to respond to the new conditions, the Grande Ligne Mission passed control of its work to the newly formed Union of French Baptist Churches in Canada, which at the time included 8 churches. By 1987, the French Canadian Baptist move-

ment has grown to include 22 churches, plus a few nucleus congregations.

The Union d'Eglises Baptistes Françaises au Canada is a member body of the Canadian Baptist Federation and thus is affiliated with the Baptist World Alliance.

Headquarters: 2285 avenue Papineau, Montreal, Quebec H2K 4J5. Tel. (514)526-6643. Gen. Sec., Rev. John Gilmour

Churches: 22; Inclusive Membership: 1,091; Sunday or Sabbath Schools: 22; Total Enrollment: 1,305; Ordained Clergy: 16

Note: *The above statistics are a subtotal for the Baptist Federation of Canada whose total statistics are reported initially.*

Canadian Convention of Southern Baptists

The Canadian Convention of Southern Baptists was formed at the Annual Meeting, May 7-9, 1985, in Kelowna, British Columbia. It was formerly known as the Canadian Baptist Conference, founded in Kamloops, British Columbia, in 1959 by pastors of existing churches.

Churches: 81; Inclusive Membership: 5,200; Sunday or Sabbath Schools: 81; Total Enrollment: 6,000; Ordained Clergy: 67

Office: #210, 5403 Crowchild Trail N.W., Calvary, Alberta T3B 4Z1. Tel. (403)247-3113

OFFICERS

Exec. Dir.-Treas., Allen E. Schmidt, Box 7, Site 4, R. R. 1, Cochrane, Alberta T0L 0W0
Pres., Philip Yung, Goodnews Baptist Church, Box 67716, Vancouver, British Columbia V5W 3V2

The Canadian Yearly Meeting of the Religious Society of Friends

Founded in Canada as an offshoot of the Quaker movement in colonial America. Genesee Yearly Meeting, founded 1834, Canada Yearly Meeting (Orthodox), founded in 1867, and Canada Yearly Meeting, founded in 1881, united in 1955 to form the Canadian Yearly Meeting. The Canadian Yearly Meeting is affiliated with the Friends United Meeting and the Friends General Conference.

Churches: 28; Inclusive Membership: 1,866; Sunday or Sabbath Schools: N.R.; Total Enrollment: 184; Ordained Clergy: None

GENERAL ORGANIZATION

Meeting: annual
Headquarters: 60 Lowther Ave., Toronto, Ontario M5R 1C7. Tel. (416)922-2632

CLERK

Donald Laitin, 60 Lowther Ave., Toronto, Ontario M5R 1C7

PERIODICAL

The Canadian Friend, Dorothy Parshall, Ed.

The Christian and Missionary Alliance in Canada

A Canadian movement, dedicated to the teaching of Jesus Christ the Saviour, Sanctifier, Healer and Coming King, commenced in Toronto in 1887 under the leadership of the Rev. John Salmon. Two years later the movement united with The Christian Alliance of New York, founded by Rev. A. B. Simpson, becoming the Dominion Auxiliary

of the Christian Alliance, Toronto, under the presidency of the Hon. William H. Howland. Its four founding branches were Toronto, Hamilton, Montreal and Quebec.

In 1980 the Christian and Missionary Alliance in Canada became autonomous. Its General Assembly is held every two years.

Churches: 289; Inclusive Membership: 59,733; Sunday or Sabbath Schools: 289; Total Enrollment: 43,942; Ordained Clergy: N.R.

NATIONAL LEADERSHIP

Pres., Rev. Melvin Sylvester, Box 7900, Postal Sta. B, Willowdale, Ontario M2K 2R6
Exec. Vice-Pres., Mr. Gerald L. Fowler
Dir. of Pers. and Missions, Rev. Arnold L. Cook
Dir. of Stewardship, Rev. Ronald L. Frentz
Sec., Rev. Donald P. Olsen
Treas., Mr. Milton H. Quigg

CTS

Canadian Pacific: Rev. Gordon R. Fowler, Supt.
Western Canadian: Rev. Harvey A. Town, Supt.
Canadian Midwest: Rev. Arnold Downey, Supt.
Eastern and Central: Rev. Robert J. Gould, Supt.
St. Lawrence: Rev. Jesse D. Jespersen, Supt.

Christian Brethren (Also known as Plymouth Brethren)

An orthodox and evangelical movement which began in the British Isles in the 1820's and is now worldwide. Congregations are usually simply called "assemblies." The name "Plymouth Brethren" was given by others because the group in Plymouth, England was a large congregation. In recent years the term Christian Brethren has replaced Plymouth Brethren for the "open" branch of the movement in Canada and British Commonwealth countries, and to some extent in the U.S.

Unwillingness to establish a denominational structure makes the autonomy of local congregations an important feature of the movement. Other features are weekly observance of the Lord's Supper and adherence to the doctrinal position of conservative, evangelical Christianity.

In the 1840's the movement divided. The "exclusive" branch, led by John Darby, stressed the interdependence of congregations. Since disciplinary decisions were held to be binding on all assemblies, exclusives had sub-divided into seven or eight main groups by the end of the century. Since 1925 a trend toward reunification has reduced that number to three or four. Canadian congregations number approximately 150, with an inclusive membership estimated at 11,000.

The "open" branch of the movement, stressing evangelism and foreign missions, is now the larger of the two. Following the leadership of George Muller in rejecting the "Exclusive" principle of binding discipline, this branch has escaped large-scale division. Canadian congregations number approximately 450, with an inclusive membership estimated at 41,000. There are 200 "commended" full-time ministers, not including foreign missionaries.

GENERAL ORGANIZATION

For Quebec: Christian Brethren Church in the Province of Quebec, 222 Alexander St., Sherbrooke, Quebec J1H 4S7, Norman R. Buchanan, Sec. (No General Organization for other provinces)Tel. (819)562-9198
Correspondent for North America: Interest Ministries, Bruce R. McNicol, Pres., 218 W. Willow, Wheaton, IL 60187. Tel. (312)653-6573

OTHER ORGANIZATIONS

Missionary Service Committee, William Coffey, Exec.

Dir., 1562A Danforth Ave., Toronto, Ontario M4J 1N4. Tel. (416)469-2012

PERIODICALS

Interest Magazine (m), 218 W. Willow, Wheaton, IL 60187

Missions Magazine (m), 1562A Danforth Ave., Toronto, Ontario M4J 1N4

News of Quebec (q), 222 Alexander St., Sherbrooke, Quebec J1H 4S7, Richard Strout, Ed.

Christian Church (Disciples of Christ) in Canada

Disciples have been in Canada since 1810 but were organized nationally in 1922 when the All-Canada Committee was formed. It seeks to serve the Canadian context as part of the whole Christian Church (Disciples of Christ)in the United States and Canada.

Churches: 37; Inclusive Membership: 4,665; Sunday or Sabbath Schools: 37; Total Enrollment: 1,008; Ordained Clergy: 49

Headquarters: 55 Cork St. E., Ste. 303, Guelph, Ontario N1H 2W7. Tel. (519)823-5190

OFFICERS

Moderator, Rev. Steven Dobbins, c/o Westlock Community Church of Christ, Box 1126, Westlock, Alberta T0G 2L0

Vice-Moderator, Mrs. Marilyn Hodgson, 3228 Crosstree Ct., Mississauga, Ontario L5L 1G7

Exec. Reg. Min., Rev. Robert W. Steffer, 7 Lynwood Dr., Guelph, Ontario N1G 1P8

PERIODICAL

Canadian Disciple (4/yr.), 240 Home St., Winnipeg, Manitoba R3G 1X3. Rev. Raymond Cuthbert, Ed.

Christian Churches and Churches of Christ in Canada

This fellowship, dedicated to the "restoration of the New Testament Church in doctrine, ordinances and life," has been operating in Canada since 1820. There is no general organization. Each church within the fellowship is completely independent. For detailed information see: Directory of the Ministry, Christian Churches and Churches of Christ, 1525 Cherry Rd., Springfield, IL 62704, U.S.A.

Churches: 70; Inclusive Membership; 5,946; Sunday or Sabbath Schools: N.R.; Total Enrollment: N.R.; Ordained Clergy: 75

Christian Reformed Church in North America

The Christian Reformed Church in North America represents the historic faith of Protestantism and is creedally united in the Belgic Confession (1561), the Heidelberg Catechism (1563), and the Canons of Dort (1618-19). The denomination was founded in the U.S. in 1857. Canadian congregations have been formed since 1908.

Churches: 199; Inclusive Membership: 83,662; Sunday or Sabbath Schools: 197; Total Enrollment: 19,181; Ordained Clergy: 231

GENERAL ORGANIZATION

Synod: Annual (June)
United States Office: 2850 Kalamazoo Ave., S.E., Grand Rapids, MI 49560. Tel. (616)246-0744.

Canadian Office: 3475 Mainway P.O. Box 5070, Burlington, Ontario L7R 3Y8. Tel. (416)336-2920

OFFICERS

Stated Clerk, Rev. Leonard J. Hofman, 2850 Kalamazoo Ave., S.E., Grand Rapids, MI 49560

Denomination Financial Coordinator, Harry J. Vander Meer, 2850 Kalamazoo Ave. S.E., Grand Rapids, MI 49560

Council of Christian Reformed Churches in Canada: Exec. Sec., Arie G. Van Eek, 3475 Mainway PO Box 5070, Burlington, Ontario L7R 3Y8. Tel. (416)336-2920

Church of God (Anderson, Ind.)

This body is one of the largest of the groups which have taken the name "Church of God." Its headquarters are at Anderson, Indiana. It originated about 1880 and emphasizes Christian unity.

Churches: 53; Inclusive Membership 3,244; Sunday or Sabbath Schools: 51; Total Enrollment: 3,187; Ordained Clergy: 57

GENERAL ORGANIZATION

Ontario Assembly: Chpsn., E. Sonnenburg, 319 Winston Blvd., Cambridge, Ontario N3C 3C4

Western Canada Assembly: Exec. Sec., Lewis E. Hyslip, 4717 56th St., Camrose, Alberta T4V 2C4

PERIODICALS

Ontario Messenger (m), 85 Emmett Ave., #1109, Toronto, Ontario M6M 5A2. Paul Kilburn, Ed.

The Gospel Contact (m), 5807 47th Ave., Camrose, Alberta T4V 0G7. Richard N. Yamabe, Ed.

Church of God (Cleveland, Tenn.)

This body began in the U.S. in 1886 as the outgrowth of the holiness revival under the name Christian Union, and in 1902 it was reorganized as the Holiness Church. In 1907, the church adopted the name Church of God. Its doctrine is fundamental and Pentecostal, it maintains a centralized form of government and an evangelistic and missionary program.

The first church in Canada was established in 1919 in Scotland Farm, Manitoba. Paul H. Walker became the first overseer of Canada in 1931.

Churches: 86; Inclusive Membership: 4,996; Sunday or Sabbath Schools: 76; Total Enrollment: 2,975; Ordained Clergy: 198

GENERAL ORGANIZATION

General Assembly: biennial (Next Meeting, 1988)
International Offices: Keith St. at 25th, N.W., Cleveland, TN 37311. Tel. (615) 472-3361

Exec. Office in Canada: Rev. S. A. Lankford, P.O. Box 2036, Bramalea, Ontario L6T 3S3. Tel. (416) 459-6588; Western Canada: Rev. Philip F. Siggelkon, 175 Rogers Rd., Regina; Saskatchewan S4R 6V1. Tel. (306) 545-5771

PERIODICAL

Church of God Beacon (m), P.O. Box 2036, Bramalea, Ontario L6T 3S3

The Church of God of Prophecy in Canada

In the late nineteenth century, men seeking God's eternal plan as they followed the Reformation spirit began to delve further for scriptural light concerning Christ and his church. On June 13, 1903, a small group gathered in Cherokee County, North Carolina, for prayer and further study of God's Word.

At that historic meeting the divine principles and purposes for the church as outlined in the Holy Scriptures began to shine through. Today that church is a visible, organized body, operating in all 50 states of the United States. In 1911 the first missionary effort was launched in the Bahamas; that outreach has continued, and today the church is represented in 81 countries and territories around the world.

In Canada, the first Church of God of Prophecy congregation was organized in Swan River, Manitoba, in 1937. Churches are now established in British Columbia, Manitoba, Alberta, Saskatchewan, Ontario, and Quebec.

The church accepts the whole Bible rightly divided, with the New Testament as the rule of faith and practice, government, and discipline. The membership upholds the Bible as the inspired Word of God and believes that its truths are known by illuminative revelation of the Holy Scriptures. The Trinity is recognized as one supreme Godhead in three persons—Father, Son, and Holy Ghost. Jesus Christ, the virgin-born Son of God, lived a sinless life, fulfilled his ministry on earth, was crucified, resurrected, and later ascended to the right hand of God.

Churches: 40; Inclusive Membership: 2,208; Sunday or Sabbath Schools: 45; Total Enrollment: 2,892; Ordained Clergy: 66

GENERAL ORGANIZATION

National headquarters for the Church of God of Prophecy in Canada is located at 1st Line East, R.R. 2, Brampton, Ontario L6V 1A1. Tel. (416) 843-2379

World Headquarters: Bible Place, Cleveland, TN U.S.A. 37311

General Meetings: National and Provincial (by district) annually

OFFICERS

Natl. Overseer, Canada East, Bishop Richard E. Davis, P.O. Box 457, Brampton, Ontario L6V 2L4. Tel. (416)843-2379

Natl. Overseer, Canada West, Bishop John Doroshuk, Box 952, Strathmore, Alberta T0J 3H0. Tel. (403) 934-4787

BOARD OF DIRECTORS

Pres., Bishop John Doroshuk
Vice Pres., Bishop Richard E. Davis
Sec., Bishop H. L. Martin
Member, Bishop M. A. Tomlinson
Member, Bishop Adrian Varlack
Member, Bishop Wendell Miller
Member, Bishop Vernon VanDeventer

PERIODICALS

Canadian Trumpeter Canada-West, John Doroshuk, Ed.
Maple Leaf Communque Canada-East, Richard E. Davis, Ed.

The Church of Jesus Christ of Latter-day Saints in Canada

This body has no central headquarters in Canada, only stake and mission offices. Elders Rex. C. Reeve and A. Theodore Tuttle of the First Quorum of the Seventy oversee the Church's activities in Canada. They reside in Salt Lake City, Utah. All General Authorities may be reached at 47 East South Temple St., Salt Lake City, UT 84150. [See U. S. Directory, "Religious Bodies in the United States" in this edition for further details.]

In Canada, there are 30 stakes, 6 missions, 15 districts, 178 branches and 189 wards.

For further information contact: Richard R. Robertson, The Church of Jesus Christ of Latter-day Saints in Canada, 7181 Woodbine Ave., #234, Markham, Ontario L3R 1A3

Church of the Lutheran Brethren

Organized in Milwaukee, Wis. in 1900. It adheres to the Lutheran Confessions and accepts into membership those who profess a personal faith in Jesus Christ. It practices congregational autonomy and conducts its services in a nonliturgical pattern. The synod has an advisory rather than ruling function on the congregational level, but in the cooperative efforts of all congregations (Education, American and World Missions, Publications, and Youth Ministries)it exercises a ruling function.

GENERAL ORGANIZATION

Convention: annual in June
Headquarters: 1007 Westside Dr., Box 655, Fergus Falls, MN 56537. Tel. (218)736-5666

OFFICERS

Pres., Rev. Robert M. Overgaard, 1007 Westside Dr., Box 655, Fergus Falls, MN 56537
1st Vice Pres., Rev. Theodore Thompson, 17 Apache Dr., Mount Bethel, PA 18343
2nd Vice Pres., Rev. Bruce Vallevik, Rte. 2, P.O. Box 2394, Sidney, MT 59270
Sec., Rev. Richard Vettrus, 707 Crestview Dr., West Union, IA 52175
Exec. Dir. of Finance, Ronald Egge, 1007 Westside Dr., Box 655, Fergus Falls, MN 56537

Church of the Nazarene

The first Church of the Nazarene in Canada was organized in November, 1902, by Dr. H. F. Reynolds. It was in Oxford, Nova Scotia. The Church of the Nazarene is Wesleyan Arminian in theology, representative in church government, and warmly evangelistic.

Churches: 151; Inclusive Membership: 10,054; Sunday or Sabbath Schools: 145; Total Enrollment: 15,389; Ordained Clergy: 227

GENERAL ORGANIZATION

Executive Board: meets annually in January.
Exec. Adm., Rudy Pedersen, Box 30080 Stn. B, Calgary, Alberta T2M 2N7

OFFICERS

Pres., Rev. William Stewart, 14 Hollywood Dr., Moncton, New Brunswick E1E 2R5
Vice-Pres. Charles Muxworthy, 5443 Meadedale Dr., Burnaby, British Columbia V5B 2E6
Sec., Dr. Robert Collier, 5710 Sherwood Blvd., Delta, British Columbia V4L 2C6
Treas., Robert Rimington, 6516 Lombardy Cres., S. W., Sta. B, Calgary, Alberta T3E 5R4

Churches of Christ in Canada

Churches of Christ are autonomous congregations, whose members appeal to the Bible alone to determine matters of faith and practice. There are no central offices or officers. Publications and institutions related to the churches are either under local congregational control or independent of any one congregation.

Churches of Christ shared a common fellowship in the 19th century with the Christian Churches/Churches of Christ and the Christian Church (Disciples of Christ). Fellowship was broken after the introduction of instrumental music in worship and centralization of church-wide activities through a missionary society. Churches of Christ began in Canada soon after 1800 largely in the middle provinces. The few pioneer congregations were greatly strengthened in the mid-1800s, growing in size and number.

Members of Churches of Christ believe in the inspiration of the Scriptures, the divinity of Jesus Christ, and immersion into Christ for the remission of sins. The New Testament pattern is followed in worship and church organization.

Mr. Eugene C. Perry, Beamsville, Ontario L0R 1B0

Conference of Mennonites in Canada

The Conference of Mennonites in Canada began in 1902 as an organized fellowship of Mennonite immigrants from Russia clustered in southern Manitoba and around Rosthern, Saskatchewan. The first annual sessions were held in July, 1903. Its members hold to traditional Christian beliefs, believer's baptism, and congregational polity. They emphasize practical Christianity: opposition to war, service to others, and personal ethics. Further immigration from Russia in the 1920s and 1940s increased the group which is now located in all provinces from Quebec to British Columbia. This conference is affiliated with the General Conference Mennonite Church whose offices are at Newton, Kansas.
Churches: 150; Inclusive Membership: 28,573; Sunday or Sabbath Schools: N.R.; Total Enrollment: N.R.; Ordained Clergy: 452

GENERAL ORGANIZATION
Conference of Mennonites in Canada meets annually in July.
Headquarters: 600 Shaftesbury Blvd., Winnipeg, Manitoba R3P 0M4. Tel. (204)888-6781
OFFICERS
Chpsn., Walter Franz, Box 90, Altona, Manitoba R0G 0B0
Vice-Chpsn., George Richert, 3504 Gordon Rd., Regina, Saskatchewan S4S 2V4
Sec., Ruth Enns, 2425 Haultain Ave., Saskatoon, Saskatchewan S7J 1R2
Gen. Sec., Larry Kehler, 600 Shaftesbury Blvd., Winnipeg, Manitoba R3P 0M4

Congregational Christian Churches in Ontario, The Conference of

This body originated in the early 19th century when devout Christians within several denominations in the northern and eastern United States, dissatisfied with sectarian controversy, broke away from their own denominations and took the simple title "Christians."
First organized in Canada at Keswick, Ontario, these churches became affiliated with the Conservative Congregational Christian Conference in the U.S.A.
In doctrine the body is evangelical, being governed by the Bible as the final authority in faith and practice; it believes that Christian character must be expressed in daily living; it aims at the unity of all true believers in Christ that others may believe in Him and be saved.
In church polity, the body is democratic and autonomous.
Churches: 5; Inclusive Membership: 278; Sunday or Sabbath Schools: 5; Total Enrollment: 148; Ordained Clergy: 12

GENERAL ORGANIZATION
Headquarters: Conservative Congregational Christian Conference, 7582 Currell Blvd., Ste. 108, St. Paul, MN 55125. Tel. (612)739-1474
Canadian Headquarters: 44 Virginia Beach Blvd., Gen. Del., Sutton West, Ontario L0E 1R0
OFFICERS
Pres., Mr. William Bastedo, 45 Glenwood Ave., Toronto, Ontario M6P 3C7
1st Vice-Pres., Rev. Walter Reigert, 154 First Ave., Keswick, Ontario L4P 3E1
2nd Vice-Pres., Mr. Keith McMinn, R. R. #1, Goodwood, Ontario L0C 1A0

Clerk, Mrs. Dolores Byrne, 44 Virginia Beach Blvd., Gen. Del., Sutton West, Ontario L0E 1R0
Area Representative, Mr. Bill Bastedo, 45 Glenwood Ave., Toronto, Ontario M6P 3C7

PERIODICAL
Tidings, Mr. Clare Hart, Ed.

The Coptic Church in Canada

The Coptic Church in Canada was begun in Canada in 1964 and was registered in the Province of Ontario in 1965. The Coptic Church has spread since then to a number of locations in Canada.
The governing body of each local church is an elected Board of Deacons. The Diocesan Council is the national governing body and meets at least once a year.
Churches: 7; Inclusive membership: 40,000; Sunday or Sabbath Schools: N.R.; Total Enrollment: N.R.; Ordained Clergy: 7

OFFICER
Archpriest, Fr. M. A. Marcos, St. Mark's Coptic Orthodox Church, 41 Glendinning Ave., Agincourt, Ontario M1S 3B2. Tel. (416)494-4449, (416)298-3355

†Elim Fellowship of Evangelical Churches and Ministers

The Elim Fellowship of Evangelical Churches and Ministers, a Pentecostal body, was established in 1984 as a sister organization of Elim Fellowship in the U.S.
This is an association of churches, ministers, and missionaries seeking to serve the whole body of Christ. It is Pentecostal and has a charismatic orientation.

GENERAL ORGANIZATION
Annual Representational Assemblies: Bd. of Dirs. meets quarterly; Council of Elders, bi-monthly
OFFICERS
Pres., Carlton Spencer, 7245 College St., Lima, NY 14485.
Vice Pres., Winston Nunes, 4 Palamino Cres., Willowdale, North York, Ontario M2K 1W1. Tel. (416)225-4824
Sec., Paul Heidt, 1303 Murphy Rd., Sarnia, Ontario N7S 2Y7. Tel. (519)542-8938
Treas. Errol Alchin, 15 Melissa Cres., Hamilton, Ontario L9J 1J1. Tel. (416)689-7301

The Estonian Evangelical Lutheran Church

The Estonian Evangelical Lutheran Church (EELC) was founded in 1917 in Estonia and reorganized in Sweden in 1944. The teachings of the EELC are based on the Old and New Testaments, explained through the Apostolic, Nicean and Athanasian confessions, the unaltered Confession of Augsburg and other teachings found in the Book of Concord.
Churches: 13; Inclusive Membership: 7,222; Sunday or Sabbath Schools: N.R.; Total Enrollment: N.R.; Ordained Clergy: 14

GENERAL ORGANIZATION
Executive Board headed by the Archbishop, Consistorium, Auditing Committee and District Conference.
Headquarters: Wallingatan 32, Box 45074, 10430 Stockholm 45, Sweden.

OFFICERS
Bishop in North America, Rev. Karl Raudsepp, 30 Sunrise Ave., Apt. 216, Toronto, Ontario M4A 2R3.
Assts. to the Bishop: Dr. Arthur Vööbus, 230 So. Euclid Ave., Oak Park, IL 60302. Tel. (312)386-6274; Dean

Rudolf Reinaru, 607 E. 7th St., Lakewood, NJ 08701. Tel. (201)364-9860.

PERIODICAL

Eesti Kirik (m), Box 45074, S-104, 30 Stockholm 45, Sweden. Dr. E. Putsep, ed.

Evangelical Baptist Churches in Canada, The Fellowship of

Formed in 1953 by the merging of the Union of Regular Baptist Churches of Ontario and Quebec with the Fellowship of Independent Baptist Churches of Canada.

Churches: 464; Inclusive Membership: 56,627; Sunday or Sabbath Schools: N.R.; Total Enrollment: N.R.; Ordained Clergy: N.R.

Headquarters: 3034 Bayview Ave., Willowdale, Ontario M2N 6J5. Tel. (416)223-8696

OFFICERS

Pres., Rev. John S. H. Bonham
Gen. Sec.-Treas., Dr. R. W. Lawson

PERIODICALS

Evangelical Baptist, 3034 Bayview Ave., Willowdale, Ontario, M2N 6J5, Dr. R. W. Lawson, Ed.
Intercom, Dr. R. W. Lawson, Ed.

The Evangelical Church in Canada

Founded early in the 19th century by Jacob Albright and William Otterbein in Pennsylvania as the Evangelical Church, this body became known later as the Evangelical United Brethren Church, which in the U.S. became a part of The United Methodist Church in 1968. This Canadian body is Methodist in organization and Arminian, Wesleyan, and Methodist in doctrine. It was incorporated in 1928 by Dominion Charter as The Northwest Canada Conference Evangelical Church. In 1970, this Canadian Conference was granted autonomy and became a separate denomination. In 1982 The Evangelical Church in Canada joined with The Evangelical Church of North America.

Churches: 48; Inclusive Membership: 3,665; Sunday or Sabbath Schools: 46; Total Enrollment: 3,700; Ordained Clergy: 69

GENERAL ORGANIZATION

Council of Administration: Meets 2 to 4 times each year. Annual Conference. Quadrennial Conference, next meeting, June, 1988

Headquarters: Evangelical Church Office Bldg., 2805 13th Ave., S.E., Medicine Hat, Alberta T1A 3R1

OFFICERS

General Supt., Dr. George K. Millen, 7525 S. E. Lake Rd., Ste. 7, Milwaukie, OR 97222
Conference Supt., Rev. Walter H. Erion, 30 Larkspur Ct., S.E., Medicine Hat, Alberta T1B 2J7
Conference Chpsn., Dr. G. K. Millen, 7525 Lake Rd., Ste. 7, Milwaukee, OR 97222
Conference Sec., Rev. Richard Kopanke, 480 McKenzie St., Winnipeg, Manitoba R2W 5B9

PERIODICAL

Northwest Canada Echoes (m), c/o 2805-13th Ave., S.E., Medicine Hat, Alberta T1A 3R1. A.W. Riegel, Ed.

The Evangelical Covenant Church of Canada

A Canadian denomination organized in Canada at Winnipeg in 1904 which is affiliated with the Evangelical Covenant Church of America and with the International Federation of Free Evangelical Churches, which includes churches in eleven European countries.

This body believes in the one triune God as confessed in the Apostles' Creed, that salvation is received through faith in Christ as Saviour, that the Bible is the authoritative guide in all matters of faith and practice. Christian Baptism and the Lord's Supper are accepted as divinely ordained sacraments of the church. As descendants of the 19th century pietistic awakening, the group believes in the need of a personal experience of commitment to Christ, the development of a virtuous life, and the urgency of spreading the gospel to the "ends of the world."

Most of the members of this group came from Northern Europe originally, primarily from Scandinavia.

Churches: 23; Inclusive Membership: 1,232; Sunday or Sabbath Schools: 17; Total Enrollment: 1,547; Ordained Clergy: 26

GENERAL ORGANIZATION

Headquarters: 245 21st St. E., Prince Albert, Saskatchewan S6V 1L9
Mailing Address: same as above
Conference: annual.

OFFICERS

Supt. Rev. Gerald V. Stenberg, 245 21st St. E., Prince Albert, Saskatchewan S6V 1L9
Chpsn., Mr. Willard Schneider, 3007-43A Ave., Edmonton, Alberta T6T 1A8
Sec., Miss Myrtle Augustson, 120 Coach Grove Pl. S.W., Calgary, Alberta T3H 1J2
Treas., Mr. David Peterson, Box 328, Norquay, Saskatchewan S0A 2V0

PERIODICAL

The Covenant Messenger (m), 245 21st St. E., Prince Albert, Saskatchewan S6V 1L9. Mrs. Donna Wilson, Ed.

Evangelical Free Church of Canada

The Evangelical Free Churches in Canada celebrated 50 years of Free Church work under the American Evangelical Free Church by becoming incorporated as a Canadian organization on March 21, 1967. On July 8, 1984, the Evangelical Free Church of Canada was given its autonomy as a self-governing Canadian denomination.

Churches: 106; Inclusive Membership: 5,600; Sunday or Sabbath Schools: N.R.; Total Enrollment: N.R.; Ordained Clergy: 154

GENERAL ORGANIZATION

Board of Directors
Home Office: #4, 10008 - 29A Ave., Edmonton, Alberta T6N 1A8

OFFICERS

Pres., Rev. Ronald Swanson, # 4, 10008-29A Ave., Edmonton, Alberta T6N 1A8
Mod., Mr. Henry Wiebe, 14203 - 60 Ave., Edmonton, Alberta T6H 1J6
Vice-Mod., Dr. Austin Stouffer, 954 John St., Thunder Bay, Ontario P7B 5V7
Fin. Chmn., Mr. Dave Smithers, Box 760, Three Hills, Alberta T0M 2A0

Evangelical Lutheran Church in Canada

The Evangelical Lutheran Church in Canada was organized in 1985 through a merger of The Evangelical-Lutheran Church of Canada (ELCC) and the Lutheran Church in America—Canada Section. The merger is a result of an invitation issued in 1972 by the ELCC to the Lutheran Church in America—Canada Section and the

Lutheran Church—Canada (LC-MS). Three-way merger discussions took place until 1978 when it was decided that only a two-way merger was possible. The ELCC was the Canada District of the ALC until autonomy in 1967.

The Lutheran Church in Canada traces its history back more than 200 years. Congregations were organized by German Lutherans in Halifax and Lunenburg County in Nova Scotia in 1749. German Lutherans, including many United Empire Loyalists, also settled in large numbers along the St. Lawrence and in Upper Canada. In the late nineteenth century immigrants arrived from Scandinavia, Germany, and other central European countries, many via the U.S.A. The Lutheran synods in the U.S.A. have provided the pastoral support and needed help for the Canadian church.

The Evangelical Lutheran Church in Canada is a member of the Canadian Council of Churches, the Lutheran Council in Canada, the Lutheran World Federation, and the World Council of Churches.

GENERAL ORGANIZATION

Convention: biennial. Next meeting, 1989

Headquarters: 1512 St. James St., Winnipeg, Manitoba R3H 0L2. Tel. (204)786-6707

OFFICERS

Pres., Rev. Dr. Donald W. Sjoberg
Vice-Pres., Joan Meyer
Sec., Rev. Leon C. Gilbertson
Treas., Ernest A. Kurbis

DIVISIONS AND OFFICES

Division for Canadian Missions, Exec. Dir., Rev. James A. Chell
Division for Church and Society, Exec. Dir., Rev. Ruth Blaser
Division for College and University Services, Exec. Dir., _____
Division for Parish Life, Exec. Dir., Rev. Dr. Lawrence Denef
Division for Theological Education and Leadership, Exec. Dir., Rev. William Stouffer
Division for World Mission, Exec. Dir., Rev. Paul G. Nostbakken
Office for Communication, _____
Office for Finance & Management and Committee of Pensions, Exec. Dir., Daniel A. Skaret
Office for Resource Development, Exec. Dir., Peter K. Schmidt
Evangelical Lutheran Women, Pres., Jackie Schmitt; Exec. Dir. Diane Doth Rehbein

SYNODS

Alberta-North: 10014-81 Ave., Edmonton, Alberta T6E 1W8. Tel. (403) 439-2636. Bishop: Rev. J. Robert Jacobson
Eastern: 50 Queen St. N., Kitchener, Ontario N2H 6P4. Tel. (519) 743-1461. Bishop: Rev. Dr. William D. Huras
British Columbia: 80-10th Ave., E., New Westminster, British Columbia V3L 4R5. Tel. (604) 524-1318. Bishop: Rev. Dr. Marlin Aadland
Manitoba/Northwestern Ontario:201-3657 Roblin Blvd., Winnipeg, Manitoba R3G 0E2. Tel. (204)889-3760. Bishop: Rev. G. W. Luetkehoelter
Saskatchewan: Rm. 707, Bessborough Towers, 601 Spadina Cres. E., Saskatoon, Saskatchewan S7K 3G8. Tel. (306)244-2474. Bishop: Rev. Telmor G. Sartison

PERIODICAL

Canada Lutheran (11/yr.), 1512 St. James St., Winnipeg, Manitoba R3H 0L2. Fergy E. Baglo, ed.

The Evangelical Mennonite Conference

The Evangelical Mennonite Conference (EMC) was founded in 1812-14 in southern Russia and began as a renewal movement in the larger Mennonite church. One of the key figures in this secession was Klaas Reimer, who also became the first elder. The beginning years were difficult, partly because of the attitude of the church they had left. In 1843, a decree was issued that the group be recognized as a church.

In 1874-75, almost the entire group, consisting of about 200 families, came to North America, most to Manitoba and the remainder to Nebraska. The reason for the migration was that their faith, especially their stand on nonresistance, was being threatened.

Soon after coming to Canada, a schism occurred and about one-third of the members formed another church.

Another secession occurred around 1945 when most of the U.S. members formed their own fellowship and others joined another existing church.

Churches: 48; Inclusive Membership: 5,639; Sunday or Sabbath Schools: 48; Total Enrollment: 5,766; Ordained Clergy: 104

GENERAL ORGANIZATION

Annual Meeting
Headquarters: Box 1268, 440 Main St., Steinbach, Manitoba R0A 2A0. Tel. (204) 326-6401

OFFICERS

Conf. Mod., Arden Thiessen, Box 144, Blumenort, Manitoba R0A 0C0
Bd. of Missions, Exec. Sec., Henry Klassen, Box 1268, Steinbach, Manitoba R0A 2A0

PERIODICALS

The Messenger (bi-w), Box 1268, Steinbach, Manitoba R0A 2A0. Menno Hamm, Ed.

Evangelical Mennonite Mission Conference

Founded in 1936 as the Rudnerwelder Mennonite Church in Southern Manitoba and organized as the Evangelical Mennonite Mission Conference in 1959. It was incorporated in 1962.

GENERAL ORGANIZATION

Annual Conference meeting in July
Headquarters: 526 McMillan Ave., Winnipeg Manitoba R3L 0N5. Tel. (204) 477-1213

OFFICERS

Mod., Rev. Wilf Loewen, Box 311, Hague, Saskatchewan S0K 1X0. Tel. (306)225-2214
Vice-Mod., Rev. Jack Hoeppner, Box 1420, Steinbach, Manitoba R0A 2A0. Tel. (204)326-6788
Sec., Mr. Bill Thiessen, Box 12, Randolph, Manitoba R0A 1L0
Exec. Sec., Henry Dueck. Tel. (204)489-2616

OTHER ORGANIZATIONS

Missions Dir., Mr. Lawrence Giesbrecht, Box 927, Altona, Manitoba R0G 0B0. Tel. (204)324-6179
The Gospel Message: Box 1622, Saskatoon, Saskatchewan S7K 3R8; 1712 Ave. E North, Saskatoon, Saskatchewan S7L 1V4. Tel. (306)242-5001; Radio Pastor, John D. Friesen, Tel. (306)242-5001; Radio Administrator, Ernest Friesen, Tel. (306)384-7243

PERIODICAL

The Recorder (m), Box 126, Winnipeg, Manitoba R3C 2G1. Dave and Gladys Penner, Co-Eds.

Foursquare Gospel Church of Canada

The Western Canada District was formed in 1964 with the Rev. Roy Hicks as supervisor. Prior to 1964 it had been a part of the Northwest District of the International

Church of the Foursquare Gospel with headquarters in Portland, Oregon.

A Provincial Society, The Church of the Foursquare Gospel of Western Canada, was formed in 1976; a Federal corporation, the Foursquare Gospel Church of Canada was incorporated in 1981, and a national church formed.

Churches: 39; Inclusive Membership: 2,391; Sunday or Sabbath Schools: 26; Total Enrollment: 1,505; Ordained Clergy: 92

GENERAL ORGANIZATION

National Convention, Annual.

Headquarters: 7895 Welsley Dr., Burnaby, British Columbia V5E 3X4

OFFICER

Pres. and Gen. Supervisor, Victor F. Gardner, 7875 Welsley Dr., V5E 3X4

PERIODICALS

The Canadian Challenge (1/yr.)
News & Views (3/yr.)

Free Methodist Church in Canada

The Free Methodist Church was founded in New York State in 1860 and expanded to Canada in 1880. It is Methodist in doctrine, evangelical in ministry, and emphasizes the teaching of holiness of life through faith in Jesus Christ.

The Canadian Executive Board was organized in 1927. The Free Methodist Church in Canada was incorporated in 1959 when the Holiness Movement Church merged with the Free Methodist Church. The Canadian Jurisdictional Conference in 1974 was another step toward fuller autonomy.

Churches: 133; Inclusive Membership: 6,856; Sunday or Sabbath Schools: 133; Total Enrollment: 9,538; Ordained Clergy: 214

GENERAL ORGANIZATION

Canadian Jurisdictional Conference, meets annually in July. Three geographical conferences meet annually in June and July.

Headquarters: 4315 Village Centre Ct., Mississauga, Ontario L4Z 1S2. Tel. (416) 848-2600.

OFFICERS

Pres., Bishop Donald N. Bastian, 96 Elmbrook Crescent, Etobicoke, Ontario M9C 5E2. Tel. (416) 622-4157

Ex. Dir.-Treas., Rev. Paul G. Johnston, 3020 Oka Rd., Mississauga, Ontario L5N 3A5. Tel. (416) 824-0740.

Canada East Conference Supt.: Rev. Robert J. Buchanan, Box 670 Belleville. Ontario K8N 5B3. Tel. (613)968-8511

Canada Great Lakes Conference Supt.: Rev. Glen M. Buffram, 30 King St., Brantford, Ontario N3T 3C5. Tel. (519)753-7390

Canada West Conference Supt.: Rev. Joseph F. James, Box 268, Moose Jaw, Saskatchewan S6H 4N9. Tel. (306)693-4500

PERIODICAL

The Free Methodist Herald (m), 69 Browning Ave., Toronto, Ontario M4K 1W1. Donald Gregory Bastian, Ed. Tel. (416)463-4536.

Free Will Baptists

As revival fires burned throughout New England in the mid- and late 1700s, Benjamin Randall proclaimed his doctrine of Free Will to large crowds of seekers. In due time a number of Randall's converts moved to Nova Scotia. One such believer was Asa McGray, who was to become instrumental in the establishment of several Free Baptist churches. Local congregations were organized in New Brunswick, and for several years all went smoothly,

with gains being made numerically and geographically.

However, disagreements surfaced over the question of music, Sunday school, church offerings, salaried clergy, and several other issues. When the situation remained irresolute, adherents of the more progressive element decided to form their own fellowship. Led by George Orser, they declared their intentions to become known as Free Christian Baptists. This the parent group strongly protested, arguing that the inclusion of the word Christian in the name had a negative connotation toward the original group.

Upon petitioning the province of New Brunswick for incorporation in 1898, a government official suggested the problem be resolved by employing the name Primitive Baptist Conference (to convey the idea of *first* by use of the term *Primitive*.)

Although the new group rejected some particular elements in the worship and practice of the Free Baptists, it faithfully adhered to the truths and doctrines which embodied the theological basis of Free Will Baptists. One may conclude that it has always been Free Will Baptist in doctrine and deportment, if not always in name.

Largely through the efforts of Archibald Hatfield, contact was made with Free Will Baptists in the United States, resulting in fellowship through visits of denominational leaders, the arranging of special services, and such. This contact began in the early 1960s and continues today.

Desiring to become more effective in missions, evangelism, and church growth, the association petitioned the National Association for affiliation and fellowship and was officially welcomed into the Free Will Baptist "family" in July 1981, when the National Association was in conference in Louisville, Kentucky.

GENERAL ORGANIZATION

Annual Conference convenes in early July at Hartland, New Brunswick. Also quarterly meetings in October, January and April.

OFFICER

Conference moderator, Rev. Fred D. Hanson, Box 355, Hartland, New Brunswick E0J 1N0. Tel. (506) 375-6735

PERIODICAL

The Gospel Standard, Box 355, Hartland, New Brunswick E0J 1N0. Mrs. Blanche Rideout, Ed.

General Church of the New Jerusalem

The Church of the New Jerusalem is founded on the Writings of Emanuel Swedenborg (1688-1772). These were first brought to Ontario in 1835 by Christian Enslin.

GENERAL ORGANIZATION

Annual Meeting General Church of the New Jerusalem in Canada each spring in Toronto or Kitchener.

Headquarters: 279 Burnhamthorpe Rd., Islington, Ontario M9B 1Z6. Tel. (416) 239-3054

OFFICERS

Pres., Rt. Rev. L. B. King Bryn Athyn, PA 19009

Exec. Vice-Pres., Rev. Louis D. Synnestvedt, 58 Chapel Hill Dr., Kitchener, Ontario N3G 3W5

Sec., Walter Bellinger, 110 Chapel Hill Dr., Kitchener, Ontario N2G 3W5

Treas., John Wyncoll, 19 Hampshire Heights, Islington, Ontario M9B 2J9

PERIODICAL

New Church Life (m), Bryn Athyn, PA 19009, Rev. Donald L. Rose, Ed.

New Church Canadian, 279 Burnhamthrope Rd., Islington, Ontario M9B 1Z6

The Gospel Missionary Association

Initially organized in 1951 under the chairmanship of Rev. W. J. Laing of the Bethel Baptist Church and a group of clergymen of independent missions and churches; then incorporated by the Province of Alberta in 1956. This Association consists of a body of affiliated churches, 10 in Alberta and 1 in the Yukon.

The doctrines of this body are fundamental and evangelical.

Annual Meeting: March

OFFICER

Pres., Rev. Chris Wilson, Innisfail Baptist Church, Box 773, Innisfail, Alberta T0M 1A0

Greek Orthodox Diocese of Toronto (Canada)

Greek Orthodox Christians in Canada under the jurisdiction of the Ecumenical Patriarchate of Constantinople (Istanbul).

GENERAL ORGANIZATION

Headquarters: 40 Donlands Ave., Toronto, Ontario M4J 3N6. Tel. (416)462-0833

OFFICERS

Primate of the Archdiocese of North and South America: The Most Rev. Iakovos. (See U.S. listing.)
Bishop of the Diocese of Toronto: The Rt. Rev. Bishop Sotirios 40 Donlands Ave., Toronto, Ontario M4J 3N6. Tel. (416)462-0833

Independent Assemblies of God—Canada

This fellowship of churches has been operating in Canada for over twenty-five years. It is a branch of the Pentecostal Church in Sweden. Each church within the fellowship is completely independent.

GENERAL ORGANIZATION

General Convention, annual
Headquarters: 1920 Huron St., London, Ontario N5V 3A7. Tel. (519)452-3480

OFFICER

Gen. Sec., Rev. Harry Wuerch, 1211 Lancaster St., London, Ontario N5V 2L4.

PERIODICAL

The Mantle (m), 3840 5th Ave., San Diego, CA 92103. Rev. A. W. Rassmussen, Ed.

Independent Holiness Church

The former Holiness Movement of Canada merged with the Free Methodist Church in 1958. Some churches remained independent of this merger and they formed the Independent Holiness Church in 1960, in Kingston, Ontario. The doctrines are Methodist and Wesleyan.

Churches: 13; Inclusive Membership: 600; Sunday or Sabbath Schools: N.R.; Total Enrollment: N.R.; Ordained Clergy: 21

General Conference: every three years, next meeting, 1989

OFFICERS

Gen. Supt., Rev. R. E. Votary, Sydenham, Ontario K0H 2T0. Tel. (613) 376-3114
Dist., Supt., Rev. Clifford G. Votary, Box 1433, Nipawin, Saskatchewan S0E 1E0
Gen. Sec., Mr. Dwayne Reaney, Manotick, Ontario K0A 2N0.

PERIODICAL

Gospel Tidings (m)

The Italian Pentecostal Church of Canada

This body had its beginnings in Hamilton, Ontario, in 1912 when a few people of an Italian Presbyterian Church banded themselves together for prayer and received a Pentecostal experience of the Baptism in the Holy Spirit. Since 1912, there has been a close association with the teachings and practices of the Pentecostal Assemblies of Canada.

From Hamilton the work spread to Toronto, which became a center for all of Southern Ontario. The Church then spread to Montreal, where it also flourished.

In 1959, the Church was incorporated under its present name, in the Province of Quebec, Canada, and authorized by charter and Letters' Patent.

The early leaders of this body were the Rev. Luigi Ippolito and the Rev. Ferdinand Zaffuto. The churches have carried on active missionary work in Italy and among many thousands of immigrants recently arrived in Canada.

GENERAL ORGANIZATION

General Conference, annual, Oct.
Headquarters: 6724 Fabre St., Montreal, Quebec H2G 2Z6. Tel. (514) 721-5614

OFFICERS

Gen. Supt. Rev. Alberico DeVito, 7685 Tremblay St., Boussard, Quebec J4W 2W2
Gen. Sec., Rev. David DiStaulo, 6550 Maurice Duplesis, Montreal, Quebec H1G 6K9 Tel. (514) 323-3087
Gen. Treas., Mr. Joseph Manafò, 6730 Fabre St., Montreal, Quebec H1G 2Z6. Tel. (514) 721-5614
Overseers, Rev. Daniel Ippolito, 384 Sunnyside Ave., Toronto, Ontario M6R 2S1. Tel. (416) 766-6692; Rev. Mario Spiridigliozzi, 505 Nanaimo St., Vancouver, British Columbia V5L 4S2. Tel. (604) 524-9624

PERIODICAL

Voce Evangelica (Evangel Voice) (q) Joseph Manafo, Daniel Ippolito, Eds.

Jehovah's Witnesses

For details on Jehovah's Witnesses see the directory in this edition "Religious Bodies in the United States."

Churches: 1,189; Inclusive Membership: 88,130; Sunday or Sabbath Schools: None; Total Enrollment: None; Ordained Clergy: None

GENERAL ORGANIZATION

Headquarters: 25 Columbia Heights, Brooklyn, NY 11201. Tel. (718) 625-3600
Canadian Branch Office: Box 4100, Halton Hills, Ontario L7G 4Y4

Jewish Organizations in Canada

The Jewish community of Canada numbered 296,425 persons in 1981 according to Statistics Canada. Jews are spread from coast to coast with organized communities ranging from Saint John's, Newfoundland, to Victoria, British Columbia. The largest concentration is in Montreal (some 95,000) and in Toronto (approximately 104,000).

The history of the Jewish Community began in 1760 with the conquest of Quebec by the British during the Seven Years War, although a few Jews had come north to Halifax from the Atlantic Colonies as early as 1752. The Colony of Lower Canada (new Quebec) had the first considerable settlement and it was there that, in 1768, a synagogue was organized, cemeteries established, rabbis were invited to officiate, and the community won its battles for official legal status and civic equality.

The first synagogue, Shearith Israel of Montreal, was affiliated with the Spanish-Portuguese Congregation in London and follows its rite to the present day. In 1846 the east European tradition was formally established by the issuance of a charter to the Congregation of Polish and German Jews (now Shaar Hashomayim) and in 1882 the Reform Temple Emanu-El was organized. In mid-19th century the Toronto community was formed with the establishment of a congregation (the present Holy Blossom Temple) and the consecration of a cemetery. At the same time the Hamilton community set up its facilities for worship and for the interment of its dead.

After 1880 a large number of immigrants from eastern Europe came to Canada and the present-day community took shape. Its social history parallels that of the United States, with its story of immigrant reception and settlement, industrial life in the garment industries of the large cities, the implantation of synagogues in the Russian tradition, and the slow integration and development of the community on every level.

In 1919 the Canadian Jewish community united in the Canadian Jewish Congress (CJC) which was only of short duration, but it was revived in 1934 in the face of the internal threat of anti-semitism and the world-wide problems of Jewry, which the Canadian community sought to ameliorate. In the years since, the Canadian Jewish Congress became a unique nation-wide institution which arranged for the reception of over 40,000 immigrants in the years following World War II. The Canadian Jewish Congress fought anti-semitism, coordinated the development of an admirable school system and voiced the concerns of the Jewish community of Canada in many areas. During the past decades the Jewish community developed a remarkable press and literature which bolstered civic pride among its members and ensured articulation and dignity for the entire community.

Among the CJC's important activities is the National Religious Department, which speaks for the varied and far-flung religious institutions of the community and participates in their behalf in the tripartite commission which unites Jews, Catholics and Protestants in a common program to make the voice of the community of faith heard in the councils of the nation, and also to strengthen the bonds of friendship between the adherents of the Judeo-Christian revelation.

In addition to the national interfaith program, a Committee of Dialogue, established on the initiative of the Archbishop of Montreal, brings together Jews, Protestants and Catholics for the purpose of closer understanding in the particular context of French Canada.

A census being compiled by the Religious Department of the Canadian Jewish Congress indicates 112 synagogues across the country, of which approximately 53 are Orthodox, 43 are Conservative, 14 are Reform and 2 are Reconstructionist.

Synagogues: 112; Inclusive Membership: 310,000; No. of Rabbis: N.R.

Note: *The Congregational and Rabbinical Organizations pertaining to Canada are the same as those for the United States and are listed in Directory 3, "Religious Bodies in the United States" under Jewish Organizations.*

EDUCATIONAL AND SOCIAL SERVICE ORGANIZATIONS

Canada-Israel Securities, Ltd., State of Israel Bonds: 1255 University St., Montreal, Quebec H3B 3B2. Tel. (514)878-1871. Pres., Thomas O. Hecht; Nat'l Exec. Vice-Pres., Julius Briskin

Canadian Foundation for Jewish Culture: 4600 Bathurst St., Willowdale, Ontario M2R 3V2. Tel. (416) 635-2883. Pres., Mira Koschitzky; Exec. Sec., Edmond Y. Lipsitz

Canadian Jewish Congress: 1590 Ave. Docteur Penfield, Montreal, Quebec H3G 1C5. Tel. (514) 931-7531. Pres., Dorothy Reitman; Exec. Vice-Pres., Alan Rose

Canadian ORT Organization (Organization of Rehabilitation Through Training): 5165 Sherbrooke St., W., Ste. 208, Montreal, Quebec H4A 1T6. Tel. (514) 481-2787. Pres., J. A. Lyone Heppner; Exec. Dir., Mac Silver

Canadian Sephardi Federation: 345 Wilson Ave., Ste. 303, Downsview, Ontario M3H 5W1. Te. (416)630-7136. Pres., Leon Oziel; Sec. Laeticia Benabou

Canadian Zionist Federation: 1310 Greene Ave., Montreal, Quebec H3Z 2B8. Tel. (514) 934-0804. Pres., Neri J. Bloomfield; Exec. Vice-Pres., Rabbi Meyer Krentzman

Hadassah-WIZO Organization of Canada: 1310 Greene Ave., 9th fl., Montreal, Quebec H3Z 2B8. Tel. (514) 937-9431. Pres., Cecily Peters; Exec. Vice-Pres., Lily Frank

Jewish Immigrant Aid Services of Canada (JIAS): 5151 Cote Ste. Catherine Rd., Montreal, Quebec H3W 1M6. Tel. (514) 342-9351. Pres., Daniel Morris; Exec. Vice-Pres., Herb Abrams

Jewish National Fund of Canada (Keren Kayemeth Le' Israel, Inc.): 1980 Sherbrooke St., W., Ste. 500, Montreal, Quebec H3H 2M7. Pres., Saul B. Zitzerman; Exec. Vice-Pres., Michael Goldstein

Labor Zionist Movement of Canada: 4770 Kent Ave., Montreal, Quebec H3W 1H2. Tel. (514) 342-9710. Nat'l Exec., Abraham Shurem

National Council of Jewish Women of Canada: 1111 Finch Ave. W., Ste., 401, Willowdale, Ontario M3J 2E5. Tel. (416) 665-8251. Pres., Sheila Freeman; Exec. Dir., Eleanor Appleby

National Joint Community Relations Committee of Canadian Jewish Congress: 4600 Bathurst St., Willowdale, Ontario M2R 3V2. Tel. (416) 635-2883. Co-Chair, Victor Goldbloom, Joseph L. Wilder; Nat'l. Exec. Dir., Manuel Prutschi

United Jewish Teachers' Seminary: 5237 Clanranald Ave., Montreal, Quebec H3X 2S5. Tel. (514) 489-4401. Dir., A. Aisenbach

Zionist Organization of Canada: 788 Marlee Ave., Toronto, Ontario M6B 3K1. Tel. (416) 781-3571. Pres., Max Goody; Exec. Vice-Pres., George Liban

JEWISH WELFARE FUNDS, COMMUNITY COUNCILS

Calgary, Alberta: Calgary Jewish Community Council, 1607 90th Ave., S.W. (T2V 4V7). Tel. (403) 253-8600. Pres. Morris Dancyger; Exec. Dir., Drew Stauffenberg

Edmonton, Alberta: Jewish Federation of Edmonton, 7200-156th St. (T5R 1X3). Tel. (403)487-5120. Pres., Judith Goldsand; Exec. Dir., Howard Bloom

Hamilton, Ontario: Hamilton Jewish Federation, 57 Delaware Ave. (L8M 1T6). Tel. (416)528-8570. Pres., Andrea Stringer; Exec. Dir., Sid Brail

London, Ontario: London Jewish Community Council, 536 Huron St. (N5Y 4J5). Tel. (519)673-3310. Pres., Allan Richman; Exec. Dir., Gerald Enchin

Montreal, Quebec: Allied Jewish Community Services, 5151 Cote Ste. Catherine Rd. (H3W 1M6). Tel. (514)735-3541. Pres., Carl Laxer; Exec. Vice-Pres., John Fishel

Ottawa, Ontario: Jewish Community Council of Ottawa, 151 Chapel St. (K1N 7Y2). Tel. (613)232-7306. Pres., Gerald Berger; Exec. Dir., Gittel Tatz

Toronto, Ontario: Toronto Jewish Congress, 4600 Bathurst St., Willowdale (M2R 3V2). Tel. (416)635-2883. Pres., Ronald Appleby; Exec. Dir., Steven Ain

Vancouver, British Columbia: Jewish Federation of Greater Vancouver, 950 W. 41st Ave. (V5Z 2N7). Tel. (604)266-8371. Pres., Ronald Coleman; Exec. Dir., Steve Drysdale

Windsor, Ontario: Jewish Community Council, 1641 Ouellette Ave. (N8X 1K9). Tel. (519)973-1772. Pres., Richard Rosenthal; Exec. Dir., Joseph Eisenberg

Winnipeg, Manitoba: Winnipeg Jewish Community Council, 370 Hargrave St. (R3B 2K1). Tel. (204)943-0406. Pres., Evelyn Katz; Exec. Dir., Robert Freedman

PERIODICALS

Bulletin du Congres Juif de Langue Française du Congres Juif Canadien (q), 1590 Ave. Docteur Penfield, Montreal, Quebec H3G 1C5. Tel. (514)931-7531. M. Mayer Lévy, Ed. French.

Canadian Jewish Herald (Irregular), 17 Anselme Lavigne Blvd., Dollard des Ormeaux, Quebec H9A 1N3. Tel. (514)684-7667. Dan Nimrod, Ed.

Canadian Jewish News (w), 562 Eglinton Ave., E., Ste. 401, Toronto, Ontario M4P 1P1. Tel. (416)483-9331. Maurice Lucow, Ed.

Canadian Jewish Outlook (m), 6184 Ash St., #3, Vancouver, British Columbia V5Z 3G9. Tel. (604)324-5101. Ben Chud, Henry Rosenthal, Eds.

Canadian Zionist (bi-m), 1310 Greene Ave., Ste. 800, Montreal, Quebec H3Z 2B2. Tel. (514)934-0804. Glenna Vline, Ed.

Jewish Eagle (w), 4180 De Courtrai, Ste. 218, Montreal, Quebec H3S 1C3. Tel. (514)735-6577. B. Hershtal, Ed. Yiddish-Hebrew-French

Jewish Post (w), 117 Hutchings St., Winnipeg, Manitoba R2X 2V4. Tel. (204)694-3332. Matt Bellan, Ed.

Jewish Standard (semi-m), 67 Mowat Ave., Ste. 319, Toronto, Ontario M6K 3E3. Tel (416)537-2696. Julius Hayman, Ed.

Jewish Western Bulletin (w), 3268 Heather St., Vancouver, British Columbia V5Z 3K5. Tel. (604)879-6575. Samuel Kaplan, Ed.

Ottawa Jewish Bulletin & Review (bi-w), 151 Chapel St., Ottawa, Ontario K1H 7Y2. Tel. (613)232-7306. Cynthia Engel, Ed.

Undzer Veg (q), 272 Codsell Ave., Downsview, Ontario M3H 3X2. Tel. (416)636-4024. Joseph Kligman, Ed. Yiddish-English

Western Jewish News (w), 400-259 Portage Ave., Winnipeg, Manitoba R3C 2G6. Tel. (204)942-6361. Cheryl Fogel, Ed.

Windsor Jewish Community Council Bulletin (irregular), 1641 Ouellette Ave., Windsor, Ontario N8X 1K9. Tel. (519)973-1772. Joseph Eisenberg, Ed.

Note: *For details concerning many aspects of Jewish life and organization in Canada and throughout the world, consult the American Jewish Year Book, 1987, edited by David Singer and published by the American Jewish Committee, New York, and the Jewish Publication Society of America, Philadelphia.*

The Latvian Evangelical Lutheran Church in America

This body was organized into a denomination on April 10, 1976, after having existed as the Federation of Latvian Evangelical Lutheran Churches since 1957. This church is a regional constituent part of the Lutheran Church of Latvia in Exile, a member of the Lutheran World Federation and the World Council of Churches.

The Latvian Evangelical Lutheran Church in America works to foster religious life, tradition and customs in its congregations in harmony with the Holy Scriptures, the Apostles', Nicaean, and Athanasian Creeds, the unaltered Augsburg Confession, Martin Luther's Small and Large Catechisms and other documents of the Book of Concord.

The LELCA is ordered by its Synod, executive board, auditing committee, and district conferences.

Churches: 9; Inclusive Membership: 2,669; Sunday or Sabbath Schools: 5; Total Enrollment 125; Ordained Clergy: 6

GENERAL ORGANIZATION

Synod: Meets every three years. Next meeting, 1987

Headquarters: 6551 West Montrose Ave., Chicago, IL 60634.

OFFICERS

Pres., Rev. Vilis Varsbergs, 6551 West Montrose Ave., Chicago, IL 60634. Tel. (312)725-3820.

Vice-Pres., Rev. Janis Calitis, 8 Rolland Rd., Toronto, Ontario M4G 1V5. Tel. (416)482-8403.

2nd Vice-Pres., Dr. Janis Robins, 11 Ludlow Ave., St. Paul, MN 55108. Tel. (612)646-1980.

Sec., Dr. Ernests Reinbergs, 32 Hales Cres., Guelph, Ontario N1G 1P6. Tel. (519)822-6842

Treas., Mr. Alfreds Trautmanis, 103 Rose St., Freeport, NY 11520. Tel. (516)623-2646

PERIODICAL

Cela Biedrs (10/yr.), Dean A. Voitkus, 26 Chippewa Ave., Ottawa, Ontario K2G 1X7

Lutheran Church—Canada

Founded April 23, 1959, at Edmonton, Alberta, by the Canadian congregations of the Lutheran Church—Missouri Synod.

Churches: 360; Inclusive Membership: 94,627; Sunday or Sabbath Schools: 280; Total Enrollment: 19,233; Ordained Clergy: 332

GENERAL ORGANIZATION

Biennial Convention. Next meeting, 1987

Headquarters: #203, 2727 Portage Ave., Winnipeg, Manitoba, P. O. Box 55, Sta. A., Winnipeg, Manitoba R3Z 1K9. Tel. (204)885-3273

Exec. Dir., William Buller

OFFICERS

Pres., Rev. Elroy Treit, 3022 E. 49th Ave., Vancouver, British Columbia V5S 1K9

Vice-Pres., Rev. R. Holm, 1927 Grant Dr., Regina, Saskatchewan S4S 4V6

Sec., Rev. E. Lehman, # 35, 9912 106 St., Edmonton, Alberta T5K 1C5

Treas., Mr. Ken Werschler, 1927 Grant Dr., Regina, Saskatchewan S4S 4V6

Dirs., Rev. A. Stanfel, 149 Queen St. S., Kitchener, Ontario N2G 4A2; Mr. Walter Seehagel, 440 Parkridge Crescent S.E., Calgary, Alberta T2J 5A9; Rev. H. Ruf, #35-9912 106 St., Edmonton, Alberta T5K 1C5; Mr. John Fuge, 51 Roselawn Bay, Winnipeg, Manitoba R2G 1W5; Mr. A. Schmitt, 303 Highgate Ave., Oshawa, Ontario L1G 7S9; Rev. M.R.L. Krey, 160 Giles Blvd. W., Windsor, Ontario N9A 6G9; Mr. Art Timm, 1130- 8 St., Saskatoon, Saskatchewan S7H 0S4

†Mennonite Brethren Churches, Canadian Conference of

Incorporated November 22, 1945

Churches: 162; Inclusive Membership: 23,306; Sunday or Sabbath Schools: N.R.; Total Enrollment: N.R.; Ordained Clergy: N.R.

GENERAL ORGANIZATION

Annual Conference: next meeting July

Headquarters: 3-169 Riverton Ave., Winnipeg, Manitoba R2L 2E5. Tel. (204) 669-6575

OFFICERS

Mod., Dr. John Redekop, 298 Ferndale Ave., Waterloo, Ontario N2J 3X9

Asst. Mod., Rev. Herbert Neufeld, 4812 Willington Ave., Burnaby, British Columbia V5G 3H6
Sec., Rev. Robert Friesen, 46611 Maple Ave., Chilliwack, British Columbia V2P 2K3

PERIODICALS

Mennonite Brethren Herald (bi-w), 3-169 Riverton Ave., Winnipeg, Manitoba R2L 2E5. Herb Kopp, Ed.
Mennonitische Rundschau: 3-169 Riverton Ave., Manitoba R2L 1L4. Abe Schellenberg, Ed.

Mennonite Church (Canada)

This body had its origins in Europe in 1525 as an outgrowth of the Anabaptist movement. It was organized in North America in 1898. Canada has been considered Region 1 of the North American Mennonite Church since 1971. In 1983, Regions were dropped and the Mennonite Church (Canada) consists of three conferences in Canada

Churches: 85; Inclusive Membership: 9,400; Sunday or Sabbath Schools: 80; Total Enrollment: 9,937; Ordained Clergy: 156

GENERAL ORGANIZATION

Mennonite Church (Canada) consists mainly of three conferences which are part of the 22-Conference network of the Mennonite Church with general offices in Lombard, IL. (See listing in the section "Religious Bodies in the U.S." of this edition.) The General Assembly of the Mennonite Church meets biennially. Next meeting is 1987.

Mailing Address: 131 Erb St., W., Waterloo, Ontario N2L 1T7

OFFICERS

Chpsn., Nelson Scheifele
Vice-Chpsn., Tim Burkholder
Sec., J. Lester Kehl
Treas., Darrell Jantzi

PERIODICAL

Mennonite Reporter (bi-w), Waterloo, Ontario. Ron Rempel, Ed.

Metropolitan Community Churches, Universal Fellowship of

The Universal Fellowship of Metropolitan Community Churches is a Christian church which directs a special ministry within, and on behalf of, the homosexual community.

Founded in 1968 in Los Angeles by the Rev. Troy Perry, the "U.F.M.C.C." has 200 member congregations worldwide. Ten congregations are in Canada, in Vancouver, Edmonton, Calgary, Toronto, London, Ottawa, Winnipeg, Kingston, and Montreal.

Theologically, the Metropolitan Community Churches stand within the mainstream of Christian doctrine, being "ecumenical" or "interdenominational" in stance (albeit a "denomination" in their own right).

The Metropolitan Community Churches are characterized by their belief that a) the love of God is a gift, freely offered to all people, regardless of "sexual orientation"and that b) no incompatability exists between human sexuality and the Christian faith.

The Metropolitan Community Churches in Canada were founded in Toronto in 1973 by the Rev. Robert Wolfe.

GENERAL ORGANIZATION

General Conference (International), biennial, next meeting, 1987.
District Conferences (Regional), annual.

OFFICERS

Western Canadian District, P. O. Box 245, Maple Rdge, British Columbia V2X 7G1. Tel. (604)534-9221. District Coordinator, Mr. Arthur Pearson.
Eastern Canadian District, P. O. Box 2979, Sta. D, Ottawa, Ontario K1P 5W9. Tel. (613)232-0241. District Coordinator, Rev. Ron Bergeron

The Missionary Church of Canada

This denomination in Canada is affiliated with the worldwide body of the Missionary Church. Historically part of the Anabaptist, Mennonite movement, it changed its name to the United Missionary Church in 1947 and in 1969 it merged with the Missionary Church Association of Fort Wayne, IN. It is an evangelical, missionary church.

GENERAL ORGANIZATION

The Missionary Church of Canada meets biennially and the General Conference of the International Missionary Church meets biennially on alternate years. District Conferences meet annually.

OFFICERS

Missionary Church of Canada:
Pres., Rev. Alfred W. Rees, Banfield Memorial Church, 89 Centre Ave., North York, Ontario M2M 2L7
Canada East District: Dist. Supt., Rev. C. E. Prosser, 130 Fergus Ave., Kitchener, Ontario N2A 2H2
Canada West District: Dist. Supt., Rev. David Crouse, Box 640, Midnapore, Alberta T0L 1J0

Moravian Church in America, Northern Province, Canadian District of the

Note: The work in Canada is under the general oversight and rules of the Moravian Church, Northern Province, general offices for which are located at 1021 Center St., P.O. Box 1245, Bethlehem, PA 18016

Churches: 9; Inclusive Membership: 2,025; Sunday or Sabbath Schools: 9; Total Enrollment: 681; Ordained Clergy: 13

OFFICER

Pres., Mr. Elmer F. Kadatz, R.R. 1, Site 4, Box 8, Edmonton, Alberta T6H 4N6. Tel. (403)988-5096

†Muslims

There are many thousands of Muslims in Canada, primarily in the larger cities. The Muslim community in Canada is gathered together by Islamic societies and Muslim Mosques. These societies and other organizations are not regarded as religious sects or divisions. Their multiplication arises from the needs of each group in a given area, long distances between groups, and the absence in Islam of organized hierarchy. All the groups hold the same beliefs, aspire to practice the same rituals; namely, prayers, fasting, almsgiving, and pilgrimage to Makkah Almukarramah (Mecca).

REGIONAL AND NATIONAL GROUPS

A number of regional and national groups exist which were started with the objective of helping local groups, coordinating their work, and promoting closer unity among them.
These include:
The Federation of Islamic Associations in the United States and Canada, 25341 Five Mile Rd., Redford Township, MI 48239.Sec. Gen., Nihad Namid. Publication: *The Muslim Star,* 17514 Woodward Ave., Detroit, MI 48203

143

The Muslim Students Association of the United States and Canada, P. O. Box 38, Plainfield, Indianapolis, IN 46168. Tel. (317) 839-8157. Publications: *The Islamic Horizons* (m); *Al-Ittihad* (q)

Council of Muslim Communities of Canada, 229 Younge St., Ste. 404, Toronto, Ontario M5B 1N9. Tel. (416)384-7542. Pres., Dr. Fuad Sahin; Sec. Gen., Dr. Imtaiz Ali. Publication: *Islam Canada,* 203-500 James St. N., 2nd Fl., Hamilton, Ontario L8L 1J1. Tel. (416)529-2621.

Council of Masajid (Mosques) in the U.S.A., 300 E. 44th St., New York City, NY 10017. Sec. Gen., Dawud A. Assad. Tel. (212) 986-6824. Publication: *Majallat Al-Masjid* (newsletter).

Netherlands Reformed Congregations of North America

The Netherlands Reformed Church, presently numbering 158 congregations in the Netherlands (83,000 members), 25 congregations in North America (8,300 members), and a handful of congregations in various other countries, organized denominationally in 1907. The so-called Churches Under the Cross (established in 1839, after breaking away from the 1834 secession congregations) and the so-called Ledeboerian churches (established in 1841 under the leadership of Rev. Ledeboer who seceded from the Reformed state church), united in 1907 under the leadership of the then 25-year-old Rev. G. H. Kersten to form the Netherlands Reformed Congregations (*Gereformeerde Gemeenten*). Many of the North American congregations left the Christian Reformed Church to join the Netherlands Reformed Congregations after the Kuyperian presupposed regeneration doctrine began making serious inroads into that denomination.

All Netherlands Reformed congregations, office bearers, and members subscribe to three Reformed Forms of Unity: the *Belgic Confession of Faith* (by DeBres), the *Heidelberg Catechism* and the *Canons of Dordt. The Belgic Confession* and *Canons of Dordt* are read regularly at worship services, and the *Heidelberg Catechism* is preached weekly except on church feast days.

The NRC stresses the traditional Reformed doctrines of grace, such as the sovereignty of God, responsibility of humankind, the necessity of the new birth, and the experience of God's sanctifying grace.

GENERAL ORGANIZATION
Clk. of Synod, Rev. J. R. Beeke, 2115 Romence St. N.E., Grand Rapids, MI 49503

North American Baptist Conference

Churches belonging to this conference emanated from German Baptist immigrants of more than a century ago. Although scattered across Canada and the U.S., they are bound together by a common heritage, a strong spiritual unity, a Bible-centered faith, and a deep interest in missions.

Note: The details of general organization, officers, and periodicals of this body will be found in the North American Baptist Conference directory in the United States section of this *Yearbook.* The international office at 1 S. 210 Summit Ave., Oakbrook Terrace, IL 60181, serves the Canadian and U.S. churches.

The Old Catholic Church of Canada

Founded in 1948 in Hamilton, Ontario. The first bishop was the Rt. Rev. Georges Davis. The Old Catholic Church of Canada accepts all the doctrines of the Eastern Orthodox Churches and, therefore, not Papal Infallibility or the Immaculate Conception. The ritual is Western (Latin Rite) and is in the vernacular. Celibacy is optional. The Old Catholic Church of Canada is affiliated with the North American Old Roman Catholic Church, whose Presiding Bishop is Most Rev. John E. Schweikert of Chicago (see U.S. directory).

GENERAL ORGANIZATION
Headquarters: R. R. #1, Midland, Ontario L4R 4K3. Tel. (705)835-3526

OFFICERS
Bishop (Retired), Rt. Rev. Robert Ritchie, 216 Tragina Ave., N., Hamilton, Ontario L8H 5E1
Bishop-Elect, Rev. David Thomson, R. R. 1, Midland, Ontario L4R 4K3

Old Order Amish Church

This is the most conservative branch of the Mennonite Church and direct descendants of Swiss Brethren (Anabaptists) who emerged from the Reformation in Switzerland in 1525. The Amish, followers of Bishop Jacob Ammann, became a distinct group in 1693. They began migrating to America about 1720 where 95 percent of them still reside. They first migrated to Ontario in 1824 directly from Bavaria, Germany and also from Pennsylvania and Alsace-Lorraine. Since 1953 many Amish have migrated to Ontario from Ohio, Indiana, and Iowa.

In 1987, there were 16 congregations in Ontario, each being autonomous. No membership figures are kept by this group but membership has been estimated at 775. Being congregational in structure, there is no central headquarters. Each congregation is served by a bishop, two ministers, and a deacon, all of whom are chosen from among the male members by lot for life.

Churches: 16; Inclusive Membership: 775; Sunday or Sabbath Schools: N.R.; Total Enrollment: N.R.; Ordained Clergy: N.R.

CORRESPONDENT
Mr. David Luthy, Pathway Publishers, Rte. 4, Aylmer, Ontario, N5H 2R3

PERIODICALS
Blackboard Bulletin; The Budget; The Diary; Die Botschaft; Family Life; Herold der Wahrheit; Young Companion

The Open Bible Standard Churches of Canada

This is the Canadian branch of the Open Bible Standard Churches, Inc., USA of Des Moines, Iowa. It is an evangelical, full gospel denomination emphasizing evangelism, missions, and the message of the Open Bible. The Canadian Branch was chartered January 7, 1982.

Churches: 4; Inclusive Membership: 1,000; Sunday or Sabbath Schools: 4; Total Enrollment: 500; Ordained Clergy: 6

GENERAL ORGANIZATION
General Conference: Annual (April)
Headquarters: 4545 Jane St., Toronto (Downsview), Ontario M3N 2K7. Tel. (416)661-6770

OFFICERS
Supt. and Gen. Overseer, Rev. C. Russell Archer, P. O. Box 306, Dayton, OH 45401
Prov. Supt., Rev. Richard Lewis, 82 Northland Rd., Toronto, Ontario M4B 2E5. Tel. (416)752-6479
Vice-Pres., Rev. Peter Morgan, Lot 17, RR #4,

Bramalea, Ontario L6T 3S1. Tel. (416)846-5153
Sec.-Treas., _____

The Pentecostal Assemblies of Canada

This body is incorporated under the Dominion Charter of 1919 and is also recognized in the Province of Quebec as an ecclesiastical corporation. Its beginnings are to be found in the revivals at the turn of the century, and most of the first Canadian Pentecostal leaders came from a religious background rooted in the Holiness movements.

The original incorporation of 1919 was implemented among churches of eastern Canada only. In the same year, a conference was called in Moose Jaw, Saskatchewan, to which the late Rev. J. M. Welsh, gen. supt. of the then-organized Assemblies of God in the U.S., was invited. The churches of Manitoba and Saskatchewan were organized as the Western District Council of the Assemblies of God. They were joined later by Alberta and British Columbia. In 1921, a conference was held in Montreal, to which the general chairman of the Assemblies of God was invited. Eastern Canada also became a district of the Assemblies of God, joining Eastern and Western Canada as two districts in a single organizational union.

In 1922, at Kitchener, Ontario, a special committee met with a delegation from both eastern and western churches, at which time it was agreed to dissolve the Canadian District of the Assemblies of God and unite under the name The Pentecostal Assemblies of Canada.

Today, the Pentecostal Assemblies of Canada operate throughout the nation, and religious services are conducted in more than 27 languages, in more than 200 ethnic churches. There are 107 native churches.

Churches: 1,052; Inclusive Membership: 185,208; Sunday or Sabbath Schools: N.R.; Total Enrollment: N.R.; Ordained Clergy: N.R.

OFFICERS

Gen. Supt., Rev. James M. MacKnight
Gen. Sec., Rev. Charles Yates
Gen. Treas., Rev. John Totafurno
Exec. Dir. Overseas Missions, Rev. W. C. Cornelius
Exec. Dir. Church Ministries, Rev. W. A. Griffin
Exec. Dir. Home Missions and Bible Colleges, Rev. Gordon R. Upton
Dir. Women's Ministries, Mrs. Eileen Stewart
Mgr. Full Gospel Publishing House, Mr. Harry E. Anderson

DISTRICT SUPERINTENDENTS

British Columbia, Rev. Reuben L. Schmunk, 5641 176 A St., Surrey, British Columbia, V3S 4G8
Alberta, Rev. John A. Keys, 10585-111 st., #101, Edmonton, Alberta, T5H 3E8
Saskatchewan, Rev. L. Calvin King, 1219 Idylwyld Ave., Saskatoon, Saskatchewan S7L 1A1
Manitoba, Rev. Vernon W. Taylor, 3081 Ness Ave., Winnipeg, Manitoba R2Y 2G3
Western Ontario, Rev. Earl K. Young, 3419 Mainway, Burlington, Ontario L7M 1A9
Eastern Ontario and Quebec, Rev. E. Stewart Hunter, Box 1600, Belleville, Ontario K8N 5J3
Maritime Provinces, Rev. A. Donald Moore, Box 1184, Truro, Nova Scotia B2N 5H1

CONFERENCES

German Conference, Rev. Gustav Kurtz, 5 Manitou Dr., Kitchener, Ontario N2C 2J6
French Conference, Rev. Oscar Masseau, 4770 boul. Lalande, Pierrefonds, Quebec H8Y 1V2
Slavic Conference: Eastern District, Rev. Walter Senko, R.R. 1, Wilsonville, Ontario N0E 1Z0; Western District, Rev. Michael Brandebura, Box 180, Glendon, Alberta T0A 1P0

Finnish Conference, Rev. A. Wirkkala, 1920 Argyle Dr., Vancouver, British Columbia V5P 2A8

PERIODICAL

The Pentecostal Testimony, 10 Overlea Blvd., Toronto, Ontario M4H 1A5. Rev. Robert J. Skinner, Ed.

Pentecostal Assemblies of Newfoundland

This body began in 1910 and held its first assembly at the Bethesda Pentecostal Mission at St. John's. It was incorporated in 1925 as the Bethesda Pentecostal Assemblies and changed its name in 1930 to the Pentecostal Assemblies of Newfoundland.

GENERAL ORGANIZATION

Headquarters: 57 Thorburn Rd., St. John's, Newfoundland A1B 3N4. Tel. (709)753-6314
General Conference: Bi-Annual, Next meeting, June, 1988

OFFICERS

Pres. and Gen. Supt., Roy D. King, 50 Brownsdale St., St. John's, Newfoundland A1E 4R2
Asst. Supts: A. W. Rowe, P. O. Box 542, Lewisporte, Newfoundland A0G 3A0; B. Q. Grimes, 14 Chamberlain St., Grand Falls, Newfoundland A2A 2G4
Gen. Sec.-Treas., F. V. Rideout, 59 Wishingwell Rd., St. John's, Newfoundland A1B 1G6
Youth and S.S. Dir., R. H. Dewling, 26 Wicklow St., St. John's, Newfoundland A1B 3H2

PERIODICALS

Good Tidings (m), 57 Thorburn Rd., St. John's Newfoundland A1B 3N4, Roy D. King, Ed.
Reach (bi-m), 57 Thorburn Rd., St. John's, Newfoundland A1B 3N4, R.H. Dewling, Ed.

†Pentecostal Holiness Church of Canada

The first General Conference convened in May, 1971 in Toronto. Prior to this, the Canadian churches were under the leadership of the Pentecostal Holiness Church in the U.S.A.

GENERAL ORGANIZATION

General Conference every four years. Next meeting, 1986
Headquarters: Box 442, Waterloo, Ontario N2J 4A9. Tel. (519) 746-1310

OFFICERS

Gen. Supt., G. H. Nunn, Box 442, Waterloo, Ontario N2J 4A9
Asst. Supt., Rev. E. A. Gagnon, P.O. Box 395, Athens, Ontario K0E 1B0; Don Tosh, 210 Scott Dr., Kentville, Nova Scotia B4N 4C1; W. Longard, 132 Henderson Ave., Chilliwack, British Columbia V2P 2Y1
Sec. Treas., Clarence Wood, R. R. # 1, Minden, Ontario K0M 2K0
Comptroller, W. Head, 35 Appalachian Cres., Kitchener, Ontario N2E 1A3

PERIODICAL

Impact (q), Dept. of Publications, Box 442, Waterloo, Ontario N2J 4A9

Plymouth Brethren
(Also known as Christian Brethren, see above)

Polish National Catholic Church of Canada

This Diocese was created at the XII General Synod of the Polish National Catholic Church of America in October, 1967. Formerly, the Canadian parishes were a part of the

Western Diocese and Buffalo-Pittsburgh Diocese of the Polish National Catholic Church in America.

GENERAL ORGANIZATION

Headquarters: 186 Cowan Ave., Toronto, Ontario M6K 2N6

OFFICER

The Rt. Rev. Joseph Nieminski, Bishop Ordinary, 186 Cowan Ave., Toronto, Ontario M6K 2N6. Tel. (416) 532-8249

Presbyterian Church in America (Canadian Section)

Canadian congregations of the Reformed Presbyterian Church, Evangelical Synod, became a part of the Presbyterian Church in America when the RPCES joined PCA in June 1982. Some of the churches were in predecessor bodies of the RPCES, which was the product of a 1965 merger of the Reformed Presbyterian Church in North America, General Synod, and the Evangelical Presbyterian Church. Others came into existence later as a part of the home missions work of RPCES. Congregations are located in six provinces, and the PCA is continuing church extension work in Canada. The denomination is committed to world evangelization and to a continuation of historic Presbyterianism. Its officers are required to subscribe, without reservation, to the Reformed faith as set forth in the Westminster Confession of Faith and Catechisms.

Churches: 15; Inclusive Membership: 1,000; Sunday or Sabbath Schools: 15; Total Enrollment: 420; Ordained Clergy: 20

CORRESPONDENT

Rev. Douglas Codling, 10120 Lassam Rd., Richmond, British Columbia V7E 2C2

The Presbyterian Church in Canada

The nonconcurring portion of the Presbyterian Church in Canada that did not become a part of The United Church of Canada in 1925.

Churches: 1,028; Inclusive Membership: 213,483; Sunday or Sabbath Schools: 637; Total Enrollment: 34,594; Ordained Clergy: 1,102

Offices: 50 Wynford Dr., Don Mills, Ontario M3C 1J7. Tel. (416)441-1111

OFFICERS

Mod., Rev. T. Plomp

Clerks of Assembly: Principal Clerk, Dr. E. F. Roberts; Deputy Clerks, Dr. E. H. Bean, Dr. D. B. Lowry; Rev. T. Plomp Principal Clerk Emeritus, Dr. D. C. MacDonald

Adm. Council: Sec., Dr. E. F. Roberts; Treas., Mr. H.W.F. McKay; Comp., Mr. D. A. Taylor

NATIONAL BOARDS

Board of World Missions: Gen. Sec., Rev. C. M. Costerus; Sec. for Africa, Adm. and Fin., Rev. C. R. Talbot; Sec., Edu. for Mission, Rev. M. L. Garvin; Sec., Canada Operations, Miss G. G. Kelly; Sec., Overseas Rel., Rev. H. G. Davis; Sec. for Mission Personnel & Univ. Ministries, Dr. A. G. MacDougall

Board of Congregational Life: Gen. Sec., Rev. H. E. Waite; Sec. for Worship, Rev. E. M. MacNaughton; Sec. for Lay Ministries & Church Edu., Miss H. G. Tetley; Sec. for Church and Society, Dr. R. Hodgson; Sec. for Camping & Outdoor Min., Mrs. S. Ford; Sec. for Evangelism, Dr. A. N. McCombie

Communication Services: Consultant, Mr. Donald Stephens

Board of Ministry: Gen. Sec., Rev. T. Gemmell

Presbyterian World Service and Development: Dir., Miss Jean Davidson

Presbyterian Church Building Corp.: Dir., Rev. F. R. Kendall

Women's Missionary Society (WD): Pres., Mrs. G. Jess, Oshawa, Ontario

Women's Missionary Society (ED): Pres., Mrs. E. H. Bean, Sydney, Nova Scotia

PERIODICAL

The Presbyterian Record (m), 50 Wynford Ave., Don Mills, Ontario M3C 1J7. Rev. James Ross Dickey, Ed.

Reformed Church in Canada

The Canadian branch of the Reformed Church in America consists of 29 churches organized under the Council of the Reformed Church in Canada and within the classis of Ontario (19 churches), Cascades (9 churches), Lake Erie (1 church). The Reformed Church in America was established in 1628 by the earliest Dutch settlers in America as the Reformed Protestant Dutch Church. It is evangelical in theology and presbyterian in government.

Churches: 29; Inclusive Membership: 6,487; Sunday or Sabbath Schools: 29; Total Enrollment: 1,725; Ordained Clergy: 40

GENERAL ORGANIZATION

Gen. Sec., Rev. Edwin G. Mulder, 475 Riverside Dr., New York, NY 10115. Tel (212) 870-2841

Council of the Reformed Church in Canada; Reformed Church Center, R.R. #4, Cambridge, Ontario N1R 5S5. Tel. (519) 623-4860.

PERIODICAL

Pioneer Christian Monthly (m), Reformed Church Center, R.R. #4 Cambridge, Ontario N1R 5S5. Tel. (519) 623-4860. Rev. Cor Bons, Ed.

Reformed Doukhobors, Christian Community and Brotherhood of

Doukhobors were founded in the late 17th century in Russia. Their doctrine is the "Living Book," which is based on traditional songs and chants and on contents of the Bible. The Living Book is memorized by each generation.

Churches; 1; Inclusive Membership; 2,108; Sunday or Sabbath Schools: 1; Total Enrollment; 181; Ordained Clergy: None

GENERAL ORGANIZATION

Headquarters: Site 8, Comp. 50, R.R. 1, Crescent Valley, British Columbia V0G 1H0

OFFICERS

Pastor, Stephan S. Sorokin (assisted by a 11-member Fraternal Council)

The Reformed Episcopal Church

The Canadian jurisdiction of the Reformed Episcopal Church (see U.S. listing in Directory 3, "Religious Bodies in the United States") maintains the founding principles of episcopacy (in historic succession from the apostles), Anglican liturgy, Reformed doctrine and evangelical zeal, and in its practice, continues to recognize the validity of certain nonepiscopal orders of evangelical ministry.

OFFICERS

Pres., Bishop W. W. Lyle, 1544 Broadview Ct., Coquitlam, British Columbia V3J 5X9

Vice Pres., Laurence Jackson, 600 Foul Bay Rd., Victoria, British Columbia V8S 4H3

Sec., Miss E. R. MacQueen, 736-13th St., New Westminster, British Columbia V3M 4M7. Tel. (604) 521-3580

Treas., J. A. Hill, 1209 Crown Cres., Victoria, British Columbia V8P 1M5

Reinlaender Mennonite Church

This group was founded in 1958 when ten ministers and approximately 600 members separated from the Sommerfelder Mennonite Church. In 1968, four ministers and about 200 members migrated to Bolivia. The church has work in Winkler, Altona, Blumenfeld, Austin, Grunthal and Stuartburn, Manitoba.

Churches: 6; Inclusive Membership: 700; Sunday or Sabbath Schools: N.R.; Total Enrollment: N.R.; Ordained Clergy: 10.

CORRESPONDENT
Bishop P. A. Rempel, 223rd St. S., Winkler, Manitoba R6W 2V9

Reorganized Church of Jesus Christ of Latter Day Saints

Founded April 6, 1830, by Joseph Smith, Jr., and reorganized under the leadership of the founder's son, Joseph Smith III, in 1860. The Church is established in 35 countries in addition to the United States and Canada. A biennial world conference is held in Independence, Mo. The current president is Wallace B. Smith, greatgrandson of the original founder.

Churches: 52; Inclusive Membership: 12,465; Sunday or Sabbath Schools: N.R.; Total Enrollment: N.R.; Ordained Clergy: 1,058

Headquarters: World Headquarters, The Auditorium, Independence, Mo.; Canadian Office, 390 Speedvale Ave., E., Guelph, Ontario N1E 1N5

CHURCH OFFICERS IN CANADA
Region Admin., Donald H. Comer, 390 Speedvale Ave., E., Guelph, Ontario N1E 1N5
District Presidents:
Alberta, G. Ivan Millar, #13, 20 Laval Blvd., Lethbridge, Alberta T1K 4E4
British Columbia, E. Carl Bolger, 410-1005 McKenzie Ave., Victoria, British Columbia V8X 4A9
Chatham, Ontario, John S. Scherer, 87 Glenwood Dr., Chatham, Ontario N7L 3X3
London, Ontario, John S. Wright, 303 Commissioners Rd., W.,London, Ontario N6J 1Y4
Niagara, Ontario, L. Neil McLean, #25 1422 Tyandaga Park Dr., Burlington, Ontario L7P 1N3
Northern Ontario, Donald Arrowsmith, 917 Woodbine Ave., Sudbury, Ontario P3A 2L8
Ottawa Missionary District, Roy A. Young, RR #4, Odessa, Ontario K0H 2H0
Owen Sound, Ontario, Robert G. Butcher, 409-860 9th St., E., Owen Sound, Ontario N4K 1R2
Saskatchewan, Frank W. Ward, 411 Preston Ave., Saskatoon, Saskatchewan S7H 2V1
Toronto, Ontario, Larry D. Windland, 1443 Bathhurst St., Toronto, Ontario M5R 3J2
Grand River, A. J. David Snell, 49-121 University Ave. E., Waterloo, Ontario N2J 4J1

The Roman Catholic Church in Canada

The largest single body of Christians in Canada, the Roman Catholic Church is under the spiritual leadership of His Holiness the Pope. Catholicism in Canada dates back to 1534, when the first Mass was celebrated on the Gaspé Peninsula on July 7, by a priest accompanying Jacques Cartier. There seems little doubt that Catholicism had been implanted earlier by fishermen and sailors from Europe. Priests came to Acadia as early as 1604. Traces of a regular colony go back to 1608 when Champlain settled in Quebec City. The Recollets (1615), followed by the Jesuits (1625) and the Sulpicians (1657), began the missions among the native population. The first official Roman document relative to the Canadian missions dates from March 20, 1618. Bishop Francois de Montmorency-Laval, the first bishop, arrived in Quebec in 1659. The church developed in the East but not until 1818 did systematic missionary work begin in western Canada.

In the latter 1700s, English-speaking Roman Catholics, mainly from Ireland and Scotland, began to arrive in Canada's Atlantic provinces. After 1815 Irish Catholics settled in large numbers in what is now Ontario. The Irish potato famine of 1847 greatly increased that population in all parts of eastern Canada.

By the 1850s the Catholic Church in both English- and French-speaking Canada had begun to erect new dioceses and found many religious communities. These communities did educational, medical, and charitable work among their own people as well as among Canada's native peoples. By the 1890s large numbers of non-English and non-French-speaking Catholics had settled in Canada, especially in the Western provinces. In the 20th century the pastoral horizons have continued to expand to meet the needs of what has now become a very multiracial church.

INTERNATIONAL ORGANIZATION

His Holiness the Pope, Bishop of Rome, Vicar of Jesus Christ, Supreme Pontiff of the Catholic Church.
POPE JOHN PAUL II, Karol Wojtyla (born May 18, 1920; installed October 22, 1978)
APOSTOLIC PRO NUNCIO TO CANADA Archbishop Angelo Palmas, 724 Manor Ave., Rockcliffe Park, Ottawa, Ontario K1M 0E3. Tel. (613)746-4914

Churches: 5,981; Inclusive Membership: 10,999,964; Sunday or Sabbath Schools: N.R.; Total Enrollment: N.R.; Ordained Clergy: 11,835

CANADIAN ORGANIZATION

Canadian Conference of Catholic Bishops (Conférence des évêques catholiques du Canada) 90 Parent Ave. Ottawa, Ontario, K1N 7B1. Tel. (613)236-9461. (All offices below are at this address and telephone number unless otherwise stated.)
The Canadian Conference of Catholic Bishops is an Association of Cardinals, Archbishops, and Bishops of Canada established to assure the progress of the Church and the Coordination of Catholic activities in Canada.
The Canadian Hierarchy is divided along linquistic lines between French and English.

OFFICERS

General Secretariat of the Episcopacy
Secrétaire général (French Sector) Msgr Denis Rabitaille
General Secretary (English Sector) Rev. William J. Ryan
Assistant General Secretary (English Sector), Mr. Bernard Daly
Secrétaire général adjoint (French Sector), P. Roland Denis

EXECUTIVE COMMITTEE

National Level
Pres., Mgr Bernard Hubert
Vice Pres., Most Rev. James Hayes
Co. Treas., Most Rev. Thomas Fulton; Mgr Robert Lebel

EPISCOPAL COMMISSIONS

National Level
Social Affairs, Most Rev. Paul J. O'Byrne
Canon Law—Inter-rite, Mgr Louis-de-Gonzague Langevin

Ministries, Most Rev. Raymond Saint-Gelais
Missions, Most Rev. Hubert O'Connor
Ecumenism, Most Rev. Antoine Hacault
Theology, Most Rev. James H. MacDonald
Sector Level
Communications Sociales, Mgr Charles Valois
Social Communications, Most Rev. Alphonsus Penney
Education Chrétien, Mgr Donat Chiasson
Christian Education, Most Rev. Marcel Gervais
Liturgie, Mgr Maurice Couture
Liturgy, Most Rev. James L. Doyle

OFFICES

Secteur Francais
Office des Missions, Dir., Père Claude Pagé
Office des Communications Sociales, Dir., Abbé Lucien Labelle, 4005 rue de Bellechasse, Montreal, Québec. H1X 1J6. Tel. (514)729-6391
Office National de liturgie, coordonnateur: M. Jean-Bernard Allard, p.s.s., 1225 est, boul. St. Joseph, Montréal, Québec H2J 1L7. Tel. (514)277-2133
Office pour le Dialogue avec les Non-Croyants, Dir., Père Léopold de Reyès, ss.cc., 2930 Lacombe, Montréal, Québec H3T 1L4. Tel. (514)735-1565
Office National d'Ocumenisme, Rev. Thomas Ryan, C.S.P., 2065 ouest rue Sherbrooke, Montréal, Québec H3H 1G6. Tel. (514)937-9176
Services des Relations Publiques, Dir., M. Jacques Binet
Service des Editions, Dir., Mlle Claire Dubé.
English Sector
National Liturgical Office, Dir., Rev. Murray Kroetsch; Msgr. P. Byrne
National Office of Religious Education, Dir., Mrs. Bernadette Tourangeau
Office for Missions, Dir., Rev. Michael Murray, S.J.L
Public Information Office, Dir., Miss Bonnie Brennan
Social Affairs, Dir., Mr. Tony Clarke

REGIONAL EPISCOPAL ASSEMBLIES

Atlantic Episcopal Assembly, Pres., Mgr Austin E. Burke; Vice-Pres., Most Rev. James MacDonald; Sec., Rev. Guy Léger, C.S.C., P.O. Box 700, Sainte-Anne du Ruisseau, Yarmouth County, Nova Scotia B0W 2X0. Tel. (902)648-2315
Assemblée des Évêques du Quebec, Prés., Mgr Jean-Marie Fortier; Vice-Pres., Mgr Gilles Ouellet; Sécretaire général, L'abbé Michel Buron; Secrétariat: 1225 boulevard Saint Joseph est, Montréal, Québec H2J 1L7. Tél. (514)274-4323
Ontario Conference of Catholic Bishops, Pres., Most Rev. John O'Mara; Vice-Pres., Mgr Eugene LaRocque; Sec., Rev. Angus J. Macdougall, S.J.; Secretariat: 67 Bond St., Ste. 304, Toronto, Ontario M5B 1X5. Tel. (416)368-1804
Western Catholic Conference, Pres., Most Rev. Remi De Roo; Vice-Pres., Most Rev. Emmett Doyle; Sec., Mgr Hubert O'Connor, 2935 Highway 16 West, P.O. Box 7000, Prince George, British Columbia V2N 3Z2. Tel. (604)964-4424

MILITARY VICARIATE (VICARIAT MILITAIRE)

Vicaire aux Forces canadiennes (Military Vicar), Most Rev. Francis J. Spence, 279 Johnson St., Kingston, Ontario K7L 1Y5. Tel. (613)546-5521
Canadian Religious Conference, 324 Laurier Ave., East, Ottawa, Ontario K1N 6P6. Tel. (613)236-0824. Sec. Gen., Fr. Albert Dumont, O.P.

ARCHDIOCESES AND DIOCESES

The Roman Catholic Church in Canada has 17 Archdioceses and 47 Dioceses of the Latin rite; 3 Archeparchies, 5 Eparchies and 1 Exarchate of the Oriental rite; 1 Abbacy Nullius; and the Military Vicariate. Each of these ecclesiastical jurisdictions appears alphabetically in the following list and contains this information in sequence: Name of incumbent bishop, address of Chancery office (Evêché) or other headquarters, and telephone number.

Cardinals are addressed as "His Eminence" (in French as "Son Eminence") and Archbishops and Bishops as "Most Reverend" (in French as "Son Excellence").

LATIN RITE

Alexandria-Cornwall, Mgr Eugéne P. LaRocque. Centre diocésain, 220 Chemin Montréal, C. P. 1388 Cornwall, Ontario K6H 5V4. Tel. (613) 933-1138
Amos, Mgr Gérard Drainville. Evêché, 450, Principale Nord, Amos, Québec J9T 2M1. Tel. (819) 732-6515
Antigonish, Bishop Colin Campbell. Chancery Office, 155 Main St., P.O. Box 1330, Antigonish, Nova Scotia B2G 2L7. Tel. (902) 863-4818
Baie-Comeau, Mgr Roger Ebacher. Evêché, 639 Rue de Bretagne, Baie-Comeau, Québec G5C 1X2. Tel. (418) 589-5744
Bathurst, Mgr Arsène Richard. Evêché, 645, avenue Murray, C. P. 460, Bathurst, New Brunswick E2A 3Z4. Tel. (506) 546-3493
Calgary, Bishop Paul J. O'Byrne. Bishop's Office, 1916 Second St. S.W., Calgary, Alberta T2S 1S3. Tel. (403) 228-4501
Charlottetown, Bishop James H. MacDonald. Bishop's Residence, P.O. Box 907, Charlottetown, Prince Edward Island C1A 7L9. Tel. (902) 892-1357
Chicoutimi, Mgr Jean-Guy Couture. Evêché, 602 est, rue Racine, C.P. 278, Chicoutimi,Québec G7H 6J6. Tel. (418) 543-0783
Churchill-Baie D'Hudson, Mgr Reynald Rouleau, O.M.I. Evêché, C.P. 10, Churchill, Manitoba, R0B 0E0. Tel. (204) 675-2541
Archdiocese of Edmonton, Archbishop Joseph N. MacNeil. Archdiocesan Office, 10044-113th St., Edmonton, Alberta T5K 1N8 Tel. (403) 488-0118
Edmundston, Mgr Gérard Dionne. Evêché, Centre diocesain, Edmundston, New Brunswick E3V 3K1. Tel. (506) 735-5578
Gaspé, Mgr Bertrand Blanchet. Evêché, C.P. 440, Gaspé, Québec G0C 1R0. Tel. (418) 368-2274
Gatineau-Hull, Mgr Adolphe Proulx. Evêché, 119, rue Carillon, Hull, Québec J8X 2P8. Tel. (819) 771-8391
Grand Falls, Bishop Joseph Faber MacDonald. Chancery Office: P.O. Box 397, Grand Falls, Newfoundland, A2A 2J8. Tel. (709) 489-4019
Gravelbourg, Mgr Noel Delaquis. Secrétariat, C.P. 690, Gravelbourg, Saskatchewan S0H 1X0. Tel. (306) 648-2235
Archdiocèse de Grouard-McLennan, Mgr Henri Légaré. Archevêché, C.P. 388, McLennan, Alberta T0H 2L0, Tel. (403) 324-3002
Archdiocese of Halifax, Archbishop James M. Hayes. Archbishop's Residence, 6541 Coburg Rd., P.O. Box 1527, Halifax, Nova Scotia B3J 2Y3. Tel. (902) 429-9388
Hamilton, Bishop Anthony Tonnos. Chancery Office, 700 King St. W., Hamilton, Ontario L8P 1C7. Tel. (416) 528-7988
Hearst, Mgr Roger A. Despatie. Evêché, C.P. 1330, Hearst, Ontario P0L 1N0. Tel. (705) 362-4903
Joliette, Mgr René Audet. Evêché, 2, rue St.-Charles Borromée, Nord. C.P. 470, Joliette, Québec J6E 6H6. Tel. (514) 753-7596
Kamloops, Bishop Lawrence Sabatini. Bishop's Residence, 635A Tranquille Rd., Kamloops, British Columbia V2B 3H5. Tel. (604) 376-3351
Archidiocèse de Keewatin-LePas, Archbishop Peter-Alfred Sutton. Résidence, 108 1st St. W., C.P. 270, Le Pas, Manitoba R9A 1K4. Tel. (204) 623-3529

Archdioceses of Kingston, Archbishop Francis J. Spence. P. O. Box 997, 390 Palace Rd., Kingston, Ontario K7L 4X8. Tel. (613) 548-4461

Labrador-Schefferville, Mgr Henri Goudreault. Evêché, 318 Ave. Elizabeth, Labrador City, Labrador A2V 2K7. Tel. (709) 944-2046

London, Bishop John M. Sherlock. Chancery Office, 1070 Waterloo St., London Ontario N6A 3Y2, Tel. (519) 433-0658

Mackenzie-Fort Smith (T.No.O.), Mgr Denis Croteau. Evêché, C.P. 3, Fort Smith, T.N.O. X0E 0P0. Tel. (403)872-2302

Archidiocèse de Moncton, Mgr Donat Chiasson. Archevêché, C.P. 248, Moncton, New Brunswick E1C 8K9. Tel. (506) 389-9531

Mont-Laurier, Mgr Jean Gratton. Evêché, 435, rue de la Madone, C.P. 1290, Mont Laurier, Québec J9L 1S1. Tel. (819) 623-5530

Archidiocèse de Montréal, Mgr Paul Grégoire. Archevêché, 2000 ouest, rue Sherbrooke, Montréal, Québec H3H 1G4. Tel. (514) 931-7311

Moosonee, Mgr Jules LeGuerrier. Résidence, C.P. 40, Moosonee, Ontario P0L 1Y0. Tel. (705) 336-2908

Abbatia Nullius of Muenster, Abbot Ordinary Jerome Weber, OSB. Abbot's Residence, St. Peter's Abbey, Muenster, Saskatchewan S0K 2Y0. Tel. (306) 682-5521

Nelson, Bishop W. Emmett Doyle. Chancery Office, 813 Ward St., Nelson, British Columbia V1L 1T4. Tel. (604) 352-6921

Nicolet, Mgr J. Albertus Martin. Evêché, C.P. 820, Nicolet, Québec J0G 1E0. Tel. (819) 293-4234

Archidiocèse D'Ottawa, Mgr Joseph-Auréle Plourde. Chancellerie, 1247, avenue Kilborn, Ottawa, Ontario K1H 6K9 Tel. (613)738-5025

Pembroke, Bishop J. R. Windle. Bishop's Residence, 188 Renfrew St., P.O. Box 7, Pembroke, Ontario K8A 6X1. Tel. (613) 732-3895

Peterborough, Bishop James L. Doyle. Bishop's Residence, 350 Hunter St. W., Peterborough, Ontario K9J 6Y8. Tel. (705) 745-5123

Prince-Albert, Mgr Blaise Morand. Evêché, 1415-ouest, 4e Ave., Prince-Albert, Saskatchewan S6V 5H1. Tel. (306) 922-4747.

Prince-George, Bishop Hubert O'Connor. Chancery Office, 2935 Highway 16 West, P.O. Box 7000, Prince George, British Columbia V2N 3Z2. Tel. (604) 964-4424

Archidiocèse de Québec, Mgr Louis-Albert Vachon. Archevêché, 2, rue Port Dauphin, C.P. 459, Québec, Québec G1R 4R6. Tel. (418) 692-3935

Archdiocese of Regina, Archbishop Charles A. Halpin, Chancery Office, 3225 13th Ave., Regina, Saskatchewan S4T 1P5. Tel. (306)352-1651

Archidiocèse de Rimouski, Mgr Gilles Quellet. Archevêché, 34 ouest, rue de L'evêché, C.P. 730, Rimouski, Québec. G5L 7C7. Tel. (418) 723-3320

Rouyn-Noranda, Mgr Jean-Guy Hamelin, Evêché, 515, rue Cuddihy, C.P. 1060, Rouyn, Québec J9X 5W9. Tel. (819) 764-4660

Ste-Anne de la, Pocatière, Mgr André Gaumond. Evêché, C.P. 430 La Pocatière, Québec G0R 1Z0. Tel. (418) 856-1811

Archidiocèse de Saint-Boniface, Mgr Antoine Hacault. Archevêché, 151, ave de la Cathédrale, St-Boniface Manitoba R2H 0H6. Tel. (204) 237-9851

St. Catharine's, Bishop Thomas B. Fulton. Bishop's Residence, 122 Riverdale Ave., St. Catharines, Ontario L2R 4C2. Tel. (416) 684-0154

St. George's, Bishop Raymond J. Lahey. Bishop's Residence, 16 Hammond Dr., Corner Brook, Newfoundland A2H 2W2. Tel. (709) 639-7073

Saint Hyacinthe, Mgr Louis-de-Gonzague Langevin. Evêché 1900 ouest, Girouard, C. P. 190, Saint-Hyacinthe, Québec J2S 7B4. Tel. (514) 773-8581

Saint-Jean-de-Longueuil, Mgr Bernard Hubert. Evêché, 740 boul. Ste-Foy, C.P. 40, Longueuil, Québec J4K 4X8. Tel. (514) 679-1100

Saint-Jérôme, Mgr Charles Valois, Evêché, 355, rue St-Georges, C.P. 580, Saint-Jérôme, Québec J7Z 5V3. Tel. (514) 432-9741

Saint John, Bishop J. Edward Troy. Chancery Office, 1 Bayard Dr., Saint John, New Brunswick E2L 3L5. Tel. (506) 693-4418

Archdiocese of St. John's, Archbishop Alphonsus Penney. Archbishop's Residence, P.O. Box 37, Basilica Residence, St. John's, Newfoundland A1C 5H5. Tel. (709) 726-3660

Saint-Paul, Mgr Raymond Roy. Evêché, 4410 51e Ave., C.P. 339, St-Paul, Alberta T0A 3A0. Tel. (403) 645-3277

Saskatoon, Bishop James P. Mahoney. Chancery Office, 106-5th Ave., N., Saskatoon. Saskatchewan S7K 2N7. Tel. (306) 242-7831

Sault Ste. Marie, Bishop Marcel Gervais. Bishop's Residence, 480 McIntyre St., W., P.O. Box 510, North Bay, Ontario, P1B 8J1 Tel. (705) 476-1300

Archidiocèse de Sherbrooke, Mgr Jean-Marie Fortier, Archevêché, 130, rue de la Cathedrale, C.P. 430, Sherbrooke, Québec J1H 5K1. Tel. (819) 563-9934

Thunder Bay, Bishop John A. O'Mara. Bishop's Residence, 1306 Ridgeway St., Thunder Bay, Ontario PC7 4V5. Tel. (807) 623-6633

Timmins, Mgr Jacques Landriault. Centre diocésain, 65, avenue Jubilee est, Timmins, Ontario P4N 5W4. Tel. (705) 267-6224

Archdiocese of Toronto, Archbishop G. Emmett Cardinal Carter, Chancery Office, 355 Church St., Toronto, Ontario M5B 1Z8. Tel. (416) 977-1500

Trois-Rivières, Mgr Laurent Noël. Evêché, 362, rue Bonaventure, C.P. 879, Trois-Rivièrès, Québec G9A 5J9. Tel. (819) 374-9847

Valleyfield, Mgr Robert Lebel. Evêché, 31 rue Fabrique, C.P. 338, Valleyfield, Québec J6T 4G9. Tel. (514) 373-8122

Archdiocese of Vancouver, Archbishop James F. Carney, Chancery Office, 150 Robson St., Vancouver, British Columbia, V6B 2A7. Tel. (604) 683-0281

Victoria, Bishop Remi J. De Roo. Bishop's Office, 230-1555 McKenzie Ave., Victoria, British-Columbia V8N 1A4. Tel. (604) 721-4423

Whitehorse (Yukon), _____. Bishop's Residence, 5119 5th Ave., Whitehorse, Yukon Y1A 1L5. Tel. (403) 667-2052

Archdiocese of Winnipeg, Archbishop Adam Exner. Chancery Office 50 Stafford Street, Winnipeg, Manitoba R3M 2V7. Tel. (204) 474-2361

Yarmouth, Mgr Austin-Emile Burke. Evêché, 53, rue Park, Yarmouth, Nova Scotia B5A 4B2. Tel. (902) 742-7163

EASTERN RITES

The Hierarchy for Ukrainian Catholics of the Byzantine Rite in All of Canada

Eparchy of Edmonton, Eparch: Most Rev. Martin Greschuk. Eparch's Residence, 6240 Ada Blvd., Edmonton, Alberta T5W 4P1. Tel. (403) 479-0381

Eparchy of New Westminster, Eparch: Most Rev. Jerome I. Chimy. Eparch's Residence, 502 5th Ave., New Westminster, British Columbia V3L 1S2. Tel. (604) 521-8015

Eparchy of Saskatoon, Eparch: Most Rev. Basil Filevich. Eparch's Residence, 866 Saskatchewan. Crescent East, Saskatoon, Saskatchewan S7N 0L4. Tel. (306) 653-0138

Eparchy of Toronto, Eparch: Most Rev. Isidore Borecky. Eparch's Residence, 61 Glen Edyth Dr., Toronto, Ontario M4V 2V8. Tel. (416) 924-2381

Archeparchy of Winnipeg, Archeparch: Most Rev. Maxim Hermaniuk. Archeparch's Residence, 235 Sco-

149

tia St., Winnipeg, Manitoba R2V 1V7. Tel. (204) 339-7457

The Eparchy for Slovak Catholics of the Byzantine Rite in All of Canada
Toronto, Ontario Eparchy, Eparch: Most Rev. Michael Rusnak. Chancery Office, Box 70, Unionville, Ontario L3R 2L8. Tel. (416) 477-4867.

The Melkite Archeparchy for All of Canada
Montréal (Qué) Archéparchie, Archéparque, Mgr Michel Hakim; Chancelier: Mgr Georges Coriaty. Chancellerie: 34 Maplewood, Montréal, Québec H2V 2M1. Tél. (514) 272-6430

The Maronite Archeparchy for All of Canada
Archéparchie de Montréal, Archéparque, Mgr Elias Shaheen. Chancellerie, 12475 rue Grenet, Montréal, Québec H4J 2K4. Tél. (514) 336-4220

Romanian Orthodox Church in America (Canadian Parishes)

The first Romanian Orthodox immigrants in Canada called for Orthodox priests from their native country of Romania. Between 1902-1914, they organized the first Romanian parish communities and built Orthodox churches in different cities and farming regions of western Canada (Alberta, Saskatchewan, Manitoba) as well as in the eastern part (Ontario and Quebec).

In 1929, the Romanian Orthodox parishes from Canada joined with those of the U.S. in a Congress held in Detroit, Mich., and asked the Holy Synod of the Romanian Orthodox Church of Romania to establish a Romanian Orthodox Missionary Episcopate in America (which was the legal title of this body). The first Bishop, Policarp (Morushca), was elected and consecrated by the Holy Synod of the Romanian Orthodox Church and came to the U.S. in 1935. He established his headquarters in Detroit with jurisdiction over all the Romanian Orthodox parishes in the U.S. and Canada.

In 1950, the Romanian Orthodox Church in America (i.e. the Romanian Orthodox Missionary Episcopate in America) was granted administrative autonomy by the Holy Synod of the Romanian Orthodox Church of Romania, and only doctrinal and canonical ties remain with this latter body.

The Holy Synod of the Romanian Orthodox Church of Romania, in its session of Dec. 12, 1974, recognized and approved the Decision taken by the Annual Congress of the Romanian Church in America, held on July 21, 1973, at Edmonton-Boian, Alberta, relating to the elevation of the Episcopate to the rank of "Archdiocese" with the official title **The Romanian Orthodox Missionary Archdiocese in America**, renewing at the same time its status of Ecclesiastical Autonomy.

The 46th Annual Church Congress of the Archdiocese approved the amendment that the Archdiocese will be known as The Romanian Orthodox Missionary Archdiocese in America and Canada

GENERAL ORGANIZATION

Archbishop assisted by his Vicar and the Canadian Diocesan Council. Annual Congress for both U.S. and Canada.
Canadian Office: St. Demetrios Romanian Orthodox Church, 103 Furby St., Winnipeg, Manitoba R3C 2A4. Tel. (204) 775-3701

OFFICERS

Archbishop: Most Rev. Archbishop Victorin, 19959 Riopelle St., Detroit, MI 48203. Tel. (313) 893-7191
Vicar, V. Rev. Archim, Dr. Vasile Vasilachi 19959 Riopelle St., Detroit, MI 48203. Tel. (313) 893-7191
Cultural Councilor, V. Rev. Fr. Nicolae Ciurea, 19

Murray St., W., Hamilton, Ontario, Tel. (416) 529-1663
Administrative Councilor, V. Rev. Fr. Mircea Panciuk, 11024-165th Ave., Edmonton, Alberta T5X 1X9
Sec., V. Rev. Arhim Felix Dubneac, 19959 Riopelle St., Detroit, MI 48203. Tel. (313) 893-7191

PERIODICALS

Credinta—The Faith (m), and Calendarul Credinta (Yearbook with the Church Directory of the Archdiocese) (a). 19959 Riopelle St., Detroit, MI 48203. V. Rev. Archim., Dr. Vasile Vasilachi, Ed.

The Romanian Orthodox Episcopate of America (Jackson, Michigan)

This body of Eastern Orthodox Christians of Romanian descent was organized in 1929 as an autonomous Diocese under the jurisdiction of the Romanian Patriarchate. In 1951, it served all relations with the Orthodox Church of Romania. Now under the canonical jurisdiction of the autocephalous Orthodox Church in America, it enjoys full administrative autonomy and is headed by its own Bishop.

Churches: 13; Inclusive Membership: 8,600; Sunday or Sabbath Schools: 10; Total Enrollment: 663; Ordained Clergy: 11

GENERAL ORGANIZATION

Church Congress, held annually in July
Headquarters: 2522 Grey Tower Rd., Jackson, MI 49201

OFFICERS

Ruling Bishop: Rt. Rev. Nathaniel (Popp).
Dean of all Canada: Very Rev. Archim. Martinian Ivanovici, Romanian Orthodox Christian Missionary Centre, Box 636, Ft. Qu'Appelle, Saskatchewan S0G 1S0. Tel. (306)332-6620

OTHER ORGANIZATIONS

The American Romanian Orthodox Youth (AROY), Patrick Roach, 3739 W. 165th St., Cleveland, OH 44111
Association of Romanian Orthodox Ladies Auxiliaries (ARFORA), Pauline Trutza, 1446 Waterbury Ave., Lakewood, OH 44107
Orthodox Brotherhood of Canada, Pres., Trian Lascu, Site 1, Box 8, Assinibola, Saskatchewan S0H 0B0

PERIODICAL

Solia, Romanian News (m), 146 W. Cortland St., Jackson, MI 49201. Tel. (517)789-9088
Solia Calendar (a)

Russian Orthodox Church in Canada, Patriarchal Parishes of the

Diocese of Canada of the former Exarchate of North and South America of the Russian Orthodox Church. Originally founded in 1897 by the Russian Orthodox Archdiocese in North America.

Churches: 24; Inclusive Membership: 8,000; Sunday or Sabbath Schools: 1; Total Enrollment: 21; Ordained Clergy: 7

GENERAL ORGANIZATION

General Conference: Meets annually at call from Bishop, St. Barbara's Russian Orthodox Cathedral, 10105—96th St., Edmonton, Alberta T5H 2G3.

OFFICERS

Administrator: Most Rev. Archbishop Nicholas, St.

Barbara's Complex, #303, 9566 - 101 Ave., Edmonton, Alberta T5H 0B4

The Salvation Army in Canada

The Salvation Army is an international religious movement whose members are motivated by love for God and people. An evangelical branch of the Christian church, its membership includes officers (clergy) and laity. Its spiritual ministry comes from commitment to Jesus Christ and reveals itself in practical service, regardless of race, color, creed, sex, or age.

The goals of The Salvation Army are to preach the gospel, disseminate Christian truths, instill Christian values, enrich family life, and improve the quality of all life.

The organization provides personal counseling, supplies basic human necessities, and undertakes the spiritual and moral rehabilitation of all in need who come within its sphere of influence.

An evangelistic organization with a military government, it was first set up by General William Booth (1829-1912) in England in 1865. Converts from England started Salvation Army work in London, Ontario, in 1882. In 1884, Canada became a separate command which also has included Bermuda since 1933. An act to incorporate the Governing Council of The Salvation Army in Canada received royal assent on May 19, 1909.

Headquarters for Canada and Bermuda: 20 Albert St., Toronto, Ontario; P. O. Box 4021 Postal Sta. A, Toronto, Ontario M5W 2B1 Tel. (416) 598-2071

Churches: 378; Inclusive Membership: 102,018; Sunday or Sabbath Schools: 359; Total Enrollment: 26,919; Ordained Clergy: 2,057

OFFICERS

Territorial Commander, Commissioner Will Pratt
Territorial Pres., Women's Organizations, Mrs. Commissioner, Will Pratt
Chief Sec., Col. Arthur E. Waters
Field Sec. for Personnel, Col. Roy Calvert
Program Sec., Lt. Col. Edwin Brown
Bus. Adm. Sec., Major Ivor Rich
Fin. Sec., Maj. Douglas Kerr
Pub. Relations Sec., Lt. Col. Howard Moore
Property Sec., Lt. Col. Ralph Stanley
Information Services Sec., Major Mel Bond

PERIODICAL

War Cry, Maj. Maxwell Ryan, Ed-in-Chief.

Serbian Orthodox Church in the U.S.A. and Canada, Diocese of Canada

The Serbian Orthodox Church is an organic part of the Eastern Orthodox Church. As a local church it received its autocephaly from Constantinople in 1219 A.D. The Patriarchal seat of the church today is in Belgrade, Yugoslavia. In 1921, a Serbian Orthodox Diocese in the United States of America and Canada was organized. In 1963, it was reorganized into three dioceses and in 1983 a fourth diocese was created for the Canadian part of the church. The Serbian Orthodox Church is in absolute doctrinal unity with all other local Orthodox Churches.

GENERAL ORGANIZATION

The Serbian Orthodox Diocese of Canada, 5a Stockbridge Ave., Toronto, Ontario H8Z 4M6. Tel. (416) 231-4409.

OFFICERS

Rt. Rev. Georgije, Serbian Orthodox Bishop of Canada, 5a Stockbridge Ave., Toronto, Ontario H8Z 4M6. Tel. (416) 231-4409

Dean of Western Deanery. Rev. Miroslav Dejanov, 620 E. 63rd Ave., Vancouver, British Columbia V5X 2K4. Tel. (604) 321-9750.

Dean of Eastern Deanery, Rev. Stevo Stojsavljevich, 143 Nash Rd., S., Hamilton, Ontario L8K 4J9. Tel. (416) 560-9424

PERIODICAL

The Path of Orthodoxy, P. O. Box 36, Leetsdale, PA 15056. Tel (412) 741-8660. Rev. Rade Merick, Eng. Ed.; V. Rev. Uros Ocokoljic, V. Rev. Nedeljko Lunich, Rev. Vasilije Tomic, Serbian Eds.

Seventh-day Adventist Church in Canada

The Seventh-day Adventist Church in Canada is part of the worldwide Seventh-day Adventist Church with headquarters in Washington, D.C. The Seventh-day Adventist Church in Canada was organized in 1901 and reorganized in 1932.

Churches: 289; Inclusive Membership: 35,992; Sunday or Sabbath Schools: 319; Total Enrollment: 27,300; Ordained Clergy: 263

GENERAL ORGANIZATION

Headquarters: 1148 King St., E., Oshawa, Ontario L1H 1H8. Tel. (416) 433-0011

OFFICERS

Pres., J. W. Wilson
Vice Pres., L. G. Lowe
Treas., G. B. DeBoer
Sec., G.E. Maxson

DEPARTMENTS

A.S.I.: L. G. Lowe
Education: J. D. V. Fitch
Assoc. Educ. Dir., J. Saliba
Personal Ministries: E. R. Bacchus
Communication Dept.: G. E. Maxson
Public Affairs: D. D. Devnich
Publishing: Paul Cordray
Actg. Trust Services Dir., E. Skula
Consultant to Health Care Institutions: A. G. Rodgers

PERIODICAL

Canadian Adventist Messenger, (m), Maracle Press, 1148 King St. E.,Oshawa, Ontario L1H 1H8. G.E. Maxson, Ed.

Sikhs

Sikhism was born in the northwestern part of the Indo-Pakistan sub-continent in Punjab province about five hundred years ago. Guru Nanak, founder of the religion, was born in 1469. He was followed by nine successor Gurus. The Guruship was then bestowed on the Sikh Holy Book, popularly known as the Guru Granth. The Granth contains writings of the Sikh Gurus and some Hindu and Muslim saints and was compiled by the fifth Guru, Arjan Dev. For the Sikhs, the Granth is the only object of worship. It contains, mostly, hymns of praise of God, the Formless One.

Sikhs started migrating from India more than a half century ago. A number of them settled on the West coast of North America, in British Columbia and California. More recently, a sizeable group has settled in the Eastern part of the Continent as well, particularly in Ontario, New York and Michigan. Sikhs are found in all major cities of the U.S. and Canada.

When Sikhs settle, they soon establish a Gurdwara, or Sikh temple, for worship and social gathering. Gurdwaras are found, among other places, in Toronto, Vancouver, Victoria, and Yuba City, California. At other places, they meet for worship in schools and community centers.

The First Sikh Conference was held on March 24-25, 1979 in Toronto. This is the first step in establishing a federation of all the Sikh Associations in Canada, and, if possible, in USA as well. A Sikh Heritage Conference was held September 19-21, 1981 in Toronto.

There are approximately 120-150,000 Sikhs in North America.

CORRESPONDENT

The Sikh Social and Educational Society, 70 Cairnside Crescent, Willowdale, Ontario M2J 3M8

Syrian Orthodox Church of Antioch (Archdiocese of the United States and Canada)

An archdiocese of the Syrian Orthodox Church of Antioch in North America, the Syrian Orthodox Church professes the faith of the first three ecumenical councils of Nicaea, Constantinople, and Ephesus and numbers faithful in the Middle East, India, the Americas, Europe, and Australia. It traces its origin to the Patriarchate established in Antioch by St. Peter the Apostle and is under the supreme ecclesiastical jurisdiction of His Holiness the Syrian Orthodox Patriarch of Antioch and All the East, now residing in Damascus, Syria.

The Archdiocese of the Syrian Orthodox Church in the U.S. and Canada was formally established in 1957. The first Syrian Orthodox faithful came to Canada in the 1890s and formed the first Canadian parish in Sherbrooke, Quebec. Today five official parishes of the Archdiocese exist in Canada—two in the Province of Quebec and three in the Province of Ontario.

ORGANIZATION

Archdiocese of the U.S. and Canada, 49 Kipp Ave., Lodi, NJ 07644. Tel. (201)778-0638
Archdiocesan Convention: Annual

OFFICERS

Primate: Archbishop Mar Athanasius Y. Samuel, 49 Kipp Ave., Lodi, NJ 07644. Tel. (201)778-0638
Archdiocesan Gen. Sec., Very Rev. Chorepiscopus John Meno, 45 Fairmount Ave., Hackensack, NJ 07601. Tel. (201)646-9443

Ukrainian Greek-Orthodox Church of Canada

Toward the end of the 19th century the Ukrainian people began leaving their homeland, and many immigrated to Canada, which has been their homeland for 90 years. At Saskatoon, in 1918, the Ukrainian pioneers organized this Church. The Ukrainian Orthodox Church of Canada has grown rapidly in the past 67 years so that today it is the largest Ukrainian Orthodox Church beyond the borders of the Ukraine.

GENERAL ORGANIZATION

General Organization: Sobor (General Council) meets every five years, Presidium meets monthly, Full Consistory, semi-annually
Headquarters: Consistory of the Ukrainian Orthodox Church of Canada, 9 St. John's Ave., Winnipeg, Manitoba R2W 1G8. Tel. (204) 586-3093

OFFICERS

Presidium, Chpsn., V. Rev. Dr. S. Jarmus, 9 St. John's Ave., Winnipeg, Manitoba R2W 1G8

Primate, Mt. Rev. Metropolitan Wasyly, 174 Seven Oaks Ave., Winnipeg, Manitoba R2V 0K8

PERIODICALS

Visnyk (s-m), 9 St. John's Ave., Winnipeg, Manitoba, R2W 1G8.

Union of Spiritual Communities of Christ (Orthodox Doukhobors in Canada)

Groups of Canadians of Russian origin living in the western provinces of Canada whose beginnings in Russia are unknown. The name "Doukhobors," or "Spirit Wrestlers," was given in derision by the Russian Orthodox clergy in Russia as far back as 1785. Victims of decades of persecution in Russia, about 7,500 Doukhobors finally arrived in Canada in 1899.

The whole teaching of the Doukhobors is penetrated with the Gospel spirit of love; worshiping God in the spirit they affirm that the outward Church and all that is performed in it and concerns it has no importance for them; the Church is where two or three are gathered together, united in the name of Christ. Their teaching is founded on tradition, which is called among them the "Book of Life," because it lives in their memory and hearts. In this book are recorded sacred songs or chants, partly composed independently, partly formed out of the contents of the Bible, and these are committed to memory by each succeeding generation. Doukhobors observe complete pacifism and non-violence.

The Doukhobors were reorganized in 1938 by their leader, Peter P. Verigin, shortly before his death, into the Union of Spiritual Communities of Christ, commonly called Orthodox Doukhobors. It is headed by a democratically elected Executive Committee which executes the will and protects the interests of the people.

In the present day at least 99 percent of the Doukhobors are law-abiding, pay taxes, and definitely "do not burn or bomb or parade in the nude" as they say a fanatical offshoot called the "Sons of Freedom" does.

GENERAL ORGANIZATION

General Meeting: Annual in February
· Headquarters: USCC Central Office, Box 760, Grand Forks, British Columbia V0H 1H0. Tel. (604) 442-8252

OFFICERS

Honorary Chpsn. of the Exec. Comm., John J. Verigin, Box 760, Grand Forks, British Columbia V0H 1H0
Chpsn., John K. Novokshonoff
Adm., S. W. Babakaiff

PERIODICAL

Iskra (bi-w) in Russian with part of Youth Section in English, Box 760, Grand Forks, British Columbia, V0H 1H0. D. E. (Jim) Popoff, Ed.

Unitarian Universalist Association

The headquarters of the Unitarian Universalist Association is located at 25 Beacon St., Boston, MA 02108. Tel. (617) 742-2100. Three of the twenty-three districts of the UUA are located partly or wholly in Canada, as are 46 of the 1,002 congregations. There is a Canadian Unitarian Council—Conseil Unitaire Canadien which handles matters of particular concern to Canadian churches and fellowships. Its office is located at 175 St. Clair Ave. W. Toronto, Ontario M4V 1P7

Churches: 46; Inclusive Membership: 6,294; Sunday or Sabbath Schools: 36; Total Enrollment: 1,260; Ordained Clergy: 18

Pacific Northwest, Mr. Alan Deale, 1011 S.W. 12th Ave., Portland OR 97205

St. Lawrence, Mr. Richard D. Hogan, 936 Hill Ave., Endicott NY 13760

PrairieStar/Western Canada, Drusilla Cummins, 4238 Sheridan Ave., South Minneapolis, MN 55410

Trustee-at-Large from Canada, Bert Christensen, 135-10 Livonia Pl., West Hill, Ontario M1E 4W6

United Brethren in Christ, Ontario Conference

Founded in 1767 in Lancaster Bounty, PA, missionaries came to Canada about 1850. The first class was held in Kitchener in 1855, and the first building was erected in Port Elgin in 1867.

The Church of the United Brethren in Christ had its beginning with Philip William Otterbein and Martin Boehm who were leaders in the revivalistic movement in Pennsylvania and Maryland during the late 1760s.

GENERAL ORGANIZATION

Ontario conference, Annual. Quadrennial conference: Next meeting, June 1989

Headquarters: 302 Lake St., Huntington, IN 46750

Conf. Supt., Rev. Martin Magnus, 118 Ross Ave., Kitchener, Ontario N2A 1V4. Tel. (519)576-7647

Treas., Mr. Don Nash, 1 Checkendon Dr., Rexdale, Ontario M9W 2Y4

PERIODICAL

The United Brethren (m), 302 Lake St., Huntington, IN 46750. Steve Dennie, Ed.

The United Church of Canada

The United Church of Canada was formed on June 10, 1925, through the union of the Methodist Church, Canada; the congregational Union of Canada; the Council of Local Union Churches; and 70 percent of the Presbyterian Church in Canada. The union culminated years of negotiation between the churches, all of which had integral associations with the development and history of the nation. In fulfillment of its mandate to be a uniting as well as a United Church, the denomination has been enriched by other unions during its history. The Wesleyan Methodist Church of Bermuda joined in 1930. On January 1, 1968, the Canada Conference of the Evangelical United Brethren became part of The United Church of Canada. At various times, congregations of other christian communions have also become congregations of the United Church. The United Church of Canada is a full member of the World Methodist Council, the World Alliance of Reformed Churches (Presbyterian and Congregational), and the Canadian and World Councils of Churches. The United Church is the largest Protestant denomination in Canada.

Churches: 4,192; Inclusive Membership: 2,185,531; Sunday or Sabbath Schools: 3,565; Total Enrollment: 231,996; Ordained Clergy: 3,891

GENERAL ORGANIZATION

Headquarters: The United Church House, 85 St. Clair Ave. E., Toronto, Ontario M4T 1M8, Tel. (416) 925-5931

General Council, meets every two years. Next meeting, 1988 in Victoria, British Columbia.

THE GENERAL COUNCIL

The General Council is the highest legislative body of The United Church of Canada. The Moderator is elected at each meeting of the General Council to hold office until the following Council.

Mod., Dr. Anne M. Squire

Sec., Dr. Howard M. Mills

Deputy Sec., (Regionalism and Personnel), _____, (Theology, Faith, and Ecumenism), Rev. Hallett E. Llewellyn

Personnel Officer, Margaret C. Scriven

Archivist, Jean E. Dryden, 73 Queen's Park Cr., E., Toronto, Ontario M5C 1K7. Tel. (416) 585-4563

Information Officer, Douglas L. Flanders

ADMINISTRATIVE DIVISIONS

Communication: Gen. Sec., Rev. Randolph L. Naylor; Dir. of Fin. and Admn., Alice E. Foster; Dept. of Media Resources, Rev. Rodney M. Booth

The United Church Publishing House: Dir., William G. Park

Productions (Berkeley Studo): Media Services: 315 Queen St. E., Toronto, Ontario M5A 1S7, Tel. (416) 366-9221

Finance: Gen. Sec., William R. Davis

Dept. of the Treasury: Treas., Kenneth H. Ward

Dept. of Pensions and Group Insurance: Sec., Janet E. Petrie

Dept. of Stewardship Services: Sec., Rev. Vincent D. Alfano

Ministry Personnel and Education: Gen. Sec., Rev. Richard H. Moffatt

Basic and Continuing Education, _____

Personnel Services and Career Development, Rev. Barry F. H. Cooke

Student Services and Internships, Mary E. Sanderson

Diaconal Ministry, K. Virginia Coleman

Women in Ministry, J. Ann Naylor

Administrator, S. George Shehata

Mission in Canada: Gen. Sec., Rev. Howard L. Brox; Deputy Sec. (Ofc. of Christian Dev.), S. Ruth Evans; Deputy Sec. (Ofc. of Church in Society), Bonnie M. Greene; Deputy Sec. (Ofc. of Adm. and Fin.), Amy M. Downs.

Adult Prog. (Men), Rev. Dale S. Perkins; Adult Prog. (Women), Deborah S. Marshall; Adult Resources, Lynda L. Newmarch; Children, Jean Olthius, Rev. Robin D. Wardlaw

Cong. & Mission Support, Morris O. Bartlett; Evangelism, Rev. Gordon B. Turner.

Human Rights and Justice: (Economic Policy and Coalitions), John W. Foster; (Human Rights, International Affairs, and Peace), Pierre Le Blanc; (Native Concerns, Immigration, Refugees, Racism), Helga Kutz-Harder; (Energy and Environment, Persons with Special Needs); David G. Hallman.

Program and Leadership Dev., Mardi A. Tindel; Marriage and Family Life, Rev. Robin Smith; Planning, Dixie Kee; Resources, Rev. Gordon J. Freer; Senior Adults, Social Services, Elaine P. Kaye; Worship, Rev. Fred W. McNally; Youth & Recreational Ministries, Robyn L. Brown-Hewitt, Raymond D. McGinnis

World Outreach: Gen. Sec., Rev. Frederick M. Bayliss Africa, Rev. James A. Kirkwood; Caribbean and Latin America, Rev. Thomas C. Edmonds; Asia and Pacific, Rhea M. Whitehead, Inter-Faith Dialogue, John H. Berthrong; Personnel, Rev. George H. Lavery

Development, Lee R. Holland; Finance and Administration, Johanna Jamieson

CONFERENCE EXECUTIVE SECRETARIES

Alberta and Northwest: Rev. William F. A. Phipps, 9911 48 Ave., Edmonton, Alberta T6E 5V6, Tel. (403) 435-3995

Bay of Quinte: Rev. Peter M. McKellar, 218 Barrie St., Kingston, Ontario K7L 3K3, Tel. (613) 549-2503

British Columbia: Rev. Gordon C. How, 1955 W. 4th Ave., Vancouver, British Columbia V6J 1M7, Tel. (604) 734-0434

Hamilton: Rev. D. Bruce MacDougall, Box 100, Carlisle, Ontario L0R 1H0 (416) 659-3343
London: Rev. Douglas H. Ross, 359 Windermere Rd., London, Ontario N6G 2K3, Tel. (519) 672-1930
Manitoba and Northwestern Ontario: Mrs. H. Dianne Cooper, 120 Maryland St., Winnipeg, Manitoba R3G 1L1, Tel. (204) 786-8911
Manitou: Rev. J. Stewart Bell, 366 McIntyre St. W., North Bay, Ontario P1B 2Z1, Tel. (705) 474-3350
Maritime: Rev. J. Henry Tye, Box 1560, Sackville, Nova Scotia E0A 3C0, Tel. (506) 536-1334
Montreal and Ottawa: Rev. Richard E. Allen, 225-50 Ave., Lachine, Quebec H8T 2T7, Tel. (514) 613-8594
Newfoundland and Labrador: Rev. Boyd L. Hiscock, 320 Elizabeth Ave., St. John's, Newfoundland, A1B 1T9, Tel. (709) 754-0386
Saskatchewan: Rev. Wilbert R. Wall, 1805 Rae St., Regina, Saskatchewan S4T 2E3, Tel. (306) 525-9155
Toronto: Rev. Lorne H. Taylor-Walsh, Rm. 404, 85 St. Clair Ave. E., Toronto, Ontario M4T 1L8, Tel. (416) 967-1880

PERIODICAL

United Church Observer, 85 St. Clair Ave. E., Toronto, Ontario M4T 1M8. Hugh B. McCullum, Ed. and Publ. Tel. (416)960-8500

United Pentecostal Church in Canada

This body, which is affiliated with the United Pentecostal Church, International with headquarters in Hazelwood, Missouri, accepts the Bible standard of full salvation, which is repentance, baptism by immersion in the Name of the Lord Jesus Christ for the remission of sins, and the baptism of the Holy Ghost with the initial signs of speaking in tongues as the Spirit gives utterance. Other tenets of faith include the Oneness of God in Christ, holiness, divine healing and the second coming of Jesus Christ.

Churches: 196; Inclusive Membership: 23,000; Sunday or Sabbath Schools: N.R.; Total Enrollment: N.R.; Ordained Clergy: N.R.

ORGANIZATION

Atlantic District, Dist. Supt., Rev. R. A. Beesley, Box 965, Sussex, New Brunswick E0E 1P0
British Columbia District, Dist. Supt., Rev. Paul V. Reynolds, 13447-112th Ave., Surrey, British Columbia V3R 2E7
Canadian Plains District, Dist. Supt., Rev. Johnny King, 300 Midvalley Dr., SE, Calgary, Alberta T2X 1L9
Manitoba/Northwestern Ontario District, Dist. Supt., Rev. J. E. Yonts, 8855 Dunn Rd., Hazelwood, MO 63042 (Home Missions Director)
Nova Scotia-Newfoundland District, Dist. Supt., Rev. John D. Mean, P.O. Box 2183, D.E.P.S., Dartmouth, Nova Scotia B2W 3Y2
Ontario District, Dist. Supt., Rev. William V. Cooling, Box 651, Brockville, Ontario K6V 5V8

The Wesleyan Church of Canada

The Canadian portion of The Wesleyan Church which consists of the Atlantic and Central Canada districts. The Central Canada District of the former Wesleyan Methodist Church of America was organized at Winchester, Ontario, in 1889 and the Atlantic District was founded in 1888 as the Alliance of the Reformed Baptist Church which merged with the Wesleyan Methodist Church in July, 1966. In 1984 a Canada West District with pioneer status was inaugurated under the direction of the Department of Extension and Evangelism.

The Wesleyan Methodist Church and the Pilgrim Holiness Church merged in June, 1968, to become The Wesleyan Church. The doctrine is evangelical and Arminian and stresses holiness beliefs. For more details, consult the U.S. listing under The Wesleyan Church.

Churches: 75; Inclusive Membership: 4,961; Sunday or Sabbath Schools: 75; Total Enrollment: 8,187; Ordained Clergy: 183

GENERAL ORGANIZATION

Central Canada District Conference: meets the third week in July at Silver Lake Campgrounds, Maberly, Ontario, (613) 268-2770. Office and Mailing Address: Ste. 102, 3 Applewood Dr., Belleville, Ontario K8P 4E3. Tel. (613) 966-7527
Atlantic District Conference: meets the first week in July. Office: 41 Summit Ave., Sussex, New Brunswick. Mailing Address: Box 20, Sussex, New Brunswick E0E 1PO. Tel: (506) 433-1007.

OFFICERS

District Supt. (Central Canada District), Rev. W. W. Jewell, Ste. 102, 3 Applewood Dr., Belleville, Ontario K8P 4E3. Tel. (613)966-7527
District Supt. (Atlantic District), Rev. H. R. Ingersoll, P.O. Box 20, Sussex, New Brunswick E0E 1P0
Western Canada Pioneer District: Dist. Supt., Dr. Thomas Phillippe, Gen. Sec., Extension and Evangelism, The Wesleyan Ch. Liaison: Rev. Walter W. Jewell, Ste. 102, 3 Applewood Dr., Belleville, Ontario K8P 4E3. Tel. (613)966-7527

PERIODICALS

Wesleyan Advocate (s-m), P. O. Box 2000, Marion, IN 46952. Dr. Wayne F. Caldwell, Ed.
Central Canada Clarion (bi-m), Ste. 102, 3 Applewood Dr., Belleville, Ontario K8P 4E3. Rev. W. W. Jewell, Ed.
Atlantic Wesleyan (m), Box 20, Sussex, New Brunswick E0E 1P0. Rev. H. R. Ingersoll, Ed.

Wisconsin Evangelical Lutheran Synod

The W.E.L.S. was founded in Milwaukee, WI, in 1850. The Synod believes in a verbally inspired, inerrant Bible and embraces without reservation the Lutheran Confessions as found in the Book of Concord.

Churches: 9; Inclusive Membership: 1,146; Sunday or Sabbath Schools: 9; Total Enrollment: 232; Ordained Clergy: 8

GENERAL ORGANIZATION

No separate Canadian organization. National Convention meets biennially. Next meeting in 1989.
For additional details, consult Wisconsin Evangelical Lutheran Synod listing in Directory 3, "Religious Bodies in the U.S."

OTHER RELIGIOUS BODIES IN CANADA

Although a sizable majority of Canadian religious bodies, having most of the Canadian church membership, is accounted for by denominations providing directory materials in the sectin immediately preceding, a number of important groups have not yet provided directory information.

For the sake of completeness, an alphabetical listing of these religious bodies not yet supplying directory information appears below.

The editor of the **Yearbook of American and Canadian Churches** would be grateful for any information concerning significant omissions from this listing of Religious Bodies in Canada as well as for any other information concerning this section.

African Methodist Episcopal Church in Canada, 765 Lawrence Ave. W., Toronto, Ontario M6A 1B7. Rev. William J. Daniel (9 churches)

Beachy Amish Mennonite Churches, 9675 Iams Rd., Plain City, OH 43064. Tel. (614) 873-8140 (6 congregations, 378 members)

Bergthaler (Mennonite) Congregations, John Neudorf, LaCrete, Alberta T0H 2H0.

Canadian Reformed Churches, 9210-132A St., Surrey, British Columbia V3V 7E1 (10,228 members)

Chortitzer (Mennonite) Conference, Bishop Wilhelm Hildebrandt Box 452, Steinbach, Manitoba R0A 2A0 (2,000 members)

Christadelphians in Canada, P.O. Box 221, Weston, Ontario M9N 3M7

Christian Science in Canada, Mr. J. Donald Fulton, 696 Yonge St., Ste. 403. Toronto, Ontario M4Y 2A7. Tel. (416) 922-7473

Church of God in Christ, Mennonite (Holdeman), Moundridge, KS 67107. Tel. (316) 345-2533 (2,513 members)

Evangelical Mennonite Brethren Conference, P.O. Box 456, Steinbach, Manitoba R0A 2A0. Tel. (204) 326-2108 (20 congregations, 1,987 members)

Hutterian Brethren, Elder Jacob Kleinsasser, Crystal Sprint Colony, Ste. Agatha, Manitoba R0G 1Y0 (246 congregations, 9,213 members)

New Apostolic Church of North America in Canada, c/o Rev. Michael Kraus, President, 267 Lincoln Rd., Waterloo, Ontario N2J 2P6

Old Colony Mennonite Church in Canada, Alberta, Deacon Herman Geisbrecht, La Crete, Alberta T0H 2H0 (650 members); British Columbia, Deacon Jacob Giesbrecht, Ft. St. John, British Columbia V0C P20 (320 members); Manitoba, Deacon Abram Driedger, Box 601, Winkler, Manitoba R0G 2X0 (930 members); Ontario, Bishop Henry Reimer, R. R. 3, Wheatley, Ontario N0P 2P0 (260 members); Saskatchewan, Deacon Klass Dyck, R. R. 4, Saskatoon, Saskatchewan (1,087 members)

Old Order Mennonite Church, R. 1, Fergus, Ontario N1M 2W3 (28 congregations, 3,280 members)

Orthodox Church in America (Canada Section), Archbishop Metropolitan Theodosius, The Rt. Rev. Seraphim, Bishop of Edmonton, 55 Clarey Ave., Ottawa, Ontario K1F 2R6

Reformed Presbyterian Church of North America, Louis D. Hutmire, 7418 Penn Ave., Pittsburg, PA 15208. Tel. (412) 731-1177

Sommerfelder (Mennonite) Church, Bishop John A. Friesen, Lowe Farm, Manitoba R0G 1E0 (3,650 members)

Standard Church of America (Canadian Section), 243 Perth St., Brockville, Ontario K6V 5E7

RELIGIOUS BODIES IN CANADA ARRANGED BY FAMILIES

The following list of religious bodies appearing in Directory 4, "Religious Bodies in Canada," including "Other Religious Bodies in Canada," shows the "families" or related clusters into which Canadian religious bodies can be grouped. For example, there are many bodies that can be grouped under the heading "Baptist" for historical and theological reasons. It is not to be assumed, however, that all denominations under one family heading are necessarily similar in belief or practice. Often any similarity is purely coincidental since ethnicity, theological divergence, and even political and personality factors have shaped the directions denominational groups have taken.

Family categories provide one of the major pitfalls of church statistics because of the tendency to combine statistics by "families" for analytical and comparative purposes. Such combined totals are almost meaningless, although often used as variables for sociological analysis.

The editor would be grateful for any additions or corrections in the family table below. **Religious bodies not grouped under family headings appear alphabetically and are not indented in the following list.**

The Anglican Church of Canada
Apostolic Christian Church (Nazarene)
Armenian Evangelical Church
Associated Gospel Churches
Baha'i Faith

BAPTIST BODIES

The Association of Regular Baptist Churches (Canada)
Baptist General Conference of Canada
　The Central Canada Baptist Conference
　Baptist General Conference of Alberta
　British Columbia Baptist Conference
Canadian Baptist Federation
　Baptist Convention of Ontario and Quebec
　Baptist Union of Western Canada
　Union of French Baptist Churches in Canada
　United Baptist Convention of the Atlantic
　Provinces
Canadian Convention of Southern Baptists
*Evangelical Baptist Churches in Canada, The
Fellowship of*

Free Will Baptists
North American Baptist Conference
Bible Holiness Movement
Brethren in Christ Church, Canadian Conference
Buddhist Churches of Canada
The Canadian Yearly Meeting of the Religious Society of Friends
Christadelphians in Canada
The Christian and Missionary Alliance in Canada
Christian Brethren (aka Plymouth Brethren)
Christian Science in Canada
Church of God, (Anderson, Ind.)
Church of the Nazarene

**CHURCHES OF CHRIST—
CHRISTIAN CHURCHES**

　Christian Church (Disciples of Christ) in Canada
　Christian Churches and Churches of Christ in Canada
　Churches of Christ in Canada

Congregational Christian Churches in Ontario, The Conference of

DOUKHOBORS

Reformed Doukhobors, Christian Community and
  Brotherhood of
Union of Spiritual Communities of Christ (Orthodox
  Doukhobors in Canada)

EASTERN CHURCHES

The Antiochian Orthodox Christian Archdiocese of
  North America
The Armenian Church of North America, Diocese of
  Canada
The Coptic Church in Canada
Greek Orthodox Diocese of Toronto, Canada
Orthodox Church in America (Canada Section)
Romanian Orthodox Church in America (Canadian
  Parishes)
The Romanian Orthodox Episcopate of America (Jack-
  son, Michigan)
Russian Orthodox Church in Canada, Patriarchal
  Parishes of the
Serbian Orthodox Church in the U.S.A. and Canada,
  Diocese of Canada
Syrian Orthodox Church of Antioch (Archdiocese of the
  United States and Canada)
Ukrainian Greek-Orthodox Church of Canada

The Evangelical Covenant Church of Canada
Evangelical Free Church of Canada
General Church of the New Jerusalem
Gospel Missionary Association
Independent Holiness Church
Jehovah's Witnesses
Jewish Organizations in Canada

LATTER DAY SAINTS

The Church of Jesus Christ of Latter-day Saints
Reorganized Church of Jesus Christ of Latter Day Saints

LUTHERANS

Church of the Lutheran Brethren
The Estonian Evangelical Lutheran Church
The Evangelical Lutheran Church in Canada
The Latvian Evangelical Lutheran Church in America
Lutheran Church—Canada
Wisconsin Evangelical Lutheran Synod

MENNONITE BODIES

Beachy Amish Mennonite Churches
Bergthaler Congregations
Chortitz Congregations
Church of God in Christ, Mennonite (Holdeman)
Conference of Mennonites in Canada
Evangelical Mennonite Brethren Conference
The Evangelical Mennonite Conference
Evangelical Mennonite Mission Conference
Hutterian Brethren
Mennonite Brethren Churches, Canadian Conference
  of
Mennonite Church (Canada)

Old Colony Mennonite Church in Canada
Old Order Amish Church
Old Order Mennonite Church
Reinlaender Mennonite Church
Sommerfelder (Mennonite) Church

METHODIST BODIES

African Methodist Episcopal Church in Canada
British Methodist Episcopal Church of Canada
The Evangelical Church in Canada
Free Methodist Church in Canada
The Wesleyan Church of Canada

Metropolitan Community Churches, Universal Fellowship
  of
The Missionary Church of Canada
Moravian Church in America, Northern Province
Muslims
New Apostolic Church of North America in Canada
The Old Catholic Church of Canada

PENTECOSTAL BODIES

The Apostolic Church in Canada
Apostolic Church of Pentecost of Canada
Church of God (Cleveland, Tenn.)
The Church of God of Prophecy in Canada
Elim Felowship of Evangelical Churches and Ministers
Foursquare Gospel Church of Canada
Independent Assemblies of God—Canada
The Italian Pentecostal Church of Canada
The Open Bible Standard Churches of Canada
The Pentecostal Assemblies of Canada
Pentecostal Assemblies of Newfoundland
Pentecostal Holiness Church of Canada
United Pentecostal Church in Canada

Polish National Catholic Church of Canada

PRESBYTERIAN BODIES

Presbyterian Church in America (Canadian Section)
The Presbyterian Church in Canada
Reformed Presbyterian Church of North America

REFORMED BODIES

Canadian Reformed Churches
Christian Reformed Church in North America
Netherlands Reformed Congregations of North America
Reformed Church in Canada
The United Church of Canada

The Reformed Episcopal Church
The Roman Catholic Church in Canada
The Salvation Army in Canada
Seventh-day Adventist Church in Canada
Sikhs
Standard Church of America (Canadian Section)
Unitarian Universalist Association
United Brethren in Christ, Ontario Conference

5. INTERNATIONAL AGENCIES: CONFESSIONAL, INTERDENOMINATIONAL, COOPERATIVE

A listing of major confessional, interdenominational, and cooperative international agencies follows. The editor of the **Yearbook of American and Canadian Churches** would be grateful for details on major groups omitted from this listing.

WORLD COUNCIL OF CHURCHES

The World Council of Churches is a fellowship of more than 300 churches of the Protestant, Anglican, Orthodox, and Old Catholic traditions banded together for study, witness, service, and the advancement of unity. It includes in its membership churches in more than 100 countries with various forms of government, and its life reflects the immense richness and variety of Christian faith and practice.

The World Council of Churches came into being after many years of preparation on August 23, 1948, when its First Assembly was held in Amsterdam, The Netherlands.

The basis for World Council membership is: "The World Council of Churches is a fellowship of Churches which confess the Lord Jesus Christ as God and Saviour according to the Scriptures and therefore seek to fulfill together their common calling to the glory of the one God, Father, Son, and Holy Spirit."

Membership is open to churches which express their agreement with this basis and satisfy such criteria as the Assembly or Central Committee may prescribe.

Headquarters: 150 route de Ferney (P.O. Box 66), 1211. Geneva, 20, Switzerland. Tel. (022) 91 61 11
U.S. Office: 475 Riverside Dr., Rm. 1062, New York, NY 10115. Tel. (212) 870-2533
New York Office, CCIA: 777 United Nations Plz., New York, NY 10017. Tel. (212) 867-5890

PRESIDENTS

Most Rev. W. P. K. Makhulu, Botswana
Metropolitan Paulos Mar Gregorios, India
Dame R. Nita Barrow, Barbados
Bishop Johannes Hempel, GDR
Dr. Marga Buehrig, Switzerland
Dr. Lois Wilson, Canada
Patriarch Ignatios IV, Syria

CENTRAL COMMITTEE

Moderator, Rev. Dr. Heinz Joachim Held, FRG
Vice-moderators, Metropolitan Chrysostomos, Turkey; Dr. Sylvia Talbot, USA

GENERAL SECRETARIAT

Gen. Sec., Rev. Emilio Castro.
Deputy Gen. Secs. Ms. Mercy Oduyoye; Dr. Todor Sabev; Ms. Ruth Sovik; Asst. Gen. Sec. for Finance and Administration, Mr. Patrick Coidan; Asst. to Gen. Sec., Rev. William Perkins.
Income Coordination and Development, Dir., Ms. M. Béguin-Austin
Librarian, Mr. Pierre Beffa
Office for Resource Sharing, Mr. Huibert van Beek
Personnel Dir., Mr. Trevor Davies
Ecumenical Institute: Dir., Rev. Dr. Adrian Geense,
Communication:Mr. Jan Kok
U. S. Office, Exec. Dir.: Rev. Joan Campbell

PROGRAM UNIT I— FAITH AND WITNESS

Staff Moderator: Dr. Todor Sabev

Commission on Faith and Order: Dir., Günther Gassman.
Commission on World Mission and Evangelism: Dir., Dr. Eugene Stockwell.

Sub-Unit on Church and Society: Dir., Dr. David Gosling
Sub-Unit on Dialogue with People of Living Faiths: Dir., Rev. Wesley Ariarajah

PROGRAM UNIT II— JUSTICE AND SERVICE

Staff Moderator: Ms. Ruth Sovik

Commission on Inter-Church Aid, Refugee and World Service: Dir., Dr. Klaus Poser
Commission of the Churches on International Affairs: Dir.: Mr. Ninan Koshy; Exec. Sec., New York Office, Dr. A. Barkat
Human Rights Resources Officer for Latin America: Rev. Charles Harper
Commission on the Churches' Participation in Development: Dir.: Mr. Oh Jae Shik
Program to Combat Racism: Dir., _____;
Christian Medical Commission: Dir., Dr. Eric Ram

PROGRAM UNIT III— EDUCATION AND RENEWAL

Staff Moderator: Ms. Mercy Oduyoye

Sub-Unit on Women in Church and Society: Dir., Rev. Anna Karin Hammar
Sub-Unit on Renewal & Congregational Life: Dir., Rev. Ion Bria
Sub-Unit on Education: Dir., Dr. Clifford Payne; Portfolio on Biblical Studies, _____
Sub-Unit on Youth: Dir., Rev. Heikki Huttunen
Program on Theological Education Dir., Dr. Samuel Amirtham

PERIODICALS

The Ecumenical Review (q), Rev. Emilio Castro.
The Ecumenical Press Service (w), Mr. Thomas H. Dorris, Ed., English edition.
International Review of Mission (q), Rev. Eugene Stockwell.
One World, Mr. Marlin VanElderen, Ed.

Constituent Bodies of the World Council of Churches and Associate Member Churches

MEMBER CHURCHES

Angola
Evangelical Congregational Church in Angola

Argentina
Iglesia Evangélica del Río de la Plata (Evangelical Church of the River Plata)

Iglesia Evangélica Metodista Argentina (Evangelical Methodist Church of Argentina)

Australia
The Anglican Church of Australia

Churches of Christ in Australia

The Uniting Church in Australia

Austria
Alt-katholische Kirche Österreichs (Old Catholic Church of Austria)

Evangelische Kirche Augsburgischen u. Helvetischen Bekenntnisses (A.u.H.B.) (Evangelical Church of the Augsburg and Helvetic Confession)

Bahamas
Church in the Province of the West Indies
(see under *West Indies*)

Methodist Church in the Caribbean and the Americas
(see under *West Indies*)

Bangladesh
Bangladesh Baptist Sangha

Barbados
Church in the Province of the West Indies
(see under *West Indies*)

Methodist Church in the Caribbean and the Americas
(see under *West Indies*)

Moravian Church, Eastern West Indies Province
(see under *West Indies*)

Belgium
Eglise protestante unie de Belgique (United Protestant Church of Belgium)

Benin (People's Republic of)
Eglise protestante méthodiste en République populaire du Bénin (Protestant Methodist Church in the People's Republic of Benin)

Botswana
Church of the Province of Central Africa

(see under *Central Africa*)

Brazil
Igreja Episcopal do Brasil (Episcopal Church of Brazil)

Igreja Evangélica de Confissão Luterana no Brasil (Evangelical Church of Lutheran Confession in Brazil)

Igreja Metodista do Brasil (Methodist Church in Brazil)

Igreja Reformada Latino Americana (The Latin American Reformed Church)

Bulgaria
Bulgarian Orthodox Church

Burma
Burma Baptist Convention

Church of the Province of Burma

Methodist Church, Upper Burma

Burundi
Church of the Province of Burundi, Rwanda and Zaire

Cameroon
Eglise évangélique du Cameroun (Evangelical Church of Cameroon)

Eglise presbytérienne camérounaise (Presbyterian Church of Cameroon)

Presbyterian Church in Cameroon

Union des Eglises baptistes du Cameroun (Union of Baptist Churches of Cameroon)

Canada
The Anglican Church of Canada

Canadian Yearly Meeting of the Society of Friends

Christian Church (Disciples of Christ)

The Evangelical Lutheran Church of Canada

The Presbyterian Church in Canada

The United Church of Canada

Central Africa
Church of the Province of Central Africa
(covers Botswana, Malawi, Zambia, Zimbabwe)

Chile
Iglesia Evangélica Luterana en Chile (Evangelical Lutheran Church in Chile)

Iglesia Pentecostal de Chile (Pentecostal Church of Chile)

Misión Iglesia Pentecosta (Pentecostal Mission Church)

Congo (People's Republic of the)
Eglise évangélique du Congo (Evangelical Church of the Congo)

Cook Islands
Cook Islands Christian Church

Costa Rica
Methodist Church in the Caribbean and the Americas
(see under *West Indies*)

Cyprus
Church of Cyprus

Episcopal Church in Jerusalem and the Middle East
(see under *Jerusalem*)

Czechoslovakia
Ceskobratrská církev evangelická (Evangelical Church of Czech Brethren)

Ceskoslovenská církev husitská (Czechoslovak Hussite Church)

Pravoslavná církev v CSSR (Orthodox Church of Czechoslovakia)

Ref. krest. církev na Slovensku (Reformed Christian Church in Slovakia)

Slezská církev evangelická a.v. (Silesian Evangelical Church of the Augsburg Confession)

Slovenská evanjelická církev a.v. v CSSR (Slovak Evangelical Church of the Augsburg Confession in the CSSR)

Denmark
Det danske Baptistsamfund (The Baptist Union of Denmark)

Den evangelisk-lutherske Folkekirke i Danmark (The Church of Denmark)

East Africa
Presbyterian Church of East Africa
(covers Kenya, Tanzania, Uganda)

Egypt
Coptic Orthodox Church

Coptic Evangelical Church—The Synod of the Nile

Episcopal Church in Jerusalem and the Middle East
(see under *Jerusalem*)
Greek Orthodox Patriarchate of Alexandria and All
Africa
Ethiopia
Ethiopian Orthodox Church
The Ethiopian Evangelical Church Mekane Yesus
Europe
Europaïsch-Festländische Brüder-Unität, Distrikt Bad
Boll (European Continental Province of the Mora-
vian Church—Western District)
Fiji
Methodist Church in Fiji
Finland
Suomen evankelis-luterilainen kirkko (Evangelical-Lu-
theran Church of Finland)
Orthodox Church of Finland
France
Eglise de la Confession d'Augsbourg d'Alsace et de
Lorraine (Evangelical Church of the Augsburg
Confession of Alsace and Lorraine)
Eglise évangélique luthérienne de France (Evangelical
Lutheran Church of France)
Eglise réformée d'Alsace et de Lorraine (Reformed
Church of Alsace and Lorraine)
Eglise réformée de France (Reformed Church of
France)
French Polynesia (formerly Tahiti)
Eglise évangélique de Polynésie française (Evangelical
Church of French Polynesia)
Gabonese Republic
Eglise évangélique du Gabon (Evangelical Church of
Gabon)
The Gambia
Church of the Province of West Africa
(see under *West Africa*)
German Churches
Federal Republic of Germany
Katholisches Bistum der Alt-Katholiken in Deutschland
(Catholic Diocese of the Old Catholics in Germany)
Europaïsch-Festländische Brüder-Unität, Distrikt Bad
Boll (see under *Europe*)
Evangelische Kirche in Deutschland (Evangelical Church
in Germany)
Evangelische Landeskirche in Baden
Evangelisch-Lutherische Kirche in Bayern*
Evangelische Kirche in Berlin-Brandenburg (Berlin
West)
Evangelisch-Lutherische Landeskirche in Braunsch-
weig*
Bremische Evangelische Kirche
Evangelisch-Lutherische Landeskirche Hannovers*
Evangelische Kirche in Hessen und Nassau
Evangelische Kirche von Kurhessen-Waldeck
Lippische Landeskirche
Nordelbische Evangelisch-Lutherische Kirche*
Evangelisch-Reformierte Kirche in Nordwestdeutsch-
land
Evangelisch-Lutherische Kirche in Oldenburg
Evangelische Christliche Kirche der Pfalz
Evangelische Kirche im Rheinland
Evangelisch-Lutherische Landeskirche Schaumburg-
Lippe*
Evangelische Kirche von Westfalen
Evangelische Landeskirche in Württemberg
Vereiningung der Deutschen Mennonitengemeinden
(Mennonite Church)

*This church is directly a member of the World Council of
Churches in accordance with the resolution of the General

Synod of the United Evangelical Lutheran Church of
Germany, dated 27 January, 1949, which recommended
that the member churches of the United Evangelical
Lutheran Church should make the following declaration to
the Council of the Evangelical Church in Germany
concerning their relation to the World Council of
Churches:

"The Evangelical Church in Germany has made it clear
through its constitution that it is a federation (Bund) of
confessionally determined churches. Moreover, the
conditions of membership of the World Council of
Churches have been determined at the Assembly at
Amsterdam. Therefore, this Evangelical Lutheran
Church declares concerning its membership in the
World Council of Churches:
  i) It is represented in the World Council as a church
     of the Evangelical Lutheran confession.
 ii) Representatives which it sends to the World
     Council are to be identified as Evangelical
     Lutherans.
iii) Within the limits of the competence of the
     Evangelical Church in Germany it is represented
     in the World Council through the intermediary of
     the Council of the Evangelical Church in Ger-
     many."

German Democratic Republic
Bund der Evangelischen Kirchen in der Deutschen
Demokratischen Republik (Federation of the
Evangelical Churches in the GDR)
Evangelische Landeskirche Anhalts†
Evangelische Kirche in Berlin-Brandenburg†
Evangelische Kirche des Görlitzer Kirchengebietes†
Evangelische Landeskirche Greifswald†
Evangelisch-Lutherische Landeskirche Mecklen-
burgs†
Evangelische Kirche der Kirchenprovinz Sachsen†
Evangelisch-Lutherische Landeskirche Sachsens†
Evangelisch-Lutherische Kirche in Thüringen†
Evangelische Brüder-Unität (Distrikt Herrnhut)
(Moravian Church)
Gemeindeverband der Alt-Katholischen Kirche in der
Deutschen Demokratischen Republik (Federation
of the Old Catholic Church in the GDR)

†United in a fellowship of Christian witness and service in
the Federation of Evangelical Churches in the GDR, these
churches are represented in the Council through agencies
of the Federation of Evangelical Churches in the GDR.

Ghana
Church of the Province of West Africa
(see under *West Africa*)
Evangelical Presbyterian Church
The Methodist Church, Ghana
Presbyterian Church of Ghana
Greece
Ekklesia tes Ellados (Church of Greece)
Helleniki Evangeliki Ekklesia (Greek Evangelical
Church)
Guyana
Church in the Province of the West Indies
(see under *West Indies*)
Methodist Church in the Caribbean and the Americas
(see under *West Indies*)
Haiti
Methodist Church in the Caribbean and the Americas
(see under *West Indies*)
Honduras
Methodist Church in the Caribbean and the Americas
(see under *West Indies*)
Hong Kong
The Church of Christ in China, The Hong Kong Council

Hungary
Magyarországi Baptista Egyház
(Baptist Church of Hungary)
Magyarországi Evangélikus Egyház
(Lutheran Church in Hungary)
Magyarországi Reformatus Egyház
(Reformed Church in Hungary)

Iceland
Evangelical Lutheran Church of Iceland

India
Church of North India
Church of South India
United Evangelical Lutheran Church in India
Mar Thoma Syrian Church of Malabar
Malankara Orthodox Syrian Church
Methodist Church in India
The Samavesam of Telugu Baptist Churches

Indian Ocean
Church of the Province of the Indian Ocean
(covers Mauritius, Madagascar, Seychelles)

Indonesia
Gereja Batak Karo Protestan (Karo Batak Protestant Church)
Huria Kristen Batak Protestan (Batak Protestant Christian Church)
Gereja Kristen Protestan Indonesia (G.K.P.I.) (Christian Protestant Church in Indonesia)
The Evangelical Christian Church in Halmahera
Huria Kristen Indonesia (H.K.I.) (The Indonesian Christian Church)
Gereja Kristen Indonesia (Indonesian Christian Church)
Gereja Protestan di Indonesia (Protestant Church in Indonesia)
Gereja Kristen Injili di Irian Jaya (Evangelical Christian Church in West Irian)
Gereja Kristen Jawi Wetan (Christian Church of East Java)
Gereja-Gereja Kristen Java (Javanese Christian Churches)
Gereja Kalimantan Evangelis (Kalimantan Evangelical Church)
Gereja Protestan Maluku (Protestant Church in the Moluccas)
Gereja Masehi Injili Minahasa (Christian Evangelical Church in Minahasa)
Banua Niha Keriso Protestan (Nias Protestant Christian Church)
Gereja Kristen Pasundan (Pasundan Christian Church)
Gereja Masehi Injili Sangihe Talaud (GMIST) (Evangelical Church of Sangir Talaud)
Gereja Kristen Protestan Simalungun (Simalungun Protestant Christian Church)
Gereja Kristen Sulawesi Tengah (Christian Church in Central Sulawesi)
Gereja Masehi Injili di Timor (Protestant Evangelical Church in Timor)
Gereja Toraja (Toraja Church)

Iran
Apostolic Catholic Assyrian Church of the East
(see under *U.S.A.*)
Episcopal Church in Jerusalem and the Middle East
(see under *Jerusalem*)
Synod of the Evangelical Church of Iran

Italy
Chiesa Evangelica Metodista d'Italia (Evangelical Methodist Church of Italy)
Chiesa Evangelica Valdese (Waldensian Church)

Ivory Coast
Methodist Church, Ivory Coast

Jamaica
Church in the Province of the West Indies
(see under *West Indies*)
Methodist Church in the Caribbean and the Americas
(see under *West Indies*)
The Moravian Church in Jamaica
The United Church of Jamaica and Grand Cayman

Japan
Japanese Orthodox Church
Nippon Kirisuto Kyodan (The United Church of Christ in Japan)
Nippon Sei Ko Kai (Anglican-Episcopal Church in Japan)

Jerusalem
Episcopal Church in Jerusalem and the Middle East
(covers Jerusalem, Egypt, Iran, Cyprus, the Gulf)
Greek Orthodox Patriarchate of Jerusalem

Kenya
African Christian Church and Schools
African Israel Church, Nineveh
Church of the Province of Kenya
The Methodist Church in Kenya
Presbyterian Church of East Africa
(see under *East Africa*)

Korea
The Korean Methodist Church
The Presbyterian Church in the Republic of Korea
The Presbyterian Church of Korea

Lebanon
Armenian Apostolic Church
National Evangelical Synod of Syria and Lebanon
Greek Orthodox Patriarchate of Antioch and All the East
(see under *Syria*)
Union of the Armenian Evangelical Churches in the Near East

Lesotho
Lesotho Evangelical Church

Liberia
The Church of the Province of West Africa
(see under *West Africa*)
Lutheran Church in Liberia

Madagascar
Church of the Province of the Indian Ocean
(see under *Indian Ocean*)
Eglise de Jésus Christ à Madagascar (Church of Jesus Christ in Madagascar)
Eglise luthérienne malgache (Malagasy Lutheran Church)

Malawi
Church of the Province of Central Africa
(see under *Central Africa*)

Malaysia
The Methodist Church in Malaysia

Mauritius
Church of the Province of the Indian Ocean
(see under *Indian Ocean*)

Melanesia
Church of Melanesia
(see under *Solomon Islands*)

Mexico
Iglesia Metodista de México (Methodist Church of Mexico)

Netherlands
Algemene Doopsgezinde Sociëteit (General Mennonite Society)
Evangelisch Lutherse Kerk (Evangelical Lutheran Church)
De Gereformeerde Kerken in Nederland (The Reformed Churches in the Netherlands)

Nederlandse Hervormde Kerk (Netherlands Reformed Church)
Oud-Katholieke Kerk van Nederland (Old Catholic Church of the Netherlands)
Remonstrantse Broederschap (Remonstrant Brotherhood)

New Caledonia
Eglise évangélique en Nouvelle Calédonie et aux Iles Loyauté (Evangelical Church in New Caledonia and the Loyalty Isles)

New Zealand
Associated Churches of Christ in New Zealand
The Baptist Union of New Zealand
Church of the Province of New Zealand
The Methodist Church of New Zealand
The Presbyterian Church of New Zealand

Nicaragua
Convención Bautista de Nicaragua (Baptist Convention of Nicaragua)
Iglesia Morava en Nicaragua (Moravian Church in Nicaragua)

Nigeria
Church of the Lord Aladura
Church of the Province of Nigeria
Methodist Church, Nigeria
Nigerian Baptist Convention
The Presbyterian Church of Nigeria
Brethren Church of Nigeria

Norway
Den Norske Kirke (Church of Norway)

Pakistan
The Church of Pakistan
United Presbyterian Church of Pakistan

Papua New Guinea
The United Church in Papua New Guinea and the Solomon Islands

Philippines
Iglesia Filipina Independiente (Philippine Independent Church)
United Church of Christ in the Philippines
Iglesia Evangelica Metodista en las Islas Filipinas (The Evangelical Methodist Church in the Philippines)

Poland
Autocephalic Orthodox Church in Poland
Kosciola Ewangelicko-Augsburskiego w PRL (Evangelical Church of the Augsburg Confession in Poland)
Kosciola Polskokatolickiego w PRL (Polish Catholic Church in Poland)
Staro-Katolickiego Kosciola Mariatowitow w PRL (Old Catholic Mariavite Church in Poland)

Romania
Evangelische Kirche A.B. in der Sozialistischen Republik Rumänien (Evangelical Church of the Augsburg Confession in the Socialist Republic of Romania)
Biserica Ortodoxa Romana (Romanian Orthodox Church)
Reformed Church of Romania
Evangelical Synodal Presbyterial Church of the Augsburg Confession in the Socialist Republic of Romania

Rwanda
Church of the Province of Burundi, Rwanda and Zaïre (see under Burundi)
Eglise presbytérienne au Rwanda (Presbyterian Church of Rwanda)

Samoa
Congregational Christian Church in American Samoa
The Congregational Christian Church in Samoa
The Methodist Church in Samoa

Seychelles
Church of the Province of the Indian Ocean (see under Indian Ocean)

Sierra Leone
Church of the Province of West Africa (see under West Africa)
The Methodist Church of Sierra Leone

Solomon Islands
Church of Melanesia

South Africa (Republic of)
Church of the Province of Southern Africa
Evangelical Lutheran Church in Southern Africa
Evangelical Presbyterian Church in South Africa
The Methodist Church of Southern Africa
Moravian Church in South Africa
Presbyterian Church of Africa
The Presbyterian Church of Southern Africa
The Reformed Presbyterian Church of Southern Africa
The United Congregational Church of Southern Africa

Spain
Iglesia Evangélica Española (Spanish Evangelical Church)

Sri Lanka
The Church of Ceylon
Methodist Church

Sudan
Presbyterian Church in the Sudan
Province of the Episcopal Church of the Sudan

Surinam
Moravian Church in Surinam

Sweden
Estonian Evangelical Lutheran Church (see under Other Churches)
Svenska Kyrkan (Church of Sweden)
Svenska Missionsförbundet (The Mission Covenant Church of Sweden)

Switzerland
Christkatholische Kirche der Schweiz (Old Catholic Church of Switzerland)
Schweizerischer Evangelischer Kirchenbund, Fédération des Eglises protestantes de la Suisse (Swiss Protestant Church Federation)

Syria
The National Evangelical Synod of Syria and Lebanon (see under Lebanon)
Patriarcat Grec-Orthodoxe d'Antioche et de tout l'Orient (Greek Orthodox Patriarchate of Antioch and All the East)
Syrian Orthodox Patriarchate of Antioch and All the East

Taiwan
The Presbyterian Church in Taiwan

Tanzania
Church of the Province of Tanzania
Evangelical Lutheran Church in Tanzania
Joint Board of the Moravian Church in Tanzania
Presbyterian Church of East Africa (see under East Africa)

Thailand
The Church of Christ in Thailand

Togo
Eglise évangélique du Togo (Evangelical Church of Togo)

Tonga
Methodist Church in Tonga (Free Wesleyan Church of Tonga)

Trinidad
Church in the Province of the West Indies
(see under *West Indies*)
Methodist Church in the Caribbean and the Americas
(see under *West Indies*)
Moravian Church, Eastern West Indies Province
(see under *West Indies*)
The Presbyterian Church in Trinidad and Grenada

Turkey
Ecumenical Patriarchate of Constantinople

Tuvalu
Church of Tuvalu

Uganda
The Church of Uganda
Presbyterian Church of East Africa
(see under *East Africa*)

Union of Soviet Socialist Republics
Russian Orthodox Church
The Union of Evangelical Christian Baptists of USSR
Eglise apostolique arménienne (Armenian Apostolic Church)
Eesti Evangeelne Luterlik Kirik (Estonian Evangelical Lutheran Church)
Georgian Orthodox Church
Latvijas Evangeliska-Luteriski Baznica (Evangelical Lutheran Church of Latvia)

United Kingdom (of Great Britain and Northern Ireland) and Republic of Ireland

Churches with headquarters in England
The Baptist Union of Great Britain and Ireland
The Church of England
The Methodist Church
The Moravian Church in Great Britain and Ireland
The United Reformed Church in the United Kingdom

Churches with headquarters in Ireland
The Church of Ireland
The Methodist Church in Ireland

Churches with headquarters in Scotland
The Church of Scotland
The Congregational Union of Scotland
The Scottish Episcopal Church
United Free Church of Scotland

Churches with headquarters in Wales
The Church in Wales
The Presbyterian Church of Wales
Union of Welsh Independents

United States of America
African Methodist Episcopal Church
African Methodist Episcopal Zion Church
American Baptist Churches in the U.S.A.
Apostolic Catholic Assyrian Church of the East
Christian Church (Disciples of Christ)
Christian Methodist Episcopal Church
Church of the Brethren
The Episcopal Church
Evangelical Lutheran Church in America
Hungarian Reformed Church in America
International Council of Community Churches
International Evangelical Church
Moravian Church in America (Northern Province)
Moravian Church in America (Southern Province)
National Baptist Convention of America
National Baptist Convention, U.S.A., Inc.
The Orthodox Church in America
Polish National Catholic Church of America
Presbyterian Church (U.S.A.)

Progressive National Baptist Convention
Reformed Church in America
Religious Society of Friends
Friends General Conference
Friends United Meeting
United Church of Christ
The United Methodist Church

Uruguay
Iglesia Evangélica Valdense del Rio de la Plata
(part of the Waldensian Church—see under *Italy*)

Vanuatu
Presbyterian Church of Vanuatu

Venezuela
Church of the Province of the West Indies
(see under *West Indies*)

West Africa
The Church of the Province of West Africa
(covers The Gambia, Ghana, Liberia, Sierra Leone)

West Indies
The Church in the Province of the West Indies
The Methodist Church in the Caribbean and the Americas
Moravian Church, Eastern West Indies Province

Yugoslavia
Reformatska Crkve u SFRJ (The Reformed Church in Yugoslavia)
Serbian Orthodox Church
Slovenska ev.-kr. a.v. cirkev v. Juhuslavii (Slovak Evangelical Church of the Augsburg Confession in Yugoslavia)

Zaïre (Republic of)
Church of the Province of Burundi, Rwanda and Zaïre
(see under *Burundi*)
Eglise du Christ au Zaïre (Communauté baptiste du Zaïre Ouest [CBZO]) (Church of Christ in Zaïre—Baptist Community of Western Zaïre)
Eglise du Christ au Zaïre (Communauté épiscopale baptiste en Afrique [CEBA]) (Church of Christ in Zaire—Episcopal Baptist Community)
Eglise du Christ au Zaïre (Communauté des Disciples) (Church of Christ in Zaïre—Community of Disciples)
Eglise du Christ au Zaire (Commauté évangélique) (Church of Christ in Zaïre—Evangelical Community)
Eglise du Christ au Zaïre (Communauté lumière) (Church of Christ in Zaïre—Community of Light)
Eglise du Christ au Zaïre (Communauté mennonite au Zaïre) (Church of Christ in Zaïre-Mennonite Community)
Eglise du Christ au Zaïre (Communauté presbytérienne) (Church of Christ in Zaïre—Presbyterian Community)
Eglise du Jésus Christ sur la Terre par le Prophète Simon Kimbangu (Church of Jesus Christ on Earth by the Prophet Simon Kimbangu)

Zambia
Church of the Province of Central Africa
(see under *Central Africa*)
United Church of Zambia

Zimbabwe
Church of the Province of Central Africa
(see under *Central Africa*)
Methodist Church in Zimbabwe

Other Churches
Eesti Evangeeliumi Luteri Usu Kirik
(Estonian Evangelical Lutheran Church)
Latvijas Evangeliski Luteriska baznica eklisa
(Evangelical Lutheran Church of Latvia in Exile)

Algeria
Eglise protestante d'Algérie (Protestant Church of Algeria)

Angola
United Evangelical Church of Angola
Evangelical Pentecostal Church of Angola

Argentina
La Iglesia de Dios (Church of God)
Iglesia Evangélica Luterana Unida (United Evangelical Lutheran Church)
Iglesia de los Discípulos de Cristo (Church of the Disciples of Christ)

Bangladesh
Church of Bangladesh

Bolivia
Iglesia Evangélica Metodista en Bolivie (Evangelical Methodist Church in Bolivia)

Brazil
Igreja Presbiteriana Unida do Brasil (United Presbyterian Church of Brazil)

Cameroon
Eglise Protestante Africaine (African Protestant Church)

Chile
Iglesia Metodista de Chile (The Methodist Church of Chile)

Costa Rica
Iglesia Evangélica Metodista de Costa Rica (Evangelical Methodist Church of Costa Rica)

Cuba
Iglesia Metodista en Cuba (Methodist Church in Cuba)
Iglesia Presbiteriana-Reformada en Cuba (Presbyterian-Reformed Church in Cuba)

Equatorial Guinea
Iglesia Reformada de Guinea Ecuatorial (Reformed Church of Equatorial Guinea)

India
Bengal-Orissa-Bihar Baptist Convention

Indonesia
Gereja Kristen Protestan di Bali (Protestant Christian Church in Bali)
Gereja Punguan Kristen Batak (GPKB) (Batak Christian Community Church)

Italy
Baptist Union of Italy

Japan
The Korean Christian Church in Japan

Kenya
African Church of the Holy Spirit

Liberia
Presbytery of Liberia

Malaysia
Protestant Church in Sabah

Mozambique
Igreja Presbiteriana de Moçambique (Presbyterian Church of Mozambique)

Netherlands Antilles
Iglesia Protestant Uni (United Protestant Church)

Peru
Iglesia Metodista del Peru (The Methodist Church of Peru)

Portugal
Igreja Evangélica Presbiteriana de Portugal (Evangelical Presbyterian Church of Portugal)
Igreja Lusitana Catolica Apostolica Evangélica (Lusitanian Catholic-Apostolic Evangelical Church)

Singapore
Methodist Church in Singapore

Spain
Iglesia Española Reformada Episcopal (Spanish Reformed Episcopal Church)

Uruguay
Iglesia Evangélica Metodista en el Uruguay (The Evangelical Methodist Church in Uruguay)

Alliance World Fellowship

The Alliance World Fellowship, founded in 1975, at Nyack, New York, is a nonlegislative body whose members are the national churches raised up through the ministry of The Christian and Missionary Alliance and found under a variety of names in 53 nations of the world.

The purpose of the Fellowship is to provide a means of fellowship, consultation, cooperation and encouragement in the task of missions and evangelism which we understand to be the special calling of the church.

The AWF has a plenary convocation quadrennially. The first was in Nyack, NY, in 1975; the second in Hong Kong in 1979; the third in Lima, Peru, in 1983; the fourth in St. Paul, MN in 1987; and the fifth to be held in Abidjan, Ivory Coast in 1991.

Headquarters: 350 North Highland Ave., Nyack, NY 10960

OFFICERS

Pres., Dr. Benjamin de Jesus, Box 649, Manila, Republic of the Philippines 2800

Vice-Pres., Dr. Melvin P. Sylvester, Box 7900, Postal Sta. B, Willowdale, Ontario M2K 2R6

Sec., Rev. Arni Shareski, 350 N. Highland Ave., Nyack, NY 10960

Treas., Rev. Roger Lang, P. O. Box 120, French's Forest, New South Wales, Australia 2686

Anglican Consultative Council

The Anglican Consultative Council is the central council for the worldwide Anglican Communion. Its creation was proposed by the Lambeth Conference of Bishops of the Anglican Communion in 1968, and came into being by the end of 1969 with the consent of all the Provinces (or member Churches). Council meetings are held in different parts of the world. Its first meeting was held in Limuru, Kenya, in 1971; the second in Dublin, Ireland, in July 1973; the third in Trinidad, April 1976; the fourth in Canada May 1979; the fifth in Newcastle, England, September 1981; the sixth meeting in

Badagry, Nigeria, July, 1984. The seventh meeting was held in Singapore, April 25 - May 7, 1987. Its report is titled "Many Gifts, One Spirit."

The membership includes bishops, priests, and lay people. Each Province (or member Church) is represented by up to three members and meetings are held every second or third year; the Standing Committee meets every year.

True to the Anglican Communion's style of working, the Council has no legislative powers. It fills a liaison role, consulting and recommending, and at times representing the Anglican Communion. Among its functions are "to share information about developments in one or more provinces with the other parts of the Communion and to serve as needed as an instrument of common action"; "to develop as far as possible agreed Anglican policies in the world mission of the Church and to encourage national and regional Churches to engage together in developing and implementing such policies by sharing their resources of manpower, money, and experience to the best advantage of all"; "to encourage and guide Anglican participation in the Ecumenical Movement and the ecumenical organizations." It is responsible for international dialogues with other world communions.

OFFICERS

Pres., The Archbishop of Canterbury, Most Rev. Robert Runcie, Lambeth Palace, London, SE1 7JU., England.
Chpsn., The Ven. Yong Ping Chung, P.O. Box 17, Sandakan, Sabah, Malayaia.
Sec. Gen., Rev., Canon Samuel Van Culin, 14 Great Peter St., London SW1P 3NQ, England.

Baptist World Alliance

The Baptist World Alliance is a voluntary association of Baptist conventions and unions which was formed at the first world gathering of Baptists in Exeter Hall, London, England, July 11-18, 1905. There have been fifteen meetings of the Alliance's Baptist World Congress, the most recent of which was held in Los Angeles, California, July 1985.

One hundred thirty-four Baptist bodies around the world participate in the Alliance, and these bodies represent approximately 34 million baptized, communicant members. Each body retains its autonomy.

BWA functions as: 1) An agency of communications between Baptists through publications, dissemination of news, film, radio, personal visits, and correspondence; 2) A forum for study and fraternal discussion of doctrines, practice and ways of witness to the world; 3) A channel of world aid to the hungry and victims of disaster, for development projects and fraternal assistance to those in need; 4) A vigilant force for safeguarding religious liberty and other God-given rights; 5) a sponsor of regional and worldwide gatherings for the furtherance of the gospel; 6) an agency for promotion consultation and cooperation among Baptists; 7) an agency for promotion of evangelism and education; and 8) a sponsor of program for lay development.

Headquarters: 6733 Curran St., McLean, VA 22101. Tel. (703) 790-8980. Next Congress: Seoul, Korea, July 10-15, 1990.

OFFICERS

Pres., Dr. G. Noel Vose, Baptist Theological College, Hayman Rd.,Bentley 6102, Western Australia
Gen. Sec.-Treas., _____
Division Dirs., Dr. Reinhold J. Kerstan, Dr. Denton Lotz, Dr. Archibald B. Goldie, Rev. John M. Wilkes, 6733 Curran St., McLean, VA 22101. Tel. (703) 790-8980
Regional Secs., Africa, Dr. Samuel T. Ola, Akande, Nigeria; Asia, Rev. Edwin I. Lopez, Philippines; Caribbean, Rev. Azariah McKenzie, Jamaica; Europe, Rev. Knud Wümpelmann, Denmark; North America, Dr. Archibald R. Goldie, U.S.A.; South America, Rev. Jose Missena, Paraguay

Disciples Ecumenical Consultative Council (DECC)

The Disciples Ecumenical Consultative Council is an international body of Disciples of Christ Churches, established in 1975, which has four major objectives: 1) to deepen the fellowship of Disciples with each other and with other Churches on the way to the visible unity God wills for his people; 2) to encourage participation in the ecumenical movement through joint theological study, church union conversations and other forms of dialogue, and programs of joint action and witness; 3) to gather, share and evaluate information about Disciples ecumenical activities in local, national and regional situations around the world; 4) to appoint fraternal representatives of Disciples to the assemblies of ecumenical bodies such as the World Council of Churches, and of other world families of churches, including the Roman Catholic Church.

OFFICERS

Moderator, Dr. Trevor A. Banks, 13 Eton Rd., Belmont 3216, Victoria, Australia
Gen. Sec., Dr. Paul A. Crow, Jr., P.O. Box 1986, Indianapolis, IN 46206. Tel. (317) 353-1491

ADVISORY COMMITTEE

Dr. Trevor Banks (Australia), Ms. Hazel Byfield (Jamaica), Rev. Carmelo Alvarez (Puerto Rico), Dr. Paul A. Crow, Jr. (U.S.A.)

MEMBERSHIP

Disciples of Christ Churches in Argentina, Canada, Great Britain, Jamaica, Mexico, New Zealand, Paraguay, Puerto Rico, Southern Africa, United States of America, Vanuatu and Zaire.

Friends World Committee for Consultation
Section of the Americas

The Friends World Committee for Consultation (FWCC) was formed in 1937. There has been an American Section as well as a European Section from the early days and an African Section was organized in 1971. In 1974 the name Section of the Americas was adopted by that part of the FWCC with constituency in North, Central and South America and in the Caribbean area. The purposes of the Section of the Americas can be summarized as follows:

1) To encourage and strengthen the spiritual life within the Society of Friends through such measures as the promotion of intervisitation, study, conferences, and a wide sharing of experience on the deepest spiritual level.
2) To help Friends to gain a better understanding of the worldwide character of the Society of Friends and its vocation in the world today.

3) To promote consultation amongst Friends of all cultures, countries, and languages. The Committee seeks to bring the different groups of Friends into intimate touch with one another on the basis of their common Quaker heritage, with a view to sharing experience and coming to some measure of agreement in regard to their attitude to modern world problems.
4) To promote understanding between Friends of all countries and members of other branches of the Christian Church and members of other religious faiths, and to interpret the specific Quaker message to those who seek for further religious experience.
5) To keep under review the Quaker contribution in world affairs and to facilitate both the examination and presentation of Quaker thinking and concern.

Headquarters: 1506 Race St., Philadelphia, PA 19102. Tel. (215) 241-7250.
Other Officers: P.O. Box 1797, Richmond IN 47375. Tel. (317) 935-1967; P.O. Box 11715, Denver, CO 80211. Tel. (303)433-0509; P.O. Box 923, Oregon City, OR 97045. Tel. (503)635-3779.
Latin American Office: Casa de los Amigos, Ignacio Mariscal 132, Mexico. Tel. (905)705-0521.

Heads of Orthodox Churches

Among the churches that are referred to as "Orthodox" there are three distinct groups defined by the recognition of different ecumenical councils. Divisions of this family of churches stem from seven ecumenical councils held from the fourth to the eighth centuries. The Apostolic and Catholic Assyrian Church of the East accepts the first two ecumenical councils. The Oriental Orthodox Churches, The Armenian Apostolic Church, the Coptic Orthodox Church of Alexandria (Egypt), the Ethiopian Orthodox Church and the Syrian Orthodox Church, accept the first three ecumenical councils. The eighteen local churches referred to as "Eastern Orthodox" embody the teachings of all the seven ecumenical councils. The Ecumenical Patriarch of Constantinople is regarded by all as "first among equals," the first in honor and distinction without direct authority over churches other than his own.

ASSYRIAN CHURCH OF THE EAST
Patriarchate of the Apostolic and Catholic Assyrian Church of the East: His Holiness Mar Dinkha IV, Darya Now, Third Avenue No. 32, Tehran 14, Iran. (Presently residing at 7444 North Kildare, Chicago, Illinois 60076).

ORIENTAL ORTHODOX CHURCHES
Catholicossate of the Armenian Apostolic Church: His Holiness Vazken I, Supreme Patriarch and Catholicos of All Armenians, Etchmiadzin, Armenia, USSR.
Catholicossate of the Armenian Apostolic Church, See of Cilicia: His Holiness Karekin II, Catholicos of Cilicia Antelias, Lebanon.
Patriarchate of the Coptic Orthodox Church: His Holiness Pope Shenouda III, Pope of Alexandria and Patriarch of the See of St. Mark, Anba Rueiss Building, Ramses Street, Abbasyia, Cairo, Arab Republic of Egypt.
Patriarchate of the Ethiopian Orthodox Church: His Holiness Abuna Tekle Haimanot, Patriarch of the Ethiopian Orthodox Church, Post Office Box 1283, Addis Ababa, Ethiopia.
Patriarchate of Antioch and All the East of the Syrian Orthodox Church: His Holiness Moran Mor Ignatius Zakka I, Patriarch of Antioch and All the East, Supreme Head of the Universal Syrian Orthodox Church, Bab Tooma, Damascus, Syria.

EASTERN ORTHODOX CHURCHES
Ecumenical Patriarchate: His All-Holiness Demetrios I, Archbishop of Constantinople, and Ecumenical Patriarch, Rum Patrikhanesi, Fener, Istanbul, Turkey
Patriarchate of Alexandria: His Beatitude Parthenios, Patriarch of Alexandria, Greek Orthodox Patriarchate, P. O. Box 2006, Alexandria, Egypt
Patriarchate of Antioch: His Beatitude Ignatius IV, Patriarch of Antioch, Greek Orthodox Patriarchate, P. O. Box 9, Damascus, Syria
Patriarchate of Jerusalem: His Beatitude Diodoros, Patriarch of Jerusalem, P. O. Box 19, Jerusalem, Old City, Israel
Patriarchate of Russia: His Holiness Pimen, Patriarch of Moscow and All Russia, 5 Tchisty Pereulok, Moscow 34, U.S.S.R.
Patriarchate of Serbia: His Holiness German, Patriarch of the Serbian Orthodox Church, 7 Juli 5, Belgrade, Yugoslavia
Patriarchate of Romania: His Holiness Teoctist, Patriarch of Romania, 29 Strada Antim, Bucharest, Romania
Patriarchate of Bulgaria: His Holiness Maxim, Patriarch of the Bulgarian Orthodox Church, The Orthodox Patriarchate, Sofia, Bulgaria
Church of Georgia: His Holiness Ilya II, Catholicos Patriarch of Georgia, Tiflis, Georgia, U.S.S.R.
Church of Cyprus: His Beatitude Chrysostomos, Archbishop of Cyprus, Nicosia, Cyprus
Church of Greece: His Beatitude Seraphim, Archbishop of Athens and All Greece, Athens, Greece
Church of Albania: _____, Tirana, Albania
Church of Poland: His Beatitude Vasilios, Metropolitan of Warsaw and All Poland, Aleja Generala K, Swiercewskiego 52, Warsaw 4, Poland
Church of Czechoslovakia: His Beatitude Dorotheos, Metropolitan of Prague and All Czechoslovakia V Jame 6, Prague 1, Czechoslovakia
Orthodox Church in America: His Beatitude Metropolitan Theodosius, Metropolitan of All America and Canada, P.O. Box 675, Syosset, NY 11791, U.S.A.
Church of Sinai: The Archbishop-Abbott Damian, Mt. Sinai, Egypt
Church of Finland: Most Rev. Archbishop John, Archbishop of Karelia and All Finland, Kupio, Finland
Church of Japan: His Eminence Metropolitan Theodosius, Metropolitan of All Japan, 3-1-4 Surugadai Kanda, Chiyoda Ku, Tokyo, Japan

Hierarchy of the Roman Catholic Church

The Hierarchy of the Roman Catholic Church consists of His Holiness, the Pope, Supreme Pastor of the Roman Catholic Church and the various bishops from around the world joined with the Pope in one apostolic body to care for the Church. Cardinals, now always bishops, number about one hundred and fifty. They serve as the chief counselors to the Pope.
The Supreme Pastor is further assisted by the Roman Curia, which consists of the Secretariat of State or the Papal Secretariat, and the Council for the Public Affairs of the Church, various Sacred Congregations, Secretariats, Tribunals, and Offices. The bishops, some bearing the title of Patriarch or Archbishop, are united with the Supreme Pastor in the

government of the whole Church. The bishops, when assigned to particular sees, are individually responsible for the teaching, sanctification and governance of their particular jurisdictions of the Church.

The Papal territorial possessions are called the State of Vatican City situated within the city of Rome and occupying 108.7 acres. It is the smallest sovereign state in the world. Papal authority is recognized as supreme by virtue of a Concordat reached with the Italian state and ratified June 7, 1929. Included in Vatican City are the Vatican Palace, various museums, art galleries, libraries, apartments, officers, a radio station, post office and St. Peter's Basilica.

HIS HOLINESS THE POPE

John Paul II, Karol Wojtyla, Supreme Pastor of the Roman Catholic Church (born May 18, 1920, installed, October 22, 1978.)

THE ROMAN CURIA

(A few sections of the Roman Curia relevant to ecclesiastical bodies outside the Roman Catholic Church and to other groups and individuals are listed below.)

The Secretariat for Promoting Christian Unity. This Secretariat has responsibility for relations with non–Roman Catholic Christian religious bodies, is concerned with the observance of the principles of ecumenism, promotes bilateral conversations on Christian unity both on national and international levels; institutes colloquies on ecumenical questions and activities with churches and ecclesiastical communities separated from the Holy See; deputes Catholic observers for Christian congresses; invites to Catholic gatherings observers of the separated churches and orders into practice conciliar degrees on ecumenical matters. The Secretariat for Promoting Christian Unity deals with all questions concerning religious relations with Judaism. Cardinal Praeses: Jan Cardinal Willebrands; Vice. Pres., Most Rev. Ramon Torrella Cascante. Office: 1 via dell'Erba, Rome, Italy.

Secretariat for Non-Christians. This Secretariat deals with those who are outside the Christian religion, profess some religion, or have a religious sense. It fosters studies and promotes relations with non-Christians to bring about an increase in mutual respect and seeks ways to establish a dialogue with them. President: Francis Cardinal Arinze; Sec., Rev. Marcello Zago, O.M.I. Office: 1 via dell'Erba, Rome, Italy.

Secretariat for Non-Believers. This Secretariat studies atheism in order to expore more fully its nature and to establish a dialogue with non-believers who sincerely wish to collaborate. President: Paul Cardinal Poupard; Sec., Rev. Jordan Gallego-Salvadores, O.P.; Undersecretary, Rev. Franc Rode, C.M. Office: 16 Palazza S. Calisto, Vatican City State.

(Note: For a complete description and listing of the Hierarchy of the Roman Catholic Church see: the Official Catholic *Directory, 1987,* P. J. Kenedy & Sons, 3004 Glenview Rd., Wilmette IL 60091, pp. ix-xiv. For a description of the Roman Catholic Church in the United States and in Canada, see under Directory 3, "Religious Bodies in the United States," and Directory 4, "Religious Bodies in Canada," appearing in this **Yearbook**.)

International Congregational Fellowship

ICF is a voluntary association, first formed at a world gathering of Congregationalists in Chrislehurst, England, in 1975. It is a successor to the International Congregational Council (formed in London, England, in 1891 and merged into the World Alliance of Reformed Churches in 1966, during which time it held 10 international meetings). The ICF has held additional meetings, the most recent at Endicott College, Beverly, Mass. It is in contact with Congregational-related bodies and individuals, each autonomous, in 52 countries.

ICF functions as: 1) an agency of communication between Congregationalists through publications, dissemination of news, personal visits, and correspondence; 2) a forum for study and fraternal discussion of doctrines, practice, and ways of witnessing to the world; 3) a channel of cooperation in extending help to one another and those in need; 4) a vigilant force for safeguarding religious liberty and other God-given rights; 5) a sponsor of regional and worldwide gatherings for the furtherance of the gospel; 6) an agency for promotion, consultation, and cooperation among Congregationalists.

GENERAL ORGANIZATION

Headquarters: Correspondence to: 61 Oakroyd Ave., Potters Bar, Herts. EN6 2EN, United Kingdom
Next meeting: The Netherlands, August, 1989.

OFFICERS

Chpsn.: Dr. Manfred W. Kohl, Limes Strasse 12, 6382, Friedrichsdorf 2, West Germany.
Regional Secretaries: United Kingdom, Mr. David S. Watson, 61 Oakroyd Ave., Potters Bar, Herts. EN6 2EN; North America: Dr. Leslie Deinstadt, 12 Valencia Circle, De Bary, FL 32713; Pacific and Australia: Rev. Jim Chambers, P.O. Box 2047, Raumati Beach, New Zealand; Central and Southern America, Pastor Teodoro Stricker, Primera Junta 286, 3315 Leandro N. Alem, Misiones, Republica Argentina; Africa and Central Europe, Rev. Phaedon Cambouropoulos, 82 Amissou St., New Smyrna, Athens, Greece.

International Council of Christian Churches

Founded in 1948 and consisting of denominations of Bible-believing churches throughout the world, the ICCC promotes worldwide fellowship of evangelical churches and councils, encourages member bodies to foster a loyal and aggressive revival of Bible Christianity, seeks to awaken Christians to the dangers of modernism and to call them to unity of mind and effort against unbelief and compromise with modernism.

GENERAL ORGANIZATION

Headquarters: 756 Haddon Ave., Collingswood, NJ 08108. Tel. (609) 858-0700.
Triennial Plenary Congress, July 27-August 5, 1988. Amsterdam, Netherlands.

OFFICER

Sec., Suzanne L. DiCanio

ORGANIZATIONS

Commissions: Christian Education; Evangelism; Information and Publication; International Affairs; International Christian Youth; Justice and Freedom; Missions; New Contacts; Radio; Social and Relief

PUBLICATIONS

Getrouw (m, in Dutch)   The Reformation Review (q)

Lambeth Conference of Bishops of the Anglican Communion

The Lambeth Conference consists of all the diocesan bishops and a limited number of other members of the Anglican Communion, and is called together by the personal invitation of the Archbishop of Canterbury.

The first Lambeth Conference was held in 1867 at the request of the bishops in Canada and the United States, and it became a recurring event at approximately ten-year intervals.

The Anglican Communion has no central legislative body but in 1968 the Lambeth Conference agreed to the formation of the Anglican Consultative Council, a body with a permanent office in London. It brings together clergy, lay, and episcopal representatives once every two or three years. This practice of consultation and acknowledged interdependence ensures the validity of the Anglican Communion as a worldwide family of autonomous churches and provinces in communion with the See of Canterbury.

After the Lambeth Conference of 1958, a full-time officer, who became known as the Anglican Executive Officer, was appointed "to collect and disseminate information, keep open lines of communication, and make contact when necessary with responsible authority." The next Lambeth Conference in 1968 proposed the setting up of an Anglican Consultative Council, which, with the consent of all the provinces (or member churches), came into being at the end of 1969. The appointment of Secretary General of the Council replaced that of Anglican Executive Officer. The Lambeth Conference of 1978 proposed regular meetings of the Primates of the Anglican Communion. These have taken place in England in 1979, in America in 1981, in Kenya in 1983, and in Canada in 1986.

Pres., The Archbishop of Canterbury, Most Rev. Robert Runcie, Lambeth Palace, London, SE1 7JU., England.

Lutheran World Federation

The Lutheran World Federation is the successor to an earlier organization of Lutheran churches named the Lutheran World Convention and organized in Eisenach, Germany, in 1923. World War II inflicted such tremendous damage upon the spiritual and welfare activities of Lutheran and other churches in western Europe and elsewhere in the world that it was felt necessary to establish a more functional organization. Thus, the Lutheran World Federation was organized on July 1, 1947, at Lund, Sweden, and plunged immediately into programs of emergency relief, interchurch aid, and studies. Currently it functions between assemblies through major departments of Communication, Studies, Church Cooperation, and World Service. The 1986 membership consists of 104 member churches from all parts of the world with constituencies approaching 55 million persons.

The LWF is incorporated under Swiss law and has its headquarters in Geneva. Its constitution stipulates that "the Lutheran World Federation shall be a free association of Lutheran Churches. It shall act as their agent in such matters as they assign to it. It shall not exercise churchly functions on its own authority, nor shall it have power to legislate for the Churches belonging to it or to limit the autonomy of any Member Church.

"In accord with the preceding paragraphs, the Lutheran World Federation shall:
(a) Further a united witness before the world to the Gospel of Jesus Christ as the power of God for salvation.
(b) Cultivate unity of faith and confession among the Lutheran Churches of the world.
(c) Develop fellowship and cooperation in study among Lutherans.
(d) Foster Lutheran interest in, concern for, and participation in ecumenical movements.
(e) Support Lutheran Churches and groups as they endeavor to extend the gospel and carry out the church's mission.
(f) Help Lutheran churches and groups, as a sharing community, to serve human need and to promote social and economic justice and human rights."

Headquarters: 150 Route de Ferney, 1211 Geneva 20, Switzerland. Meets every 5-7 years. Last meeting July 22-Aug. 5, 1984, Budapest, Hungary. Next Assembly: Jan. 20-Feb. 10, 1990, Curitiba, Brazil.

OFFICERS

Interim Pres: Rt. Rev.Dr. Johannes Hanselman, Evangelical Lutheran Church in Bavaria, Munich, Federal Republic of Germany.

Vice-Presidents: Rev. Dr. Augusto Ernesto Kunert, Evangelical Church of the Lutheran Confession in Brazil, Porto Alegre, Brazil; Rev. Dr. Soritua Nababan, Protestant Christian Batak Church, Jakarta, Indonesia; Ms. Susannah B. Telewoda, Lutheran Church in Liberia, Monrovia, Liberia.

Treas., Mr. Carl-Gustav Von Ehrenheim, Sweden

Gen. Sec., Rev. Dr. Gunnar Staalsett, Geneva, Switzerland.

Gen. Sec., U.S. National Committee, Mr. Harold T. Hanson, Office of Ecumenical Affairs, Evangelical Lutheran Church in America, 8765 W. Higgins Rd., Chicago, IL 60631. Tel. (312)380-2700

PERIODICALS

Lutheran Reports and Documentation.   LWF Information (news service in English, German, French)

Mennonite World Conference

The first Conference was held in Basel, Switzerland, in 1925 under the leadership of Christian Neff, elder of the Weierhof, Palatinate, Germany. All the major Mennonite and Brethren in Christ Church bodies around the world participate in the program of the World Conference and these bodies represent approximately 800,000 baptized members. The MWC does not legislate for the member churches; it convenes basically for inspiration and discussion. Each of the participating Mennonite church bodies retains its autonomy. The Mennonite World Conference normally meets every six years.

OFFICERS

Pres., Ross T. Bender, 11480 W. Virginia Ave., Lakewood, CO 80226

Exec. Sec., Paul N. Kraybill, 465 Gundersen Dr., Ste. 200, Carol Stream, IL 60188.

Pentecostal World Conference

The Pentecostal World Conference was organized in 1947 at Zurich, Switzerland, where Pentecostal leaders met in conference seeking ways to help bring about greater understanding and cooperation among their churches.

Formed and continuing as a nonlegislative body, the conference provides a forum for exchanging ideas, sharing information, and participating in fellowship together.

The main event of the organization is the triennial worldwide convention. Past conventions have been in Zurich, Switzerland; Paris, France; London, England; Stockholm, Sweden; Toronto, Canada; Jerusalem, Israel; Helsinki, Finland; Rio de Janeiro, Brazil; Dallas, Texas; Seoul, Korea; London, England; Vancouver, Canada; Nairobi, Kenya; and Zurich, Switzerland. The next conference will be held in 1989.

Between conventions the World Conference Advisory Committee supervises the work of the conference and plans the next convention. The 25-member committee is elected at each Pentecostal World Conference convention and has members from around the world.

OFFICERS

Chpsn., Dr. Thomas F. Zimmerman, P.O. Box 904 HSJ, Springfield MO 65801
Sec., Rev. Jakob Zopfi, Heimstatte SPM, 6376 Emmetten NW, Switzerland

PERIODICAL

World Pentecost, (q), Rev. Jacob Zopfi, Ed.

United Bible Societies

The United Bible Societies is a world fellowship of 70 national Bible Societies and 38 national offices which, through its national, regional, and global organization, coordinates the efforts of Bible Societies and their staff in over 180 countries, territories, and colonies.

The UBS was founded in 1946 to facilitate consultation and mutual support between its then 16 member Societies, thus helping them to carry out the translation, production and distribution of the Scriptures with ever-increasing effectiveness. In fulfilling this purpose the UBS has evolved over the years, and is now a single partnership of Societies—some old-established, some very recently formed—responsible corporately through national and regional representation in the operation of a World Service Budget (now totaling some $36 million annually), for planning, policy making, financing, and carrying out the worldwide work.

The UBS has functional subcommittees (on translation, production, personnel, etc.) and a team of technical consultants working in the four Regions of Africa, Americas, Asia-Pacific, and Europe. The UBS organizes training institutes and publishes technical helps for translators; coordinates and advises on the most efficient and economical production of the Scriptures; makes known and stimulates new methods of Scripture distribution, especially by church members, for whom training courses are organized; is currently working on the New Readers Project, a graded series of Scriptures for the millions who study in the worldwide literacy campaigns and have no reading material at the end of their courses; represents Bible Society interests at world and regional interdenominational conferences and committees; and when necessary coordinates arrangements to provide Scriptures in emergency situations.

Office of the Gen. Sec.: P.O. Box 810340, D-7000 Stuttgart 80, West Germany
Council meeting at least once every eight years.

OFFICERS

Pres., The Rev. Dr. Oswald C. J. Hoffmann
Gen. Sec., The Rev. Dr. Ulrich Fick.

PERIODICALS

United Bible Societies Bulletin (q); The Bible Translator (q); Technical Papers (1 & 3), Practical Papers (2 & 4); The Bible Distributor (q); World Report (m); Nouvelles Bibliques (m); Prayer Booklet; La Biblia en America Latina.

World Alliance of Reformed Churches
(Presbyterian and Congregational)

The World Alliance of Reformed Churches (Presbyterian and Congregational) was formed in 1970 at Nairobi, Kenya, with the union of the former World Alliance of Reformed Churches and the former International Congregational Council. Both organizations were composed of member churches whose origins lie mainly in the Reformation with which the names of Calvin and Zwingli are linked.

Member churches constituent to WARC number 157 in more than 82 different countries with a total estimated 70 million people as members.

The constitution provides that *ordinarily* once in five years delegates from member churches will meet in General Council (Assembly). Only this Assembly has the authority to make and administer policies and plans, and to speak as the Alliance. Between Assemblies, the Executive Committee exercises general oversight of the Alliance work; it meets annually. The next General Council will be held in 1989.

The Executive Committee consists of the president, three vice-presidents, department heads, and fifteen members, WARC headquarters are in the ecumenical center in Geneva, Switzerland, and its staff members maintain close contact with departments and agencies of the World Council of Churches and with the executives of other world confessional organizations.

Regional needs and growing membership in all parts of the world have produced area organizations within the Alliance. Two areas are fully organized: the European and the Caribbean and North American; and an informal consultative group is at work in Latin America. The major object of such area organizations is to provide means of cooperation, fellowship, and study in specific regions of the world.

THE ALLIANCE OFFICERS

Pres., Rev. Dr. Allan A. Boesak, 6 Hoex St., Glenhaven, Capetown, Box 182, 7530, Republic of South Africa
Vice Presidents: Dr. Chung Hyun Ro, Korea; Rev. Ms. Ansley C. Throckmorton, U.S.A; Rev. Karoly Toth, Hungary
Gen. Sec., Rev. Dr. Edmond Perret, 150 route de Ferney, 1211 Geneva 20, Switzerland.
North American Sec., Rev. James E. Andrews, 100 Witherspoon St., Louisville, KY 40202
Gen. Treas., Mr. Jean Francois Rochette, 11, Corraterie, 1204 Geneva, Switzerland

CARIBBEAN AND NORTH AMERICAN AREA COUNCIL OFFICERS

Chpsn., Rev. R. Stanley Wood, 226 Church St. N.W., Huntsville, AL 35801
Vice Chpsn., Mrs. Sally Mackey, 2127 S.W. 162nd St., Seattle, WA 98166
North American Sec., Rev. James E. Andrews, 100 Witherspoon St., Louisville, KY 40202
Sec., Dr. Roy Blakeburn, 1978 Union Ave., Memphis, TN 38104
Treas., John MacFarlane, 99 Acacia Ave., Ottawa, Ontario KIM OP8

World Alliance of Young Men's Christian Associations

The World Alliance of YMCAs was constituted at the First World Conference of Young Men's Christian Associations, held in Paris in 1855. Geneva, Switzerland, was designated as its headquarters, and in the early years the work was largely undertaken by lay and honorary officers, using the professional assistance of the staff of some National Movements. In 1878 a permanent office was acquired and the first General Secretary, with related staff, was appointed.

The World Alliance is basically a confederation, its members being the National YMCAs around the world. At present 79 National YMCA Movements maintain membership in the Alliance, and in addition to these, the World Alliance cooperates with YMCAs in 11 other countries where National Movements have not yet been organized. Thus the World Alliance provides the coordination and service functions for National Movements which National Movements in turn provide for the Member Associations in their several countries.

The basis of the World Alliance, popularly known as the Paris Basis, because it was at the 1855 Conference in Paris that it was formulated, is as follows:

"The Young Men's Christian Association seek to unite those young men who, regarding Jesus Christ as their God and Saviour according to the Holy Scriptures, desire to be His disciples in their faith and in their life, and to associate their efforts for the extension of His Kingdom amongst young men.

"Any differences of opinion on other subjects, however important in themselves, shall not interfere with the harmonious relations of the Constituent Members and Associates of the World Alliance."

The World Alliance is governed by a World Council of YMCAs, which is held every three years to decide the future policy of the Alliance, determine its programs and elect an Executive Committee. The World Alliance helps to coordinate intermovement cooperation, particularly to extend the movement into new fields. It represents the YMCA at the United Nations and its agencies, and cooperates with churches and other world Christian bodies.

Headquarters: 37 Quai Wilson, 1201 Geneva, Switzerland. Tel. (022) 32-31-00

OFFICERS

Pres., James R. Bellatti
Sec. Gen., Lee Soo-Min, 37 Quai Wilson, 1201 Geneva, Switzerland.

World Association for Christian Communication

The World Association for Christian Communication (WACC) is a professional service organization working with churches and other groups in more than 50 countries to use media for the proclamation of the Christian values in their relevance to all of life.

WACC channels nearly $3 million yearly to more than 100 communication projects mainly in developing nations as well as providing professional services for management, planning and coordination. Funds come from churches and development agencies.

WACC also helps communicators improve skills through training, consultations, research and information exchange.

WACC's 240 corporate members include Protestant, Catholic and Orthodox churches and related groups as well as secular organizations. (WACC also has more than 300 personal members.) Members are divided into regional associations: Africa, Asia, Europe, Latin America-Caribbean, Middle East, Pacific and North America.

Headquarters: 357 Kennington Lane, London SE11 5QY, England. Tel. (01) 582-9139

OFFICERS

Pres., Dr. William F. Fore (USA)
Vice Pres., Nancy Mwendamseke (Tanzania)
Sec., Dr. Judo Poerwowidagdo (Indonesia)
Treas., Ian McNeil (U.K.)
Chpsns. of Regional Associations, Africa, Rev. Daniel Ako'o (Cameroun); Asia, Judo Poerwowidagdo (Indonesia); Europe, James Keegan (U.K.); Latin America-Caribbean, Rev. Hilmar Kannenberg (Brazil); Middle East, Gabriel Habib (Lebanon); Pacific, Seru Verebalavu (Fiji); North America, Rev. Randy Naylor (Canada).

STAFF

Gen. Sec., Rev. Carlos Valle (Argentina)
Dir., Studies & Planning, Mr. Neville D. Jayaweera (Sri Lanka)
Dir. Project Evaluation, Dr. Albert D. Manuel (India)
Dir., Funding, Rev. Don Roper (USA)
Dir., Publications, Dr. Michael Traber (Switzerland)
Dir., Communication Education, Teresita Hermano (Philippines)
Information Coordinator, Editor of *Action,* Ann Shakespeare (U.K.)

PERIODICALS

Media Development (q), Philip Lee, Ed.
Action Newsletter (10/yr.), Ann Shakespeare, Ed.

World Convention of Churches of Christ

The World Convention of Churches of Christ was organized in 1930 in Washington, D.C. It normally meets every four years and is an international confessional grouping including churches and work in 60 countries of the world. It uses the name "Churches of Christ" because it is the name used by many of its churches in various parts of the world. The World Convention is aligned with the Christian Church (Disciples of Christ), Christian Churches/Churches of Christ.

This organization, according to its constitution, "may in no way interfere with the independence of the churches or assume the administrative functions of existing ongoing organizations among us." It exists "in order, more fully to show the essential oneness of the churches in the Lord Jesus Christ; impart inspiration to the world brotherhood; cultivate the spirit of fellowship; provide unity among the churches; and to cooperate with Christians everywhere toward the unity of the Church upon the basis of the New Testament."

Headquarters: First City Bank Center, 100 N. Central Expressway, Ste. 804, Richardson TX 75080
Next Convention: Auckland, New Zealand, November 2-6, 1988.

OFFICERS

Pres., Lyndsay Jacobs, Christchurch, New Zealand
First Vice-Pres., Peggy Owen Clark, Los Angeles, CA, USA
Gen. Sec., Dr. Allan W. Lee, Richardson, Texas, USA.

World Council of Synagogues (Conservative)

The World Council of Synagogues (Conservative) was organized in 1957 as an alliance of Conservative synagogues and synagogue organizations throughout the world. Its purpose is to extend fellowship and mutual aid to each other and to foster the growth and development of Conservative Judaism abroad.

OFFICERS

Pres., Mr. Marshall Wolke, 1212 N. Lake Shore Dr., Chicago IL 60610, Tel. (312) 922-9012
Exec. Dir., Barbara Kessel, 155 Fifth Ave., New York, NY 10010, Tel. (212)533-7693

World Evangelical Fellowship

Founded in 1951 in the Netherlands, the World Evangelical Fellowship traces its roots to the Evangelical Alliance founded in 1846 in Britain. It is an international alliance of autonomous national and regional bodies serving as a resource and catalyst through these bodies to encourage, motivate, and help the local church fulfill its scriptural mandate.

International Headquarters: 07-09 Peace Centre, 1 Sophia Rd., Singapore 0922
European Office: Dreve de Nivelles, 53, B-1150 Bruxelles, Belgium. Tel. 2/771-14-37.
North American Office: P. O. Box WEF, Wheaton, IL 60189. Tel. (312) 668-0440

OFFICERS

Gen. Dir., Dr. David M. Howard
Executive Council: Chpsn., Dr. Tokunboh Adeyemo, Nigeria; Pres., Dr. Theodore Williams, India; Sec., Rev. Alfred C. H. Yeo, Singapore; Treas., Mr. John E. Langlois, Channel Islands; Rev. David Ho, Jamaica; Dr. Emilio A. Nunez C., Guatemala; Pfarrer Hans-Winrich Scheffbuch, Fed. Rep. of Germany; Rev. Brian C. Stiller, Canada; Rev. Agustin B. Vencer, Jr., Philippines; Dr. Raymond V. J. Windsor, New Zealand.

WORLD EVANGELICAL FELLOWSHIP MEMBER BODIES

Association of Evangelical Christians (Sudan)
Association of Evangelicals of Angola
Argentine Alliance of Christian Churches
Australian Evangelical Alliance
National Christian Fellowship of Bangladesh
Evangelical Fellowship of Botswana
Federation of Evangelical Churches and Missions in Burkina Faso
Association of Evangelicals in Burundi
Evangelical Fellowship of Canada
Association of Central African Evangelical Churches
China Evangelical Fellowship (Taiwan)
Evangelical Alliance of Denmark
Dutch Evangelical Alliance
Fellowship of Evangelicals in Egypt
French Evangelical Alliance
German Evangelical Alliance
Evangelical Alliance in the German Democratic Republic
National Association of Evangelicals of Ghana
Evangelical Alliance of Great Britain
Evangelical Alliance of Guatemala
Evangelical Protestant Church of Guinea
Guyana Evangelical Fellowship
Council of Evangelical Churches of Haiti
Pan-Hellenic Evangelical Alliance
Evangelical Fellowship of India
Indonesia Evangelical Fellowship
Evangelical Federation of the Ivory Coast

Jamaica Association of Evangelicals
Japan Evangelical Association
Evangelical Fellowship of Kenya
Liberia Evangelical Fellowship
Evangelical Fellowship of Malawi
National Evangelical Christian Fellowship, Malaysia
Association of Evangelical Protestants of Mali
Evangelical Fellowship of New Zealand
Nigeria Evangelical Fellowship
Evangelical Fellowship of Pakistan
Philippine Council of Evangelical Churches
Portugese Evangelical Alliance
Evangelical Fraternity of Senegal
Evangelical Fellowship of Singapore
Evangelical Fellowship, Sierra Leone
Evangelical Fellowship of South Africa
Evangelical Alliance of the South Pacific Islands
Spanish Evangelical Alliance
Evangelical Alliance of Sri Lanka
Swaziland Conference of Churches
Swiss Evangelical Alliance
Evangelical Fellowship of Thailand
Trinidad and Tobago Council of Evangelical Churches
National Association of Evangelicals, U.S.A.
Evangelical Fellowship of Vietnam
Evangelical Fellowship of Zambia
Evangelical Fellowship of Zimbabwe

REGIONAL MEMBERS

Association of Evangelicals of Africa and Madagascar
Evangelical Association of the Caribbean
Evangelical Fellowship of Asia
European Evangelical Alliance

PERIODICALS

Global Report (bi-m), P. O. Box WEF, Wheaton, IL 60189
Evangelical Review of Theology (q), P.O. Box 1943, Birmingham, AL 35201

World Jewish Congress

The World Jewish Congress was organized in 1936 and, in the United States, in 1939. The WJC seeks to intensify bonds of world Jewry with Israel as a cultural force in Jewish life; to strengthen solidarity among Jews everywhere and secure their rights, status, and interests as individuals and communities; to encourage development of Jewish social, religious and cultural life throughout the world and coordinate efforts by Jewish communities and organizations to cope with any Jewish problems; to work for human rights generally.

Headquarters: 1 Park Ave., Ste. 418, New York, NY 10016. Tel. (212) 679-0600.

OFFICERS

Pres., Edgar M. Bronfman
Chmn., N. Amer. Branch, Senator Leo Kolber
Chmn., American Sect., Rabbi Wolfe Kelman

Sec.-Gen., Israel Singer
Dir., American Sect., Elan Steinberg

World Methodist Council

The World Methodist Council is an association of 64 different Methodist, or Methodist-related groups at work in 90 countries of the world. According to its constitution, "it does not seek to legislate for them nor to invade their autonomy. Rather it exists to serve them and to give unity to their witness and enterprise."

Although the name World Methodist Council was adopted in 1951 at Oxford, England, the Council dates from 1881, when the first Ecumenical Methodist Conference met in London, England. As the Ecumenical Methodist Conference, this world organization convened at ensuing ten-year intervals with the exception of the 1941 Conference, which because of World War II was not held until 1947. Since 1951, meetings have been held every five years.

The membership of the Council is composed of autonomous churches or such units of international church organizations as have attained a significant degree of autonomy.

The World Methodist Council seeks: to deepen the fellowship of the Methodist peoples over the barriers of race, nationality, color, and language; to foster Methodist participation in the ecumenical movement and to promote the unity of Methodist witness and service in that movement; to advance unity of theological and moral standards in the Methodist churches of the world; to suggest priorities in Methodist activity; to promote the most effective use of Methodist resources in the Christian mission throughout the world; to encourage evangelism in every land; to promote Christian education and the church's care for youth; to uphold and relieve persecuted or needy Christian minorities; to provide a means of consultation and cooperation between world Methodism and the other world communions of the Christian Church; to study union and reunion proposals which affect Methodist member churches and to offer advice and help as needed; to arrange the exchange of ministers, youth and laity through a program of world exchange; to train and equip men and women from the nations of the world as evangelists in their own culture through the Council's new Institute for World Evangelism.

World Methodists number 25,141,663 with the sphere of church influence reaching a community of more than 54 million.

OFFICERS

Chpsn., Exec. Cmte., Bishop Lawi Imathiu, Kenya; Vice-Chpsn., Dr. Donald English, U.K.; Treas., Mr. John R. Harper, U.S.A.
Presidium: Mr. Baltron A. Archer, Bahamas; Mr. Charles Boayue, Liberia; Dr. Phyllis Guthardt, New Zealand; Bishop Isaias Gutierrez, Chile; Bishop Ben R. Oliphant, UM, U.S.A.
Mrs. Sinta Sitorus, Indonesia; Bishop William M. Smith, AMEZ, U.S.A.; Dr. Melitta Tenner, German Democratic Republic; Mrs. Edith W. Ming, WFMW, U.S.A.;
Gen. Sec., Dr. Joe Hale, P.O. Box 518, Lake Junaluska, NC 28745, Tel.(704)456-9432; Geneva Sec., Mr. Ralph C. Young, 150 Route de Ferney, 1211 Geneva 20, Switzerland, Tel. 91-61-11; Asst. Treas. (Hdq. Operation), Mrs. Edna Alsdurf; Hon. Pres., Bishop William R. Cannon; Past Chpsns., Dr. Kenneth G. Greet, Bishop Prince A. Taylor, Jr.; Gen. Sec. Emeritus, Dr. Lee F. Tuttle.

World Student Christian Federation

The World Student Christian Association was founded in 1895 by a group of Student Christian Movement leaders, John R. Mott prominent among them.

WSCF now has movements in more than 90 countries with constituency at all levels of education: secondary schools, university and graduate institutions and the wider academic community. For many years, WSCF published the quarterly *Student World,* which has been replaced by regional publications, the *WSCF Journal*, and the quarterly *Federation News.* Information and subscriptions can be obtained by contacting the WSCF interregional office in Geneva, Switzerland.

At the General Assembly in Helsinki, Finland, in 1968, a decision was made to regionalize the WSCF. Now, six regional, continental offices serve to coordinate regional and interregional programs which seek to promote Christian community and a just world.

At the General Assembly, in San Francisco, California in August 1981, the WSCF adopted four major foci for the next quadrennium: education, human rights and solidarity, theology and ecumenism, and women. These program areas are a further development of WSCF's previous commitment to provide Christian witness in the struggle for liberation. Further development of these four program areas occurred at the XXIX WSCF General Assembly in Mexico City, March 1986, under the theme "That They May Have Life in All Its Fullness: Our Commitment to Peace with Justice." Continued and vigorous commitment to theological reflection and involvement in the church universal undergirds the programs. The next General Assembly is planned for 1990.

Interregional Office: 27, ch. des Crêts-de-Pregny, 1218 Grand-Saconnex, Switzerland. Tel. (022) 98 89 53
WSCF North America, 475 Riverside Dr., Rm. 1244 J, New York, NY 10115. Tel. (212)870-2976

OFFICERS

Co-Gen. Secs., Manuel Quintero, Christine Ledger
Chpsn., Bishop Paulose mar Paulose
North American Regional Sec., Mr. John O'Brian

World Union for Progressive Judaism

The World Union for Progressive Judaism was established in London, England, in 1926, by representatives of Liberal, Progressive, and Reform congregational associations and individual synagogues from six nations. The movement has grown, and today the World Union stimulates the development of a worldwide movement and its congregations in 25 countries. The membership of these congregations totals approximately 1.1 million Jewish men, women, and children.

The World Union operates a secondary school in Haifa, Israel, and a college for training rabbis in London. It extends organizational and financial assistance to new congregations in many countries, assigns and employs rabbis wherever Jews are in search of their religious heritage, operates religious and social youth programs in Israel and Europe, publishes prayer books and other texts in many languages, holds biennial conferences for Jewish leaders and scholars from all corners of the world.

Offices: 838 5th Ave., New York, NY 10021. Tel. (212)249-0100; 13 King David St., Jerusalem, Israel. Tel. 02-203-452

OFFICERS

Pres., Mr. Gerard Daniel
Exec. Dir., Rabbi Richard G. Hirsch.
North American Dir., Mr. Martin Strelzer

World Young Women's Christian Association

The World YWCA was founded in 1894 by four of the existing National YWCAs: the Associations of Great Britain, Norway, Sweden, and the United States. During the first years of its history the world movement, reflecting the patterns of its national affiliates, was primarily made up of members of various Protestant denominations. However, as the work spread around the world, Roman Catholic and Orthodox Christians joined the Association and the World YWCA became consciously ecumenical. Today it includes large numbers of women from all confessions and serves women and girls of many faiths. The latest World YWCA constitution was adopted in 1955 and expressed the functions of the World Association as follows:

"The World YWCA provides a channel for the sharing of resources and the exchange of experience among its affiliated associations.

It helps its affiliated associations with the development of their leadership and programme.

It surveys new fields and promotes work to meet the needs therein.

It acts in cooperation with world voluntary movements and with intergovernmental organizations in matters of common concern.

It works for international understanding for improved social and economic conditions and for basic human rights for all people.

In times of emergency it undertakes and sponsors international humanitarian, welfare, and relief work, in accordance with Christian principles, irrespective of religious, social, political, national or racial differences."

The YWCA is now at work in 88 countries with programs including a variety of development projects with emphasis on self-reliance and appropriate technology, educational activities, vocational training programs for women and girls, hostels, rural projects, and programs of study and action in relation to social and economic issues. A wide network of sharing of financial resources and personnel between Associations and of financial aid from other sources forms the World YWCA program of development aid. The World YWCA also carries on refugee services in cooperation with other international agencies bodies and with its own member associations.

The World YWCA has a legislative Council which brings together representatives of its national affiliates every four years and an Executive Committee made up of twenty members from all parts of the world which meets annually. An international staff works at the headquarters in Geneva.

Headquarters: 37 Quai Wilson, 1201 Geneva, Switzerland. Tel. (022) 32-31-00.

OFFICERS

Pres., Ann Northcote
Gen. Sec., Elaine Hesse Greif

World's Christian Endeavor Union

Christian Endeavor is a movement composed of committed followers of Jesus Christ, organized in groups usually called societies, for the purpose of: leading young people (also children and adults) to accept Jesus Christ as Saviour and Lord; bringing them into the life of the church; sustaining and training them for the service of Christ and his cause; releasing them through all channels of human activity in the service of God and man.

Christian Endeavor societies are generally sponsored by a local church, which determines theology, program, activities, and relationships. In most countries it is a graded program including organizational pattern and materials for various age groups.

The first society was organized February 2, 1881, in Portland, Maine. The idea spread rapidly, and by 1895 Christian Endeavor had become a worldwide movement and the World's Christian Endeavor Union was organized in Boston, Mass. As the movement spread to other lands, many national unions were formed. Presently, Christian Endeavor operates in 78 nations and islands and is used by 93 different Christian groups; there are approximately 2 million members worldwide. The World's Union is composed of two areas for the effective promotion of the work—Area I (the Americas, Caribbean, Pacific Region, and Asia) and Area II (Europe, Africa, India, Pakistan, and the Near East). World conventions are held quadrennially and Area conferences in the intervening years. The union is incorporated and is governed by a Council which meets every four years, a Board of Trustees which meets annually, and an Executive Committee which meets on call. There are no full-time paid employees. Most of the work is carried on by volunteer service.

Headquarters: 1221 E. Broad St., P.O. Box 1110. Columbus, OH 43216. Tel. (614) 258-9545
Area II Office: 18 Leam Terrace, Leamington Spa, Warwickshire CV31 1BB, England. Tel. 44-926-21347
Next convention: 1986, Seoul, Korea

OFFICERS

Pres., Rev. Konrad Brandt
Treas., Mrs. Phyllis Meadows
Gen. Sec., Rev. David G. Jackson
Area II. Gen. Sec., Rev. James Heron

6. NATIONAL CHRISTIAN COUNCILS AND REGIONAL AND INTER-REGIONAL CONFERENCES

The following directory material is taken from the *Directory of Christian Councils, Fourth Edition, 1985*, published by the World Council of Churches, 150 route de Ferney, 1211 Geneva 20, Switzerland. Supplementary material supplied by the WCC was also used. This directory is produced in this abridged form by permission of the World Council of Churches.
Listings below follow a geographical arrangement and within geographical area alphabetically by country. Each listing gives the name and address of the Christian Council or Interregional Conference, telephone number, cable and/or Telex, name of chief executive officer, President or other responsible person.

NATIONAL CHRISTIAN COUNCILS

AFRICA

Angola—Conselho Angolano de Igrejas Evangelicas (Angolan Council of Evangelical Churches), Caixa Postal 1659, Rua Amilcar Cabral No. 182, 1 andar 11, Luanda, People's Republic of Angola. Cable: CAIE, Luanda. Gen. Sec., _____.

Botswana—Botswana Christian Council, P. O. Box 355, Gaborone, Botswana. Tel 51981, Cable: KOPANYO. Gen. Sec., Mr. N.T.K. Mmono.

Burundi—Conseil des Eglises du Burundi (Council of Churches of Burundi), B.P. 17, Bujumbura, Burundi. Tel.: 24216. Gen. Sec., Rev. Noé Nzeyimana.

Cameroun—Fédération des Eglises et Missions Evangéliques du Cameroun (Federation of Protestant Churches and Missions in Cameroun), B.P. 491, Yaoundé, Cameroun. Tel.: 22 30 78, Cable: FEMEC B.P. 491 Yaoundé. Gen. Sec., Rev. Grégoire Ambadiang.

The Gambia—Christian Council of The Gambia, P. O. Box 27, Banjul, The Gambia, West Africa. Gen. Sec., J. Tunde Taylor-Thomas.

Ghana—Christian Council of Ghana, P. O. Box 919, Accra, Ghana. Tel.: 76678/76725; Cable: CHRISTCON. Gen. Sec., Rev. Anselm Kofi Zormelo.

Kenya—National Council of Churches of Kenya, P. O. Box 45009, Nairobi, Kenya, East Africa. Tel.: 338211/ 336763, Cable: OIKOUMENE. Gen. Sec., Rev. Samuel Kobia.

Lesotho—Christian Council of Lesotho, P. O. Box 547, 100 Maseru, Lesotho. Tel.: 323639, Cable: CHRISTCOL Maseru. Gen. Sec., Fr. Ramolulela Michael Taole.

Liberia—Liberian Council of Churches, 182 Tubman Blvd., P.O. Box 2191, Monrovia, Liberia. Tel. 262820. Gen. Sec., Mrs. Imogene M. Collins.

Madagascar—Fiombonan'ny Fiangonana Protestanta eto Madagascar, Fédération des Eglises Protestantes à Madagascar (Federation of the Protestant Churches in Madagascar), Vohipiraisana Ambohijatovo-Sud, 101-Antananarivo, Madagascar. Tel.: 201.44. Gen. Sec., Pasteur Charles Rakotoson. Fiombonan'ny Fiangonana Kristiana eto Madagasikara (Christian Council of Churches in Madagascar), B.P. 798, 101-Antananarivo, Madagascar. Tel. 290.52. Exec. Sec., Rev. Lala Andriamiharisoa.

Malawi—Christian Council of Malawi, P. O. Box 30068, Capital City, Lilongwe 3, Malawi, Tel.: 730499, Cable: EKLESIAS. Gen. Sec. Rev. Maxwell Maputwa.

Mozambique—Christian Council of Mozambique, Av. Afonso de Albuquerque No. 1822, P. O. Box 108, Maputo, Mozambique. Tel.: 25103-3,22836, Cable: COCRIMO, Maputo, Telex: 6-199 cocri mo. Maputo. Gen. Sec., Rev. Filipe Sique Banze.

Namibia—Council of Churches of Namibia, P. O. Box 41, Windhoek 9000, Namibia. Tel. 37510/36511/37512/ 32976, Telex: 56834 wk. Gen. Sec., Dr. Abisai Shejavali.

Nigeria—Christian Council of Nigeria, 139 Ogunlana Dr., Surulere, P. O. Box 2838, Marina, Lagos, Nigeria. Tel. Lagos 836019, Cable: CHURCHCON, Lagos. Gen. Sec., Mr. C. O. Williams.

Rwanda—Conseil Protestant du Rwanda (Protestant Council of Rwanda) B.P. 79, Kigali, Rwanda. Tel.: 5825. Gen. Sec., Mr. Jean Utumabahutu.

Sierra Leone—The United Christian Council of Sierra Leone, 4 A Kingharman Rd., Brookfields, P. O. Box 404, Freetown, Sierra Leone. Tel.: 40568, Cable: UNCED, Freetown. Gen. Sec., Rev. Dr. Eustace L. Renner.

South Africa—South African Council of Churches, P. O. Box 4921, Johannesburg, 2000, South Africa. Tel.: (011) 28 22 51/8, Cable: Ecunews, Johannesburg, Telex: 4-86519 sa. Gen Sec., Rev. Frank Chikane.

Sudan—Sudan Council of Churches, P. O. Box 469 Khartoum. Sudan, Tel.: 42859/42855/41137, Cable: SUDCHURCH, Khartoum, Telex: 24099 scc, sd. Khartoum. Gen. Sec., Rev. Clement Janda.

Swaziland—Council of Swaziland Churches, P. O. Box 1095, Manzini, Swaziland. Gen. Sec., Mrs. Eunice Nokuthula Sowazi.

Tanzania—Christian Council of Tanzania, P.O. Box 372, Dodoma, Tanzania. Tel:20445, Cable: UNITAS. Sec., Rev. Canon Stanford A. Shauri.

Zambia—Christian Council of Zambia, P. O. Box 30315, Lusaka, Zambia. Tel.: 214308/219379/219380, Telex: 45160 christ 2a. Gen. Sec., Mr. Philip Mudenda.

Zimbabwe—Zimbabwe Christian Council, 128 Victoria St., P.O. Box 3566, Harare, Zimbabwe. Tel.: 791208; Cable: OIKOUMENE; Telex: 4752 C CARE ZW. Gen. Sec., Rev. M. C. Kuchera.

ASIA

Bangladesh—Jatiya Church Parishad, Bangladesh (National Council of Churches, Bangladesh), 395 New Eskaton Rd., P. O. Box 220, Moghbazar, Dhaka-2, Bangladesh. Tel.: 402869, Cable: CHURCHSERV Dhaka. Gen Sec.-in-Charge, Mr. Subodh Adhikary

Burma—Burma Council of Churches, 263 Maha Bandoola St., GPO Box 1400, Rangoon, Burma. Tel.: 73290, Cable: OIKOUMENE, Rangoon. Gen. Sec., Rev. Canon Andrew Mya Han.

China—China Christian Council, 169 Yuen Ming Yuan Rd., Shanghai, China. Tel: 213396 and 13 Da Jian Yin Xiang, Nanjing, China. Tel: 41439/49053; Cable: 4377

Nanjing; Telex: 34136 glynj cn ccc. Assoc. Gen. Sec., (contact) Mr. Han Wenzao (Nanjing address).

Hong Kong—Hong Kong Christian Council, 33 Granville Rd., Tsim Sha Tsui, Kowloon, Hong Kong. Tel.: 3-670071. Gen. Sec., Rev. Kwok Nai Wang.

India—National Council of Churches in India, Christian Council Lodge, Civil Lines, Nagpur 440 001, India. Tel.: 31312, Cable: AIKYA. Gen. Sec., Mr. Mathai Zachariah.

Indonesia—Communion of Churches in Indonesia, Jalan Salemba Raya 10, Jakarta Pusat, Indonesia. Tel.: 884321, Cable.: OIKOUMENE Jakarta. Gen. Sec., Rev. Dr. Fridolin Ukur.

Japan—National Christian Council of Japan, Japan Christian Center, 2-3-18-24 Nishiwaseda, Shinjuku-ku, Tokyo, Japan 160. Tel. (03) 203-0372 to 4, Cable: JAPACONCIL Tokyo; Telex: 27890 ccrai-j. Gen. Sec., Rev. Maejima Munetoshi.

Korea—National Council of Churches in Korea, Rm. 706 Christian Building, 136-46 Yunchi Dong, Chrongro-Ku, Seoul 110, Korea. Tel.: 763-8427, 763-7323, Cable: KOCOUNCIL, Telex: Korencc K 26840. Gen. Sec., Rev. Kim So Young.

Malaysia—Majlis Gereja-Gereja Malaysia (Council of Churches of Malaysia), 26 Jalan University, Petaling Jaya, Selangor, Malaysia. Tel.: 03.567092, Cable: ECUMENICAL PETALING JAYA. Hon. Gen. Sec., Rev. Dr. Denis C. Dutton.

Pakistan—National Council of Churches in Pakistan, P. O. Box 357, 32-B Shar-e-Fatima Jinna, Lahore-4, Pakistan. Tel.: 57307, Cable: ECUMENICAL, Lahore. Exec. Sec., Mr. William K. Mall.

Philippines—National Council of Churches in the Philippines (Sangguniang Pambansa ng mga Simbahan sa Pilipinas) 879 Epifanio de los Santos Ave., Quezon City (P. O. Box 1767, Manila D-406), Republic of the Philippines. Tel.: 99-86-36, Cable: OIKOUMENE, Manila. Gen. Sec., Bishop La Verne D. Mercado.

Singapore—National Council of Churches, Singapore, Paza Lebar, P. O. Box 80, Singapore 9154. Tel.: 7322631. Hon. Gen. Sec., Sam C. P. Goh.

Sri Lanka—National Christian Council of Sri Lanka, 490/2 Havelock Rd., Colombo 6, Sri Lanka. Tel. 587285. Gen. Sec., Mr. Shirley J. S. Peiris.

AUSTRALASIA

Australia—Australian Council of Churches, 379 Kent St., Sydney, N.S.W. 2000, P. O. Box C 199 Clarence St., Sydney, N.S.W.2000. Tel.: (02) 29.2215, Cable: ECUMENICAL, Sydney, Telex: aa 171715 Sydacc, Sydney. Gen. Sec., _____.

New Zealand—National Council of Churches in New Zealand, Box 297, Christchurch, New Zealand, 1st Floor, 176 Hereford St., Christchurch 1, New Zealand. Tel.: 69-274, Cable: UNITY Christchurch. Gen. Sec., Mrs. Jocelyn A. Armstrong. Te Runanga Whakawhanaunga I Nga Haahi O Aotearoa (Maori Council of Churches), P.O. Box 9573, Newmarket, Auckland, New Zealand. Gen. Sec., Rev. Rua Rakena.

CARIBBEAN, CENTRAL AMERICA & MEXICO

Antigua—Antigua Christian Council, P. O. Box 863, St. John's, Antigua, West Indies. Tel.: 20261. Exec. Sec., Miss Edris Roberts.

Bahamas—The Bahamas Christian Council, P. O. Box SS-5863, The Shirley Street Post Office, Nassau, Bahamas. Tel. 32153/31441 Sec., Rev. Charles A. Sweeting.

Belize—Belize Christian Council, P. O. Box 508, 149

Allenby St., Belize City, Belize, C.A. Tel.: 02-7077. Exec. Sec., Ms. J. A. Jeffries.

Cuba—Consejo Ecuménico de Cuba (Ecumenical Council of Cuba), Calle 6, No. 273, entre 12 y 13, Vedado, La Habana 4, Cuba. Tel.: 3-7404, Cable: IGLEPICUBA. Gen. Sec., Rev. Raul Suarez Ramos.

Curaçao—Curaçao Council of Churches, Fortkerk, Fort Amsterdam, Curaçao, Netherlands Antilles. Tel. 611139. Exec. Sec. Rev. E. G. Stockmann

Jamaica—The Jamaica Council of Churches, 14 South Avenue, P. O. Box 30, Kingston 10, Jamaica, West Indies. Tel.: 092-60974; Cable: CILCHURCH. Actg. Gen. Sec., Mrs. Doreen Kirkcaldy.

Mexico—Federacion Evangélica de Mexico (Evangelical Federation of Mexico) Apartado 1830, Motolinia No. 8-107, Mexico 06001, D.F., Mexico. Tel.: 585-0594. Exec. Sec., Rev. Israel Ortiz Murrieta.

Puerto Rico—(See under Directory 7, "United States Regional and Local Ecumenical Agencies" in this **Yearbook.**)

St. Vincent—St. Vincent Christian Council, P. O. Box 445, Kingstown, St. Vincent, W.I. Tel.: 71809. Exec. Sec., Mr. Liley Cato.

Trinidad & Tobago—Christian Council of Trinidad & Tobago, Hayes Court, Hayes St., Port-of-Spain, Trinidad and Tobago. Tel. 809-622-2863. Exec. Sec., Mrs. Grace Steele.

EUROPE

Austria—Oekumenischer Rat der Kirchen in Öesterreich (Ecumenical Council of Churches in Austria), Dorotheergasse 16, 1010 Vienna, Austria. Tel. 52 83 93. Mod., Rev. Dr. Ernst Kreuzeder.

Czechoslovakia— Czechoslovak Ecumenical Council of Churches, 18600 Prague 8—Karlin, Vitkova 13. Tel. 227581. Sec., Rev. Prof. Anezka Ebertova.

Denmark—Ecumenical Council of Denmark, Norregade 11, DK-1165 Copenhagen K. Tel.: 01-15 59 27. Sec., Mr. Peter Lodberg.

Federal Republic of Germany—Arbeitsgemeinschaft christlicher Kirchen in der Bundesrepublik Deutschland und Berlin (West) e. V. (Council of Christian Churches in the Federal Republic of Germany and West Berlin), Friedrichstrasse 2-6, Postfach 17 02 54, 6000 Frankfurt/Main 17, FRG. Tel.: (069)7159.237. Gen. Sec., Dr. Athanasios Basdekis.

Finland—Ecumenical Council of Finland, Luotsikatu la, PL 185, SF-00161 Helsinki 16, Finland. Tel.: 3580-18021; Telex: infic 122357. Gen. Sec., Rev. Jaakko Rusama.

France—Fédération Protestante de France (French Protestant Federation), 47 rue de Clichy, Paris F-75009, France. Tel.: 1/4874. Telex: 642 380 f paribip., Gen. Sec., Rev. Louis Schweitzer

German Democratic Republic—Arbeitsgemeinschaft christlicher Kirchen in der Deutschen Demokratischen Republik (Council of Churches in the German Democratic Republic), Auguststrasse 80, 104 Berlin, GDR. Tel.: Berlin (GDR) 28860. Gen. Sec., Rev. Martin Lange.

Hungary—Ecumenical Council of Churches in Hungary, Szabadsag tér 2, H-1054 Budapest V, Hungary. Tel.: (36-1) 114-862, Cable: OIKOUMENE Budapest. Gen. Sec., Rev. Dr. Tiber Goeroeg.

Ireland—The Irish Council of Churches, Inter-Church Centre, 48 Elmwood Ave., Belfast, BT9 6AZ, Northern Ireland, Tel.: Belfast 663145. Gen. Sec., Rt. Hon. David W. Bleakley.

Italy—Federazione delle Chiese Evangeliche in Italia (Federation of Protestant Churches in Italy), via Firenze

174

38, 00184 Rome, Italy. Tel.: 47 55 120. Pres., Rev. Aurelio Sbaffi

Netherlands, Raad van Kerken in Nederland (Council of Churches in The Netherlands), Kon. Wilhelminalaan 5, 3818 HN Amersfoort, The Netherlands. Tel. (3133) 633844, Gen. Sec., Rev. W. R. van der Zee.

Poland—Polska Rada Ekumeniczna (Polish Ecumenical Council), ul. Willowa 1, 00-790 Warszawa Poland. Tel.: 49 96 79/49 73 43, Cable: OIKUMENE Warsaw, Telex: 817 875 pec pl, Warszawa. Gen. Sec., Rev. Zdzislaw Pawlik.

Portugal—Conselho Portugués de Igrejas Christas (Portuguese Council of Christian Churches), Rua de Lapa 9, Sala I, 3080 Figueira da Foz, Portugal. Tel. 033-28279. Gen. Sec., Rev. Manuel Pedro Cardoso.

Sweden—Swedish Ecumenical Council, Stortorget 3, 11129 Stockholm, Sweden. Tel.: 08/10.12.35. Sec., Rev. Rune Forsbeck

United Kingdom—British Council of Churches, Inter-Church House, 35/41, Lower Marsh, Waterloo, London SE1 7RL, Tel.: 01-620-4444, Cable; KOINONIA London SWI, Telex: 916504 CHRAID G. Gen. Sec., Rev. Dr. Philip Morgan. **Isle of Man Council of Churches**—Sec., Rev. Douglas V. Brown, The Homestead, Bay View Rd., Port Erin, Isle of Man, U.K. **Scottish Churches' Council**—Scottish Churches' House, Dunblane, Perthshire, FK15 OAJ, Scotland, UK. Tel. Dunblane 823588. Gen. Sec., Rev. Canon Kenyon E. Wright. **Cyngor Eglwysi Cymru** (Council of Churches for Wales)—First Floor, 21 St. Helen's Rd., Swansea, West Glamorgar SA1 4AP, Wales, UK. Tel. (0792)460876. Gen. Sec., Rev. Noel A. Davies.

Yugoslavia—Ecumenical Council of Churches in Yugoslavia, Secretariat, Fah 182, 1101 Belgrade, Yugoslavia. Gen. Sec., Deacon Radomir Rakic.

MIDDLE EAST

Israel—International Christian Council in Israel, P.O.B. 546, Jerusalem, 91004, Israel. Gen. Sec., Mr. Charles Kopp; Chpsn., Dr. Sami Geraisy, P. O. Box 304, Nazareth, Israel.

Jerusalem—International Christian Committee and Inter-Church Aid Committee, Sec., Mr. Elias Khouri, P. O. Box 19195, Jerusalem.

NORTH AMERICA

Canada—(See Canadian Council of Churches in Directory 2—"Canadian Cooperative Organizations, National" in this **Yearbook** for complete details.)

United States—(See National Council of the Churches of Christ in the U.S.A. in Directory 1—"United States Cooperative Organizations, National" in this **Yearbook** for complete details.)

PACIFIC

American Samoa—American Samoa Council of Christian Churches, c/o CCCAS Offices, P.O. Box 1637, American Samoa 96799. Gen. Sec., Rev. Enoka L. Alesana

Cook Islands—Religions Advisory Council of the Cook Islands, P.O. Box 93, Takamoa Rarotonga, Cook Islands. Tel. 22851. Gen. Sec., Bishop Robin Leamy.

Fiji—Fiji Council of Churches, Actg. Gen. Sec., Mrs. Davila Walker, P.O. Box 2300, Government Buildings, Suva.

Papua New Guinea—Melanesian Council of Churches, P. O. Box 1015, Boroko, National Capital District, Papua New Guinea. Tel.: 256410; Cable: Melcon Boroko; Telex: c/o 22213 Wantok. Gen. Sec., Rev. Leva Kila Pat.

Samoa—Samoa Council of Churches, P.O. Box 574, Apia, Western Samoa. Sec., Rev. Oka Fau'olo.

Solomon Islands—Solomon Islands Christian Association, P.O. Box 556, Honiara, Solomon Islands. Tel. 22898; Cable: SICA Honiara. Gen. Sec., Rev. Philemon Riti.

Tonga—Tonga National Council of Churches, P.O. Box 1205, Nuku'alofa, Tonga. Tel. 21177; Cable: UNICIL Nuku'alofa; Telex: 66237 lipons ts. Exec. Sec., Mr. Laitia Fifita.

Vanuatu—Vanuatu Christian Council, P.O. Box 379, Port Vila, Vanuatu. Tel.: 2161. Sec., Rev. Allen Nafuki.

SOUTH AMERICA

Argentina—Federacion Argentina de Iglesias Evangélicas (Argentine Federation of Evangelical Churches) José Maria Moreno 873, 1424 Buenos Aíres, Argentina. Tel.: 922-5356. Pres., Rev. Rodolfo Reinich.

Brazil—The National Council of Christian Churches in Brazil, C.P. 2876, 90.000 Porto Alegre, R.S., Brazil. Sec., Rev. Godofredo G. Boll. Tel. (0512) 24.50.10-1, Cable: ECLESIA; Telex: 512332

Guyana—The Guyana Council of Churches, 71 Murray St., Georgetown, Guyana. Tel. 66610. Sec., Mr. Michael McCormack

Surinam—Surinam Council of Churches, Verlengde Kteizerstraat 92 bov. Postbus 1683, Paramaribe, Surinam. Tel.: 76306. Exec. Sec., Mr. Johan S. P. Kraag.

Uruguay—Federacion de Iglesias Evangélicas del Uruguay (Federation of Evangelical Churches of Uruguay), Av. 8 de Octubre 3324, Montevideo, Uruguay. Tel.: 81.33.16; Cable: OIKOUMENE, Montevideo. Exec. Sec., Rev. Lothar J. Driedger.

REGIONAL AND INTER-REGIONAL CONFERENCES

Africa—All Africa Conference of Churches (Conférence des Eglises de Toute l'Afrique), Waiyaki Way, P. O. Box 14205, Westlands, Nairobi, Kenya. Tel.: 62601/ 62602/62603, Cable: CHURCHCON, Nairobi, Telex: 22175 AACC Nairobi. Gen. Sec., Rev. José Chipenda

Asia—Christian Conference of Asia, Fifth Floor, 10 New Industrial Rd., Singapore 1953. Tel. 2553671/2552889, Cable: CHRISTCONAS Singapore; Telex: rs 33733. Gen. Sec., Rev. Park Sang Jung.

Caribbean—Caribbean Conference of Churches, P. O. Box 616, Bridgetown, Barbados. Tel.: (809) 42-72681, Cable: CHRISTOS, Telex: 2335 CADEC WB. Gen. Sec., Rev. Allan F. Kirton.

Europe—Conference of European Churches, 150 route de Ferney, 1211 Geneva 20, Swizerland. Tel.: 91 61 11, Cable: OIKOUMENE Geneva, Telex: 23 423 OIK CH. Gen. Sec., Mr. Jean Fischer.

Latin America—Consejo Latinoamericano de Iglesias (CLAI), Latin American Council of Churches, Casilla, 85-22, Quito, Ecuador, South America. Tel.: 238.220; Telex: clai 2316 ietel ed. Gen. Sec., Rev. Felipe Adolf.

Middle East—The Middle East Council of Churches, Mail to: c/o P.O. Box 1021020, Limassol, Cyprus. Tel.: (51) 26 022, Telex: 5378 oik cy; Telex West Beirut Office: 22662 oik le; East Beirut Office: 22054 telesco le for mecc. Gen. Sec., Mr. Gabriel Gergi Habib.

Pacific—Pacific Conference of Churches, P. O. Box 208, 4 Thurston St., Suva, Fiji, South Pacific. Tel.: 311-335, Cable: PACFICONS, Suva. Gen. Sec., Mr. S. K. Motu'ahala.

7. UNITED STATES REGIONAL AND LOCAL ECUMENICAL AGENCIES

One of the many ways Christians and Christian churches relate to one another locally and regionally is through ecumenical agencies. The membership in these ecumenical organizations is diverse. Historically, councils of churches were formed primarily by Protestants, but many local and regional organizations now include Orthodox and Roman Catholics. Many are made up of congregations or judicatory units of churches. Some have a membership-base of individuals. Others foster cooperation between ministerial groups, community ministries, coalitions, or church agencies. While Councils of Churches is a term still commonly used to describe this form of cooperation, other terms such as "conference of churches," "ecumenical councils," "churches united," "metropolitan ministries," are coming into use.

An increasing number of ecumenical agencies have been exploring ways to strengthen the interreligious aspect of life in the context of religious pluralism in the U.S. today. Some organizations in this listing are interfaith agencies primarily through the inclusion of Jewish congregations in their membership. Other organizations are considering ways to nurture partnership with a broader base of religious groups in their communities, especially in the areas of public policy and interreligious dialogue.

The interactive network embodied in these pages demonstrates the essential interrelatedness of the one ecumenical movement in its local and global dimensions, lifts up programs of study and action, and calls attention to the witness and experience of local and regional ecumenical and interreligious organizations.

This list does not include all local and regional ecumenical and interfaith instrumentalities in existence today. No such compilation currently exists. However, the Commission on Regional and Local Ecumenism of the National Council of Churches of Christ in the U.S.A. (CORLE), the National Association of Ecumenical Staff (NAES), and the newly developing North America Interfaith Network (NAIN) are cooperating on the compilation of such data.

The terms *regional* and *local* are sometimes relative, making identification somewhat ambiguous. Regional councils may cover sections of large states or cross state borders. Local councils may be made up of several counties, towns, or clusters of congregations. State councils or state-level ecumenical contacts exits in 45 of the 50 states. One of these, at the state level, is an interfaith council—the Arkansas Council of Churches and Synagogues.

In this listing, the organizations that work primarily across state borders are listed under the "regional" heading. Others are grouped by state and listed alphabetically, with state-wide ecumenical agencies listed first; then follow metropolitan, city, or area agencies with paid staff, listed alphabetically by name of agency, using significant geographical words in the title. For councils or agencies with paid staff, the name, address, and telephone number of the agency are given, and the names of professional staff are listed, as well as officers and major activities as reported by the agency. When the name of the city is omitted from an address, the city is the same as that of the headquarters of the organization.

For additional information about community ministries, ecumenical agencies with voluntary leadership, covenant congregations, or new developments within a specific area, consult the state or local councils.

For information concerning this listing or to report changes in staff, officers, mailing addresses, and program emphases for the agencies listed here, contact: Commission on Regional and Local Ecumenism, National Council of the Churches of Christ in the USA, 475 Riverside Dr., Rm. 870, New York, NY 10115. Tel. (212)870-2158.

Information concerning NAES, a professional association for persons engaged in ecumenical service—local, state, regional, national—may be obtained through CORLE at the address and phone listed above.

Listing includes information available through January 1988.

†Indicates information repeated from a previous Yearbook, since no more recent report has been received.

REGIONAL

The Commission on Religion in Appalachia, Inc.

864 Weisgarber Rd., NW, P.O. Box 10867, Knoxville, TN 37939
Tel. (615) 584-6133
Coordinator, Jim Sessions
Adm. Sec., Lee Mynatt
Resource Coord., Jim Rugh,
Financial Sec., Pearl Jones
Chpsn., Gladys Campbell, United Methodist Church, 475 Riverside Dr., Rm. 337, New York, NY 10115
Appalachian Development Projects Cmte., Coord., Gaye Evans; Asst. Coord., Linda Selfridge; Chpsn., Barbara Greene
Social, Economic and Political Issues Task Force, Coord., Fr. John Rausch; Chpsns., John Bookser-Feister, J. William Troy
Parish Development Task Force Chpsn., Dr. Harold McSwain
Communications Coord., Jamie Harris
Northern Prog. Coord., Joyce Dukes
Volunteer Coord., John MacLean
An A 13-state regional ecumenical agency composed of 18 communions and 10 state councils of churches.

IMPACT

100 Maryland Ave., NE, Washington, DC 20002
Tel. (202) 544-8636
National Director, Gretchen Eick
An interfaith legislative information and action network. Action alerts with recommendations for immediate response; network organizations with specific response objectives. Publications recommending political action on peace, human rights, economic justice, women's equity, immigration, and environmental issues.

National Farm Worker Ministry

P.O. Box 302, Delano, CA 93216
Tel. (805)725-7445
Dir., Sr. Patricia Drydyk
Continuing the National Migrant Ministry. Related to the National Council of the Churches of Christ in the U.S.A.
Major Activities: Ministry Among Pesticide Victims; Pesticide Seminars; UFW Table Grape Boycott; Farm Worker Week; Farm Labor Organizing Committee Support

North American Interfaith Network (NAIN)

Temple of Understanding
The Cathedral of St. John the Divine, 1047 Amsterdam Ave., New York, NY 10025, Tel. (212)865-9117
Dir., Rev. Daniel Anderson
Major Activities: Interfaith Directory; Interfaith Conferences: Networking between Interfaith Organizations

ALABAMA

No state council at present

ALASKA

Alaska Christian Conference

P.O. Box 441, Fairbanks 99707
Pres., Bishop George Haris, Box 441, Fairbanks 99707
Vice-Pres., Bishop Jacob Nelson, Sr., P.O. Box 9, Bethel 99559
Treas., Barbara Shaffer, 1660 Patterson St., Anchorage 99504
Newsletter Ed., John Shaffer, 1660 Patterson St., Anchorage 99504
Major Activities: Legislative & Social Concerns, Resources and Continuing Education; New Ecumenical Ministries; Communication; Alcoholism, Education & Prevention; Family Violence, Education & Prevention; Native Issues; Ecumenical, Theological Dialogue; Criminal Justice.

ARIZONA

Arizona Ecumenical Council

4423 N. 24th St., Ste. 750, Phoenix 85016
Tel. (602)468-3818
Adm., Dr. Arlo Nau
Pres., Rev. Robert Seel, 3809 E. Third St., Tuscon 85716. Tel. (602)881-6648
Major Activities: Donohoe Ecumenical Forum Series; Affordable Housing Documentary; Disaster Response Network; Political Action Team; Resident Alien Registration Assistance Taskforce; Hopi/Navajo Relocation Taskforce

Tucson Ecumenical Council

Mailing address: P.O. Box 43243, Tucson 85733
Tel. (602)323-9244
Pres., Rev. Franklin Oliver
Pres.,-Elect, Rev. Vickie Curtiss
Vice Pres., Rev. Paul Buckwalter
Sec., Rev. John Kautz
Treas., Rev. Mary Jacobs
Social Concerns, Rev. Bill Dougherty
Edu., Faith and Worship, Rev. James Stewart
Adm. Asst., Edie Lauver
Dir., Central American Task Force, Rev. Kenneth Kennon
Dir., Interfaith Coalition for the Homeless, Edie Lauver
Dir. Legal Assistance Task Force, Joan Peacock
Dir. Techo Cultural Center, _____
ERRSS, Penny Costello
Major Activities: Interfaith and Ecumenical Services; Homeless; Central America Task Force; Inter-American Educational and Cultural Project; Legal Assistance for Refugees

ARKANSAS

Arkansas Council of Churches and Synagogues

415 N. Maple St., P.O. Box 5292, North Little Rock 72119.
Tel. (501) 375-1553
Conf. Exec.,, Rev. Dale E. Bard
Pres., Rev. George Gunn, 8801 Leatrice, Little Rock, 77207
Sec., Mrs. Frances Bing, 5009 Burrow Dr., Little Rock 72114
Treas., Mr. Jim Davis, Box 7239, 72217
Major Activities: Task Forces on Hunger, Aging, Energy & Disasters; Institutional Ministry; Church World Service; Heifer Project; Ecumenical Worship Seminar; Week of Prayer for Christian Unity; Interfaith Executives' Advisory Council; Theological Studies; Mt. Sequoyah Ecumenical Mission Conference; T.V. Awareness; Communications; Liaison with State Agencies—Family Planning, Drug Abuse, Rural Health; Interfaith Relations; Church Women United; IM-PACT; Farm Crisis

CALIFORNIA

Northern California Ecumenical Council

942 Market St., No. 702, San Francisco 94102
Tel. (415) 434-0670
Exec. Dir., Rev. John C. Moyer
Co-Eds., Sequoia Newspaper, Rev. Paul Burks, Rev. Janet Burks
Dir., Nicaragua Interfaith Committee for Action, Janine Chagoya
Dir., Refugee Community Programs, John Driscoll, Interim
Dir., Human Rights in El Salvdor, Jesus Campos
Pres., Rev. Richard Lauer
Vice-Pres., Rev. Tim Boeve
Sec., Ms. Elsie Tufts
Treas., Ms. Alice Wimer
Major Activities: Peace with Justice; Faith and Witness; Ministry; Communications

California Council of Churches, Office for State Affairs

1300 N. St., Sacramento 95814
Tel. (916) 442-5447
Exec. Dir., Rev. Glen Holman
Assoc. Dir., Patti Whitney-Wise
Calif. Food Policy Advocate, Sal Alvarez, Tel. (916) 442-3676
Major Activities: Monitoring State Legislation; Calif. IMPACT Network; Farmers Markets, Preservation of Prime Agricultural Land; Legislative Principles

Southern California Ecumenical Council

1010 S. Flower, 500, Los Angeles, 90015
Tel. (213) 746-7677
Exec. Dir., Mr. Charles ("Chuck") L. Jones
Adm., Michele Prichard
Pres., Dr. Frederick Beebe
Dir., El Rescate, Lauren McMahon; Dir., Interfaith Coalition, Rev. Kathy Cooper; Dir., Homeless Health Care Proj., Michael Cousineau; Dir., Ecumedia, Rev. Max Perrow; Dir., Interfaith Taskforce on Central Am., Mary Brent Wehrli

Major Activities: Faith and Order; Christian Unity; Ecumenical Education and Interpretation; Peace with Justice; Legislation and Other Advocacy; Services to Central American Refugees; Other Immigration and Refugee Resettlement; Hunger Coordination; Welfare Advocacy, Emergency Food; Shelter; Health Care; Clergy and Laity Concerned; Disaster Readiness; ECUMEDIA; Interreligious Concerns; Church/State; Human Rights

Pacific and Asian American Center for Theology and Strategies (PACTS)

1798 Scenic Ave. Berkeley 94709
Tel. (415) 848-0173
Dir., Julia K. Estrella
Pres., Rev. Katie Choy-Wong
Treas., Toshi Yamamoto
Fin. Sec., Rev. Benjamin Wu
Major Activities: Collect and Disseminate Resource Materials; Training Conferences; Public Seminars, Communication, Network and Advocacy Center for Women in Ministry; Human Rights; Migration Issues; Lay Ministry; Continuing Educations; Racial and Ethnic Minority Concerns.

Council of Churches of Contra Costa County

1543 Sunnyvale Ave., Walnut Creek 94596
Tel. (415) 933-6030
Adm. Dir., Consuelo F. Bennett
Chaplains: Rev. Keith Spooner; Rev. Norman Behrmann; Rev. J. Richard Flowers; Rev. Harry Washburn
Pres., Mrs. Ann Scott, 50 El Paseo, Walnut Creek 94596
Treas., Mr. Tom Tousignant, 3719 Oakpark Ct., Concord 94519
Major Activities: Institutional Ministries; Social Education and Action; Christian Education

Fresno Metropolitan Ministry

4411 E. Tulare Ave., Fresno 93702
Tel. (209) 252-1889
Exec. Dir., Rev. Walter P. Parry
Adm. Asst., Jackie Church
Pres., Audrey Brouwer
Major Activities: Hunger Relief Advocacy; Human Relations; Convalescent Home Visitation & Advocacy; Urban Education; Biblical & Theological Education for Laity; County Hospital Advocacy; Mental Health; Women and Health

South Coast Ecumenical Council

3326 Magnolia Ave., Long Beach 90806
Tel. (213) 595-0268
Exec. Dir., Rev. Don E. Lindblom
Dir. of Aging, Mrs. Roberta Stabbert
Dir. of Cmty. Action, Rev. Grace Moore
Dir. of Counseling, Dr. Lester Kim
Pres., Mr. L. Duane Eberhardt
Treas., Rev. V. K. Vose
Major Activities: Weekday Christian Education; Immigration and Refugee Support Services; Interfaith Action for Aging; Farmers' Markets; Hunger Projects; Shelters for the Homeless; Lay Academy of Religion; Church Athletic Leagues

Ecumedia/Los Angeles

3300 Wilshire Blvd., Los Angeles 90010
Tel. (213) 380-0460
Exec. Dir., Dr. Maxwell V. Perrow

Major Activities: Ecumenical Communication; Secular and Religious Media Coordination; News and Information Office; Video Production

The Ecumenical Council of the Pasadena Area Churches

444 E. Washington Blvd., Pasadena 91104
Tel. (818) 797-2402
Exec. Dir., Rev. Charles B. Milburn
Pres., Constance H. Smith
Major Activities: Christian Education; Community Worship; Community Concerns; Christian Unity; Youth; Ethnic Ministries; Hunger; Peace; Friends in Deed; Emergency Shelter Line Alternative Christmas Markets; Campus Ministry; Chaplaincy

Pomona Valley Council of Churches

1753 N. Park Ave., Pomona 91768
Tel. (714) 622-3806
Pres. Rev. Richard Landrum
Exec. Dir., _____
Sec., Gene Jordon
Treas., Charles Ralston
Major Activities: Advocacy and Education for Social Justice; Ecumenical Celebratons; Interfaith Legislative Action; Hunger Advocacy; Emergency Food and Shelter Assistance; Farmer's Market; Low Income Housing; Hospital Chaplaincy; Pastoral Counseling; Coalition to Combat Racism

San Fernando Valley Interfaith Council

10824 Toponga Canyon Blvd., No. 7, Chatsworth 91311
Tel. (818) 718-6460
Actg. Exec., Lois Hamer
Pres., _____
Major Activities: Seniors' Multi-Purpose Centers; Nutrition & Services; Meals to the Homebound; "Interfaith Reporter"; Task Forces on Interreligious Concerns, Emergency Needs, Peace and Justice, Aging, Hunger; Human Relations

Interfaith Service Bureau

3720 Folsom Blvd., Sacramento 95816
Tel. (916) 456-3815
Exec. Dir., Mary Deuel
Pres., Rev. Scott Anderson, Tel. (916)718-6460
Major Activities: Chaplaincy; Food Closet Coalition; Mass Media; Credit Union; Interfaith Voice; Indo-Chinese Assistance Center; Clergy Concerns Committee; Cable Television and Religious Channel; International Boutique

San Diego County Ecumenical Conference

4075 Park Blvd., P. O. Box 3628, San Diego 92103
Tel. (619) 296-4557
Exec. Dir., Rev. E. Vaughn Lyons
Dirs. of Communication, Rev. Bernard Filmyer
Admin. Asst., Patricia R. Munley
Pres., Rev. Dr. Faith Conklin
Treas., Mr. Joseph Ramsey
Major Activities: Emerging Issues; Communications; Faith Order & Witness; Worship & Celebration; Youth; Ecumenical Tribute Dinner; Advent Prayer Breakfast; Clergy Continuing Education Seminars; AIDS Chaplaincy Project; Third World Opportunities Maritime Ministry; Sunday Focus TV News; Religion in the News Radio

San Francisco Council of Churches

942 Market St., Rm. 402, San Francisco 94102
Tel. (415) 433-3024
Exec. Dir., Rev. Dr. Norman E. Leach
Pres., Rev. Roland Gordon
Treas., Mr. Charles Oliver
Major Activities: Ecumenical and Interfaith Program; Annual Easter Sunrise Services; Services to Seniors; Child Development; Prisoner-Mother Program; Placement Service for Church Musicians; Night Ministry; Healing Community; Holiday Connection; Job Training/ Placement for Developmentally Disabled Adults; Information and Referral; Project Opportunity (Employment for Handicapped)

The Council of Churches of Santa Clara County

1229 Naglee Ave., P. O. Box 26308, San Jose 95159
Tel. (408) 297-2660
Exec. Min., Rev. Bill Kirlin-Hackett
Dir., Senior Services, Dona Reddy
Coord., Emergency Assistance, Rev. Harold Zimmerman
Correctional Chpsn., Rev. Charles Walker
Pres., Rev. Paul Dirdak
Major Activities: Services for Aging; Social Education/ Action; Correctional Inst. Chaplaincies; Hunger and Emergency Services; Ecumenical and Interfaith Witness; Head Trauma Rehabilitation

Westside Ecumenical Conference

P.O. Box 1402, Santa Monica 90406
Tel. (213) 394-1518
Exec. Dir., Rev. David McAllister
Major Activities: Convalescent Hospital Visiting; Meals on Wheels; Community Religious Services; Convalescent Hospital Chaplaincy

COLORADO

Colorado Council of Churches

1370 Pennsylvania Ste. 100, Denver 80203
Tel. (303)861-1884
Pres., Rt. Rev. William C. Frey
Exec. Dir., Rev. Gilbert Horn
Major Activities: Ecumenical Witness and Religious Dialogue; Institutional Ministries; Human Needs and Economic Issues (Includes Homelessness, Rural Crisis, Justice in the Workplace); World Peace and Global Affairs; Communication, Media and the Arts

Boulder Council of Churches and Synagogues

2650 Table Mesa Dr., Boulder 80303
Tel. (303) 499-5611
Exec. Dir., Marsha Caplan
Major Activities: Interfaith Dialogue and Programs; Thanksgiving Worship Services; Food for the Hungry

CONNECTICUT

Christian Conference of Connecticut (CHRISCON)

60 Lorraine St., Hartford 06105
Tel. (203) 236-4281
Exec. Kir., Rev. Stephen J. Sidorak, Jr.
Exec. Asst., Betty Anderson
Operation Fuel Mgr., Diane Casey
Adm. Asst., Mildred Robinson

Pres., Dr. Carroll Kann
Treas., Gerald Lamb, CBT, 1 Constitution Plaza 06115
Major Activities: Communications; Education; Institutional Ministries; Peace and Social Justice Issues; Legislation; Conn. Bible Society; Conn. Council on Alcohol Problems; Ecumenical Forum, Operation Fuel; Faith & Order

Council of Churches of Greater Bridgeport, Inc.

126 Washington Ave., Bridgeport 06604
Tel. (203) 334-1121
Exec. Dir., Rev. John S. Kidd
Pres., Rev. George Bland
Sec., Mrs. Dorothy Allsop
Treas., Thomas Holloway
Major Activities: Runaway and Homeless Youth; Nursing Home, Hospital, and Prison Ministries; Feeding Programs and Food Bank; Tutoring; Ecumenical Activities

Association of Religious Communities

213 Main St., Danbury 06810
Tel. (203) 792-9450
Exec. Dir., Samuel E. Deibler, Jr.
Pres., Rev. Martha Larsen

The Capitol Region Conference of Churches

30 Arbor St., Hartford 06106
Tel. (203) 236-1295
Exec. Dir., Rev. Roger W. Floyd
Dir. Pastoral Care & Training and Anna M. Fulling Chaplain, Rev. John Swift
Dir. Social Concerns, Rev. William Watson
Dir., B.T.A., Rev. Robert Feldmann
Dir. Retired Senior Volunteer Program, Ms. Pamela Morrill
Dir., Foster Grandparents Prog., Mr. Robert Dembek
Community Organizer, Mr. Joseph Wasserman
Housing Advocate, Ms. Annette Carter
Foster Grandparents Prog. Volunteer Coord., Barbara Cecchini
Hartford Correctional Center Chaplain, Rev. John Melendez, Rev. Larry Williams
R.S.V.P. Field Coordinators: Roberta Renson
Broadcast Ministry Consultant, Ivor T. Hugh
Pres., Mr. William Metzgar
Major Activities: Organizing for Peace and Justice; Chaplaincy; Aging; Legislative Action; Cooperative Broadcast Ministry. Retired Senior Volunteer Program; Foster Grandparent Program; Ecumenical Cooperation

Center City Churches

170 Main St., Hartford 06106
Tel. (203) 728-3201
Exec. Dir., Paul C. Christie
Pres., Frank Hoffman
Sec., Sabrina Saunders
Treas., Betty Fairchild
Major Activities: Aging; Youth and Community Resources; Tutorial Program; Food Pantry; Outreach Ministry; Community Mental Health; Indigent; Advocacy; AIDS Residency

Manchester Area Conference of Churches

736 East Middle Tpke., Box 773, Manchester 06040
Tel. (203) 649-2093
Exec. Dir., Nancy P. Carr

Dir., Dept. of Human Needs, Elizabeth Harlow
Coord., Project Reentry, Jeffrey Cox
Chaplain, Rev. James Rush
Dir., Shelter Services, Priscilla Burt
Pres., Rev. Dr. Shephard Johnson
Treas., Florence Noyes
Major Activities: Provision of Basic Needs (Food, Fuel, Clothing, Furniture); Emergency Aid Assistance; Reentry Assistance to Ex-Offenders; Pastoral Care in Local Institutions; Interfaith Day Camp; Advocacy; Ecumenical Education and Worship

New Britain Area Conference of Churches (NEWBRACC)

19 Chestnut St. New Britain 06051
Tel. (203) 229-3751
Exec. Minister, Rev. Dr. David D. Mellon
Pastoral Care/Chaplaincy, Rev. Hudson R. Richard; Rev. Dr. Lydia E. Rivera
Pres., Mary Pacinda-Turner
Treas., Margaret Fletcher
Major Activities: Worship; Social Concerns; Emergency Food Bank; Communications-Mass Media

The Downtown Cooperative Ministry in New Haven

57 Olive St., New Haven 06511
Tel. (203) 776-9526
Coord., Rev. Samuel N. Slie
Pres., Rev. Ellen Tillotson, 129 Church St., New Haven 06510
Treas., Richard Snyder, P.O. Box 1721, New Haven 06507
Major Activities: Mission to Poor and Dispossessed; Criminal Justice; Elderly; Sheltering Homeless; Soup Kitchen; Low Income Housing

Wider City Parish

48 Howe St., New Haven 06511
Tel. (203) 624-6515
Exec. Dir., Rev. Robert Forsberg
Chair, Rev. Dr. Edwin Edmonds, 217 Dixwell Ave., 06511
Major Activities: Community Organization; Work With Children in Public Housing; Peace Education and Action; Bread for the World Congressional District Coordination; Public Education; Computer Literacy

Christian Community Action

98 South Main St., South Norwalk 06854
Tel. (203) 854-1811
Coord., Eleanor Crystal
Major Activities: Emergency Food Program; Used Furniture & Clothing; Loans for Rent, Security, and Fuel

Stamford Area Council of Churches and Synagogues

628 Main St., Stamford 06901
Tel. (203) 348-2800
Exec. Dir., Rev. Brenda J. Stiers
Administrator, Mrs. Nancy Martell
Associate, John Sapora
Ofc. Mgr., Barbara Dordelman
Hospital Chaplain, Rev. William Scrivener
Pres., Mr. Stephen Alpert
Treas., Mr. Roger Cromwell
Major Activities: Prison Visitation; Counseling, Senior Neighborhood Support Services; Ecumenical Services; Interfaith Dialogues; Food Bank and Salvage Program;

Media Commission/Cable/TV; Fuel Assistance; Peace Center; Elderly Visitation Programs

Waterbury Area Council of Churches

24 Central Ave., Waterbury 06702
Tel. (203) 756-7831
Coordinator, Mrs. Virginia B. Tillson
Adm. Asst., Evelyn Hanneman
Pres., Rev. David Halmers
Major Activities: Emergency Food Program; Emergency Fuel Program; Soup Kitchens; Ecumenical Worship; Christmas Toy Sale

DELAWARE

Delmarva Ecumenical Agency

1626 N. Union St., Wilmington 19806,
Tel. (302) 655-6151; Dir., Dr. George F. Cora
Adm. Sec., Mrs. Judith G. Berry
Pres., Rt. Rev. Elliott L. Sorge, P.O. Box 1027, Easton, MD 21601. Tel. (301)822-1919
Major Activities: Facilitates and coordinates the work of churches and public and private agencies in urban, rural, social concerns, education, and worship ministries

DISTRICT OF COLUMBIA

Interfaith Conference of Metropolitan Washington

1419 V St., N.W. 20009
Tel. (202) 234-6300
Exec. Dir., Rev. Clark Lobenstine
Admin. Sec., Jynnifer V. Jemison
Staff Assoc. for Issues and Advocacy, Susan Donahue
Staff Associate, Lisa Iversen
Pres., Rev. John V. O'Connor
1st Vice Pres., Rev. Frank Tucker
Vice Pres., Rabbi Andrew Baker
Vice Pres., Dr. Ibrahim M. Fofanah
Vice Pres., The Most Rev. James A. Hickey; Elder L. Ralph Mecham
Sec., Rev. Carl Nissen
Treas., Ms. Dorothy Knight
Major Activities: Interfaith Dialogue; Health; Employment/Economic Development; Hate Violence-Group Hatred; Interfaith Concert

The Council of Churches of Greater Washington

411 Rittenhouse St., N.W., Washington 20011
Tel. (202)722-9240
Exec. Dir., Rev. Ernest R. Gibson
Dir. for Prog., City, Rev. Rodney L. Young
D.C. Communities Ministries, Rev. H. Wesley Wiley
Res. Dir., Hope Valley Camp, Mr. Steven Owens
Pres., Rev. Edward Castner
Major Activities: Development of Group and Community Ministries; Church Development and Redevelopment; Liaison with Public Agencies; Work Training Employment Programs: Year-round Ex-offenders; Aid to Families With Dependent Children; Training and Retraining for the Homeless; In-school Youth Employment; Summer Youth Employment; Hope Valley Camp; Institutional Ministry; Hunger Relief; Sheltering and Rehabilitation of the Homeless; Vision to Action—Community Revitalization; Health Ministries

FLORIDA

Florida Council of Churches

1794 N. Mills Ave., Orlando 32803
Tel. (305) 898-7746
Exec. Dir., Walter F. Horlander
Admin., Asst., Mrs Joyce Neese
Assoc. Dir. for Refugee Services, John F. White
Assoc. Dir. for Development, Shelburn M. Wilkes
Assoc. Dir. for Prog., Voris G. Brookshire
Major Activities: Faith and Order; Education and Renewal; Evangelism and Mission; Justice and Peace

Christian Service Center for Central Florida, Inc.

808 West Central Blvd., P.O. Bos 232, Orlando 32802
Tel. (305)425-2523
Exec. Dir., Earl W. Scarbeary
Bus. Adm., Richard D. Black
Family Emergency Services, Dir., Melinda Castillo
Family Life Counseling, Dir., William Hasenyager
Daily Bread, Dir., Charles G. Parkhouse
Social Justice Ministry, Dir., Robert Land
Thrift Service, Dir., De'Borah Scott
Respite, Dir., Patricia Riffle
Meals on Wheels, Dir., Anderson Knight
Fresh Start, Dir., Robert Land
Pres., Donald E. C. Crismon
Vice-Pres., Flossie Hellinger
Treas., James S. Hunt
Sec., Dorothy J. Clements
Major Activities: Provision of Basic Needs (food, clothing, shelter); Emergency Assistance; Professional Counseling. Noon-time Meals; Sunday Church Services at Walt Disney World; Research and Development in Social Issues; Collection and Distribution of Used Clothing; Shelter for Homeless, Meals on Wheels.

GEORGIA

Georgia Christian Council

P.O. Box 7193, Macon 31209
Tel. (912) 474-3906
Exec. Dir., Rev. Donald E. Leiter
Pres., Mrs. Patricia Evans, 115 River Park Dr., NW, 30328
Treas., Rev. James Cantrell, 28 Woosley Rd., Hampton 30228
Major Activities: Local Ecumenical Support and Resourcing; Legislation (GRAIN); Rural Development; Racial Justice; Networking for Migrant Coalition and Aging Coalition

Christian Council of Metropolitan Atlanta

465 Boulevard, S.E., Atlanta 30312
Tel. (404) 622-2235
Exec. Dir., Dr. Perry Ginn
Deputy Dir., Mrs. Margaret Koehler
Pres., Dr. William J. Hinson
Treas., Mr. Waymon Ahart
Editor, Mr. Neal P. Ponder, Jr.
Major Activities: Refugee Services; Emergency Assistance; Hunger Programs; Christian Education; Chronically Medically Ill; Voluntary Service; Employment; Racism; Homeless; Elderly; Ecumenical and Interreligious Events; Peace and Justice Ministries; Computerized Action-Information Ministry and Human Needs Network; AIDS Education; Interchurch Ministry Planning

Atlanta Interfaith Broadcasters

1580 Peachtree St., NE, Atlanta 30309
Tel. (404) 892-0454
Pres., Rev. John H. Allen
Station Mgr., Ms. O'Lynn J. Allen
Chpsn. of Bd., John A. Conant
Major Activities: Cable TV Operation; TV Production; Satellite Receiving; Production of Slide Shows, Film Strips, and Audio Cassettes; Media Ministries Training, Seminary Internships; Public Relations Consulting; National Religious Cable Connection

HAWAII

Hawaii Council of Churches

1300 Kailua Rd., Kailua 96734
Tel. (808)263-9788
Coordinators, Ms. Pat Mumford, Rev. John T. Norris
Major Activities: Laity and Clergy Education; Ecumenical Worship; Religious Art, Music, Drama; Legislative Concerns; Interfaith TV and Radio Ministry; Social Action; AIDS Education; Advocacy for Peace with Justice

IDAHO

The Regional Council for Christian Ministry, Inc.

P.O. Box 2236, Rm. 10 Trinity United Methodist Church, Idaho Falls 83403
Tel. (208) 522-7921
Exec. Sec., Kathy Knauts
Major Activities: Island Park Ministry; Community Food Bank; Community Observances; Community Information and Referral Service; F.I.S.H.; Refugee Assistance Program

ILLINOIS

Illinois Conference of Churches

615 S. 5th St., Springfield 62703
Tel. (217) 544-3423
Exec. Sec., Rev. James P. Ebbers
Dir. Governmental Concerns, Rev. Richard R. Wood
Dir. Farm Worker Ministry, Ms. Olgha Sandman, 935 Curtiss, Rm. 8, Downers Grove 60515, Tel. (312) 964-7474
Dir., Refugee Resettlement Coordination Task Force, Ms. Mary Caroline Dana
Supervisor Chicago Refugee Services Ofc., Ms. May Campbell, 2320 W. Peterson, Ste. 505, Chicago 60659, Tel. (312) 764-0008
Dir., Community Care Toll Free Telephone Prog., Barbara Manning
Dir., Domestic Violence Prog., Mrs. Jacqueline Clingan
Dir., Human Services Ministry, Mr. Richard Brumleve
Pres., Rev. J. Robert Sandman, 1840 Westchester Blvd., Box 7208, Westchester 60153
Treas., Rev. Donald Lowe, 501 E. Capitol Ave., Ste. 230, Springfield 62701
Major Activities: Poverty & Race; Migrant & Farm Worker Ministry; Chaplaincy in Institutions; Governmental Concerns and Illinois Impact; Ecumenical Courier; Ministry to Mentally Handicapped; Ministry with Aging; Church-Community Development; Hunger and Welfare Reform; Immigration and Refugee Resettlement; Peace Action; Domestic Violence

Calumet Community Relations Conference

833 Hirsh Ave., Calument City 60409
Tel. (312) 862-3200
Exec. Dir., Rev. Leo T. Mahon

The Church Federation of Greater Chicago

111 E. Wacker Dr., Ste. 510, 60601
Tel. (312) 565-1100
Exec. Dir., Rev. David M. Whitermore
Broadcasting Dir., Lydia Talbot
Hunger Dir., Beverly Decker
Pres., Ms. Carolyn Oehler
Treas., Mr. George Sisler
Major Activities: Radio, Television, Cable, Inter-faith/Ecumenical Development; Social/Justice Concerns; Christian Education; Hunger Ministry/Community Organization; Literacy Program; Chaplaincy

The Hyde Park & Kenwood Interfaith Council

1448 East 53rd St., Chicago 60615
Tel. (312) 363-1620
Exec. Dir., Mr. Werner H. Heymann
Pres., Rev. Neil W. Gerdes
Treas., Ms. Beverly Morris Armstrong

Evanston Ecumenical Action Council

P. O. Box 1414, Evanston 60201
Tel. (312) 475-1150
Exec. Dir., Tecla Sund Reklau
Pres., Sandy Hubbard
Treas., Connie Magistrelli, 833 Madison, Evanston 70202
Major Activities: Interchurch Communication and Education; Peace and Justice Ministries; Coordinated Social Action; Soup Kitchen; Multi-Purpose Hospitality Center for the Homeless; Worship and Renewal

Oak Park-River Forest Community of Churches

324 N. Oak Park Ave., Oak Park 60302
Exec. Sec. for the Council, Miss Ruth E. McNutt
Pres., Rev. Robert A. Cross
Major Activities: Community Affairs; Ecumenical Affairs; Youth; Education; Food Pantry; Senior Citizens Worship Services; Laity; Interfaith Thanksgiving Services; Good Friday Services, UNICEF; ASSIST; Workshops on Pornography; Sexual Exploitation of Youth; Christian Unity Week Pulpit Exchange; Peace and Justice; Hunger Walkathon

Churches United of Scott County, Iowa & Rock Island County, Illinois

630 9th St., Rock Island 61201
Tel. (309) 786-6494
Exec. Dir., Thomas N. Kalshoven
Assoc. Exec. Dir., Sheila D. Fitts
Pres., Rev. Emmett Wiseman
Treas., G. Pierson Brauch
Major Activities: Jail Ministry; Hunger Projects; Minority Enablement; Criminal Justice; Migrant Ministry; Radio-TV; Peace; Aging; Local Church Development

Contact Ministries of Springfield

401 E. Washington, Springfield 62701
Tel. (217) 753-3939

Dir., Ethel Butcher
Major Activities: Information; Referral and Advocacy; Ecumenical Coordination; Low Income Housing Referral; Food Pantry Coordination; Low Income Budget Counseling; Police Dept. Social Services

INDIANA

Indiana Council of Churches

1100 W. 42nd St. Rm. 225, Indianapolis 46208
Tel. (317) 923-3674
Exec. Dir., Rev. Scott Schieswohl
Pres., Rev. Carl R. Smith
Sec., Rev. Robert Stauffer
Treas., Mary Ann Spengler
Major Activities: Educational Ministries; Public Media Ministries; Social Ministries; Peace and Justice; Farmworker Ministries; Institutional Ministries; Ecumenical Concerns

Ecumenical Assembly of Bartholomew County Churches

Love Chapel, 311 Center St.,
P.O. Box 1420, Columbus 47202
Tel. (812) 372-9421
Exec. Dir., Carole Hyneman

Christian Ministries of Delaware County

806 W. White River Blvd., Muncie 47303
Tel. (317) 288-0601
Exec. Sec., Donna Watson
Pres., Douglas Bakken, 4801 N. Everett Rd., 47304
Treas., John Wilson, 4232 N. Lancaster, 47309
Major Activities: Migrant Ministry, Christian Education, Feed-the-Baby Program; Youth Ministry at Detention Center; Community Church Festivals; Community Pantry; Community Assistance Fund

Church Community Services

1703 Benham Ave., Elkhart 46516
Tel. (219)295-3673
Exec. Dir., Mary Jane Carpenter

Evansville Area Council of Churches, Inc.

119 N.W. Sixth St., Evansville 47708
Tel. (812) 425-3524
Interim Dir., Ms. Sue Woodson
Weekday Supervisor, Mrs. Walter Foster
Pres., Mrs. Evelyn Cave
Sec., Clarence Clarke
Fin. Chpsn., Rev. Conrad Grosenick
Major Activities: Christian Education; Community Responsibility & Service; Public Relations; Interpretation; Church Women United; Institutional Ministries; Interchurch Foundation; Hunger Program; Housing Program; Jail Ministry; Emergency Shelter

The Associated Churches of Fort Wayne & Allen County, Inc.

227 E. Washington Blvd., Ste. 102, Fort Wayne 46802
Tel. (219) 422-3528
Exec. Min., Rev. Melvin R. Phillips
Adm. Asst., Lisa Kumfer
WRE Coord., Ruth Proctor
Pres., JoAnne Valentine, 2101 Cimarron Pass 46815
Treas., Melvin McFall, 1300 S. Clinton 46802
Major Activities: Weekday Religious Education; Radio & TV; Church Clusters; Church and Society Division;

Education for Christian Life Division; Clergy United for Action; Single/Young Adult Ministries; Faith and Order Commission; Christian Education; Widowed-to-Widowed; CROP; Campus Ministry; Food Bank System; Peace Education; Welfare Reform; Endowment Development

The Church Federation
of Greater Indianapolis, Inc.

1100 W. 42nd St., Indianapolis 46208
Tel. (317) 926-5371
Exec. Dir., Rev. C. Bruce Naylor
Adm. Sec., Marilyn V. Wilkes
Dir., Social Service, Rev. Donald Carpenter
Consultant—TV-Radio, Rev. Alfred R. Edyvean
Chaplains, Rev. Frank O. Carlson, Rev. Wendell Abel; Rev. Wilbert Cunningham, Rev. John Merriweather, Rev. Glen Calkins
Pres., Dr. Harry N. Huxhold
Treas., Elmer Faulk
Major Activities: Congregational Concerns; Communications; Special Ministries; Urban Affairs

Indiana Interreligious Commission
on Human Equality

1100 W. 42nd St., Indianapolis 46208
Tel. (317) 924-4226
Interim Dir., Dorothea S. Green
Pres., Bp. Leroy C. Hodapp
Treas., Rev. John McKune
Major Activities: Project Equality; Anti-Racism Training; Racism/Sexism Inventory; Cultural and Religious Intolerance

Indiana Office for Campus Ministries

1100 W. 42nd St., Indianapolis 46208
Tel. (317)923-4839
Exec. Dir., Dr. E. Max Case
Major Activities: Resourcing for Campus Ministry (Seminars, Continuing Education)

Monroe County United
Ministries, Inc.

827 W. 14th St.
Bloomington 47401
Tel. (812) 339-3429
Administrator, Meri Reinhold
Preschool Dir., Joyce Grubb
Major Activities: Clergy Luncheons; Preschool; Summer Youth Camp; After School Program; Adult Education for Seniors; Emergency Services for Poor and Needy

Lafayette Urban Ministry

12 North 8th St., Lafayette 47901
Tel. (317) 423-2691
Dir. Rev. Jud Dolphin
Advocate Coord., Sara Bowling
Public Policy Coord., Joe Micon
Pres., Tom Hull
Treas., Evelyn Miller
Major Activities: Social Justice Ministries With and Among the Poor

Interfaith Community
Council, Inc. (of So. Indiana)

702 E. Market St., New Albany 47150
Tel. (812) 948-9248
Exec. Dir., Rev. Dr. George Venable Beury
Adm. Asst., Mrs. Marion Nunemacher
Dir., Child Dev. Center, Nancy Leediker

Dir., Deaf Relay, Ms. Susan Wagner
Dir. RSVP, Mary Ann Sodrel
Chpsn., Donald L. Sodrel, 1032 Cliffwood 47150
Treas., Robert Craig, Sr., 1624 Hedden Ct. 47150
Major Activities: Child Development Center; Deaf Relay Teletype Center; Hospice; Emergency Assistance; Hedden House (Half Way Home for Recovering Alcoholic Women); Retired Senior Volunteer Program; New Clothing and Toy Drives; Job Training; Convalescent Sitter & Mother's Aides; Senior Day College

United Religious Community
of St. Joseph County

2015 Western Ave., South Bend 46629
Tel. (219) 282-2397
Exec. Dir., Dr. James J. Fisko
Chaplain at County Jail, Fr. Patrick Logan, S.S.B.
Coord., State Prison Visitation, Sr. Susan Kintzele, CSC
Coord., Victim Offender Reconciliation Prog. (VORP), Rev. Daniel Stoltzfus
Coord., Religious Arts Min., Phyllis Wezeman
Coord., Shelter for the Homeless, Eugene Foust
Coord., Volunteer Advocacy Project, Sara Goetz
Dir., Refugee Day Care, Carolyn Hornbuckle
Pres., Sr. Monica Brown, O.P.
Major Activities: Religious Understanding; Social and Pastoral Ministries; Congregational Ministries

IOWA

Iowa Inter-Church Forum

3816 36th St., Des Moines 50310
Tel. (515) 255-5905
Exec. Coord., Dr. Boyd Mather
Major Activities: A forum dialogue related to theological faith issues and social concerns; opportunity to develop responses to discern needs and join in common mission

Iowa Inter-Church Agency
for Peace and Justice

3816 36th St., Des Moines 50310
Tel. (515)255-5905
Prog. Coordinators: Roz Ostendorf, Suzanne Peterson, and Paul Stanfield
Major Activities: International Peace; Human Needs; Governmental Concerns; Chaplaincy; Ministry to Handicapped

Iowa Religious Media Services

3816 36th St., Des Moines 50310
Tel. (515)277-2920
Dir., Sue Sonner
Edu. Consultant, JoAnne Talarico
Prod. Mgr., Rich Harbart
Major Activities: Distribute AV Resources; Media Workshops; Provide Studio for Production, Satellite Taping and Programming

Churches United, Inc.

222 29th St. Drive, SE, Cedar Rapids 52403
Tel. (319) 366-7163
Adm. Sec., Mrs. Maurice Wilson
Pres., Rev. Carolyn Myers, First Luth. Ch., 1000 3rd Ave., SE 52403
Treas., Bruce Jorth, 1015 MNB Bldg. 52401
Major Activities: Community Food Bank; L.E.A.F. (Local Emergency Assistance Fund; CROP; Cooperative Low Income Store (O.N.E. Store); Community Information and Referral; Jail Chaplaincy; World

Hunger; Nursing Home Ministry; Radio and TV Ministry; Ecumenical City-Wide Celebrations

Des Moines Area Religious Council

3816 36th St., Des Moines 50310
Tel. (515) 277-6969
Exec. Dir., Harold A. Varce
Pres., James Lesher
Treas., Lavon Aten
Major Activities: Evangelism, Education; Social Concerns; Mission; Worship; Emergency Food Pantry; Ministry to Widowed; Child Care Assistance

KANSAS

Kansas Ecumenical Ministries

3615 S.W. 29th St., Topeka 66614
Tel. (913) 272-9531
Exec. Dir., Dorothy G. Berry
Pres., Rev. Fred Ansell
Vice Pres., Jeanne Goddard
Sec., Rev. John Tomlonson
Treas., Rev. Jay Henderson
Major Activities: Legislative Activities; Program Facilitation and Coordination; World Hunger; Lakes Ministry; Higher Education Concerns; Interfaith Rural Life Committee; Education; Mother-to-Mother Program; Peacemaking

Cross-Lines Cooperative Council

1620 S. 37th St., Kansas City 66106
Tel. (913)432-5497
Exec. Dir., Rev. Donald C. Bakely
Program Dir., Rev. Robert Moore
Pres., Charlotte Withrow
Treas., Jim White
Major Activities: Emergency Assistance; Housing Repair; Wood Shop; Adult School Work Camps; Christmas Store; Clothing Store; Education; Homeless Assistance; Volunteer Services

Inter-Faith Ministries—Wichita

216 E. 2nd St., Wichita 67202
Tel. (316) 264-9303
Exec. Dir., Rev. James M. Bell
Ofc. Mgr., Carolyn A. Bell
Coord. Operation Holiday, Marilyn Harp
Dir., Indian Ministries, Mrs. Irene Heinze
Dir. Cmty. Min., Patrick Cameron
Dir., Homeless Shelter, Carol Cook
Ed., The Forum, Lucerne Montague
Pres., Rev. George Bever
Major Activities: Communications; Urban Education; Inter-religious Understanding; Community Needs and Issues; Theology and Worship; Hunger; Advocacy

KENTUCKY

Kentucky Council of Churches

1039 Goodwin Dr., Lexington 40505
Tel. (606) 253-3027
Exec. Dir., Dr. John C. Bush
Coord., Kentucky Hunger Task Force, Ms. Anne Joseph
Coord., Disaster Recovery Prog., C. Nelson Hostetter
Ed., INTERCOM, Dr. David Berg
Pres., Dr. Tecumseh X. Graham, Broadway Temple A.M.E. Zion Ch., 662 S. 13th St., Louisville 40203. Tel. (502)442-0077
Major Activities: Institutional Ministry; Hunger, Church and Government; Media; Disaster Response; Christian Unity; Peace Issues; Racism; Church Property Taxa-

tion; Health Care Issues; Local Ecumenism; Rural Land/Farm Issues

Human/Economic Appalachian Development (HEAD) Corporation

Box 504, Berea 40403
Tel. (606) 986-1651
Dir., Tom DelSavio
Mgr. Credit Union, Thomas DelSavio
Major Activities: Development of Credit Union and providing financial assistance to members of groups of HEAD Corp; Community Loan Fund

Highlands Community Ministries

1140 Cherokee Rd., Louisville 40204
Tel. (502) 451-3695
Exec. Dir., Stan Esterle
Pres., Rev. Sr. Borromeo Walker
Vice Pres., Rev. Glen Sea
Sec., Peter Glauber
Treas., Rev. Richard Teaford
Major Activities: Welfare Assistance; Day Care; Counseling with Youth, Parents and Adults; Social Services for Elderly; Housing for Elderly and Handicapped; Ecumenical Programs; Community Classes; Activities for Children

Interreligious Coalition on Human Services

400 East Chestnut St., Louisville 40202
Tel. (502) 584-2343
Exec. Dir., _____
Pres., J. Michael Jupin
Treas., Jim Holladay
Major Activities: Communication between County and Religious Groups; Religious Community Networking; Social Concerns Consultancy; Educational Resource Provider to Church and Community Groups; Legislative Advocacy for Low-Income Population

Kentuckiana Interfaith Community

P.O. Box 4671, Louisville 40204
Tel. (502) 458-4076
. Exec. Dir., Rev. Kenneth D. MacHarg
Pres., Rev. John Bassett
Vice Pres., Ms. Marilyn Markwell
Sec., Rev. Joyce Seaman
Treas., Rev. Stephen Hampton
Mod., Mr. Mark Issacs
Major Activities: Religious Workers Insurance Plan; Radio and TV; Interfaith Dialogue; Religion and Race; Ecumenical Newspaper; Religion & Labor Council; Church and State Committee; Heating Assistance Program; Ecumenical Cable TV Channel

South East Associated Ministries (SEAM)

3728 Taylorsville Rd., Louisville 40220
Tel. (502)454-0380
Exec. Dir., Rev. Robert F. Owens
Program Coordinator, Life Skills Center, Martha Hinson
Volunteer Coordinator, Life Skills Center, Pat Osborne
Coordinator, Youth Services, Jackie Town
Pres., Rev. Maurice LeFevre
Treas., Joe Hays
Major Activities: Emergency Food and Financial Assistance; Life Skills Center (Programs of Prevention and Self-Sufficiency Through Education, Empowerment, Support Groups, etc.); Juvenile Court Diversion Program; Bloodmobile; Ecumenical Education and Worship

South Louisville Community Ministries

801 Camden Ave., Louisville 40215
Tel.(502)367-6445
Exec. Dir., J. Michael Jupin
Bd. Chair, George Buck
Bd. Vice Chair, Rev. Ernie Gross
Bd. Treas., Eugene Wells
Major Activities: Food, Clothing & Financial Assistance;
Home Delivered Meals, Transportation, Homemakers
for Elderly; Ecumenical Worship; Juvenile Diversion
Program

Northern Kentucky Interfaith Commission, Inc.

601 Greenup St. Covington 41011
Tel. (606) 581-2237
Exec. Dir., Rev. William C. Neuroth
Major Activities: Spiritual; Disaster Ministries; Interracial
and Intercultural Awareness; Peace & Justice

St. Matthews Area Ministries

4006 Shelbyville Rd., Louisville 40207
Tel. (502) 893-0205
Exec. Dir., A. David Bos
Dir., Youth Services, Patricia Emery
Dir. After-School Care Centers, Janet Hennessey
Major Activities: After-School Care; Youth Services;
Ecumenical Worship

Paducah Cooperative Ministry

1359 South Sixth St. Paducah 42001
Tel. (502) 442-6795
Dir., JoAnn Ross
Chpsn., Rev. Jerry Bell
Major Activities: The P.C.M. is a cooperative venture of
29 local churches and six denominational judicatories,
serving the community's hungry, elderly, poor, prison-
ers, alcoholics, handicapped and mentally retarded

LOUISIANA

Louisiana Interchurch Conference

440 North Foster Dr., Ste. 106, Baton Rouge 70806
Tel. (504)924-0213
Exec. Dir., Rev. James L. Stovall
Pres., Dr. Francis Williams, 1410 Hano Rd., Indepen-
dence 70443
Treas., Mr. Winter Trapolin, 119 Audubon Blvd., New
Orleans 70118
Major Activities: Ministries to Aging; Prison Reform;
Liaison with State Agencies; Ecumenical Dialogue;
Institutional Chaplains; Peace Education

Greater New Orleans Federation of Churches

301 Camp St., New Orleans 70130
Tel. (504) 524-0246
Pres./Exec. Dir., Dr. Tom S. Roote, Jr.
O.M.F.S., Mrs. Johanna Schlater
Gen. Sec., Mrs. Lucille Francis
REACH (Cable TV Channel), Dr. Charles Sommervill,
Exec. Dir., Mr. Kerry Towsen, Production Mgr.
TV Coordinator, Rev. Eugene Coleman
Chaplain Coordinator, Rev. Gene Huffstutler
Police Chaplain, Rev. Sam Allen
Fire Chaplancy Coord., _____
Fin. Sec., Sue Sadler
Newsletter Editor, _____
Operation Mainstream-Literacy, Mrs. Jackie Abreu

Chmn. of Bd., Dr. Tom Morgan
Treas., Mr. Norman Kerth, Jr.
Major Activities: Radio-TV Programs; Central Business
District Task Force; Regional Suburban Network;
Leadership Training; Senior Citizens; Social Action;
Public Information; Child Abuse; Religious Census and
Survey; Nutritional Programs; Literacy; Counseling
Coordination; Cable T.V. Channel; Video Series on the
Whole Bible; Teenage Pregnancy; Emergency Food
and Shelter; Non-Profit Management; Community
Awareness; Evangelism; Hunger; Religion and the
Arts; Public Events: Crime Prevention; Comfort
Ministry to Widows and other Bereaved Persons;
Ministry to Nursing Homes; Church Growth; "Prayer
Line"; Gospel Music Festival

MAINE

Maine Council of Churches

15 Pleasant Ave., Portland 04103
Tel. (207)772-1918
Pres., Rev. James Connor
Exec. Dir., Thomas C. Ewell

MARYLAND

Central Maryland Ecumenical Council

Cathedral House, 4 East University Pkwy., Baltimore
21218
Tel. (301) 467-6194
Exec. Dir., Richard M. Kelly
Pres., Rev. Myron Manzuk
Asst. Dir., Lynn A. Bopp
AIDS Proj. Dir., Sharon M. K. Kugler
Major Activities: Interchurch Communications and Col-
laboration; Information Systems; Ecumenical Rela-
tions; Urban Mission and Advocacy; Staff Judicatory
Leadership Council; Interfaith Residential Services for
Persons with AIDS

MASSACHUSETTS

Massachusetts Council of Churches

14 Beacon St., Boston 02108
Tel. (617) 523-2771
Exec. Dir., Rev. Dr. James A. Nash
Assoc. Dir. for Strategy and Action, Rev. Diane C. Kessler
Assoc. Dir., Regional Ecumenism, Rev. David A. Ander-
son

Attleboro Area Council of Churches, Inc.

505 N. Main St., Attleboro 02703
Tel. (617) 222-2933
Exec. Dir., Carolyn L. Bronkar
Admin. Sec., Joan H. Lindstrom
Program Aide, Lynne F. Sias
Hosp. Chpln., Rev. Linnea Prefontaine
Pres., Rev. David B. Roberts, 516 Newport Ave. 02703
Treas., David Quinlan, 20 Everett St., Plainville 02762
Major Activities: Hospital Chaplaincy; Radio Ministry;
Personal Growth/Skill Workshops; Ecumenical Worship;
Media Resource Center; Referral Center; Communica-
tions/Publications; Community Social Action; Food'n
Friends Kitchen; Emergency Food and Shelter Fund

The Cape Cod Council of Churches, Inc.

397 Main St., Hyannis 02601
Tel. (617) 775-5073
Exec. Dir., Rev. James M. Webb

Adm. Sec., Muriel L. Eggers
Pres., Alexandra MacCallum Clark
Chaplain, House of Correction & Jail, Rev. Thomas
Shepherd
Chaplain, Friends of Prisoners House, Rev. James Taylor
Chaplain, Cape Cod Hospital, Rev. William Wilcox
Chaplain, Barnstable County Hospital, David Loomis;
Chaplain, Falmouth Hospital, _____Nursing Home
Coord., _____
Dir., Service Center and Thrift Shop, Joan McCurdy, Box
981 W. Dennis 02670. Tel. (617)394-6361
Dir., Friends of Prisoners, Rev. Thomas Shepherd
Major Activities: Stewardship & Finance; Pastoral Serv-
ices; Social Concerns; Communications; Christian
Education; Youth; Church World Service; Interfaith
Relations; Friends of Prisoners; Emergency Distribu-
tion of Food, Clothing, Furniture

Massachusetts Commission on
Christian Unity

82 Luce St., Lowell 01852
Tel. (617)453-5423
Exec. Sec., Rev. K. Gordon White
Major Activity: Faith and Order Dialogue with Church
Judicatories.

Inter-Church Council
of Greater New Bedford

412 County St., New Bedford 02740
Tel. (617) 993-6242
Exec. Min., Dr. Lawrence van Heerden
Adm. Asst., Andrea Lentz
Pres., Eric Lindell
Treas., William Reed
Major Activities: Pastoral Counseling; Chaplaincy; Hous-
ing for Elderly; Urban Affairs; Parent-Child Center;
Social Rehabilitation Club

Cooperative
Metropolitan Ministries

474 Centre St., Newton 02158
Tel. (617) 244-3650
Cncl. Chpsn., Robert Borden
Board Pres., Odessa Smith
Treas. Richard Knibbs
Sec., D. Diane Chambers
Major Activities: Low Income, Elderly, Family Shelter
Housing; Emergency Food Program; Nursing Home
Information; Legislative Advocacy

Council of Churches
of Greater Springfield

152 Sumner Ave. Springfield 01108
Tel. (413) 733-2149
Exec. Dir., Rev. Ann Geer
Dir. of Urban Min., Kathleen Del Pino
Dir. Nursing Home Min., Patrick McMahon
Pres., Mr. William Wildey
Treas., Mr. Jerre Hoffman
Major Activities: Christian Education Resource Center;
Urban and Downtown Ministry; Emergency Fuel Fund;
World Peace and Justice; Visitor Ombudspersons to
Nursing Homes; Task Force on Aging; Hospital
Chaplaincy; Pastoral Service; Christian Social Rela-
tions; Crisis Counseling; Relief Collections; Ecumenical
and Interfaith Relations; Ecumenical Dialogue with
Roman Catholic Diocese; Mass Media; Church/Com-
munity Projects and Dialog

Worcester County
Ecumenical Council

63 Wachusett St., Worcester 01609
Tel. (617) 757-8385
Exec. Dir., Rev. Richard A. Hennigar
Asst. to Dir., Ms. Carol Casey
Pres., Rev. John Kelliher
Major Activities: Clusters of Churches; Mass Media;
Economic Justice; Youth Ministries; Ecumenical Wor-
ship and Dialog; Interfaith Activities; Nursing Home
Chaplaincies, Assistance to Churches; Peace; Hunger
Ministries

MICHIGAN

Michigan Ecumenical Forum

P.O. Box 10206, Lansing 48901
Tel. (517) 485-4395
Ecumenical Coordinator/Exec. Dir., Rev. Dr. Gustav
Kopka, Jr.
Prog. Dir., Carol Ingells
Staff Assoc., Nancy Kopka
Major Activities: Communication and Coordination;
Studies and Fellowship; Church and Society Issues;
School For Ministry

Area Christian Churches
on Renewed Dedication

72 E. Michigan Mall, Battle Creek 49017
Tel. (616) 963-2280
Dir., Pamela V. Sten
Pres., Ray Francisco
Vice-Pres./Church, Rev. Robert J. Eckert
Vice Pres/Admin., Dennis Stansbery
Vice-Pres./Community, Rev. Erick Johnson
Major Activities: CROP Walk; Thanksgiving Interna-
tional Student Homestay; Food Closet; Christian
Sports; Week of Prayer for Christian Unity; Nursing
Home Vesper Services; Ecumenical Worship

Christian Communication Council
of Metropolitan Detroit Churches

1300 Mutual Building, 28 W. Adams, Detroit 48226
Tel. (313) 962-0340
Exec. Dir., Rev. Edward Willingham
Adm. Assoc., Mrs. Angie Willingham
Media Assoc., Sr. Helen Bishop
Prog. Dir., Meals for Shut-Ins, Mr. Reginald Williams
Services Dir., Meals for Shut-ins, Mr. Clark Churchill
Coord., Summer Feeding Prog., Mrs. Karen Reedy
Major Activities: Educational Services; Ecumenical Wor-
ship; Meals for Shut-Ins; Summer Feeding Program;
Theological and Social Concerns; Electronic Media;
Print Media; Contact Lifeline Telephone Ministry

Greater Flint Council of Churches

927 Church St., Flint 48502
Tel. (313) 238-3691
Ofc. Adm., _____
Pres., _____
Treas., _____
Major Activities: Christian Education; Christian Unity;
Christian Missions; Filmstrip Library; Hospital and
Nursing Home Chaplaincy; Church in Society; Ameri-
can Bible Society Materials

Grand Rapids Area Center for Ecumenism (GRACE)

38 West Fulton, Grand Rapids 49503
Tel. (616) 774-2042
Exec. Dir., Rev. David P. Baak
Prog. Dir., Ms. Betty Zilstra
Major Activities: Plant Hope (Hunger); Shelter Ministry Council; Aging Ministry Committee; AIDS Religious Support Network; Clergy Interracial Forum; Christian Unity. Affiliates: ACCESS (All County Churches Emergency Support System); FISH for My People (Transportation); Habitat for Humanity/GR; Widowed Persons Service. *Grace Notes*

Jackson County Interfaith Council

425 Oakwood Dr., Box 156, Clarklake 49234
Tel. (517) 529-9721
Exec. Dir., Rev. Loyal H. Wiemer
Major Activities: Chaplaincy; Radio & TV; Education; Caring Ministries; Worship Services at Rest Homes and Hospitals; Ecumenical Activities

MINNESOTA

Minnesota Council of Churches

122 W. Franklin Avenue, #230, Minneapolis 55404.
Tel. (612) 870-3600
Exec. Dir., Rev. Margaret J. Thomas
Dir. of Life and Work and Hispanic Ministry, Carlos Mariani-Rosa
Dir. of Faith and Order, Rev. Rebecca Tollefson
Dir. Refugee Services, Shannon Bevans; Caseworkers, Shareth Prum and Teng Ly
Dir., of Indian Ministry, Mary Ann Walt
Dir. of Facilities, Gus Margellos
Dir. Twin Cities Metropolitan Church Commission, Rev. Sally Hill
Dir. Joint Religious Legislative Coalition, Samuel I. Horowitz
Pres., Mr. Earl Branum
Major Activities: Minnesota Church Center; Local Ecumenism; Life and Work: Black Ministries, Hispanic Ministries, Indian Ministries, Youth Ministry, State Fair Ministry, Minnesota Impact, Refugee Services, Regional Life Transformation, Violence in Significant Relationships; Faith and Order: Baptism, Eucharist and Ministry, Jewish Christian Relations, Consultation on Church Union; Spirituality; Communications

Community Emergency Assistance Program (CEAP)

7321 Brooklyn Blvd., Brooklyn Center 55429
Tel. (612 566-9600
Exec. Dir., Edward T. Eide
Major Activities: Provision of Basic Needs (Food, Clothing, Furnityre); Emergency Financial Assistance for Shelter; Home Delivered Meals; Chore Services and Homemaking Assistance; Single Parent Loan Program; Volunteer Services

Arrowhead Council of Churches

230 E Skyline Pkwy., Duluth 55811
Tel. (218) 727-5020
Exec. Dir., Betsy Coons
Pres., Tab Baumgartner
Major Activities: Christian Education; Inter-Church Evangelism; Community Concerns; Joint Religious Legis-

lative Coalition; Downtown Ecumenical Good Friday Service; Jail Ministry; Food Shelf; Soup Kitchen; Emergency Housing; Forum for Interfaith dialogue; Church Women United; Community Seminars

Greater Minneapolis Council of Churches

122 W. Franklin Ave., Rm. 218 Minneapolis 55404
Tel. (612) 870-3660
Exec. Dir., Rev. Thomas H. Quigley
Assoc. Dir., Twin Cities Metropolitan Church Commission, Rev. Sally Hill
Juvenile Court Chaplain; Rev. William Baldridge
Dir. of Indian Work, Mrs. Mary Ellen Dumas
Pres., Rev. John Chell
Treas., Mr. Roger Heegaard
Major Activities: Chaplaincy Services; Church Women United; Educational Ministries; Faith in Dialogue; Indian Work; Social Ministries; Aging Services; PIE Tutoring Program; Minnesota FoodShare; Metro Paint-A-Thon

The Joint Religious Legislative Coalition

122 West Franklin Ave., Minneapolis 55404
Tel. (612)870-3670
Exec. Dir., Samuel I. Horowitz
Adm. Ass't., Gwendolyn T. Green
Major Activities: Lobbying at State Legislature; Researching Social Justice Issues and Preparing Position Statements; Organizing Grassroots Citizen's Lobby

Twin Cities Metropolitan Church Commission

122 West Franklin, Rm. 218, Minneapolis 55404
Tel. (612) 870-3662
Exec. Dir., Rev. Sally L. Hill
Pres., Rev. Thomas Van Leer, 1182 Hillcrest Dr., Woodbury 55125
Major Activities: Education; Criminal Justice Coordinating Committee; Nursing Homes Project; Peacemaking Education; Peace Child Project; Interreligious Committee on Central America; Faith in Dialogue Seminars; Ecumenical Travel-Study Seminars; Child Care Ecumenical Network

St. Paul Area Council of Churches

1671 Summit Ave., St. Paul 55105
Tel. (612)646-8805
Exec. Dir., Rev. Thomas Duke
Ecumenical Education, Assoc. Dir., Rev. Sally Hill
Juvenile Court Chaplain, Rev. John Gilmore
Institutional Chaplain, Dr. Fred A. Hueners
Pres., Rev. George A. Toren
Treas., Arthur Sternberg
Major Activities: Religious Services and Counseling for Prisoners at Detention and Corrections Authority Institutions; Delinquency Prevention Counseling; Kinship Program for Youth; Educational Development; Ecumenical Encounters and Activities; Indian Ministries

MISSISSIPPI

Mississippi Religious Leadership Conference

Woodland Hills Bldg., Ste. 260, 3000 Old Canton Rd., Jackson, 39216
Tel. (601)981-6752

Exec. Dir., Rev. Thomas E. Tiller, Jr.
Chair, Rev. Elvin Sunds
Treas., Mrs. Lisa Hall
Major Activities: Foster trust, understanding and cooperation among religious leaders; Lay/Clergy Retreats; Social Concerns Seminars; Disaster Task Force; Advocacy for Disadvantaged

MISSOURI

Ecumedia of Kansas City

201 Westport Rd., Kansas City 64111
Tel. (816) 531-1345
Dir., Shirley Koritnik, S.C.L.
Major Activities: Production; Media Education; Ecumenical/Cooperative Communication; Local Media Placement

Springfield Area Council of Churches

Box 3947, Springfield 65808
Tel. (417) 862-3586
Exec. Dir., Rev. Dorsey E. Levell
Assoc. Dir., Rosanna Bradshaw
Major Activities: Poverty Program; Community Treatment Program for Ex-Public Offenders; Legislative Affairs; Ministerial Alliance; Hospital Chaplains' Fellowship; Retired Senior Volunteer Program; Treatment Center for Alcoholics and Drug Abuse; Refugee Program; Helping Elderly Live More Productively; Ombudsman for Nursing Homes; Family Day Care Homes; USDA Food Program; Youth Ministry; Disaster Aid and Counseling; Homebound Shoppers; Community Service Program as an Alternative to Incarceration; Food and Clothing Pantry; Ozarks Food Harvest; Homesharing

Interfaith Community Services

200 Cherokee, St. Joseph 64504
Tel. (816) 238-4511
Exec. Dir., David G. Berger
Major Activities: Child Development; Neighborhood Family Services; Group Home for Girls and Boys; Retired Senior Volunteer Program; Nutrition Program; Mobile Meals; Southside Youth Program; Church and Community; Housing Development

MONTANA

Montana Association of Churches

1511 Poly Dr. Billings 59102
Tel. (406) 252-5138
Exec. Dir., Rev. Dr. Lawrence F. Small
Pres., Rev. David W. Peters, 120 Treasure St. Dr., Great Falls 59404
Treas., Mrs. Claris Peterson, 2033 Green Terrace Dr., Billings 59102
Rural Ministry Coord., Mrs. Mary Lou Heiken, 935 S. 72nd St., W., Billings 59106
Legislative Liaison, Mrs. Mignon Waterman, 530 Hazelgreen, Helena 59601

Major Activities: Christian Education; Montana Religious Legislative Coalition; Christian Unity; Junior Citizen Camp; Public Information; Ministries Development; Social Ministry; Rural Ministry

NEBRASKA

Interchurch Ministries of Nebraska

215 Centennial Mall S., Room 411, Lincoln 68508
Tel. (402) 476-3391
Exec. Sec., Dr. Mel H. Luetchens
Admin. Asst., Sharon K. Kalcik
Pres., Rev. Dr. N. Dwain Acker
Treas., Ms. Ima Stapleman
Major Activities: Interchurch Planning and Development; Comity; Indian Ministry; Television Ministry; Teacher Training; Audio-Visual Center; Rural Church Strategy; World Hunger; CWS Refugee Coordination; United Ministries in Higher Education; Small Church Leadership Development; Human Needs; Disaster Response; Christian in Society Forum; Clergy Consultations; Farm Families Crisis Response Network; Video Technology; Visioning Ministry; Interim Ministry Network; Pantry Network; Rural Theological Education Network; Farm Mediation Services; Hispanic Ministry

Lincoln Fellowship of Churches

215 Centennial Mall South, Room 411, Lincoln 68508
Tel. (402) 474-3017
Exec. Sec., Rev. Stephen C. Evans
Pres., Mrs. Pearl Goldenstein, 2201 N. 61st, 68505
Treas., Mrs. Velma Struthers, 441 S. 41st, Lincoln 68801
Media Specialist, Laura Hayes
Major Activities: Media Ministry; Emergency Food Service; Community Liaison; Indian Concerns; Police and Fire Chaplaincy Corps; Church Directory; Ministerial Fellowship; Center for Christian Growth; Ecumenical Events; Crime and the Community; Jail Worship; Barrier-Free Playground Project; High School Baccalaureate; New Clergy Orientation; Urban Ministries; Housing Coalition

Interchurch Ministries of Nebraska Farm Crisis Hotline/Response

Box 383, Walthill, 68067
Tel. (402)846-5578
Coord., Kathleen Severens
Staff, Judith Dye
Chpsn. of I.M.N. Cncl., Rev. Ken Wittrock
Dir. of I.M.N., Dr. Melvin Leutchens, Ste 411, Lincoln Center Bldg., 215 Centennial Mall South Lincoln, 68508
Tel. (402)476-3391
Major Activities: Financial, Legal and Emotional Counseling for Farm Families in Economic Distress.

NEVADA

(No current information)

NEW HAMPSHIRE

New Hampshire Council of Churches

24 Warren St., P.O. Box 1107, Concord 03302
Tel. (603) 224-1352
Exec. Sec., Rev. Frank H. Gross
Pres., Rev. Philip Crane, 19 Norwich St. 03301
Treas., Timothy Woodman, 63 Green St. 03301
Major Activities: Facilitating cooperative work of member denominations

NEW JERSEY

New Jersey
Council of Churches

116 N. Oraton Pkwy., East Orange 07017
Tel. (201) 675-8600
176 W. State St., Trenton 08608
Tel. (609) 396-9546
Exec. Dir., Rev. Charles W. Rawlings
Adm. Assoc., Mrs. Alice Schuler
Commission Community Life, Rev. Dudley E. Sarfaty
Commissions on Research & Church Development and
  Pastoral and Institutional Ministries, Rev. Jean Paul
  Richter
Dir., IMPACT Ms. Joan Diefenbach
Pres., Mrs. Christine E. Trigg
Treas., Rev. William Jewett
Major Activities: Consultancy; Public Advocacy; Service

Bergen County Council
of Churches

165 Burton Ave., Hasbrouck Heights 07604
Tel. (201) 288-3784
Exec. Sec., Neila Vander Vliet

Council of Churches
of Greater Camden

Box 1208, Merchantville 08109
Tel. (609) 665-1919
Exec. Sec., Dr. Samuel A. Jeanes
Pres., Rev. Lawrence L. Dunn
Treas., Mr. Ray Hunniford
Major Activities: Radio & TV; Hospital Chaplaincy;
  United Services; Good Friday Breakfast; Mayors'
  Prayer Breakfast; Public Affairs; Easter Sunrise Service

Metropolitan
Ecumenical Ministry

404 University Ave., Newark 07102
Tel. (201) 623-9259
Exec. Dir., David S. Burgess
Coord., Proj. Schools, Mr. Stephen Jones
Coord., Signs of Hope, Rev. David A. Robinson
Coord., Youth Employment, Mr. Walter Doward
Ed., Voices of Hope, Stephen Moctezuma
Coord., Project Read, Ms. Claudia Connor
Chpsn. of Board, Msgr. John Maloney
Sec., Ms. Nancy Zak
Treas., M. Esther Brome
Major Activities: Project Read; Project Schools; Task
  Forces: Public Education; Employment; Housing;
  Toxic Waste

Trenton Ecumenical Area
Ministry (TEAM)

2 Prospect St., 08618
Tel. (609) 396-9166 or 393-3636
Exec. Dir., Rev. Angelique Walker-Smith
Sec., Mrs. Ann Wilson
Chpsn., Rev. Frederick Wilkes
Major Activities: Racial Justice; Children & Youth
  Ministries; Advocacy; CROP Walk; Ecumenical Wor-
  ship; Hospital Chaplains

NEW MEXICO

New Mexico Conference
of Churches

124 Hermosa SE, Albuquerque 87108

Tel. (505) 255-1509
Exec. Sec., Dr. Wallace Ford
Pres., Rev. C. Richard Brown, Presbytery of Sierra
  Blanca, Box 1434, Roswell 88201
Treas., Mr. Roy Nials, 3901 Indian School Rd., NE,
  A-401, Albuquerque 87110
Major Activities: State Task Forces: Peace With Justice;
  Poverty; Caring Inclusive Congregations; Legislative
  Concerns/Impact; Faith and Order; AIDS; Correctional
  Ministries; Public Education. Regional Task Forces:
  Aging; Ecumenical Worship; Refugees; Emergency
  Care; Alcoholism; Rural Support Network

Inter-Faith Council of Santa Fe

P.O. Box 4637, Santa Fe 87502
Pres., Carol Decker
Treas. Ms. Donna Elliot
Chpsn. Peace with Justice Force, Hib Sabin
Chpsn. Hunger/Shelter Task Force, Barbara Robinson
Exec. Sec., Mr. Hank Hughes
Major Activities: Hunger Walk, Interfaith Dialogues/Cel-
  ebrations/Visitations; Community Forums; Music Fes-
  tival; Art Show; Peace Symposium; Service Projects;
  Inter-Faith Consciousness-Raising/Community-Build-
  ing; Newsletter

NEW YORK

New York State Council
of Churches, Inc.

362 State St., Albany 12210
Tel. (518) 436-9319
3049 E. Genesee St., Syracuse 13224
Tel. (315) 446-6151
Exec. Dir., Dr. Arleon L. Kelley
Pres., Dr. John E. Hiemstra
1st Vice Pres., Dr. Judith E. Hjorth
2nd Vice Pres., Rev. James H. Miller
Sec., Ms. Mary Lu Bowen
Treas., Dr. George H. DeHority
Major Activities: Public Policy and Ecumenical Minis-
  tries; Rural Poor and Migrants; Homeless; AIDS;
  U.S.-Canadian Border Concerns; Single Parent Fami-
  lies; Chaplaincy in State Institutions; Faith and Order

Christians United in Mission, Inc.

40 N. Main Ave., Albany, 12203
Tel. (518) 438-6681
Prog. Dir., Mr. Ronald K. Willis
Communications Dir., Mrs. Zenna Barrett
Major Activities: To promote cooperation/coordination
  among member judicatories in the areas of urban
  ministries, media communications, social action, crimi-
  nal justice; emergency food and program development

Broome County Council
of Churches, Inc.

81 Main St., Binghamton 13905
Tel. (607) 724-9130
Exec. Dir., Mr. Kenneth A. Cable
Admin. Asst., Mrs. Marilyn F. Sweet
Hospital Chaplains, Rev. LeRoy Flohr, Mrs. Betty
  Pomeroy
Jail Chaplain, Rev. Philip Singer
Campus Chaplains, Rev. C. James Jones, Rev. George
  Hanssen
CREW (Youth Project) Dir., Mr. Barry Foster
Aging Ministry Coord., Mrs. Betty Pomeroy
CHOW Prog. Coord., Mrs. Rachel Dunn
Pres., Rev. H. Arthur Doersam

Treas., Mr. Hayden Myers
Major Activities: Campus, Hospital and Jail Chaplains; Youth and Aging Ministries; CHOW (Emergency Hunger Program; Christian Education; Ecumenical Worship and Fellowship; Media; Community Affairs

Buffalo Area Council of Churches

1272 Delaware Ave., Buffalo 14209
Tel. (716) 882-4793
Exec. Dir., _____
Dir. Church Supply Agency, Mrs Leona Drumstra
Admin. Sec., Church Women United, Mrs. Norma Roscover
Chpsn, Radio-TV Ministry, Rev. Ivan Crossno
Pres., Rev. Robert Leach
Treas., Mr. Charles R. Banks
Major Activities: Radio-TV; Social Services; Hospital Chaplains; Church Women United; Ecumenical Relations

Buffalo Area Metropolitan Ministries, Inc.

100 Wadsworth, Buffalo 14201
Tel. (716) 883-7717
Exec. Dir., Rev. Charles R. White
Pres., Rev. Francis X. Mazur
Vice Pres., _____
Sec., Mrs. Barbara Hora
Chair., of the Commission on Inter-Religious Dialogue, Rev. Daniel Palys, Mr. Harold Axlerod, Imam Abdel Nurridin
Chair, Task Force on Shelter and Sanctuary, Mr. Ted. Hengerer
Chair Food for All Prog., Rev. Kay Woike
Chair., Council on Eco. Justice and Work, Mr. Roger Cook
Major Activities: Shelter; Sanctuary; Hunger; Economic Issues; Interreligious Dialogue

Capital Area Council of Churches, Inc.

901 Madison Ave., Albany 12208
Tel. (518) 489-8441
Exec. Dir., Rev. Mr. James H. Snedeker, Jr.
Adm. Asst., Mrs. Su-Anne White
Pres., Hon. Morton M. Z. Lynn
Treas., Mr. Alan Spencer
Major Activities: Hospital Chaplaincy; Food Pantries; CROP Walk; Jail and Nursing Home Ministries; Martin Luther King Memorial Service and Scholarship Fund; Emergency Shelter for the Homeless; Campus Relations; Forums on Social Concerns; Community Worship; Peace and Justice Education; Inter-Faith Programs; Legislative Concerns; Half-Way House for Ex-Offenders; Annual Ecumenical Musical Celebration

Council of Churches of Chemung County Inc.

330 W. Church St., Elmira 14901
Exec. Dir., Mrs. Joan Geldmacher
Pres., Mr. George Barchet
Major Activities: CWS Clothing Collection; CROP Walk; UNICEF; Institutional Chaplaincies; Radio; Easter Dawn Service; Preaching Mission; Communications Network; Representation on Community Boards and Agencies; Meals on Wheels; Campus Ministry; Food Cupboards; Ecumenical Services

The Cortland County Council of Churches, Inc.

7 Calvert St., Cortland 13045
Tel. (607) 753-1002
Exec. Dir., Rev. Donald M. Wilcox
Major Activities: College Campus Ministry; Jail Ministry; Hospital Chaplaincy; Nursing Home Ministry; Newspaper Column; Interfaith Relationships; Hunger Relief; Family Life (Sexuality Education, Adoption, Child Abuse Prevention); UNICEF; CWS; Leadership Education; Community Issues; Peace Task Force; Criminal Justice; Mental Health Chaplaincy

Dutchess Interfaith Council, Inc.

9 Vassar St., Poughkeepsie 12601
Tel. (914) 471-7333
Exec. Dir., Mrs. Martha S. Miller
Protestant Chaplain, Rev. Dr. Charles E. Byrd
Roman Catholic Chaplain, Rev. Ernest D'Onofrio
Pres., Robert H. Lipschutz
Treas., Rev. Jeff M. Archer
Major Activities: County Jail Chaplaincy; Radio; CROP Hunger Walk; Interfaith Music Festival; Public Worship Events; Indochinese Refugee Sponsorship; Interfaith Dialog; Christian Unity; Interfaith Forum; Oil Purchase Group; Volunteer Caregiver Program

Genesee Ecumenical Ministries

17 South Fitzhugh St., Rochester 14614
Tel. (716) 232-6530
Exec. Dir., Rev. Lawrence E. Witmer
Adm. Asst., Marie E. Gibson
Fin. Adm., Ilse Kearney
Pres., Rev. James Rice, 216 Thurston Rd. 14619
Treas., Mr. Russell L. Olson
Major Activities: Criminal Justice (Alternatives to Incarceration); Legislative IMPACT Network; Mission Education & Training; Refugee Resettlement; Hospital Chaplaincies; Hunger and Food Policies; Habitat for Humanity; Respite Cares (developmental disabilities)

The Long Island Council of Churches

Western Office: 249 Merrick Rd. Box 105, Rockville Centre 11571 (Nassau Co.) Tel. (516) 536-8707
Eastern Office: 235 Sweezy Ave., Riverhead 11901 (Suffolk Co.) Tel. (516) 727-2210
Exec. Dir., Rev. Robert L. Pierce
Exec. Asst., Ms. Carolynn Winters-Hazelton
Dir., Pastoral Care & CPE, Rev. Thomas F. Kennedy, Jr.
Dir., Social Services, Mrs. Lillian Sharik
Dir., Project REAL, Mr. Stephen Gervais
Dir., Counseling Services, LICC, Rev. S. Bruce Wagner
Suffolk Aid Secs., Mrs. Deborah Scott, Mrs. Carolyn Brown
Nassau Aid Sec., Ms. Paula Carnevale
Major Activities: Pastoral Care in Hospitals and Jails; Clinical Pastoral Education; Emergency Aid and Food; Advocacy for Domestic and International Peace & Justice; Blood Donor Coordination; Church World Service; Central American Refugee Ministry; Worship; Inter-faith Cooperation; Radio Program; Church Directory; Newsletter; Counseling Service; Project REAL; Special Projects

Council of Churches of the Mohawk Valley Area, Inc.

1644 Genesee St., Utica 13502
Tel. (315) 733-4661

Exec., Blanche E. Liess
Adm. Sec., Elizabeth E. Liess
Pres., David Mathis
Treas., Mr. James Turnbull IV
Major Activities: Christian Education; Social Action; Urban Ministry; Ecumenical Relations; Ministry in Higher Education; Church Women United; Radio and TV; Teen Centers; Personal Care Service Aides; Summer Day Camping; CROP; Clothing Collections

The Council of Churches of the City of New York

490 Riverside Dr., 10th Fl. Twr., New York 10027
Tel. (212) 749-1214
Exec. Dir., Rev. Robert L. Polk
Div. Dir., Dept. Pastoral Care, Rev. Erik Korbell
Div. Dir., Dept. Communications, Rev. Roy Lloyd
Chaplain, Protestant Ecumenical Chapel, Kennedy Airport, Dr. Lars J. Silverness
Ministries in Higher Education, Rev. Erik Korbell
Pres., Douglas Ades
Treas., Dwight Bush
Major Activities: Radio & TV; Church Women United; Youth Services; Pastoral Care; Protestant Chapel, Kennedy International Airport; Public Relations; Family of Man; Response to AIDS; Homeless Shelter; Center for the City

Bronx Division of the Council of Churches of the City of New York

2427 Morris Ave., Bronx 10468
Tel. (212)365-7370
Pres., Mrs. Maizie Bruce
Divisional Dir., Rev. David Hill
Major Activities: Pastoral Care; Christian Education & Youth Ministry; Welfare & Advocacy; Substance Abuse

Brooklyn Division of the Council of Churches of the City of New York

125 Ft. Greene Pl. 11217
Tel. (718) 625-5851
Dir., Rev. Phyllis Byrd
Pres., Charles E. Batson
Treas., Rev. Albert J. Berube
Major Activities: Education Ministry; Justice Ministry; Hunger Ministry; Local Ecumenism; Pastoral Care; Community Issues; Youth Ministry; Women's Advocate; Chaplains Associates

Manhattan Division of the Council of Churches of the City of New York

490 Riverside Drive 10th Fl. Twr., New York 10027
Tel. (212)749-1214
Dir., Rev. Erik Kolbell
Pres., Mr. Lee Nattress
Major Activities: Christian Education; Pastoral Care; Social Concerns

Staten Island Division of the Council of Churches of the City of New York

2187 Victory Blvd., Staten Island 10314
Tel. (718) 761-6782
Ofc. Mgr., Mrs. Marjorie R. Bergendale
Div. Dir. ____
Pres., Rev. Dr. Lowell B. Johnson, 2187 Victory Blvd. 10314
Major Activities: Support; Christian Education; Pastoral Care; Congregational Concerns; Urban Affairs

Queens Federation of Churches

86-17 105th St., Richmond Hill 11418
Tel. (718) 847-6764
Exec. Dir., Rev. N. J. L'Heureux, Jr.
Adm. Asst., Kevin Murphy
York College Chaplain, Rev. Irvine A. Bryer, Jr.
Pres., Mrs. Lorna Valencia
Treas., Lloyd W. Patterson, Jr.
Major Activities: Emergency Food Service; Pastoral Counseling at Family Court; York College Campus Ministry; Blood Bank; Scouting; Christian Education Workshops; Planning and Strategy; Church Women United; Community Consultations; Seminars for Church Leaders; Directory of Churches and Synagogues; Christian Relations (Prot/RC), Chaplaincies; Public Policy Issues; N.Y.S. Interfaith Commission on Landmarking of Religious Property; Queens Interfaith Hunger Network

East Harlem Interfaith

2050 2nd Ave., New York 10029
Tel. (212) 427-1500
Dir., Rev. John Vaughn
Bd. Chmn., Jackie Johnson
Major Activities: Ecumenical Worship; Welfare and Hunger Advocacy; Health Advocacy; Community Organizing; Economic Development (Community Reinvestment)

Metro New York Project Equality, Inc.

85 South Oxford St., Brooklyn 11217
Exec. Dir., ____
Pres., Msgr. William F. Burke
Major Activities: An interfaith organization using purchasing power to promote equal opportunity and affirmative action for all

The Niagara Council of Churches

Rainbow Blvd. & 2nd St.
Niagara Falls 14303
Tel. (716) 285-7505
Exec. Dir., Ms. Claudia L. MacDonald
Pres., Ms. Ruth Human, 1617 South Ave. 14305
Treas., Mrs. Ida Read, 209-59th St. 14304
Major Activities: Ecumenical Worship; Bible Study; Christian Education and Social Concerns; Church Women United; Evangelism and Mission; Institutional Ministries Interfaith Concert; Week of Prayer for Christian Unity; Church World Service Projects; Store for Church Supplies and Audio-Visual Library

Rochester: see Genesee Ecumenical Ministries

Schenectady Inner City Ministry

5 Catherine St., Schenectady 12307
Tel. (518)374-2683
Exec. Dir., Rev. Phillip N. Grigsby
Adm. Asst., Ms. Karen Rembert
Emergency Food Liaison, Ms. Patricia Obrecht
Project SAFE Dir., Ms. Delores Edmonds-McIntosh
Pres., Ms. Robin Stocks
Major Activities: Emergency Food; Advocacy; Housing; Child Care; Alternatives to Prostitution for Runaway and At-Risk Youth; Family Court Ministries; Drop-In Senior Center; Neighborhood and Economic Issues; Ecumenical Worship and Fellowship; Community Research; Education in Churches on Faith Responses to Social Concerns; Legislative Advocacy

Syracuse Area
Interreligious Council

910 Madison St., Syracuse 13210
Tel. (315)476-2001
Exec. Dir., Dorothy F. Rose
Pres., Nancy Sullivan Murray
Dir. Pastoral Care, Rev. Dr. John Regier
Dir. of Prog. and Cmty. Rel., Rev. Dale Hindmarsh
Dir. of Refugee Resettlement, Ms. Nona Stewart
Dir., Senior Companion Prog., Kathleen Rupprecht
Dir., Nutrition Ed./Food Stamp Outreach, Ken Klein
Dir., Food Bank, Barton Feinberg
Camp Adelphi Dir., Preston and Becky Mattix
Project Exodus, Frank Woolever
Major Activities: Direct Services; Advocacy; Education;
Community & Social Concerns; Interreligious Dialog;
Celebration and Worship

NORTH CAROLINA

North Carolina Council
of Churches

Bryan Bldg., Ste. 201A, Raleigh 27605
Tel. (919)828-6501
Exec. Dir., Rev. S. Collins Kilburn
Prg. Assoc., Evelyn Mattern, S.F.C.C.
Pres., Rev. George M. Kloster, 2210 N. Elm St.,
Greensboro 27408
Treas., Dr. W. C. Smith, Jr., 400 Radiance Dr.,
Greensboro 27403
Major Activities: Christian Nurture; Christian Unity;
Christian Social Ministries; Legislative Program; Crimi-
nal Justice; Migrant Farmworkers; Peace; Hunger

Asheville-Buncombe Community
Christian Ministry (ABCCM)

24 Cumberland AVe., Asheville 28801
Tel. (704)252-2752
Exec. Dir., Rev. Scott Rogers
Pres., Dr. Marion Starr

Greensboro Urban Ministry

407 N. Eugene St., Greensboro 27401
Tel. (919)273-6916
Exec. Dir., Rev. Mike Aiken
Major Activities: Emergency Financial Assistance; Hous-
ing, Hunger Relief; Inter-Faith and Inter-Racial Un-
derstanding; Justice Ministry

Urban Ministry Center of Raleigh

310 W. Edenton St., Raleigh 27603
Tel. (919)834-4707
Exec. Dir., Anne M. Burke
Assoc. Dir., Dr. Sheila H. Parker
Dir., Ark Shelters, Dorothy Lane Ellis
Dir., Open Door Clinic, Dr. Sheila H. Parker
Admin. Asst., Nancy K. Evans
Major Activities: Provision of Basic Needs (Financial
Assistance for Fuel, Utilities, Rent, Medications,
Food); Emergency Shelter for Homeless Men and
Women; Free Medical and Dental Clinic for Medically
Indigent Population

NORTH DAKOTA

North Dakota Conference
of Churches

218 N. Fourth St., Bismarck 58501
Tel. (701)255-0604
Pres., Rev. Charles R. Freuden
Treas., Vye Elmer
Ofc. Mgr., Eunice Brinckerhoff
Major Activities: Prison Chaplaincy; Legislative Con-
cerns; Rural Life Crisis Ministry; Peace and Justice;
Promotion of Christian Unity

OHIO

Ohio Council of Churches, Inc.

89 E. Wilson Bridge Rd., Columbus 43085
Tel. (614)885-9590
Exec. Dir., Rev. Carlton N. Weber
Assoc. Dir., Rev. Keene R. Lebold
Legislative Representative, Ms. Kay Keller
Min. of Black Church and Cmty. Rel., Rev. Kujenga Ashe
Dir. of Refugee Services, Rev. Robin Tetzloff
Sponsorship Developer, _____
Sponsorship Coord., Ms. Thi Tuyet Nga Nguyen
Pres., Rev. Dr. Joseph M. Mason
Treas., Rev. Forrest Nees
Major Activities: Economic Justice; Minority Church
Empowerment; Ecumenical Development; Public Poli-
cy Issues; Criminal Justice Issues; Refugee Resettle-
ment

Akron Area Association
of Churches

750 Work Dr., Akron 44320
Tel. (216)535-3112
Exec. Sec., _____
Pres. Bd. of Trustees, Rev. Forrest Nees
Vice-Pres., Mrs. Katharine Chapman
Sec., Mr. Howard Rookard, Jr.
Treas., Dr. Stephen Laning
Telecommunications, Mr. George Bozeka
Community Ministry, David Boerner
Worship and Fellowship Ministry, Ms. Patricia Spriggel
Resource Center Cons., Rev. Rebecca Wolf
Ofc. Sec., Mrs. Elaine Tietz
Major Activities: Messiah Sing; Interfaith Council;
Newsletters; S. E. Asian Refugee Resettlement; Re-
source Center; Community Worship; Training of Local
Church Leadership; Hunger; Radio Programs; Adult
Learning Fairs; Cable TV; Clergy Forum; Assistance to
Elderly

Alliance Area Council
of Churches

470 E. Broadway, Alliance 44601
Tel. (216)821-6648
Dir., Carol DeGrange
Pres., Paul Goodrich
Treas., Ms. Marjorie Stargen
Major Activities: Christian Education; Community Rela-
tions & Service; Ecumenical Worship; Community
Ministry; Peacemaking; Medical Transportation for
Elderly

Council of Christian Communions of Greater Cincinnati

2439 Auburn Ave., Cincinnati 45219
Tel. (513)579-0099
Exec. Dir., Dr. Richard P. Jameson
Interim Assoc. Dir., Coord. of Justice Chaplaincies, Rev. Jack Marsh
Assoc. Dir., Rel. Edu., Terry R. Keeney
Asst. Dir., Communication, John H. Gassett
Chaplain, Juvenile Court, Rev. J. Donald Mosley
Chaplain, Rollman Psychiatric Inst., Rev. Dwight Wilkins
Pres., Rev. James Lewis
Major Activities: Christian Unity & Interfaith Cooperation; Justice Chaplaincies; Police-Clergy Team; Adult and Juvenile Jail Chaplains; Religious Education; Broadcasting and Communications; Information Service

Metropolitan Area Religious Coalition of Cincinnati (MARCC)

1035 Enquirer Bldg., 617 Vine St., Cincinnati 45202
Tel. (513)721-4843
Dir., Rev. Duane Holm
Pres., Dr. Peter Rentos
Major Activities: Minorities in Local Government; Public Education; Human Services

Greater Cleveland Interchurch Council

2230 Euclid Ave., Cleveland 44115
Tel. (216)621-5925
Exec. Dir., Rev. Thomas Olcott
Assoc. Dir. and Dir., Church and Society, Ms. Mylion Waite
Assoc. Dir. and Dir., Communications, Ms. Janice Giering
Pres., Rev. Kenneth Ehrman
Chmn. of the Assembly, Bertha Ingram
Major Activities: Church and Society; Communications; Hunger; Project Learn; Christian Education; Legislation; Faith and Order; Urban Crisis; Public Education; Interchurch News; Tutoring; Parent-Child Books Program; Books for People; Anti-Apartheid; Adult Literacy; Teen Pregnancy Prevention; Shelter for Homeless Women and Children; Radio and TV; Interracial Cooperation; Interfaith Cooperation

Inner City Renewal Society

2230 Euclid Ave., Cleveland 44115
Tel. (216)781-3913
Exec. Dir., Myrtle L. Mitchell
Dir., Friendly Town Prog., Rev. Jerry Wilkins
Dir., J.O.I.N. Prog., James Martin
Dir., Alcoholism Prog., Rev. Thomas Chapman
Pres., Rev. Dr. Allison Phillips
Treas., William Bennett
Major Activities: To serve as the "Extended Arm of the Church in reaching humankind (especially poor & oppressed, wounded of spirit, and afflicted).

West Side Ecumenical Ministry

4315 Bridge Ave, Cleveland 44113
Tel. (216)651-2037
Exec. Dir., Robert T. Begin
Major Activities: Emergency Food Distribution Centers; Senior Meals Programs; Day Care Centers: Youth Counselling and Enrichment; Community Organization; Advocacy; Church Clusters

Metropolitan Area Church Board

760 E. Broad St., Columbus 43205
Tel. (614)461-7103
Exec. Dir., Dr. Robert Lee Erickson
Support Service Coord., Marcia Verhoff
Chmn. Bd., Rev. John Edgar
Vice Chmn., Mrs. Marilyn Shreffler
Sec., Rev. James Miner
Treas., Mrs. Dolores Eyerman
Major Activities: Weekly Radio and Cable TV Programs; Newsletter; Liaison with Other Community Organizations; Annual Congregational Assembly; Week of Prayer for Christian Unity; Support for Ministerial Associations and Church Councils; Enrichment Seminars; Community Bible Study; Prayer Groups; "Emerging Social Issues Forums"; CROP Walk; Habitat for Humanity; Black Business Expo

Metropolitan Churches United

212 Belmonte Park E., Dayton 45405
Tel. (513)222-8654
Exec. Dir., Rev. Robert E. Kolze
Exec. Asst., _____
Coord., Montgomery County Voluntary Jail Prog., Sr. Mary Jean Foppe, R.S.M.
Pres., Dr. Patricia Torvick
Hosp. Notification Service, Mrs. Carrie Beasley
Major Activities: Communications: Service to the Churches and Community; Social Action and Legislation

Churchpeople for Change and Reconciliation

221 W. North St., Lima 45801
Tel. (419) 229-6949
Exec. Dir., Betsy Bouska
Major Activities: New programs for minorities, poor, alienated, and despairing and spinning them off as independent agencies

Mahoning Valley Association of Churches

631 Wick Ave., Youngstown 44502
Tel. (216) 744-8946
Exec. Dir., Rev. Richard D. Speicher
Pres., Rev. William Brewster
Treas., Mr. Paul Fryman, 42 Venloe Dr., Poland 44514
Major Activities: Communications; Christian Education; Ecumenism; Social Action; Advocacy

Pike County Outreach Council

122 East Second St., Waverly 45690
Tel. (614) 947-7151
Fieldworker, Joy A. DeCamp

Metro-Toledo Churches United

444 Floyd St. Toledo 43620
Tel. (419) 242-7401
Adm., Ms. Nancy Lee Atkins
Prog. Dir., Ms. Polly White
Ecumenical Liaison, Rev. John McKissick
Exec. Dir., Toledo Campus Ministry, Rev. Glenn B. Hosman, Jr.
Exec. Dir., Toledo Metropolitan Mission, Ms. Nancy Atkins
Pres., Rev. Peter Martyn
Treas., Fred Plassman
Major Activities: Social Service; Christian Education; Hunger; Interfaith Relations; Christian Unity Campus Ministry; Social Action (Public Education; Mental

Retardation; Voter Registration/Education; Health Care; Community Economic Development; Urban Ministry; Employment; Community Organization; Welfare Rights; Housing; Refugee Assistance.)

Ecumenical Communication Commission of N.W. Ohio (Toledo)

P. O. Box 351, 1011 Sandusky, Ste. M., Perrysburg 43551
Tel. (419) 874-3932
Dir. Ms. Margaret Hoepfl
Major Activities: Ecumenical/Cooperative Communication; TV Production

Tuscarawas County Council for Church and Community

120 First Dr. SE, New Philadelphia 44663
Tel. (216) 343-6012
Exec. Dir., Barbara E. Lauer
Pres., Mr. Thomas L. Kane, Jr., 1221 Crater Ave., Dover 44622
Treas., Mr. James Barnhouse, 120 N. Broadway, New Philadelphia 44663
Major Activities: Human Services; Health; Family Life; Child Abuse; Housing; Educational Programs; Emergency Assistance; Legislative Concerns; Juvenile Prevention Program; Teen Pregnancy Prevention Program; Prevention Program for High Risk Children (The Council acts as a facilitator of the above.)

Youngstown: see Mahoning Valley

OKLAHOMA

Oklahoma Conference of Churches

P. O. Box 60288, Oklahoma City 73146
Tel. (405) 525-2928
Exec. Dir., Rev. Dr. Max E. Glenn
Pres., Mr. Chester Gipson, 1901 Washington Blvd. 73121
Treas., Dr. Robert Elliott
Major Activities: Priority is Church and Unity Concerns with "BEM" Studies; Community Building Among Denominations; Cooperative Community Ministries; Church and Society; IMPACT; Disaster Response; Minority Affairs; Rural Farm Crisis

Tulsa Metropolitan Ministry

240 East Apache, Tulsa 74106
Tel. (918) 582-3147
Exec. Dir., Mr. Marvin L. Cooke
Assoc. Dir., Sr. Sylvia Schmidt, S.C.C.
Dir., Jail Ministry, Rev. Gerald Davis
Dir., Homeless Programs, Marcia Sharp
Pres., Rev. David C. Fox
Sec., John Kontogianes
Treas., Sandra Alexander
Major Activities: Corrections Ministry; Jewish-Christian Understanding; Weatherization Program; Police-Community Relations; Shelter for the Homeless; Women's Issues; Shelter for Mentally Ill; Outreach and Advocacy for Public Housing; Spirituality and Aging; Collective Buying for Congregations and Nonprofits; Legislative Issues; Interfaith Dialogue TV Series

OREGON

Ecumenical Ministries of Oregon

0245 S. W. Bancroft St., Ste. B, Portland 97201
Tel. (503) 221-1054
Exec. Dir., Rev. Rodney I. Page
Assoc. Dir., Barbara J. George
Dir. of Center for Urban Education, Mr. David Lansky
Dir., Legislative and Governmental Ofc., Ellen C. Lowe
Fin. Dev., Michael Keys
Dir., Alcohol and Drugs Ministries, Richard Milsom
Police Chaplain, Rev. Greg Kammann
Sponsors Organized to Assist Refugees, Mrs. Ellen Martin
Dir., Proj. Linkage, Barbara Swicegood
Dir. Emergency Food, Rev. Douglas Wirt
Dir., Folk-Time (Socialization Program for Chronically Mentall Ill), Jenny Steward
Dir., Job Opportunity Bank, Norene Goplen
Pres., Bishop Calvin McConnell
Pres.-Elect, Dr. Wayne Bryant
Treas., Mr. Burke Mims
Major Activities: Educational Ministries; Legislation; Urban Ministries; Refugees; Chaplaincy; Social Concerns; Direct Services; Jewish-Christian Relations; Farm Ministry; Alcohol and Drug Ministry; Welfare Advocacy; Faith & Order; Peace Ministries; IMPACT; Communications; AIDS Ministry; Prostitution Ministry

PENNSYLVANIA

The Pennsylvania Council of Churches

900 S. Arlington Ave., Rm. 100, Harrisburg 17109
Tel. (717) 545-4761
Exec. Dir., Rev. Albert E. Myers
Asst. to the Exec. Dir. for Ethnic Cooperation and Institutional Ministries, Rev. Andrew T. Holtz, Jr.
Asst. to the Exec. Dir. for Special Min., Rev. Charles E. Dorsey
Asst. to the Exec. Dir., for Soc. Min., Rev. Paul D. Gehris
Pres., Rev. Paul L. Westcoat, Jr., 320 S. Maple Ave., Greensburg 15601
Vice Pres., Rhebena T. Castleberry
Sec., Hon Gorham L. Black, Jr.
Treas., Roger P. Anderson
Bus. Mgr., Pascal L. Foucault
Major Activities: Institutional Ministry; Migrant Ministry; Social Ministry; Park Ministry; Inter-Church Planning and Dialog; Conferences; Disaster Response; Trade Association Activities; Church Education; Radio Newscript Service; Ethnic Cooperation

Pennsylvania Conference on Interchurch Cooperation

P. O. Box 2835, Harrisburg 17105
Tel. (717) 545-4761
Co-Staff: Dr. Howard Fetterhoff, Rev. Albert E. Myers
Co-Chairpersons: Bishop William H. Keeler and Bishop Charlie F. McNutt, Jr.
Major Activities: Theological Consultation; Social Concerns; Inter-Church Planning; Conferences and Seminars; Disaster Response Preparedness

Allentown; see Lehigh County Conference

Ecumenical Conference of Greater Altoona

1208 Thirteenth St., P. O. Box 305, Altoona 16603
Exec. Dir., Ms. Eileen Becker
Major Activities: Religious Education; Workshops; Ecumenical Activities; TV; Religious Christmas Parade; Campus Ministry; Community Concerns; Peace Forum; Religious Education for Mentally Handicapped

Christians United in Beaver County

1098 Third Street, Beaver 15009
Tel. (412) 774-1446
Exec. Sec., Mrs. Lois L. Smith
Chaplains, Rev. Clark Olson-Sawyer, Mrs. Erika Bruner, Rev. Edward O. Poole, Rev. Frank Churchill, Mr. Jack Kirkpatrick, Rev. Elaine Solomon
Pres., Mrs. Erika Bruner, 1320 Third Ave., Beaver Falls 15010
Treas., Mr. Eugene Wilson, 162 Wm. Penn Way, New Brighton 15066
Major Activities: Christian Education; Evangelism; Radio; Social Action; Church Women United; United Church Men; Ecumenism

Greater Bethlehem Area Council of Churches

520 E. Broad St., Bethlehem 18018
Tel. (215) 867-8671
Coord., Mrs. Audrey Bertsch
Pres., Rev. Dr. Earl Shay, 3554 Chesterfield La. 18017
Treas., Mrs. Polly McClure, 7 W. Washington Ave. 18018
Major Activities: Hospital Chaplaincy; Support Ministry; Low-Cost Housing Development; Institutional Ministry to Elderly and Infirm; Community-Wide Christian Education

Delaware Valley Media Ministry

1501 Cherry St., Philadelphia 19102
Tel (215) 563-7854
Exec. Dir., Ms. Nancy Nolde
Major Activities: Interfaith Communication and Television Production Agency

Easton Area Council of Churches

330 Ferry St., Easton 18042
Tel. (215) 258-4955
Exec. Sec., Mirian Fretzo

Inter-Church Ministries of Northwestern Pennsylvania

252 W. 7th St., Erie 16501
Tel. (814) 454-2411
Exec. Dir., Dr. Harry Souders
Assoc. Dir., Rev. Deborah R. Dockstader
Pres., Rev. J. David Mumford, 252 W. 7th St., 16501
Treas., Rev. Richard E. Kneller, 1249 W. 10th St. 16502
Major Activities: Local Ecumenism; Ministry with Aging; Social Ministry; Interchurch TV; Pastoral Counseling; Continuing Education; N.W. Pa. Conf. of Bishops and Judicatory Execs.; Institute of Pastoral Care

Christian Churches United of the Tri-County Area

900 S. Arlington Ave., Rm. 128, Harrisburg 17109
Tel. (717) 652-2771
Exec. Dir., _____
Pres., Rev. Richard Dowhower
Treas., _____

Major Activities: Institutional Ministries to Prisons and Hospitals; Communications; Resources for Parish Ministry; Interreligious Forum; HELP (Harrisburg Emergency Life Survival Program); ENTER (Employment Now Through Education, Effort, Responsibility); La Casa de Amistad

Lancaster County Council of Churches

447 E. King St., Lancaster 17602
Tel. (717) 291-2261
Exec. Dir., Dr. Barry L. Snowden
Prison Chaplain, Rev. David F. Myer
Dir. Community Church Rel.; Rev. Joseph N. Peacock
Dir. Prescott House, Terrence Muzzi
Child Abuse, Elsbeth Duke
Dir. CONTACT, Janet Sandham
Dir., Shared Holiday, Ellen Mellinger-Blouch
Pres., Stephen Gibble, 127 E. Main St., Lititz 17543
Treas., John W. Zook, 1724 Niblick Ave., Lancaster 17602
Major Activities: Hospital Chaplaincy; Christian Social Ministry; Residential Ministry to Youthful Offenders; Prison Ministry; Housing; CONTACT; Widow Support

Lebanon County Christian Ministries

818 Water St., P.O.Box 654, Lebanon 17042
Tel. (717)274-2601
Exec. Dir., Mrs. Elizabeth F. Greer
Food & Clothing Bank Dir., Mrs. Sally M. Jackson
H.O.P.E. Services Dir., Mrs. Ruth Shenk
Noon Meals Coord., Mrs. Glenda Wenger
Major Activities: H.O.P.E. (Helping Our People in Emergencies—Emergency Material Needs Clearinghouse); Food & Clothing Bank; Free Noon Meal Program; Surplus Federal Commodity Distribution Program; Worship Chaplaincy at County Institutions; Ecumenical Activities

Lehigh County Conference; Counseling; Child Abuse Prevention of Churches

36 S. 6th St., Allentown 18101
Tel. (215) 433-6421
Exec. Dir., Rev. William A. Seaman
Pres., Dr. Blaine Bogert
Treas., Mr. James Hottenstein, 152 E. South St. 18103
Major Activities: Chaplaincy Program; Migrant Ministry; Social Concerns and Action; Clergy Dialogues; Drop-In-Center for De-Institutionalized Adults; Ecumenical Food Kitchen; Housing Advocacy Program

TELERAD (South Central Pennsylvania Television and Radio Ministry)

140 N. Penn St., Manheim 17545
Tel. (717) 665-2331
Program Coord., Rev. Donald Zechman
Major Activities: Ecumenical/Cooperative Broadcasting

United Churches of Northeastern Pennsylvania

550 Madison Ave., Scranton 18510
Tel. (717) 347-4730
Exec. Dir., _____
Chaplain (Cmty. Min.), Rev. Paul W. Gere
Ofc. Sec., Mrs. Paul A. Knorr
Pres., Rev. George J. Matthews, Jr.
Treas., Raymond P. Wytovich

Major Activities: Chaplaincy in Hospitals, Nursing Homes, Detox Unit; "United in Service" Newsletter; Christian Education for Retarded and Deaf; United Churches Book Store; "Religion in the News" Radio Broadcasts; Emergency Rent/Mortgage Funds; Crisis Intervention Ministry; Human Services Fair; Vacation Bible School Preview; Tri-County Migrant Ministry

Metropolitan Christian Council of Philadelphia

1501 Cherry St., Philadelphia 19102
Tel. (215) 563-7854
Exec. Dir., Rev. C. Edward Geiger
Assoc., Communications, Ms. Nancy L. Nolde
Adm. Asst., Mrs. Joan G. Shipman
Chairperson: Samuel D. Caldwell
Pres., Dr. William J. Shaw
Treas., John A. Clark, 1 Franklin Plz. 19102
Major Activities: Congregational Clusters; Public Policy Advocacy; Communication; Interfaith Dialogue

Northwest Interfaith Movement

Greene Street at Westview, Philadelphia 19119
Tel. (215) 843-5600
Dir., Rev. Richard R. Fernandez
Coord. Nursing Home Prog., Mary Fallon
Chairperson, Eddilera E. Kinzer
Major Activities: Community Development & Community Reinvestment; Older Adult Concerns; Nursing Home Program; Unemployment; Economic Issues; Public Education; Peace

Christian Associates of Southwest Pennsylvania

239 Fourth Ave., Pittsburgh 15222
Tel. (412) 281-1515
Exec. Dir., Dr. W. Lee Hicks
Assoc. Exec. and Dir. of Planning. Rev. Bruce H. Swenson
Cable TV Co-ordinator, Andrew James
Adm. Asst., Mrs. Barbara Kovach
Pres., Canon Richard W. Davies
Treas., Fr. John M. O'Toole
Major Activities: Communications; Planning; Church and Community; Leadership Development; Theological Dialogue; Evangelism/Church Growth

East End Cooperative Ministry

250 N. Highland Ave., Pittsburgh 15206
Tel. (412) 361-5549
Exec. Dir., Mrs. Judith Marker
Major Activities: Food Pantry; Soup Kitchen; Men's Emergency Shelter; Meals on Wheels; Casework and Supportive Services; Supportive Services for Elderly; Information and Referral; Program for Children and Youth; Bridge Housing Program

Ecumenical Urban Ministries

100 N. Bellefield at Fifth Ave., Pittsburgh 15213
Tel. (412)682-2751
Exec. Dir., Rev. Gail Buchwalter King
Pres. of EUM Bd., Dr. Wendell Paull
Major Activities: Revitalization of Local Urban Churches; Ethics Panels; Advocacy Networks; Learning Opportunities

North Hills Youth Ministry

1566 Northway Mall, Pittsburgh 15237
Tel. (412) 366-1300
Exec. Dir., Ronald B. Barnes

South Hills Interfaith Ministries

5171 Park Ave., Bethel Park 15102
Tel. (412) 833-6177
Exec. Dir., Robert Laird Brashear
Psychological Services, Mr. Don Zandier, Dr. Charles Lockwood, Ms. Hilda Schorr-Ribera
Cmty. Services, Ms. Suzanne Kelley, Mrs. Marie Shumovich
Adm. Asst., Ms. Cassandra Southworth
Interfaith Reemployment Job Advocate, Mr. David Bates
Pres., Ms. Josephine Kelly
Treas., Thomas Serpa
Major Activities: Basic Human Needs; Unemployment; Community Organization and Development Inter-Faith Cooperation; Family Hospice; Personal Growth

The Greater Reading Council of Churches

54 N. 8th St., Reading 19601
Tel. (215) 375-6108
Exec. Dir., Rev. Warren P. Wilfert, Jr.
Adm. Asst., Constance B. Reinholz
Pres., Helen Mengel
Rec. Sec., Mrs. Virginia Chudgar
Treas., Mr. Lee M. LeVan
Major Activities: Institutional Ministry; CWU; Social Action; Migrant Ministry; CWS; CROP Walk for Hunger; Emergency Assistance

Reading Urban Ministry

430 N. Second St., Reading 19601
Tel. (215) 374-6917
Exec. Dir., Rev. Douglas L. Shaffer
Pres., Mary Ann Cope
Vice Pres., _____
Sec., Fianna Holt
Treas., Dorothy Breitegarn
Major Activities: Community Clothing Center; Friendly Visitor Program to Elderly; Caring When It Counts (Emergency Intervention with Elderly); Reading Emergency Shelter for Homeless Men; Summer Youth Program

United Churches of Williamsport and Lycoming County

202 E. Third St., Williamsport 17701
Tel. (717) 322-1110
Exec. Dir., Rev. Dr. Alton M. Motter
Ofc. Sec., Mrs. Linda Winter
Pres., Rev. James W. Grubb, 2 Ross St. 17701
Treas., Mr. Howard R. Baldwin, Jr., R.D. 2 17701
Dir., Ecumenism and Evangelism, Msgr. William J. Fleming, 410 Walnut St. 17701
Dir., Institutional Ministry, Rev. David W. Schmuck, 1427 Memorial Ave.
Dir., Radio-TV, Rev. Robert H Logan, 369 Broad St., Montoursville 17754
Dir., Social Concerns, Rev. Mark A. Santucci, 426 Mulberry St.
Dir., Prison Ministry, Rev. John N. Mostoller, 1200 Almond St. 17701
Major Activities: Ecumenism; Educational Ministries; Evangelization and Church Renewal; Church Women United; Church World Service and CROP; Prison Ministry; Radio-TV; Nursing Homes; Fuel Bank; Food Pantry; UNICEF; Hospice; Pornography; Family Life; Shepherd of the Streets Urban Ministry

Wyoming Valley Council of Churches

35 S. Franklin St., Wilkes-Barre 18701

Tel. (717); 825-8543
Exec. Dir., Rev. Anita J. Ambrose
Ofc. Sec., Ms. Sandra Karrott
Pres., Wesley Simmers
Treas., Miss Marjorie Trethaway
Major Activities: Hospital and Nursing Home Chaplaincy; Church Women United; High Rise Apartment Ministry; Hospital Referral Service; Emergency Response; Food Bank; Migrant Ministry; Meals on Wheels; Dial-A-Driver; Radio and TV; Leadership Schools; Interfaith Programs; Shepherd of the Streets Ministry

York County Council of Churches

145 S. Duke St., York 17403
Tel. (717) 854-9504
Exec. Dir., Rev. Robert B. Ketcham
CONTACT-York Teleministry Dir., Mrs. Lois Wetzler
Pres., Mrs. Jesse Schaefer
Treas., Mr. James Stein
Major Activities: Educational Development; Spiritual Growth and Renewal; Worship and Witness; Congregational Resourcing; Outreach and Mission

PUERTO RICO

Evangelical Council of Puerto Rico (Concilio Evangélico de Puerto Rico)

P.O. Box 21343, Río Piedras 00928
Tel. (809) 765-5977
Exec. Sec., _____
Treas., Pres., _____
Pres., Rev. Paulita Garcia
Major Activities: Christian Social Action; Chaplaincy; Evangelism; Ecumenism; Public Relations; Radio-TV; Head Start Program; FEMA Program

RHODE ISLAND

Rhode Island State Council of Churches

743 Hope St., Providence 02906
Tel. (401) 861-1700
Exec. Minister, Rev. Dr. Richard C. Brown
Adm. Asst., Peggy Macnie
Pres., Rev. Kate Penfield
Treas., Mr. Robert A. Mitchell
Major Activities: Urban Ministries; Radio-TV; Institutional Chaplaincy; Advocacy/Justice & Service: Legislative Liaison; Faith & Order; CWS; Leadership Development; Campus Ministries

SOUTH CAROLINA

South Carolina Christian Action Council, Inc.

P.O. Box 3663, Columbia 29230
Tel. (803) 786-7115
Exec. Minister, Rev. Dr. Russell B. Norris, Jr.
Pres., Rev. Carnell Hampton
Major Activities: Advocacy and Ecumenism; Continuing Education; Interfaith Dialogue; Citizenship and Public Affairs; Publications

United Ministries

606 Pendleton St., P.O. Box 17307, Greenville 29606
Te. (803) 232-6463
Exec. Dir., Rev. Beth Templeton
Chpsn. of Bd., Eugene Fitzgerald
V. Chair of Bd., Frank Williams
Sec. of Bd., Jane Hicks
Treas. of Bd., Barry Edwards
Major Activities: Caring Volunteers; H.E.A.T. (Heat for Elderly and Toddlers); Congregate Dining; Caring for Unemployed People (C.U.P.); M.E.D. (Medication, Education; Dedication); Emergency Assistance; Hunger Pantry

SOUTH DAKOTA

Association of Christian Churches

200 W. 18th St., Sioux Falls 57104
Tel. (605) 334-1980
Exec. Dir., Dr. Bruce Gray
Pres., Rev. Richard Lounsbery
Sec., Ms. Bev Berry
Major Activities: Ecumenical Forums; Continuing Education for Clergy; Church and Community Relations; Legislative Information; Resourcing Local Ecumenism

TENNESSEE

Tennessee Association of Churches

1785 Hayden Rd., Germantown 38138
Tel. (901)754-1716
Exec. Dir., Dr. C. Ray Dobbins, 1785 Hayden, Germantown 38118. Tel. (901)755-1716
Pres., Rev. Herbert W. Carlock
Major Activities: Faith and Order; Christian Unity; Social Concern Ministries; Legislative Concerns

Metropolitan Inter Faith Association (MIFA)

P.O. Box 3130, Memphis, 38173
Tel. (901) 527-0208
Exec. Dir., Rev. Gid Smith

TEXAS

Texas Conference of Churches

2704 Rio Grande #9, Austin 78705
Tel. (512) 478-7491
Exec. Dir., Rev. Dr. Frank H. Dietz
Assoc. Dir., Ms. Annmarie Jensen
Dir. TX IMPACT, Ms. Linda B. Team
Pres., Msgr. Robert Rehkemper
Major Activities: Church and Society; Ecumenism; Education; Communication; Christian-Jewish Relations; Texas Church Women United; Domestic Violence; Disaster Response; Texas Church World Service/CROP; Alcoholism-Addiction Education; Peace; Central American Issues; Texas IMPACT

Austin Area Conference of Churches

1110 Guadalupe, Austin 78701
Tel. (512)472-7627
Pres., Fr. Walter J. Dalton, C.S.P.
Pres-Elect, Dr. William Jaap

Treas., Mr. David E. Erickson, Jr.
Chaplain, Rev. H. Rex Lewis (Brackenridge Hospital)
Chaplain, Rev. Charles I. Fay (Travis Co. Jails)
Major Activities: Pastoral Care in Hospital and Jails;
Monthly Fellowship and Program; Interfaith Services;
Emergency Services Directory; Occasional Educational
Workshops

Metro-Ministries of Austin (United Urban Council of Austin, Inc.)

100 East 27th St., Austin 78705
Tel. (512) 478-5353
Dir., Rev. Carl Siegenthaler
Major Activities: Situation Analysis; Community Self-Development; Direct Services; Constituency and Social Policy Advocacy

Corpus Christi Metro-Ministries

1906 Leopard, Corpus Christi 78408
Tel. (512)887-0151
Exec. Dir., Rev. Dr. Richard C. Duncan
Dir., Programs, Rev. Dr. James Smith-Farris
Dir., Operations, Ann Schiro
Admin., Sue McCown
Dir., Loaves and Fishes, Joe Jaimes
Dir., Counseling, Amie Harrell
Dir., Employment, Frank Johnson
Dir., Bethany House, Bill Moyes
Dir., Rainbow House, Cheral Flugel
Dir., Child Abuse Prevention, Ellen Myers
Dir., Child Abuse Prevention, Ellen Myers
Major Activities: Food Center; Shelters; Counseling; Job Readiness; Job Placement; Abuse Prevention and Intervention

Greater Dallas Community of Churches

2800 Swiss Ave., Dallas 75204
Tel. (214) 824-8680
Exec. Dir., _____
Assoc. Exec. Dir., Oeita Bottorff
Dir., Hospital Chaplaincy, Dr. Benjamin H. E. Breitkreuz
Dir., County Jail Chaplaincy, Rev. Holsey Hickman
Dir., Community College Ministry, Rev. Georjean Blanton
Prog. Assoc., John Stoesz
Devel. Dir., Margaret M. Hogan
Communications Dir., Ellen Lindsey Key
Pres., Ernest R. Higginbotham
Treas., Hector Escamilla
Major Activities: Center for Urban Ministry; Hospital Chaplaincy; Community College Ministry; Jail Chaplaincy; Housing; Hunger; Peacemaking; Faith and Life; Jewish-Christian Relations; Congregational Action; Racial Ethnic Justice; Public Policy

Border Association for Refugees from Central America (BARCA)

P.O. Box 715, Edinburg 78540
Tel. (512)381-0002; 425-7447
Exec. Dir., Ninfa O. Krueger
Dir., Refugee Children Serv., Jesse Rodriguez
Major Activities: Food, Shelter, Clothing, to Central Americans; Medical and Other Emergency Aid; Legal Advocacy; Special Services to Children; Speakers on Refugee Concerns for Church Groups.

Tarrant Area Community of Churches

807 Texas St., Ste. 101, Fort Worth 76102
Tel. (817) 335-9341
Exec. Dir., Dr. Samuel P. Auslam
Adm. Asst., Verna Deene Keene
Pres., Mrs. Virginia Richards
Treas., Rev. Bert Honea
Major Activities: Developing Community Resources; Workshops and Seminars; Ecumenical Celebrations; Airport Chaplaincy; Nursing Home Ministry; Aging; Hunger; Faith & Life; Jewish-Christian Relations; Teenage Pregnancy Prevention Program; Jail Ministry

Northside Inter-Church Agency (NICA)

506 NW 15th St., Fort Worth 76106
Tel. (817) 626-1102
Dir., Francine Esposito Pratt

Southeast Area Churches (SEARCH)

P.O. Box 51256, 1405 Campbell St., Fort Worth 76105
Tel. (817) 531-2211
Dir., Ms. Dorothy Anderson

Southside Area Ministries (SAM)

305 W. Broadway, Fort Worth 76104
Tel. (817) 332-3778
Exec. Dir., Rev. Janice Kreitner Cain
Major Activities: Refugee Assistance; Community Development; Language Development; Tutoring

Houston Metropolitan Ministries

3217 Montrose Blvd., Houston 77006
Tel. (713) 522-3955
Exec. Dir., Rev. Bruce Theunissen
Dir. of Cong. Rel., Rev. Edward B. Seeger
Dir. of Dev. and Publ. Rel., Mr. James Maxwell
Dir., Adm. and Fin., Ms. Deborah Lackey
Dir. RSVP, Ms. Candice Twyman
Dir., Bordersville Cmty. Cntr., Mr. Douglas J. Samuel
Dir., Senior Health Care, Ms. Susann L. Wilkinson
Dir., Cottage Industries, Ms. Jeanne Sickman
Dir., Youth Victim/Witness, Ms. Pamela R. Hobbs
Dir., Family Connection Shelter, Mr. Vincent Manning
Dir., EDGE for Youth, John O. Holmes
Dir., Meals on Wheels, Ms. Thelma Pierre
Dir., Houston Interfaith Hunger Coalition, Ms. Ellen Mitchell
Dir., Refugee Resettlement, Bill Thomas
Jail Chaplains, Rev. George Cordova, Rev. Everett Fredholm, Rev. Rebecca Lewis
Pres., Betty Mathis
Treas., Nancy Williams
Major Activities: Opportunities for the Aging; Combating Hunger; Community Self-Development; Criminal Justice; Interfaith Relations; Youth Services

United Board of Missions

1701 Bluebonnet Ave., P. O. Box 3856, Port Arthur 77643
Exec. Dir., Clark Moore
Pres., Rev. Don Sheffield
Major Activities: Emergency Assistance, i.e., Food and Clothing, Rent and Utility, Medical, Dental, Transportation; Share a Toy at Christmas; Counseling; Back to School Clothing Assistance; Information and Referral; Hearing Aid Bank; Meals on Wheels; Scholarships; Energy Conservation Programs

Project Dignidad, San Angelo

313 W. Ave. "N", San Angelo 76903
Dir., Dr. Tomas Chavez
Major Activities: Hunger Ministry; Medical Ministry; La Escuelita Pre-school; Ministry to Illegal Aliens

San Antonio Community of Churches

1101 W. Woodlawn, San Antonio 78201
Tel. (512)733-9159
Exec. Dir., Rev. Dr. C. Don Baugh
Instit. Chaplain, Rev. Michael De Gerolami
Pres., Rev. Ernest Lantz
Vice Pres., Mr. William Morse
Sec., Mr. Robert Green
Treas., Fred Knight
Major Activities: Christian Educ.; Missions; Social Relations; Radio-TV; Battered Women's Shelter; Refugee Language School; Continuing Education; Resource Center

San Antonio Urban Council

1602-A Goliad Rd., San Antonio 78223
Tel. (512)337-8550
Exec. Dir., L. C. (Jim) Harrier
Pres., Rev. Leslie Ellison
Major Activities: Homes for Discharged Mental Patients; After School Care for Latch Key Children; Christian Base Community

VERMONT

Vermont Ecumenical Council and Bible Society

285 Maple St., Burlington 05402
Tel. (802) 864-7723
Exec. Sec., Rev. John E. Nutting
Pres., Rev. D. Curtis Minter
Treas., Most Rev. John A. Marshall
Major Activities: Peace; Legislative Liaison; Christian Unity; Bible Distribution; Social Justice

VIRGINIA

Virginia Council of Churches, Inc.

2321 Westwood Ave., Richmond 23230
Tel. (804) 353-5587
Exec. Dir., _____
Dir. of Prog. Ministries, _____
Coord., Weekday Rel. Ed., Miss Olive Clark, 137 Robin Rd., Waynesboro 22980
Coord., Refugee Resettlement, Rev. Dorothy D. France
Coord., Campus Ministry Forum, Rev. James McDonald, 1908 Lewis Mountain Rd., Charlottesville 22903
Major Activities: Educational Development; Church and Society; Direct Ministries; Ecumenical Affairs; Communications; Refugee Resettlement; Legislative Concerns and Public Witness; Park Ministries; Migrant Ministries; Day Care; Disaster Coordination

Community Ministry of Fairfax County

1920 Association Dr., Rm. 507, Reston 22091
Tel. (703)620-5014
Exec. Dir., Rev. Frederick S. Lowry
Newsletter Ed., James Vining
Chpsn., Russell Stevens
Sec., Debra Haraldson

Treas., Harry Hoft
Major Activities: Ecumenical Social Ministry; Elderly; Criminal Justice; Housing; Public Education

Virginia Interfaith Center for Public Policy

6 North 6th St., Richmond 23219
Tel. (804) 780-2703
Exec. Dir., Rev. James A. Payne
Chpsn., Dr. Paul Nichols
Sec.-Treas., Mark E. Rubin
Major Activities: Interfaith Dialogue and Legislative Witness in Virginia; Interact (Legislative Bulletin); Legislative Agenda (Annual Publication); Interfaith Legislative Education; State-Wide Seminars

WASHINGTON

Washington Association of Churches

4759 15th Ave., NE, Seattle 98105
Tel. (206) 525-1988
Exec., Min., Rev. Loren E. Arnett
Dir., Refugee Resettlement and Job Program, Ms. Sally Mackey, 3902 South Ferdinand St. 98118. Tel. (206)721-5288
Dir., Salvadoran/Guatemalan Refugee Prog., Mrs. Hermalinda Gonzales, 225 N. 70th 98103. Tel. (206) 789-7297
Pres., Rev. Dr. William F. Walles, 4035 Olympic Blvd. W., Tacoma 98466. Tel. (206)564-2200
Treas., Rev. Dr. Robert C. Brock, 6558 35th Ave., S.W., Seattle 98126 Tel. (206) 938-1008
Major Activities: Faith and Order; Poverty Programs; Hunger Action; Legislation; Denominational-Ecumenical Coordination; Congregational Renewal; Refugee Resettlement; Peace Education

Center for the Prevention of Sexual and Domestic Violence

1914 N. 34th St., Ste. 105, Seattle
Tel. (206)634-1903
Exec. Dir., Rev. Marie M. Fortune
Program Dir., Frances W. Wood
Admin. Dir., Jay Anton
Admin. Assoc., Sandra Barone
Clerical Asst., Lorna Newgent
Major Activities: Educational Ministry; Clergy and Lay Training; Social Action.

Church Council of Greater Seattle

4759 15th Ave., NE, Seattle 98105
Tel. (206) 525-1213
Pres.-Dir., Rev. Dr. William B. Cate
Assoc. Dir.-Urban Min., Rev. David C. Bloom
Assoc. Dir.-Adm., Alice M. Woldt
Assoc. Dir.-Dev., Sharon L. Edberg
Adm. Asst., Angela W. Ford
Dir., Central Amer. Task Force, Beth Brunton
Dir., Emerg. Feeding Prog., Rev. Dr. O. J. Moore
Dir., Friend-to-Friend, Joe Rust
Dir., Peace Task Force, Paul Riley; Consl, Charles Meconis
Vice-Pres., Laura Bailey
Treas., Donald Bell
Major Activities: Racial Justice; Peace Action; Pastoral Ministry; Hunger; Religious Education; Women in the Church; Housing; Employment; Mental Health; Gay Rights; Aging; Family; Central America; South Africa; Native Americans; Pacific Rim

Ecumenical Metropolitan Ministry

P.O. Box 12272, Seattle 98102
Tel. (206) 625-0755
Exec. Dir., Ruth Sterling Velozo
Chpsn., Phillip L. Burton
Major Activities: Northwest Harvest (Hunger Response); Northwest Infants Corner (Special Nutrititional Products for Infants and Babies); Northwest Caring Ministry (Individuals and Family Crisis Intervention and Advocacy); Northwest Senior Nutrition (Special Food Needs for the Elderly); E.M.M. (Advocacy, Education, Communications Relative to Programs and Economic Justice).

Religious Broadcasting Commission

500 Wall St., Ste. 415, Seattle 98121
Tel. (206)441-6110
Exec. Dir., Rev. J. Graley Taylor
Major Activities: Motion Picture and TV Production; Slide Films; Graphic Art; Media Service; Film & Video Rental Library; Ecumenical Broadcasting

†Spokane Christian Coalition

E. 245-13th Ave., Spokane 99202
Tel. (509) 624-5156
Exec. Dir., Rev. John A. Olson
Pres., Rev. Flora Bowers, E. 1526 11th Ave. 99202
Treas., Lula Hage, N. 1413 Superior 99202
Major Activities: Forums on Issues; Friend to Friend Visitation with Nursing Home Patients; "Fig Tree" Newspaper; Interstate Task Foce on Human Relations; U.S. Economy/Poverty Task Force

Associated Ministries of Tacoma-Pierce County

2520 Sixth Ave., Tacoma 98406
Tel. (206) 383-3056
Exec. Dir., Rev. David T. Alger, 650 N. Hawthorne 98406
Assoc. Dir., Janet E. Leng, 1809 N. Lexington 98406
Pres., Ms. Sharon Verharen
Sec., Rev. Dick Tietjen
Treas., Ms. Shelby Scherer
Major Activities: Friend to Friend (Nursing Home Visitation); FISH/Food Banks; Hunger Awareness; Coordination of Refugee Resettlement; Economic Justice; Christian Education; Shalom (Peacemaking) Resource Center; Social Service Program Advocacy; Communication and Networking of Churches; Habitat for Humanity; Emergency Housing; Pierce Cnty AIDS Foundation

Associated Ministries of Thurston County

Box 895, Olympia 98507
Tel. (206) 357-7224
Exec. Adm., Nancy Hoff
Pres., Paul Zech
Treas., Steve Davis
Major Activities: Church Information and Referral; Interfaith Worship; Workshops; Social and Health Concerns; Legislation

WEST VIRGINIA

West Virginia Council of Churches

1608 Virginia St. E., Charleston 25311
Tel. (304) 344-3141

Exec. Dir., Rev. John F. Price
Dir., Support Services Network, Janet Harmon
Pres., Rev. Dr. H. Davis Yeuell, Synod of the Virginias, 4841 Williamson Rd., N.W. Roanoke, VA 24012
Treas., Warren Moyer, 4205 Seventh Ave., Vienna 26105
Major Activities: Leisure Ministry; Correctional Reform; Ecumenical Events; Disaster Response; Faith and Order; Family Concerns; Inter-Faith Relations; Peace and Justice; Campus Ministry; Public Policy Issues

The Greater Wheeling Council of Churches

110 Methodist Bldg., Wheeling 26003
Tel. (304) 232-5315
Exec. Sec., Mrs. Mabel Griffith
Hospital Notification Sec., Mrs. Ruth Fletcher
Pres., Rev. Kenneth Price, Jr.
Treas., Dr. Beryl Hart
Major Activities: Christian Education; Evangelism; Vespers; Television; Institutional Ministry; Religious Film Library; Church Women United; Volunteer Pastor Care at OVMC Hospital; School of Religion; Hospital Notification; Hymn Sing in the Park; Free Lunch Program

WISCONSIN

Wisconsin Conference of Churches

1955 West Broadway, Ste. 104, Madison 53713
Tel. (608) 222-9779
Exec. Dir., Rev. John D. Fischer
Adm. Asst. and Asst. Treas., Mrs. Phyllis Brinkman
Public Policy Dir. and IMPACT Dir., Ms. Bonnee Voss
Dir. Broadcasting Ministry Commission, Rev. Robert P. Seater, 4240 N. 78th St., Milwaukee 53222. Tel. (414) 461-1774
Dir. Ofc. of Pastoral Services, Rev. G. Lloyd Rediger, 222 N. Midvale Blvd., Madison 53705. Tel. (608) 231-1550
Peace and Justice Ecumenical Partnership, Co-Dirs., Jane Hammatt-Kavaloski and Vincent Kavaloski, Rt. #3, Box 228 E, Dodgeville 53533
Pres., Rev. Frederick Trost
Treas., Mr. Chester Spangler, 625 Crandall, Madison 53711
Major Activities: Church and Society; Religion and Leisure; Migrant Ministry; Pastoral Services; Broadcasting Ministry; Aging; IMPACT; Institutional Chaplaincy; Peace and Justice; Faith and Order; Rural Concerns Forum

Christian Youth Council

1715—52nd St., Kenosha 53140
Tel. (414) 652-9543
Exec. Dir., Ron Stevens
Christian Education, Rev. Mrs. Paul Mitchell
Sports Dir., Krisp Jensen
Outreach Dir., Linda Osborne
Pres., William Stone
Major Activities: Christian Education; Leisure Time Ministry; Institutional Ministries; Ecumenical Committee; Social Concerns

Interfaith Conference of Greater Milwaukee

1442 N. Farwell Ave., Ste. 208, 53202
Tel. (414) 276-9050
Exec. Dir., Mr. Patrick M. Flood
Program Dir., Mr. Jack Murtaugh
Coalition on Food and Shelter Issues, Mrs. Mary Strecker

Adm. Asst., Mrs. Charlotte Holloman
Dir., Interfaith Prog. for the Elderly, _____
Consultant in Communications, Rev. Robert Seater
Chpsn., Rt. Rev. Roger White
Treas., Mrs. Ruth Olsen
Major Activities: Economic Issues - Unemployment; Emergency Assistance - Public Policy; Religion and Labor Committee; Economic Concerns - Private Sector Committee; Criminal Justice Task Force: Public Education Committee; TV Programming; Peace and International Issues Committee; Annual Membership Luncheon

Project Equality of Wisconsin

1442 North Farwell Ave., Ste. 210, Milwaukee 53202
Tel. (414) 272-2642
Exec. Dir., Mrs. Betty J. Thompson
Major Activities: Change systematic causes of employment discrimination against minorities, women and other protected groups.

Center for Community Concerns

1501 Villa St. Racine 53403
Exec. Dir., Mrs. Jean Mandli
Tel. (414) 637-9176
Skillbank Coord., _____
Volunteer Prog. Coord., Chris Udell-Solberg
VIPS (Volunteers for Intergenerational Programs in Schools) Coord., Chris Udell-Solberg
Major Activities: Advocacy; Direct Services; Research; Community Consultant; Criminal Justice; Volunteerism; Senior Citizen Services

WYOMING

Wyoming Church Coalition

1215 Gibbon, Laramie 82070
Tel. (307)745-6000
Exec. Sec., Adm. Coord., Anne Ludlow
Major Activities: Christian Education and Leadership Development; Higher Education; Impacted Areas; Christian Camping; Social Concerns; Legislative Concerns; Media; Penitentiary Chaplaincy; Peace and Justice; Hunger; Agricultural and Rural Crisis Concerns

Wyoming Ministries in Higher Education

Dir., Rev. Willis Ludlow, 1115 Grand Ave., Laramie 82070. Tel. (307) 742-5969
Facilitator, Northwest Community College, _____, 1118 Barrows Rd., Rt. 1, Powell 82435. Tel (307)754-4000
Facilitator for Campus Ministry, Western Wyoming College, Rev. David Wade, 1275 Adams St., Rock Springs 82901; Rev. H. Eugene Warren, Box 517, Rock Springs 89201
Facilitator, Sheridan College, Georgia Huckeby, 903 Big Horn Ave., Sheridan 82801
Facilitator for Campus Ministry, Laramie County Community College, _____
Facilitator for Campus Ministry, Central Wyoming College, Mr. Roger Thomas, 33 North View Dr., HC 31, Box 2746H, Riverton 82501
Facilitator for Campus Ministry, Eastern Wyoming College, Peggy Sewell, 359 Rio Vista, Torrington 82240
Facilitator, Casper College, Scott Wilson, 2408 E. 10th St., Casper 82601. Tel. (307)237-5851

8. CANADIAN REGIONAL AND LOCAL ECUMENICAL AGENCIES

Most of the organizations listed below are councils of churches in which churches participate officially, whether at the parish or judicatory level. They operate at either the city, metropolitan area, or county level. Parish clusters within urban areas are not included.

Canadian local ecumenical bodies operate without paid staff, with the exception a few which have part-time staff. In most cases the name and address of the president or chairperson is listed. As these offices change from year to year, some of this information may be out of date by the time the **Yearbook of American and Canadian Churches** is published. However, a letter to the address listed will be forwarded. Up-to-date information may be secured from the Canadian Council of Churches, 40 St. Clair Ave., E., Toronto, Ontario M4T 1M9.

ALBERTA

Calgary Inter-Faith Community Action Committee
1916 - 2nd St. S.W., Calgary, Alberta T2S 1S3

Calgary Council of Churches
Mrs. Molly Mainman, 616 - 47th Ave. S.W., Calgary, Alberta T2S 1C6

Edmonton & District Council of Churches
Rev. Ken Walker, 11304-78th Ave., Edmonton, Alberta T6G 0M9

ATLANTIC PROVINCES

Atlantic Ecumenical Council of Churches
Pres., Rev. John E. Boyd, P. O. Box 637, 90 Victoria St., Amherst, Nova Scotia B4H 4B4

BRITISH COLUMBIA

Canadian Ecumenical Action (Formerly POEM)
Coordinator, 1410 West 12th Ave., Vancouver, British Columbia V6H 1M8

Greater Victoria Council of Churches
Pres., Mr. H. de Zwager, 1457 Clifford St., Victoria, British Columbia V8S 1M1

MANITOBA

Manitoba Provincial Interfaith Council
Rev. Canon W. J. G. Ayers, #8 - 400 Carpathia St., Winnipeg, Manitoba R3N 1Y4

The Ecumenical Committee of Manitoba
Rev. Ray Cuthbert, 1104 Mulvey Ave., Winnipeg, Manitoba R3M 1J5

NEW BRUNSWICK

Moncton Area Council of Churches
Ms. Faye L. MacKay, Site 9. Comp. 7, R.R. #1, Hillsborough, New Brunswick EOA 1XO

First Miramichi Inter-Church Council
Mrs. Victor Ross, Boiestown, New Brunswick E0H 1A0

NOVA SCOTIA

Amherst and Area Council of Churches
Rev. W. T. Slaney, Joggins, Nova Scotia B0L 1A0

Annapolis Royal Council of Churches
Rev. David Stokes, P. O. Box 7, Annapolis Royal, Nova Scotia BOS 1AO

Atlantic Baptist Fellowship
Rev. Donald Jackson, Tideways, Apt. 207, Wolfville, Nova Scotia BOP 1XO

Bedford and Sackville Church Association
Ms. Dianne Swineman, P. O. Box 585, Lower Sackville, Nova Scotia B4C 3J1

Bridgewater Inter-Church Council
Pres., Ms. Carroll Young, 159 High St., Bridgewater, Nova Scotia B4V 1W2

Cornwallis District Inter-Church Council
Pres., Mr. Tom Regan, Centreville, R.R. #2, Kings County, Nova Scotia BOT 1JO

Halifax-Dartmouth Council of Churches
Rev. Robert L. Johnson, 2021 Oxford St., Halifax, Nova Scotia B3L 2T3

Industrial Cape Breton Council of Churches
Mr. Allison Turnbull, 1736 George St., Sydney, Nova Scotia B1P 1P4

Kentville and District Council of Churches

Mrs. R. A. McNamara, 673 West Main St., Kentville, Nova Scotia B4N 1L6

Mahone Bay Inter-Church Council

Mrs. Phyllis Smeltzer, R. R. 1, Mahone Bay, Nova Scotia B0J 2E0

Pictou County Council of Churches

Mr. Alan Flemming, 265 Meadowlark Dr., New Glasgow, Nova Scotia B2H 1S2

Queen's County Council of Churches

Rev. Robert L. Johnson, P.O. Box 394, Milton, Nova Scotia B0T 1P0

Wolfville Inter-Church Council

Rev. D. H. Stokes, Box 89, St. Francis of Assisi Church, Wolfville, Nova Scotia B0P 1X0

ONTARIO

Burlington Inter-Church Council

Ms. Albert Nutt, 208-2289 Fairview St., Burlington, Ontario L7R 2E3

Ottawa Christian Council of the Capital Area

Rev. Don Frieson, 301-56 Spraks St., Ottawa, Ontario K1P 1A9

Glengarry-Prescott-Russell Christian Council

Pres., Rev. G. Labrosse, St.-Eugene, Prescott, Ontario K0B 1P0

Hamilton and District Christian Churches Association

Chpsn., Rev. Dr. John A. Johnston, 147 Chedoke Ave., Hamilton, Ontario L8P 4P2

Kitchener-Waterloo Council of Churches

Rev. Eric Reble, Box 803, Kitchener, Ontario N2G 4C5

London Inter-Church Council

Rev. R. Breitwieser, 172 High St., London, Ontario N6C 4K6

Manitoulin (Western Manitoulin Inter-Church Council)

Mrs. Peggy Noble, Silver Water, Ontario P0P 1Y0

Massey Inter-Church Council

Rev. Hope Jackson, Box 248, Massey, Ontario P0P 1P0

Stratford & District Council of Churches

Sr. Mary Teresa Antaya, 36 Well St., Stratford, Ontario N5A 3L7

Thorold Inter-Faith Council

Sec., Mrs. Ruth Pett, 1 Dunn St., St. Catharines, Ontario L2T 1P3

PRINCE EDWARD ISLAND

Charlottetown Christian Council

Miss Bernice Rowland, 131 North River Rd., Apt. C3, Charlottetown, Prince Edward Island C1A 3K9

Summerside Christian Council

Mr. James A. Connell, 329 Argyle St., Summerside, Prince Edward Island C1N 1Y8

West Prince Christian Council

Rev. Kenneth C. Jones, Box S, Ellerslie, Prince Edward Island C0B 1J0

QUÉBEC

Montréal Council of Churches

Rev. Stéphane Valiquette, 2065 Sherbrooke St., W., Montréal, Québec H3H 1G6

Ecumenical Council of Churches/ Downtown Montreal

Rev. Vernon Wishart, 3407 Avenue de Musee, Montréal, Québec H3G 2C6

SASKATCHEWAN

Saskatoon Council of Churches

Sr. M. Flory, 816 Spadina Cres., E.,Saskatoon, Saskatchewan S7K 3H4

9. THEOLOGICAL SEMINARIES AND BIBLE COLLEGES IN THE UNITED STATES

The following list of theological seminaries also includes certain departments of colleges and universities in which ministerial training is given. This list has been checked with the *Education Directory* published by the U. S. Office of Education, and with other directories. The compilation is fairly complete for Protestant and Jewish institutions and for the larger Roman Catholic seminaries. The listing of accredited Bible Colleges comes from the American Association of Bible Colleges.

The listings follow this order: Institution, affiliation, location, head, telephone number.

Abilene Christian University, Chs. of Chr. Abilene TX 79699. William J. Teague. Tel. (915)674-2000.

Academy of the New Church (Theol. Sch.), Gen. Ch. of the New Jerusalem. 2815 Huntingdon Pike, Bryn Athyn PA 19009. R. S. Junge. Tel. (215)947-4200

Alabama Christian School of Religion, Chs. of Chr. 7500 Taylor Rd., P.O. Box 17096, Montgomery AL 36117. Rex A. Turner, Jr. Tel. (205)277-2277; 1-800-351-3939.

Alaska Bible College, interdenom. P.O. Box 289, Glennallen AK 99588. Gene Mayhew. Tel. (907)822-3201.

Alliance Theological Seminary, Nyack College, Chr. and Miss. All. Nyack NY 10960. David L. Rambo. Tel. (914)358-1710

American Baptist College, Natl. Bapt., U.S.A., Inc.; So. Bapt. Conv. 1800 White's Creek Pike, Nashville TN 37207. Odell McGlothian, Sr. Tel. (615)262-1369.

American Baptist Seminary of the West, Amer. Bapt. 2515 Hillegass, Berkeley CA 94704. Wesley H. Brown. Tel. (415)841-1905.

Anderson School of Theology, Ch. of God. Anderson IN 46012. Jerry C. Grubbs. Tel. (317)641-4032

Andover Newton Theol. Sch., Amer. Bapt.; U. Ch. of Christ. 210 Herrick Rd., Newton Centre MA 02159. George Peck. Tel. (617)964-1100

Appalachian Bible College, indep. Bradley WV 25818. Daniel L. Anderson. Tel. (304)877-6428

Aquinas Institute of Theology, 3642 Lindell Blvd., St. Louis MO 63108. John F. Taylor. Tel. (314)658-3882

Arizona College of the Bible, nondenom. 2045 W. Northern Ave., Phoenix AZ 85021. Leonard W. Fleming. Tel. (602)995-2670

Arlington Baptist College. 3001 W. Division, Arlington TX 76012. Wayne Martin. Tel. (817)461-8741

Asbury Theol. Sem., interdenom. Wilmore KY 40390. David McKenna. Tel. (606)858-3581

Ashland Theol. Sem., Breth. Ch. Ashland OH 44805. Joseph R. Shultz. Tel. (419)289-4142

Assemblies of God Theological Seminary, Assemblies of God. 1445 Boonville Ave., Springfield MO 65802. H. Glynn Hall. Tel. (417)862-3344

Atlanta Christian College, Ch. of Christ. 2605 Ben Hill Rd., East Point GA 30344. James C. Donovan. Tel. (404)761-8861

Austin Presbyterian Theol. Sem., PCUSA. 100 E. 27th St., Austin TX 78705. Jack L. Stotts. Tel. (512)472-6736

Azusa Pacific University, interdenom. Citrus and Alosta, Azusa CA 91702. Paul E. Sago. Tel. (818)969-3434

Bangor Theol. Sem., U. Ch. of Christ. 300 Union St., Bangor ME 04401. Malcolm Warford. Tel. (207)942-6781

Baptist Bible College, Bapt. 628 E. Kearney, Springfield MO 65803. Leland Kennedy. Tel. (417)869-9811

Baptist Bible College and Seminary, Bapt. 538 Venard Rd., Clarks Summit PA 18411. Milo Thompson, Jr. Tel. (717)587-1172

Baptist Missionary Association Theol. Sem., Bapt. Missionary Assoc. of Amer. 1410 E. Pine, Jacksonville TX 75766. Philip R. Bryan. Tel. (214)586-2501

Berean Christian College, interdenom. 6801 Millmark Ave., Long Beach CA 90805. A. A. Bachman. Tel. (213)438-9302

Berkeley Divinity Sch. at Yale, Epis. New Haven CT 06511. James E. Annand. Tel. (203)432-6106

Bethany Bible College, Assem. of God. 800 Bethany Dr., Scotts Valley, CA 95066. Richard Foth. Tel. (408)438-3800

Bethany Lutheran Theol. Sem., Evang. Luth. Synod. 447 N. Division St., Mankato MN 56001. W. W. Petersen. Tel. (507)625-2977

Bethany Theol. Sem., Ch. of Breth. Butterfield and Meyers Rd., Oak Brook IL 60521. Warren F. Groff. Tel. (312)620-2200

Bethel Theol. Sem., Bapt. Gen. Conf. St. Paul MN 55112. George K. Brushaber. Tel. (612)638-6230

Beulah Heights Bible College, Pentecostal. 892-906 Berne St. S.E., Atlanta GA 30316. James B. Keiller. Tel. (404)627-2681

Biblical Theological Seminary, interdenom. 200 N. Main St., Hatfield PA 19440. David G. Dunbar. Tel. (215)368-5000

Biola University, Interdenom., 13800 Biola Ave., La-Miranda, CA 90639. Clyde Cook. Tel. (213)944-0351.

Boston University (Sch. of Theol.), U. Meth. 745 Commonwealth Ave., Boston MA 02215. Richard Nesmith. Tel. (617)353-3051

Brite Divinity Sch., Texas Christian University, Christian Ch. (Disc.). P.O. Box 32923, Fort Worth TX 76129. M. Jack Suggs. Tel. (817)921-7575

Calvary Bible College, nondenom. Kansas City MO 64147. Leslie Madison. Tel. (816)322-0110

Calvin Theol. Sem., Christian Ref. Grand Rapids MI 49506. J. A. DeJong. Tel. (616)957-6036

Catholic Theological Union, Cath. 5401 S. Cornell Ave., Chicago IL 60615. John E. Linnan. Tel. (312)324-8000

Catholic University of America (Theol. College), 401 Michigan Ave. N.E., Washington DC 20017. Lawrence B. Terrien. Tel. (202)635-5900

Central Baptist College, Bapt. CBC Station, Conway AR 72032. James R. Raines. Tel. (501)329-6872

Central Baptist Theol. Sem. in Indiana, Natl. Bapt., U.S.A.; Natl. Bapt. Conv. of America; Prog. Natl. Bapt. 1519-65 Martindale Ave., Indianapolis IN 46202. F. Benjamin Davis. Tel. (317)636-6622

Central Baptist Theol. Sem., Amer. Bapt. Kansas City KS 66102. John R. Landgraf. Tel. (913)371-5313

Central Bible College, Assem. of God. 3000 N. Grant Ave., Springfield MO 65803. H. Maurice Lednicky. Tel. (417)833-2551

Central Christian Col. of the Bible, Chr. Chs. 911 E. Urbandale, Moberly MO 65270. Lloyd M. Pelfrey. Tel. (816)263-3900

Central Wesleyan College, Wesleyan Ch. Wesleyan Dr., Central SC 29630. John Newby. Tel. (803)639-2453

Chicago Theol. Sem., U. Ch. of Christ. 5757 University Ave., Chicago IL 60637. Kenneth B. Smith. Tel. (312)752-5757

Christ the King Sem., Cath. 711 Knox Rd., P.O. Box 607, East Aurora NY 14052. Kevin E. Macklin. Tel. (716)652-8900

Christ the Savior Sem., Am. Carpatho-Russ; Orth. Greek Cath. Diocese. 225 Chandler Ave., Johnstown PA 15906. John R. Martin. Tel. (814)539-8086

Christian Theol. Sem., Christian Ch. (Disc.). 1000 W. 42nd St., Indianapolis IN 46208. Richard D. N. Dickinson. Tel. (317)924-1331

Church Divinity Sch. of the Pacific, Epis. 2451 Ridge Rd., Berkeley CA 94709. William S. Pregnall. Tel. (415)848-3282

Cincinnati Bible College, CC/CC. 2700 Glenway Ave., Cincinnati OH 45204. Ronald G. Geary. Tel. (513)244-8100

Circleville Bible College, Chs. of Chr. in Christian Union. P.O. Box 458, Circleville OH 43113. Douglas Carter. Tel. (614)474-8896

Clear Creek Baptist Bible College, So. Bapt., 300 Clear Creek Rd., Pineville, KY 40977. Leon Simpson. Tel. (606)337-3196.

Colgate Rochester Divinity School/Bexley Hall/Crozer Theological Seminary, multidenom. 1100 S. Goodman St., Rochester NY 14620. Larry L. Greenfield. Tel. (716)271-1320

Colorado Christian College, interdenom. 180 S. Garrison St., Lakewood, CO 80226. Joe L. Wall. Tel. (303)238-5386

Columbia Biblical Seminary and Graduate School of Missions, interdenom. P.O. Box 3122, Columbia SC 29230. J. Robertson McQuilkin. Tel. (803)754-4100

Columbia Theol. Sem., PCUSA. Decatur GA 30031. Douglas Oldenburg. Tel. (404)378-8821

Concordia Sem., Luth. Ch.—Mo. Synod. St. Louis (Clayton) MO 63105. Karl L. Barth. Tel. (314)721-5934

Concordia Theol. Sem., Luth. Ch.—Mo. Synod. Ft. Wayne IN 46825. Robert Preus. Tel. (219)482-9611

Covenant Theol. Sem., Presb. Ch. in Amer. 12330 Conway Rd., St. Louis MO 63141. Paul Kooistra. Tel. (314)434-4044

The Criswell College, Bapt. 525 N. Ervay, Dallas TX 75201. L. Paige Patterson. Tel. (214)954-0012

Dallas Christian College, Chr. Chs. 2700 Christian Pky., Dallas TX 75234. Gene Shepherd. Tel. (214)241-3371

Dallas Theol. Sem., interdenom. 3909 Swiss Ave., Dallas TX 75204. Donald K. Campbell. Tel. (214)824-3094

De Sales School of Theology, Cath. 721 Lawrence St. N.E., Washington DC 20017. John W. Crossin. Tel. (202)269-9412

Denver Conservative Bapt. Sem., Cons. Bapt. Box 10,000, Denver CO 80210. Haddon Robinson. Tel. (303)761-2482

Disciples Divinity House, Univ. of Chicago, Chr. Ch. (Disc. of Christ). 1156 E. 57th St., Chicago IL 60637. W. Clark Gilpin. Tel. (312)643-4411

Dominican House of Studies (Pontifical Faculty of the Immaculate Conception). 487 Michigan Ave. N.E., Washington DC 20017. William C. Dettling. Tel. (202)529-5300

Drew University (Theol. School), U. Meth. Madison NJ 07940. Thomas W. Ogletree. Tel. (201)377-3000

Dubuque, Univ. of (Theol. Sem.), PCUSA. 2000 University, Dubuque IA 52001. Walter F. Peterson. Tel. (319)589-3222

Duke University (Divinity Sch.), U. Meth. Durham NC 27706. Dennis M. Campbell. Tel. (919)684-4041

Earlham School of Religion, Friends (Quakers). Richmond IN 47374. Tom Mullen. Tel. (317)983-1423

East Coast Bible College, Ch. of God, 6900 Wilkinson Blvd., Charlotte, NC 28214. Ronald Martin. Tel. (704)394-2307

Eastern Baptist Theol. Sem., Amer. Bapt. City Line and Lancaster Ave., Philadelphia PA 19151. Robert A. Seiple. Tel. (215)896-5000

Eastern Mennonite Seminary, Menn. Ch. Harrisonburg VA 22801. Joseph L. Lapp. Tel. (703)433-2771

Eden Theol. Sem., U. Ch. of Christ. 475 E. Lockwood Ave., St. Louis MO 63119. Vacant. Tel. (314)961-3627

Emmanuel Col. Sch. of Chr. Ministries, Pent. Holiness. P.O. Box 129, Franklin Springs GA 30639. David Hopkins. Tel. (404)245-7226

Emmaus Bible College, Indep., 2570 Asbury Rd., Dubuque, IA. Daniel Smith. Tel. (319)588-8000

Emory University (The Candler Sch. of Theol.), U. Meth. Atlanta GA 30322. Jim L. Waits. Tel. (404)727-6324

Episcopal Divinity Sch., Epis. 99 Brattle St., Cambridge MA 02138. Otis Charles. Tel. (617)868-3450

Episcopal Theol. Sem. of the Southwest, Epis. P.O. Box 2247, Austin TX 78768. Durstan R. McDonald. Tel. (512)472-4133

Erskine Theol. Sem., Assoc. Ref. Presb. P.O. Box 171, Due West SC 29639. R. T. Ruble. Tel. (803)379-8885

Eugene Bible College. 2155 Bailey Hill Rd., Eugene OR 97405. Donald R. Bryan. Tel. (503)485-1780

Evangelical Sch. of Theol., Evangel. Congreg. Ch. 121 S. College St., Myerstown PA 17067. Ray A. Seilhamer. Tel. (717)866-5775

Evangelical Theol. Sem., Inc., 2302-2400 E. Ash St., Goldsboro NC 27530. William Ralph Painter. Tel. (919) 735-0831

Faith Baptist Bible College and Seminary, Bapt. 1900 N.W. 4th St., Ankeny IA 50021. Robert Domokos. Tel. (515)964-0601

Florida Christian College, Chr. Ch. 1011 Osceola Blvd., Kissimmee, FL 32743. A. Wayne Lowen. Tel. (305) 847-8966

Fort Wayne Bible College, Miss. Ch. 1025 W. Rudisill Blvd., Fort Wayne IN 46807. Donald D. Gerig. Tel. (219)456-2111

Franciscan Sch. of Theol., Cath. 1712 Euclid Ave., Berkeley CA 94709. Xavier J. Harris. Tel. (415)848-5232

Free Will Baptist Bible College, Free Will Bapt. 3606 West End Ave., Nashville TN 37205. Charles A. Thigpen. Tel. (615)383-1340

Friends Bible College, Friends. P.O. Box 288, Haviland KS 67059. Robin W. Johnston. Tel. (316)862-5252

Fuller Theol. Sem., multidenom. 135 N. Oakland Ave., Pasadena CA 91182. David A. Hubbard. Tel. (818)584-5200

Garrett-Evangelical Theol. Sem., U. Meth. 2121 Sheridan Rd., Evanston IL 60201. Neal F. Fisher. Tel. (312)866-3900

General Theol. Sem., Epis. 175 Ninth Ave., New York NY 10011. James C. Fenhagen. Tel. (212)243-5150

George Mercer, Jr., Memorial Sch. of Theol., Epis. 65 Fourth St., Garden City NY 11530. George Hill. Tel. (516)248-4800

God's Bible School and College, Indep., 1810 Young St., Cincinnait, OH 45210. Bence Miller. Tel. (513)721-7944

Golden Gate Bapt. Theol. Sem., S. Bapt. Strawberry Point, Mill Valley CA 94941. Harold K. Graves, Interim. Tel. (415)388-8080

Gordon-Conwell Theological Seminary, interdenom. South Hamilton MA 01982. Robert E. Cooley. Tel. (617)468-7111

Goshen Biblical Sem., Menn. 3003 Benham Ave., Elkhart IN 46517. Marlin E. Miller. Tel. (219)295-3726

Grace Bible College, Grace Gospel Fell. P.O. Box 910, Grand Rapids MI 49509. Samuel R. Vinton, Jr. Tel. (616)538-2330

Grace College of the Bible, indep. 1515 S. 10th St., Omaha 68108. Warren E. Bathke. Tel. (402)449-2800

Grace Theol. Sem., Fellowship of Grace Breth. 200 Seminary Dr., Winona Lake IN 46590. John J. Davis. Tel. (219)372-5100

Graduate Theol. Union, nondenom. 2400 Ridge Rd., Berkeley CA 94709. Michael J. Blecker. Tel. (415)649-2000

Great Lakes Bible College, Ch. of Christ/Chr. Ch. P.O. Box 40060, Lansing MI 48901. Vacant. Tel. (517)321-0242

Greenville College, Free Meth. 315 E. College Ave., Greenville IL 62246. W. Richard Stephens. Tel. (618)664-1840

Harding University Graduate School of Religion, Chs. of Chr. 1000 Cherry Rd., Memphis TN 38117. C. Philip Slate. Tel. (901)761-1352.

Hartford Seminary, interdenom. Hartford CT 06105. Michael R. Rion. Tel. (203)232-4451

Harvard Divinity School, nondenom. 45 Francis Ave., Cambridge MA 02138. Ronald F. Thiemann. Tel. (617)495-5761

Hebrew Union College—Jewish Inst. of Religion, Jewish. 3101 Clifton Ave., Cincinnati OH 45220, Tel. (513)221-1875; 1 W. 4th St., New York NY 10012, Tel. (212)674-5300; 3077 University, Los Angeles CA 90007, Tel. (213)749-3424; 13 King David St., Jerusalem, Israel, Tel. 02-232444. Alfred Gottschalk

Hobe Sound Bible College, Indep., P. O. Box 1065, Hobe Sound, FL 33455. Robert Whitaker. Tel. (305)546-5534

Holy Cross School of Theology (Hellenic College), Greek Orthodox. 50 Goddard Ave., Brookline MA 02146. Alkiviadis Calivas. Tel. (617)731-3500

Holy Trinity Orthodox Seminary, Russian Orthodox. Jordanville NY 13361. Archbishop Laurus (Skurla). Tel. (315)858-0940

Hood Theological Seminary, A.M.E. Zion. Salisbury NC 28144. William F. Lawrence, Jr. Tel. (704)633-7960

Howard University Divinity School, interdenom. 1400 Shepherd St., N.E., Washington DC 20017. Tel. (202)269-1122

Huntington College, Graduate School of Christian Ministries, U. B. in Christ. Huntington IN 46750. Paul R. Fetters. Tel. (219)356-6000

Iliff School of Theol., The, U. Meth. 2201 S. University Blvd., Denver CO 80210. Donald Edward Messer. Tel. (303)744-1287

Immaculate Conception Sem. at Seton Hall Univ., Cath. South Orange NJ 07079. Richard M. Liddy. Tel. (201)761-9575

Interdenominational Theol. Center. 671 Beckwith St. S.W., Atlanta GA 30314. James H. Costen. Tel. (404)527-7702

Jesuit School of Theology at Berkeley, Cath. 1735 LeRoy Ave., Berkeley CA 94709. Thomas F. Gleeson. Tel. (415)841-8804

Jewish Theol. Sem. of America, Jewish. 3080 Broadway, New York NY 10027. Ismar Schorsch. Tel. (212)678-8000

John Wesley College. 2314 N. Centennial St., High Point NC 27260. Brian C. Donley. Tel. (919)889-2262

Johnson Bible College, Christian Chs. Kimberlin Hts., Knoxville TN 37998. David L. Eubanks. Tel. (615)573-4517

Kentucky Christian College, Chr. Ch. Grayson KY 41143. L. Palmer Young. Tel. (606)474-6613

Lancaster Bible College, interdenom. 901 Eden Rd., Lancaster PA 17601. Gilbert A. Peterson. Tel. (717)569-7071

Lancaster Theol. Sem. of the U. Ch. of Christ. Lancaster PA 17603. Peter M. Schmiechen. Tel. (717)393-0654

Lexington Theol. Sem. (formerly College of the Bible, The), Chr. Ch. (Disc.). 631 S. Limestone, Lexington KY 40508. _____. Tel. (606)252-0361

L.I.F.E. Bible College, Intl. Ch. Foursquare Gospel. 1100 Glendale Blvd., Los Angeles CA 90026. Jack E. Hamilton. Tel. (213)413-1234

Lincoln Christian College and Seminary, CC/CC. Box 178, Lincoln IL 62656. Charles A. McNeely. Tel. (217)732-3168

Loma Linda University, Seventh-day Adv. Loma Linda Campus, Loma Linda CA 92350, Tel. (714)824-4300; La Sierra Campus, Riverside CA 92515. Norman J. Woods. Tel. (714)785-2022

Louisville Presbyterian Theol. Sem., PCUSA. 1044 Alta Vista Rd., Louisville KY 40205. John M. Mulder. Tel. (502)895-3411

Luther Northwestern Theological Sem., Ev. Luth. Ch. in Am., 2481 Como Ave. W., St. Paul MN 55108. David L. Tiede. Tel. (612)641-3456

Lutheran Bible Institute in California, Luth., 641 S. Western Ave., Anaheim, CA 92804. Clifton Pederson

Luther Bible Institute of Seattle, Luth. Providence Heights, Issaquah WA 98027. C. Jack Eichhorst. Tel. (206)392-0400

Lutheran Brethren Seminary, Ch. of the Luth. Breth. Fergus Falls MN 56537. Rev. O. Gjerness. Tel. (218)739-3375

Lutheran Sch. of Theol. at Chicago, Ev. Luth. Ch. in Amer. 1100 E. 55th St., Chicago IL 60615. William E. Lesher. Tel. (312)753-0700

Lutheran Theol. Sem., Ev. Luth. Ch. in Amer. Gettysburg PA 17325. Herman G. Stuempfle. Tel. (717)334-6286

Lutheran Theol. Sem. at Philadelphia, Ev. Luth. Ch. in Amer. 7301 Germantown Ave., Mt. Airy, Philadelphia PA 19119. John W. Vannorsdall. Tel. (215)248-4616

Lutheran Theol. Southern Sem., Ev. Luth. Ch. in Amer. Columbia SC 29203. Mack C. Branham, Jr. Tel. (803)786-5150

Manhattan Christian College, Christian Churches. 1407 Anderson, Manhattan KS 66502. Kenneth Cable. Tel. (913)539-3571

Marion College (Div. of Religion and Philosophy), Wesleyan Ch. 4201 S. Washington, Marion IN 46953. R. Duane Thompson. Tel. (317)674-6901

Mary Immaculate Sem., Cath. 300 Cherryville Rd., Box 27, Northampton PA 18067. Thomas F. Hoar. Tel. (215)262-7866

Maryknoll School of Theology (Cath. For. Miss. Soc. of Amer., Inc.). Maryknoll NY 10545. John J. Casey. Tel. (914)941-7590

McCormick Theol. Sem., PCUSA. 5555 S. Woodlawm Ave., Chicago IL 60637. David Ramage, Jr. Tel. (312)241-7800

Meadville/Lombard Theol. Sch., Unit. Univ. 5701 S. Woodlawn Ave., Chicago IL 60637. Gene Reeves. Tel. (312)753-3195

Memphis Theol. Sem. of the Cumberland Presbyterian Church, 168 E. Parkway S., Memphis TN 38104. J. David Hester. Tel. (901)458-8232

Mennonite Biblical Sem., Gen. Conf. Menn. 3003 Benham Ave., Elkhart IN 46517. Henry Poettcker. Tel. (219)295-3726

Mennonite Brethren Biblical Sem., Menn. Breth. Ch. 4824 E. Butler at Chestnut Ave., Fresno CA 93727. Larry D. Martens. Tel. (209)251-8628

Meth. Theol. Sch. in Ohio, U. Meth. 3081 Columbus Pike, Delaware OH 43015. Norman E. DeWire. Tel. (614)363-1146

Miami Christian College, interdenom. 2300 N.W. 135th St., Miami FL 33167. George S. Pearson. Tel. (305)685-7431

Mid-America Bible College, Ch. of God, 3500 SW 119th St., Oklahoma City, OK 73170. John Conley. Tel. (405)691-3800

Mid-South Bible College, non-affiliated. 2485 Union Ave., P.O. Box 12144, Memphis TN 38112. Robert J. Hilgenberg. Tel. (901)458-7466

Midwestern Bapt. Theol. Sem., S. Bapt. 5001 N. Oak Trafficway, Kansas City MO 64118. Milton Ferguson. Tel. (816)453-4600

Minnesota Bible College, Ch. of Christ. 920 Mayowood Rd. S.W., Rochester MN 55902. Donald Lloyd. Tel. (507)288-4563

Moody Bible Institute, interdenom. 820 N. La Salle Dr., Chicago IL 60610. Joseph M. Stowell, III. Tel. (312)329-4000

Moravian Theol. Sem., Morav. Bethlehem PA 18018. William W. Matz. Tel. (215)861-1516

Moreau Sem. (Holy Cross Fathers), Cath. Notre Dame IN 46556. John C. Gerber. Tel. (219)283-7735

Morehouse School of Religion, Amer. Bapt.; Prog. Natl. Bapt.; Natl. Bapt. Conv. of Amer.; Natl. Bapt. Conv., U.S.A., Inc.; So. Bapt. Conv. 645 Beckwith St. S.W., Atlanta GA 30314. Edward L. Wheeler. Tel. (404)688-6743

Mt. Angel Sem., Cath. St. Benedict OR 97373. J. Terrence Fitzgerald. Tel. (503)845-3030

Mt. St. Mary's Sem., Cath. Emmitsburg MD 21727. Richard M. McGuinness. Tel. (301)447-5295

Mt. St. Mary's Sem. of the West, Cath. 6616 Beechmont Ave., Cincinnati OH 45230. James J. Walsh.

Multnomah School of the Bible, interdenom. 8435 N.E. Glisan St., Portland OR 97220. Joseph C. Aldrich. Tel. (503)255-0332

Mundelein Seminary of the Univ. of St. Mary-of-the-Lake, Cath. Mundelein IL 60060. Gerald F. Kicanas. Tel. (312)566-6401

Nashotah House (Theol. Sem.), Epis. Nashotah WI 53058. Jack C. Knight. Tel. (414)646-3371

Nazarene Bible College, Naz. Box 15749, Colorado Springs CO 80935. Jerry Lambert. Tel. (303)596-5110

Nazarene Theol. Sem., Naz. 1700 E. Meyer Blvd., Kansas City MO 64131. Terrell C. Sanders, Jr. Tel. (816)333-6254

Nebraska Christian College, Chr. Ch. 1800 Syracuse Ave., Norfolk, NE 68701. Richard Wamsley. Tel. (402)371-5960

New Brunswick Theol. Sem., Ref. Amer. 17 Seminary Pl., New Brunswick NJ 08901. Robert A. White. Tel.(201)247-5241

New Orleans Baptist Theol. Sem., S. Bapt. New Orleans LA 70126. Landrum P. Leavell II. Tel. (504)282-4455

New York Theol. Sem., interdenom. 5 W. 29th St., New York NY 10001. Keith A. Russell. Tel. (212)532-4012

North American Baptist Sem., N. Amer. Bapt. Conf. 1321 W. 22nd St., Sioux Falls SD 57105. Charles M. Hiatt. Tel. (605)336-6588

North Central Bible College, Assem. of God. 910 Elliot Ave. S., Minneapolis MN 55404. Don Argue. Tel. (612)332-3491

North Park Theol. Sem., Ev. Cov. Ch. 3225 W. Foster Ave., Chicago IL 60625. David G. Horner. Tel. (312)478-2696

Northeastern Bible College, interdenom. 12 Oak La., Essex Fells NJ 07021. Robert W. Benton. Tel. (201)226-1074

Northern Bapt. Theol. Sem., Amer. Bapt. 660 E. Butterfield Rd., Lombard IL 60148. William R. Myers. Tel. (312)620-2101

Northwest Col. of the Assemb. of God, Assem. of God. P.O. Box 579, Kirkland WA 98083. D. V. Hurst. Tel. (206)822-8266

Notre Dame Sem., Cath. 2901 S. Carrollton Ave., New Orleans LA 70118. Robert J. Stahl. Tel. (504)866-7426

Oblate College, Cath. 391 Michigan Ave. N.E., Washington DC 20017. Richard J. Murphy. Tel. (202)529-6544

Oblate School of Theology, Cath. 285 Oblate Dr., San Antonio TX 78216. Patrick Guidon. Tel. (512)341-1366

Ozark Christian College, CC/CC. 1111 N. Main St., Joplin MO 64801. Ken Idleman. Tel. (417)624-2518

Pacific Christian College, nondenom. 2500 E. Nutwood Ave., Fullerton CA 92631. Knofel L. Staton. Tel. (714)879-3901

Pacific Lutheran Theol. Sem., Ev. Luth. Ch. in Am., 2770 Marin Ave., Berkeley CA 94708. Walter M. Stuhr. Tel. (415)524-5264

Pacific Sch. of Religion, interdenom. 1798 Berkeley CA 94709. Neely D. McCarter. Tel. (415)848-0528

Payne Theol. Sem., A.M.E. P.O. Box 474, Wilberforce OH 45384. John E. Brandon. Tel. (513)376-2946

Pepperdine Univ., Chs. of Chr. Malibu CA 90265. David Davenport. Tel. (213)456-4500

Perkins Sch. of Theol. (Southern Methodist Univ.), U. Meth. Dallas TX 75275. James E. Kirby, Jr. Tel. (214)692-2138

Philadelphia College of Bible, interdenom. Langhorne Manor, Langhorne PA 19047. W. Sherrill Babb. Tel. (215)752-5800

Phillips University Graduate Seminary, Chr. Chs. (Disc.). Box 2000, University Sta., Enid OK 73702. Roger Sizemore. Tel. (405)237-4433

Piedmont Bible College, Bapt. 716 Franklin St., Winston-Salem NC 27101. Donald K. Drake. Tel. (919)725-8344

Pittsburgh Theol. Sem., PCUSA. Pittsburgh PA 15206. Carnegie Samuel Calian. Tel. (412)362-5610

Point Loma Nazarene College, Naz. San Diego CA 92106. Jim Bond. Tel. (619)221-2200

Pontifical College Josephinum, Cath. 7625 N. High St., Columbus OH 43085. Dennis F. Sheehan. Tel. (614)885-5585

Pope John XXIII National Seminary, Cath. 558 South Ave., Weston MA 02193. Cornelius M. McRae. Tel. (617)899-5500

Practical Bible Training School, Independent. Drawer A, Bible School Park, NY 13737. Woodrow Kroll. Tel. (607)729-1581

Presbyterian School of Christian Education, PCUSA. 1205 Palmyra Ave., Richmond VA 23227. Heath K. Rada. Tel. (804)359-5031

Princeton Theol. Sem., PCUSA. CN821, Princeton NJ 08542. Thomas W. Gillespie. Tel. (609)921-8300

Protestant Episcopal Theol. Sem. in Virginia, Epis. Alexandria VA 22304. Richard Reid. Tel. (703)370-6600

Puget Sound Christian College, Chr. Chs. 410 Fourth Ave. N., Edmonds WA 98020. Glen R. Basey. Tel. (206)775-8686

Rabbi Isaac Elchanan Theol. Sem. (affil. of Yeshiva Univ.), Orth. Jewish. 2540 Amsterdam Ave., New York NY 10033. Zevulun Charlop. Tel. (212)960-5344

Reconstructionist Rabbinical College, Jewish. Church Rd. and Greenwood Ave., Wyncote PA 19095. Arthur Green. Tel. (215)576-0800

Reformed Bible College, Interdenom., 1869 Robinson Rd. S.E., Grand Rapids MI 49506. Edwin D. Roels. Tel. (616)458-0404

Reformed Presbyterian Theol. Sem., Ref. Presb. Ch. of N. Amer. 7418 Penn Ave., Pittsburgh PA 15208. Bruce C. Stewart. Tel. (412)731-8690

Reformed Theol. Sem., interdenom. 5422 Clinton Blvd., Jackson MS 39209. Luder G. Whitlock, Jr. Tel. (601)922-4988

Roanoke Bible College, Chs. of Ch. P.O. Box 387, Elizabeth City NC 27909. William A. Griffin. Tel. (919)338-5191

Saint Bernard's Institute, Cath. 1100 S. Goodman St., Rochester NY 14620. Sebastian A. Falcone. Tel. (716)271-1320

St. Charles Borromeo Sem., Cath. Overbrook, Philadelphia PA 19151. Francis X. DiLorenzo. Tel. (215)839-3760

St. Francis Seminary School of Pastoral Ministry, Cath. 3257 S. Lake Dr., Milwaukee WI 53207. Daniel J. Packenham. Tel. (414)744-1730

St. John's Sem., Cath. Brighton MA 02135. Thomas J. Daly. Tel. (617)254-2610

St. John's Sem., Cath. Camarillo CA 93010. George H. Niederauer. Tel. (805)482-2755

St. John's University, School of Theology, Cath. Collegeville MN 56321. Daniel R. Finn. Tel. (612)363-2100

St. Joseph's Sem., Cath. 201 Seminary Ave., (Dunwoodie), Yonkers NY 10704. Edwin F. O'Brien. Tel. (914)968-6200

St. Louis Christian College, Chr. Chs. 1360 Grandview Dr., Florissant MO 63033. Thomas W. McGee. Tel. (314)837-6777

St. Louis Roman Cath. Theol. Sem. (Kenrick Sem.), Cath. 5200 Glennon Dr., St. Louis MO 63119. Ronald W. Ramson. Tel. (314)644-0266

St. Mary Sem., Cath. 1227 Ansel Rd., Cleveland OH 44108, Allan R. Laubenthal. Tel. (216)721-2100

St. Mary's Sem., Cath. 9845 Memorial Dr., Houston TX 77024. Chester L. Borski. Tel. (713)686-4345

St. Mary's Sem. and Univ., Cath. 5400 Roland Ave., Baltimore MD 21210. Robert F. Leavitt. Tel. (301)323-3200

St. Meinrad School of Theology, Cath. St. Meinrad IN 47577. Eugene Hensell. Tel. (812)357-6611

St. Patrick's Sem., Cath. 320 Middlefield Rd., Menlo Park CA 94025. Howard P. Bleichner. Tel. (415)325-5621

St. Paul Bible College, Chr. and Miss. All., Bible College MN 55375. Bill W. Lanpher. Tel. (612)446-1411

Saint Paul Sch. of Theol., U. Meth. 5123 Truman Rd., Kansas City MO 64127. Lovett H. Weems. Tel. (816)483-9600

St. Paul Sem. School of Divinity, Cath. 2260 Summit Ave., St. Paul MN 55105. Charles Froehle. Tel. (612)698-0323

St. Thomas Sem., Cath. Denver CO 80210. John E. Rybolt. Tel. (303)722-4687

St. Tikhon's Orthodox Theol. Sem., Russian Orth. South Canaan PA 18459. Bishop Herman. Tel. (717)937-4686

St. Vincent de Paul Regional Seminary, Cath. 10701 S. Military Trail, Box 460, Boynton Beach FL 33436. Joseph L. Cunningham. Tel. (305)732-4424

St. Vincent Sem., Cath., Latrobe PA 15650. John E. Haag. Tel. (412)539-9761

St. Vladimir's Orth. Theol. Sem., Eastern Orth. 575 Scarsdale Rd., Crestwood NY 10707. Metropolitan Theodosius. Tel. (914)961-8313

SS. Cyril and Methodius Sem., Cath. Orchard Lake MI 48033. Stanley E. Milewski. Tel. (313)682-1885

San Francisco Theol. Sem., PCUSA. San Anselmo CA 94960. J. Randolph Taylor. Tel. (415)258-6500

San Jose Bible College, nondenom. 790 South 12th St., P.O. Box 1090, San Jose CA 95108. Bryce L. Jessup. Tel. (408)293-9058

Savonarola Theol. Sem., Pol. Natl. Cath. 1031 Cedar Ave., Scranton PA 18505. Thaddeus F. Zielinski. Tel. (717)343-0100

Sch. of Theol. at Claremont, U. Meth.; Christian Ch. (Disc.); Epis. Claremont CA 91711. Richard W. Cain. Tel. (714)626-3521

Seabury-Western Theol. Sem., Epis. 2122 Sheridan Rd., Evanston IL 60201. M. S. Sisk. Tel. (312)328-9300

Seminario Evangelico de Puerto Rico, interdemon., 776 Ponce de Leon Ave., Hato Rey, PR 00918. Luis Fidel Mercado. Tel. (809)751-6483

Seminary of the Immaculate Conception, Cath. West Neck Rd., Huntington NY 11743. John J. Strynkowski. Tel. (516)423-0483

Seventh-day Adventist Theol. Sem., Andrews Univ., Seventh-day Adv. Berrien Springs MI 49104. Gerhard F. Hasel. Tel. (616)471-3536

Seventh Day Bapt. Center on Ministry, Seventh Day Bapt. Gen. Conf. 3120 Kennedy Rd., P.O. Box 1678, Janesville WI 53547. J. Paul Green. Tel. (608)752-5055

Shaw Divinity School, Natl. Bapt. Raleigh NC 27611. James Z. Alexander. Tel. (919)755-4846

Simpson College, Chr. and Miss. All. 801 Silver Ave., San Francisco CA 94134. Francis Grubbs. Tel. (415)334-7400

Southeastern Baptist Theol. Sem., S. Bapt. Wake Forest NC 27587. W. Randall Lolley. Tel. (919)556-3101

Southeastern Bible College, interdenom. 2901 Pawnee Ave., Birmingham AL 35256. James G. Kallam. Tel. (205)251-2311

Southeastern College of the A/G, Assem. of God. 1000 Longfellow Blvd., Lakeland FL 33801. James L. Hennesy. Tel. (813)665-4404

Southern Baptist Theol. Sem., S. Bapt. Louisville KY 40280. Roy Lee Honeycutt, Jr. Tel. (502)897-4011

Southwestern Assemblies of God College, Assemb. of God. 1200 Sycamore St., Waxahachie TX 75165. Paul Savell. Tel. (214)937-4010

Southwestern Baptist Theol. Sem., S. Bapt. P.O.Box 22000, Fort Worth TX 76122. Russell H. Dilday. Tel. (817)923-1921

Southwestern Conservative Baptist Bible College, Bapt. 2625 East Cactus Rd., Phoenix AZ 85032. Wesley A. Olsen. Tel. (602)992-6101

Starr King Sch. for the Ministry, Unit. Berkeley CA 94709. Gordon B. McKeeman. Tel. (415)845-6232

Swedenborg Sch. of Religion (formerly New Church Theol. Sch.), Genl. Conv., Swedenborgian Ch. 48 Sargent St., Newton MA 02158. Mary Kay Klein. Tel. (617)244-0504

Talbot School of Theology, interdenom. 13800 Biola Ave., La Mirada CA 90639. W. Bingham Hunter. Tel. (213)944-0351

Tennessee Temple Univ., Bapt. 1815 Union Ave., Chattanooga TN 37404. Don Jennings. Tel. (615)698-4100

Theol. Sem. of the Ref. Epis. Ch., Ref. Epis. 4225 Chestnut St., Philadelphia PA 19104. Leonard W. Riches. Tel. (215)222-5158

Toccoa Falls College, Chr. and Miss. All. Toccoa Falls GA 30598. Paul L. Alford. Tel. (404)886-6831

Trevecca Nazarene College (Relig. Dept.), Naz. 333 Murfreesboro Rd., Nashville TN 37203. H. Ray Dunning. Tel. (615)248-1387

Trinity Bible College, Assem. of God. Ellendale ND 58436. Lowell Lundstrom. Tel. 349-3621 (ND); 1-800-523-1603

Trinity Evangel. Divinity Sch., Evangel. Free Ch. of Amer. 2065 Half Day Rd., Deerfield IL 60015. Kenneth M. Meyer. Tel. (312)945-8800

Trinity Lutheran Seminary, Ev. Luth. Ch. in Am. 2199 East Main St., Columbus OH 43209. Fred W. Meuser. Tel. (614)235-4136

Union Theol. Sem., interdenom. 3041 Broadway, New York NY 10027. Donald W. Shriver, Jr. Tel. (212)662-7100

Union Theol. Sem. in Va., PCUSA. 3401 Brook Rd., Richmond VA 23227. T. Hartley Hall IV. Tel. (804)355-0671

United Theol. Sem., U. Meth. 1810 Harvard Blvd., Dayton OH 45406. Leonard I. Sweet. Tel. (513)278-5817

United Theol. Sem. of the Twin Cities, U. Ch. of Christ. 3000 Fifth St. N.W., New Brighton MN 55112. Benjamin Griffin. Tel. (612)633-4311

United Wesleyan College, Wes. Ch. 1414 East Cedar St., Allentown PA 18103. John P. Ragsdale. Tel. (215)439-8709

University of Chicago (Divinity Sch.), interdenom. Swift Hall, Chicago IL 60637. Franklin I. Gamwell. Tel. (312)702-8221

University of Notre Dame, Dept. of Theology, Cath. Notre Dame IN 46556. Richard P. McBrien. Tel. (219)239-7811

University of St. Thomas, School of Theology, Cath. St. Mary's Campus, 9845 Memorial Dr., Houston TX 77024. Virgile Blanchard. Tel. (713)686-4345

University of the South (Sch. of Theol.), Epis. Sewanee TN 37375. Robert Giannini. Tel. (615)598-5931

Valley Forge Christian College, Assem. of God. Charlestown Rd., Phoenixville PA 19460, Wesley W. Smith. Tel. (215)935-0450

Vanderbilt University (Divinity Sch.), interdenom. Nashville TN 37240. H. Jackson Forstman. Tel. (615)322-2776

Vennard College, interdenom. University Park IA 52595. Warthen T. Isreal. Tel. (515)673-8391

Virginia Union University (Sch. of Theol.), Bapt. 1601 W. Leigh St., Richmond VA 23220. Henry H. Mitchell. Tel. (804)257-5715

Walla Walla College (Sch. of Theol.), Seventh-day Adv. College Pl., Walla Walla WA 99324. John Brunt. Tel. (509)527-2195

Wartburg Theol. Sem., Ev. Luth. Ch. in Am., 333 Wartburg Pl., Dubuque IA 52001. Roger Fjeld, actg. Tel. (319)589-0200

Washington Bible College/Capital Bible Seminary, interdenom. 6511 Princess Garden Pkwy., Lanham MD 20706. Harry E. Fletcher. Tel. (301)552-1400

Washington Theological Consortium and Washington Institute of Ecumenics, 487 Michigan Ave. N.E., Washington DC 20017. Daniel Martensen. Tel. (202)832-2675.

Washington Theological Union, Cath. 9001 New Hampshire Ave., Silver Spring MD 20903. Vincent D. Cushing. Tel. (301)439-0551

Wesley College, Cong. Meth. P.O. Box 70, Florence MS 39073. Roman J. Miller. Tel. (601)845-2265

Wesley Theol. Sem., U. Meth. 4500 Massachusetts Ave. N.W., Washington DC 20016. Douglass Lewis. Tel. (202)885-8600

West Coast Christian College, Ch. of God. 6901 N. Maple Ave., Fresno CA 93710. Allen McCray. Tel. (209)299-7201

Western Baptist College. 5000 Deer Park Dr. S.E., Salem OR 97301. John G. Balyo. Tel. (503)581-8600

Western Conservative Baptist Sem., Cons. Bapt. 5511 S.E. Hawthorne Blvd., Portland OR 97215. Earl D. Radmacher. Tel. (503)233-8561

Western Evangelical Seminary, interdenom. 4200 S.E. Jennings Ave., Portland OR 97267. Leo M. Thornton. Tel. (503)654-5466

Western Theol. Sem., Ref. Ch. in Amer. Holland MI 49423. Marvin D. Hoff. Tel. (616)392-8555

Westminster Theol. Sem., Presb. Chestnut Hill, Philadelphia PA 19118. George C. Fuller. Tel. (215)887-5511

Weston School of Theol., Cath. 3 Phillips Pl., Cambridge MA 02138. Edward M. O'Flaherty. Tel. (617)492-1960

William Tyndale College, interdenom. 35700 W. Twelve Mile Rd., Farmington Hills MI 48018. William A. Shoemaker. Tel. (313)553-7200

Winebrenner Theol. Sem., Churches of God, Gen. Conf. 701 E. Melrose Ave., P.O. Box 478, Findlay OH 45839. G. E. Weaver. Tel. (419)422-4824

Wisconsin Lutheran Sem., Luth. (Wis.). 11831 N. Seminary Dr., 65W, Mequon WI 53092. Armin Panning. Tel. (414)242-7200

Yale University (Divinity Sch.), nondenom. New Haven CT 06510. Leander E. Keck. Tel. (203)432-5307

10. CANADIAN THEOLOGICAL SEMINARIES AND FACULTIES, AND BIBLE SCHOOLS

The following list has been developed by direct correspondence with the institutions involved and is, therefore, a current and reasonably comprehensive list of the major Canadian theological seminaries and faculties, and Bible schools. The editor of the **Yearbook** would be grateful for knowledge of any significant omissions from this compilation. Listings are alphabetical by name of institution and generally have the following order: Institution, affiliation, location, head, telephone number.

Acadia Divinity College, Un. Bapt. Conv. of the Atlantic Provinces. Wolfville, Nova Scotia B0P 1X0. Andrew D. MacRae. Tel. (902)542-2285

Alberta Bible College, CC/CC. 599 Northmount Dr. N.W., Calgary, Alberta T2K 3J6. Tel. (403)282-2994

Aldersgate College, Free Meth. Ch. Box 460, Moose Jaw, Saskatchewan S6H 4P1. Norman Swanson, Interim. Tel. (306)693-7773

Arthur Turner Training School, Ang. Ch. of Canada. Pangnirtung, Northwest Territories X0A 0R0. Tel. (819)473-8768

Atlantic Baptist College, Un. Bapt. Conv. of the Atlantic Provinces. Box 1004, Moncton, New Brunswick EIC 8P4. W. Ralph Richardson. Tel. (506)858-8970

Atlantic School of Theology, ecumenical (Ang. Ch. of Canada; Cath.; Un. Ch. of Canada). Halifax, Nova Scotia B3H 3B5. G. Russell Hatton. Tel. (902)423-6801

Baptist Leadership Training School, Bapt. Un. of Western Canada. 4330 16th St. S.W., Calgary, Alberta T2T 4H9. Kenneth W. Bellous. Tel. (403)243-3770

Bethany Bible College—Canada. Main St., Sussex, New Brunswick E0E 1P0. Ronald E. Mitchell. Tel. (506)433-3668

Bethany Bible Institute, Menn. Br. Chs. Box 160, Hepburn, Saskatchewan S0K 1Z0. Cliff Jantzen. Tel. (306)947-2175

Briercrest Bible College, interdenom. Caronport, Saskatchewan S0H 0S0. Henry H. Budd. Tel. (306)756-2321

Brockville Bible College, Stand. Ch. of Am. Box 1900, Brockville, Ontario K6V 6N4. Tel. (613)342-2730

Canadian Bible College, Chr. and Miss. All. 4400-4th Ave., Regina, Saskatchewan S4T 0H8. Rexford Boda. Tel. (306)545-1515

Canadian Lutheran Bible Institute, Luth. 4837 52A St., Camrose, Alberta T4V 1W5. Tel. (403)672-4454

Canadian Mennonite Bible College. 600 Shaftesbury Blvd., Winnipeg, Manitoba R3P 0M4. John H. Neufeld. Tel. (204)888-6781

Canadian Nazarene College, Ch. of the Naz. 1301 Lee Blvd., Winnipeg, Manitoba R3T 2P7. Neil E. Hightower. Tel. (204)269-2120

Canadian Reformed Churches, Theol. College of the, Can. Ref. Chs. 110 West 27th St., Hamilton, Ontario L9C 5A1. J. Faber.

Canadian Theological Seminary, Chr. and Miss. All. 4400-4th Ave., Regina, Saskatchewan S4T 0H8. Rexford Boda. Tel. (306)545-1515

Catherine Booth Bible College, Salv. Army. 340 Assiniboine Ave., Winnipeg, Manitoba R3C 0Y1. Major Earl Robinson. Tel. (204)947-6701

Central Baptist Seminary and Bible College, Fell. of Evan. Bapt. Chs.in Canada. 95 Jonesville Cres., Toronto, Ontario M4A 1H3. George D. Bell. Tel. (416)752-1976

Central Pentecostal College, Pent. Assem. of Canada. 1303 Jackson Ave., Saskatoon, Saskatchewan S7H 2M9. J. Harry Faught. Tel. (306)374-6655

Centre d'Etudes Théologiques Evangéliques, Un. d' Eglises Bapt. Françaises au Canada. 2285, avenue Papineau, Montréal, Québec H2K 4J5. W. N. Thomson. Tél. (514)526-6643

Centre for Christian Studies, Ang. Ch. of Canada; Un. Ch. of Canada. 77 Charles St. W., Toronto, Ontario M5S 1K5. Gwyneth Griffith. Tel. (416)923-1168

Christianview Bible College, Pent. Holiness Chs. of Canada. 164 George St., Ailsa Craig, Ontario N0M 1A0. Tel. (519)293-3506

Church Army Training College, Ang. Ch. of Canada. 397 Brunswick Ave., Toronto, Ontario M5R 2Z2. Capt. P. Noll. Tel. (416)924-9279

College Dominicain de Philosophie et de Théologie, Cath. 96 avenue Empress, Ottawa, Ontario K1R 7G3. Gilles D. Mailhiot. Tel. (613)233-5696

College of Emmanuel and St. Chad, Ang. Ch. of Canada. Saskatoon, Saskatchewan S7N 0W6. J. Russell Brown. Tel. (306)343-1353

Columbia Bible College, Menn. Breth.; Gen. Conf. Menn. 2940 Clearbrook Rd., Clearbrook, British Columbia V2T 2Z8. Walter Unger. Tel. (604)853-3358

Concordia Lutheran Seminary, Luth. Ch.-Canada. 7040 Ada Blvd., Edmonton, Alberta T5B 4E3. Milton L. Rudnick. Tel. (403)474-1468

Concordia Lutheran Theological Seminary, Luth. Ch.-Canada. 470 Glenridge Ave., Box 1117, St. Catharines, Ontario L2R 7A3. Howard Kramer. Tel. (416)688-2362

Covenant Bible College, Ev. Cov. Ch. of Canada. 245-21st St. E., Prince Albert, Saskatchewan S6V 1L9. W. B. Anderson. Tel. (306)922-3443

Eastern Pentecostal Bible College, Pent. Assem. of Canada. 780 Argyle St., Peterborough, Ontario K9H 5T2. R. W. Taitinger. Tel. (705)748-9111

Elim Bible Institute, Conf. of Menn. in Manitoba. Box 120 Altona, Manitoba R0G 0B0. Victor Kliewer. Tel. (204)324-8631

Emmanuel Bible College, Miss. Ch. 100 Fergus Ave., Kitchener, Ontario N2A 2H2. Ellis A. Lageer. Tel. (519)742-3572

Emmanuel College (see **Toronto School of Theology**)

Ewart College, Presby. Ch. in Canada. 156 St. George St., Toronto, Ontario M5S 2G1. Irene Dickson. Tel. (416)979-2501.

Full Gospel Bible Institute, Apost. Ch. of Pent. Box 579, Eston, Saskatchewan S0L 1A0. A. B. Mortensen. Tel. (306)962-3621

Gardner Bible College, Ch. of God (And.). 4704 55th St., Camrose, Alberta T4V 2B6. Robert Hazen. Tel. (403)672-0171

Great Lakes Christian College, Chs. of Christ. 310 King St. E., Box 399, Beamsville, Ontario L0R 1B0. Edwin L. Broadus. Tel. (416)563-5374

Hillcrest Christian College, Ev. Ch. 2801-13th Ave. S.E., Medicine Hat, Alberta T1A 3R1. Kervin Raugust. Tel. (403)526-6951

Huron College, Ang. Ch. of Canada. Faculty of Theology, London, Ontario N6G 1H3. Charles Jago. Tel. (519)438-7224

Institut Biblique Béthel, transdenom. C.P. 1600, Sherbrooke, Québec J1H 5M4. Tel. (819)569-3257

Institut Biblique Laval, Menn. Breth. 1775, boul. Edouard-Laurin, Ville Saint-Laurent, Québec H4L 2B9. Tél. (514)332-9326

International Bible College, Ch. of God (Cleveland, TN). 401 Trinity La., Moose Jaw, Saskatchewan S6H 0E3. Tel. (306)692-4041

Knox College (see Toronto School of Theology)

Lutheran Theological Seminary, Ev. Luth. Ch. in Canada. Saskatoon, Saskatchewan S7N 0X3. Roger Nostbakken. Tel. (306)343-8204

Maritime Christian College, CC/CC. Box 1145, 223 Kent St., Charlottetown, Prince Edward Island C1A 7M8. Stewart J. Lewis. Tel. (902)894-3828

McMaster Divinity College, Bapt. Conv. of Ontario and Quebec. Hamilton, Ontario L8S 4K1. Melvyn R. Hillmer. Tel. (416)525-9140

Mennonite Brethren Bible College, Menn. Br. 1-169 Riverton Ave., Winnipeg, Manitoba R2L 2E5. David Ewert. Tel. (204)669-6575

Montreal Diocesan Theological College, Ang. Ch. of Canada. 3473 University St., Montreal, Quebec H3A 2A8. A. C. Capon. Tel. (514)849-3004

Mountain View Bible College, Miss. Ch. Box 190, Didsbury, Alberta T0M 0W0. Edward Oke. Tel. (403)335-3337

Newman Theological College, Cath. RR 8, Edmonton, Alberta T5L 4H8. W. Murchland. Tel. (403)459-6656

Nipawin Bible Institute, interdenom. Box 1986, Nipawin, Saskatchewan S0E 1E0. Jake Rempel. Tel. (306)862-3651

North American Baptist College and Divinity School, N. Amer. Bapt. Conf. 11525 - 23rd Ave., Edmonton, Alberta T6J 4T3. J. Walter Goltz. Tel. (403)437-1960

Northwest Baptist Theological College and Seminary, Fell. Bapt. 3358 S.E. Marine Dr., Vancouver, British Columbia V5S 3W3. Doug Harris. Tel. (604)433-2475

Northwest Bible College, Pent. Assem. of Canada. 11617-106 Ave., Edmonton, Alberta T5H 0S1. M. O. Dynna. Tel. (403)452-0808

Okanagan Bible College, interdenom. Box 407, Kelowna, British Columbia V1Y 7N8. Dan Kelly. Tel. (604)860-8080

Ontario Christian Seminary, CC/CC. 260 High Park Ave., Box 324, Sta. D, Toronto, Ontario M6P 3J9. Donald Stevenson. Tel. (416)769-7115

Ontario Theological Seminary, multidenom. 25 Ballyconnor Ct., Willowdale, Ontario M2M 4B3. Wm. J. McRae. Tel. (416)226-6380

Peace River Bible Institute. Box 99, Sexsmith, Alberta T0H 3C0. Harold Peters. Tel. (403)568-3962

Prairie Bible Institute, interdenom. Three Hills, Alberta T0M 2A0. Ted S. Rendall. Tel. (403)443-5511

Presbyterian College. 3495 University St., Montreal, Quebec H3A 2A8. W. J. Klempa. Tel. (514)288-5256

Queen's Theological College, Un. Ch. of Canada. Kingston, Ontario K7L 3N6. Tel. (613)545-2110

Regent College, transdenom. 2130 Wesbrook Mall, Vancouver, British Columbia V6T 1W6. Carl E. Armerding. Tel. (604)224-3245

Regis College (see Toronto School of Theology).

St. Andrew's College, Un. Ch. of Canada. 1121 College Dr., Saskatoon, Saskatchewan S7N 0W3. Tel. (306)966-8970

St. Augustine Seminary (see Toronto School of Theology)

St. John's College, Univ. of Manitoba, Faculty of Theology, Ang. Ch. of Canada. Winnipeg, Manitoba R3T 2M5. Canon James Draper. Tel. (204)474-8518

St. Michael's College, Faculty of Theology (see Toronto School of Theology)

St. Peter's Seminary, Cath. 1040 Waterloo St., London, Ontario N6A 3Y1. P. W. Fuerth. Tel. (519)432-1824

St. Stephen's College, Graduate and Continuing Theological Education for Clergy and Laity, Un. Ch. of Canada. University of Alberta Campus, Edmonton, Alberta T6G 2J6. Garth I. Mundle. Tel. (403)439-7311

Salvation Army College for Officer Traning, The, Salv. Army. 2130 Bayview Ave., Toronto, Ontario M4N 3K6. Donald Kerr. Tel (416)481-6131

Steinbach Bible College, Menn. Box 1420, Steinbach, Manitoba R0A 2A0. Ben Eidse. Tel. (204)326-6451

Swift Current Bible Institute, Menn. Box 1268, Swift Current, Saskatchewan S9H 3X4. David Hall. Tel. (306)773-0604

Toronto Baptist Seminary and Bible College, Bapt. 337 Jarvis St., Toronto, Ontario M5B 2C7. Norman Street, G. A. Adams. Tel. (416)925-3263

Toronto School of Theology (a federation of 7 theological colleges: 3 Roman Catholic, 2 Anglican, 1 Presbyterian, and 1 United Church of Canada. Affiliated with the University of Toronto. McMaster Divinity College is an associate member.). 47 Queen's Park Crescent E., Toronto, Ontario M5S 2C3. E. James Reed. Tel. (416)978-4039

Emmanuel College, Un. Ch. of Canada. 75 Queen's Park Crescent, Toronto, Ontario M5S 1K7. C. Douglas Jay. Tel. (416)585-4539

Knox College, Presb. Ch. in Canada. 59 St. George St., Toronto, Ontario M5S 2E6. Donald J. M. Corbett. Tel. (416)978-4500

Regis College, Cath. 15 St. Mary St., Toronto, Ontario M4Y 2R5. Jacques Monet. Tel. (416)922-5474

St. Augustine's Seminary of Toronto, Cath. 2661 Kingston Rd., Scarborough, Ontario M1M 1M3. James Wingle. Tel. (416)261-7207.

Trinity College, Faculty of Divinity, Ang. Ch. of Canada. 6 Hoskin Ave., Toronto, Ontario M5S 1H8. E. R. Fairweather. Tel. (416)978-2525

University of St. Michael's College, Faculty of Theology, Cath. 81 St. Mary St., Toronto, Ontario M5S 1J4. Michael A. Fahey. Tel. (416)926-7140

Wycliffe College, Ang. Ch. of Canada. 5 Hoskin Ave., Toronto, Ontario M5S 1H7. P. R. Mason. Tel. (416)979-2870

Trinity College (see Toronto School of Theology)

United Theological College, Un. Ch. of Can. 3521 University St., Montreal, Quebec H3A 2A9

Université de Montréal, Faculté de théologie, Cath. C. P.

211

6128, Montréal Québec H3C 3J7. André Charron. Tel. (514)343-7167

Université de Sherbrooke, Faculté de théologie, Cath. Cité Universitaire, 2500 Boulevard de l' Université, Sherbrooke, Quebec J1K 2R1. Lucien Vachon. Tél. (819)821-7600

Université Laval, Faculté de théologie, Cath. Cité Universitaire Ste-Foy, Québec G1K 4P7. Jacques Racine. Tel. (418)656-2131

University of Winnipeg, Faculty of Theology, Un. Ch. of Canada. Winnipeg, Manitoba R3B 2E9. H. J. King. Tel. (204)786-9390

Université Saint-Paul, Faculté de théologie, Cath. 223 rue Main, Ottawa, Ontario K1S 1C4. M. Achiel Peelman. Tél. (613)236-1393

Vancouver School of Theology, ecumen. 6000 Iona Dr., Vancouver, British Columbia V6T 1L4. Arthur Van Seters. Tel. (604)228-9031

Waterloo Lutheran Seminary, Ev. Luth. Ch. in Canada. Waterloo, Ontario N2L 3C5. Richard C. Crossman. Tel. (519)884-1970

Western Christian College, Chs. of Christ. North Weyburn, Saskatchewan S0C 1X0. E. Dan Wieb.

Western Pentecostal Bible College, Pent. Assem. of Canada. Box 1000, Clayburn, British Columbia V0X 1E0. James G. Richards. Tel. (604)853-7491

Winkler Bible Institute, Menn. Breth. 121 7th St., South, Winkler, Manitoba R6W 2N4. Eldon DeFehr. Tel. (204)325-4242

Winnipeg Bible College and Theological Seminary. Otterburne, Manitoba R0A 1G0. William R. Eichhorst. Tel. (204)284-2923

Wycliffe College (see **Toronto School of Theology**)

11. CHURCH-RELATED AND ACCREDITED COLLEGES AND UNIVERSITIES IN THE UNITED STATES

The following 680 alphabetically listed Protestant, Catholic, Jewish, and other religious colleges and universities have been identified as four-year, church-related, accredited institutions offering a bachelor's degree. The list does not include junior colleges, teachers' or other professional schools, or bible colleges.

Although there are no up-to-date statistics, it was discovered by the U. S. Office of Education in 1981 that there were 1,978 four-year institutions of higher learning in the U. S. and that 1,420 of these were private. About 51 percent of these private colleges and universities were church-related, and most of the church-related institutions were identified as Protestant, outnumbering the Roman Catholic by roughly two to one.

The term *church-related* is difficult to define since it can mean many different things: church-owned and controlled; colleges and universities with independent boards of trustees, having a relationship to individual denominations through such forms as covenants; denominational representation on boards of trustees, and so on. For a detailed examination of the concept of church-relatedness, see *Church-Related Higher Education: Perceptions and Perspectives,* edited by Robert Rue Parsonage (Valley Forge, Pa.: Judson Press, 1978).

A majority of church-related colleges and universities identify themselves in various directories of higher education as church-controlled or affiliated. Many colleges and universities not so identified nevertheless maintain a degree of church-relatedness to a specific denomination or group of denominations. These institutions can be identified only by consulting denominational records or other private sources. This was done in the preparation of the list that follows. Abbreviations for nationally recognized regional Accrediting Associations are as follows:

MS   Middle States Association of Colleges and Schools
NC   North Central Association of Colleges and Schools
NE   New England Association of Schools and Colleges
NW   Northwest Association of Schools and Colleges
S   Southern Association of Schools and Colleges
West   Western Association of Schools and Colleges

Other abbreviations are as follows:
C   Coeducational   W   Women
M   Men   Co-Ord.   Coordinate

Each item in the listing below has the following order: Name of institution, address, telephone number, head of institution, nature of student body, accrediting, denominational relationship, enrollment.

Abilene Christian University, Abilene TX 97699. Tel. (915) 674-2000. John C. Stevens, C S, Chs. of Christ, 4,505

Academy of the New Church, Byrn Athyn, PA 19009, Tel. (215) 947-4200. Geoffrey S. Childs, C MS, Ch. of New Jerusalem, 156

Adrian College, Adrian, MI 49221, Tel. (517) 265-5161. Donald S. Stanton, C NC, Un. Meth. 1,139

Agnes Scott College, Decatur, GA 30030, Tel. (404) 371-6000. Ruth A. Schmidt, W S, PCUSA, 495

Alaska Pacific University, Anchorage, AK 99508, Tel. (907) 561-1266. Dr. Glenn A. Olds, C NW, Un. Meth., 699

Albertus Magnus College, New Haven, CT 06511, Tel. (203) 773-8550. Sr. Julia McNamara, C NE, Cath., 490

Albion College, Albion, MI 49224, Tel. (517) 629-5511. Melvin L. Vulgamore, C NC, Un. Meth., 1,571

Albright College, Reading, PA 19612, Tel. (215) 921-2381. David G. Ruffer, C MS, Un. Meth., 2,053

Alderson-Broaddus College, Philippi, WV 26416, Tel. (304) 457-1700. W. Christian Sizemore, C NC, Am. Bapt., 742

Allegheny College, Meadville, PA 16335, Tel. (814) 724-3100. Daniel F. Sullivan, C MS, Un. Meth., 1,905

Allentown College of Saint Francis de Sales, Center Valley, PA 18034, Tel. (215) 282-1100. Daniel G. Gambet, C MS, Cath., 1,407

Alma College, Alma, MI 48801, Tel. (517) 463-7111. Gordon E. Areen, Interim, C NC, PCUSA, 1,012

Alvernia College, Reading, PA 19607, Tel. (215) 777-5411. Sr. M. Dolorey, C MS, Cath., 779

Alverno College, Milwaukee, WI 53215, Tel. (414) 382-6000. Sr. M. Joel Read, W NC, Cath., 1,704

Amber University, 1700 Eastgate Dr., Garland, TX 75041. Tel. (214) 279-6511. Douglas W. Warner, C S, Chs. of Christ, 858

American University, The, Washington, DC 20016, Tel. (202) 885-1000. Richard Berendzen, C MS, Un. Meth., 10,662

Anderson University, Anderson, IN 46012, Tel. (317) 649-9071. Robert A. Nicholson, C NC, Ch. of God, (And.), 1,970

Andrews University, Berrien Springs, MI 49104, Tel. (616) 471-7771. W. Richard Lescher, C NC, S.D.A., 3,032

Anna Maria College, Paxton, MA 01612, Tel. (617) 757-4586. Sr. Bernadette Madore, C NE, Cath., 1,447

Antillian College, Mayaguez, PR 00709, Tel. (918) 834-9595. James D. Unger, C MS, S.D.A., 867

Aquinas College, Grand Rapids, MI 49506, Tel. (616) 459-8281. Peter D. O'Connor, C NC, Cath., 2,724

Arkansas College, Batesville, AR 72503, Tel. (501) 793-9813. Dan C. West, C NC, PCUSA, 705

Ashland College, Ashland, OH 44805, Tel. (419) 289-4142. Joseph R. Schultz, C NC, Breth. Ch., 3,486

Assumption College, Worcester, MA 01609, Tel. (617) 752-5615. Joseph H. Hagen, C NE, Cath., 2,629

Atlantic Christian College, Wilson, NC 27893, Tel. (919) 237-3161. James B. Hemby, Jr., C S, Christian Church (Disc.), 1,278

Atlantic Union College, South Lancaster, MA 01561, Tel. (617) 365-4561. Lawrence T. Geraty, C NE, S.D.A., 548

Augsburg College, Minneapolis, MN 55454, Tel. (612) 330-1000. Charles S. Anderson, C NC, ELCA, 1,802

Augustana College, Rock Island, IL 61201, Tel. (309) 794-7000. J. Thomas Tredway, C NC, ELCA, 2,160

Augustana College, Sioux Falls, SD 57197, Tel. (605) 336-0770. Lloyd Svendsbye, C NC, ELCA, 1,866

Aurora University, Aurora, IL 60507, Tel. (312) 892-6431. Alan J. Stone, C NC, Adv. Chr. Ch., 1,489

Austin College, Sherman, TX 75090, Tel. (214) 892-9101. Harry E. Smith, C S, PCUSA, 1,198

Averett College, Danville, VA 24541, Tel. (804) 793-7811. Frank R. Campbell, C S, Bapt., 953

Avila College, Kansas City, MO 64145, Tel. (816) 942-8400. Larry Kramer, C NC, Cath., 1,499

Baker University, Baldwin City, KS 66006, Tel. (913) 594-6451. Daniel M. Lambert, C NC, Un. Meth., 840

Baldwin-Wallace College, Berea, OH 44017, Tel. (216) 826-2900. Neal Malicky, C NC, Un. Meth., 4,071

Baltimore Hebrew College, Baltimore, MD 21215, Tel. (301) 578-6900. Leivy Smolar, C MS, Jewish, 211

Baptist College at Charleston, Charleston, SC 29411, Tel. (803) 797-4011. Jairy C. Hunter, C S, So. Bapt., 1,459

Barat College, Lake Forest, IL 60045, Tel. (312) 234-3000. Richard Soter, C NC, Cath., 606

Barber-Scotia College, Concord, NC 28025, Tel. (704) 786-5171. Mable P. McLean, C S, PCUSA, 379

Bard College, Annandale-on-Hudson, NY 12504, Tel. (914) 758-6822. Leon Botstein, C MS, Epis., 710

Barry University, Miami, FL 33161, Tel. (305) 758-3392. Sr. Jeanne O'Laughlin, C S, Cath., 3,930

Bartlesville Wesleyan College, Bartlesville, OK 74006, Tel. (918) 333-6151. Paul R. Mills, C NC, Wesleyan Ch., 516

Bayamon Central University, Bayamon, PR 00621, Tel. (809) 786-3030. Vincent A. M. Van Rooij, C MS, Cath., 2,801

Baylor University, Waco, TX 76798, Tel. (817) 755-1011. Herbert H. Reynolds, C S, So. Bapt., 11,481

Beaver College, Glenside, PA 19038, Tel. (215) 572-2900. Bette E. Landman, C MS, PCUSA, 2,004

Belhaven College, Jackson, MS 39202, Tel. (601) 968-5919. Newton Wilson, C S, PCUSA, 737

Bellarmine College, Louisville, KY 40205, Tel. (502) 452-8211. Eugene V. Petrik, C S, Cath., 2,664

Belmont Abbey College, Belmont, NC 28012, Tel. (704) 825-3711. John R. Dempsey, C S, Cath., 936

Belmont College, Nashville, TN 37203, Tel. (615) 383-7001. William E. Troutt, C S, So. Bapt., 2,257

Beloit College, Beloit, WI 53511, Tel. (608) 365-3391. Roger Hull, C NC, U. Ch. of Christ, 1,027

Benedict College, Columbia, SC 29204, Tel. (803) 256-4220. Marshall C. Grigsby, C S, Am. Bapt., 1,373

Benedictine College, Atchison, KS 66002. Tel. (913) 367-6110. Sr. Katherine Deloney, C NC, Cath., 860

Bennett College, Greensboro, NC 27401, Tel. (919) 273-4431. Gloria R. Scott, W S, Un. Meth. 566

Bethany College, Bethany, WV 26032, Tel. (304) 829-7000. Todd H. Bullard, C NC, Christian Church (Disc.), 774

Bethany College, Lindsborg, KS 67456, Tel. (913) 227-3311. Peter J. Ristuben, C NC, ELCA, 731

Bethany Nazarene College, Bethany, OK 73708, Tel. (405) 789-6400. Ponder W. Gilliland, C NC, Nazarene, 1,287

Bethel College, McKenzie, TN 38201, Tel. (901) 352-5321. William L. Odom, C S, Cumb. Presb., 469

Bethel College, North Newton, KS 67117, Tel. (316) 283-2500. Harold J. Schultz, C NC, Gen. Conf. Menn. Ch., 623

Bethel College, Mishawaka, IN 46545, Tel. (219) 259-8511. James A. Bennett, C NC, Miss. Ch., 573

Bethel College, St. Paul, MN, 55112, Tel. (612) 638-6400. George K. Brushaber, C NC, Bapt. Gen'l Conf., 1,791

Bethune-Cookman College, Daytona Beach, FL 32015, Tel. (904) 255-1401. Oswald P. Bronson, C S, Un. Meth., 1,781

Birmingham-Southern College, Birmingham, AL 35254, Tel. (205) 266-4600. Neil B. Berte, C S, Un. Meth., 1,656

Blackburn College, Carlinville, IL 62626, Tel. (217) 854-3231. William F. Denman, C NC, PCUSA, 468

Bloomfield College, Bloomfield, NJ 07003, Tel. (201) 748-9000. John F. Noonan, C MS, PCUSA, 1,436

Blue Mountain College, Blue Mountain, MS 38610, Tel. (601) 685-4771. E. Harold Fisher, W S, So. Bapt., 276

Bluefield College, Bluefield, VA 24605, Tel. (703) 326-3682. Charles L. Tyer, C S, So. Bapt., 335

Bluffton College, Bluffton, OH 45817, Tel. (419) 358-8015. Elmer Neufeld, C NC, Menn. Ch., 594

Borromeo College of Ohio, Wickliffe, OH 44092, Tel. (216) 585-5900. James L. Caddy, M NC, Cath., 94

Boston College, Chestnut Hill, MA 02167, Tel. (617) 552-8000. J. Donald Monan, C NE, Cath., 14,473

Brescia College, Owensboro, KY 42301, Tel. (502) 685-3131. Sr. Ruth Gehres, C S, Cath., 744

Briar Cliff College, Sioux City, IA 51104, Tel. (712) 279-5321. Sr. Margaret Wick, Interim, C NC, Cath., 1,313

Bridgewater College, Bridgewater, VA 22812, Tel. (703) 828-2501. Wayne F. Geisert, C S, Ch. Breth., 739

Brigham Young University, Provo, UT 84602 Tel. (801) 378-1211. Jeffrey R. Holland, C NW, L.D.S., 29,800

Brigham Young University, Hawaii Campus, Laie Oahu, HI 96762, Tel. (808) 233-3211. Alton L. Wade, L.D.S., 1,936

Buena Vista College, Storm Lake, IA 50588, Tel. (712) 749-2351. Keith G. Briscoe, C NC PCUSA, 2,009

Cabrini College, Radnor, PA 19087, Tel. (215) 687-2100. Sr. Eileen Currie, C MS, Cath., 1,000

Caldwell College, Caldwell, NJ 07006, Tel. (201) 228-4424. Sr. Vivian Jennings, C MS, Cath., 669

California Baptist College, Riverside, CA 92504, Tel. (714) 689-5771. Russell R. Tuck, C West, So. Bapt., 597

California Lutheran University, Thousand Oaks, CA 91360, Tel. (805) 492-2411. Jerry H. Miller, C West, ELCA, 2,274

Calumet College of St. Joseph, Whiting, IN 46394, Tel. (219) 473-7770. Dennis C. Rittenmeyer, C NC, Cath., 1,073

Calvin College, Grand Rapids, MI 49506, Tel. (616) 957-6000. Anthony J. Diekema, C NC, Christ. Ref., 4,012

Campbell University, Buies Creek, NC 27506, Tel. (919) 893-4111. Norman A. Wiggins, C S, So. Bapt., 3,238

Campbellsville College, Campbellsville, KY 42718, Tel. (502) 465-8158. W. R. Davenport, C S, So. Bapt., 641

Canisius College, Buffalo, NY 14208, Tel. (716) 883-7000. James M. Demske, C MS, Cath., 4,155

Capital University, Columbus, OH 43209, Tel. (614) 236-6011. Josiah H. Blackmore, Interim, CNC, ELCA, 2,594

Cardinal Stritch College, Milwaukee, WI 53217, Tel. (414) 352-5400. Sr. M. Camille Kliebhan, C NC, Cath., 2,123

Carleton College, Northfield, MN 55057, Tel. (507) 663-4000. David H. Porter, C NC, U. Ch. of Christ, 1,877

Carlow College, Pittsburgh, PA 15213. Tel. (412) 578-6000. Sr. Marylouise Fennell, W MS, Cath., 1,174

Carroll College, Helena, MT 59625, Tel. (406) 442-3450. Francis J. Kerins, C NW, Cath., 1,501

Carroll College, Waukesha, WI 53186, Tel. (414) 547-1211. Robert V. Cramer, C NC, PCUSA, 1,705

Carson-Newman College, Jefferson City, TN 37760, Tel. (615) 475-9061. J. Cordell Maddox, C S, So. Bapt., 1,631

Carthage College, Kenosha, WI 53141, Tel. (414) 551-8500. F. Gregory Campbell, C NC, ELCA, 1,473

Catawba College, Salisbury, NC 28144, Tel. (704) 637-4111. Stephen H. Wurster, C S, U. Ch. of Christ, 905

Cathedral College of the Immaculate Conception, Douglaston, NY 11362, Tel. (212) 631-4600. James P. Grace, M MS, Cath., 83

Catholic University of America, Washington, DC 20064, Tel. (202) 635-5000. William J. Byron, C MS, Cath., 6,651

Catholic University of Puerto Rico, Ponce, PR 00732, Tel. (809) 844-4150. Tosello Giangiacomo, C MS, Cath., 13,308

Cedar Crest College, Allentown, PA 18104, Tel. (215) 437-4471. Gene S. Cesari, W MS, U. Ch. of Christ, 1,157

Cedarville College, Cedarville, OH 45314, Tel. (513) 766-2211. Paul H. Dixon, C NC, Bapt., 1,817

Centenary College of Louisiana, Shreveport, LA 71134, Tel. (318) 869-5011. Donald A. Webb, C S., Un. Meth., 965

Centenary College, Hackettstown, NJ 07840. Tel. (201) 852-1400. Stephanie M. Bennett, W MS, Un. Meth., 1,063

Central Methodist College, Fayette, MO 65248, Tel. (816) 248-3391. Joseph A. Howell, C NC, Un. Meth., 646

Central University of Iowa, Pella, IA 50219, Tel. (515) 628-4151 Kenneth J. Weller, C NC, Ref. in Am., 1,557

Central Wesleyan College, Central, SC 29630, Tel. (803) 639-2453. John M. Newby, C S, Wesleyan Ch., 418

Centre College of Kentucky, Danville, KY 40422, Tel. (606) 236-5211. Richard L. Morrill, C S, PCUSA, 804

Chaminade University of Honolulu, Honolulu, HI 96816, Tel. (808) 735-4711. Raymond A. Roesch, C West, Cath., 2,512

Chapman College, Orange, CA 92666, Tel. (714) 997-6815. G. T. Smith, C West, Christian Church (Disc.), 1,699

Chestnut Hill College, Philadelphia, PA 19118, Tel. (215) 248-7000. Sr. Matthew Anita MacDonald, W MS, Cath., 925

Christ College Irvine, Irvine, CA 92715. Tel. (714) 854-8002. D. Ray Halm, C West, Luth. (Mo.), 394

Christian Brothers College, Memphis, TN 38104, Tel. (901) 722-0200. Bro. Theodore Drahmann, C S, Cath., 1,543

Claflin College, Orangeburg, SC 29115, Tel. (803) 534-2710. Oscar A. Rogers, Jr., C S, Un. Meth., 760

Clark College, Atlanta, GA 30314, Tel. (404) 681-3080 Winifred Harris, Actg., C S, Un. Meth., 1,860

Clarke College, Dubuque, IA 52001, Tel. (319) 588-6300. Catherine Dunn, C NC, Cath., 857

Coe College, Cedar Rapids, IA 52402, Tel. (319) 399-8000. John Brown, C NC, PCUSA, 1,186

College Misericordia, Dallas, PA 18612, Tel. (717) 675-2181. Joseph R. Fink, C MS, Cath., 1,268

College of Great Falls, Great Falls, MT 59405, Tel. (406) 761-8210. William A. Shields, C NW, Cath., 1,078

College of Idaho, Caldwell, ID 83605, Tel. (208) 459-5011. Robert L. Hendron, C NW, PCUSA, 975

College of Mt. St. Joseph, Mt. St. Joseph, OH 45051, Tel. (513) 244-4200. Sr. Francis M. Thrailkill, W NC, Cath., 1,868

College of Mt. St. Vincent, Riverdale, NY 10471, Tel. (718) 549-8000. Sr. Doris Smith, C MS, Cath., 1,050

College of New Rochelle, New Rochelle, NY 10801, Tel. (914) 632-5300. Sr. Dorothy A. Kelly, C MS, Cath., 4,648

College of Notre Dame, Belmont, CA 94002, Tel. (415) 593-1601. Sr. Veronica Skillin, C West, Cath., 1,077

College of Notre Dame of Md., Baltimore, MD 21210. Tel. (301) 435-0100. Sr. Kathleen Feeley, W MS, Cath., 1,712

College of Our Lady of the Elms, Chicopee, MA 01013, Tel. (413) 598-8351. Sr. Mary A. Dooley, W NE, Cath., 865

College of St. Benedict, St. Joseph, MN 56374, Tel. (612) 363-5011. Sr. Colman O'Connell, Co-Ord. NC, Cath., 2,042

College of St. Catherine, St. Paul, MN 55105, Tel. (612) 690-6000. Sr. Anita Pompusch, W NC, Cath., 2,405

College of St. Elizabeth, Convent Sta., NJ 07961, Tel. (201) 292-6300. Sr. Jacqueline Burns, W MS, Cath., 991

College of St. Francis, Joliet, IL 60435, Tel. (815) 740-3360. John C. Orr, C NC, Cath., 4,030

College of St. Joseph, Rutland, VT 05701, Tel. (802) 773-5900. Frank J. Miglorie, Jr., C NE, Cath., 376

College of St. Mary, Omaha, NE 68124, Tel. (402) 399-2400. Kenneth Nielsen, W NC, Cath., 1,009

College of St. Rose, Albany, NY 12203, Tel. (518) 454-5111. Louis Vaccaro, C MS, Cath., 2,886

College of St. Scholastica, Duluth, MN 55811, Tel. (218) 723-6000, Daniel H. Pilon, C NC, Cath., 1,449

College of St. Teresa, Winona, MN 55987, Tel. (507) 454-2930. Sr. Michaea Byron, W NC, Cath., 422

College of St. Thomas, St. Paul, MN 55105, Tel. (612) 647-5000. Terrence J. Murphy, C NC, Cath., 6,765

College of Santa Fe, Santa Fe, NM 87501, Tel. (505) 982-6011. Bill Welch, C NC, Cath., 844

College of the Holy Cross, Worcester, MA 01610, Tel. (617) 793-2011. John E. Brooks, C NE, Cath., 2,695

College of Wooster, Wooster, OH 44691, Tel. (216) 263-2000. Henry J. Copeland, C NC, PCUSA, 1,711

Columbia College, Columbia, SC 29203, Tel. (803) 786-3012. Ralph T. Mirse, W S, Un. Meth., 1,180

Columbia College, Columbia, MO 65216. Tel. (314) 875-8700, Donald B. Ruthenberg, C NC, Christian Ch. (Disc.), 2,950

Columbia Christian College, Portland, OR 97216, Tel. (503) 255-7060. Gary D. Elliott, C NW, Chs. of Christ, 267

Columbia Union College, Takoma Park, MD 20912, Tel. (301) 270-9200, William A. Loveless, C MS, S.D.A., 611

Conception Seminary College, Conception, MO 64433, Tel. (816) 944-2218. Gregory Polen, M NC, Cath., 114

Concordia College, River Forest, IL 60305, Tel. (312) 771-8300. Eugene L. Krentz, C NC, Luth. (Mo.) 1,239

Concordia College, Bronxville, NY 10708, Tel. (914) 337-9300. Ralph C. Schultz, C MS, Luth. (Mo.), 542

Concordia College, Ann Arbor, MI 48105, Tel. (313) 995-7300. David G. Schmiel, C NC, Luth. (Mo.), 433

Concordia College, Portland, OR 97211, Tel. (503) 288-9371. Charles E. Schlimpert, C NW, Luth. (Mo.), 481

Concordia College at Moorhead, Moorhead, MN 56542, Tel. (218) 299-3000. Paul J. Dovre, C NC, ELCA, 2,481

Concordia College—St. Paul, St. Paul, MN 55104, Tel. (612) 641-8278. Alan F. Harre, C NC, Luth. (Mo.), 768

Concordia Lutheran College, Austin, TX 78705, Tel. (512) 452-7661. Ray F. Martens, C S, Luth. (Mo.), 445

Cornell College, Mt. Vernon, IA 52314, Tel. (319) 895-8784. David G. Marker, C NC, Un. Meth., 1,101

Covenant College, Lookout Mountain, TN 30750, Tel. (404) 820-1542. Frank A. Brock, Interim, C S, Preby. Ch in Am., 569

Creighton University, Omaha, NE 68178, Tel. (402) 280-2700. Michael G. Morrison, C NC, Cath., 5,927

Culver-Stockton College, Canton, MO 63435, Tel. (314) 288-5221. Robert W. Brown, C NC, Christian Church (Disc.), 729

Cumberland College, Williamsburg, KY 40769, Tel. (606) 549-2200. James Taylor, C S, So. Bapt., 2,094

Dakota Wesleyan University, Mitchell, SD 57301, Tel. (605) 996-6511. James B. Beddow, C NC, Un. Meth., 692

Dallas Baptist University, Dallas, TX 75211, Tel. (214) 331-8311. W. Marvin Watson, C S, So. Bapt., 1,626

Dallas, University of, Irving, TX 75061, Tel. (214) 519-5000. Robert F. Sasseen, C S, Cath., 2,553

Dana College, Blair, NE 68008, Tel. (402) 426-4101. Myrvin F. Christopherson, C NC, ELCA, 414

David Lipscomb College, Nashville, TN 37204, Tel. (615) 385-3855. Harold Hazelip, C S, Chs. of Christ, 2,232

Davidson College, Davidson, NC 28036, Tel. (704) 892-2000. John W. Kuykendall, , C S, PCUSA, 1,400

Davis and Elkins College, Elkins, WV 26241, Tel. (304) 636-1900. Dorothy I. MacConkey, C NC, PCUSA, 892

Dayton, University of, Dayton, OH 45469, Tel. (513) 229-1000. Bro. Raymond L. Fitz, C NC, Cath., 10,300

Defiance College, Defiance, OH 43512, Tel. (419) 784-4010. Marvin Ludwig, C NC, U. Ch. of Christ, 913

Denver, University of, Denver, CO 80208, Tel. (303) 871-2000. Dwight Smith, C NC, Un. Meth., 7,078

DePaul University, Chicago, IL 60604, Tel. (312) 321-8000. John T. Richardson, C NC, Cath., 12,836

DePauw University, Greencastle, IN 41435, Tel. (317) 658-4800. Robert G. Bottoms, C NC, Un. Meth., 2,398

Detroit, University of, Detroit, MI 48221, Tel. (313) 927-1000. Robert A. Mitchell, C NC, Cath., 5,866

Dickinson College, Carlisle, PA 17013, Tel. (717) 243-5121. A. Lee Fritschler, C MS, Un. Meth. 1,937

Dillard University, New Orleans, LA 70122, Tel. (504) 283-8822. Samuel Dubois Cook, C S., U. Ch. of Christ, Un. Meth., 1,194

Divine Word College, Epworth, IA 52045, Tel. (319) 876-3353. Joseph D. Simon, M NC, Cath., 71

Doane College, Crete, NB 68333, Tel. (402) 826-2161. Frederic D. Brown, C NC, U. Ch. of Christ, 787

Dominican College of Blauvelt, Orangeburg, NY 10962, Tel. (914) 359-7800. Sr. Kathleen Sullivan, C MS, Cath., 1,654

Dominican College of San Rafael, San Rafael, CA 94901, Tel. (415) 457-4440. Neal Webb, C West, Cath., 722

Don Bosco College, Newton, NJ 07860, Tel. (201) 383-3900. Kenneth A. McAlice, M MS, Cath., 62

Dordt College, Sioux Center, IA 51250, Tel. (712) 722-3771. John B. Hulst, C NC, Christ. Ref. Ch., 1,021

Dr. Martin Luther College, New Ulm, MN 54273, Tel. (507) 354-8221. Lloyd C. Huebner, C NC, Wis. Ev. Luth. Synod., 520

Drew University, Madison, NJ 07940, Tel. (201) 377-3000. Paul Hardin, C MS, Un. Meth., 2,354

Drury College, Springfield, MO 65802, Tel. (417) 865-8731. John E. Moore,, Jr., C NC, U. Ch. of Christ, 2,577

Dubuque, University of, Dubuque, IA 52001, Tel. (319) 589-3000. Walter F. Peterson, C NC, PCUSA, 1,157

Duke University, Durham, NC 27706, Tel. (877) 684-7841. Keith H. Brodie, C S, Un. Meth., 10,253

Duquesne University, Pittsburgh, PA 15282, Tel. (412) 434-6000. Donald S. Nesti, C MS, Cath., 6,528

D'Youville College, Buffalo, NY 14201, Tel. (716) 881-3200. Sr. Denise Roche, C MS, Cath., 1,182

Earlham College, Richmond, IN 47374. Tel. (317) 983-1200. Richard Wood, C NC, Friends, 1,084

East Texas Baptist University, Marshall, TX 75670, Tel. (214) 935-7963. Robert E. Craig, C S. So. Bapt., 705

Eastern College, St. Davids, PA 19087, Tel. (215) 341-5810. Roberta Hestenes, C MS, Am. Bapt., 959

Eastern Mennonite College, Harrisonburg, VA 22801, Tel. (703) 433-2771. Joseph L. Lapp, C S, Menn. Ch., 877

Eastern Nazarene College, Wollaston, MA 02170, Tel. (617) 773-6350. Stephen W. Nease, C NE, Nazarene, 903

Eckerd College, St. Petersburg, FL 33733, Tel. (813) 867-1166. Peter H. Armacost, C S, PCUSA, 1,136

Edgewood College, Madison, WI 53711, Tel. (608) 257-4861. James A. Ebben, C NC, Cath., 890

Edward Waters College, Jacksonville, Fl 32209, Tel. (904) 355-3030. Cecil W. Cone, C S, A.M.E., 748.

Elizabethtown College, Elizabethtown, PA 17022, Tel. (717) 367-1151. Gerhard E. Spiegler, C MS, Ch. Breth., 1,608

Elmhurst College, Elmhurst, IL 60126, Tel. (312) 279-4100. Ivan Frick, C NC, U. Ch. of Christ, 3,383

Elon College, Elon College, NC 27244, Tel. (919) 584-9711. J. Fred Young, C S, U. Ch. of Christ, 2,929

Emmanuel College, Boston, MA 02115, Tel. (617) 277-9340. Sr. Janet Eisner, W NE, Cath., 937

Emory and Henry College, Emory, VA 24327, Tel. (703) 944-3121. Charles W. Sydnor, Jr. C S, Un. Meth., 771

Emory University, Atlanta, GA 30322, Tel. (404) 727-6123. James T. Laney, C S, Un. Meth., 8,421

Erskine College, Due West, SC 29578, Tel. (803) 379-2131. William Bruce Ezell, Jr., C S, Asso. Ref. Presb., 578

Eureka College, Eureka, IL 61530, Tel. (309) 467-3721. George A. Hearne, C NC, Christian Church (Disc.), 444

Evangel College, Springfield, MO 65802, Tel. (417) 865-2811. Robert H. Spence, C NC, Assem. of God, 1,622

Evansville, University of, Evansville, IN 47722, Tel. (812) 477-6241, James S. Vinson, C S, Un. Meth., 4,033

Fairfield University, Fairfield, CT 06430, Tel. (203) 254-4000. Aloysius P. Kelley, C NE, Cath., 5,077

Faulkner University, Montgomery, AL 36193. Billy D. Hiyler, Interim, CS, Chs. of Christ, 1,432

Felician College, Lodi, NJ 07644, Tel. (201) 778-1190, Sr. Theresa M. Martin, C MS, Cath., 551

Ferrum College, Ferrum, VA 24088, Tel. (703) 365-2121. Jerry M. Boone, C S, Un. Meth., 1,337

Findlay College, Findlay, OH 45840, Tel. (419) 422-8313. Kenneth E. Zirkle, C NC, Ch. of God, Gen. Eldership, 1,385

Fisk University, Nashville, TN 37203, Tel. (615) 329-8500. Harry Ponder, C S, U. Ch. of Christ, 694

Florida Memorial College, Miami, FL 33054, Tel. (305) 625-4141. Willie C. Robinson, C S, Am. Bapt., 1,960

Florida Southern College, Lakeland, FL 33801, Tel. (813) 680-4111. Robert A. Davis, C S, Un. Meth., 2,984

Fontbonne College, St. Louis, MO 63105, Tel. (314) 862-3456. Maneve Dunham, C NC, Cath., 952

Fordham University, Bronx, NY 10458, Tel. (212) 579-2000. Joseph A. O'Hare, C MS, Cath., 12,228

Franciscan University of Steubenville, Steubenville, OH 43952, Tel. (614) 283-3771. Michael Scanlan, C NC, Cath., 907

Franklin College of Indiana, Franklin, IN 46131, Tel. (317) 736-8441. William B. Martin, C NC, Am. Bapt., 711

Franklin & Marshall College, Lancaster, PA 17604, Tel. (717) 291-3911. James L. Powell, C MS, U. Ch. of Christ, 2,794

Freed-Hardeman College, Henderson, TN 38340, Tel. (901) 989-6000. E. C. Gardner, C S, Chs. of Christ, 1,038

Fresno Pacific College, Fresno, CA 93702, Tel. (209) 453-2000. Richard Kriegbaum, C West., Menn. Breth. Ch., 1,040

Friends University, Wichita, KS 67213, Tel. (316) 261-5800. Richard E. Felix, C NC, Friends, 868

Furman University, Greenville, SC 29613, Tel. (803) 294-2000. John E. Johns, C S, So. Bapt., 2,952

Gannon University, Erie, PA 16541, Tel. (814) 871-7000. M. Daniel Henry, C MS, Cath., 4,096

Gardner-Webb College, Boiling Springs, NC 28017, Tel. (704) 434-2361. Christopher White, C S, So. Bapt., 1,826

Geneva College, Beaver Falls, PA 15010, Tel. (412) 846-5100. Joe McFarland, C MS, Ref. Presby. Ch., 1,191

George Fox College, Newberg, OR 97132, Tel. (503) 538-8383. Edward F. Stevens, C NW, Friends, 694

Georgetown College, Georgetown, KY 40324, Tel. (502) 863-8011. W. Morgan Patterson, C S, So. Bapt., 1,315

Georgetown University, Washington, DC 20057, Tel. (202) 625-0100. Timothy S. Healy, C MS, Cath., 11,985

Georgian Court College, Lakewood, NJ 08701, Tel. (201) 364-2200. Sr. Barbara Williams, W MS, Cath., 1,608

Gettysburg College, Gettysburg, PA 17325, Tel. (717) 337-6000. Charles E. Glassick, C MS, ELCA, 1,978

Gonzaga University, Spokane, WA 99258, Tel. (509) 328-4220. Bernard J. Coughlin, C NW, Cath., 3,117

Gordon College, Wenham, MA 01984, Tel. (617) 927-2300. Richard F. Gross, C NE, Interdenom, 1,258

Goshen College, Goshen, IN 46526, Tel. (219) 533-3161. J. Victor Stoltzfus, C NC, Menn. Ch., 951

Grace College, Winona Lake, IN 46590, Tel. (219) 372-5100. John J. Davis, C NC, Breth. in Christ, 783

Graceland College, Lamoni, IA 50140, Tel. (515) 784-5000. Barbara J. Higdon, C NC, Reorg. L.D.S., 952

Grand Canyon College, Phoenix, AZ 85017, Tel. (602) 249-3300. Bill Williams, C NC, So. Bapt., 1,515

Grand Rapids Baptist College and Seminary, Grand Rapids, MI 49505, Tel. (616) 949-5300. Charles U. Wagner, C NC, Bapt., 910

Grand View College, Des Moines, IA 50316, Tel. (515) 263-2800. Karl F. Langrock, C NC, ELCA, 1,323

Greensboro College, Greensboro, NC 27401 Tel. (919) 272-7102. William H. Likins, C S, Un. Meth., 562

Greenville College, Greenville, IL 62246, Tel. (618) 664-1840. W. Richard Stephens, C NC, Free Meth., 615

Grinnell College, Grinnell, IA 51526, Tel. (515) 236-2500. George A. Drake, C NC, U. Ch. of Christ, 1,277

Grove City College, Grove City, PA 16127, Tel. (412) 458-6600, Charles S. MacKenzie, C MS, PCUSA, 2,162

Guilford College, Greensboro, NC 27410, Tel. (919) 292-5511. William R. Rogers, C S, Friends, 1,643

Gustavus Adolphus College, St. Peter, MN 56082, Tel. (507) 931-8000. John Kendall, C NC, ELCA, 2,190

Gwynedd-Mercy College, Gwynedd Valley, PA 19437, Tel. (215) 646-7300. Sr. Isabelle Keiss, C MS, Cath., 2,007

Hamline University, St. Paul, MN 55104, Tel. (612) 641-2800. Charles J. Graham, C NC, Un. Meth., 1,864

Hampden-Sydney College, Hampden-Sydney, VA 23943. Tel. (804) 223-4381. James R. Leutze, III, M S, PCUSA, 828

Hannibal-La Grange College, Hannibal, MO 63401, Tel. (314) 221-3675. Paul E. Brown, Actg., C NC, So. Bapt., 687

Hanover College, Hanover, IN 47243, Tel. (812) 866-2151. Russell L. Nichols, C NC, PCUSA, 1,005

Hardin-Simmons University, Abilene, TX 79698, Tel. (915) 677-7281. Jesse C. Fletcher, C S, So. Bapt., 1,817

Harding University, Searcy, AR 72143, Tel. (501) 268-6161. David B. Burks, C NC, Chs. of Christ., 2,772

Hastings College, Hastings, NE 68901, Tel. (402) 463-2402. Thomas J. Reeves, C NC, PCUSA, 825

Haverford College, Haverford, PA 19041, Tel. (215) 896-1000. Harry C. Payne, Actg., C MS, Friends, 1,101

Hawaii Loa College, Kaneohe, HI 96744. Tel. (808) 235-3641. Marvin J. Anderson, C West., Interdenom., 472

Hebrew College, Brookline, MA 02146. Tel. (617) 232-8710. Samuel Schafler, C NE, Jewish, 64

Hebrew Union College, New York Branch, New York, NY 10012, Tel. (212) 674-5300. Paul M. Steinberg, C MS, Jewish, 100

Heidelberg College, Tiffin, OH 44883, Tel. (419) 448-2000. William C. Cassell, C NC, U. Ch. of Christ, 989

Hellenic College, Brookline, MA 02146. Tel. (617) 731-3500. Alkiviades Calivas, C NE, Greek Orth., 161

Hendrix College, Conway, AR 72032, Tel. (501) 329-6811. Joe B. Hatcher, C NC, Un. Meth., 995

High Point College, High Point, NC 27262, Tel. (919) 841-9000. Jacob C. Martinson, C S, Un. Meth., 1,353

Hiram College, Hiram, OH 44234, Tel. (216) 569-3211. Russell Aiuto, C NC, Christian Church (Disc.), 1,072

Hobart and William Smith Colleges, Geneva, NY 14456, Tel. (315) 789-5500. Carroll W. Brewster, Co. Ord. MS, Epis., 1,960

Holy Apostles College, Cromwell, CT 06416, Tel. (203) 635-5311. Francis J. Lescoe, C NE, Cath., 190

Holy Family College, Philadelphia, PA 19114, Tel. (215) 637-7700. Sr. M. Francesca Onley, C MS, Cath., 1,525

Holy Names College, Oakland, CA 94619. Tel. (415) 436-0111. Sr. Lois MacGillivray, C West, Cath., 582

Hood College, Frederick, MD 21701, Tel. (301) 663-3131. Martha E. Church, W MS, U. Ch. of Christ, 1,711

Hope College, Holland, MI 49423, Tel. (616) 392-5111. John H. Jacobson, Jr., C NC, Ref. Am., 2,522

Houghton College, Houghton, NY 14744, Tel. (716) 567-2211. Daniel R. Chamberlain, C MS, Wes. Ch., 1,273

Houston Baptist University, Houston, TX 77074, Tel. (713) 774-7661. William H. Hinton, C S, So. Bapt., 2,775

Howard Payne University, Brownwood, TX 76801, Tel. (915) 646-2502. Don Newbury, C S, So. Bapt., 850

Huntingdon College, Montgomery, AL 36194, Tel. (205) 265-0511. Allen Keith Jackson, C S, Un. Meth., 762

Huntington College, Huntington, IN 46750, Tel. (161) 356-6000. Eugene B. Habecker, C NC, U. Breth., 447

Huston-Tillotson College, Austin, TX 78702, Tel. (512) 476-7421. John T. King, C S, Un. Meth. and U. Ch. of Christ, 524

Illinois Benedictine College, Lisle, IL 60532, Tel. (312) 960-1500. Hugh Anderson, C NC, Cath., 2,150

Illinois College, Jacksonville, IL 62650. Tel. (217) 245-7126. Donald C. Mundinger, C NC, PCUSA, 761

Illinois Wesleyan University, Bloomington, IL 6170 2 Tel. (309) 556-3131. Wayne Anderson, C NC, Un. Meth. 1,588

Immaculata College, Immaculata, PA 19345, Tel. (215) 647-4400. Sr. Marian William, W MS, Cath., 1,912

Incarnate Word College, San Antonio, TX 78209. Tel. (512) 828-1261. Sr. Margaret P. Slattery, C S, Cath., 1,296

Indianapolis, The University of, Indianapolis, IN 46227. Tel. (317) 788-3368. Gene E. Sease, C NC, Un. Meth., 2,964

Iona College, New Rochelle, NY 10801. Tel. (914) 633-2000. Br. John G. Driscoll, C MS, Cath., 6,050

Iowa Wesleyan College, Mt. Pleasant, IA 52641, Tel. (319) 385-8021. Robert J. Prins, C NC, Un. Meth., 639

Jamestown College, Jamestown, ND 58401, Tel. (701) 252-3467. James S. Walker, C NC, PCUSA, 503

Jarvis Christian College, Hawkins, TX 75765, Tel. (214) 769-2174. C. A. Berry, C S, Christian Ch. (Disc.), 472

John Carroll University, Cleveland, OH 44118, Tel. (216) 397-1886. Thomas P. O'Malley, C NC, Cath., 3,583

Johnson C. Smith University, Charlotte, NC 28216, Tel. (704) 378-1000. Robert L. Albright, C S, PCUSA, 1,272

Judaism, University of, Los Angeles, CA 90077, Tel. (213) 476-9777. David L. Lieber, C West, Jewish, 179

Judson College, Elgin, IL 60123, Tel. (312) 695-2500. Harm A. Weber, C NC, Am. Bapt., 480

Judson College, Marion, AL 36756, Tel. (205) 683-6161. Norman H. McCrummen, W S, So. Bapt., 305

Juniata College, Huntingdon, PA 16652, Tel. (814) 643-4310. Robert W. Neff, C MS, Ch. Breth., 1,127

Kalamazoo College, Kalamazoo, MI 49007, Tel. (616) 383-8400, David W. Breneman, C NC, Am. Bapt., 1,115

Kansas Newman College, Wichita, KS 67213, Tel. (316) 942-4291. Robert J. Giroux, C NC, Cath., 819

Kansas Wesleyan University, Salina, KS 67401, Tel. (913) 827-5541. Marshall P. Stanton, C NC, Un. Meth., 639

Kendall College, Evanston, IL 60201, Tel. (312) 866-1300. Andrew N. Cothran, C NC. Un. Meth., 239

Kentucky Christian College, Grayson, KY 41143, Tel. (606) 474-6613. Keith P. Keeran, C S, Chr. Chs./Chs. of Christ, 536

Kentucky Wesleyan College, Owensboro, KY 42301, Tel. (502) 926-3111. Luther W. White, III, C S, Un. Meth., 798

Kenyon College, Gambier, OH 43022, Tel. (614) 427-5000. Philip H. Jordan, Jr., C NC, Epis., 1,493

Keuka College, Keuka Park, NY 14478, Tel. (315) 536-4411. Arthur F. Kirk, Jr., C MS, Am. Bapt., 435

King College, Bristol, TN 37620, Tel. (615) 989-1187. Don R. Mitchell, C S, PCUSA, 588

King's College, Wilkes-Barre, PA 18711, Tel. (717) 826-5900. James Lackenmier, C MS Cath., 2,327

Lafayette College, Easton, PA 18042, Tel. (215) 250-5000. David W. Ellis, C MS, PCUSA, 2,375

LaGrange College, LaGrange, GA 30240, Tel. (404) 882-2911. Walter Y. Murphy, C S, Un. Meth., 955

Lake Forest College, Lake Forest, IL 60045, Tel. (312) 234-3100. Eugene Hotchkiss, III, C NC, PCUSA, 1,156

Lakeland College, Sheboygan, WI 53081, Tel. (414) 565-2111. Richard E. Hill, C NC, U. Ch. of Christ, 1,077

Lambuth College, Jackson, TN 38301, Tel. (901) 427-1500, Thomas F. Boyd, C S, Un. Meth., 677

Lane College, Jackson, TN 38301, Tel. (901) 424-4600 Alex Chambers, C S, Chr. M.E., 632

La Roche College, Pittsburgh, PA 15237, Tel. (412) 367-9300. Sr. Margaret Huber, C MS, Cath., 1,751

La Salle University, Philadelphia, PA 19141, Tel. (215) 951-1000. Br. F. Patrick Ellis, C MS, Cath., 6,340

La Verne University of, La Verne, CA 91750, Tel. (714) 593-3511. Stephen C. Morgan, C West. Ch. of Breth., 4,783

Lebanon Valley College, Annville, PA 17003, Tel. (717) 867-6100. William J. McGill, Actg., C MS, Un. Meth., 1,210

Lee College, Cleveland, TN 37311, Tel. (615) 472-2111. Paul Conn, C S, Ch. of God, 1,204

Le Moyne College, Syracuse, N.Y. 13214, Tel. (315) 445-4100. Frank R. Haig, C MS, Cath., 2,140

LeMoyne-Owen College, Memphis, TN 38126, Tel. (901) 774-9090. Irving P. McPhail, C S, interdenom., 951

Lenoir-Rhyne College, Hickory, NC 28603, Tel. (704) 328-1741. John E. Trainer, Jr., C S, ELCA, 1,563

Lewis University, Romeoville, Il 60441, Tel. (815) 838-0500. Br. David Delahanty, C NC, Cath., 3,076

Lewis & Clark College, Portland, OR 97219, Tel. (503) 293-2651. James A. Gardner, C NW, PCUSA, 2,837

Liberty University, Lynchburg, VA 24506, Tel. (804) 582-2000. A. Pierre Guillermin, C S, Bapt. 7,288

Lindenwood College, St. Charles, MO 63301, Tel. (314) 949-2000. James I. Spainhower, C NC, PCUSA, 1,995

Linfield College, McMinnville, OR 97128, Tel. (503) 472-4121. Charles U. Walker, C NW, Amer. Bapt. 1,800

Livingstone College, Salisbury, NC 28144, Tel. (704) 633-7960. William H. Greene, C S, A.M.E. Zion, 630

Loma Linda University, Loma Linda, CA 92350, Tel. (714) 824-4300. Norman J. Woods, C West, S.D.A., 4,390

Loras College, Dubuque, IA 52004, Tel. (319) 588-7100 James Barta, Actg., C NC, Cath., 1,998

Loretto Heights College, Denver, CO 80236, Tel. (303) 936-8441. Thomas K. Craine, C NC, Cath., 779

Louisiana College, Pineville, LA 71359, Tel. (318) 487-7011. Robert L. Lynn, C S, So. Bapt., 1,022

Lourdes College, Sylvania, OH 43560, Tel. (419) 885-3211. Sr. Ann Francis Klimkowski, C NC, Cath., 773

Loyola College, Baltimore, MD 21210, Tel. (301) 323-1010. Joseph A. Sellinger, C MS, Cath., 5,157

Loyola University of Chicago, Chicago, IL 60611, Tel. (312) 670-3000. Raymond C. Baumhart, C NC, Cath., 14,027

Loyola University, New Orleans, LA 70118, Tel. (504) 865-2011. James C. Carter, C S. Cath., 4,748

Loyola Marymount University, Los Angeles, CA 90045, Tel. (213) 642-2700. James N. Loughran, C West, Cath., 6,598

Lubbock Christian University, Lubbock, TX 79407, Tel. (806) 792-3221. Steven S. Lemley, C S, Chs. of Christ, 1,035

Luther College, Decorah, IA 52101, Tel. (319) 387-2000. H. George Anderson, C NC, ELCA, 2,029

Lycoming College, Williamsport, PA 17701, Tel. (717) 321-4000. Frederick E. Blumer, C MS, Un. Meth. 1,208

Lynchburg College, Lynchburg, VA 24501, Tel. (804) 522-8100. George N. Rainsford, C S, Christian Church (Disc.), 2,175

Macalester College, St. Paul, MN 55105, Tel. (612) 696-6207. Robert M. Gavin, Jr., C NC, PCUSA, 1,703

MacMurray College, Jacksonville, IL 62650, Tel. (217) 245-6151. Edward J. Mitchell, C NC, Un. Meth., 831

Madonna College, Livonia, MI 48150, Tel. (313) 591-5000. Sr. Mary Francilene, C NC, Cath., 3,969

Mallinkrodt College Of The North Shore, Wilmette, IL 60091, Tel. (312) 256-1094. Sr. M. Patrice Noterman, C NC, Cath., 259

Malone College, Canton, OH 44709, Tel. (216) 489-0800. Gordon R. Werkema, C NC, Friends, 1,022

Manchester College, North Manchester, IN 46962, Tel. (219) 982-2141. William P. Robinson, C NC, Ch. Breth., 960

Manhattan College, Bronx, NY 10471, Tel. (212) 920-0100. Br. Thomas J. Scanlan, C MS, Cath., 4,533

Manhattanville College, Purchase, NY 10577, Tel. (914) 694-2200. Marcia A. Savage, C MS, Cath., 1,306

Marian College, Indianapolis, IN 46222, Tel. (317) 929-0123. Louis Gatto, C NC, Cath., 1,060

Marian College of Fond du Lac, Fond du Lac, WI 54935, Tel. (414) 923-7600. Ed L. Henry, C NC, Cath., 378

Marion College, Marion, IN 46952, Tel. (317) 674-6901. James Barnes, C NC, Wes. Ch., 1,061

Marist College, Poughkeepsie, NY 12601, Tel. (914) 471-3240. Dennis J. Murray, C MS, Cath., 4,471

Marquette University, Milwaukee, WI 53233, Tel. (414) 224-7700. John P. Raynor, C NC, Cath., 11,442

Mars Hill College, Mars Hill, NC 28754, Tel. (704) 689-1111. Fred B. Bentley, C S, So. Bapt., 1,419

Mary Baldwin College, Staunton, VA 24401, Tel. (703) 887-7000. Cynthia H. Tyson, W S, PCUSA, 902

Mary University of, Bismarck, ND 58501, Tel. (701) 255-7500. Sr. Thomas Welder, C NC, Cath., 1,195

Mary Hardin-Baylor, University of, Belton, TX 76513, Tel. (817) 939-5811. Bobby E. Parker, C S, So. Bapt., 1,302

Marycrest College, Davenport, IA 52804, Tel. (319) 326-9512. Wanda D. Bigham, C NC, Cath., 1,600

Marygrove College, Detroit, MI 48221, Tel. (313) 862-8000. John E. Shay, Jr., C NC, Cath., 1,232

Marylhurst College for Lifelong Learning, Marylhurst, OR 97036, Tel. (503) 636-8141. Nancy Wilgenbusch, C NW, Cath, 759

Marymount College of Kansas, Salina, KS 67401, Tel. (913) 825-2101. Dan Johnson, C NC, Cath., 606

Marymount College, Tarrytown, NY 10591, Tel. (914) 631-3200. Sr. Brigid Driscoll, W MS, Cath., 1,233

Marymount University, Arlington, VA 22207, Tel. (703) 522-5600. Sr. M. Majella Berg, C S, Cath., 2,210

Marymount Manhattan College, New York, NY 10021, Tel. (212) 517-0400. Sr. Colette Mahoney, W MS, Cath., 1,551

Maryville College, Maryville, TN 37801, Tel. (615) 982-6412. Richard I. Ferrin, C S, PCUSA, 654

Maryville College, St. Louis, MO 63141, Tel. (314) 576-9300. Claudius X. Pritchard, C NC, Cath., 2,395

Marywood College, Scranton, PA 18509, Tel. (717) 348-6211. Sr. M. Coleman Nee, W MS, Cath., 3,194

Master's College, The, Newhall, CA 91322, Tel. (805) 259-3540. John MacArthur, Jr., C West, Bapt., 304

McKendree College, Lebanon, IL 62254, Tel. (618) 537-4481. Garrit Tenbrink, C NC, Un. Meth., 952

McMurry College, Abilene, TX 79697, Tel. (915) 691-6200. Thomas K. Kim, C S, Un. Meth., 1,657

McPherson College, McPherson, KS 67460, Tel. (316) 241-0731. Paul W. Hoffman, C NC, Ch. Breth., 467

Medaille College, Buffalo, NY 14214, Tel. (716) 884-3281. Kevin I. Sullivan, C MS, Cath., 911

Mercer University Atlanta, Atlanta, GA 30341, Tel. (404) 451-0331, R. Kirby Godsey, C S, So. Bapt., 2,332

Mercer University Macon, Macon, GA 31207, Tel. (912) 744-2700. R. Kirby Godsey, C S, So. Bapt. 2,905

Mercy College, Dobbs Ferry, NY 10522, Tel. (914) 693-4500, Wilbert J. Lemelle, C MS, Cath., 8,374

Mercy College of Detroit, Detroit, MI 48219, Tel. (313) 592-6000. Sr. Maureen A. Fay, C NC, Cath., 2,402

Mercyhurst College, Erie, PA 16546, Tel. (814) 825-0200 William P. Garvey, C MS, Cath., 1,653

Meredith College, Raleigh, NC 27607, Tel. (919) 829-8600. John E. Weems, W S, So. Bapt., 1,848

Merrimack College, North Andover, MA 01845, Tel. (617) 683-7111. John E. Deegan, C NE, Cath., 3,548

Messiah College, Grantham, PA 17027, Tel. (717) 766-2511. D. Ray Hostetter, C MS, Breth. in Christ, 1,846

Methodist College, Fayetteville, NC 28301, Tel. (919) 488-7110 M. Elton Hendricks, C S, Un. Meth., 1,226

Mid-America Nazarene College, Olathe, KS 66061, Tel. (913) 782-3750. Donald D. Owens, C NC, Nazarene, 1,040

Midland Lutheran College, Fremont, NE 68025, Tel. (402) 721-5480. Carl. L. Hansen, C NC, ELCA, 801

Miles College, Birmingham, AL 35208, Tel. (205) 923-2771. Le Roy Johnson, C S, CME, 517

Milligan College, Milligan College, TN 37682, Tel. (615) 929-0116. Marshall J. Leggett, C S, CC/CC, 603

Millikin University, Decatur, IL 62522, Tel. (217) 424-6211. J. Roger Miller, C NC, PCUSA, 1,556

Millsaps College, Jackson, MS 39210, Tel. (601) 354-5201. George M. Harmon, C S, Un. Meth., 1,310

Mississippi College, Clinton, MS 39058, Tel. (601) 925-3000. Lewis Nobles, C S, So. Bapt. 2,799

Missouri Baptist College, St. Louis, MO 63141, Tel. (314) 434-1115. Patrick O. Copley, C NC, So. Bapt., 386

Missouri Valley College, Marshall, MO 65340, Tel. (816) 886-6924. Earl J. Reeves, C NC, PCUSA, 566

Mobile College, Mobile, AL 36613, Tel. (205) 675-5990. Michael A. Magnoli, C S, So. Bapt., 804

Molloy College, Rockville Centre, NY 11570, Tel. (516) 678-5000. Sr. Janet A. Fitzgerald, C MS, Cath., 1,593

Monmouth College, Monmouth, IL 61462, Tel. (309) 457-2311. Bruce Haywood, C NC, PCUSA, 699

Moravian College, Bethlehem, PA 18018, Tel. (215) 861-1300. Roger H. Martin, C MS, Morav, 1,692

Morningside College, Sioux City, IA 51106, Tel. (712) 274-5000. Miles Tommeraasen, C NC, Un. Meth., 1,172

Morris College, Sumter, SC 29150, Tel. (803) 775-9371. Luns C. Richardson, C S, Bapt., 597

Morris Brown College, Atlanta, GA 30314, Tel. (404) 525-7831. Calvert H. Smith, C S, A.M.E., 1,257

Mt. Angel Seminary, Saint Benedict, OR 97373, Tel. (503) 845-3030. Bonaventure Zerr, M NW, Cath., 136

Mt. Marty College, Yankton, SD 57078, Tel. (605) 668-1011. Sr. Jacquelyn Ernster, C NC, Cath., 805

Mt. Mary College, Milwaukee, WI 53222, Tel. (414) 258-4810. Sr. Ruth Hollenbach, W NC, Cath., 1,278

Mt. Mercy College, Cedar Rapids, IA 52402, Tel. (319) 363-8213. Thomas R. Feld, C NC, Cath., 1,321

Mt. St. Mary College, Newburgh, NY 12550, Tel. (914) 561-0800. Sr. Ann V. Sakac, C MS, Cath., 1,138

Mt. St. Mary's College, Emmitsburg, MD 21727, Tel. (301) 447-6122. Robert J. Wickenheiser, C MS, Cath., 1,779

Mt. St. Mary's College, Los Angeles, CA 90049, Tel. (213) 476-2237. Sr. Magdalen Coughlin, W West, Cath., 1,222

Mount Saint Claire College, Clinton, IA 52732, Tel. (319) 242-4023. Charles E. Lang, C NC, Cath., 355

Mount Union College, Alliance, OH 44601, Tel. (216) 821-5320. Harold M. Kolenbrander, C NC, Un. Meth., 975

Mount Vernon, Nazarene College, Mount Vernon, OH 43050. Tel. (614) 397-1244. William J. Prince, C NC, Nazarene 1,056

Muhlenberg College, Allentown, PA 18104, Tel. (215) 433-3191. Johnathan C. Messerli, C MS, ELCA 2,133

Mundelein College, Chicago, IL 60660, Tel. (312) 262-8100. Sr. Mary Breslin, W NC, Cath., 1,182

Muskingum College, New Concord, OH 43762, Tel. (614) 826-8211. Arthur J. De Jong, C NC, PCUSA, 1,025

Nazareth College in Kalamazoo, Nazareth, MI 49001, Tel. (616) 349-4200. Patrick Smith, C NC, Cath., 853

Nazareth College of Rochester, Rochester, NY 14610, Tel. (716) 586-2525. Rose Marie Beston, C MS, Cath., 2,620

Nebraska Wesleyan University, Lincoln, NE 68504, Tel. (402) 466-2371. John W. White, C NC, Un. Meth., 1,285

Neumann College, Aston, PA 19014, Tel. (215) 459-0905. Sr. Margarella O'Neill, C MS, Cath., 1,016

Newberry College, Newberry, SC 29108, Tel. (803) 276-5010. Hubert H. Setzler, Jr., C S, ELCA, 583

New England, University of, Biddleford, ME 04005, Tel. (207) 283-0171. Charles W. Ford, C NC, Cath., 943

Niagara University, Niagara University, NY 14109, Tel. (716) 285-1212. Donald G. Harrington, C MS, Cath., 3,264

North Carolina Wesleyan College, Rocky Mount, NC 27804, Tel. (919) 977-7171. Leslie H. Garner, Jr., C S, Un. Meth., 1,174

North Central College, Naperville, IL 60566, Tel. (312) 420-3400. Gael D. Swing, C NC, Un. Meth., 1,787

North Park College, Chicago IL 60625, Tel. (312) 583-2700. David G. Horner, C NC, Evan. Cov. Ch. of Amer., 1,539

Northland College, Ashland, WI 54806, Tel. (715) 682-4531. Robert Parsonage, C NC, U. Ch. of Christ, 558

Northwest Christian College, Eugene, OR 97401, Tel. (503) 343-1641. James E. Womack, C NW, Christian Church (Disc.), 250

Northwest College of the Assemblies of God, Kirkland, WA 98083, Tel. (206) 822-8266, D. V. Hurst, C NW, Assem. of God, 671

Northwest Nazarene College, Nampa, ID 83651, Tel. (208) 467-8011. A. Gordon Wetmore, C NW, Nazarene, 1,091

Northwestern College, Orange City, IA 51041, Tel. (712) 737-4821. James E. Bultman C NC, Ref. Am., 859

Northwestern College, Watertown, WI 53094, Tel. (414) 261-4352. Robert J. Voss, M NC, ELCA, 210

Notre Dame College, Manchester, NH 03104, Tel. (603) 669-4298 Sr. Carol Descoteaux, C NE, Cath., 810

Notre Dame College, Cleveland, OH 44121, Tel. (216) 381-1680. Sr. Mary Marthe Reinhard, W NC, Cath., 748

Notre Dame, University of, Notre Dame, IN 46556, Tel. (219) 239-5000. Edward A. Malloy, C NC, Cath., 9,588

Nyack College, Nyack, NY 10960. Tel. (914) 358-1710. Paul D. Collord, Actg., C MS, Chr. and and Miss. All., 874

Oakland City College, Oakland City, IN 47660. Tel. (812) 749-4781. James W. Murray, C NC, Baptist, 624

Oakwood College, Huntsville, AL 35896, Tel. (205) 837-1630 Benjamin F. Reaves, C S, S.D.A., 1,141

Oblate College, Washington, DC 20017, Tel. (202) 529-6544. Joseph C. Schwab, C MS, Cath., 46

Occidental College, Los Angeles, CA 90041, Tel. (213) 259-2500. Richard C. Gilman, C West, PCUSA, 1,649

Ohio Dominican College, Columbus, OH 43219, Tel. (614) 253-2741, Sr. Mary Andrew Matesich, C NC, Cath., 1,129

Ohio Northern University, Ada, OH 45810, Tel. (419) 772-2000. De Bow Freed, C NC, Un. Meth., 2,422

Ohio Wesleyan University, Delaware, OH 43015, Tel. (614) 369-4431. David L. Warren, C NC, Un. Meth., 1,349

Oklahoma Baptist University, Shawnee, OK 74801, Tel. (405) 275-2850. Bob R. Agee, C NC, So. Bapt., 1,559

Oklahoma Christian College, Oklahoma City, OK 73111, Tel. (405) 478-1661. Terry Johnson, C NC, Chs. of Christ 1,515

Oklahoma City University, Oklahoma City, OK 73106, Tel. (405) 521-5000. Jerald C. Walker, C NC, Un. Meth., 2,787

Olivet College, Olivet, MI 49076, Tel. (616) 749-7000. Donald A. Morris, C NC, U. Ch. of Christ, 680

Olivet Nazarene College, Kankakee, IL 60901, Tel. (815) 939-5011. Leslie W. Parrott, C NC, Nazarene, 1,634

Oral Roberts University, Tulsa, OK 74171, Tel. (918) 495-6161. G. Oral Roberts, C NC, interdenom, 4,351

Ottawa University, Ottawa, KS 66067, Tel. (913) 242-5200. Wilbur D. Wheaton, C NC, Amer. Bapt., 1,681

Otterbein College, Westerville, OH 43081, Tel. (614) 890-3000. C. Brent Devore, C NC, Un. Meth., 1,675

Ouachita Baptist University, Arkadelphia, AR 71923 Tel. (501) 246-4531. Daniel R. Grant, C NC, So. Bapt., 1,414

Our Lady of the Holy Cross College, New Orleans, LA 70131, Tel. (504) 394-7744, Thomas E. Chambers, C S, Cath., 646

Our Lady of the Lake University of San Antonio, San Antonio, TX 78285, Tel. (512) 434-6711. Sr. Elizabeth A. Sueltenfuss, C S, Cath., 1,695

Ozarks, University of the, Clarksville, AR 72830, Tel. (501) 754-3839. Fritz H. Ehren, C NC, PCUSA, 629

Ozarks, School of the, Point Lookout, MO 65726, Tel. (417) 334-6411. William D. Todd, C NC, PCUSA, 1,201

Pacific Christian College, Fullerton, CA 92631. Tel. (714) 879-3901. Knofel Staton, C West, Ch. of Christ, 483

Pacific Lutheran University, Tacoma, WA 98447, Tel. (206) 531-6900. William O. Rieke, C NW, ELCA, 3,758

Pacific Union College, Angwin, CA 94508, Tel. (707) 965-6211. D. Malcolm Maxwell, C West, S.D.A., 1,402

Pacific, University of the, Stockton, CA 95211. Tel. (209) 946-2011. Bill L. Atchley, C West, Un. Meth., 5,622

Pacific University, Forest Grove, OR 97116, Tel. (503) 357-6151. Robert F. Duvall, C NW, U. Ch. of Christ, 1,138

Paine College, Augusta, GA 30910, Tel. (404) 722-4471. William H. Harris, Jr., C S, Protestant Denoms., 752

Palm Beach Atlantic College, West Palm Beach, FL 33401, Tel. (305) 833-8592. Claude H. Rhea, C S, Bapt., 1,091

Park College, Parkville, MO 64152, Tel. (816) 741-2000. Arnold J. Breckon, C NC, Reorg. L.D.S., 3,565

Paul Quinn College, Waco, TX 76704, Tel. (817) 753-6415. Warren W. Morgan, C S, A.M.E., 365

Pepperdine University, Malibu, CA 90265, Tel. (213) 456-4000. David Davenport, C West, Chs. of Christ, 6,836

Pfeiffer College, Misenheimer, NC 28109, Tel. (704) 463-7343. Cameron P. West, C S, Un. Meth., 827

Philander Smith College, Little Rock, AR 72202, Tel. (501) 375-9845. Hazo W. Carter, C NC, Un. Meth., 565

Phillips University, Enid, OK 73701, Tel. (405) 237-4433. Joe Jones, C NC, Christian Church (Disc.), 1,057

Pikeville College, Pikeville, KY 41501, Tel. (606) 432-9200. William H. Owens, C S, PCUSA, 600

Point Loma Nazarene College, San Diego CA 92106, Tel. (619) 221-2200. Jim L. Bond, C West, Nazarene, 1,930

Pontifical College Josephinum, Columbus, OH 43085, Tel. (614) 885-5585. Dennis F. Sheehan, M NC, Cath., 193

Portland, University of, Portland, OR 97203. Tel. (503) 283-7911, Thomas C. Oddo, C NW, Cath., 2,792

Presbyterian College, Clinton, SC 29325, Tel. (803) 833-2820. Kenneth B. Orr, C S, PCUSA, 920

Providence College, Providence, RI 02918, Tel. (401) 865-1000. John F. Cunningham, C NE, Cath., 5,570

Puget Sound, University of, Tacoma, WA 98416, Tel. (206) 756-3100. Philip M. Phibbs, C NW, Un. Meth. 4,041

Queens College, Charlotte, NC 28274, Tel. (704) 337-2200. Billy O. Wireman, C S, PCUSA, 1,258

Quincy College, Quincy, IL 62301, Tel. (217) 222-8020. James Toal, C NC, Cath., 867

Randolph-Macon College, Ashland, VA 23005, Tel. (804) 798-8372. Ladell Payne, C S, Un. Meth., 991

Randolph-Macon Woman's College, Lynchburg, VA 24503, Tel. (804) 846-7392. Linda K. Lorimer, W S, Un. Meth., 764

Redlands, University of, Redlands, CA 92373, Tel. (714) 793-2121. William M. Jones, Interim, C West, Am. Bapt., 2,646

Regis College, Denver, CO 80221, Tel. (303) 458-4100. David M. Clarke, C NC Cath., 3,529

Regis College, Weston, MA 02193, Tel. (617) 893-1820. Sr. Therese Higgins, W NE, Cath., 1,069

Rhodes College, Memphis, TN 38112, Tel. (901) 726-3000. James H. Daughdrill, Jr., C S, PCUSA, 1,063

Richmond, University of, Richmond, VA 23173, Tel. (804) 289-8000. Samuel A. Banks, Co. Ord., C S, So. Bapt. 4,609

Ripon College, Ripon, WI 54971, Tel. (414) 748-8115. William R. Stott, Jr., C NC, U. Ch. of Christ, 872

Rivier College, Nashua, NH 03060, Tel. (603) 888-1311 Sr. Jeanne Perreault, W NE, Cath., 2,294

Roanoke College, Salem, VA 24153, Tel. (703) 375-2500. Norman D. Fintel, C S, ELCA, 1,511

Roberts Wesleyan College, Rochester, NY 14624, Tel. (716) 594-9471. William C. Crothers, C MS, Free Meth., 698

Rockhurst College, Kansas City, MO 64110, Tel. (816) 926-4000. Robert F. Weiss, C NC, Cath., 2,888

Rocky Mountain College, Billings, MT 59102, Tel. (406) 657-1000. Arthur H. Derosier, Jr., C NW, Un. Meth., U. Ch. of Christ, PCUSA, 428

Rosary College, River Forest, IL 60305, Tel. (312) 366-2490. Sr. Jean Murray, C NC, Cath., 1,558

Rosemont College, Rosemont, PA 19010, Tel. (215) 527-0200. Dorothy Brown, W MS, Cath., 519

Rust College, Holly Springs, MS 38635, Tel. (601) 252-4661. William A. McMillan, C S, Un. Meth., 900

Sacred Heart Seminary College, Detroit, MI 48206, Tel. (313) 868-2700. F. Gerald Martin, NC, Cath., 318

Sacred Heart University, Bridgeport, CT 06606, Tel. (203) 371-7999. Robert A. Preston, C NE, Cath., 4,808

Sacred Heart, University of the, Santurce, PR 00914, Tel. (809) 728-1515. Jose A. Morales, C MS, Cath., 8,453

St. Alphonsus College, Suffield, CT 06078, Tel. (203) 668-7393. Patrick McGarrity, M NE, Cath., 36

St. Ambrose College, Davenport, IA 52803, Tel. (319) 383-8765. Edward J. Rogalski, C NC, Cath., 2,221

St. Andrews Presbyterian College, Laurinburg, NC 28352, Tel. (919) 276-3652. Alvin P. Perkinson, C S, PCUSA, 772

St. Anselm College, Manchester, NH 03102, Tel. (603) 669-1030. Br. Joachim W. Froehlich, C NE, Cath., 1,933

St. Augustine's College, Raleigh, NC 27611, Tel. (919) 828-4451. Prezell R. Robinson, C S, Epis., 1,701

St. Bonaventure University, St. Bonaventure, NY 14778, Tel. (716) 375-2000. Mathias Doyle, C MS, Cath., 2,656

St. Charles Borromeo Seminary, Philadelphia, PA 19151 Tel. (215) 839-3760. Frances X. DiLorenzo, M MS Cath., 504

St. Edward's University, Austin, TX 78704, Tel. (512) 448-8400. Patricia A. Hayes, C S, Cath., 2,502

St. Francis College, Brooklyn, NY 11201, Tel. (212) 522-2300. Br. Donald Sullivan, C MS, Cath., 2,436

St. Francis College, Fort Wayne, IN 46808, Tel. (219) 432-3551. Sr. Joellen Scheetz, C NC, Cath., 1,306

St. Francis College, Loretto, PA 15940, Tel. (814) 472-7000. Christian R. Oravec, C MS, Cath., 1,604

St. Hyacinth College, Granby, MA 01033, Tel. (413) 467-7191. Alexander Cymerman, M NE, Cath., 52

St. John Fisher College, Rochester, NY 14618, Tel. (716) 385-8000. William L. Pickett, C MS, Cath., 2,348

St. John Vianney College Seminary, Miami, FL 33165, Tel. (305) 223-4561. Thomas O'Dwyer, M S, Cath. 65

St. John's Seminary College, Camarillo, CA 93010, Tel. (805) 482-4697. Sylvester Ryan, M West, Cath., 108

St. John's Seminary, Brighton, MA 02135. Tel. (617) 254-2610. Thomas J. Daly, M NE, Cath., 197

St. John's University, Collegeville, MN 56321, Tel. (612) 363-2011. Hilary Thimmesh, Coord. NC, Cath., 1,938

St. John's University, Jamaica, NY 11439, Tel. (212) 990-6161. Joseph T. Cahill, C MS, Cath. 19,248

St. Joseph College, W. Hartford, CT 06117, Tel. (203) 232-4571. M. Payton Ryan, W NE, Cath., 1,465

St. Joseph's College, Rensselaer, IN 47978, Tel. (219) 866-7111. Charles H. Banet, C NC, Cath., 847

St. Joseph's College, North Windham, ME 04062, Tel. (207) 892-6766. Loring E. Hart, C NE, Cath., 7,821

St. Joseph's College, Brooklyn, NY 11205 Tel. (718) 636-6800. Sr. George A. O'Connor, C MS, Cath., 873

St. Joseph's University, Philadelphia, PA 19131, Tel. (215) 879-7300. Nicholas S. Rashford, C MS, Cath., 5,705

St. Joseph's College, Mountain View, CA 94039, Tel. (415) 967-9501. Gerald D. Coleman, M West, Cath., 114

St. Joseph Seminary College, Saint Benedict, LA 70457, Tel. (504) 892-1800. Pius Lartique, M Cath., 168

St. Leo College, St. Leo, FL 33574, Tel. (904) 588-8200. Frank M. Mouch C S, Cath., 5,786

St. Louis University, St. Louis, MO 63103, Tel. (314) 658-2222. Lawrence Boinoi, C NC, Cath., 8,334

St. Louis University-Parks College, Cahokia, IL 62206, Tel. (618) 337-7500. Paul A. Whelan, C NC, Cath., 1,036

St. Martin's College, Lacey, WA 98503, Tel. (206) 491-4700. Conrad Rausch, C NW, Cath., 603

St. Mary College, Leavenworth, KS 66048, Tel. (913) 682-5151. Sr. Mary Janet McGilley, W NC, Cath., 961

St. Mary of the Plains College, Dodge City, KS 67801. Tel. (316) 225-4171. Michael J. McCarthy, C NC, Cath., 622

St. Mary-of-the-Woods College, St. Mary-of-the-Woods, IN 47876, Tel. (812) 535-5151. Sr. Barbara Doherty, W NC, Cath., 691

St. Mary's College, Notre Dame, IN 46556, Tel. (219) 284-4000. William A. Hickey, W NC, Cath., 1,740

St. Mary's College, Winona, MN 55987, Tel. (507) 452-4430. Br. Louis Dethomasis, C NC, Cath., 1,542

St. Mary's College, Orchard Lake, MI 48033, Tel. (313) 682-1885. Stanley E. Milewski, C NC, Cath., 221

St. Mary's College of California, Moraga, CA 94575, Tel. (415) 376-4411. Br. Mel Anderson, C West, Cath., 3,590

St. Mary's Seminary and University, Baltimore, MD 21210. Tel. (301) 323-3200. Robert F. Leavitt, C MS, Cath., 388

St. Mary's University of San Antonio, San Antonio, TX 78284, Tel. (512) 436-3722. John A. Leies, C S, Cath., 3,298

St. Meinrad College, St. Meinrad, IN 47577, Tel. (812) 357-6611. Eugene Hensell, M NC, Cath., 168

St. Michael's College, Winooski, VT 05404, Tel. (802) 655-2000. Paul T. Reiss, C NE, Cath., 2,076

St. Norbert College, De Pere, WI 54115, Tel. (414) 337-3181. Thomas A. Manion, C NC, Cath., 1,717

St. Olaf College, Northfield, MN 55057, Tel. (507) 663-2222. Melvin D. George, C NC, ELCA, 2,999

St. Paul's College, Lawrenceville, VA 23868, Tel. (804) 848-3111. Marvin B. Scott, C S, Epis., 712

St. Peter's College, Jersey City, NJ 07306, Tel. (201) 333-4400. Edward R. Glynn, C MS, Cath., 3,757

St. Thomas, University of, Houston, TX 77006, Tel. (713) 522-7911. William J. Young, C S, Cath., 1,811

St. Thomas Aquinas College, Sparkhill, NY 10976. Tel. (914) 359-9500. Donald T. McNelis, C MS, Cath., 2,081

St. Thomas University, Miami, FL 33054, Tel. (305) 625-6000. Pasquale Di Pasquale, C S, Cath., 3,353

St. Vincent College and Seminary, Latrobe, PA 15650, Tel. (412) 539-9761. John F. Murtha, C MS, Cath., 1,300

St. Xavier College, Chicago, IL 60655, Tel. (312) 779-3300. Ronald O. Champagne, C NC, Cath., 2,566

Salem College, Salem, WV 26426, Tel. (304) 782-5011. Ronald E. Ohl, C NC, 7th Day Bapt., 973

Salem College, Winston-Salem, NC 27108, Tel. (919) 721-2600. Thomas V. Litzenburg, Jr., W S, Morav, 660

Salve Regina-The Newport College, Newport, RI 02840, Tel. (401) 847-6650, Sr. M. Lucille McKillop, C NE, Cath., 2,046

Samford University, Birmingham, AL 35229, Tel. (205) 870-2011. Thomas E. Corts, C S, So. Bapt., 3,669

San Diego, University of, San Diego, CA 92110, Tel. (619) 260-4600. Author E. Hughes, C West, Cath., 5,264

San Francisco, University of, San Francisco, CA 94117, Tel. (415) 666-6886. John J. LoSchiavo, C West, Cath., 5,202

Santa Clara University Santa Clara, CA 95053, Tel. (408) 544-4764. William J. Rewak, C West, Cath., 7,453

Scranton, University of, Scranton, PA 18510, Tel. (717) 961-7400. J. A. Panuska, C MS, Cath., 4,688

Schreiner College, Kerrville, TX 78028, Tel. (512) 896-5411. Sam M. Junkin, C S, PCUSA, 518

Seattle Pacific University, Seattle, WA 98119, Tel. (206) 281-2000. David C. LeShana, C NW, Free Meth., 2,975

Seattle University, Seattle, WA 98122, Tel. (206) 296-6000. William J. Sullivan, C NW, Cath., 4,394

Seton Hall University, South Orange, NJ 07079, Tel. (201) 761-9000. John J. Petillo, C MS, Cath., 8,964

Seton Hill College, Greensburg, PA 15601, Tel. (412) 834-2200. JoAnne W. Boyle, W MS, Cath., 892

Shaw University, Raleigh, NC 27611, Tel. (919) 755-4800. John H. Lucas, C S, Am. Bapt., 1,736

Shenandoah College, Winchester, VA 22601, Tel. (703) 665-4500. James A. Davis, C S, Un. Meth., 902

Shorter College, Rome, GA 30161, Tel. (404) 291-2121. James D. Jordan, C S, So. Bapt., 726

Siena College, Loudonville, NY 12211, Tel. (518) 783-2300. Hugh Hines, C MS, Cath., 3,355

Siena Heights College, Adrian, MI 49221, Tel. (517) 263-0731. Sr. Cathleen C. Real, C NC, Cath., 1,487

Silver Lake College, Manitowoc, WI 54220, Tel. (414) 684-6691. Sr. Barbara Belinske, C NC, Cath., 457

Simpson College, San Francisco CA 94134. Tel. (415) 334-7400. Francis Grubbs, C West, Chr. and Miss. All., 323

Simpson College, Indianola, IA 50125, Tel. (515) 961-6251. Stephen G. Jennings, C NC, Un. Meth., 1,316

Sioux Falls College, Sioux Falls, SD 57105, Tel. (605) 331-5000. Owen P. Halleen, C NC, Am. Bapt., 854

South, University of the, Sewanee, TN 37375, Tel. (615) 598-5931, Robert M. Ayres, Jr., C S, Epis., 1,179

Southeastern College of The Assemblies of God, Lakeland, FL 33801, Tel. (813) 665-4404. James L. Hennesy, C S, Assemb. of God, 1,043

Southern Baptist College, Walnut Ridge, AR 72476, Tel. (501) 886-6741. D. Jack Nicholas, C NC, So. Bapt., 423

Southern California College, Costa Mesa, CA 92626, Tel. (714) 556-3610. Wayne E. Kraiss, C West, Assem. of God., 886

Southern College of Seventh-Day Adventists, Collegedale, TN 37315, Tel. (615) 238-2111. Donald R. Sahly C S, S.D.A., 1,468

Southern Methodist University, Dallas, TX 75275, Tel. (214) 692-2000. A. Kenneth Pye, C S, Un. Meth., 9,049

Southern Nazarene University, Bethany, OK 73008, Tel. (405) 789-6400. Ponder W. Gilliland, C NC, Nazarene, 1,175

Southwest Baptist University, Bolivar, MO 65613, Tel. (417) 326-5281. James L. Sells, C NC, So. Bapt., 1,691

Southwestern College, Winfield, KS 67156, Tel. (316) 221-4150. Bruce Blake, C NC, Un. Meth., 529

Southwestern Adventist College, Keene, TX 76059, Tel. (817) 645-3921. Marvin Anderson, C S, S.D.A., 734

Southwestern Assemblies of God College, Waxahachie, TX 75165, Tel. (214) 937-4010. Paul Savell, C S, Assemb. of God, 635

Southwestern Christian College, Terrell, TX 75160, Tel. (214) 563-3341. Jack Evans, C NC. Chs. of Christ, 222

Southwestern University, Georgetown, TX 78627. Tel. (512) 863-6511. Roy B. Shilling, Jr., C S, Un. Meth., 1,081

Spalding University, Louisville, KY 40203, Tel. (502) 585-9911, Eileen M. Egan, C S, Cath., 1,138

Spelman College, Atlanta, Ga 30314, Tel. (404) 681-3643. Johnneta B. Cole, Bapt., 1,687

Spertus College of Judaica, Chicago, IL 60605. Tel. (312) 922-9012. Howard A. Sulkin, C NC, Jewish, 98

Spring Arbor College, Spring Arbor, MI 49283, Tel. (517) 750-1200. Dorsey W. Brause, C NC, Free Meth., 1,072

Spring Hill College, Mobile, AL 36608, Tel. (205) 460-2121. Paul S. Tipton, C S, Cath., 1,080

Sterling College, Sterling, KS 67579, Tel. (316) 278-2173. Robert A. Veitch, C NC, PCUSA, 436

Stetson University, Deland, FL 32720, Tel. (904) 734-4121. Pope A. Duncan, C S, So. Bapt., 2,794

Stillman College, Tuscaloosa, AL 35403, Tel. (205) 349-4240. Cordell Wynn, C S, PCUSA, 745

Stonehill College, North Easton, MA 02357, Tel. (617) 238-1081. Bartley Mac Phaidin, C NE, Cath., 2,838

Susquehanna University, Selinsgrove, PA 17870, Tel. (717) 374-0101, Joel L. Cunningham, C MS, ELCA, 1,720

Swarthmore College, Swarthmore, PA 19081, Tel. (215) 328 = 8000. David W. Fraser C MS, Friends, 1,322

Tabor College, Hillsboro, KS 67063, Tel. (316) 947-3121. Vernon R. Wiebe, Interim, C NC, Menn. Breth., 399

Talladega College, Talladega, AL 35160, Tel. (205) 362-0206. Paul B. Mohr, Sr., C S, U. Ch. of Christ, 548

Tarkio College, Tarkio, MO 64491, Tel. (816) 736-4131. Roy McIntosh, C NC, PCUSA, 1,621

Tennessee Wesleyan College, Athens, TN 37303, Tel. (615) 745-7504. James E. Cheek II, C S, Un. Meth., 503

Texas Christian University, Fort Worth, TX 76129, Tel. (817) 921-7000. William E. Tucker, C S, Christian Church (Disc.), 6,925

Texas College, Tyler, TX 75702, Tel. (214) 593-8311. David H. Johnson, C S, Chr. Meth. Epis., 512

Texas Lutheran College, Seguin, TX 78155, Tel. (512) 379-4161. Charles H. Oestreich, C S, ELCA, 1,296

Texas Wesleyan College, Fort Worth, TX 76105, Tel. (817) 534-0251. Jerry Bawcom, C S, Un. Meth., 1,437

Thiel College, Greenville, PA 16125, Tel. (412) 588-7700. Louis T. Almen, C MS, ELCA, 854

Thomas More College, Fort Mitchell, Ky 41017, Tel. (606) 341-5800. Charles J. Bensman, C S, Cath., 1,167

Tougaloo College, Tougaloo, MS 39174, Tel. (601) 956-4941. Charles A. Baldwin, Interim, C S, U. Ch. of Christ, 782

Transylvania University, Lexington, KY 40508, Tel. (606) 233-8111. Charles L. Shearer, C S, Christian Church (Disc.), 856

Trevecca Nazarene College, Nashville, TN 37203. Tel. (615) 248-1200. Homer J. Adams, C S, Nazarene, 1,058

Trinity College, Washington, DC 20017. Tel. (202) 939-5000. Marie V. Tarpey, Actg., C MS, Cath., 941

Trinity College, Deerfield, IL 60015, Tel. (312) 948-8980. Kenneth M. Meyer, C NC, Evan. Free Ch. of Am., 626

Trinity College, Burlington, VT 05401, Tel. (802) 658-0337. Sr. Janice E. Ryan, W NE, Cath., 915

Trinity University, San Antonio TX 78284, Tel. (512)

736-7011. Ronald Calgaard, C S, PCUSA, 2,687

Tusculum College, Greeneville, TN 37743, Tel. (615) 638-1111. Earl B. Mezoff, C S, PCUSA, 652

Union College, Barbourville, KY 40906, Tel. (606) 546-4151. Jack C. Phillips, C S, Un. Meth., 905

Union College, Lincoln, NE 68506, Tel. (402) 488-2331. John H. Wagner, C NC, S.D.A., 700

Union University, Jackson, TN 38305, Tel. (901) 668-1818. Hyran E. Barefoot, C S, So. Bapt., 1,511

Upsala College, E. Orange, NJ 07019, Tel. (201) 266-7000. David E. Schramm, ELCA, 1,786

Ursinus College, Collegeville, PA 19426, Tel. (215) 489-4111. Richard P. Richter, C MS, U. Ch. of Christ, 2,127

Ursuline College, Cleveland, OH 44124, Tel. (216) 449-4200. Sr. Anne Marie Diederich, W NC, Cath., 1,514

Valparaiso University, Valparaiso, IN 46383, Tel. (219) 464-5000. Robert V. Schnabel, C NC, Luth. (Mo.), 3,906

Villa Maria College, Erie, PA 16505, Tel. (814) 838-1966. Sr. M. Lawrence Antoun, W MS, Cath., 596

Villanova University, Villanova, PA 19085, Tel. (215) 645-4500. John M. Driscoll, C MS, Cath., 11,956

Virginia Intermont College, Bristol, VA 24201, Tel. (703) 669-6101. Gary M. Poulton, C S, So. Bapt., 517

Virginia Union University, Richmond, VA 23220, Tel. (804) 257-5600. S. Dallas Simmons, C S, Am. Bapt., 1,311

Virginia Wesleyan College, Norfolk, VA 23502, Tel. (804) 461-3232. Lambuth M. Clarke, C S, Un. Meth., 1,000

Viterbo College, La Crosse, WI 54601, Tel. (608) 784-0040. Robert E. Gibbons, C NC, Cath., 1,038

Voorhees College, Denmark, SC 29042, Tel. (803) 793-3351. Leonard E. Dawson, C S, Epis., 612

Wadham's Hall Seminary and College, Ogdensburg, NY 13669, Tel. (315) 393-4231. Thomas J. Thottumkal, M MS, Cath. 52

Wagner College, Staten Island, NY 10301 Tel. (718) 390-3100. Sam H. Frank, C MS, ELCA, 1,980

Wake Forest University, Winston-Salem, NC 27109, Tel. (919) 761-5000. Thomas K. Hearn, C S, So. Bapt., 5,062

Walla Walla College, College Place, WA 99324, Tel. (509) 527-2615. H. J. Bergman, C NW, S.D.A., 1,550

Walsh College, Canton, OH 44720, Tel. (216) 499-7090. Br. Francis Blouin, C NC, Cath., 1,269

Warner Southern College, Lake Wales, FL 33853, Tel. (813) 638-1426. Leroy M. Fulton, C S, Church of God, 294

Warner Pacific College, Portland, OR 97215. Tel. (503) 775-4366. Marshall K. Christensen, C NW, Ch. of God, 392

Warren Wilson College, Swannanoa, NC 28778, Tel. (704) 298-3325. John J. Carey, C S, PCUSA, 489

Wartburg College, Waverly, IA 50677, Tel. (319) 352-8200. Robert Vogel, C NC, ELCA, 1,311

Wayland Baptist University, Plainview, TX 79072, Tel. (806) 296-5521. Glenn E. Barnett, Interim, C S, So. Bapt., 1,799

Waynesburg College, Waynesburg, PA 15370, Tel. (412) 627-8191. J. Thomas Mills, Jr., C MS, PCUSA, 869

Wesley College, Dover, DE 19901, Tel. (302) 736-2300. Reed M. Stewart, C MS, Un. Meth., 1,083

Wesleyan College, Macon, GA 31297, Tel. (912) 477-1110. Robert K. Ackerman, W S, Un. Meth., 358

West Virginia Wesleyan College, Buckhannon, WV, 26201, Tel. (304) 473-8000, Thomas B. Courtice, C NC, Un. Meth., 1,481

Western Baptist College, Salem, OR 97301, Tel. (503) 581-8600. John G. Balyo, C NC, Bapt., 257

Westmar College, Le Mars, IA 51031, Tel. (712) 546-7081. Arthur W. Richardson, C NC, Un. Meth., 512

Westminster College, Fulton, MO 65251, Tel. (314) 642-3361. J. Harvey L. Saunders, C NC, PCUSA, 616

Westminster College, New Wilmington, PA 16172, Tel. (412) 946-8761. Oscar E. Remick, C MS, PCUSA, 1,297

Westminster College, of Salt Lake City, Salt Lake City, UT 84105, Tel. (801) 484-7651. Charles H. Dick, C NW, Interdenom., 1,361

Wheaton College, Wheaton, IL 60187. Tel. (312) 260-5000. J. Richard Chase, C NC, Interdenom., 2,597

Wheeling Jesuit College, Wheeling, WV 26003, Tel. (304) 243-2000. Thomas S. Acker, C NC, Cath., 1,018

Whittier College, Whittier, CA 90608, Tel. (213) 693-0771. Eugene S. Mills, C West, Friends 1,525

Whitworth College, Spokane, WA 99251, Tel. (509) 466-1000. Joseph P. H. Black, Actg., C NW, PCUSA, 1,803

Wilberforce University, Wilberforce, OH 45384, Tel. (513) 376-2911. Yvonne Walker-Taylor, C NC, A.M.E., 788

Wiley College, Marshall, TX 75670. Tel. (214) 938-8341. David L. Beckley, C S, Un. Meth., 481

Willamette University, Salem, OR 97301, Tel. (503) 370-6300. Jerry E. Hudson, C NW, Un. Meth., 1,940

William Carey College, Hattiesburg, MS 39401, Tel. (601) 582-5051. J. Ralph Noonkester, C S, So. Bapt., 1,778

William Jewell College, Liberty, MO 64068, Tel. (816) 781-7700. J. Gordon Kingsley, C NC, Am. Bapt. and So. Bapt., 2,026

William Penn College, Oskaloosa, IA 52577, Tel. (515) 673-8311. John Wagoner, C NC, Friends, 510

William Woods College, Fulton, MO 65251, Tel. (314) 642-2251. John M. Bartholomy, W NC, Christian Church (Disc.), 757

Wilmington College, Wilmington, OH 45177, Tel. (513) 382-6661. Neil Thorburn, C NC, Friends Un. Mtg., 1,256

Wilson College, Chambersburg, PA 17201, Tel. (717) 264-4141. Mary-Linda Merriam, W MS, PCUSA, 328

Wingate College, Wingate, NC 28174, Tel. (704) 233-8000. Paul R. Corts, C S, So. Bapt., 1,666

Wittenberg University, Springfield, OH 45501, Tel. (513) 327-6231. William A. Kinnison, C NC, ELCA, 2,117

Wofford College, Spartanburg, SC 29301, Tel. (803) 585-4821. Joab M. Lesesne C S, Un. Meth., 1,093

Xavier University, Cincinnati, OH 45207, Tel. (513) 745-3000. Albert J. Diulio, C NC, Cath., 6,237

Xavier University of Louisiana, New Orleans, LA 70125, Tel. (504) 486-7411, Norman C. Francis, C S, Cath., 1,959

Yeshiva University, New York, NY 10033, Tel. (212) 960-5400. Norman Lamm, Co. Ord. MS, Jewish, 4,360

12. CHURCH-RELATED COLLEGES AND UNIVERSITIES IN CANADA

The majority of the colleges and universities established in Canada in the 19th century were church-related. In subsequent reorganizations of higher education, especially after World War II, a number of these institutions were secularized and a large number of new, entirely non-denominational institutions of higher learning were established.

A uniquely Canadian solution to church-state problems over educational jurisdiction has evolved which permits denominational colleges to affiliate with larger provincial universities. The former thereby obtain some government grants while retaining some independence of action. Also, the advantages of smallness and largeness are combined; that is, the old religious traditions are maintained while students are also exposed to the new trends from the outside world in a larger setting.

In Canada education is a provincial responsibility and each of the ten provinces has worked out its own particular solution as to how the state will support the church in their respective educational endeavors. The provincial governments by establishing and funding all colleges and universities within their jurisdiction thereby accredit them.

Despite the recent secularization of some formerly religiously oriented colleges and universities, there is often a pronounced residue of religious atmosphere remaining in them, especially in the French Canadian universities. There individual students can choose between a Roman Catholic or secular humanist approach to their studies. Even in the large non-denominational provincial universities, the major denominations in the area usually provide chaplaincy services for those students who wish them.

Following is a list of those Canadian colleges and universities which still claim to offer a religious atmosphere for their students, spiritually, intellectually and socially, even if it is only by providing denominationally operated residences for them. Canadian universities are either English or French speaking and a few are bilingual. In the listing below the English or French title of each university indicates the language used therein. All French universities are Roman Catholic and secular.

This list was drawn mainly from the 1986-87 edition of the *Directory of Canadian Universities,* published by the Association of Universities and Colleges of Canada, 151 Slater St., Ottawa, Ontario K1P 5N1. Enrollment figures are for full-time undergraduates only. The colleges and universities are listed geographically from east to west with affiliated institutions listed under the major provincial university with which they are associated.

Abbreviations used are as follows: C-Coeducational, M-Men, W-Women. Each item in the listing below has the following order: Name of institution, address, telephone number, head of institution, nature of student body, denominational relationship, enrollment.

NEWFOUNDLAND

Memorial University of Newfoundland, Elizabeth Ave., St. John's Newfoundland A1C 5S7, Tel. (709) 737-8000. L. Harris, secular, C. (Has residences operated by the Anglican Church of Canada, the Roman Catholic Church, and United Church of Canada) 10,072

NOVA SCOTIA

Acadia University, Wolfville, Nova Scotia, B0P 1X0, Tel. (902) 542-2201. J. R. C. Perkin, C, Baptist, 3,133.

Dalhousie University, Halifax, Nova Scotia B3H 3J5, Tel. (902) 424-2211. Howard C. Clark, C, secular, 8,133. Associated universities: **The University of King's College,** Halifax, Nova Scotia B3H 2A1, Tel. (902) 422-1271. J.F. Godfrey, C, Anglican Church of Canada, 530. **Mount Saint Vincent University,** Halifax, Nova Scotia B3M 2J6, Tel. (902) 443-4450. Naomi Hersom, mostly W, Roman Catholic, 2,156.

Saint Francis Xavier University, Antigonish, Nova Scotia B2G 1C0, Tel. (902) 863-3300. Rev. G.A. MacKinnon, C, Roman Catholic, 2,483. Constituent college: **Mount Saint Bernard College,** Antigonish, Nova Scotia B2G 1C0, Tel. (902) 863-4960. Sr. M. MacDonnell, Roman Catholic. Residential accommodation for women.

St. Mary's University, Halifax, Nova Scotia B3H 3C3, Tel. (902) 429-9780. K. L. Ozmon, C, Roman Catholic/secular, 3,224.

Université Sainte-Anne, Church Point, Nova Scotia B0W 1M0, Tel. (902) 769-2114. R. Runte, C, 185.

University College of Cape Breton, P.O. Box 5300, Sydney, Nova Scotia B1P 6L2, Tel. (902) 539-5300. W. M. Reid, C, Roman Catholic, and Protestant, 1,288.

PRINCE EDWARD ISLAND

University of Prince Edward Island, 550 University Ave., Charlottetown, Prince Edward Island C1A 4P3, Tel (902) 566-0439. C. W. J. Eliot, C (secular, but has some residually religiously oriented residences), 1,768.

NEW BRUNSWICK

Mount Allison University, Sackville, New Brunswick E0A 3C0. Tel. (506) 364-2200. Donald O. Wells, C, United Church of Canada, 1,734.

Saint Thomas University, Fredericton, New Brunswick, E3B 5G3, Tel. (506) 452-7700. Rev. G.W. Martin, C, Roman Catholic, 1,235. (Shares facilities with the Fredericton campus of the University of New Brunswick.)

St. Stephen's University, St. Stephen, New Brunswick, C, Interdenominational.

Université de Moncton, Moncton, New Brunswick, E1A 3E9, Tel. (506) 858-4129. Louis-Philippe Blanchard, C, 3,965, (Branches at Moncton, Shippagan and Edmunston, New Brunswick.)

QUEBEC

Concordia University—Loyola Campus, 7141 Sherbrooke St., W., Montréal, Québec H4B 1R6, Tel. (514) 848-2424. P. J. Kenniff, C, Roman Catholic, 11,599.

Université Laval, Cité Universitaire, Québec, Québec G1K 7P4. Tél. (418) 656-2131. J. G. Pacquet, C, 17,461.

Université de Montréal, Case Postale 6128, Succursale A, Montréal, Québec H3C 3J7, Tel. (514) 343-6111. Gilles G. Cloutier, C, 19,184.

Université de Sherbrooke, Cité Universitaire, boulevard de l'Université, Sherbrooke, Québec J1K 2R1, Tél. (819) 821-7680. Aldée Cabana, C, 7,224.

Université du Québec, 2875 Boulevard Laurier, Ste-Foy, Québec G1V 2M3, Tel. (418) 657-3551. G. Boulet, C, 25,185. There are branches of the Université du Québec at the following locations in the Province of Québec: Rimouski, Chicoutimi, Québec, Ste-Foy, Three Rivers, Montréal, Laval, Hull, Rouyn.

ONTARIO

The Institute for Christian Studies, 229 College St., Toronto, Ontario M5T 1R4, Tel. (416) 979-2331. Dr. Clifford Pitt, C, non-denom., 40.

Laurentian University of Sudbury, Ramsey Lake Road, Sudbury, Ontario P3E 2C6, Tel. (705) 675-1151. John Daniel, C, secular 4,025. Three federated universities: **Huntington University,** Sudbury, Ontario P3E 2C6, Tel. (705) 675-1151, ext. 1051, L.J. Winckel, C, United Church of Canada. **L'Université de Sudbury/The Un-**

225

sity of Sudbury, Chemin du Lac Ramsey, Sudbury, Ontario P3E 2C6, Tel. (705) 673-5661. Rev. L. Larouche, C, Roman Catholic. **Thorneloe University,** Sudbury, Ontario P3E 2C6, Tel. (705) 675-1151, ext. 1052, J. W. K. Sandys-Wunsch, C, Anglican Church of Canada

McMaster University, Hamilton, Ontario L8S 4L8, Tel. (416) 525-9140. A. A. Lee, C. Baptist/secular, 10,104.

Université d'Ottawa/University of Ottawa, Ottawa, Ontario K1N 6N5, Tel. (613) 564-3311. A. D'Iorio, C, Roman Catholic/secular, 11,686.

The University of Toronto, Toronto, Ontario M5S 1A1, Tel. (416) 978-2011. G. E. Connell, C, secular, 28,878. Three federated universities: **The University of St. Michael's College,** 81 St. Mary St., Toronto, Ontario M5S 1J4, Tel. (416) 926-1300. Rev. J. McConica, C, Roman Catholic, 2,571. Two constituent residential colleges for women: **Loretto College,** 70 St. Mary St., Toronto, Ontario M5S 1J3, Tel. (416) 925-2833. Sr. J. D'Agostino, W, Roman Catholic. **St. Joseph's College,** 90 Wellesley St., West, Toronto, Ontario M5S 1C5, Tel. (416) 924-2121. Sr. Mary Anne McCarthy, W, Roman Catholic. **The University of Trinity College,** Toronto, Ontario M5S 1H8, Tel. (416) 978-2522. F.K. Hare, C, Anglican Church of Canada, 1,007. Constituent residential college for women; **St. Hilda's College,** 44 Devonshire Pl., Toronto, Ontario M5S 2E2, Tel. (416) 978-3562. E.M. Rowlinson, W, Anglican Church of Canada. **Victoria University,** 73 Queen's Park, Toronto, Ontario M5S 1K7, Tel. (416) 978-3801. G.S. French, C, United Church of Canada, 2,435. Residences for men and women.

The University of Waterloo, Waterloo, Ontario N2L 3G1, Tel. (519) 885-1211. D. T. Wright, C, secular, 14,541. Three affiliated colleges: **Renison College,** Waterloo, Ontario N2L 3G4, Tel. (519) 884-4400. Ian L. Campbell, C, Anglican Church of Canada. **St. Paul's College,** Westmount Rd., N., Waterloo, Ontario N2L 3G5, Tel. (519) 885-1460. F.C. Gérard, C, United Church of Canada. **Conrad Grebel College,** Waterloo, Ontario N2L 3G6, Tel. (519) 885-0220. R. Lebold, C, Mennonite. Federated with the University of Waterloo: **University of St. Jerome's College,** Waterloo, Ontario N2L 3G3, Tel. (519) 884-8110. N. L. Choate, C, Roman Catholic, 545. Attached to St. Jerome's is **Notre Dame College,** a women's residence run by the School Sisters of Notre Dame.

The University of Western Ontario, London, Ontario N6A 3K7, Tel. (519) 679-2111. K. George Pedersen, C, secular, 18,179. Three affiliated colleges: **Brescia College,** 1285 Western Rd., London, Ontario N6G 1H2, Tel. (519) 432-8353. Sr. Dolores Kuntz, W, Roman Catholic, 578. **Huron College,** London, Ontario N6G 1H3, Tel. (519) 438-7224. Frederick W. Bird, C, Anglican Church of Canada, 594. **King's College,** 266 Epworth Ave., London, Ontario N6A 2M3, Tel. (519) 433-3491. J.D. Morgan, C, Roman Catholic, 1,325.

The University of Windsor, Windsor, Ontario N9B 3P4, Tel. (519) 253-4232. Ronald Ianni, C, secular, 7,282. Two affiliated colleges: **Canterbury College,** 172 Patricia Rd., Windsor, Ontario N9B 3P4, Tel. (519) 256-6442. Rev. F.T. Kingston, C, Anglican Church of Canada. **Iona College,** 208 Sunset Ave., Windsor, Ontario N9B 3P4, Tel. (519)253-7257. Dr. J. Murray MacInnes, C, United Church of Canada. Federated university: **Assumption University,** Windsor, Ontario N9B 3P4, Tel. (519) 254-3783. Rev. David Gordon Heath, C, Roman Catholic.

MANITOBA

The University of Winnipeg, 515 Portage Ave., Winnipeg, Manitoba R3B 2E9, Tel. (204) 786-7811. R.H. Farquhar, C, United Church of Canada, 2,969. Associated institution: **Mennonite Brethren College of Arts,** 1-169 Riverton Ave., Winnipeg, Manitoba R2L 2E5, Tel. (204) 669-6575. D. Ewert, C, Canadian Mennonite Brethren Conference.

The University of Manitoba, Winnipeg, Manitoba R3T 2N2, Tel. (204) 474-8880. Arnold Naimark, C, secular, 13,481. Four affiliated colleges: **Collège universitaire de Saint Boniface,** 200 avenue Cathédrale, Saint-Boniface, Manitoba R2H 0H7, Tel. (204) 233-0210. P. Ruest, C, Roman Catholic, **St. John's College,** 400 Dysart Rd., Winnipeg, Manitoba R3T 2M5, Tel. (204) 474-8531. Rev. M. McLean, C, Anglican Church of Canada. **St. Paul's College,** 430 Dysart Rd., Winnipeg, Manitoba R3T 2M6, Tel. (204) 474-8575. D. J. Lawless, C, Roman Catholic. **St. Andrew's College,** 475 Dysart Rd., Winnipeg, Manitoba R3T 2M7, Tel. (204) 269-3565. Rev. O. A. Krawchenko, C, Ukrainian Greek Orthodox Church of Canada. Two approved teaching centres: **Canadian Mennonite Bible College,** 600 Shaftesbury Blvd., Winnipeg, Manitoba R3P 0M4, Tel. (204) 888-6781. Rev. J. Neufeld, C, Mennonite. **Canadian Nazarene College,** 1301 Lee Blvd., Winnipeg, Manitoba R3T 2P7, Tel. (204) 269-2120. N. Hightower, C, Church of the Nazarene.

SASKATCHEWAN

The University of Regina, Regina, Saskatchewan S4S 0A2, Tel. (306) 584-4111. L.I. Barber, C, secular, 5,369. Two federated colleges: **Campion College,** c/o University of Regina, Regina, Saskatchewan S4S 0A2, Tel. (306) 586-4242. Rev. Joseph Schner, sj, C, Roman Catholic, 598. **Luther College,** University of Regina, Regina, Saskatchewan S4S 0A2, Tel. (306) 584-0255. Donald G. Lee, C, Lutheran, 357.

Athol Murray College of Notre Dame, Wilcox, Saskatchewan S0G 5E0, Tel. (306) 732-2080. R. M. Kenney, C, Roman Catholic.

The University of Saskatchewan, Saskatoon, Saskatchewan S7N 0W0, Tel. (306) 244-4343. L. F. Kristjanson, C, secular, 11,485. Federated college: **Saint Thomas More College,** 1437 College Dr., Saskatoon, Saskatchewan S7N 0W6, Tel. (306) 966-8900. Rev. J. Hanrahan, csb, C, Roman Catholic, 1,058. Affiliated college: **St. Peter's College,** Muenster, Saskatchewan S0K 2Y0, Tel. (306) 682-5431. Rev. M. R. Weber, C, Roman Catholic.

ALBERTA

The University of Alberta, Edmonton, Alberta T6G 2E5, Tel. (403) 432-3111. M. Horowitz, C, secular, 21,063. Five affiliated colleges: **Camrose Lutheran College,** Camrose, Alberta T4V 2R3, Tel. (403) 679-1100. K.G. Johnson, C, Lutheran. **Canadian Union College,** Lacombe, Alberta T0C 0Z0, Tel. (403) 782-3381. Malcolm S. Graham, C, Seventh-Day Adventist. **Concordia Lutheran College,** 7128 Ada Blvd., Edmonton, Alberta T5B 4E4, Tel. (403) 479-8481. O. Walz, C, Lutheran. **The King's College,** 10766 - 97 St., Edmonton, Alberta T5H 2M1, Tel. (403) 428-0727. H. W. H. Van Andel, C, Nondenom. **St. Joseph's College,** 11325 89 Ave., Edmonton, Alberta T6G 2M7, Tel. (403) 433-1569. Rev. P. W. Platt, C, Roman Catholic. **St. Stephen's College,** Edmonton, Alberta T6G 2M7, Tel. (403) 439-7311. G. I. Mundle, C, United Church of Canada.

BRITISH COLUMBIA

Trinity Western College, 7600 Glover Rd., Langley, British Columbia V3A 4R9, Tel. (604) 888-7511, Neil Snider, C, Non-denominational/ Evangelical.

The University of British Columbia, 2075 Westbrook Mall, Vancouver, British Columbia V6T 1W5, Tel. (604) 228-2211. David Strongway, C, secular, 18,211. Three residences for men: **Carey Hall,** 5920 Iona, Vancouver, British Columbia, V6T 1J6, Tel. (604) 224-4308. Philip Collins, M, Baptist. **St. Andrew's Hall,** 6040 Iona, Vancouver, British Columbia, V6T 1J6, Tel. (604) 224-7720. Rev. B. J. Fraser, M, Presbyterian. **St. Mark's College,** 5935 Iona, Vancouver, British Columbia V6T 1J7, Tel. (604) 224-5935. Rev. Paul C. Burns, M, Roman Catholic.

13. RELIGIOUS PERIODICALS IN THE UNITED STATES

This list has been compiled for those who may wish to utilize a relatively large, representative group of religious periodicals. Many additional titles appear in the directories of religious bodies presented in this book. Probably the most inclusive list of religious periodicals published in the United States can be found in the *Gale Directory of Publications, 1988, Rev. Ed.* (IMS Press, 426 Pennsylvania Ave., Ft. Washington, PA 19034).

Each entry lists, in this order: Title of periodical, frequency of publication, religious affiliation, editor's name, address, and telephone number.

ADRIS Newsletter (q), non-sect., Richard F. Smith, Dept. of Theology, Fordham University, Bronx, NY 10458 Tel. (212)579-2400

Adventist Review (w), Seventh-day Adv., W. G. Johnson, 6840 Eastern Ave., N.W., Washington, DC 20012. Tel. (202)722-6965

Alliance Life (bi-w), The Christian and Missionary Alliance, Maurice Irvin, 350 N. Highland Ave., Nyack, NY 10960. Tel. (914)353-0750

Alliance Witness, The (bi-w), The Christian & Missionary Alliance, Maurice Irvin, 350 N. Highland Ave., Nyack, NY 10960. Tel. (914)353-0750

America (w), Cath., George W. Hunt, 106 W. 56th St., New York, NY 10019. Tel. (212)581-4640

American Baptist, The (bi-m), Am. Bapt., P.O. Box 851, Philip E. Jenks, American Baptist Churches, U.S.A., Valley Forge, PA 19482. Tel. (215)768-2216

American Bible Society Record (10/yr.), nondenom., Amer. Bible Society, Clifford P. Macdonald, 1865 Broadway, New York, NY. 10023,. Tel. (212)581-7400

American Journal of Theology & Philosophy (3/yr), Larry E. Axel and W. Creighton Peden, Dept. of Philosophy, Purdue Univ., West Lafayette, IN 47907 and Dept. of Philosophy, Augusta College, Augusta, GA 30910. Tel. (317)494-4286; Tel. (404)737-1709

American Presbyterians: Journal of Presbyterian History (q), PCUSA, James H. Smylie, 425 Lombard St., Philadelphia, PA 19147. Tel. (215)627-1852

Anglican and Episcopal History (q), Epis., John F. Woolverton, Trinity Church, 113 Coyle St., Portland, ME 04013

Arkansas United Methodist, (semi-m), U. Meth., Georgia M. Daily, P.O. Box 3547, Little Rock, AR 72203. Tel. (501)374-4831

Banner, The (w), Chr. Ref., Andrew Kuyvenhoven, 2850 Kalamazoo Ave., S.E., Grand Rapids, MI 49560. Tel. (616)246-0732

Baptist, The—A Monthly Magazine (q) Bapt., David N. Licorish, 18 W. 123rd St., New York, NY 10027. Tel. (212)876-2399

Baptist and Reflector (w), S. Bapt., W. Fletcher Allen, P.O. Box 728, Brentwood, TN 37024. Tel. (615)373-2255

Baptist Bulletin (m), Gen. Assoc. Reg. Bapt. Chs., Vernon D. Miller, 1300 N. Meacham Rd., Schaumburg, IL 60173

Baptist Courier (w), S. Bapt., John E. Roberts, P.O. Box 2168, Greenville, SC 29602. Tel. (803)232-8736

Baptist Herald (m), N. A. Bapt. Conf., Barbara J. Binder, 1 S. 210 Summit Ave., Oakbrook Terrace, IL 60181

Baptist History and Heritage (q), S. Bapt., Lynn E. May, Jr., 901 Commerce St., Ste. 400, Nashville, TN 37203. Tel. (615)244-0344

Baptist Leader (m), Am. Bapt., Linda Isham, Valley Forge, PA 19482. Tel. (215)768-2153

Baptist Messenger (w), S. Bapt., Glenn A. Brown, Box 25816, Oklahoma City, OK 73125. Tel. (405)236-4341

Baptist Record (w), S. Bapt., Donald T. McGregor, Box 530, Jackson, MS 39205. Tel. (601)968-3800

Baptist Standard (w), S. Bapt., Presnall H. Wood, 2343 Lone Star Dr., P.O. Box 660267, Dallas TX 75266. Tel. (214)630-4571

Biblical Recorder (w), S. Bapt., R. Gene Puckett, P.O. Box 26568, Raleigh, NC 27611. Tel. (919)847-2127

Brethren Journal, The (m), Unity of Brethren, Milton Maly Rt. 3, Box 766, Brenham, TX 77833

Catholic Chronicle (bi-w), Cath., Daniel J. McCarthy, 2130 Madison Ave., P.O. Box 1866, Toledo, OH 43603. Tel. (419)243-4178

Catholic Digest (m), Cath., Henry Lexau, P. O. Box 64090, St. Paul, MN 55164. Tel. (612)647-5296

Catholic Herald (w), Cath., Ethel M. Gintoft, 3501 S. Lake Dr., Milwaukee, WI 53207. Tel. (414)769-3500

Catholic Light (bi-w), Cath., Arthur F. Perry, The Chancery Bldg., 300 Wyoming Ave., Scranton, PA 18503

Catholic Review, The (w), Cath., Martin J. Cone, 320 Cathedral St., Baltimore, MD 21203. Tel. (301)547-5327

Catholic Standard and Times (w), Cath., David W. Givey, 222 N. 17th St., Philadelphia, PA 19103. Tel. (215)587-3660

Catholic Transcript, The (w), Cath., Vivian R. Stephenson, 785 Asylum Ave., Hartford, CT 06105. Tel. (203)527-1175

Catholic Universe Bulletin (w), Cath., Michael G. Dimengo, 1027 Superior Ave., N.E., Cleveland, OH 44114. Tel. (216)696-6525

Catholic Worker (8/yr.), Cath., Tim Lambert, 36 E. First St., New York, NY 10003. Tel. (212)254-1640

Celebration: A Creative Worship Service (m), Cath., William Freburger, P.O. Box 414293, Kansas City, MO 64141. Tel. (816)531-0538

Chicago Catholic, The, (w), Cath., Robert L. Johnston, 1144 W. Jackson Blvd., Chicago, IL 60607. Tel. (312)243-1300

Christian Bookseller (m), undenom., Karen M. Ball, 396 E. St. Charles Rd., Wheaton, IL 60188. Tel. (312) 653-4200

Christian Century, The (42/yr.), ecumen., James M. Wall, 407 S. Dearborn St., Chicago, IL 60605. Tel. (312) 427-5380

Christian Community, The (m, except Feb., June, Aug., and Sept.), International Council of Community Churches, J. Ralph Shotwell, 900 Ridge Rd., Homewood, IL 60430. Tel. (312)798-2264

Christian Endeavor World, The (q), interdenom., David G. Jackson, 1221 E. Broad St., P.O. Box 1110, Columbus, OH 43216. Tel. (614)258-9545

Christian Herald (m), interdenom., Dean Merrill, 40 Overlook Dr., Chappaqua, NY 10514 Tel. (914) 769-9000

Christian Index, The (w), S. Bapt., Jack U. Harwell, 2930 Flowers Rd., S., Atlanta, GA 30341.Tel. (404)455-0404

Christian Index, The (bi-m), Chr. Meth. Epis., Lawrence L. Reddick, III, P. O. Box 665, Memphis, TN 38101. Tel. (901)785-0222

Christian Life Magazine (m), undenom., Robert Walker, 396 East St. Charles Rd., Wheaton, IL 60188. Tel. (312)653-4200

Christian Ministry, The (6/yr.), James M. Wall, 407 S. Dearborn St., Chicago, IL 60605. Tel. (312)427-5380

Christian Reader, The (bi-m), non-denom., Dwight Hooten, 336 Gundersen Dr., P.O. Box 220, Wheaton, IL 60189. Tel. (312)668-8300

Christian Science Journal, The (m), Chr. Sc., A. W. Phinney, Jr., One Norway St., Boston, MA 02115. Tel. (617)450-2701

Christian Science Quarterly-Bible Lessons, Chr. Sc., (English, Danish, Dutch, French, German, Greek, Indonesian, available in Indonesia only), Italian, Japanese, Norwegian, Polish, Portuguese, Spanish, Swedish, and English Braille editions (q), One Norway St., Boston, MA 02115. Tel. (617)262-2300

Christian Science Sentinel (w), Chr. Sc., A. W. Phinney, Jr., One Norway St., Boston, MA 02115. Tel. (617)450-2701

Christian Standard (w), Christian Churches/Churches of Christ, Sam E. Stone, 8121 Hamilton Ave., Cincinnati, OH 45231

Christianity and Crisis (bi-w), ecumen., Leon Howell,537 W. 121st St., New York, NY 10027. Tel. (212)662-5907

Christianity Today (18/yr.), indepdt., Terry C. Muck, 465 Gunderson Dr., Carol Stream, IL 60188. Tel. (312)260-6200

Church Advocate, The (m), Chs. of God, Gen. Conf., Linda M. Draper, 700 E. Melrose Ave., P. O. Box 926, Findlay, OH 45839. Tel. (419)424-1961

Church and Society (bi-m), PCUSA, Kathy Lancaster and Gaspar B. Langella, 100 Witherspoon St., Louisville, KY 40202

Church Herald, The (22/yr.), Ref. Ch. in Am., John Stapert, 6157-28th St., SE, Grand Rapids, MI 49506 Tel. (616)957-1351

Church History (q), undenom., Robert M. Grant, Martin E. Marty, and Jerald C. Brauer, Swift Hall, The Univ. of Chicago, Chicago, IL 60637. Tel. (312)962-8215

Church Management: The Clergy Journal (10/yr), non-denom., Manfred Holck, Jr. P.O. Box 162527, Austin, TX 78716. Tel. (512)327-8501

Churchman, The (m), interdenom., Edna Ruth Johnson, 1074 23rd Ave., N., St. Petersburg, FL 33704. Tel. (813)894-0097

Church Woman, The (q), ecumen., Church Women United, Margaret Schiffert, 475 Riverside Dr., New York, NY 10115. Tel. (212)870-2344

Clarion Herald (w), Cath., Emile M. Comar, Jr., 523 Natchez St. P. O. Box 53247, New Orleans, 70153. Tel. (504)523-7731

Columban Mission (10/yr.), Cath., Richard Steinhilber, St. Columbans, NE 68056

Columbia (m), Cath., Elmer Von Feldt, P. O. Drawer 1670, New Haven, CT 06507

Commonweal (bi-w), Cath., Peter Steinfels, 15 Dutch St., New York, NY 10038. Tel. (212)732-0800

Concern Magazine/Newsfold, (q and 6/yr.), PCUSA, U. Presby. Women, Barbara Roche, 475 Riverside Dr., Rm. 454, New York, NY 10115. Tel. (212)870-2661

Congregationalist, The (bi-m), Congr. Chr. Chs., Natl. Assn. of, Mary Woolsey, 6134 Kerry Ave., Cheyenne, WY 82009. Tel. (307)634-1432

Congregational Journal, (3/yr.), Congr. Chr. Chs., Am. Cong. Cntr., Henry David Gray, 298 Fairfax Ave., Ventura, CA 93003. Tel. (805)644-3397

Conservative Judaism (q), Jewish, David Wolf Silverman, 3080 Broadway, New York, NY 10027. Tel. (212)678-8863

Courage in the Struggle for Justice and Peace (10/yr), Office for Church in Society, UCC, Russell, G. Claussen, 105 Madison Ave., New York, NY 10016. Tel. (212)683-5656

Criterion, The (w), Cath., John F. Fink, 1400 N. Meridian, P. O. Box 1717, Indianapolis, IN 46206. Tel. (317)236-1570

Cumberland Presbyterian, The (bi-w, ex. July and Dec., m), Cumb. Presb., Mark Brown, Interim, 1978 Union Ave., Memphis, TN 38104. Tel. (901)276-4572

Currents in Theology and Mission (6/yr.), Christ Sem.-Seminex, Ralph W. Klein, 1100 E. 55th St., Chicago, Il 60615. Tel. (312)753-0763.

Decision (11/yr.), Billy Graham Evangelistic Assn., Roger C. Palms, 1300 Harmon Pl., Minneapolis, MN 55403

Disciple, The (m), Chr. Ch. (Disc.), James L. Merrell, Box 179, St. Louis, MO 63166. Tel. (314)231-8500

Ecumenical Courier (q), U.S. Conference for the World Council of Churches, Rm. 1062, 475 Riverside Dr., New York, NY 10115. Tel. (212)870-2533

Ecumenical Review, The (q), interdenom., Emilio Castro, World Council of Churches, 150 Route de Ferney, CH-1211 Geneva 20, Switzerland

Ecumenical Trends (m), ecum., Patrick J. Cogan, Graymoor Ecumenical Institute, 475 Riverside Dr., Rm. 528, New York, NY 10115. Tel. (212)870-2330

Emphasis on Faith and Living (m), Missionary Ch. Michael Reynolds, 3901 S. Wayne Ave., Fort Wayne, IN 46807

Engage/Social Action (m), U. Meth., Lee Ranck, 100 Maryland Ave., N. E., Washington, DC 20002. Tel. (202)488-5632

Episcopal Recorder (m), Ref. Epis., George B. Fincke, 4225 Chestnut St., Philadelphia, PA 19104. Tel. (215)222-5158

Episcopalian, The (m), Epis., Richard L. Crawford, 1201 Chestnut St., Philadelphia, PA 19107. Tel. (215)564-2010

Eternity (m), interdenom., James M. Boice, 1716 Spruce St., Philadelphia, PA 19103. Tel. (215)546-3696

Evangelist, The (w), Cath., James Breig, 39 Philip St., Albany, NY 12207. Tel. (518)434-0107

Extension (10/yr), Cath., Bradley Collins, 35 East Wacker Dr., Chicago, IL 60601. Tel. (312)236-7240

Firm Foundation (semi-m), Chs. of Christ, William S. Cline, Box 17200, Pensacola, FL 32522

Forum Letter (m), Luth., Richard J. Neuhaus, 338 E. 19th St., New York, NY 10003. Tel. (212)532-4320

Franciscan Herald (m), Cath., Gabriel Brinkman, 1434 W. 51st. St., Chicago, IL 60609. Tel. (312)254-4462

Free Will Baptist, The (w), Original Free Will Bapt., Janie Jones Sowers, Free Will Baptist Press, P. O. Box 159, Ayden, NC 28513. Tel. (919)746-6128

Friends Journal (s-m), Friends (Quakers), Vinton Deming, 1501 Cherry St., Philadelphia, PA 19102. Tel. (215)241-7277

Gospel Advocate (semi-m), Chs. of Christ, Furman Kearley, Box 150, Nashville, TN 37202

Gospel Herald (w), Menn., Daniel Hertzler, Scottdale, PA 15683. Tel. (412)887-8500

Grapevine (10/yr.), Joint Strategy and Action Committee, James E. Solheim, 475 Riverside Dr., Rm. 450, New York, NY 10115. Tel. (212)870-3105

Herald of Christian Science, The, Chr. Sc., French, German, Portugese, and Spanish editions (m); Danish, Dutch, Greek, Indonesian, Italian, Japanese, Norwegian, Swedish editions (q), A. W. Phinney, One Norway St., Boston, MA 02115. Tel. (617)450-2701

Herald of Holiness (semi-m), Nazarene, W. E. McCumber, 6401 The Paseo, Kansas City, MO 64131. Tel. (816)333-7000.

Heritage (q), Assem. of God, Wayne E. Warner, 1445 Boonville Ave., Springfield, MO 65802. Tel. (417)862-2781.

Homiletic and Pastoral Review (m), Cath., Kenneth Baker, 86 Riverside Dr., New York, NY 10024. Tel. (212)799-2600

Image (semi-m), Chs. of Chr., Reuel Lemmons, 115 Warren Dr., Ste. D., West Monroe, LA 71291. Tel. (318)396-4366.

Interest (m), Christian Breth., William W. Conard, 218 W. Willow, Wheaton, IL 60187. Tel. (312)653-6573

International Bulletin of Missionary Research (q), nondenom., Gerald H. Anderson, 490 Prospect St., New Haven, CT 06511. Tel. (203)624-6672.

International Christian Digest (10/yr.), nondenom., J. Richard Peck, P.O. Box 801, Nashville, TN 37202. Tel. (615)749-6488.

International Review of Mission (q), Commission on World Mission and Evangelism, World Council of Churches, Eugene Stockwell, 150 Route de Ferney, P. O. Box 66, CH-1211 Geneva 20, Switzerland

Interpretation (q), Union Theol. Sem. in Va., Paul J. Achtemeier, 3401 Brook Rd., Richmond, VA 23227. Tel. (804)355-0671

Interpreter, The (m), U. Meth., Darrell R. Shamblin, 810 Twelfth Ave. S., Nashville, TN 37202. Tel. (615)742-5400

Jewish Action (q), Jewish, Heidi Tenzer, 45 W. 36 St., New York, NY 10018. Tel. (212)244-2011

Journal of Christian Education of the African Methodist Episcopal Church, A.M.E. Edgar L. Mack, 500-8th Ave., S., Nashville, TN 37203. Tel. (615)242-1420

Journal of Ecumenical Studies (q), Leonard Swidler, Temple Univ. (022-38), Philadelphia, PA 19122. Tel. (215)787-7714

Journal of Pastoral Care, The (q), nondenom., Orlo Strunk, Jr., P.O. Box 2967, 901 N. Kings Hwy., Myrtle Beach, SC 29578. Tel. (803)448-4820.

Journal of Religion (q), undenom., 1025 E. 58th St., Chicago, IL 60637. Tel. (312)702-8216

Journal of the American Academy of Religion (q), undenom., William Scott Green, Univ. of Rochester, Rochester, NY 14627. Tel. (716)275-5378

Journal of the American Scientific Affiliation (See: Perspectives on Science and Christian Faith)

Judaism (q), Jewish, Robert Gordis, 15 E. 84th St., New York, NY 10028. Tel. (212)879-4500

Liguorian (m), Cath., Norman J. Muckerman, Liguori, MO 63057. Tel. (314)464-2500

Living Church, The (w), Epis., H. Boone Porter, 816 E. Juneau Ave., Milwaukee, WI 53202. Tel. (414)276-5420

Long Island Catholic, The (51/yr.), Cath., Francis J. Maniscalco, 115 Greenwich St., P. O. Box 700, Hempstead, NY 11551. Tel. (516)538-8800

Lookout, The (w), Christian Churches/Churches of Christ, Mark Taylor, 8121 Hamilton Ave., Cincinnati, OH 45231. Tel. (513)931-4050

Louisiana United Methodist, The (w), U. Meth., Harvey G. Williamson, 527 North Blvd., Baton Rouge, LA 70802

Lutheran, The (s-m), Ev. Luth. Ch. in Am., Edgar R. Trexler, 8765 W. Higgins Rd., Chicago, IL 60631. Tel. (312)380-2700

Lutheran Forum (q), Luth., Glenn C. Stone, 308 W. 46 St., New York, NY 10036. Tel. (212)757-1292

Lutheran Witness (m), Luth., Mo, Synod, 1333 S. Kirkwood Rd., St. Louis, MO 63122. Tel. (314)965-9000

Maryknoll (m), Cath., Ronald R. Saucci, Maryknoll Fathers and Brothers, Maryknoll, NY 10545. Tel. (914)941-7590

Media & and Values (q), nondenom., Elizabeth Thoman, 1962 S. Shenandoah St., Los Angeles, CA 90034. Tel. (213)559-2944

Mennonite, The, (semi-m), Gen. Conf. Menn., Muriel T. Stackley, Box 347, Newton, KS 67114. Tel. (316)283-5100

Message Magazine, The (bi-m), Seventh-day Adv., Delbert W. Baker, 55 West Oak Ridge Dr., Hagerstown, MD 21740. Tel. (301)791-7000

Messenger (m), Ch. Breth., Kermon Thomasson, Ch. Breth., 1451 Dundee Ave., Elgin, IL 60120. Tel. (312)742-5100

Messenger, The (m), Swedenborgian, James Lawrence, 2107 Lyon St., San Francisco, CA 94114.

Mid-Stream: An Ecumenical Journal, (q), Chr. Ch. (Disc.), Paul A. Crow, Jr., P. O. Box 1986 Indianapolis, IN 46206. Tel. (317)353-1491

Mission Herald (bi-m), Natl. Bapt., Wm. J. Harvey, III, 701 S. 19th St., Philadelphia, PA 19146

Missionary Monthly (m), Chr. Ref. and Ref. Chs. Dick L. Van Halsema, (P.O. Box 6181), Grand Rapids, MI 49506. Tel. (616)957-4673

Missionary Seer, The (m), A.M.E. Zion, Kermit J. DeGraffenreidt, 475 Riverside Dr., Ste. 1910 New York, NY 10115. Tel. (212)870-2952

Missions USA, (m), S. Bapt., Phyllis Thompson, 1350 Spring St., N.W., Atlanta, GA 30367. Tel. (404)873-4041

Mississippi United Methodist Advocate (bi-w), U. Meth., J. Rayford Woodrick, P. O. Box 1093, Jackson, MS 39205. Tel. (601)354-0515

Moody Monthly (m), interdenom., Robert Flood, 2101 W. Howard, Chicago, IL 60645. Tel. (312)508-6820

Muslim World, The (q), undenom., Willem A. Bijlefeld, Duncan Black Macdonald Center, Hartford Seminary, 77 Sherman St., Hartford, CT 06105. Tel. (203)232-4451

National Catholic Reporter (w, Sept.-May; bi-w, June-Aug.), Cath., Thomas C. Fox, P.O. Box 419281, Kansas City, MO 64141. Tel. (816)531-0538

National Christian Reporter, The, (w), interdenom., Spurgeon M. Dunnam, III, P. O. Box 222198, Dallas, TX 75222. Tel. (214)630-6495.

New Catholic World (bi-m), Cath., Laurie Felknor, 997 Macarthur Blvd., Mahwah, NJ 07430.

New Oxford Review (10/yr.), Cath., Dale Vree, 1069 Kains Ave., Berkeley, CA 94706. Tel. (415)526-5374

New World Outlook (m), U. Meth., George M. Daniels, 475 Riverside Dr., New York, NY 10115. Tel. (212)870-3765

North American Moravian, The (m), Morav., Hermann I. Weinlick, 1021 Center St., P.O. Box 1245, Bethlehem, PA 18016. Tel. (215)867-0594

North Carolina Christian Advocate (w), U. Meth., C. A. Simonton, Jr., P. O. Box 508, Greensboro, NC 27402. Tel. (919)272-1196

Orthodox Observer, The (bi-w), Greek Orth., P. J. Gazouleas, 8 E. 79th St., New York, NY 10021. Tel. (212)628-2590

Our Sunday Visitor (w), Cath., Robert Lockwood, Noll Plaza, Huntington, IN 46750. Tel. (219)356-8400

Pastoral Life (m), Cath., Jeffrey Mickler, Canfield, OH 44406. Tel. (216)533-5503

PCA Messenger, The (m), PCA, Paul R. Gilcrest, 4319-F Memorial Dr., Decatur, GA 30032. Tel. (404)292-6102.

Pentecostal Evangel (w), Assem. of God, Richard G. Champion, 1445 Boonville Ave., Springfield, MO 65802. Tel. (417)862-2781

Perspectives on Science and Christian Faith (Journal of the American Scientific Affiliation) (q), Interdenom., Wilbur L. Bullock, P. O. Box 668, Ipswich, MA 01938

Pilot, The (w), Cath. Philip F. Lawler, 49 Franklin St., Boston, MA 02110. Tel. (617)482-4316

Praying (bi-m), Cath., Art Winter, P.O. Box 410335, Kansas City, MO 64141. Tel. (816)531-0538

Presbyterian Layman, The (6/yr.), Presbyterian Lay Committee, James J. Cochran, 1489 Baltimore Pike, Ste. 301, Springfield, PA 19064. Tel. (215)543-0227

Presbyterian Outlook (w), PCUSA, George L. Hunt, Box C-32071, Richmond, VA 23261. Tel. (804)359-8442

Presbyterian Survey (m), PCUSA, Vic Jameson, 341 Ponce de Leon Ave., N.E., Atlanta, GA 30365

Providence Visitor (w), Cath., Gloria Barone, 184 Broad St., Providence, RI 02903. Tel. (401)272-1010

Pulpit Digest, The (bi-m), interdenom., David A. Farmer, % Harper & Row, San Francisco, CA 94111

Quaker Life (m), Friends United Mtg., J. Stanley Banker, 101 Quaker Hill Dr., Richmond, IN 47374. Tel. (317)962-7573

Quarterly Review, The (q), S. Bapt., K. Gail Merritt, 127 Ninth Ave. N., Nashville, TN 37234. Tel. (615)251-2516

Quarterly Review, U. Meth., Charles E. Cole, Box 871, Nashville, TN 37202

Reform Judaism (4/yr.), Ref. Jewish, Aron Hirt-Manheimer, 838 Fifth Ave., New York, NY 10021. Tel. (212)249-0100

Religion and Society Report (m), Richard J Neuhaus, Rockford Institute Center on Religion & Society, 152 Madison Ave., 24th Fl., New York, NY 10016. Tel. (212)532-4320.

Religion Index One: Periodicals (formerly Index to Religious Periodical Literature) and Religion Index Two: Multi-Author Works. American Theological Library Association, Index Board. Albert E. Hurd, Exec. Dir., 5600 S. Woodlawn Ave., Chicago, IL 60637

Religious Broadcasting (11/yr.), National Religious Broadcasters, Ben Armstrong, CN1926, Morristown, NJ 07960. Tel. (201)428-5400

Religious Education (q), multi-faith, Jack D. Spiro, Virginia Commonwealth Univ., Richmond, VA 23284. Tel. (804)257-1224

Research in Ministry (an index to Doctor of Ministry Projects and Reports—, 1981, American Theological Library Association Index Board, Albert E. Hurd, Exec. Dir., 5600 South Woodlawn Ave., Chicago, IL 60637

Reporter/Alive (w), Luth. Mo. Synod, David Mahsman, 1333 S. Kirkwood Rd., St. Louis, MO 63122. Tel. (314)965-9000

Resources for Youth Ministry (q), Luth., Mo. Synod, LeRoy Wilke, 1333 S. Kirkwood Rd., St. Louis, MO 63122. Tel. (314)965-9000

Response (11/yr.), U. Meth., Carol Marie Herb, 475 Riverside Dr., Rm. 1344, New York, NY 10115. Tel. (212)870-3755

Restoration Herald (m), Christian Chs., Ch. of Christ, Thomas D. Thurman, 5664 Cheviot Rd., Cincinnati, OH 45247. Tel. (513)385-0461

Restoration Quarterly (q), Chs. of Christ, Everett Ferguson, Box 8227, Abilene, TX 79699

Review for Religious (bi-m), Cath., Daniel F. X. Meenan, 3601 Lindell Blvd., St. Louis, MO 63108. Tel. (314)535-3048

Review of Religious Research (4/yr.), The Religious Research Assoc., Edward Lehman, Jr., Dept. of Sociology, SUNY, Brockport, NY 14420. Tel. (716)395-5664

Sabbath Recorder, The (m), Seventh Day Bapt., D. Scott Smith, P.O. Box 1678, Janesville, WI 53547. Tel. (608)752-5055

Saint Anthony Messenger (m), Cath., Norman Perry, 1615 Republic St., Cincinnati, OH 45210. Tel. (513)241-5616

Saints' Herald (m), Reorg. Ch. of Jesus Christ of, L.D.S., Roger Yarrington, P.O. Box HH, Independence, MO 64055

Salt (m), Cath., Mark J. Brummel, 205 W. Monroe St., Chicago, IL 60606. Tel. (312)236-7782

Second Century, The (q), W. Everett Ferguson, Box 8227, Abilene, TX 79699.

Signs of the Times (m), Seventh-day Adv., K. J. Holland, Box 7000, Boise, ID 83707.

Social Questions Bulletin (bi-m), Methodist Fed. for Social Action (independent), Rev. George McClain, Shalom House, 76 Clinton Ave., Staten Island, NY 10301. Tel. (718)273-4941

Sojourners (11/yr.), nondemom., Jim Wallis, Box 29272, Washington, DC 20017. Tel. (202)636-3637

South Carolina United Methodist Advocate (w), U. Meth., Maryneal Jones, 4908 Colonial Dr., Ste. 207, Columbia, SC 29203. Tel. (803)786-9483

Southern New England United Methodist Reporter (w), U. Meth.; Ann Whiting, The United Methodist Center, 566 Commonwealth Ave., Boston, MA 02215. Tel. (617)266-9038

Southwestern News (m, except Aug.), S. Bapt., John Earl Seelig, Southwestern Bapt. Theol. Sem., Box 22,000-3E, Fort Worth, TX 76122

Spirituality Today (q), Cath., Richard Woods, 7200 W. Division St., River Forest, IL 60305. Tel. (312)771-4270

Standard, The (m), Bapt. Gen. Conf., Donald E. Anderson, 2002 S. Arlington Heights Rd., Arlington Heights, IL 60005. Tel. (312)228-0200, (1-800)323-4215

Star of Zion (w), A.M.E. Zion, Morgan W. Tann, P.O. Box 31005, Charlotte, NC 28230. Tel. (704)377-4329

Stewardship USA, Raymond B. Knudsen II, 31 Langerfeld Rd., Hillsdale, NJ 07642. Tel. (201)664-8890

Sunday (q), interdenom., James P. Wesberry, 2930 Flowers Rd., S., Atlanta, GA 30341. Tel. (404)451-7315

Tablet, The (w), Cath., Ed Wilkinson, 1 Hanson Pl., Brooklyn, NY 11243. Tel. (718)789-1500

Theological Education (semi-a), undenom., Leon Pacala, Association of Theological Schools in the United States and Canada, P. O. Box 130, Vandalia, OH 45377

Theology Digest (q), Cath., Bernhard A. Asen, Rosemary Jermann, 3634 Lindell Blvd., St. Louis, MO 63108, Tel. (314)658-2857

Theology Today (q), undenom., Hugh T. Kerr, P. O. Box 29, Princeton, NJ 08542

This World (q), Richard J. Neuhaus, Rockford Institute Center on Religion & Society, 152 MadisonAve., 24th Fl., New York, NY 10016. Tel. (212)532-4320

Thought (q), Cath., G. Richard Dimler, Fordham Univ., Bronx, NY 10458. Tel. (212)579-2322

Tidings, The (w), Cath., Alphonse J. Antczak, 1530 W. Ninth St., Los Angeles, CA 90015. Tel. (213)251-3360

Tradition (4/yr.), Jewish (Rabbinical Council of America), W. S. Wurzburger, 275 7th Ave., New York, NY 10001. Tel. (212)807-7888

Unitarian Universalist World (9/yr.), David B. Parke, 25 Beacon St., Boston, MA 02108

United Evangelical, The (m), David H. Reed, Evang. Congreg. Ch., E. C. Church Center, 100 W. Park Ave. Box 186, Myerstown, PA 17067. Tel. (717)866-7581

United Evangelical Action (bi-m), interdenom., Donald R. Brown, 450 E. Gundersen Drive, Carol Stream, IL 60188; P. O. Box 28, Wheaton, IL 60189. Tel. (312)665-0500

United Methodist Christian Advocate, The (bi-w), U. Meth., Paul E. Ruark, 909 9th Ave. W., Birmingham, AL 35204. Tel. (205)251-9279

United Methodist Review, The (bi-w), U. Meth., Spurgeon, M. Dunnam, III, P. O. Box 660275, Dallas, TX 75266. Tel. (214)630-6495

Upreach (sm), Chs. of Christ, Harold Hazelip, Box 2001, Abilene, TX 79604

U.S. Catholic (m), Cath., Mark J. Brummel, 205 W. Monroe St., Chicago, IL 60606. Tel. (312)236-7782

Virginia Advocate (bi-m), U. Meth., Alvin J. Horton, 4016 W. Broad St., Rm. 208, P. O. Box 11367, Richmond, VA 23230. Tel. (804)359-9451, Ext. 65

Vital Christianity (20/yr.), Ch. of God (Anderson, Ind.), Arlo F. Newell, Box 2499, Anderson, IN 46018. Tel. (317)644-7721

Voice of Missions (bi-m), Afr. Meth. Epis., Maeola Herring, 475 Riverside Dr., Rm. 1926, New York, NY 10115. Tel. (212)870-2258

War Cry, The (w), Salv. Army, Lt. Col. Henry Gariepy, 799 Bloomfield Ave., Verona, NJ 07044. Tel. (201)239-0606

Wesleyan Christian Advocate (w), U. Meth., G. Ross Freeman, 410-411 Methodist Center, 159 Ralph McGill Blvd., N. E., Atlanta, GA 30308. Tel. (404)659-0002

Western Recorder (w), S. Bapt., Jack D. Sanford, Box 43401, Middletown, KY 40243. Tel. (502)245-4101

White Wing Messenger, The (bi-w), Ch. of God of Prophecy, M. A. Tomlinson, Bible Pl., Cleveland, TN 37311

Word and Work (m), undenom., Alex V. Wilson, 2518 Portland Ave., Louisville, KY 40212

World Vision (bi-m), nondenom., David Olson, 919 W. Huntington Dr., Monrovia, CA 91016. Tel. (818)357-7979

Worship (6/yr.) Cath., Aelred Tegels, St. John's Abbey, Collegeville, MN 56321. Tel. (612) 363-2011

Your Church (bi-m), undenom., Phyllis Mather Rice, 198 Allendale Rd., King of Prussia, PA 19406

Zion's Herald (m), U. Meth., Ann Whiting, The United Methodist Center, 566 Commonwealth Ave., Boston, MA 02215. Tel. (617) 266-9038

14. RELIGIOUS PERIODICALS IN CANADA

The religious periodicals below constitute a basic core of important newspapers, journals, and periodicals circulated in Canada. For additional publications treating religion and religious affairs in Canada, the reader should check the denominational directories in this **Yearbook** in Directory 4, "Religious Bodies in Canada." Details on other religious periodicals circulating in Canada can also be found in Directory 3, "Religious Bodies in the United States" in this **Yearbook.**

Each entry generally appears in this order: title of periodical, frequency of publication, religious affiliation, editor's name, address, and telephone number.

Action (m), Pent. Assem. of Canada, The Overseas Mission Dept., 10 Overlea Blvd., Toronto, Ontario M4H 1A5. Tel. (416) 425-1010

Actionews (m), J. Don Scott, World Vision Canada, 6630 Turner Valley Rd., Mississauga, Ontario L5N 2S4. Tel. (416)821-3030

Advance (bi-m), Assoc. Gospel Chs., Wayne Foster, 8 Silver St., Paris, Ontario N3L 1T6. Tel. (519)442-6220

ALbERTa, The, Bapt. Gen. Conf., Rev. Virgil Olson, #4, 9825-44 Ave, Edmonton, Alberta T6E 5E3. Tel. (403) 438-9126

Anakainosis (q), Institute for Christian Studies, 229 College St., Toronto, Ontario M5T 1R4. Tel. (416) 979-2331

Anglican, The (10/yr.), Debbie Dimmick, 135 Adelaide St., E., Toronto, Ontario M5C 1L8. Tel. (416)363-6021

Annals of the Propagation of the Faith (bi-m), Cath., Bernard Prince, 2661 Kingston Rd., Scarborough, Ontario M1M 1M3. Tel. (416)266-4535

ARC (2/yr), Fac. of Rel. Stud., McGill Univ., 3520 University St., Montreal, Quebec H3A 2A7. Tel. (514) 398-4121

Atlantic Baptist, The (m), Un. Bapt. Conv. of the Atlantic Provinces, Michael Lipe, Box 756, Kentville, Nova Scotia B4N 3X9. Tel. (902)678-6868

Atlantic Wesleyan (m), Wes. Ch., Rev. H. R. Ingersoll, Box 20, Sussex, New Brunswick E0E 1P0. Tel. (506) 433-1007

Bible Tidings (q), Canadian Luth. Bible Inst., 4837-52A, Camrose, Alberta T4V 1W5. Tel. (403)672-4454

B. C. Fellowship Baptist (m), Fellowship of Reg. Bapt. Chs. of B. C., Donald W. Reed 1420 E. 2nd Ave., Vancouver, British Columbia V5N 5L9. Tel. (604) 255-5471

Briarcrest Echo, The, (q), Klaus Thon, Briarcrest Bible College, Caronport, Saskatchewan S0H 0S0. Tel. (306)756-2321

British Columbia Catholic, The (w), Cath., Vincent J. Hawkswell, 150 Robson St., Vancouver, British Columbia V6B 2A7. Tel. (604) 683-0281

Bulletin nationale de liturgie (bi-m), Cath., Office national de liturgie, 3530, rue Adam, Montréal, Québec H1W 1Y8

Cahiers de Josephologie (2/yr), Cath., Roland Gauthier, Centre de recherche, 3800 Ch. Reine-Marie, Montréal, Québec H3V 1H6. Tel. (514)733-8211

Cahiers de Spiritualité Ignatienne (q), Cath., Centre de Spiritualité Ignatienne, 2370 Rue Nicolas-Pinel, Ste. Foy, Québec G1V 4L6. Tel. (418)653-6353

Caledonia Times (10/yr.) Bill Graham, Ang. Ch. of Canada, Box 339, Burns Lake, British Columbia V0J 1E0

Calvinist-Contact (w), Ref., Bert Witvoet, 261 Martindale Rd., Unit 4, St. Catharines, Ontario L2R 6P9. Tel. (416) 682-8311

Campus News: Western Pentecostal Bible College (4/yr),

West. Pent. Bible College, Box 1000, Clayburn, British Columbia V0X 1E0

Canada Armenian Press (q), Y. Sarmazian, 42 Glenforest Rd., Toronto, Ontario M4N 1Z8. Tel. (416) 485-4336

Canada Asia Currents (See: Currents)

Canada Lutheran, The (11/yr), Ev. Luth. Ch. in Canada, Ferdy Baglo, 1512 St. James St., Winnipeg, Manitoba R3H 0L2. Tel. (204)786-6707

Canadian Adventist Messenger (12/yr), Seventh-day Adv. Ch. in Canada, G. E. Maxson, Maracle Press, 1156 King St. E., Oshawa, Ontario L1H 1H8. Tel. (416)686-2700

Canadian Baptist, The (m), Bapt. Conv. of Ontario and Quebec, Bapt. Un. of West. Canada and Canadian Bapt. Fed., William H. Jones, 217 St. George St., Toronto, Ontario M5R 2M2. Tel. (416)922-5163

Canadian Bible Society Quarterly Newsletter (q), William R. Russell,10 Carnforth, Toronto, Ontario M4A 2S4. Tel. (416)757-4171

Canadian Buddhist (m), Buddhist Chs. of Canada, 220 Jackson Ave., Vancouver, British Columbia V6A 3B3. Tel. (603) 253-7033

Canadian C. S. Lewis Journal (q), Stephen Scofield, Dunsfold Godaiming, Surrey GU8 4PF, England

Canadian Challenge (a), Foursquare Gospel Church of Canada, 7895 Welsley Dr., Burnaby, British Columbia V5E 3X4

Canadian Christian Harbinger (m), Chs. of Chr. and Chr. Chs., Don Lewis, Canadian Christian Press, P.O. Box 460, Vernon, British Columbia V1T 6M4

Canadian Churchman (m), Ang. Ch. of Canada, Jerrold F. Hames, 600 Jarvis St., Toronto, Ontario M4Y 2J6. Tel. (416) 924-9192

Canadian Council of Churches News Bulletin/Bulletin de nouvelles du Conseil canadien des Eglises (q), Canadian Council of Churches, 40 St. Clair Ave. E., Toronto, Ontario M4T 1M9. Tel. (416)921-4152

Canadian Disciple (q), Chr. Ch. (Disc. of Chr.) Raymond A. Cuthbert, 240 Home St., Winnipeg, Manitoba R3G 1X3. Tel. (204)783-5881

Canadian Ecumenical News (9/yr.), Jim Pence, 1410 W. 12th Ave., Vancouver, British Columbia V6H 1M8. Tel. (604)736-1613

Canadian Friend, The, The Canadian Yearly Mtg. of the Rel. Soc. of Friends, Dorothy Parshall, 3417 Rue Ste. Famille, #1, Montréal, Québec H2X 2K6. Tél. (514)281-6207

Canadian Lutheran (bi-m), Frances A. Wershler, Luth Ch. Canada, Box 163, Stn. A., Winnipeg, Manitoba R3K 2A1. Tel. (204)832-0123

Canadian Trumpeter Canada-West, Ch. of God of Prophecy in Canada, John and Ruth Doroshuk, Box 952, Strathmore, Alberta T0J 3H0

Candle, The (m), Cath., Velma Brown, 2-B John St., Dartmouth, Nova Scotia B3A 1L4

Caravan (q), CCCB, Joanne Chafe, 90 Parent Ave., Ottawa, Ontario K1N 7B1. Tel. (613)236-9461

Catalyst (8/yr.), Citizens for Public Justice, Virginia

Smith, 229 College St., #311, Toronto, Ontario M5T 1R4. Tel. (416) 979-2443

Catholic New Times (bi-w), Cath., Frances Ryan, 80 Sackville St., Toronto, Ontario M5A 3E5. Tel. (416) 361-0761

Catholic Register, The (w), Cath., Sean O'Sullivan, 67 Bond St., Toronto, Ontario M5B 1X6. Tel. (416) 362-6822

Catholic Times, The, (10/yr), Cath., Leo MacGillivray, 2005 St. Marc St., Montreal, Quebec H3H 2G8. Tel. (514)937-2301

Central Canada Clarion (bi-m), Wes. Ch., W. W. Jewell, 15 Robertson Lane, Belleville, Ontario K8P 4C2

Channels (q), Renewal Fellowship, Presby. Ch. in Canada, J. H. (Hans) Kouvenberg, 2130 Wesbrook Mall, Vancouver, British Columbia V6T 1W6. Tel. (604)224-3245

China and Ourselves (q), Ecum., Canada China Prog., 40 St. Clair Ave. E., Toronto, Ontario M5T 1M9. Tel. (416)921-4152

Christian Communications (6/yr). Cath., 223 Main St., Ottawa, Ontario K1S 1C4

Christian Info (bi-w), cross-denom., Debra Fieguth, 250-195 W. 2nd Ave., Vancouver, British Columbia V5Y 1B8. Tel. (604)872-4535

Church of God Beacon (m), Ch. of God (Cleveland, Tenn.), P.O. Box 2036, Bramalea, Ontario L6T 3S3. Tel. (416)793-2213

Clarion (bi-w), Canadian Ref., 9210-132A St., Surrey, British Columbia V3V 7E1. Tel. (604)581-2290

College Bulletin (q), Menn. Breth. Bible College, 1-169 Riverton Ave., Winnipeg, Manitoba R2L 2E5. Tel. (204)669-6575.

Communauté Chrétienne (6/yr), unaffil., Gilles Thibault, Institut de pastorale, 2715, chemin de la Côte Sainte-Catherine, Montréal, Québec H3T 1B6. Tel. (514) 739-9797

Companion Magazine (m), Conv. Franciscan Friars, Fr. Philip Kelly, P. O. Box 535, Stn. F, Toronto, Ontario M4Y 2L8. Tel. (416)924-6349

Companion Magazine (m), Conv. Franciscan Friars, Fr. Philip Kelly, P. O. Box 535, Stn.F, Toronto, Ontario M4Y 2L8. Tel. (416)924-6349

Communicator, The (5/yr) Assoc. of R.C. Communicators of Can., Margaret Knott, 355 Church St., Toronto, Ontario M5B 1Z8. Tel. (416)977-1500

Connexions (4/yr), 427 Bloor St. W., Toronto, Ontario M5S 1X7. Tel. (416)960-3903

Consensus: A Canadian Lutheran Journal of Theology (bi-a), Luth., Luth. Theol. Sem. and Waterloo Luth. Sem., 75 University Ave. W., Waterloo, Ontario N2L 3C5

Contact, The, Menn., Bethany Bible Institute, Box 160, Hepburn, Saskatchewan S0K 1Z0. Tel. (306)947-2175

Continental Reflections (bi-m), Continental Mission Inc., Box 98, Thompson, Manitoba R8N 1M9

Council Communicator (See: Canadian Council of Churches News Bulletin/Bulletin de nouvelles du Conseil canadien des Eglises)

Covenant Messenger, The (m), Evan. Cov. Ch. of Canada, Donna Wilson, 245 21st St. E., Prince Albert, Saskatchewan S6V 6Z1

Credo (French m), Église unie du Canada (United Church of Canada), Gérard Gautier, 3480 Boul. Décarie, Montréal, Québec H4A 3J5. Tél. (514)486-9213

Crosstalk (10/yr), Ang. Ch. of Can., W. A. Gilbert, 71 Bronson Ave., Ottawa, Ontario K1R 6G6. Tel. (613)233-6271

Crusader, The (2/yr), Ang. Ch. of Canada, Capt. Ray

Taylor, 397 Brunswick Ave., Toronto, Ontario M5R 2Z2. Tel. (416)924-9279

Crux (q), Klaus Bockmuehl, Regent College, 2130 Wesbrook Mall, Vancouver, British Columbia V6T 1W6

Currents (q), Canada Asia Working Group, 11 Madison Ave., Toronto, Ontario M5R 2S2. Tel. (416)921-5626

Dimanche et fête (6/yr), Cath., 1073 boul. St-Cyrille ouest, Sillery, Québec G1S 4R5. Tél. (418)688-1211

Direction (bi-a), Menn. Breth., Allen Guenther, 4824 E. Butler Ave., Fresno, CA 93727. Tel. (209)251-8628

Discover the Bible (w), Cath., Walter Bedard, Archdiocese of Montreal Bible Center, 2065 Sherbrooke St. W., Montreal, Quebec H3H 1G6. Tel. (514)931-7311

Echo, The (See: Briarcrest Echo)

Ecumenism/Oecuménisme, (q), Thomas Ryan, Canadian Centre for Ecumenism, 2065 Sherbrooke St. W., Montreal, Quebec H3H 1G6. Tel. (514)937-9176

Educational Ideabank (q), Menn. Br., Christian Education Coord., Christian Education Office of Mennonite Brethren Churches, 3-169 Riverton Ave., Winnipeg, Manitoba R2L 2E5

L'Eglise Canadienne (bi-m), Cath., Jacques Barnard, 1073, boulevard Saint-Cyrille ouest, Québec, Québec G1S 4R5. Tél. (418)681-8109

Eglise et Theologie (3/yr), Cath., Leo Laberge, Faculté de théologie, St. Paul Univ., 223 Main St. Ottawa, Ontario K1S 1C4

Elim Contact (q), Elim Bible Institute, Box 120, Altona Manitoba R0G 0B0. Tel. (204) 324-8631

EMMC Recorder (m), Menn., Gladys Penner, Evangelical Mennonite Mission Conference, Box 126, Winnipeg, Manitoba R3C 2G1

End Times' Messenger (11/yr), Apost. Ch. of Pent. of Canada, 1. W. Ellis, Bldg. #3, 31 Manning Cres. N.E., Calgary, Alberta T2E 7M9

Enterprise (q), Bapt., Frank Byrne, Canadian Baptist Overseas Mission Board, 7185 Millcreek Dr., Mississauga, Ontario L5N 5R4. Tel. (416)922-5163

Esprit (bi-m), Év. Luth. Women, Gwen Hawkins, Box 19, R.R. #1, Madeira Park, British Columbia VON 2H0. Tel. (604)883-2778

Evangelical Baptist (m), Bapt., R. W. Lawson, Fell. of Evang. Bapt. Churches in Canada, 3034 Bayview Ave., Willowdale, Ontario M2N 6J5. Tel. (416)223-8696

Exchange (3/yr), Un. Ch. of Canada, Lynda Newmarch, Div. of Mission in Canada, 85 St. Clair Ave. E., Toronto, Ontario M4T 1M8. Tel. (416)925-5931

Faith Today (bi-m), Evan. Fell. of Canada, Brian C. Stiller, Box 8800, Sta. B, Willowdale, Ontario M2K 2R6. Tel. (416)479-5885

Fish Eye Lens (4/yr), The Ecumenical Forum of Canada, 11 Madison Ave., Toronto, Ontario M5R 2S2. Tel. (416)924-9351

Focus on Social Justice (4/yr), Cath., Canadian Religious Conference-Ontario, 101-146 Laird Dr., Toronto, Ontario M4G 3V7. Tel. (416) 424-4664

Food for the Flock: Ministry in Focus (6/yr), Board of Food for the Flock, Box 353, Etobicoke, Ontario M9C 4V3

For the Record, Luth., John M. Cobb, Canadian Luth. Hist. Assn., Box 86, Gen. Del., Wildwood, Alberta T0E 2M0

Free Methodist Herald, The (q), Free Meth., D. G. Bastian, 69 Browning Ave., Toronto, Ontario M4K 1W1. Tel. (416)463-4536

Gardner Insights and Alumni News (q), Ch. of God in West. Canada, 4704 55th St., Camrose, Alberta T4V 2B6

Glad Tidings (10/yr), Women's Miss. Soc., Presby. Ch. in Can., L. June Stevenson, 50 Wynford Dr., Rm. 100, Don Mills, Ontario M3C 1J7. Tel. (416)441-2840

Global Village Voice (q), Cath., Canadian Catholic

Organization for Development and Peace, 3028 Dan forth Ave., Toronto, Ontario M4C 1N2. Tel. (416) 698-7770

Godshow, Ang., Bapt., Luth., Presby., R.C., Un. Ch., Peter Reynolds, 315 Queen St. E., Toronto, Ontario M5A 1S7. Tel. (416)366-9221

Good Tidings (m), Pent. Assemb. of Nfld., Roy D. King, 57 Thorburn Rd., P.O. Box 8895, Stn.A., St. John's, Newfoundland A1B 3T2

Gospel Contact, The (10/yr), Ch. of God in West. Canada, Gospel Contact Press, 5005-49th St., Camrose, Alberta T4V 1N5

Gospel Herald (m), Chs. of Christ, Eugene C. Perry, Box 94, Beamsville, Ontario L0R 1BO

Gospel Standard, The (m), Fundamental, Perry F. Rockwood, Box 1660, Halifax, Nova Scotia B3J 3A1. Tel. (902)423-5540

Gospel Witness, The (22/yr.), Reg. Bapt., Jarvis St. Baptist Church, 130 Gerrard St. E., Toronto, Ontario M5A 3T4

Grail (q), Cath., Univ. of St. Jerome's Col., Douglas Letson, Waterloo, Ontario N2L 3G3. Tel. (519)884-8100

Guide, The (9/yr.), Edward Vanderkloet, Christian Labour Association of Canada, 821 Albion Rd., Rexdale, Ontario M9V 1A3. Tel. (416)744-2340

Hamilton Diocesan News, Cath., 700 King St. West, Hamilton, Ontario L8P 1C7.

His Dominion (4/yr), Chr. & Miss. All., Franklin Pyles, Faculty of Canadian Theological Seminary, 4400 4th Ave., Regina Saskatchewan S4T 0H8. Tel. (306) 545-1515

Huron Church News (10/yr). Ang. Ch. of Canada, Geoffrey Dibbs, 4-220 Dundas St., London, Ontario N6A 1H3. Tel. (519)434-6893

Intercom (q), Fell. of Evang. Bapt. Churches in Canada, R. W. Lawson, 3034 Bayview Ave., Willowdale, Ontario M2N 6J5. Tel. (416)223-8696

Insight•Insound•Intouch, (6/yr, q,q), John Milton Soc., Muriel Israel, 40 St. Clair Ave., E. Ste. 202, Toronto, Ontario M4T1 M9. Tel. (416)960-3953

Iskra (bi-w), Un. of Spiritual Communities in Christ (Orth. Doukhobors in Canada), D.E. (Jim) Popoff, Box 760, Grand Forks, British Columbia V0H 1H0

Journal of the Canadian Church Historical Society (2/yr), Ang., c/o The General Synod Archives, Anglican Church of Canada, 600 Jarvis St., Toronto, Ontario M4Y 2J6. Tel. (416)924-9192

Laval Theologique et Philosophique (3/yr), Cath., René-Michel Roberge, Pavillon Félix Antoine-Savard, Université Laval, Québec, Québec G1K 7P4 Tel. (418) 656-3576

Liberation (formerly Encounter) (bi-m), Ken Campbell, Box 100, Milton, Ontario L9T 2Y3. Tel. (416)878-8461

Link & Visitor, The, (9/yr), Bapt. Women's Miss. Soc. of Ont. and Que., Esther Barnes, 10 Pembroke Cres., Chatham, Ontario N7G 2J3. Tel. (519)352-4309

Living Message: The Anglican Magazine, (10/yr). Ang. Ch. of Can., John Bird, Box 820, Petrolia, Ontario N0N 1R0. Tel. (519)882-2497

Mandate (7/yr), Un. Ch. of Canada, Dean Salter, Division of Communication, The United Church of Canada, 85 St. Clair Ave. E., Toronto, Ontario M4T 1M8 Tel. (416) 925-5931

Maple Leaf Communique Canada-East, Ch. of God of Prophecy, Richard E. Davis, P.O. Box 457, Brampton, Ontario L6V 2L4. Tel. (416)843-2379

Marketplace, The: A Magazine for Christians in Business (m), Menn., Wally Kroeker, 402-280 Smith St., Winnipeg, Manitoba R3C 1K2. Tel. (204)944-1995

Martyrs' Shrine Message (m), Cath., Martyrs' Shrine, Midland, Ontario L4R 4K5. Tel. (416)526-3788

MCC Contact (m), Mennonite Central Committee (Canada), 134 Plaza Dr., Winnipeg, Manitoba R3T 5K9. Tel. (204)261-6381

Mennonite, The, (semi-m), Gen. Conf. Menn., Muriel T. Stackley Box 347, 722 Main, Newton, KS 67114. Tel. (316)283-5100

Mennonite Brethren Communications Expression (q), Dan Block, Mennonite Brethren Communications, Box 2, Sta. F, Winnipeg, Manitoba R2L 2A5. Tel. (214) 667-9576

Mennonite Brethren Herald (semi-m), Menn. Breth. Ch., Herb Kopp, 3-169 Riverton Ave., Winnipeg, Manitoba R2L 2E5. Tel. (204)669-6575

Mennonite Historian (q) Menn. Breth. Hist. Soc. and Menn. Heritage Centre, Conf. of Menn. in Canada, Kenneth Reddig, Center for Mennonite Brethren Studies in Canada, 169 Riverton Ave., Winnipeg, Manitoba R2L 2E5

Mennonite Mirror (10/yr), Inter-Menn., Al Reimer, Mennonite Literary Society, 207-1317A Portage Ave., Winnipeg, Manitoba R3G 0V3. Tel. (204)786-2289

Mennonite Reporter (bi-w), Inter-Menn., Ron Rempel, 3 - 312 Marsland Dr., Waterloo, Ontario N2J 3Z1. Tel. (519)884-3810

Die Mennonitische Post (bi-m), Inter-Menn., Abe Warkentin, Box 1120, Steinbach, Manitoba R0A 2A0. Tel. (204)326-6790

Mennonitische Rundschau (German bi-w), Mennonite Brethren, Herb Kopp, 3-169 Riverton Ave., Winnipeg, Manitoba R2L 2E5

Messenger, The (bi-w), Evang. Menn. Conf., Menno Hamm, Board of Education and Publication, Box 1268, Steinbach, Manitoba R0A 2A0

Messenger (Of the Sacred Heart) (m), Cath., F. J. Power, Apostleship of Prayer, 661 Greenwood Ave., Toronto, Ontario M4J 4B3. Tel. (416)466-1195

Missions Magazine (m), Ply. Br., 27 Charles St. E., Toronto, Ontario M4Y 1R9. Tel. (416)920-4391

Monitor, The (m), Cath., William Callahan, actg., P.O. Box 986, St. John's, Newfoundland A1C 5M3. Tel. (709)739-6553

MPE News (2/yr.), Un. Ch. of Can., Jim Taylor, Div of Ministry Personnel and Edu., 85 St. Clair Ave. E., Toronto, Ontario M4T 1M8. Tel. (416)925-5931

Montreal Churchman (m), Ang. Ch. of Can., David Yarrow, Box 158, Stn. A, Montréal, Québec H3B 3J5. Tel. (514)879-1722

Music Maker, The (q), Menn. Br., Chr. Edu. Coordinator, Christian Education Office, Canadian Conference of Mennonite Brethren Churches, 3-169 Riverton Ave., Winnipeg, Manitoba R2L 2E5

National Bulletin on Liturgy (5/yr), Cath., Patrick Byrne, Canadian Conference of Catholic Bishops (Concacan) Publications Service, 90 Parent Ave., Ottawa, Ontario K1N 7B1. Tel. (613)236-9461

Newfoundland Churchmen (m), Ang. Ch. of Canada, Hollis Hiscock, 26 Empire Ave., St. John's, Newfoundland A1C 3E6. Tel. (709)726-3487

New Freeman, The (w), Cath., Robert G. Merzetti, One Bayard Dr., Saint John, New Brunswick E2L 3L5. Tel. (506)652-3667

Newsletter of the Diocese of London (q), Cath., Ron Pickersgill, P. O. Box 2400, London, Ontario N6A 4G3. Tel. (519)439-7211

News & Views (3/yr), Foursquare Gospel Ch. of Canada, 7895 Welsley Dr., Burnaby, British Columbia V5E 3X4

News of Quebec (q), Breth., Richard Strout, P.O. Box 1054, Sherbrooke, Quebec. Tel. (819)562-3447

Nor Serount (m, in Armenian and English), Holy Trinity Armenian Church of Toronto, Diocese of Canada, 14 Woodlawn Ave., Toronto, Ontario M4V 1G7

Northern Lights (bi-m), interdenom., Northern Canada Evangelical Mission, P.O. Box 3030, Prince Albert, Saskatchewan S6V 7V4. Tel. (306)764-3388

Northland, The (q), Ang. Ch. of Can., Mrs. M. Lawrence, P. O. Box 841 Schumacher, Ontario P0N 1G0. Tel. (705)267-1129

Northwest Canada Echoes (m), Evang. Ch. in Canada, A. W. Riegel, 2805 - 13th Ave., S.E., Medicine Hat, Alberta T1A 3R1. Tel. (403)527-4101

Ontario Messenger (m), Ch. of God (Anderson, Ind.), Paul Kilburn, 85 Emmett Ave., #1109, Toronto, Ontario M6M 5A2

Our Diocese, Cath., 22 Sutherland Dr., Grand Falls, Newfoundland A2A 2G1.

Our Family (q), Ang. Ch. of Can., J.C.R. Williams, Box 276, 4907-52nd St., Yellowknife, Northwest Territories X1A 2N2. Tel. (403)873-4517

Pentecostal Testimony (m), Pent. Assemblies of Canada, R. J. Skinner, 10 Overlea Blvd., Toronto, Ontario M4H 1A5. Tel. (416)425-1010

Peoples' Magazine, The, People's Church, Paul B. Smith, 374 Sheppard Ave. E., Toronto, Ontario M2N 3B6. Tel. (416)222-3341

Pioneer Christian Monthly (m), Ref. Ch. in Am., Reformed Church Center, R. R. #4, Cambridge, Ontario N1R 5S5. Tel. (519)623-4860

PMC: The Practice of Ministry in Canada (4/yr.), Jim Taylor, PMC Board, 60 St. Clair Ave. E., Ste. 500, Toronto, Ontario M4T IN5. Tel. (416)928-3223

Prairie Messenger (w), Cath., Andrew Britz, Box 190, Muenster, Saskatchewan S0K 2Y0. Tel. (306)682-5215

Prairie Overcomer (11/yr), interdenom., Ted S. Rendall, Prairie Bible Institute, Three Hills, Alberta T0M 2A0. Tel. (403)443-5511

Presbyterian Message, The (10/yr), Women's Miss. Soc., Eastern Div., Mrs. John Posno, 140 North Ave., #5, New Glasgow, Nova Scotia B2H 2E3. Tel. (902)752-4718

Presbyterian Record (m), James R. Dickey, Presby. Ch. in Canada, 50 Wynford Dr., Don Mills, Ontario M3C 1J7. Tel. (416)441-1111

Reach (bi-m), Pent. Assemb. of Nfld., R. H. Dewling, 57 Thorburn Rd., St. John's, Newfoundland A1B 3N4

Regent College Bulletin (m), Regent College, 2130 Wesbrook Mall, Vancouver, British Columbia V6T 1W6

Relations (m), Cath., Compagnie de Jésus, 8100 boul. St. Laurent, Montréal, Québec H2P 2L9. Tel. (514) 387-2541

Religious Studies amd Theology (3/yr), P. Joseph Cahill, University of Alberta, Religious Studies, Edmonton, Alberta T6G 2E5. Tel. (403)432-2173.

Revival Fellowship (m), interdenom., Canadian Revival Fellowship, Box 584, Regina, Saskatchewan S4P 3A3. Tel. (306)522-3685

Rivers of Living Water (q), interdenom., Nipawin Bible Institute, Box 1986, Nipawin, Saskatchewan S0E 1E0. Tel. (306)862-3651

Scarboro Missions (11/yr), Scarboro For. Miss. Soc., Joseph M. Young, 2685 Kingston Rd., Scarborough, Ontario M1M 1M4. Tel. (416)261-7135

Rupert's Land News (10/yr), Ang. Ch. of Can., Anita Schmidt, 935 Nesbitt Bay, Winnipeg, Manitoba R3T 1W6. Tel. (214)453-6130

Saskatchewan Anglican (10/yr), Ang. Ch. of Can., W. Patrick Tomalin, 1501 College Ave., Regina, Saskatchewan S4P 1B8. Tel. (316)522-1608

Science et Esprit (3/yr), Cath., Science et Esprit, 5605 avenue Decelles, Montréal, Québec H3T 1W4

Servant, The (bi-m), Inter-Menn., Jerry Hildebrand, Steinbach Bible College, Box 1420, Steinbach, Manitoba R0A 2A0

Shantyman, The (m), Non-denom., George M. Bowman, 29 Point Grey Cres., Scarborough, Ontario M1G 2L1

Small Voice, The (q), indep., The United Church Renewal Fellowship, 240 Bayview Dr., Unit 5, Barrie, Ontario L4N 4Y8

Solidarités (5/yr), Cath., Francois-A. Thuot, 2111 rue Centre, Montréal, Québec H3K 1J5. Tel. (514) 932-5136

Stevite, The (q), Un. Ch. of Canada, St. Stephen's College, Graduate and Continuing Theological Education for Clergy and Laity, University of Alberta Campus, Edmonton, Alberta T6G 2J6. Tel. (403) 439-7311

Studia Canonica (semi-a), Cath., Francis G. Morrisey, Faculty of Canon Law, Saint Paul Univ., 223 Main St., Ottawa, Ontario K1S 1C4. Tel. (613)236-1393

SR: Studies in Religion: Sciences religieuses (q), Tom Sinclair-Faulkner, c/o Wilfrid Laurier University Press, Waterloo, Ontario N2L 3C5

Theodolite: A Journal of Christian Thought and Practice (2/yr), Bapt., T. R. Hobbs, McMaster Divinity College, Hamilton, Ontario L8S 4K1. Tel. (416)525-9140, x4401

Tidings, Cong. Chr. Chrs. in Ontario. Diane Bastedo, 45 Glenwood Ave., Toronto, Ontario M6P 3C7

Tidings (10/yr), Un. Bapt. Missy. Un. of the Atlantic Prov., H. May Bartlett, 225 Massey St., Frederickton, New Brunswick E3B 2T5. Tel. (506)455-9674

Topic (m), Ang. Dioc. of New Westminster, Joanne Leslie, #302-814 Richards St., Vancouver, British Columbia V6B 3A7. Tel. (604)684-6306

Touchstone (3/yr), A. M. Watts, Faculty of Theology, University of Winnipeg, Winnipeg, Manitoba R3B 2E9. Tel. (204)786-9390

Truth on Fire (bi-m), Bible Holiness Movement, W. H. Wakefield, Box 223, Sta. A, Vancouver, British Columbia V6C 2M3. Tel. (604)498-3895

United Church Observer (m), Un. Ch. of Canada, Hugh McCullum, 85 St. Clair Ave. E., Toronto, Ontario M4T 1M8. Tel. (416)960-8500

Update (q), multidenom., Wm. J. McRae, Ontario Bible College and Theological Seminary, 25 Ballyconnor Ct., Willowdale, Ontario M2M 4B3. Tel. (416)226-6380

Update/A Jour (2/yr). Ch. Cncl. on Justice and Corrections, Vern Redekop, 507 Bank St., Ottawa, Ontario K2P 1Z5. Tel. (613)563-1688

La Vie Chrétienne (French, m), Presby. Ch. in Canada, Jean Porret, 2302 Goyer, Montréal, Québec H3S 1G9. Tel. (514)737-4168

La Vie des Communautés religieuses (5/yr), Cath., Laurent Boisvert, 5750 boulevard Rosemont, Montréal, Québec H1T 2H2

La Vie Liturgique (10/yr), Cath., 1073 boul. Saint-Cyrille ouest, Sillery, Québec G1S 4R5. Tél. (418)837-1407

Visnyk (semi-m), Ukrainian Greek Orthodox Ch. of Canada, 9 St. John's Ave., Winnipeg, Manitoba R2W 1G8

Voce Evangelica (q), Italian Pent. Ch. of Canada, Joseph Manafo and Daniel Ippolito, P.O. Box 599, Station

Beaubien, Montreal, Quebec H2G 3E2. Tel. (514) 593-1944 or (416)766-6692.

War Cry, The (w), Salv. Army in Canada and Bermuda, Maj. Maxwell Ryan, 455 N. Service Rd. E., Oakville, Ontario L6H 1A5. Tel. (416)845-9235

Way, The (q), Faith at Work, Frank Kennedy, P. O. Box 135, Thornhill, Ontario L3T 3N1. Tel. (416)889-0172.

Wesleyan Advocate (semi-m), Wes. Ch., Wayne Caldwell, P.O. Box 2000, Marion, IN 46952

Western Catholic Reporter (w), Cath., Shirley Pfister, Great Western Press, 10562 - 109 St., Edmonton, Alberta T5H 3B2. Tel. (403) 420-1330

Western Tract News (bi-m), interdenom. Western Tract Mission, 401 - 33rd St. W., Saskatoon, Saskatchewan S7L 0V5

Word Alive (bi-m), Interdenon., Wycliffe Bible Transla-

tors of Canada, Box 3068, Stn. B., Calgary, Alberta T2M 4L6. Tel. (403) 250-5411

World Concern Canada (semi-m), World Concern of Canada, Box 11000, Vancouver, British Columbia V6B 4V7. Tel. (604) 270-6555

World Wind/World View (3/yr), Un. Ch. of Can., Rebekah Chevalier, 85 St. Clair Ave., E., Toronto, Ontario M4T 1M8. Tel. (416)925-5931

Worth Reading (bi-m), Ch. of God in Can., 4704 - 55th St., Camrose, Alberta T4V 2B6

Young Pilot (11/yr), Ted S. Rendall, Prairie Press, Three Hills, Alberta T0M 2A0. Tel. (403) 443-5511

Youth Incites (q), Menn. Br., A. Ben Thiessen, Christian Education Coord., Chr. Edu. Ofc., Canadian Conference of Mennonite Brethren Churches, 3-169 Riverton Ave., Winnipeg, Manitoba R2L 2E5

15. UNITED STATES SERVICE AGENCIES: SOCIAL, CIVIC, RELIGIOUS

The Yearbook of American and Canadian Churches offers the following selected list of Service Agencies for two purposes. The first purpose is to direct attention to a number of major agencies which can provide resources of information and service to the churches. No attempt is made to produce a complete listing of such agencies. The second purpose is to illustrate the types of resources that are available. There are many agencies providing services which can be of assistance to local, regional or national church groups. It is suggested that a valuable tool in locating such service agencies is *The Encyclopedia of Associations*, Vol. I, *National Organizations of the United States*. The organizations are listed in Parts 1 and 2, and Part 3 is a name and keyword index. It is published by Gale Research Co., Book Tower, Detroit, Michigan 48277.

ADRIS (Association for the Development of Religious Information Systems): Dept. of Sociology and Anthropology, Marquette Univ., Milwaukee, WI 53233. Tel. (414)224-6838. Coordinator, Dr. David O. Moberg; Ed., Rev. Richard F. Smith, Dept. of Theology, Fordham Univ., Bronx, NY 10458. Tel. (212)579-2400
Periodical: ADRIS Newsletter.

Alban Institute: 4125 Nebraska Ave. N.W., Washington, DC 20016. Tel. (202)244-7320. Exec. Dir., Loren B. Mead.

Periodical: Action Information (6/yr)

American Academy of Political and Social Science, The: 3937 Chestnut St., Philadelphia, PA 19104. Tel. (215)386-4594. Pres., Marvin E. Wolfgang

Periodical: The Annals of the American Academy of Political and Social Science (bi-m)

American Association for Adult and Continuing Education: 1201 Sixteenth St., N.W., Ste. 230, Washington, DC 20036. Tel. (202)822-7866. Pres., Mary G. Williams; Exec. Dir., Judith Ann Koloski

Periodicals: Adult Education (4/yr); Lifelong Learning: an Omnibus of Practice and Research (8/yr)

American Association of Bible Colleges: P. O. Box 1523, Fayetteville, AR 72701. Tel. (501)521-8164. Exec. Dir., Randall E. Bell

American Association of Retired Persons: 1909 K St. N.W., Washington, DC 20049. Tel. (202)872-4700. Exec. Dir., Cyril F. Brickfield

Periodicals: AARP News Bulletin (m); Modern Maturity (bi-m)

American Civil Liberties Union: 132 West 43rd St., New York, NY 10036. Tel. (212)944-9800. Pres., Norman Dorsen; Exec. Dir., Ira Glasser

Periodical: Civil Liberties (m).

American Council on Alcohol Problems: 3426 Bridgeland Dr., Bridgeton, MO 63044. Tel. (314)739-5944. Curt Scarborough

American Farm Bureau Federation: 225 Touhy Ave., Park Ridge, IL 60068. Washington office, 600 Maryland Ave., S.W., Washington, DC 20024. Pres. and Admin., Dean R. Kleckner; Sec. and Dir., Washington Ofc., John C. Datt; Treas., William H. Broderick.

Periodical: Farm Bureau News(w)

American Federation of Labor and Congress of Industrial Organizations: AFL-CIO Bldg., 815 16th St. N.W., Washington, DC 20006. Pres., Lane Kirkland

Periodicals: American Federationist (m); News (w)

American Friends Service Committee: 1501 Cherry St., Philadelphia, PA 19102. Tel. (215)241-7000. Chmn., Stephen G. Cary; Exec. Sec., Asia Alderson Bennett.

Periodical: Quaker Service Bulletin (3/yr.)

American Guild of Religious Historiographers: 3500 Fuller, N.E., Grand Rapids, MI 49505. Tel. (616)361-0694. Correspondent, Ms. Jean Heibel.

American Library Association: 50 E. Huron St., Chicago, IL 60611. Tel. (312)944-6780. Exec Dir., Thomas J. Galvin

Periodicals: American Libraries (m except July-Aug. bi-m); Booklist (semi-m); Choice (11/yr.); College and Research Libraries (bi-m); ALA Washington Newsletter (m); Information Technology and Libraries (q); Library Resources and Technical Services (q); RQ: School Library Media Quarterly (q); Top of the News (q)

American Medical Association: 535 N. Dearborn St., Chicago, IL 60610. Tel. (312)645-5000. Pres., John J. Coury, Jr., M.D.; Exec. Vice-Pres., James H. Sammons, M.D.

Periodicals: The Journal of the American Medical Association (w); The Citation (bi-w); American Medical News (w); Specialty Scientific Journals (m); Legislative Roundup (w); Facets (q)

American Protestant Health Association: 1 Woodfield Pl., 1701 E. Woodfield Rd., Ste. 311, Schaumburg, IL 60173. Tel. (312)843-2701. Pres., Charles D. Phillips.

American Public Health Association: 1015 15th St., N.W., Washington, DC 20005. Tel. (202)789-5600. Exec. Dir., William H. McBeath, M.D.

Periodical: American Journal of Public Health (m); The Nation's Health (m)

American Public Welfare Association: 1125 15th St., N.W., Ste. 300, Washington, DC 20005. Tel. (202)293-7550

Periodicals: Public Welfare (q); This Week in Washington (50/yr): W-Memo. (30-40/yr); Public Welfare Directory (a)

American Red Cross, The: 17th & D Sts., N.W., Washington, DC 20006. Chpsn., George F. Moody; Pres., Richard F. Schubert

Periodical: Red Cross News (m)

American Theological Library Association: Office of the Exec. Sec., St. Meinrad School of Theology, St. Meinrad, IN 47577. Pres., Miss Rosalyn Lewis, United Methodist Publishing House, 201 8th Ave., S., Lib. Rm. 122, Nashville, TN 37202; ATLA Exec. Sec., Rev. Simeon Daly, O.S.B.; Preservation Bd. Chair, John Bollier; Dir. of Program, Robert Markham, 1118 E. 54th Pl., Chicago, IL 60615; Religion Index Board Chair, Norman J. Kansfield; Dir., Albert Hurd, 5600 S. Woodlawn Ave., Chicago, IL 60637

American Waldensian Society, The: Rm. 1850, 475 Riverside Dr., New York, NY 10115. Tel. (212)870-2671. Exec. Dir., Rev. Frank G. Gibson, Jr.

Periodical: Newsletter

Americans United for Separation of Church and State: 8120 Fenton St., Silver Spring, MD 20910. Tel. (301)589-3707. Exec. Dir., Robert L. Maddox; Ed., Joseph L. Conn

Periodical: Church & State (m)

Association for Clinical Pastoral Education: 1549 Clairmont Rd., Ste. 103, Decatur, GA 30030. Exec. Dir., Duane F. Parker.

Periodical: Journal of Pastoral Care (q)

Association of Jewish Chaplains of the Armed Forces: 15 E. 26th St., New York, NY 10010. Tel. (212)532-4949. Dir., David Lapp

Association of Theological Schools in the United States and Canada: P.O. Box 130, Vandalia, OH 45377. Tel. (513)898-4654. Pres., Barbara Brown Zikmund, Pacific School of Religion, 1798 Scenic Ave., Berkeley CA 94709; Exec. Dir., Leon Pacala; Asso. Dirs., David S. Schuller, and William L. Baumgaertner

Baptist Joint Committee on Public Affairs: 200 Maryland Ave., N.E., Washington, DC 20002. Tel. (202)544-4226. Exec. Dir., James M. Dunn
Periodical: Report from the Capital (10/yr.)

Bible Sabbath Association: Fairview, OK 73737. Pres., Leroy Bass; Sec.-Treas., Lawrence Burrell.
Periodical: The Sabbath Sentinel (w), Richard A. Wiedenhebt

B'nai B'rith International: B'nai B'rith Bldg., 1640 Rhode Island Ave., N. W., Washington, DC 20036. Tel. (202)857-6600. Pres., Gerald Kraft; Exec. Vice-Pres., Daniel Thursz
Periodical: B'nai B'rith International Jewish Monthly

Boy Scouts of America: 1325 Walnut Hill Lane, Irving TX 75038. Tel. (214)580-2000. Pres., Charles M. Pigott; Chief Scout Exec., Ben. H. Love
Periodicals: Scouting Magazine (6/year); Boys' Life (m); BSA Today (q); Exploring (4/year); Scouting Bulletin of the Catholic Committee on Scouting (q); Hatsofe (Jewish) (m); Scouting Ministry (Protestant) (q); New Trail (Baptist)

Boys Clubs of America: 771 First Ave., New York, NY 10017. Tel. (212)351-5900. Chmn. of Bd., John L. Burns; Pres., Jeremiah Milbank: Nat'l. Dir., William R. Bricker
Periodicals: *Connections* Magazine (q); Annual Report; Bulletin (bi-a)

Bread for the World: 802 Rhode Island Ave. N.E., Washington, DC 20018. Tel. (202)269-0200. Exec. Dir., Arthur Simon.
Periodicals: Action Alert Newsletter (m); Bread (q); Leaven (q); Background Papers on Hunger Related Issues (occ.)

Camp Fire Inc.: 4601 Madison Ave., Kansas City, MO 64112, Tel. (816)756-1950. Natl. Exec. Dir., David W. Bahlmann.
Periodical: Camp Fire Leadership (3/yr)

Campus Crusade for Christ International: Arrowhead Springs, San Bernardino, CA 92414. Pres., William R. Bright.
Periodical: Worldwide Challenge (bi-m)

CARE: 660 First Ave., New York, NY 10016, Tel. (212)686-3110. Exec. Dir., Philip Johnston

Carnegie Council on Ethics and International Affairs: 170 E. 64th St., New York, NY 10021. Tel. (212)838-4120. Chpsn., Donald P. Moriarty; Vice Chpsn., Mrs. Helen Maguire Muller; Pres., Robert J. Myers
Periodicals: Ethics and International Affairs

Center for Applied Research in the Apostolate (CARA): 3700 Oakview Terr., NE, Washington, DC 20017. Tel. (202)832-2300. Pres., William P. Clark; Dir. of Research, Francis Gillespie

Center for Parish Development: 5407 S. University Ave., Chicago, IL 60615. Tel. (312)752-1596; Genesis Division, 207 E. Buffalo, Ste. 326, Milwaukee, WI 53202. Tel. (414)224-1050. Dir., Paul Dietterich
Periodical: The Center Letter (m)

Christian Camping International (USA): P.O. Box 646, 5407 S. University Ave., Wheaton, IL 60189. Tel. (312)462-0300. Exec. Dir., John Pearson.
Periodicals: Journal of Christian Camping (bi-m); Official Guide to Christian Camps and Conference Centers

Christian Children's Fund, Inc.: P.O. Box 26511, Richmond, VA 23261. Tel. (804)644-4654. Pres., C. Hobson Goddin; Exec. Dir., Dr. James MacCracken
Periodicals: Childworld (m); Field Notes (m)

Christian Ministries Management Association: P.O. Box 4638, Diamond Bar, CA 91765. Tel. (714)861-8861. Exec. Dir., Sylvia Flaten.
Periodical: Christian Management Report (bi-m)

Church Growth Center: Corunna, IN 46730. Tel. (219)281-2452. Dir., Dr. Kent R. Hunter

Churches' Center for Theology and Public Policy, 4500 Massachusetts Ave., N.W., Washington, DC 20016. Tel. (202)885-9100.Actg. Dir., Ron Pasquariello,
Periodicals: Shalom Paper (Occ.); Center Circles (Occ.)

Committee of Southern Churchmen, The: P.O. Box 140215, Nashville, TN 37214, Tel. (615)758-7862. Pres., Gene L. Davenport; Dir., Will D. Campbell

Congress of National Black Churches: 1919 Pennsylvania Ave. N.W., Ste. 501, Washington, DC 20006. Tel. (202)429-0714. Chpsn., Bishop John Adams; Exec. Dir., Mr. Joseph P. Eaglin, Jr.

CONTACT Teleministries USA, Inc.: Pouch A, Harrisburg, PA 17105. Actg. Exec. Dir., Dennis R. Gable.

Council for Health and Human Service Ministries, The: 543 College Ave., Lancaster, PA 17603. Tel. (717)299-9945; outside PA 1-800-822-4476. Exec. Dir., J. Robert Achtermann.
Periodicals: Directory of Services (bi-a); The Link (q); President's Newsetter (q); Shoptalk (m); Employment Opportunities (m); CHHSM Report: Papers on Public Policy Issues (2-3 a).

Council of the Southern Mountains, Inc.: P.O. Box 1188, Clintwood, VA 24228. Tel. (703)926-4347. Adm. Dir., Cathy Stanley.
Periodical: Mountain Life and Work (m)

Counselor Association, Inc., The: 31 Langerfeld Rd., Hillsdale, NJ 07642. Tel. (201)664-8890. Chmn., Raymond B. Knudsen; Pres., Raymond B. Knudsen II.

Credit Union National Association: P.O. Box 431, Madison, WI 53701. Tel. (608)231-4000
Periodicals: Credit Union Magazine (m); Everybody's Money (q); Credit Union Executive (q); Credit Union Manager Newsletter (bi-w); Credit Union Newsletter for Directors (m); Credit Union Newswatch (w).

Evangelical Council for Financial Accountability (ECFA): P.O. Box 17511,Washington, DC 20041. Tel. (703)938-6006. Pres., Arthur C. Borden.

Fellowship of Reconciliation, The: Box 271, Nyack, NY 10960. Tel. (914)358-4601. Chpsn., Shelley Mae Douglass; Exec. Sec., Doug Hostetter.
Periodicals: Fellowship (m); Reconciliation International (q)

Foreign Policy Association: 729 Seventh Ave., New York, NY 10019. Tel. (212)764-4050. Pres. and C.E.O., John W. Kiermaier
Periodicals: Headline Series (5/yr.); Great Decisions Book (a)

Friends Committee on National Legislation: 245 Second St., N.E., Washington, DC 20002. Tel. (202)547-6000. Clerk of Gen. Comm., Walter Schutt; Exec. Sec., Edward F. Snyder
Periodical: FCNL Washington Newsletter (m)

General Federation of Women's Clubs: 1734 N St. N.W., Washington, DC 20036. Tel. (202)347-3168. Pres., Phyllis Roberts
Periodical: GFWC Clubwomen Magazine (bi-m)

Girl Scouts of the U.S.A.: 830 Third Ave., New York, NY 10022. Tel. (212)940-7500. Pres., Mrs. Betty F. Pilsbury; Nat'l. Exec. Dir., Mrs. Frances R. Hesselbein
Periodicals: Girl Scout Leader (4/yr)

Glenmary Research Center: 750 Piedmont Ave., N.E., Atlanta, GA 30308. Tel. (404)876-6518. Dir., Lou McNeil

Healing Community: 139 Walworth Ave., White Plains,

NY 10606. Tel. (914)761-4986. Dir., Dr. Harold Wilke. Periodical: The Caring Congregation.

Institute of International Education: 809 United Nations Plaza, New York, NY 10017. Tel. (212)883-8200. Pres., Richard M. Krasno

Institutes of Religion and Health: 3 W. 29th St., New York, NY 10001. Tel. (212)725-7850. Exec. Dir., Roger W. Plantikow

Periodical: Journal of Religion and Health (q)

Interfaith Forum on Religion, Art and Architecture: 1913 Architects Bldg., Philadelphia, PA 19103, Tel. (215)568-0960. Dir., Henry Jung.

Periodicals: Newsletter (q.), Faith and Forum (semi-a)

Japan International Christian University Foundation, Inc., The: 475 Riverside Dr., Rm. 1848, New York, NY 10115. Tel. (212)870-2893. Pres., David H. C. Read; Chmn, Exec. Comm., James A. Cogswell; Exec. Dir., Betty Gray

John Milton Society for the Blind: A Worldwide Ministry, 475 Riverside Dr., Rm. 249, New York, NY 10115. Tel. (212)870-3335. Gen. Sec., Richard Preston

Periodicals: (Braille); John Milton Magazine, for Adults (m); Discovery, for Boys and Girls (m); John Milton Sunday School Quarterly (q)

Periodicals (recorded): John Milton Talking Book Magazine (bi-m, 8rpm); John Milton Recorded Sunday School Lessons (q, 8rpm). Other Recorded Publications: New English Bible-New Testament (16 rpm); Paul—an Ambassador for Christ (Acts) (16 rpm).

Periodicals (large type): John Milton Magazine-Large Type Edition (m); World Day of Prayer (a)

All publications free on request to persons who cannot see to read ordinary printed matter

LAOS/Partners for Global Justice: 4920 Piney Branch Rd. NW, Washington, DC 20011. Exec. Dir., Kathy Penrose; Educ. Dir., Jean Martensen

Periodicals: Conversations (4/yr.)

Laymen's National Bible Association: 815 Second Ave., New York, NY 10017. Tel., (212)687-0555. Pres., Victor W. Eimicke; Exec. Dir., Reuben Gums

Periodical: Newsletter (q); Annual Report

League of Women Voters of the U.S.: 1730 M St., N.W., Washington, DC 20036. Tel. (202)429-1965. Pres., Nancy M. Neuman

Periodical: The National Voter (bi-m)

Lutheran Church Library Association: 122 West Franklin Ave., Minneapolis, MN 55404. Tel. (612)870-3623. Exec. Dir., Wilma W. Jensen.

Periodicals: Lutheran Libraries (q)

Lutheran Educational Conference of North America: 122 C St., NW, Ste. 300, Washington, DC 20001. Tel. (202)783-7501. Pres., Norman F. Fintel; Exec. Dir., Arthur E. Puotinen

Lutheran Immigration and Refugee Service: 360 Park Ave. S., New York, NY 10010.Exec. Dir., Donald H. Larsen.

Periodical: LIRS Bulletin

Lutheran Resources Commission–Washington: The Woodward Bldg., Ste. 900, 733 Fifteenth St. NW, Washington, DC 20005. Tel. (202)639-8280. Chpsn., Kenneth C. Senft, Luther. Ch. in Am.; Vice-Chpsns., Eugene Linse, Luth. Ch.–Mo. Synod, and Norman E. Neumann, Am. Luth. Ch.; Treas., Floyd E. Anderson, Luth. Ch. in Am.; Exec. Dir., Lloyd Foerster.

(A grants consultation agency serving units of the Lutheran Church bodies, the Presbyterian Church (U.S.A.), and The United Methodist Church.)

Lutheran World Relief: 360 Park Ave., S., New York, NY 10010. Tel. (212)532-6350. Pres., Robert J. Marshall; Exec. Dir., Norman E. Barth

National Association for the Advancement of Colored

People: 4805 Mt. Hope Dr., Baltimore, MD 21215. Tel. (301)358-8900. Pres., Enolia McMillan; Exec. Dir., Benjamin L. Hooks; Chpsn. of the Bd., William F.Gibson.

Periodical: Crisis (10/yr.)

National Association of Church Business Administration, Inc.: 7001 Grapevine Hwy. #324, Fort Worth, TX 76180. Tel. (817)284-1732. Pres., Richard L. Hardy, FCBA, First Assembly of God, 2725 Merle Hay Rd., Des Moines, IA 50310. Tel. (515)279-9766; Exec. Dir., F. Marvin Myers, FCBA, 7001 Grapevine Hwy., Ste. 324, Fort Worth, TX 76180. Tel. (817)284-1732

National Association of Human Rights Workers (NAHRW): Pres., Earl Williams Dir., Community Relations Bd., 601 Lakeside Ave., Cleveland, OH 44114. Tel. (216)664-2287

National Assoc. of Pastoral Musicians: 225 Sheridan St., N.W., Washington, DC 20011. Tel. (202)723-5800. Pres., Rev. Virgil C. Funk.

Periodical: Pastoral Music (6/yr)

National Association of Social Workers, Inc.: 7981 Eastern Ave., Silver Spring, MD 20910 . Pres., Suzanne Dworak-Peck; Exec. Dir., Mark G. Battle.

National Catholic Educational Association: 1077 30th St., N.W., Ste., 100, Washington, DC 20007. Tel. (202)337-6232. Pres., Catherine T. McNamee

Periodical: Momentum

National Conference of Black Churchmen: P.O. Box 24431, Nashville, TN 37202. Tel. (615)254-7972. Pres. Harold Jackson; Exec. Dir., Cedric Earl Gibb

National Consultation on Financial Development, 31 Langerfeld Rd., Hillsdale, NJ 07642. Tel. (201)664-8890. Chmn. Raymond B. Knudsen; Pres., Raymond B. Knudsen II

National Consumers League: 815 15th St., N.W., Ste. 516, Washington, DC 20005. Tel. (202)639-8140. Pres., Jack A. Blum; Exec. Dir., Linda F. Golodner

Periodicals: NCL Bulletin (bi-m)

National Cooperative Business Associaton: Pres., E. Morgan Williams, 1401 New York Ave. NW, Ste. 1100, Washington, DC 20005. Tel. (202)638-6222.

Periodical: In League (bi-m)

National Council on Alcoholism: 12 W. 21st St., New York, NY 10010. Tel. (212)206-6770, Pres: Martha B. Baker; Exec. Dir., Thomas Seessel; Chmn. of Bd.: Dr. James Kelsey

Periodicals: Currents (5/yr); Bulletins, Alerts, Fact Sheets

National Council on Crime and Delinquency: 77 Maiden Lane, 4th Fl., San Francisco, CA 94108. Tel. (415)956-5651. Chpsn., Allen F. Breed; Pres., Barry Krisberg

Periodicals: Crime and Delinquency (q); Journal of Research in Crime and Delinquency (semi-a)

National Education Association: 1201 16th St., N.W., Washington, DC 20036. Pres., Mary Hatwood Futrell; Exec. Dir., Don Cameron

Periodical: Today's Education (a); NEA Today (8/yr.)

National Farmers Union: 10065 E. Harvard Ave., Denver, CO 80251. Tel. (303)337-5500. Pres., Cy Carpenter

Periodical: Washington Newsletter (m)

National Federation of Business and Professional Women's Clubs, Inc.: 2012 Massachusetts Ave., N.W., Washington, DC 20036. Tel. (202)293-1100. E$xec. Dir., Linda Colvard Dorian

Periodical: National Business Woman (6/yr)

National Grange: 1616 H Street, N.W., Washington, DC 20006. Tel. (202)628-3507. Edward Andersen, Master

National Housing Conference: 1126 16th St., N.W., Washington, DC 20036. Tel. (202)223-4844. Dir., Juliette Madison

National Interreligious Task Force on Soviet Jewry: 1307 South Wabash Ave., #221, Chicago, IL 60605. Tel. (312)922-1983. Exec. Dir., Sr. Ann Gillen

National Mental Health Association, The: 1021 Prince St., Alexandria, VA 22314.

National Planning Association: 1616 P St. N.W., Ste. 400, Washington, DC 20036. Tel. (202)265-7685. Chpsn., Walter Sterling Surrey; Pres., Edward E. Masters
Periodicals: Looking Ahead (q)

National PTA, The (National Congress of Parents and Teachers): 700 N. Rush St., Chicago, IL 60611. Tel. (312)787-0997. Pres., Mrs. Ann P. Kahn

National Urban League, Inc.: 500 E. 62nd St., New York, NY 10021. Tel. (212)310-9000 Chmn. of Bd., David T. Kearns; Pres., John E. Jacob.

Planned Parenthood Federation of America, Inc.: 810 Seventh Ave., New York, NY 10019. Tel. (212)541-7800. Pres. Faye Wattleton; Chpsn., Anne Saunier; Chpsn., Individual Rights Comm., Judith Jones
Periodical: Planned Parenthood Review (4/yr)

Protestant Health and Welfare Assembly: 1 Woodfield Pl., 1701 E. Woodfield Rd., Ste. 311, Schaumburg, IL 60173. Tel. (312)843-2701. Exec. Sec., Charles D. Phillips

Protestant Radio and TV Center: 1727 Clifton Rd., N.E., Atlanta, GA 30329. Tel. (404)634-3324. Pres., William Horlock

Public Affairs Committee: 381 Park Ave. So., New York, NY 10016. Tel. (212)683-4331. Chmn., Clifford C. Nelson; Ed. and Exec. Dir., Adele Braude
Publication: Public Affairs Pamphlets

Religious Education Association, The: 409 Prospect St., New Haven, CT 06511. Tel. (203)865-6141. Pres., Joanne Chafe; Exec. Sec., Dr. Donald T. Russo; Chpsn. of Bd., William B. Kennedy

Religious News Service: 104 W. 56th St., New York, NY 10019. Tel. (212)315-0870. Ed. and Dir., Judith L. Weidman; News Ed., Tom Roberts; Photo Ed., Kevin McLaughlin.

Religious Research Association, Inc.: Marist Hall, Rm. 108, Catholic Univ. of Am., Washington, DC 20064. Tel. (202)635-5447. Pres., Hart M. Nelsen; Treas., David Roozen; Sec., Peggy A. L. Shriver
Periodical: Review of Religious Research (4/yr.)

Society for Values in Higher Education: 409 Prospect St., New Haven, CT 06510. Exec. Dir., David C. Smith

Southern Christian Leadership Conference: 334 Auburn Ave., N.E., Atlanta, GA 30312. Tel. (404)522-1420. Pres. Joseph E. Lowery

Southern Regional Council: 2nd Fl., 60 Wolton St., NW, Atlanta, GA 30303. Tel. (404)522-8764. Pres., Paul Gaston. Exec. Dir., Steve Suitts

Theos Foundation: 1301 Clark Bldg., 717 Liberty Ave., Pittsburgh, PA 15222. Tel. (412)471-7779. Exec. Dir., Sue Kreke Rumbaugh.
Periodical: Survivors Outreach

United Nations Association of the U.S.A.: 485 Fifth Ave., New York, NY 10017. Tel. (212)697-3232. Chpsn. of the Assn., Elliot L. Richardson; Chpsn., Bd. of Governors, Orville Freeman.
Periodicals: The Inter Dependent (6/yr); Issues before the General Assembly (a); Fact Sheets on Issues.

United Way of America.: 701 North Fairfax St., Alexandria, VA 22314. Tel. (703)836-7100. Pres., William Aramony
Periodical: Community (10/yr.)

USO World Headquarters: 601 Indiana Ave., NW, Washington, DC 20004. Tel. (202)383-1517. Exec. Vice-Pres., Michael E. Menster

Vellore Christian Medical College Board Inc.: 475 Riverside Dr., Rm. 243, New York, NY 10115. Tel. (212)870-2642; Exec. Dir., Linda L. Pierce.

Woman's Christian Temperance Union (National): 1730 Chicago Ave., Evanston, IL 60201. Tel. (312)864-1396. Pres., Mrs. Kermit S. Edgar
Periodicals: The Union Signal (m); The Young Crusader (m)

Women's International League for Peace and Freedom: 1213 Race St., Philadelphia, PA 19107. Tel. (215)563-7110. Pres., Anne Ivey; Exec. Dir., Jane Midgley
Periodicals: Peace and Freedom; Program and Action/Legislative Bulletin

World Conference on Religion and Peace: 777 United Nations Plaza, New York, NY 10017. Tel. (212)687-2163.
Periodical: Religion for Peace (occ.); WCRP/USA Newsletter (occ.)

World Education, Inc.: 210 Lincoln St., Boston, MA 02111. Tel. (617)482-9485. Pres., Joel H. Lamstein; Chpsn., Bd. of Trustees, Jerry-Ann Barker
Periodical: World Education Reports (bi-a)

World Peace Foundation: 22 Batterymarch St., Boston, MA 02109. Tel. (617)482-3875. Dir., Richard J. Bloomfield.
Periodical: International Organization (q)

World Vision, Inc.: 919 W. Huntington Dr., Monrovia, CA 91016. Tel. (818)357-7979. Pres. and Chief Exec., Officer, Ted W. Engstrom.
Periodicals: Christian Leadership Letter (m); World Vision Magazine (m)

16. CANADIAN SERVICE AGENCIES: SOCIAL, CIVIC, RELIGIOUS

The following list of Canadian service agencies is offered for purposes of directing the reader's attention to a number of major Canadian agencies that can provide resources of information and service to the churches. No attempt is made to produce a complete listing of such agencies, and the reader is referred to the *Canadian Almanac and Directory for 1988* and The *1988 Corpus Almanac and Canadian Source Book*, Vols. 1 & 2, for comprehensive listings of Canadian organizations.

Listings are alphabetical by name of institution and generally have the following order: Name of institution, address, telephone number, principal officers, periodical.

Alcohol and Drug Concerns: 11 Progress Ave., Ste. 200, Scarborough, Ontario M1P 4S7, Exec. Dir., Karl Burden. Tel. (416)293-3400
Periodical: Concerns (q)

Alcoholics Anonymous: 234 Eglinton Ave., E., Toronto, Ontario M4P 1K5. Tel. (416)487-5591 (there are approx. 4,000 A.A. Groups in Canada). Correspondence to: Exec. Sec.

Alliance for Life: B1 - 90 Garry St., Winnipeg, Manitoba R3C 4H1. Tel. (204)942-4772

L'Association canadienne des périodiques catholiques: 9795, boul. Ste-Anne-de-Beaupré, C.P. 1000, Ste-Anne-de-Beaupré, Québec, Québec G0A 3C0. Tél. (418)827-4538. Prés., Jean Paré.
Périodique: Annuaire

Association of Canadian Bible Colleges, The: 100 Fergus Ave., Kitchener, Ontario N2A 2H2. Sec.-Treas., Tom Dow. Tel. (519)745-2446
Periodical: Directory and Informational Survey of Member Schools (a)

Association of Universities and Colleges of Canada: 151 Slater, Ottawa, Ontario K1P 5N1. Tel. (613)563-1236. Exec. Dir., A. K. Gillmore.
Periodicals: University Affairs (10/yr.); Directory of Canadian Universities (bi-a); Canadian Directory of Awards for Graduate Study (bi-a); Academic and Administrative Officers at Canadian Universities (a); Compendium of University Statistics (a); Directory of University Resources for International Development (tri-a); Canadian Universities in International Development (4/yr.)

B'nai B'rith Canada, The League for Human Rights of: 15 Hove St., Downsview, Ontario M3H 4Y8. Tel (416)633-6224. Exec. Vice-Pres., Frank Dimant
Periodical: The Review of Anti-Semitism in Canada (a)

Boy Scouts of Canada, National Council: 1345 Baseline Rd., P.O. Box 5151, Sta. F., Ottawa, Ontario K2C 3G7. Tel. (613)224-5131. Chief Exec., J. Blain
Periodicals: The Canadian Leader (m)

Boys' Brigade in Canada, The: 115 St. Andrews Rd., Scarborough, Ontario M1P 4N2. Tel. (416)431-6052. Pres., Wayne Rogers
Periodicals: Hotline (q);

Boys and Girls Clubs of Canada: 250 Consumers Rd., Ste. 505, Willowdale, Ontario M2J 4V6. Tel. (416)494-1212. Natl. Dir., Dr. Charles A. Griffith
Periodical: Stafflines; President's Newsletter

Canada China Programme: 40 St. Clair Ave. E. Ste. 201, Toronto, Ontario M4T 1M9. Tel. (416)921-4152. Dir., Theresa Chu

Canadian Association for Adult Education: 29 Prince Arthur Ave., Toronto, Ontario M5R 1B2. Exec. Dir., Ian Morrison, Tel. (416)964-0559
Periodicals: Learning (occ.), Learning Resources Kit

Canadian Association for Community Living: Kinsmen Bldg., York Univ. Campus, 4700 Keele St., Downsview, Ontario M3J 1P3. Tel. (416)661-9611
Periodical: Entourage (q)

Canadian Association for Pastoral Education: P.O. Box 96, Roxboro, Quebec H8Y 3E8. Mrs. Verda Rochon. Tel. (514)694-0893

Canadian Association in Solidarity with the Native Peoples: 16 Spadina Rd., Toronto Ontario M5R 2S7, Tel. (416)964-0169.
Periodical: Phoenix (newsletter)

Canadian Association of Schools of Social Work: 151 Slater St., Rm. 909, Ottawa, Ontario K1P 5N1. Exec. Dir., Dennis Kimberly. Tel. (613)563-1217

Canadian Association of Social Workers: 55 Parkdale Ave., Ottawa, Ontario, K1Y 1E5. Tel. (613)728-1865.
Periodicals: The Social Worker (q.)

Canadian Book Publishers' Council: 45 Charles St. E., 7th Floor Toronto, Ontario M4Y 1S2. Tel. (416)964-7231. Exec. Dir., Jacqueline Hushion

Canadian Catholic Organization for Development and Peace/Organisation Catholique Canadienne pour le Développement et la Paix: 2111 rue Centre Montréal, Québec H3K 1J5. Tél. (514)932-5136. Exec. Dir., Jacques Champagne; Assoc. Exec. Dir., Tom Johnston. English Sector Offices: 3028 Danforth Ave., Toronto, Ontario M4C 1N2. Tel. (416)698-7770. French Sector Offices: 2111 rue Centre, Montréal, Québec H3K 1J5. Tél. (514)932-5136. Projects Offices: 2111 rue Centre, Montréal.
Periodicals (French Sector): Solidarités (newspaper)
Periodicals (English Sector): Education Notes (m), The Global Village Voice (bi-m)

Canadian Center for Ecumenism: 2065 Sherbroke St. W., Montreal, Quebec H3H 1G6. Dir., Thomas Ryan. Tel. (514)937-9176
Periodical: Ecumenism (q); Oecuménisme (q)

Canadian Chamber of Commerce, The: 200 Elgin St., Ste. 301, Ottawa, Ontario K2P 2J7. Tel. (613)238-4000. Pres., Roger B. Hamel.

Canadian Civil Liberties Association: 229 Yonge St., Ste. 403, Toronto, Ontario M5B 1N9. Tel. (416)363-0321. Gen. Counsel., A. Alan Borovoy

Canadian Co-operative Credit Society Limited: 300 The East Mall, Islington, Ontario M9B 6B7. Tel. (416)232-1262. National Credit Union Organization, Chief Exec. Off., Norm A. Bromberger
Periodicals: Briefs (bi-w)

Canadian Council of Crisis Centres: c/o Distress Centre, Inc. Box 393, Postal Sta. K, Toronto, Ontario M4P 2G7. Tel. (416)486-6766. Exec. Dir., Patricia Harnisch

Canadian Council on Social Development, The: 55 Parkdale Ave., Box 3505, Sta. C, Ottawa, Ontario K1Y 4G1. Tel (613)728-1865. Exec. Dir., Terrance M. Hunsley
Periodicals: Perception (5/yr.); Overview (4/yr.); Catalogue of Publications

Canadian Education Association/Association canadienne d' éducation: Ste., 8-200, 252 Bloor St. W., Toronto, Ontario M5S 1V5. Exec. Dir., Robert Blair. Tel. (416)924-7721
Periodicals: CEA Newsletter (9/yr.) Education Canada (q); Bulletin (9/année)

Canadian Girls in Training: Rm. 200, 40 St. Clair Ave., E., Toronto, Ontario M4T 1M9. Tel. (416)961-2036. Exec. Dir., Jean M. Day

Canadian Institute of Planners: 30-46 Elgin St., Ottawa, Ontario K1P 5K6. Tel. (613)233-2105. Exec. Dir., David Sherwood.
Periodical: Plan Canada (10/yr)

Canadian Institute of Religion and Gerontology: 40 St. Clair Ave., East, Ste. 203, Toronto, Ontario M4T 1M9. Dir., Rev. Donald H. Powell. Tel. (416)924-5865.

Canadian Labour Congress: 2841 Riverside Dr., Ottawa, Ontario, K1V 8X7. Tel. (613)521-3400. Pres., Shirley G. E. Carr
Periodical: Canadian Labour (m)

Canadian Medical Association, The: 1867 Alta Vista Dr., Box 8650, Ottawa, Ontario K1G 0G8. Tel. (613)731-9331. Sec. Gen., Leo Paul Landry, M.D.

Canadian Mental Health Association: 2160 Yonge St., Toronto, Ontario M4S 2Z3. Tel. (416)484-7750. Gen. Dir., George Rohn

Canadian Prisoner's Aid Societies:
Elizabeth Fry Society of Toronto, 215 Wellesley St. E., Toronto, Ontario M4X 1G1. Tel. (416)924-3708. Exec. Dir., Ms. Darlene Lawson

John Howard Society of Ontario, 46 St. Clair Ave., E., 3rd Fl., Toronto, Ontario M4T 1M9. Tel. (416)925-2205. Exec. Dir. Gordon C. MacFarlane
Periodicals: Newsletter (4/yr.); Reform Bulletin (4/yr)

The St. Leonard's Society of Canada, 104-525 Windsor Ave., Windsor, Ontario N9A 1J4. Tel. (519)254-9430. Exec. Dir., L. A. Drouillard
Periodical: Annual Report; Report on Objectives

Canadian Red Cross Society: 95 Wellesley St. E. Toronto, Ontario M4Y 1H6. Tel. (416)923-6692. Sec. Gen., George Weber
Periodical: Service (4/yr)

Canadian Society of Biblical Studies: Exec. Sec., Wayne O. McCready,. Dept. of Religious Studies, Univ . of Calgary, Calgary, Alberta T2N 1N4. Pres., Paul Dion, Dept. of Near Eastern Studies, Univ. of Toronto, Toronto, Ontario M5S 1A1
Periodicals: The Bulletin of the Canadian Society of Biblical Studies (a); Newsletter for Ugaritic Studies (3/yr); Newsletter for Targumic and Cognate Studies (3/yr.)

Canadian Society of Church History: c/o John Brian Scott, Dept. of Religious Studies, Univ. of Ottawa, 177 Waller St., Ottawa, Ontario K1N 6N5

Canadian UNICEF Committee: 443 Mount Pleasant Rd., Toronto, Ontario M4S 2L8. Tel. (416)482-4444. Exec. Dir., Harry S. Black
Periodicals: Communiqué Unicef Canada (q);

Canadian Unitarian Council, 175 St. Clair Ave. W., Toronto, Ontario M4V 1P7. Tel. (416)921-4506. Pres., Elinor R. Knight; Exec. Dir., Kathleen D. Hunter

Canadian Woman's Christian Temperance Union: #302 - 30 Gloucester St., Toronto, Ontario M4Y 1L6. Tel. (416)922-0757. Natl. Pres., Mrs. Brig. A. Rawlings, 875 Sunset Blvd., Woodstock, Ontario N4S 4A5
Periodical: Canadian White Ribbon Tidings (q)

CARE Canada: 1312 Bank St., Ottawa, Ontario K1S 5H7. Tel. (613)521-7081. Exec. Dir., A. John Watson.

Publication: CARE Donor Newsletter (q); Annual Report

Catholic Women's League of Canada, The: 3081 Ness Ave., Winnipeg, Manitoba R2Y 2G3. Tel. (204)885-4856. Exec. Dir., Miss Valerie J. Fall
Periodical: The Canadian League (q)

Christian Service Brigade of Canada: 1254 Plains Rd. E., Burlington, Ontario L7S 1W6. Tel. (416)634-1841. Gen. Dir., Robert A. Clayton
Periodical: The Torch Runner (q)

Church Army in Canada, The: 397 Brunswick Ave., Toronto, Ontario M5R 2Z2. Canadian Dir., Capt. Ray Taylor. Tel. (416)924-9279.
Periodical: The Crusader (q).

Church Council on Justice and Corrections, The: 507 Bank St., 2nd Fl., Ottawa, Ontario K2P 1Z5. Tel. (613)563-1688. Prog. Coord., Rev. J. D. McCord

Churches and Corporate Responsibility, Taskforce on The: 129 St. Clair Ave. W., Toronto, Ontario M4V 1N5. Tel. (416)923-1758. Coordinator, Moira Hutchinson

Churches' Council on Theological Education in Canada, The 60 St. Clair Ave. E., Ste. 500, Toronto, Ontario M4T 1N5. Tel. (416)921-4860. Chpsn., Rev. Jean Armstrong; Exec. Dir., Lloyd Gesner

Consumers' Association of Canada: Level 3, 2660 Southvale Crescent, Ottawa, Ontario K1B 5C4. Tel. (613)733-9450. Pres., Sally Hall

Couchiching Institute on Public Affairs: 25 Adelaide St., E., #1711, Toronto, Ontario M5C 1H7. Exec. Sec., Lee Walsh

CUSO: 135 Rideau St. Ottawa, Ontario K1N 9K7. Tel. (613)563-1242.
Periodicals: CUSO Forum (5/yr); CUSO Journal (a)

Evangelical Theological Society of Canada: McMaster Divinity College, Hamilton, Ontario L8S 4K1. Tel. (416)525-9140. Pres., Clark H. Pinnock

Frontiers Foundation/Operation Beaver: 2615 Danforth Ave., Ste. 203, Toronto, Ontario M4C 1L6. Tel. (416)690-3930. Exec. Dir., Charles R. Catto
Periodical: Annual Report

GATT-Fly, A Project of Canadian Churches for Global Economic Justice: 11 Madison Ave., Toronto, Ontario M5R 2S2. Tel. (416)921-4615. Co-ordinator, John Dillon
Periodical: GATT-Fly Report (4/yr.)

Gideons International in Canada: 501 Imperial Rd. N., Guelph, Ontario N1H 7A2. Tel. (519)823-1140. Exec. Dir., H. Braun
Periodical: Canadian Gideon Magazine (6/yr.)

Girl Guides of Canada—Guides du Canada: 50 Merton St., Toronto, Ontario M4S 1A3. Tel. (416)487-5281. Exec. Dir., Mrs. Margaret Ringland.
Periodical: Canadian Guider (5/yr.)

Health League of Canada, The: 1560 Bayview Ave., Ste. 304, Toronto, Ontario M4G 3B9. Dir., Dr. Donald F. Damude
Periodical: Health News Digest

Institute for Christian Studies: 229 College St., Toronto, Ontario M5T 1R4. Tel. (416)979-2331. Pres., Dr. Clifford Pitt
Periodical: Perspective Newsletter (bi-m); Anakainosis (q)

Inter-Church Committee on Human Rights in Latin America: 40 St. Clair Ave. E., Ste. 201. Toronto, Ontario M4T 1M9. Tel. (416)921-4152. Exec. Dir., Tim Ryan
Periodical: Newsletter

Inter-Church Committee for Refugees: 40 St. Clair Ave. E., Toronto, Ontario M4T 1M9. Tel. (416)921-4152. Officer: Dr. Tom Clark.

Interchurch Committee for World Development Education (Ten Days for World Development): 85 St. Clair Ave. E., Toronto, Ontario M4T 1M8, Nat'l Co-Ord., Jeanne Moffat

Inter-Church Communications: Berkeley Studio, The United Church of Canada, 315 Queen St., E., Toronto, Ontario M5A 1S7. Tel. (416)925-5931. Chmn. Larry Jones

Inter-Church Fund for International Development (ICFID): 85 St. Clair Ave. E., Ste. 204, Toronto, Ontario M4T 1M8. Tel. (416)968-1411. Exec. Sec., Dr. Robert Fugere

Interfaith Committee on Chaplaincy in the Correctional Service of Canada: 40 St. Clair Ave. E., Toronto, Ontario M4T 1M9. Tel. (416)921-4152. Sec.-Treas., Edith B. Shore

John Milton Society for the Blind in Canada: 40 St. Clair Ave., E., Ste. 202, Toronto, Ontario M4T 1M9. Tel. (416)960-3953.
Periodicals: Insight (Large Print magazine bi-m); Insound (cassette magazine); In Touch (Braille magazine for Adults); National Library in Sound (Bible series, commentary and music); Meeting Place

Organisation Catholique Canadienne pour le Developpement et la Paix (see: Canadian Catholic Organization for Development and Peace)

Oxfam-Canada/National Office: 251 Laurier W., Ste. 301, Ottawa, Ontario K1P 5J6. Tel. (613)237-5236

Pioneer Clubs Canada, Inc.: Box 447, Burlington, Ontario L7R 3Y3. Tel. (416)681-2883. Nat'l. Dir., Richard G. Beurling
Periodicals: Lampion (q); Perspective (q)

Planned Parenthood Federation of Canada: 323 Chapel St., 3rd Fl., Ottawa, Ontario K1N 7Z2. Tel. (613)238-4474

PLURA (Inter-Church Association to Promote Social Justice in Canada): Box 1023, New Hamburg, Ontario N0B 2G0. Tel. (519)662-3450. Sec., Roy Shepherd

Project North: 80 Sackville St., Toronto, Ontario M5A 3E5. Tel. (416)366-6493. Staff Contact: Karmel Taylor McCullum
Periodical: Newsletter (q)

Project Ploughshares: Conrad Grebel College, Waterloo, Ontario N2L 3G6. Res. Coord., Ernie Regehr, Tel. (519)888-6541; Edu. Coord., David Pollack
Periodical: Ploughshares Monitor (q)

Religious Television Associates: Berkeley Studio, 315 Queen St. East, Toronto, Ontario M5A 1S7. Tel. (416)366-9221. Dir., Rev. Rod Booth

Save the Children (Aide à l'enfance Canada): 3080 Yonge St., Ste. 6020, Toronto, Ontario M4N 3P4. Tel. (416)960-3190. Natl. Dir., Gordon Ramsay
Periodical: Network (Fr. Liaison) (q)

Scripture Union: 300 Steelcase Rd. W., #19, Markham, Ontario L3R 2W2. Tel. (416)475-0890. Gen. Dir., John F. Booker
Periodicals: S.U. News (q); Daily Bible Readng Guides

Shantymen's Christian Association of North America: 2110 Argentia Rd., Ste. 301, Mississauga, Ontario L5N 2K7. Tel. (416)821-1175. Pres., W. D. Morrison; Gen. Dir., Arthur C. Dixon
Periodical: The Shantyman (m)

Social Science Federation of Canada and Canadian Federation for the Humanities: 151 Slater St., Ste. 407, Ottawa, Ontario K1P 5H3. Tel. (613)236-4686. Exec. Dir., Dr. Christian Pouyez (Social Science Fed. of Canada); Exec. Dir., Viviane Launay (Canadian Federation for the Humanities)

TELECARE Teleministries of Canada, Inc.: P.O. Box 695, Midland, Ontario L4R 4P4. Tel. (705)526-8058. Coord: Rev. James Manuel

Unitarian Service Committee of Canada: 56 Sparks St., Ottawa, Ontario K1P 5B1. Tel. (613)234-6827. Founding Dir., Lotta Hirschmanova

United Nations Association in Canada: 63 Sparks St., Ste., 808 Ottawa, Ontario K1P 5A6. Tel. (613)232-5751. Pres., David Cadman; Exec. Dir., Firdaus James Kharas

Vanier Institute of the Family, The—l'institut Vanier de la famille: 120 Holland Ave., 3rd Fl., Ottawa, Ontario K1Y 0X6. Tel. (613)722-4007. Coord. of Adm. and Communication/Inf., Alan Mirabelli; Coord. of Prog. and Rsch., Dr. Robert Glossop
Periodical: Transition (q)

Voice of Women/La Voix des Femmes: 736 Bathurst St., Toronto, Ontario M5S 2R4. Tel. (416)537-9343. Natl. Staff: Vera de Jong
Periodical: Voice of Women (q)

World University Service of Canada: P. O. Box 3000, Stn. C. Ottawa, Ontario K1Y 4M8.Tel. (613)725-3121. Exec. Dir., William W. McNeill

World Vision Canada: 6630 Turner Valley Rd., Mississauga, Ontario L5N 2S4. Exec. Dir., J. Don Scott
Periodicals: Actionews (m)—English Sector; Vision Mondiale (6/yr)—French Sector; Christian Leadership Letter (m), International Intercessors (m); MARC (6/yr)

Youth for Christ/Canada: 1180A Martin Grove Rd., Rexdale, Ontario M9W 5M9. Tel. (416)243-3420. Pres., Robert E. Simpson

III
STATISTICAL AND HISTORICAL SECTION

This section of the **Yearbook** provides various types of statistical data and information on depositories of church history material for the U.S. and Canada. It is hoped that these materials will be useful in describing some major dimensions of religious life.

Much of the data presented here are unique, at least in form of presentation, and can be used judiciously to interpret developments in the religious life of the U.S. and Canada. Whenever necessary, qualifying statements have been made to warn the user of some of the pitfalls in the data.

Information in this section of the **Yearbook,** when compared with that of previous editions, suggests a number of interesting subjects for students, journalists, and church researchers to analyze and interpret. For the most part, generalizations on trends reflected in the data are left up to the reader.

The following information is contained in this Statistical and Historical Section.

1. **Current and Non-Current Statistical Data.** This section contains nine tables, numbered 1-A through 1-I, as follows: 1-A, United States Current and Non-Current Statistics, arranged alphabetically for 220 United States religious bodies. Included is information on Number of Churches, Inclusive Membership, Full, Communicant or Confirmed Members (current data only), Number of Pastors Serving Parishes, Total Number of Clergy, Number of Sunday or Sabbath Schools (current data only), and Total Enrollment (current data only). Table 1-B, Summary of United States Current and Non-Current Statistics, provides totals for 220 bodies in the above categories and compares these totals with those in the previous **Yearbook** for 1987. Table 1-C, Some Comparative United States Church Statistics, compares data mainly for 1986 with those mainly for 1985 with regard to Church Membership as a Percent of U.S. Population, Membership Gain and Percentage of Gain over Previous Year. Table 1-D, Current and Non-Current Canadian Statistics provides the same data for Canadian bodies as those described above for Table 1-A. Table 1-E provides a Summary of Canadian Current and Non-Current Statistics. Table 1-F, Number of United States Churches, and of Members, by Religious Groups, is continued from the previous year with all the necessary qualifications. Table 1-G, Constituency of the National Council of the Churches of Christ in the U.S.A., is followed by Table 1-H, Church Membership Statistics, 1940-1986, for Selected U.S. Denominations. Table 1-I, Inclusive Membership, 58 Compilations, concludes this section.

2. **Church Financial Statistics and Related Data.** Complete data on contributions of members of 71 United States and Canadian religious bodies are supplied in the following categories: Total Contributions, Total Congregational Finances, and Benevolences. Per-capita contributions based on both Inclusive and Full or Confirmed Membership are supplemented by some related data.

3. **Some Trends and Developments.** This section of the **Yearbook** begins with "Religious Affiliation in Canada," an article excerpted and summarized from the Autumn 1987 *Canadian Social Trends,* from the original by George A. Mori, on the staff of Statistics Canada, Ottawa. Data from *The 1987 Official Catholic Directory,* providing statistical trends for the Roman Catholic Church, follow. "Trends in Seminary Enrollment: 1980–1987" by Dr. William L. Baumgaertner, associate director of The Association of Theological Schools in the United States and Canada, concludes the section.

4. **Surveys of Religion in American Life.** Three survey articles comprise this section. The first, "Costs of Professional Parish Leadership: A Cross-Denominational Survey" by Dr. Jackson W. Carroll, vice president of Religion and Society, Hartford Seminary; Dr. Dean R. Hoge, professor of Sociology, Catholic University; and Dr. Francis K. Scheets, a Crosier Father, is followed by a roundup of selected Church Attendance and Other Polls. "Value of New Construction of Religious Buildings" concludes this section.

5. **Main Depositories of Church History Material and Sources.** This is a listing, by denomination, of various major depositories of historical and archival materials in the United States and Canada, including a bibliographical guide to information on church archives.

1. CURRENT AND NON-CURRENT STATISTICAL DATA, UNITED STATES AND CANADA

Tables 1-A through 1-I in this section, containing current and non-current data, have been compiled from questionnaires returned to the **Yearbook of American and Canadian Churches** by statisticians and other officials of religious bodies. These statistics have been checked carefully, but in no case have they been "adjusted" by the editor in any way for any purpose. What is reported here are official reports.

In keeping with the bi-national organization of the **Yearbook**, statistical totals are given in separate tables for the United States and Canada for the 305 denominations or parts of denominations reporting. In some cases, therefore, statistical tables for a denomination with headquarters in the U.S., and which has a Canadian section, will vary slightly from officially reported statistics of that denomination, and it will be necessary to add the two parts together. For example, the Brethren in Christ Church had an official membership in 1986 of 20,133, of which 16,693 was in the United States and 3,440 in the Brethren in Christ Church, Canadian Conference.

In Table 1-A, the religious bodies in the U.S. are listed alphabetically and current data appear in **bold face** type. Non-current data appear in the light face type. Current data are those compiled and reported in 1987 or 1986. Non-current data are those for 1985 or earlier. Table 1-A contains 108 current and 112 non-current reports, making a total of 220. Current reports, comprising 49.1 percent of all reports, account for 74.6 percent of reported membership.

Statistics appearing in Table 1-G, Constituency of the National Council of Churches of Christ in the U.S.A., do not show the distinction between current and non-current data, although the date of the last statistical report received is noted for each religious body. This year Table 1-D, Canadian Current and Non-Current Statistics, contains statistical reports from 85 Canadian bodies, one more than the previous edition of the **Yearbook**.

Caution should be exercised in interpreting Table 1-B, Summary of United States Current and Non-Current Statistics, which indicates the general trends shown by the data in the 1988 and 1987 **Yearbooks.** Since current and non-current statistics are combined for this comparison, the dangers of elaborate generalizations are obvious. The same is true for Table 1-C, Some Comparative United States Church Statistics.

Users of church statistics are referred to "A Guide for the User of Church Statistics," found at the front of this **Yearbook.** It is essential reading for all who intend to work with and interpret statistics contained in this volume. The Guide is placed in this prominent position to highlight its importance, and its chief function is to state candidly the many qualifications that must be taken into account when using church statistics.

TABLE 1-A: UNITED STATES CURRENT AND NON-CURRENT STATISTICS

The following table provides current and non-current statistics for United States religious bodies listed alphabetically. Current statistics are defined as those gathered and reported for 1987 and 1986. Those bodies having current statistics, and the statistics themselves, are shown in **bold face** type. Non-current statistics are those for 1985 or earlier. They appear in light face type. No statistics for "Full, Communicant, or Confirmed members," "Number of Sunday or Sabbath Schools," and "Total Enrollment" are reported for bodies having non-current statistics.

Religious Body	Year Reported	No. of Churches	Inclusive Membership	Full, Communicant or Confirmed Members	No. of Pastors Serving Parishes	Total No. of Clergy	No. of Sunday or Sabbath Schools	Total Enrollment
ADVENT CHRISTIAN CHURCH	**1986**	**352**	**19,946**	**19,946**	**300**	**568**	**300**	**18,874**
African Methodist Episcopal Church	1981	6,200	2,210,000		6,050	6,550		
AFRICAN METHODIST EPISCOPAL ZION CHURCH	**1986**	**6,057**	**1,195,173**	**1,098,949**	**6,000**	**6,396**	**6,057**	**217,000**
Albanian Orthodox Archdiocese in America	1978	16	40,000		18	25		
Albanian Orthodox Diocese of America	1982	10	5,250		2	3		
ALLEGHENY WESLEYAN METHODIST CONNECTION (ORIGINAL ALLEGHENY CONFERENCE)	**1986**	**122**	**2,474**	**2,302**	**102**	**199**	**126**	**6,755**
AMANA CHURCH SOCIETY	**1986**	**4**	**890**	**612**	**13**	**14**	**4**	**83**
AMERICAN BAPTIST ASSOCIATION	**1986**	**1,705**	**250,000**	**250,000**	**1,740**	**1,760**	**N.R.**	**N.R.**
AMERICAN BAPTIST CHURCHES IN THE U.S.A	**1986**	**5,864**	**1,576,483**	**1,576,483**	**4,836**	**7,678**	**N.R.**	**384,477**
American Carpatho-Russian Orthodox Greek Catholic Church	1976	70	100,000		61	66		
THE AMERICAN LUTHERAN CHURCH	**1986**	**4,959**	**2,319,443**	**1,740,439**	**4,720**	**7,671**	**4,569**	**581,938**
American Rescue Workers	1984	20	2,700		35	53		
The Anglican Orthodox Church	1983	40	6,000		8	8		
The Antiochian Orthodox Christian Archdiocese of North America	1984	120	280,000		155	180		
Apostolic Catholic Assyrian Church of the East, North American Diocese	1984	24	80,000		54	57		
Apostolic Christian Church (Nazarene)	1985	48	2,799		178	178		
APOSTOLIC CHRISTIAN CHURCHES OF AMERICA	**1986**	**80**	**16,916**	**10,916**	**269**	**347**	**79**	**6,197**
Apostolic Faith Mission of Portland Oregon	1985	45	4,100		74	84		
Apostolic Faith Mission Church of God	1983	17	1,500		28	38		
APOSTOLIC LUTHERAN CHURCH OF AMERICA	**1986**	**51**	**6,353**	**5,455**	**27**	**39**	**39**	**2,646**
APOSTOLIC OVERCOMING HOLY CHURCH OF GOD	**1987**	**175**	**12,310**	**12,310**	**250**	**295**	**N.R.**	**N.R.**
ARMENIAN APOSTOLIC CHURCH OF AMERICA	**1986**	**18**	**29,070**	**29,070**	**16**	**19**	**13**	**500**
Armenian Church of America, Diocese of	1979	66	450,000		45	61		
ASSEMBLIES OF GOD	**1986**	**10,886**	**2,135,104**	**1,258,724**	**15,221**	**26,837**	**10,572**	**1,404,974**
Associate Reformed Presbyterian Church, General Synod	1985	172	36,543		139	214		
BAPTIST BIBLE FELLOWSHIP, INTERNATIONAL	**1986**	**3,449**	**1,405,900**	**1,405,900**	**3,400**	**4,500**	**3,400**	**750,000**
BAPTIST GENERAL CONFERENCE	**1987**	**762**	**131,480**	**131,480**	**1,200**	**1,700**	**762**	**74,611**

TABLE 1-A: UNITED STATES CURRENT AND NON-CURRENT STATISTICS—Continued

Religious Body	Year Reported	No. of Churches	Inclusive Membership	Full, Communicant or Confirmed Members	No. of Pastors Serving Parishes	Total No. of Clergy	No. of Sunday or Sabbath Schools	Total Enrollment
BAPTIST MISSIONARY ASSOCIATION OF AMERICA	1986	1,359	228,125	228,125	1,500	2,450	1,357	97,564
BEACHY AMISH MENNONITE CHURCH	1986	83	5,862	5,862	271	271	N.R.	N.R.
Berean Fundamental Church	1981	49	3,350		51	53		
Bethel Ministerial Association	1983	15	3,500		40	57		
THE BIBLE CHURCH OF CHRIST	1987	6	6,400	4,800	6	40	6	644
Bible Way Church of Our Lord Jesus Christ, World Wide, Inc.	1970	350	30,000		350	350		
Brethren Church (Ashland, Ohio)	1984	122	14,229		N.R.	N.R.		
BRETHREN IN CHRIST CHURCH	1986	183	16,693	15,911	185	227	167	9,516
Buddhist Churches of America	1984	100	100,000		70	115		
Bulgarian Eastern Orthodox Church (Diocese of N. & S. America and Australia)	1971	13	86,000		N.R.	11		
CHRIST CATHOLIC CHURCH	1986	8	1,320	1,088	11	13	1	9
Christadelphians	1964	850	15,800		None	None		
THE CHRISTIAN AND MISSIONARY ALLIANCE	1986	1,691	238,734	130,116	1,654	2,154	1,538	168,380
Christian Brethren (a.k.a. (Plymouth Brethren)	1984	1,150	98,000		N.R.	500		
CHRISTIAN CATHOLIC CHURCH (EVANGELICAL PROTESTANT)	1987	6	2,500	2,500	6	16	6	1,050
CHRISTIAN CHURCH (DISCIPLES OF CHRIST)	1986	4,221	1,106,692	732,466	4,002	6,806	4,221	337,595
Christian Church of North America, General Council	1985	104	13,500		107	159		
CHRISTIAN CHURCHES AND CHURCHES OF CHRIST	1986	5,566	1,063,469	1,063,469	N.R.	5,476	N.R.	N.R.
THE CHRISTIAN CONGREGATION	1986	1,450	105,478	105,478	1,448	1,455	1,316	57,563
Christian Methodist Episcopal Church	1983	2,340	718,922		2,340	2,650		
CHRISTIAN NATION CHURCH, U.S.A.	1986	5	200	200	5	23	5	170
Christian Reformed Church in North America	1985	650	219,988		N.R.	1,077		
Christian Union	1984	114	6,000		80	114		
Church of Christ	1972	32	2,400		169	188		
Church of Daniel's Band	1951	4	200		4	10		
The Church of God	1978	2,035	75,890		1,910	2,737		
CHURCH OF GOD (ANDERSON, IND.)	1986	2,296	188,662	185,662	1,994	3,313	2,245	200,180
Church of God by Faith	1973	105	4,500		125	150		
Church of God (Cleveland, Tenn.)	1984	5,346	505,775		6,341	9,638		
CHURCH OF GOD GENERAL CONFERENCE (OREGON, ILL.)	1987	89	5,652	4,348	65	84	89	3,737
The Church of God in Christ	1982	9,982	3,709,661		9,204	10,425		
The Church of God in Christ, International	1982	300	200,000		700	1,600		

TABLE 1-A: UNITED STATES CURRENT AND NON-CURRENT STATISTICS—Continued

Religious Body	Year Reported	No. of Churches	Inclusive Membership	Full, Communicant or Confirmed Members	No. of Pastors Serving Parishes	Total No. of Clergy	No. of Sunday or Sabbath Schools	Total Enrollment
Church of God in Christ (Mennonite)	1985	88	7,753		N.R.	N.R.		
THE CHURCH OF GOD OF PROPHECY	1986	2,062	74,122	74,122	5,517	7,573	2,094	95,312
The Church of God of the Mountain Assembly	1977	105	3,125		162	162		
CHURCH OF GOD (SEVENTH DAY) DENVER, COLO.	1986	135	6,178	5,528	73	92	135	6,250
CHURCH OF GOD (WHICH HE PURCHASED WITH HIS OWN BLOOD)	1986	7	800	800	10	10	N.R.	N.R.
Church of Illumination	1983	4	9,000		60	60		
The Church of Jesus Christ (Bickertonites)	1981	53	2,654		243	243		
The Church of Jesus Christ of Latter-day Saints	1985	8,396	3,860,000		25,188	28,598		
Church of Our Lord Jesus Christ of the Apostolic Faith	1954	155	45,000		150	185		
CHURCH OF THE BRETHREN	1986	1,059	155,967	155,967	984	1,963	971	59,410
Church of the Living God (C.W.F.F.)	1985	170	42,000		N.R.	170		
CHURCH OF THE LUTHERAN BRETHREN OF AMERICA	1986	118	11,778	11,778	113	184	107	10,035
CHURCH OF THE LUTHERAN CONFESSION	1986	68	8,852	6,410	55	78	63	1,473
CHURCH OF THE NAZARENE	1986	5,018	530,912	529,192	4,088	8,667	4,854	835,353
CHURCHES OF CHRIST	1987	13,364	1,623,754	1,275,533	N.R.	N.R.	N.R.	N.R.
CHURCHES OF CHRIST IN CHRISTIAN UNION	1987	260	11,400	11,400	171	373	260	19,100
Churches of God, General Conference	1985	353	34,870		300	458		
COMMUNITY CHURCHES, INTERNATIONAL COUNCIL OF	1987	350	200,000	200,000	N.R.	350	N.R.	N.R.
Congregational Christian Churches, National Association of	1985	464	108,115		563	826		
Congregational Holiness Church	1981	174	8,347		176	488		
Conservative Baptist Association of America	1982	1,140	225,000		N.R.	N.R.		
CONSERVATIVE CONGREGATIONAL CHRISTIAN CONFERENCE	1986	170	28,948	28,948	274	424	161	8,641
COPTIC ORTHODOX CHURCH	1986	28	115,000	115,000	28	28	N.R.	N.R.
CUMBERLAND PRESBYTERIAN CHURCH	1986	811	98,103	91,556	573	776	734	46,334
Duck River (and Kindred) Associations of Baptists	1975	85	8,632		148	148		
Elim Fellowship	1983	36	N.R.		144	185		
THE EPISCOPAL CHURCH	1986	7,054	2,504,507	1,756,120	7,887	14,111	N.R.	557,863
THE ESTONIAN EVANGELICAL LUTHERAN CHURCH	1986	24	7,191	N.R.	22	23	N.R.	N.R.
ETHICAL CULTURE MOVEMENT	1986	21	3,500	3,500	15	45	14	500
EVANGELICAL CHURCH OF NORTH AMERICA	1987	186	17,440	17,440	178	306	N.R.	19,255
EVANGELICAL CONGREGATIONAL CHURCH	1986	160	41,237	25,625	122	211	159	19,029
EVANGELICAL COVENANT CHURCH	1986	570	86,079	86,079	517	930	524	71,424
EVANGELICAL FREE CHURCH OF AMERICA	1986	880	95,722	95,722	N.R.	1,484	N.R.	N.R.
Evangelical Friends Alliance	1982	217	24,095		192	483		

TABLE 1-A: UNITED STATES CURRENT AND NON-CURRENT STATISTICS—Continued

Religious Body	Year Reported	No. of Churches	Inclusive Membership	Full, Communicant or Confirmed Members	No. of Pastors Serving Parishes	Total No. of Clergy	No. of Sunday or Sabbath Schools	Total Enrollment
EVANGELICAL LUTHERAN CHURCHES, THE ASSOCIATION OF	1986	250	103,263	77,448	298	672	N.R.	N.R.
EVANGELICAL LUTHERAN SYNOD	1986	120	19,938	15,082	96	128	104	3,483
EVANGELICAL MENNONITE CHURCH	1987	25	3,841	3,841	40	66	25	4,397
Evangelical Methodist Church	1985	126	9,040		126	N.R.		
EVANGELICAL PRESBYTERIAN CHURCH	1986	106	30,000	30,000	135	177	N.R.	N.R.
FELLOWSHIP OF EVANGELICAL BIBLE CHURCHES	1986	14	2,107	2,107	14	46	14	1,418
Fellowship of Fundamental Bible Churches	1984	31	1,840		31	52		
The Fire Baptized Holiness Church (Wesleyan)	1958	53	998		N.R.	N.R.		
Free Christian Zion Church of Christ	1956	742	22,260		321	420		
FREE LUTHERAN CONGREGATIONS, THE ASSOCIATION OF	1986	160	19,508	14,867	90	160	141	6,898
FREE METHODIST CHURCH OF NORTH AMERICA	1986	1,048	71,682	56,243	1,079	1,765	1,000	109,844
FREE WILL BAPTISTS, NATIONAL ASSOCIATION OF	1986	2,483	205,546	205,546	2,800	2,895	2,483	155,766
Friends General Conference	1983	505	31,600		None	None		
FRIENDS UNITED MEETING	1986	533	56,495	48,143	297	595	398	25,766
Full Gospel Assemblies, International	1984	150	3,800		122	399		
Full Gospel Fellowship of Churches and Ministers, International	1985	450	65,000		850	850		
FUNDAMENTAL METHODIST CHURCH, INC.	1986	13	698	698	16	23	13	515
General Association of Regular Baptist Churches	1981	1,571	300,839		2,000	2,045		
GENERAL BAPTISTS (GENERAL ASSOCIATION OF)	1986	871	72,263	72,263	N.R.	1,444	N.R.	N.R.
General Church of the New Jerusalem	1971	33	2,143		17	31		
General Conference of Mennonite Brethren Churches	1985	128	16,942		N.R.	N.R.		
General Conference of the Evangelical Baptist Church, Inc.	1952	31	2,200		22	37		
General Convention, The Swedenborgian Church	1985	49	2,245		35	51		
General Six Principle Baptists	1970	7	175		4	7		
Grace Brethren Churches, Fellowship of	1985	312	41,767		424	519		
GRACE GOSPEL FELLOWSHIP	1986	52	4,400	2,400	73	122	N.R.	N.R.
Greek Orthodox Archdiocese of North and South America	1977	535	1,950,000		610	655		
The Holiness Church of God, Inc.	1968	28	927		25	36		
Holy Ukrainian Autocephalic Church in Exile	1965	15	4,800		15	24		
House of God, Which is the Church of the Living God, the Pillar and Ground of the Truth, Inc.	1956	107	2,350		80	120		
Hungarian Reformed Church in America	1982	31	11,000		27	43		
Hutterian Brethren	1985	77	3,968		N.R.	N.R.		
Independent Assemblies of God, International	1962	136	N.R.		136	367		

TABLE 1-A: UNITED STATES CURRENT AND NON-CURRENT STATISTICS—Continued

Religious Body	Year Reported	No. of Churches	Inclusive Membership	Full, Communicant or Confirmed Members	No. of Pastors Serving Parishes	Total No. of Clergy	No. of Sunday or Sabbath Schools	Total Enrollment
Independent Fundamental Churches of America	1980	1,019	120,446		782	1,366	959	42,694
INTERNATIONAL CHURCH OF THE FOURSQUARE GOSPEL	1986	1,250	186,213	181,470	1,264	3,482	75	4,202
INTERNATIONAL PENTECOSTAL CHURCH OF CHRIST	1987	75	2,743	2,743	128	128	None	None
JEHOVAH'S WITNESSES	1986	8,336	752,404	752,404	None	None	None	None
JEWS**	1986	3,416	5,814,000	3,750,000	N.R.	6,500	N.R.	N.R.
KOREAN PRESBYTERIAN CHURCH IN AMERICA, GENERAL ASSEMBLY OF THE	1986	180	24,000	21,000	200	225	150	6,500
Kodesh Church of Immanuel	1980	5	326		5	28		
LATVIAN EVANGELICAL LUTHERAN CHURCH IN AMERICA, THE	1986	62	13,838	12,515	28	40	20	560
LIBERAL CATHOLIC CHURCH—PROVINCE OF THE UNITED STATES OF AMERICA	1987	34	2,800	2,600	64	127	3	22
Liberty Baptist Fellowship	1983	267	130,000		374	374		
THE LUTHERAN CHURCH IN AMERICA*	1986	5,832	2,896,138	2,157,701	5,226	8,586	5,355	622,627
THE LUTHERAN CHURCH—MISSOURI SYNOD	1986	5,897	2,630,588	1,974,798	5,261	8,044	N.R.	657,992
MENNONITE CHURCH	1987	989	91,167	91,167	1,562	2,399	973	112,381
MENNONITE CHURCH, THE GENERAL CONFERENCE	1986	215	35,170	35,170	180	365	N.R.	15,705
Metropolitan Church Association, Inc.	1958	15	443		13	62		
Metropolitan Community Churches, Universal Fellowship of	1985	230	34,000		240	266		
THE MISSIONARY CHURCH	1986	295	26,869	26,869	339	616	282	39,933
MORAVIAN CHURCH—NORTHERN PROVINCE	1986	101	32,180	24,611	98	174	98	7,440
MORAVIAN CHURCH—SOUTHERN PROVINCE	1986	56	21,722	17,660	53	83	57	8,850
National Baptist Convention of America	1956	11,398	2,668,799		7,598	28,574		
National Baptist Convention, U.S.A., Inc.	1958	26,000	5,500,000		26,000	27,500		
National Primitive Baptist Convention, Inc.	1975	606	250,000		460	636		
National Spiritualist Association of Churches	1984	142	5,558		128	142		
Netherlands Reformed Congregations	1984	14	5,520		3	4		
NEW APOSTOLIC CHURCH OF NORTH AMERICA	1986	473	34,726	34,726	703	795	473	2,062
NORTH AMERICAN BAPTIST CONFERENCE	1986	253	42,084	42,084	253	381	253	22,644
NORTH AMERICAN OLD ROMAN CATHOLIC CHURCH	1986	133	62,611	53,321	109	150	54	8,660
NORTH AMERICAN OLD ROMAN CATHOLIC CHURCH (ARCHDIOCESE OF NEW YORK)	1986	5	750	750	9	12	4	81
Old German Baptist Brethren	1982	52	4,254		236	236		
OLD ORDER AMISH CHURCH	1986	696	62,640	62,640	N.R.	N.R.	N.R.	N.R.
Old Order (Wisler) Mennonite Church	1980	38	9,731		N.R.	N.R.		
OPEN BIBLE STANDARD CHURCHES, INC.	1986	281	46,000	42,000	559	883	270	25,000
The (Original) Church of God	1971	70	20,000		50	124		

TABLE 1-A: UNITED STATES CURRENT AND NON-CURRENT STATISTICS—Continued

Religious Body	Year Reported	No. of Churches	Inclusive Membership	Full, Communicant or Confirmed Members	No. of Pastors Serving Parishes	Total No. of Clergy	No. of Sunday or Sabbath Schools	Total Enrollment
The Orthodox Presbyterian Church	1985	171	18,502		177	319		
Pentecostal Assemblies of the World, Inc.	1960	550	4,500		450	600		
PENTECOSTAL CHURCH OF GOD, INC.	1986	1,144	90,900	42,255	N.R.	1,595	N.R.	68,000
Pentecostal Fire-Baptized Holiness Church	1969	41	545		80	80		
The Pentecostal Free Will Baptist Church, Inc.	1985	130	10,700		116	171		
Pentecostal Holiness Church, International	1984	1,461	113,000		1,530	3,422		
Pillar of Fire	1949	61	5,100		N.R.	N.R.		
Polish National Catholic Church of America	1960	162	282,411		141	141		
PRESBYTERIAN CHURCH IN AMERICA	1986	913	188,083	158,645	N.R.	1,702	913	90,710
PRESBYTERIAN CHURCH (U.S.A.)	1986	11,531	3,007,322	3,007,322	10,925	19,514	11,531	1,098,362
Primitive Advent Christian Church	1984	10	546		11	11		
Primitive Baptists	1960	1,000	72,000		N.R.	N.R.		
PRIMITIVE METHODIST CHURCH, U.S.A.	1986	86	8,625	5,942	66	105	82	5,030
Progressive National Baptist Convention, Inc.	1967	655	521,692		N.R.	863		
THE PROTESTANT CONFERENCE (LUTHERAN)	1986	7	979	728	6	7	4	118
Protestant Reformed Churches in America	1980	21	4,544		19	31		
REFORMED CHURCH IN AMERICA	1986	928	340,359	207,933	852	1,636	900	101,569
Reformed Church in the United States	1985	34	3,778		28	34		
REFORMED EPISCOPAL CHURCH	1987	81	5,733	5,733	65	116	76	3,163
Reformed Mennonite Church	1970	12	500		18	21		
Reformed Methodist Union Episcopal Church	1983	18	3,800		24	33		
REFORMED PRESBYTERIAN CHURCH IN NORTH AMERICA	1986	71	5,111	3,757	57	121	71	2,898
Reformed Zion Union Apostolic Church	1965	50	16,000		23	N.R.		
Religious Society of Friends (Conservative)	1984	28	1,744		N.R.	17		
Religious Society of Friends (Unaffiliated Meetings)	1980	112	6,386		N.R.	N.R.		
REORGANIZED CHURCH OF JESUS CHRIST OF LATTER DAY SAINTS	1986	1,094	192,077	192,077	16,585	16,585	N.R.	N.R.
THE ROMAN CATHOLIC CHURCH	1986	23,561	52,893,217	N.R.	34,471	53,382	N.R.	7,215,948
THE ROMANIAN ORTHODOX EPISCOPATE OF AMERICA	1986	34	60,000	60,000	28	67	28	1,612
Russian Orthodox Church in the U.S.A., Patriarchal Parishes	1985	38	9,780		37	45		
The Russian Orthodox Church Outside of Russia	1955	81	55,000		92	168		
THE SALVATION ARMY	1986	1,092	432,893	126,440	2,509	5,195	1,113	108,659
THE SCHWENKFELDER CHURCH	1986	5	2,647	2,647	7	10	5	882

TABLE 1-A: UNITED STATES CURRENT AND NON-CURRENT STATISTICS—Continued

Religious Body	Year Reported	No. of Churches	Inclusive Membership	Full, Communicant or Confirmed Members	No. of Pastors Serving Parishes	Total No. of Clergy	No. of Sunday or Sabbath Schools	Total Enrollment
Second Cumberland Presbyterian Church in the U.S.	1959	121	30,000		121	125		
Separate Baptists in Christ	1983	101	9,051		175	175		
SERBIAN EASTERN ORTHODOX CHURCH IN THE U.S.A. AND CANADA	1986	68	67,000	65,000	60	82	56	5,010
SEVENTH-DAY ADVENTISTS	1986	4,055	666,199	666,199	3,069	5,481	4,180	464,307
Seventh Day Baptist General Conference	1980	60	5,008		33	69		
Social Brethren	1975	40	1,784		47	47		
SOUTHERN BAPTIST CONVENTION	1986	37,072	14,613,618	14,613,618	37,000	63,200	35,975	7,938,479
The Southern Methodist Church	1985	150	7,231		80	94	250	
SOVEREIGN GRACE BAPTISTS	1986	250	2,000	2,000	300	325	250	3,025
SYRIAN ORTHODOX CHURCH OF ANTIOCH (ARCHDIOCESE OF THE U.S.A. AND CANADA)	1986	22	30,000	N.R.	20	25	N.R.	N.R.
Triumph The Church and Kingdom of God in Christ (International)	1972	475	54,307		860	1,375		
TRUE (OLD CALENDAR) ORTHODOX CHURCH OF GREECE (SYNOD OF METROPOLITAN CYPRIAN), AMERICAN EXARCHATE	1986	14	4,532	4,532	13	21	None	None
Ukrainian Orthodox Church in the U.S.A.	1966	107	87,745		107	131		
UKRAINIAN ORTHODOX CHURCH OF AMERICA (ECUMENICAL PATRIARCHATE)	1986	27	5,000	5,000	35	37	17	645
UNITARIAN UNIVERSALIST ASSOCIATION	1986	956	173,167	139,531	N.R.	1,069	N.R.	38,899
United Brethren in Christ	1982	256	26,869		320	382		
UNITED CHRISTIAN CHURCH	1987	12	420	420	8	11	12	684
UNITED CHURCH OF CHRIST	1986	6,406	1,676,105	1,676,105	5,127	10,071	6,406	441,547
United Holy Church of America	1960	470	28,890		379	400		
The United Methodist Church	1985	37,876	9,192,172		21,589	37,808		
UNITED PENTECOSTAL CHURCH, INTERNATIONAL	1986	3,410	500,000	500,000	N.R.	6,984	N.R.	N.R.
United Zion Church	1983	13	929		17	20		
UNITY OF THE BRETHREN	1986	26	3,581	2,978	18	21	22	1,055
VEDANTA SOCIETY	1986	13	2,500	2,500	14	14	N.R.	N.R.
Volunteers of America	1978	607	36,634		704	704		
THE WESLEYAN CHURCH	1986	1,704	109,196	99,997	1,342	2,596	1,704	188,620
WISCONSIN EVANGELICAL LUTHERAN SYNOD	1986	1,180	416,493	316,416	1,086	1,497	1,146	48,461
WORLD CONFESSIONAL LUTHERAN ASSOCIATION	1986	11	1,385	982	18	24	11	389

*The American Lutheran Church, The Association of Evangelical Lutheran Churches and the Lutheran Church in America merged to form the Evangelical Lutheran Church in America (ECLA) during the period April 30-May 3, 1987. Since the statistics reported here are for 1986, these bodies reported separately for the last time.

**Inclusive membership represents estimates of the total number of lay persons as an ethnic, social, and religious community. Full membership is the number of lay persons estimated to be associated with

Table 1-B: SUMMARY OF UNITED STATES CURRENT AND NON-CURRENT STATISTICS

Current statistics are those reported for the years 1987 or 1986. Non-current statistics are those for the years 1985 and earlier. Only current totals are provided in the categories: Full, Communicant, or Confirmed Members; Number of Sunday or Sabbath Schools; Total Enrollment.

	No. of Bodies	No. of Churches	Inclusive Membership	Full, Communicant or Confirmed Members	No. of Pastors Serving Parishes	Total No. of Clergy	No. of Sunday or Sabbath Schools	Total Enrollment
1988 Yearbook								
Current............	108	213,819	106,560,345	46,237,955	204,523	350,555	124,654	25,787,954
Non-Current........	112	132,283	36,239,317	N.R.	124,033	182,142	N.R.	N.R.
Totals.............	220	346,102	142,799,662		328,566	532,697		
1987 Yearbook								
Current............	116	217,328	109,403,175	48,502,059	222,927	375,262	135,059	29,660,252
Non-Current........	102	128,633	33,523,188	N.R.	102,184	155,501	N.R.	N.R.
Totals.............	218	345,961	142,926,363		325,111	530,763		

TABLE 1-C: SOME COMPARATIVE UNITED STATES CHURCH STATISTICS

	1986	1987
Church Membership as a Percent of U.S. Population........	59.3	58.7
Membership Gain or Loss over Previous Year..............	754,225	-126,701
Percentage of Gain or Loss over Previous Year...........	0.53	-0.09

TABLE 1-D: CANADIAN CURRENT AND NON-CURRENT STATISTICS

The following table provides current and non-current statistics for Canadian denominations listed alphabetically. Current statistics, defined as those gathered and reported for 1987 and 1986 are shown in **bold face** type. Non-current statistics are those for 1985 and earlier, and appear in light face.

Religious Body	Year Reported	No. of Churches	Inclusive Membership	Full, Communi- cant or Con- firmed Members	No. of Pastors Serv- ing Parishes	Total No. of Clergy	No. of Sunday or Sabbath Schools	Total Enrollment
THE ANGLICAN CHURCH OF CANADA	**1986**	**3,169**	**851,032**	**558,405**	**1,788**	**3,180**	**1,913**	**95,440**
The Antiochian Orthodox Christian Archdiocese of North America	1985	10	20,000		12	12		
Apostolic Christian Church (Nazarene)	1985	14	830		49	49		
Apostolic Church in Canada	1982	9	810		9	13		
Apostolic Church of Pentecost of Canada	1984	143	15,000		150	352		
Armenian Church of North America, Diocese of Canada	1979	7	25,000		3	3		
Associated Gospel Churches	1977	102	11,558		78	174		
Baptist General Conference	1984	71	6,128		70	90		
BIBLE HOLINESS MOVEMENT	**1986**	**11**	**632**	**393**	**6**	**10**	**N.R.**	**N.R.**
BRETHREN IN CHRIST CHURCH, CANADIAN CONFERENCE	**1986**	**34**	**3,440**	**2,768**	**37**	**48**	**31**	**2,941**
British Methodist Episcopal Church	1978	13	2,000		9	9		
Buddhist Churches of Canada	1979	15	2,543		10	10		
CANADIAN BAPTIST FEDERATION	**1985**	**1,131**	**129,757**	**111,881**	**566**	**1,107**	**935**	**71,944**
CANADIAN CONVENTION OF SOUTHERN BAPTISTS	**1986**	**81**	**5,200**	**5,200**	**56**	**67**	**81**	**6,000**
CANADIAN YEARLY MEETING OF THE RELIGIOUS SOCIETY OF FRIENDS	1987	28	1,866	1,176	None	None	N.R.	184
THE CHRISTIAN AND MISSIONARY ALLIANCE IN CANADA	**1986**	**289**	**59,733**	**23,843**	**N.R.**	**N.R.**	**289**	**43,942**
Christian Brethren (a.k.a. Plymouth Brethren)	1985	600	52,000		N.R.	250		
CHRISTIAN CHURCH (DISCIPLES OF CHRIST) IN CANADA	**1986**	**37**	**4,665**	**2,876**	**25**	**49**	**37**	**1,008**
CHRISTIAN CHURCHES AND CHURCHES OF CHRIST	**1986**	**70**	**5,946**	**5,946**	**N.R.**	**75**	**N.R.**	**N.R.**
CHRISTIAN REFORMED CHURCH IN NORTH AMERICA	**1986**	**199**	**83,622**	**46,939**	**194**	**231**	**197**	**19,181**
CHURCH OF GOD (ANDERSON, IND.)	**1986**	**53**	**3,244**	**3,244**	**38**	**57**	**51**	**3,187**
CHURCH OF GOD (CLEVELAND, TENN.)	**1987**	**86**	**4,996**	**4,996**	**86**	**198**	**76**	**2,975**
THE CHURCH OF GOD OF PROPHECY OF CANADA	**1986**	**40**	**2,208**	**2,208**	**40**	**66**	**45**	**2,892**
The Church of Jesus Christ of Latter-Day Saints in Canada	1985	373	113,000		1,119	1,275		
Church of the Lutheran Brethren	1984	10	579		8	9		
CHURCH OF THE NAZARENE	**1986**	**151**	**10,054**	**10,034**	**110**	**227**	**145**	**15,389**
Churches of Christ in Canada	1985	149	9,962		103	113		
CONFERENCE OF MENNONITES IN CANADA	**1986**	**150**	**28,573**	**28,573**	**347**	**452**	**N.R.**	**N.R.**
CONGREGATIONAL CHRISTIAN CHURCHES IN ONTARIO, **THE CONFERENCE OF**	**1986**	**5**	**278**	**278**	**5**	**12**	**5**	**148**
THE COPTIC CHURCH IN CANADA	**1986**	**7**	**40,000**	**40,000**	**7**	**7**	**N.R.**	**N.R.**

254

TABLE 1-D: CANADIAN CURRENT AND NON-CURRENT STATISTICS—Continued

Religious Body	Year Reported	No. of Churches	Inclusive Membership	Full, Communicant or Confirmed Members	No. of Pastors Serving Parishes	Total No. of Clergy	No. of Sunday or Sabbath Schools	Total Enrollment
					12	13		
THE ESTONIAN EVANGELICAL LUTHERAN CHURCH	1986	13	7,183	N.R.	N.R.	13	N.R.	N.R.
EVANGELICAL BAPTIST CHURCHES IN CANADA, THE FELLOWSHIP OF	1986	475	56,371	56,371	N.R.	N.R.	N.R.	N.R.
THE EVANGELICAL CHURCH IN CANADA	1986	48	3,665	3,665	39	69	46	3,700
THE EVANGELICAL COVENANT CHURCH OF CANADA	1986	23	1,232	1,232	18	26	17	1,547
EVANGELICAL FREE CHURCH OF CANADA	1987	106	5,600	5,600	124	154	N.R.	N.R.
THE EVANGELICAL LUTHERAN CHURCH OF CANADA*	1985	653	207,674	152,024	476	744	N.R.	31,335
EVANGELICAL MENNONITE CONFERENCE	1986	48	5,639	5,639	103	104	48	5,766
Evangelical Mennonite Mission Conference	1985	30	3,039		N.R.	N.R.		
FOURSQUARE GOSPEL CHURCH OF CANADA	1986	39	2,391	2,391	72	92	26	1,505
FREE METHODIST CHURCH IN CANADA	1986	133	6,865	5,329	125	214	133	9,538
Free Will Baptists	1985	17	1,895		8	10		
General Church of the New Jerusalem	1985	3	540		5	7		
The Gospel Missionary Association	1981	13	N.R.		10	44		
Greek Orthodox Diocese of Toronto (Canada)	1984	58	230,000		45	49		
Independent Assemblies of God—Canada	1977	45	4,500		125	166		
INDEPENDENT HOLINESS CHURCH	1987	13	600	600	13	21	N.R.	N.R.
The Italian Pentecostal Church of Canada	1985	17	3,600		24	26		
JEHOVAH'S WITNESSES	1986	1,189	88,130	88,130	None	None	None	None
Jews	1981	112	296,425		N.R.	N.R.		
THE LATVIAN EVANGELICAL LUTHERAN CHURCH IN AMERICA	1986	9	2,210	2,010	4	6	5	130
LUTHERAN CHURCH—CANADA	1986	359	93,168	68,955	226	328	289	18,992
Mennonite Brethren Churches, Canadian Conference of	1985	162	23,306		N.R.	N.R.		
MENNONITE CHURCH (CANADA)	1986	85	9,400	9,400	92	156	80	9,937
Metropolitan Community Churches, Universal Fellowship of	1984	11	1,600		10	10		
The Missionary Church of Canada	1984	92	6,431		73	129		
MORAVIAN CHURCH IN AMERICA—NORTHERN PROVINCE, CANADIAN DISTRICT OF THE	1986	9	2,025	1,407	10	13	9	681
Netherlands Reformed Congregations of North America	1984	10	3,750		N.R.	N.R.		
North American Baptist Conference	1985	114	17,403		101	157		
OLD ORDER AMISH CHURCH	1987	16	775	775	N.R.	N.R.	N.R.	N.R.
THE OPEN BIBLE STANDARD CHURCHES OF CANADA	1987	4	1,000	1,000	5	6	4	500
THE PENTECOSTAL ASSEMBLIES OF CANADA	1986	1,052	185,208	185,208	N.R.	N.R.	N.R.	N.R.
Pentecostal Assemblies of Newfoundland	1982	163	34,000		128	188		

TABLE 1-D: CANADIAN CURRENT AND NON-CURRENT STATISTICS—Continued

Religious Body	Year Reported	No. of Churches	Inclusive Membership	Full, Communicant or Confirmed Members	No. of Pastors Serving Parishes	Total No. of Clergy	No. of Sunday or Sabbath Schools	Total Enrollment
Polish National Catholic Church	1982	13	6,000		11	14		
PRESBYTERIAN CHURCH IN AMERICA (CANADA SECTION)	1986	15	1,000	550	15	20	15	420
THE PRESBYTERIAN CHURCH IN CANADA	1986	1,028	213,483	159,179	1,102	1,102	637	34,594
REFORMED CHURCH IN CANADA	1986	29	6,487	3,897	24	40	29	1,725
REFORMED DOUKHOBORS, CHRISTIAN COMMUNITY AND BROTHERHOOD OF	1986	1	2,108	2,108	None	None	1	181
REFORMED EPISCOPAL CHURCH, THE FIRST SYNOD IN THE DOMINION OF CANADA	1986	2	369	212	4	6	N.R.	N.R.
REINLAENDER MENNONITE CHURCH	1986	6	700	700	10	10	N.R.	N.R.
REORGANIZED CHURCH OF JESUS CHRIST OF LATTER DAY SAINTS	1986	52	12,465	12,465	1,058	1,058	N.R.	N.R.
THE ROMAN CATHOLIC CHURCH IN CANADA	1986	5,981	10,999,964	N.R.	7,118	11,835	N.R.	N.R.
The Romanian Orthodox Church in America (Canadian Parishes)	1972	19	16,000		19	19		
THE ROMANIAN ORTHODOX EPISCOPATE OF AMERICA (JACKSON, MICH.)	1986	13	8,600	8,600	11	11	10	663
RUSSIAN ORTHODOX CHURCH IN CANADA, PATRIARCHAL PARISHES OF THE	1986	25	8,000	6,000	6	7	N.R.	N.R.
THE SALVATION ARMY IN CANADA	1986	378	102,018	N.R.	756	2,057	359	26,919
Serbian Orthodox Church in the U.S.A. and Canada, Diocese of Canada	1983	17	18,494		11	13		
SEVENTH-DAY ADVENTIST CHURCH IN CANADA	1986	289	35,992	35,992	153	263	319	27,300
Ukrainian Greek-Orthodox Church of Canada	1970	118	140,000		N.R.	75		
Union of Spiritual Communities of Christ (Orthodox Doukhobors in Canada)	1972	25	21,300		None	None		
UNITARIAN UNIVERSALIST ASSOCIATION	1986	46	6,294	5,034	N.R.	18	36	1,260
United Brethren in Christ, Ontario Conference	1983	10	910		10	13		
THE UNITED CHURCH OF CANADA	1986	4,192	2,185,531	872,290	2,089	3,891	3,565	231,996
UNITED PENTECOSTAL CHURCH IN CANADA	1987	196	23,000	23,000	N.R.	N.R.	N.R.	N.R.
THE WESLEYAN CHURCH	1986	75	4,961	4,698	67	183	75	8,187
WISCONSIN EVANGELICAL LUTHERAN SYNOD	1986	9	1,146	826	8	8	9	232

TABLE 1-E: SUMMARY OF CANADIAN CURRENT AND NON-CURRENT STATISTICS

Current statistics are those reported for the year 1987 or 1986. Non-current statistics are those for the years 1985 and earlier. Only current totals are provided in the categories: Full, Communicant or Confirmed Members; Number of Sunday or Sabbath Schools; Total Enrollment.

	No. of Bodies	No. of Churches	Inclusive Membership	Full, Communicant or Confirmed Members	No. of Pastors Serving Parishes	Total No. of Clergy	No. of Sunday or Sabbath Schools	Total Enrollment
1988 Yearbook								
Current..................	52	22,152	15,526,491	2,574,047	17,045	28,241	9,517	682,339
Non-Current...........	33	2,565	1,088,603	N.R.	2,200	3,279	N.R.	N.R.
Totals...................	85	24,717	16,615,094		19,245	31,520		
1987 Yearbook								
Current..................	57	23,301	15,664,321	2,751,656	18,725	30,219	10,487	809,466
Non-Current...........	27	1,336	862,402	N.R.	1,018	1,651	N.R.	N.R.
Totals...................	84	24,637	16,526,723		19,743	31,870		

257

TABLE 1-F: NUMBER OF UNITED STATES CHURCHES, AND OF MEMBERS, BY RELIGIOUS GROUPS

The 220 U.S. religious bodies reporting in this edition of the **Yearbook** may be classifie somewhat arbitrarily, into seven major categories.

It should be reiterated that comparisons of statistics of the various religious groups tabulate below are not meaningful because definitions of membership vary greatly from one religio body to another. For example, Roman Catholics count all baptized individuals, including infa members, as do many Protestant bodies. Some Protestant bodies, however, count as membe those who have been received into the church at baptism, which can take place as early as age thereby leaving out of official counts of membership many millions of children. Jewish statisti are estimates of the number of individuals in households in which one or more Jews reside an therefore, include non-Jews living in such households as the result of intermarriage. The tot number of persons in Jewish households is estimated to be 7 percent larger than the number Jewish persons residing in these households.

The definition of membership in each case is of necessity left up to the religious body itsel and the statistics reported by various religious bodies are not adjusted by the editor of t **Yearbook.**

	Number Bodies Reporting	Number of Churches	Number of Members
Buddhists..	1	100	100,000
Eastern Churches.................................	18	1,662	3,980,107
Jews*...	1	3,416	5,814,000
Old Catholic, Polish National Catholic, Armenian Churches......................	7	426	828,962
Protestants**.....................................	187	315,810	78,991,261
Roman Catholics.................................	1	23,561	52,893,217
Miscellaneous***...............................	5	1,127	192,115
Totals..	220	346,102	142,799,662

*Including Orthodox, Conservative, and Reformed branches.

**Some bodies included here such as various Latter-Day Saints groups and Jehovah's Witnesse are, strictly speaking, not "Protestant" in the usual sense.

***This is a grouping of bodies officially non-Christian, including those such as Spiritualis Ethical Culture Movement, and Unitarian-Universalists.

TABLE 1-G: CONSTITUENCY OF THE NATIONAL COUNCIL OF THE CHURCHES OF CHRIST IN THE U.S.A.

A separate tabulation has been made of the constituent bodies of the National Council of Churches of Christ in the U.S.A. and is given below:

Religious Body	Year	Number of Churches	Inclusive Membership	Pastors Serving Parishes
African Methodist Episcopal Church	1981	6,200	2,210,000	6,050
African Methodist Episcopal Zion Church	1986	6,057	1,195,173	6,000
American Baptist Churches in the U.S.A.	1986	5,864	1,576,483	4,836
The Antiochian Orthodox Christian Archdiocese of North America	1984	120	280,000	155
Armenian Church of America, Diocese of the	1979	66	450,000	45
Christian Church (Disciples of Christ)	1986	4,221	1,106,692	4,002
Christian Methodist Episcopal Church	1983	2,340	718,922	2,340
Church of the Brethren	1986	1,059	155,967	984
Community Churches, International Council of	1987	350	200,000	N.R.
Coptic Orthodox Church	1986	28	115,000	28
The Episcopal Church	1986	7,054	2,504,507	7,887
Friends United Meeting	1986	533	56,495	297
General Convention, the Swedenborgian Church	1985	49	2,245	35
Greek Orthodox Archdiocese of North and South America	1977	535	1,950,000	610
Hungarian Reformed Church in America	1982	31	11,000	27
Korean Presbyterian Church in America, General Assembly of the	1986	180	24,000	200
Lutheran Church in America*	1986	5,832	2,896,138	5,226
Moravian Church in America				
Northern Province	1986	101	32,180	98
Southern Province	1986	56	21,722	53
National Baptist Convention of America	1956	11,398	2,668,799	7,598
National Baptist Convention, U.S.A., Inc.	1958	26,000	5,500,000	26,000
Orthodox Church in America	1978	440	1,000,000	457
Philadelphia Yearly Meeting of the Religious Society of Friends	1967	202	(1965) 16,965	(1965) 23
Polish National Catholic Church of America	1960	162	282,411	141
Presbyterian Church (U.S.A.)	1986	11,531	3,007,322	10,925
Progressive National Baptist Convention, Inc.	1967	655	521,692	N.R.
Reformed Church in America	1986	928	340,359	852
Russian Orthodox Church in the U.S.A., Patriarchal Parishes of the	1985	38	9,780	37
Serbian Orthodox Church for the U.S.A. and Canada	1986	68	67,000	60
Syrian Orthodox Church of Antioch (Archdiocese of the U.S.A. and Canada)	1986	22	30,000	20
Ukrainian Orthodox Church in America (Ecumenical Patriarchate)	1986	27	5,000	35
United Church of Christ	1986	6,406	1,676,105	5,127
The United Methodist Church	1985	37,876	9,192,172	21,589
Total (32) bodies.		136,429	39,824,129	111,737

*The Lutheran Church in America, together with The American Lutheran Church and the Association of Evangelical Lutheran Church in America (ECLA) which began operations on January 1, 1988. The ECLA was accepted into membership in the National Council of Churches as of January 1, 1988 by action of the NCC Governing Board in November, 1987. The Evangelical Lutheran Church in America is estimated to have 11,041 churches, an inclusive membership of 5,318,844, and 10,244 pastors serving parishes. Since the data reported here are for 1986, however, only the Lutheran Church in America statistics are included. Future compilations will include the statistics from the ECLA as a whole.

259

TABLE 1-H: CHURCH MEMBERSHIP STATISTICS, 1940–1986

Compiled by Constant H. Jacquet Jr., Editor,

The following statistical time series for 29 U.S. denominations is presented in this edition of the **Yearbook of American and Canadian Churches** as a response to a number of requests for such a tabulation. The denominations selected represent a cross-section of theological orientations, ecclesiastical structures, and geographical foci. Reliability and completeness in statistical reporting were the criteria used in selecting the bodies. Many conclusions can be drawn from the material presented below but interpretations are left to the user of the statistics. The reader is referred to the qualifications relating to statistical data stated throughout this statistical and historical section and in "A Guide for the User of Church Statistics."

Denomination	1940	1947*	1950	1955
American Lutheran Church	(1,129,349)	N.A.	(1,587,152)	(1,911,641)
Assemblies of God[(b)]	198,834	241,782	318,478	400,047
Baptist General Conference	N.A.	N.A.	48,647[(c)]	54,000
Christian and Missionary Alliance**	22,832[(d)]	N.A.	58,347	57,109[(e)]
Christian Church (Disciples of Christ)	1,658,966	1,889,066	1,767,964	1,897,736
Church of God (Anderson, Ind.)	74,497	95,325	107,094	123,523
Church of God (Cleveland, Tenn.)	63,216	N.A.	121,706[(f)]	142,668
Church of Jesus Christ of Latter-day Saints	724,401[(d)]	911,279	1,111,314	1,230,021
Church of the Brethren	176,908	182,497	186,201	195,609
Church of the Nazarene	165,532	201,487[(g)]	226,684	270,576
Cumberland Presbyterian Church	73,357	75,427	81,806	84,990
Episcopal Church	1,996,434	2,155,514	2,417,464	2,852,965[(h)]
Evangelical Covenant Church of America	45,634	N.A.	51,850	55,311
Free Methodist Church of North America	45,890	46,783[(g)]	48,574	51,437
Jehovah's Witnesses	N.A.	N.A.	N.A.	187,120
Lutheran Church in America	(1,988,277)	N.A.	(2,395,356)	(2,760,442)
Lutheran Church—Missouri Synod	1,277,097	1,422,513	1,674,901	2,004,110
Mennonite Church	51,304	52,596	56,480	70,283
North American Baptist Conference	N.A.	N.A.	41,560	47,319
Presbyterian Church (U.S.A.)	(2,690,969)	(2,969,382)	(3,210,635)	(3,701,635)
Reformed Church in America	255,107	274,455	284,504	319,593
Reorganized Church of Jesus Christ of Latter-Day Saints	106,554	116,888	124,925	137,856
Roman Catholic Church	21,284,455	24,402,124	28,634,878	33,396,647
Salvation Army	238,357	205,881	209,341	249,641
Seventh-day Adventists	176,218	208,030	237,168	277,162
Southern Baptist Convention	4,949,174	6,079,305	7,079,889	8,467,439
United Church of Christ	(1,708,146)	(1,835,853)	(1,977,418)	(2,116,322)
United Methodist Church	(8,043,454)	(9,135,248)	(9,653,178)	(10,029,535)
Wisconsin Evangelical Lutheran Synod	256,007[(d)]	259,097	307,216	328,969

*Reported in the **Christian Herald,** June 1947. Only bodies of 50,000 or more reported.
(a) Data for 1966
(b) Assemblies of God statistics for 1971 and later are full membership statistics.
(c) Data for 1952
(d) Data for 1939
(e) Data for 1954
(f) Data for 1951
(g) Data for 1945
(h) Data for 1956
(j) Data for 1961
(k) Adjusted downward to eliminate Canadian membership previously reported.
**A change in the basis of reporting occurred in this body; statistics from 1970 are inclusive statistics, as opposed to those reported earlier.

FOR SELECTED U.S. DENOMINATIONS

Yearbook of American and Canadian Churches

Note: Statistics contained in parentheses are composite totals for the denominations listed prior to merger of the several component bodies. The symbol NA means "Not Available." Most recent titles are used in the case of denominations listed. For information concerning dates and circumstances of merger, see the historical sketches for these denominations in Directory 3, "Religious Bodies in the United States" in this edition.

1960	1965	1970	1975	1980	1985	1986
2,242,259	2,541,546	2,543,293	2,415,687	2,353,229	2,332,316	2,319,443
508,602	572,123	625,027	785,348	1,064,490	2,082,878	2,135,104
72,056	86,719	103,955	115,340	133,385	132,546	131,480
59,657	64,586	112,519	145,833	189,710	227,846	238,734
1,801,821	1,918,471	1,424,479	1,302,164	1,177,984	1,116,326	1,106,692
142,796	143,231	150,198	166,257	176,429	185,593	188,662
170,261	205,465	272,278	343,249	435,012	N.A.	N.A.
1,486,887	1,789,175	2,073,146	2,336,715	2,811,000	3,860,000	N.A.
199,947	194,815	182,614	179,336	170,839	159,184	155,967
307,629	343,380	383,284	441,093	484,276	522,082	530,912
88,452	78,917	92,095	94,050	96,553	98,037	98,103
3,269,325	3,429,153(a)	3,285,826	2,857,513	2,786,004	2,739,422	2,504,507
60,090	65,780	67,441	71,808	77,737	84,150	86,079
55,338	59,415	64,901	67,043	68,477	72,223	71,682
250,000	330,358	388,920	560,897	565,309	730,441	752,404
(3,053,243)	3,142,752	3,106,844	2,986,078	2,923,260	2,898,202	2,896,138
2,391,195	2,692,889	2,788,536	2,763,545	2,625,650	2,628,164	2,630,588
73,125	80,087	88,522	94,209	99,511	91,167	91,167
50,646	53,711	55,080	42,122(k)	43,041	42,863	42,084
(4,161,860)	(3,984,460)	(4,045,408)	(3,535,825)	(3,362,086)	3,048,235	3,007,322
354,621	385,754	367,606	355,052	345,532	342,375	340,359
155,291	168,355	152,670	157,762	190,087	192,082	192,077
42,104,900	46,246,175	48,214,729	48,881,872	50,449,842	52,654,908	52,893,217
254,141	287,991	326,934	384,817	417,359	427,825	432,893
317,852	364,666	420,419	495,699	571,141	651,954	666,199
9,731,591	10,770,573	11,628,032	12,733,124	13,600,126	14,477,364	14,613,618
(2,241,134)	2,070,413	1,960,608	1,818,762	1,736,244	1,683,777	1,676,105
(10,641,310)	(11,067,497)	10,509,198	9,861,028	9,519,407	9,192,172	N.A.
348,184(i)	358,466	381,321	395,440	407,043	415,389	416,493

TABLE 1-I: INCLUSIVE MEMBERSHIP, 58 COMPILATIONS

The following are the figures reported on inclusive membership in religious bodies in the U.S. in 58 compilations, between 1890 and 1986 as reported in the Census of Religious Bodies, as indicated, and by private publications. For years omitted no compilations were made.

1890	41,699,342	(CRB)[1]	1957	104,189,678	(YBAC)
1906	35,068,058	(CRB)	1958	109,557,741	(YBAC)
1916	41,926,852	(CRB)	1959	112,226,905	(YBAC)
1926	54,576,346	(CRB)	1960	114,449,217	(YBAC)
1931	59,268,764	(CH)[2]	1961	116,109,929	(YBAC)
1932	60,157,392	(CH)	1962	117,946,002	(YBAC)
1933	60,812,624	(CH)	1963	120,965,238	(YBAC)
1934	62,007,376	(CH)	1964	123,307,449	(YBAC)
1935	62,678,177	(CH)	1965	124,682,422	(YBAC)
1936	55,807,366	(CRB)	1966	125,778,656	(YBAC)
1936	63,221,996	(CH)	1967	126,445,110	(YBAC)
1937	63,848,094	(CH)[3]	1968	128,469,636	(YBAC)
1938	64,156,895	(YBAC)[3]	1969	128,505,084	(YBAC)
1940	64,501,594	(YBAC)	1970	131,045,053	(YBAC)
1942	68,501,186	(YBAC)	1971	131,389,642	(YBAC)
1944	72,492,699	(YBAC)	1972	131,424,564	(YBAC)
1945	71,700,142*	(CH)	1973	131,245,139	(YBAC)
1946	73,673,182*	(CH)	1974	131,871,743	(YBAC)
1947	77,386,188	(CH)	1975	131,012,953	(YBACC)[4]
1948	79,435,605	(CH)	1976	131,897,539	(YBACC)
1949	81,862,328	(CH)	1977	131,812,470	(YBACC)
1950	86,830,490	(YBAC)	1978	133,388,776	(YBACC)
1951	88,673,005	(YBAC)	1979	133,469,690	(YBACC)
1952	92,277,129	(YBAC)	1980	134,816,943	(YBACC)
1953	94,842,845	(YBAC)	1981	138,452,614	(YBACC)
1954	97,482,611	(YBAC)	1982	139,603,059	(YBACC)
1955	100,162,529	(YBAC)	1983	140,816,385	(YBACC)
1956	103,224,954	(YBAC)	1984	142,172,138	(YBACC)
			1985	142,926,363	(YBACC)
			1986	142,799,662	(YBACC)

Note: For certain other years *Christian Herald*, New York, published compilations of "communicant" or adult membership only. These totals are not included in the table because they are not comparable with the inclusive figures here noted.
[1] CRB—*Census of Religious Bodies*, Bureau of the Census, Washington.
[2] CH—*The Christian Herald*, New York.
[3] YBAC—*Yearbook of American Churches*, New York.
[4] YBACC—*Yearbook of American and Canadian Churches*, New York.
*Including only bodies with over 50,000 members.

As a general record of the trends in church membership since 1890, the above table is very useful since it presents the results of fifty-six compilations made by various statisticians. It is the only record existing on church membership. Although the table follows a logical progression upwards over time, it is by no means without its faults.

There are certain qualifications relating to the above data that should be kept in mind. First of all, aggregate data on inclusive membership, while accounting for the bulk of church membership, is always incomplete. A small number of religious bodies do not have membership statistics. Further, some religious groups, but not many major ones, are excluded from these totals by virtue of the definitions used for a "religious body" by the various compilers of these data.

Second, the totals here reported are additions of both current and non-current data which is made necessary because not all religious bodies gather and report statistics each year yet all bodies in the total must be aggregated each year for sake of completeness.

Third, definitions of inclusive membership vary from one religious body to another. Some count only full members and exclude probationary members, children, and those nominally related while other religious bodies include this wider grouping. Occasionally an individual body will go from the more restrictive to the more inclusive definition over time. A third category of religious bodies has no actual statistical records and only make estimates of inclusive membership which roughly parallel the ethnic and cultural community to which they relate.

Last, these compilations were made by three different organizations from data derived from the religious bodies themselves; the U.S. Bureau of the Census made five compilations, *The Christian Herald* made twelve, and the **Yearbook of American and Canadian Churches** (formerly Yearbook of American Churches), made forty-one. Criteria for defining inclusive membership has not been completely standard over the 96-year period of these compilations.

2. CHURCH FINANCIAL STATISTICS AND RELATED DATA, UNITED STATES AND CANADA

For this edition of the **Yearbook of American and Canadian Churches,** complete financial data were supplied by 44 United States communions. The results are presented in the table entitled "Some Statistics of Church Finances—United States Churches." The data are complete for each communion in the three major categories of reporting. It will be noted that Total Contributions are the sum total of Total Congregational Finances and Total Benevolences.

Similarly, data were supplied by 27 Canadian church bodies. The information is included in the table "Some Statistics of Church Finances—Canadian Churches." Both the U.S. and Canadian data are current, and incomplete information submitted by denominations has been excluded from the tables.

A third table, "Summary Statistics of Church Finances," provides totals for the U.S. and Canadian bodies. The 44 U.S. bodies report total contributions of $14,519,966,515 and the 27 Canadian groups $805,867,911 (Canadian). It must be remembered however, that some of the Canadian groups are not wholly Canadian denominations but, rather, sections of denominations existing and headquartered in the U.S. A majority of the 27 bodies listed in the table "Some Statistics of Church Finances—Canadian Churches" are strictly Canadian denominations. Per capita contributions for full membership of U.S. communions amounted to $344.42 and for the Canadian bodies, $388.72 (Canadian). Benevolences as a percentage of total contributions amounted to 19.06 percent for the U.S. bodies and 23.05 percent for the Canadian.

Readers of the tables should be aware that the Canadian and U.S. financial data appearing in this section are only a significant part of total contributions from members of all communions. Not all bodies in the U.S. and Canada gather church financial data centrally, and some have information but do not reveal it publicly. Additionally, little is known about other major segments of church financial income such as earned income, interest from investments, and bequests.

Comparisons between this year's aggregate financial data and those in previous editions of the **Yearbook** should not be made, since the same bodies do not report financial data each year. However, for an individual denomination or groups of denominations reporting annually over time, comparisons can be made.

Comparative data for nine major Protestant denominations in the U.S. among the 44 listed in this section show a total 1986 full membership of 23,813,606, or 268,496 fewer members than the same churches' total for 1985. These members increased total giving in the nine denominations by 2.35 percent. When this is compared with a 1.1 percent inflation in the U.S. in 1986, the total effect is increased real income for these denominations. For Canada, comparative statistics for nine communions indicate a decrease in membership from 1985 to 1986 to a total of 1,831,075, and an increase in giving of $65,835,018 (Canadian) to a total of $690,683,962 (Canadian). Assuming an inflation rate in Canada of 4.1 percent for 1986, the total contributions of these nine communions show an increase, after inflation, of $40,841,060 (Canadian).

SOME STATISTICS OF CHURCH FINANC

				TOTAL CONTRIBUTIONS		
COMMUNION	Year	Full or* Confirmed Membership	Inclusive** Membership	Total Contributions	Per Capita Full or Confirmed Membership	Per Cap Inclus Members
American Baptist Churches in the U.S.A.	1985	1,576,483	1,576,483	$314,895,803	$199.75	$199.
The American Lutheran Church#	1986	1,740,439	2,319,443	530,788,865	304.97	228.
Baptist General Conference	1987	131,480	131,480	96,785,070	736.12	736.
Baptist Missionary Association of America	1986	228,125	228,125	51,627,407	226.31	226.
Brethren in Christ Church	1986	15,911	16,693	12,997,441	816.88	778.
Christian and Missionary Alliance	1986	130,116	238,734	132,492,973	1,018.27	554.
Christian Church (Disciples of Christ)	1986	732,466	1,106,692	330,304,890	450.95	298.
Church of God (Anderson, Ind.)	1986	188,662	188,662	107,905,502	571.95	571.
Church of God General Conference (Oregon, Ill.)	1987	4,348	5,652	3,176,596	730.59	562.
Church of the Brethren	1986	155,967	155,967	61,390,394	393.61	393.
Church of the Nazarene	1986	529,192	530,912	327,849,894	619.53	617.
Conservative Congregational Christian Conference	1986	28,948	28,948	19,607,896	677.35	677.
Cumberland Presbyterian Church	1986	91,556	98,103	26,774,907	292.44	272.
The Episcopal Church	1986	1,756,120	2,504,507	1,134,455,479	646.00	452.
Evangelical Church of North America	1987	17,440	17,440	11,194,311	641.88	641.
Evangelical Congregational Church	1986	25,625	41,237	10,019,579	391.01	242.
Evangelical Covenant Church	1986	86,079	86,079	72,003,279	836.48	836.
Evangelical Lutheran Synod	1986	15,082	19,938	5,970,891	395.90	299.
Evangelical Mennonite Church	1987	3,841	3,841	3,658,927	952.60	952.
Free Methodist Church of North America	1986	56,243	71,682	55,597,001	988.51	775.
Free Will Baptists, National Association of	1986	205,546	205,546	75,200,000	365.86	365.
Friends United Meeting	1986	48,143	56,495	15,707,779	326.28	278.
Fundamental Methodist Church	1986	698	698	168,724	241.73	241.
General Association of General Baptists	1986	72,263	72,263	21,627,091	299.28	299.
International Pentecostal Church of Christ	1987	2,743	2,743	2,035,193	741.96	741.
The Latvian Evangelical Lutheran Church in America	1986	12,515	13,838	2,593,000	207.19	187.
Lutheran Church in America	1986	2,157,701	2,896,138	681,121,693	315.67	235.
Lutheran Church–Missouri Synod	1986	1,974,798	2,630,588	717,706,885	363.43	272.
Mennonite Church	1987	91,167	91,167	64,501,700	707.51	707.
Mennonite Church—The General Conference	1986	35,170	35,170	17,477,406	496.94	496.
The Missionary Church	1986	26,869	26,869	20,934,021	779.11	779.
Moravian Church in America, Northern Province	1986	24,260	31,593	9,288,477	382.87	294.
North American Baptist Conference	1986	42,084	42,084	26,944,190	640.24	640.
Presbyterian Church (U.S.A.)	1986	3,007,322	3,007,322	1,567,474,145	521.22	521.
Presbyterian Church in America	1986	158,645	188,083	143,842,638	906.69	764.
Primitive Methodist Church in the U.S.A.	1986	5,942	8,625	4,190,662	705.26	485.
Reformed Church in America	1986	207,993	340,359	137,186,025	659.57	403.
Reformed Episcopal Church	1987	5,733	5,733	7,388,584	1,288.78	1,288.
Seventh-day Adventists	1986	666,199	666,199	528,009,727	792.57	792.
Southern Baptist Convention	1986	14,613,638	14,613,638	4,116,321,455	281.68	281.
United Church of Christ	1986	1,676,105	1,676,105	493,148,330	294.22	294.
The United Methodist Church	1985	9,192,172	9,192,172	2,333,928,274	253.90	253.
The Wesleyan Church	1986	99,997	109,196	92,238,792	922.41	844.
Wisconsin Evangelical Lutheran Synod	1986	316,416	416,493	131,434,619	415.39	315.

*Full or Confirmed Membership refers to those with full, communicant, or confirmed status.
**Inclusive Membership refers to those who are full, communicant, or confirmed members, plus other members listed baptized, nonconfirmed, or noncommunicant.
#The American Lutheran Church, The Association of Evangelical Lutheran Churches and the Lutheran Church in America merged to form the Evangelical Lutheran Church in America (ELCA) during the period April 30–May 3, 1987. Since the statistic reported here are for 1986, two of the merging denominations reporting statistics provided data for 1986, the last year prior the merger.

—UNITED STATES CHURCHES

	CONGREGATIONAL FINANCES			BENEVOLENCES		
Total Congregational Contributions	Per Capita Full or Confirmed Membership	Per Capita Inclusive Membership	Total Benevolences	Per Capita Full or Confirmed Membership	Per Capita Inclusive Membership	Benevolences As a Percentage of Total Contributions
$267,694,684	$169.80	$169.80	$47,201,119	$ 29.95	$ 29.95	14.99%
434,641,736	249.73	187.39	96,147,129	55.24	41.45	18.11
80,188,545	609.89	609.89	16,596,525	126.23	126.23	17.15
43,323,837	189.91	189.91	8,303,570	36.40	36.40	16.08
10,533,883	662.05	631.04	2,463,558	154.83	147.58	18.95
107,994,530	829.99	452.36	24,498,443	188.28	102.62	18.491
288,277,386	393.57	260.49	42,027,504	57.38	37.98	12.72
91,768,855	486.42	486.42	16,136,647	85.53	85.53	14.95
2,437,778	560.17	431.31	738,818	169.92	130.72	23.26
43,531,293	279.11	279.11	17,859,101	114.50	114.50	29.09
283,189,977	535.14	533.40	44,659,917	84.39	84.12	13.62
15,646,859	540.52	540.52	3,961,037	136.83	136.83	20.20
22,992,625	251.13	234.37	3,782,282	41.31	38.55	14.13
955,668,993	544.19	381.58	178,786,486	101.81	71.39	15.76
8,816,995	505.57	505.57	2,377,316	136.31	136.31	21.24
8,619,708	336.38	209.03	1,399,871	54.63	33.95	13.97
57,628,572	669.48	669.48	14,374,707	167.00	167.00	19.96
4,941,917	327.67	247.86	1,028,974	68.23	51.61	17.23
2,332,216	607.19	607.19	1,326,711	345.41	345.41	36.26
46,150,881	820.56	643.83	9,446,120	167.95	131.78	16.99
64,800,000	315.26	315.26	10,400,000	50.60	50.60	13.83
12,790,909	265.69	226.41	2,916,870	60.59	51.63	18.57
152,196	218.05	218.05	16,528	23.68	23.68	9.80
19,743,265	273.21	273.21	1,883,826	26.07	26.07	8.71
1,732,128	631.47	631.47	303,065	110.49	110.49	14.89
2,310,000	184.58	166.93	283,000	22.61	20.45	10.91
569,250,519	263.82	196.56	111,871,174	51.85	38.63	16.42
605,768,688	306.75	230.28	111,938,197	56.68	42.55	15.60
40,097,500	439.82	439.82	24,404,200	267.69	267.69	37.83
9,927,515	282.27	282.27	7,549,891	214.67	214.67	43.20
16,238,388	604.35	604.35	4,695,633	174.76	174.76	22.43
8,133,127	335.25	257.43	1,155,350	47.62	36.57	12.44
20,961,799	498.09	498.09	5,982,391	142.15	142.15	22.02
1,318,440,264	438.41	438.41	249,033,881	82.81	82.81	15.89
106,233,795	669.63	564.82	37,608,843	237.06	199.96	26.15
3,564,020	599.80	413.22	626,642	105.46	72.65	14.95
114,231,429	549.21	335.62	22,954,596	110.36	67.44	16.73
6,014,350	1,049.08	1,049.08	1,374,234	239.71	239.71	18.60
166,692,974	250.21	250.21	361,316,753	542.36	542.36	68.43
3,481,124,471	238.21	238.21	635,196,984	43.47	43.47	15.43
429,340,239	256.15	256.15	63,808,091	38.07	38.07	12.94
1,789,454,589	194.67	194.67	544,473,685	59.23	59.23	23.33
79,697,014	796.99	729.85	12,541,778	125.42	114.86	13.60
108,985,699	344.44	261.67	22,448,920	70.95	53.90	17.08

SOME STATISTICS OF CHURCH FINANC

				TOTAL CONTRIBUTIONS		
COMMUNION	Year	Full or* Confirmed Membership	Inclusive** Membership	Total Contributions	Per Capita Full or Confirmed Membership	Per Cap Inclus Members
The Anglican Church of Canada	1986	558,405	851,032	$171,054,228	$306.32	$201
Baptist Convention of Ontario and Quebec	1986	33,138	45,397	31,827,880	960.47	701
Baptist Union of Western Canada	1986	15,680	21,297	17,163,843	1,094.63	805
Brethren in Christ Church	1986	2,768	3,440	3,168,57	1,444.71	921
The Christian and Missionary Alliance in Canada	1986	22,843	59,733	45,628,272	1,913.70	763
Christian Church (Disciples of Christ) in Canada	1986	2,876	4,665	1,481,716	515.20	317
Church of the Nazarene	1986	10,034	10,054	8,636,189	860.70	858
Conference of Mennonites in Canada	1986	29,000	29,000	18,060,253	622.77	622
Congregational Christian Churches in Ontario, The Conference of	1986	278	278	190,305	684.55	684
Evangelical Church in Canada	1986	3,665	3,665	3,529,431	963.01	963
The Evangelical Covenant Church of Canada	1986	1,232	1,232	1,393,542	1,131.12	1,131
The Evangelical Lutheran Church in Canada**	1985	152,024	207,674	37,350,188	245.69	179
Foursquare Gospel Church of Canada	1986	2,391	2,391	3,470,632	1,451.54	1,451
Lutheran Church–Canada	1986	68,955	93,168	31,144,548	451.67	334
Mennonite Church (Canada)	1987	9,400	9,400	7,189,200	764.81	764
Moravian Church in America, Northern Province, Canadian District	1986	1,407	2,025	1,257,028	893.41	620
North American Baptist Conference	1986	17,301	17,301	20,121,924	1,163.05	1,163
Presbyterian Church in America (Canada Section)	1986	550	1,000	765,000	1,390.91	765
The Presbyterian Church in Canada	1986	159,179	213,483	68,040,295	427.44	318
Reformed Church in Canada	1986	3,897	6,487	2,790,818	716.15	430
Reformed Episcopal Church	1986	212	369	122,435	577.52	331
Seventh-day Adventist Church in Canada	1986	35,992	35,992	38,455,408	1,068.45	1,068
Union d'Églises Baptistes Françaises au Canada	1986	1,091	1,091	573,520	525.68	525
United Baptist Convention of the Atlantic Provinces	1986	61,972	61,972	29,040,438	468.61	468
The United Church of Canada	1986	872,290	2,185,531	255,370,969	292.76	116
The Wesleyan Church	1986	4,698	4,961	7,455,945	1,587.05	1,502
Wisconsin Evangelical Lutheran Synod	1986	826	1,146	585,333	708.64	510

(a) Although most denominations reported Canadian dollars for this table, certain denominations reported U.S. dollars. In orc to standardize these amounts, U.S. dollars were multiplied by 1.3736, a factor which represents the average differentia exchange rates in 1986; thus all totals are expressed in Canadian dollars.

SUMMARY STATISTI

	Total Bodies	Full or* Confirmed Membership	Inclusive** Membership	TOTAL CONTRIBUTIONS		
				Total Contributions	Per Capita Full or Confirmed Membership	Per Cap Inclus Members
United States Communions	44	42,158,242	45,699,735	$14,519,966,515	$344.42	$317
Canadian Communions(b)	27	2,073,104	3,873,784	805,867,911	388.72	208

*Full or Confirmed Membership refers to those with full, communicant, or confirmed status.
**Inclusive Membership refers to those who are full, communicant, or confirmed members, plus other members baptize nonconfirmed, or noncommunicant.
(b)Shown in Canadian dollars.

266

	CONGREGATIONAL FINANCES			BENEVOLENCES			
Total Congregational Contributions	Per Capita Full or Confirmed Membership	Per Capita Inclusive Membership	Total Benevolences	Per Capita Full or Confirmed Membership	Per Capita Inclusive Membership	Benevolences As a Percentage of Total Contributions
$127,764,943	$228.80	$150.13	$43,289,285	$ 77.52	$ 50.87	25.31%
27,527,653	830.70	606.38	4,300,227	129.77	94.72	13.51
13,906,933	886.92	653.00	3,256,910	207.71	152.93	18.98
2,452,838	886.14	713.03	715,733	258.57	208.06	22.59
36,292,830	1,522.16	607.58	9,335,442	391.54	156.29	20.46
1,289,978	448.53	276.52	191,738	66.67	41.10	12.94
7,933,942	790.71	789.13	702,247	69.99	69.85	8.13
9,759,643	336.54	336.54	8,300,610	286.23	286.23	45.96
141,570	509.24	509.24	48,735	175.31	175.31	25.61
2,704,256	737.86	737.86	825,175	225.15	225.15	23.38
1,077,939	874.95	874.95	315,603	256.17	256.17	22.65
29,895,456	196.65	143.95	7,454,732	49.04	35.90	19.96
3,363,861	1,406.88	1,406.88	106,771	44.66	44.66	3.08
23,970,550	347.63	257.28	7,173,998	104.04	77.00	23.03
4,461,500	474.63	474.63	2,727,700	290.18	290.18	37.94
1,142,957	812.34	564.42	114,071	81.07	56.33	9.07
14,237,311	822.92	822.92	5,844,613	340.13	340.13	29.24
450,000	818.18	450.00	315,000	572.73	315.00	41.18
58,425,662	367.04	273.68	9,614,633	60.40	45.04	14.13
2,303,903	591.20	355.16	486,915	124.95	75.06	17.45
103,435	487.90	280.31	19,000	89.62	51.49	15.52
9,791,492	272.05	272.05	28,663,916	796.40	796.40	74.54
490,000	449.13	449.13	83,520	76.55	76.55	14.56
21,502,383	346.97	346.97	7,538,055	121.64	121.64	25.96
212,429,897	243.53	97.20	42,941,072	49.23	19.65	16.82
6,247,107	1,329.74	1,259.24	1,208,838	257.31	243.67	16.21
460,145	557.08	401.52	125,188	151.56	109.24	21.39

OF CHURCH FINANCES

	CONGREGATIONAL FINANCES			BENEVOLENCES			
Total Congregational Contributions	Per Capita Full or Confirmed Membership	Per Capita Inclusive Membership	Total Benevolences	Per Capita Full or Confirmed Membership	Per Capita Inclusive Membership	Benevolences As a Percentage of Total Contributions
$11,752,066,148	$278.76	$257.16	$2,767,900,367	$65.66	$60.57	19.06%
620,128,184	299.13	160.08	185,739,727	89.59	47.95	23.05

EFFECTS OF INFLATION ON PER CAPITA GIVING
1961–1986

Constant H. Jacquet, Jr.
Office of Research and Evaluation
National Council of Churches

Somewhere between 38 and 52 religious bodies have been able to supply annually complete financial data on total contributions received. Total contributions are the sum of all benevolences, plus all congregational finances. Representing roughly 20 percent of the total number of U.S. denominations and 30 percent of total U.S. membership reported to the *Yearbook of American and Canadian Churches*, giving to these bodies is approximately 40 percent of total church contributions in the U.S. in any given year.

At least four reasons why more denominations do not supply statistical data on church finanes are: 1) the desire to keep the information confidential, 2) a belief that there are biblical restrictions against this type of accounting, 3) a lack of adequate statistical programs in denominations to report accurate membership and financial data, and 4) denominational polities that do not require full reporting to a central office.

The fragmentary information currently received, however, provides a good sample that helps to determine what is happening in the area of U.S. church contributions. It should be remembered that these are aggregate data, and the experiences of individual denominations may vary from those presented here.

Organized religion, like other privately financed agencies, is, on the whole, struggling with powerful forces of inflation in the U.S. Although the dollar amounts of giving have increased from $69.00 per capita full member in 1961 to $344.42 in 1986, an increase of 399.2 percent in constant 1967 dollars, the increase is only from $77.01 in 1961 to $104.88 in 1986, an increase in real terms of only 36.2 percent, or slightly more than 1.4 percent a year on average. Therefore much education and action in the area of stewardship has been necessary to defend the financial structure of organized religion.

DENOMINATIONAL PER CAPITA
FULL MEMBER CONTRIBUTIONS
AND ADJUSTED TO 1967 DOLLARS, 1961–1986

Year	No. of Denoms.	Per Capita Full Member	Constant 1967 Dollars	Year	No. of Denoms.	Per Capita Full Member	Constant 1967 Dollars
1961	46	$69.00	$77.01	1974	44	$127.16	$86.09
1962	42	68.76	75.89	1975	43	138.54	85.94
1963	41	69.87	76.19	1976	43	149.07	87.43
1964	41	72.04	77.55	1977	45	159.33	87.78
1965	38	77.75	82.38	1978	42	176.37	90.26
1966		(Not Reported)		1979	44	197.44	90.82
1967		(Not Reported)		1980	40	213.41	86.47
1968	52	95.31	91.47	1981	45	239.71	88.00
1969	48	99.68	90.78	1982	40	261.95	90.60
1970	45	96.84	83.27	1983	40	278.67	93.39
1971	42	103.94	85.69	1984	39	300.40	96.56
1972	39	110.29	88.02	1985	42	321.77	99.87
1973	40	118.16	88.77	1986	44	344.42	104.88

3. SOME TRENDS AND DEVELOPMENTS

This section begins with "Religious Affiliation in Canada," followed by data from *The 1987 Official Catholic Directory.* "Trends in Seminary Enrollment, 1980–1987," concludes the section.

RELIGIOUS AFFILIATION IN CANADA

The Autumn 1987 issue of *Canadian Social Trends,* a quarterly journal of Statistics Canada (Jean Talon Bldg., Ottawa, Ontario K1A 0T6) contains the article "Religious Affiliation in Canada" by George A. Mori, an analyst with the Housing, Family, and Social Statistics Division of Statistics Canada. The article refers only to stated religious *preference* of Canadians, not to their actual *membership* in a religious denomination.

Mori observes that historically, most Canadians have been either Protestant or Catholic but that over the years a major change has occurred in the distribution of these two groups: "Through the late 1800s and the first few decades of this century, Protestants clearly outnumbered Catholics. In the last several decades, though, this has been reversed. The percentage of the population affiliated with a Protestant denomination fell from 54% in 1931 to just over 40% in 1981. The population affiliated with the Catholic Church increased from 41% to 47% between 1931 and 1961 and remained at that level in both 1971 and 1981."

The decline in the Protestant portion of the population, Mori believes, has been accounted for by decreases in the mainline Protestant groups. "In 1981, 35% of all Canadians were affiliated with either the Anglican, Baptist, Lutheran, Presbyterian, or United Church denominations. This, however, was down from 40% in 1971 and 49% in 1941." Between 1971 and 1981, the total number of persons affiliated with the Presbyterian Church fell 7%, the Anglican Church 4%, and the Lutheran 2%. The decline in the number affiliated with The United Church of Canada was less than 1%. Baptists, however, increased 4% over this decade.

"On the other hand," Mori notes, "the share of the population affiliated with Protestant denominations other than the mainline groups has increased. In 1981, these other Protestant denominations accounted for 6% of the Canadian population, up from 5% in 1971 and 3% in 1941."

The fastest growing of these denominations has been the Pentecostal churches. In the 1971–1981 period, for example, the Pentecostal population recorded an increase of 54%, increasing from 220,000 to 339,000, Mori reports. [*Ed. Note:* It is interesting to observe the similarity in trends between the United States and Canada in religious preference, as well as in othr areas such as church attendance, financial contributions, and lower church affiliation in the western areas of the two countries. In the United States, the proportion of those preferring the Protestant faith, relative to the Roman Catholic, have declined, though Protestants remain heavily in the majority. Most of the Protestant decline is due to losses suffered by mainline bodies, offset to some degree by increases in preference for conservative and evangelical denominations such as the Pentecostal churches, certain Baptists groups, and others.]

Mori also points out that preferences for several smaller religious groups have declined. Over the period 1971–1981, Unitarian-Universalists have declined 31%; Doukhobors by 27%; Jehovah's Witnesses by 17%. "The decline in the number of Jehovah's Witnesses is particularly notable in that his group was among the fastest growing Christian denominations in Canada between 1941 and 1971. However, in the 1971–1981 period, the number of Canadians reporting affiliation with the Jehovah's Witnesses declined from 173,000 to 143,-000."

In the 1961 census of population, less than 1% of Canadians reported no religious preference. By 1981 this grew to 7%, an increase from less than 100,000 persons in 1961 to 1.8 million in 1981. In 1981, however, only 11,000 reported themselves as agnostics and only 4,000 as atheists.

Other religious groupings in Canada include the Eastern Orthodox denominations, Eastern non-Christian religions, and Judaism, as well as small groups that do not fall into convenient religious categories. The Canadian census found that in 1981 these groupings accounted for almost one million Canadians, about 4% of the total population. "The overall percentage of the population affiliated with these groups has been relatively stable most of this century," Mori notes.

"In 1981, there were 362,000 persons affiliated with the Christian Eastern Orthodox denominations. The vast majority of these, almost 90%, were Greek Orthodox. There were just over 300,000 persons affiliated with one of the Eastern non-Christian religions in 1981. The largest of these groups in Canada were Islam, Hinduism, Sikhism, and Buddhism. Also in 1984, there were 296,000 persons of the Jewish faith in Canada. They represented 1.3% of the total population, down slightly from 1.5% in 1951." Mori observes that the data show that "the number of followers of cults or sect religions in Canada appears to be minimal, compared to the overwhelming number of Canadians who subscribe to the Christian, Judaic, or Eastern non-Christian religions, or subscribe to no religion at all."

Since the 1981 Canadian census, a General Social Survey was conducted by Statistics Canada in 1985. Direct comparisons between these two surveys can be made,

Statistics Canada says, only with caution. "Nevertheless," Mori writes, "several general trends are apparent." In the period 1981–1985, "the Roman Catholic population increased 3.5% while the number of persons affiliated with the mainline Protestant denominaions declined 3.0%. Persons reporting 'other' religions, a category which includes the smaller Protestant denominations and other Catholics, increased 13.3%." The percentage of the population age 15 years and over reporting no religious preference increased from 7% in 1981 to 10% in 1985.

Considerable variation in the religious composition of Canadian provinces is evident. In 1981, 88% of the people in Quebec were affiliated with the Roman Catholic Church; 53% were affiliated in New Brunswick, the only other province with a Catholic majority. Protestants made up more than half the total population in all other provinces in 1981, ranging from 51% in Prince Edward Island to 63% in Newfoundland. The following table shows the religious affiliation of Canadians in 1981, by province:

RELIGIOUS AFFILIATION OF THE POPULATION, BY PROVINCE, 1981

	Catholic	Protes-tant	Other religious groupings	No religious preference	Total
			%		
Newfoundland	36.3	62.6	0.1	1.0	100.0
Prince Edward Island	46,6	50.5	0.3	2.7	100.0
Nova Scotia	37.0	58.0	0.9	4.1	100.0
New Brunswick	53.9	42.9	0.4	2.9	100.0
Quebec	88.2	6.4	3.4	2.1	100.0
Ontario	35.6	51.8	5.4	7.2	100.0
Manitoba	31.5	56.6	4.4	7.5	100.0
Saskatchewan	32.4	58.3	3.1	6.3	100.0
Alberta	27.7	56.0	4.5	11.7	100.0
British Columbia	19.8	54.7	4.5	20.9	100.0
Canada	**47.3**	**41.2**	**4.1**	**7.4**	**100.0**

Source: Statistics Canada, Catalogue 92-912, *1981 Census of Canada, Population: Religion.*

Socio-demographic details in the 1981 census indicated that religious affiliation still reflects underlying social differences among Canadians as the following table shows:

SOCIO-DEMOGRAPHIC PROFILE OF SELECTED RELIGIOUS GROUPS, 1981

	Total population	Median age	Median years of schooling	Average income[1]	Unemployment rate[2]
	000s		$		%
Catholic	11,403	28.2	11.4	12,300	9.0
Protestant	9,915	31.6	12.0	13,200	5.8
Eastern Orthodox	362	33.8	10.8	12,400	5.7
Eastern Non-Christian	306	27.0	12.7	12,900	7.2
Jewish	296	35.1	13.3	19,500	5.3
Other groups	13	30.5	12.9	12,200	9.4
No religious preference	1,784	26.3	12.6	14,900	6.5
Total population[3]	**24,084**	**29.4**	**11.8**	**13,000**	**7.4**

1. Weighted 1980 average total income of population aged 15 and over with income.
2. Percentage of persons aged 15 and over in the labour force who were unemployed in the week prior to June 3, 1981.
3. Includes 5,500 persons not classified elsewhere.
Source: Statistics Canada, 1981 Census of Canada, unpublished data.

The above data indicate, among other things, that Protestants, on average, were older, had more median years of schooling, higher average incomes, and lower unemployment rates than Catholics. The average income of Catholics was among the lowest of all religious groups, and their unemployment rate was among the highest.

"Persons of the Jewish faith had the highest median age, the most schooling, the highest average income, and the lowest unemployment rate of any religious group," Mori observes.

The General Social Survey conducted in 1985 by Statistics Canada also discovered that "only 30% of Canadians with a stated religious preference attended a religious service or meeting on a weekly basis, while a further 17% did so at least once a month. On the other hand, more than one in five persons (21%) with a stated religion never attended a service or meeting.

"Among Baptists and Roman Catholics, around 40% attended a religious service at least once a week, while over half attended once a month. More than half of those affiliated with Eastern Orthodox denominations also attended a service at least monthly. In comparison, much smaller percentages of those affiliated with the Anglican and United Churches, as well as those of the Jewish faith attended religious services on a regular basis." It was pointed out that in the case of the Jewish statistics, this figure should be used with caution due to a higher sampling variability.

Comparing 1975 data from R. W. Bibby's "State of Collective Religiosity in Canada," *Canadian Review of Sociology and Anthropology* (16)1, 1979, with data from the 1985 General Social Survey, Mori concludes: "There has also been a decline in the frequency of religious attendance at religious services in the last decade. Between 1975 and 1985, the percentage reporting weekly attendance at religious services or meetings declined from 25% to 15% for members of the United Church, from 45% to 36% for Roman Catholics, and from 24% to 17% for Anglicans. On the other hand, there was little or no change in the frequency of attendance for Presbyterians, Lutherans, Baptists, and among persons of the Jewish faith."

THE 1987 OFFICIAL CATHOLIC DATA

Catholics in the 50 states, including all families in the defense forces both at home and abroad, and diplomatic and other services abroad, now number 52,893,217, according to *The Official Catholic Directory* for 1987 issued by P. J. Kenedy & Sons, Wilmette, Ill. The new total represents an increase over last year of 238,309.

Archdioceses and Dioceses

There are now 34 archdioceses in the United States with a Catholic population of 23,527,475, and 152 dioceses, recording a Catholic population of 29,365,742—for a total Catholic population of 52,893,217.

Los Angeles remains the largest archdiocese, with a Catholic population of 2,659,000, followed by Chicago with 2,350,000. Over one million are: Boston, 1,848,232; New York, 1,824,040; Detroit, 1,473,941; Philadelphia, 1,353,004; and Newark, 1,344,070. Brooklyn continues as the largest diocese with a Catholic population of 1,445,783, followed by Rockville Centre, reporting 1,333,487. In addition, eight archdioceses and six dioceses reported a Catholic population of over 1.5 million. Thirteen sees reported no change in Catholic population; 59 reflected decreases; and advances were reported by 113. The largest increases have been noted in Austin, 59,668; Galveston-Houston, 38,523 and St. Paul/Minneapolis, 35,276. The largest decreases were noted in Boston, 70,483 and Hartford, 45,886.

Hierarchy and Clergy

The 1986 *Directory* lists 391 members of the hierarchy—a decrease of 5 over the 396 listed a year ago.

A decrease of 3,801 brings the total of ordained priests to 53,382. There are now 34,471, or 684 fewer diocesan or secular priests, and 18,911 religious order priests, a decrease of 3,117. Permanent deacons increased 419 during the past year, to bring the current total to 7,981, for a total of 61,333 clergy. Professed religious personnel include 7,418 Brothers, a decrease of 11, and 112,489 Sisters, a decrease of 1,169.

	1956	1966	1976	1987
Priests	48,349	59,193	58,847	53,382
Deacons	. . .	. . .	. . .	7,981
Brothers	8,868	12,255	8,563	7,418
Sisters	159,545	181,421	130,995	112,489

The *Directory* reports a total of 19,546 Catholic parishes in the 50 states, up 416. Also listed are 3,185 missions, down 235.

Educational Institutions

There are a total of 9,657 separate educational institutions, 177 fewer than reported in 1985. Included are 76 diocesan seminaries; 163 religious order seminaries or novitiates and scholasticates; 238 colleges and universities; 850 diocesan and parish high schools; 558 private high schools; 7,485 parish elementary schools; and 287 private elementary schools. There are, in addition, 97 protective institutions, with 13,259 youths in attendance.

Teachers

Full-time teaching staffs of all educational institutions under Catholic auspices have decreased by 197 to a total of 170,486, comprising 3,738 priests; 199 scholastics; 2,265 Brothers; 26,574 Sisters; and 137,170 lay teachers. There are 498 fewer priests, 38 more scholastics, 226 fewer Brothers, 1,064 fewer Sisters, and 1,013 more lay teachers than a year ago.

Today lay teachers number 137,170 and represent 80.5 percent of all teachers in Catholic schools. There are 77,867 (74.6%) fewer Sisters teaching than the 104,441 recorded at their peak in 1964.

Seminaries and Seminarians

During 1986, there were in operation 14 fewer diocesan and 66 fewer religious order seminaries. The 76 diocesan seminaries report an enrollment of 5,138 seminarians, a decrease of 1,880; the 163 novitiates and scholasticates of the religious orders have 3,418 students, four fewer, indicating a total of 8,556 candidates for the priesthood, down 1,884 from a year ago.

Colleges and Students

The 238 Catholic colleges and universities, down five from the 243 reported in 1986, show an enrollment of 556,337, up 10,876.

Children in Catholic Schools

The number of full-time pupils in Catholic elementary and high schools decreased 90,860 during the past year. The 850 parish and diocesan high schools, seven fewer, report 449,815 pupils, a decrease of 6,168; the 558 private high schools, three fewer, report 304,899, a decrease of 5,862 in one year. Pupils in 7,485 parish elementary schools, down 79, now number 1,972,639, or 65,400 fewer, while students in the 287 private elementary schools now total 57,959, a decrease of 3,381 in 14 fewer schools.

Youth Under Religious Instruction

Religious instruction to children under Confraternity of Christian Doctrine schools and other classes, in 1987 accounted for 888,452 high school pupils, and 2,972,588 elementary students, for a total of 3,861,040 public school children receiving religious instruction, indicating a decrease of 73,806 pupils. There is an aggregate, including dependent children, of 7,215,948 American youth of all grades under Catholic instruction, a decrease of 148,911 over comparable figures for 1986.

Baptisms, Converts, Marriages

The 941,898 baptisms recorded show a decrease of 11,425 over 1986. The number of converts decreased by 7,293, to a total of 80,703.

Marriages recorded decreased by 5,860, to 342,440. During the same period, 430,352 Catholics died in the U.S., 16,470 fewer than in the previous year.

TRENDS IN SEMINARY ENROLLMENT 1980–1987

Seminary enrollment in ATS member schools has suffered a decline of 1% this year with an opening fall 1987 enrollment of 55,766. This is slightly greater than the overall decline last year of −0.6%. Excluding, however, the six new schools which were added in 1986, the decline for 1986 would have been −1.2%, slightly larger than the 1987 decline. This is the third straight year of a gradual decrease in enrollment, reversing a long-time trend of growth since 1970. Canadian member schools likewise experienced a decrease of −3.3% in overall enrollment. The same decline of −3.3% was found in the ordinary pre-ordination programs in the Canadian schools. The largest drop in the schools was found in the Northeast region (−6.6%). The Far West region experienced a decline of −3.6% and Canada, as noted above a decline of −3.3%. The only growth was that in the Great Lakes region which experienced an increase of +3.4%, all but 1% of which was accounted for by the first time reporting of a program which had been in existence for a number of years at one of the member schools. Except for the regions noted above, enrollment was stable across the country. The decline of enrollment in those programs which normally lead to ordained ministries was −3.1%, greater than the overall average of 1% for all programs. A trend which was noted last year, namely, a growth in the number of first year students, was again noted this year with a growth of +4%, up from 12,944 students to 13,459. Schools hope that this trend will continue and will be reflected eventually in overall statistics. The retention rate of students may be a greater concern in coming years.

TABLE 1
Autumn Enrollments in ATS Member Schools

	1980	1982	1983	1984	1985	1986	1987
Number of Schools	194	196	195	197	196	201	201
Total Enrollment	49,611	52,620	55,112	56,466	56,377	56,335	55,766
By Nation							
Canada	2,731	2,961	3,081	3,352	3,583	3,696	3,572
United States	46,880	49,659	52,031	53,114	52,794	52,639	52,194
By Membership							
Accredited	45,952	48,887	51,495	52,091	52,581	52,864	52,464
Not Accredited	3,659	3,733	3,617	4,375	3,796	3,471	3,302

The fall of 1987 experienced a fractional growth in Full-Time equivalent (FTE) enrollment of +0.1%. This follows a decline of −1.4% for the past year. The percentage of FTE (68.6%) in relation to total head-count was also up this year from 68.0% to 68.6%. This reverses a long-time trend of a declining ratio. Schools have been making a major effort to increase endowment dedicated to financial aid for students in order to free more students for full-time studies. Perhaps the impact of this effort is finally being felt. The trend to a lower percentage in the FTE enrollment has at least been arrested. But given a percentage of error in reporting, this slow-down is not enough in one year to constitute a reversal.

TABLE 2
Comparisons of Total Enrollment, 1978–1987
Total Number of Individuals and Their Full-time Equivalents

Year	Total Persons	% Change	FTE Enrollment	% Change	FTE % of Total Person Enrollment
1978	46,460		36,219		78.0%
1979	48,433	+4.2%	36,795	+1.6%	76.0%
1980	49,611	+2.4%	37,245	+1.2%	75.1%
1981	50,559	+1.9%	37,254	+0.02%	73.7%
1982	52,620	+4.1%	37,705	+1.2%	71.7%
1983	55,112	+4.7%	38,923	+3.3%	70.6%
1984	56,466	+2.5%	39,414	+1.3%	69.8%
1985	56,377	−0.16%	38,841	−1.5%	68.9%
1986	56,328	−0.09%	38,286	−1.4%	68.0%
1987	55,766	−1.0%	38,329	−1.1%	68.6%

Table 3 reports the increase in numbers and ratio of women seminary students for each year since 1972 when the collection of data was begun. Thirteen years ago women constituted only 10.2% of the total student population. This year they constituted 27% of the student group. The actual head count has grown by 446 or +3%. The average increase for the past six years was +4.6%. The growth for the current year (3%) is significant especially in light of the continuing decline in overall enrollment.

TABLE 3
Women Theological Students

	Number of Women	% Annual Increase	% Total Enrollment
1972	3,358		10.2%
1973	4,021	+19.7%	11.8%
1974	5,255	+30.7%	14.3%
1975	6,505	+23.8%	15.9%
1976	7,349	+13.0%	17.1%
1977	8,371	+13.9%	18.5%
1978	8,972	+ 7.2%	19.3%
1979	10,204	+13.7%	21.1%
1980	10,830	+ 6.1%	21.8%
1981	11,683	+ 7.9%	23.1%
1982	12,473	+ 6.8%	23.7%
1983	13,451	+ 7.8%	24.4%
1984	14,142	+ 5.1%	25.0%
1985	14,572	+ 3.0%	25.8%
1986	14,864	+ 2.0%	26.4%
1987	15,310	+ 3.0%	27.0%

TABLE 4
Black Student Enrollment

	Number of Black Students	% Annual Increase	% Total Enrollment
1970	808		2.6%
1971	908	+12.4%	2.8%
1972	1,061	+16.9%	3.2%
1973	1,210	+14.0%	3.6%
1974	1,246	+ 3.0%	3.4%
1975	1,365	+ 9.6%	3.3%
1976	1,524	+11.6%	3.5%
1977	1,759	+15.4%	3.9%
1978	1,919	+ 9.1%	4.1%
1979	2,043	+ 6.5%	4.2%
1980	2,205	+ 7.9%	4.4%
1981	2,371	+ 7.5%	4.7%
1982	2,576	+ 8.6%	4.9%
1983	2,881	+11.8%	5.2%
1984	2,917	+ 1.2%	5.2%
1985	3,046	+ 4.4%	5.4%
1986	3,277	+ 7.6%	5.8%
1987	3,379	+ 3.1%	6.0%

Table 4 provides data on the black student population in theological seminaries, which the Association has collected only since 1970. The total enrollment in 1987 rose by +3.1% (102 students), lower than last year's increase of +7.6%. If, however, the six new schools added in 1986 had been excluded from the calculations, the 1986 percentage of increase would have been +1.7%, less than this year's figure of +3.1%. The percentage of blacks in the total student body is now up to 6%, an encouraging growth but still small in proportion to the percentage of blacks in the total population. The average increase for the past six years was +6.1%. In light of the reported decline of black students in colleges across the country, there is reason for encouragement in the steady growth of black enrollment in theological schools.

Table 5 provides data on the enrollment of Hispanics in schools of theology. The increase in enrollment of +6.8% is encouraging in light of significant efforts on the part of many denominations to support this group in preparation for ministry and for advanced graduate level degrees. What is of even greater importance is the growth of +3% of candidates enrolled in programs ordinarily leading to ordained ministry. With this increase in numbers, the proportion of Hispanics in the total student body grew to 2.5%.

TABLE 5
Hispanic Student Enrollment

	Number of Hispanic Students	% Annual Increase	% Total Enrollment
1972	264		0.8%
1973	387	+46.8%	1.1%
1974	448	+15.8%	1.2%
1975	524	+17.0%	1.3%
1976	541	+ 3.2%	1.3%
1977	601	+11.1%	1.3%
1978	681	+13.3%	1.5%
1979	822	+20.7%	1.7%
1980	894	+ 8.8%	1.8%
1981	955	+ 6.8%	1.9%
1982	1,180	+23.6%	2.2%
1983	1,381	+17.0%	2.5%
1984	1,314	− 4.9%	2.3%
1985	1,454	+10.6%	2.6%
1986	1,297	−10.8%	2.3%
1987	1,385	+ 6.8%	2.5%

Table 6 provides data on the enrollment of persons of Pacific/Asian American ancestry. Though the numbers are quite small, they are already greater than thos of Hispanic students. The growth this year of +18% is substantial. With this Pacific/Asian Americans constitute 2.9% of the total student body. The determination of this group to provide an educated ministry is obvious in these statistics.

TABLE 6
Pacific/Asian American Students

	Number of Students	% Annual Increase	% Total Enrollment
1977	494		1.1%
1978	499	+ 1.0%	1.1%
1979	577	+15.6%	1.2%
1980	602	+ 4.3%	1.2%
1981	716	+18.9%	1.4%
1982	707	− 1.3%	1.3%
1983	779	+10.2%	1.4%
1984	1,130	+45.1%	2.0%
1985	1,195	+ 5.8%	2.1%
1986	1,393	+16.6%	2.5%
1987	1,645	+18.0%	2.9%

Full details regarding these enrollment data and other statistical information are available from the annual *Fact Book on Theological Education (1987-1988)* published by the Association of Theological Schools, P.O. Box 130, Vandalia, OH 45377.

4. SURVEYS OF RELIGION IN AMERICAN LIFE

In this section are three recently completed surveys which come from a variety of sources. The first is "Costs of Professional Parish Leadership: A Cross-Denominational Survey." This is followed by a roundup of selected Church Attendance and Other Polls. The last survey is "Value of New Construction of Religious Buildings," which has been a yearly report in the **Yearbook** for many years.

COSTS OF PROFESSIONAL PARISH LEADERSHIP: A CROSS-DENOMINATIONAL STUDY

Jackson W. Carroll,
Dean R. Hoge,
and Francis K. Scheets, O.S.C.*

Catholics and Protestants face difficult issues of ordained leadership. On the surface, the issues seem quite different, but in some ways, mirror images of each other. For Catholics, the core issue, already manifest in some parts of the country, is one of a priest shortage that will grow dramatically by the end of the century unless changes are made in key institutional policies regarding the priesthood. Careful estimates suggest that there will be a 40 percent decline in the number of diocesan priests between 1980 and 2000 (Schoenherr and Sorensen, 1982; Hoge, 1987), and if priests who are members of religious orders were counted, the decline would be even greater. The number of Catholic seminarians enrolled in the Theologate (the final four years before ordination) declined from 8,885 in 1965 to 4,063 in 1985, while the number of Catholics continued to grow. There were 5,137 Catholics per seminarian in 1965; twenty years later, there were 12,869 (Hoge, 1987:228-29). Thus the issue of providing professional leadership for Catholic parishes is a critical one, and Catholic leaders are exploring various options, including the growing use of deacons (usually unpaid) and full-time professionally trained lay ministers.

In contrast to the Catholic situation, Protestants—or more precisely—some mainline Protestant denominations—have experienced an oversupply (or at least a considerable "tightness" in the numbers) or ordained clergy (Carroll and Wilson, 1980; Roozen and Lummis, 1987). At the same time, these denominations have had a growing number of small parishes that are unable to afford full-time ordained leadership and, in some instances, unable to attract ordained leadership, full- or part-time. Lyle Schaller (1987:8) reports that in The United Methodist Church, one of the denominations we examine in this study, 9,741 of its congregations in 1974 had an average Sunday worship attendance of 35 or fewer persons (Schaller's definition of a small congregation). Ten years later, in spite of closing or merging approximately 1,500 congregations, the number of small congregations grew to 10,127. He notes further that fewer than one-third of United Methodist congregations in the United States presently have a full-time resident pastor who does not serve any other churches, does not have any other appointment, does not attend school on a part-time basis, and is not officially retired. While we do not have entirely comparable data on the other two Protestant denominations included in our study, the situation is not too far different. Approximately 7 percent of Lutheran Church in America congregations have an average worship attendance of fewer than 35, and 37 percent have an average attendance of fewer than 100 (Schaller:8). A recent study of Episcopal theological education estimated that approximately 38 percent of Episcopal parishes had fewer than 100 communicant members (Roozen and Lummis 1987), which would probably translate to a worship attendance of approximately 35. In the three denominations, and in

---

*Jackson W. Carroll, Ph.D., is vice-president and professor of religion and society, Hartford Seminary; Dean R. Hoge, Ph.D., is professor of sociology, Catholic University; Francis K. Scheets, Ph.D., is a Crosier Father and specialist in church planning and management information.

other Protestant denominations as well, the question not only is one of how to deploy available ordained clergy in congregations that can afford to support them, but it is also how to provide trained leadership for this growing number of congregations that cannot afford full-time, ordained clergy.

Thus while the respective situations for Catholics and Protestants seems manifestly different, common elements exist. Both must develop alternatives to the use of full-time, ordained clergy in meeting parish leadership needs. Also, the problems they face have cost implications in finances and effectiveness. What does it cost to have a full-time, ordained clergyperson in a parish—not just in cash salary but in total compensation? What do part-time clergy cost? What, also, are the costs of using paid lay professional staff in place of, or as a supplement for, ordained leadership? How do laity perceive the various alternative forms of parish leadership in terms of desirability and effectiveness?

The research we report here aims to provide information about these questions. Our purpose has been to gather data about the financial costs and perceptions of desirability of various patterns of professional leadership, ordained and lay, in Catholic and Protestant parishes or congregations.[1] Protestant denominations studied include The Episcopal Church, Lutheran Church in America (before its recent merger), and The United Methodist Church. Episcopal and Lutheran denominations, like the Catholic, have strong sacramental traditions; all four denominations are episcopal in polity; and United Methodist and Catholic bishops function somewhat similarly in assigning pastors to parishes. Here we report some of our findings. A full report will be available approximately mid-year 1988. The Lilly Endowment, Inc., has generously provided funding for our research.

Methods and Data

We gathered data for the study from Catholic and Protestant parishes in a randomly selected Metropolitan Statistical Area (MSA) in each of eight regions across the country. (We combined the Rocky Mountain and North Central regions be-

cause of relatively sparse population). The eight MSAs are: Nashua, NH; Trenton, NJ; Orlando, FL; Mobile, AL; Dallas, TX; Cleveland, OH; Colorado Springs, CO; and Bremerton, WA.

We contacted the denominational heads of the four communions in each of the eight sites. With their assistance, we enlisted in each site 26 parishes representing differing staffing patterns. There are eight Catholic parishes in each location: usually three with more than one full-time priest, three with only one full-time priest, and two with no full-time priest. For each of the three Protestant denominations, we usually selected two parishes in each of the staffing categories. (There was some variation due to availability in each region.) We then enlisted and trained on-site researchers in each region to visit the parishes, secure the relevant financial information (some of which is not available in published statistics), and distribute questionnaires to members of the lay governing boards.

Financial data included all costs associated with ordained and lay professional leadership, both direct and indirect, including housing costs. The questionnaire dealt with attitudes about various patterns of leadership, ordained and lay professional. We were especially interested in openness to alternatives to full-time ordained leaders and to perceptions about leader effectiveness. We did not concern ourselves in the study with unpaid deacons, since we were primarily interested in leaders who are paid for their services. We also secured relevant cost information at the middle and national judicatory levels. This included monies expended for such things as support for theological seminaries, clergy continuing education, and various other forms of counseling and support costs related to parish leadership, whether for clergy or professionally trained laity.

Of the 208 parishes invited to participate, 201 (97%) agreed to cooperate. We also received 1,829 completed surveys of the 2,209 that were mailed to lay governing board members of the parishes, for an 83 percent return, evenly distributed across the four denominations.

As we present the findings, we would caution the reader that *neither the financial nor the attitudinal data come from a true*

1. While we recognize that the words *parish* and *congregation* have different meanings in Catholic and Protestant usage, we use them interchangeably here to designate local religious organizations which gather for worship, fellowship, and various types of programs.

random sample of all U.S. Catholic or Protestant parishes. Due to difficulties of securing cooperation, we were unable to study a true random sample. In some places, probable uncooperative parishes were never invited. We believe, nevertheless, that the parishes we chose for study are not atypical, that they adequately reflect regional variations and differing staffing patterns, and that our data provide accurate information about costs and perceived effectiveness of ministry professionals in these parishes. While one cannot extrapolate the findings to all parishes as if they came from a true random sample, it is possible, we believe, to generalize from them with appropriate caution. Here we report some of our findings, both financial and attitudinal, and reflect briefly on their implications.

Selected Findings
About Compensation Patterns

In Table 1, we summarize basic findings regarding compensation for *full-time* ordained clergy in each denomination. Readers should note that full-time clergy in congregations designated as having no full-time ordained minister are those who receive *all* their compensation from church sources, though only part comes from the parish we studied. The tables include costs only at the parish level. Later, we note additional costs contributed to the support of clergy or lay professional leadership by regional or national judicatories. The first subtable shows a weighted national average for all clergy in each denomination; the other subtables break down the findings by denomination and staffing pattern.[2]

Total compensation includes the cost of housing and other allowances and benefits paid by the congregation. The dollar income reflects actual cash salary received, plus fees for weddings, funerals, etc., received during a typical year. For housing costs, we secured estimates of the fair rental value of parsonages and rectories, if the parish or congregation provided them, and other housing expenses, including food and housekeeping expenses (usually for Catho-

lic priests), if the parish provided them in addition to the clergy's cash salary. Allowances include automobile expenses, continuing-education fees, conference participation, and the purchase of books and journals. Benefits include pension, Social Security, and insurance payments made by the parish. The final column shows the total compensation divided by the number of households in the parish to get an average figure for compensation per household.

The average dollar salary paid full-time clergy (Table 1) in the three Protestant denominations is not substantially different: between $20,833 and $22,174. Catholic priests, however, receive considerably less: $7,525 on average, or just over one-third that of Protestants. When we add other sources of compensation—housing, travel, continuing education, health care and retirement benefits—the total compensation for all denominations is considerably higher. Catholic priests still receive less total compensation ($26,376 on average) than their Protestant counterparts. Among the three Protestant groups, Episcopal priests receive the highest average total compensation ($45,005), followed by Lutherans ($39,059) and United Methodists ($35,308). Of the four denominations, housing for Catholic priests is most costly, while retirement benefits for Protestant clergy are substantially higher than for priests.

In the breakdowns by parish-staffing type for each denomination, the average total compensation for full-time Episcopal clergy in parishes with two or more ordained priests is almost twice that of Catholic priests in similar parishes and substantially greater than for Lutherans or United Methodists.[3] These differences are primarily the result of substantially higher health and retirement benefits for Episcopal clergy. The actual dollar income of the three Protestant groups is close, with Lutherans making slightly less than the other two.

In parishes with one full-time ordained person, Catholic clergy still lag considerably behind their Protestant counterparts in total compensation. United Methodists in these parishes receive more than $5,000 less in

2. As noted above, our sample of parishes was divided into three types (those with more than one full-time clergy; those with one full-time clergy; those with less than one full-time clergy), and all financial data were gathered within each type. An estimate of the overall national situation in each denomination needs to be based on weighted figures, in which the correct proportions of each type in each denomination are used. The overall or national denominational figures in this article are weighted data based on the best available information for each denomination.

3. Note that the figure is the *average* cost of full-time ordained clergy in multiple-staff parishes. Full-time senior pastors would cost more; full-time associates and assistants would cost less.

total compensation than either Episcopal or Lutheran clergy. Cash salary in the three groups is similar.

When we look at parishes with no full-time ordained pastor, the Catholic Protestant differences continue. Catholic priests (recall that we include only those whose full salaries come from church sources) receive an average total compensation of just under $20,000. Total compensation for Protestant clergy varies between $28,976 for Lutherans and $31,636 for United Methodists. The actual cash salary for Catholic priests in these parishes averages only $5,749, as compared with approximately $20,000 for each of the three Protestant groups.

Look, finally, at the last column of Table 1—the average compensation per household. Catholics, whose parishes are typically much larger than Protestant congregations, pay substantially less per household ($28) for clergy leadership than do Protestants. Overall, Lutherans pay the most ($342). The subtables show a substantial size penalty for parishes with less than a full-time ordained minister (typically, small parishes). The per-household contribution for ordained leadership rises sharply in these churches. The Episcopal figure ($1,-590 per household) is especially high in comparison to the other denominations and more than ten times greater than Episcopal parishes with two or more ordained persons. It may be accidentally higher, since it is based on only ten cases.

Table 2 reports additional costs of clergy leadership borne by the regional or national judicatories. While some of the money spent on clergy leadership at the judicatory level comes from assessments to local parishes, we excluded these costs in the figures in Table 1. Of the four communions, United Methodist judicatories contribute most for clergy support—approximately $3,747 per clergy per year. That denomination also contributes $583 per clergy annually for support of theological seminaries. These figures reflect in large part the assessment (Ministerial Education Fund) levied by Methodists on each congregation for basic and continuing theological education.[4] They also bring the total costs of full-time leadership for United Methodists (Tables 1 and 2 combined) more in line with

the other two Protestant denominations.

Table 3 reports compensation data for full-time lay professionals, broken down first by denomination, second by type of parish staffing pattern and denomination, and third by type of position, regardless of denomination. Average dollar income overall varies from $13,531 for Episcopalians to $18,632 for United Methodists. Total compensation follows the same pattern. When we compare the dollar income for full-time Protestant lay professionals with full-time ordained clergy (Tables 1 and 3), lay professionals receive less, ranging from almost $10,000 for Episcopalians to $4,000 less for United Methodists. The total compensation gap, however, is substantially greater. For Catholics the difference is smaller, approximately $5,000.

The second subtable of Table 3 breaks down full-time lay professional compensation by denomination and type of staffing pattern. For the three Protestant denominations, compensation is highest for those lay professionals in parishes with two or more ordained clergy—usually parishes with larger memberships. There are no lay professionals in the sample Protestant parishes with less than one full-time ordained pastor. For Catholics, there are two cases. Two parishes in the study are "priestless" and served by lay professionals—in this case by Sisters. A priest relates to the parish on a part-time basis, but the lay professionals carry out the day-to-day work of the parish. The Sisters receive considerably less dollar income than lay professionals in larger parishes, and somewhat less total compensation.

In the final subtable of Table 3, we report average compensation for lay professionals by position, regardless of denomination. The position titles are mostly self-explanatory, with the possible exception of Administrative Assistant, which involves parish business and property management, and Pastoral Associate, which includes such responsibilities as parish visitation and outreach, and coordination of lay volunteers. In the parishes we studied, Music Directors, on average, received the highest dollar income and total compensation, followed by Administrative Assistants and Youth Directors. Organists and Pastoral Associates received the lowest income and

4. Readers should note that the denomination uses a portion of this assessment for various overhead costs related to the support of ordained clergy, which may inflate the figure to some degree when compared with the other denominations.

total compensation. Whether the higher income paid Youth Directors than Christian Education Directors is an artifact of our sample or reflects the actual situation nationally is impossible to say.

Selected Findings for Attitudes About Professional Leadership

Space prohibits presenting summary tables or detailed findings regarding attitudes about various forms of professional leadership. Generally, three things stand out.

1. The majority sentiment in all four traditions is a desire for ordained ministers rather than professionally trained lay leadership. Approximately 60 percent in each denomination express strong or moderate agreement that members' morale in their parish or congregation would be adversely affected, were they not able to secure a full-time, ordained pastor. This is especially the case, as one might imagine, in parishes that already have at least one full-time ordained person; however, it is true for approximately 40 or more percent in parishes with less than a full-time clergy-person. Also, except for Lutherans (52 percent), over 60 percent of all respondents agree that the average lay person responds best to ordained leadership. Even in parishes with less than a full-time clergy—parishes most likely to have a lay rather than an ordained professional-over half the respondents agree with this statement.

When asked to choose among several options for ministry leadership, if they could not afford a full-time ordained person, a substantial majority (over 80 percent in most instances), preferred some form of ordained, part-time leadership to either full- or part-time trained lay leadership. In a similar vein, we also asked the three Protestant groups to express their feelings about "tent-making," or nonstipendiary clergy, whose principal income derives from nonchurch sources. There is little enthusiasm for this pattern among any Protestant laity. Less than 7 percent thought it an exciting development; and between one-fourth and one-third thought it should be encouraged, but not generally.

We note finally that many lay Catholics showed, in written comments, their preference for opening the ordained ministry to married persons and women as a means of ensuring ordained leadership in the face of the shortage of priests. As one lay woman expressed it: "I feel I would not be satisfied with my religion anymore if it gets to a point where only lay people are involved [in parish leadership] or more involved than the priest." They are not, however, asking for a priest-dominated church; rather, they are expressing their preference for ordained leadership.

Overall, therefore, the data show that the majority sentiment among lay governing-board members is for some form of ordained leadership, full- or part-time, but preferably not nonstipendiary.

2. In spite of the preference for ordained leadership, Catholics are less "hung up" about ordained leadership for a variety of parish ministry tasks than are Protestants. This came as something of a surprise. Three-fourths of the Catholic lay leaders, in contrast to approximately half the Protestants, believe that "most of the tasks currently done by ordained pastors can be done equally well by lay persons with special competence for the task." In another question, we listed some functions of parish leadership such as preaching, conducting a funeral, counseling, and so forth. (The list did not include celebration of the sacraments, which is restricted to ordained clergy in all the denominations.) We asked respondents to indicate for each function, whether they prefer that it be done by an ordained or a lay person, or whether it does not matter. Overall, Protestants are much more likely to prefer an ordained person for most of the functions. Catholics, on the other hand, have a strong desire for an ordained person for only one of the listed functions: conducting a funeral (81 percent prefer a priest). Just over half the Catholics, but three-fourths or more Protestants, prefer that ordained clergy preach. About equal numbers of Catholics and Protestants (approximately half) prefer an ordained person to counsel with them and visit them in the hospital. Only a fourth of Catholics, but almost two-thirds of Protestants, prefer an ordained person to teach confirmation classes. For other functions listed (leading pastoral prayers, reading lessons, teaching adult-education classes), Protestants and Catholics, for the most part, say it does not matter. Only for managing the organizational affairs of the parish is there, for Catholics and Lutherans, slightly more

sentiment for a lay than an ordained leader. Episcopalians and United Methodists, by a small margin, still prefer clergy leadership in parish management.

3. While lay governing-board members prefer ordained leaders for their parishes, they express considerable concern over ordained leaders' effectiveness in various tasks of ministry. We listed twelve leadership tasks and asked how important they think each task is and how effective they judge their current staff to be in carrying out the tasks. While there is a considerable gap between ratings of importance and effectiveness on most tasks within most denominations, Catholic laity are especially critical in rating their parish staff's effectiveness. For preaching, liturgical leadership, pastoral counseling, directing religious education, parish evangelization, and parish planning, the gap between importance and effectiveness ranges from 30 to 40 percent. For the three Protestant groups, the gap between importance and effectiveness ratings for most of the tasks is somewhat smaller, yet it usually ranges between 20 and 30 percent.

For both Protestants and Catholics, the greatest difference between importance and effectiveness ratings is in "deepening parishioners' spiritual lives." The difference is over 60 percent for Catholics, almost 50 percent for Episcopalians and United Methodists, and 42 percent for Lutherans. There is apparently considerable desire for a deeper spiritual experience than lay leaders are presently finding in their church participation.

Some Concluding Observations

We will not attempt to summarize the findings we have reported here. Rather, we conclude with four observations about the findings.

1. Our salary data confirm what other research has shown: Clergy and full-time lay professional salaries, especially in cash income, are low relative to other professions. Without going into detail, we note several comparisons. The average 1985 cash salary for secondary school teachers was $24,300; for college professors (all ranks and disciplines), $33,400. Social workers with a Master's degree earned $27,700, and general practitioners (the lowest-earning M.D.s) earned an average of $68,600 (1984 figure).[5] Catholic priests, in particular, in our study, receive significantly lower dollar income than any of the professions noted. Our findings for total clergy compensation show, however, that many clergy (but not lay professionals) receive substantial compensation beyond their salaries. This improves the picture to some extent, although clergy compensation still seems somewhat low, given the lengthy preparation required for ordination. Even when we consider total compensation, Catholic priests receive only slightly more compensation than the cash salary of secondary school teachers, the lowest paid of the professions we compared. It is true that neither clergy nor lay professionals enter the ministry (ordained or lay) on the basis of rational calculation about potential earnings. It would be surprising, however, if compensation considerations did not play some role, however slight, in the decision.

2. The use of full-time lay professionals by Catholics in nonsacramental leadership roles will cost slightly less, in total compensation, than the use of full-time priests. For most Protestants, use of part-time ordained clergy in small parishes appears to be slightly less costly than full-time lay professionals, although the potential gain in the range of services a full-time lay professional might provide, in contrast to a part-time ordained leader, merits consideration.

3. The clear preference among lay leaders for ordained clergy, even part-time, over lay professionals as primary parish leaders suggests that a major educational task is necessary if lay professionals are to be so deployed. On this score, Catholics face a less serious educational task than Protestants. As we noted, Catholic laity seem more open to lay professionals undertaking many parish ministry tasks than are Protestants. Still, for all groups, there is strong preference for ordained leadership.

4. We simply reiterate our finding that lay leaders are critical of the effectiveness of their ordained leaders, even though they prefer ordained over lay leadership. This obviously has implications for candidate selection, basic seminary training, and

5. Data for secondary school teachers, college professors and M.D.s are from the *Statistical Abstract of the United States, 1986* (U.S. Census, 1986). Social work salary data were supplied by the National Association of Social Workers.

continuing education of clergy. It is also interesting to speculate about the relation between the perceived low clergy effectiveness and the compensation they receive. Would clergy compensation be higher if the parishes thought they were getting more effective leadership by their clergy? Or, conversely, would an increase in clergy compensation attract persons of greater competence into the ministry? Such issues are clearly matters of speculation and beyond the scope of our study.

References

Carroll, Jackson W., and Robert L. Wilson
    1980 *Too Many Pastors? The Clergy Job Market.* New York: Pilgrim Press.

Census, U.S. Bureau of the
    1986 *Statistical Abstract of the United States: 1986.* Washington, D.C.: U.S. Government Printing Office.

Hoge, Dean
    1987 *Future of Catholic Leadership: Responses to the Priest Shortage.* Kansas City: Sheed & Ward.

Roozen, David A., and Adair T. Lummis
    1987 *Leadership and Theological Education in The Episcopal Church.* Hartford: Hartford Seminary Center for Social and Religious Research.

Schaller, Lyle
    1987 "UMC: What's the Future of the Small-church Denomination?" *Circuit Rider* 11(Dec-Jan):8-10.

Schoenherr, Richard, and Annemette Sorensen
    1982 "Social Change in Religious Organizations: Consequences of Clergy Decline in the U.S. Catholic Church." *Sociological Analysis* 43(Spring):23-52.

TABLE 1: Average Total Compensation, Income, Housing, Allowances & Benefits: Full-Time Ordained Clergy by Denomination

	Number Persons	Total Compensation	Dollar Income	Housing Rent	Travel	Education	Retirement	Health	Compensation per household
WEIGHTED NATIONAL AVERAGE									
Roman Catholic	98	26,376	7,526	12,767	3,169	535	1,011	1,369	28
Episcopal	58	45,005	22,174	10,543	2,937	765	5,598	2,988	201
Lutheran	51	39,059	21,688	8,548	3,000	544	3,629	1,649	342
United Methodist	59	35,308	20,833	6,717	2,822	473	3,018	1,444	268
	328								
ROMAN CATHOLIC									
Two or More Clergy	69	25,041	7,243	11,532	3,410	498	1,026	1,332	15
One Full-time Clergy	25	28,201	7,917	14,405	2,887	584	998	1,410	40
No Full-time Clergy	4	19,464	5,749	8,633	2,346	375	748	1,613	115
EPISCOPAL									
Two or more Clergy	37	48,707	23,908	10,781	3,443	1,063	6,429	3,083	116
One Full-time Clergy	19	43,672	21,473	10,562	2,726	659	5,304	2,957	280
No Full-time Clergy	2	30,996	20,938	2,358	3,000	200	2,100	2,400	866
LUTHERAN									
Two or More Clergy	27	40,094	21,691	9,500	2,973	636	3,745	1,549	127
One Full-time Clergy	22	42,795	22,725	10,485	3,169	569	4,275	1,572	406
No Full-time Clergy	2	28,976	19,399	2,575	2,677	325	2,000	2,000	375
UNITED METHODIST									
Two or More Clergy	41	39,997	23,154	8,289	2,843	575	3,440	1,676	66
One Full-time Clergy	16	37,630	20,887	8,168	2,609	552	3,898	1,516	235
No Full-time Clergy	2	31,636	19,961	4,900	3,000	369	2,106	1,300	354

TABLE 2: Denominational Contributions to Clergy Support

	PASTORAL SUPPORT PROGRAMS							
	Personal Personal Counseling	Continuing Education	Career Assistance	Insurance Personal Medical	Retirement	Other	Support COST PER CLERGY	Seminary Theological Education
NATIONAL AVERAGE:								
Roman Catholic	290	303	9	366	440	19	1,428	1,039
Episcopal	44	60	74	457	78	654	1,366	355

284

TABLE 3: Average Total Compensation & Housings, Allowances & Benefits: Full Time Lay Professionals by Denomination

	Number	Total Compensation	Dollar Income	Housing/FICA	Allowances Travel	Allowances Education	Benefits Retirement	Benefits Health	Compensation Per Hsld
NATIONAL AVERAGE:									
Roman Catholic	91	$18,527	$14,426	$1,719	$514	$293	611	966	14
Episcopal	31	16,754	13,531	1,207	283	78	376	1,279	49
Lutheran	17	19,462	15,977	1,645	735	315	318	472	62
United Methodist	22	23,246	18,632	2,522	165	251	736	940	30
	161								
ROMAN CATHOLIC:									
Two or More Clergy	70	18,442	14,306	1,651	629	236	601	1,019	11
One Full-time Clergy	19	19,195	15,437	1,732	18	507	675	826	24
No Full-time Clergy	2	15,140	8,900	3,989	1,200	240	380	431	32
EPISCOPAL:									
Two or More Clergy	22	18,168	14,518	1,464	380	51	342	1,413	48
One Full-time Clergy	9	13,298	11,119	579	47	144	458	951	50
No Full-time Clergy									
LUTHERAN:									
Two or More Clergy	10	21,147	18,443	906	660	204	428	506	64
One Full-time Clergy	7	17,055	12,454	2,700	842	474	161	424	60
No Full-time Clergy									
METHODIST:									
Two or More Clergy	19	23,578	18,982	2,335	171	249	853	988	24
One Full-time Clergy	3	21,144	16,416	3,696	133	266		633	64
No Full-time Clergy									
NATIONAL AVERAGE:									
Christian Ed. Director	39	18,937	14,884	2,582	584	887			
Youth Director	20	20,442	16,404	2,466	514	1,058			
Worship Director	5	20,404	14,738	4,126	635	905			
Music Director	17	22,653	18,510	1,995	776	1,372			
Organist	7	14,051	12,013	1,084	428	526			
Administrative Assistant	34	19,668	16,745	1,387	524	1,012			
Pastoral Associate	18	17,148	11,856	3,942	443	907			
Other	21	16,065	11,896	2,794	505	870			
	161								

CHURCH ATTENDANCE AND OTHER POLLS

Four adults in every ten (40%) attended church or synagogue in a typical week in 1986, according to three in=person surveys conducted in more than 300 scientifically selected localities across the nation, and two telephone surveys during five selected weeks. A total of 6,633 adults, 18 years of age and older, were interviewed.

The findings of these surveys were reported in *Religion in America,* The Gallup Report, April 1987, Report No. 259 (P.O. Box 628, Princeton, NJ 08542, $25).

Gallup notes that "Churchgoing has remained remarkably constant since 1969 after having declined from the high point of 49 percent recorded in 1955 and 1958."

Responding to the question *"Did you, yourself, happen to attend church or synagogue during the last seven days?"* 6,633 adults responded in the following manner:

CHURCH/SYNAGOGUE ATTENDANCE
1986

NATIONAL.. 40%

Men	33
Women	46
Protestants	41
Catholics	49
Jews	20
18–24 years	33
25–29	33
30–49	39
50–64	47
65 & older	49
East	39
Midwest	42
South	43
West	35
College graduates	42
College incomplete	41
High school graduates	40
Not H.S. graduates	38
Whites	40
Blacks	43
Hispanics	46

Denominational Preferences of Americans

"The percentage of adults who give their denominational preferences as Methodist, Presbyterian, or Episcopalian has leveled off in the last few years after sharp declines in the 1970s and 1960s" according to a report in *PRRC emerging trends,* Vol. 9, No. 2, Feb. 1987 (Princeton Religion Research Center, PO.Box 310, 53 Bank St., Princeton, NJ 08542).

In the table below, the data indicate that those having a Baptist preference have shown little change over the period 1967–86, whereas those in the Methodist and Episcopal group have fallen about one-third. Presbyterians have declined by two-thirds and Lutherans by a little more than one-quarter.

Gallup points out that "It is important to bear in mind that the annual Gallup audits focus on *preference* and not *membership.*"

Protestant Church Preferences

	Baptist %	Methodist %	Lutheran %	Presbyterian %	Episcopalian %
1986	20	9	5	2	2
1985	20	10	6	2	2
1984	20	9	7	2	3
1983	21	10	7	3	2
1982	19	10	6	4	2
1981	19	10	6	4	2
1980	19	10	6	4	2
1979	19	11	6	4	2
1978	19	11	6	4	2
1976	21	11	7	5	3
1975	20	11	7	5	3
1974	21	14	7	6	3
1969	20	14	7	6	3
1967	21	14	7	6	3

Little Change in Major Faiths

Gallup's 1986 audit shows little change in recent years in the relative strength of major faiths in the country with 59 percent giving their religious preference as Protestant, 27 percent as Roman Catholic, 2 percent as Jewish, and 2 percent indicating their religious preference to be the Church of Jesus Christ of Latter Day Saints (Mormon). The 1986 figures are based on in-person interviews with 8,203 adults, 18 and older, conducted in more than 300 scientifically selected localities across the nation.

Responses to the question *"What is your religious preference—Protestant, Roman Catholic, Jewish, Mormon, or an Orthodox Church such as Greek or Russian Orthodox Church?"* produced the following results:

Religious Preferences

Protestant..59%
Roman Catholic..27
Jewish... 2
Mormon (The Church of Jesus Christ of Latter-day Saints)........................ 2
Orthodox Church.. *
Other.. 2
None... 9

*Less than one percent.

Interviewing on religious preference began in 1947, and over the four-decade period there have been some significant changes in religious preference. The Protestant category declined from 69 percent to 59, and the Roman Catholic increased from 20 to 27 percent. In the table below, Mormon and Orthodox churches are omitted because of insufficient historical data and are included under the "other" category, Gallup notes.

Religious Preferences
-Yearly-

	Protestant %	Catholic %	Jewish %	Otner %	None %
1986	59	27	2	4	8
1985	57	28	2	4	9
1984	57	28	2	4	9
1983	56	29	2	4	9
1982.	57	29	2	4	8
1981	59	28	2	4	7
1980	61	28	2	2	7
1979	59	29	2	2	8
1977-78	60	29	2	1	8
1976	61	27	2	4	6
1975	62	27	2	4	6

-By 5-year periods-

1972	63	26	2	4	5
1967	67	25	3	3	2
1962	70	23	3	2	2
1957	66	26	3	1	3
1952	67	25	4	1	2
1947	69	20	5	1	6

VALUE OF NEW CONSTRUCTION OF RELIGIOUS BUILDINGS IN CURRENT AND CONSTANT 1982 DOLLARS
(In Millions of Dollars)

Year	Current Dollars	1982 Dollars	Year	Current Dollars	1982 Dollars
1964	$ 992	$3,605	1975	$ 867	$1,543
1965	1,201	4,220	1976	956	1,631
1966	1,145	3,869	1977	1,046	1,659
1967	1,063	3,491	1978	1,248	1,779
1968	1,079	3,336	1979	1,548	1,996
1969	989	2,827	1980	1,637	1,884
1970	929	2,488	1981	1,665	1,746
1971	813	2,004	1982	1,543	1,541
1972	845	1,947	1983	1,780	1,712
1973	814	1,734	1984	2,132	1,968
1974	918	1,707	1985	2,409	2,161
			1986	2,676	2,345

Source: U. S. Department of Commerce, *Annual Value of New Construction Put in Place in the United States: 1982 to 1986*, "Current Construction Reports, C-30, Value of New Construction Put in Place," Table 1.

In constant 1982 dollars the peak year for the value of new construction of religious buildings was 1965, when the value in real terms was almost twice that of 1985. The amount expended in 1986, however, was higher than for any year since 1970.

5. MAIN DEPOSITORIES OF CHURCH HISTORY MATERIAL AND SOURCES

The **Yearbook** is grateful for useful revisions of the United States listing below made by Kenneth E. Rowe, Librarian, Methodist Archives & History Center, Drew University Library, Madison, NJ 07940

Many denominations have established central archival-manuscript depositories and, in addition, are dealing with regional, diocesan, synodical, or provincial subdivisions. Communions functioning through this type of structure especially are the Roman Catholic, Episcopal, Baptist, Lutheran, and Methodist.

Some denominations with headquarters in the United States also have churches in Canada. Historical material on Canadian sections of these denominations will occasionally be found at the various locations cited below. The reader is also referred to the section "In Canada," which follows.

IN THE UNITED STATES

Adventist:

Adventual Library, Aurora College, Aurora, IL 60507 (Advent Christian Church)

Dr. Linden J. Carter Library, Berkshire Christian College, Lenox, MA 01240

Andrews University, Berrien Springs, MI 49104

General Conference of Seventh-day Adventists, 6840 Eastern Ave. NW, Washington, DC 20012

Baptist:

American Baptist Historical Society (including Samuel Colgate Baptist Historical Collection), 1100 South Goodman St., Rochester, NY 14620

Andover Newton Theological School (including Backus Historical Society), Newton Centre, MA 02159

Bethel Seminary (Swedish Baptist material), 3949 Bethel Dr., St. Paul, MN 55112

Historical Commission, Southern Baptist Convention, 901 Commerce St., Suite 400, Nashville TN 37203

Seventh Day Baptist Historical Society, 3120 Kennedy Rd., P.O. Box 1678, Janesville, WI 53547

Primitive Baptist Archives, Elon College, Elon, NC 27244

Brethren in Christ Church:

Archives of the Brethren in Christ Church, Messiah College, Grantham, PA 17027

Church of the Brethren:

Bethany Theological Seminary, Butterfield and Meyers Roads, Oak Brook, IL 60521

Brethren Historical Library and Archives, 1451 Dundee Ave., Elgin, IL 60120

Juniata College, Huntingdon, PA 16652

Churches of Christ:

Abilene Christian University Library, Abilene, TX 79699

Harding Graduate School of Religion Library, 1000 Cherry Rd., Memphis, TN 38117

Pepperline University Library, Malibu, CA 90265

Churches of God, General Conference:

Archives/Museum of the Churches of God, General Conference, 700 E. Melrose Ave., P.O. Box 926, Findlay, OH 45839

Congregationalist:

(See United Church of Christ)

Disciples:

The Disciples of Christ Historical Society, 1101 Nineteenth Ave., S., Nashville, TN 37212

Christian Theological Seminary, Indianapolis, IN 46208

Lexington Theological Seminary, Lexington, KY 40508

The Disciples Divinity House, University of Chicago, Chicago, IL 60637

Texas Christian University, Fort Worth, TX 76219

Culver-Stockton College, Canton, MO 63435

Episcopalian:

National Council, Protestant Episcopal Church, 815 2nd Ave., New York, NY 10017

Library and Archives of the Church Historical Society, 606 Rathervue Pl., Austin, TX 78767

Berkeley Divinity School at Yale, New Haven, CT 06510

General Theological Seminary, 175 Ninth Ave., New York, NY 10011

Evangelical United Brethren:

(see United Methodist Church)

Evangelical Congregational Church:

Historical Society of the Evangelical Congregational Church, 121 S. College St., Myerstown, PA 17067

Friends:

Friends' Historical Library, Swarthmore College, Swarthmore, PA 19081

Haverford College, Quaker Collection, Magill Library, Haverford, PA 19041

Jewish:

American Jewish Archives, 3101 Clifton Ave., Cincinnati, OH 45220

Yiddish Scientific Institute—YIVO, 1048 Fifth Ave., New York, NY 10028

American Jewish Historical Society, 2 Thornton Rd., Waltham, MA 02154

Latter Day Saints:

Historian's Office, Church Archives, Historical Department, 50 East North Temple St., Salt Lake City, UT 84150

The Genealogical Society, 50 E. North Temple, Salt Lake City, UT 84150

Lutheran:

Concordia Historical Institute, Dept. of Archives and History. The Lutheran Church-Missouri Synod, Historical Library, Archives and Museum on Lutheranism, 801 De Mun Ave., St. Louis, MO 63105.

Archives of American Lutheran Church, Wartburg Theological Seminary, 333 Wartburg Place, Dubuque, IA 52001

Archives of the Lutheran Church in America, Lutheran School of Theology at Chicago, 1100 East 55th St., Chicago, IL 60615

Luther College, Decorah, IA 52101

Lutheran Archives Center at Philadelphia, 7301 Germantown Ave., Philadelphia, PA 19119

Lutheran Theological Seminary, Gettysburg, PA 17325

Concordia Theological Seminary, St. Louis, MO 63105

Finnish-American Historical Archives, Hancock, MI 49930

St. Olaf College (Norwegian), Northfield, MN 55057

Archives of Cooperative Lutheranism, Office of the Secretary, Evangelical Lutheran Church in America, 8765 West Higgins Rd., Chicago, IL 60631

Lutheran Theological Southern Seminary, 4201 N. Main St., Columbia, SC 29203

Mennonite:

Bethel College, Historical Library, N. Newton, KS 67117

Centre for MB Studies, 4824 E. Butler, Fresno, CA 93727

The Archives of the Mennonite Church, 1700 South Main, Goshen, IN 46526

Menno Simons Historical Library and Archives, Eastern Mennonite College, Harrisonburg, VA 22801

Mennonite Historical Library, Bluffton College, Bluffton, OH 45817

Methodist:

Archives and Historical Library, The Wesleyan Church, P. O. Box 50434, Indianapolis, IN 46520. Daniel L. Burnett, Dir.

B. L. Fisher Library, Asbury Theological Seminary, Wilmore, KY 40390; David W. Faupel, Dir.

Bridwell Library Center for Methodist Studies, Perkins School of Theology, Southern Methodist University, Dallas, TX 75275. Dr. Richard P. Heitzenrater, Dir.

Center for Evangelical United Brethren Studies, United Theological Seminary, 1810 Harvard Blvd., Dayton, OH 45406. Elmer J. O'Brien, Lib.

Drew University Library, Madison, NJ 07940, Kenneth E. Rowe, Methodist Lib.

Duke Divinity School Library, Duke University, Durham, NC 27706. Harriet V. Leonard, Ref. Lib.

General Commission on Archives and History, The United Methodist Church, PO. Box 127, Madison, NJ 07940. Arthur W. Swarthout, Asst. Gen. Sec.

Indiana United Methodist Archives, Roy O. West Library, DePauw University, Greencastle, IN 46135

Interdenominational Theological Center Library, 671 Beckwith Street, S.W., Atlanta, GA 30314. (black Methodism)

Marston Memorial Historical Center, Free Methodist World Headquarters, Winona Lake, IN 46590.Evelyn Mottweiler, Lib.

New England Methodist Historical Society Library, Boston University School of Theology, 745 Commonwealth Ave., Boston, MA 02215.William Zimpfer, Lib.

Nippert Memorial Library, German Methodist Collection, Cincinnati Historical Society, Eden Park, Cincinnati, OH 45402

Pitts Theology Library, Candler School of Theology, Emory University, Atlanta, GA 30322.Channing Jeschke, Lib.

The United Library, (Garrett-Evangelical and Seabury Western Theological Seminaries) 2121 Sheridan Road, Evanston, IL 60201. David K. Himrod, Ref. Lib.

United Methodist Historical Library, Beeghley Library, Ohio Wesleyan University, Delaware, OH 43015

United Methodist Publishing House Library, Room 122, 201 Eighth Ave., South, Nashville, TN 37202. Rosalyn Lewis, Librarian

The Upper Room Library, 1908 Grand Avenue, Nashville, TN 37203

World Methodist Council Library, P.O. Box 518, Lake Junaluska, NC 28745. Evelyn Sutton, Lib.

Moravian:

The Archives of the Moravian Church, 1228 Main St., Bethlehem, PA 18018

Moravian Archives, Southern Province of the Moravian Church, Drawer M., Salem Station, Winston-Salem, NC 27108

Nazarene:

Nazarene Theological Seminary, 1700 East Meyer Blvd., Kansas City, MO 64131. William C. Miller, Librarian

Pentecostal:

Oral Roberts University Library, 7777 South Lewis, Tulsa, OK 74105

Assemblies of God Archives, 1445 Boonville Ave., Springfield, MO 65802. Dir., Wayne Warner

Polish National Catholic:

Commission on History and Archives, Polish National Catholic Church, 1031 Cedar Ave., Scranton, PA 18505. Chmn., Joseph Wielczerzak

Presbyterian:

Presbyterian Historical Society and Department of History, United Presbyterian Church in the U.S.A., 425 Lombard St., Philadelphia, PA 19147

Historical Foundation Montreat, NC 28757

Princeton Theological Seminary, Speer Library, Princeton, NJ 08540

McCormack Theological Seminary, 800 West Belden Ave., Chicago, IL 60614

Reformed:

Calvin College, Grand Rapids, MI 49056 (Christian Reformed)

Commission on History, Reformed Church in America, New Brunswick Theological Seminary, New Brunswick, NJ 08901

Evangelical and Reformed Historical Society, Lancaster Theological Seminary, Lancaster, PA 17603. (Reformed in the U.S., Evangelical and Reformed)

Roman Catholic:

Archives of the American Catholic Historical Society of Philadelphia, St. Charles Boromeo Seminary, Overbrook, Philadelphia, PA 19151

Department of Archives and Manuscripts, Catholic University of America, Washington, DC 20017

University of Notre Dame Archives, Box 513, Notre Dame, IN 46556

St. Mary's Sem. & Univ., Roland Park, Baltimore, MD 21210

Georgetown University, Washington, DC 20007

St. Louis University, St. Louis, MO 63103

Salvation Army:

The Salvation Army Archives and Research Center, 120 W. 14th St., New York, NY 10011

Schwenkfelder:

Schwenkfelder Library, Seminary Ave., Pennsburg, PA 18073

Shaker:

Western Reserve Historical Society, Cleveland, OH 44106

Ohio Historical Society, Division of Archives & Manuscripts, Columbus, OH 43211

Swendenborgian:

Academy of the New Church Library, Bryn Athyn, PA 19009

Unitarian and Universalist:

Harvard Divinity School Library, 45 Francis Ave., Cambridge, MA 02138

Rhode Island Historical Society, Providence, RI

Meadville Theological School, 5701 S. Woodlawn Ave., Chicago, IL 60637

Archives of the Unitarian-Universalist Association, 25 Beacon St., Boston, MA 02108

The United Church of Christ:

Archives of the United Church of Christ, 555 W. James St., Lancaster, PA 17603

Congregational Library, 14 Beacon St., Boston, MA 02108

Chicago Theological Seminary, 5757 University Ave., Chicago, IL 60637

Divinity Library, and University Library, Yale University, New Haven, CT 06520

Library of Hartford Theological Seminary, Hartford, CT 06105

Harvard Divinity School Library, Cambridge, MA 02138

Eden Archives, 475 E. Lockwood Ave., Webster Groves, MO 63119. (Evangelical and Reformed)

STANDARD GUIDES TO CHURCH ARCHIVES

William Henry Allison, **Inventory of Unpublished Material for American Religious History in Protestant Church Archives and other Depositories** (Washington, D. C., Carnegie Institution of Washington, 1910, 254 pp.).

John Graves Barrow, **A Bibliography of Bibliographies in Religion** (Ann Arbor, Mich., 1955), pp. 185-198.

Edmund L. Binsfield, "Church Archives in the United States and Canada: a Bibliography," in **American Archivist**, V. 21, No. 3 (July 1958) pp. 311-332, 219 entries.

Nelson R. Burr, "Sources for the Study of American Church History in the Library of Congress," 1953. 13 pp. Reprinted from **Church History**, Vol. XXII, No. 3 (Sept. 1953).

Homer L. Calkin, **Catalog of Methodist Archival and Manuscript Collections.** Mont Alto, PA: World Methodist Historical Society, 1982—(4 vols. to date)

Church Records Symposium, **American Archivist**, Vol. 24, October 1961, pp. 387-456.

Mable Deutrich, "Supplement to Church Archives in the United States and Canada, a Bibliography," Washington, DC: 1964.

Andrea Hinding, ed. **Women's History Sources: A Guide to Archives and Manuscript Collections in the U.S.** New York: Bowker, 1979. 2 vols.

E. Kay Kirkham, **A Survey of American Church Records, for the Period Before The Civil War, East of the Mississippi River** (Salt Lake City, 1959-60, 2 vols.). Includes the depositories and bibliographies.

Peter G. Mode, **Source Book and Bibliographical Guide for American Church History** (Menasha, Wisc., George Banta Publishing Co., 1921, 735 pp.).

Society of American Archivists. **American Archivist**, 1936/37 (continuing). Has articles on church records and depositories.

Aug. R. Suelflow, **A Preliminary Guide to Church Records Repositories,** Society of American Archivists, Church Archives Committee, 1969. Lists more than 500 historical-archival depositories with denominational and religious history in America.

U. S. National Historical Publications and Records Commission, **Directory of Archives and Manuscript Repositories in the United States.** Washington: NHPRC, 1978

United States, Library of Congress, Division of Manuscripts, **Manuscripts in Public and Private Collections in the United States** (Washington, D.C., 1924).

U. S. Library of Congress, Washington, D. C.: **The National Union Catalog of Manuscript Collections**, A59—22 vols., 1959-1986. Based on reports from American repositories of manuscripts.

Contains many entries for collections of church archives. This series is continuing. Extremely valuable collection. Researchers must consult the cumulative indexes.

Notes

The Libraries of the University of Chicago, Chicago; Union Theological Seminary, New York; and Yale Divinity School, New Haven, have large collections.

Day Missions Library, Yale Divinity School, 409 Prospect St., New Haven, CT 06510

The Archives of the National Council of the Churches of Christ in the U.S.A., and predecessor agencies, are located in the Presbyterian Historical Society, 425 Lombard St., Philadelphia, PA 19147. Tel. (215)627-1852.

The Missionary Research Library Collection of the Union Theological Seminary Library, 3041 Broadway, New York, NY 10027, has a large collection of interdenominational material.

The Library of the American Bible Society, Broadway at 61st St., New York, NY 10023, has material on the history of transmission of the Bible text, Bible translation, etc.

The Archives of the Billy Graham Center, Wheaton College, Wheaton, IL 60187, Tel. (312)260-5910, has a large collection of North American nondenominational missions and evangelism materials.

Zion Research Library, Boston University, 771 Commonwealth Ave., Boston, MA 02215 has a noteworthy archival collection.

"Specialized Research Libraries in Missions" are described by Frank W. Price in **Library Trends**, Oct, 1960, V. 9, No 2, University of Illinois Graduate School of Library Science, Urbana, IL 61801.

IN CANADA

The list of depositories of church history material which follows was reviewed recently by Dr. Neil Semple, Senior Archivist—Manuscripts, The United Church of Canada, to whom the editor is grateful.

A few small Canadian religious bodies have headquarters in the United States, and therefore the reader is advised to consult "Main Depositories of Church History Material and Sources in the United States," which immediately precedes this section for possible sources of information on Canadian religious groups. Another source: *Directory of Canadian Archives*, edited by Marcel Caya.

The use of the term "main" depositories in this section implies that there are some smaller communions with archival collections not listed below and also that practically every judicatory of large religious bodies (e.g., diocese, presbytery, conference) has archives excluded from this listing. For information on these collections, write directly to the denominational headquarters or to the judicatory involved.

The major libraries in the United States listed above under "Notes" contain material relating to Canadian Church history. Most American Protestant denominational archives have important primary and secondary source material relating to missionary work in Canada during the pioneer era.

Anglican:

General Synod Archives, 600 Jarvis St., Toronto, Ontario M4Y 2J6. Archivist: Mrs. Terry Thompson. Also Archives.

Baptist:

Canadian Baptist Archives, McMaster Divinity College, Hamilton, Ontario L8S 4K1. Librarian: Judith Colwell

Evangelical Baptist Historical Library, 3034 Bayview Ave., Willowdale, Ontario M2N 6J5

Baptist Historical Collection, Vaughan Memorial library, Acadia University, Wolfville, Nova Scotia BOP 1XO. Archivist: Mrs. Pat Thompson

Disciples of Christ:

Canadian Disciples Archives, 39 Arkell Rd., R.R. 2, Guelph, Ontario N1H 6H8. Archivist: James A. Whitehead

Reuben Butchart Collection, Victoria, University, Toronto, Ontario M5S1K7

Jewish:

Jewish Historical Society of Western Canada, 404-365 Hargrave St., Winnipeg, Manitoba R3B 2K3. Archivist: Dorothy Hershfield

Canadian Jewish Congress (Central Region) Archives, 4600 Bathurst St., Toronto, Ontario M5T 1Y6. Archivist: Stephen A. Speisman

Lutheran:

Lutheran Council in Canada, 500-365 Hargrave St., Winnipeg, Manitoba R3B 2K3. Archivist: Rev. N. J. Threinen

Evangelical Lutheran Church in Canada, 1512 St. James St., Winnipeg, Manitoba R3H 0L2. Archivist: Rev. Leon C. Gilbertson (incorporating archives of the Evangelical Lutheran Church of Canada, the Lutheran Church in America—Canada Section's Central Synod Archives and those of the Western Canada Synod) The Eastern Synod Archives are housed at Wilfrid Laurier University, Waterloo, Ontario N2L 3C5. Archivist: Rev. E.R.W. Schultz.

Lutheran Church—Canada, Ontario District, 149 Queen St., S., Kitchener, Ontario N2H 1W2. Archivist: Rev. W. W. Wentzlaff; Manitoba-Saskatchewan District, 411 Leighton Ave., Winnipeg, Monitoba R2K 0J8. Archivist Mr. Harry Laudin.

Concordia College, Edmonton, Alberta T5B 4E4. Archivist: Mrs. Hilda Robinson.

Mennonite:

Conrad Grebel College, Archives Centre, Waterloo, Ontario N2L 3G6. Archivist: Sam Steiner

Mennonite Brethren Bible College, Center for Mennonite Brethren Studies in Canada, 1-169 Riverton Ave., Winnipeg, Manitoba R2L 2E5. Archivist: Kenneth Reddig

Mennonite Heritage Centre. Archives of the General Conference of Mennonites in Canada, 600 Shaftesbury Blvd., Winnipeg, Manitoba R3P 0M4. Tel (204) 888-6781. Historian-archivist: Lawrence Klippenstein

Free Methodist:

4315 Village Centre Ct., Mississauga, Ontario L4Z 1S2

Pentecostal:

The Pentecostal Assemblies of Canada, 10 Overlea Blvd., Toronto Ontario M4H 1A5.

Presbyterian:

Presbyterian Archives, Knox College, University of Toronto, 59 St. George St., Toronto, Ontario M5S 2E6. Archivist: Rev. T. M. Bailey; Deputy Archivist, Mrs. Kim Moir

Roman Catholic:

For guides to many Canadian Catholic diocesan religious community, and institutional archives, write: Rev. Pierre Hurtubise, O.M.I., Dir. of the Research Center in Religious History in Canada, St. Paul Univ., 223 Main St., Ottawa, Ontario K1S 1C4.

Salvation Army:

The George Scott Railton Heritage Centre, 2130 Bayview Ave., Toronto, Ontario M4N 3K6. Contact: Catherine Sequin.

The United Church of Canada:

Central Archives, Victoria University, Toronto, Ontario M5S 1K7. Archivist-Historian: Miss Jean Dryden. (Methodist, Presbyterian, Congregational, Evangelical United Brethren.) Also Regional Conference Archives.

Note: The archives of the Canadian Council of Churches and related organizations have been deposited in the Public Archives of Canada, 395 Wellington, Ottawa, Ontario K1A 0N3. Some remain at the Canadian Council of Churches located at 40 St. Clair Ave. E., Toronto, Ontario M4T 1M9. The Public Archives of Canada also contains a large number of records and personal papers related to the various churches.

IV: INDEX

Baptist Missionary Association of America, 33
Baptist Union of Western Canada, 132
Baptist World Alliance, 164
Beachy Amish Mennonite Churches, 34
Beachy Amish Mennonite Churches (Canada), 155
Berean Fundamental Church, 34
Bergthaler (Mennonite) Congregations, 155
Bethel Ministerial Association, Inc., 34
Bible Church of Christ, Inc., The, 35
Bible Colleges in the U.S., 204-09
Bible Holiness Movement (Canada), 130
Bible Sabbath Association, 238
Bible Schools in Canada, 210-12
Bible Way Church of Our Lord Jesus Christ World Wide, Inc., 35
Black Students Enrollment, 275
B'nai B'rith, (Canada), 241
B'nai B'rith International, 238
Boy Scouts of America, 238
Boy Scouts of Canada, 241
Boys and Girls Clubs of Canada, 241
Boys Brigade in Canada, The, 241
Boys' Clubs of America, 238
Bread for the World, 238
Brethren (German Baptists) U.S.
  Brethren Church (Ashland, Ohio), 35
  Church of the Brethren, 50
  Grace Brethren Churches, Fellowship of, 72
  Old German Baptist Brethren, 85
Brethren, River (U.S.)
  Brethren in Christ Church, 35
  United Zion Church, 121
Brethren Church (Ashland, Ohio), 35
Brethren in Christ Church, 35
Brethren in Christ Church, Canadian Conference, 131
British Columbia Baptist Conference, 130
British Methodist Episcopal Church of Canada, 131
Buddhist Churches of America, 36
Buddhist Churches of Canada, 131
Buildings, Religious, Value of New Construction, 288
Bulgarian Eastern Orthodox Church, 36

Calendar for Church Use, A, 1-2
Camp Fire, Inc., 238
Campus Crusade for Christ, International, 238
Canada China Programme, 241
Canada, Religious Affiliation, 269
Canada, Religious Bodies in, Arranged by Families, 155-56
Canadian Association for Adult Education, 221
Canadian Association for Community Living, 241
Canadian Association for Pastoral Education, 241
Canadian Association in Solidarity with the Native Peoples, 241
Canadian Association of Schools of Social Work, 241
Canadian Association of Social Workers, 241
Canadian Baptist Federation, 131
Canadian Bible Schools, 210-12
Canadian Bible Society, 18
Canadian Book Publishers' Council, 241
Canadian Catholic Organization for Development and Peace, 241
Canadian Center for Ecumenism, 241
Canadian Chamber of Commerce, The, 241
Canadian Churches, Finances, 266-67
Canadian Civil Liberties Association, 241
Canadian Conference of Catholic Bishops, 147
Canadian Convention of Southern Baptists, 133
Canadian Co-operative Credit Society, 241
Canadian Cooperative Organizations, National, 18-20
Canadian Council of Christians and Jews, 18
Canadian Council of Churches, 18
Canadian Council of Crisis Centers, 241
Canadian Council on Social Development, The, 241
Canadian Current and Non-Current Statistics, 254-57

Canadian Education Association, 242
Canadian Girls in Training, 242
Canadian Institute of Planners, 242
Canadian Institute of Religion and Gerontology, 242
Canadian Labour Congress, 242
Canadian Medical Association, The, 242
Canadian Mental Health Association, 242
Canadian Prisoner's Aid Societies, 242
Canadian Red Cross Society, 242
Canadian Reformed Churches, 155
Canadian Regional, Local Ecumenical Agencies, 202-03
Canadian Religious Periodicals, 232-36
Canadian Service Agencies: Social, Civic, Religious, 241-43
Canadian Society of Biblical Studies, 242
Canadian Society of Church History, 242
Canadian Theological Seminaries, 210-12
Canadian Tract Society, 18
Canadian UNICEF Committee, 242
Canadian Unitarian Council, 242
Canadian Woman's Christian Temperance Union, 242
Canadian Yearly Meeting of the Religious Society of Friends, 133
CARE Canada, 242
CARE, 238
Catholic Statistics, 1987, 272-73
Catholic Women's League of Canada, The, 242
Center for Applied Research in the Apostolate (CARA), 238
Center for Parish Development, 238
Central Canada Baptist Conference, The, 129
Chortitz (Mennonite) Congregations, 155
Christ Catholic Church, 37
Christadelphians, 37
Christadelphians in Canada, 155
Christian and Missionary Alliance, The, 37
Christian and Missionary Alliance in Canada, The, 133
Christian Brethren (Canada), 133
Christian Brethren, U.S., 38
Christian Camping, International (U.S. Division), 238
Christian Catholic Church, 38
Christian Children's Fund, 238
Christian Church (Disciples of Christ), 38
Christian Church (Disciples of Christ), in Canada, 134
Christian Church of North America, General Council, 40
Christian Churches and Churches of Christ, 40
Christian Churches and Churches of Christ in Canada, 134
Christian Congregation, Inc., The, 41
Christian Endeavor, International Society of, 9
Christian Endeavor Union, World's, 172
Christian Holiness Association, 7
Christian Methodist Episcopal Church, 41
Christian Ministries Management Association, 238
Christian Ministry in the National Parks, A, 7
Christian Nation Church U.S.A., 41
Christian Reformed Church in North America, 41
Christian Reformed Church in North America (Canada), 134
Christian Science in Canada, 155
Christian Service Brigade of Canada, 242
Christian Union, 42
Church Army in Canada, 242
Church Attendance Polls, U.S., 286-87
Church Building, Value of New, 288
Church Council on Justice and Corrections, The, 242
Church Finances, Statistics, 263
Church Financial Statistics and Related Data U.S. and Canada, 263-68
Church Growth Center, 238
Church History Material and Sources, Main Depositories in Canada, 292-93
Church History Material and Sources, Main Depositories of, U.S., 289-92
Church Membership Statistics, 245-56
Church Membership Statistics, 1940-86, Selected U.S. Denominations, 260-61
Church of Christ, 42
Church of Christ, Scientist, 42

Greek Orthodox Archdiocese of North and South America, 72
Holy Ukrainian Autocephalic Orthodox Church in Exile, 73
Orthodox Church in América, The, 86
Romanian Orthodox Church in America, 103
Romanian Orthodox Episcopate of America, The, 103
Russian Orthodox Church in the U.S.A., Patriarchal Parishes of the, 104
Russian Orthodox Church Outside of Russia, The, 104
Serbian Orthodox Church in the U.S.A. and Canada, 105
Syrian Orthodox Church of Antioch (Archdiocese of the U.S.A. and Canada), 110
True (Old Calendar) Orthodox Church of Greece (Synod of Metropolitan Cyprian), American Exarchate, 111
Ukrainian Orthodox Church in America (Ecumenical Patriarchate), 111
Ukrainian Orthodox Church of the U.S.A., 111
Eastern Orthodox Churches, 165
Ecumenical Agencies, 176-201
Ecumenical Agencies, Canada, 202-03
Elim Fellowship, 56
Elim Fellowship of Evangelical Churches and Ministers, 136
Elizabeth Fry of Toronto, 242
Enrollment, Seminaries, Full Time Equivalent, 1978-87, 274
Episcopal Church, The, 56
Estonian Evangelical Lutheran Church, The, 59
Estonian Evangelical Lutheran Church, The (Canada), 136
Ethical Culture Movement, 59
Ethical Union, American, 59
Evangelical Baptist Churches in Canada, The Fellowship of, 137
Evangelical Church Alliance, The, 9
Evangelical Church in Canada, The, 137
Evangelical Church, The, 60
Evangelical Congregational Church, 60
Evangelical Council for Financial Accountability, 238
Evangelical Covenant Church, The, 60
Evangelical Covenant Church of Canada, The, 137
Evangelical Fellowship of Canada, 18
Evangelical Free Church of America, The, 61
Evangelical Free Church of Canada, 137
Evangelical Friends Alliance, 61
Evangelical Lutheran in Canada, 137
Evangelical Lutheran Synod, 64
Evangelical Mennonite Brethren Conference, 64
Evangelical Mennonite Brethren Conference (Canada), 138
Evangelical Mennonite Church, Inc., 64
Evangelical Mennonite Conference (Canada), 138
Evangelical Mennonite Mission Conference (Canada), 138
Evangelical Methodist Church, 64
Evangelical Presbyterian Church, 65
Evangelical Press Association, 9
Evangelical Theological Society of Canada, 242
Evangelistic Associations (U.S.)
    Apostolic Christian Church (Nazarean), 28
    Apostolic Christian Churches in America, 28
    Apostolic Faith Mission of Portland, Oregon, 28
    Christian Congregation, Inc., The, 41
    Church of Daniel's Band, 43

Fellowship of Evangelical Baptist Churches in Canada, The, 137
Fellowship of Fundamental Bible Churches, 66
Fellowship of Reconciliation, The, 238
Finances, Church, 263-68
Fire-Baptized Holiness Church (Wesleyan), The, 66
Foreign Policy Association, 238
Foursquare Gospel Church of Canada, 138
Free Christian Zion Church of Christ, 66
Free Lutheran Congregations, The Association of, 66

Free Methodist Church in Canada, The, 139
Free Methodist Church of North America, 67
Free Will Baptists, 67
Free Will Baptists (Canada), 139
French Baptist Union (Canada), 132
Friends (U.S.)
    Evangelical Friends Alliance, 61
    Friends General Conference, 68
    Friends United Meeting, 68
    Religious Society of Friends (Conservative), 96
    Religious Society of Friends (Unaffiliated Meetings), 96
Friends Committee on National Legislation, 238
Friends General Conference, 68
Friends United Meeting, 68
Friends World Committee for Consultation, Section of the Americas, 164
Frontiers Foundation/Operation Beaver, 242
Full Gospel Assemblies, International, 69
Full Gospel Fellowship of Churches and Ministers, International, 69
Fundamental Methodist Church, Inc., 70

GATT-Fly, 242
General Association of Regular Baptist Churches, 70
General Baptists, General Association of, 70
General Church of the New Jerusalem, 70
General Church of the New Jerusalem (Canada), 139
General Conference of Mennonite Brethren Churches, 71
General Conference of the Evangelical Baptist Church, Inc., 71
General Convention The Swedenborgian Church, 71
General Federation of Women's Clubs, 238
General Six-Principle Baptists, 71
Gideons International in Canada, 242
Girl Guides of Canada—Guides du Canada, 242
Girl Scouts of the U.S.A., 238
Giving, per Capita, Effects of Inflation on, 1961-1986, 268
Glenmary Research Center, 238
Gospel Missionary Association, The (Canada), 140
Grace Brethren Churches, Fellowship of, 72
Grace Gospel Fellowship, 72
Greek Orthodox Archdiocese of North and South America, 72
Greek Orthodox Diocese of Toronto, 140
Guide for the User of Church Statistics, ix

Heads of Orthodox Churches, 165
Health League of Canada, The, 242
Hierarchy of the Roman Catholic Church, 165
Hispanic Students Enrollment, 276
Holiness Church of God, Inc., The, 73
Holy Ukrainian Autocephalic Orthodox Church in Exile, 73
House of God, Which Is the Church of the Living God, the Pillar and Ground of the Truth, Inc., 73
Hungarian Reformed Church in America, 73
Hutterian Brethren, 74
Hutterian Brethren (Canada), 155

Inclusive Membership 1890-1986, 262
Independent Assemblies of God—Canada, 140
Independent Assemblies of God, International, 74
Independent Fundamental Churches of America, 74
Independent Holiness Church (Canada), 140
Inflation, Effects of on Per Capita Giving, 1961-1986, 268
Institute for Christian Studies, 242
Institute of International Education, 239
Institutes of Religion and Health, 239
Inter-Church Committee for Refugees, 243
Interchurch Committee for World Development Education, 243
Inter-Church Committee on Human Rights in Latin America, 243
Inter-Church Communications, 243
Inter-Church Consultative Committee on Development and Relief (Canada), 19
Inter-Church Fund for International Development (Canada), 243
Interdenominational International Agencies, 157-72
Interfaith Committee on Chaplaincy in the Correctional Service of Canada, 243
Interfaith Forum on Religion, Art and Architecture, 239

International Agencies, Confessional Interdenomination-
al Cooperative, 157-72
International Christian Youth Exchange, 9
International Church of the Foursquare Gospel, 74
International Congregational Fellowship, 166
International Council of Christian Churches, 166
International Pentecostal Church of Christ, The, 75
International Society of Christian Endeavor, 9
Inter-Varsity Christian Fellowship of Canada, 19
Inter-Varsity Christian Fellowship of the U.S.A., 10
Interreligious Foundation for Community Organization, 9
Israelite House of David, 75
Italian Pentecostal Church of Canada, The, 140

Japan International Christian Unity Foundation, 239
Jehovah's Witnesses, 75
Jehovah's Witnesses (Canada), 140
Jewish Organizations, 76
Jewish Organizations in Canada, 140
John Howard Society of Ontario, 242
John Milton Society for the Blind, 239
John Milton Society for the Blind, Canada, 243
Joint Strategy and Action Committee, 10

Kodesh Church of Immanuel, 77
Korean Presbyterian Church in America, General Assembly of the, 77

Lambeth Conference of Bishops of the Anglican Commu-
nion, 166
LAOS/Partners for Global Justice, 239
Latter Day Saints (Canada)
    Church of Jesus Christ of Latter-day Saints, The, 138
    Reorganized Church of Jesus Christ of Latter Day
        Saints, 147
Latter Day Saints (U.S.)
    Church of Christ, 42
    Church of Jesus Christ (Bickertonites), The, 49
    Church of Jesus Christ of Latter-day Saints, The, 49
    Reorganized Church of Jesus Christ of Latter Day
        Saints, 96
Latvian Evangelical Lutheran Church in America, The
    (Canada), 142
Latvian Evangelical Lutheran Church in America, The, 78
Laymen's National Bible Association, 239
Leadership, Professional Church, Attitude Toward, 281
League of Women Voters, The, 239
Liberal Catholic Church—Province of the U.S.A., The, 78
Liberty Baptist Fellowship, 78
Liturgical Conference, The, 10
Lord's Day Alliance of the United States, The, 11
Lutheran Church—Canada, 142
Lutheran Church Library Association, 239
Lutheran Church—Missouri Synod, The, 78
Lutheran Council in Canada, 19
Lutheran Resources Commission—Washington, 239
Lutheran World Federation, 167
Lutheran (Canada)
    Church of the Lutheran Brethren, 135
    Estonian Evangelical Lutheran Church, The, 136
    Evangelical Lutheran Church in Canada, The, 137
    Latvian Evangelical Lutheran Church in America, 142
    Lutheran Church—Canada, 142
    Wisconsin Evangelical Lutheran Synod, 154
Lutherans (U.S.)
    Apostolic Lutheran Church of America, 29
    Church of the Lutheran Brethren of America, 51
    Church of the Lutheran Confession, 52
    Estonian Evangelical Lutheran Church, The, 59
    Evangelical Lutheran Church in America, 62
    Evangelical Lutheran Synod, 64
    Free Lutheran Congregations, The Association of, 66
    Latvian Evangelical Lutheran Church in America, The,
        78
    Lutheran Church in America, 75
    Lutheran Church—Missouri Synod, The, 78
    Protestant Conference (Lutheran), The, 93
    Wisconsin Evangelical Lutheran Synod, 122

World Confessional Lutheran Association, 123

Main Depositories of Church History Material in Canada,
    292
Main Depositories of Church History Material in the
    United States, 289-91
Membership, Inclusive, 1890-1986, 262
Mennonite Bodies (Canada)
    Beachy Amish Menonites Churches, 155
    Bergthaler Congregations, 155
    Chortitz Congregations, 155
    Church of God in Christ Mennonite (Holdeman),
        Canada, 155
    Conference of Mennonites in Canada, 136
    Evangelical Mennonite Brethren Conference, 155
    Evangelical Mennonite Conference, 138
    Evangelical Mennonite Mission Conference, 138
    Hutterian Brethren, 155
    Mennonite Brethren Churches, Canadian Conference
        of, 142
    Mennonite Church (Canada), 142
    Old Colony Mennonite Church in Canada, 155
    Old Order Amish Church, 144
    Old Order Mennonite Church, 155
    Reinlaender Mennonite Church, 147
    Sommerfelder (Mennonite) Church, 155
Mennonite Bodies (U.S.)
    Beachy Amish Mennonite Churches, 34
    Church of God in Christ (Mennonite), 47
    Evangelical Mennonite Church, 64
    Fellowship of Evangelical Bible Churches, 65
    General Conference of Mennonite Brethren Churches,
        71
    Hutterian Brethren, 74
    Mennonite Church, 79
    Mennonite Church, The General Conference, 80
    Old Order Amish Church, 85
    Old Order Mennonite Church, 155
    Old Order (Wisler) Mennonite Church, 86
    Reformed Mennonite Church, 95
Mennonite Brethren Churches, Canadian Conference of,
    142
Mennonite Central Committee, 11
Mennonite Central Committee (Canada), 19
Mennonite Church, 79
Mennonite Church (Canada), 143
Mennonite Church, The General Conference, 80
Mennonite World Conference, 167
Methodist Bodies (Canada)
    African Methodist Episcopal Church in Canada, 155
    British Methodist Episcopal Church of Canada, 131
    Evangelical Church in Canada, The, 137
    Free Methodist Church in Canada, 139
    Wesleyan Church, 154
Methodist Bodies (U.S.)
    African Methodist Episcopal Church, 21
    African Methodist Episcopal Zion Church, 22
    Allegheny Wesleyan Methodist Connection (Original
        Allegheny Conference), 23
    Christian Methodist Episcopal Church, 41
    Evangelical Methodist Church, 64
    Free Methodist Church of North America, 67
    Fundamental Methodist Church, Inc., 70L† Primitive
        Methodist Church, U.S.A., 92
    Reformed Methodist Union Episcopal Church, 95
    Reformed Zion Union Apostolic Church, 96
    Southern Methodist Church, 109
    United Methodist Church, The, 116
    Wesleyan Church, 121
Metropolitan Church Association, The, 80
Metropolitan Community Churches, Universal Fellow-
    ship of, 81
Metropolitan Community Churches, Universal Fellow-
    ship of (Canada), 143
Missionary Church, The, 81
Missionary Church of Canada, The, 143
Moravian Bodies (U.S.)
    Moravian Church in America (Unitas Fratrum), 82
    Unity of the Brethren, 121

300